THE YEAR'S WORK IN MODERN LANGUAGE STUDIES

THE YEAR'S WORK IN MODERN LANGUAGE STUDIES

GENERAL EDITOR
STEPHEN PARKINSON

ASSISTANT EDITOR
LISA BARBER

SECTION EDITORS

LATIN, FRENCH, OCCITAN
LISA BARBER, M.A., D.PHIL

ITALIAN, ROMANIAN, RHETO-ROMANCE
JOHN M. A. LINDON, M.A.
Professor of Italian Studies, University College London

ROMANCE LINGUISTICS, SPANISH, CATALAN, PORTUGUESE, GALICIAN, LATIN AMERICAN, SLAVONIC
STEPHEN PARKINSON, M.A., PH.D.
Lecturer in Portuguese Language and Linguistics, University of Oxford

CELTIC
DAVID A. THORNE, M.A., PH.D.
Professor of Welsh, University of Wales, Lampeter

GERMANIC
DAVID A. WELLS, M.A., PH.D.
Professor of German, Birkbeck College, University of London

VOLUME 64

2002

MANEY PUBLISHING
for the
MODERN HUMANITIES RESEARCH ASSOCIATION
2004

The Year's Work in Modern Language Studies may be ordered from the Subscriptions Department, Maney Publishing, Hudson Road, Leeds LS9 7DL, UK.

ISBN 1 904350 16 X

ISSN 0084-4152

Produced in Great Britain by
MANEY PUBLISHING
HUDSON ROAD LEEDS LS9 7DL UK

CONTENTS

PREFACE *page* xi

1 LATIN

I MEDIEVAL LATIN, Postponed

II NEO-LATIN, Postponed

2 ROMANCE LANGUAGES

I ROMANCE LINGUISTICS 3
by PROFESSOR J. N. GREEN, M.A., D.PHIL.

II FRENCH STUDIES

Language, 19
by PROFESSOR GLANVILLE PRICE, M.A., DOCT. DE L'UNIV.

Early Medieval Literature, 35
by SARA I. JAMES, B.A., M.A., PH.D.
and ADRIAN P. TUDOR, B.A., M.A., PH.D.

Late Medieval Literature, 65
by NICOLE LASSAHN, PH.D.

The Sixteenth Century, 96
by GILLES BANDERIER, D. ÈS L.

The Seventeenth Century, 125
by JOHN TRETHEWEY, B.A., PH.D.
and †J. P. SHORT, B.A.

The Eighteenth Century, Postponed

The Romantic Era, 169
by JOHN WHITTAKER, B.A., PH.D., M.A.

The Nineteenth Century (Post-Romantic), 189
by LARRY DUFFY, B.A., L. ÈS L., M.A., PH.D.

The Twentieth Century, 1900–1945, Postponed

Literature, 1945 to the Present Day, Postponed

French Canadian Literature, 207
by C. D. ROLFE, M.A.

Caribbean Literature, 216
by MAEVE MCCUSKER, M.A., PH.D.

African and Maghreb Literature, Postponed

III OCCITAN STUDIES
Language, 221
by PROFESSOR KATHRYN KLINGEBIEL, M.A., PH.D.
Literature, 231
by MIRIAM CABRÉ, LLIC.FIL., PH.D.,
SADURNÍ MARTÍ, LLIC.FIL., D.FIL.,
and STANLEY F. LEVINE, PH.D., L. ÈS L.

IV SPANISH STUDIES
Language, 246
by PROFESSOR STEVEN DWORKIN, M.A., PH.D.
and MIRANDA STEWART, B.A., M. ÈS L., PH.D.
Medieval Literature, Postponed
Aljamiado Literature, Postponed
Literature, 1490–1700 (Prose and Poetry), 265
by CARMEN PERAITA, LIC.FIL., PH.D.
Literature, 1490–1700 (Drama), Postponed
Literature, 1700–1823, 275
by GABRIEL SÁNCHEZ ESPINOSA, D.PHIL.
Literature, 1823–1898, Postponed
Literature, 1898–1936, 279
by PROFESSOR K. M. SIBBALD, M.A., PH.D.
Literature, 1936 to the Present Day, Postponed

V CATALAN STUDIES
Language, Postponed
Medieval Literature, 296
by PROFESSOR LOLA BADIA, LLIC.FIL., D.FIL.
and MIRIAM CABRÉ, LLIC.FIL., PH.D.
Literature (Modern), Postponed

VI PORTUGUESE STUDIES
Language, Postponed
Medieval Literature, Postponed
Literature, 1500 to the Present Day, Postponed

VII GALICIAN STUDIES
Language, 304
by PROFESSOR DAVID MACKENZIE, M.A., PH.D.,
FRANCISCO DUBERT GARCÍA, LIC.FIL., PH.D.,
and XULIO SOUSA FERNÁNDEZ, LIC.FIL., PH.D.

Literature, 313
by DOLORES VILAVEDRA, PH.D.
and DEREK FLITTER, M.A., D.PHIL.

VIII LATIN AMERICAN STUDIES

Spanish-American Literature: The Colonial Period, Postponed

The Nineteenth Century, 318
by ANNELLA MCDERMOTT, M.A.

The Twentieth Century, 321
by VICTORIA CARPENTER, B.SC., PH.D.
and FIONA J. MACKINTOSH, M.A., M.PHIL., PH.D.

Brazilian Literature, 343
by MARK DINNEEN, M.A., PH.D.

IX ITALIAN STUDIES

Language, 351
by ROBERTA MIDDLETON, DOTT. LETT., D.PHIL.
and SIMONE BACCHINI, B.A., M.ST.

Duecento and Trecento I (Dante), 364
by PAOLA NASTI, B.A.

Duecento and Trecento II (excluding Dante), 381
by ROBERTA CAPELLI, DOTT. LETT., DOTT. RICERCA.
and ATTILIO MOTTA, DOTT. LETT., DOTT. RICERCA.

Humanism and the Renaissance, Postponed

Seicento, Postponed

Settecento, 400
by G. W. SLOWEY, M.A.

Ottocento, 421
by PROFESSOR J. M. A. LINDON, M.A.

Novecento, 450
by ROBERTO BERTONI, DOTT. LETT.
and PROFESSOR CATHERINE O'BRIEN, M.A., DOTT. LETT.

X ROMANIAN STUDIES

Language, 495
by PROFESSOR MARTIN MAIDEN, M.A., M.PHIL., PH.D.

Literature, 507
by PROFESSOR MIRCEA ANGHELESCU, PH.D.

XI RHETO-ROMANCE STUDIES 518
by INGMAR SÖHRMAN, M.A., PH.D.

3 CELTIC LANGUAGES

I WELSH STUDIES

Language, 525
by DAVID THORNE, M.A., PH.D.

Early and Medieval Literature, 527
by OWEN THOMAS, B.A., LL.B., M.ST.

Literature since 1500, 533
by A. CYNFAEL LAKE, M.A., PH.D.

II BRETON AND CORNISH STUDIES, Postponed

III IRISH STUDIES

Early Irish, 538
by KEVIN MURRAY, B.A., PH.D.

Modern Irish, Postponed

IV SCOTTISH GAELIC STUDIES, Postponed

4 GERMANIC LANGUAGES

I GERMAN STUDIES

Language, 543
by CHARLES V. J. RUSS, M.A., M.LITT., PH.D.

Medieval Literature, 576
by NIGEL W. HARRIS, B.A., D.PHIL.

The Sixteenth Century, 621
by MARK TAPLIN, B.A., M.LITT., PH.D.

The Seventeenth Century, 637
by ANNA CARRDUS, B.A., PH.D.

The Classical Era, Postponed

The Romantic Era, 647
by CAROL TULLY, B.A., PH.D.

Literature, 1830–1880, 667
by BARBARA BURNS, M.A., PH.D.

Literature, 1880–1945, 699
by MALCOLM HUMBLE, M.A., PH.D.

Literature from 1945 to the Present Day, 733
by JOANNE LEAL, B.A., PH.D.

II DUTCH STUDIES

Language, Postponed

Literature, Postponed

III DANISH STUDIES

Language, 755
by TOM LUNDSKÆR-NIELSEN, M.PHIL., PH.D.

Literature, 763
by JENS LOHFERT JØRGENSEN, CAND.MAG

IV NORWEGIAN STUDIES

Language, Postponed

Literature since the Reformation, 774
by ØYSTEN ROTTEM, CAND.PHILOL.

V SWEDISH STUDIES

Language, Postponed

Literature, Postponed

5 SLAVONIC LANGUAGES

I CZECH STUDIES

Language, 781
by PH.DR. MARIE NOVÁKOVÁ
and PH.DR. JANA PAPCUNOVÁ

Literature, Postponed

II SLOVAK STUDIES

Language, Postponed

Literature, Postponed

III POLISH STUDIES

Language, 789
by NIGEL GOTTERI, M.A.

Literature, Postponed

IV RUSSIAN STUDIES

Language, Postponed

Literature from the beginning to 1700, Postponed

Literature, 1700–1800, Postponed

Literature, 1800–1848, 806
by BORIS LANIN, M.A., PH.D.

Literature, 1848–1917, 819
by BORIS LANIN, M.A., PH.D.

Literature from 1917 to the Present Day, 831
by BORIS LANIN, M.A., PH.D.

V UKRAINIAN STUDIES, Postponed

VI BELARUSIAN STUDIES, Postponed

VII SERBO-CROAT STUDIES
Language, Postponed
Literature, Postponed

VIII BULGARIAN STUDIES, Postponed

ABBREVIATIONS

I ACTA, FESTSCHRIFTEN AND OTHER COLLECTIVE AND GENERAL WORKS 859

II GENERAL 871

III PLACE NAMES 873

IV PERIODICALS, INSTITUTIONS, PUBLISHERS 873

INDEX 925

PREFACE

This volume surveys work, published in 2002, unless otherwise stated, in the fields of Romance, Celtic, Germanic, and Slavonic languages and literatures. An asterisk before the title of a book or article indicates that the item in question has not been seen by the contributor.

The attention of users is drawn to the lists of abbreviations at the end of the volume, which are also available on-line via the MHRA's WWW site (http://www.mhra.org.uk/Publications/Journals/ywmls.html).

The Editors wish to record with sorrow the deaths of Joseph Cremona, doyen of British Romance Linguistics and founder of the Romance Linguistics section of this journal, and of Pat Short, contributor to the section on 17th-century French literature, who continued to work for this volume through his last illness. They are individually commemorated in the sections they enriched.

Many authors, editors and publishers supply review copies and offprints of their publications. To these we and our contributors are grateful, and we would invite others to follow their example, especially in the case of work issuing from unusual, unexpected, or inaccessible sources of publication. We would ask that, whenever possible, items for review be sent directly to the appropriate contributor; where no obvious recipient can be identified, as in the case of books or journal issues relating to a number of fields, the item should be sent to one of the editors, who will distribute the contents accordingly.

The compilation of a contribution to the volume, especially in the field of the major languages and periods of literature, is a substantial research task requiring wide-ranging and specialized knowledge of the subject besides a huge reading effort accompanied by the constant exercise of critical judgement. We are deeply grateful to the authors who have devoted significant amounts of increasingly precious research time to this enterprise. The measure of their task is indicated by the number of sections for which the editors have failed to find contributors; we encourage approaches from potential contributors or groups of contributors for future volumes.

The completion of this volume would not have been possible without the ever-increasing contribution of Lisa Barber, Assistant Editor and compiler of the Index. Thanks are also due to the other institutions and individuals who have contributed in one way or another to the making of the volume, in particular, Paolo Ranbelli, Luca Baldoni, Evgeniia Drozdova, the secretarial and administrative staff of the Faculty of Modern Languages of Oxford University, and our printers, Maney Publishing, particularly Liz Rosindale and Anna Thrush, whose expertise has been invaluable in the completion of this complex operation.

January 2004 S.R.P., L.B., J.M.A.L., D.A.T., D.A.W.

PREFACE

1

LATIN

I. MEDIEVAL LATIN

POSTPONED

NEO-LATIN

POSTPONED

2
ROMANCE LANGUAGES
I. ROMANCE LINGUISTICS

By John N. Green, *University of Bradford*

To the memory of Joseph A. Cremona (1922–2003)
who founded this section in 1957

1. Acta, Festschriften

Such is the interest in Romance as a source of data and challenges to formal linguistics that a fairly lean year for conferences now betokens three substantial items. Wiltshire, *Romance Phonology*, the second volume of papers from the 30th meeting of the annual American symposium (the first was discussed in *YWMLS*, 63: 15, as *LSRL 30*), coincides with *LSRL 29*, the still substantial but only single-volume publication from the previous, Ann Arbor meeting, in which Spanish takes pole position. The matching European venture, having now notched up 14 meetings but only published two as formal proceedings, is represented by *Going Romance 2000*, a tidy collection of 16 mostly monolingual papers on aspects of clitics, focus, specificity, and edge phenomena.

Marking their recipients' 60th birthdays, *Fest. Lüdtke* assembles 40 essays on language variation and linguistic change, mainly within Ibero-Romance; and *Renzi Vol.* contains 16 articles mostly on the generative syntax of Italian but with some comparative items mentioned below. Intended as a Festschrift but sadly appearing as a memorial, Jacques Monfrin, *Études de philologie romane*, ed. Geneviève Hasenohr et al. (PRF, 230), 2001, xii + 1035 pp., reprints 39 of M.'s sometimes inaccessible essays, largely on philology and textual scholarship, together with a full bibliography of his writings (981–97). Appearing as a memorial to Alarcos Llorach, *La corónica*, 29.2, 2001, ed. A. Cortijo Ocaña and F. Marcos Marín, includes a CV and full bibliography compiled by his widow Josefina Martínez (7–22) and an evaluation by S. Gutiérrez Ordóñez, 'La obra lingüística de Emilio Alarcos Llorach' (95–123).

2. General Romance and Latin

Fernando Sánchez-Miret, *Proyecto de gramática histórica y comparada de las lenguas romances*, 2 vols, Munich, LinCom Europa, 2001, [vi +] 370, 371–790 pp., offers an extraordinarily comprehensive panorama, based on advanced lectures and with copious references, prepared under the provisions of Spanish law in support of an application to establish a Chair of the discipline — ¡Que tenga suerte! Long announced, Jürgen Klausenburger, *A Coursebook in Romance Linguistics*, Munich, LinCom Europa, 2001, [x +] 203 pp., gives prominence to morphosyntax, verb inflection, and sandhi phenomena, with a somewhat propagandist emphasis on K.'s own 'morphocentricity' (*YWMLS*, 62 : 16; see also p. 10 below). Compact, neo-traditional, and thoroughly commendable, Jacques Allières, *Manuel de linguistique romane*, Paris, Champion, 2001, xxii + 323 pp., seeks to reposition linguistic geography and to rescue the 'minor' languages. *Language, Ethnicity and the State*, ed. Camille C. O'Reilly, Basingstoke, Palgrave, 2001, 2 vols, x + 183, xii + 228 pp., presents a series of case studies, including A. Jaffe on Corsica (1 : 40–55), S. DiGiacomo on Catalan (1 : 56–77), L. Timm on Brittany (1 : 104–27), and T. J. Hegarty on Moldova (2 : 123–54). *Sociolinguistica*, 15, 2001, ed. K. J. Mattheier et al., defiantly devoted to 'Lingua francas in Europe — except English', has a thoughtful overview by W. F. Mackay, 'Conflicting languages in a United Europe' (1–17), and includes case studies by C. Truchot, 'Le français langue véhiculaire en Europe' (18–31), F. J. Zamora, 'Spanish' (59–71), and G. Berruto 'Italienisch' (72–95). *CILL*, 27.3–4, 2001, and 28.1–2, ed. J. C. Herreras, under the title 'Les langues de grande diffusion de l'union européenne', surveys the rise and status of individual languages, their speaker statistics, and — less systematically — their interactions.

Joseph Farrell, *Latin Language and Latin Culture. From Ancient to Modern Times*, CUP, 2001, xiv + 148 pp., studies the metaphors conventionally applied to Latin ('masculine', 'Imperial', 'classical', 'dead') which, willy nilly, still affect our reading of Latin texts and our ideological conception of the transition to Romance; it is, as P. Baldi says in a tolerant review (*LSo*, 31 : 460–66), not a linguist's book. Gärtner, *Skripta*, assembles 23 papers from the 1998 Trier colloquium on medieval scribal practice and codification, including: J. Wüest, 'Sind Schreibdialekte phonologisch interpretierbar?' (37–51), replying with a cautious yes, but remembering that scribes would have been writing their own, different, pronunciations; M. Selig, 'Überlegungen zur Erforschung der romanischen Urkundensprachen' (53–73), on the need to read texts from the perspective of gradual codification with some divergent local practice; and A. Monjour, 'Scriptologie et analyse du discours' (147–67), on the desirability of applying modern (post-structuralist and post-Chomskyan) discourse analysis to medieval textology.

Banniard, *Langages*, the proceedings of a 1997 colloquium on medieval identities, has a prologue by B. (7–12) on the 'barbarisation' of Latin and the search for names for emergent identities; and 12 other papers, mostly on Romance, including G. Hasenohr, 'Écrire en latin, écrire en roman' (79–110), on MS abbreviations; M. van Uytfange, 'Aux confins de la romanité et de la germanité du VIIIe siècle' (209–59), on a method for dating texts intended for oral performance; and R. Wright, 'La chronologie relative des nouvelles *scripta* et des nouvelles langues' (261–69), on the persistence of functional intercommunication long after the appearance of the first distinctive scripts and tentative differentiations. W. also contributes: 'La sociolingüística y la sociofilología del siglo XII', *CIHCE 6*, 15–38, on the riches to be struck in truly diplomatic editions of various text types; and 'Early medieval pan-Romance comprehension', Conreni, *Word*, 25–42, which infers continuing intelligibility from the 9th-c. expedition of Eulogio de Córdoba, intentionally to Strasbourg but aborted some way north of the Pyrenees, only after he had made firm friends with monastic brethren with whom he could manifestly communicate and later corresponded. Moreover, with LUPU(M) > *lobo* as a case-study, W. asks '¿Qué cambia?', *Fest. Lüdtke*, 17–24, answering that a revised lexical entry is propagated and becomes socially acceptable; change need not have extended to any other linguistic level, much less to 'the language', as implied by classical phonemic split.

G. Marotta, 'The features of the Romance alphabet', *RivL*, 12, 2000[2001]: 283–306, reviews sympathetically but eventually rejects Mounin's approach based on a limited number of basic geometric shapes, in favour of a dot-matrix model; she convincingly shows that a 3x5 matrix gives an adequate account, while 5x5 offers both functionality and elegance. G. Salvi, 'The two sentence structures of Early Romance', *Renzi Vol.*, 297–312, finds that the new V_2 pattern, though well established in subordinate clauses by the emergence of the first Romance texts, was nevertheless in competition with an older word order which, in focalized contexts like *quant li barun ço orent fait*, could give rise to three variants. Comparing monosemic and ambiguous syntactic structures, L. Schøsler, 'Passage du système valentiel latin au système de l'ancien français', Banniard, *Langages*, 187–208, concludes that valency (marked by the presence of a direct object, a support verb, or prepositional accusative), rather than nominal inflection, becomes the most effective means of disambiguation. For S. Pieroni, after an upsurge in the use of impersonal structures, 'Voice shifts in Late Latin', *IF*, 106, 2001:216–28, came to be correlated with action type: non-agentive states generally required active morphology, and agentive verbs in passive guise conveyed impersonal semantics. The 7th-c. *Liber Historiae Francorum*, which incorporates passages from Gregory of Tours but removes all Gregory's passives and deponents, provides J. Herman with evidence to date 'La disparition du passif synthétique latin', *ER*, 24:31–46; even so, other sources point to continuing if infrequent use later in the century.

And the consequences? Noting that Romance languages have moved further away from synthetic structure than all other I-E families, yet within Romance not all have moved as quickly or as consistently, M. Gawełko, 'Sobre la tendencia analítica de algunas lenguas romances', *RELing*, 31, 2001:393–412, devises a series of tests for analytic structure in running prose, from which Spanish emerges as the most synthetic, followed by Italian, with Portuguese by far the most analytic of the three.

3. History of Romance Linguistics

Drawing on one of the richest archival sources in the world, Jürgen Storost, *300 Jahre romanische Sprachen und Literaturen an der Berliner Akademie der Wissenschaften*, 2 vols, Frankfurt, Lang, 2001, xviii + 606, xvi + 455 pp., edits a huge array of over 200 documents (in vol. 2), preceded by his own thematic interpretation of Romance languages and literatures in the Leibniz-dominated 18th c., the institutionalization of Romanistik in the 19th c., the era of Adolf Tobler, and the conflict-torn 20th c., under Weimar, the Third Reich, and the Soviet-dominated DDR. An appreciative review article of Hausmann's *Vom Strudel der Ereignisse verschlungen* (*YWMLS*, 63:18), by K.-H. Ehlers, 'Die Entwicklung einer nationalsozialistischen Romanistik', *BGS*, 12:187–92, praises the painstaking documentation but questions why German Romanistik escaped relatively unscathed from the purges of 1935–41, suggesting it was perhaps because it had already adapted and was subtly complicit with the regime. J. M. Meisel and C. Schwarze, reflecting on the state of German 'Romanistische Linguistik heute', *RF*, 114:423–44, advocate severing the withered links with Romance literatures and making much fuller use of the rich comparative data in contributing to research on universals and corpus linguistics.

Originally a plenary at the 2001 Salamanca Congress, J. M. Lipski, 'La lingüística románica en los Estados Unidos', *RLiR*, 66:367–401, surveys the achievements of the past half century in historical grammar, phonology of various vintages, contrastive analysis, applied linguistics, sociolinguistics, and the role of Spanish in the US, concluding optimistically that these amount to 'incredible vitality'. A short but thought-provoking section in Klausenburger's *Coursebook* (10–11; see p. 4), however, distinguishes sharply between classical Romance linguistics and the applied-theoretical orientation of the Linguistic Symposia; he predicts that the classical version, already in decline, will be absorbed by the new vibrancy — history almost repeating itself with a century's time lag. By contrast, emblematic of the marginalization of Romance linguistics in the UK, is *Linguistics in Britain: Personal Histories*, ed. Keith Brown and Vivien Law (Publications of the Philological Society, 36), Oxford, Blackwell, in which the late 'Joseph Cremona' (78–90) is the only acknowledged Romanist to merit inclusion among the movers and shakers, despite the service of eminent Romanists in the roster of the Society's own Presidents.

Celebrating an approximate centenary, *RLaR*, 105.2, 2001 [2002, incorrectly numbered 105.1], ed. Philippe Martel and Pierre Boutan, brings together ten papers from the 2000 Montpellier colloquium 'Autour de la *Revue des Langues Romanes*', among which G. Bergounioux chronicles its difficult launch at the end of the Franco–Prussian War, when German comparativism was deeply suspect (385–407); M. Décimo points to the symbolic choice of Montpellier as a focus for Romance philology in the south, vying with the Paris–Meyer axis in the north (409–27); J. Thomas analyses the early contents, often poorly indexed (477–89); G. Brun-Trigaud contrasts the editorial style of *RLaR* with that of its arch rival *Romania* (429–54); P. Boutan reflects on exchanges between Bréal and Grammont, and especially on G.'s later preoccupation with second language learning (455–76); A.-M. Frýba-Reber publishes extracts from correspondence between student friends Grammont and Meillet on the establishment of linguistics in France (503–15); and the once highly influential scholars Ronjat and Millardet are portrayed as worthy of rehabilitation by J.-C. Bouvier and P. Swiggers (491–502 and 517–35 respectively).

With a little help from Malkiel, E. F. K. Koerner investigates 'William Labov and the origins of sociolinguistics', *FLinHist*, 22, 2001[2002]: 1–40, finding sources in three strands of dialectological and historical studies prominently represented by Jaberg and Martinet, whose crucial role was to recognize the *necessarily* semiotic nature of language. E. Radtke contrasts the continuing vigour of the notion 'Der Polymorphismus in der romanischen Dialektologie und Sprachgeschichte', *Fest Lüdtke*, 45–51, with its problematic application elsewhere. H. Geckeler, 'Zu den Auswirkungen des Sprachwandels in sprachlichen Teilsystemen', *ib.*, 37–43, catalogues some of the trials of Saussure, Trier, and Coseriu in accommodating change within a modular synchronic framework. With some wry reflections on Nebrija's working methods, M. Rivas Zancarrón, 'Desde una sintaxis histórica hasta una morfología sincrónica', *ZRP*, 118:376–91, believes that the visual imperative of finding a term for a non-classical entity led to the coining of 'auxiliary' and the assignment of the new category to syntax, with a resultant schism between what ought to have been merely old and new morphology.

Finally, a book with much wider implications than its title, *The Battle over Spanish between 1800 and 2000*, ed. José del Valle and Luis Gabriel-Stheeman, London–NY, Routledge, xiv + 237 pp., examines the role of intellectuals in creating a monolingual (and hegemonic) ideology for the Spanish language that has more recently been embodied in the monarchy and ruthlessly promoted by commercial interests.

4. Phonology

In the best Romance tradition, Thomas D. Cravens, *Comparative Historical Dialectology. Romance Clues to Ibero-Romance Sound Change* (CILT, 231), Amsterdam, Benjamins, xii + 163 pp., offers a methodology for reconstructing elusive changes from fragmentary evidence: elimination of geminates, once pan-Romance, may be the common cause underlying lenition of /-p-, -t-, -k-/ and palatalization of initial /l-, n-/. Complementary and enormously detailed, M. De Martino, 'I suoni di L ed LL latine secondo i grammatici d'età imperiale', *IF*, 106, 2001:164–203 (following on from *ib.*, 105, 2000:213–54), concentrates on the likely meaning of the common terms EXILIS / PINGUIS, deciding that the geminate was once a heterosyllabic palatal. Likewise relevant to the historical problem is a modern corpus-based study by A. M. Lewis of 'Contrast maintenance and intervocalic stop lenition', *LSRL 29*, 160–71, who finds almost equal numbers of voiceless and voiced tokens of /-p-, -t-, -k-/ but far fewer fricative, approximant or zero realizations, and speculates that voicing and closure might be independent variables. Again drawing on multiple dialectological and textual sources, F. Möhren, '"Guai victis!" Le problème du GU initial roman', *MedRom*, 24, 2000[2001]:5–81, rejects the hypothesis of Germanic influence, largely owing to geolinguistic mismatch; instead, /w-/ > [g^w] was a spontaneous change, competing with /w-/ > [v-], whose spread to some regions took longer than is often supposed (with significant consequences for some etymological dictionaries).

Contrary to accepted wisdom, regular metathesis can be gradual, argues K. J. Wireback, whose three contributions accept that sporadic metathesis can still be sudden, as can its consequential severing of delicate analogical links: 'A gradual approach to sibilant + /j/ metathesis in Hispano-Romance', *La corónica*, 30.1, 2001 : 159–203, 'On the metathesis of labials + /j/', *HR*, 70 : 311–31, and 'Consonant + yod metathesis', *RF*, 114 : 133–59. Also gradual, both phonetically and lexically, was the split of /tj/ and /kj/, according to J. M. Aski, 'Prototype categorization and phonological split', *Diachronica*, 18, 2001[2002] : 205–39, whose cognitive framework is said to improve on Labov's in portraying innovation and propagation.

The seven articles on 'Intonation in Romance' comprising *Probus*, 14.1, ed. J. I. Hualde, though individually monolingual, together offer a thorough and uncommonly consistent coverage of the synchronic intonational structures of Italian, French, Catalan, Spanish, and European Portuguese, within an autosegmental–metrical model. H. also contributes 'Intonation in Spanish and the other Ibero-Romance languages', Wiltshire, *Romance Phonology*, 101–15, concentrating on the imperfect correlation of pitch and stress, especially in contrastive environments. Reviewing major work by Zubizaretta (*YWMLS*, 60 : 22), S. Winkler, and E. Göbbel, 'Focus, p-movement, and the nuclear stress rule', *Linguistics*, 40 : 1185–1242, find much to praise in her analysis of Romance, to which the NSR is clearly applicable, but have more reservations about its suitability for Germanic. Similarly, but with narrower proxies, R. Gutiérrez-Bravo, 'Focus, word order variation and intonation', Wiltshire, *Romance Phonology*, 39–53, argues that the NSR in Spanish dominates the subject constraint, while English has the opposite ranking, gamely concluding — as Optimality allows — that the NSR can be maintained provided it is classed as violable. Commenting on the pioneering work of Trubetzkoy and Jakobson, W. L. Wetzels, 'On the relation between quantity-sensitive stress and distinctive vowel length', *ib.*, 219–34, decides that they had not fully understood that stress assignment might require the recognition of morae, even in languages without long vowels. Finally, on the basis of some troublesome edge phenomena like definite article substitution and *h-aspiré*, B. Tranel and F. Del Gobbo, 'Local conjunction in Italian and French phonology', *ib.*, 191–218, make a novel case for the recognition of {ONSET&NOCODA} as a legitimate 'conjoined constraint' within Optimality — the ultimate in non-adjacency!

5. Morphosyntax and Typology

Nunzio La Fauci, *Forme romanze della funzione predicativa. Teorie, testi, tassonomie*, Pisa, ETS, 2000, 143 pp., develops the theory of predicate twinning through a series of thought-provoking but rather loosely connected essays on auxiliary selection in existential, middle, and passive structures. *Clitics in Phonology, Morphology and Syntax*, ed. Birgit Gerlach and Janet Grijzenhout, Amsterdam, Benjamins, 2000, xii + 441 pp., a collection of papers from a 1999 workshop in Konstanz highlighting the multifaceted and often transitional status of clitics, draws quite extensively on Romance data and includes a good overview by the editors, 'Clitics from different perspectives' (1–29). Richard S. Kayne, *Parameters and Universals*, OUP, 2000, xiv + 369 pp., largely a convenient collection of K.'s recent writing on Romance clitics, auxiliaries, and negation, also contains his more traditional 'Person morphemes and reflexives in Italian, French and related languages' (131–62), proposing that *moi/toi/soi* and congeners are bimorphemic, with {-wa}, but not necessarily {m-, t-, s-}, marking singular. This emphasis on the semiotic value of the morpheme might even placate E. C. García, a seasoned opponent of generative analyses of Romance clitics that end up positing twin or multiple lexical entries for what is patently one morpheme; but this time, it is E. Bonet (*YWMLS*, 57:26) who is in the firing line of G.'s 'Deconstructed morphology vs. constructive syntax', *NMi*, 103:73–101.

In a radical version of his 'Grammaticalization within a theory of morphocentricity', Wischer, *Grammaticalization*, 31–43, J. Klausenburger presents Romance changes as a flight from phonological, syntactic, and lexical characteristics back into the minimal structure of the morphology. A long review article by H.-J. Sasse, 'Recent activity in the theory of aspect', *Linguistic Typology*, 6:199–271, covering work by Bertinetto among others (*YWMLS*, 62:23), praises achievements within morphosyntax but considers that aspectual distinctions in the lexicon and other subsystems have been unjustly neglected. Contrasting Ibero-Romance with French and Italian, G. Hassler, 'Crosslinguistic and diachronic remarks on the grammaticalization of aspect', Wischer, *Grammaticalization*, 163–79, finds that *estar* + gerund periphrases in Spanish are gaining ground over those construed with verbs of motion, which in turn are effectively restricted to modal senses in Italian. Expecting a close link 'Entre l'auxiliaire et le participe passé', *RFP*, 17:11–27, P. Cappeau actually found a rich variety of adverbials attested in the 'wrong' place, in both French and Spanish. In most Romance colligations of 'Verbes et prépositions', *Verbum* (Nancy), 23, 2001[2002]:415–27, E. Castagne finds that the verb has the greater semantic weight, though a few constructions in modern French and more so Italian (notably *andare* + *addosso, attorno, avanti, fuori*) may point to a countervailing trend.

Taking issue with Dardel's analysis (*YWMLS*, 62:17–18), W. Mańczak, 'Origine du parfait fort dans les langues romanes', *KN*, 48, 2001:273–76, avers that D.'s chronononology is wrong and that the strong perfects can be explained by the frequency principle. Careful examination of the histories of QUIUIS/QUILUBET and the suffixes -FER/-GER by H. Rosén, 'Grammaticalization in Latin?' *Glotta*, 76, 2000[2002]:94–112, reveals gradual specialization (in particular of -FER for inanimates and -GER for animates or personifications) but no morphophonemic or semantic attrition that would tempt one to invoke categorial shift. O. Spevak, 'La distribution des morphèmes concessifs en latin tardif', *ib.*, 113–32, finds that LICET is the most frequent and neutral, QUAMLIBET is spontaneous, QUAMUIS is found in philosophy and didactic poetry, while QUAMQUAM and TAMETSI are both by now high-register and archaizing. According to E. Dickey, 'The vocative problems of Latin words ending in -EUS', *ib.*, 32–49, were solved by Probus and have been obscured by modern scholars: all words on the pattern of MEUS are disyllabic throughout (save for the trisyllabic genitive plural) and therefore happily accept MEE as their vocative. A. Elizaincín, 'Port. *Você/Van(n)cê* y *A gente* en perspectiva histórica comparada con el español', *Fest. Lüdtke*, 295–301, considers *a gente* a new grammaticalized pronoun which has largely kept its high register, although one non-standard colligation, in *a gente vamos*, resembles French more than Ibero-Romance. Finally, C. Schapira, 'Un pronom *on* en roumain', *RLiR*, 66:513–22, tracing the spread of *omul*, pertinently asks whether this gives a plausible historical model for Fr. *on*, without recourse to Germanic influence.

6. Generative Syntax

Seven well focused papers from a 1998 Amsterdam colloquium are published as Hulk, *Inversion*, with a lead article by A. Hulk and J.-Y. Pollock, 'Subject positions in Romance and the theory of universal grammar' (3–19), on newer, discoursal approaches to atypical stylistic inversion in French; P. Barbosa, 'On inversion in WH-questions in Romance' (20–59), claiming that embedded questions are bare IPs in Romance but not in Germanic; A. Belletti, '"Inversion" as focalization' (60–90), on VS order largely in Italian; J. Costa, 'Marked versus unmarked inversion' (91–106), on the virtues of an optimality-style analysis with minor re-rankings of constraints; R. S. Kayne and J.-Y. Pollock, 'New thoughts on stylistic inversion' (107–62), seeking to limit the application of SI to a narrow range of constructions; while K. T. Taraldsen, 'Subject extraction, the distribution of expletives and stylistic inversion' (163–82), proposes that SI is the key to all extractions from WH- clauses; and M. L. Zubizaretta, 'The constraint on preverbal subjects in Romance interrogatives' (183–204), offers a minimalist account based on 'the ph-lexicalization of the Q-feature that expresses the force of the sentence'. In addition to left detachment and focus movement, J. Quer, 'Edging quantifiers', *Going Romance 2000*, 253–70, finds a third type of fronting peculiar to Ibero-Romance quantifiers, as in *muitos livros lhe ofreci eu!* Reanalysing critical evidence from clitic doubling in dislocation structures, A. Cardinaletti argues 'Against optional and null clitics', *SL*, 56 : 29–57; what appears to be right dislocation, entailing an optional resumptive clitic, is none other than 'marginalization', when the constituent is defocalized, destressed, and generally relaxed out of existence.

Two items examine the once-popular 'Arb-indexing' and conclude that it has outlived its usefulness: L. Alonso-Ovalle, 'Arbitrary pronouns are not that indefinite', *Going Romance 2000*, 1–14, and R. Aranovich, 'Impersonal constructions, control and second-order predication', *ib.*, 41–55. A. Munn and C. Schmitt, 'Bare nouns and the morphosyntax of number', *LSRL 29*, 225–39, claim that Romance interpretable number, which is not obligatorily specified, can be captured by the Free-Agr parameter. M. T. Guasti and A. Moro, 'Romance causatives and dynamic antisymmetry', *Renzi Vol.*, 173–88, propose to treat the material following the causative as a small clause. An HPSG account of the readings that can be generated from combinations of negative indefinites, like *personne n'a rien fait*, is offered by H. De Swart and I. A. Sag, 'Negation and negative concord in Romance', *LPh*, 25 : 373–417. Some parallels are drawn by F. Benucci between 'Aspect prefixes in verbal periphrases', *Renzi Vol.*, 65–96, such as event-related *re-*, and the emergence of passivizing *si*. E. Torrego, 'Aspects in the prepositional system of Romance', *LSRL 29*, 337–57, seeks to bring together under one parameter the absence of BE/HAVE alternations, clitic doubling, and the marking of accusatives with the dative preposition. J. Rafel, 'Selecting atomic cells from temporal domains', *ib.*, 255–69, neatly tabulates the equivalents of *Juan está corriendo / *a correr / *que corre* as descriptions for events in progress; he finds that among European and Brazilian Portuguese, Spanish, Catalan, and Italian, no two languages have exactly the same pattern of acceptability, leading to the conclusion that parametric feature selection operates here in much the same way as has been attested for nominal domains.

A critique of recent minimalist accounts of Romance, Laura Brugè, *Categorie funzionali del nome nelle lingue romanze*, Milan, Cisalpino, 2000, 320 pp., concentrates on demonstratives within the projection of the noun, and on the marking of accusatives, concluding that Sp. *a* is a case-marker that assigns accusative to the least prominent argument of the verb. Supporting Kayne's analysis of direct objects as independent elements adjoined to functional heads, is C. Tortora, 'Romance enclisis, prepositions and aspect', *NLLT*, 20:725–58, which nonetheless finds challenging data in the little-known Piedmontese variety of Bergomanerese. D. Vermandere achieves 'A unified analysis of French and Italian *en / ne*', *LSRL 29*, 359–73, by underspecifying the categorial features of EN-clitic. Offering a formal minimalist account of the split of ILLE into article and pronoun, G. Giusti, 'The birth of a functional category', *Renzi Vol.*, 157–71, ventures the claim that outcomes of ECCUM-ILLE in certain Italian dialects are recapitulating earlier changes. An incorporation account of the development of possessive pronouns by N. M. Antrim, 'On becoming a clitic', *LSRL 29*, 1–15, neatly shows that the diachronic grouping of Spanish-Italian vs. French has been replaced synchronically by French–Spanish vs. Italian. No doubt parameters have been reset.

7. Discourse and Pragmatics

Seeking a thoroughgoing reappraisal of so-called 'reported speech', which does not always report prior speech or even speech, S. Marnette, 'Aux frontières du discours rapporté', *RevR*, 37:3–30, points to systematic but overlooked distinctions between speech and thought, and between narrative and argumentative sequences. In praise of Construction Grammar, K. Lambrecht, 'Topic, focus and secondary predication', *Going Romance 2000*, 171–212, deals with presentational relatives like *il y a le facteur qui arrive*, more frequent in French than elsewhere in Romance because they address a particular conjunction of word order and focus problems. L. Stage, 'Les modalités épistémique et déontique dans les énoncés au futur', *RevR*, 37:44–66, comparing future tense-form and *devoir* usage in French, Spanish, and Italian, decides that the potential modal readings are quite similar, but in each case can only be actualized in well-delimited pragmatic contexts. Hans-Ingo Radatz's cognitive approach to *Die Semantik der Adjektivstellung* (Beiheft zur *ZRP*, 312), Tübingen, Niemeyer, 2001, xii + 161 pp., concludes that N-Adj is unmarked (74% of his corpus in French, 72% in Spanish, 71% in Portuguese, 70% in Catalan, and 61% in Italian) and that non-rhematic Adj-N, producing a range of stylistic effects, is driven by discoursal not syntactic processes.

Though not specifically comparative, Hellinger, *Gender*, contains three Romance case studies from which quite a coherent picture emerges of intralinguistic change, social and legislative pressures, and their discoursal effects: F. Maurice, 'Deconstructing gender. The case of Romanian' (1, 229–52), G. Marcato and E.-M. Thüne, 'Gender and female visibility in Italian' (2, 187–217), and U. K. Nissen,

'Gender in Spanish. Tradition and innovation' (2, 251–79), this last disappointed by the rate of progress.

8. Lexis

Advancing their concept of proprionyms, Jean-Claude Boulanger and Monique C. Cormier, *Le Nom propre dans l'espace dictionnairique général. Études de métalexicographie*, Tübingen, Niemeyer, 2001, xvi + 214 pp., sketch the route by which proper nouns, usually regarded as meaningless but 'singularizing', acquire related forms and semantic content; contrary to popular belief and sometimes explicit editorial policy, embedded proper nouns like *eau de Javel* have always been well represented in dictionaries. Reflecting on an 11th-c. north-Italian treatise, S. Lazard, 'La structuration du lexique dans le *Vocabularium* de Papias', *RLiR*, 66:221–43, is impressed by P.'s emphasis on multiple networks of derivational and semantic links, which can still serve as an object lesson to lexicologists today. The contrasting distribution and semantics of *mismo* and *mateix* lead M. L. Juge, 'Polysemy patterns in semi-lexical elements in Spanish and Catalan', *StLa*, 26:315–35, to propose a trifold division of the lexicon into lexical, semi-lexical, and grammatical sub-parts. Likewise contrasting frozen adverbials like *à bras ouverts / a braccia aperte* in French and Italian, M. De Gioia, 'Adverbes figés en contraste', *LInv*, 24, 2001[2002]: 183–202, extols the capability of the Lamiroy model to establish semantic equivalence when there is not a perfect morphosyntactic match. The same model, however, works less well for R. Kailuweit, 'Verbes de sentiment "figurés"', *ib.*, 227–43, who finds that L.'s proposal for predicting the metaphorical extensions of polysemous verbs from their reduced syntactic flexibility is much less reliable than separate lexical entries.

Now published are the remaining comprehensive but somewhat dated volumes of *Onomastik. Akten des 18 internationalen Kongresses für Namenforschung, Trier 12–17 April 1993*, ed. Dieter Kremer, Tübingen, Niemeyer (see *YWMLS*, 61:27): I: *Namenetymologie und Namengeschichte*, ed. M. G. Arcamone, xxxiv + 366 pp., V: *Onomastik und Lexikographie. Deonomastik*, ed. J.-P. Chambon and W. Schweickard, viii + 369 pp., and VI: *Namenforschung und Geschichtswissenschaften*, ed. M. Bourin, W. F. Nicolaisen, and W. Seibicke, x + 544 pp. Partly a reappraisal of Vincent's classic *Toponymie* of 1937, J.-P. Chambon, 'Le système latin de dénomination des localités', *RLiR*, 66:119–29, shows that Latin toponyms can be decomposed into a small number of semantic primitives, with 'deanthroponyms', characterized as [+ agricultural, + private, – collective, – urban], privileged above other types.

J. Grzega contributes a theoretical piece, 'Some aspects of modern diachronic onomasiology', *Linguistics*, 40:1021–45, advocating a cognitive approach to motivation, giving due weight to prototypicality, salience, and fuzziness. Grzega, *Romania*, a case study of Celticisms in North Italy and Rhaeto-Romance, distinguishes true Celticisms from dialect relict words, and also in-loco items from 'Wanderwörter'; careful application of his criteria draws a clear isogloss between the northern varieties including the Veneto, and Emilia-Romagna, where Celticisms are less in evidence. In 'Pilgerfahrten and Kreuzzüge als Entlehnungsquelle für Gallizismen', *ZRP*, 118:1–24, C. Glanemann and U. Hoinkes point out that pilgrimages — which sanctioned much travel in the Middle Ages — were a powerful conduit for socio-linguistic exchange; such common words as *viaggio*, *forestiero*, *ostale*, and *lega* reached Italy by this route. Almost a monograph, R. M. Medina Granda, 'Expresiones de valor mínimo y polaridad negativa', *Archivum*, 50–51, 2000–01, 279–362, traces NP items in Old Occitan and neighbouring Romance, finding 82 words capable of acting as negative reinforcers, mostly small objects of little intrinsic worth and usually with some obvious semantic bond to the reported activity.

Max Pfister and Antonio Lupis, *Introduzione all'etimologia romanza*, Soveria Mannelli, Rubbettino, 2001, 342 pp., a revised and extended translation of P.'s 1980 German original, receives a long and often unsympathetic review from F. Toso, *ZRP*, 118:497–503, complaining that the lessons of the *LEI* and other more recent work in etymology have been inadequately learned. A. Peţan, 'Sur les mots latins hérités seulement en roumain', *RLiR*, 66:215–19, documents the gradual erosion of Puşcariu's controversial category as more and better comparative etymologies are published, speculating on whether it might disappear altogether. Converging phonetic and semantic evidence leads F. J. Ledo-Lemos to a novel proposal on 'The etymology of Latin UIRGŌ', *IF*, 107:219–39 — VIR originally meant not 'man' but 'young', so that VIR-G^{W}EN simply meant 'young woman' on the same model as German *Jungfrau*. Lastly comes the most famous of all weasel words: M. Bettini, 'The origin of Latin *mustela*', *Glotta*, 76, 2000[2002]:1–19, acknowledges the formal proximity of MUS, but believes the real etymon is MUSTA, 'fresh, fragrant' and also 'young woman, bride', so anticipating euphemistic replacements such as *belette* in Romance.

In a thorough comparative study, Andreas Gather, *Romanische Verb-Nomen-Komposita. Wortbildung zwischen Lexikon, Morphologie und Syntax* (TBL, 452), x + 245 pp., dwells on the indeterminate status of coinings like *tire-bouchon* / *sacacorchos* / *saca-rolhas* / *llevataps* and the means by which 'lexicalization' is achieved. According to M. Fruyt, the 'Constraints and productivity in Latin nominal compounding', *TPS*, 100:259–87, are unlike those of other Indo-European languages, requiring fairly short words with limited numbers of morphemes, which in turn places strict limits on derivational productivity. The derivational role of Latin SEMI- is investigated by J.-F. Thomas, 'La lexicalisation de l'idée de moitié', *BSLP*, 27:219–44; productive but vague, it contrasted with its more precise counterparts DIMIDIUS/-ATUS and DIMIDIUM, all of which presuppose calculations already completed. Focusing on the improbable derivational morphology of '*Libertas/libertus* et *uestustas/uestustus*', *HSp*, 115:79–89, J.-P. Brachet decides that the nouns are original and ancient, not de-adjectivals using the later -ITAS suffix, though possibly revived and extended in 1st-c. BC debates on slavery and freedom.

Twin articles by N. Grandi, 'Su alcune presunte anomalie della morfologia valutativa', *AGI*, 86, 2001:25–56, and 'I suffissi valutativi tra derivazione e flessione', *ib.*, 129–73, respectively ask why diminutives and augmentatives often change the gender of their base form (because there is a close link between evaluation and animacy), and propose that evaluatives are 'non-prototypical derivations' which should otherwise not be distinguished from the morphological mainstream. G.'s first concern is also investigated by M. Roché, 'Gender inversion in Romance derivatives with *-arius*', *Morphology 2000*, 283–91, who avers that GI is seldom due to noun ellipsis, but rather to a semantic relationship between the base and derivative, usually collection and element or container and thing contained; his statistics for GI in this class of derivatives are arresting — 62% in Portuguese, 72% in French, and 82% in Castilian.

9. Sociolinguistics and Dialectology

Alinei's 'continuity' theory (*YWMLS*, 63:26) courts controversy by making dialectology serve the needs of archaeology at a time depth that traditional dialectologists find inconceivable. A measured critique by I.-X. Adiego, 'Indo-europeïzació al paleolític?', *ER*, 24:7–29, questions the implied excessive immobility of populations and worries about the status of loanwords traditionally reconstructed for IE but unlikely to have existed in the Paleolithic. By contrast, Gilliéron seems very recent, and H. Goebl is anxious to persuade us that this is no illusion: his magnificently presented 'Analyse dialectométrique des structures de profondeur de l'*ALF*', *RLiR*, 66:5–63, explains the digitization of the still rich data of the *ALF* and its formal statistical reinterpretation, which largely vindicates the traditional subgrouping of Gallo-Romance. Welcome detective work by D. Heap, 'Segunda noticia histórica del *ALPI*', *RFE*, 82:5–19, reveals that the 527 missing *cuadernos* of the original investigation, allotted by region to the intending editors, have all been recovered and could be Web-published, even if they do not reach print.

J. Cremona, drawing some macrosociolinguistic parallels between 'Latin and Arabic evolutionary processes', Jones, *Language Change*, 201–07, nonetheless cautions against inferring too much from the contact: there was certainly not a *Sprachbund*, and some matching internal processes seem to have been independent. For the contemporary instance of 'Italienischer Einfluss auf das Maltesische', *Fest. Lüdtke*, 365–73, R. Kontzi finds massive effects on vocabulary but surprisingly little elsewhere. Wary of carving out a permanent disciplinary space between traditional dialectology and modern sociolinguistics, R. Sornicola, 'Sulla dialettologia sociolinguistica', *RLiR*, 66:79–117, draws a parallel with the renewal of history through sociology; eventually, there should just be 'renewed' dialectology. Nevertheless, in future, dialogue between specialists and the lay public will be essential in resolving sociolinguistic problems, according to R. Kailuweit, '"Lingüística lega", un enfoque para tratar la historia de la normativa', *Fest. Lüdtke*, 53–62; Catalan and Galician have both benefited from a considerable lay input that has largely been denied to Spanish, already commodified into a market with its norm and ideology.

H. Aschenberg's harrowing reconstruction of 'Sprachterror. Kommunikation im nationalsozialistischen Konzentrationslager', *ZRP*, 118: 529–72, shows how victims desperately needing access to German, but also multilingual support and identity, created a German–Romance sabir with severe grammatical reduction; she does not explicitly call this pidginization, but the parallels are self-evident. *Creolization and Contact*, ed. Norval Smith and Tonjes Veenstra, Amsterdam, Benjamins, 2001, vi + 323 pp., contains two papers explicitly linking theoretical debates and Romance data: C. Lefebvre, 'Relexification in creole genesis and its effects on the development of the creole' (9–42), on the close but controversial ties between Haitian and Fongbe (*YWMLS*, 60:26); and N. Smith, 'Differential substrate effects in Saramaccan and Haitian' (43–80), which marshalls demographic evidence to show why two creoles with a shared substrate could diverge so markedly — Saramaccan was subject to heavy adstrate influence from Judeo-Portuguese plantation owners in the late 17th c., though this was not sufficient to change its status as an English-lexifier creole. Finally, for readers bemused by some of the arcane debates within creolistics, *ECre* 25.1, ed. A. Valdman, and pithily titled 'La créolisation: à chacun sa vérité', pulls no punches in its confrontation of 'superstratists' with their opponents; V.'s own 'Comment distinguer la créolisation du changement linguistique ordinaire?' (123–41) is a model of sober clarity.

II. FRENCH STUDIES*

LANGUAGE

By Glanville Price,
University of Wales Aberystwyth

1. General and Bibliographical

IG, 94, ed. Anna Jaubert, is a thematic number devoted to 'La langue française au XXe siècle'; it includes B. Laks, 'Description de l'oral et variation: la phonologie et la norme' (5–10), C. Blanche-Benveniste, 'Quel est le rôle du français parlé dans les évolutions syntaxiques?' (11–17), R. Éluerd, 'Pavane pour des vocabulaires défunts. Quelques remarques *fin de siècle* sur la richesse lexicale' (18–21), J.-M. Klinkenberg, 'La légitimation de la variation linguistique' (22–26), L. Rosier, 'La presse et les modalités du discours rapporté: l'effet d'*hyperréalisme* du discours direct surmarqué' (27–32), M. Bonhomme, 'La publicité comme laboratoire du français actuel' (33–38), and four items of primarily literary interest.

D. Naguschewski, 'Zur Bedeutung und Rezeption eines Sprachgesetzes: die *Loi 118 du 2 Thermidor, l'an II de la République française*', *ZRP*, 118:31–46, considers this law to be the second significant legal text relating to the French language, the first being the *Ordonnances de Villers-Cotterêts* of 1539, and both of them as forerunners of a tradition leading to the *loi Toubon* of 1994.

La Langue française au féminin: le sexe et le genre affectent-ils la variation linguistique?, ed. Nigel Armstrong et al., L'Harmattan, 2001, 236 pp., falls into three parts: I, 'Variation phonique', includes C. Bauvois, 'L'assourdissement des sonores finales en français: une distribution sexolectale atypique' (19–36), N. Armstrong, 'Variantes féminines, langue standard et mobilité socio-géographique' (37–52), T. Pooley, 'Les variantes sociolinguistiques féminines: essai de synthèse' (53–73); II, 'Variation discursive', includes S. Bailly, 'Les hommes et les femmes: deux communautés ethno-linguistiques?' (77–100), K. Beeching, 'La fonction de la particule pragmatique *enfin* dans le discours des hommes et des femmes' (101–22), J.-M. Dewaele, 'Stéréotype à l'épreuve: le discours oral des femmes est-il plus émotionnel et déictique que celui des hommes?' (123–47); and III, 'Féminisation', includes M.-M. Gervais, 'Le monde et la féminisation des titres: étude comparative 1997–98' (151–66), J. Lamothe, 'Les

* The place of publication of books is Paris unless otherwise stated.

mots masculins désignent-ils aussi des femmes? Les effets sur la langue de la culture et de la politique au Québec et en Belgique' (167–85), and S. Decamps, 'Faut-il féminiser les termes de profession? L'interprétation des offres d'emploi' (187–204).

**French in and out of France. Language Policies, Intercultural Antagonisms and Dialogue*, ed. Kamal Salhi, Berne, Lang, viii + 487 pp. Zeina el-Tibi, **La Francophonie et le dialogue des cultures*, Lausanne, Âge d'homme, 2001, 192 pp. Bernard Cerquiglini, **Les Langues de la France*, PUF, 368 pp. **Le Français dans tous ses états*, ed. Benoît Peeters et al., Flammarion, 416 pp.

2. History of Grammar and of Linguistic Theory

CFS, 54, 2001, is mainly devoted to the proceedings of two colloquia, each, though ranging more widely than the specific field of French studies, dealing with the thought, work, and influence of an eminent scholar in that field; the *Actes du Colloque international 'Charles Bally'*, 5 et 6 décembre, 1997, 'De la stylistique à la linguistique générale', include R. Amacker, 'Charles Bally juge de la *Grammaire des fautes* d'Henri Frei' (5–20), P. Caussat, 'Charles Bally face à la psychologie allemande de la fin du siècle' (21–42), S. Durer, 'Note sur la politesse selon Charles Bally' (43–60), R. Englier, 'Entre Bally, Spitzer, . . . Saussure' (61–81), C.-A. Forel, 'Une base de données pour servir à la connaissance des inédits de Charles Bally' (83–123), and A.-M. Frýba-Reber, 'La revanche de la stylistique: hommage d'Albert Sechehaye à son prédécesseur et ami Charles Bally' (125–44); the *Actes du colloque international 'Ferdinand de Sausssure et l'interdisciplinarité des sciences du langage'*, 12–13 novembre 1999, include S. Bouquet, 'Linguistique et sémiologie: le projet de Saussure et l'interdisciplinarité' (155–61), C. Normand, 'De quelques effets de la théorie saussurienne sur une description sémantique' (163–75), F. Rastier, 'Du signe aux plans du langage' (177–200), J.-M. Adam, 'Discours et interdisciplinarité. Benveniste lecteur de Saussure' (201–18), C. Stetter, 'Am Ende des Chomsky-Paradigmas — zurück zu Saussure?' (219–67), J. Trabant, 'Signe et articulation. La solution humboldtienne d'un mystère saussurien' (269–88), and L. Jäger, 'Neurosemiologie. Das transdisziplinäre Fundament der saussureschen Sprachidee' (289–337). P. Lauwers writes on 'Forces centripète et centrifuge. Autour du *complément circonstanciel* dans la grammaire "traditionnelle" de la première moitié du XXe siècle', *TrL*, 44:115–42.

3. History of the Language

Mireille Huchon, *Histoire de la langue française*, LGF, 315 pp., is reasonably comprehensive within its limited scope but does not go deeply into anything. Michèle Perret, *Introduction à l'histoire de la langue française*, Armand Colin, 2001, 192 pp., is significantly better.

Most (not quite all) of the items in *Rickard Vol.* are important contributions to scholarship and the volume is a worthy tribute to its honorand. S. Marnette, 'The evolution of reported discourse in medieval French: an overview' (3–34), studies, on the basis of 34 texts representative of different genres, the use of direct discourse and indirect discourse, either of them introduced or not by *que*, and 'free indirect discourse' which incorporates features of direct discourse; C. R. Sneddon, 'Rewriting the *Old French Bible*: the New Testament and evolving reader expectations in the thirteenth and early fourteenth centuries' (35–59), explores the possibility that scribes or their correctors changed their source text to improve its quality, and the implications of this for the concept of a 'Standard Old French'; J.-P. Saint-Gérand, 'Mediæval French, ou, comment le français prit conscience de son histoire à l'époque romantique' (61–91); Y. C. Morin, 'The phonological status of nasal vowels in sixteenth-century French' (95–129), is based on the evidence provided by, inter alia, the writings of J.-A. de Baïf, L. Meigret, H. Rambaud, P. de la Ramée, and by O. de Lanoue's *Dictionnaire des rimes françoises* (1596); R. Sampson, 'A transient vowel in early Modern French: *i nasal*' (131–49), shows that J. Hindret (1687) and L. Dangeau (1694) clearly consider the initial vowel of words in *im-* and *in-* (e.g. *importun, insolent*) to be different from that of *pin, pain, peint*, etc., but that a century later the distinction had gone; C. Schmitt, 'Aspects historiques de la normalisation du système verbal français: le point de vue extra-hexagonal' (151–79), considers that, 'comparées aux grammaires parisiennes', 17th-c. grammars published outside France (and mainly in Germany) are 'moins normatives' and, consequently, 'plus proches de l'usage réel'; M. Wilmet, 'L'accord du *participe passé* avant la grammaire scolaire' (181–93), is a witty and cogent follow-up to his 1999 book (see *YWMLS*, 61:39–40), demonstrating that 'la grammaire scolaire, de servante promue maîtresse, ne supporte plus qu'on ait raison contre elle ou sans elle'; L. Schøsler, 'La variation linguistique: le cas de l'expression du sujet' (195–212), is a *multum in parvo* that one hopes she will find the opportunity to develop further elsewhere; W. Kemp, 'L'introduction et la diffusion de *patrie* en français au seizième siècle' (213–42), offers 'un portrait de ce qui semble être l'intégration progressive de *patrie* dans le vocabulaire français entre les années 1510 et le début des années 1570'; D. Singleton, 'Crosslinguistic operations in the mental lexicon and lexical change' (243–57), generalizes rather too much in seeking to explain the mechanics of lexical change in language contact situations on the basis of one particular situation, namely that in northern Gaul after the 5th-c. Salian Frank invasion; A. Lodge, 'The medieval sources of standardisation in French' (261–96), is a well-documented and well-argued article that tackles the problem of the much contested definition of the term *francien* and distinguishes helpfully between the concepts of koinéization and standardization; in comparison, J. Wüest, 'Marques d'oralité et conventions littéraires dans les anciens textes en français populaire' (297–311), comes across as somewhat light-weight — and there is no more than a passing reference to just one of Lodge's articles and none to his book, *French: from Dialect to Standard*, London, Routledge, 1993 (French translation, *Le Français: histoire d'un dialecte devenu langue*, Fayard, 1997), which, *mea maxima culpa*, escaped mention in *YWMLS*, a lapse for which I make belated and inadequate amends now; D. A. Kibbee, 'Growing pains: territorial expansion and language policy in France from Villers-Cotterêts to the Revolution' (313–28), though claiming to study how French became 'the language of non-Romance speakers living within the French state', deals only with Alsace and Flanders, dismissing Brittany and the *pays basque* in a footnote, on the (in my view inadequate) grounds that official acts were not written in Breton or Basque; in a thought-provoking article, P. Caron, 'Vers la notion de chronolecte? Quelques jalons à propos du français préclassique' (329–52), argues persuasively that the problem of periodization of a language, its division into 'chronolects', is as important as and even more delicate than the problem of defining dialects, with which it has certain analogies; taking as a test case the French of the early 17th c., C. shows that the period 1610–1620 (which, interestingly, precedes the setting up of the Académie française) marks a transition between two chronolects; W. Ayres-Bennett, 'An evolving genre: seventeenth-century *Remarques* and *Observations* on the French language' (353–68), argues, on the basis of 13 volumes of *Remarques* and *Observations* (mainly from the period 1672–93), that the order of presentation, the length of the entries, and the citation of sources became increasingly important and that, in general, the *remarqueurs* orientated their work in relation to that of others and notably to Vaugelas.

4. Texts and Documents

The following contributions to Gärtner, *Skripta*, relate specifically or primarily to French documents: J. Wüest, 'Sind Schreibdialekte phonologisch interpretierbar?' (37–51), M. Selig, 'Überlegungen zur

Erforschung der romanischen Urkundensprachen im Mittelalter' (53–73), H. Völker, 'Die Skriptaforschung als eine Philologie der Varietäten. Zur Negation mit *(ne) . . . nient* in den altfranzösischen Urkunden der Grafen von Luxemburg (1237–1281)' (75–104), A. Monjour, 'Scriptologie et analyse du discours. Éléments textuels caractéristiques dans des chartes médiévales' (147–67), H. Goebl and G. Schilz, 'Der *Atlas des formes et des constructions des chartes françaises du 13e siecle* von Anthonij Dees (1980) — dialektometrisch betrachtet' (169–221), M. Pfister, 'Nordöstliche Skripten im Grenzbereich Germania-Romania vor 1300' (223–44), W. Müller, 'Die Urkundensprache von Fribourg im 14. und 15. Jahrhundert' (245–56), M.-D. Glessgen, 'Das altfranzösische Geschäftsschriftum im Oberlothringen: Quellenanlage und Deutungsansätze' (257–94), M. Pitz, 'Volkssprachige Originalurkunden aus Metzer Archiven bis zum Jahr 1270' (295–392), A. Körner, 'Kontinuität oder Variation? Die Sprache der Luxemburger Grafenurkunden des 13. Jahrhunderts in Original und Kartularabschrift' (393–417), M.-G. Boutier, 'Études sur des chartes luxembourgeoises' (419–47), and G. Holtus and A. Körner, 'Sprachvariation und Sprachwandel *in statu nascendi*. Zur Analyse der Kopialüberlieferung einer altfranzösischen Urkunde (1273) in den "Balduineen"' (449–73).

Textes français privés des XVIIe et XVIIIe siècles, ed. Gerhard Ernst and Barbara Wolf, Tübingen, Niemeyer, 2 CDs, constitutes Beiheft 310 to *ZRP*.

5. Phonetics and Phonology

Douglas C. Walker, **French Sound Structure*, Calgary U.P., 2001, xii + 229 pp. + CD-ROM.

A. B. Hansen, 'Lexical diffusion as a factor of phonetic change: the case of Modern French nasal vowels', *LVC*, 13, 2001 : 209–52, sees the need to revise W. Labov's classification of types of sound change. Y. Ellis, 'Identifying a French-specific laughter particle', *JFLS*, 12 : 263–77, draws attention to 'a voiceless palatal fricative following a word-final high fronted vowel [i]'. I. Racine and F. Grosjean ask 'La production du E caduc facultatif est-elle prévisible?', *ib.*, 307–26 — answer: 'en partie'.

6. Orthography and Acronyms

G. Kremnitz, *Allières Vol.*, 419–25, asks 'Pourquoi les réformes de l'orthographe ont-elles tant de problèmes aujourd'hui?'.

Georges Himelfarb, *Sigles et acronymes*, Belin, 639 pp., is a somewhat unusual but particularly welcome addition to the series 'Le français retrouvé' (see also pp. 28–29 below); listing as it does (on a rough calculation) between 3500 and 4000 items, many of them having multiple applications (*CES*, for example, has seven) and including some that, while not being originally French, are likely to be met with in the French press and elsewhere (e.g. *BBC*, *BMW*, *Goulag*, *SPQR*). It is likely to prove a most useful reference work.

Jean Léance Doneux, **L'Écriture du français, prédictabilité et aléa*, Aix-en-Provence, Univ. de Provence, 200 pp.

7. Grammar

OLD AND MIDDLE FRENCH

G. Ferraresi and M. Goldbach, 'V2 syntax and topicalisation in Old French', *LBer*, 189: 3–25, argue that Old French has more in common with Celtic than with modern Germanic languages. U. Jokinen 'Tout sur *tout*', *Allières Vol.*, 409–17, offers 'réflexions sur *tout* déterminant dans le syntagme nominal en moyen français'.

MODERN FRENCH

Roland Éluerd, **Grammaire descriptive de la langue française*, Nathan, v + 249 pp. Christopher Gledhill, **Fundamentals of French Syntax*, Munich, Lincom Europa, 200 pp. **Syntaxe et sémantique*. 3, *Les Grammaires du français et les mots-outils*, ed. Gudrun Ledegen and Nathalie Rossi-Gensane, Caen U.P., 146 pp.

FM, 70.1, is largely devoted to three articles discussing well-worn topics in some depth without however opening any striking new vistas, viz. C. Molinier, 'Morpho-syntaxe des pronoms interrogatifs et des pronoms relatifs sans antécédent' (3–19), C. Vandeloise, 'La prédication de la matière entre prédicats nominaux et prédicats adjectivaux' (20–44), and V. Lenepveu, 'Adjectifs et adverbes: une corrélation syntactico-sémantique' (45–70). **LaF*, 136, ed. Catherine Schnecker, is devoted to 'L'adjectif sans qualité(s)'. J.-P. Colin studies 'La pluri-antéposition de l'adjectif dans l'oeuvre de Gaston Leroux', *CLe*, 81 : 187–202.

Danielle-Leeman Bouix, **Grammaire du verbe français: des formes au sens: modes, aspects, temps, auxiliaires*, Nathan, 224 pp. A. Abeillé and D. Godard, 'The syntactic structure of French auxiliaries', *Language*, 78: 404–52, is unlikely to be widely consulted by those unfamiliar with the head-driven phrase structure grammar framework within which the authors work.

J. B. Makamina, 'De "subjonctif" à "virtualisatif personnel": essai de dénomination sémantique formelle', *ZRP*, 118: 351–59, draws in particular on the work of G. Guillaume and M. Wilmet.

Les Temps du passé français et leur enseignement, ed. Emmanuelle Labeau and Pierre Larrivée (*Cahiers Chronos*, 9), Amsterdam, Rodopi, 241 pp., includes D. M. Engel, 'Les nouveaux temps du passé?' (1–13), D. L. Rideout, 'L'opposition perfectif/imperfectif dans le passé français' (15–29), M.-E. Ritz, 'The semantics of the *passé composé* in contemporary French: towards a unified representation' (31–50), P. Larrivée, 'Sémantique conceptuelle et sémantique référentielle du passé composé' (51–69), F. Labelle, 'Point de vue et aspect en français et en anglais' (71–89), A. Molendijk, 'La structuration logico-temporelle du texte: le passé composé et l'imparfait du français' (91–104), B. Facques, 'Passé composé, imparfait et présent dans les récits journalistiques: des alternances aux ruptures temporelles' (105–33), and four others which, being concerned with language teaching and language learning, are outside the scope of *YWMLS*. Michaela Krell, **L'Imparfait qui commente. Analyse d'un corpus journalistique*, Vienna, Praesens, 2001, 308 pp.

M. L. Wales, 'The relative frequency of the synthetic and composite futures in the newspaper *Ouest-France* and some observations on distribution', *JFLS*, 12:73–93, finds that the synthetic future is dominant and suggests reasons. I. Evrard, 'Le temps, c'est de l'agent! *Être* + participe passé: structure prédicative et référence aspecto-temporelle', *RLiR*, 66:245–59, compresses too much into the available space. N. Furukawa, 'Construction grammaticale et sous-détermination structurelle: autour de l'emploi attributif du verbe *avoir*', *FM*, 70:129–44, is on the construction *elle a les yeux bleus, elle a son mari malade*. L. Abouda, 'Négation, interrogation et alternance indicatif — subjonctif', *JFLS*, 12:1–22, dealing with the mood in clauses dependent on a 'verbe d'opinion' (*croire*, *douter*, etc.), is a GB-based study.

Jung-Hae Lim, *La Fréquence et son expression en français*, Champion, 261 pp., is an original and penetrating study, analysing the different lexical and grammatical procedures, involving members of various syntactic categories, at the disposal of the language for expressing up to ten different types of repetition. M.-B. Mosegaard Hansen discusses 'La polysémie de l'adverbe *encore*', *TrL*, 44:143–66. Y. Otaka, 'La tournure adverbiale *aussi vrai que*', *Allières Vol.*, 515–25, traces the history of the expression.

TrL, 44, ed. Lucien Kupferman, Eva Katz, and Maria Asnès, continues the publication, under the title 'La préposition', of the proceedings of a colloquium held at Tel Aviv in September, 2000 (see *YWMLS*, 63:38); this third part includes, under the overall heading 'Sémantique et pragmatique de la préposition': P. Cadiot, 'Schémas et motifs en sémantique prépositionnelle: vers une description renouvelée des prépositions dites "spatiales"' (9–24), S. Feigenbaum,

'Le rapport entre *selon* et *suivant*' (25–34), E. Katz, 'Systématique de la triade spatiale *à*, *en*, *dans*' (35–49), D. Paillard, 'Prépositions et rection verbale' (51–67), M. Pierrard, '*Comme* préposition? Observations sur le statut catégoriel des prépositions et des conjonctions' (69–78), L. Rosier, '*Genre*: le nuancier de sa grammaticalisation' (79–88), C. Schapira, 'Préposition et conjonction? Le cas de *avec*' (89–100), and C. Schnedecker, 'A propos des emplois régis d'*avec*' (101–13). P.-A. Buvet, 'Analyse de compléments du nom en termes de classes d'objets', *FM*, 70: 187–29, modestly claims to do no more than 'esquisser ce que serait une analyse exhaustive des suites *DET Na de DET Nb* du point de vue des classes d'objets'. M. Aurnague and D. Stosic discuss 'La préposition *par* et l'expression du déplacement', *CLe*, 81: 113–39.

Aidan Coveney, *Variability in Spoken French; A Sociolinguistic Study of Interrogation and Negation* (see *YWMLS*, 58: 36), is reissued, Bristol–Portland, OR, Elm Bank, vi + 296 pp., with, as a supplement, 'A critical survey of recent research on grammatical variability, negation and interrogation in French' (pp. 272–96). N. Armstrong and A. Smith discuss 'The influence of linguistic and social factors on the recent decline of French *ne*', *JFLS*, 12: 23–41, on the basis of radio corpora dating from 1973 and 1997 respectively. S. Marnette, 'Aux frontières du discours rapporté', *RevR*, 37: 3–30, deals, in relation to spoken French, with aspects of the definition of reported speech.

8. Lexicography

Jean Pruvost, *Les Dictionnaires de langue française* (Que sais-je?, 3622), PUF, 127 pp., gives both a historical and a typological survey, together with a chronological listing, from 1502 (A. Calepino's *Dictionarum*) to 2000, of over 400 dictionaries, including 14 online dictionaries.

The Tobler-Lommatzsch *Altfranzösisches Wörterbuch*, which began publication in 1915, is at last complete with the appearance of fascicle 96, Wiesbaden, Steiner, cols 769–938, which proclaims itself, doubtless with relief, to be the 'fünfte und letzte Lieferung des XI. Bandes', and covers VONJEMENT—ZURE. It is also available both on *DVD (ISBN 3–515–08199–2) and on *four CDs (3–515–08176–4), both edited by Peter Blumenthal and Achim Stein, Stuttgart, Steiner. W. Rothwell, 'The semantic field of Old French *Astele*: the pitfalls of the medieval gloss in lexicography', *JFLS*, 12: 203–20, takes a few well-aimed sideswipes at *TL* in particular. Meanwhile, vol. 'H' of Kurt Baldinger's *Dictionnaire étymologique de l'ancien français* is completed with *Index H*, prepared by Sabine Tittel, Tübingen, Niemeyer, 2000, vii + 136 pp. H. Goebl presents an 'Analyse dialectométrique des structures de profondeur de l'*ALF*', *RLiR*, 66:5–63. *CLe*, 79, 2001, includes M. C. Cormier, 'Abel Boyer, lexicographe. Genèse d'une oeuvre' (95–42), on the two-way French and English *Royal Dictionary* (London, 1699), and F. Gaudin, 'Lettres à André Clas à propos du *Nouveau dictionnaire universel* de Maurice Lachâtre' (43–54), publishing two letters from F. G. to A. C. on a 19th-c. French lexicographer.

Jacqueline Picoche and Jean-Claude Rolland, *Dictionnaire du français usuel: 15 000 mots utiles en 442 articles*, Brussels, De Boeck–Duculot, 1064 pp., is, as the authors say, not 'un dictionnaire comme les autres'; defining *usuel* by what it is not, they inform us that the term excludes in general such categories (among others) as regionalisms, specialized technical terms, archaisms, and neologisms, though some learned, colloquial, argot, and technical terms are admitted (and are marked as such) when they can be considered to be in widespread use; pronouns, articles, conjunctions, and most prepositions are also excluded; more positively, they aim to present 'un trésor de mots relativement modeste permettant à tous les francophones de communiquer aisément à travers le monde'; the coverage is, in consequence, limited to some 15,000 words, as compared with some 70,000 in Littré and some 50,000 in the *Petit Robert*; the choice of words for inclusion is based primarily on the *Dictionnaire de fréquences du Trésor de la Langue Française*; there are not, however, 15,000 entries but a mere 442, this being achieved by grouping together semantically related words in a single article: the article 'pierre', for example, includes (among many others) the words *minéral*, *rocher*, *caillou*, *gravier*, *sable*, *émeraude*, *fossile*, *pétrole*, *écueil*, *carrière*, *paléolithique*, *menhir*, *lapider*, *stèle*, *monolithique*, and *lithographe* — these and other words not themselves headwords are all listed in an index; despite the authors' view that this is 'un dictionnaire d'apprentissage plutôt qu'un dictionnaire de consultation', it seems to be eminently 'un dictionnaire de consultation'; it is likely, however, that even greater consultation will be made of the admirably devised CD version, which is available either as an accompaniment to the printed version or separately; all in all, this is, in both its forms, an excellent reference work on which the authors and publishers are to be congratulated.

Jacqueline Picoche, **Dictionnaire étymologique du français*, new edn, Le Robert, xiii + 739 pp. J. Schön, 'Pour un traitement systématique des acceptions *familières* dans les dictionnaires', *Allières Vol.*, 605–15, looks at four dictionaries of modern French. *CLe*, 78, 2000, includes D. Candel, 'De l'usage des dictionnaires de spécialité. (Une enquête 1985–2000)' (81–98), and J. Picoche, 'L'outillage lexical' (127–38), explaining the methodology of her *Dictionnaire du français usuel* (see above). *CLe*, 81, includes M. Mathieu-Colas, 'La représentation des verbes dans un dictionnaire électronique. De la langue générale aux langues spécialisées' (51–67), and M. Kramer, '*Jarnac* et *bilboquet*: deux curiosités lexicographiques vues à travers des attestations textuelles' (69–82).

9. Lexicology

**LaF*, 133, ed. Jean-Jacques Franckel, is devoted to 'Le lexique, entre identité et variation'. Despite its title, *Cahiers de lexicologie* has recently been including a number of articles that seem to be well outside the scope of this section of *YWMLS* (but see also under 'Grammar: Modern French', 'Lexicography' and 'French in Canada') and, indeed, in some cases outside the field of *YWMLS*. Relatively few contributions to the last four issues are directly relevant to this subsection, and some of those that are relevant are of only minor importance; of direct relevance to this subsection, no. 78, 2000, includes only A. Clas, '*Abelle* et *Rose-Épine!* Mots-valises et méronymie' (99–106), on the importance of lexical creativity in the form of portmanteau words, specifically in the field of chemistry, and no. 79, 2001, only M. Pires, 'Les abréviations des titres de civilité en français. Prescriptions et usages' (85–111); no. 80, subtitled *L'Espace lexical: d'hier à aujourd'hui. Hommage à André Clas*, ed. M. C. Cormier, includes R. Goffin, 'L'eurolecte. Analyse contrastive de quinze eurolexies néologiques' (167–78) (the contrasted languages being English and German), G. Gross and F. Guenthner, 'Comment décrire une langue de spécialité' (179–99), and S. Mejri, 'Le figement lexical; nouvelles tendances' (213–25); no. 81 includes F. Gobert, 'La dénomination *étymologie populaire* ou l'utopie d'une terminologie non ambigüe' (5–37), and O. Anokhina, 'Sur le mécanisme de référence des noms abstraits' (39–49).

New additions to the series 'Le français retrouvé' (see *YWMLS*, 63:40 and also pp. 23–24 above) include two particularly substantial volumes: Christophe Hardy, *Les Mots de la mer*, Belin, 623 pp., ranges widely, including not only terms in widespread use and standard technical terms but also others that are characteristic particularly of the informal speech of sea-going folk (e.g. *(faire) capsaille* 'chavirer', *gargouillou* 'aide-cuisinier', *sinago(t)* 'chaloupe traditionnelle du golfe de Morbihan', to quote only three that are not in the *Petit Larousse*); most entries provide explanatory and/or etymological notes and many include also examples from literary texts; Alain (Georges) Leduc, *Les Mots de la peinture*, Belin, 622 pp., has fewer entries than *Les Mots de la mer* but many take the form of extended essays running to a page or more and occasionally (as in the case, for example, of such entries as *art*, *école*, *peinture*) to several pages; entries range from such wide-ranging studies as these to highly technical terms such as *Blauer Reiter*, *cut-up*, *feuilliste*, *maginois*, *zinzolin*.

Pierre Merle, **Précis de français précieux au XXIe siècle*, Tournai, Renaissance du livre, 176 pp.

L'Extension du féminin: les incertitudes de la langue, ed. Marie-Jo Mathieu, Champion, 142 pp., derives ultimately from a Prime Ministerial request for 'un rapport sur les conditions linguistiques de la féminisation des noms de métiers'; they fall under different subheadings of this survey but, for convenience, are grouped together here: A.-M. Houdebine-Gravaud, 'Différenciations sexuelles dans les langues et identification sociale des femmes ou de la féminisation des noms de métiers' (13–23), E. Khaznadar, 'Métalangage du genre: un flou artistique' (25–44), N. Cholewka, 'Féminin et familier' (45–58), M. Yaguello, 'Le féminin comme catégorie biologique, sociale et grammaticale: étude comparée du français et de l'anglais' (59–67), M. Coutier, 'Le féminin des noms de personne en *-(t)eur*: résistances et concurrences' (69–93), and M.-J. Mathieu, 'Le féminin n'est pas neutre' (95–126). N. Brick and C. Wilks, 'Les partis politiques et la féminisation des noms de métier', *JFLS*, 12:45–53, identify a sharp division between 'les partis qui reconnaissent la notion de langue discriminatoire' and those that do not. M. Camprubi, 'Vous avez dit exception? Le genre de certaines dénominations', *Allières Vol.*, 345–50, discusses the gender of names such as *la Caravelle*, *le Concorde*.

Anne Schlömer, **Phraseologische Wortpaare im Französischen: 'sitôt dit, sitôt fait' und Vergleichbares*, Tübingen, Niemeyer, xi + 193 pp.

G. M. Cropp, '*Le Char saint Martin*: désignation de la Grande Ourse', *ZRP*, 118:173–81, studies a rarely attested 14th-c. term. W. Hasenkamp discusses 'Fr. *étymologie populaire* "Volksetymologie" und seine Terminusgeschichte', *ib.*, 587–92. Denis Apothéloz, **La Construction du lexique français: principes et morphologie dérivationnelle*, Gap, Ophrys, iii + 164 pp. M. Roché, *Allières Vol.*, 561–72, finds multiple origins for the suffix *-ouille(r)*.

10. Semantics

TrL, 45, 'La notion d'invariant sémantique', ed. Pierre Larrivée, includes: J. Lamarche, 'Invariance et contingence' (15–44), which takes *être* and *aller* as illustrative examples for detailed analysis; P. Péroz, 'Régularités de la variation sémantique du verbe *lutter*' (45–66); P. Larrivée, 'Invariants sémantiques et constructions syntaxiques' (67–82), concludes that 'la notion d'unité linguistique repose sur celle de stabilité dans le rapport entre sens et forme'; B. Peeters, 'La *Métalangue sémantique naturelle* au service de l'étude du transculturel' (83–101), contrasts features of French and of Australian

English; D. Philps, 'Le concept de marqueur sub-lexical et la notion d'invariant sémantique' (103–23), is mainly on English; C. Rittaud-Hutinet, 'L'invariant en prosodie: la question orale' (125–56), includes a critical survey of work on French intonation in the period 1992–2001; E. Labeau, 'L'unité de l'imparfait: vues théoriques et perspectives pour les apprenants du français, langue étrangère' (157–84).

11. Onomastics

**La Toponymie urbaine: significations et enjeux*, ed. Jean-Claude Bouvier and Jean-Marie Guillon, L'Harmattan, 2001, 254 pp. J.-P. Chambon, 'Sur le système latin de dénomination des localités (toponymie de la Gaule)', *RLiR*, 66: 119–29, proposes a different typology from that provided by A. Vincent's *Toponymie de la France* (Brussels, 1937, and considered by C. to be 'le manuel de toponymie française le plus sûr'). Alain Noël, *Les Lieux-dits. Essai d'archéologie verbale. La forêt d'Othe à l'âge moderne*, Champion, 316 pp., is a strikingly original and informative study of the information to be derived from a thorough and pluridimensional survey of the place-names of a given locality; the area covered (east of the Yonne between Joigny and Sens) is inevitably restricted but this work could well serve as a model for similar studies of other areas (and not only in France).

Pierre-Gabriel Gonzalez, **Grand dictionnaire des noms de famille*, Ambre, 2001, 504 pp. M. Pitz offers 'Nouvelles données pour l'anthroponymie de la Galloromania: les toponymes mérovingiens du type *(A)vricourt*', *RLiR*, 66: 421–49. Frank Paulikat, **Eigennamen in Pressetexten. Studien su Formen und Funktionen des Eigennamengebrauchs in der französischen Pressesprache* (EH, 21: 230), 2001, xii + 252 pp.

12. Dialects and Regional French

**French Accents: Phonological and Sociolinguistic Perspectives*, ed. Marie-Anne Hintze, Tim Pooley, and Anne Judge, London, AFLS–CILT, 2001, 345 pp. J. Lechanteur, *Allières Vol.*, 437–45, discusses 'La *mouche* d'un fruit: un belgisme méconnu'. Alain Dawson, **Le Chtimi de poche (parler du Nord et du Pas-de-Calais)*, Assimil, x + 182 pp. Offering evidence from word-initial vowel epenthesis in Vimeu Picard, J. Auger discusses 'Phonological variation and optimality theory', *LVC*, 13, 2001: 253–303, while W. Cardoso gives an 'Optimality theoretical account' of 'Variation patterns in across-word regressive assimilation', *ib.*, 305–41. D. Hornsby, 'Dialect contact and konéization: the case of northern France', Jones, *Language Change*, 19–28, contrasts the interplay of extra-linguistic factors and internal processes of linguistic change in Avion (Pas-de-Calais) with a contact situation in northern Sweden. T. Pooley discusses 'The depicardization of the vernaculars of the Lille conurbation', *ib.*, 29–62. Leon Zeliqzon, **Dictionnaire des parlers romans de la Moselle*, Woippy, Serpenoise, 835 pp.

Pierrette Dubuisson and Marcel Bonin, *Le Parler du Berry et du Bourbonnais: dictionnaire du français régional*, Bonneton, 142 pp., is a 2nd edn, 'revue et corrigée', of a work first published in 1993 (see *YWMLS*, 55 : 62–63). Frantz Brunet, **Dictionnaire du parler bourbonnais et des régions voisines*, Clermont-Ferrand, De Borée, l + 258 pp. Colette Dondaine, *Trésor étymologique des mots de la Franche-Comté*, Strasbourg, SLR, xvi + 581 pp., is the first volume in a new series, 'Bibliothèque de linguistique romane', to be published by the SLR; it itemizes in dictionary form, with references to the *FEW* and the *GPSR*, 'la quasi-totalité des formes dialectales' contained in the 1220 maps of the *Atlas linguistique et ethnographique de la Franche-Comté*.

A. Borrell, *Allières Vol.*, 337–44, wonders why the nasal vowel of *bon*, etc., is less open in Paris than in Toulouse.

13. Channel Islands French

M. C. Jones, 'Mette a haout dauve la grippe des Angllaïs: convergence on the island of Guernsey', Jones, *Language Change*, 143–68, concludes that Guernésiais and the English spoken on the island 'display a high degree of isomorphism' and argues that this is to be explained by a period of convergence before the linguistic situation was drastically changed to the detriment of Guernésiais by the evacuation of most of the island's children during the Second World War.

14. French in Canada

L. Beaulieu and P. Balcom, 'La structure des propositions adverbiales du français: arguments sociolinguistiques', *JFLS*, 12 : 241–62, is on the French of north-eastern New Brunswick. M. Starets, 'The complementizer C with the WH-word *quo* in a Franco-Ontarian vernacular of south-western Ontario', *ib.*, 55–71, is a thoroughgoing analysis of a feature that is unlikely to be of interest to a wide readership. G. Dostie, 'L'exemplarité de *par exemple*. Un cas de pragmaticalisation en français québécois', *ib.*, 149–67, deals with a discourse marker whose use differs significantly from that which it has in standard French.

A. Farina, 'Féminisme et dictionnaires québécois: des femmes reconstruites dans des définitions politiquement correctes', *FM*,

70:79, looks at three dictionaries, while L. Mercier and C. Verreault, 'Opposer français "standard" et français québécois pour mieux se comprendre entre francophones?', *ib.*, 87–108, express serious reservations about Lionel Meney's *Dictionnaire québécois français* (Montreal, Guérin, 1999, xxxiv + 1884 pp.). *CLe*, 80, includes C. Poirier and G. Saint-Yves, 'La lexicographie du français canadien de 1860 à 1930: les conséquences d'un mythe' (55–76), and J. Bossé-Andrieu and R. P. Roberts, 'Le *Dictionnaire canadien bilingue*: reflet d'une culture en évolution' (77–88). M. Drescher, '*Eh tabarnouche! c'était bon.* Für eine kommunikative Sicht frankokanadianischer Flüche', *ZFSL*, 112:4–25, studies religious oaths in Quebec French.

15. French in Africa and Asia

Le Français en Algérie; lexique et dynamique des langues, ed. Ambroise Queffélec et al. (Champs linguistiques), Louvain-la-Neuve, Duculot, 590 pp., which derives from a wider research project into the spoken and written French of the Maghreb, falls into two clearly differentiated parts; I, 'Sociolinguistique de l'Algérie' (9–141), primarily due to Yacine Derradji, covers *inter alia* the historical and cultural background to the present situation in Algeria, the coexistence of various languages (principally, of course, Berber, Arabic, and French), linguistic policy in Algeria since independence, the official status of French and its role in education, the media, and public life generally, and includes also a chapter on the typological characteristics of Algerian French; II, 'Inventaire lexical' (143–560), itemizes, with definitions and a commendable wealth of examples, some 1500 Algerianisms, the great majority of them of Arabic origin but also including specialized derivatives or uses of French words (e.g. *blondiste* 'personne qui fume des cigarettes blondes', *permaniser* 'titulariser dans un poste de travail'). K. Ploog, **Le Français à Abidjan: pour une approche syntaxique du non-standard*, CNRS, 384 pp. Christian Seignobos and Henry Tourneux, **Le Nord-Cameroun à travers ses mots*, Karthala, 334 pp. *La Culture francophone en Israël*, ed. David Mendelson, L'Harmattan, 2 vols, 351 + 337 pp.

16. Registers

Choix de textes du français parlé: 36 extraits, ed. Claire Blanche-Benveniste, Christine Rouget, and Frédéric Sabio, Champion, 224 pp. + 1 CD, includes interviews with or role-plays by children, accounts of their work by a range of manual and professional workers and others, a selection of *récits* (accounts of a road accident, of *la chasse au sanglier*, of an encounter with a dodgy car-repairer, wartime memories, etc.), and miscellaneous *témoignages*; this is a book that is likely to have a multiplicity of uses. Christina Lindqvist, **Corpus transcrit de quelques journaux télévisés français*, Uppsala U.P., 2001, 289 pp. L. Oakes, 'Phonostylistique des annonceurs de la radio', *JFLS*, 12:279–306, is an 'étude prosodique de textes radiophoniques'.

La Linguistique, 38.1, devoted to 'Argots et argotologie', includes J.-P. Goudaillier, 'De l'argot traditionnel au français contemporain des cités' (5–23), M. Sourdot, 'L'argotologie: entre forme et fonction' (25–39), E. Logier, 'Quelles approches théoriques pour la description du français parlé par les jeunes des cités?' (41–52), B. Turpin, 'Le jargon, figure du multiple' (53–68), M. Ayzanneau, M. Bento, and V. Fayolle, 'De la diversité lexicale dans le rap au Gabon et au Sénegal' (69–98), and A. Sokolija, 'Étude comparative des argots de Sarajevo et de Paris, aspects méthodologiques' (99–112). Alice Becker-Ho, **Du jargon héritier en Bastardie*, Gallimard, 168 pp. Aurélie Dejond, **La Cyberlangue française*, Brussels, Renaissance du livre, 250 pp. Pierre Perret, **Le Parler des métiers: dictionnaire thématique alphabétique*, Laffont, 1100 pp.

17. Discourse Analysis and Pragmatics

Anne Grobet, *L'Identification des topiques dans les dialogues* (Champs linguistiques), Louvain-la-Neuve, Duculot, 422 pp., is a deeply thoughtful work devoted specifically only to French but whose theoretical basis, methodology, and conclusions are of much wider applicability. A lengthy first part, consisting of a critical survey of earlier relevant work (much of it by British or American scholars) and a detailed statement of working hypotheses, leads to a penetrating analysis of linguistic (lexical and syntactic) and discursive factors in the identification of the topic, the interrelationship between the two being the subject of the final part. Kate Beeching, **Gender, Politeness and Pragmatic Particles in French*, Amsterdam, Benjamins, 240 pp. J. van Baardewijk-Rességuier, 'Analyse polyphonique de *bien*, marqueur du discours', *JFLS*, 12:327–48, distinguishes between '*bien*, marqueur du discours' and '*bien*, adverbe de manière ou d'intensité'.

Isabel González Rey, **La Phraséologie du français*, Toulouse, Mirail U.P., 267 pp.

Danielle Bouvet and Mary-Annick Morel, **Le Ballet et la musique de la parole: le geste et l'intonation dans le dialogue oral en français*, Gap, Ophrys, 135 pp.

18. Contrastive Studies

Raija Solatie, **Étude contrastive sur l'impersonnel en allemand et en français*, Vienna, Braumüller, 2001, 150 pp. P. Frath, 'Étude du verbe *commencer* en contexte', *JFLS*, 12:169–80, proposes a semiotic analysis of *commencer* and of *to begin* with a direct object. P. Blumenthal, 'Profil combinatoire des noms. Synonymie distinctive et analyse contrastive', *ZFSL*, 112:115–38, contrasts German *Angst/Furcht* and French *peur/crainte* and generalizes therefrom.

EARLY MEDIEVAL LITERATURE

By Sara I. James, *University of Hull*, and
Adrian P. Tudor, *University of Hull*

I. General

Corpus de la littérature médiévale en langue d'oïl des origines à la fin du XVe siècle: Prose narrative — Poésie — Théâtre, Champion, 2001, is a CD-ROM containing over 500 complete texts in OF. Editions are drawn from Champion, Droz, SATF, and others and are divided into the following sections: i. Œuvres narratives de fiction; ii. Chansons de geste; iii. Poésie; iv. Théâtre. There are complex search functions — words, contexts, author, title, date, editor, etc. — and a user-friendly passage from one genre, work, author, edition, version, or text to another. This CD-ROM makes a wealth of materials easily accessible and offers a solution to those in need of an instant and comprehensive library of OF texts.

Dictionnaire du Moyen Age, ed. Claude Gauvard, Alain de Libera, and Michel Zink, Quadrige–PUF, li + 1548 pp., is a comprehensive yet accessible reference work covering all aspects of medieval life and work: authors, texts, genres, events, concepts and beliefs, rites and rituals, objects, places, arts, social structures, philosophy, and science. It includes French, English, German, and Arabic material, and handily provides an index of cross-references.

Sarah Kay, *Courtly Contradictions: The Emergence of the Literary Object in the Twelfth Century* (Figurae: Reading Medieval Culture), Stanford U.P., 2001, xii + 380 pp., is a challenging and rewarding study of the development of courtly literature in the 12th century. K. studies what has primarily been seen as an historical problem from a theoretical viewpoint, arguing that contradiction is central to the makeup of courtly literature, to the intellectual environment which gave rise to it, and to its modern critical reception. She asks what it is about the courtly text which makes it foster contradiction and wonders why contradictory texts continue to influence the subjectivities of modern readers. The introduction explains the role and place of contradiction in medieval and psychoanalytical thought, but often difficult theoretical frameworks, in particular those of Lacan and Kristeva, are also defined throughout the book. Romance — *romans antiques*, Chrétien, Marie de France, *Partonopeus de Blois* — is central to K.'s study, but she equally examines in detail the roles of hagiography and lyric in the generation of what we call 'courtly literature'. The book concludes with the suggestion that the historical importance of courtly literature lies in its capacity to mediate the transfer from medieval to modern structures of thought, thereby shaping modern forms of enjoyment.

J. A. Burrow, *Gestures and Looks in Medieval Narrative*, CUP, xi + 200 pp., studies Chrétien, the prose *Lancelot*, Froissart, Machaut, *La Queste del Saint Graal*, *Eneas*, and *Le Roman de la Rose* alongside *Troilus and Criseyde*, *Sir Gawain and the Green Knight*, Malory's *Morte D'Arthur*, Boccaccio, and Dante. B. argues that since non-verbal signs are in general less subject to change than words, many of the behaviours recorded in these texts, such as pointing and amorous gazing, are familiar in themselves; yet many prove easy to misread, either because they are no longer common, like bowing, or because their use has changed, like winking.

Keith Busby, *Codex and Context: Reading Old French Verse Narrative in Manuscript* (Faux Titre, 221–222), 2 vols, Amsterdam–NY, Rodopi, xii + 484, 485–941 pp., represents a major contribution to our understanding of medieval literature, its textuality and reception, and is likely to become essential reading for scholars of all genres of the early period. B. insists that the alterity of medieval literature is largely due to its preservation and transmission in MS form — our best and only means of contact with medieval textual reality — and that this alterity should be both stressed and extolled. B. limits his study to 12th- and 13th-c. verse narratives and, with the exceptions of the *Vie des pères* and Gautier de Coinci, mainly to secular texts. He begins by considering the practical ramifications of manufacture and sale and then studies, with reference in particular to *fabliaux*, Chrétien, *Rigomer*, *Renart*, the crusade cycle, and the Alexander romances, the many ways in which scribal behaviour, page layout, and the interaction between text and image can manipulate reader response. Reading in sequence in collections or cyclical MSS, the 'geography of the codex', and the evidence of ownership are examined in the second volume. Much of B.'s work is ground-breaking with regard to vernacular literature and he asks a number of fundamental questions concerning not only how medieval texts were produced and consumed, but also how we should read them today. Posing rather similar questions, Andrew Taylor, *Textual Situations: Three Medieval Manuscripts and Their Readers*, Philadelphia, Pennsylvania U.P., 300 pp., focuses on Bodleian MS Digby 23 (*La Chanson de Roland* being its most famous text), British Library MS Harley 978 (Marie de France's *lais* and *fables*) and British Library MS Royal 10.E.4 (Latin texts). T. claims that previous editorial work on these texts 'has been conducted with [. . .] comprehensive disregard for [their] manuscripts' and seeks to re-establish the textual context of these works, including the history of their medieval ownership and readers. With reference to the (highly emotional) discovery of Digby 23 and the *Roland*, T. (quoting

Francisque Michel's correspondence in English translation for some reason) queries the objectivity of many of the contemporary and subsequent assessments of the MS. However, he concludes, they are no more 'wishful thinking' than that indulged in by the original scribes, whose work he perceives as suffused with nostalgic longing for an idealized past. P. Ménard, 'Réflexions sur l'édition du texte', *SMV*, 48 : 3–32, provides a valuable overview of editorial approaches to and debates about the edition of late prose works, *fabliaux* and travel writing. M. insists on the value of addressing the practical over the theoretical and strongly questions the usefulness of current electronic tools and editions.

Jacques Ribard, *Symbolisme et Christianisme dans la littérature médiévale* (Essais sur le Moyen Age, 25), Champion, 2001, 308 pp., is a characteristically rich and provocative collection of 24 essays in which R. applies the critical approach he has long since championed; namely, the symbolic interpretation of texts where, between the lines, a deliberately religious tone can be identified. The essays, most of which have been published elsewhere quite recently, are grouped into six sections: 'Orientations générales'; 'Les romans de Tristan'; 'Les *Lais* de Marie de France'; 'Les romans de Chrétien de Troyes'; 'Les oeuvres romanesques du XIIIème siècle'; 'Les poésies de François Villon'.

David Coward, *A History of French Literature: From 'Chanson de Geste' to Cinema*, Oxford, Blackwell, xxviii + 606 pp., includes a first chapter on medieval literature that, although brief (perhaps destined for undergraduates?), is relatively comprehensive in scope and appropriate detail. Francis Gingras, *Erotisme et merveilles dans le récit français des XIIe et XIIIe siècles* (Nouvelle Bibliothèque du Moyen Age, 63), Champion, 524 pp., is an admirably comprehensive work on two key themes of OF literature. G. establishes five driving forces in the literary conjunction of the magical with love: transformation of literary types; folkloric elements; *lieux communs* in the spatial and literary senses; adaptation of great themes; and reaffirmation of a new esthetic and new ethics within vernacular literature. According to G., the development of the hero signifies a move away from the 'je' of the *grand chant courtois* towards a more complex exploration of relationships. This is a broad and coherent study of the strange, otherworldly and frankly Other within the context of another dauntingly broad literary theme, love.

Armand Strubel, *'Grant senefiance a': allégorie et littérature au Moyen Age* (Moyen Age: Outils de Synthèse, 3), Champion, 464 pp., is an equally ambitious work, covering works from the Classical period through to the 15th century. A significant part of this study focuses on medieval Latin works and their philosophical underpinnings, before moving on to vernacular works, of which the *Roman de la rose* is the most lengthily discussed. The bibliography is thematically organized, preceded by a four-page outline of the bibliography that mirrors to some extent the content of the book. The index combines all entries and, with a rather unusual listing convention for proper names, could initially confuse some readers.

Lynne Tarte Ramey's *Christian, Saracen and Genre in Medieval French Literature* (Medieval History and Culture, 3), NY, Routledge, 2001, xiv + 120 pp., examines the topic of French identity and self as depicted by 'interethnic' (French/Saracen) couples, whether lovers or friends, opposite- or same-sex. This focus, and the rather small corpus of works studied (11 *chansons de geste*, *Aucassin et Nicolette*, and travel literature), narrows down a topic that would otherwise be far too broad and unwieldy for one slim volume. R. admirably covers both the variety and complexity of the 'types' under examination, 'types' that have far too often suffered from a broad-brushstroke approach.

L. Harf-Lancner, 'Les malheurs des intellectuels à la cour: les clercs curiaux d'Henri II Plantagenêt', *ICLS 10*, 3–18, detects in the entourage of Henry II a conflict between the cleric and the court, which, she argues, is too radical to be harmonized. This conflict, which traditionally finds expression in court satire, will run like a thread throughout the entire Middle Ages.

K. Kong, 'Guilty as charged? Subjectivity and the law in *La Chanson de Roland* and *Lanval*', *EMS*, 17, 2001 : 35–46, examines the trial scenes of Ganelon and Lanval in order to explore the definitions of, respectively, 'traitor' and 'felon', their identities in relation to a society structured by sovereign rule, and their literary representations. Both characters demonstrate what K. calls 'culpable subjectivity': they defend themselves using self-interest and individual position, concepts at odds with the collective identity and justice that has accused them. R. L. Krueger, 'Beyond debate: gender in play in old French courtly fiction', Fenster, *Gender*, 79–96, proposes that OF literature (Marie de France's *Lais*, *Aucassin et Nicolette* and *Le Roman de Silence*) provided a context in which social constructs and assumptions about gender and gender roles could be questioned or criticized.

2. Epic

ROLAND AND CHARLEMAGNE. Marianne J. Ailes, *The Song of Roland — On Absolutes and Relative Values* (Studies in Mediaeval Literature, 20), Lampeter, Mellen, vi + 177 pp., is a work examining religious and ethical values as expressed specifically within the *Roland*. In immmersing the discussion fully within the 12th-c. Christian context, and providing extremely close readings of the text, A. brings out both the complexity of the characters and, by extension, the full impact of their conflicts, choices, and consequences. This is a strong and detailed study that seeks to provide definitions of concepts such as tragedy, justice, and love, so as to help modern audiences understand the *Roland* on its own terms and appreciate its original resonance. She has also produced '*Fierabras* and the *Chanson de Roland*: an intertextual diptych', *RMS*, 18:3–22, which explores the possibility of humorous aspects to the portrayals of Ganelon and Roland; and 'Ganelon in the middle English *Fierabras* romances', Hardman, *Identity*, 73–85, which quotes extensively from both the *Chanson de Roland* and the OF *Fierabras*, concluding that the ME adaptation of the latter provides a relatively more nuanced Ganelon.

H. M. Adrien, '"Baligant" ou l'effet paratextuel du *Roland*', *DFS*, 57:3–9, contends that the Baligant episode, far from being a later addition to an already coherent text, is in fact the element that completes it, confirms it as a *chanson de geste* (rather than as a *chanson de défaite*) and elevates it to an account of ultimate victory. Id., '*La Chanson de Roland*, ou l'hymne de la fournaise', *Olifant*, 21.3–4:11–40, draws on critics as diverse as Roland Barthes and Marianne Cramer Vos in an attempt to read the *Roland* for (somewhat evangelical) Biblical symbols.

J.-P. Carton, 'A contribution to the study of *laisses similaires* in the *Chanson de Roland*: repetition and narrative progression in laisses 133–35', *Olifant*, 21.3–4:65–84, is an intensive and rather technical demonstration of how this specific use of the *laisse similaire* gives momentum to the text, increasing dramatic tension for the audience. M. Pantazakos, *'From epic to romance: the literary transformation of private blood feud into societal *ressentiment*', *Comitatus*, 33:37–57.

GUILLAUME D'ORANGE AND THE GARIN CYCLE. P. Black, 'The gendered world of the *Chanson de Guillaume*', *Olifant*, 21.3–4:41–63, sees Guibourc's actions as displaying a need to fill gaps created by Guillaume's absence; unlike Blancheflor, condemned for crossing gender roles and boundaries with her public actions, Guibourc is praised. J.-C. Herbin, 'La rédaction *C* de la *Chevalerie Vivien*', Herbin, *Richesses*, 11–23, explores the possibility of proper names being common not only within the Vivien 'cycle', but also between the Vivien poems and other epics such as *Herviz de Metz* and *Garin le Loherain*. H. refrains, however, from forcing conclusions about inter-cyclical influence from his observations.

OTHER EPICS. *Orson de Beauvais, chanson de geste du XIIe siècle* (CFMA, 140), ed. J.-P. Martin, Champion, 259 pp., edited from a single extant MS, does not present a particularly remarkable plot, and thematic commonplaces abound throughout; M. interprets this as evidence of the poem's influence on other works of the same genre. Id., 'Notes lexicographiques sur *Orson de Beauvais*', *Romania*, 119:231–41, examines the terms *fronté*, *sanc*, *port*, *don*, and *destroit*. Many OF words are uniquely attested in this work. J.-C. Cossard, 'Propositions pour une lecture historique croisée du *Roman d'Aiquin*', *CCMe*, 45:111–27, explores the work not as a *chanson de geste* of any particular literary interest, but as potentially revelatory of Breton history, assumptions, and political agendas. John Victor Tolan, *Saracens: Islam in the Medieval European Imagination*, NY, Columbia U.P., xxiii + 372 pp., includes a chapter 'Saracens and Pagans' (pp. 105–134), which examines in part the *chansons de croisade* and their portrayal of the Saracen to contemporary audiences. Works such as the *Chanson d'Antioche* place the crusader's struggle within an historico-religious context: the conquest of the pagan has been preordained, thus defining the crusader's task and clearing his conscience for him.

3. Romance

GENERAL. Keith Nickolaus, *Marriage Fictions in Old French Secular Narratives, 1170–1250: A Critical Re-evaluation of the Courtly Love Debate* (Studies in Medieval History and Culture, 6), NY–London, Routledge, xxiv + 255 pp., provides a critical discussion of the 'courtly love' debate. It offers a broad historical and comparative analysis and proposes a model which explains, at the level of plot, rhetoric, and ideology, the proper place of amorous motifs in the context of prevailing Christian doctrines and attitudes. By reviewing modern critical debates on the origin and nature of courtliness, examining historical context and Latin prototypes, and considering a deliberately broad range of authors and texts — Tristan stories, *Partonopeus de Blois*, Chrétien, Marie de France, Jean de Meun, *romans antiques*, *Girart de Roussillon* — N. aims to put forward a new, more meaningful definition of what 'courtly love' actually meant to authors and readers of romance. E. Jane Burns, *Courtly Love Undressed: Reading through Clothes in Medieval French Culture* (The Middle Ages Series), Philadelphia, Pennsylvania U.P., 326 pp., offers a reassessment of courtly love through the lens of the elaborate garments which typify literary accounts of court life. Although it is generally agreed that sumptuous clothes provide social definition for key players, B.'s study questions common perceptions of courtly desire, gender issues, the negotiability of class, and even the symbolic location of the western court itself. B. identifies specific instances where medieval discussions of clothing convey cultural anxieties whilst also insisting upon a crucial easternness within the lush fabrics of courtly love protagonists. She concludes that in dressing up its subjects, courtly love substantially undoes and shakes up a number of key cultural paradigms on which medieval amorous attachment has been thought to rely. This absorbing book studies a broad range of 12th-c. and 13th-c. OF courtly texts: vernacular sermons, sumptuary legislation, didactic literature, lyric (*chansons de toile*, Provençal texts) and romance (*Roman de la Rose*, Chrétien, Jean Renart, Gautier d'Arras, Arthurian texts, Marie de France). Dennis H. Green, *The Beginnings of Medieval Romance: Fact and Fiction, 1150–1220*, CUP, 308 pp., explores how and why romance emerged and examines a period of crucial importance for the birth of the romance and the genesis of medieval fiction in the vernacular. Although the crucial innovative role of writers in Germany is G.'s main concern, he also takes literature in Latin, French and A-N into account. He offers a definition of medieval fictionality in its first formative period in the 12th c., and underlines the difficulties encountered in finding a place for the fictional romance within earlier literary traditions.

CHRÉTIEN DE TROYES. Douglas Kelly, *Chrétien de Troyes: Supplement 1* (Research Bibliographies and Checklists: n.s., 3), Woodbridge, Tamesis, 582 pp., is the much-awaited updating of K.'s 1976 bibliography. Items included cover the period to 2001 and encompass scholarship not only from Western Europe and North America but also from Eastern and Central Europe, Africa, Central and South America, and Japan. There are 22 thematic sections, each divided into user-friendly sub-sections. The numbering system is essentially the same as in the 1976 volume; there are useful cross-postings; brief introductions to each section explain new developments and directions in Chrétien scholarship; and references are given to items for which summaries can be found in the *Bulletin Bibliographique de la Société Internationale Arthurienne*. It is always possible to ask for more (e.g. reviews of monographs) but it would be churlish not to recognize the enormous contribution this invaluable volume makes to Chrétien studies.

V. Gontero, 'Les gemmes dans l'oeuvre de Chrétien de Troyes (*Erec et Enide, Cligès, le Chevalier de la charrette, le Chevalier au lion, Perceval*)', *CCMe*, 45:237–54, notes that colour and light are central to Arthurian symbolism and discusses how this extends into the literary object of the gemstone. C. exploits this *topos*, but also renews the portrait of women by 'mineralizing' it through comparisons with and metaphors of precious stones. J. Mandel, 'The idea of family in Chrétien de Troyes and Sir Thomas Malory', *Arthuriana*, 12.4:90–99, remarks that the construction of family in each author's work does not reflect historical accuracy but aesthetic need. For Malory, the family provides the source of political antagonism and narrative tension that invigorates the romance. For Chrétien, the family provides an ideal alternative to chivalric adventurism that deconstructs the ideal of romance.

A. de Mandach, 'Les modèles anglo-normands de Chrétien: Chrétien en Angleterre', *RZLG*, 25, 2001 : 283–93, offers a number of examples confirming his assertion that the A-N *Erec* and the Welsh *Gereint ac Enid* share a much more substantial common source than the conserved *Gereint ac Enid*.

M. Mancini, *'*Yvain*: Chretien de Troyes e il sacerdoto di Nemi', *SMV*, 48 : 143–56. H. Andersen and H. Nolke, *'Style oral et connexion dans *Lancelot*', *(Pre)Publications*, 182, 2001 : 29–43. L. J. Getty, *'Lancelot and the Cathars: heresy in Chretien de Troyes' *Le Chevalier de la Charrette*', *RoN*, 42 : 139–50. G. Heyworth, 'Love and honor in *Cligès*', *Romania*, 120 : 99–117, identifies a coherent recoding of medieval *mores* in C.'s use of *los*. By 'ironizing' the formal vocabulary of honour, C. manages to bring the ideals of knightly behaviour down to the reality of a nobility with time on its hands. Also, by invoking Ovidian authority, in itself parodic of epic *mores*, C. redrafts romance sensibilities, rebutting his opening dictum: 'Ne s'acordent pas bien ansanble / repos et los'.

Perceval ou le Conte du graal, ed. Hervé-François Fournier (Etonnants Classiques), Flammarion, 2001, 157 pp., is an attractive volume intended for adolescents. Jean Dufournet's translation is preceded by a brief introduction to Chrétien, courtly society and literature, and by a *chronologie*. Following the glossary is a nine-page *dossier jeu* offering a variety of activities based on the text. Danielle Buschinger, *Parzival, Arthur et le Graal* (Médiévales, 18), Amiens, Presses du Centre d'Etudes Médiévales, Univ. de Picardie-Jules Verne, 2001, 162 pp., is a collection of lectures, some of which have been partially published elsewhere, which will interest scholars of the *Conte del Graal*. Buschinger investigates courtly adaptations and creative re-writings of C.'s *Conte del Graal* and of the *Lancelot-Graal* in chapters 1, 3, 4, and 7. The introduction, 'Traduire le Moyen Age: la réécriture des textes médiévaux', is especially useful. C. Dona, *'Il prologo del *Conte del Graal* e il senso del romanzo', *SMV*, 48 : 33–44. M. Vauthier, 'Biographie et hagiographie chez Chrétien de Troyes: quelques ambiguïtés d'un genre littéraire', *BDBA*, 20 : 183–94, considers the prologue to the *Conte du Graal*, which is neither simple biography nor standard hagiography: it is above all an artistic work suggesting a conversion whose historical veracity the reader must accept. In the light of its prologue, the *Conte* can be read as a representation of the metaphorical movements of a soul. K. Stierle, '*A te convien tenere altro vïaggio*: Dantes *Commedia* und Chrétiens *Contes del Graal*', *RZLG*, 25, 2001 : 39–64, examines the similarities between the 'quests' of Dante and Perceval. It is clear that the 'seed' which C. discusses in his prologue has found a fertile soil in Dante. M. Gaillard, 'Etude sémantique d'un stéréotype médiéval: Les trois "gotes de sanc" dans *Le Conte du Graal*', *Poétique*, 131:285–308, considers the episode of the drops of blood in order to explore how a critic can find, analyse, and describe a literary stereotype in a tradition which constantly relies on formulas and re-writings. A.-M. Ferguson, *'Percival and the Grail: always ask the foolish question', *Parabola*, 26, 2001:44–47.

OTHER ARTHURIAN. **Romans de la table ronde*, ed. Jean-Marie Fritz et al. (Classiques de Poche), LP, 734 pp. **Lancelot du Lac*, vol. IV, ed. Marie-Louise Ollier (Lettres Gothiques), LP, 480 pp.

Frédérique Le Nan, *Le Secret dans la littérature arthurienne (1150–1250): Du lexique au motif* (Nouvelle Bibliothèque du Moyen Age, 62), Champion, 463 pp., is a dense study of all types of secrets, both 'religious' and 'profane', in Arthurian romance. These include 'marvels' and 'miracles' (in particular surrounding the Grail) as well as human 'mysteries' and secrets (such as illegitimate births, disguises, and forbidden love) which may be intentional or unintentional. Romance is an ideal place for the expansion of the *topos* of secrecy in all its guises. It uses secrets to bring together many narrative strands at an appropriate moment but also to reveal character traits, motivation, and even inner truths. Texts covered include both verse and prose vernacular narratives: 'Grail literature' in the broadest sense, and *Tristan* texts prior to the *Tristan en prose*. Michel Stanesco, **D'armes et d'amours: Études de littérature arthurienne*, Paradigme, Orléans, 446 pp. V. Greene, 'Qui croit au retour d'Arthur', *CCMe*, 45:321–40, is a broad study of the motif which concludes that medieval sources repeat a stereotype rather than report an actual fact and that this belief was not significant outside of Arthurian fiction. **ArLit*, 19, 'Comedy in Arthurian Literature', includes essays by E. Archibald, F. Brandsma, C. Ferlampin-Acher, L. Gowans, D. L. Hoffman, M. Hogenbirk, N. J. Lacy, M. Lawrence, B. Milland-Bove, P. S. Noble, K. Pratt, A. Rieger, E. S. Sklar, and F. Zambon. **New Directions in Arthurian Studies*, ed. A. Lupack (Arthurian Studies, 51), Cambridge, Brewer, ix + 168 pp. Denis Hue, **Le Monde et l'Autre Monde*, Paradigme, Orléans, 460 pp., offers many examples of otherworldly themes and motifs in Arthurian narrative.

Arthuriana, 12.1, is devoted to the *Roman de Silence*. S. Roche-Mahdi, 'A reappraisal of the role of Merlin in the *Roman de Silence*' (6–21), argues that an intertextual reading of 'Grisandole' and other passages from the *Prose Vulgate* establishes Merlin as manipulator of the action of the *Roman de Silence* long before the dénouement. The fact that Merlin subjects Silence to the prevailing cultural norms of what is 'natural' for a female does not mean that the *Silence* poet is an arch-conservative misogynist. Merlin is merely being true to his character, and his laughter is anything but liberating. L. Kochanske Stock, 'Civilisation and its discontents: cultural primitivism and the depiction of Merlin as a wild man in the *Roman de Silence*' (22–36), notes that by depicting Merlin as a Wild Man and referring allusively to Dangiers in the *Roman de la Rose*, Heldris engages ambivalently with the discourse of cultural primitivism, which expresses discontent with civilization and promotes a 'natural' lifestyle as preferable to the corruption inherent in 'nurtured' civilized life. If not utterly cynical, Heldris is at least disconcertingly pragmatic in suggesting that roasted meat, however decadent its origin or associations, does taste better than raw roots. R. S. Sturges, 'The crossdresser and the *juventus*: category crisis in *Silence*' (37–49), examines the problematics of class and gender which intersect in the crossdressing heroines of medieval romance. Silence can be read as an alternative version of the high medieval disinherited younger son, the *juvenis*, supporting the claim that the crossdresser often represents displaced anxieties about categories other than gender. R. L. A. Clark, 'Queering gender and naturalising class in the *Roman de Silence*' (50–63), argues that a queer reading allows us to see how the text's sodomitic moments not only serve to destabilize sex–gender categories but also point to a more general anxiety about the coherence of categories of race and class. Noble birth emerges as the only stable referent, the only work of Nature not undone by Nurture. S. Kinoshita, 'Male-order brides: marriage, patriarchy, and monarchy in the *Roman de Silence*' (64–75), analyses two specific mechanisms through which Ebain enhances monarchical power: exchanging an adulterous, exogamous wife for a chaste, endogamous one; and dispossessing the earl of Chester, a great baron of the realm. The king's restoration of female succession spells Silence's capitulation to his feudal politics of lineage. R. Omar Khan, 'Genealogy and cross-gendering in *Le Roman de Silence* and *Ariake no Wakare* (*Parting at Dawn*)' (76–84), compares *Silence* and the 12th-c. Japanese court tale *Ariake no Wakare*. Both feature similar constellations of themes, narrativization, and reception history. They link aristocratic inheritance anxieties and female-to-male crossdressing with extraordinary musical abilities and services to a sovereign, reflecting parallel preoccupations. K. M. Krause, 'Li mireor du monde: specularity in the *Roman de Silence*' (85–91), notes that Silence, twice called 'le miroir du monde', embodies both positive and negative symbolic aspects of the medieval mirror. She exemplifies courtly and chivalric virtue, and reveals hidden truths, but she is also a 'miroir trompeur', reflecting surface appearances while hiding her real identity. K. Blumreich, 'Strategies for teaching the *Roman de Silence*' (92–100), offers a variety of approaches for teaching the *Roman de Silence*, including ideas for small group, whole class, and research assignments. M. Bolduc, 'Images of romance: the miniatures of *Erec et Enide* and *Le Roman de Silence*' (101–12), comments that, if the MS illuminations of chivalric romance are typically active and courtly, those of the *Roman de Silence* visually highlight the romance's preoccupation with language and gender. She concludes that *Silence's* narrative images visually re-enact the ambiguity of language at the heart of the romance. L. Dahmen, 'Sacred romance: *Silence* and the hagiographical tradition' (113–22), insists that the tradition of *vitae*, specifically of crossdressing female saints, serves as an important source and point of reference for this didactic romance. The poet consciously creates a hybrid text by combining contemporary narrative traditions associated with romance and saints' Lives. C. Callahan, 'Lyric discourse and female vocality: on the unsilencing of Silence' (123–31), highlights how the practice of lyric allows both Silence and *Aucassin's* Nicolette to transcend the limits of gender, by validating both their male and female personae at once. Whether purely literary convention or reality, this empowerment is characteristic of medieval lyric discourse. Id., *'Canon law, primogeniture and the marriage of Ebain and Silence', *RoQ*, 49: 12–20.

V. Greene, 'How the demoiselle d'Escalot became a picture', *Arthuriana*, 12.3: 31–48, examines the *Mort Artu's* story of the demoiselle d'Escalot and notes that it displays through its narrative and descriptive peculiarities the difficulty of representing a woman in romance. The *demoiselle* represents the haunting presence of female reality in a masculine imaginary world; she creates in the text a lasting pattern of aesthetic disturbance. Id., 'The bed and the boat: illustrations of the demoiselle d'Escalot's story in illuminated manuscripts of *La Mort Artu*', *ib.*, 12.4: 50–73, studies the visual sequences representing the story of the *demoiselle* in ten 13th-c. to 15th-c. illustrated manuscripts. Although many of these images can be related to two common types of scenes (the conversation scene and the bed scene), the introduction of a 'boat scene' seems to have forced illustrators to become inventive. A. Berthelot, 'Un nouveau modèle de clerc: Merlin', *ICLS 10*, 105–20, interprets the romance figure of Merlin as a cleric who, as magician, counsellor, and lover, is far removed from historical reality. In the medium of the French romance the role of *clericus curialis* is restyled and finally dispensed with altogether.

J.-J. Vincensini, 'Temps perdu, temps retrouvé: rythme et sens da la mémoire dans le *Haut livre du Graal*', *MA*, 108: 43–60, studies 'organic ties' represented by time and *remembrance* as veritable and effective structural tools. V. examines the characters of Arthur, Gauvain, Lancelot, and Perlesvaus and concludes that remembering and forgetting are critical moments of the narrative which regulate the rhythm and organize the presentation of the adventures. A. Berthelot, '"L'épée qui décolla saint Jean-Baptiste" dans *Perlesvaus: le Haut livre du Graal*', *Senefiance*, 48: 17–28, traces the history of the sword associated with Gauvain from its origins as an obscure artifact into its elevation as a holy relic. B. concludes that the sword is a purely literary creation conceived to complete the Grail assemblage. B. Ramm, 'Two for one? A case of mistaken identity in the *Perlesvaus*', *FSB*, 85: 2–4, highlights a case in which the narrative assigns the same meaning/identity (Joseph of Arimathea) to two different agents whilst allowing for the possibility of deriving a number of different significations (e.g. Joseph, Nicodemus) from a single agent.

A. Combes, 'Le prologue en blanc du *Lancelot* en prose', Baumgartner, *Seuils*, 1, 21–52, examines the *absence* of a prologue for this work, which is not interpreted as 'editorial' (i.e., because of the text's inclusion within a larger cycle). Rather, the absence of a prologue *sets* the contract with the reader, announcing the originality of what is to follow. Id., 'From quest to quest: Perceval and Galahad in the Prose *Lancelot*', *Arthuriana*, 12.3: 7–30, points out that the *Lancelot's* long-standing 'internal contradiction' is generated by a long-term strategy that not only authorizes a double reading, but also holds the key to the work's mysterious construction of Lancelot's genealogy. A. P. Longley, 'Guinevere as lord', *ib.*, 49–62, studies the Prose *Lancelot* and notes that the two most important women in Lancelot's life, Guinevere and the Lady of the Lake, are his 'female lord' and his 'female master'. Their female roles are examined in relation to the love theme and in the context of decoding female authority. J. Looper, '*L'Estoire de Merlin* and the mirage of patrilineage', *ib.*, 63–85, remarks that *Merlin* contains the *Lancelot-Grail* Cycle's most extensive re-evaluation of father figures in both the aristocratic family and literary lineages. The author's simultaneous acceptance and dismissal of male hegemony as a stabilizing force in these two domains reveals his ambivalent attitude toward the subject. M. Séguy, 'Naming and renaming: on two Grail scenes in *L'Estoire del Saint Graal*', *ib.*, 87–102, comments that the *Estoire del Saint Graal* is crafted with a concern for precise naming which is authenticated by divine transcendence and/or etymological explications. The Grail, like the castle where it resides, is given a series of names. This is more than a matter of accumulating names. Rather, they are the means whereby the romance overwrites the divine word, and thereby appropriates for fictional representation the power to convey meaning.

Joanne Rittey, *Amplification as Gloss in Two Twelfth-Century Texts: Robert de Boron's Joseph d'Arimathie and Renaut de Beaujeu's Li Biaus Descouneüs* (Studies in the Humanities, Literature–Politics–Society, 59), NY–Berne, Lang, 352 pp., concentrates on the author as the motivating agent of the text. The material selected acts as the vehicle for the authors' central ideas. Structure and amplification clarify the authors' intentions and offer a framework that, rather than being contrived and restrictive, defines fiction as a craft organizing and glossing material and creating unity through authorial perspective. R. studies plot, process and character — the rhetorical techniques the authors use to control the way in which the reader understands the text — and concludes that both authors were fully aware of the manipulative power of literature. D. B. Schwartz, 'Guinglain and Lancelot: the nightmares in *Le Bel Inconnu*', *Arthuriana*, 12.2:3–31, notes that the Lancelot of Chrétien's *Charrette* is the primary intertextual model for the Unknown Knight Guinglain in Renaut de Beaujeu's *Bel Inconnu*. Guinglain's Lancelotian nightmares parody the Sword Bridge and Future Cemetery episodes of the *Charrette*, link the narratives of poet and hero, and offer a medieval example of the 'anxiety of influence'.

TRISTAN AND ISEUT. D. Buschinger, 'L'histoire de Riwalin et Blanchefleur dans les romans de Tristan de Thomas d'Angleterre et de Gottfried von Strassburg', Buschinger, *Travail*, 71–77, notes how Gottfried reworked and intensified Thomas's model to turn the story into a hymn in praise of true love. B. Franceschini, *'Ephemeros: per un'analisi dei caratteri nel Tristano di Thomas e di Beroul', *CN*, 61, 2001:275–99.

S. Huot, 'Unspeakable horror, ineffable bliss: riddles and marvels in the Prose *Tristan*', *MAe*, 71:47–65, examines the function and unity of riddles, with particular reference to the opening section of the text. F. Bogdanow, 'Intertextuality and the problem of the relationship of the first and second versions of the Prose *Tristan* to the Post-Vulgate *Queste del Saint Graal*, third part of the *Post-Vulgate Roman du Graal*', *Arthuriana*, 12.2:32–68, highlights a close relationship between the *Post-Vulgate Queste* and the *Queste* incorporated into the 'second version' of the Prose *Tristan (Tr. II)*. Textual evidence would suggest that the compiler of *Tr. II* incorporated large sections of the *P-V Queste*.

ROMANS D'ANTIQUITÉ. *Narcisus et Dané* (LivOS, 6), ed. Penny Eley, <http://www.liv.ac.uk/www/french/LOS/Narcisus.pdf>, 94 pp., offers a critical edition and facing page, line-by-line translation into English. The introduction and *mise-en-contexte* include an extremely useful and detailed thematic commentary. Notes to the carefully edited text are equally detailed. Valérie Gontero, *Parures d'or et de gemmes: l'orfèvrerie dans les romans antiques du XIIe siècle*, Aix-en-Provence, Univ. de Provence, 308 pp., is an abridged version of the author's doctoral thesis (2000). G. studies the *amplificationes* relating to gold and precious stones, noting that the *ekphraseis* that marks *romans antiques* renews a number of techniques, including that of the portrait, and descriptions of the town and the tomb. Links are established between the *romans antiques* and lapidaries, bestiaries, encyclopaedias, and the art of rhetoric. There are two useful appendices listing occurrences of precious stones in the texts studied. G. concludes that these '*romans orfévrés*' represent a *mise en abyme* of romanesque art and thought: not only is a broad décor revealed to the reader, but also the silhouette of the author.

P. Logié, 'Mythe et biographie dans quelques épisodes des romans antiques du XIIe siècle', *BDBA*, 20: 115–23, examines to what extent details given as historical should be considered as fiction. Myth and anachronism are not synonymous with fiction, and the mixing of myths with the contemporary world of the narrators offers in fact a coherent vision of the universe, inspired by both Christian and pagan sources. Id., 'L'oubli d'Hésione ou le fatal aveuglement: le jeu du *tort* et du *droit* dans le *Roman de Thèbes* de Benoît de Sainte-Maure', *MA*, 108: 235–52, notes how B. introduced a chain of human cause and effect, where the myth allowed for the intervention of a particular god, to give Christian meaning to events and passages that would otherwise have appeared shockingly pagan to his audience. Deliberate anachronism is therefore an effective way of bridging the gap between two very different cultures.

Ribémont, *Etudes*, is a volume on the *Roman de Thèbes* destined for *agrégation* students (2002–03), with a 47-page introduction covering major questions of *auctoritas*, omissions and additions to the original *Thébaïde*, etc. It takes the stance that the text itself distances itself from the epic register in order to 'inaugurate' the romance genre. The majority of articles are reprints, originally published from the 1970s onwards; three new articles have been written specifically for this collection. C. Croizy-Naquet, 'Mères, filles et soeurs: amantes, épouses et veuves dans le *Roman de Thèbes*' (159–74), examines the medieval author's considerable development of female characters. C.-N. perceives not only vertical solidarity and coherence (i.e., the tracing of a woman's destiny, from girl/lover to queen/wife to widow), but also horizontal solidarity in the suffering of women across the warring city boundaries. Women's place is not an exclusively private one; they act in and on men and cities, as well as on narrative. G. Giordanengo, 'Le *Roman de Thèbes*, un "roman féodal"?' (192–99), considers the work as displaying the author's consciousness of social structures developing at the time; however, G. rightly emphasizes the degree to which 'feudal' practice was still in flux. It would be dangerous to (over-)interpret the text as referring directly to ranks and functions that were yet to be established. A. Petit, 'L'épisode des jeux dans le *Roman de Thèbes*' (175–92), examines MS S (the oldest), in which the death of the serpent responsible for killing Archémore follows the original *Thébaïde*, yet differs from other MSS; similarly, the funerary games are omitted in the original and in MS S. There follows a brief edition and comparison of the varying texts, with P. concluding that the later reinsertion of the games demonstrates an appreciation of Antiquity. Id., 'Wauchier de Denain et la matière du *Roman de Thèbes* dans l'*Histoire ancienne jusqu'à César*', Herbin, *Richesses*, 243–52, notes that in the *Thèbes* section of the *Histoire ancienne* Wauchier treats his historico-romanesque subject as an admirer of *mirabilia* and adventure stories. P. concludes that a comparison of Wauchier's *mise-en-prose* of the *Thèbes* story and his known source reveal him to be as much a writer of romance as of history. L. Harf-Lancner, 'Translation et création: l'histoire de Daire le Roux dans le *Roman de Thèbes*', Buschinger, *Travail*, 51–59, studies this episode, an addition to the story by the *Thèbes* poet and dealing with the duties of vassal and family, and compares it to a similar episode in *Raoul de Cambrai*. This is the only instance in *Thèbes* where the author's source is mentioned, presumably to add *auctoritas* to the new material and to claim the invention's equality with the translation. The number of different versions of the episode, ranging from 900 to 2500 lines, allow us to examine closely the processes of re-writing the past and writing the present.

C. Gaullier-Bougassas, 'L'*Alexandre décasyllabique*: l'adaptation du roman d'Albéric et la naissance du roman médiéval', Buschinger, *Travail*, 11–18, notes the fundamental role played by the two earliest vernacular Alexander texts in the birth of romance. In particular, their use and adaptation of Latin sources and their celebration of a new concept of royalty are highlighted. Maddox, *Alexander*, brings together work by distinguished scholars from the United States, France, Britain, and the Netherlands. It offers a systematic, collective study of Alexander's thematic prominence in medieval culture, from the early 12th c. to the end of the Middle Ages. A variety of methodological perspectives informs the 16 studies found here. These include anthropology, art history, codicology, the history of mentalities, postcolonial theory, and sociology. The topics addressed include issues of genre; the ideological implications of successive rewritings of ancient history; the 13th-c. *mise-en-prose* of the heroic story; the 14th-c. cyclification of the legend's components; questions pertaining to *auctoritas*; and medieval beliefs concerning the fabulous and the exotic. M. Zink, 'The prologue to the *Historia de Preliis*: a pagan model of spiritual struggle' (21–28), explores an early example of the Alexander legend being recognized by clerical authors as an apt vehicle for addressing a wide range of contemporary concerns. The figurative implementation of the legend found in the *Historia de Preliis* reappears in the prologue to Chrétien's *Conte du Graal*, where Chrétien's patron, Philip of Flanders, is favourably compared to Alexander in terms of the practice of largesse. E. Baumgartner, 'The raid on Gaza in Alexandre de Paris's romance' (29–38), examines an episode redolent of OF epic in a larger work generally studied for its affinities with romance. B. shows that, while in terms of its generic properties the episode in many ways compares favourably with the *chansons de geste*, it conveys a didactic and ideological perspective that is fundamentally at odds with an epic worldview. D. Kelly, 'Alexander's *Clergie*' (39–56), considers the interplay of ideals of *clergie* and *chevalerie* in the Vulgate *Alexandre* and the *Roman de toute chevalerie*. Although *clergie* is vital to to the hero's brilliant education as well as to his active life, the intellectual component ultimately facilitates and glorifies the vast agenda of militant conquest. K. concludes that it is *chevalerie*, not *clergie*, that prevails as an ideal. C. Gaullier-Bougassas, 'Alexander and Aristotle in the French Alexander romances' (57–74), also studies an aspect of Alexander's education, in a selection of texts from the 12th to the 15th centuries. At times, Aristotle serves to project a favourable view of the influence of clerics on rulers, but he later acquires less positive traits. In the *Lai d'Aristote* he is even subjected to pitiless ridicule. F. Suard, 'Alexander's gabs' (75–88), notes how Alexandre de Paris individualizes and nuances the traditional image of the omnipotent conqueror. The medieval author's rewriting of two scenes of *déguisement* introduces the humourous vein of *gab* found in the early epico-romanesque tradition. His aim is both literary and didactic: it heightens the exemplary nature of the scenes by suggesting them to the reader as instructive. R. T. Pickens, '"Mout est proz e vassaus"/"Mout es corteis": *Vasselage* and courtesy in the *Roman d'Alexandre*' (89–110), demonstrates that subtle semantic changes in the 12th-c. romances, detectable within a modest, though culturally charged, lexicon inherited from early epic discourse, can provide valuable indices of social change. This marks out a major transition from the epic celebration of *vasselage* to a more courtly concept of *courtoisie*. W. W. Kibler, '"A paine a on bon arbre de malvaise raïs": counsel for kings in the *Roman d'Alexandre*' (111–26), identifies in the Vulgate *Alexandre* striking reflections of the profound institutional changes taking place on the French political horizon. The romance offers a conservative ideal of kingship valorizing traditional forms of largesse while also repeatedly emphasizing the perils of reliance on low-born men rather than the higher aristocracy. S. D. White, 'Giving fiefs and honor: largesse, avarice, and the problem of "feudalism" in Alexander's testament' (127–42), considers the *Roman d'Alexandre* in the light of current theoretical discussions of models for the study of feudal society. He concludes that the romance reproduces and mystifies, but fails to resolve, a fundamental underlying ambiguity between honorable fief-giving and bribery camouflaged as largesse. M. R. Warren, 'Take the world by prose: modes of possession in the *Roman d'Alexandre*' (143–60), whose essay is informed by contemporary postcolonial studies, suggests that the prose *Alexandre* moves significantly away from courtly concerns towards the embodiment of a more resolutely expansionist ideology, and that prose is especially suited to this new discourse. C. Croizy-Naquet, 'Alexander and Caesar in the *Faits des Romains*' (161–74), shows how the figure of Alexander comes into prominence in the emergence of prose and of writing history in the vernacular. The compiler of the *Faits des Romains* redefines contours of two exemplary figures, Alexander and Caesar, thereby playing an important role in the development of medieval historiography. K. Busby, '"Codices manuscriptos nudos tenemus": Alexander and the new codicology' (259–74), is a wide-ranging enquiry which makes the codex containing each known version of a work the central object of study. Codicological features may cast light on the reception of the legend within the historical context that produced a given manuscript. Our understanding of the intrinsic significance of a text, and its larger implications, may depend on the MS's material properties. A. Varvaro, *'Considerazioni sulle edizioni facsimile di codici letterari (a proposito del Roman d'Alexandre' del Museo Correr, ms. 1493)', *MedRom*, 25:481–91.

OTHER ROMANCES. M. Dickson, 'Female doubling and male identity in medieval romance', Hardman, *Identity*, 59–72, takes Thomas's *Tristan* as her starting point in an examination of the archetypal romance approach to the question of identity, which is the doubling of female characters. She then extends her study to *Le Roman de Horn*, *Beuve de Hantone*, and *Eliduc*. The doubling of a character suggests replacement or substitution, and this impression of interchangeability (from a male perspective) points to the conclusion that the doubling of female characters exists primarily to enhance the establishment of a specifically male identity.

P. Eley, 'Sex and writing: Hue de Rotelande's *Ipomedon* and Alan of Lille's *De planctu naturae*', *ICLS 10*, 93–104, analyses the reciprocity of of courtly and clerical culture on the level of intertextuality. *Ipomedon*'s quoting of Alain de Lille represents a playful subversion, literature demonstrating its own sovereignty through irony and parody. This implies also the presence in Hue's audience of clerks familiar with current intellectual and literary developments. F. Mora, 'Les prologues et les epilogues de Hue de Rotelande', Baumgartner, *Seuils*, 1, 97–114, argues that Hue's prologues establish his proximity to Latin *auctores*, whilst his endings (in M.'s view) are far more accomplished than Chrétien's.

K. L. Burr, 'Re-creating the body: Euriaut's tales in *Le Roman de la violette*', *Symposium*, 56:3–16, explains how through the series of stories, based on marks on her body, the heroine of *Violette* refuses the passivity that male characters attempt to impose on her. Gerbert de Montreuil's Euriaut's tales simultaneously assert her right to determine her body's significance and modify its role in courtly society. K. M. Krause, 'The material erotic: the clothed and unclothed female body in the *Roman de la violette*', Curtis, *Material Culture*, 17–35, examines the roles of nudity and clothing; when seen nude in her bath, Euriaut is not sexualized in the same manner as when she later appears clothed. K. attributes this to the fact that the bath scene provides knowledge (of Euriaut's birthmark), rather than sexual experience, to Lisiart. Her appearance when clothed is commented upon in a highly sexualized fashion; however, her body is decorated with clothing and jewels that recall heroines famous for their virtue, thus protecting the seemingly exposed heroine.

A. Corbellari, 'Onirisme et bestialité: le roman de *Guillaume de Palerne*', *Neophilologus*, 86:353–62, argues that the motif of the werewolf and the important place given to dreams jointly express a 'return of the repressed'. Centuries before Freud, the Middle Ages understood that dreams bring together the civilized and animal aspects of human nature. K. M. Talarico, '"Un merveilleux contraire": public and private desire in *Galeran de Bretagne*', *DFS*, 59:3–20, suggests that insights into the changes occurring in romance in the 13th c. can be clearly gained through a study of public and private desire. It is important to situate *romans d'aventure* in the history of textual development since they offer a more realistic, if stylized, view of reality, courtly life and society than the *roman arthurien*. The *merveilleux contraire* places *Galeran de Bretagne* at the crossroads of the development of the medieval *roman* since the author turns away from the divine comedy of human nature to begin exploring more fully the human comedy. N. A. Jones, 'The daughter's text and the thread of lineage in the old French *Philomena*', Robertson, *Rape*, 161–87, sees the tale as a critique of the brutality and decadence of 12th-c. courtly society; at the same time, both the text and society (according to J.) recognize the role of the tapestry as a medium of female expression.

Gautier d'Arras, *Eracle*, trans. André Eskénazi (TCMA, 54), Champion, 247 pp., offers a translation of Guy Raynaud de Lage's edition (CFMA, 102). There is an introduction, by Corinne Pierreville, which discusses sources and Gautier's preference for '*réalité*' over '*merveilleux*', but in particular presents the case for considering the author a worthy rival to Chrétien. If Gautier did not enjoy the success of Chrétien, it was because he was ahead of his time in both subject matter and form. A long 'Note sur la traduction' precedes the prose translation, for which references to the OF text are given every dozen-or-so lines. The translation follows the OF closely, resulting at times in rather over-complicated syntax. More serious, however, is the lack of notes, a vital reading aid even when offering a text in translation.

Alcuin Blamires and Gail C. Holian, *The Romance of the Rose Illuminated: Manuscripts at the National Library of Wales, Aberystwyth* (MRTS, 223), Tempe, Arizona State U.P. — Cardiff, Univ. of Wales, 137 pp., offers fresh insights into the history and reception of the *Roman de la Rose* by reproducing all the miniatures from the seven unpublished illuminated MSS found in the National Library of Wales. In addition to providing a full commentary on the illuminations, the authors also discuss the practicalities of medieval book illustration, survey previous scholarship on the poem's iconography and offer comparisons with reproductions from other MSS of the *Romance*. There are 49 superb colour reproductions, 16 b/w plates and some absorbing contextual discussions, all of which which help further to explain the poem and its derivatives. The book is of particular interest to scholars of reception theory.

Heller, *Philippe de Remy*, mainly contains material dealing with the father. B. Sargent-Baur, 'Dating the romances of Philippe de Remi: between an improbable source and a dubious adaptation' (21–46), questions the assumption that P. relied faithfully on a source text and strengthens the argument for dating the romances to the second quarter of the 13th century. L. C. Brook, 'Falling in love and wooing in Philippe de Rémi's romances' (47–68), deals with issues of gender, conjugal and family relations, and the *arts d'aimer*. P.'s romances are deeply concerned with relations between the sexes, condemning such practices as incest, arranged unions, and sex outside marriage while celebrating dutiful courtship and committed, loving couples. B. analyses the techniques used to represent the experience of love and its role in P.'s ideal of conduct. C. Harvey, 'Time and space in *La Manekine*' (69–94), notes that P.'s conception of space contrives a unique balance between the symbolic and the realistic. The structure of time within which he works is intricately framed by the rhythms of the liturgical year and folklore traditions. D. K. Wrisley, 'Narrating and performing the saintly in romance: the case of Philippe de Remi's *La Manekine*' (95–118), compares *La Manekine* and Rutebeuf's *Vie de sainte Elysabel* in order to explore the 13th-c. vogue for portrayals of saintly women. Subjects covered include sainthood, royal conduct, and marriage. F. R. P. Akehurst, 'Courtly text and erotic subtext in *Jehan et Blonde*' (119–30), challenges the notion that P. de R. was an unsophisticated, prudish realist and reveals passages suggesting erotic nuances beneath their literal meaning. J. Dufournet contibutes two essays, 'Philippe de Rémy and rewriting I: *Jehan et Blonde* and *Joufroi de Poitiers*. From one English romance to another' (131–56), and 'Philippe de Rémy and rewriting II: *Jehan et Blonde* and the *Roman de la Rose*' (157–72). The first essay shows *Jehan et Blonde* to be a romance of social adventure which includes political ideas and erases many of the 'traditional' romance motifs found in its source. The second essay illustrates how *Jehan et Blonde* recasts in an original manner the numerous motifs it borrows from the literary tradition, in particular the *Roman de la Rose*. D. advocates a recognition of *Jean et Blonde*'s many highly modern aspects, from its new attitudes about marriage to its inclusion of all social classes. Barbara N. Sargent-Baur, *Philippe de Remi* (see below, p. 59), presents an edition of *Jehan et Blonde*, a complement to the author's study of *La Manekine* (Faux Titre, 159). S.-B. offers a summary of the romance, a commentary and detailed *mise-en-contexte*, a somewhat conservative edition with facing line-by-line English translation, and notes. The edition contains many errors and should be read with prudence.

4. Lais

Marie de France, **Le Lai du rossignol et autres lais courtois*, trans. Françoise Morvan (Coll. Librio, 258), Librio, 2001, 155 pp. J. Barban, 'The case for a possible acrostic in the *lais* of Marie de France', *Le Cygne*, n.s. 1 : 25–44, reminds us, in the light of Margaret Boland's 1995 *Architectural Structure in the Lais of Marie de France* (see *YWMLS*, 58 : 66), of the importance Marie placed on *remembrance* and suggests a possible acrostic which sheds light on M.'s lifespan. B. lists in some detail acrostics in the Christian tradition with which M. may have been acquainted, before suggesting an acrostic formed by the initial letter of the noun in each title as set out in the Harley manuscript. With one small change, this gives: GE FABLAY MCC G + G, 'I told stories (in the year) 1200 G + G'. A number of intriguing possible solutions are listed for the problematic 'G + G', some of which may require a re-thinking of M.'s biography. H. M. Arden, 'The end game in Marie de France's *lais*: the search for a solution', *DFS*, 61 : 3–10, explores M.'s female characters and suggests that the ultimate resolution of the *Lais* are determined by their men. This pattern of male solutions taking precedence over female ones may reflect M.'s pessimism about women's sphere of action in a society where men traditionally have the last word. A. concludes that it is possible to discern M.'s perception of differences in how women and men respond to life's crises, and also her realization that men and women will respond to her *Lais* in strikingly different ways.

5. Religious Writings

The Voyage of St. Brendan: Representative Versions of the Legend in English Translation, ed. W. R. J. Barron and G. S. Burgess (Exeter Medieval Texts and Studies), Exeter U.P., xii + 377 pp., offers a general introduction to the legendary Brendan, an extensive bibliography, and English translations of the Latin, A-N, Dutch, German, Venetian, Occitan, Catalan, Middle English, and Norse redactions. Benedeit's A-N version (pp. 105–02) is succinctly introduced (MSS, editions and translations; authorship; patron and date; content and structure; source; genre; the author's purpose) and translated into extremely readable prose by Burgess. The editors of this excellent volume, of interest to scholars in a number of fields, stress how, in recasting the original Brendan material, the writers of vernacular medieval versions of the legend seized the opportunity to explore the culture and spiritual needs of their own age. D. Maddox, 'Exordes, épilogues, et réécriture hagiographique: *La Vie de saint Alexis* (XIe s.-XIVe s.)', Baumgartner, *Seuils*, II, 129–57, is a diachronic study of how prologues and epilogues allow legendary material to be renewed and re-evaluated. The *mouvance* of the Alexis legend in French reveals a remarkable elasticity, allowing each re-writing to reconceptualize the legend's *senefiance*. Prologues and epilogues play a crucial role in mediating between the 'original' material and whatever meaning a particular re-writing may afford the legend. Guernes de Pont-Sainte-Maxence, **La Vie de saint Thomas de Canterbury*, ed. Jacques T. E. Thomas (Ktemata, 15 + 16), 2 vols, Paris–Louvain, Peeters, 352, 423 pp. T. Hunt, *'The miracle of Ildefonsus in the version of Everard of Gateley', *MedRom*, 25:25–43. M.-G. Grossel, 'Quand dans les cours on rêvait d'ascèse et de vie solitaire: la traduction romane des *Vies des pères* de Wauchier de Denain', Herbin, *Richesses*, 47–64, studies in particular the relationship between the text (content and translation) and the milieu for and which it was produced, namely the court of Philippe de Namur. G. equally situates Wauchier's work in the tradition of translations of the *Vitae Patrum*, or purporting to be such. Wauchier presents models to be followed that are exemplary but also accessible to his audience. T. Matsumura, *'Sur le texte de la *Vie des Peres*', *RLiR*, 66:65–78. M. Powell, 'Translating scripture for ma dame de Champagne: the old French "paraphrase" of Psalm 44 (Eructavit)', Blumenfeld-Kosinski, *Spirit*, 83–103, considers the cultural work of biblical translation for members of the French nobility during the high Middle Ages. P. focuses on the implications of psalm translation for the larger phenomenology of early vernacular literature and argues that in, translating Psalm 44 (widely read as the heavenly epithalamion of

Christ and Holy Church) for Marie de Champagne, the clerical translator transformed scripture by combining the modes of instruction and courtly performance. N. Andrieux-Reix, 'Un clerc médiéval au travail: le *Sermon sur Jonas* (Valenciennes, B.M., Ms 521)', Herbin, *Richesses*, 125–138, studies part of the text ('une page de brouillon') as an object representing the preparation for an oral delivery. Since we witness a stage between the source texts and the sermon to be delivered, a stage of adaptation, it is possible to discern a *méthode de travail*. There are two written forms and two languages, all of which are inextricably mixed as the clerk seeks ways to design techniques of expression.

L. A. Whalan, 'A knight in hell: the poetics of memory for clerical and courtly worlds in Marie de France's *Espurgatoire saint Patrice*', *ICLS 10*, 19–28, is a sensitive reminder of a constructive literary attempt to bridge the gap between court and cleric. Taking as starting-point the notion of *memoria*, he shows how M. retells the story of Henry of Saltry's *Tractatus de Purgatorio sanctii Patricii* in such a way as to make it accessible to a courtly and lay audience. Not only did she translate the story into a language that the new audience could understand, but also she invokes the rhetoric of literary composition and invention to which they were accustomed. In an important article, 'Marie de France as translatrix', *Le Cygne*, n.s. 1:7–24, R. T. Pickens situates the *Espurgatoire Seint Patriz* in the context of M.'s other works. In particular, P. seeks what attracted M. to 'H' of Saltry's *Tractatus de Purgatorio Sancti Patricii* and how she has taken it over and made it her own. He studies how M. advances a poetics of *translatio*; how her poetry champions vernacular literature over Latin; how she promotes the hegemony of Francophone culture in Plantagenet England; how her narratives enact translation and textual transmission; and how she personalizes her role as poet and translator. He concludes that her *translatio* removes the Latin work from the monastery and relocates it in the vernacular noble court, thereby finding the resources to refashion a man's world to her own liking. J. H. McCash, *'*La Vie seinte Audree*: a fourth text by Marie de France?', *Speculum*, 77:744–77.

T. Hunt, '"Monachus curialis": Gautier de Coinci and courtoisie', *ICLS 10*, 121–36, shows how literary patterns of courtly love are exploited to serve the purposes of spiritual edification in the *Miracles de Nostre Dame*. G. does not attack courtly culture but appropriates it for a higher cause. F. Laurent, '*Si douz miracle enseveli dedens la letre ont trop esté*: Le *Livre des Miracles* de Gautier de Coinci', Baumgartner, *Seuils*, II, 219–243, examines the structure of the collection: G. composed autonomous items, then ordered and collected them in such a way to lend unity to the entire work. Through a study of prologues and *queues*, and of the general epilogue, L. questions the notion of the *livre* and concludes that G. af23's evident desire to structure the collection allows us to consider the *Miracles* an autonomous whole displaying internal and organic unity.

E. Pinto-Mathieu, '"Quant amors la parole amaine": réminiscences et allégorie dans l'adaptation française du *Cantique des cantiques* (XIIe siècle)', *Zink Vol.*, 99–117, demonstrates how the version retains its links to Church doctrine and tradition and yet innovates through providing a vernacular translation of controversial allegory. In recalling within his translation the Church's warning about its falling into unsuitable hands, the author takes a radical, and seemingly contradictory, position.

6. Lyric

Ardis Butterfield, *Poetry and Music in Medieval France from Jean Renart to Guillaume de Machaut* (Cambridge Studies in Medieval Literature, 49), CUP, xx + 375 pp., describes the wide range of contexts in which vernacular, secular songs were quoted and copied in narrative romances, satires, and love poetry. Basing her comments on MS evidence, she sheds light on medieval perceptions of how music and poetry were composed and interpreted. B. reassesses the importance of formalism with regard to 13th-c. writing and analyses the changes context require of a song. The book is broadly chronological: it begins with a detailed study of sources, performance, and Jean Renart's *Rose*, and continues with an examination of the refrain and the movement from secular to sacred by Gautier de Coinci; an analysis of the role played by urban culture, particularly Arras; and an assessment of the codicological evidence (especially *Aucassin* and *Fauvel*). The final two sections deal with Guillaume de Machaut, issues of citation and authorship, and the *formes fixes* from Adam de la Halle to Machaut. This book is an extremely rich contribution to the study of medieval song, performance, and textuality. A. M. Babbi, 'L'insertion lyrique entre interprétation et art de la mémoire', *Zink Vol.*, 11–22, proposes that Jean Renart's technique of lyric insertion serves both to develop and enhance the narrative, and to preserve the audience's memory of old songs through the fragments he includes and the melodies they evoke. S. Lefèvre, 'De la naissance du chant à l'envoi', *ib.*, 67–81, briefly cites *envois* from Charles d'Orléans, Gace Brulé, Thibaut de Champagne, Brunetto Latini, *Floire et Blancheflor*, Gontier de Soignies, and Occitan texts, in order to trace the *envoi*'s structure, its dedicatory function, and eventual rhetorical redundancy. P. Bracken, 'The myth of the medieval minstrel: an interdisciplinary approach to the performers of the *chansonnier* repertory', *Viator*, 33:100–116, examines evidence from a wide range of contemporary vernacular descriptions of performances, considers a number of modern critical arguments, and suggests that the currently blurred picture derived from these sources could be improved when supplemented by more conventional historical evidence, including administrative records and relevant iconography. C. Léglu, 'Vernacular poems and inquisitors in Languedoc and Champagne, ca. 1242–1249', *ib.*, 33:117–32, suggests that two Occitan pieces occupying the grey area between poetry and preaching may be in dialogue with a similar poem produced in Champagne at the same period, the 'Chantepleure', which may be the product of the inquisitorial activity of Robert le Bougre. J.-M. Fritz, 'Temps du souvenir et espace de la mémoire chez Thibaut de Champagne et Richard de Fournival', *Zink Vol.*, 23–41, examines the themes (common to both writers) of animal imagery and the importance of remembrance. According to F., the animals' poses and purported traits can be read as commentary upon women's ability and desire to remember their lovers. The bestiary effectively becomes an *art de mémoire*.

E. J. Burns, 'Sewing like a girl: working women in the *chanson de toile*', Klinck, *Woman's Song*, 99–126, identifies the role of the female singer/lover/sewer and examines the significance of sewing as a vehicle for portraying women who are much less passive and lovelorn than has previously been thought. The *chansons de toile* refigure the subjectivity of the singing, loving lady through the exercise of women's work. B. concludes by labelling this 'the poetics of touch'. C. Callahan, 'Hybrid discourse and performance in the Old French *pastourelle*', *FrF*, 27:1–22, highlights the hybrid lyrico-narrative character of the OF *pastourelle*, considering this distinguishing feature to be the key to its long-term success as motet voice, farce, and moralizing pastorale. M. T. Bruckner, 'What short tales does Jehan Bodel's political pastourelle tell?', *Romania*, 120:118–31, asks why Bodel chose the form of the *pastourelle* to tell his short tale of historical and political exploitation and aims to recreate the instantaneous reception Bodel might have anticipated in the immediacy of performance. S. Santoni, 'Due pastorelle di Jean Bodel', *QFLR*, 16:51–91, offers an edition from MS. fr. 12615, detailed notes, and an Italian translation of *L'autre jor les un boschel* and *Entre le bos et le plainte.* S. carefully situates B.'s *pastourelles* in the literary tradition, studies the MS tradition and provides a commentary for the two edited texts. C. Deschapper, 'La lèpre des *Congès*: naissance, stabilité et dégénérescence du genre', *LR*, 55, 2001:5–18, notes how the *Congés* cover the complete cycle outlined in the title. The first part of the article deals with Jean Bodel and his sources; the second, with Baude Fastoul; the third, with Adam de la Halle. Bodel unknowingly creates a new literary form that will be both developed and perverted.

Barbara N. Sargent-Baur, *Philippe de Remi, Jehan et Blonde, Poems and Songs: Edited from Paris BNF fr. 1588, Paris BNF fr. 24006 and Paris BNF fr. 837* (Faux Titre, 201), Amsterdam–Atlanta, Rodopi, 2001, ii + 586 pp., contains P.'s works as preserved in the unique MS, Paris BNF fr. 1588: eight substantial verse compositions offering much variety in length, tone, and content. As well as the edition of *Jehan et Blonde* (see above, p. 54), two other bodies of work are also included: 11 songs in BNF fr. 24006 (of which ten are surely by him) and the series of *Resveries* in BNF fr. 837 now generally ascribed to him. The introduction to the miscellaneous poems is very brief, although references to recent studies are given. Presentation reproduces the poems' appearance in manuscripts. The notes to the poems are especially useful. As with the poems, there is no translation of the songs or *Resveries*, the introductions are short, offering references to other editions and studies. There is a short glossary pertaining only to the poems, songs, and *Resveries*. Thanks to S.-B. the complete works of Philippe de Remi are now available. S. N. Rosenberg, 'The lyric poetry of Philippe de Remy', Heller, *Philippe de Remy*, 173–88, highlights how, by using what very probably may be his second wife's name in his love poems, P. proves once again to be a unique poet, breaking with the tradition of using cryptic *senhals* or generic names to address the beloved.

J.-J. Vincensini, 'Rhétorique de la fraîcheur et valeurs de l'idylle dans *Aucassin et Nicolette*', *Zink Vol.*, 151–175, examines the text's claims to innovation to established traditions, and the work's relationship to other (supposedly fixed?) genres.

M. Tyssens, *'Amors tencon en la bataille (R-S 121)', *CN*, 62:19–42. R. Crespo, *'Richard de Fournival, *Puis k'il m'estuet de ma dolour kanter* (R. 805): edizione e commento', *ib.*, 61, 2001:75–157. Id., *'Le liriche di Richard de Fournival: Questioni attributive,' *ib.*, 62:43–56. Id., 'Richard de Fournival, *Qant la justice est saisie* (R. 1206)', *Romania*, 120:149–75, offers an extremely detailed, line-by-line analysis of the text.

7. Roman de Renart

A. Barre, 'L'image du texte: L'enluminure au seuil du manuscrit O', *Reinardus*, 15:17–31, examines a miniature preceding Branche XVII but illustrating a different episode. B. reads the illustration as a subtle discourse on the text, one which confirms a pact with the reader. Renart's adventures are condensed in this deceptive, ironic, and metaphorical visual image. B. Zumbült, 'Approaching the medieval illustration cycles of the fox-epic as an art historian: problems and perspectives', *ib.*, 191–204, includes *Renart* amongst the central texts of an intertextual, comparative, and iconographical study.

8. Fabliaux

B. J. Levy, 'Du fabliau à la farce? Encore la question performencielle?', *Reinardus*, 15:87–100, is a comparative study of *Le Pet au vilain* and *Le Prestre crucefié* and the 15th-c. farces they inspired. The later farces are in no way superior to the *fabliaux*, nor do the older texts ignore what we now understand to be the conventions of comic theatre. L. insists that these short narrative texts, rich in images and vigorous dialogues, always liable to shock, and full of performance potential, offer a clear example of how the skilled *jongleur*-narrator 'plays the text' before his audience, concluding that any dramatization of a *fabliau*, medieval or modern, will inevitably lessen its comic effect. A. Corbellari, 'Rêves et fabliaux: un autre aspect de la ruse féminine', *ib.*, 53–62, notes how the *fabliaux* reject the idealistic use of dreams in other genres. Rather than placing the dreamer in contact with an invisible, future world, *fabliau* dreams concentrate on the past or the present. This allows C. to consider *fabliau* dreams as a precursor to more modern interpretative frameworks. G. D. Mole, 'Du bacon et de la femme: pour une relecture de *Barat et Haimet* de Jean Bodel', *Neophilologus*, 86:17–31, notes that the ham occupying the second part of the *fabliau* is interchangeable with the woman and that the story of theft is one of illicit, non-consensual sex in which Bodel both endorses and toys with the misogynistic discourse inherent in the *fabliau* genre. This ambiguity arises from Bodel's subtle use of inversion and suggestion and cannot be reduced to the text's most explicit meanings and parodic intent. E. Baumgartner, 'Titre et nom d'auteur: le cas des fabliaux,' Baumgartner, *Seuils*, I, 53–75, treats, in the particular case of *fabliaux*, the complex question of titles: the ways in which these titles are and are not assigned by the author, the medieval reception history, and the work of modern critical editors.

9. Moral, Didactic, and Allegorical Works

C. Connochie-Bourgne, 'Les *Vies des philosofes* dans la seconde rédaction de l'*Image du monde*: Fragments d'une chronique universelle', *BDBA*, 20:25–38, studies how telling of the past helps to construct the present. The inclusion of biographical material such as the *philosofes* both establish a moral order and celebrate the pedigree of men of science in the manner of aristocratic lineages. M. Gally, 'Pourquoi écrit-on des *Arts d'aimer*? ou les prologues d'un genre inclassable', Baumgartner, *Seuils*, II, 199–218, studies northern *Arts* in relation to the Ovidian text and to contemporary society. She examines a number of rhetorical strategies and wonders whether in composing such a text the poet is exploiting a means of obtaining the favours of his lady. R. Trachsler, 'La tortue, la limace et la welke: le dossier iconographique de la fable de l'aigle et de la corneille', *Reinardus*, 15: 161–74, is an interesting study of different interpretations of *testudo*. T. examines MSS of Marie de France's *Fables* and considers the different medieval transcriptions and illustrations, concluding that interpretative problems are not limited to modern readers. J. Barban, *'Lai ester: acceptance of the status quo in the fables of Marie de France', *RoQ*, 49: 3–11. M. Fantoni, *'Una riedizione del *Dit des XII mois*', *MedRom*, 25: 44–62.

Y. Foehr-Jannsens, H. Bellon-Méguelle, and S. Schaller Wu, 'L'honneur de la clergie dans les *Fables* de Pierre Alphonse: à propos d'une des traductions françaises de la *Disciplina clericalis*', *ICLS 10*, 149–60, observe how the French translations of the *Disciplina* are invaded by a profane concept of honour which is then reinterpreted as an expression of courtly claims to recognition by recourse to the norm of 'enobling virtue'. D. Maddox, 'Avatars courtois d'un genre du discours clérical: le *chastoiement*, *ICLS 10*, 161–76, perceives the unfolding development of an originally classical, then medieval-clerical literary form into a varied typology of vernacular genres with a primarily didactic function. This is the case even when this function is subverted.

R. L. A. Clark, 'Jousting without a lance: the condemnation of female homoeroticism in the *Livre des manières*', Sautman, *Love*, 143–77, analyses the only medieval French vernacular work to mention female homoeroticism; in doing so, the cleric Etienne de Fougères sees it as similar to *fin'amors*, in that both are inherently immoral and threatening to good social order. S. Amer, 'Lesbian sex and the military: from the medieval Arabic tradition to French literature', *ib.*, 179–98, also examines Etienne de Fougères' work and its similarities (especially in imagery) to medieval Arabic works.

10. Drama

Dunbar H. Ogden, *The Staging of Drama in the Medieval Church*, Delaware U.P., 2001, 256 pp., covers the period from the 10th c. to about 1600 when the liturgical drama was staged in churches. The volume reproduces ground plans and traces on them the performers' paths in a number of cathedrals. R. Brusegan, 'L'évolution du prologue de théâtre en France au Moyen Age (XIIe–XIIIe siècles)', Baumgartner, *Seuils*, II, 159–77, aims to establish a typology and description of dramatic prologues which link internal structure with theoretical concepts underpinning it. The lyrical prologue belongs to liturgical drama, the *prologue-rubrique* to paraliturgical plays. A detailed examination of the 'independent prologue' to the *Jeu de saint Nicolas* reveals how it sets out both the edifying value and dramatic nature of the play. B. concludes that the need to provide such a prologue would only be felt when a theatrical work begins also to be read. M. R. Warren, 'The flavour of sin in the *Ordo representacionis Ade*', *Neophilologus*, 86: 179–95, argues that the *Ordo*, allied with both Lent and predication, represents gustatory desire as the source of both sin and salvation. The drama figures illicit 'gourmandisme' as a social danger born of both pride and avarice, whilst at the same time offering itself as a source of aesthetic pleasure. As spectators rather than sinners, the audience can be distracted from pious messages by aesthetic pleasures. The play therefore maintains the fundamental tensions between individual tastes and communal responsibilities. M. Fries, 'The evolution of Eve in medieval French and English religious drama', *SP*, 99: 1–16, notes that as religious drama developed separately in England and France, Eve changed too. In fact, we can almost speak of an 'English Eve' and a 'French Eve'. The 'French Eve' grew in womanliness but lost her prophetic vision, whereas the 'English Eve' failed both to develop as a living woman and also to function as a prophet of redemption.

11. Historiography and Chronicle

Wace, *The Roman de Rou*, trans. Glyn S. Burgess, St. Helier, Société Jersiaise, xlix + 408 pp., is a handsome volume containing a co-authored introduction (with E. van Houts), an up-to-date bibliography, and Burgess's characteristically readable translation facing Anthony J. Holden's SATF edition of the A-N text. The introduction considers questions of authorship, examines Wace's relationship with the Plantagenet court, surveys the MS tradition and modern editions, studies the principal written sources, and reflects on the dual roles of the writer and historian. B. posits that the work was eventually abandoned by its author since Wace was more interested in truth than in propaganda. The prose translation follows the A-N text closely and is accompanied by an Index of Place Names and brief but useful notes. It is carefully divided into paragraphs, each giving line numbers, which faithfully match the A-N text. This is the first complete translation of Wace's *Rou* and as such represents a major contribution to the study of OF and A-N literature. L. Mathey-Maille, 'L'écriture des commencements: le *Roman de Rou* de Wace et la Chronique des ducs de Normandie de Benoît de Sainte-Maure,' Baumgartner, *Seuils*, 1, 79–95, examines the same material used in both texts, concluding that whilst a preface can be an autonomous work, a prologue is directly linked to the text.

Wace's Roman de Brut — A History of the British. Text and Translation, trans. Judith Weiss, Exeter U.P., xxix + 385 pp., is a revised version of her 1999 work, with Ivor Arnold's 1938 SATF edition reproduced (and emended) *en face*. L. Mathey-Maille, 'De l'*Historia Regum Britanniae* de Geoffroy de Monmouth au *Roman de Brut* de Wace: la naissance du roman', Buschinger, *Travail*, 5–10, argues that *Brut* constitutes the beginning of romance through its innovations in the use of speech (direct and individualistic), interventions that signal the advent of debate, and the introduction of the *merveilleux*.

J. Weiss, 'Emperors and Antichrists: reflections of empire in insular narrative, 1130–1250', Hardman, *Identity*, 87–101, examines (*inter alia*) *Beuve de Hantone*, *Waldef*, *Gui de Warewick*, and the *Roman de Brut*, in order to see how historiography draws on previous eschatological texts (e.g., Sibylline Oracle, Biblical commentary) to provide complex views of empire in both chronicles and romance. C. Gaullier-Bougassas, 'Origines d'un lignage et l'écriture romanesque: les romans lignagers anglo-normands', Baumgartner, *Seuils*, II, 19–36, studies Thomas's *Roman de Horn*, *Beuve de Hantone*, *Waldef*, *Gui de Warewick* (all late 12th-c. to mid-13th-c.), and *Fouke le Fitz Waryn* (14th c.). All are considered romances, although the authors insist on historico-epic elements in them, never once using the term '*romanz*'. These texts exploit the sources and conventions of both romance and historiography, creating (in G.-B.'s view) a new genre of historical fiction.

C. Croizy-Naquet, 'De la *translation* à la *compilation*: le cas de l'*Estoire des Engleis* de Geiffrei Gaimar', Buschinger, *Travail*, 19–27, studies the skill with which Gaimar provides both translation of the sources and literary creation by using diverse models within a coherent text. Furthermore, G. combines annalistic sections of his *estoire* with romanesque insertions. C.-N. has also published 'Les festivités dans l'*Estoire de la Guerre Sainte d'Ambroise*', *MA*, 108:61–82. C.-N. states that Ambroise deliberately places references to feast days in order to structure and drive his narrative. His unusual (for a chronicler) insistence on feasts and festivities can be explained by their function as a princely mirror, reflecting Richard's glory. F. Vielliard, 'Richard Coeur de Lion et son entourage normand: le témoignage de l'*Estoire de la Guerre Sainte*', *BEC*, 160:5–52, suggests that the 'Norman' identity of the author may have as much to do with borrowings from the *Itinerarium regis Ricardi* as with the supposed Norman emphasis of the author's 'original' text. S. Loutchitskaja, 'L'idée de conversion dans les chroniques de la première croisade', *CCMe*, 45:39–53, compares *chansons de geste* with chronicle in order to underline the common oral tradition producing one genre whilst influencing another. Chronicle treatment of conversion in particular is aligned more closely to the literary model than to historical reality, even by eyewitnesses, as well as being heavily influenced by the rhetoric of martyrologies. P. Noble, 'Eyewitnesses of the fourth crusade: the reign of Alexius V', Kooper, *Chronicle* II, 178–189, examines the accounts of Alexius' short-lived reign of 1204, as given by Geoffrey de Villehardouin, Robert de Clari, and Nicetas Choniates; N.'s summary, though brief, does provide a clear and compelling analysis of all three accounts.

In 'La culture des historiens anglo-normands: l'exemple de Thomas de Kent', Buschinger, *Travail*, 29–40, V. proposes a typology of auctorial references by which texts can be classified as historical or not; thus, Thomas of Kent's *Roman de toute chevalerie*, presenting one reference per 200 verses, would be historical (V. asserting that the average ratio for such works is one reference per 340 verses).

E. Baumgartner, 'Ecrire et penser l'histoire selon l'*Histoire des ducs de Normandie* de Benoît de Sainte-Maure', Buschinger, *Travail*, 41–50, touches on diverse aspects of the composition and reception of Benoît's 'historical' work, returning most frequently to the point that his concept of history is one overtly linking past to present, present to future. In each case, the former presages the latter as the latter fulfils the former.

LATE MEDIEVAL LITERATURE

By Nicole Lassahn, *University of Chicago*

1. Epic

A. Labbé, 'Les stratégies de la famine dans la *Chanson de Bertrand du Guesclin*', *Littératures*, 42, 2000: 5–36, argues that hunger and food have a double signification when situated in the context of the open battlefield of Najera. G. Allaire, 'Considerations on *Huon d'Auvergne/Ugo d'Alvernia*', *Viator*, 32, 2001: 185–204, traces the complex transmission of this epic romance through Franco-Italian manuscripts and various versions, some in prose. L. Brook, 'Allusions à l'antiquité gréco-latine dans l'*Entrée d'Espagne*', *ZRP*, 118: 573–86, argues that this, though late, is still truly a *chanson de geste*, despite allusions clearly gleaned from romance. D. Collomp, 'Un singulier ermite dans *Dieudonné de Hongrie*', *Senefiance*, 45, 2000: 51–65, examines the role of the hermit Moisan (Moïsant) in the unedited part of the text, linking it to difficulties encountered by the author in composing a late epic. M. de Combarieu du Grès, 'Les deux morts de Renaut de Montauban (d'après les manuscrits Douce et La Vallière)', *ib.*, 67–81, compares these two versions, especially the prologue and the episode of Renaut's death. I. Weill, 'Les "merveilles" de la cour de Flandre dans la chanson de geste d'*Auberi le Bourgoin*', Herbin, *Richesses*, 37–47, examining the lack of 'fit' of this episode with the rest of the narrative, argues that the whole makes a point about the value of prowess and love over riches, power, and beauty. H.-E. Keller, 'La chanson de geste au XVe siècle: bilan', *MoyFr*, 44–45, 2000: 297–307, overviews the characteristics of the late 14th-c. and 15th-c. epic, including their links to noble tastes. M.-J. Pinvidic, 'Les noms propres dans *La Geste de Garin de Monglane* en prose', *Senefiance*, 45, 2000: 217–41, is a concordance of these proper names with an account of the project's difficulties.

Editions. *Baudouin de Sebourc*, ed. Larry S. Crist and Robert F. Cook, 2 vols, SATF, 1227 pp., was mistakenly published under Crist's name alone; this edition (containing 25,778 lines) is based on Paris, BNF, MS fr. 12552 with some additions and corrections from Paris, BNF, MS fr. 12553; it is intended to replace L.-N. Boca's 1841 edition.

2. Drama

G. Smith, 'Marion's merry resistance: implications of theatralization in Adam de la Halle's *Le Jeu de Robin et Marion*', *WIFS*, 8, 2000: 16–30, argues that when the *pastourelle* becomes drama, Marion's physical presence on stage evens out the previously unequal status of men and women. G. Runnalls, 'Medieval actors and the invention of printing in late medieval France', *Early Drama, Art, and Music Review*, 22, 2000: 58–80, explores how printing influenced late medieval French mystery plays, especially their circulation and performance. P. Happé, 'The management of narrative in the performance of cycle plays: the Cornish *Ordinalia, La Passion d'Auvergne,* and *N-Town*', *ib.*, 24: 105–21, compares cycle plays from England and France, linking differences in staging to the use of a flexible cyclic form. M. Carlson, 'Spectator responses to an image of violence: seeing Apollonia', *FCS*, 27: 7–19, challenges the notion of a single, unified cultural response to violence by devising six speculative, hypothetical audience responses. E. DuBruck, 'Lazarus's vision of Hell: a significant passage in late-medieval passion plays', *ib.*, 44–55, links Lazarus's report from hell with contemporary judicial violence. J. Enders, 'The music of the medieval body in pain', *ib.*, 93–112, argues that Old French medieval drama developed a 'shared lexicon of torture, rhetoric, and music' because judicial culture is partly about a performance of pleasure and pain. Jody Enders, *Death by Drama and Other Medieval Urban Legends*, Chicago U.P., 324 pp., examines the social circumstances of late medieval French theatre, especially in performance, arguing for a shift from the 15th c. to a new early modern theological sensibility; the same author's 'Dramatic memories and tortured spaces in the *Mistere de la sainte Hostie*', Hanawalt, *Space*, 199–222, argues that the play suggests to its Christian audience that it be suspicious of activities in the private spaces (homes) of Jews. S. Le Briz-Orgeur, 'Le *Mystère de la Passion* d'Arnoul Gréban, un atelier du dialogue', *MoyFr*, 46–47, 2000: 327–46, examines the relationship between formal considerations and performance, especially dialogue as a means to dramatic success. J.-P. Bordier, 'Le rôle de Jean-Baptiste chez Arnoul Gréban et Jean Michel', *Senefiance*, 48: 43–59, examines violence as part of a tradition of theological thinking about the person of Christ, linking Gréban to Thomas Aquinas and Michel to William of Ockham. J. Subrenat, 'La mission de Jean-Baptiste dans les *Passions* du XVe siècle: l'exemple du *Mystère de la passion* d'Arras', *ib.*, 185–99, considers dramatological evidence for what the author had in mind as John's mission. V. Hamblin, 'Orleans on stage: reconstructing the performance history of the French *Mistere du siege d'Orleans*', *Parergon*, 19: 69–80, examines evidence that this play was performed in the late 15th c. despite the fact that the events depicted were somewhat earlier. E. Birge Vitz, 'La liturgie dans les *Mystères* de la Passion et les *Mystères* en tant que liturgie', *MoyFr*, 46–47, 2000: 591–608, studies the influence of the liturgy on 14th-c. and 15th-c. French theatre. O. A.

Duhl, 'À la recherche du jeu médiéval comique: texte, théorie et spectacle virtuel', *ib.*, 44–45, 2000: 209–21, overviews research on late medieval theatre. C. Harvey, '*La Manekine* de Philippe de Remy et ses avatars: *La fille du roy de Hongrie*', *ib.*, 265–77, studies the relationship between the original *Manekine* and this adaptation into dramatic form, part of the *Miracles de Nostre Dame par personnages.*

EDITIONS. *Le Mystère du Jour du Jugement*, ed. Jean-Pierre Perrot and Jean-Jacques Nonot, Chambéry, Comp'Act, 2000, 277 pp., edits this 14th-c. drama from a single 15th-c. manuscript, Bibliothèque municipale de Besançon, MS 579; it includes plates of the miniatures, an introduction, notes, and a facing-page translation into modern French prose.

3. Lyric

D. Nelson, 'From twelfth-century *cortezia* to fifteenth-century *courtoisie*: evolution of a concept or continuation of a tradition?' *FCS*, 25, 2000: 86–96, traces the related, but discrete, meanings of these terms through the 15th c. in the works of Charles d'Orléans, Christine de Pizan, Alain Chartier, and Villon. S. Rosenberg, 'An unrecognized Old French *ballade*', *RPh*, 54, 2000: 51–55, ties this *ballade* from Baltimore, MD, Walters Art Gallery, MS W.132 to the *ballade* tradition in Oxford, Bodleian Library, Douce 308 and Paris, BNF, MS fr. 146, and includes a transcription. In J. Tansey, 'A strategy for translating medieval lyric: Rutebeuf's "La Griesche d'yver" ', *Metamorphoses: Journal of the Five-College Seminar on Literary Translation*, 8, 2000: 248–55, problems of translation lead to a reading of Rutebeuf that includes tracking manuscript variants as a key to the sites of polysemy, dialect as a gauge of social register, and the multiplicity of first-person voices and poetic stances. H. Solterer, 'The freedoms of fiction for gender in premodern France', Fenster, *Gender*, 135–63, examines a shift in the meaning of *franchise* and the idea of freedom in the 15th-c. controversy over the 'Belle dame sans merci.' G. Peters, 'Urban minstrels in late medieval southern France: opportunities, status and professional relationships', *EMH*, 19, 2000: 201–35, examines minstrels' freelance activities, socio-economic status, and professional relationships. W. A. Davenport, 'Ballades, French and English, and Chaucer's "scarcity" of rhyme', *Parergon*, 18, 2001: 181–201, examines English transformations of the French *ballade* into a looser, but more flexible, form. B. Roy, 'Sur deux poèmes de Robert Regnaud, grand bedeau de l'Université d'Angers', *MoyFr*, 46–47, 2000: 469–96, presents a transcription with an introduction to the author and the context of these two 15th-c. lyrics: *Ballade faitte touchant la grant deception des Angloys*, and *Lay de confession.*

C. Thiry, 'Prospections et prospectives sur la Rhétorique seconde', *ib.*, 541–62, overviews studies and editions of poetry of the second rhetoric period.

LYRIC AND GENRE. C. Page, 'Around the performance of a 13th-century motet', *EMus*, 28, 2000:343–57, treats the question of performance and multiple text in 'Par un matinet/Hé, sire/Hé, bergier'. P. argues that the three upper-voice texts in the *pastourelle* form create a conversation which is not discernable in polyphonic performance; he also treats the larger question of polyphony in performance, especially 4-part polyphony. Four articles in *LR*, 55, 2001, all consider the *congé* as a genre *per se* in the face of the small number of examples: a brief introduction by M. Watthée-Delmotte, 'Frontières génériques: le cas des congés' (3–4); C. Deschepper, 'La lèpre des congés: naissance, stabilité, et dégénérescence du genre' (5–17), argues that the available examples do form a complete generic cycle; V. Minet-Mahy, 'Récupération lyrique et courtoise d'un genre: observations sur quelques "congés d'amours" en moyen français' (19–37), argues for a reconsideration of the generic criteria themselves; and C. Thiry, 'Vie et survie des congés' (39–52), argues for later, perhaps 'perverted or denatured' examples of the genre. M. Bruckner, 'What short tale does Jehan Bodel's political pastourelle tell?' *Romania*, 120:118–31, argues that the open-ended form of this *pastourelle* inscribes a multiplicity of potential future political events.

4. Romance

M. Szkilnik, 'Un exercice de style au XIIIe siècle: *Hunbaut*', *RPh*, 54, 2000:29–42, argues that the author exaggerates *ad absurdam* the Gawain portions of the *Conte du Graal* in a burlesque of his exploits. L. Walters, 'Parody and the parrot: Lancelot reference in the *Chevalier du papegau*', *Uitti Vol.*, 331–44, argues that, since the parrot is both linked to Arthur and the opponent of the nightingale, the *Papegau* works as a parody of romance conventions, especially Chrétien's *Lancelot*. W. Azzam, 'La charade des *Quinze Joies de Mariage*: un sobriquet', *Romania*, 120:234–38, quickly reconsiders the possible solutions to the word-game attribution near the end of the *QJM*. K. Pratt, 'The strains of defence: the many voices of Jean Le Fèvre's *Livre de leesche*', Fenster, *Gender*, 113–33, argues that L. uses textual strategies to undermine the authority of his female advocate, and that his real audience is male even though he invokes a Parisian lady. A. Martineau, 'De la laideur à la beauté: la métamorphose de Tronc en Aubéron dans le roman *d'Ysaÿe le triste*', *Senefiance*, 43, 2000:371–81, studies this transformation as a key for the complex structures of opposition of the text as a whole. L. Brook, 'De la *Demande* à l'*Arrêt*:

Martial d'Auvergne', *MoyFr*, 44–45, 2000:63–74, examines the relationship of the *Arrêts d'Amour* to the tradition of the *demande d'amour.* R. Fajen, 'Malincolia di un lignaggio: lo *Chevalier Errant* nel castello della Manta', *Romania*, 118, 2000:105–37, explores the relationship between literature and family history using a genealogical 'key'.

Catherine Batt, *Malory's Morte Darthur: Remaking Arthurian Tradition*, NY, Palgrave, 264 pp., contains an extensive treatment of French source material for Malory including the later and much less-studied narratives, e.g. *Guiron le Courtois*, the second prose *Tristan*, the Arthurian collection of Paris, BNF, MS fr.112. Michael St. John, *Chaucer's Dream Visions: Courtliness and Individual Identity*, Aldershot, Ashgate, 2000, 226 pp., examines the dream vision's importation into England as a site of 'cultural transition', and treats Machaut, Froissart, and the *Rose*, but only *passim*. Christine Ferlampin-Acher, *Fées, bestes et luitons: croyances et merveilles dans les romans français en prose (XIIIe–XIVe siècles)*, Sorbonne U.P., 513 pp., traces the evolution of *merveilles* using a literary approach combined with folklore and centered around the concept of belief; she includes chapters on marvellous time, magicians, monsters, marvellous objects, and the idea of foreign lands, hell, and heaven. Miha Pintaric, *Le Sentiment du temps dans la littérature française (XIIe s.- fin du XVIe s.)*, Champion, 342 pp., traces a change from 'medieval' time ('moral time') to a new sense of objective time; the book includes chapters on the *Rose*, Rutebeuf, and Villon (as well as earlier works: *Roland*, the troubadours, Chrétien de Troyes, and the Lancelot-Grail cycle). Ana Pairet, *Les Mutacions des fables: figures de la métamorphose dans la littérature française du Moyen Âge*, Champion, 197 pp., traces Ovidian stories through the 14th c., treating, among other things, the relationship of the idea of change in literary work to its theological contructions; she includes chapters on the *Ovide moralisé*, the *Voyage en Béarn*, and the *Livre de la Mutacion de Fortune*. Nadine Bordessoule, *De proies et d'ombres: écritures de la chasse dans la littérature française du XIVe siècle*, NY, Lang, 2000, 145 pp., examines images of hunting in both courtly poetry and manuals for hunting; she relates them to changes in authorial stance and the poetic use of desire and self-representation; she includes discussion of Machaut, Froissart, and Acart de Hesdin.

A. Ballor, 'Il mito di Giasone e Medea nel medioevo francese (XII–XIV secolo)', *SFr*, 44, 2000:455–71, traces the story through the *Roman de Troie*, the *Roman de la Rose* of Jean de Meun, the *Ovide moralisé*, Machaut's *Jugement du Roi de Navarre*, and the lyrics of Froissart and Deschamps, arguing that those who follow Benoît are interested not only in the golden fleece, but also in Jason's return to his homeland and his relationship to Medea. S. Lefèvre, 'Prologues de recueils et mise en oeuvre des textes: Robert de Blois, Christine de

Pizan et Antoine de la Sale', Baumgartner, *Seuils*, II, 89–125, studies those cases where a prologue connects to the construction of a whole codex. J. Merceron, '*Paternoster* et *Patenostre*: de la liturgie à la sanctification érotique', *Romania*, 120:132–48, adds new examples to the theory of J. Ziolkowski that 'paternoster' is a *double entendre*; examples include *Renart* branch I and Rutebeuf's *La Dame qui ala .iii. fois entour le moulier*. J. Cerquiglini-Toulet, 'Polyphème et Prométhée: deux voies de la "création" au XIVe siècle', Zimmerman, *Auctor*, 401–10, considers these images of poetic creation both as voice (song) and as hand (writing); she treats Jean Le Fèvre, Brunetto Latini, Martin le Franc, Froissart, Machaut, Christine de Pizan, and the *Ovide moralisé*. D. Lechat, 'Prolixité et silences dans les prologues de quelques dits de Machaut et de Froissart', Baumgartner, *Seuils*, I, 131–46, argues that these prologues differ from typical prologues partly in that they mix the formal characteristics of the lyric with the motifs of overture to narrative. M. Jeay, 'Ruser avec la mort: trois lectures médiévales d'une séquence topique', Grodek, *Ruse*, 283–96, examines a shared *topos* in Philippe de Rémi's *La Manekine*, Jean Maillart's *Le Roman du comte d'Anjou*, and *La Belle Hélène de Constantinople*, in order to illustrate the heuristic value of the *topos*. J. L. Picherit, 'L'hôtellerie, les hôteliers et hôtelières dans quelques oeuvres de la fin du Moyen Âge', *MA*, 108:301–32, explores evidence for commercial hostelry in literary sources, especially the *Roman du Comte d'Anjou* and *Guillaume de Dôle*. C. Müller, 'Le rôle intellectuel et l'écriture poétique dans les cours princières au passage du XVe au XVIe siècle', *ICLS 10*, 221–30, examines the role of French queens as writers and patrons at the courts of Burgundy and France, especially Margaret of Burgundy and Anne de Graville. J. Koopmans, 'Du text à la diffusion; de la diffusion au texte: l'exemple des farces et des sotties', *MoyFr*, 44–45, 2000:309–26, studies the effects of textual transmission on the medieval farce.

TEXTUAL TRADITIONS. Emma Dillon, *Medieval Music-Making and the 'Roman de Fauvel'*, CUP, 304 pp., is geared toward musicologists, but covers a lot of introductory ground; readers working in literary studies will probably find most useful her arguments about the music itself, which she treats, interestingly, as part of the physical text and *mise-en-page*. S. Huot, 'The *Chastelaine de Vergi* at the crossroads of courtly, moral, and devotional literature', *Dembowski Vol.*, 269–79, uses manuscript tradition and varied readership as a means to solve the problem of the story's multiple genres and competing themes. C. Carroll, 'Transformations d'un texte: les premières éditions du *Chevalier deliveré*', *MoyFr*, 44–45, 2000:75–85, traces an instance of *mouvance* through both manuscript and early printed versions. S. Schwam-Baird, 'Terror and laughter in the images of the Wild Man: the case of the 1489 *Valentin et Orson*', *FCS*, 27:238–56, places the 1489 edition of this tale and its illustrations in the wild man tradition, while her 'The crucified heart of René d'Anjou in text and image', *ib.*, 25, 2000:228–52, situates the image of the crucified heart from the *Mortifiement de vaine plaisance* in the practices of lay piety and devotional literature. E. Rosenthal, '*Theseus de Cologne*: les différentes versions, l'auteur et la date', *Senefiance*, 45, 2000:243–52, is an overview of versions, date, and author. R. Rouse and M. Rouse, 'Publishing Watriquet's *Dits*', *Viator*, 32, 2001:127–76, examines five manuscript collections which were produced by a single, identifiable Parisian *libraire*; their research shows that W. kept copies of his own texts and also explores a relationship to the *Roman de Fauvel*. N. Virtue, 'Rereading rape in two versions of *La Fille du Comte de Pontieu*', *FCS*, 27:257–72, compares two versions of the same tale, that of the 15th c. and that of the 13th c.; building on Vitz's 1992 article on medieval rape, V. argues that the differences between the two versions affect both the way that the stories entertain and an evolving concept of subjectivity. T. Adams, 'Making 'sens' in BNF fr. 19152', *NZJFS*, 23:22–33, connects the dissimilar contents of this manuscript using the idea of *sens* and the practice of ethical analysis as ordering principles.

THE HUNDRED YEARS WAR. Susan Crane, *The Performance of Self: Ritual, Clothing, and Identity During the Hundred Years War*, Philadephia, Pennsylavania U.P., 268 pp. C. treats dress as a formalized, ritual, ceremonial practice associated with the construction of self, especially a courtly self; she includes chapters on Joan of Arc and the *Roman de Fauvel*. R. Blumenfeld-Kosinski, 'Alain Chartier and the crisis in France: courtly and clerical responses', *ICLS 10*, 211–20, argues that Chartier 'fills' the courtly love-debate form with political content and that his persona transforms itself from courtly to clerical in his writings after the Treaty of Troyes (1420). I. Guyot-Bachy, 'La diffusion du *Roman des roys* avant la Guerre de Cent Ans: le manuscrit de Pierre Honoré, serviteur de Charles de Valois', Kooper, *Chronicle* II, 90–102, is an account of the sources and author of this text (Paris, BNF, MS fr. 10132) which argues that his proximity to Charles de Valois affected his account of the beginning of the Valois dynasty. R. F. Yeager, 'Politics and the French language in England during the Hundred Years' War: the case of John Gower', Baker, *Hundred Years' War*, 127–57, argues that G.'s French works were written for Henry IV (not Richard II), and that they are necessarily political simply by being written in French. M. Szkilnik, 'A pacifist utopia: *Cleriadus et Meliadice*', *ib.*, 221–35, argues that this romance is a response to Froissart's *Chroniques*: both share an ideal of chivalric society which can be realized only in the fictive mode of the romance. P. DeMarco, 'Inscribing the body with meaning: chivalric culture and the norms of violence in *The Vows of the Heron*', *ib.*, 27–53, argues that Queen Philippa's vow is the most affective because of gendered norms of violence. N. Lacy, 'Warmongering in verse: *Les Voeux du heron*', *ib.*, 17–25, is a contextualization which aims at recuperating the poem as literature. S. Crane, 'Clothing and gender definition: Joan of Arc', *ib.*, 195–219, reads J.'s cross-dressing not in the political and military sphere, but as linked to sexual identity. Deborah Fraioli, *Joan of Arc: The Early Debate*, Woodbridge–Rochester, NY, Boydell and Brewer, 2000, x + 235 pp., introduces text by text the documents debating J.'s claim to divine mission, many of which are unedited, and some of which are in French; she also argues that this claim, and not just the military and political situation, partly underlies the debate about her.

MISES EN PROSE. C. Brucker, 'Mises en prose et genres littéraires à la fin du Moyen Age: la quête du vraisemblable', *TLit*, 13, 2000: 29–47, argues that these later rewritings eliminate the characteristic features of the original genres for the stories, aiming instead at an idea of verisimilitude. S. Huot, 'Unspeakable horror, ineffable bliss: riddles and marvels in the Prose *Tristan*', *MAe*, 71: 47–65, treats life choices made by the two nephews of Joseph of Arimathea — desire for God and desire for the princess Celinde — in relation to abject sin and divine grace. M. Gil, 'Le cycle d'illustrations du *Roman de Troie en prose* de Benoît de Sainte-Maure dans le milieu bourguignon: le cas du ms. f. 26 de l'abbaye de Mardesous (Arras ou Cambrai, vers 1450)', Herbin, *Richesses*, 155–71, considers this cycle as part of a recontextualization of the matter of Troy in a Burgundian context, especially the idea of the reconquest of the holy land. F. Suard, 'Le *Chastellain de Coucy*: du vers à la prose', *ib.*, 25–36, studies this transformation as an example of Fortune's mutability and as a piteous adventure. G. Roques, 'Les régionalismes dans les diverses versions du *Chastelain de Coucy et de la Dame du Fayel*', *ib.*, 229–42, argues for the examination of regional words as part of the estimation of the value of manuscripts. M. C. Timelli, 'Sur l'édition des mises en prose de romans (XVe siècle): bilan et perspectives', *MoyFr*, 44–45, 2000: 87–106, explores editorial difficulties with these texts, especially the author's own, using the example of the *Erec en prose*.

EDITIONS. Thomas d'Aleran, *Le Chevalier errant*, ed. Daniel Chaubet, Turin, Centro interuniversitario di ricerche sul viaggio in Italia, 2001, 419 pp. takes the text from Paris, BNF, MS fr. 12559, and presents it translated and abridged, but since there is no other extant edition it may be useful. *Les Faicts et les conquestes d'Alexandre le Grand de Jehan Wauquelin (XVe siècle)*, ed. Sandrine Hériché, Geneva, Droz, 2000; cl + 704 pp., uses as a base text Paris, Bibliothèque du Petit Palais, Collection Dutuit, 456, and includes an introduction placing the work in its context at the Burgundian court of Philippe le Bon

(1419–1467) and in the Alexander romance traditions. Octovien de Saint-Gelais, *Le Séjour d'honeur*, ed. Frédéric Duval, Geneva, Droz, 534 pp., edits from Paris, BNF, MS fr. 12783, and includes notes, a glossary, and an extensive literary introduction. George Chastelain, Jean Robertet, and Jean de Montferrant, *Les douze dames de rhétorique*, ed. David Cowling, Geneva, Droz, 279 pp., uses as a base text Cambridge University Library, MS Nn.III.2, which was made for Montferrant himself. M. Fantoni, 'Una riedizione du "Dit des XII mois"', *MedRom*, 25, 2001:44–62, is re-edited because of the discovery of two new manuscripts since the 1926 edition, and includes a description of all seven manuscripts extant. M. Colomba-Timelli, '*Le Purgatoire des mauvais maris* et l'*Enfer des mauvaises femmes*: deuxième partie: édition', *Romania*, 120:192–225, includes a glossary. F. Vielliard and B. Merrilees, 'La vaillance des Marseillaises: un poème français du XVe siècle en l'honneur des femmes (Angers, Bibl. mun. 498, ff. 428–433)', *ib.*, 28–62, presents a poem of 250 lines in octosyllabic couplets, found in a manuscript which contains part of a French-Latin *lexique*; the edition includes an introduction linking the poem to the *louange des femmes* tradition. D. Burrows, '*Le Chastiement des Clers*: a *dit* concerning the nations of the University of Paris, edited from Paris, Bibliothèque Nationale, MS f.fr. 837', *MAe*, 69, 2000:211–26, includes an introduction dealing with the historical and literary context.

COMMENTARY AND TRANSLATION. M.-H. Tesnière, 'À propos de la traduction de Tite-Live par Pierre Bersuire: le manuscrit Oxford, Bibliothèque Bodléienne, Rawlinson C447', *Romania*, 118, 2000:449–98, argues on the basis of this manuscript for two versions which reflect two successive stages of translation. B. Ribémont, 'Encyclopédie et traduction: le double prologue du *Livre des proprietés des choses*', Baumgartner, *Seuils* II, 59–87, argues that the dual prologues respond to the twofold needs of translation and encyclopedia. G. M. Cropp, 'Le char saint Martin: désignation de la Grande Ourse', *ZRP*, 118:173–81, traces the association of Saint Martin with this constellation through versions of Boethius and Vegetius. Kathryn L. McKinley, *Reading the Ovidian Heroine: 'Metamorphoses' Commentaries 1100–1618*, Leiden, Brill, 2001, 187 pp., treats subjectivity and gender: the French work treated is the *Ovide moralisé*.

5. Chronicles and Travel Narratives

E. DuBruck, 'Violence and late-medieval justice', *FCS*, 27:56–67, explores judicial violence in, among other things, miniatures in French historical texts and in conjunction with Villon's 1461 legal troubles. S. Zale, 'The French kill their king: the assassination of

Childeric II in late-medieval French historiography', *ib.*, 273–94, examines accounts of this 7th-c. murder written between 1380 and 1515, when it was ideologically necessary to claim that the entirety of French history was free of regicides; Z. concludes that while some history writers omitted any account for this reason, most, deciding as historians, did not. C. Beaune and M. Lequain, 'Femmes et histoire en France au XVe siècle: Gabrielle de la Tour et ses contemporaines', *Médiévales*, 38, 2000: 111–36, considering that women were enjoined to read historical work, check G.'s library for evidence of female reading pratices and the relationship to historical genres. D. Tyson, 'Olivier de la Marche: l'homme dans l'oeuvre', *Neophilologus*, 86: 507–23, argues that, even though he is usually treated as a source of historical information, O. worked more as a memorialist than as a chronicler: that his aims and descriptions were fundamentally personal; the same author's 'The *Siege of Caerlaverock*: a re-examination', *NMS*, 46: 45–69, is a survey of manuscripts and editions of this OF verse account of Edward I's Scottish campaign of 1300, which argues it is an occasional piece composed by a herald of continental origin in Edward's retinue. P. Lewis, 'Note on the fifteenth-century *Grande Chronique de Normandie*', *ib.*, 185–98, considers the 1487 printing by Guillaume Le Talleur and its relationship to the late manuscript tradition. D. Quéruel, 'Jean d'Avesnes: histoire ou légende d'un seigneur du Hainaut', Herbin, *Richesses*, 199–215, examines the interaction between history and fiction in the 15th-c. *L'istoire de tres vaillans princez monseigneur Jehan d'Avennez*, whose hero was the 13th-c. Jean D'Avesnes; while A. M. Finoli, 'Le cycle de *Jehan d'Avennes* : réflexions et perspectives', *MoyFr*, 44–45, 2000: 223–41, overviews studies and editions. C. Croizy-Naquet, 'Contantes et variantes de l'exorde chez Jean de Vignay', Baumgartner, *Seuils* II, 37–57, argues that J.'s theory of translation relates to his hierarchical vision of the world. P. Noble, 'Perspectives nouvelles sur deux textes historiques du quinzième siècle', *MoyFr*, 46–47, 2000: 377–86, contrasts the two authors' lives, their attitudes to history and the hundred years' war, and social status; the works treated are *Le Voyage d'outremer en Jherusalem* and *La Petite Chronique de la Guyenne*.

M. Guéret-Laferté, 'Le prologue d'un pseudo-voyageur: Jean de Mandeville', Baumgartner, *Seuils*, I, 179–200, argues that de Mandeville works from two sources: Guillaume de Boldensele, *Traité de l'estat de la terre sainte* and Odoric de Pordenone, *Voyages en Orient*. V. Bertolucci-Pizzorusso, 'Pour commencer à raconter de voyage: le prologue du *Devisement du Monde* de Marco Polo', *ib.*, 115–130, explores the textual relationships between Marco Polo and *Méliadus* (a romance) through Rusticien of Pisa, author of the latter and compilator of the former.

EDITIONS. Jean de Mandeville, *Le Livre des merveilles du monde*, ed. Christiane Deluz, CNRS, 2000, 528 pp., includes an extended discussion of the complicated manuscript tradition of the three French versions. Marco Polo, *Le Devisement du monde*, ed. Philippe Ménard, vol. I: *Départ des voyageurs et traversée de la Perse*, Geneva, Droz, 2001, 287pp., is based on M.'s previous work on the entirety of the manuscript tradition, and includes an account of the relationships between the different versions, especially the French and the Franco-Italian. M. plans to publish the whole of the text in six volumes.

6. Paradise and Pilgrimage Narratives

Fabienne Pomel, *Les Voies de l'au-delà et l'essor de l'allégorie au moyen âge*, Champion, 2001, 649 pp., treats these narratives as a genre, with particular attention to Guillaume de Digulleville's narratives; the book traces changes in form (dream frame, first person) and purpose, i.e. as documents which function in various structures and with ideas of mediation. M. Boulton, 'Digulleville's *Pélerinage de Jésus Christ*: a poem of courtly devotion', Blumenfeld-Kosinski, *Spirit*, 125–44, argues that this text — third in a series that includes both religious and literary writing — has adapted the techniques of the courtly *dit* to the life of Christ in a way that marks a departure from earlier vernacular religious writing; the same author's 'La passion pour la Passion: un aspect de la littérature religieuse, 1300–1500', *MoyFr*, 44–45, 2000:45–62, explores genres of writing the Passion other than drama, including sermons and narrative works. M. Rus, 'Sur le paradis au Moyen Age: les mots pour le dire', *Poétique*, 132:415–28, concerns strategies for describing the indescribable in depictions of paradise from the 12th c. to 1501. A.-M. Legaré, 'Les rapports du maître d'Antoine Rolin avec l'imprimé: l'exemple du *Pèlerinage de vie humaine* en prose', Herbin, *Richesses*, 65–79, considers textual organization and the iconographic programme in the latest manuscripts and the earliest printed editions.

7. Biblical and Hagiographical Narratives

C. Sneddon, 'Rewriting the Old French Bible: the New Testament and evolving reader expectations in the thirteenth and early fourteenth centuries', *Rickard Vol.*, 35–59, argues that one explanation for variation in texts of the OF Bible is that scribes deliberately changed the text in order to improve it, and that this means that they had an idea of 'standard' OF; Id., 'On the creation of the Old French Bible', *NMS*, 46:25–44, is a textual study of the OF Bible aimed at discovering the origins of its production: its relationship to the *Bible moralisée*, patronage, and place of production. A. Komada, 'Particularités des manuscrits de la *Bible historiale* enluminés dans le Nord: le cas de la *Bible* de Philippe de Croÿ, comte de Chimay', Herbin, *Richesses*, 185–98, argues that the particulars of Nothern production in this manuscript differ from those to be found in the centralized production of Paris.

G. Hasenohr, 'Les prologues des textes du dévotion en langue française (XIIIe – XVe siècles): formes et fonctions', pp. 593–638 of *Les Prologues Médiévaux*, ed. Jacqueline Hamesse, Turnhout, Brepols, 2000, 691 pp., examines the prologues of religious and devotional literature with the question of what constitutes a prologue in mind. M. Thiry-Stasssin, 'Les légendiers en prose française écrits dans la Belgique actuelle: le cas du Leiden BPL 46A (Huy) et du BRB II 2243 (Namur)', *MoyFr*, 46–47, 2000: 563–75, studies two 15th-c. *légendiers* in relation to local saints. G. Hesketh, 'An unpublished Anglo-Norman *Life* of Saint Katherine of Alexandria from MS London, BL, Add. 40143', *Romania*, 118, 2000: 33–82, is an edition of this text. R. Thompson, E. Friesen, and R. Taylor, '"C'est li riule de vo vie . . .": texte d'instruction pieuse du XIIIe siècle', *ZRP*, 118: 333–50, is a critical edition from a unique copy, MS Arsenal 2058, with gloss, bibliography, and introduction. Pierre de Nesson, *Les Vigiles des morts (XVe s.)*, ed. Alain Collet, Champion, 125 pp., edits this verse version of Job from base text Paris, BNF, MS fr. 578. *The Life of Saint Douceline, a Beguine of Provence*, trans. Kathleen Garay and Madeleine Jeay, Cambridge, Brewer, 2001, 180 pp., presents an English translation of a late 13th-c. life from the unique copy in Paris, BNF, MS fr. 13503; it is not an edition, but it does include an interpretive essay examining Douceline's theology, asceticism, and the issue of female co-authorship, and an introduction providing a historical overview of Douceline and of beguinage. A.-F. Leurquin-Labie, 'La promotion de l'hagiographie régionale au XVe siècle: l'exemple du Hainaut et du Cambrésis', Herbin, *Richesses*, 253–67, argues that from the 15th c. hagiographical narratives began to include local saints.

F. Gingras, '"Un autre temps viendra . . .": permanence et imitations des motifs narratifs dans différentes versions de la *Vie de saint Jean-Baptiste*, entre la figure de l'hagiographie médiévale et celle du saint patron des Canadiens français', *Senefiance*, 48: 79–91, studies conjoined motifs, such as silence/speech, love/death, obedience/revolt, arguing that they vary though the narrative frame is fixed. M.-G. Grossel, 'Vies de saint Jean-Baptiste en vers et récits: permanence et muances d'un culte', *ib.*, 93–109, studies J.'s cultural role as intercessor across a variety of 13th-c. and 14th-c. texts. D. Hüe, 'Le Baptiste et Marie: images et résonances', *ib.*, 111–30, arguing that J. operates between the Old and the New Testaments, examines echoes of Moses and links to Mary. F. Laurent, '"Une voix crie dans le désert . . .": parole sainte et parole inspirée dans la *Vie* versifiée de saint Jean-Baptiste composée dans le premier tiers du XIVe siècle', *ib.*, 149–65, arguing that this narrative transforms its material into speech, examines ties to text and gloss, and to preaching. A.-J. Surdel, 'L'hagiographie médiévale de saint Jean-Baptiste: evangiles, légendiers sanctoraux et récits de voyage en terre sainte', *ib*,. 201–16, looks at J. in narratives of pilgrimage to the holy land.

8. Instructional Manuals and Conduct Books

A. Smets, 'La traduction en moyen français des traités cynégétiques latins: le cas du *De Falconibus* d'Albert le Grand', Paravicini Bagliani, *Chasse*, 71–85, overviews those 14th-c. French translations of falconry texts which come from Albert's Latin version. A. Strubel, 'La chasse à la *senefiance*: Henri de Ferrières et la moralisation du traité cynégétique', *ib.*, 221–35, argues that hunting fits into the world of the prophetic dream in *Les Livres du roy Modus et de la royne Ratio* (1354–77). S. Udry, 'Robert de Blois and Geoffroy de la Tour Landry on feminine beauty: two late medieval French conduct books for women', *EMS*, 19:90–102, examines the relationship between conduct manuals and the idea of feminine beauty, both as a practical concern and as a theoretical construct of identity and gender roles. S. Lécuyer, 'A social, political and religious ideal passed from father to son: from the romance of *Jehan et Blonde* to the *Coutumes de Beauvaisis*', Heller, *Philippe de Remy*, 189–203, argues that the *roman* creates an ideal model of society seen also in the *Coutumes*. M. J. Schenck, 'The role of narration in Philippe de Beaumanoir's *Coutumes de Beauvaisis*', *ib.*, 205–20, treats the narratives within the *Coutumes* as both closed (law) and open (*exempla*) texts. R. Jacob, 'Beaumanoir vs. Révigny: the two faces of customary law in Philip the Bold's France', *ib.*, 221–76, is a study of Beaumanoir's biography, his relationship to sources in common law, and contrasts his concept of customary law with other contemporary concepts. S. L'Engle, 'Justice in the margins: punishment in medieval Toulouse', *Viator*, 33:133–65, concerns a programme of illustrations in Paris, BNF, MS lat. 91877, which contains both the *Coutumes de Toulouse* and a commentary on it. L. argues that the author of the commentary, Arnaud Arpadelle, was also responsible for the design of these pictures, which act as a second gloss.

9. Individual Authors and Texts

ALEXANDER ROMANCES. M. Gosman, 'Alexander the Great as the icon of perfection in the epigones of the *Roman d'Alexandre*', Maddox,

Alexander, 175–91, argues that these writers transform the A. legend in ways related to changing theories of monarchy. R. Blumenfeld-Kosinski, 'Ekphrasis and memory in the fourteenth-century *Parfait du Paon*', *ib.*, 193–202, reads the murals in the *chambre amoureuse* episode from this Jean de la Mote poem as part of a poetic enterprise of nostalgia. M. Szkilnik, 'Conquering Alexander: *Perceforest* and the Alexandrian tradition', *ib.*, 203–17, argues that *P.* integrates Alexander into the Arthurian tradition both in terms of lineage and in terms of values. J. Taylor, 'Alexander amoroso: rethinking Alexander in the *Roman de Perceforest*', *ib.*, 219–34, argues that A. as lover makes explicit the tensions between erotic, private love and public empire building. L. Harf-Lancner, 'From Alexander to Marco Polo, from text to image: the marvels of India, *ib.*, 235–57, compares A. as a means of engaging other cultures to Marco Polo's *Devisement du monde*, which classifies rather than wonders at the marvels of the East. C. Ridoux, 'Astres et désastres dans le *Perceforest*', Herbin, *Richesses*, 217–27, looks at the comet as one of several fractures in the larger frame of a narrative which marches toward an ideal civilization typified by the Arthurian world. M. Szkilnik, 'David Aubert chroniqueur: le prologue du *Perceforest* dans la compilation de l'Arsénal', Baumgartner, *Seuils*, 1, 201–21, argues that Aubert's compilational interventions in the text (marginialia, rubrics, prologues, etc.) form a coherent programme to present the romance as a chronicle for his patron: a reader interested in history.

JEAN D'ARRAS. F. C. Colombani, 'Le beau et le laid dans le Roman de Mélusine', *Senefiance*, 43, 2000:81–103, argues that transformations from ugly to beautiful are linked to M.'s transformation from a *fée* and her reintegration into a Christian system; P. Victorin, 'Le nombril de Mélusine ou la laideur en partage dans la *Mélusine* de Jean d'Arras', *ib.*, 533–46, treats M.'s hybrid nature, linking it to monstrous ancestry and noble lineage and viewing it as both the punishment for fault and a means to its redemption. P. Mayer, 'Melusine: the Romantic appropriation of a medieval tale', *GRM*, 52:189–302, argues that Romantic appropriations transform Melusine from tragic heroine to abstract, modern symbol.

CENT NOUVELLES NOUVELLES. M. Jeay, 'Ruse ou obsession? La "coucherie par substitution" dans les *Cent nouvelles nouvelles*', Grodek, *Ruse*, 297–307, argues for the *Cent nouvelles nouvelles* as a series of stories with the same structure: the substitution of a sexual partner. B. Beardsmore, 'A study of two Middle French horror stories', *NMS*, 46:84–101, treats espisodes in *Ysaÿe le Triste* and the *Cent nouvelles nouvelles* of spending the night alone in a haunted house as part of the horror story genre. D. Fein, 'The plague as a sexually-transmitted disease: a commentary on the fifty-fifth tale of *Les cent nouvelles*

nouvelles', *NZJFS*, 23:5–13, reads this tale in the context of the plague outbreak of the 1450s and 1460s, and as linked with female sexuality. Y. Foehr, 'Pour une littérature du derrière: licence du corps féminin et stratégie du sens dans les trois premiers récits des *Cent nouvelles nouvelles*', *Hicks Vol.*, 277–91, using themes of the feminine and sexuality, reads the first three tales as an introductory unit. M. Olsen, 'L'amour puni: quelques considérations narratologiques', *MoyFr*, 46–47, 2000:387–98, explores narratological concerns through images of punished and unpunished adultery. M. Baker, 'Spinning out the story in the *Cent nouvelles nouvelles*', *ib.*, 44–45, 2000:21–8, looks for the subtle differences among the stories in *Cent nouvelles nouvelles* usually overlooked because they share similar structures or plots.

CHARLES D'ORLÉANS. J.-C. Mühlethaler, 'Ouvertures, clôtures, paratexte — réfléxions sur le montage d'un recueil: *La Chasse et le Depart d'Amours*, imprimé en 1509 par Antoine Vérard', Baumgartner, *Seuils*, 1, 223–47, examines the recontextualization of the poems in this edition; she argues that the compiler suppresses no longer relevant political and historical particulars. The same author's 'Récrire *Le Roman de la Rose* au XVe siecle: les commandements d'amour chez Charles d'Orléans et ses lecteurs', *Hicks Vol.*, 105–19, explores C.'s reworking of the relationship between dream-frame and personification. J.-C. Mühlethaler and P. Wegmann, 'Le soupir ineffable: aux limites de la parole poétique: réflexions sur l'esthétique de la maîtrise à l'aube des temps modernes: Charles d'Orléans et Maurice Scève,' *Versants*, 38, 2000:169–92, examine the role of the sigh as part of the link between body and heart that underlies the tradition of love-sickness. A. E. B. Coldiron, *Canon, Period, and the Poetry of Charles of Orleans: Found in Translation*, Ann Arbor, Michigan U.P., 2000, 232 pp., studies Charles as bilingual, examining particularly London, BL, MS Harley 682 — the only single-author love-lyric sequence in English — and also studying him as self-translator. She argues for Charles as unique, neither bringing French practice to England nor doing the same work as post-Chaucerian English authors. Chapter 4 of this book is an earlier version of 'Translation, canons, and cultural capital: manuscripts and reception of Charles d'Orléans's English poetry', pp. 183–214 of *Charles d'Orléans in England (1415–1440)*, ed. Mary-Jo Arn, Cambridge, Brewer, 2000, 231 pp. It traces historical reception in a comparative context (French and English) and the relationship to English canon formation. W. Askins, 'The brothers Orléans and their keepers', *ib.*, 27–45, basing itself on the dates of C.'s poetic production, re-examines the notion that only the duke of Suffolk was a hospitable captor. M. Jones, ' "Gardez mon corps, sauvez ma terre": immunity from war and the lands of a captive knight; the siege of Orléans (1428–29) revisited', *ib.*, 9–26, argues that C.'s historical role in the siege is understudied and underestimated because of an image of him lost in an interior world and oblivious of exterior events that comes from his poetry. G. Ouy, 'Charles d'Orléans and his brother Jean d'Angoulême in England: what their manuscripts have to tell', *ib.*, 47–60, studies manuscripts belonging to the two brothers with suggestions for future research. M.-J. Arn, 'Two manuscripts, one mind: Charles d'Orléans and the production of manuscripts in two languages (Paris, BNF, MS fr. 25458 and London, BL, MS Harley 682)', *ib.*, 61–78, argues that the differences between the manuscripts indicate a difference in attitude toward the two languages as well as a difference in intended audience. C. Galderisi, 'Charles d'Orléans et l'"autre" langue: ce *français* que son "cuer amer doit"', *ib.*, 79–87, argues that the English poems are a translation of an idea of poetry and the poet tied to C.'s rehabilitation of the forms of *ballade* and *rondeau*. J. Fox, 'Glanures', *ib.*, 89–108, uses C.'s self-translation and macaronic poems to track his changing attitudes to language over time. R. Cholakian, 'Le monde vivant', *ib.*, 109–21, compares C.'s captivity poems to those written afterwards to check for a change in authorial stance, especially towards the world outside and physical description. A. C. Spearing, 'Dreams in *The Kingis Quair* and the duke's book', *ib.*, 123–44, argues for a change from the general, abstract allegory of earlier dream poetry to a more specific, historical content; he calls C.'s work a 'literary fiction of the private life.' D. Pearsall, 'The literary milieu of Charles of Orléans and the duke of Suffolk, and the authorship of the Fairfax sequence', *ib.*, 145–56, looks at this open authorship question and evidence of shared literary interests and personal historical connections between the two men in order to evoke a general literary environment and culture. J. Backhouse, 'Charles of Orléans illuminated', *ib.*, 157–63, is an account of the three miniatures, each linked to a particular poem, of London, BL, MS Royal 16.F.ii. J.-C. Mühlethaler, 'Charles d'Orléans, une prison en porte-à faux: co-texte courtois et ancrage référentiel: les ballades de la captivité dans l'édition d'Antoine Vérard (1509)', *ib.*, 165–82, concerns the relationship between historical and fictional in late medieval narratives of prison; she also treats Machaut's *Fonteinne amoureuse* and Froissart's *Prison amoureuse*.

CHRISTINE DE PIZAN. Hicks, *Christine*, contains the following essays: B. Altmann (693–708), on illuminations of David in the *Livre du Debat de deux amans*; C. Heck (709–21), on images of the celestial realm in *Le Livre du chemin de long estude*; S. Jeanneret (723–36), on the images in l'*Epistre Othea* as political reading; M. McMunn (737–53), on illuminated manuscripts of the *Rose* belonging to those in C.'s circle; A. Kennedy (759–70), on the dating and redating of the *Ditié de Jehanne d'Arc*; J. Laidlaw (771–80), on the manuscripts and C.'s relationships; C. Reno (781–87), on marginalia in Paris, BNF, MS fr. 1197; E. J. Richards (789–816), on his edition of the *Cité des dames*; P. Davies (819–32) on C.'s rhymes; and M. Quereuil (833–43), on her vocabulary; K. Brownlee (5–23), on the self-portrait as authorial/ authorizing strategy; D. McGrady, (25–40), on author portraits *versus* authorial self-presentation in C.'s construction as author and as court-poet; J. Monhan (41–49), on gender, authority, marginalization, the power of the written word itself; A. Paupert (51–71), on the difference between literary construction and autobiography proper; P. Romagnoli (73–90), on C.'s creation of her own literary mothers; D. Ruhe (91–109) on C.'s use of martyrs; N. Wandruszka (111–30), on C.'s historical family; P. Caraffi (133–47), on the figure of Medea; J. S. Holderness (149–60), on her conflations of historical personages; F. Huber (161–74), on *L'Histoire ancienne jusqu'à César* as a source for the *Mutacion*; D. Lechat (175–96), on C. and Valerius Maximus; and L. Walters (197–215), on C. and Augustine; M. Lacassagne (219–30), on C. and Deschamps; S. Lefèvre (231–50), on C. and Oresme; N. Nabert (251–68), on C. and Gerson; N. Margolis (269–308), on C. and Nicolas de Clamages; C. McWebb (309–24), on the *querelle*; and A. Tarnowski (325–33), on C. and Philippe de Mézières; L. A. Callahan (481–91), on the figure of the daughter; A. Echtermann and S. Nagel (493–515), on C.'s representations of the variety of women's voices; J. Nephew (517–32), on C.'s gender transformation in the *Mutacion*; J. Walker (533–48), reads the *Book of Three Virtues* in political context; X. Zhang (549–60), on female community and social order; M. Zimmerman (561–78), on cultural memory and female canon; J. Cerquiglini-Toulet (597–608), on images of taste, hunger, food; L. Dulac (609–26), on C.'s use of the gesture; R. Reisinger (627–37), on fiction and pseudo-fiction; E. Schreiner (639–50), on images of nature; G. Smith (651–61), argues that C. subverts the courtly ideal; T. Van Hemelryck (663–89), on the rhetoric of C.'s theory of peace; B. Carroll (337–58), examines C.'s theory of peace; K. L. Forhan (359–81), on C.'s use of Aristotle; C. Nederman (383–97), on C. and political economy; M. Niederoest (399–410), on female violence; T. Adams (413–24), on the dangers of interpretation and C.'s depiction of love; G. Angeli (425–38), on poverty and charity; E. Benkov (439–48), on agency and gender; M. L. Brown (449–59), on reputation and politics; and T. Fenster (461–77), on personal honour and *médisance*.

Kennedy, *Christine*, contains essays by J. Boulton (87–98), on heraldry in the *Livre des fais d'armes et de chevalerie*; C. Bozzolo (115–28), on civil war in the work of C. and her contemporaries; N. Chareyron

(243–56), on nostalgia in the *Dit de Poissy*; S. Dudash (315–30), on C. and the third estate; T. Lassabatère (483–504), on the personification of France in C. and Deschamps; D. Lechat (515–29), on C.'s portrayal of Charles V; N. Margolis (561–73), on history and fiction in C. and Froissart; J. Quillet (685–91), on the *Corps de policie* ; E. J. Richards (747–66), on C. and jurisprudence; M. Richarz (767–76), on the idea of *concorde* in C.; and P. A. Sigal (811–28), on C.'s notion of the *peuple* ; B. Altman (17–30), on C. as a medieval icon; S. Bell (51–64), on C. in 16th-c. tapestries; T. Brandenberger (129–40), on C.'s reception in 15th-c. and 16th-c. Portugal; M. Brink (141–54), on the adaptation of the theme of *amour-passion*; D. Buschinger (171–73), on the *Livre des fais d'armes et de chevalerie* in Germany; J. Dufournet (331–54), on Commynes's *Mémoires*; M. Lacassagne (453–65), on the epistolary exchange between C. and Deschamps; S. Lawson (505–14), on the change of spelling from Pisan to Pizan for modern scholars; C. Müller (603–19), on C. and other 15th-c. female poets; G. Parussa and R. Trachsler (621–43), on C.'s orthography; C. Reno and G. Ouy (723–30), also on C.'s orthography; E. Schreiner (795–810), on early-modern Spanish texts defending women; G. Stedman (829–41), on an early feminist reception of C.; N. Wandruszka (889–906), on C.'s family; T. Adams (1–15), on gender, love poetry, and enjoyment; H. Arden (31–41), on the roles of C.'s parents in her life; J. Beer (43–50), compares the *querelle* over the *Rose* to that over Richard de Fournival; R. Blumenfeld-Kosinski (75–85), compares C. to Alain Chartier; M. Boulton (99–113), on the *Heures de contemplacion de la Passion* and late-medieval devotion; R. Brown-Grant (155–69), on C.'s language and the defence of women; P. Caraffi (175–86), on Boccaccio and the *Cité des dames*; J. Chance (203–29), on images of women in manuscripts of the *Cité des dames*; L. Cheney (257–72), on painting and poetry in the *Cité des dames*; C. Clark-Evans (287–300), on C.'s female *exempla* from the Near East and Egypt; G. Cropp (301–13), on Alexander in C. and Deschamps; T. Fenster (355–66), on paradoxes of sexual difference; M. W. Gibbons (367–80), on self-portraits, literary and pictorial; S. V. Gibbs (397–408), on the *Epistre Othea* in England; K. Hall (409–20), on C.'s view of the mixed life; J. Kellogg (431–41), on the body politic in the *Cité des dames*; C. Kiehl (443–52), on a change in C.'s use of Fortune; J. Lemaire (531–44), on miniatures in the manuscripts in Lille; M.-T. Lorcin (549–60), on solitude in C.'s works; J. Monahan (575–84), on *querelles* medieval and modern; J.-C. Mühlethaler (585–601), on virtue and mirrors for princes; A. Paupert (645–62), on C. and Boethius; M. Posturzynnska (663–70), on anaphor and association in C.; K. Pratt (671–84), compares rhetorical strategy in the *Livre des trois vertus* and the *Corps de policie*; A. Ramsay (693–703), on the link between war and rape in the *Cité des dames*; R. Reisinger (705–21), sees the *Advision* in its context; B. Ribémont (731–45), on C. and newness; S. Sasaki (777–93), on the poetics of journeys in C. and in a 13th-c. Japanese poet; B. Wagner (855–67), on text and miniature in the *Mutacion*; L. Walters (873–88), on C.'s self-presentation as patron-saint; J. Weinstein (907–17), on the sibyl in the *Duc des vrais amans*; M. Zimmerman (919–30), on C. and the art of memory.

B. Ribémont, 'Christine de Pizan et la figure de la mère', *Kennedy Vol.*, 149–61, 324, examining the role of the mother in C.'s political works, argues that she addresses herself to an abstract woman in the role of mother who is associated with peace and social equilibrium. L. Dulac, 'Quelques éléments d'une poétique de l'exemple dans le *Corps de policie*', *ib.*, 91–104, 316–17, treats the use of examples, arguing that their form is a new use of material C. had already treated and a break with contemporary topical content. C. C. Willard, 'The Dominican abbey of Poissy in 1400', *ib.*, 209–18, 330–31, examines the first section of the *Dit de Poissy* as a source for an historical account of life at Poissy. E. Hicks, 'Excerpts and originality: authorial purpose in the *Fais et bonnes meurs*', *ib.*, 221–31, 331–34, re-examines the question of citation from male-authored sources as part of a 'feminist–ideological' project. G. Ouy and C. Reno, 'Où mène le chemin de long estude? Christine de Pizan, Ambrogio Migli, et les ambitions impériales de Louis d'Orléans (A propos du ms. BNF fr. 1643)', *ib.*, 177–95, 325–28, based on recently-discovered Latin poems of Migli, secretary and advisor to Louis d'Orléans, argues that C. proposed Orléans for the imperial crown. G. Cropp, 'Christine de Pizan and Alexander the Great', *ib.*, 125–34, 320–22, examining 'l'istoire d'Alixandre abrigee' included in the *Mutacion de Fortune*, argues that Alexander is used as a warning against the mutability of Fortune, and to suggest self-knowledge as an alternative to trust therein. A. Tarnowski, 'Perspectives on the *Advision*', *ib.*, 105–14, 317–18, treats the use of allegory in C.'s text as a means to explore how allegory works as 'unity-in-plurality', an idea opposed to modern notions of multiplicity.

C. Brucker, 'Mouvement et fragilité humaine dans quelques oeuvres de Christine de Pizan', *Hicks Vol.*, 161–80, explores themes of movement, change, and stoicism in C.'s life and writings. E. J. Richards, 'Virile woman and womanchrist: the meaning of gender metamorphosis in Christine', *ib.*, 239–52, argues for a detailed and informed response in C. to medieval philosophy, particularly Thomas Aquinas. L. Dulac, 'Sur les fonctions du bestiaire dans quelques oeuvres didactiques de Christine de Pizan', *ib.*, 181–94, examines the functions of beast images both fantastic and allegorical in the *Advision, Mutacion,* and *Livre de la Paix*. L. Walters, 'Fortune's double face:

gender and the transformations of Christine de Pizan, Augustine, and Perpetua', *FCS*, 25, 2000:97–114, argues that C.'s own transformation (gender) is based in the narratives of transformation of Perpetua and Augustine. A. Dziedzic, 'A la recherche d'une figure maternelle: l'image de la mère dans l'oeuvre de Christine de Pizan', *Neophilologus*, 86:493–506, examines the problematic depictions of Christine's mother in her writings both in terms of her own biography and as a way to understand the allegorical female figures that populate her works. B. Stevenson, 'Re-visioning the widow Christine de Pizan' pp. 29–44 of *Crossing the Bridge: Comparative Essays on Medieval European and Heian Japanese Women Writers*, ed. Barbara Stevenson and Cynthia Ho, NY, Palgrave, 2000, xiv + 234 pp., argues that debates about feminism and subjectivity obscure C.'s self-presentation as widow, a stance that she uses to construct her authority to speak. C. Harding, '"True lovers": love and irony in Murasaki Shikibu and Christine de Pizan', *ib.*, 153–73, compares the *Livre du duc des vrais amants* to the Japanese *Tale of Genji*, reading both as critiques of coutly love ideals. T. Fenster, 'Christine at Carnant: reading Christine de Pizan reading Chrétien de Troyes's *Erec et Enide*', *Kennedy Vol.*, 135–48; 322–24, argues that C.'s reading of Chrétien's formulation of *mésdisance* creates also a new form of (female) self. K. Varty, 'Christine's guided tour of the *sale merveilleuse*: on reactions to reading and being guided round medieval murals in real and imaginary buildings', *ib.*, 163–73, 325, compares characters' reactions to explanations of paintings in C.'s work to those in other medieval works. E. Benkov, 'Unmanning Hercules: myth and gender in the *Dit de la pastoure*', Kennedy, *Christine*, 65–74, considers C.'s citation of Ovid's *Heroides* in the *Dit de la pastoure*.

J. Wisman, 'D'une cité l'autre: modernité de Christine de Pizan gynéphile', *RF*, 112, 2000:61–71, examines both the literal and the allegorical city in the *Cité des dames* as *urbs* and *civitas*, countering over-emphasis on allegorical, especially Augustinian, readings. E. J. Richards, 'Where are the men in Christine de Pizan's *City of Ladies*?: architectural and allegorical structures in Christine de Pizan's *Livre de la Cité des dames*', *Uitti Vol.*, 221–43, examining the book as annunciation, the city as a legal space, and the ladies as noble by nature rather than birth, argues that the *Cité des dames* 'looks forward to a reconciliation of the sexes at the moment of the realization of women's freedom.' L. Sylvester, 'Reading narratives of rape: the story of Lucretia in Chaucer, Gower and Christine de Pizan', *Leeds Studies in English*, 31, 2000:115–44, reads this account in all three tale collections (C.'s is in the *Cité des dames*) as a narrative that opens a space to explore 'relationships between sexual pleasure and the literary conventions of male and female desire', including an erotic response to rape. L. Walters, '"Translating" Petrarch: *Cité des dames*

II.7.1, Jean Daudin, and vernacular authority', *Kennedy Vol.*, 283–97; 347–50, shows how, by citing Petrarch in French and via an intermediary French text, C. makes him part of her political programme to strengthen the monarchy, as well as femininizing the vernacular by inhabiting a genre/place of male literary authority. M. Bose, 'The annunciation to Pecock: clerical *Imitatio* in the fifteenth century', *NQ*, 47:172–76, examining the relationship between prologue and authority, finds a source for Pecock in Christine's *Cité des dames*. D. Gray, '"A fulle wyse gentyl-woman of Fraunce": the *Epistle of Othea* and later medieval English literary culture', *ib.*, 237–49, uses C.'s reception, looking particularly at Stephen Scrope's translation (1440–59) of the *EO*, to rethink the traditional opposition between humanism and chivalry and argue for a wider diversity in late-medieval intellectual culture than an emphasis on humanism alone allows for.

A. Lutkus and J. Walker, Baker, *Hundred Years War*, 177–94, read in C.'s *Ditié de Jehanne d'Arc* evidence of hostility between Charles VII and Joan over whether to take Paris in 1429. B. Cornford, 'Christine de Pizan's *Ditié de Jehanne d'Arc*: poetry and propaganda at the court of Charles VII', *Parergon*, 17, 2000:75–106, given a later date for its composition (1429), explores why and for whom could it have been written, especially given its immediate, topical reference. C. also re-assesses Gerson's *De quadam puella*, Jacques Gelu, and *De mirabili victoria* in terms of political context, using Christine's poem as a backdrop to understand why and how Joan of Arc was transformed into a national hero.

N. Margolis, 'The poem's progress: Christine's *Autres Balades* no. 42 and the fortunes of a text', *Kennedy Vol.*, 251–62; 336–38, describes C.'s sources and their implications for knowledge of Latin among writers in the French vernacular, as well as the reception of the *balade* as political propaganda. J. Taylor, 'Mimesis meets artifice: two lyrics by Christine de Pizan', *ib.*, 115–22, 319–20, argues that C. recasts the same bestiary images to accommodate the needs of two different lyric forms in the rondeau 'Cum turtre suis' and the ballade 'Seulette m'a laissée.' P. Davies, '"Si bas suis qu'a peine / Releveray": Christine de Pizan's use of enjambement', *ib.*, 77–90, 308–15, is an analysis and classification of *enjambement* in two sample poems. B. Altmann, 'Through the byways of lyric and narrative: the *voiage d'oultremer* in the *ballade* cycles of Christine de Pizan', *ib.*, 49–64, 303–06, argues that this lover's voyage becomes the central metaphor over the course of three of C.'s collections of poetry. G. Mombello, 'Pour la réception de Christine de Pizan en Italie: l'*Arte del rimare* de Giovanni M. Barbieri', *ib.*, 263–81, 338–47, transcribes chapter 9 of this 1572 treatise as evidence of the early reception of C. and her son,

Jean Castel. M.-C. Gérard-Zai, '*Le Dit de la pastoure* de Christine de Pizan: quelques réflexions sur l'aspect formel', *Hicks Vol.*, 209–15, is a detailed reading especially of lyric intercalation. J. Cerquiglini-Toulet, 'Voix et figures du lyrisme dans l'oeuvre de Christine de Pizan', Kennedy, *Christine*, 187–202, considers 'lyrical' figures in C.'s poetry. J. S. Holderness, 'Fiction and truth in Ballad 15 of the *Cent balades*', *ib.*, 421–29, explores the question of truth and fiction in terms of history and genre. J. Laidlaw, 'Christine's lays — does practice make perfect?' *ib.*, 467–81, tracks the change in C.'s composition of this most difficult of the *formes fixes* in conjunction with the question of the autograph manuscripts. J. Taylor, 'Christine de Pizan and the poetics of the *envoi*', *ib.*, 843–54, considers C.'s response to and transformation of the novel poetic *envoi.*

K. Forhan, *The Political Theory of Christine de Pizan*, Aldershot–Burlington, VT, Ashgate, 2001, xvi, 187 pp., treats over a dozen of Christine's works in order to argue that she had 'a sustained and internally consistent political theory.' The book is written with the discipline and questions of political philosophy in mind, and is organized thematically on that basis, with chapters treating political community, kingship and tyranny, justice, and peace and the just war. E. Wheeler, 'Christine de Pizan's *Livre des fais d'armes et de chevalerie*: gender and the prefaces', *NMS*, 46: 119–61, examines how C.'s reception (and alteration) until the year 1527 affects the way her use of sources is treated in secondary criticism and her place within Western military theory. L. Walters, 'The royal vernacular: poet and patron in Christine de Pizan's *Charles V* and the *Sept psaumes allégorisés*', Blumenfeld-Kosinski, *Spirit*, 145–82, reads these two works together in the context of the translation programme of her patron, Charles le Noble of Navarre, as well as her own translation programme which is set in relationship to Dante in order to argue for the superiority of the French vernacular (her adopted language) over Italian (her native language). A. Kennedy, 'The Châtellerault manuscript of Book VII of Christine de Pizan's *Mutacion de Fortune* and the *Epistre a la Reine*', *Hicks Vol.*, 25–36, gives a complete account of the manuscript itself, its relationship to the late tradition, and recent scholarship on the question. C. C. Willard, 'Christine de Pizan's concept of the just war', *ib.*, 253–60, examines this concept found in the *Faits d'armes et de chevalerie* in the light of historical events.

R. Brown-Grant, 'Christine de Pizan: feminist linguist *avant la lettre*', *Kennedy Vol.*, 65–76; 306–07, compares the use of feminine nouns in the *Cité des Dames* to a 1401 translation of Boccaccio's *De claris mulieribis* (*Des cleres et nobles femmes*), arguing that the differences are deliberate and linked to C.'s anti-misogynist thinking. S. Huot, 'Confronting misogyny: Christine de Pizan and the *Roman de la Rose*',

Uitti Vol., 169–87, treats the role of the female reader both in the *Rose* itself and in the *Querelle*, examining especially how C. positions herself as a female reader and how Pierre Col and Jean de Montreuil seek to undermine her readings. J. Laidlaw, 'Maurice Roy (1856–1932)', *ib.*, 233–50, 334–36, examines the papers of Maurice Roy, a 19th-c. editor of C., with transcriptions from MS 4106 of the library of the Institut de France. N. Margolis, 'Maurice Roy, maverick editor, and the making of the Christinian corpus', *Hicks Vol.*, 217–27, argues that R.'s work is related to concepts of *mouvance* and *variance*, and his fame to Christine's own; C. Brown, 'The "famous-women" *topos* in early sixteenth-century France: echoes of Christine de Pizan', *ib.*, 149–60, examines this *topos* and its relation to the *querelle* in co-existing literary and print cultures; T. Fenster and C. Reno, '*Demoiselle* Christine and Heloise *La Grande Amoureuse*: reading Christine de Pizan and Heloise in the nineteenth-century feminine press', *ib.*, 195–207, examines C. as historical role model in the feminine press; B. Ribémont, 'Jeanne de Schomberg, lectrice de Christine de Pizan?: à propos de l'éducation des enfants', *ib*,. 229–38, is on the 17th-c. use of C. in moral education for children.

Christine de Pizan, *Le Livre de l'advision Cristine*, ed. Christine Reno and Liliane Dulac, Champion, 2001, xcix + 261 pp., use as base text a previously unedited manuscript, formerly Phillipps 128, sold by Sotheby's in 1972 and currently in a private collection. This manuscript gives a corrected version of the text that also includes a preface explaining the three allegorical levels of the first part: the editors present it as an example of auto-exegesis. A codicological description of the three extant manuscripts is provided.

DESCHAMPS. A. Roberts, 'The "homicidal women" stories in the *Roman de Thèbes*, the *Brut Chronicles*, and Deschamps's "Ballade 285" ', Salisbury, *Violence*, 205–22, traces the motif of the 'homicidal woman' through three, chronologically disparate, medieval French texts. R. argues that the motif is rare because it is confined to texts which narrate a foundation legend and which, hence, contain its threatening and disruptive presence. M. Lacassagne, 'Présence de l'épopée dans l'oeuvre d'Eustache Deschamps', *Senefiance*, 45, 2000: 141–51, examining crusade themes in Deschamps, broadly considered (including for example prophecies of the reconquest of Jerusalem), argues for the poetry's engagement with its context and political circumstances. E. J. Richards, 'The uncertainty in defining France as a nation in the works of Eustache Descamps', Baker, *Hundred Years' War*, 159–75, finds contradiction between a tradition of accidental national difference and a new model of patriotism which calls France ontologically and metaphyscially better in representations of France and England in works written between 1385 and 1405.

FROISSART. *Jean Froissart: An Anthology of Narrative and Lyric Poetry*, ed. Kristen M. Figg, with R. Barton Palmer, NY, Routledge, 2001, xx + 700 pp., is a new edition of many of Froissart's poetic works which renders them accessible both by collecting them together in print and by providing a facing-page English translation. The editors have also included an introduction and an up-to-date bibliography. The collection includes poems edited from two manuscripts: Paris, BNF, MSS fr. 830 and 831 (*Le Paradis d'amours*, *L'Espinette amoureuse*, *Le Joli Buisson de jonece*, *Le Dit de la margheritte*, *Le Debat du cheval et du levrier*, *Le Dit dou Florin*, etc.), as well as an excerpt from the *Meliador*, 'The story of Agamanor the painter', edited from Paris, BNF, MS fr. 12557, ff. 145b–170a. K. Figg, 'Froissart's "Debate of the horse and the greyhound": companion animals and signs of social status in the fourteenth century', pp. 85–107 of *Marvels, Monsters, and Miracles : Studies in the Medieval and Early Modern Imaginations*, ed. Timothy S. Jones and David A. Sprunger, Kalamazoo, MI, Medieval Institute Publications, xxv + 306 pp., examines F.'s short *dit* as evidence for animal-human relations as a way of marking upper-class behaviour; F. specifically links social class and nationality as the poem pits civilized English against barbaric Scots. P. Cherchi, '*L'Orloge amoureus* di Jean Froissart', *Dembowski Vol.*, 339–51, argues that F. uses the model of the clock to create a model of general courtliness outside lyric time.

L. Harf-Lancner, 'De la prouesse du chevalier à la gloire du clerc: les prologues des *Chroniques* de Froissart', Baumgartner, *Seuils*, 1, 147–75, looks for an evolution in F.'s idea of the function of the historical text in the prologues to books 1, 2, and 4 in the various textual redactions of the *Chroniques*. L. Stock, 'Froissart's *Chroniques* and its illustrators: historicity and ficticity in the verbal and visual imaging of Charles VI's "Bal des ardents" ', *Studies in Iconography*, 21, 2000: 123–80, argues that F. adopts literary (rather than historical) techniques to create a true-to-life account of the Bal des Ardents of 28 January 1393. S. Huot, 'Unruly bodies, unspeakable acts: Pierre de Béarn, Camel de Camois, and Actaeon in the writings of Jean Froissart', *Exemplaria*, 14: 79–98, examines various representations, in *Méliador*, the *Chroniques*, the *Voyage en Béarn*, of Pierre de Béarn and Gaston Phébus, literary constructions which simultaneously acknowledge and deny 'Gaston's traumatic potency'; while K. Brownlee, 'Mimesis, authority, and murder: Jean Froissart's *Voyage en Béarn*', *Uitti Vol.*, 65–85, examines a contrast between authority and mimetic stance of the author and the protagonist in the presentation of two murders committed by Gaston Phébus; and M.-A. Bossy, 'Donnant, donnant: les échanges entre Froissart et ses interlocuteurs à la cour de Gaston Phébus', *ICLS 10*, 29–38, argues that, as F. moves from transcriber to investigator in his historical writing, his new, ironic, clerkly persona means we should read this murder as part of ingrained courtly corruption. O. Ellena, 'La noblesse face à la violence: arrestations, exécutions et assassinats dans les *Chroniques* de Jean Froissart commandées par Louis de Gruuthuse (Paris, BNF, mss. fr. 2643–46)', *FCS*, 27:68–92, argues that the images of extreme violence found in these manuscripts reinscribe this 14th-c. work in 15th-c. Burgundian history during a time when Charles le Téméraire of Burgundy was using fear to enforce his idea of justice. G. Croenen, M. Rouse, and R. Rouse, 'Pierre de Liffol and the manuscripts of Froissart's *Chronicles*', *Viator*, 33:261–93, concerns a new examination under ultra-violet light of the flyleaf of Paris, BNF, MS fr. 2663 which reveals that this illuminated manuscript of Book I of the *Chroniques* was produced by the Parisian bookseller Pierre de Liffol *c.* 1411–18. The authors argue from textual affiliations and the use of the same frontispiece that two other manuscripts were also produced by Liffol: Besançon, Bibliothèque municipale, 864 and Stonyhurst College, MS I; they hope to be able to atttributefive more manuscripts on these same grounds in the future. O. Ellena, 'Temps, représentation, identité: l'image de la guerre dans les *Chroniques* de Froissart (ms. fr. 2643 à 2646 de la B.N.F., Paris)', Kooper, *Chronicle*, II, 78–89, examines the representation of war in the illustrations of the copy of the four books of the *Chroniques* made for Louis de Gruuthuse.

GERSON. G. Ouy and C. Gauvard, 'Gerson et l'infanticide: défense des femmes et critique de la pénitence publique (ms. London, BL Add. 29279, f. 19v–20v)', *Hicks Vol.*, 45–66, uses new evidence from this manuscript to explore a relationship between infanticide and the status of women in both lay and clerical courts, and looks also at public and private penance. M. A. Edsall, 'Like wise master builders: Jean Gerson's ecclesiology, *lectio divina*, and Christine de Pizan's *Livre de la cité des dames*', *MH*, 27, 2000:33–56, argues that C. and G. knew each other, and that parts of the *Cité des dames* respond to G.'s constructions of Church, the soul, and reform. E. J. Richards, 'Christine de Pizan and Jean Gerson: an intellectual friendship', *Kennedy Vol.*, 197–208, 328–30, re-examines C.'s relationship with G. based on several textual source-influence connections.

MACHAUT. Anne Walters Robertson, *Guillaume de Machaut and Reims: Context and Meaning in his Musical Works*, CUP, 456 pp., examines a number of M.'s lyric poems in their 'local contexts', especially that of Rheims itself; she treats the motets in series in the context of the sacred and secular sources from the Rheims library and the 'David Hocket's' relationship to French kingship. J. Boogaart, 'Encompassing past and present: quotations and their function in Machaut's motets', *EMH*, 20, 2001:1–86, against the claim that musical quotation gradually replaced textual allusion, argues that literary quotation continued into the 14th c. and combined with formal, intertextual references to music. E. Leach, 'Fortune's demesne: the interrelation of text and music in Machaut's *Il mest avis* (B22), *De fortune* (B23) and two related anonymous balades', *ib.*, 47–79, argues that these two form a diptych on fortune; that their musical setting encourages reading them together. S. Lefèvre, '*Longue de mouvee fait changier ami*: de la lettre close à la lyrique dans le *Voir Dit* de Guillaume de Machaut', *Romania*, 120:226–34, concerns the envoi of *lettre* 30, and argues that epistolary writing is a replacement for a lyric production which has become problematic after the events of the narrative. J. Coleman, 'The text recontextualized in performance: Deschamps' prelection of the *Voir Dit* to the Count of Flanders', *Viator*, 31, 2000:233–48, concerns a (rare) report of a public reading; C. treats this performance as a recontextualization of the original, written text to the particulars of the setting, a 1375 meeting of John of Gaunt and Philip the Bold in Bruges to treat at the Court of Louis de Mâle, count of Flanders. D. Leech-Wilkinson, '"Rose, lis" revisité', Cerquiglini-Toulet, *Machaut*, 53–69, examines interactions between contrapuntal music and poetic composition, especially the choice and placement of vowels. M.-B. Dufourcet Hakim, 'Figures et symboles dans les motets de Guillaume de Machaut', *ib.*, 71–94, is an aesthetic reading of symbols, especially those of unity, the universe, and other abstractions, in the text and musical structure of the motets. I. Bétemps, 'Les lais de plour: Guillaume de Machaut et Oton de Grandson', *ib.*, 95–106, examines M.'s influence on later 14th-c. poets, seeing both similarity and difference: 'rupture et continuation.' M. Switten, 'L'oeuvre poético-musicale de Machaut: paroles sans musique ou de la musique avant toute chose?', *ib.*, 119–35, explores relationships between text and music in the organization of the principal manuscripts, the structure of the *Remede de Fortune*, and the conception of M.'s *oeuvre*. K. Brownlee, 'La polyphonie textuelle dans le Motet 7 de Machaut: Narcisse, la *Rose*, et la voix féminine', *ib.*, 137–46, examines three forms of dialogism or 'textual polyphony': triplum vs. motetus, triplum and motetus vs. tenor, and literary context and intertextuality.

G. M. Roccati, 'Guillaume de Machaut, "Prologue" aux oeuvres: la disposition du texte dans le ms. A (Paris, BNF, fr. 1584)', *SFr*, 44, 2000:535–40, concludes that because the 'Prologue' is arranged differently in ms. A than elsewhere, the opening *cahiers* were made in conference with M., while the overall plan escaped his control somewhat. M. Hasselman, 'Teaching Machaut's *Remede de Fortune* in an undergraduate humanities course', *Studies in Medieval and Renaissance Teaching*, 8, 2000:27–36, is an account of teaching Machaut, which relates him to a longer tradition of *fin'amors*. S. Huot, 'Guillaume de Machaut and the consolation of poetry', *MP*, 100:169–95, through the intermediary of the *Rose*, explores Machaut's response to and reworking of the Boethian model of poetry and its proper relationship to suffering. R. Boenig, 'Musical instruments as iconographical artifacts in medieval poetry', Perry, *Material Culture*, 1–15, argues that the relationship between physical objects and their representations is skewed by allegorical overlaid meanings. C. Atwood, 'Temps et lieux de Souvenir: le *Voir Dit* de Guillaume de Machaut', pp. 235–56 of *'Comme mon coeur désire': Guillaume de Machaut's 'Le Livre du Voir Dit'*, ed. Denis Hüe, Orleans, Paradigme, 2001, 282 pp., examines the spatial and temporal situations of Souvenir, seeing her not as past, but as perpetually becoming. N. Lassahn, 'Vérité historique et vérité fictionalle dans le *Voir Dit* de Guillaume de Machaut', *ib.*, 257–80, argues that the model of ideal kingship shifts between the *Confort d'Ami* and the *Voir Dit* in response to the events of the hundred years' war. J. Cerquiglini-Toulet, *Guillaume de Machaut 'Le Livre du Voir Dit': un art d'aimer; un art d'écrire*, Sedes, 2001, 108 pp., was published in conjunction with the *agrégation*, and is an up-to-date account of fundamental *Voir Dit* questions: history, fiction, autobiography, metadiscourse about poetry, music, and reading. Her 'Lyrisme de désir et lyrisme d'espérance dans la poésie de Guillaume de Machaut', Cerquiglini-Toulet, *Machaut*, 41–51, examines music as a theme which resolves (or at least addresses) certain oppositions within M.'s narrative poetry. W. Arlt, 'Machaut in context', *ib.*, 147–62, concerns the question of M. as innovator, poet, and composer. A. Hurworth, 'Le corps remembré: hagiographie et historiographie dans *La Prise d'Alixandrie* ', *ib.*, 107–18, studies the 'microtext' of the signature containing Machaut's and Pierre de Lusignan's names as an investigation of the making of the whole (historical) text. L. Earp, 'Machaut's music in the early nineteenth century: the work of Perne, Bottée de Toulmon, and Fétis', *ib.*, 9–40, treats the history of the earliest scholarly work on medieval polyphony.

JEAN DE MEUN. S. Huot, 'Bodily peril: sexuality and the subversion of order in Jean de Meun's *Roman de la Rose*', *MLR*, 95, 2000:41–61, considers the problem of Genius's sermon, which medieval readers both marked out textually and often misattributed to the narrator, in the larger context of J.'s project and his view of heterosexuality as something which aims at conjoining opposites. S.-G. Heller, 'Fashioning a woman: the vernacular Pygmalion in the *Roman de la Rose*', *MH*, 27, 2000:1–18, argues that Jean's Pygmalion differs from Ovid's because he exploits 'cultural codes of dress to both exploit and deride fantasies of ownership.' G. Raimondi, 'Lectio Boetiana:

l'example di Nerone e Seneca nel *Roman de la Rose*', *Romania*, 120:63–98, explores a link between poetry and philosophy in Jean's *Rose* and his *Boethius*. W. Calin, 'Is Jean de Meun antifeminist?', *Hicks Vol.*, 81–90, overviews modern criticism on the question. E. Baumgartner, ' "Batailles que li con esmurent" (*Roman de la Rose*, v. 13894): de la banalisation du mythe antique dans l'oeuvre de Jean de Meun', *ib.*, 69–79, using Helen of Troy as an example, explores J.'s use of mythological figures as *exempla*. L. Walters, 'Who was Gui de Mori?', *ib.*, 133–46, argues the case that Guibert de Tournai was Gui, a reader who made the *Rose* more didactic and spriritual. Alistair Minnis, *Magister amoris: The Roman de la Rose and Vernacular Hermeneutics*, OUP, 2001, 352 pp., examines medieval literary theory and the reception and interpretations of Jean's *Rose*, in particular the *querelle*. He treats Jean's appropriation of the ironic idea of *magister amoris* from Ovid, and the tradition of French vernacular hermenuetics. Denis Billotte, *Le Vocabulaire de la traduction par Jean de Meun de la 'Consolatio Philosophiae' de Boèce*, 2 vols, Champion, 2000, 501 + 580 pp., is a bilingual dictionary and concordance to J.'s *Boethius*; the introduction addresses the problem of building an abstract, philosophical vocabulary in the vernacular and hence the status of the French vernacular more generally.

PHILIPPE DE MÉZIÈRES. C. Collette, 'Chaucer and the French tradition revisited: Philippe de Mézières and the Good Wife', pp. 151–68 of *Medieval Women: Text and Contexts in Late Medieval Britain: Essays for Felicity Riddy*, ed. Jocelyn Wogan-Browne et al., Turnhout, Brepols, 2000, 436 pp., argues for a third French literary influence on Chaucer, in addition to Muscatine's categories of courtly and bourgeois: advice books for women; here Philippe's *Le Livre de la vertu du sacrement de mariage et du reconfort des dames maries* (1384–89). R. Brown-Grant, 'Mirroring the court: clerkly advice to noble men and women in the works of Philippe de Mézières and Christine de Pizan', *ICLS 10*, 39–53, argues that both P. and C. advised men and women, but while P. offered advice for the good of the immortal soul, C. aimed at a good reputation in the mortal world.

MARGUERITE PORETE. B. Newman, 'The mirror and the rose: Marguerite Porete's encounter with the dieu d'Amours', Blumenfeld-Kosinski, *Spirit*, 105–23, responding to work that argues for a vague or generic relationship between women's vernacular mysticism in terms of the vocabulary and ideas of *fin'amors*, posits an intertextual relationship between Porete's text and the Roman de la Rose, (perhaps via Gérard of Liège's *Quinque incitamenta ad deum amandum ardenter*). C. Müller, ' "La lettre et la figure": lecture allégorique du *Mirouer* de Marguerite Porete dans *Les Prisons* de Marguerite de Navarre', *Versants*, 38, 2000: 153–67, identifies Porete as the unnamed source for *Les Prisons*. M. Cré, 'Women in the Charterhouse? Julian of Norwich's revelations of divine love and Marguerite Porete's *Mirror of Simple Souls* in British Library, MS Additional 37790', pp. 43–62 of *Writing Religious Women: Female Spiritual and Textual Practices in Late Medieval England*, ed. Denis Renevey and Christiana Whitehead, Toronto U.P., 2000, 270 pp., argues that the context of this manuscript collection places Marguerite (and Julian of Norwich) outside a place where the primary hermeneutic is gender. J. Arsenault, 'Authority, autonomy, and antinomianism: the mystical and ethical piety of Marguerite Porete in *The Mirror of Simple Souls*', *StMy*, 21, 2000: 65–94, explores P.'s constructions of the self and of the virtues in terms of conflict between her authority and church authority. A. Hollywood, *Sensible Ecstasy: Mysticism, Sexual Difference, and the Demands of History*, Chicago U.P., 371 pp., is primarily concerned with a highly theoretical construction of mysticism and gender; however since one of her three major medieval examples is Marguerite Porete, those working on P. will certainly find the book useful.

ANTOINE DE LA SALE. R. Dubuis, 'Introduction: pour une lecture "moderne" de Saintré', *RLaR*, 105, 2001: 1–29, revisits the question of literary genre: *roman* or *histoire*? D. Lalande, 'Violence et courtoisie dans le roman de *Saintré*', *ib.*, 31–49, argues that de la Sale opposes Saintré, a warrior, to Boucicaut, a diplomat, in order to depict the gradual detachment of violence from the world of chivalric honour. E. Gaucher, 'Le chevalier, la femme et l'abbé: la structure du *Saintré*', *ib.*, 51–70, argues that the multiplicity of genres reflects the contradictions of a society in crisis. L. Louison and P. Servet, '*Saintré*, roman réaliste', *ib.*, 71–98, argues that certain techniques in S. prefigure those of 18th-c. and 19th-c. realism. M. Santucci, 'Les gestes dans *Jean de Saintré*', *ib.*, 99–128, uses an analysis of gestures within the text to argue that the opposition between court and abbey is less pronounced than one might think. D. Quéruel, 'Veuvage, amour et liberté: la Dame des Belles Cousines dans le roman de *Jehan de Saintré*', *ib.*, 129–42, argues that the character's ambiguity is linked to her widowhood, and to the larger ambiguity of widowhood in the Middle Ages. L. Pierdominici, '"Chose vraye faict a doubter": *Saintré*, ou l'invitation au mensonge', *ib.*, 143–69, argues that formal and ideological ruptures in the *roman* come from an attempt to reconcile the ideal with the real. P. Demarolle, 'Individus et société dans *Saintré*', *ib.*, 165–179, examines *Saintré* both as a work of fiction and as it was read by a 15th-c. audience, while his 'Saintré: langue, style, écriture', *ib.*, 181–194, argues that, though de la Sale's usage seems to differ from that of his contemporaries, each seemingly new thing comes from a recognizable social model. D. Heitsch, '*Jehan de Saintré*: questioning a historical phenomenon', *BHR*, 64: 241–50, argues that

Saintré is a literary version of the biography found also in *Le Livre des faits du bon chevalier, messire Jacques de Lalaigne* (*c.* 1468).

VILLON. I. Roche, 'The use and abuse of legality in Villon's *Testament*', *FR*, 76:78–87, examines V.'s use of legal terms, forms, and practices, especially that of the *testament.* R. Pickens, 'Villon on the edge/Villon at the center: Paris in the *Testament* once again', *Lacy Vol.*, 385–403, focuses on discourse of the centre and margin, especially Villon's use of Paris as a spatial category. E. Ormsby, 'Orpheus with arsenic', *NC*, 20:63–68, treats the problem of how vengeance in the *Legacy* and the *Testament* is both concerned with memory and crafted so as to seem spontaneous; he also evaluates L. Simpson's translation in these terms. J. Koopmans, 'Villon et Jacquet Cardon', *FS*, 54, 2000:277–86, against studies that compare Villon to canonical but non-contemporary work (e.g. 13th-c. theology), argues for an approach which is more precise, historically and philologically; he reads the references to Cardon in the *Testament* and the *Lais* as much less innocent than is commonly thought because of the circular way in which his biography is constructed from Villon's references. P. Walter, 'Le fardeau de Saturne ou la mélancolie de François Villon dans le *Lais*', *Hicks Vol.*, 307–20, treats V.'s relationship to theories of melancholy (especially astrological) as a means of addressing the question of autobiographical fiction. T. Conley, 'Erotic islands: contours of Villon's printed *Testament* (1489)', pp. 136–56 of *Historicism, Psychoanalysis, and Early Modern Culture*, ed. Carla Mazzio and Douglas Trevor, NY, Routledge, 2000, 417 pp., examines V.'s use of Paris and city space through a comparison between spatial relationships in the first printed *Testament* and those found in early cartography; Id., 'Poetic mapping: on Villon's "Contredictz de Franc Gontier"', Hanawalt, *Space*, 242–60, reads this poem as a map of the city of Paris. Jane H. M. Taylor, *The Poetry of François Villon: Text and Context*, CUP, 2001, xii + 234 pp., argues, against an idea of V. as single, speaking subject, that he — and 15th-c. poetry more generally — uses a social construction of self from his participation in contemporary 'poetics of dialectic and debate'. The same author's 'Lire l'illisible: le *Lay* et la *Bergeronnecte* du *Testament* de Villon', *MoyFr*, 46–47, 2000:526–39, argues for treating the *Testament* as a whole. R. Van Deyck, 'Pour un panorama des études villoniennes', *ib.*, 577–90, is an overview of the text and criticism. G. Angeli, 'Comique et cruauté à la fin du moyen âge: Panurge et Villon', *ib.*, 44–45, 2000:9–20, treats tricksters, cruelty, and humour in V. in comparison with Rabelais. Michael Freeman, *François Villon in His Works: The Villain's Tale*, Amsterdam, Rodopi, 2000, 269 pp., is a general study of V. in his works and in his times meant for a general audience or one new to Villon, but with notes and scholarly apparatus. Aubrey Burl, *Danse Macabre: François Villon: Poetry and Murder in Medieval France*, Stroud, Sutton, 2000, xiii + 242 pp., is a yet more general and accessible biography. M. Holton, 'Poets and gaol-birds: Pound, Lowell, and Villon', pp. 15–28 of *Ezra Pound and Poetic Influence*, ed. Helen M. Dennis, Amsterdam, Rodopi, xii + 282 pp., treats the influence of Pound's model of translation on Lowell's translation of Villon.

THE SIXTEENTH CENTURY

By Gilles Banderier, *Basle*

1. General

William J. Bouwsma, *The Waning of the Renaissance, 1550–1640*, New Haven–London, Yale U.P., 2000, xii + 288 pp., describes how men of the Renaissance escaped chaos and managed to build a new political and spiritual order. G. Dotoli, 'D'un siècle à l'autre', Desan, *Littérature*, 11–48, also studies the darker side of the Renaissance. Reinhard Krüger, *Die französische Renaissance. Literatur, Gesellschaft und Kultur des 14. bis 16. Jahrhunderts*, Stuttgart, Klett, 192 pp., is a stimulating handbook, with general chapters and more detailed ones on certain writers and literary genres (poetry, epic, drama). The use of *manchettes* is an amusing feature. Considering that there was no border between the Middle Ages and modern times, K. has a very broad concept of the Renaissance, for the first author taken into account is Nicolas Oresme (c. 1320–1382). Richard Crescenzo, *Histoire de la littérature française du XVIe siècle*, Champion, 2001, 240 pp., is a concise and brillant introduction to the subject, including good consideration of the history of the book. It is divided into two parts, the first one dealing with 'Littérature et société', 'Production, édition et médiations des oeuvres littéraires', 'Littérature, idéologies et esthétique'; the second with 'Les écrivains, les oeuvres, les mouvements', 'Formes et genres littéraires dominants', 'Littérature et univers artistique'.

The transition between the Middle Ages and the Renaissance was not a passage from darkness to light, and this is made clear in François Rigolot, *L'Erreur de la Renaissance. Perspectives littéraires*, Champion, 418 pp., an eminently readable book, which examines the important role of lapses of memory, as well as religious, philological, scientific, or trivial mistakes of the 16th century. Patricia Eichel-Lojkine, *Excentricité et humanisme. Parodie, dérision et détournement des codes à la Renaissance*, Geneva, Droz, 348 pp., charts the rise and evolution of the 16th-c. sense of parody or disrespect, from Alberti's *Momus* and Erasmus's *Stultitia* to Rabelais and d'Aubigné's love-poetry. Michael G. Paulson, *Catherine de Medici. Five portraits*, NY, Lang, 126 pp., shows how as both a Renaissance Italian learned woman and an adept of dark sciences, the Queen raised contrary opinions. P.'s biography closely follows that of I. Cloulas and studies C.'s image in *La Princesse de Clèves*, Balzac's *Catherine de M.*, A. Dumas's *Reine Margot*, and Mérimée's *Chronique du règne de Charles IX*. The bibliography is unfortunately not up to full modern scholarly standards.

Jean-Paul Poisson, *Essais de notarialogie*, Economica, x + 436 pp., is a collection of articles, some of them dealing with the 16th century (the *Minutier central des notaires* in Paris is a gold mine for scholars). Miha Pintarič's study on *Le Sentiment du temps dans la littérature française (XIIe s. - fin du XVIe s.)*, Champion, 342 pp., provides an interesting and detailed analysis, with chapters on Rabelais, Du Bellay, Ronsard, and Montaigne. Floyd Gray, *Gender, Rhetoric, and Print Culture in French Renaissance Writing*, CUP, 2000, viii + 228 pp., describes how literature was shaped by rhetorical conventions and the publishing business, has sections on Rabelais and Montaigne, and reminds us that the books we enjoy reading deal more with fiction than with reality. Renaissance literature should always be considered within the context of its historical background. Mario Turchetti, *Tyrannie et tyrannicide de l'Antiquité à nos jours*, PUF, 2001, 1048 pp., is an immense book, offering a section of relevance to the 16th century (409–511): the author's erudition is daunting, dazzling, but often depressing.

Viallon-Schoneveld, *Histoire*, includes: E. Vaucheret, 'L'historien G. Paradin, source de Brantôme' (125–31), W. J. A. Bots, 'Montaigne historien et/ou conteur d'historiettes' (133–40), and J. Boucher, 'Henri III et le recours à l'histoire dans la vie publique' (157–67). *L'Histoire en marge de l'histoire à la Renaissance* (Cahiers Saulnier, 19), PENS, 224 pp., presents important and new contributions by M.-D. Couzinet, 'La bibliographie de l'histoire dans la *Methodus* de Bodin' (49–60), T. Conley, 'Bernard Salomon en Esclavonie' (85–105), A. Grewe, 'L'historiographie des femmes. L'exemple de Brantôme' (113–27), and B. Conconi, 'L'historien protestant face au devoir d'une nouvelle méthode' (156–76).

W. Monter studies 'The fate of the English and French Reformations, 1554–1563', *BHR*, 64:7–19, showing how, paradoxally, during this decisive period, French protestantism was stronger than its English counterpart, but its strengh was actually a weakness, for it caused French protestants to plunge into a civil war. Ronsard, d'Aubigné, and Montaigne wrote accounts of these tragical events, obviously from different viewpoints, as seen by F. Rigolot, 'Trois "mises en scène" littéraires du politique', Hempfer, *Spielwelten*, 147–63. Calvin was initially a lawyer and his works display an interesting distinction between public and private life, as studied by O. Millet, 'Sphère publique et sphère privée dans l'oeuvre et la pensée de Calvin', *Kwansei Gakuin University School of Sociology Journal*, 89, 2001:41–51. On the birth of the modern state, one may read T. Berns, 'Le regard du censeur et la naissance de la statistique à la fin de la Renaissance', *BHR*, 64:317–26, and C. Randall, 'Masculinity, monarchy, and metaphysics. A crisis of authority in early modern France', Long, *Masculinity*, 211–31.

COLLECTIONS, CONFERENCES, AND WORKS OF REFERENCE. If Renaissance rhetoric is of increasing interest to scholars, it is in a large part due to an already classic work, Marc Fumaroli's *Age de l'Eloquence*. Published originally in 1980, it was reissued in paperback in 1994, and is now available in a third, updated, paperback edition: Geneva, Droz, xxiv + 882 pp. The revised second edition of Jean Jehasse's *La Renaissance de la critique. L'essor de l'humanisme érudit de 1560 à 1614*, Champion, xxviii + 776 pp., shows that the book stands up well to the test of time and offers further insights into the works of Henri Estienne II, Scaliger, and Casaubon. Bernard Quilliet, *La Tradition humaniste*, Fayard, 544 pp., is a magisterial synthesis on European humanism. Danièle Duport, *Le Jardin et la nature. Ordre et variété dans la littérature de la Renaissance* (THR, 363), 408 pp. studies a wide range of topics, such as the garden as *locus amoenus*, its role in alchemy, the praise of country life and gardens abroad; see also Id., 'La variété botanique dans les récits de voyage au XVIe siècle: une glorification du Créateur', *RHLF*, 101, 2001 : 195–212, and 'L'oisif en ses terres ou le repos géorgique', Jones-Davies, *Oisiveté*, 233–48. Renaissance France was no closed world and among major influences we have to take that of Melanchthon into account: Kees Meerhoff, *Entre logique et littérature. Autour de Philippe Melanchton*, Orléans, Paradigme, 2001, 228 pp., is a collection of papers on subjects such as 'Rhétorique néo-latine et culture vernaculaire' (39–57), 'Eloquence ou silence' (151–69), and 'La lecture humaniste' (171–89). Patricia Eichel-Lojkine, *Le Siècle des grands hommes. Les recueils de vies d'hommes illustres avec portraits du XVIe siècle*, Leuven–Paris, Peeters, 2001, 448 pp., deals with the 16th-c. concept of the requirements of biography. Renaissance men (and sometimes women) were fascinated by Antiquity and biographies of 'hommes illustres.' They printed large books with luxurious portrait engravings. This exciting and clear-sighted study covers a wide range of sources, including Giovio, Vasari, Thevet, and Bèze, and the translation of Plutarch by Amyot, and will be standard for a long time. Among great men, the image of Socrates in 16th-c. France (and in the works of Rabelais, Montaigne, Tahureau) is studied by G. Huppert, 'Under the shadow of Socrates', Sandy, *Heritage*, 281–95. S. Perkinson, 'From an "art de mémoire" to the art of portraiture : printed effigy books of the 16th century', *SCJ*, 33:687–723, examines the development of modern conceptions of portraiture in Renaissance France. Some of these books derive their understanding of likeness from medieval arts of memory. Lionello Sozzi, *Rome n'est plus Rome. La polémique anti-italienne et autres essais sur la Renaissance*, Champion, 538 pp., is a useful distillation of articles, only two of which have not been published before. French attitudes toward Italy then were rather similar to attitudes toward the USA today:

writers praised Italian culture and way of life, but endlessly claimed the land was in decline. The second part of this collection deals with the complex notion of *dignitas hominis*, on which one may also read J.-L. Martinet, 'La *dignitas hominis* dans les traités médicaux de Bretonnayau', Viallon-Schoneveld, *Médecins*, 51–63. B.'s *Génération de l'homme* is a collection of medical verse treatises on eyes, heart, liver, kidneys.

There have been recent translations of two important books. Tom Conley's original work was published in 1992 (*YWMLS* 54:84); it now appears, with a new foreword, as *L'Inconscient graphique. Essai sur l'écriture de la Renaissance (Marot, Ronsard, Rabelais, Montaigne)*, Saint-Denis, Vincennes U.P., 2000, 246 pp. C. makes clever use of disciplines as disparate as psychoanalysis and book history. Ann Moss's seminal study (*YWMLS*, 60:95–96), now appears in paper-back translation: *Les Recueils de lieux communs. Apprendre à penser à la Renaissance*, Geneva, Droz, 548 pp. Montaigne himself was greatly indebted to these collections of *loci communes rerum*, useful both to students and to men of mature years.

Figurations du volcan à la Renaissance, ed. Dominique Bertrand, Champion, 2001, 332 pp. contains contributions on Boaistuau, Palissy, Garnier, Rabelais, emblem books, and alchemy. This last discipline is often despised by literary scholars, who are wrong to do so, as excellently demonstrated by D. Kahn, 'Architecture, réforme et alchimie en Franche-Comté vers 1560', *Faivre Vol.*, 91–99.

2. Book History

Henri-Jean Martin et al., *La Naissance du livre moderne (XIVe–XVIIe siècle). Mise en page et mise en texte du livre français*, Cercle de la Librarie, 2000, viii + 492 pp., is probably the work of the decade, and even superlatives fall short when describing this masterpiece of erudition and typography, this gorgeous art book. Renaissance scholars will especially enjoy the chapters dealing with humanist MSS, the role of the *devotio moderna*, printing during the reign of François I, and Italian influences. Jean Balsamo and Michel Simonin, *Abel L'Angelier et Françoise Louvain (1574–1620)* (THR, 358), 636 pp., is an extraordinarily precise catalogue of almost 600 editions, printed by one of the most notorious and prolific French stationers, a clever businessman and a champion of the French language. J. Balsamo is also interested in 'La collection des anciens poètes français de Galliot du Pré (1528–1533)', *Analisi linguistica e letteraria*, 8, 2000:177–94.

Women were active in the book trade, as is shown by S. Broomhall, 'Re-assessing female representation in the print trade in 16th-c. France', *Parergon*, 18.2, 2001:55–73. *Books and the Sciences in History*, ed. Marina Frasca-Spada and Nick Jardine, CUP, 2000, xiv + 438 pp., contains articles by A. Grafton on Geniture collections, A. Blair on the uses (and sometimes abuses) of indexes, and S. Kusukawa on book illustration. Robert Weeda, *Le Psautier de Calvin*, Turnhout, Brepols, 230 pp., is concerned with a European bestseller. *De la publication entre Renaissance et Lumières*, ed. Christian Jouhaud and Alain Viala, Fayard, 368 pp. covers the 16th to 18th centuries. Publishing and purchasing a book was not as easy as today: printing was a lengthy process, paper expensive, and the book a fine object. Some concrete cases (for instance, rhetorical speeches) are discussed in this highly recommended synthesis.

Printers were active in other cities than Paris, and W. Kemp examines 'Une édition clandestine du *Jugement d'amour* de J. de Florès (vers 1530) dans l'univers du livre à Caen et à Rouen', *Memini*, 4, 2000: 137–57; Id., 'Printing Erasmus in italic in Lyons: J. Moderne to S. Gryphius', *Yale University Library Gazette*, 75.1, 2000: 22–36; T. Peach, 'Une collaboration éditoriale à Poitiers au XVIe siècle', *Mémoires de la Société des Antiquaires de l'Ouest*, 5th ser., 13, 1999: 91–132.

In some respects, book history is a cross-disciplinary field. F. Higman, 'Histoire du livre et histoire de la Réforme', *BSHPF*, 148: 837–50, traces a programme including physical bibliography, the history of printers, and the relevance for Reformation studies. I. de Conihout and P. Ract-Madoux, in their beautifully illustrated article on 'Veuves, pénitents et tombeaux. Reliures françaises du XVIe siècle à motifs funèbres', *SFDES 12*, 225–68, show the links between the history of bookbinding and the history of ideas. D. Pallier, 'L'office de libraire juré de l'Université de Paris pendant les guerres de religion', *BBib*, 1, 47–69 gives the dates of appointment of 104 booksellers active from 1550 to the eve of 17th century. The office played a part in both censorship and commercial propriety. A. Armstrong, 'Paratexte et autorité(s) chez les Grands Rhétoriqueurs', *TLit*, 14, 2001: 61–89, and G. Defaux, 'Trois cas d'écrivains éditeurs: Marot, Rabelais, Dolet', *ib.*, 91–118, examine how writers faced the Gutenberg revolution. Wallace Kirsop, *Manuscrits et imprimés: une cohabitation équivoque*, Monash, Centre for the Book, 2001, 20 pp., is a useful synthesis on marginalia and marks in books.

A. Saunders, '16th-c. book illustration: the classical heritage', Sandy, *Heritage*, 503–32, is a study that ranges widely, from books of hours to royal entries, showing that, after the wars of religion, France was no longer a centre for illustrated printing. M. Vasselin, 'Les métamorphoses d'une déesse antique: les figures de Diane dans les gravures du XVIe siècle', *Albineana*, 14: 247–77, is on mythological engravings. J. Balsamo, 'Quelques remarques sur les collections d'éditions anciennes de Pétrarque conservées en France et les conditions éditoriales du pétrarquisme', *CEFI 36*, 87–97, presents the results of an investigation made in 160 French public libraries and confirming the wide diffusion of Petrarch in France: no less than 640 examples of Italian and Latin works still exist.

The Estiennes were a long-reigning dynasty of stationers and printers. On Henri Estienne I, read P. Way, 'J. de Mouveaux's *Primum exemplar*. A model copy made for H. Estienne's 1512 edition of Eusebius' *Chronicon*', *Quaerendo*, 32:60–98, and E. Armstrong, 'J. B. Monzetti's consolation for Mary Tudor, Queen of France: a little known edition of H. Estienne', *BHR*, 64:251–70. Another printer, Simon de Colines, belonged to the family of H. Estienne I (he married his widow and was his successor): H. D. L. Vervliet, 'The printing types of the young S. de Colines (1518–1522)', *BBib*, 2:269–99, shows which Estienne fonts can be attributed to Colines. Several studies are devoted to Henri Estienne II: H. Cazes, 'Le livre et son objet: une poétique selon E. dans les *Parodiae morales*', Rouget, *L'Objet*, 185–200 (on a curious collection, forgotten even by its author); Id., 'Les mille et une pages d'E. et de ses lecteurs: un recueil infini', Beaulieu, *Disposition*, 71–80 ; and B. Boudou, 'La place de la mémoire dans la composition chez E.', *NRSS*, 20.2:57–72. We may also note the second edition of an important book on the history of reading, Thomas Kock's *Die Buchkultur der 'Devotio moderna'. Handschriftenproduktion, Literaturversorgung und Bibliothekaufbau im Zeitalter des Medienwechsels*, Frankfurt, Lang, 474 pp.

F. Roudaut, 'Classements et bibliothèques à la Renaissance. Quelques éléments', *Babel*, 6, 2001 : 151–68 gives some hints on how to classify all these new books produced by the printing industry. Numerous books used the word 'theatre' in their titles and L. van Delft, 'L'idée de théâtre (XVIe–XVIIIe siècles)', *RHLF*, 101, 2001 : 1349–65, and 'Théâtre du monde et cyberculture', *RZLG*, 26:63–75, reminds us that 'la composante spirituelle de la notion est infiniment plus présente que notre culture moderne ne nous prépare à le pressentir.' Between *miseria* and *dignitas hominis*, D. shows how Christian doctrine stands behind books as different as Boaistuau's *Théatre du monde* and Boissard's *Theatrum vitae humanae*, and studies the present decline of religion and classical culture.

3. Humanism, Theology, and the History of Ideas

The influence of St Augustine on Renaissance thought is generally underestimated, although deep and lasting. Åke Bergvall, *Augustinian Perspectives in the Renaissance*, AUU, 2001, 234 pp., carefully studies the impact of Augustine on 16th-c. psychology, epistemology, semiology, and politics. This excellent book is primarily intended for students of

English literature, but it deserves to be read by every Renaissance scholar. Guillaume Budé, *Philologie / De Philologia*, ed. Marie-Madeleine de La Garanderie, Les Belles Lettres, 2001, xliv + 370 pp., is a new translation which uses B.'s personal copy, with abundant autograph marginalia (BnF, Rés. Z.13). The dialogue between the King and B. was first published in 1532 (the same year as *Pantagruel*). This plea for the humanities stands as a 'jalon essentiel dans l'histoire de la politique culturelle' of the reign of François I. According to B. (who is neither the first nor the last to use such an argument), the King's fame depends on the writer's good will. Thanks to this editor, an interesting moment in cultural history, when Latin is getting purer, but French growing stronger, is now accessible to both lay readers and specialists. B. probably knew that the King himself wrote poetry, even if, for the sake of France, François I was a better King than poet: J.-M. Colard, 'La "veine royale" de François Ier poète', Cogitore, *Devenir roi*, 119–45. B. also wrote for François I a *Livre de l'Institution du Prince* (1519, with close links to *De Philologia*), carefully studied by Christina Rohwetter, *Zur Typologie des Herrschers im französischen Humanismus*, Frankfurt, Lang, 144 pp. B. was one of the greatest intellectual authorities in 16th-c. France, as seen by G. Sandy, 'B.: philologist and polymath. A preliminary study', Sandy, *Heritage*, 79–108. Even so, he found time to marry and leave a widow after his death, whose biography is sketched out by M.-M. de La Garanderie, 'Roberte, veuve B.', *Cazauran Vol.*, 717–30.

Un professeur-poète humaniste: J. Vaccaeus, la 'Sylve parisienne' (1522), ed. Perrine Galand-Hallyn et al. (THR, 369), lxxxviii + 122 pp. V., who may not be well known to non-specialist readers, was a humanist, born in Spain, who came to Paris, where he stayed for a decade, in order to learn eloquence. His *Sylva Parrhisia* is a eulogy of this science, a didactic Latin poem dedicated to Budé and imitated from Poliziano, translated into French and annotated for the first time since its publication. The translation of famous or neglected works is a typically humanist activity. Sylvius and La Boderie turned into French Ficino's *Commentarium in Convivium Platonis, De Amore*, a work essential for a good understanding of the Renaissance, and now translated anew by Pierre Laurens, Les Belles Lettres, cxxxvi + 320 pp. On Ficino's influence, see C. Margellos, 'Le modèle ficinien dans le *Sympose* de Louis Le Roy', Petris, *Sources*, 67–75. P. Cherchi, 'I *Dubbi* di Ortensio Lando in inglese erroneamente attribuiti ad Alain Chartier', *La Bibliofilia*, 104.2: 189–97, sheds light on a false attribution. V. Worth-Stylianou, 'Translations from Latin into French in the Renaissance', Sandy, *Heritage*, 137–64, states that 'over the 150 years following the advent of printing in Western Europe, new translations were produced on a hitherto unprecedented scale', and studies their pedagogic role, the relations between translation and creative writing, using a practical case (O. de Saint-Gelais, H. de Crenne, Des Masures, Du Bellay, and M. de Gournay all translated *Aeneid*, IV, vv. 693–705). Further examples are examined by F. Nies, 'Das Land der Griechen in Italien suchend. Bereicherung durch Übersetzen im Frankreich des 16. Jahrhunderts', *ZFSL*, 111, 2001: 249–59. On the French translations of Plutarch before and after Amyot, one may read A. Billaut's study on 'Plutarch's *Lives*', Sandy, *Heritage*, 219–35. A prolific and versatile translator, Amyot also turned into French the *Aethiopica* and *Daphnis and Chloe*: L. Plazenet, 'Amyot and the Greek novel', *ib.*, 237–80.

On translations from Spanish, mainly chivalric novels such as the *Amadis*, see M. Huchon, 'Les clefs du château d'Apolidon', *Cazauran Vol.*, 167–90, which deals with the translation by Herberay des Essarts and some alterations he brought to the text. The *Amadis* was a bestseller with great influence on French writers, as brilliantly studied by Charles Dédéyan, *Le Chevalier Berger ou de l''Amadis' à l''Astrée'*, Sorbonne U.P., 324 pp. Jacques Gohory was a French translator of Machiavelli and alchemist, as R. Gorris reminds us in 'Diane de Guindaye, Pentasilée et les autres, ou les Diane de J. Gohory', *Albineana*, 14: 291–332. Humanists however failed to translate hieroglyphics, but never gave up using them, as seen by C. Balavoine, 'De la perversion du signe égyptien dans le langage iconique de la Renaissance', Grell, *Egypte*, 27–48. James Veazie Skalnik, *Ramus and Reform. University and Church at the End of the Renaissance*, Kirksville, Truman State U.P., xii + 172 pp., a precise and delightful biography, begins with the words: 'Ramus was a difficult man' and continues to reveal that this is no understatement. Unbearable to his colleagues, a heretic for the Catholics and a rebel for the Protestants, he was destined for his premature death. But this logician who continuously fought Aristotle's influence may deserve to be compared to Wittgenstein.

Langer, *Aristotle*, is a valuable collection of papers on this highly important figure, in which Renaissance scholars will read with great interest the contributions by F. Goyet, 'Le machiavélisme est-il aristotélicien' (13–34), J. O'Brien, 'A.'s prudence, and Pyrrho's' (35–45, on Montaigne and Zwinger), F. Rigolot, 'Montaigne et A.' (47–63), I. Maclean, 'A.'s infinities in the late Renaissance' (123–37), and M.-L. Demonet, 'Scolastique française et mondes possibles à la fin de la Renaissance' (139–60). On the Aristotelian conception of prudence, see also F. Goyet, 'Entre sublime et raison d'Etat', Cogitore, *Devenir roi*, 163–78. Stella P. Reward, *Pindar and the Renaissance Hymn-Ode, 1450–1700* (MRTS 221), 2001, xiv + 384 pp., and Jean-Eudes Girot, *Pindare avant Ronsard. De l'émergence du grec à la publication des 'Quatre premiers livres des Odes' de Ronsard* (THR, 355), 496 pp., both study the history of Pindar's reception. 'Pindariser' was a 16th-c. neologism, stressing the importance of the Greek poet, before and for Ronsard who, despite his claims for originality, owed much to his precursors. Both monographs also contain precious data on the beginnings of the teaching of Greek in France and on the different editions or translations of Pindar (by Zwingli, Lonicer, and Melanchthon), underlining his importance for the development of classical and Christian hymnology during the Renaissance.

R. Mouren, 'La *varietas* des philologues au XVIe siècle', Courcelles, *Varietas*, 5–31, is an interesting inquiry into the 'small world' of Renaissance philologists, tormented by variants of ancient texts. They sought them passionately and produced massive volumes of *adversaria*, *miscellanea*, and philological notes. Their comparisons between Greek and Latin writers may be regarded as the dawn of comparative literature. No trouble with variants for the Anacreontic corpus, preserved in a single MS, printed by Henri Estienne II: some poems were adapted by Ronsard, Belleau, and Baïf, as discussed in P. Rosenmeyer, 'The Greek Anacreontics and 16th-c. French lyric poetry', Sandy, *Heritage*, 393–424. On the rediscovery of pagan gods, see the valuable contributions by R. Cooper, 'Dionysos exhumé: les archéologues français à la Renaissance', Zinguer, *Dionysos*, 123–35, and P. Eichel-Lojkine, 'De Dionysos l'étranger au sage Bacchus: l'assimilation humaniste', *ib.*, 137–18. M.-D. Couzinet, 'La variété dans la philosophie de la nature', Courcelles, *Varietas*, 105–17, compares Cardano's *De varietate* and Bodin's *Universae naturae theatrum*, a scientific treaty in the form of a dialogue. On Richard Le Blanc's translation of Cardano (reprinted often until 1642), see F. Epée, 'R. Le Blanc traducteur du *De subtilitate* de Cardan', Viallon-Schoneveld, *Traduction*, 123–37.

Before being imitated by several great writers, Petrarch, the master of European humanism, was translated into French by humble translators such as G. de La Forge, V. Philieul, and J. Maynier, as studied by D. Ménager, 'Le "Triomphe de la Mort" dans deux traductions françaises du XVIe siècle', *CEFI 36*, 347–61. On Maynier see P. Cifarelli, 'M. traduttore di Petrarca. Aspetti linguistici e stilistici di una traduzione francese cinquecentesca dei *Trionfi*', *ib.*, 363–81. O. Millet, 'Variations humanistes: les dialogues de Pétrarque (*De Remediis*) et de Des Périers sur la danse', *Cazauran Vol.*, 151–65, shows that Des P.'s 38th short-story is a reply to Petrarch's condemnation of dancing. See also G. Mathieu-Castellani, 'L'écriture à la première personne et le modèle de la narration humaniste', *Le Fablier*, 13, 2001:79–89. O. Deroint-Allaire, 'Le dialogue dans les *Nouvelles récréations et joyeux devis* de Des P.', *RHR*, 54:31–51, is written in a barely comprehensible jargon.

Renaissance scholars are gradually taking more interest in the history of science and a special issue of *NRSS*, 20.1, is devoted to the 'Renaissance des savoirs scientifiques et techniques?' (medecine, astronomy, ballistics, botany). J.-M. Mandosio, 'Les lexiques bilingues philosophiques, scientifiques et notamment alchimiques à la Renaissance', Hamesse, *Lexiques*, 175–226, shows that humanists paid attention to Greek and Latin vocabulary. Alchemy stood at the crossroads of several sciences and thus alchemists needed a precise vocabulary. On 16th-c. physicians, read G.-A. Pérouse, '"Docteurs" et "médecins". Situation de la médecine au 16e siècle', Viallon-Schoneveld, *Médecins*, 8–22. Guillaume Rondelet, *L'Histoire entière des poissons*, Comité des travaux historiques et scientifiques, 28 pp. + vi ff. + 418 pp. + xv ff. + 182 pp + 4 ff., is a handsome reprint, making available to the modern reader a great monument in the history of ichtiology and literature. A model of a Renaissance man, Rondelet was a friend of Rabelais. As a physician, he carried out the autopsy of his own still-born son. First published in Latin, this work was translated by L. Joubert and remained a compendium of Renaissance ichtyology, influencing Du Bartas's *Sepmaine*. On the comparative viewpoint, an interesting collection of essays is *Esthétiques de la nouveauté à la Renaissance*, ed. F. Laroque and F. Lessay, Sorbonne Nouvelle U.P., 2001, iv + 190 pp.

4. Poetry and Prose

Jean Paul Barbier, *Ma bibliothèque poétique*, part 4, vol. III: 'Contemporains et successeurs de Ronsard. De La Gessée à Malherbe', Geneva, Droz, 558 pp., illus., is compelling and fascinating to read even for non-specialists. J. Balsamo, 'Les poètes français et les anthologies lyriques italiennes', *Italiques*, 5:9–32, proves how instructive a close look at anthologies may be. François Rigolot, *Poésie et Renaissance*, Le Seuil, 406 pp., is a careful presentation of poetry from the late Middle Ages to the eve of 17th century, with individual chapters on Marot, Scève, Ronsard, and Du Bellay. F. Rigolot rightly reminds us that scarcely anyone in the Renaissance made a living out of writing, and J. Lemaire, 'J. Fossetier, poète arthois thuriféraire de Charles Quint', *BCLSMP*, 12, 2001:287–316, reminds us that some poets were compelled to fawn upon kings, and gives us a critical edition of the poem on *La glorieuse victoire obtenue devant Pavie par l'empereur Charles Quint*. On a royal entry see J. Nassichuk, 'Poétique de la diplomatie: Hugues Salel et l'entrée de Charles-Quint en France, 1539–1540', *RHR*, 55:51–67. Jean Lemaire de Belges,

Chronique de 1507, ed. Anne Schoysman, Bruxelles, Académie royale de Belgique, 2001, 226 pp., is an excellent critical edition, publishing a first draft in Lemaire's own hand, an exceptional testimony (BnF, Ms. Dupuy 503). Id., *Epistre du roy à Hector et autres pièces de circonstances (1511–1513)*, ed. Adrian Armstrong and Jennifer Britnell, STFM, 2000, lxxxviii + 144 pp., is presented with the *Epistre d'Hector au roy* by Jean d'Auton. E. A. Brown, 'Refreshment of the dead: *post mortem* meals, Anne de Bretagne, J. Lemaire de Belges, and the influence of antiquity on royal ceremonial', *SFDES 12*, 113–30, studies the strangest element in French royal funeral ceremony, the service of meals to the dead person's corpse, put into practice for the last time at Henri IV's death.

16th-c. French prose was not always *Kunstprosa*, but sometimes humble journalistic style: G. Guilleminot-Chrétien, 'La destruction de Malines en 1546: du fait divers à l'histoire prodigieuse', *Cazauran Vol.*, 191–99, is an edition of an unknown *canard* relating the explosion of a powder magazine.

5. Theatre and Rhetoric

The latest volume of the 'Théâtre français de la Renaissance' is *La Tragédie à l'époque d'Henri III*, 2nd ser., vol. 3 (1582–84), Florence, Olschki — Paris, PUF, 578 pp., contains such plays as P. de Bousy's *Meleagre* (ed. L. Zilli), P. Heyns's *Jokebed* and *Holoferne* (ed. J. Manley and M. Miotti), C. Mermet's *Sophonisbe* (ed. F. Caldari Bevilacqua and A. Bettoni), J. Robelin's *Thebaide*, and the more famous *Juives* by Garnier (ed. B. Gallina). The spelling and punctuation are modernized, following the principles of the collection. On the last play, see also D. Di Mauro, 'Le *Credo* de Sédécie dans *Les Juifves* de Garnier', *RHR*, 55:69–85. Garnier's *Cornélie* is reissued by Jean-Claude Ternaux, Champion, 178 pp. Charles Mazouer, *Le Théâtre français de la Renaissance*, Champion, 496 pp., is a valuable synthesis on a still barely explored subject, dealing with the birth of modern dramaturgy, school theatre, and Italian influences. Illustrations are reproduced from manuscript or printed books and a 52-page long bibliography completes this book. Classical influences on French tragedies and comedies are studied by G. Jondorf, 'Drama', Sandy, *Heritage*, 453–70. D. Di Mauro, 'L'unité religieuse des *Tragédies sainctes* de L. Des Masures', *BHR*, 64:271–94, shows that his trilogy is linked by an over-arching religious idea, mixed with Stoician moral virtue (courage, patience, magnanimity) and theological virtues (faith, hope, charity). A strange example of revenge tragedy, taking place in Persia, is studied by G. Banderier, 'Une tragédie persane au XVIe siècle: l'*Orbecc-Oronte* de Du Monin', *Luqmān*, 18.1:57–65.

6. Emblematica

In the constantly increasing body of critical material piling up on the desk of the patient, if sometimes distressed, bibliographer, one may especially note two studies: *A Bibliography of French Emblem Books*, ed. Alison Adams, Stephen Rawles, and Alison Saunders (THR, 362), vol. II, xxii + 762 pp., is a well-illustrated and well-argued book, especially valuable to those needing information on surviving copies. John Manning, *The Emblem*, London, Reaktion, 398 pp., sets the emblem against the background of a European and neo-Latin culture of festive celebration. He provides us with a remarkable historical survey of this amazing form, from the Renaissance (when it becomes a genre of its own) to the mutations of the present day. H. Campangne, 'Fonction et poétique de l'objet dans les livres d'emblèmes et de devises', Rouget, *L'Objet*, 167–83, points out that 'pour l'historien ou l'archéologue qui chercherait à reconstituer l'univers quotidien des hommes et des femmes des XVIe et XVIIe siècles, les livres d'emblèmes et de devises contiennent des renseignements significatifs'. We must however not forget that, in spite of the sometimes beautiful realism of their engravings, emblems are not a descriptive genre. C. Zecher, 'Musical instruments and public life in mid-16th-c. French emblem books', Brooks, *Poetry*, 111–39, notes how 'in early French emblematics, scenes of music-making with musical instruments express political and moral values'.

7. Individual Authors

D'AUBIGNÉ. G. Banderier, 'Un chapitre inédit du *Debvoir mutuel*', *BHR*, 64:369–76, edits a hitherto unknown draft of the *Debvoir mutuel des roys et des subjects*, a political treatise written during A.'s Genevan exile, and gives an annotated edition of this sketch, interesting in so far as A. raised the topic of tyrannicide. Id., 'L'*Advis aux princes chrestiens*: un texte inédit d'A.', *BSHPF*, 148:309–35, deals with a printed booklet, issued four times before being reprinted in a compendium published by P. Aubert, A.'s printer in Geneva. This work, probably written between 1628 and 1629, is in content and form not far from the *Advis au Roy de la Grande Bretagne*, positively attributed to A. J.-R. Fanlo, 'L'imagination dans la polémique anti-jésuite', *LitC*, 45:91–108, also prints some unpublished verses in footnotes. Other texts sent or related to A. are edited by G. Banderier, 'A. et la tradition des poésies liminaires', *RevAR*, 15:85–106; Id., 'A. et Dieppe: un document en marge de l'*Histoire Universelle*', *AnN*, 52:3–13, 361–62; Id., 'Une lettre adressée à A.', *FSB*, 84:2–4; and Id., 'Une lettre inédite de Constant d'Aubigné à son père', *BHR*,

64:689–93. B. has also studied a new MS of an already well-known text, A.'s autobiography: 'Un nouveau manuscrit de *Sa vie à ses enfants*', *Codices Manuscripti*, 39–40:45–50.

Two articles deal with the *Tragiques*: M. Pintarič, '*Ut pictura tempus*', *Babel*, 4, 2000:53–63, and S. Junod, 'Résurgences et surgissement: deux modalités de la parole dans *Les Tragiques* ', Petris, *Sources*, 39–48. On A.'s love-poetry, see S. Murphy, 'Idoles et statues poétiques à la Renaissance', Rouget, *L'Objet*, 83–93 (studying the brass bull of Phalaris, built by Pérille, who was also the first victim of his invention); and J.-R. Fanlo, 'Pygmalion et Erostrate, ou les deux visages du *Printemps* d'A.', *Albineana*, 14:131–48. A.'s religious poetry is examined by V. Ferrer, 'Les *vers mesurés* d'A.: voies et détours d'une poésie religieuse', *Cazauran Vol.*, 639–53. S. Murphy, 'Du Bartas, A. et le triomphe militant', *CEFI 36*, 325–33, studies Du Bartas's *Triomfe de la Foy* and the 4th book of A.'s *Faeneste*.

BÈZE. *Correspondance de Théodore de Bèze*, vol. 24, ed. Alain Dufour, Béatrice Nicollier, and Hervé Genton, (THR, 366), xxviii + 432 pp., provides the minutely annotated text of 87 letters and 11 annexes, for the year 1583 only, including one important letter from Jean de Léry. Bèze was an outstanding person, not only in the literary world, and though written in Latin, his *Iuvenilia* are important for the history of French Renaissance poetry, even if (or because) Bèze later disowned them: '*The Muses of Helicon give way to the Holy Spirit'. A View from the Palatine: The 'Iuvenilia' of B.*, ed. and trans. Kirk M. Summers (MRTS 237), 2001, xxxvi + 462 pp., is an important edition. S. has established the Latin text, translated it into English, and provides full scholarly apparatus.

DU BARTAS. It is well-known that this Protestant poet was, surprisingly, an avid reader of Lucretius. S. Lamacz, 'La construction du savoir et la réécriture du *De Rerum Natura* dans *La Sepmaine*', *BHR*, 64:617–38, cannot be said to break new ground. The best study (and the only one available) on Du B.'s reception in Germany is due to G. Banderier, 'Du B. et l'Allemagne', *SN*, 74:171–79. Unpublished documents are edited by Id., 'Notes et documents sur Du B. (1)', *BSAHLSG*, 102:170–78. Id., 'L'intégration des sciences naturelles dans la poésie encyclopédique du XVIe siècle', Arambasin, *Médiations*, 21–37, studies how Du B. and two epigones, Christofle de Gamon and the unkonwn author of *La Création*, managed (or failed) to unite science and poetry. Jean Weisgerber, *La Muse des Jardins. Jardins de l'Europe littéraire*, Brussels, Lang, 218 pp., contains an important comparative chapter on 'Trois exemples de topographie édénique: Du B., Vondel et Milton' (179–90), reminding us of the great influence of Du B. on European literature.

DU BELLAY. François Roudaut provides a good edition (with more than a hundred pages of notes and useful appendices) of *Les Regrets — Antiquités de Rome — Songe*, Librairie Générale Française, 380 pp. Barbara Vinken, *Du Bellay und Petrarca. Das Rom der Renaissance* (Mimesis, 37), Tübingen, Niemeyer, 2001, viii + 256 pp., is an important and clever book on the Renaissance attitude toward the *Urbs*: a rebirth to come, according to Petrarch (who was referred to as 'a Virgil without Rome' — against the medieval tradition of the *contemptus Romae*) — or a decline to come for Du B. The true 16th-c. Rome was probably something between Petrarch's imperial dream of *restauratio* and Du B.'s disillusion. Did the French poet anticipate the fall of the Renaissance in the turmoil of the wars of religion? The place of Du B. in the tradition of *translatio studii*, more or less linked with the *translatio imperii*, is studied by R. Regosin, 'Rewriting Babel: history, cultural memory, and the reuse of metaphor in Du B.'s *Deffence*', *La Charité Vol.*, 211–27. K. W. Hempfer, 'Diskurstraditionen und fragmentarisierte Rezeption: Ariosts *Orlando Furioso* in Du B.s *L'Olive*', *ZFSL*, 112.3:264–83, discusses how Du B. was an avid reader of Italian poetry, and examines the influence of the epic poet on Du B.'s sonnet sequence.

On the 16th-c. French research scene, epistolography is a kind of waste land. Marc Bizer, *Les lettres romaines de Du Bellay*, Montreal U.P., 2001, 304 pp., studies Du B.'s Roman sonnets as verse epistles, the expression of a circle of friends. On Du B.'s theory of imitation, one may read T. Chevrolet, 'L'impossible imitation: tradition et découverte dans quelques traités théoriques de la Renaissance', Petris, *Sources*, 9–18. Du B. was himself imitated by other poets, as described in S. Aubert-Gillet, 'Les *Imitations chrétiennes* de S. Goulart: une réécriture réformée de *L'Olive*', *ib.*, 31–38, and P. Sudan, 'Des *Regrets* au désenchantement', *ib.*, 157–66. A mythographic study is given by O. Pot, 'Le mythe de Diane chez Du B.: de la symbolique lunaire à l'emblème de cour', *Albineana*, 14:57–80. P. J. Smith, 'Architecture et typographie dans les *Antiquitez* de Du B.', Rouget, *L'Objet*, 119–38, is a very interesting comparison of Du B.'s sonnets, the topographical guides of Rome (Fulvio, Marliani, Palladio, Calvo) and architectural treatises (Alberti, Serlio). Smith observes that 'Du B. est le seul [. . .] à faire coïncider, de façon systématique, thématique architecturale et disposition architecturale'. C. Magnien, 'J.-P. de Mesmes, son épithalame christianisé de H. de Mesmes et de J. Hennequin, avec commentaire et une ode de Du B.', *Cazauran Vol.*, 549–65. On Du B.'s iconography, see K. M. MacDonald, 'Un exemplaire illustré des *Elogia Gallorum Doctrina Illustrium* (1602) de S. de Sainte-Marthe et l'iconographie de Du B.: un portrait inconnu?', *BHR*, 64:79–95.

MARGUERITE DE NAVARRE. *Oeuvres complètes*, IV: *Théâtre*, ed. Geneviève Hasenohr and Olivier Millet, Champion, 674 pp., is the joint work of a recognized medievalist and of an eminent Calvin scholar. The biblical and worldly comedies are carefully edited, following the *Marguerites de la Marguerite* (Lyons, de Tournes, 1547). Britt-Marie Karlsson, *Sagesse divine et folie humaine. Etude sur les structures antithétiques dans l'Heptaméron* (*Rgo*, 47), 2001, 286 pp., a study of the use of antithetical expressions, the chiasmus, the oxymoron, and the paradox, is a valuable key to M.'s *Weltanschauung*. N. Cazauran, 'Boaistuau et Gruget éditeurs de l'*Heptaméron*: à chacun sa part', *TLit*, 14, 2001: 149–69, describes how, a decade after the Queen's death (1549), her collection was published by two different editors (1558–59). One of them, Pierre Boaistuau, censored the text. But, censored or integral, the *Heptaméron* was by no means a bestseller, as shown by M. Simonin, 'De la prime fortune éditoriale des nouvelles de M. (XVIe et début du XVIIe s.)', *La Charité Vol.*, 155–66, on the diffusion of the first edition (with a valuable bibliographical appendix). As a complement, read A. Parent-Charon, 'Présence des livres de M. dans la boutique d'un marchant libraire parisien', *Cazauran Vol.*, 465–71, on Galliot du Pré. M. B. McKinley, 'Agony, ecstasy, and the mulekeeper's wife: a reading of *Heptaméron* 2', *La Charité Vol.*, 129–42, studies the evangelical background of the story. Fine philological observations on the third story are to be found in S. Lefèvre, 'Les cornes du cerf ou les leçons de la variante', *Cazauran Vol.*, 403–16. On the 26th story, see F. Charpentier, 'La rhétorique des dames', *ib.*, 435–43. The concepts of patience and prudence are studied by I. Morrison, 'Quelques remarques sur la patience et la prudence dans l'*Heptaméron* de M. (à propos des nouvelles 35 et 36)', *SN*, 74: 113–20. The same scholar challenges U. Langer's commentaries of the 22nd story in 'An aspect of justice in the *Heptaméron*', *FSB*, 76, 2000: 13–15. A very interesting inquiry into M.'s sources (Latin historians and poets, Italian storytellers) is provided by J. Leeker, 'M.s Novelle von der tugenhaften Françoise (*Heptaméron* 42) im Spiegel der Tradition', *WRM*, 26.1: 1–25. The blending of fiction and reality in the tales are examined by C. Freccero, 'Archives in the fiction: M.'s *Heptaméron*', Kahn, *Rhetoric*, 73–94; V. Montagne, '*L'Heptaméron* de M.: éléments pour une poétique du dialogue inséré', *RHR*, 54: 53–78; G. Mathieu-Castellani, '*L'Heptaméron* ou la malice contre la malice', *Cazauran Vol.*, 417–33. A chapter on the *Heptaméron* may be found in Armine Kotin Mortimer's *Writing Realism. Representations in French Fiction*, Baltimore–London, Johns Hopkins U.P., 2000, xiv + 254 pp. A new study of the religious and philosophical beliefs of the Queen (a vexed question) is M. Soulié's 'Les convictions religieuses de M. d'après le *Dialogue en forme de vision nocturne* (1524)',

Cazauran Vol., 329–45. Marial devotion in her theatre is studied by C. Martineau-Génieys, 'La vierge et son Dieu dans les *Comédies bibliques* de M.', *ib.*, 347–67. On Stoic influences, read J. Lecointe, 'Le devis des larmes: polémique anti-stoïcienne et dialogicité, autour de *La Navire* de M.', *ib.*, 369–84, and I. Pantin, 'L'ordre des fables: l'allégorie dans *Les Prisons* de M.', *ib.*, 385–401. R. Cooper devotes his paper on 'Deux admirateurs grecs des trois Marguerite de Valois', *ib.*, 473–89, to M.'s relations to contemporary Greece. J. Grimm, 'L'expression morale dans l'*Heptaméron* et dans les *Fables*', *Le Fablier*, 13, 2001 : 90–95, makes a close comparison of the two works, drawing similar and contrastive parallels between them. Only a few studies have been devoted to M.'s letters, which makes all the more noticeable J.-P. Beaulieu, 'Postures épistolaires et effets de *dispositio* dans la correspondance entre M. et Briçonnet', Beaulieu, *Disposition*, 43–54.

MAROT. *Index des 'Oeuvres' de Clément Marot*, ed. Dominique Bertrand, Gilles Proust, and François Rouget, Champion, 800 pp., is a computer-generated index, following the two-volume edition provided by G. Defaux. An unpublished piece of poetry comes to light in G. Defaux, 'De la traduction du *Courtisan* à celle de l'*Hecatomphile*', *BHR*, 64 : 513–48. On M.'s quiet symmetry, read H. Orii, 'La structure de l'*Enfer* de M.', *RHR*, 55 : 7–24, and E. M. Duval, 'L'*Adolescence Clementine* et l'oeuvre de M.', Beaulieu, *Disposition*, 12–24. M. was the editor of Villon's poetry and of his own father, as studied by F. Preisig, 'M. éditeur de son père', *TLit*, 14, 2001 : 119–37. On M.'s reception, read J.-C. Monferran, 'M., le marotique et La Fontaine', *Le Fablier*, 13, 2001 : 25–35.

MONTAIGNE. No new edition of the *Essais* this year, but a wonderful colour reproduction of the 'Bordeaux copy', *L'Exemplaire avec notes manuscrites marginales des 'Essais' de Montaigne (exemplaire de Bordeaux)*, ed. Philippe Desan, Fasano, Schena, 508 ff. The academic quarrel over the authentic text of the *Essais* remains alive and well, and some recent editions have been closely examined by G. Hoffmann, 'New editions of M.'s *Essais*: a test for editorial principles', *MonS*, 12, 2000 : 209–30. Ken Keffer, *A publication history of the rival transcriptions of M.'s 'Essays'*, Lampeter, Mellen, 2001, xiv + 264 pp., is a scholarly study, full of original documents and discoveries on the making of the first critical editions of the *Essais* (following the 'Bordeaux copy'), but may be read as a novel on university life at the beginning of the 20th century. The re-edition of John O'Neill's important study, *Essaying M.: A Study of the Renaissance Institution of Writing and Reading*, Liverpool U.P., 2001, viii + 264 pp. is presented as 'revised', but the bibliography has not really been updated. Géralde Nakam, *Les 'Essais' de M., miroir et procès de leur temps*,

Champion, 2001, xvi + 540 pp., is a re-edition of an excellent book, first published in 1984, with a new foreword and a bibliographical supplement. Id., *Le dernier M.*, Champion, 318 pp., is a remarkably coherent work, in spite of the fact that the different chapters are taken from already published articles. N. focuses her attention on the C stage of M.'s text (see also *NRSS*, 20.2: 119–34). *Lire les 'Essais' de M.*, ed. Noël Peacock and James J. Supple, Champion, 2001, 334 pp., consists of the papers from a 1997 conference in Glasgow and presents contributions by J. Brody, D. Ménager, T. Cave, A. Tournon, and P. Desan on M.'s sources of inspiration (St Augustine, Ronsard). P. Desan, 'De l'*exemplar* à l'exemplaire de Bordeaux', is also available in his collection, *M. dans tous ses états*, Fasano, Schena, 2001, iv + 404 pp., with 15 other essays on the *Essais* which study the different editions of M.'s masterwork, the roles of La Boétie and M. de Gournay in the birth and fate of this unusual book, its reception from the 16th century to the Empire, the influence of Aristotle and Seneca, etc. On the influence of Tacitus, see S. W. Farquhar, 'M.: the *Essais* and a Tacitean discourse', Sandy, *Heritage*, 187–218.

Olivier Guerrier, *Quand 'les poètes feignent': 'fantasie' et fiction dans les 'Essais'*, Champion, 518 pp., is a study of the dynamic of poetical quotations. On M.'s attitude toward writing, read N. Kuperty-Tsur, 'De la pensée à l'écriture dans les *Essais*', Dornier, *Ecriture*, 15–32. Two important contributions to the study of M. and Nature come from Japan: N. Tsutui, 'Le mot de nature dans le chapitre "De l'expérience"', *Bulletin d'études françaises*, 31, 2000: 89–102, and 'La nature et la "seconde nature" chez M.', *ib.*, 32, 2001: 81–94. A special issue of *MonS*, 13, 2001, is devoted to the writer's *familia*, which does not only mean his wife and daughters, but his teachers, friends, and relations. This brilliant volume includes contributions on the Portuguese scholar André de Gouvea (R. Gorris Camos), the Scottish humanist George Buchanan (P. Ford), the Spanish Jesuit Juan Maldonado (A. Legros), the maréchal de Matignon (R. Cooper), M.'s brother-in-law Geoffroy de La Chassaigne, sieur de Pressac (J. Balsamo), François d'Amboise (D. Costa), Claude Expilly (A. Preda), Antoine de Laval (G. Hoffmann), Jacques-Auguste de Thou (I. A. R. de Smet), Anthony Bacon (W. Boutcher), Etienne Pasquier (C. Magnien), and Bernard Automne (M. Simonin). A study on another acquaintance, Torquato Tasso, is to be found in J. Balsamo, 'M. et le "saut" du Tasse', *RLMC*, 54, 2001: 389–407. Sophie Jama, *L'Histoire juive de M.*, Flammarion, 2001, 240 pp., is a puzzling book. It is well known that M.'s parents had Jewish origins, and their influence, and those of the Jewish religion, on M. is a matter of debate. Despite the proliferation of arguments and counter-arguments, none of the various discussions ever manages to be decisive. J. claims that M. was a crypto-Jew, citing for instance that, in the first edition of the *Essais*, the note 'Au lecteur' is dated 1 March 1580, the day of the *Purim* festival; this book may, one fears, contribute further to misunderstandings about M. and his work. In a very persuasive article, G. Defaux, 'M., la vie, les livres: naissance d'un philosophe sceptique et "imprémédité"', *MLN*, 117:780–807, traces M.'s relations to medieval scepticism and shows that his thought is remarkably coherent and non-evolutive. One thing is sure: M. was a sick man, suffering all his life from kidney stones, as discussed once more by W. J. A. Bots, 'M., écrivain et voyageur malade, devant la médecine', Viallon-Schoneveld, *Médecins*, 105–12. He was not the only one to suffer from such a disease, even if it is only a poor consolation: A. Jacobson Schutte, 'Suffering from the stone: the accounts of M. and C. Ferrazzi', *BHR*, 64:21–36.

Thomas Berns, *Violence de la loi à la Renaissance. L'originaire du politique chez Machiavel et M.*, Kimé, 2000, 454 pp., is a stimulating book, examining what happens to law in a world 'ondoyant et divers'. M. considered law and political order as two historical artifacts, as discussed in C. Jordan, 'Law and political reference in M.'s *Apologie de Raimond Sebond*', Kahn, *Rhetoric*, 199–219. The fruits of a seminar in Rouen on 'Montaigne et la justice' are published in the *BSAM*, 8th ser., 21–22, 276 pp. On a related topic, *MonS*, 14, is devoted to 'M. and ethics'. M.'s attitude toward the New World is excellently studied by G. Hoffmann, 'Anatomy of the mass: M.'s "Cannibals"', *PMLA*, 117:207–21. T. Conley, 'M. moqueur. "Virgile" and its geographies of gender', Long, *Masculinity*, 93–106, is a study of *Essais* III, 5 from a special angle.

It is not easy to write on M. without writing on La Boétie. His *Discours de la servitude volontaire* is usually regarded as a manifesto for liberty against tyranny. In a fine study, E. Buron, 'Le *Discours de la servitude volontaire* et son double', *StF*, 135, 2001:498–532, reminds us of the values to which La Boétie refers, freedom and tyranny. His little book was more an attack against Protestant democraticism. B. also sheds a new light on the date of publication. A minor writer, but a genuine *femme savante*, Marie de Gournay became part of history as M.'s 'fille d'alliance'. On her own work, read G. Devincenzo, 'Une femme de lettres dans une période de transition', Desan, *Littérature*, 219–31. Her prefaces to the *Essais* are reprinted in her *Oeuvres complètes*, ed. Jean-Claude Arnould et al., Champion, 2 vols, 2076 pp. On M.'s reception in England, see N. Myers, 'M. en Angleterre au XVIIe siècle', Viallon-Schoneveld, *Traduction*, 159–71.

RABELAIS. Kurt Baldinger, *Etymologisches Wörterbuch zu R. (Gargantua)* (*ZRP*, Beiheft 306) Tübingen, Niemeyer, 2001, vi + 452 pp., is a treasure-trove of philological data, not only for Rabelaisian scholars.

Florence Weinberg, *R. et les leçons du rire. Paraboles évangéliques et néoplatoniciennes*, Orléans, Paradigme, 2000, 246 pp., is a jumble of articles (sometimes rejuvenated), with chapters on R. and Erasmus, Fischart, and on allegorical readings. C. Deloince-Louette, 'Frère Jean des Entommeures: chasseur et cynique', *RHLF*, 101, 2001: 3–20, studies chapter 39 of *Gargantua* and shows how this monk subverted humanist wisdom. On another fascinating character see J. C. Nash, 'Further reflections on the character portrayal of Panurge as the Devil', *La Charité Vol.*, 77–85. V. Zaercher plunges into the 'dialogues héroïques' of the *Quart Livre*, *RHR*, 54: 79–93. How R. used and rewrote in a burlesque way tales by Aesop is examined by F. Weinberg, 'Extreme means to talk about moderation: Priapus and Couillatris in R.'s *Quart Livre*', *La Charité Vol.*, 87–92, and J.-M. Boivin, 'Le bucheron Couillatris et Mercure: R. fabuliste', *Cazauran Vol.*, 201–24. Some articles, challenging Bakhtin's interpretation, remind us that R. was a scholar and a humanist, with a consummate knowledge of Antiquity: B. Pinchard, 'Trois notes sur le mystère et une invocation à Bacchus', Zinguer, *Dionysos*, 67–77, Y. Tsutsui, 'Le *Gargantua* — découverte du génie', *Meiji-gakuïn-Ronso*, 620: 1–33, and J. Parkin, Sandy, *Heritage*, 165–86. H. Glidden, 'Le *nostos* épique dans le *Cinquiesme Livre* de R.', *La Charité Vol.*, 93–106, and R. Chevallier, 'R., lecteur de Virgile', *RBPH*, 79.1, 2001: 119–26, are both on the inspiration R. drew from epic poetry and the return to the native for Pantagruel and his friends. R.'s misogyny is tackled by A. Staples, 'Primal scenes/primal screens. The homosocial economy of dirty jokes', Long, *Masculinity*, 37–54, who so much challenges W. Booth's view on R. that she almost forgets to speak of R., who of course had his tongue in his cheek when he praised intolerance, as shown by F. Rigolot, 'R. et l'éloge paradoxal de l'intolérance', *La Charité Vol.*, 57–68. On his apparently sincere condemnation of idleness, see M. Marrache, 'R. et les périls de l'oisiveté', Jones-Davies, *Oisiveté*, 133–56. L. K. Donaldson-Evans, '"Comme chemise et cul": reflections on an article of Renaissance dress in R., M. de Navarre and Montaigne', *La Charité Vol.*, 69–76, discusses how 'a precise knowledge of what men and women in the Renaissance wore, as well as the social significance of their costume and the role played by clothes in Renaissance society, often provides valuable insights into texts in which clothing figures.' The *chemise* was not an equivalent of the modern shirt, but was an undergarment. To wear nothing but a *chemise* is a sign that one is in dire need. On memory and oblivion, see M. Marrache, 'R., l'écriture et l'oubli', Jones-Davies, *Mémoire*, 121–36.

New elements of biography have been discovered by J. Dupèbe, 'Remarques critiques sur la date de la naissance de R.', *Cazauran Vol.*,

731–46, and S. Geonget, 'R. et son ami Boysonné', *RHR*, 55:41–50. Catherine Sevestre, *Le Roman des contes. Contes merveilleux et récits animaliers, histoire et évolution, du Moyen Age à nos jours*, Etampes, Cedis, 2001, x + 382 pp., has a section (103–24) on R.

RONSARD. Anne-Pascale Pouey-Mounou, *L'Imaginaire cosmologique de Ronsard* (THR, 357), 864 pp., is a hefty monograph on the 'retentissement mutuel du monde et du langage dans la poétique de Ronsard', and on the invariants (themes, archetypes, imagery) of his poetry. On a related field, see D. Ménager, 'Anges et démons dans la poésie de R.', *Cazauran Vol.*, 567–77. *Ronsard, figure de la variété. En mémoire d'Isidore Silver*, ed. Colette H. Winn (THR, 368), 328 pp., a tribute to a great scholar, consists of the papers from a 1999 conference in Washington University, bringing together specialists from Europe, the U.S.A., and Canada. It offers important perspectives on a variety of aspects and is divided as follows: 'Le chantre des amours' (contributions by G. Defaux, J. C. Nash, C. Yandell), 'Prochain Homère, nouveau Virgile' (F. Rigolot, P. Ford, A. Moss, R. Wooldridge), 'Le R. des palais' (M. Engammare, Y. Bellenger, C. Skenazi, H. Campangne, S. Davidson), 'Le prince des poètes français' (M.-D. Legrand, J.-C. Carron, D. Martin, C. H. Winn), and 'Le poète au travail' (C. Jomphe, R. Campo, F. Rouget).

Three neat little books for students are Marie-Claire Thomine's *Pierre de Ronsard. Les 'Amours'*, PUF, 2001, 128 pp. (an introduction to R.'s *canzoniere*); *Lecture des 'Odes' de R.*, ed. Julien Goeury, Rennes U.P., 2001, 196 pp.; and *Lire les 'Odes' de R.*, ed. Dominique Bertrand, Clermont-Ferrand U.P., 230 pp., which includes 15 papers under the headings 'Une "Muse publicitaire"', 'Hommages littéraires', 'A "l'image de la Nature": une "copieuse diversité"', and 'La mort transfigurée'. It is becoming ever harder to say something new on prominent writers, but D. Maira's scholarly and important study, 'Le titre des *Amours* de R. (1552) dans son contexte éditorial et littéraire', *BHR*, 64:653–68, shows that R. did not derive his title from Ovid's *Amores*, but from Neo-Latin or Italian collections, such as that of Bernardo Tasso. D. Cecchetti, 'L'appello ai lettori. I sonetti proemiali del *Canzoniere* di Petrarca e delle *Amours* di R.', *CEFI 36*, 291–305, is a new contribution to an old question (R.'s debt to P.). S. Sturm-Maddox, '*In morte de Laura*, "Sur la mort de Marie"', *ib.*, 307–16, shows that R. returned to Petrarch at the end of his life, in the *Second livre des Amours* (1578). A close study of 'Le pin' is provided by S. Murphy, 'Catherine, Cybele, and R.'s witnesses', Long, *Masculinity*, 55–70. On R. and Du Bellay's poetical innovations, see E. M. Duval, 'Poetic genres and lyric forms, 1549–1552', Brooks, *Poetry*, 53–77, and K. van Orden, 'La *chanson vulgaire* and R.'s poetry for music', *ib.*, 79–109. Both Muret and Belleau commented on R.'s poetry, giving mythological explanations and tracing imitations, and this is examined by F. Gray, 'Les commentaires de Muret et de Belleau ou la critique des difficultés', *La Charité Vol.*, 229–40: 'Muret et Belleau continuent le travail de défense et d'illustration de la Pléiade, soulignant dans et par leurs commentaires les principes d'un art qui est nouveau dans la mesure où il relève de l'Antiquité, source de toute vraie inspiration et d'authentique invention.' Interesting studies on the great French scholar Muret, who died in Rome at the peak of his fame, are given by T. Tunberg, 'De Mureto oratore et Gallo et Romano', *HL*, 50, 2001 : 303–27, K. Inomata, 'Cicéronianisme et rhétorique dans la Rome tridentine', *RevAR*, 15 : 27–51 (in Japanese), and D. C. Andersson, 'Muret's moral philosophy: the Renaissance contest of the disciplines?', *BHR*, 64 : 669–78.

On R.'s use of classical or national mythology, one may read G. Demerson, 'Diane pour R.: un mythe taciturne et toujours menacé', *Albineana*, 14 : 81–106, and D. Bjaï, 'Ronsard et les "vieux Gaulois"', *RevAR*, 15 : 69–83. R. was the pupil of Jean Dorat, whose important interpretative methods are described in P. Ford's 'Classical myth and its interpretation in 16th-c. France', Sandy, *Heritage*, 331–49. Christoph O. Mayer, *R. und die Herausbildung des 'premier champ littéraire'*, Herne, Schäfer, 2001, 318 pp., is a sociological analysis, inspired by Pierre Bourdieu. The author has probably tried harder to impress a dean than inform the learned world.

8. Minor Writers

POETRY. The *Puys de palinods de Rouen* were a poetical competition, which took place from 1486 to the French Revolution, to celebrate the Immaculate Conception. They continued the medieval tradition into modern times, and Denis Hüe's magisterial book on *La poésie palinodique à Rouen (1486–1550)*, Champion, 1054 pp., is an important contribution to our knowledge. Not only did minor writers compete, but also Marot. This book comes with a lengthy bibliography and a study of the MS tradition, poetical imagery, and metrical analysis.

Renaissance poets were the inheritors of the medieval forms, and this is studied by S. Garnier, 'Rhétorique de la consolation dans la déploration funèbre des grands rhétoriqueurs', *SFDES 12*, 389–402. Gisela Febel, *Poesia ambigua oder vom Alphabet zum Gedicht* (Analecta Romanica, 62), Frankfurt, Klostermann, 2001, 610 pp., is a minutely detailed study on the poetry of the 'Grands Rhétoriqueurs' and its links to oral and printed culture. The reader will find new light is shed on Lemaire de Belges, Bouchet, and even Ronsard. The analysis is persuasive, well-expressed, and easily comprehensible. On Bouchet, see also C. La Charité, 'Les *Epistres morales et familieres* (1545) de B.: de la hiérarchie médiévale au diaogue humaniste', Beaulieu, *Disposition*, 25–42. Mühlethaler, *Poétiques*, essentially devoted to the late Middle Ages, includes contributions by M.-R. Jung, 'La ballade à la fin du XVe et au début du XVIe s.' (23–41), and F. Cornillat, 'Figures de l'échec de J. Molinet à E. Jodelle' (129–61). Silvia D'Amico, *'Heureux qui comme Ulysse . . .'. Ulisse nella poesia francese e neolatina del XVI secolo*, Milan, LED, 226 pp., is an excellent reference work, examining the various dimensions of the character, either courtier, lover, wanderer, or warrior. Yvonne Bellenger, *Le temps et les jours dans quelques recueils poétiques du XVIe siècle*, Champion, 244 pp. is a mixed bag of already published articles on Scève, Louise Labé, Du Bellay, Ronsard, Desportes, d'Aubigné, Du Bartas.

Hécatomphile, ou les Fleurs de Poesie Françoyse, ed. Gérard Defaux, STFM, cxlii + 244 pp. is a new and scholarly edition of a collection published in 1534 by the famous stationer Galliot du Pré. *Lettres et poèmes de Ch. de Bovelles*, ed. Jean-Claude Margolin, Champion, 1000 pp., edits poetry by Charles de Bovelles and Pierre Crespet found in the MS 1134 of the Paris University Library. On Bovelles's historical works, see J.-C. Margolin, 'Temps et histoire', Viallon-Schoneveld, *Histoire*, 183–204. Catherine d'Amboise, *Les devotes Epistres*, ed. Yves Giraud, Fribourg U.P., xxviii + 76 pp., edits from the unique MS (BnF f. fr. 2282) the poetry of Catherine d'Amboise (*c.* 1481–1550), which was never printed before the mid-19th century. G. provides an excellent photograph of the MS with a transcription and critical notes on the facing page.

J. McClelland, 'Measuring poetry, measuring music: from the Rhétoriqueurs to the Pléiade', Brooks, *Poetry*, 17–32, examines the attempts of French poets who tried to find equivalents to the quantitative rhythms of Greek and Latin poetry. The motifs of 'Et in Arcadia ego' and of the irruption of death in a pastoral landscape are examined by D. Ménager, 'L'églogue funèbre de la Renaissance', *SFDES 12*, 403–13, A. Flègès, '"Et moy chetif, je vy!", Magny, Ronsard, et l'*Ombre de Salel* (1554)', *ib.*, 425–42 (on Salel's commemoration, to which Ronsard, Jodelle, Tahureau, and Magny collaborated), and J. Castonguay Bélanger, 'L'édification d'un tombeau poétique : du rituel au recueil', Beaulieu, *Disposition*, 55–69. On another aspect of pastoral poetry, read N. Dauvois, 'La Diane pastorale', *Albineana*, 14: 279–90.

N. Frelick, 'Poétique du transfert et objet (a): l'exemple de la *Délie*', Rouget, *L'Objet*, 73–82, offers a Lacanian decoding of Scève. Taking a different aspect, G. Defaux stresses the importance of Marial poetry in his article, 'Du nouveau sur *Délie*: Scève et la poésie mariale', *La Charité Vol.*, 179–94. J. A. Della Neva, 'Petrarchan peregrinations in Scève's *Délie*', *ib.*, 195–209, relates that Scève was proud of having discovered the so-called grave of Petrarch's beloved Laura in Avignon. On a formal aspect of Scève's poetry, read X. Bonnier, 'Les dizains dialogués de la *Délie* de Scève', *BHR*, 64:579–604. D. Ménager, 'Le mythe du Léthé dans quelques oeuvres de la Renaissance', Jones-Davies, *Mémoire*, 107–20, and J.-C. Margolin, 'Sur quelques figures d'Actéon à la Renaissance', *Fest. Guthmuller*, 129–39, study the development of various myths during the Renaissance, and especially in French poetry (Scève, Du Bellay, Sponde, Ronsard, Desportes). See also several contributions in *Albineana*, 14: P. Martin, 'De Maurice Scève à Pernette du Guillet, ou le jeu d'Actéon' (39–55), G. Mathieu-Castellani, 'La figure de Diane dans la poésie baroque et maniériste: de la dramatisation du mythe à sa décoloration' (149–68), H. Campangne, 'Diane/Actéon: les métamorphoses d'une parénèse' (171–87), P. Marechaux, 'La Diane des commençants: sur quelques pédagogies d'un mythe' (213–26). One may also read V. Montagne, 'Antoine Héroët et l'*Aultre invention extraicte de Platon*: remarques sur les inventions d'un poète-philosophe', *BHR*, 64:549–77.

There are two articles on Louise Labé: C. Yandell, 'L.'s transgressions', Long, *Masculinity*, 1–17, on her love-poetry, and C. Skenazi, 'L. Labé et la musique', Brooks, *Poetry*, 33–51 (the daughter of a ropemaker was a fine musician).

Eva Kushner, *Pontus de Tyard et son oeuvre poétique*, Champion, 2001, 354 pp. is a very complete study of T.'s poetical work. After an almost 100–page-long biography, a chapter is devoted to each collection, from the 1549 *Erreurs amoureuses* to the 1585 *Douze fables de fleuves ou fontaines*. S. Alyn-Stacey, 'Pétrarque et le pétrarquisme plurilinguistique : émergence d'un texte européen', *CEFI 36*, 259–73, shows T. as a disciple of Petrarch. G. Banderier, 'A propos d'un sonnet attribué à T.', *BHR*, 64:71–77 discusses the attribution of a piece of poetry, ascribed both to T. and to Du Perron.

An edition of Belleau's complete works are in progress: *Oeuvres poétiques*, IV: *La Bergerie* (1572), ed. Guy Demerson and Maurice-F. Verdier, Champion, 2001, 418 pp. B.'s poetry has inspired three articles: F. Rigolot, 'Poétiques de l'huître : Francis Ponge correcteur de B.?', Rouget, *L'Objet*, 231–45; R. Campo, 'Du miroir à la mémoire: sur les jeux ecphrastiques dans *La Bergerie* de B.', *NRSS*, 20.2:5–23; J. Persels, 'Masculine rhetoric and the French *Blason anatomique*', Long, *Masculinity*, 19–35.

Du Monin's *Uranologie* was more of an adaptation than a translation of Buchanan's *De Sphaera*. This work of didactic and hardly readable poetry is studied by M. Fraimout-Auda, 'La prophétie sur le décès du monde dans *l'Uranologie* de Du M.', *Babel*, 4, 2000:91–103. The brutal and tragic death of Du M., at the age of 27, raised intense emotion in the Parisian learned world. No less than seven *tumuli* were devoted to the young poet's memory. This clumsy poetry is reviewed by I. Pantin and M. Magnien, 'Du M. au miroir de ses tombeaux', *SFDES 12*, 443–67 (with a valuable bibliography of ancient editions).

On Desportes: F. Rouget, 'Le mythe de Diane dans l'oeuvre poétique de D.', *Albineana*, 14: 107–18; Id., 'De nouveaux documents sur D.', *BHR*, 64: 347–52, which deals with an unknown edition of the *Premières Oeuvres* and with a book belonging to the poet. On another book from his library, see G. Banderier, *Nouvelles du livre ancien*, 110: 19. B. Petey-Girard, 'Bible et tradition liturgique dans les prières françaises de la fin du XVIe siècle', *BHR*, 64: 353–68, and '1574–1589: littérature de spiritualité et "commandement du Roy"', *NRSS*, 20.2: 73–86, both deal with D.'s religious compositions.

A well-educated woman, Nicole Liébault-Estienne wrote an interesting description of the torments she endured throughout her life as a married woman and R. Reynolds-Cornell, '*Les misères de la femme mariée*: another look at N. Liébault and a few questions about the woes of the married woman', *BHR*, 64: 37–54, suggests a re-evaluation of her recently acquired reputation. H. Cazes, 'N. Estienne à ses miroirs, les "Felicitez de mariage" et les *Misères de la femme mariée*', *Cazauran Vol.*, 747–66, shows that her work was more a reply to Desportes's *Stances contre le mariage* than a verse biography. On Petrarch and Renaissance French love-poetry, one may read G. Mathieu-Castellani, 'Les enfants de Pétrarque (1540–1640)', *CEFI 36*, 623–42, claiming that 'les vrais héritiers seront les infidèles, un d'Aubigné, un Sponde, qui, s'éloignant des modèles et traçant leur sentier à l'écart, sauront retrouver la belle ambition de Pétrarque'; and Id., '"Avoir l'object plus vifvement empreint en l'ame": le statut de l'objet dans la poétique de la Renaissance', Rouget, *L'Objet*, 21–36.

Nicolas Rapin, known as one of the authors of the *Satire Ménipée*, is the subject of J. Brunel's *thèse de doctorat*, defended in 1989, and now published: *Un poitevin poète, humaniste et soldat à l'époque des guerres de religion. Nicolas Rapin (1539–1608). La carrière, les milieux, l'œuvre*, Champion, 2 vols, 1678 pp., is the work of a lifetime and a labour of love, a detailed inquiry into Rapin's life and works. Even the smallest piece of poetry is examined and placed against its background.

Etienne Pasquier, *Les Jeux poetiques*, ed. Jean-Pierre Dupouy, Champion, 2001, 480 pp. Pasquier is essentially remembered as the author of *Les Recherches de la France*, yet he was also a poet: in 1610, the 81-year old republished some of his *juvenilia*, written two generations before, between 1555 and 1578. He was also a biting critic, seeing, for instance, in Jean-Antoine de Baïf a learned man, but with no feeling for poetry. This abrupt verdict is always quoted in handbooks for students, but the two men were in conflict and there may be more than literary taste in P.'s judgment, as discussed by Y. Roberts, 'P.

versus Baïf. The case for a retrial', *FSB*, 83:8–10. We will soon be able to judge for ourselves, for a nine-volume edition of Baïf's poetical works is in progress, the first volume of which has appeared: *Euvres en rime. Neuf livres des Poemes*, ed. Jean Vignes et al., Champion, 1010 pp. An astonishing dabbler, B. did not collect his own works and left this ingrate task to modern scholars.

Even if the 16th c. was not the greatest age for epistolary writers, what survives deserves to be studied. The son of Etienne Pasquier, Nicolas, published a collection of letters, examined by D. Carabin, 'Les *Lettres* de N. Pasquier: la lettre de consolation', *RHLF*, 102:15–31; and Id., 'La réception posthume des *Commentaires* de Blaise de Monluc chez E. et N. Pasquier: naissance d'une symbolique politique', *ib.*, 102:179–90. See also C. H. Winn, 'L'épitre consolatoire au XVIe siècle: un genre en voie de définition', *SFDES 12*, 485–97.

Epic poetry is the French Renaissance's most splendid failure. Its dominant themes and the view of theoreticians are studied by J. Braybrook, 'The epic in 16th-c. France', Sandy, *Heritage*, 351–91, and B. Méniel, 'Territoire de l'épique. Définition du genre de la poésie épique', *RevAR*, 15:107–26, and Id., 'Le dialogue dans la poésie héroïque, en France, à la fin de la Renaissance', *RHR*, 54:95–113.

The Renaissance did not ignore the poetical genre of fables. Y. Giraud, 'Un album de fables au temps de François Ier', *Le Fablier*, 13, 2001:69–78, studies Pierre Sala's *Fables en quatrains* (whose text is given at the end of the article, from the MSS in the Pierpont Morgan Library and the British Library). P. Cifarelli, 'Fables: Aesop and Babrius', Sandy, *Heritage*, 425–52, contains a valuable chronological table of French Aesopic collections (15th and 16th cs); Id., 'Le fablier de Rinuccio d'Arezzo et ses traductions françaises au XVIe siècle', *Le Fablier*, 13, 2001:53–67, and 'Quelques réflexions sur l'utilisation des locutions et des proverbes dans la fable ésopique du 16e siècle', *Reinardus*, 15:33–51.

Scévole de Sainte-Marthe wrote biographies of French poets and scholars, and was also a poet himself: J. Brunel, 'Les *Poësies chrestiennes* de S. de Sainte-Marthe', *Cazauran Vol.*, 597–623. Another prose writer, Béroalde de Verville, wrote didactic poetry: *L'Histoire des vers qui filent la soye*, ed. Michel Renaud, Champion, 2001, 224 pp. This piece, also known under the not very appealing title of *Sérodokimasie*, has survived in two copies (BnF and British Library). Texts on the silkworm by Vida and Olivier de Serres are given in appendix. *RHAM*, 20, 2000, contains three contributions on the versatile Jacques Peletier du Mans, forerunner of natural descriptions: T. Peach, 'P. et son poème *La Savoye*, 1572' (253–72); I. Pantin, 'P. et la médecine. Le traité sur la peste de 1563' (273–88), which discusses two treatises published in Paris and Basle; and G. Cifoletti, 'P. entre humanisme et mathématiques. Notes historiques' (289–99), which sees him as one of the most important mathematicians of his time. See also F. Loget, 'P. mathématicien: l'angle de contact', *NRSS*, 20.2:37–55.

A Savoyard lawyer, friend of St François de Sales and grandfather of Vaugelas, Antoine Favre was also a religious poet, perhaps as great as Jean de Sponde, in his *Entretiens spirituels*, ed. Lance K. Donaldson-Evans, STFM, 316 pp.

On the Renaissance ode and its relations to other poetical forms, one may read P. Galand-Hallyn's studies on 'L'ode latine comme genre "tempéré": le lyrisme familial de Macrin dans les *Hymnes* de 1537', *HL*, 50, 2001:221–65, and 'Le "jour en trop" de Macrin (l'ode liminaire des *Naeniae* de 1550: grandeur et plasticité)', *Cazauran Vol.*, 525–47.

PROSE. Loris Petris, *La Plume et la tribune. Michel de L'Hospital et ses discours (1559–1562)* (THR, 360), xxviii + 610 pp., is an elegant and enlightening study of this neglected yet important figure, icon of religious tolerance. After a biography, P. studies L'Hospital's work from a rhetorical viewpoint. A rich range of sources are covered and almost 200 pages of texts are edited or translated in appendix. A complement is given by Id., '*De pace*. Autour d'un inédit de Michel de L'Hospital', *BHR*, 64:327–46, an edition and translation with a fine analysis of an autograph Latin text, critical of any violence carried out for religious motives.

Philippe Duplessis-Mornay had little to do with tolerance. A friend of Coligny, he left France after the massacre of Saint-Barthélemy and was later at the head of the French Protestant party. Putting his versatile talents to the service of Henri de Navarre, he nevertheless fell short in his goal of establishing a 'France protestante'. Agrippa d'Aubigné was almost ready to consider him as a renegade. Hugues Daussy, *Les Huguenots et le Roi. Le combat politique de Ph. Duplessis-Mornay (1572–1600)* (THR, 364), 694 pp., has read D.-M.'s abundant and dispersed correspondence, as well as his memoirs, and examines with the closest scrutiny the religious and political conceptions of the 'protestant pope', a failed statesman, a man not easily understood by the modern reader. This book is a joy to read and will be useful to historians as well as literary scholars. On religious controversy, see P. Blum-Cuny, 'Fondements argumentatifs de la polémique contre Baronius dans *Le mystère d'iniquité* de Ph. Duplessis-Mornay', *Cazauran Vol.*, 855–65, and M. Tetel, 'Marnix de Sainte-Aldegonde entre deux feux', Desan, *Littérature*, 283–96.

Monica Barsi, *L'Énigme de la chronique de Pierre Belon*, Milan, LED, 390 pp., is a careful edition of Paris, Arsenal, MS 4651. A traveller and ornithologist, Belon pondered upon the wars of religion and wrote an interesting testimony, now at our disposal. U. Langer, 'Variété et prudence dans le traité moral: les *Oeuvres morales et diversifiées en histoires* (1575), de Jean des Caurres', Courcelles, *Varietas*, 119–30. Des Caurres, a friend of Dorat, was the head of a college in Amiens. His book was honoured by a liminary piece of poetry by Ronsard himself. His conception of *varietas* may be a precursor of scepticism or uncertainty.

Less moral is Béroalde de Verville's weird novel, studied by B. Bowen, '"Il faut donner dedans": sexe ou/et rhétorique dans le *Moyen de parvenir*', *La Charité Vol.*, 107–14, and I. Zinguer, 'Un dionysisme particulier: banquet de paroles alimentaires au XVIe siècle', Zinguer, *Dionysos*, 115–21. A synthesis is provided by D. Mauri, 'L'ermite détenteur du savoir dans l'oeuvre romanesque de B. de Verville', *Babel*, 4, 2000: 37–52. On Verville's first novel, the *Avantures de Floride*, see S. Bokdam, 'Du fait-divers au personnage romanesque', *Cazauran Vol.*, 295–325.

Guillaume Du Vair, *Premières oeuvres de piété*, ed. Bruno Petey-Girard, Champion, 406 pp. Du Vair is representative of both the Counter-Reformation and Stoic renewal. This edition gives the carefully annotated text of *La saincte philosophie* and of some religious meditations. A. Tarrête, 'La *Consolation* de Du Vair sur la mort de sa soeur (1584)', *SFDES 12*, 499–516, examines a short text published in 1606. Du Vair's contribution to French *Kunstprosa* was first a consolation for himself. On French meditative prose, read S. Lardon, 'Les *Meditations sur les Pseaumes* de Jean de Sponde: le modèle calviniste et le modèle psalmique', *Cazauran Vol.*, 625–37. Sponde was a scholar, as C. Deloince-Louette reminds us in 'Poésie et politique dans les préfaces à l'"Homère" de Sponde', Cogitore, *Devenir roi*, 147–62, 266–73.

Autobiography occupies a relatively small space in the Renaissance literary output. N. Kuperty-Tsur, 'Justice historique et écriture mémorialiste', Kuperty-Tsur, *Ecriture*, 47–64, examines autobiographical writings as trials. A concrete case is discussed by M.-D. Legrand, 'La narration autobiographique chez Bernard Palissy ou l'argument du martyr(e)', *Cazauran Vol.*, 279–93. Pierre de l'Estoile, *Registre-Journal du règne de Henri III*, vol. v, ed. Madeleine Lazard and Gilbert Schrenck (TLF, 542), 2001, 416 pp., is a valuable and sometimes hilarious source of information. F. Marin, 'La fortune éditoriale des *Registres-Journaux* de P. de L'Estoile', *NRSS*, 20.2: 87–108, provides a second-hand bibliography. See also M. Lazard, 'P. de l'Estoile et l'exécution de Marie-Stuart', *Cazauran Vol.*,

803–12. W. McCuaig, 'Paris / Jerusalem in P. de l'Estoile, the *Satyre Ménipée* and Louis Dorléans', *BHR*, 64:295–315, traces parallels between the siege and famine in Paris (1589–90) and the revolt of the Jewish zealots against the Romans.

In *Jean Bodin et le dilemme de la philosophie politique moderne*, Copenhagen, Museum Tusculanum, 2000, 184 pp., Mogens C. Jacobsen studies from a Kantian viewpoint the contradictions in the *Six livres de la République*, the opposition between natural and individual right, divine and natural law, freedom and sovereignty. Marie-Dominique Couzinet, *Jean Bodin*, Paris–Rome, Memini, 2001, 366 pp., will provide a useful guide, with some 1500 bibliographical references. Just published and already incomplete — such is the common fate of bibliographies, and so one must add A. Tenenti, 'Il doppio volto della storia comparata nella *Methodus* di Bodin', *RLMC*, 54, 2001:3–15, a new study of B.'s historical thought.

On Renaissance dialogue, one may read R. I. Vulcan, 'Le dialogue humaniste et la persuasion', Petris, *Sources*, 57–65, and V. Zaercher, 'Entre dispute et conciliation: stratégies et figures du *consensus* dans le dialogue de la seconde moitié du XVIe siècle', *RHLF*, 101, 2001:1331–48, who focuses her attention on Peletier du Mans and Henri Estienne II, and examines the influences of Cicero and of civility treatises.

In spite of the increasing popularity of the travelogue, scant critical attention has been given to Marc Lescarbot, but we now have Eric Thierry's more or less revised doctoral dissertation, *Marc Lescarbot (vers 1570–1641). Un homme de plume au service de la Nouvelle-France*, Champion, 2001, 440 pp., which discusses how L., trying to escape the French wars of religion, became a pioneer in the French colonization of North America. Serge Elmalan, *Nicolas Durand de Villegagnon ou l'utopie tropicale*, Lausanne, Favre, 298 pp. is a valuable biography of the admiral, founder of the short-lived 'France antarctique'.

C. H. Winn, '*Les Angoysses douloureuses* d'Hélisenne de Crenne (1ère partie): déterminisme physiologique et symbolisme chrétien', *La Charité Vol.*, 115–28, asks whether this long novel is something more than a sentimental novel, and whether it had links with the *devotio moderna*. G.-A. Pérouse, 'Une lecture de *L'Amant ressuscité de la mort d'amour* ',*Cazauran Vol.*, 225–37, studies a novel attributed to Nicolas Denisot. On this writer, see also V. Duché, 'Vers un colloque sentimental', *RHR*, 54:115–37. M.-C. Thomine, 'Les jeux sur le poncif dans *La Nouvelle Fabrique des excellents traicts de verité* de Philippe d'Alcripe', *Cazauran Vol.*, 239–63, studies the use of commonplaces and their parody. On a pastoral novel written by Nicolas de Montreux, see M. Bideaux, 'Le chevalier Filistel chez les bergers de Juliette', *ib.*, 265–77.

THE SEVENTEENTH CENTURY

By J. Trethewey, *University of Wales, Aberystwyth*, and J. P. Short†, *formerly Senior Lecturer in French at the University of Sheffield*

1. General

Dotoli, *Méditerranées*, contains the following colloquium papers: A. Viala, 'Des mythes cythéréens et galants' (25–32), which cites three Watteau paintings referring to Cythera and depicting 'fêtes galantes', and then reviews similar references and depictions in 17th-c. writers from Mlle de Scudéry to Fénelon; S. Poli, 'Toutes les couleurs de la mer lexicographique' (33–48), seeking out seascape descriptions in the poetry of Saint-Amant and Tristan, in *Les Entretiens d'Ariste et d'Eugène* by Bouhours, and consulting 17th-c. dictionaries for maritime definitions; M. Majorano, 'Pages d'eau: mers exemplaires' (157–68), pointing to the way water manifests itself in *Polexandre*, in *Bérénice* (tears mostly), in *Dom Juan*, and in Sorel's *Nouvelles françoises* and *Francion*; A. Baccar, 'De Grenade à Tunis: itinéraire des modèles arabo-musulmans en Méditerranée au XVIIe siècle français' (287–94), tracing the influence of the French translation of Ginés Perez de Hita's *Histoire des guerres civiles de Grenade* and other Spanish works on 'le grand nombre d'ouvrages dont le sujet puise la matière dans le monde arabo-musulman'; F. Assaf, 'Voyageurs dans le Levant au XVIIe siècle: regard(s) sur/de l'Autre' (295–308), reading the travel writings of Pietro Della Valle, Jean de Thévenot, and Laurent d'Arvieux; S. Allam, 'Peut-on parler d'un stéréotype dans la perception de la Méditerranée au XVIIe siècle? L'exemple des turqueries' (309–17), claiming that much literature on the Orient 'nous en apprend en définitive moins sur l'objet "Orient" décrit que sur le sujet "Occident" ayant écrit', and that 'tout se passe [. . .] comme si les Occidentaux n'avaient découvert en Orient que ce qu'ils y cherchaient ou ce qu'ils y projetaient'; A.'s chief example is Molière's *Bourgeois gentilhomme*.

Koch, *Unities*, prints congress *actes*: D. Vaillancourt, 'Faire rouler le carrosse ou comment le XVIIe siècle ne marche pas' (45–55), finds 'un croisement entre façons de dire, art de converser, hygiène sociale et culturelle et façons d'habiter', and chooses 'le carrosse' as 'un bon objet pour rendre compte de cette interaction entre différentes pratiques culturelles' and to study La Bruyère's *Les Caractères* and

† Pat Short died on 13 June, 2003. Despite illness, he made considerable contributions in this chapter to his usual subsections — 2, Poetry, and 3, Drama. His ready advice and cheerful co-operation will be sorely missed in future surveys. J.T.

Rousseau's *Rêveries du promeneur solitaire* with this preoccupation in mind; L. C. Seifert, 'L'homme de ruelle chez les dames: civility and masculinity in the salon' (95–111), asserts that since men play a role as important as do women in 17th-c. French salons, 'salon femininity must continue to be explored, but *along with* salon masculinity'; S. confines his investigations to the period 1630–60, and mainly to effeminate men, 'the chief masculine counterpart of the *précieuse*', taking examples from Sorel, Sarasin, Mlle de Scudéry, and Somaize's *Grand Dictionnaire*; S. E. Melzer, 'The underside of France's civilizing mission: assimilationist politics in "New France"' (151–64), pursues her theme through Colbert's letters, Joseph Le Mercier's *Relations jésuites*, Champlain's *Voyages*, and others; M. Gutwirth, 'Classicisme pas mort?' (171–77), surveys the works thus labelled and finds their beauty and fascination eternally renewed and renewable; P. Gethner, 'Two views on women's education: Molière and Poullain' (241–50), looks at M.'s *Les femmes savantes* and compares it with Poullain de la Barre's views in his *De l'égalité des deux sexes* and his *De la conduite de l'esprit dans les sciences et dans les moeurs*; M. Taormina, 'Decorum: the intersection of eloquence and action' (363–69), notes a 17th-c. shift in views about decorum 'from a Ciceronian balance of polish and power to an Aristotelian emphasis on vividness and *vraisemblance*', but without there being a clear break between the two: rather 'these two modes of eloquence depend on one another'. Christian Jouhaud, *Les Pouvoirs de la littérature: histoire d'un paradoxe* (NRF Essais), Gallimard, 2000, 450 pp., is intrigued by the paradox that at a moment in history when writers' dependence on state power and political ambitions was never so restricting, they benefited 'd'une reconnaissance nouvelle et d'une croissante autonomie où se dessinent les contours d'un statut social en gestation — naissance de l'écrivain'. To explain the paradox, J. reviews the cultural aims of Richelieu and the activities in their various fields of a number of key writers of the first half of the 17th c., most notably Scipion Dupleix, Chapelain, Sorel, Desmarets, Corneille, and particularly Guez de Balzac.

Marchal, *Salons*, prints colloquium papers: N. Hepp, 'Féminité, culture de l'esprit et vie mondaine au XVIIe siècle' (9–18), starts with Racine's acknowledgment of Henriette d'Angleterre's influence in his 'Dédicace' to her of *Andromaque*, and goes on to cite examples of 'les qualités d'esprit et les qualités de caractère' required in a woman who presides over a salon; R. Duchêne, 'De la chambre au salon: réalités et représentations' (21–28), notes a change in usage leading to the first recorded appearance in 1664 of the word *salon* to signify a room in which to receive company; D. then evokes the activities pursued there, particularly the discussing and promoting of literature; A. Cullière, 'Autour de Catherine de Bourbon à Nancy (1599–1604), l'art de la "Marqueterie"' (203–14), recalls poets patronized by the Duchesse de Bar, such as Claude Billard de Courgenay, Du Gallas, and François Du Souhait, whose *Marqueteries ou oeuvres diverses* (1601) are reviewed in some detail; D. Aris, 'Une province très "parisienne": le Maine et ses milieux littéraires au XVIIe siècle' (215–26), quotes disobliging references to the province from Scarron and Roland Le Vayer de Boutigny, but points to the positive influence of the Comte de Belin, patron of Mairet, Rotrou, and the Scudérys, and that of the Duc de Tresme, patron of Charles Rosteau; R. Aulotte, 'Ruelles, activités intellectuelles et mondaines en Bordelais, dans le dernier tiers du XVIIe siècle' (227–31), finds intellectual life in religious establishments which influenced lay centres like the home of the Président Salomon de Virelade, and also literary works like those of Jean d'Intras, Pierre Trichet, Jean-Léon de Métivier, and, above all, Jean Benech de Cantenac.

LitC, 44, is devoted to *L'illusion au XVIIe siècle*: P. Choné, 'L'oeil charmé et l'oeil instruit' (35–50), discusses the views of theorists on *trompe l'oeil* and 'le plaisir d'être trompé', such as Roland Fréart de Chambray, Jean-Pierre Niceron, Jean Du Breuil, and above all Roger de Piles. Other papers are reviewed below. *LitC*, 45, tackles collectively *L'imagination au XVIIe siècle*: N. Doiron, 'L'Enfer du Sage. L'imagination et la philosophie stoïcienne' (29–45), follows the claims and counterclaims of stoics and sceptics from ancient classical times to Montaigne, Charron, Descartes, and others, and looks at dramatic representations of 'la chute aux enfers' from Garnier to Desmarets de Saint-Sorlin; R. Scholar, 'La force de l'imagination de Montaigne: Camus, Malebranche, Pascal' (127–38), studies the reactions to Montaigne ('imagination forte par excellence') of three 17th-c. figures, 'qui lisent les *Essais* dans une perspective augustinienne'; N. Négroni, 'Le champ sémantique et métaphorique de l'imagination au XVIIe siècle: un état des lieux' (259–76), points to the century's problems with imagination, at once 'moyen' and 'organe du savoir', but also associated with 'la chimère' and 'l'illusion', and proposes a complex series of 'interprétations de cet état de fait' via the faculty's 'représentations sémantiques, métaphoriques et épistémologiques'; P.-J. Salazar, 'Rhétorique et "expérience fictive": l'Académie' (297–307), surveys three addresses to the Académie Française: Tallemant's *Panégyrique sur l'heureux retour de la santé du Roy* (1687), La Bruyère's *discours de réception* (1693) and that of Huet (1674); K. Lanini, 'L'imaginaire gelé: codes, règles et modèles dans les traités de peinture du XVIIe siècle' (309–22), studies works, listed at the end of the paper, which all display one purpose: 'il s'agit bien de *guider* la peinture'; at first these works are concerned with theory only, but from the foundation of the Académie Royale de Peinture et de Sculpture (1648), they become more and more prescriptive.

Laurence Grove, *Emblematics and Seventeenth-Century French Literature: Descartes, Tristan, La Fontaine and Perrault*, Charlottesville, VA, Rookwood, 2000, 284 pp., proposes 'a reconsideration of our attitude towards major writings of the 17th c. in the light of information that until recently had been unavailable or grossly neglected'. All of G.'s writers were influenced in their own ways by emblematics (and, in the case of T. and P., expressed their own opinions on the subject), and are studied both for their intrinsic interest and as examples to promote further research. Alison Adams, Alison Saunders, and Stephen Rawles, **A Bibliography of French Emblem Books of the Sixteenth and Seventeenth Centuries, 2: L-Z* (THR, 362), Geneva, Droz, xxii + 762 pp., with illustrations, covers the period 1534–1700, and over 700 printed editions. *Le Point de vue de l'emblème*, ed. Paulette Choné (Écritures), Dijon U.P., 2001, 216 pp., prints 12 essays by nine 'historiens de systèmes symboliques'. Their interests cover the whole of Europe, and their emphasis is mainly on the pictorial rather than on verse. Contributions on French material (wholly or in part) are: D. Russell, 'Emblématique et anamorphose' (9–28); B. Gaulard, 'Le vocabulaire de la paix: concorde de la paix et amitié dans l'emblème du *Siège de Dole*' (141–51), B. Teyssandier, '*La Doctrine des Moeurs*, roman emblématique pour l'instruction d'un jeune prince' (153–69), on the collaboration between Gomberville and the engraver Pierre Daret; Id., '*La Doctrine des Moeurs* ou les lunettes de l'académicien: correction optique pour une galerie politique' (171–84); and J.-M. Chatelain, 'La devise héroïque et l'amitié des grandes âmes' (185–93), on the difference between the *emblème moral* and the *devise héroïque.* F. Dumora-Mabille, 'Le centaure et l'homoncule', *LitC*, 45:243–58, examines the use to which these two emblematic figures are put by Descartes (in his *Dioptrique*), Cureau de la Chambre (*Traité de la connaissance des animaux*) and Pierre Chanet (*Traité de l'esprit de l'homme*).

Landry, *Dialogue*, prints papers on 'la rivalité et/ou la concorde entre les arts': A. Saunders, 'Modèles artistiques réciproques: le livre d'emblèmes comme source d'oeuvres d'art et vice versa' (185–206), cites graphic and printed evidence from England and France for 'ce processus réciproque'; A.-E. Spica, 'L'emblématique, une poétique de la peinture' (207–21), examines a crisis of confidence in words and images, brought about by the Council of Trent and the Counter-Reformation, and the remedies proposed to 'incarner véridiquement l'intelligible', among them books of emblems and Aesopic fables which had their influence on d'Urfé, Mlle de Scudéry, and La Fontaine; A. Gaillard, 'Des yeux et des oreilles: le parallèle entre les arts aux XVIIe et XVIIIe siècles' (267–84), discusses attitudes to this theme, naming in passing Cesare Ripa, Jean Baudouin, Charles Perrault, La Fontaine, Félibien, Roger de Piles, Jean-Baptiste Du Bos, and Lessing. Jean Weisgerber, *La Muse des jardins: jardins de l'Europe littéraire (1580–1700)* (Nouvelle poétique comparatiste, 5), Berne–NY, Lang, 216 pp., looks at the way in which European writers celebrate gardens noting a Cartesian desire to control nature with science (or sometimes, like Saint-Simon, deplore the violence done to nature). The French writers most in evidence are Mlle de Scudéry, La Fontaine, and Louis XIV who is credited with the *Manière de montrer les Jardins de Versailles.*

Christian Biet, *Droit et littérature sous l'Ancien Régime: le jeu de la valeur et de la loi* (Lumière classique, 41), Champion, 415 pp., covers law viewed by literature from the mid-16th c. to the end of the 18th c., noting 'à la fois une illustration fictionnelle des règles et des procédures du droit, et un moyen de les mettre en question, d'en déterminer les lacunes et d'en analyser les failles', and also the expectations of a reading public conditioned by a familiar legal system. All forms of literature are considered, though particular attention is paid to Corneille, La Fontaine, Mme de La Fayette, Molière, Racine, Regnard, and Mme de Villedieu.

Jean Rohou, *Le XVIIe siècle, une révolution de la condition humaine*, Seuil, 670 pp., surveys all aspects of literature, theatre, law, philosophy; economic, social religious and artistic life, from the late 16th to the early 18th c., in order to trace 'une révolution et de la personnalité humaine et de la conception qu'on s'en faisait', which took place, paradoxically, in a period which 'passe pour une époque de stabilisation conservatrice'. This revolution, says R., did not have an immediate political or social impact, but 's'est produite [. . .] chez une petite minorité socio-culturelle déterminante pour l'avenir', that future being the enormous political and industrial transformations of the next two centuries. The complexities of this 'inversion (ou révolution au sens premier)' are analysed and laid before us with admirable clarity. Id., 'La périodisation: une reconstruction révélatrice et explicatrice', *RHLF*, 102:707–32, confirms that R. has firm views in favour of *périodisation*, even if it means downgrading in certain writers (like Pascal and La Rochefoucauld) the importance attributed to the 'vérités éternelles sur la nature humaine [. . .]. C'est sans doute les relativiser; mais c'est retrouver leur véritable raison d'être, et préciser leur signification'. A. Maral, 'Portrait religieux de Louis XIV', *DSS*, 54:697–723, collects the opinions and memoirs of many of the king's contemporaries, among them the Princesse Palatine, Saint-Simon, the Abbé de Choisy, and Louis XIV himself in his *Mémoires pour l'instruction du dauphin.* M. C. Canova-Green, 'Espace et pouvoir dans *Les Plaisirs de l'Île enchantée* (1664)', *SCFS*, 23,

2001:121–38, describes some of the activities at the *fête* ordered by Louis XIV to represent absolutism, and point to his own near magical power to transform the world. A. Henshaw, 'Descartes and Corneille: a re-examination', *Neophilologus*, 86:45–56, offers explanations of how the two might have undergone the same influences, suggesting linking agents — St François de Sales, Honoré d'Urfé, and the Jesuit schoolteachers of all four — quoting from Jesuit pedagogical texts of the period, and comparing them with quotations from them all. D. Orsini, 'L'approche pragmatique du récit théâtral: une propédeutique du roman-mémoires (*Cinna* de Corneille et *Mémoires de Madame la marquise de Frêne* de Courtilz de Sandras)', *QLL*, 26, 2001:41–59, compares the methods of narration used by a dramatist and a writer of *mémoires*. He chooses a *récit* from *Cinna* for the first and one by Mme de Frêne from C. de S.'s fictional work for the second. He shows that in both cases the speaker is using a technique that will distance him/herself from their questionable actions.

Pister, *Image du prêtre*, prints 17 colloquium papers, none of which study classical literature *per se*, and nearly all of which comment approvingly on works of piety by 17th-c. writers (the most notable being François de Sales and Saint-Cyran) who worked for the success of the Counter-Reformation. **Dieu au XVIIe siècle: crises et renouvellements du discours, une approche interdisciplinaire, philosophie, esthétique, théologie mystique*, ed. Henri Laux and Dominique Salin, Éditions des Facultés jésuites de Paris, 295 pp., prints conference papers on Augustinianism and philosophy, Jansenism, Molière's *Tartuffe*, and the 'invasion mystique'. B. Guion, 'De la vérité avant toute chose: fables, fiction et histoire à Port-Royal', *Delmas Vol.*, 297–322, is concerned with Jansenist pedagogical methods, as opposed to those of the Jesuits, particularly at the turn of the 17th-18th c., when the latter 'délaissent l'histoire pour orienter leurs élèves vers les belles-lettres', while Port-Royal displays 'une exigence de vérité' which involves a rejection of fiction and a concentration on history in which is seen, 'non pas une invitation à égaler la grandeur d'âme des héros, mais une révélation de la condition humaine'.

Strategic Rewriting, ed. David Lee Rubin (Studies in Early Modern France, 8), Charlottesville, Rookwood, 288 pp., includes articles on La Ceppède's *Théorèmes*, Théophile's *Pyrame et Thisbé*, Mairet's and Corneille's versions of *Sophonisbe*, d'Aubignac's *Histoire du temps*, the Psyche myth, epistolary novels by Villedieu and Boursault, Anne Dacier and the 'Homer debate', La Fontaine's 'La Clochette', and Diderot on painting. Benedetta Papàsogli, **Volti della memoria nel 'Grand Siècle' e oltre*, Rome, Bulzoni, 2000, 343 pp., studies reference to memory, particularly in Corneille's *Cinna*, Mme de La Fayette's *La Princesse de Clèves*, Pascal's *Pensées* and Fénelon's *Télémaque*. Madeleine de Scudéry et al., **Chroniques du Samedi suivies de pièces diverses (1653–1654)*, ed. Alain Niderst et al. (Sources classiques, 43), Champion, 400 pp., is the first complete edition of this 'manuscrit légendaire'.

Stéphane Haffemayer, *L'Information dans la France du XVIIe siècle. La Gazette de Renaudot de 1647 à 1663* (Bibliothèque de l'histoire moderne et contemporaine, 6), Champion, 848 pp., analyses 22,200 pages containing 20,327 items of news from all over Europe, relating them to the historical events which inspired them, and illustrating their frequency and provenance with maps and graphs. The 'valeur informative de la Gazette' is found on the whole to be 'incontestable', though a certain amount of manipulation, it is noticed, takes place 'afin de servir les buts de la politique étrangère de la France', and there is the inevitable praise and exaltation of Louis XIV, as well as a decided pro-Catholic bias on the part of R., himself a convert.

Les Ventes de livres et leurs catalogues XVIIe–XXe siècle, ed. Annie Charon and Elisabeth Parinet (Études et rencontres, 5), École des Chartes, 2000, 205 pp., prints *actes* from *journées d'étude*, including the following: D. Varry, 'Les ventes publiques de livres à Lyon aux XVIIe et XVIIIe siècles et leurs catalogues' (29–48); G. Mandelbrote, 'La nouvelle édition de Graham Pollard et Albert Ehrman, *The distribution of books by catalogue from the invention of printing to AD 1800*: bilan des travaux préparatoires: catalogue français' (49–76); F. Bléchet, 'Glanes bibliographiques sur quelques grandes ventes publiques: la politique d'acquisition de la Bibliothèque du Roi' (77–96).

2. Poetry

**L'Épopée et ses modèles de la Renaissance aux Lumières*, ed. Franck Greiner and Jean-Claude Ternaux (Colloques, congrès et conférences sur la Renaissance, 29), Champion, 368 pp., collects conference papers. G. Banderier, 'Note sur un sonnet baroque ("Tourment sans passion, passion sans pointure")', *FSB*, 85:4–6, locates 17th-c. printed appearances of this sonnet which had been thought to exist only in MS. M.-O. Sweetser, 'The art of praise from Malherbe to La Fontaine', *Rubin Vol.*, 119–39, points to La F.'s acknowledgment of M.'s influence in his composition of encomiastic poems, and views examples of the tradition that links the two poets, via Théophile, Saint-Amant, and Tristan L'Hermite. G. Bosco, 'Les merveilles de la mer dans les poèmes épiques français du XVIIe siècle', Dotoli, *Méditerranées*, 93–105, discusses the role of the sea in epic poetry, showing it as the setting where representations of the conflict between good and evil can take place. Scudéry's *Alaric* and Saint-Amant's *Moyse sauvé* are used, with others, to illustrate this point. P. Ronzeaud,

'Du mauvais genre à la subversion des genres: l'Autre femme au XVIIe siècle', Hodgson, *Femme*, 33–52, takes an unapologetic look, in satirical poetry and comic novels, at repulsive female stereotypes such as 'la paysanne grossière', 'la courtisane lubrique', 'la muse mégère' and 'la harangère harangueuse', all of them, in his view, fertile 'productrices de formes nouvelles d'écriture'.

BOILEAU. R. T. Corum, Jr., 'The rhetoric of disgust and contempt in Boileau', *Rubin Vol.*, 163–78, examines 'the range of sentiments and emotions experienced by Boileau's speaker and consequently aroused in the reader', the emotions being 'bemused pity, contempt, righteous indignation, or the visceral depths of disgust'.

CHAPELAIN. L. Goupillaud, 'Chapelain recoiffé par Perrault: une apologie paradoxale de *La Pucelle*', *DSS*, 54:343–68, deplores the general denigration of this epic, which, G. believes, is incompatible with praise for C. the critic and literary theorist. G. brings to C.'s rescue the judicious assessment of the poem made by P. in his *Parallèle des Anciens et des Modernes*.

DESMARETS DE SAINT-SORLIN. *Marie-Madeleine ou le triomphe de la grâce, 1669*, ed. Gilles Banderier, Grenoble, Jérôme Millon, 2001, 219 pp. The editor's introduction places this 'poème héroïque' in the context of D.'s life and development as writer and polemicist, and in that of the considerable number of works in verse and prose devoted to Mary Magdalene. B. also discusses the role and nature of the fiction that D. felt it necessary to add to the biblical story, and the religious convictions that make of D. a *moderne* in the *Querelle des Anciens et des Modernes*. Y. Loskoutoff, '*Mazarini's Desmarets*. Addenda au *Corpus Maresianum*', *DSS*, 54:741–48, refers to the *Corpus* which opens H. G. Hall's *Richelieu's Desmarets and the century of Louis XIV*, 1990 (see *YWMLS*, 52:100), and to an ode, the text of which could not be found by H., but of which L. has unearthed an edition. Other poets writing on behalf of Mazarin are also quoted, notably Cyrano, Tristan, François Maynard, and the Abbé Perrin.

LA FONTAINE. Olivier Leplatre, *Le Pouvoir et la parole dans les* Fables *de La Fontaine*, Lyons U.P., 367 pp., claims that in the *Fables* 'cohabitent une pensée et une sagesse', the first being in 'l'intelligence du politique et de sa parole', the second in 'l'expérience du poétique, dans l'affirmation que l'écriture est une manière cultivée de vivre et d'exister'. L. finds no alternative political system proposed by La F., rather 'il se replie sur l'idéal de la pensée et du corps s'écrivant'. M.-O. Sweetser, 'Vaux et son goût: son exemplarité chez La Fontaine', Marchal, *Salons*, 173–88, produces almost a collage of quotations from recent writers about Vaux, its proprietor and his literary clientèle, and follows it up with a survey of La F.'s poetic evocations of the château, and other poems influenced by it.

J. Morgante, 'À la croisée des genres: les "Lettres à sa femme" de La Fontaine', *ib.*, 271–83, analyses the six letters (also known as *Relation de voyage*) that La F. addressed to his wife from Limousin in 1663, and discerns in them a subtle plea to the king on behalf of the imprisoned Fouquet. S.-O. Stiker-Metral, '"Ainsi parla le solitaire". Itinéraire augustinien dans les *Fables* de La Fontaine', *CPR*, 51:325–46, begins by quoting the whole of 'Le juge arbitre, l'hospitalier et le solitaire', the last fable of La F.'s last book, and points to its source, an extract from Arnauld d'Andilly's translation of *Les Vies des Pères des Déserts.* Noting thus the 'présence de Port-Royal en ce lieu stratégique des *Fables*', S.-M. sets out to 'déterminer précisément la place et la fonction de l'anthropologie augustinienne dans les *Fables*'. S. Gruffat, 'Les fables illustrées de La Fontaine: de l'évidence morale à la suggestion poétique', Landry, *Dialogue*, 251–66, sees in Chauveau's and Oudry's illustrations to the *Fables*, not so much a deliberate intention to 'gloser la signification symbolique des vers', as a 'système iconique' which contributes to the 'fonctionnement heuristique et ludique de la fable'.

The following papers appear in *Rubin Vol.*: J. Brody, '"L'alouette et ses petits" (4.22): reflections on La Fontaine's "esprit critique"' (181–95), quotes the fable in full, and then sets out to show how La F. combines 'an almost superstitious respect for the fable's traditional data with bold, personal touches calculated to point the new version [. . .] in a direction all its own'; R. Danner, 'Monkey rhetoric and donkey discourse: irony and relativism in "Le lion, le singe et les deux ânes" (*Fables*, 11.5)' (197–216), uses this poem to remind us that a fable — or any poem — is 'more than what it *says*', and that its meanings should be 'determined by what the poem actually does, in the labyrinthine territory of its lines and the often expressive spaces between them'; J. D. Hubert, 'Displacement in La Fontaine's *Fables* from metaphor to theater' (217–37), finds fables where 'metaphor helps reduce the gap separating discourse from the state of nature while at the same time directing both of them toward role playing'; C. M. Grisé, 'La Fontaine's "Les filles de Minée": weaving a poetic narrative' (239–63), proposes to uncover in this poem a narrative passage that confers a new level of meaning contained in the tapestry which is described for us — 'a meta-narrative device positioned at the core of the four diegetic tales' told by the daughters; M. Vincent, 'Illustration, image, and emblem in La Fontaine's *Fables*' (265–85), discusses to what extent and in what ways illustrations — above all those of Chauveau — contribute to the fables; N. Cronk, 'Reading La Fontaine and writing literary history in the eighteenth century: the problem of Voltaire' (287–314), asks to what extent 18th-c. readers understand the mechanisms of La F.'s poetry, and answers by referring us to the writings of 'two dissidents': Voltaire and the Comte de Caylus; R. Albanese, Jr., 'La Fontaine and the teaching of Frenchness' (315–35), surveys the poet's role as cultural model and purveyor of 'normative cultural values', helping, by his constant presence in the school curriculum, to 'strengthen the political and moral ideology' particularly of the Third Republic.

LESCARBOT. Eric Thierry, *Marc Lescarbot (vers 1570–1641): un homme au service de la Nouvelle-France* (Les Géographies du Monde, 4), Champion, 2001, 440 pp., charts the stages in L.'s life, as a lawyer-servant of the Counter Reformation, as a poet and historian of Nouvelle France, and as a poet who celebrated his discovery of the Swiss Alps. Bernard Emont, **Marc Lescarbot: mythes et rêves fondateurs de la Nouvelle-France: avec une biographie nouvelle de l'auteur*, L'Harmattan, 362 pp.

ANNE DE MARQUETS. R. Ganim, 'Variations on the Virgin: Anne de Marquets's depiction of Mary in the *Sonets spirituels*', Hodgson, *Femme*, 407–17. These poems, published at the beginning of the 17th c., show a much more active and positive Mother of God than the one normally depicted. Marquets's feminism leads her to seek out her own shrewd way of reaffirming the cult of the Virgin.

SAINT-AMANT. A. L. Birberick, 'Drink, eat and write: Saint-Amant's gastronomic discourse', *Rubin Vol.*, 141–61, views the poet's gastronomic and bacchic poems, less as evidence of *dévergondage* on his part, and more for their professionalism and skill in handling motifs and imagery. N. Négroni, '*Le passage de Gibraltar* de Saint-Amant: entre navigation "capricieuse" et voyage spiritueux', Dotoli, *Méditerranées*, 195–208, shows that the poem mixes genres and is itself an elaborate metaphor.

SCARRON. D. Bertrand, 'Travestissement d'un haut lieu virgilien: l'Etna revisité par Scarron', Dotoli, *Méditerranées*, 49–62, studies S.'s burlesque version in his *Virgile travesty* of 34 lines of Canto III of the *Aeneid*, expanded by him to 146 lines, and sees in this irreverent description evidence concerning 17th-c. mental attitudes.

TRISTAN L'HERMITE. S. Berregard, 'Tristan ou l'image d'un poète mélancolique', *CTH*, 24:15–29, explores the implications of her assertion that 'Tristan fait figure de poète mélancolique — au point d'apparaître comme le type même du poète mélancolique'. A. Howe, 'Du nouveau sur les *Vers héroïques*, *L'Office de la sainte Vierge* et *La mort de Chrispe*: trois documents inédits', *ib.*, 38–52, introduces and prints for the first time three *actes* from the Minutier central which give information on the reception of *La mort de Chrispe*, throw light on T.'s relations with Gaston d'Orléans, and point to an evolution in his religious ideas. A. Mansau, 'La mort et la foi: à propos d'Isabelle-Claire-Eugénie, héroïne de Tristan L'Hermite', *ib.*, 68–76, reviews appreciatively the poems written in exile in Brussels by T. in honour of the Infanta, and mourning her death in 1633. L. Grove, 'Les *Poésies héroïques et burlesques* (1650): Jean-Baptiste et/ou Tristan?', *ib.*, 77–97, wishes to support the cause of Jean-Baptiste L'Hermite, the much maligned younger brother of T., whose 'poésies ne sont pas dénuées d'intérêt'. *Oeuvres complètes,* II. *Poésie* (I), ed. Jean-Pierre Chauveau et al. (Sources classiques, 41), Champion, 562 pp. contains *Les Amours* (1638), ed. Véronique Adam; *La Lyre* (1641), ed. Alain Génetiot; and, as *annexes, Annotations sur les Plaintes d'Acante* (1633), *Principes de Cosmographie* (1637), and the *Carte du Royaume d'Amour* (1658).

THÉOPHILE DE VIAU. *'Après m'avoir fait tant mourir': Oeuvres choisies,* ed. Jean-Pierre Chauveau (Poésie, 374), Gallimard, 298 pp., keeps the chronological order of original publication and, in addition to verse, includes extracts from prose works (*Traité de l'immortalité de l'âme, Première journée,* letters) and scenes from *Pyrame et Thisbé.* C. contributes an enthusiastic and highly readable preface, and a 'Dossier' full of information, insights, and comparisons which provide a historical context to the works. H. Merlin, 'Théophile de Viau: moi libertin, moi abandonné', *La Licorne,* 61 : 123–36, feels uneasy with some of the ideas of this 'libertin héroïque': 'par certains de ses aspects essentiels, le cas Théophile fait entrer dans la *liberté de penser* chère à nos consciences modernes des éléments dérangeants'. G. Matthieu-Castellani, 'Éros et ses masques: images de la femme dans la poésie de Théophile de Viau', Hodgson, *Femme,* 11–32, discusses the ambiguity of the representation of women in T.'s poetry, many of the images suggesting to M.-C. that it was young men who were being discreetly evoked. N. Négroni, 'Femmes au bord de la crise de vers', *ib.*, 225–39, undertakes a minute and delicate exploration of T.'s presentation of women which finds the poet engaged 'dans des enjeux esthétiques et génériques complexes'.

3. Drama

Femmes dramaturges en France (1650–1750). Pièces choisies, vol. II, ed. Perry Gethner (Biblio 17, 136), Tübingen, Narr, 472 pp., presents six more plays from the period covered by the first volume of 1993 (see *YWMLS,* 55 : 148). Two of the dramatists in that volume are represented in this: Françoise Pascal, with *Endymion,* a tragi-comedy of 1657, a *pièce à machines,* and Marie-Catherine Desjardins (Mme de Villedieu) with *Nitétis,* a tragedy of 1664. Others represented are Antoinette Deshouliers, *Genséric* (1680); Catherine Durand, *Comédies en proverbes,* 1699; Marguerite-Jeanne de Staal, *La Mode,* a comedy of 1755; and Anne-Marie Du Boccage, *Les Amazones,* a tragedy of 1749.

Delmas Vol., in its first part prints 11 articles by C. Delmas, ten already published between 1987 and 1999, and one 'à paraître': 'Histoire et mythe' (161–68), in which he wishes to correct his own past belief in history as the predominant element in drama by showing that, particularly in Racine, 'la tragédie historique est elle-même ouverte au mythe'. The second part contains contributions by various authors: R. Zuber, 'Le théâtre classique et l'honnête homme: histoire ou mythe?' (181–83), opts for 'histoire' for the not entirely convincing reason that in general classical theatre 'donnait le modèle d'un art de vivre en société'; J.-P. Grosperrin, 'Furies de théâtre. Mythologies et dramaturgie des *fureurs* dans la tragédie classique' (261–81), examines evocations of the Furies in 17th-c. plays, notably by Corneille, Rotrou, and Racine; H. Visentin, 'La tragédie à machines ou l'art d'un théâtre bien ajusté' (417–29), compares the generally unfavourable reception given to this form of theatre by the theorists La Mesnardière and d'Aubignac with the more balanced view of the practising dramatist Pierre Corneille.

E. Hénin, 'Poétique de l'illusion scénique. Des poétiques italiennes de la Renaissance à la doctrine classique (ou: de la Renaissance italienne à Corneille)', *LitC*, 44:15–34, starts in Italy in 1550 with 'l'image théâtrale' which 'n'a de réalité qu'optique' and is 'étroitement liée à l'illusionnisme picturale', but in the end, 'la théorie de l'illusion à l'âge classique n'est ni complète ni autosuffisante, mais elle constitue une antichambre ouvrant sur la plus grave interrogation de toutes les poétiques: la question de la *catharsis*'. N. Courtès, 'Polistène et Alcandre ou l'illusion magique', *ib.*, 83–96, notes the importance of magic and magicians in pastoral, particularly in theatre, and concentrates on the persons and activities of the magicians in Racan's *Bergeries* and Corneille's *Illusion comique*, Alcandre also serving, in the latter play, C.'s purpose of defending and justifying theatre. G. Revaz, 'L'illusion dans l'énonciation comique (Corneille et Marivaux)', *ib.*, 97–114, is struck by current 'avancées de la linguistique de l'énonciation' and wishes to apply them to C.'s *L'Illusion comique* and *Le Menteur* and M.'s *Les Fausses Confidences*. J.-P. Grosperrin, 'La glorieuse, la songeuse et les magiciens. Séductions de l'illusion dans la tragédie lyrique (1675–1710)', *ib.*, 115–39, studies the genre from Quinault's *Thésée*, via Thomas Corneille's *Médée*, to Houdard de La Motte's tragedies, ending with a return to Quinault's *Armide*', finding in the genre a tendency to 'affectionner durablement les enchanteurs, et surtout les enchanteresses'; J. D. Lyons, 'L'illusion porteuse de vérité', *ib.*, 143–55, first notes two levels of illusion in Corneille's *L'Illusion comique*: that of the spectators, and that of the deceived father Pridamant, and then seeks out other plays where characters are deceived, citing *Le Cid*, *Horace*, *Tartuffe*, and *Phèdre*. E. Marpeau, 'Le théâtre au miroir: jeux d'optique, champ aveugle et illusions dans la comédie de la première moitié du XVIIe siècle', *ib.*, 157–74, looks for dramatic use of 'apparences trompeuses' and finds it in *Le Menteur* and Desmarets de Saint-Sorlin's *Les Visionnaires*. C. Biet, 'L'avenir des illusions, ou le théâtre et l'illusion perdue', *ib.*, 175–214, asks 'quelle sorte de spectacle les spectateurs des années 1635–1660 ont-ils été en mesure de voir, et à quel niveau se situe leur illusion?' and answers by citing evidence from various sources including Tallemant des Réaux, Michel de Pure and Marmontel. J.-Y. Vialleton, 'À propos de la mort "tragique" de Montfleury: la poésie dramatique entre illusion prosaïque et folie poétique', *ib.*, 215–37, quotes at length from Guéret's *Le Parnasse réformé* with its use of a 'dialogue des morts' in which dead authors are granted posthumous debating time, but concentrates on a fantastic intervention by the late actor Montfleury. V. then cites tales from similar fictional sources. L. Thirouin, 'Le moraliste et les fantômes: la controverse classique autour de l'illusion théâtrale', *ib.*, 265–83, examines the sources in Plato and St Augustine of the moral condemnations of theatre expressed by 17th-c. polemicists, particularly Nicole, based on convictions concerning the dangers of 'les fantômes et tout ce qui en ce monde relève du simulacre'.

**Langues, codes et conventions de l'ancien théâtre*, ed. Jean-Pierre Bordier (Le Savoir de Mantice, 8), Champion, 256 pp., prints conference papers covering the 10th to the 17th c. on Latin, French, German, and Castilian theatre. R. F. Amonoo, 'Les rapports entre le salon et la tragédie au XVIIe siècle: Pierre Corneille et Jean Racine devant le public des salons', Marchal, *Salons*, 285–92, is interested 'aux activités dans les salons, aux séances de lecture privées au cours de la genèse des pièces', and cites with comments reactions at the Hôtel de Rambouillet and elsewhere to readings from *Le Cid*, *Horace*, and *Polyeucte*, and at the Hôtel de Nevers to a reading of *Alexandre*, also to Henriette d'Angleterre's comments on the MS of *Andromaque*, and those of Colbert on *Britannicus*. G. Revaz, 'Peut-on parler de tragédie "galante" (1656–1667)?' *DSS*, 54:469–84, gives the answer: yes — a genre provided by Thomas Corneille and Quinault for the entertainment of the young Louis XIV. C. Biet, 'Actions et tragédie au XVIIe siècle, ordre et des ordres', Koch, *Unities*, 285–309, draws our attention to the potential complexities implicit in classical theatrical conventions by reading commentators other than Chapelain and d'Aubignac, 'pour en saisir toutes les facettes, quitte à douter un peu des *doxas* qui enveloppent le genre'. He proposes as examples Saint-Évremond for whom 'l'admiration' is a 'notion contestant radicalement la catharsis', and Saint-Réal who sees pleasure in the representation of cruelty.

G. Snaith, 'Dom Japhet d'Arménie and other descendants of Noah', Connon, *Drama*, 11–28, examines Scarron's comedies, and also Thomas Corneille's *Le Baron d'Albikrac* and Antoine de Montfleury's *La Femme juge et partie*, the latter two following *Don Japhet* in being examples of plays constructed round an eccentric or grotesque central character, using farce and including scenes 'getting laughs through the more *risqué* domains of sexual innuendo and scatology'. *Sept traités sur le jeu du comédien et autres textes. De l'action oratoire à l'art dramatique (1657–1750)*, ed. Sabine Chaouche (Sources classiques, 28), Champion, 2001, 872 pp., contains Michel Le Faucheur, *Traité de l'action de l'orateur ou de la prononciation et du geste* (1657), René Bary, *Méthode pour bien prononcer un discours et pour le bien animer* (1679), Grimarest, *Traité du récitatif* (1707), Jean Poisson, *Réflexions sur l'art de parler en public* (1717), Luigi Riccoboni, *Pensées sur la déclamation* (1738), Pierre-Raymond de Sainte-Albine, *Le comédien* (1747) and Antoine-François Riccoboni, *L'art du théâtre à Madame* *** (1750). Each *traité* is accompanied by extracts from other works published at about the same time on rhetoric and theatrical arts in general.

D'AUBIGNAC. C. Biet, 'Le martyre de la sainte vraisemblance: Hédelin d'Aubignac et *La Pucelle d'Orléans*', *Delmas Vol.*, 219–41, regards A.'s tragedy as a significant stage in the creation of 'l'idée de nation telle qu'elle fut lentement constituée durant l'Ancien Régime'.

BRUSCAMBILLE. A. Tomarken, '"Un beau petit encomion": Bruscambille and the satirical eulogy on stage', *Mayer Vol.*, 247–67, points to B.'s debt to Lucian of Samosata, evident from direct mention, from the nature of his style veering between obscenities and 'serious exhortation and admonition', from his 'choice of topics for his speeches and his approach to those topics', and from his displaying a similar attitude in his chosen themes to that adopted by L.

CAMPISTRON. *Tragédies (1684–1685): Arminius, Andronic, Alcibiade*, ed. Jean-Philippe Grosperrin and Jean-Noël Pascal, Toulouse, Société de Littératures Classiques, xliii + 209 pp., uses as *texte de base* the collective edition of 1715. Each play is followed by a 'Notice' covering details of first production, sources, comparisons with other dramatists, particularly Corneille and Racine. The Introduction includes a biography, a general study of the tragedies, and a survey of their success, which seems not to have outlived C. himself.

DENYS COPPÉE. J. Enders, 'The theatrical memory of Denis Coppée's *Sanglante et pitoyable tragédie de nostre sauveur et rédempteur Jesu-Christ*', *Rubin Vol.*, 1–21, shows how this dramatist from the province of Liège tackled the problem of producing in 1624 a performable version of this story without violating classical taboos.

PIERRE CORNEILLE. Milorad R. Margitić, *Cornelian Power Games: Variations on a Theme in Pierre Corneille's Theatre from 'Mélite' to 'Polyeucte'*

(Biblio 17, 133), Tübingen, Narr, 258 pp., devotes a chapter to each play in this sequence, allocating to each a one-word heading evoking a sub-theme which is an aspect of the main theme of power. M. finds that these sub-themes have in common a 'game-like quality' which enhances their striking 'theatricality'. Mariette Cuénin-Lieber, *Corneille et le monologue: une interrogation sur le héros* (Biblio 17, 134), Tübingen, Narr, 466 pp., provides us with a history of the monologue, its theory and its theatrical uses, before arriving at C., first the theorist and then the dramatist, whose plays are considered chronologically in three parts. The first division is *Mélite* to *Le Cid* 'ou Corneille et la tradition du monologue', the second, *Horace* to *Rodogune* ('fluctuations du monologue et variations sur le thème du héros'), and the third, *Théodore* to *Suréna* with the question: 'Que reste-t-il du monologue?' C.-L. is aware that changes in fashion influenced C. and led him to use the monologue forms more sparingly in later years, but she stresses that an evolution in the nature of the Cornelian hero also modifies form and frequency as time passes.

C. J. Gossip, 'Corneille as self-critic', *SCFS*, 23, 2001: 101–10, notes 'apparent inconsistencies within the author's comments on certain of his own plays', and, with his comments on *Le Cid* particularly in mind, reviews the circumstances in which the *Examens* and the *Discours* were written and published, concluding that 'his remarks in the *Examen* to *Le Cid* and the *Discours* are complementary rather than self-contradictory'. N. Ekstein, 'Metaphors of mathematics in Corneille's theater', *Neophilologus*, 86: 197–214, feels, reading C.'s plays, that she is 'entering a world of calculations, equations, geometric figures, variables and rigidly logical combinations'. The metaphors that she notes are either, 'those dealing with identities' or 'those dealing with combinatories', and she concentrates on *Don Sanche d'Aragon* which makes exceptional use of both. E. also suggests (of C.'s theatre in general) that 'the presence of mathematical figures can be linked to the curious absence of sexual passion in this dramatic universe, or conversely, to the omnipresence of self-control'. B. Louvat-Molozay, 'De l'oracle de tragédie comme procédé dramaturgique: l'exemple de Corneille', *Delmas Vol.*, 395–416, claims that the oracle in French classical tragedy 'possède ses règles et protocoles spécifiques, distincts de ceux de l'oracle de la tragédie antique, et que Corneille a très largement contribué à fixer'. L.-M. studies the roles of oracles in *Horace*, *Andromède* and *Oedipe*, and more briefly in *La Toison d'or* and *Psyche*.

C. Triau, '*Cinna*: catastrophe finale et catastrophe initiale', *SCFS*, 23, 2001: 81–89, suggests that Émilie's opening soliloquy 'se pose en inverse directement symétrique du tableau final': 'volonté de vengeance' opposed to 'clémence', 'lexique de la ruine et de la destruction' opposed to 'la pacification et l'établissement d'un empire solide et unificateur'. This soliloquy could also be read as 'une "catastrophe" qui paradoxalement semble se situer avant la pièce' like the dénouement of a tragedy 'que l'on aurait pu intituler *Toranius* ou encore *Octave* — tragédie de l'ascension du tyran'. J.-P. Landry, '*Cinna* ou le paradoxe de la clémence', *RHLF*, 102:443–59, adds to recent discussions by redefining Auguste's 'pardon' which must be at once 'un effet dramatique — un "coup de théâtre"' and 'un acte d'une portée morale profonde, qui révèle toute une philosophie de l'existence'. M. Escola, 'Récrire *Horace*', *DSS*, 54:445–67, is worried, like so many before him, about the 'dualité' of the central character. Is this play a 'tragédie de l'inhumanité' or a 'tragédie de la vertu héroïque'? E. traces the history of the argument, and imagines C. writing a version 'au lendemain des *Discours* de 1660' in which the roles of Valère and Camille are developed to justify more firmly the latter's death. M. R. Margitić, 'Fins et débuts cornéliens: une analyse comparée de *Suréna*', *SCFS*, 23, 2001:91–100, questions the traditional comparisons of this play with those of Racine, preferring to emphasize the 'air de famille' linking it with early plays from *Mélite* to *Polyeucte*.

THOMAS CORNEILLE. C. J. Gossip, 'Thomas Corneille and the comic tradition', Connon, *Drama*, 29–41, surveys C.'s comedies, particularly from *Les Engagements du hasard* to *La Comtesse d'Orgueil*, and considers that they are perhaps essential to the development of a 'national comic tradition'.

PIERRE DU RYER. D. Moncond'huy, '*Scévole* ou de la nécessité de trancher', *Delmas Vol.*, 285–95, explains why he is dissatisfied with Du R.'s most successful play.

MOLIÈRE. Gerry McCarthy, *The Theatres of Molière*, London–NY, Routledge, xvii + 238 pp., is a book, with illustrations, for students of theatre as much as for those of French; it sidelines the idea of M. as a moralist, and emphasizes his role as a man of the theatre, or indeed of many theatres. McC. reviews M.'s career from his apprenticeship and early experiences to his maturity as a supremely professional court and public entertainer, and examines in detail the theatres themselves and what they taught him regarding the stage's possibilities and limitations. Watching his plays, McC. claims, we realize his ability 'to define with extraordinary incisiveness the elements of performance as they are to be assembled on specific occasions by specific performers'. Olivier Bloch, *Molière/Philosophie*, Albin Michel, 2000, 189 pp., examines what is known about M.'s relations with Gassendi, with *libertins* and libertinage, and with Cartesianism. Brice Parent, *Variations comiques ou Les réécritures de Molière par lui-même*, Klincksieck, 2000, 200 pp., studies M.'s rewritings in order to 'mieux traquer le cheminement intellectuel qui présida à l'invention et à la confection de certaines de ses pièces'. R. E. Hong, *L'Impossible social selon Molière* (Biblio 17, 135), Tübingen, Narr, 198 pp., looks at the social identity that underpins the characters in comedies which reflect, more than those of any other dramatists, the problems of social mobility in a rigidly stratified society. M. reveals pitilessly the absurd pretensions of those who, like George Dandin or M. Jourdain, attempt to move out of their social class. H. refers particularly to M.'s use of costume and linguistic register in his examination of the relationship between the comedies and the society which they reflect.

P. Ronzeaud, 'Pour une lecture non galante des comédies de Molière', *Delmas Vol.*, 323–35, wishes to 'relativiser cette omnipotence "galante"' by pointing to 'la gauloiserie, la farce ou la polémique', and particularly to 'la satire sociale et la critique philosophique'. A. Viala, '"Un défaut [. . .] qui ne cause ni douleur ni destruction"', *ib.*, 337–48, takes issue with Ronzeaud by presenting *Le Bourgeois gentilhomme* as a study of *galanterie.* He then looks at other Molière plays and gauges how far *galanterie* is in each 'une catégorie d'analyse pertinente'. J. Serroy, 'Molière méditerranéen', Dotoli, *Méditerranées*, 219–30, discusses those plays, such as *L'Étourdi*, *L'Avare*, and *Les Fourberies de Scapin*, which refer to the Mediterranean, principally because of their various connections with Italy. K. Waterson, 'Recensement de la population féminine des comédies de Molière', Hodgson, *Femme*, 85–96, lists M.'s female characters, dividing them according to age, family, and social status. W. promises a commentary on her findings in a future publication.

F. Népote-Desmarres, '"[. . .] Amphitryon [. . .] Chez toi doit naître un fils qui, sous le nom d'Hercule"', *Delmas Vol.*, 243–260, looks for political reasons why this play, with its mocking portrayal of the powerful, should be welcomed by Louis XIV. J. F. Gaines, 'Molière's uncanonical miser', Koch, *Unities*, 201–11, claims that the French cannot take wholeheartedly to capitalism, but excepts Harpagon who displays an admirable 'familiarity with the world of dark finance'. M.-C. Canova-Green, 'Feinte et comédie dans *La Comtesse d'Escarbagnas* de Molière', Connon, *Drama*, 71–86, notes references made by characters in this and similar plays by M. to persons and events in the real world, particularly to the Court into which some characters seem able to stray. J. Harris, 'Engendering female subjectivity in Molière's *Dépit amoureux*', *SCFS*, 23, 2001 : 111–20, deplores the convention of ending comedies with a marriage, rejecting the defence that such endings are merely a 'means of textual closure'. He uses *Dépit amoureux*'s plot to lay bare 'the hierarchical power structure present but often unnoticed in something as apparently innocuous as the conclusion to a play'. G. Molinié, '*Dom Juan* mis en scène', *Delmas Vol.*, 185–87, is intrigued by 'le spectaculaire' in this play. P. Dandrey, 'Dom Juan, fils de Francion? Les leçons d'un parallèle', *ib.*, 191–217, claims that reading the three versions of Sorel's *Francion* will help us to understand 'les ombres du *Dom Juan* et de son énigmatique héros'. S. H. Fleck, 'Rustic games: *George Dandin* at the limits of genre', Koch, *Unities*, 179–89, suggests that this play is an uneasy mixture of *pastorale* and farce. R. E. Goodkin, 'Le suicide de Molière: quand dire, c'est faire dans *Le Malade imaginaire*', *ib.*, 447–56, dwells, as many have done, on 'cette conjonction extraordinaire qui cristallise les rapports complexes entre littérature et vie, littérature et mort'. J. Prest, 'The problem of praise and the first prologue to *Le Malade imaginaire*', *SCFS*, 23, 2001 : 139–49, brings out the difficulties encountered by authors of comedies who needed to praise Louis XIV. P. shows convincingly that *Le Malade imaginaire*, which was not considered as suitable for a court entertainment because of the 'problem', can be seen as a link between the plays which praise sincerely and those which sacrifice sincerity in order to praise extravagantly. N. Hammond, 'Authorship and authority in Molière's *Le Misanthrope*', Connon, *Drama*, 55–70, finds that in M.'s plays 'notions of authorship are rarely stable', that authority is frequently mocked, particularly when embodied in a character played by M. himself. H. dwells on those scenes in *Le Misanthrope* where authorship and authority are the subjects of debate, as in the sonnet scene (I.ii), the portrait scene (II.iv), the scene about Célimène's letter (IV.iii), and the dénouement. A. McKenna, 'Molière et l'imposture dévote', McKenna, *Libertins*, 97–129, looks for a 'unité d'intention' in M.'s plays, finding it in the theme of *imposture.* He concentrates on chosen 'pièces cruciales', linked by a certain 'cohérence': *L'École des femmes, Tartuffe, Don Juan*, and *Le Misanthrope.* C. Braider, 'Image and *imaginaire* in Molière's *Sganarelle, ou le cocu imaginaire*', *PMLA*, 117 : 1142–57, focuses on Lélie's portrait and the complex of emotions it arouses in various characters, and the assumptions made about it at various moments in the course of the play. This article, unsurprisingly, is not unlike Id., '*Image* and *imaginaire* in *Le Cocu imaginaire*', Koch, *Unities*, 409–19. F. Lecercle, 'Jeux avec la césure: Molière et la stratégie de l'obscène (à propos de *Tartuffe*, IV.5)', *La Licorne*, 61 : 157–84, starts with M.'s games with the word *obscénité* in *La Critique de l'École des femmes*, recalls the roots of the Church's objections to theatre, and ends with *Tartuffe*, III.3 and IV.5, where imputations of *obscénité* can only be levelled at T. the 'représentant patenté de la censure dévote'. M. has learned 'jusqu'où aller trop loin'.

QUINAULT. W. Brooks, 'Quinault and *La Mère coquette*', Connon, *Drama*, 43–54, favourably compares this comedy with a rival piece of the same name by Donneau de Visé, and then, using the play as example, extols Q.'s qualities as a comic dramatist, above all his skilful use of the genre's conventions and his ability to explore 'the use and misuse of imformation'.

RACINE. B. Norman, 'Racine, 1674, and the "Querelle d'Alceste"', Koch, *Unities*, 251–62, would clear up misunderstanding of this quarrel and its role in the *Querelle des anciens et des modernes* by persuading us to 'consider it in the context of the literary — and especially the theatrical — scene in 1674'. We are urged to read R.'s prefaces to the 1676 collected edition of his plays and to appreciate his indignation that *Alceste* and other musical dramas by Quinault and Lully should be called *tragédies*. F. Berlan, 'Entre mythe et Histoire: images de l'enfance chez Racine, de l'*innocence* à l'*ingénuité*', *Delmas Vol.*, 371–94, looks for sources of each quality in turn, first in R.'s annotations of Homer, and then in the plays, and concludes that 'la thématique de l'enfance [. . .] s'échelonne sur toute sa production dramatique du triple point de vue d'une évolution du siècle, d'une aventure personnelle et d'un infléchissement de la tragédie comme genre', pointing to the emergence of 'un nouveau mythe de la modernité, celui de l'*ingénuité* enfantine ou juvénile'. R. Pensom, 'Racine: ce que la tragédie n'est pas', *RR*, 91:397–415, claims that while there is no such thing as a typical Racinian tragedy, nevertheless R. 'a innové dans les limites des perspectives théoriques imaginées par Aristote et ses commentateurs'. P. pursues this double theme through all R.'s tragedies.

T. J. Reiss, '*Andromaque* and the search for unique sovereignty', *Rubin Vol.*, 23–51, looks into this play (as he has done elsewhere) for a political agenda intended to influence Louis XIV and his ministers. Z. Elmarsafy, '"O homines ad servitutem paratos!": *Bajazet* and the scandal of slave rule', *RR*, 91:417–31, quotes from Paul Rycaut's *History of the Present State of the Ottoman Empire* in which Racine, like any French reader in 1670, 'would be struck by [. . .] the uncanny similarity between Turkish and French modes of governance', and goes on to defend his contention that R. 'chose this particular place and this particular time as a setting for his play precisely because of what they had in common with absolutist France'. R. Ganim, 'Views of kingship: *Britannicus* and Louis XIV's *Mémoires*', Koch, *Unities*, 315–24, emphasizes the 'socio-political aspects' of Racine, proposing *Britannicus* as a commentary on the art of kingship. A.-L. Bucher, '*Iphigénie* de Racine: à la césure du classicisme et de l'archaïque', *ib.*, 335–45, sees this tragedy about human sacrifice as 'une des pièces qui pose de la façon la plus aiguë la question de l'intrusion de l'altérité archaïque .. sur la scène classique en général'. C. Nancy, 'Iphigénie, d'Euripide à Racine: une réécriture', *Poétique*, 129:33–50, picks Ériphile as the essential difference between E. and R. Ériphile wishes to betray Agamemnon's plan to save her rival Iphigénie: 'cette faute "heureuse" d'Ériphile'. S. E. Melzer, 'Incest and the Minotaur in *Phèdre*: the monsters of France's assimilationist politics', *ib.*, 431–45, dwells on the two monstrous concepts: exogamy, 'a socially censured desire for too much difference', and endogamy: 'Phèdre's incestuous desire for her step-son', and proposes them as 'figures of two conflicting needs in the formation of the seventeenth-century French absolutist state — expansion and unification'. R. Brabant, 'Gloire et ironie circonstancielle dans la *Phèdre* de Racine', *RevR*, 37.1:67–86, argues that for Phèdre it is the possible loss of her *gloire* that makes her suffer, rather than the loss of her virtue. The circumstances in which she finds herself are shown by cruel irony to add to her suffering, as is similarly the case with Thésée, Hippolyte, and Oenone. H. Cohen, 'Cocteau's *Les Parents terribles* as an ironic *remaniement* of Racine's *Phèdre*', *DFS*, 59:56–66, is an ingenious linking of the two works, comparing various characters and their roles. While throwing little light on Racine, Cohen does illuminate the intentions and motives which animate *Les Parents terribles*.

ROTROU. C. Dumas, 'Les paradoxes du roi et du bouffon dans *La bague de l'oubli* de Rotrou (1629)', *DSS*, 54:323–42, compares the 'real' madness of the king under the influence of the magic ring, with the 'professional' madness of his jester, and the use to which these juxtaposed forms are put.

TABARIN. C. Grivel, 'Tabarin des latrines', *RSH*, 261, 2001:101–17, evokes the scatological quality of these dialogues between the mocked idealistic *maître* Mondor, and the mocking, earthy, uncontrollable Tabarin.

TRISTAN L'HERMITE. C. Abraham, 'Ce fameux précurseur', *CTH*, 24:5–13, dwells on the difference between T.'s heroes and those of Corneille and Racine. To A., the voice of a T. hero is 'celle d'un dépaysé' for whom, 'le devoir est tout simplement envers un idéal, au détriment de tout, même de soi'. M. Livera, 'Autour de la mort de Chrispe et de la tragédie néo-latine: Grenaille, Tristan et leur source jésuite', *ib.*, 54–67, compares François de Grenaille's *L'Innocent malheureux, ou la mort de Chrispe* and T.'s tragedy (both of 1645) with the Latin *Crispus* (1597) by the Jesuit Bernardino Stefornio, the story of which is very similar to that of Phaedra and Hippolytus. G. Forestier, 'Mythe, histoire, et tragédie: de Crispus à *La Mort de Chrispe*', *Delmas Vol.*, 351–70, wishes to look into T.'s tragedy for its intrinsic interest rather than view it as a foreshadowing of Racine's *Phèdre*. He reviews successive versions of the story of Crispus to trace the Christian message, which emerges at the end of T.'s play and unfortunately involves T.'s abandoning the truly dramatic theme of 'le bourreau malgré lui'.

4. Prose

S. Munari, 'L'espace méditerranéen dans le roman mauresque du XVIIe siècle: mythe, symbole, stéréotype', Dotoli, *Méditerranées*, 169–78, surveys works by Catherine Bernard, Gomberville, La Calprenède, Mme de La Fayette, Mlle de Scudéry, and others. N. Oddo, 'L'invention du roman français au XVIIe siècle: littérature religieuse et matière romanesque', *DSS*, 54:221–34, in her tracing of 'l'évolution du narratif religieux vers le romanesque', concentrates on a series of portrayals of the historical figure Henri de Joyeuse, comte du Bouchage (*père* Ange de Joyeuse in religion), at first purely biographical, and finally set in a near fictional universe. A. Thiele, 'L'émergence de l'individu dans le roman comique', *ib.*, 251–61, analyses Sorel's *Francion* and Furetière's *Roman bourgeois*, examining different forms of comic depiction, especially of the protagonists and their relationships to society. A. Viala, 'De Scudéry à Courtilz de Sandras: les nouvelles historiques et galantes', *ib.*, 287–95, points out that *La Princesse de Clèves* was regarded in its time as a 'nouvelle galante', then compares it to three other examples of the same genre: S.'s *Célinte* and *La Promenade de Versailles*, and C.'s *Les Apparences trompeuses*. G. Berger, 'Genres bâtards: roman et histoire à la fin du XVIIe siècle', *ib.*, 297–305, quotes statistics and booksellers' catalogues from the last third of the century which show the immense popularity of *nouvelles historiques*, *nouvelles galantes*, *mémoires apocryphes*, and *histoires secrètes* — a popularity which continued until the mid 18th c. — and at the same time the paucity of historiographers, discouraged by the difficulties of publishing in an absolutist regime. C. Jouhaud, 'Roman historié et histoire romancée: Jean-Pierre Camus et Charles Sorel', *ib.*, 307–16, places C.'s fiction 'entre mission et direction de conscience', but points out that S. sets history above fiction whilst claiming that a good historian must have a novelist's talent. Both writers spurn pure fiction (according to J.) for christian reasons. G. Molinié, 'Perspectives sémio-culturelles sur l'invention du roman européen', *ib.*, 317–21, proposes 'une interrogation sur le Romanesque, plus que sur le roman'. C. Rolla, 'Le rapport romanciers/ salons dans les paratextes des romans de la première moitié du XVIIe siècle', Marchal, *Salons*, 253–59, concerns herself with *épîtres* and *avis au lecteur* which are the only places wherein are to be found 'les lignes de force de la théorie narrative naissante' and where one can learn about 'les rapports qui liaient le romancier à son public', particularly in authors like J.-P. Camus, Sorel and Georges de Scudéry.

Hodgson, *Femmes*, contains the following: L. Desjardins, 'Portrait et représentation de l'intériorité féminine' (201–10), consults Cureau de La Chambre on physiognomy and the passions, Rapin and La

Mesnardière on poetics, Mme de La Fayette and Racine for their subtle portrayals, in the hope of finding out how the 17th c. related feminine 'traits physiologiques' with 'qualités morales'; R. Roy, 'Une femme en colère: représentation de la colère féminine d'après trois femmes de lettres du XVIIe siècle' (211–24), reads Mlle de Scudéry, Mme de La Fayette, and Mme de Villedieu for their portrayals of 'belles irritées' and 'belles vindicatives'; L. Leibacher-Ouvrard, 'Voiles de sang et amazones de Satan: la querelle des nudités de gorge' (255–67), discovers a veritable 'querelle du sein' by reviewing the many texts concerned with female breasts: 'ces textes qui vivent du désir trouble de dévoiler le corps féminin pour exiger qu'il soit caché'; H. Trépanier, 'Entre amour-propre et anéantissement: le "jeu" des autobiographies mystiques féminines' (301–13), examines the writings of six women, from Marie de l'Incarnation to Mme Guyon, who are aware of the internal struggle between the two above contrary movements, and compares it to Pascal's *grandeur/misère*: 'il est frappant de constater que les écrits autobiographiques féminines laissent surgir un "moi" qui s'impose, à travers l'exigence radicale d'anéantissement'; D. J. Kostroun, 'Angélique Arnauld and the political significance of filial disobedience' (325–35), is concerned with accounts of the *Journée du guichet* circulated in the second half of the 17th c. which, K. claims, were oblique criticism of the crown's policies on Port-Royal; C. L. Carlin, 'Misogynie et misogamie dans les complaintes des mal mariés au XVIIe siècle' (365–78), surveys documents dating from 1600–25 attacking women, and, after 1625, 'plus subtiles' writings attacking the institution of marriage; A. Rosner, 'Un regard comparatif: le refus du mariage dans le roman du Grand Siècle' (379–90), examines J.-P. Camus's *Dorothée*, *histoires* VII and XIX of Rosset's *Histoires tragiques*, Gournay's *Le Proumenoir de Monsieur de Montaigne*, and Mlle de Scudéry's *Le Grand Cyrus*, noting that while all the novels criticize forced marriages, those by women are more fundamentally subversive of male dominated society.

Frédéric Charbonneau, *Les Silences de l'histoire. Les Mémoires français du XVIIe siècle*, Montreal, Laval U.P., 2000 (2001), xiii + 299 pp., offers as an approach to a definition of his subject the suggestion that *Mémoires* were written to fill the 'silences de l'histoire' by individuals anxious to establish their own place in history, to underline their own importance, or defend themselves against the hostility, misunderstandings or indifference of recognised historians. C. has felt obliged to give precedence, out of some 80 works, to ten which represent the others by their characteristics: social status of author, sex, age, place of origin and residence, or mode of narration. He confesses one weakness: 'le chef-d'oeuvre est toujours atypique', but he cannot resist including Retz in his 'corpus principal', along with, presumably, the lesser beings: d'Aubigné, Henri de Campion, Choisy, Fontaine, Huet, Mme de La Fayette, Lénet, Marolles, and Vignoles La Hire. His section headings indicate the sort of *triage* he has imposed on his material: 'l'antihistoire', 'les figures de la dissidence', l'écriture du secret'.

J.-P. van Elslande, 'L'illusion pastorale', *LitC*, 44:73–82, asserts that 'l'illusion est consubstantielle à la pastorale [. . .], elle en est l'âme même'. Jean-Paul Sermain, *Métafictions (1670–1730). La réflexivité dans la littérature d'imagination* (Les dix-huitièmes siècles, 65), Champion, 461 pp., studies a vast range of authors including, from the 17th c., Assoucy, Aulnoy, Bordelon, Challe, Fénelon, Foigny, Perrault, and Villedieu.

P. Bayley, 'Opposition writing: seventeenth-century memoirs and political thought', Koch, *Unities*, 267–76, makes Saint-Simon the memorialist 'heir to a tradition', and so offers 'with brutal crudity' the hypothesis that, in literature generally, 'the apparently missing third branch of oratory — the deliberative — is, so to speak, forced underground in early-modern France, but is not lost. It is in memoir writing that we may find it'. Y. Loskoutoff, '*Fascis cum sideribus* III. Le symbolisme armorial dans les éloges du cardinal Mazarin, ses prolongements, dans les mazarinades, chez Corneille, Racine et La Fontaine', *DSS*, 54:55–98, accords most space (with illustrations) to the *éloges*, but then, after the *Mazarinades*, extends his study to the three great writers 'dont la fortune fut, à un moment ou à un autre, associée à celle du cardinal'.

Sophie Raynard, *La Seconde Préciosité: floraison des conteuses de 1690 à 1756* (Biblio 17, 130), Tübingen, Narr, 512 pp., claims that the tales written by practically all the *conteuses* between Mme d'Aulnoy and Mme Leprince de Beaumont belong to the *précieuse* tradition. R. analyses their style and their themes and compares them with 'd'autres textes officiellement précieux' such as those of Mlle de Scudéry, Mlle d'Aumale, Mme de Montausier, Mme de Sablé, and others, and also contrasts them with Charles Perrault's *contes de fées*, insisting however that the contrast is due, not to sexual specificities, but to differences in education. Raymonde Robert, *Le Conte de fées littéraire en France de la fin du XVIIe siècle à la fin du XVIIIe siècle* (Lumière classique, 40), Champion, 558 pp., is the second edition of this study which first appeared in 1982 (*YWMLS*, 44:109, listed only). Most of R.'s amendments and additions are confined to footnotes, but a 'supplément bibliographique 1980–2000' has been added.

AUBIGNAC. A. Wygant, 'D'Aubignac, demonologist, I: Monkeys and monsters', *SCFS*, 23, 2001:151–71, compares the Abbé's treatment of monsters in his *Des satyres, brutes, monstres, et demons* (1627) with his treatment of the 'monstrous' in the plays he studies in *La pratique du théâtre*.

AULNOY. H. Tucker, 'Fairies, midwives, and birth spaces in the tales of Madame d'Aulnoy', Koch, *Unities*, 89–94, compares the fictional roles of fairies (good and bad) with the real-life roles of midwives. **L'Oiseau bleu et autres contes*, ed. Elisabeth Lemirre, Seuil, 124 pp. Nadine Jasmin, **Naissance du conte féminin. Mots et merveilles: les contes de fées de Madame d'Aulnoy (1690–1698)* (Lumière classique, 44), Champion, 800 pp.

BALZAC. Bernard Beugnot, *Guez de Balzac* (Bibliographie des écrivains français, 24), Paris–Rome, Memini, 2001, 261 pp., replaces and goes well beyond B.'s *Jean-Louis Guez de Balzac: bibliographie générale* (1967) and its two supplements (1969 and 1979). It not only lists all the known editions of Balzac's works, but also, as does the series generally, 'rend compte . . . de la littérature des "commentateurs"', briefly summarizing the contents of each of the 1218 entries and quoting for each a number of 'mots clés' which have their own index.

BASSOMPIERRE. Jean Castarède, *Bassompierre, 1579–1646, maréchal, gentilhomme, rival de Richelieu*, Perrin, 239 pp., is a readable biography of this *maréchal de France* and memorialist.

BAUDOIN. E. Bury, 'Jean Baudoin (1584–1650), témoin de la culture baroque et pionnier du classicisme', *DSS*, 54: 393–96, sketches briefly the life and varied interests of this *historiographe de France* and translator, and summarizes the *état présent* of B. studies. A.-E. Spica, 'Jean Baudoin et la fable', *ib.*, 417–31, finds B. revelling in all forms of figures, allegories, myths, emblems. G. Hautcoeur, 'Jean Baudoin traducteur des nouvelles espagnoles', *ib.*, 433–44, introduces us to the twelve *Nouvelles morales* by Diego de Agreda y Vargas (1621) which are something of an exception among B.'s translations from the Spanish, his predilection being for historical chronicles or works of piety. H. presents this translation as 'un cas exemplaire de "belle infidèle"'.

BÉROALDE DE VERVILLE. **L'Histoire des vers qui filent la soye*, ed. Michel Renaud (Textes de la Renaissance, 48), Champion, 2001, 224 pp.

BOILEAU. G. Banderier, 'À propos d'un autographe (perdu) de Boileau', *DSS*, 54: 155–56, has rediscovered a lost letter from B. to Claude Brossette, and transcribes it here.

BOSSUET. *LitC*, 46, is devoted to articles on 'Bossuet, *Le Carême du Louvre* (1662)', covering themes such as rhetoric and preaching, theory and practice of preaching, aspects of style and language, two articles on death, one on 'le temps et son architecture' and one on 'l'*ethos* bossuétiste'. The volume also contains a text by Bossuet himself: 'Sur le style, et la lecture des Pères de l'Église pour former un orateur' (221–29), ed. Jean-Philippe Grosperrin, who regards it as 'bref mais important'. Jean-Pierre Landry and Catherine Costentin, **Bossuet: sermons, carême du Louvre: analyse littéraire et étude de la langue*, Armand Colin, 156 pp.

JEAN-PIERRE CAMUS. *Divertissement historique (1632)*, ed. Constant Venesoen (Biblio 17, 132), Tübingen, Narr, 233 pp., chooses the first edition of C.'s 'réminiscences historiques' in preference to the last of 1642, a choice amply justified by V. in his 'Avant-propos' where he provides a biography and studies the *Divertissement*'s Spanish, Portuguese, and Italian contents, its 'édification morale', and its presentation of women. F. Lavocat, 'Ordre et désordre dans l'oeuvre de Jean-Pierre Camus. "La liberté dans le salut"', *La Licorne*, 61:137–55, finds C.'s 'conception du catholicisme aux antipodes de la version autoritaire et répressive d'un Bossuet'. He is a a writer who, although manifestly a believer, lives dangerously with ideas.

CHALLE. *Challe et/en son temps*, ed. Marie-Louise Girou Swiderski and Pierre Berthiaume (Colloques, congrès et conférences sur le dix-huitième siècle, 5), Champion, 518 pp., prints colloquium *actes* of which there are three groups, the first being devoted to *Les Illustres Françaises*, their individual stories, aspects of their style or thought, the relationship between stories and other art forms, and comparisons with the prose fiction of other authors. The second group focuses on C.'s travels, particularly on his *Journal d'un voyage fait aux Indes orientales*, but ends with one paper concerned with his memoirs: J. Cormier, '*Mémoires* de Robert Challe et *Annales de la Cour et de Paris* de Courtilz de Sandras: convergences et divergences' (327–57), comparing their 'contenu historique' and their 'procédés narratifs'. The third group is more mixed, but C.'s pronouncements on religion are to the fore with studies of the *Militaire philosophe* (F. Bessire, 359–68, and A.-R. N'Diaye, 391–407) and the *Difficultés sur la religion* (M. Benitez, 369–89), while his views on protestantism are also surveyed (P. Stewart, 459–72), and the collection ends with G. Artigas-Menant, 'La Bible dans l'oeuvre de Robert Challe' (491–514). S. R. Baker, 'Misfits, savages, and outcasts in Robert Challe's *Mémoires* (1716)', Koch, *Unities*, 277–84, picks these unfortunates to serve as examples illustrating C.'s reflections on 'what we today view as the problematic of inclusion vs exclusion, sameness vs difference, self vs other, male vs female', and 'his fascination in the face of taboo borders crossed'.

CYRANO DE BERGERAC. D. Dutton, 'La rhétorique et *L'Autre monde* de Cyrano de Bergerac', Koch, *Unities*, 383–92, claims that 'la formation de Cyrano inclut [. . .] l'étude de tous les grands maîtres de l'éloquence latine et grecque', and that, in his two novels, he exploits, parodies, and makes fun of them. D. then gives examples of 'quelques aspects de cette rhétorique cyranienne'. B. Parmentier, 'Imagination et fiction dans *Les Etats et Empires* de Cyrano de

Bergerac', *LitC*, 45:217–40, gives an enthusiastic and appreciative reading, noting the dominant fact that in both novels freedom of thought is not only an 'élément central' but also 'l'un des rares thèmes parfaitement explicites d'un récit constamment joueur et ironique'. I. Moreau, 'Mises en scène de la censure: Vanini et Descartes à l'ouverture des *États et Empires du Soleil*', *LetC*, 10, 2001:289–302, guides us through Cyrano's account of his problems during the circulation of the MS of his *États et Empires de la Lune*. A. Mothus, 'Un "duel ésotérique"? La pyrhydromachie des *Empires du Soleil*', *ib.*, 302–25, argues against any alchemical interpretation of the episode of the battle of the 'bête à feu' and the 'animal-glaçon', preferring the simple explanation that C. is mockingly exploiting the common poetic ice-fire oxymoron. M. Alcover, ' "Ah! dîtes-moi, mère-grand": l'ascension sociale des grands-parents paternels de Cyrano', *ib.*, 327–37, introduces and quotes from *actes notariés* revealing information about C.'s paternal antecedents.

DU VERDIER. M. Bannister, 'Du Verdier and the end of the *Amadis de Gaule* romances', *SCFS*, 23, 2001:71–80, emphasises qualities hitherto unnoticed by commentators, praising both *Le Romant des romans* and *Le Chevalier hipocondriaque* for their originality, despite aspects of both being borrowed from *Amadis de Gaule* and *Don Quixote*.

FÉNELON. G. Giorgi, 'La fonction des lieux méditerranéens dans les *Aventures de Télémaque*', Dotoli, *Méditerranées*, 109–19, surveys 'les étapes du vaste périple méditerranéen accompli par le fils d'Ulysse' in which the work's didactic purpose necessitates reference 'à des époques moins reculées et, en particulier, aux choses contemporaines'.

FRANÇOIS DE SALES. A. Guiderdoni-Bruslé, 'Images et emblèmes dans la spiritualité de saint François de Sales', *DSS*, 54:35–54, quotes a lengthy extract from the *Vie symbolique du bienheureux François de Sales* (1664) by Adrien Gambart, which provides a framework for a survey of the saint's 'rhétorique symbolique' and its 'fondement primordial, dans un contexte religieux, à savoir la figure christique'.

GOMBERVILLE. F. d'Ascenzo, 'L'espace marin dans la fiction narrative de Gomberville', Dotoli, *Méditerranées*, 179–91, presents the sea as the 'cadre privilégié de la narration' in *Polexandre*.

GOURNAY. **Oeuvres complètes*, ed. Jean-Claude Arnould *et al* (Textes de la Renaissance, 51), Champion, 2 vols, 2088 pp. *Apology for the Woman Writing and other works*, ed. and trans. Richard Hillman and Colette Quesnel, Chicago U.P., xxvii + 176 pp., provides English translations of the *Apologie pour celle qui escrit*, and also of *Le Proumenoir de Monsieur de Montaigne*, *L'Égalité des hommes et des femmes*, and *Le Grief des Dames*. H. writes an introduction to the whole volume, and to each of the translations. N. Frelick, '(Re)fashioning Marie de Gournay',

Hodgson, *Femmes*, 165–80, asserts that 'some discourses on Gournay [. . .] still seem invested (consciously or unconsciously) in reinscribing her in the old phallic order'. F.'s main target is Constant Venesoen.

GUILLERAGUES. V. Schröder, 'Les méditations de Mariane: la matrice mystique des *Lettres portugaises*', Hodgson, *Femmes*, 283–99, finds the nun's letters influenced ('contaminées') by another genre, the *méditation religieuse*, particularly by 'les traités d'oraison de provenance ibérique' such as the writings of Theresa of Avila.

LA BRUYÈRE. Dominique Bertrand, *'Les Caractères' de La Bruyère* (Foliothèque, 103), Gallimard, 220 pp., is divided into two sections. First comes an 'Essai' introducing the work's discontinuous form (with a brief history of that form), and examining La B.'s motivation, purpose, and technique (his 'curiosité', his 'sens du ridicule', 'peintures morales', 'théâtralité') and his subject matter. It is followed by a 'Dossier' containing biography, 'genèse', 'réception', and a select bibliography. In all, a clear, lively, vigorous presentation. E. Leveau, 'La Bruyère entre théâtre et caractère ou le risque de "faire quelque chose de rien"', Koch, *Unities*, 325–34, suggests that, when the subject of theatre arises in his work, La B. seizes the opportunity 'de poser de manière indirecte la question du pouvoir de la représentation qui est à l'oeuvre dans *Les Caractères*'.

LA FAYETTE. I. Trivisani Moreau, '*Zaïde* et l'altérité, histoire méditerranéenne', Dotoli, *Méditerranées*, 77–92, would have us appreciate the complex variety of Mediterranean places and people we encounter in this novel full of 'différences' which we must accept 'comme des richesses'. J. Cherbuliez, 'Exile and the spaces of intimacy in Lafayette's *Zayde*', Koch, *Unities*, 79–88, sees this novel as being subversive of absolutism, offering in its characters and their development 'an alternative to the elaboration of the individual court subject'. D. D. Kelley, 'Justifying the refusal: social exchange in *La Princesse de Clèves*', Hodgson, *Femme*, 139–50, argues that the Princesse's final withdrawal from society is a 'reasonable act': she is right to refuse to live on in a world that 'imposes the rules of social exchange unevenly on men and women'.

LA FORCE. M. Legault, 'Amitiés féminines dans *Plus Belle que Fée* de La Force: un modèle sapphique', Hodgson, *Femmes*, 269–79, celebrates a text which 'rend hommage quasi exclusivement non seulement à l'amitié féminine mais aussi à la sexualité ainsi qu'à l'homo-éroticisme féminine'.

LAMY. L. Roveda, 'Bernard Lamy, une poétique de l'origine du langage', *DSS*, 54: 137–53, describes L.'s 'deux versions antithétiques de l'origine du langage'; the 'mise en scène d'une troupe d'hommes découvrant le langage', and that based on the Book of Genesis. He then discusses the contradiction thus created, including L.'s explanation of it: 'les oppositions des choses contraires contribuent à l'éclaircissement d'une vérité, comme les ombres relevant l'éclat des couleurs'.

LA ROCHEFOUCAULD. **Réflexions ou Sentences et Maximes morales et Réflexions diverses*, ed. Laurence Plazenet (Sources classiques, 36), Champion, 1008 pp. M. Galland-Szymkowiak, 'Le mérite chez La Rochefoucauld ou l'héroïsme de l'honnêteté', *RHLF*, 102:799–811, feels that La R. would have had problems with merit — with its 'valeur intrinsèque' conflicting with its tendency to expect 'une reconnaissance par d'autres individus', and with his own 'tendances augustiniennes' — had it not been for his 'participation à la société des honnêtes gens'. Q. M. Hope, 'Humor in the *Maximes* of La Rochefoucauld', *DFS*, 58:3–9, strays from the *Maximes* into private letters, and even into those of Mme de Sévigné, in his search for quotable wisecracks and mocking sallies.

LA SABLIÈRE. F. Deloffre, 'Madame de La Sablière et ses familiers', Marchal, *Salons*, 117–35, gives biographical details and enumerates her interests and those of her friends: science, philosophy, travel, while 'les belles-lettres ne sont pas négligées', but most attention is given to the correspondence (quoting lengthy extracts) between La S. and Guilleragues.

LE MOYNE. A. Mantero, 'Les arts réunis dans *Les Peintures morales* et *La Gallerie des femmes fortes* du Père Le Moyne', Landry, *Dialogue*, 223–49, brings our attention to the many and various ways in which the Jesuit links the arts in his writings, and also makes use of them in the illustrations that embellish the above works. But M.'s essential purpose is to make us aware of 'la complexité de la tradition dans laquelle s'insère Le Moyne en écrivant sur, ou à propos d'une oeuvre visuelle'.

MARANA. B. Bray, 'Entre le Grand Seigneur et Louis le Grand, *L'Espion turc* de Jean-Paul Marana et ses observations méditerranéennes', Dotoli, *Méditerranées*, 243–56, confines his observations to the 'premier état' (1686) of the work, seeking to show how M. reconciles his own allegiance to Louis XIV with that of his narrator Mahmut, who 'démontre incontestablement son loyalisme et son désir de voir triompher la puissance ottomane'.

MARGUERITE DE VALOIS. G. Schrenk, 'Marguerite de Valois et son monde, ou la chambre bruissante', Marchal, *Salons*, 167–72, sees in the queen's social life an institution which 'se manifeste à la fois par son caractère permanent et discontinu; permanent dans la mesure où la princesse ne s'est jamais départie d'une présence culturelle dans son entourage immédiat, discontinu en raison des aléas de son destin malheureux de femme et de reine'.

MLLE DE MONTPENSIER. J. Garapon, 'La Grande Mademoiselle et ses divertissements littéraires', Marchal, *Salons*, 261–69, introduces us to M. as a writer conditioned by her eminent position, but also influenced by her circle of *mondains cultivés* and well-known literary figures such as Segrais and Gabriel Gilbert.

MME PALATINE. C. M. Probes, 'Feminine friendship at the end of the century: testimony from the French correspondence of Madame Palatine', *SCFS*, 23, 2001:43–54, seeks out what is distinctive in these letters: 'her insistence on continual communication and on the role of the senses and the emotions'.

NICOLAS PASQUIER. D. Carabin, '*Les Lettres* de Nicolas Pasquier: la lettre de consolation', *RHLF*, 102:15–31, studies the letters of this son of Étienne Pasquier in order to 'cerner le style et la vocation' of this particular sub-genre.

CHARLES PERRAULT. H. Neeman, 'Fairy tales and the *modernes*', Koch, *Unities*, 217–24, concentrates on P., claiming that his 'work as a fairy-tale author is intimately connected with his status as champion of the *modernes*'. J.-P. van Elslande, 'Corps éloquents et morale politique dans les contes en prose de Charles Perrault', *ib.*, 371–81, finds bodies, their qualities, their adventures, their trials and tribulations, dominant in P.'s stories, and for ideological reasons: 'à l'heure où, dès leur plus jeune âge, les corps sont appelés à s'inscrire dans l'ordre social absolutiste afin d'en mieux refléter les principes, l'écriture exemplaire des contes [. . .] propose un modèle discursive en phase avec les valeurs dominantes du moment'.

PURE. L. Leibacher-Ouvrard, 'Querelles d'autorité: les romans palimpsestueux de l'abbé de Pure', Koch, *Unities*, 225–39, considers, with *La Prétieuse* and *Épigone* providing illustrations, how an author of the mid-century 'réfléchit sur ses droits et son autorité' at a time when 'le Moderne et l'Ancien s'effrontent'. Id., *'*Épigone, histoire du siècle futur* (1659): première uchronie et politique-fiction nostalgique', *FrF*, 25, 2000:23–46.

RETZ. F. Briot, 'Illusion et citation dans les *Mémoires* du cardinal de Retz', *LitC*, 44:335–50, views R. seeing himself as 'fantasié' by everyone who comes into contact with him, as also is everyone else: 'chacun est pris, chacun est fantasié, mais ce n'est pas méchanceté, c'est faiblesse humaine'. M. Stefanovska, 'Démarches et itinéraires de la Fronde: Paris dans les *Mémoires* du cardinal de Retz', Koch, *Unities*, 355–44, points to R.'s awareness of space, and of the need to set precisely the scene of an action or episode in which he has been engaged: 'il n'y a pas à s'étonner [. . .] que la ville, lieu de rencontre, de passages, d'échanges ou de conflits, soit son milieu naturel'.

ALEXANDRE DE RHODES. M.-F. Hilgar, 'Un jésuite en Indochine', Koch, *Unities*, 135–41, surveys the life and accomplishments of R., taking much of her evidence from his *Histoire du royaume de Tonkin*.

SAINT-ÉVREMOND. *Saint-Évremond: A Voice from Exile. Newly Discovered Letters to Madame de Gouville and the Abbé de Hautefeuille (1697–1701)*, ed. Denys Potts (Research Monographs in French Studies, 10), Oxford, Legenda, xi + 91 pp., prints 23 hitherto unpublished letters together with four others, previously known but now duly corrected, all constituting 'the major part of an interlocking correspondence'. P.'s introduction is a brief 'life and works' which helps the reader to place this find in a firm context. The letters, on one level, 'unfold a saga of financial dealings [. . .] that have a quasi-Balzacian fascination of their own', but, on another, 'reveal aspects of the author's temperament and sensibility rarely to be glimpsed in his other writings'. They considerably modify the view of St-É.'s last years offered by previous commentators, based on the unsure testimony of Pierre Des Maizeaux.

SAINT-SIMON. D. de Garidel, 'La solitude vue de la Cour: quelques visages de la solitude dans les *Mémoires* de Saint-Simon', *CPR*, 51:265–81, looks at two sorts of solitude noted by St-S.: 'la retraite de certains courtisans touchés par la grâce', and that of 'les courtisans frappés de disgrâce' for whom solitude is 'signe de châtiment et de malédiction'. G. also picks out instances of St-S.'s own experiences of solitude which show it to have no personal attraction for him, no part in his scheme of things. Id., 'Les "plans-figures" dans les *Mémoires* de Saint-Simon', *RHLF*, 102:813–27, refers to rough sketches, all of 'scènes officielles', 'cérémonies', celebratory 'moments de triomphe' at court, which St-S. has added to clarify his descriptions of such scenes. F. Charbonneau, 'L'écriture du singulier. Saint-Simon et quelques mémorialistes', *ib.*, 191–209, dwells on the *monstrosity* of St-S.'s memoirs, despite the 'acuité de son observation'.

SCARRON. T. Meding, 'Translation as appropriation: the case of María de Zayas's *El prevenido engañado* and Paul Scarron's *La Précaution inutile*', *Rubin Vol.*, 91–118, shows what S. lost when he removed his translation and adaptation of Z.'s tale from the context of the story which frames all the tales of her *Novelas amorosas y ejemplares*.

MLLE DE SCUDÉRY. N. Grande, 'Du long au court: réduction de la longueur et invention des formes narratives, l'exemple de Madeleine de Scudéry', *DSS*, 54:263–71, looks at the fictional forms that replaced the old *romans-fleuves*, suggests reasons for the change in taste, and points to the features that the new *formes brèves* still had in common with the old *formes longues*. G. Penzkofer, 'L'art du mensonge dans les romans de Mlle de Scudéry', *ib.*, 273–86, looks at this 'art' and in particular 'la constitution intertextuelle des personnages', 'le caractère mensonger des signes de l'amour qui circulent dans la société courtoise du roman', and 'la mondaine "aversion pour la vérité" [. . .] qui règne dans les salons du roman'. D. Denis, 'Les samedis de Sapho: figurations littéraires de la collectivité', Marchal, *Salons*, 107–15, studies the literary influence of the 'ruelle de Madeleine de Scudéry', and of two associated salons, those of Mme Aragonnès and the Bocquet sisters. D. Kuizenga, 'Écriture à la mode/modes de réécriture: *Les Femmes illustres* de Madeleine et Georges de Scudéry', Hodgson, *Femmes*, 151–63, explores aspects of the *réécriture* of Ovid in this joint work which, K. claims, 'restent à élucider'. The writers follow O. in portraying characters whose behaviour is 'motivé par leur psychologie individuelle plutôt que par des forces extérieures', but they differ from him in opting for 'une image agrandie, héroïque des personnages'. J. D. Lyons, '*Clélie* et la pratique sociale de l'imagination', *LitC*, 45:207–16, sees 'l'imagination heureuse' in the novel as 'une pratique de groupe, une activité qui fleurit entre amis ou entre amoureux'.

Clélie. Histoire romaine, ed. Chantal Morlet-Chantalat, **Première partie, 1654* (Sources classiques, 30), Champion, 2001, 546 pp., **Seconde partie, 1655* (Sources classiques, 40), Champion, 530 pp. **Mathilde*, ed. Nathalie Grande (Sources classiques, 38), Champion, 320 pp. **La Promenade de Versailles*, ed. Marie-Gabrielle Lallemand (Sources classiques, 39), Champion, 296 pp.

SEGRAIS. J. Morgante, 'La Méditerranée dans les *Nouvelles françaises* de Segrais', Dotoli, *Méditerranées*, 137–55, focuses on two stories out of the six, which are set in different parts of the Mediterranean in order to 'diversifier le recueil' and provide local colour or background for adventures associated with the sea.

SÉVIGNÉ. D. Reguig-Naya, 'Descartes à la lettre: poétique épistolaire et philosophie mondaine chez Mme de Sévigné', *DSS*, 54:511–25, subtly probes the way in which S. and her daughter Mme de Grignan used the writings of their 'maître posthume' to season variously 'l'univers de la conversation familière' of their correspondence. C. Cartmill, 'La Providence chez Madame de Sévigné: jansénisme ou mondanité?', Hodgson, *Femme*, 315–23), claims to have found plenty of examples of a wordly use of the word *providence*.

SOREL. Reinhard Uhrig, *Changing Ideas, Changing Texts. First-Person Novels in the Early Modern Period: 'Francion', 'Courasche' and 'Moll Flanders'* (Mikrokosmos, 60), Berne–NY, Lang, 2001, 286 pp., uses these three novels as his chief examples in this study of early modern picaresque fiction, and is particularly concerned with the instability of texts, not only as a result of alterations made by authors in successive editions, but also of modifications introduced by editors and translators to meet evolving tastes or new cultural or social contexts. H. Stenzel, 'Discours Romanesque, discours utile et carrière littéraire. Roman et "anti-roman" chez Charles Sorel', *DSS*, 54:235–50, is concerned with the *Berger extravagant* and its revised version the *Anti-roman*, seeing in them 'une intention [. . .] déconstructrice, visant en premier lieu la tradition prestigieuse du roman pastoral, mais aussi les structures fondamentales du discours romanesque en général'. M. Rosellini, '*Le Berger extravagant*: critique de l'imagination ou imagination critique?', *LitC*, 45:179–205, finds S.'s novel more 'réaliste' than Cervantes's model, especially as regards the hero Lysis's 'mélancolie hypocondriaque'. We are therefore invited to 'déchiffrer, dans la mise en scène narrative de la faculté imaginative et de ses productions, les linéaments d'une critique de la fiction et d'une théorie de la lecture'. M. Alet, 'La double lecture de l'âme humaine dans *La Science universelle* de Charles Sorel', McKenna, *Libertins*, 55–72, sees in this work a surface conformity to 'la philosophie officielle de son temps' hiding a 'doctrine de l'âme humaine qui se conçoit comme un naturalisme matérialiste'.

TRISTAN L'HERMITE. C. M. Grisé, 'La rhétorique baroque de Tristan L'Hermite dans la Lettre LVIII de ses *Lettres mêlées*', *CTH*, 24:30–37, chooses one of a series of five *lettres héroïques* — a sub-genre invented by Ovid — in which historical or mythological characters address each other. The letter chosen for analysis is one 'de Thétis à une Néréide': G. is looking for traces of the elegiac and oratorical tradition founded by Ovid in his *Heroides*, and also for evidence — in the letter's complexity and allusiveness — of a baroque sensibility.

URFÉ. T. Meding, 'The conqueror and the shepherd: discovery, *habit* and costume in *L'Astrée*', *SCFS*, 23, 2001:55–69, writes of the mythology and all its accoutrements concocted by d'U. for his Forez, and their relationship to the props and artifices of theatre. P. Rossetto, 'La Méditerranée dans *L'Astrée*', Dotoli, *Méditerranées*, 121–36, sees in the 'mer sauvage, lieu de tous les dangers, lieu ouvert, lieu amer' an 'anti-Forez', recalled for the locals by travellers who make of d'U.'s romance 'un roman d'aventures, continuateur de l'épopée antique ou moderne', creating in the work as a whole the sense of 'un équilibre toujours menacé'. W. Matzat, 'Tradition et invention dans *L'Astrée* d'Honoré d'Urfé', *DSS*, 54:199–207, evokes the setting, the 'monde fictif' which must be 'doté d'une nature paradoxale': on the one hand it is an imaginary world 'marqué par une altérité radicale, and on the other 'il doit avoir l'air d'un monde familier, proche de la réalité du lecteur'. The world of *L'Astrée* is 'un très bel exemple de ce paradoxe' which is echoed in subsequent 17th-c. French romances. J.-P. van Elslande, 'Roman pastoral et crise des valeurs dans la France du premier XVIIe siècle', *ib.*, 209–19, emphasizes the theatricality of *L'Astrée*, its popularity and moral influence, reflected first, paradoxically, in François de Sales's advice on the ideal way of life for the pious, and secondly in the 'thèses libertines' preached by Hylas, and practised by his real-life disciple Vauquelin des Yveteaux. L. Giavarini, 'Du fantasme à l'expérience. Plaisir et conversion de l'imagination mélancolique dans l'*Astrée* d'Honoré d'Urfé' (1607–1619)', *LitC*, 45:157–77, dwells on Amour's tyranny, on 'l'imagination mélancolique', a pathological condition for which a cure must be found via something approaching a formal ritual.

VEIRAS. **L'Histoire des Sévarambes*, ed. Aubrey Rosenberg (Libre Pensée et littérature clandestine, 5), Champion, 2001, 336 pp.

VILLEDIEU. Gérard Letexier, **Madame de Villedieu (1640–1683): une chroniqueuse aux origines de La Princesse de Clèves* (Situation, 57), Lettres modernes Minard, 237 pp.

5. Thought

SCFS, 23, 2001, prints conference papers on 'débuts et fins': G. Ferreyrolles, 'Histoire et finalité: sur les origines du discours providentialiste au XVIIe siècle' (1–14), starts with biblical definitions and proceeds to 'la providence augustinienne' which F. first seeks out in literature, notably in La Fontaine, Pascal, and Mme de Sévigné, thence to St Thomas's views and their echoes in Bossuet and Fénelon; E. James, 'Pyrrhonism — the beginning or the end of wisdom? Pascal and Bayle' (15–25), finds both, in their different ways, ultimately defeated by scepticism; D. Conroy, 'In the beginning was the image: feminist iconography and the frontispiece in the 1640s' (27–42), reproduces four frontispieces to works by Du Bosc, Le Moyne, La Serre, and Georges and Madeleine de Scudéry, and discusses their function as prefaces to their texts and the extent to which they 'epitomise the spirit of the text and can be read as feminist'. Christian Belin, *La Conversation intérieure: la méditation en France au XVIIe siècle* (Lumière classique, 42), Champion, 422 pp., begins with Job, and after a brief grudging reference to 'les philosophes païens, de Platon à Plotin', follows the Christian 'tradition méditative' through the centuries in order to provide a foundation from which to 'suivre des itinéraires individuels et des oeuvres singulières', a chosen 'suite de monographies' — poets La Ceppède and Hopil, *prosateurs* Bérulle and Bossuet, followed by Pascal, and 'la méditation philosophique chez Descartes et Malebranche'. The final section of the work then dwells on three questions raised by what has been offered by these writers: 'Quelle intériorité?' 'Quelle mystique?' 'Quel rapport au temps?'

S. Suppa, 'Raison et passion dans le paradigme politique', Dotoli, *Méditerranées*, 257–70, studies in turn Richelieu's *Testament politique*,

Naudé's *Considérations politiques sur les coups d'État*, and Gassendi's *Traité de la philosophie d'Épicure, IIIe partie: l'éthique ou la morale*. G. Van Den Abbeele, 'The concept of colony: from Laudonnière to Iberville', Koch, *Unities*, 143–50, covers the period from 1586 (date of the publication of L.'s *Histoire notable de la Floride*) to 1699 (date of the writing by I. Of his *Mémoire de la coste de la Floride et d'une partie du Mexique*. Julie Boch, *Les Dieux désenchantés. La fable dans la pensée française de Huet à Voltaire (1680–1760)* (Les dixhuitièmes siècles, 68), Champion, 573 pp., in reviewing evolving definitions of fable, devotes a chapter to H.'s *De l'origine des romans* where she finds 'affabulation' viewed as 'une disposition naturelle au coeur de l'homme'. Another chapter covers the Oratorian Louis Thomassin who advanced 'la justification littéraire et pédagogique de la fable'. Both these writers contributed to the *Querelle des anciens et des modernes* which is also studied for its 'réflexion sur la fable'. A whole section is devoted to Bayle whose feelings about fable in classical antiquity are complicated by his upbringing: 'un pessimisme calviniste hérité de saint Augustin, [. . .] le rationalisme classique de ses immédiats prédecesseurs et [. . .] la tolérance humaniste d'un Montaigne'.

Steven Fanning, *Mystics of the Christian Tradition*, Routledge, 2001, xix + 279 pp., contains a chapter on 'French mystics of the sixteenth and seventeenth centuries' (158–74) which in particular places Marie de l'Incarnation and Mme Guyon in their historical context. S. Houdard, 'De la représentation de Dieu à la vue sans image. Hypothèse sur le rôle de l'imagination dans l'écriture mystique du XVIIe siècle', *LitC*, 45 : 109–26, surveys firstly the attempts of various writers (including Marie de l'Incarnation and François de Sales) to give some idea of their mystical experiences, and secondly those of other writers to warn against 'les artifices et tromperies, les fausses visions, les imaginaires ravissements' noted by Jeanne de Chantal. B. Guion, 'Songes et mensonges: la dénonciation de l'illusion dans l'augustinisme du Grand Siècle', *ib.*, 44 : 313–34, finds *illusion* 'une préoccupation centrale' for a host of Augustinians — 'ceux de Port-Royal . . . de l'abbé de Saint-Cyran à Pascal et à Nicole', and also 'les moralistes, catholiques et réformés': Jean de La Placette, Jacques Abbadie, and François Lamy. She examines 'la richesse sémantique du terme, susceptible de plusieurs acceptions'. P. Thouvenin, 'Les *Mémoires* de Port-Royal: bilan et perspectives', Wetsel, *Pascal*, 219–29, examines Port-Royal's 'rayonnement littéraire' in the form of the memoirs by Lancelot, Fontaine, and others, and proposes to show how they 'déjouent trois paradoxes: entre humilité et visibilité, entre écriture collective et individuelle, entre austérité et plaisir, variété stylistique et séduction'. J. A. Gallucci, 'Équivoque et mystère: autour de Boileau et Arnauld' (247–57), uses the quarrel between these two writers and Perrault to study 'un problème important de culture classique, celui de la lecture littéraire', and backs his argument with quotations from Pascal, Nicole, and the *Logique de Port-Royal*. J.-C. Darmon, 'Entre Montaigne et Malebranche: variations libertines sur la philosophie, ses fictions et ses preuves', *LitC*, 45:277–95, first examines Malebranche's attacks on Montaigne, then moves on to the views of the *libertin* Cyrano de Bergerac, which he finds more satisfying. A. Forrestal, '"Fathers, leaders, kings": episcopacy and episcopal reform in the seventeenth-century French School', *SCen*, 17:24–47, reviews the efforts of Bérulle and his successor Jean-Jacques Olier to reform the French episcopate 'through their published writings and through personal interaction'.

McKenna, *Libertins*, contains the following papers: S. Taussig, 'Les correspondances savantes comme une utopie' (37–53), which sees the letters of a man like Gassendi as projecting the portrait of 'un homme moins réel que ramené à un certain nombre de traits qui définissent la République des Lettres', and G., with his correspondents, as idealized inhabitants; B. Consarelli, 'Absolutisme, individualisme et utopie au Grand Siècle: une lecture politique des libertins' (139–50), which surveys utopias influenced by *libertinage* and the ideas of progress and of natural rights, such as the anonymous *Histoire du royaume d'Antangil* and the works of Cyrano, Foigny, Veiras, and Fontenelle.

CPR, 51, collects 'actes' from a colloquium on *La Solitude et les Solitaires de Port-Royal*: C. Delporte, 'La figure de l'ascète au siècle classique' (37–68), proposes to show how this *figure* 'participe de la modernité, en tant qu'elle est d'abord reprise de la tradition pour le présent', and to follow by way of example 'le pèlerinage ascétique' of Pascal, Vincent de Paul, Louise de Marillac, and others, in his attempted definition of 'la joyeuse spiritualité du tombeau'; F. Bonjour, 'Les morts des solitaires à Port-Royal: paradoxes et paradigmes de la "solitude"?' (69–83), regales us with extracts from writings intended to illustrate attitudes to 'la mort à soi', 'la mort de soi' and 'la mort après soi', his chosen authors including Saint-Cyran and Pascal; D. Donetzkoff, 'Sacerdoce et solitude selon Saint-Cyran' (85–119), writes of the influence, particularly, of Bérulle and Adrien Bourdoise, which can be seen in St-C.'s *Théologie familière* and in his letters; G. Duboucher, 'Ce que le dossier Achille Vallet révèle des derniers solitaires' (121–29), quotes from *actes* in this *notaire*'s dossier entered between 1679 and 1690; A. Villard, '*L'Échelle sainte* à Port-Royal-des-Champs: le moine et les trois solitaires' (143–74), traces the collaboration of Robert Arnauld d'Andilly, Antoine Le Maistre, and Pierre Thomas du Fossé in the translation of this work by St John Climacus; B. Chédozeau, 'La querelle Rancé — Mabillon: les études monastiques et la solitude du moine' (213–43), follows the stages of this dispute which began with R.'s *De la sainteté et des devoirs de la vie monastique* (1683) and revealed very different views on the question: 'que faire du livre imprimé dans la vie du moine?'; C. Cagnat-Deboeuf, 'Une "union d'amour": l'amitié entre solitaires' (361–81), finds them on the whole enthusiastic about friendship and yet uneasy that 'l'ami . . .peut agir comme un leurre et masquer Dieu'. **Jansénisme et puritanisme*, ed. Bernard Cottret et al. (Univers Port-Royal, 2), Nolin, 240 pp., prints colloquium *actes*.

Hubert Bost, *Ces messieurs de la R.P.R. Histoires et écritures de Huguenots, XVIIe–XVIIIe siècles* (Vie des Huguenots, 18), Champion, 2001, 414 pp., collects 15 papers and articles, 13 of them previously published and two 'à paraître'. All have been 'revus et actualisés', and reproduced here in the chronological order of their subject matter. The two unpublished papers are, firstly, 'Des porte-parole protestants au chevet de l'édit de Nantes moribond' (215–36), which reviews the opinions of the defenders of the Edict before its revocation, and of those who afterwards launch the 'réquisitoire contre la décision inique', including Louis Maimbourg, Claude Brousson, Henri Basnage de Beauval, and Élie Benoist; secondly, 'La superstition pire que l'athéisme? Quelques réactions aux paradoxes de Bayle dans l'Europe protestante au XVIIIe siècle' (325–47).

Jean-Pierre Cavaillé, *Dis/simulations: Jules-César Vanini, François La Mothe Le Vayer, Gabriel Naudé, Louis Machon et Torquato Accetto. Religion, morale et politique au XVIIe siècle* (Lumière classique, 37), Champion, 453 pp., gives his five dis/simulators (all but one belonging to 'la constellation libertine') a chapter each, presenting them as examples of inspired creators in their various ways of 'une écriture de la persécution et de la censure'. A. Karoui, 'Le système d'écriture des libres penseurs en France aux XVIIe et XVIIIe siècles', *La Licorne*, 61 : 197–204, examines in turn the practices of La Mothe Le Vayer, Pierre Bayle, Fontenelle, and Voltaire, describes how their readership spreads, from 'quelques privilégiés' in the early to mid-17th c., to the wide readership of V., 'le parfait vulgarisateur des idées et valeurs de son siècle'.

Protestations et revendications féminines. Textes oubliés et inédits sur l'éducation féminine (XVIe–XVIIe siècle), ed. Colette H. Winn (Textes de la Renaissance, 50), Champion, 276 pp., introduces us to eight texts dating from 1597 to 1694 which, according to the editor in her 'Introduction' (7–31), 'éclairent une prise de conscience féministe naissante'. Each of the texts (some complete, some abridged) is introduced by the editor who summarizes what is known of the life and works of each author. The best known of these is Marguerite de Valois who is represented by her posthumous *Discours docte et subtil*, published in 1618 (55–60). By far the longest work, reproduced in full, is Jacqueline de Miremont's *Apologie pour les dames* of 1602 (70–141), written in rhyming alexandrine couplets. Other authors represented are Marie Le Gendre, Charlotte de Brachart, Suzanne de Nervèze, Jacquette Guillaume, Gabrielle Suchon, and Mme de Pringy. A chronological list is appended of the *Principaux écrits sur la question féminine (Xve–XVIIe siècle)* published in French or in Latin between 1404 and 1698.

BAYLE. *Pierre Bayle: pour une histoire critique de la philosophie. Choix d'articles du 'Dictionnaire historique et critique'*, ed. Jean-Michel Gros and Jacques Chomarat (Vie des Hugenots, 16), Champion, 2001, 824 pp. The editors have printed 12 whole articles with their *remarques* and *éclaircissements*, chosen, they claim, 'par ses meilleurs lecteurs: Leibniz, Voltaire, mais aussi Hume, Kant, ou même Feuerbach et Melville'. The articles are concerned with those philosophical themes dearest to B.: 'le scepticisme, l'athéisme vertueux, le scandale théologique du mal, l'incompatibilité de la philosophie et de la religion, etc.' A relatively brief introduction traces the origins and development of B.'s thought. T. M. Lennon, 'Did Bayle read Saint-Évremond?' *JHI*, 63:225–37, claims that B. 'read Saint-Évremond only through Cotolendi, or [. . .] with him as an interpretive filter', hence believing him to be advancing a fideist conception of religion which coincided with his own. E. James, 'Pierre Bayle on the inspiration of scripture: a footnote revisited', *FSB*, 85:6–8, returns to a *remarque* on the article 'Beaulieu' in the *Dictionnaire* on 'moral demonstrations' of scriptural inspiration. J.-M. Gros, 'Pierre Bayle et la République des Lettres', McKenna, *Libertins*, 131–38, highlights this Europe-wide network which, he claims, 'a orienté toute la pratique de cet auteur'.

BOSSUET. M. Gantelet, 'La politique, de la prestige à la théorie: Bossuet dans les derniers feux de la Fronde condéenne (Metz, octobre 1653)', *DSS*, 54:485–510, looks at events and how they inspired B. the writer both of letters and of the *Panégyrique de saint François d'Assise*. Cécile Joulin, **La Mort dans les oeuvres oratoires de Bossuet*, Publications de l'Université de Saint-Étienne, 250 pp.

DESCARTES. *Règles pour la direction de l'esprit*, trans. Jacques Brunschwig, ed. Kim Sang Ong-Van-Cung, LP, 224 pp., presents, with a new preface, dossier, and glossary, the 1963 translation from the Latin of this unfinished early work, first published in Amsterdam in 1701. The editor calls it 'la matrice vivante de l'oeuvre philosophique de Descartes'. S. Giocanti, 'Descartes face au doute scandaleux des sceptiques', *DSS*, 54:663–73, studies D.'s disapproval of 'le doute sceptique' under two headings: 'le libertinage méthodologique' and 'le libertinage intellectuel', and follows this latter up by defining its 'conséquences théologico-religieuses' and its 'conséquences morales'. F. Hallyn, 'Aspects de la problématique de l'illusion chez Descartes', *LitC*, 44:285–304, confines himself to *Le Monde* and to the distinction established in that work between 'l'objet dynamique' and 'l'objet immédiat'. C. Bouriau, 'L'imagination productrice: Descartes entre Proclus et Kant', *ib.*, 45:47–62, first compares D.'s views on space and imagination with those of P., and then shows that D., 'par la fonction qu'il confère à l'imagination productrice, ouvre la voie à la perspective "transcendantale" kantienne'. S. Shapin, *'Descartes the doctor: rationalism and its therapies', *BJHS*, 33, 2000:131–54. C. Romano, 'Les trois médecines de Descartes', *DSS*, 54:675–96, reviews D.'s writings on physiology and medicine, and attempts to clarify some of the questions raised by them.

François Azouvi, *Descartes et la France: l'histoire d'une passion nationale*, Fayard, 360 pp., writes the history, not only of D.'s 'réception' and of Cartesianism through the ages, but also of 'une épisode de la constitution de l'identité culturelle et politique française', reminding us that 'on lui a prêté opinions et intentions avec une telle libéralité, une telle imagination, qu'il n'y a pas lieu de lui demander toujours des comptes'. The account is divided into five uncontroversial parts, beginning with 'le siècle de Louis XIV' and ending with 'la IIIe République fille de Descartes'. The later history of this 'passion nationale' has yet to be written. Jean-Marie Beyssade, *Études sur Descartes: l'histoire d'un esprit*, Seuil, 2001, 394 pp., is a compilation by their author of essays, introductions, and articles published between 1973 and 2000. Stéphane Van Damme, *Descartes: essai d'histoire culturelle d'une grandeur philosophique*, Presses de Sciences Po, 347 pp., studies varied and successive views of the work of D., and proposes 'deux démarches': the study of D. must firstly 'conduire certes à une analyse de la construction sociale d'une oeuvre et d'une biographie, à une "anthropologie de l'admiration" cartésienne', but secondly 'doit aussi signaler les principales étapes de la formation d'un espace herméneutique où la philosophie cartésienne prend sens et s'actualise durant ces quatre siècles'. E. Mehl, '*Dubito ergo sum*: Descartes et le *cogito* des cartésiens', *LetC*, 10, 2001:43–57, looks at the attacks of Bourdin and Voetius, and the defences of Heereboord, and D. himself in *La Recherche de la vérité*.

Le Problème des transcendantaux du XIVe au XVIIe siècle, ed. Graziella Federici Vescovini, Vrin, 288 pp., prints papers, mainly in Italian and French, on various European manifestations of the problem, including R. Perini, 'Reflets des transcendantaux scolastiques dans la Scientia cartésienne' (157–73), and J.-M. Beyssade, 'En quel sens peut-on parler de transcendantal chez Descartes?' (175–85), on the *Principia philosophiae* I, article 48. P. S. Macdonald, 'Descartes: the lost episodes', *JHP*, 40:437–60, asserts that what is known about D.'s life is 'enough to whet the appetite, but not enough to satisfy it', and suggests three episodes that might have had a formative influence on him. Richard A. Watson, **Cogito, ergo sum: The Life of René Descartes*, Lincoln, MA, Godine, 375 pp.

GARASSE. L. Godard de Donville, 'L'invention du "libertin" en 1623 et ses conséquences sur la lecture des textes', McKenna, *Libertins*, 7–17, claims that the Jesuit created, in his *Doctrine curieuse*, a synthetic 'Théophile' from 'manifestations multiples, éparses, quelquefois contradictoires' on which to stick the label *libertin*, and create a composite figure 'visant à frapper les imaginations et mobiliser les consciences'.

GASSENDI. S. Taussig, 'Gassendi et Lucrèce dans les *Lettres latines*', *DSS*, 54:527–43, emphasizes that, for G., Lucretius is not so much a poet as 'avant tout le disciple d'Épicure le plus fidèle et la meilleure source pour connaître et comprendre la philosophie du Jardin'. She studies five passages chosen from the letters, in which the views of like-minded friends such as Naudé are also referred to.

JURIEU. Emile Kappler, *Bibliographie critique de l'oeuvre imprimée de Pierre Jurieu (1637–1713)* (Vie des Huguenots, 19), Champion, 595 pp., is a meticulous piece of work divided into three main parts: 'Oeuvres imprimées', 'Oeuvres faussement attribuées . . . ou d'attribution douteuse', and 'Ouvrages satiriques écrits contre Jurieu'. *Annexes* locate and analyse holdings, public and private, throughout the world, and a select bibliography lists studies of J. and his works.

LA MOTHE LE VAYER. S. Giocanti, 'La Mothe Le Vayer et la pratique du doute', *LetC*, 10, 2001:31–42, defines the particular characteristics of this writer's doubt. He is anti-Cartesian in his mistrust of reason, and closer to Pascal, except that he will accept no constraints on the faculty, whatever the consequences. E. Bury, 'Écriture libertine et sources doxographiques: le cas La Mothe Le Vayer', McKenna, *Libertins*, 19–36, discusses the sources cited by this writer, and the use to which he puts them in his 'argumentation sceptique'.

MALEBRANCHE. M.-F. Pellegrin, 'Aristarque est-il un cartésien? Refus philosophique ou refus apologétique du doute chez Malebranche', *LetC*, 10, 2001:85–102, seeks enlightenment from a careful re-reading of the *Conversations chrétiennes*.

MÉNAGE. R. Maber, 'A publisher's nightmare: Ménage, Wetstein, and Diogenes Laertius', *SCFS*, 23, 2001:173–85, looks into the complex publishing history of the scholarly enterprises undertaken by M. during the last twenty years of his life, in particular that of his commentary, first published in Amsterdam by Henrik Wetstein in 1692, on D.L.'s *Lives of Eminent Philosophers*.

NAUDÉ. R. Damien, 'Gabriel Naudé et la lecture des romans', McKenna, *Libertins*, 73–82, looks at the *Advis pour dresser une bibliothèque* to find reasons why N. refused to allow fictional narratives in his ideal library. I. Moreau, 'Gabriel Naudé, une apologie de la prudence en matière de lecture', *ib.*, 83–95, sees the *Apologie pour tous les grands personnages qui ont été faussement soupçonnés de magie* as 'un éloge de la prudence' to be exercised especially when reading the *apologie* itself, 'conçue en trompe-l'oeil', for an élite of discerning readers.

NICOLE. R. G. Hodgson, 'Littérature morale, philosophie, politique et théologie à Port-Royal: le contrat social chez Pierre Nicole', Wetsel, *Pascal*, 101–08, summarises N.'s views on social contract as expressed in the *Essais de morale*, views which he finds as much marked 'par ses expériences dans le monde et ses observations de moraliste' as by his religious beliefs. E. R. Koch, 'Individuum: the specular self in Nicole's *De la connaissance de soi-même*', *ib.*, 259–68, starts from two definitions of *individuum*, firstly 'the most minute separate entity', and secondly 'an indivisible concatenation of parts that form a whole'. The 'atomic individual', defined by his self-interest and *amour-propre*, is the smallest piece of 'a unitary, totalizing body'. 17th-c. moralists are horrified by the developing independence of atomic individuals, whose growing importance in society nevertheless fascinates them. Béatrice Guion, **Pierre Nicole, moraliste* (Moralia, 9), Champion, 896 pp.

BLAISE PASCAL. Wetsel, *Pascal*, prints conference papers: J. Mesnard, 'Histoire secrète de la recherche pascalienne au XXe siècle' (13–38), wishes to look into 'la recherche en son cours, dans des hésitations et des tâtonnements souvent aussi instructifs que les résultats mêmes', but has only his own *hésitations* to reconsider: on the order of the *Pensées*, on P. and science, and on 'imaginaire et théologie' (39–57); A. R. Pugh, 'Imagination and the unity of the *Pensées*' (65–73), expands 'some remarks on style and syntax which [he] threw out briefly' in his book, *The Composition of Pascal's Apologia* (1984, see *YWMLS*, 46:132); A. Régent, 'La figure du juge dans les *Provinciales* et dans les *Pensées*: rupture ou continuité?' (75–90), finds a contrast in the treatment of this topic between the *Pensées* and the *Provinciales*, due to the 'nature apologétique' of the first and the 'nature polémique' of the second; F. P. Adorno, 'L'efficacité de la volonté chez Pascal et Arnauld' (91–100), believes that analysing this faculty and its effectiveness 'doit nous mettre en condition de montrer [. . .] ce qui dans leur texte semble constamment échapper à l'analyse et qui autorise de les considérer comme des réformistes à l'intérieur de la Contre-réforme'; P. Force, 'L'argumentation sceptique dans les *Pensées*' (129–36), examines P.'s possible reasons for reducing the three traditional categories — dogmatists, academicians and

Pyrrhonians — to two, omitting the second; T. M. Harrington, 'Ambiguïté et bivalence dans les *Pensées* de Pascal' (137–42), emphasizes that he is concerned with 'ambiguïtés [. . .] sémantiques et non syntaxiques' because the former were, in his view, 'voulues et destinées à jouer un rôle important dans la version définitive de l'Apologie'; he picks out for particular attention as examples the words *divertissement*, *juif*, *miracle*, *monde*, *philosophe*, and *réparateur*; L. MacKenzie, 'Évidence, regard, preuve: le poids de la vision chez Pascal' (143–48), looks at P.'s modes of persuasion, whether in the fields of science, polemics, or apologetics, and focuses on the question of the vacuum, and on fr. 230 (Sellier) where P. invites us to look directly at the sun; T. Shiokawa, 'Les limites de l'apologétique pascalienne' (149–56), asks whether P. 'aurait conçu son apologétique uniquement comme une tentative de persuasion humaine [. . .] sans s'engager dans l'ordre du coeur', but, for signs of the latter, S. looks at fragments where P. gives the impression that God speaks; H. Bjørnstad, 'The road not taken: a Benjaminian approach to a Pascalian baroque' (157–66), notes a similarity between Pascalian baroque as defined by J. Mesnard in his 'Baroque, science et religion chez Pascal' (1974), and Walter Benjamin's view of the subject in *The origin of German tragic drama* (1928); T. R. Parker, 'Intensionality and *non causa pro causa* in Pascal' (173–80), searches for examples of intensional *non causa pro causa* in P.'s scientific writings, in the *Provinciales*, and, most effectively, in the *Pensées*; S. C. Bold, 'Hyperbole in the *Pensées*' (181–87), puts again the question 'to what degree is an authentic reading of this text based in hermeneutics, in rhetoric, or in geometry?'. M. L. Jones, 'Geometry and fallen humanity in Pascal and Leibniz' (189–202), concludes that 'their contrasting visions of the wonder, incomprehension and the wisdom occasioned by mathematical infinities illustrate that Pascal had, in Leibniz, a great successor in balancing the wretchedness of humanity with its greatness'; R. Howells, 'Polemical stupidity in the *Lettres provinciales*' (231–37), takes P.'s *Lettres* as a 'founding text' for modern modes of the 'strategic failure to understand' defined by Bakhtin, based on feigned naïvety. K. Almquist, 'Individual will and contract law in Pascal's *Lettres provinciales*' (239–46), briefly describes French 17th-c. civil law of property and obligation, then shows how, according to P., the Jesuits betrayed their own prescriptions for a 'system of ethics based on obligation, intent, and individual will'; N. Hammond, 'Mémoire et éducation chez Pascal' (269–76), notes a reaction among Jansenist educationalists against the excessive emphasis on memorizing in the Jesuit education system, and points to a Jansenist encouragement of a balanced interplay of memory, judgment, and imagination, evidence of which is then found in the interest P. took in the education of members of his family, and finally in views expressed in the *Pensées.*

John F. Boitano, *The Polemics of Libertine Conversion in Pascal's Pensées. A Dialectics of Rational and Occult Libertine Beliefs* (Biblio 17, 139), Tübingen, Narr, 231 pp., starts by making the point that 'Pascal considers thoroughly both the rational and the occult beliefs of the intended seventeenth-century libertine reader of his Apology', and asks us to bear in mind that 'scientists and philosophers in the seventeenth century were quite reluctant to discard the occult precepts of Renaissance Naturalism', and any libertine reader of the *Pensées* would share this attitude. Hence P. had to take this occult component into account: his readers were not just precursors of the 18th-c. *philosophes*; they were still influenced by neo-Platonic and Pythagorean mysticism. Jean-Louis Bischoff, *Dialectique de la misère et de la grandeur chez Blaise Pascal* (Ouverture philosophique), L'Harmattan, 269 pp., furnishes an eloquent introduction to the *Pensées,* relying on the framework provided by 'misère' and 'grandeur', and concluding by emphasizing that 'c'est à la lumière de son expérience personnelle [. . .] que Pascal a élaboré sa pensée'. E. James, 'Pascal on the limits of human understanding and the possibility of apologetic', *FSB,* 82:4–6, takes issue with A. McKenna's comments on fr. 110 (Lafuma) of the *Pensées* (see *DSS,* 177:481–94, and *YWMLS,* 54:124). P. Force, '*Ad hominem* arguments in Pascal's *Pensées*', Koch, *Unities,* 393–403, agrees with previous commentators that 'the *Pensées* are fundamentally aporetic', but then proposes to show that this quality, 'far from standing in the way of its apologetic intent, is subordinated to it', and is in effect 'a tool of persuasion'. N. Hammond, 'L'illusion de la parole chez Pascal', *LitC,* 44:305–11, undertakes to analyse 'le lien entre l'illusion et le langage déchu dans les *Pensées* de Pascal'. G. Ferreyrolles, 'Compendium sur l'imagination dans les *Pensées*', *ib.,* 45:139–54, begins with P.'s assertion that imagination is the 'maîtresse d'erreur et de fausseté', but then reminds himself that imagination is God-given and that there must be a 'bon usage' for it. Dawn M. Ludwin, *Blaise Pascal's Quest for the Ineffable,* Berne–NY, Lang, xii + 159 pp., regards P. as a 'great mystic' who, haunted by 'the problem of the limits of reason', adopted 'dissonant cognitive strategies akin to the mystical tradition known as apophatic ("negative") theology'. L.'s study, she claims, 'initiates a philosophical dialogue between Pascal and Pseudo-Dionysius'. P. borrows the strategies of P.-D. in order to be able to understand the ineffable, to think what is beyond rational thought, and express what is beyond words. H. Michon, 'Pascal et la relation d'altérité', *CPR,* 51:347–59, asks a very general question of P.: 'dans quelle mesure l'homme peut-il ou doit-il chercher à nouer des relations avec ses semblables en vue de la recherche de la vérité?' Id., 'L'irreprésentable dans les *Pensées* de Pascal', *RHLF*, 102:33–43, is concerned with scientific works ('la représentation de l'espace') and apologetic works ('la représentation de l'homme dans l'espace').

RPFE, 192.1, has three articles on P.: H. Bouchilloux, 'Apologie et théologie dans les *Pensées* de Pascal' (3–19), sees much more in the *Pensées* than an apologetic purpose and doubts if that is their main one, especially since P.'s professed theology asserts that 'il n'y a aucune continuité entre la nature et la grâce, entre la raison et la foi', and since there is a relentless anti-Cartesian element in them; G. Ferreyrolles, 'Les païens dans la stratégie argumentative de Pascal' (21–40), points to P.'s adherence to the general Augustinian rejection of the notion that pagans were capable of true virtue, and sets out to 'repérer l'utilisation stratégique de ce thème dans les *Provinciales* et dans les *Pensées*; M. Le Guern, 'Le tri des papiers, le tri des arguments' (41–54), considers the implications for recent editions of the *Pensées* of the declarations made near the end of his life by P. to Fr. Beurrier on the principles which should govern the ordering of the material, emphasizing particularly 'une attention constamment centrée sur le destinataire'.

JACQUELINE PASCAL. Frédéric Delforge, **Jacqueline Pascal (1625–1661)* (Univers Port-Royal, 1), Nolin, 160 pp., is a biography.

GILBERTE PÉRIER. F. Mariner, 'Family perspectives in Gilberte Périer's *Vie de Monsieur Pascal*', Wetsel, *Pascal*, 203–17, proposes G. P.'s biography as a family portrait projecting a collective attempt to 'assert a personal identity removed from the authority of the State and other parties involved in the Jansenist Quarrel'.

POULLAIN DE LA BARRE. V. Bosley, 'A voice for women: Poullain de la Barre and the philosophical dialogue *au féminin*', Hodgson, *Femmes*, 125–37, examines *De l'éducation des dames*, a treatise in dialogue form, to show how P.'s female speakers express their point of view.

RANCÉ. B. Papasogli, 'Solitude et silence de la mémoire chez l'abbé de Rancé', *CPR*, 51:245–63, looks at the writings to 'faire ressortir [. . .] d'abord l'imaginaire de l'espace et du temps qui soustend le "nouvel ordre" de la Trappe, ensuite le discours de la mémoire et de l'oubli', and finally R.'s position on 'la querelle des méthodes de prière [. . .] où toute une tradition de spiritualité monastique est engagée'.

OLIVIER DE SERRES. Henri Gourdin, **Olivier de Serres: gentilhomme champestre*, Arles, Actes Sud, 2001, 352 pp., is a biography of this author and 'père de l'agriculture', admired by Henri IV, Sully and, a little later, by Philippe Pétain.

SORBIÈRE. *Discours sceptiques*, ed. Sophie Gouverneur (Libre pensée et littérature clandestine, 10), Champion, 106 pp., provides introductory material which almost overwhelms the text of the three *Discours*, comprising a short biography, a presentation of the sole edition of the *Discours*, and an 'Essai sur la pensée politique de Sorbière'. The length of the latter is justified, as G. explains, by the neglect from which this aspect of S.'s work has suffered.

VINCENT DE PAUL. Jean-Paul Lefebvre Filleau, **Saint Vincent de Paul contre les pirates barbaresques*, Luneray, Bertout, 211 pp., is an account of V.'s imprisonment in Tunis in 1605–07.

THE EIGHTEENTH CENTURY

POSTPONED

THE ROMANTIC ERA

By John Whittaker, *University of Hull*

1. General

D. Peyrache-Leborgne, 'Paradis mélancoliques de Jean Paul à Edgar Poe', *Romantisme*, 117:13–29, shows how the Romantics' perception of landscape and the natural world had its bases in Enlightenment sensibility, endlessly revived by the consultation of key texts. D. Roboly, 'L'Orient et l'écriture de la mort dans les récits romantiques du 19e siècle', *FSB*, 82:8–11, considers the mythical nature of the Romantic Orient, in which death is a dominant feature, and the way it was constructed through a process of rewriting. *Modernité et Romantisme*, ed. Isabelle Bour, Éric Dayre, and Patrick Née, Champion, 2001, 395 pp., contains the proceedings of the conference 'Romantisme et modernité', held at the Université de Versailles-Saint-Quentin-en-Yvelines and at the École Normale Supérieure de Fontenay-Saint-Cloud in June 1997. The main focus of most of the papers lies beyond the French literature of our period, though J.-M. Maulpoix, 'L'identité lyrique' (111–17), identifies a lyrical tradition flowing from Lamartine, Hugo, and Nerval to later poets; M. Collot, 'Paysage et subjectivité' (235–50), draws attention to the influence of Rousseau upon the landscapes of the early Romantics; J. Rancière, 'Y a-t-il un concept du romantisme?' (287–300), traces the progress of Romantic sensibility from Hegel to Flaubert and, though there is no mention of the French writers of our period, their role is implied. Pierre Laforgue, *L'Œdipe romantique, le jeune homme, le désir et l'histoire en 1830*, Grenoble U.P., 206 pp., explains the appearance of the young man in French literature from 1830 as part of the social and political history surrounding the July Revolution. Eight case studies are presented, relating to Stendhal's *Le Rouge et le Noir*, Hugo's *Lucrèce Borgia*, Musset's *Lorenzaccio*, *Fantasio*, and *La Confession d'un enfant du siècle*, and Balzac's *Le Père Goriot* and *Le Lys dans la vallée*. Vincent Laisney, *L'Arsenal romantique, le salon de Charles Nodier 1824–1834*, Champion, xiii + 839 pp., is a very thorough account of the regular Sunday meetings at Nodier's residence which began in April 1824. The evidence is assembled from a variety of sources, mainly from the reports of people who were present, and we are given a clear picture of the salons as a reflection of the literature and the society of the time. Chapters are devoted to Balzac, Gautier, Hugo, Lamartine, Musset, Nerval, and Sainte-Beuve, but attention is also given to minor writers, from Félix Arvers to Édouard Turquéty. Michel Le Bris, *Le Défi romantique*, Flammarion, 479 pp., is a revised and extended version of the work which first appeared in 1981 as *Le Journal du Romantisme*. A new conclusion resolutely brings this perspective of Romanticism, treating literature and the visual arts in France, Britain and Germany, into the 21st c., stressing the challenge of seeing beyond the clichés with which it has been surrounded.

2. Consulate Writers

CHATEAUBRIAND. L. Bouvier, 'How not to speak of incest: *Atala* and the secrets of speech', *NCFS*, 30:227–41, finds that reading *Atala* in the light of *René* illuminates crucial elements of the text, and that the problem of incest is representative of a broader question in C.'s work: how to speak of the unspeakable. L. Cantagrel, 'Dire l'absence: Chateaubriand et la mise en scène du mélancolique', *Romantisme*, 117:31–44, analyses, with reference to his early work, the distinctive shade of melancholy devised by C., and finds that it displays a striking integrity, and is even a modern concept. Bertrand Aureau, *Chateaubriand penseur de la révolution*, Champion, 2001, 349 pp., examines C.'s comparatively modern idea of the Revolution as a period of social and political change which does not necessarily impose itself on future events. The first part deals with the process of change for the individual, for society, and for the state, with reference to the situation under the *Ancien Régime*. The second part seeks to explain C.'s understanding of the historical bases of the Revolution as part of the transformation of the western world. The third considers C.'s religious standpoint in relation to Revolutionary events, and the fourth his formulation of the need for France to progress beyond the revolution. *Les Aventures du dernier Abencérage*, ed. Jean-Michel Cornu, Sète, L'Archange Minotaure, presents a work which has tended to be overshadowed by *Atala* and *René*, but which is shown to be of enduring relevance as a reflection on conflict between the western world and Islam. The text is that of the original edition of 1826.

MME DE STAËL. G. A. Levy, 'A genius for the modern era: Madame de Staël's *Corinne*', *NCFS*, 30:242–53, shows that the heroine is a combination of many different forms of genius, with traits that are both male and female, but also non-gendered, and clearly Republican.

3. Poetry

A. Boutin, '"Ring out the old, ring in the new": the symbolism of bells in nineteenth-century French poetry', *NCFS*, 30:266–80, finds that, in Romantic discourse, bells appear less often as referential signs and increasingly take on figurative meanings: for Chateaubriand as part of Catholic ritual; for Lamartine as a symbol of rootedness; for Hugo as a symbol of the poet's communion with the universe. Aimée Boutin, *Maternal Echoes, the Poetry of Marceline Desbordes-Valmore and Alphonse de Lamartine*, Newark, Delaware U.P. — London, Associated U.P., 2001, 246 pp., notes that D.-V.'s *Élégies, Marie et Romances* appeared in the year before L.'s *Méditations*, and were no less innovative. The two poets are shown to be more similar than one might expect, both seeking out the maternal voice as an object of symbolic identification. At a time when social changes were making the role of the mother more important, they established a link between motherhood and the poetic imagination which would grow stronger with succeeding generations.

GAUTIER. J. F. Hamilton and S. Champigny, '"La Basilique" de Théophile Gautier, un voyage psychologique et esthétique', *NCFS*, 31:27–40, finds that this poem of the *Poésies de 1830* represents a crucial stage in the evolution from Romanticism to Parnasse, and a crucial point in G.'s personal journey of self-discovery as a poet.

HUGO. *Victor Hugo ou les frontières effacées*, ed. Dominique Peyrache-Leborgne and Yann Jumelais, Nantes, Pleins Feux, 394 pp., includes: P. Alexandre, 'Le pacifiste Victor Hugo et l'Allemagne' (17–33), showing why the German public were slow to understand H.'s pacifist ideals; F. Wilhelm, 'Victor Hugo en Luxembourg. Effacement des frontières' (35–47), suggesting that the Grand Duchy may have provided H. with a model for the European nation of the future; J. M. Losada Goya, 'La réception du grotesque hugolien dans le théâtre espagnol du 19e siècle' (49–61), demonstrating convergence between H.'s dramatic theories and contemporary Spanish theatre; E. Roy-Reverzy, 'Hugo dans Zola' (63–77), showing the influence of H. on Z. by a comparison of *Notre-Dame de Paris* and *Le Ventre de Paris*; A. de Longevialle-Salha, 'Tombeaux de Victor Hugo' (79–91), on reactions to H.'s funeral as a representation of the position of the writer in the 19th c.; T.-V. Ton That, 'Proust lecteur de Victor Hugo dans *Jean Santeuil*' (93–104), showing the influence of the preface of the *Contemplations*; S. Ballestra-Puech, '"Car Dieu, de l'araignée, avait fait le soleil": métamorphoses d'Arachné chez Victor Hugo' (107–22), examining H.'s use of the spider motif; F. Chenet-Faugeras, 'La *Légende du beau Pécopin* revisitée' (123–36), on the considerable importance of the apparently trivial text inserted in *Le Rhin*; C. Hussherr, 'Caïn chez Victor Hugo: aspects d'un mythe personnel' (137–53), showing the profound symbolic influence of the biblical figure; Y. Jumelais, 'Actualisation d'un mythe: Caïn et Napoléon III' (155–68), continuing with the application of the myth, when H. was in exile, as a means of dealing with the Emperor's guilt; G. Zaragoza, 'Victor Hugo, metteur en scène' (169–86), drawing attention to H.'s constant awareness of the nature of dramatic performance, and its influence on his writing; P. Laforgue, 'Les zigzags de l'histoire, ou modernité et mélancolie chez Hugo' (187–95), giving particular attention to historical perspectives in *Les Misérables*; J. Friedemann, '*L'Homme qui rit* ou les voix du silence' (197–210), on the very expressive uses of silence in the novel; I. Durand-Le Guern, 'Les *Ballades* de Victor Hugo, une expérimentation romantique' (213–28), on the collection's attempt to draw on a long-standing lyrical tradition; R. Grutman, 'Hugo et l'intertextualité ibérique: l'écho du romancero dans *Notre-Dame de Paris*' (229–40), reminding us that the verses of Esmeralda's Spanish songs were borrowed from an edition by H.'s brother Abel; K. M. Grossman, 'Le Shakespeare de la France: sur la trace du Barde dans *Les Travailleurs de la mer*' (241–53), finding a significant level of intertextuality with *The Tempest*, not least in the similarities between Gilliatt and Prospero; J. Prungnaud, 'Hugo et l'imaginaire de l'architecture' (255–68), analysing the work of the writer in the description of natural phenomena; F. McIntosh, '*Quatrevingt-treize* ou le rejet de l'héritage scottien: une réflexion sur le sens de l'histoire' (269–81), suggesting that H.'s eventual rejection of the Scott tradition is linked to an ideological difference concerning the nature of revolutions; B. Franco, 'La Préface de *Cromwell*, entre Friedrich Schlegel et Walter Scott' (285–302), showing that the preface represents a personal reconciliation of the differing perspectives of German and British Romanticism; D. Peyrache-Leborgne, 'De Jean-Paul à Victor Hugo, romans baroques du romantisme' (303–33), on similarities between *L'Homme qui rit* and Richter's *Siebenkäs* and *Titan*; R. Pache, 'Insuffisances du réel: les créatures hybrides chez Hugo et Gogol' (335–49), on the similarities and differences between the two conceptions of realism; I. Cani-Wanegffien, 'Visage, masque, grimace: la nécessité des monstres (Hugo, Dumas, Mary Shelley)' (351–66), comparing H. and D. in relation to *Frankenstein*; M. Moutet, 'Concentration et dissolution du moi dans *Moby Dick* et *Les Travailleurs de la mer*' (367–83), finding that Captain Ahab and Gilliatt represent quite different philosophical viewpoints.

Jacques Eladan, *Victor Hugo, la Bible et la Kabbale*, NM7, 214 pp., raises the important question of the influence of the Bible on H.'s writing. Only in his early career did he see it as a source of Christian inspiration, and his attitude to it changed constantly with the evolution of his political and religious views. About 30 texts from H.'s poetry and prose are presented, and their relationship with the biblical source is demonstrated. Two extracts from 'Ce que dit la bouche d'ombre' are then shown to be linked to the Cabbala. Henri Meschonnic, *Hugo, la poésie contre le maintien d'ordre*, Maisonneuve et

Larose, 253 pp., shows that, even on the bicentenary of his birth, H.'s writing remains relevant to the present time. Attention is given to his perspective of the 19th c., his view of the future, his opinions on the use of language, and the influence of the Bible on his work. Chapters are devoted to 'Demain dès l'aube' and to 'Booz endormi', to the MS of *La Fin de Satan*, and to *Marion Delorme*. The volume includes an anthology. Henri Pena-Ruiz and Jean-Paul Scot, *Un poète en politique, les combats de Victor Hugo*, Flammarion, 449 pp., demonstrates the lack of a clear division between the life of the poet and the life of the political activist. Not least, the political objectives are clearly expressed in the poetry. We are shown how the young monarchist became a republican democrat and revolutionary, eventually declaring himself to be a socialist. His political debates are classified into 15 areas, many of which are strikingly modern, including: the abolition of the death penalty; the defence of freedom and of the rights of men, women, and children, in equal measure; secular state institutions; free education; the creation of a United States of Europe; the guarantee of world peace by a universal republic. Krishnâ Renou, *Victor Hugo en voyage*, Payot, 349 pp., gives an account of H.'s travels and the effect of the various journeys he made upon his writing.

Two evaluations of H.'s use of laughter present slightly different perspectives. Joë Friedemann, *Victor Hugo, un temps pour rire*, Saint-Genouph, Nizet, 2001, 204 pp., begins by examining the frequency of lexical items related to laughter in *Han d'Islande*, *Bug Jargal*, *Le Dernier Jour d'un condamné*, *Notre-Dame de Paris*, *Les Misérables*, *Les Contemplations*, and *L'Homme qui rit*, before looking closer at each in turn, along with *William Shakespeare* and the rest of the poetry, in order to define the techniques which H. uses. The conclusion suggests that, though he is not a comic writer, he is nevertheless inclined to laughter, though it is often combined with irony. Laughter is part of his belief in human values, and a demonstration of spontaneity. Maxime Prévost, *Rictus romantiques: Politiques du rire chez Victor Hugo*, Montreal U.P., 377 pp., examines in detail the phenomenon of laughter in H.'s writing, which is often sinister, perverse, forced, though also, on occasion, genuine and positive. The analysis proceeds through the novels, plays and poems, demonstrating H.'s motivation and the skill of his description, before concluding that the laughter which we encounter is a wortwhile antidote to the facile, artificial laughter that is so prevalent in the present day.

LACENAIRE. Anne-Emmanuelle Demartini, *L'Affaire Lacenaire*, Aubier, 2001, 430 pp., is chiefly a biography, but it makes a significant effort to explain the context of L.'s writing and to trace a clear path through the mythology surrounding him. A chapter is devoted to the *Mémoires*.

MUSSET. F. Lestringant, 'L'Orientalisme dévoilé: Musset, lecteur de Hugo', *RHLF*, 102:563–78, draws attention to the pastiche of H.'s orientalism in 'Namouna' and 'Mardoche', which effectively denounces it as fraudulent.

4. The Novel

C. L. Cropper, 'Playing at monarchy: *le jeu de paume* in literature of nineteenth-century France', *FR*, 75:720–29, considers the images of real tennis in Balzac's *La Maison du chat-qui-pelote* and in Mérimée's *La Vénus d'Ille*, which show that, in literature, what was formerly the sport of nobles serves as an allegory of the failure of the bourgeoisie.

BALZAC. R. M. Berrong, 'Vautrin and same-sex desire in *Le Père Goriot*', *NCFS*, 31:53–65, follows on from Berthier's 'Balzac du côté de Sodome' of 1979 (*ABa*, 147–77), carefully identifying the differences between modern perspectives of homosexuality and those of B.'s time, while showing that B. called on readers to abandon stereotypes. E. Bordas, '*Sarrasine* de Balzac, une poétique du contresens', *ib.*, 41–52, traces the path of error as the guiding feature of the story, representative of the ambiguity of male desire, and shows how the novel is constructed from illusions and half-truths. M. Brix, 'Balzac et l'héritage de Rabelais', *RHLF*, 102:829–42, finds that the influence of R. is evident in *La Peau de Chagrin*, *Le Cousin Pons*, *La Recherche de l'absolu*, *La Physiologie du mariage*, and *Le Lys dans la vallée*. A. Goulet, '"Tomber dans le phénomène": Balzac's optics of narration', *FrF*, 26.3:43–70, observes that *La Comédie humaine* registers a continual dialogue between the competing modes of vision and sight, and concludes that physical vision structures the spiritual search for truth. O. Heathcote, 'Women mediating violence in Balzac's *Les Marana* and Truffaut's *Jules et Jim*', *FS*, 56:329–44, considers the construction and deconstruction of the mechanisms of gendered, cross-gendered, and inter-gendered violence in B.'s story of the last of a dynasty of Italian courtesans. A. H. Pasco, 'The allusive complex of Balzac's *Pierrette*', *FrF*, 26.3:27–42, shows how, in this work which has received comparatively little attention, B. uses allusions to a number of texts in order not only to establish a context without using too many words, but also to add new themes of significance. P. Petitier, 'La mélancolie de *Ferragus*', *Romantisme*, 117:45–58, presents the work as a gothic novel set in a modern city, the principal features of which are representative of change, degradation, and melancholy.

ABa, 3.1, 2001, contains: J.-L. Dias, 'Portrait de Balzac en écrivain romantique. Le Balzac de Davin (1834–1835)' (7–23), examining the extent to which, in his collaboration with the 'Introductions' of Félix

Davin, B. was willing to be presented as a Romantic author; S. Vachon, 'Les "fermiers" d'Honoré de Balzac' (25–41), on B.'s view of the social position of the writer, assuming the role both of producer and of aristocrat; M. Labouret, 'Romanesque et romantique dans *Mémoires de deux jeunes mariées* et *Modeste Mignon*' (43–63), investigating the complex relationship between the terms 'roman', 'romanesque', and 'romantique'; D. Dupuis, 'Romantisme ou classicisme: l'image pathétique dans les *Scènes de la vie de province*' (65–84), noting that the originality of B.'s scenes of pathos is not in their substance but in their manner, and examining closely the use of images of animals, objects, natural elements, and people; M. Andréoli, 'Un manuel d'esthétique: *La Comédie humaine*' (85–108), finding that B.'s æsthetics are a function of the eclecticism which governed his life and work, incorporating both Romantic and Classical elements; T. Farrant, 'Balzac et le mélange des genres' (109–18), showing that B.'s mixture of genres was a reflection of his view of the unity and the variety of the real world; J.-D. Ebguy, 'D'une totalité l'autre: l'invention d'un personnage dans *Madame Firmiani*' (119–43), identifying a number of techniques which B. uses to establish a new character; J. Frølich, 'Balzac, l'objet et les archives romantiques de la création' (145–57), on the links between the description of inanimate objects and that of people; E. Bordas, 'Rythmes du récit balzacien, ou des mesures sensibles du romantisme français' (159–84), showing that the irregularity of rhythm in the language of B.'s descriptions is part of the business of telling the story; A. Lorant, 'Aspects romantiques des "premiers romans" (1822–1825) d'Honoré de Balzac' (185–204), noting that B. began his career as a novelist with parody and pastiche of the models he sought to emulate, yet he soon demonstrated a truly Romantic sensibility; W. Jung, '*L'Auberge rouge* et la vision balzacienne de la Rhénanie' (205–22), observing that B.'s description of the Rhine followed a well-established literary tradition linked to the appreciation of German Romanticism in France, yet in the novella he also made a significant contribution to the development of that tradition; F. Fiorentino, '*La Duchesse de Langeais* et la critique de la passion romantique' (223–29), on the novel's complex description of destructive passion; A. Vanoncini, 'Le sauvage dans *La Comédie humaine*' (231–47), showing that B. shared the fashionable fascination with primitive man, though his portrayal of primitive characters reflected his broader attitudes to human society; A. Michel, 'Chateaubriand, Balzac et le temps aboli' (249–64), on the feeling which both shared of living at a point of transition from one historical period to another; P. Laforgue, 'Mort et transfiguration, ou Balzac, Hugo et le romantisme en 1850' (265–75), on the nature, the motivation, and the impact of H.'s speech of the 21 August 1850 over

B.'s grave at the Père Lachaise cemetery; P. Berthier, 'Le spectateur balzacien' (279–99), on B.'s constant attraction to the theatre, and his preference for the dramatic use of visual and auditory imagery; A. Lascar, '*Vautrin*, du roman au théâtre' (301–14), on the strengths and weaknesses of the play, and the evolution of its reception; Y. Oshita, 'L'imaginaire mélodramatique dans l'œuvre de Balzac' (315–29), showing that B. was attracted to melodrama as much as to traditional drama, and that this was a significant source of inspiration, and also of narrative technique; V. Bui, 'Scénographie de la mort dans *Scènes de la vie privée*' (331–46), finding that the management of death scenes in the novels displays a skilful use of dramatic space; A.-M. Lefebvre, 'Satire sociale et création littéraire chez Balzac et chez Scribe: la mise en scène du personnage du médecin' (347–74), showing to what extent the doctors in *La Comédie humaine* are based on those in S.'s plays; F. Claudon, 'Balzac à l'opéra' (375–84), showing that, although it is far from an easy task to turn B.'s novels into opera, their dramatic nature means that the adaptation may more easily be achieved than with the novels of Stendhal or Flaubert.

ABa, 3.2, contains: P. Berthier, 'Balzac et le théâtre romantique' (7–30), showing that, although it seems that he despised the theatrical efforts of his contemporaries, B.'s contribution to the development of Romantic drama went far beyond *Le Faiseur* and, though none of his plays can be described as successful, they are worthy of consideration; P. Brunel, 'Le sublime et le grotesque chez Balzac: l'exemple du *Père Goriot*' (31–56), on B.'s predilection for pairs of dramatic opposites, and his skill in combining the sublime and the grotesque in a manner which is reminiscent of Shakespeare; J. Frølich, 'Codes du cœur, code des larmes: Balzac imagier et dramaturge de mélodrame' (57–67), on the links between the melodrama of the time and B.'s way of appealing to the emotions through an abundance of visual imagery; C. Bouillon-Mateos, 'Balzac et Frédérick Lemaître. Histoire d'une collaboration malheureuse' (69–80), on B.'s relationship with the actor who, in his role as Robert Macaire in *L'Auberge des Adrets*, may well have been the model for Vautrin; D. Dupuis, 'Entre théâtre et peinture: le tableau pathétique balzacien' (83–98), showing that B.'s scenes of pathos, though they owe much to the theatre and the visual arts, become a distinctive part of the novelist's armoury, helping to define structure and to offer opportunities for synthesis; A. Gœtz, '"Une toile de Rembrandt, marchant silencieusement et sans cadre". L'esthétique du portrait peint dans *La Comédie humaine*' (99–112), showing how the numerous portraits in B.'s novels almost become characters in their own right; A. Déruelle, 'Poétique balzacienne du pastiche' (113–39), describing what may be the most noteworthy of B.'s intertextual practices, a means of drawing attention to the originality of his writing; P. Loubier, 'Balzac et le Flâneur' (141–66), on the function of the figure in B.'s novels, not only as an observer, but also as the representative of a certain ideology; B. Grente-Méra, 'Balzac et le mythe. À propos du "Supplément mythologique" de la *Biographie Michaud*' (169–83), presenting *La Comédie humaine* as a re-reading and revision of mythology; A. Lascar, 'Caïn dans l'œuvre balzacienne' (185–98), finding that B.'s Cain has a dual personality, on the one hand representing reality, albeit fictional, and on the other representing the author's ideal; R. Borderie, 'Le corps dans *La Peau de chagrin*' (199–219), on the importance which the novel attaches to the body, and to the question of how life should be lived; M.-B. Diethelm, 'Un aspect de l'imaginaire balzacien dans les œuvres de jeunesse: la sœur-amante' (221–46), on the complex female figures, combining characteristics of the sister, lover, and mother, whose purpose is to reveal the essence of love; B. Milcent, 'Liberté intérieure et destinée féminine dans *La Comédie humaine*' (247–66), which is concerned with Augustine de Sommervieux in *La Maison du chat-qui-pelote*, Louise de Chaulieu and Renée de l'Estorade in *Les Mémoires de deux jeunes mariées*; S. Marchal, 'Une correspondance inédite de Balzac autour d'une amitié de salon: Virginie Ancelot' (269–82), on the six letters in the fonds Lovenjoul of the Bibliothèque de l'Institut de France; M. Tilby, 'Sur quelques éléments intertextuels des *Paysans*. Balzac, Walter Scott et Théophile Gautier' (283–304), on the dual function of intertextual elements, establishing external norms, but also inspiring the writer to surpass them and to make them part of his own creation; T. Takayama, 'Mauriac lecteur de Balzac' (305–16), showing the profound influence of B. on M.'s writing, not least through the character of Vautrin; S. Dali, 'Une Chine à la Balzac' (317–24), on a parallel between B.'s thinking and traditional Chinese philosophy.

Balzac pater familias, ed. Claudie Bernard and Franc Schuerewegen, Amsterdam–NY, Rodopi, 2001, 106 pp., includes the papers from a conference at the New York University Maison Française in November 1999: C. Bernard, 'Balzac: familles de chair, familles d'esprit, familles de papier' (5–17), on the position of the family in society, and the changes affecting it during B.'s lifetime; N. Mozet, 'La question biographique. Balzac ou le Génie qui n'a pas expiré dans sa mansarde' (19–28), on his parents and his family situation; R. Pyrczak, 'L'impossible symétrie de L'Enfant maudit: enfance, croissance et ordre social selon Balzac' (29–40) and P. R. Duke, 'La Muse maternelle dans *Le Lys dans la vallée* et *Albert Savarus*' (41–50), both showing the close links between B.'s life and his writing, to the extent that one needs to be aware of the biographical and historical background in order to understand the text; L. Frappier-Mazur,

'Max et les chevaliers. Famille, filiation et confrérie dans *La Rabouilleuse*' (56–61), grappling with the novel's complex genealogy; D. F. Bell, 'Effets collatéraux' (63–71), concentrating on the genealogical and sociological problems raised by *Ursule Mirouet*, and managing to relate them to the problem of excessive speed on French roads; L. R. Schehr, 'Rapports écrits: les lettres de la famille Rastignac' (73–83), on the letters which, in *Le Père Goriot*, Rastignac writes to his mother and sisters, asking for money, and the replies he receives; S. Vachon, 'Le désir de l'homme est le désir de l'autre: *Adieu* d'Honoré de Balzac' (85–94), an analysis of the novella which makes use of both genetics and Lacanian psychoanalysis; F. Schuerewegen, 'Honoré de Bouillon, un air de famille. *L'Envers de l'histoire contemporaine* et la fin de Balzac' (95–106), on the work which first appeared in the periodical *Le Musée des familles* from September 1842 to November 1844.

Anne-Marie Baron, *Balzac, ou les hiéroglyphes de l'imaginaire*, Champion, 213 pp., is concerned with B.'s fascination for hieroglyphics. Though he knew little about them, he was profoundly influenced by Champollion's discoveries, and he felt that hieroglyphics could represent the language of the subconscious. Tim Farrant, *Balzac's Shorter Fictions, Genesis and Genre*, OUP, xii + 356 pp., explores B.'s conception and practice of short fiction, with particular attention being given to the period 1830–32, when short stories constituted almost the whole of his output. The point is made that even the longest of B.'s novels started as single sentences, and that initial drafts were typically short, continuous narratives. The first half of his career was represented by a movement from short story to novel yet, during the second half, the development of short fiction continued alongside and within the novel. The relationship between shorter and longer fiction is shown to be at the heart of his work. Scott Lee, *Traces de l'excès: Essai sur la nouvelle philosophique de Balzac*, Champion, 180 pp., considers *Un drame au bord de la mer*, *Le Chef-d'œuvre inconnu*, *Adieu*, *L'Auberge rouge*, and *Melmoth réconcilié*. The excess to which the title refers is shown to be that of form over content and of signifier over signified. It is also representative of the fact that B. performs to the extreme in these texts, and that they allow him to evaluate the nature of the limits of subjectivity. Arlette Michel, *Le Réel et la beauté dans le roman balzacien*, Champion, 2001, 325 pp., sets out to demonstrate that B.'s poetics are connected with a number of complex ideas on the relationship between beauty, truth, and goodness. B. is shown to combine classical and modern æsthetic principles, maintaining a constant dialogue between hope and despair in *La Comédie humaine*. Paradoxically, his concern for beauty is part of an attempt to represent the whole of society, including the ugly. His total realism reconciles the subjective and the objective, equating beauty with truth and love. Allen Thiher, *Fiction Rivals Science: The French Novel from Balzac to Proust*, Columbia, Missouri U.P., 2001, 226 pp., includes the chapter 'Balzac and the unity of knowledge', noting that B. endorsed the view that knowledge is ultimately granted by a unified discourse, observing that the active critique of scientific disciplines in the novels is part of an ongoing debate, and showing his acceptance of the Newtonian-Laplacian view of post-Revolutionary science.

DUMAS PÈRE. Michel Cazenave, *Alexandre Dumas, le château des folies*, Saint-Cyr-sur-Loire, Pirot, 256 pp., is an account of the construction and subsequent disposal of the Château de Monte-Cristo, on the banks of the Seine. Although it can be described as a folly, it is shown to be a product of the same imagination which created *Le Comte de Monte-Cristo*. Daniel Zimmermann, *Alexandre Dumas le grand*, Phébus, 2001, 714 pp., is a revised version of the biography first published in 1993, extended by about 100 pages of new material. Daniel Compère, *D'Artagnan et Cie: Les Trois Mousquetaires, un roman à suivre*, Amiens, Encrage, 157 pp., returns to the most successful of D.'s novels. It begins with his early career, the ideas which formed the novel, and the events leading to publication. We are shown how D. turned the historical novel in a new direction, both in his representation of the period 1625–28 and in his narrative technique. There follows a survey of the novel's critical reception, from publication to the present. Close attention is then given to the numerous continuations, by D. and by other writers, and the novel's adaptation to the stage, to film, and even to cartoon strip. F. Wagner, 'Lire *Les Trois Mousquetaires* aujourd'hui', *Romantisme*, 115:53–63, argues for multiple readings of D.'s work, and discusses the possibility of a 'modern' interpretation of a 'pre-modern' text. R. Karpiak, *'Stanislaw Rzewuski and Alexandre Dumas: a case of convergence on the myth of Don Juan', *PolR*, 46, 2001:155–71. M. Prévost, '"Mesmer a vaincu Brutus": Alexandre Dumas' authorial stance on occult sciences', *RoN*, 42:205–13, discusses D.'s attitude to and representation of practitioners of the paranormal, with a nod to Barthes. Catherine Toesca, *Les 7 Monte-Cristo d'Alexandre Dumas*, Maisonneuve et Larose, 312 pp., is an account of all the phenomena in D.'s life bearing the name Monte-Cristo (the place, the boat, the château, the novel, the *feuilleton*, the play, the newspaper). K. Vassilev, *'Vengeance et récit dans *Le Comte de Monte-Cristo*', *FrF*, 26, 2001:43–66.

HUGO. *Victor Hugo, romancier de l'abîme*, ed. J. A. Hiddleston, Oxford, Legenda, xiv + 222 pp., begins with studies of the novels in chronological order: L. M. Porter, 'Politics, family and the authorial preconscious in Hugo's *Han d'Islande* and *Bug Jargal*' (4–22), considering traces of ambivalent thoughts and feelings which are partly expressed, and then repressed; F. Bowman, 'L'intertextualité du *Dernier Jour d'un condamné*' (23–40), on a number of possible sources; R. Killick, '*Notre-Dame de Paris* as cinema: from myth to commodity' (41–62), showing how successive film versions have reconstructed and extended the original story; J. Seebacher, 'Circonscription de l'abîme' (63–78), explaining the topographical references of *Les Misérables* as a function of H.'s personal reminiscences; F. Cox, ' "The dawn of a hope so horrible": Javert and the Absurd' (79–94), on the complex relationship between the police inspector and Jean Valjean; D. Gleizes, 'Genèse des formes: textes et dessins autour des *Travailleurs de la mer*' (95–118), showing the evolution of H.'s visual imagination in relation to the novel, with reference to his notes and drawings; K. M. Grossman, ' "Pleine mer, plein ciel": the wave of the future in *Les Travailleurs de la mer*' (119–36), linking the thoughts behind the two poems of the 'vingtième siècle' section of *La Légende des siècles* to the novel's vision of future freedom; E. Nœtinger, 'L'art du costume: *L'Homme qui rit* ou le drame de l'apparence' (137–55), on the use of images of clothing and disguise; Y. Gohin, 'Alternance et adhérence des contraires dans *Quatrevingt-Treize*' (156–78), on the frequent motif of juxtaposed contrasts, representing the consistency of absolute values. There follow two thematic essays: C. W. Thompson, 'Victor Hugo rôdeur de barrières et de frontières' (179–95), on H.'s fascination with borders and boundaries, perhaps due to his raised awareness of physical body limits and identity in relation to the rest of humanity; J. A. Hiddleston, 'Suicide in the novels of Victor Hugo' (196–211), treating suicide as a defining feature in H.'s novels.

Analyses et réflexions sur Victor Hugo, Quatrevingt-treize, ed. Franck Evrard, Ellipses, 192 pp., includes: C. Lieber, 'Parcours biographique de Victor Hugo: "Aimer, c'est agir" ' (7–14), setting the novel in the context of H.'s life and work; J.-C. Rouanet, 'Hugo face à l'Histoire et à la Révolution' (15–27), showing how his perspective of the Revolution was changed by the events of the Commune; D. Odier-Fraisse, '*Quatrevingt-treize*: dernier roman de Victor Hugo ou la Révolution revisitée' (29–36), on the historical background, the composition of the novel, the characters, the novel's intention and its subsequent impact; F. Evrard, 'Un humanisme critique' (37–38), introducing the second part, on the questions which the novel poses in respect of human progress beyond the Revolution, M.-H. Prouteau, 'Les armes de la non-violence' (39–47), evaluating H.'s management of the inevitable contradiction between revolutionary violence and concern for the human race; S. Alexandre, 'La paix ou la lumière qui luit dans les ténèbres' (49–57), showing that the novel's violence is fundamentally consistent with a pacifist viewpoint; F. Brin, 'L'incipit: une ouverture sur le rêve d'unité' (59–64), on the vision of unity presented in the first part of the novel; C. Horcajo, 'Les images du peuple' (65–72), on the image of the people taking charge of their own destiny; A.-G. Monot, 'Le personnage de Cimourdin' (73–78), on the character who represents most of all H.'s ideas on humanity; P. Andrès, 'Le grand homme dans *Quatrevingt-treize*' (79–85), a study of the character of Gauvin, in relation to Cimourdin and Lantenac; A. Tissut, ' "Connivence des hommes et des forêts": la nature entre guerre et paix' (87–96), showing the support which nature gives to the insurgents; A. Horcajo, 'Paternité et maternité' (97–103), on the portrayal of relationships between parents and children, and the way they are transferred to relationships between unrelated characters; C. Chevallier, 'Le sein' (105–14), showing similarities between the female sutler and the leading figure in Delacroix's *La Liberté guidant le peuple*; P.-L. Assoun, 'Fratricide et meurtre du père: le roman familial de la Paix' (115–23), on the way in which the novel reconciles Man's destructive nature with the search for peace; J.-P. Miraux, 'Du désastre de la guerre à la paix comme point d'horizon' (125–37), revealing H.'s vision of a peaceful world governed by the higher truth of the human soul; F. Evrard, 'Le roman en toute liberté' (139–40), introducing the third part, on the way H. sought to free the novel from formal constraints; A. Faucheux, 'Système et traitement des personnages' (141–52), analysing the role of the characters in the novel and the means of their portrayal; C. Durvye, 'Si vis pacem, narra bellum' (153–62), showing how far this account of civil war was intended as an argument in favour of peace; M. Lamart, '*Quatrevingt-treize*, un roman sur l'Histoire: reflet d'un feu lointain dans les miroirs de minuit' (163–69), concerning H.'s reflections on the nature of history; L. Mondor, 'Un "roi sans divertissement" ' (171–78), showing that H. freed himself from the constraints of history, rewriting it as necessary, allowing himself to dwell on preferred motifs and humorous moments; E. Seknadje-Askénazi, 'L'adaptation cinématographique de *Quatrevingt-treize* par Albert Capellani et André Antoine' (179–87), on the film which was begun in 1914 and finished in 1921.

Véronique Dufief-Sanchez, *Victor Hugo et le désir de savoir dans Quatrevingt-treize, La Forêt mouillée, La Fin de Satan*, L'Harmattan, 498 pp., relates the three works to H.'s relentless pursuit of knowledge as a paradoxical and subversive assault upon the formal world. *Quatrevingt-treize* becomes an account of a war between thinkers and the forces of ignorance,with history sweeping them into a situation in which they are powerless. The various stages of composition of *La Forêt mouillée* suggest that H. wished to confront the audience with an oxymoronic drama of creation. *La Fin de Satan* becomes a struggle to reconcile the Devil with a no-man's-land which eventually becomes impossible. The conclusion is an appreciation of H.'s attempts to grapple with the extremes of the human condition.

MÉRIMÉE. S. Carpenter, 'Supercherie et violence: Mérimée, ou le texte piégé', *Romantisme*, 116:49–57, is concerned with the numerous hoaxes in M.'s writing, which are shown often to be a representation of hidden violence.

SAND. Hortense Dufour, *George Sand la somnambule*, Monaco, Rocher, 484 pp., is a thorough and substantial biography which gives due attention both to S.'s views on the work of the writer and to the manner of her writing. Bernard Hamon, *George Sand et la politique, 'cette vilaine chose'*, L'Harmattan, 2001, 496 pp., is a thorough account of S.'s various political statements and interactions. David A. Powell, *While the Music Lasts: The Representation of Music in the Works of George Sand*, Lewisburg, Bucknell U.P. — London, Associated U.P., 2001, 381 pp., examines the ways in which S. defined her perceptions of listening to music, composing and performing, and how she made use of these ideas in her fiction. It is clear that music was important to her as a vehicle of communication between humans. *Consuelo*, which presents a model of the female musician, is shown to merit particular attention. S. Eilean Morrison, 'Restoring women's voice: feminist practice in the novels of George Sand', *RoN*, 42:187–95, discusses S.'s critique of gender inequity.

STENDHAL. K. M. Rabbitt, 'L'enfant libertine: pouvoir discursif et volonté narrative dans *Lamiel* de Stendhal', *NCFS*, 31:66–83, shows the strong links between *Lamiel* and its 18th-c. libertine precursors, drawing attention to the tension between the narrative models of the two different centuries. *AnS*, 1, includes: Y. Kasuya, 'Sur "fragments divers" de *De L'Amour*' (11–26), beginning with S.'s reception in Japan and ending with a plea for a critical edition of the work; U. Ono, 'L'art du parallélisme dans *Le Rouge et le Noir*, ou les deux ascensions de Julien Sorel' (27–44), showing that Julien's social ascension is surpassed by his progression to a point at which he truly becomes the hero of the novel; M. Matsubara, '*Les Noces de Figaro* et *Le Rouge et le Noir*' (45–56), identifying scenes in the novel which appear to derive from the opera libretto; K. Kajino, ' "Avec la vivacité et la grâce" ' (57–68), comparing Julien's first meeting with Mme de Rênal with the description of the meeting between Rousseau and Mme de Warens in the *Confessions*; M. Leoni, 'Stendhal et l'Italie, une "passion fixe" ' (69–81), on S.'s lifelong love of Italy, and the evidence of it in his writing; Y. Ansel, 'D'un nouveau complot contre la poésie' (83–102), explaining S.'s apparent dislike of poetry, or rather of the work of certain poets; J. Dürrenmatt, 'Énigmes intimes ou Stendhal crypté' (103–18), on S.'s frequent and fairly transparent encoding of information, a reflection of his attraction towards numerical classification; M. Décourt, 'A l'orée de l'œuvre de Stendhal, un roman par lettres' (119–56), on his early intention of writing an epistolary novel; M. Lavault, 'Les épigraphes d'Armance ou la "stratégie oblique"' (157–87), on the importance of epigraphs and their use to convey irony; S. Crippa, 'Au bal avec Stendhal' (189–206), on the ball which Julien Sorel attends at the Hôtel de Retz; S. Sérodes, 'Remarques sur un titre: *La Chartreuse de Parme*' (207–17), showing why S. chose to keep the title, despite Balzac's advice to abandon it; P. Laforgue, 'Son nom de Sandrino dans Parme déserte' (219–28), on the much-discussed Sandrino episode in *La Chartreuse*, reminding us that the original title was *Alexandre*, of which the diminutive is Sandrino, and identifying the character as the key to the novel; J. Houbert, 'Le dossier de presse de *La Chartreuse de Parme*' (229–53), explaining the limited critical response to the novel's publication, and the consequent importance of Balzac's contribution in the *Revue Parisienne*; S. Linkès, 'De *Letellier* à *Lamiel*, la comédie continue' (255–80), on the discovery of an early and very different version of the novel, dating from May 1839; H. Mattauch, 'Sur Henri Beyle, fonctionnaire de l'intendance, à Brunswick' (283–305), presenting some hitherto unpublished documents relating to S.'s work in Brunswick, from April 1807 to January 1808.

Stendhal journaliste anglais, ed. Philippe Berthier and Pierre-Louis Rey, Sorbonne Nouvelle U.P., 2001, 238 pp., includes: P. Berthier, 'Avant-propos' (1–4), introducing the subject of the articles written for the *Paris Monthly Review*, the *New Monthly Magazine*, and the *London Magazine*, from January 1822 to August 1829; Y. Ansel, 'Sociocritique stendhalienne' (5–19), showing that the 'chroniques anglaises' reveal a new way of approaching books, which takes into account the social environment of the reader; M. Arrous, 'Camarades et charlatans' (21–38), on S.'s *London Magazine* perspective of French literature as a product of a Parisian society based on vanity; B. Diaz, 'Paris-Londres: une comédie littéraire' (39–54), on a number of articles which take a satirical approach to the literary debates of the day; J.-L. Diaz, 'Manières d'être écrivain' (55–70), analysing S.'s role as a literary critic, exploring the standards which he used to assess the work of other writers, and suggesting that his activity as a critic helped to free him from literary convention and develop his originality; F. Spandri, 'Les *Chroniques pour l'Angleterre* et la question du comique' (71–90), finding that the attempt to understand the nature of comedy is a central strand; K. Gundersen, 'Les deux corps de la littérature' (91–98), considering S.'s appreciation of the difference between the political and the natural status of French literature; S. Esquier, 'La légende de Rossini dans le *Courrier anglais*' (99–110), on the far-reaching influence of the 1882 article on the composer; M. Reid, 'Shakespeare for ever' (111–24), tracing the path towards *Racine et Shakespeare* in *Paris-Londres*; R. Bolster, 'Stendhal et la réputation de Napoléon en Angleterre' (125–32), showing how the remarks on N. in the *London Magazine* may have been a reaction to what had been published elsewhere; M. Nerlich, 'L'Allemagne dans les contributions de Stendhal à la presse anglaise' (133–42), suggesting that S. was liable to severe misunderstandings concerning the Germans and German culture; J. Théorides, 'Les intérêts orientalistes de Stendhal' (143–62), which is mainly concerned with texts from *Paris-Londres*, but also refers to evidence of S.'s view of the Orient, which he never visited, before and after they were written; P.-L. Rey, 'Figures royales' (163–70), on the remarks in *Paris-Londres* concerning kings of France; P. Berthier, '"Mangeons du jésuite! Mangeons du jésuite!"' (171–88), explaining the reasons for S.'s reference to religious questions in *Paris-Londres*; E. Bordas, '"Censurer le style d'une duchesse": style et idéologie' (189–212), on the strong link in S.'s reviews between style and ideology; J. Dürrenmatt, 'Allusion et obscurité: violence et langage dans les chroniques stendhaliennes' (213–26), examining the nature and the import of S.'s critical discourse; A. Tibi, 'La joie d'écrire: le correspondant idéal' (227–36), giving attention to the form of S.'s contributions as correspondant, and underlining the air of liberty which is manifest in them.

A. Abassi, *Stendhal hybride, poétique du désordre et de la transgression dans Le Rouge et le Noir et La Chartreuse de Parme*, L'Harmattan, 2001, 222 pp., finds that the hybrid nature of S.'s heroes is no more and no less than a reflection of the human condition. The demonstration proceeds through commentary on four extracts from *Le Rouge et le Noir*, before comparing Julien with Fabrice in the second novel, an exercise which reveals a good measure of consistency. A chapter compares *Le Rouge et le Noir* with the painting by Delacroix of *La Liberté guidant le peuple*, before concluding that the function of the hybrid hero is to add coherence, yet the death of the hero represents a return to comparative normality. Lisa G. Algazi, *Maternal Subjectivity in the Works of Stendhal*, Lewiston, Mellen, 2001, vii + 231 pp., shows that S.'s theory of gender as something which was not entirely based on biological difference was no less than revolutionary. He could almost be described as a feminist. Attention is given to mother love in *La Vie de Henry Brulard*, traditional mother figures from *La Chartreuse de Parme*, *Lucien Leuwen*, and *Armance*, and the anti-mother in *L'Abbesse de Castro* and *Lamiel*, also with consideration of Gina del Dongo and Mathilde de la Môle, before describing the revolution of maternal desire in Clélia Conti and Mme de Rênal. Victor Del Litto, *Les Bibliothèques de*

Stendhal, Champion, 2001, 257 pp., represents a complete revision of the work which first appeared in 1980 as the preface to the *Catalogue du fonds stendhalien Bucci*. Much new material is added, and there is a list of the books owned by S. which have subsequently been preserved, along with an indication of their current location. Anne Hage, *Stendhal: deuil et symbolisation*, PUF, 2001, vii + 174 pp., is mainly concerned with *La Vie de Henry Brulard*. It begins with Freud's question, in the letter to Arthur Schnitzler in 1906, on the role of the public in artistic creation, and reveals an area of psychoanalytical enquiry in S.'s attempt to understand Henri Beyle's past through the autobiographical process. The conclusion is that S.'s literary creation is not unlike an act of mourning, transferred and addressed to the unknown readers of the future. Margherita Leoni, *Écrire le sensible, Casanova, Stendhal, Beckett*, L'Harmattan, 2001, 161 pp., includes the chapter 'Vertiges de la sensation: le spectacle impossible de Waterloo', returning to the description of the battle through the eyes of Fabrice in *La Chartreuse de Parme*. In fact, we are shown that Fabrice's perspective of the events is not the only one, for S. goes beyond this limited view in order to reveal the truth concerning the destructive nature of war. *Salons*, ed. Stéphane Guégan and Martine Reid, Gallimard, 213 pp., presents three of S.'s texts on painting: the first, as the original French has been lost, is reproduced from an English translation, and relates to the Salon of 1822; the second, 'Critique amère du Salon de 1824 par M. Van Eube de Molkirk', appeared in the *Journal de Paris* from August to December 1824; the third, 'Des beaux-arts et du caractère français', was a review of Auguste Jal's *Esquisses, croquis, pochades ou tout ce que l'on voudra sur le Salon de 1827*, appearing in the *Revue trimestrielle* of July 1828. The edition gives a valuable perspective of the novelist as art critic, and suggests that his expertise in this field may sometimes have been underestimated.

5. Drama

HUGO. S. Metzidakis and R. M. Young, 'Hugo, Shakespeare et l'enseignement des langues vivantes', *NCFS*, 31:9–26, identifies stylistic affinities between Hugo and Shakespeare, with particular reference to the drama, and demonstrates not only how H.'s admiration for S. helped to advance the cause of free public education, but also his firm belief in the value of foreign language learning for the Europe of the future.

VIGNY. N. B. Rogers, 'L'or du poète et l'or du financier: une lecture de *Chatterton*, de Vigny, avec Mallarmé', *NCFS*, 31:84–103, compares the significance of money, in relation to poetry, in *Chatterton* and in *Variations sur un sujet*, finding that the two raise similar questions regarding the convertibility of symbolic values.

6. Writers in other Genres

M. Leroy, 'La littérature française dans les instructions officielles au 19e siècle', *RHLF*, 102: 365–87, gives an interesting account of the evolution of the literary content of the school curriculum, before showing how the Romantics took their place there under the Second Empire. N. Preiss, 'De "POUFF" à "PSCHITT"!: De la blague et de la caricature politique sous la Monarchie de Juillet et après . . .', *Romantisme*, 116: 5–17, observes that this type of joke was an invention of military circles of the Napoleonic period, yet it spread to become an essential feature of 19th-c. French culture, and goes on to trace its history in publications such as *Le Charivari* and *La Caricature*. Peter Cogman, *Narration in Nineteenth-Century French Short Fiction: Prosper Mérimée to Marcel Schwob*, Durham U.P., ix + 202 pp., suggests that this was a genre which lacked confidence in its identity, tending to borrow its persona from poetry or theatre. Nevertheless, it establishes itself as a pole of disquiet against the 19th-c. novel's desire to explain, gaining potency by its ability to tell the story in a way which challenges preconceived ideas. Alain Vaillant and Marie-Ève Thérenty, *1836: l'An 1 de l'ère médiatique*, Nouveau Monde, 2001, 388 pp., is an interesting and exhaustive study of Émile de Girardin's *La Presse*. It shows the emergence of the author-journalist in an environment which allowed considerable freedom of expression.

DROUET. *Lettres familiales*, ed. Gérard Pouchain, Condé-sur-Noireau, Corlet, 515 pp., includes a total of 262 letters written by Juliette Drouet from 1850 to 1883, including those to the Hugo family, though not those written to Victor.

LUCAS. J.-F. Jeandillou, '"Mon très chier et très amé Euclides"', *Romantisme*, 116: 35–47, is concerned with the 27345 counterfeit letters produced by Vrain-Denis Lucas, who claimed them to have been handwritten by Cleopatra, Joan of Arc, Charlemagne, and others.

MICHELET. *Michelet entre naissance et renaissance (1798–1998)*, ed. Simone Bernard-Griffiths and Christian Croisille, Clermont-Ferrand, Blaise Pascal U.P., 2001, 373 pp., contains the proceedings of the bicentenary conference held at the Château de Vascœuil Musée Michelet in September 1998. It includes: S. Bernard-Griffiths, 'Michelet à l'épreuve du bicentenaire (1998): regards sur un moment de l'histoire d'une réception' (5–32), an introduction comparing the events of the bicentenary with those of the centenary, identifying M. as a strong supporter of the dialectical process, whose view of inevitable progress towards justice and freedom may now be in question, but whose unified perception of history is generally appreciated; C. Crossley, 'À propos de l'animal chez Michelet' (35–49), considering the chapter of *Le Peuple* dealing with animals and explaining the bases of M.'s attitude towards them; O. Haac, 'Michelet entre l'esprit et la matière' (51–75), examining variants of *La Mer* in order to explain M.'s philosophy concerning nature; E. K. Kaplan, 'La religion écologiste de Michelet: catéchisme, hagiographie, communion' (77–92), showing how religion and ecology were not, for M., contradictory terms, but part of his vision of the unity of the human race and the natural world; C. Rétat, 'L'aile et son héros chez Michelet: histoire naturelle et morale de la force' (93–107), on *L'Oiseau* and the way in which it renews the motif of inner strength, adding impetus to the series of works on nature; P. Laforgue, '*La Montagne*, ou révolution et fin de l'histoire' (109–27), asking how far this work of 1867 shares the approach of the three previous works of natural history, *L'Oiseau*, *L'Insecte*, and *La Mer*, and demonstrating to what extent it is different; M. Cadot, 'Les amitiés polonaises, russes et roumaines de Michelet' (131–49), on M.'s particularly strong friendship with Mickiewicz and Herzen, and his admiration for the Romanian people; I. Tieder, 'Michelet et les écrivains allemands' (151–62), on his visits to Germany, his familiarity with German culture, and the influence on his work of writers including Herder, Grimm, Schlegel, Fichte, Schelling, and Goethe; K. Oono, 'La réception de Michelet au Japon' (163–73), beginning with the translation of *Les Femmes de la Révolution* in 1948; C. Croisille, 'Regards sur la correspondance de Michelet' (175–93), on the valuable resource offered by the 1630 letters written by M. and the 3810 which he received from 1830 to 1851; R. Rioux, 'Gabriel Monod à la lumière de Jules Michelet' (195–223), on the importance of the relationship between the two and the various stages of its evolution; C. Harbaoui, 'Temps calendaire et temps légendaire dans *L'Histoire de la Révolution française*' (227–38), revealing M.'s awareness of the two different time scales in operation during the Revolutionary period; F. Laurent, 'Errance et nation dans l'*Histoire de France* et l'*Histoire de la Révolution française*' (239–71), on M.'s approach to defining and writing a national history; R. Mano, 'La fonction expiatoire de la mort dans l'*Histoire de France* au Moyen Âge: la fin de Charles le Téméraire' (273–87), explaining why M., who held that history was made by peoples and not by individuals, chose to dwell on the Duke's death; N. Roger-Taillade, 'Souffrances des peuples, passion de l'historien: les *Légendes démocratiques du Nord* dans le dialogue entre Jules Michelet et Adam Mickiewicz' (289–306), on the reasons why M. took risks with this work, and his debt to the Polish poet; M. Louâpre, 'Histoire de genèses, Michelet et les hors temps de l'histoire' (307–23), on the frequent treatment of the Genesis theme, which forms a link between the natural and the supernatural and serves as an historical model; V. Kogan, 'Michelet et le rôle public de l'intellectuel' (325–36), showing that M.'s stance marks the transition from the doctrinaire approach of 1820–40 to the role taken up by Zola at the end of the century; S.-A. Leterrier, '"La petite muse populaire": sur Michelet et la musique' (337–54), showing that, although M. made comparatively few references to music, his views on the subject were distinctive and original; R. Dalisson, 'Le centenaire de la naissance de Michelet: la République, la fête et l'historien' (355–70), on the association of the centenary and the bicentenary with the celebration of Republican progress. L. Le Guillou, 'Michelet éditeur', *TLit*, 15:83–88.

NERVAL. G. Kliebenstein, 'Une mystification absolue: sur le "souper de Cazotte"', *Romantisme*, 116:19–34, is concerned with Nerval's treatment in the *Almanach* and in *Les Illuminés* of the account by La Harpe of the prophecy of 1788 predicting certain events of the Revolution.

SAINTE-BEUVE. Michel Crépu, *Sainte-Beuve, portrait d'un sceptique*, Perrin, 2001, 263 pp., reminds us that, although Proust and others have led us to see him in negative terms, as one who set himself apart from Romanticism, this is not the best way of understanding him. If we look more closely at his life and work, we become aware of a high level of interaction with the literature of his time, though also a commitment to calm reflection and accurate synthesis.

THE NINETEENTH CENTURY (POST-ROMANTIC)

By Larry Duffy, *Lecturer in French, University of Ulster at Coleraine*

1. General

M. Brix, 'Pour un réexamen des cadres de l'histoire littéraire du XIXe siècle: l'opposition romantisme/réalisme', *SFr*, 45, 2001:268–83, argues against the imprudent use of categorizing terms, stressing that many authors routinely referred to as realists were nothing of the sort. L. M. Porter, 'The present state of nineteenth-century French Studies', *FR*, 75, 2001:1213–34, addresses transatlantic differences of approach in scholarship, and traces the development of and major achievements in the field during the 1990s. *TLit*, 15, ed. François Bessire, is on the theme of *L'Écrivain éditeur. 2. XIXe et XXe siècles*. L. Fraisse, 'Un théoricien en Sorbonne de la périodisation littéraire: Saint-René Taillandier d'après ses cours inédits (1843–1877)', *RHLF*, 102:771–88, discusses the literary historian's lectures and writings (for the *RDM*), and their continued relevance to literary periodization. L. R. Koos, 'Making angels: abortion literature in turn-of-the-century France', Grossman, *Confrontations*, 259–73.

Michael J. Dennison, *Vampirism. Literary Tropes of Decadence and Entropy*, NY, Lang, 2001, x + 156 pp., is a fascinating study of the trope of the vampire as figure of disorder in 19th-c. literature, particularly in terms of the 'root metaphor' of entropy. Authors studied include Gautier, Stoker, Poe, and Baudelaire, whose 'vampire' poems in *Les Fleurs du mal* are examined and their structural relationship with works by Poe. There is also a discussion of *fin-de-siècle* aestheticism as a 'disordering aesthetics'. Jean Bellemin-Noël, *Plaisirs de vampire*, PUF, 2001, iv + 213 pp., is a comparative study of vampirism in the work of Gautier, Gracq, and Giono, with a broadly Freudian emphasis.

S. Harismendy-Lony, 'Entre paraître et disparaître: le "testament" de Nina de Villard', *NCFS*, 30:81–91, discusses a poem by de V. (alias Callias, Manet's model for 'La Dame aux éventails'), from her *Feuillets parisiens*, and her literary salon. M. Leroy, 'La littérature française dans les instructions officielles au XIXe siècle', *RHLF*, 102:365–87, explores the curricular and critical politics of 19th-c. France. Laure Murat, *La Maison du docteur Blanche. Histoire d'un asile et de ses pensionnaires de Nerval à Maupassant*, Lattès, 2001, 424 pp. + 16 pl. is an account of a 'maison de santé' founded by Esprit Blanche and subsequently run by his son Émile (a contemporary of Charcot), which had a substantial number of famous literary patients, whose cases are discussed here. The book also says quite a lot about the contemporary perception of psychiatric illness and medicine. Alexandre Najjar, *Le Procureur de l'Empire. Ernest Pinard (1822–1909)*, Balland, 2001, 364 pp., is a biography of the prosecutor of (*inter alios*) Baudelaire and Flaubert, and contains accounts of the respective trials, as well as anecdotes about many other authors and their brushes with the law. I. Nières-Chevrel, 'Faire une place à la littérature de la jeunesse', *RHLF*, 102:97–114, is an account of youth literature up to the present day, highlighting the significance of the 19th c. in its evolution.

Prungnaud, *La Cathédrale*, examines the motif of the Cathedral in 19th-c. and 20th-c. literature, after a brief discussion of its medieval and 17th-c. antecedents. Along with an *Avant-propos* by A. Montandon and J.-M. Moura and an introduction by J. Prungnaud, it has a substantial section entitled 'L'invention de la cathédrale au XIXe siècle', containing, as well as articles on specific authors, the following: A. Ducrey, 'Le symbolisme ou les "cathédrales englouties" (125–35); J. de Palacio, 'La cathédrale décadente, monstre hybride et repaire de monstres' (137–45); J. Prungnaud, 'Nature et artifice: la Décadence et la doctrine romantique de la cathédrale gothique' (159–70). J.-M. Roulin, 'Mothers in revolution: political representations of maternity in nineteenth-century France', *YFS*, 101:182–200, reads representations of motherhood from a Freudian historiographical perspective. Dominic Rainsford, *Literature, Identity and the English Channel. Narrow Seas Expanded*, Basingstoke, Palgrave, is a cultural history of the Channel, examining its 19th- and 20th-c. manifestations in French and English literature, and arguing that it is the site of creation of a cultural space. G. Sicotte, 'Le luxe et l'horreur. Sur quelques objets précieux de la littérature fin de siècle', *NCFS*, 29, 2001:138–53, examines the motif of the luxury item in works by Huysmans, Bourges, Gourmont, Rodenbach, Rachilde, and Lorrain. I. Violante, 'Visions d'ateliers, atelier de la vision', *REI*, 47, 2001:63–79, examines Italo-Parisian artistic relations from the mid-19th c. to the First World War. Richard D. E. Burton, *Blood in the City. Violence and Revelation in Paris, 1789–1945*, Ithaca, Cornell U.P., 2001, 416 pp., is a thoughtful, thorough, highly entertaining approach to the theme of political violence at many junctures in the history of Paris, with substantial sections on 1848, the Commune, and the Dreyfus Affair. It considers historical developments in relation to specific Parisian locations, and discusses a range of literary and journalistic comment upon events.

2. Poetry

Patrick L. Day, *Saint-Georges de Bouhélier's "Naturisme". An Anti-Symbolist Movement in Late-Nineteenth-Century French Poetry*, NY, Lang, 2001, vi + 166 pp., charts one author's role in a much wider reaction to what were perceived as the elitism and hermeticism of symbolist poetry. As well as outlining the differences between the *naturiste* aesthetic and what it reacted against, the book also makes an important distinction between *naturisme* and naturalism (to which symbolism was in many respects itself a reaction), while acknowledging the key role and influence of Zola, whose endorsement of the *naturistes* B. sought and won, before the movement's demise with the arrival of Gide and others on the literary scene. S. Hartung, 'Formen und Funktionen der *obscuritas* in der modernen Lyrik: Baudelaire, Rimbaud, Mallarmé', *ZFSL*, 112:26–44, argues that the relationship between *perspicuitas* and *obscuritas* (the latter a defining feature of decadence) constantly changes throughout the late 19th c. *Les Arts de l'hallucination*, ed. D. Pesenti Campagnoni and P. Tortonese, Sorbonne Nouvelle U.P., 2001, 177 pp. + 16 pl., is a volume of essays on artistic, recreational, and 'scientific' representations of hallucination in the 19th c., and contains, among other articles, an introduction by M. Milner (7–13); T. James, 'Les hallucinés: "rêveurs tout éveillés" — ou à moitié endormis' (15–32); P. Tortonese, 'Au-delà de l'illusion: l'art sans lacunes' (33–49); M. Milner, 'Drogues, hallucination et décadence' (51–71); D. Pesenti Campagnoni, 'Les machines d'optique comme métaphores de l'esprit' (111–39); J. Rittaud-Hutinet, 'La magie et la peur: les premières projections publiques de cinéma en France (1896–1897)' (141–60).

Serrano, *Traditions*, explores intertextuality and cross-cultural transfer in poetry and writing about poetry, arguing that it is inaccurate in this context to talk of borrowing or appropriation rather than of 'forging' in its multiple senses (metallurgical, criminological, explorational). Throughout the book there is a focus on late-19th-c. French orientalism, often in relation to specific Persian, Arabic, or Chinese authors and French commentators. There are two chapters in particular devoted to Segalen and Mallarmé (see below). P. Sudan, *'Contribution à une histoire et à une rhétorique des cycles poétiques au XIXe siècle de Hugo à Mallarmé', *Versants*, 39, 2001:65–110.

BAUDELAIRE. *Baudelaire and the Poetics of Modernity*, ed. Patricia A. Ward, Nashville, Vanderbilt U.P., 2001, xiv + 230 pp., is a collection of articles based on a conference held in 1998, and deals largely with B.'s 20th-c. legacy. C. Pichois, 'Baudelaire écrivain-éditeur', *TLit*, 15:77–81. J.-C. Bailly, 'Prose and prosody: Baudelaire and the handling of genres', *Ward Vol.*, 124–33. S. Stephens,

'Contingencies and discontinuities of the lyric I: Baudelaire as poet-narrator and diarist', *ib.*, 134–43. A. Billone, '"Cette blanche agonie": Baudelaire, Mallarmé and the ice of sound', *NCFS*, 29, 2001 : 287–301, discusses 'Le Cygne' and M.'s 'Le vierge, le vivace et le bel aujourd'hui' in the light of Hugo Friedrich's *Die Struktur der modernen Lyrik*. M. Brix, 'Modern beauty versus platonist beauty', *Ward Vol.*, 1–14. Y. Bonnefoy, '"La Belle Dorothée", or poetry and painting', *ib.*, 85–97. E. S. Burt, 'Materiality and autobiography in Baudelaire's "La Pipe"', *MLN*, 116, 2001 : 941–63, considers the usefulness of materiality in reading B.'s poems. M. Deguy, 'To spear it on the mark, of mystical nature', *Ward Vol.*, 187–98. W. Franke, 'The linguistic turning of the symbol: Baudelaire and his French Symbolist heirs', *ib.*, 15–28. S. Godfrey, 'Strangers in the park: Manet, Baudelaire, and *La Musique aux Tuileries*', *ib.*, 45–60. P. G. Hadlock, 'The *other* Other: Baudelaire, melancholia, and the Dandy', *NCFS*, 30 : 58–67, explores questions of masculine desire in works by B., referring to the critical perspectives afforded by Freud, Kristeva, and Lacan. M. Miner, '(S)(m)othering Baudelaire', *Ward Vol.*, 157–71. L. C. Hamrick, 'Gautier as "seer" of the origins of modernity in Baudelaire', *ib.*, 29–41, examines contemporary definitions of modernity as much as the authors concerned. T. Raser, 'The subject of *Le Peintre de la vie moderne*', *ib.*, 61–71. K. Newmark, 'Walter Benjamin's depiction of Baudelaire', *ib.*, 72–84, examines the 'incognito' behind Benjamin's 'masks'. S. Blood, 'Modernity's curse', *ib.*, 147–56.

E. Marder, *Dead Time. Temporal Disorders in the Wake of Modernity (Baudelaire and Flaubert)*, Stanford U.P., 2001, ix + 222 pp., deals primarily with *Les Fleurs du mal* and *Madame Bovary*, but also contains much on the critical reaction to modernity by authors such as W. Benjamin. A. Jamison, 'Any where out of this verse: Baudelaire's prose poetics and the aesthetics of transgression', *NCFS*, 29, 2001 : 256–86, discusses the *Petits poèmes en prose*, *Les Fleurs du mal*, B.'s writings on the *Exposition Universelle* of 1855, Poe's poetics and B.'s translations, and Benjamin's writings on the works of B. V. Kelly, 'Suffering and expenditure. Baudelaire and Nietzsche in Char's poetic territory', *Ward Vol.*, 172–86. C. Krueger, 'Baudelaire's graphic details', *RoN*, 42 : 223–34, reads 'La Corde' as a challenge to the notion of visual representation. P. Laforgue, *'Sur la rhétorique du lyrisme dans les années 1850: "Le Flacon" de Baudelaire', *Poétique*, 126, 2001 : 245–52. Rosemary Lloyd, *Baudelaire's World*, Ithaca, Cornell U.P., xvi + 248 pp., sets B.'s poetry in its mid-19th-c. context. Ead., 'Baudelaire sonneteer: flare to the future', *Ward Vol.*, 101–23. R. Pensom, 'Le poème en prose: de Baudelaire à Rimbaud', *FS*, 56 : 15–28, argues tentatively, by way of a comparative analysis of 'Un hémisphère dans une chevelure' and 'Aube', for an evolutionary relationship between B. and R. Mario Richter, *Baudelaire. Les Fleurs du mal. Lecture intégrale*, Slatkine, 2001, 2 vols, 1705 pp., is, exactly as its title suggests, an exhaustive reading of the entirety of *Les Fleurs du mal*, in the order the poems appear in the work. Each reading is preceded by the poem in question. Id., 'Naturalismo e simbolismo di fronte a Baudelaire', *RLMC*, 55 : 257–64, examines B.'s legacy as manifested in naturalist and symbolist poetry. D. Sanyal, 'The object of poetry: commodity and critique in Baudelaire', Grossman, *Confrontations*, 158–73. Id., 'The tie that binds: violent commerce in Baudelaire's "La corde"', *YFS*, 101 : 132–49. L. Schneider, 'L'amour de l'apparence: Baudelaire, Nietzsche', *Romantisme*, 115 : 83–91, examines the respective Baudelairean and Nietzschean visions of art, as expressed in their works. A. Trouvé, 'Aragon lecteur de Baudelaire', *RHLF*, 101, 2001 : 1433–54.

CORBIÈRE. K. Lunn-Rockliffe, 'Voice-defying lyricism: Tristan Corbière's *Les Amours jaunes*', *FS*, 56 : 165–78.

HEREDIA. P. Hambly, 'Heredia et l'âge d'or: lecture de "Sur un marbre brisé"', *EFL*, 38, 2001 : 85–110, discusses H.'s sonnet and its intertextual links with Taine, Banville, Mallarmé, Leconte de Lisle, etc.

HUGO. P. Laforgue, 'Penser le XIXe siècle, écrire *La Légende des siècles*', *Littératures*, 45, 2001 : 169–79, examines the relevance of H.'s collection to the century in which it was written.

KRYSINSKA. F. Goulesque, 'Impressionnisme poétique chez Marie Krysinska: esthétique de l'ambiguïté et démarche féministe', *NCFS*, 29, 2001 : 318–33, places K.'s work in the context of scientific, philosophical, aesthetic and above all visual-art trends of the *fin de siècle*.

LAUTRÉAMONT. T. Hara, *'Répétition et univers poétique dans *Les Chants de Maldoror*', *ELLF*, 78, 2001 : 143–57. Bernard Marcadé, *Isidore Ducasse*, Seghers, 238 pp., examines L.'s work in the context of 20th-c. critical commentary on it. Leyla Perrone-Moisés and Emir Rodríguez Monegal, *Lautréamont. L'Identité culturelle. Double culture et bilinguisme chez Isidore Ducasse*, L'Harmattan, 2001, 108 pp., revisits L.'s work from the perspective of his Latin American background.

MALLARMÉ. *RTr*, 59, 2001, devotes a section to 'La langue de Mallarmé', which contains the following: F. Rouffiat, 'Mallarmé. Remarques sur les parenthèses' (157–66); M. Viegnes, '*Pas de vide nénie*. La poétique de la négation chez Mallarmé' (167–79); A. Girard, 'Le baiser murmuré. Mallarmé et la poésie amoureuse. Dématérialisation et désubjectivisation dans "Ô si chère de loin et proche de blanche"' (181–210); D. Bilous, 'Mallarmé, version française' (211–34); M. Sandras, 'La prose critique de Mallarmé ou l'éventement de la gravité' (235–54). E. Benoit, *De la crise du sens à la quête du* *sens*, Cerf, 2001, is a comparative study of Mallarmé, Bernanos, and Jabès. D. J. Code, *'Hearing Debussy reading Mallarmé: music après Wagner in the *Prélude à l'après-midi d'un faune*', *JAMS*, 54, 2001 : 493–554. Y. Delègue, 'Mallarmé, le sujet de la poésie', *RHLF*, 101, 2001 : 1423–32, considers M.'s break with tradition in terms of innovation in relation to subject matter. P. Durand, 'Auto/biographie. Le dispositif Mallarmé/Verlaine', *Littératures*, 44, 2001 : 97–119, discusses personal interaction and intertextuality between M. and Verlaine. S. Koban, **Mallarmés Schatten. Die Poetik Stéphane Mallarmés und deren Rezeption bei Yves Bonnefoy. Ein Gesprach über Dichtung und Sprache*, Bonn, Romantistischer, 294 pp. L. Lehnen, '"L'Art, ce souverain". Filiations et analogies entre les politiques poétiques de Mallarmé et de George', *RLC*, 76 : 277–99, explores links between M., Stefan George, Wagner, and Hölderlin. N. Lübecker, *'Le "triomphal renversement": le rapport entre esthétique et politique chez Mallarmé', *RevR*, 36, 2001 : 265–82. R. Lloyd, *'Mallarmé and the bounds of translation', *NFS*, 40, 2001 : 14–25. R. Serrano, 'Mallarmé's poetics of *Chine de Commande*', Serrano, *Traditions*, 184–222, considers the characteristics of M.'s work shared by classical Chinese poetry. B. Marchal, 'Mallarmé poète éditeur: le cas du *Coup de dés*', *TLit*, 15 : 351–59. D. J. Waldie, *'The ghost of an obsession: translating Mallarmé's *A throw of the dice will never abolish chance*', *Parnassus*, 26, 2001 : 180–213. H. Williams, 'Mallarmé and the language of ideas', *NCFS*, 29, 2001 : 302–17, explores the 'serious intellectual content' of M.'s work as anticipation of philosophical aspects of modern critical theory. D. A. Powell, '"La pénultième", or the next-to-last what? a musical approach to Mallarmé's "Démon"', Grossman, *Confrontations*, 144–57. G. Zachmann, 'Offensive moves in Mallarmé: dancing with *des astres*', *ib.*, 187–200. (See also BAUDELAIRE and ZOLA)

MICHEL. K. Hart, 'Oral culture and anti-colonialism in Louise Michel's *Mémoires* (1886) and *Légendes et chants de gestes canaques* (1885)', *NCFS*, 30 : 107–20, examines M.'s works in relation to the culture of the Kanak tribes in the New Caledonia of her exile, the Haute-Marne of her childhood, and the Commune of her political activism.

NERVAL. Jean-Paul Bourre, *Gérard de Nerval*, Bartillat, 2001, 182 pp., is an impressionistic biographical essay. Marc Froment-Meurice, *La Chimère. Tombeau de Nerval*, Belin, 2001, 201 pp., is in the same vein, though with more analysis of specific works by N. F. Endo, *'Rapports entre sonnet et texte en prose chez Nerval: cas des manuscrits 'rouges'', *ELLF*, 78, 2001 : 101–14. C. Erbertz, *'Der zerstuckelte Orpheus: weshalb man Gérard de Nervals *El Desdichado* als Beginn der modernen Lyrik lesen kann', *RZLG*, 25, 2001 : 339–56. J. Fornasiero, *'Fourierisme, politique et chimères chez Gérard de

Nerval', *RevR*, 36, 2001:59–80. S. Fujita, *'Gérard de Nerval et l'enchanteur Merlin', *Iris*, 21, 2001:163–72. R. Shattuck, *'Nerval and virtual reality', *Parnassus*, 25, 2001:391–402. B. Sosien, *'Les débris d'un monde éclaté: une lecture de Gérard de Nerval', *Iris*, 23:249–56. D. Wieser, 'Création théâtrale et sentiment d'identité: Nerval au miroir de Corneille', *RHLF*, 102:921–56.

RIMBAUD. O. Bivort, *'Les "Vies absentes" de Rimbaud et de Marceline Desbordes-Valmore', *RHLF*, 101, 2001:1269–73. Pierre Brunel, *Rimbaud*, LP, 288 pp., is a solid critical–biographical analysis, with firm emphasis on R.'s works rather than on psychological speculation and conjecture; it contains a bibliography, and an anthology of poems by R. and his contemporaries. Alain Jouffroy, *Rimbaud nouveau*, Rocher, 304 pp., is a collection of four essays on R. J.-J. Lefrère, *Arthur Rimbaud*, Fayard, 2001, 1243 pp. + 96 pl. is a fairly conventional literary biography, impeccable in its attention to documentary detail and containing a wealth of illustrations. E. Marty, 'A propos de "Sensation" d'Arthur Rimbaud', *Poétique*, 129:51–68, argues that R.'s poem's preoccupations are as metaphysical as they are sensorial. (See also BAUDELAIRE)

SEGALEN. R. Serrano, 'Segalen's poetics of stone and (s)hell', Serrano, *Traditions*, 146–83, reads *Stèles* against the background of S.'s writings preceding his journey to China, discussing (*inter alia*) his thesis on the representation of illness in naturalist fiction, and mentioning also Loti and Max Nordau.

VERLAINE. See MALLARMÉ.

3. Fiction

Peter Cogman, *Narration in Nineteenth-Century French Short Fiction: Prosper Mérimée to Marcel Schwob*, Durham U.P., x + 202 pp., explores the short form through analysis of stories by Mérimée, Barbey d'Aurevilly, Maupassant, Villiers, Schwob, Gautier, Balzac. A. Kotin Mortimer, 'Secrets of literature, resistance to meaning', Grossman, *Confrontations*, 55–66, discusses short stories including Maupassant's 'En Voyage'. *RLC*, 76, is a special edition entitled 'L'invention du roman pour la jeunesse au XIXe siècle', ed. and intr. by Isabelle Nières-Chevrel. Allen Thiher, *Fiction Rivals Science. The French Novel from Balzac to Proust*, Columbia, Missouri U.P., 2001, xii + 226 pp., examines the relationships with and attitudes to science of works by Balzac, Flaubert, Zola and Proust. The introduction represents a useful overview of 'literature's encounter with science', dealing with major scientific figures and discoveries and their representation by literature, and featuring by way of illustration the 'test case' of Stendhal. The most successful section on any one author is probably that on Flaubert and his use of ambiguity to undermine or at least challenge positivism. The section on Zola perhaps takes Z.'s narrator too seriously as being representative of the author's views. On the whole, though, this is a welcome volume.

BARBEY D'AUREVILLY. T. Kunieda, *'Le problème de la transmission orale de l'histoire et de la communauté dans les romans de Barbey d'Aurevilly', *ELLF*, 78, 2001 : 115–29. Fiona McIntosh, *La Vraisemblance narrative en question*, Sorbonne Nouvelle U.P., 364 pp., is a comparative study of the extent of the correspondence between fiction and reality in Walter Scott and Barbey. A. Frémiot, 'Crime et contamination dans "Le Dessous de cartes d'une partie de whist" de Barbey d'Aurevilly', Grossman, *Confrontations*, 30–41.

BERTRAND. L. Bonenfant, 'Aloysius Bertrand et les noms du genre', *UTQ*, 71 : 707–20, argues that the component parts of *Gaspard de la nuit* should be read as items of short prose fiction, and that in such readability lies the generically groundbreaking nature of the work.

BLOY. G. Guyot-Rouge, 'Léon Bloy lecteur de Juvenal: satire et compassion', *Littératures*, 44, 2001 : 121–39, identifies allusions in B.'s fiction and non-fiction to the classics, in particular to Juvenal's *Satires*. Ead., 'Byzance, la gloire et la boue', *RHLF*, 102 : 957–76, discusses B.'s reading of the Byzantine scholar Gustave Schlumberger.

CLADEL. L. Frappier-Mazur, 'Le discours épique et révolutionnaire dans *I.N.R.I.* de Léon Cladel', Grossman, *Confrontations*, 238–48.

DAUDET. N. White, 'Paternal perspectives on divorce in Alphonse Daudet's *Rose et Ninette* (1892)', *NCFS*, 30 : 131–45, considers D.'s novel in the light of the *Loi Naquet* of 1884.

FLAUBERT. *A Gustave Flaubert Encyclopedia*, ed. L. M. Porter, London, Greenwood, 2001, x + 381 pp., contains alphabetically arranged articles on personalities (writers, characters, public figures), historical events, Flaubertian preoccupations, and Flaubert criticism. Leclerc, *Bibliothèque*, consists firstly of a series of inventories, contemporary and recent, of F.'s personal library, and secondly of a series of critical articles on the general themes of the book, the library, and the inventory in his work. The section 'Inventaires', very specifically focused on Flaubert's library and posthumously inventorized belongings, contains: Y. Leclerc, 'Inventaires, mode d'emploi' (9–13); V. Maslard and J. Thébault, 'Catalogue de la bibliothèque conservée à l'Hôtel de Ville de Canteleu' (15–149); extracts from inventories compiled on F.'s death by the *notaire* Maître Bidault (151–56) and René Rouault de La Vigne (157–70); extracts from the catalogues of two 1931 auctions of property inherited and left by Mme Franklin Grout-Flaubert (171–80, 181–83); D. Fauvel,

'De Croisset à Croisset: itinéraire de la bibliothèque de Flaubert' (187–92); Y. Leclerc, 'Entretien sur la bibliothèque de Flaubert' (193–99); A. Dubois, 'La bibliothèque du Musée Flaubert et d'Histoire de la Médecine' (201–07).

A. H. Pasco, 'Trinitarian unity in *La Tentation de Saint Antoine*', *FS*, 56:457–70, explores the narrative contradictions of F.'s 'extravagant' work. É. Beaulieu, 'Silence et poésie chez Gustave Flaubert: une étude de *La Tentation de saint Antoine*', *EF*, 37, 2001:117–32. Mary Neiland, *'Les tentations de saint Antoine' and Flaubert's Fiction: A Creative Dynamic*, Amsterdam–Atlanta, Rodopi, 2001, 201 pp, explores genetic and intertextual relations between successive versions of *La Tentation de Saint-Antoine* and Flaubert's other fiction. Pierre-Marc de Biasi, *Flaubert. L'Homme-plume*, Gallimard, 128 pp., is a short, accessible compendium of manuscript facsimiles, photographs, and reproductions of works of visual art relevant to F.'s practices as a writer, with commentary on major works of F. and his contemporaries. E. Le Calvez, 'Bouvard et Pécuchet magiciens', *NCFS*, 29, 2001:100–37, is a genetic analysis (containing diplomatic manuscript transcriptions) of 'l'épisode de la magie' of chapter 8 of F.'s novel. I. Daunais, 'De "ceci" à "cela": les illuminations de Flaubert', *Romantisme*, 115:5–12, argues that the stained-glass window in Rouen cathedral which F. had wanted to include in a special edition of *Trois Contes* as illustration of *La Légende de saint Julien l'Hospitalier* can be read as illustration of all three stories in the work. S. Triaire, 'Paysager la mélancolie: rythmes flaubertiens pour un saint', *ib.*, 117:59–75, considers the theme of melancholy in Flaubert from a perspective partly informed by Kristeva, Deleuze, and Freud, using *La Légende de saint Julien l'hospitalier* as illustration.

M. Desportes, '*Hérodias* ou comment faire un cinquième évangile', Leclerc, *Bibliothèque*, 295–322. Florence Emptaz, *Aux pieds de Flaubert*, Grasset, 328 pp., is an interesting, original and witty study of the theme of feet, and everything pertaining to them (such as shoes, fetishes, and lameness) in F.'s work. Ead., 'Gustave Flaubert apprenti orthopédiste: de la bibliothèque paternelle à l'espace romanesque', Leclerc, *Bibliothèque*, 221–35.

R. A. Champagne, 'Emma's incompetence as Madame Bovary', *OL*, 57:103–19, uses Bourdieu's notions of the habitat and the hexis to interpret Emma's failure to live up to the expectations of society. H. Christiansen, *' "May I have this waltz?": *Madame Bovary* and *Nélida*', *DFS*, 55, 2001:40–52. S. Lee, 'Flaubert's blague supérieure: the secular world of Madame Bovary', *Symposium*, 54, 2001:203–17, examines the novel's implicit denunciation of religion and science. N. Sugaya, 'La bibliothèque romantique d'Emma condamnée par la bibliothèque médicale de Bouvard et Pécuchet', Leclerc, *Bibliothèque*,

237–47. S. Lubkemann Allen, 'Reflection/refraction of the dying light: narrative vision in nineteenth-century Russian and French fiction', *CL*, 54:2–22, deals with 'the dying consciousness in Russian realist fictions and their French subtexts', discussing, amongst other intertexts, the relations between Emma Bovary's death and that of Anna Karenina. J. Spires, 'Stylized ethnography? Emma Bovary's wedding(s)', *FS*, 56:345–58, examines Emma's *noce* and the ball at Vaubyessard as exemplars of the novel's ethnographical approach to provincial life. T. Bridgeman, 'Making worlds move: re-ranking textual parameters in Flaubert's *Madame Bovary* and Céline's *Voyage au bout de la nuit*', *LangLit*, 10, 2001:41–59. F. Ferguson, 'Emma, or happiness (or sex work)', *CI*, 28:749–79, might be described as a detailed study of completeness in F.'s novel. P. Gay, *Savage Reprisals*, NY, Norton, 192 pp., is a study of historical/factual reality in three realist novels, *Bleak House*, *Buddenbrooks*, and *Madame Bovary*; the section on the latter is entitled 'The phobic anatomist: Gustave Flaubert in *Madame Bovary*' (71–109).

Christophe Ippolito, *Narrative Memory in Flaubert's Works*, NY, Lang, 2001, xviii + 248 pp., explores the role of implicit cultural allusions in F.'s fiction and travel narratives, arguing that the key to their force and meaning lies less in plot than in memory of already-consumed cultural product. F. Lacoste, 'Éducation sentimentale ou éducation littéraire? (à propos de la première *Éducation sentimentale*)', Leclerc, *Bibliothèque*, 209–19. B. Donatelli, 'Flaubert: notes de lecture sur Taine', *ib.*, 279–94.; S. Dord-Crouslé, 'La face cachée de l'"impartialité" flaubertienne: le cas embarrassant de Joseph de Maistre', *ib.*, 323–46. P. M. Wetherill, 'Typologie de la lecture flaubertienne', *ib.*, 347–52. B. J. Leggett, '"A point of reference for the artist": Stevens and Flaubert, *CLS*, 39:223–39, examines intertextual relations between F. and Wallace Stevens, referring to Michel Riffaterre and Harold Bloom. Marshall C. Olds, *Au pays des perroquets. Féerie théâtrale et narration chez Flaubert*, Amsterdam–Atlanta, Rodopi, 2001, 266 pp., examines Flaubert's writings for the theatre in the light of his prose fiction. N. Rubino, 'Impotence and excess: male hysteria and androgyny in Flaubert's *Salammbô*', *NCFS*, 29, 2001:78–99, argues that F.'s coupling of hysteria and androgyny represents a trope of aesthetic modernity which emphasizes 'a dialectical process of empowerment and depletion, exaltation and fragmentation'. L. Nissim, '"Car j'y crois, à Port-Royal, et je souhaite encore moins y vivre qu'à Carthage". Flaubert lecteur de *Port-Royal* de Sainte-Beuve', Leclerc, *Bibliothèque*, 249–77. *Mémoires d'un fou/Memoirs of a Madman. Parallel translation and critical edition*, ed., trans., and introd. T. Unwin, LivOS, 2001, xxx + 89 pp., is the print version of a text available online at the LivOS website. Annette Clamor, **Flauberts Schreiblabor.*

Lesekultur und poetische Imagination in einem verkannten Jugendwerk, Berlin, Lang, 2001, 301 pp. (See also BAUDELAIRE and HUYSMANS).

FROMENTIN. Barbara Wright, *Fromentin. "Dominique"*, Glasgow Univ. French and German Publications, iv + 76 pp., is a clear exposition of F.'s novel.

GAUTIER. Jean Bellemin-Noël, *Plaisirs de vampire* (see above, p. 189), includes the chapter 'Gautier ou la fascination', dealing with Clarimonde in *La Mort amoureuse* and the female figures in *Omphale* and *Jettatura*. G. is shown to have made a singular contribution to the construction of the female vampire.

GONCOURT. P.-J. Dufief, 'Goncourt et Charpentier: le bibliophile et l'éditeur grand public', *TLit*, 15:89–101.

GOURMONT. G. Poulouin, 'Rémy de Gourmont: de *L'Ymagier* à la *Collection des plus belles pages*', *TLit*, 15:177–95.

GYP. Olivier de Brabois, **Gyp, Comtesse de Mirabeau-Martel, 1849–1932. Pasionaria nationaliste, homme de lettres et femme du monde*, Publibook, 353 pp. + 4 pl.

HUYSMANS. *Huysmans, à côté et au-delà. Actes du colloque de Cérisy-La-Salle*, ed. J.-P. Bertrand, S. Duran, and F. Grauby, Leuven, Peeters Vrin, 2001, vi + 505 pp., deals with new critical approaches to H.'s work, and with aspects of his work considered to be marginal. It contains: an introduction by the editors entitled 'A côté, au delà' (1–4); P. Berthier, 'La débâcle du genre' (5–32); P. Jourde, 'Huysmans, la structure et l'excès (33–64); F. Gaillard, 'Seul le pire arrive. Schopenhauer à la lecture d'*A vau l'eau*' (65–83); J. Dubois, 'Condition littéraire et marché sectuel dans *En ménage*' (85–103); P. Buvick, 'Fin de siècle et dégénérescence: Max Nordau lecteur de Huysmans' (105–20); C. Ridoux, 'Aspects du Moyen Age de Huysmans' (121–41); G. Sicotte, 'La chère et le verbe: une critique gastronomique de l'œuvre de Huysmans' (143–66); J. Paque, 'Belle affreusement: la femme dans l'art, un désastre sans remède' (167–85); M. Biron, 'Lettres d'un célibataire' (213–31); A. Guyaux, 'A propos des lettres de Huysmans à Verlaine et sur Verlaine' (233–44); S. Duran, 'Le Carnet vert: "Le plus émouvant alibi de la mort"' (245–77), F. Grauby, 'La faim, la femme, l'infini. Variations sur un manuscrit inachevé' (279–97); M. Lamart, 'Figures du Pierrot chez Huysmans: une voix blanche?' (299–335); G. Bonnet, 'Des ombres au tableau: mimesis et caricature', (337–59); C. Lloyd, 'Huysmans auteur comique' (361–78); J.-P. Bertrand, 'La parole de Des Esseintes' (379–94); C. Berg, '"A poisonous book": *A Rebours* dans *Le Portrait de Dorian Gray* d'Oscar Wilde' (395–412); P. Durand, 'Don pour don: Des Esseintes et sa prose' (412–40); N. Limat-Letellier, 'Enjeux de l'œuvre après la conversion' (441–61); B. Cabirol-Lacan, 'Le temps et *L'Oblat*' (463–80); J.-M. Seillan, 'Huysmans, après

L'Oblat: vers un nouvel à rebours?' (481–505). G. A. Cevasco, *The Breviary of the Decadence: J.-K. Huysmans's "A Rebours" and English Literature*, NY, AMS, 2001, xiv + 227 pp., consists of an *historique* of H.'s novel and the reaction to it, a discussion of decadence and aestheticism, and chapters on its influence on and/or appropriation by: George Moore; Oscar Wilde; Arthur Symons (coiner of the expression in the title); Aubrey Beardsley and Max Beerbohm; John Gray and André Raffalovich; Eric Stenbock and W. B. Yeats; James Joyce and Evelyn Waugh. A. Néry, 'Rouen, Bruges et Chartres: pierres poreuses des cathédrales chez Flaubert, Rodenbach et Huysmans', Prungnaud, *La Cathédrale*, 117–24. R. Ziegler, 'The seasons of the soul in J.-K. Huysmans's *La Cathédrale*', *NCFS*, 30: 148–60, considers links between natural cycles and spirituality in H.'s novel. A. Reid, 'Resisting documents: Huysmans's struggle to represent working-class women', Norman, *Documentary Impulse*, 79–95. M. Smeets, 'La proie et l'ombre. Durtal et la confusion gastro-sexuelle', *NCFS*, 30: 121–30, examines relationships between sex, food, and digestion in *Là-bas*.

LORRAIN. G. R. Heysel, 'Audacious modes and spectacular models: fashion in Jean Lorrain', Grossman, *Confrontations*, 131–43. Philippe Martin-Lau, ' "Et Narkiss se mira . . .": regard sur l'écriture hétéromosexuelle de Jean Lorrain', *DFS*, 61: 49–61, examines the theme of homosexuality in quite a wide range of L.'s works and in works by his contemporaries.

LOTI. A. Etensel-Ildem, *'La transformation de l'image de la femme turque dans les œuvres de Pierre Loti et de Claude Farrère', *Francofoni*, 13, 2001: 255–69. Edward J. Hughes, *Writing Marginality in Modern French Literature: From Loti to Genet*, CUP, 2001, xii + 209 pp., opens with a chapter on Loti's and Gauguin's appropriation of distant territories. A. Kawakami, 'Stereotype formation and sleeping women: the misreading of *Madame Chrysanthème*', *FMLS*, 38: 278–90, considers the *japonisme* of L.'s 1887 novel. Michael G. Lerner, 'Pierre Loti and Émile Vedel', *RoQ*, 48, 2001: 15–23, explores interpersonal and intertextual relations between L. and V.

LOÜYS. D. Zinszner, 'Pybrac et la Perle', *HLitt*, 3: 63–71, explores links between L.'s work and Victorian erotica. P. M. W. Cogman, 'Ambiguity and ambivalence in Pierre Loüys's *La Femme et le pantin*', *EFL*, 38, 2001: 40–61.

MALOT. Y. Pincet, 'Hector Malot, romancier de la jeunesse active et volontaire', *RLC*, 76: 479–91.

MAUPASSANT. P. G. Hadlock, '(Per)Versions of masculinity in Maupassant's *La Mère aux monstres*', *FrF*, 27: 59–79, explores monstrosity in M. via Freud, Barthes, and Judith Butler. L. Helms, 'Temps et scène intérieure dans *Notre Cœur* et dans *Un crime d'amour* de Bourget',

Littératures, 46: 124–40, compares the two novels, but does not argue merely for their similarity, as much criticism has done, but, as part of the project to rehabilitate M.'s later work, emphasizes the superiority of M.'s work over B.'s.

MIRBEAU. R. Godenne, 'Mirbeau nouvelliste', *LR*, 55: 67–73, sets M. in the context of fin-de-siècle short-story writers.

PROUST. Frank Rosengarten, *The Writings of the Young Marcel Proust (1885–1900). An Ideological Critique*, NY, Lang, 2001, xiv + 266 pp., discusses the ideological content of P.'s early fictional and critical writings in several contexts germane to it: the Lycée Condorcet, literary journalism, literary salons, personal (including sexual) relationships, P.'s aesthetic and philosopical development. It proceeds to an analysis of published critical and fictional work. T. Raser, 'The glory of the critic: Proust's preface to *La Bible d'Amiens*', Grossman, *Confrontations*, 80–87.

RACHILDE. Melanie C. Hawthorne, **Rachilde and French Women's Authorship*, Lincoln, Nebraska U.P., 2001.

SCHWOB. Agnès Lhermitte, *Palimpseste et merveilleux dans l'œuvre de Marcel Schwob*, Champion, 565 pp., is a substantial and highly systematic study of S.'s works, explored through the themes of intertextuality, parodic and self-expository appropriation of other short fiction, and appropriation of religious literature. S. Rabau, 'Inventer l'auteur, copier l'œuvre: des *Vies* d'Homère au *Pétrone* de Marcel Schwob', pp. 97–115, and J. Kany-Turpin, '*Lucrèce poète*, de Marcel Schwob', pp. 163–68 of *Fiction d'auteur? Le discours biographique sur l'auteur de l'Antiquité à nos jours*, ed. Sandrine Dubel and Sophie Rabau, Champion, 2001, 222 pp.

SÉGUR. C. Giachetti, *'Illustrating Ségur', *Neophilologus*, 85, 2001: 369–84. I. Nières-Chevrel, 'Terres étrangères, figures d'étrangers dans l'œuvre de la comtesse de Ségur', *RLC*, 76: 467–78.

VERNE. Jean Chesneaux, *Jules Verne. Un regard sur le monde*, Bayard, 2001, 298 pp., addresses the work and preoccupations of Verne through chapters focused on specific themes. D. Compère, 'Puff, bluff et humbug: de Barnum à Jules Verne', *Romantisme*, 116: 59–64, discusses the figure of Barnum in V.'s novels and short stories. Nadia Minerva, *Jules Verne aux confins de l'utopie*, L'Harmattan, 2001, 244 pp., examines Utopianism in V.'s work under 4 main headings: 'Îles' (dealing with journeys, islands, *Robinsonnades*, and the underground), 'Cités' (looking at real and imagined cities and their representation), 'Sociétés' (concerned with politics and social organization), and 'Avenirs' (exploring science-fiction issues). P. Schulman, 'The legacy of *Paris au XXème siècle*: eccentricity as defiance in Jules Verne's uneasy relationship with his era', *RoQ*, 48, 2001: 257–66, discusses the uncharacteristic scepticism about technology and progress displayed in V.'s recently discovered MS.

VILLIERS DE L'ISLE-ADAM. Jean-Paul Bourre, *Villiers de l'Isle-Adam. Splendeur et misère*, Les Belles Lettres, 194 pp., is an impressionistic biography of V. which does not contain much discussion of actual works. Chantal Collion Diérickz, *La Femme, la parole et la mort dans "Axël" et "L'Ève future" de Villiers de l'Isle-Adam*, Champion, 2001, 476 pp., explores the theme of (Greek) tragedy and the tragic heroine in the two works.

ZOLA. Colette Becker, *Zola. Le saut dans les étoiles*, Sorbonne Nouvelle U.P., 341 pp. This 'étude de l'esthétique de Zola' focuses on (and presents documents in relation to) various concrete themes, such as 'Méthodes de travail', 'Maîtres à penser et modèles', 'Invention/Logique/Expérience', '"Fantaisie", symbole, mythe', and in so doing provides a vivid account of what Zola was about. It also contains a discussion of the various attempts to define naturalism, and a representative sample of key Zola passages chosen for their relevance to key Zolian themes and preoccupations. Carlos Horcajo, *Le Naturalisme. Un mouvement littéraire et culturel du XIXe siècle*, Magnard, 160 pp. + 4 pl., although aimed at baccalauréat students (and their teachers), deals with the main issues of naturalism in a clear and simple way, and may be suitable for undergraduates encountering naturalist texts for the first time. The work contains an anthology of (often key) texts by all the major (and some minor) authors associated with naturalism, and plates of works by Manet, Caillebotte, Courbet, and Cézanne. S. Thorel-Cailleteau, *La Pertinence réaliste. Zola*, Champion, 2001, 217 pp., is a study of Z.'s work and naturalist aesthetics focused on the way in which the former resolves the apparent contradiction between lyricism and realist detail. E. Emery, 'The power of the pen: Émile Zola takes on the Sacré-Cœur Basilica' Norman, *Documentary Impulse*, 65–77 (incl. 4 pl.).

CNat, 76, is organized around two main themes, consisting of a 'Dossier littéraire. *Autour du "Rêve"*', and a series of articles entitled 'Intertextualités', preceded by a foreword by H. Mitterand (3–4). The first part contains: C. Becker, 'Le rêve d'Angélique' (7–23 + 8 pl.); J.-L. Cabanès, 'Rêver *La Légende dorée*' (25–47); S. Guermès, 'La "philosophie cachée" du *Rêve*' (49–65); K. Basilio, 'Angélique, entre Angèle et Angeline . . . Essai de ptéropsychologie zolienne' (67–83); O. Got, 'Le système des jardins dans *Le Rêve*' (85–96); C. Duboile, 'Les jeux spéculaires dans Le Rêve' (97–103); S. Disegni, 'La réception du *Rêve* en Italie entre les deux siècles' (105–19). H. Mitterand, 'Zola, l'Italie perdue et retrouvée', *REI*, 47, 2001: 89–98, looks at aspects of Z.'s relationship with Italy: his background, the Italian reception of the *Rougon-Macquart* novels, Italian motifs in his work, hostile reference to his origins at the time of the Dreyfus affair, his trips to Italy. D. Chaperon, 'L'autre cathédrale, *Le Rêve* d'Émile Zola et de Carlos Schwabe', Prungnaud, *La Cathédrale*, 99–116, contains (as indeed it discusses) illustrations by S. A.-C. Gignoux, 'L'essence de la bourgeoisie. De *Pot-Bouille* à *Passage de Milan* de Michel Butor', *CNat*, 76:127–44. P. Voilley, 'Musique et sexualité dans *Pot-Bouille*, *ib.*, 145–55. Frédéric Robert, *Zola en chansons, en poésies et en musique*, Liège, Mardaga, 2001, 216 pp., contains a wealth of fascinating (and often very amusing) contemporary songs, scores, and drawings taking Zola and his works as their subject. The essay analyses them in their historical context. S. Hiner, 'Paris pastoral: re-figuring anarchy in Zola's fin de siècle', Grossman, *Confrontations*, 248–58. C. Wilson, '*Une Page d'amour*: un panorama politique', *CNat*, 76:177–91.

L. Jouannaud, 'Des romans pour les Rougon-Macquart', *CNat*, 76:193–207. C. Loreaux-Kubler, 'Le monde intertextuel: un monde à part?', *ib.*, 209–19. M.-S. Armstrong, 'Hugo à l'aire Saint-Mittre: Zola et la problématique de la propriété littéraire', *FR*, 76:346–57, examines the relationship of Z.'s work to H.'s, specifically in the context of literary appropriation. The principal text studied is *La Fortune des Rougon*. Y. Bargues Rollins, '*Le Ventre de Paris* de Zola: il y a eu un mort dans la cuisine', *NCFS*, 30:92–106, examines the significance of rumours in Z.'s novel. Olivier Got, *Les Jardins de Zola. Psychanalyse et paysage mythique dans "Les Rougon-Macquart"*, L'Harmattan, 255 pp., is a study of the theme of the garden in Z.'s cycle, focusing primarily on *La Faute de l'abbé Mouret*, *La Fortune des Rougon*, *Le Rêve*, *La Curée* and *Le Docteur Pascal*. S. S. Hennessy, 'Killing off the mothers', *Neophilologus*, 86:215–23, examines women's deaths (figurative and actual) in the *Rougon-Macquart* novels as indices of male attempts to appropriate the female reproductive function. S. Huebner, *'Zola the Sower', *MusL*, 83:75–105. J. Loehr, '*L'Assommoir* de Zola, les *Croquis parisiens* de Huysmans: un changement d'optique', *RHLF*, 102:211–39, is a comparative study of the theme of vision in the two works. M. E. Bloom, 'The aesthetics of guilt: crime scenes and punitive portraits in Zola's *Thérèse Raquin*', *DFS*, 58:26–38, looks at theatrical and visual aspects of Z.'s novel, particularly in relation to the fantastic. D. Walker, 'Writing between fait divers and procès-verbal', *FrCS*, 12, 2001:237–51, discusses the crimes committed in *Thérèse Raquin* and *La Bête humaine* in the light of the writings of Barthes and others.

4. Non-Fictional Prose

P. Cooke, 'Critique d'art et transposition d'art: autour de *Galatée* et d'*Hélène* de Gustave Moreau (Salon de 1880)', *Romantisme*, 118:37–53, discusses critical reaction to M.'s works and its literary resonances. C. Bompaire-Evesque, 'Le procès de la rhétorique dans l'enseignement supérieur français à la fin du XIXe siècle', *RHLF*, 102:389–404, discusses political and legal aspects of French higher education in relation to the ending of the teaching of rhetoric.

ALEXIS. S. Disegni, 'Paul Alexis — Trublot: du vrai et du faux dans le naturalisme', *Romantisme*, 116:85–96, discusses Alexis's pseudonymic critical writings on naturalism, which very often relied on hoax and fabrication, but were none the less successful in disseminating the 'principles' of naturalism to a wide audience. (See also ZOLA.)

BAUDELAIRE. M. Breatnach, 'Writing about music. Baudelaire and *Tannhäuser* in Paris', Bernhart, *Song Cycle*, 49–63. J. Duprilot, 'Les souvenirs de Lorédan Larchey sur Baudelaire', *HLitt*, 3:51–62, uncovers the writings on B. of a 19th-c. archivist at the Arsénal.

BLOY. Léon Bloy, *Les Funérailles du Naturalisme*, ed. and intr. Pierre Glaudes, Les Belles Lettres, 2001, lxxxviii + 271 pp., includes a substantial introduction by P. Glaudes situating B.'s writings on naturalist authors in the context of late-19th-c. literary polemics.

BOURGET. See MAUPASSANT.

BRISSET. Walter Redfern, *All Puns Intended. The Verbal Creation of Jean-Pierre Brisset*, Oxford, Legenda, 2001, is a wonderful account of J.-P. Brisset (1837–1919), a 19th-c. autodidact, amateur linguist, theologian, sexologist, and (strictly in the scientific sense) naturalist. It is as an all-round *fou littéraire* and punster that B. is remembered, and this book, which shares his 'punophilia', argues that the madness of his writings should not lessen their literary value or interest.

COMTE. G. Chabert, 'Michel Houellebecq, lecteur d'Auguste Comte', *RevR*, 37:187–204, discusses allusions and explicit references to Comte's work in H.'s fiction, particularly in *Les Particules élémentaires*.

DREYFUS. S. Rubin Suleiman, 'Entre histoire et "roman de concierge": l'affaire Dreyfus dans l'imaginare populaire des années 1930', *CNat*, 76:157–76 (+ 4 pl.). E. Cahm, 'Moderate anti-Dreyfusism: the forgotten ideology of France's republican élite in 1898', Grossman, *Confrontations*, 203–15. E. G. Carlston, 'Secret dossiers: sexuality, race, and treason in Proust and the Dreyfus affair', *MFS*, 48:937–68, explores parallels between representations of homosexuality and Jewishness, focusing on Proust's representation of the Dreyfus affair. V. Duclert, 'Le procès Zola en 1898: l'accomplissement de "J'Accuse . . .!", Grossman, *Confrontations*, 216–37. C. E. Forth, 'Adventures of the naked truth: the Dreyfus affair and the female form', *FrCS*, 12, 2001:123–47, examines the *Affaire* from the perspective of gender, arguing that there was a specifically sexual politics attending it. It discusses activism and writing by women, as well as caricatures (by cartoonists on both sides) exploiting female stereotypes. J.-Y. Mollier, 'La propagande dreyfusarde et antidreyfusarde en France de 1894 à 1900', Grossman, *Confrontations*, 274–86. M. Perrot, '*La Fronde* des femmes au temps de l'Affaire Dreyfus', *ib.*, 287–300.

GAUTIER. J. B. Bullen, 'Ruskin, Gautier, and the feminization of Venice', pp. 64–85 of *Ruskin and Gender*, ed. D. Birch and F. O'Gorman, Basingstoke, Palgrave, ix + 211 pp., compares R.'s *Stones of Venice* and G.'s *Italia* as influential figurations of Venice. J. Patty, *'Théophile Gautier et Tannhaüser: une lecture baudelairienne', *BBaud*, 36, 2001 : 71–79.

LAZARE. *Figures contemporaines. Ceux d'aujourd'hui, ceux de demain*, ed. Hélène Millot, Grenoble U.P., 174 pp., a reissue of L.'s essays on major contemporary figures first published in *Le Figaro* in 1894, contains a substantial introduction by H. Millot entitled 'Bernard Lazare et la jeune critique fin de siècle' (9–31). Jean Philippe, *Bernard Lazare tel que Péguy l'aimait*, L'Agasse, 2001, 157 pp., is an account of the friendship between Péguy and an author whose campaigning journalism on the Dreyfus affair was somewhat eclipsed by Zola's.

MALLARMÉ. P. Dayan, 'Do Mallarmé's *Divagations* tell us not to write about musical works?', Bernhart, *Song Cycle*, 65–80. H. Williams, 'Mallarmé's early correspondence: the language of crisis', *RoS*, 19 : 148–59, reads M.'s letters as text rather than as exegetical tool, arguing not so much for their relevance to his poetry, but for their meaning in relation to other lexical contexts.

MIRBEAU. Sylvie Thiéblemont-Dollet, *Octave Mirbeau. Un journaliste faiseur d'opinion*, Nancy U.P., 2001, 108 pp., is a well-documented study of M.'s journalism.

NERVAL. H. Mizuno, 'Nerval, écrivain de la vie moderne, et la peinture flamande et hollandaise', *RHLF*, 102 : 601–16, argues tentatively for an appraisal of N. as interpreter of modernity, analysing his art criticism by way of analogy with Baudelaire's *Le Peintre de la vie moderne*.

RENOUVIER. L. Fedi, 'Philosophiser et républicaniser: la *Critique philosophique* de Renouvier et Pillon, 1872–1889', *Romantisme*, 115 : 65–82.

SAINTE-BEUVE. P. Laforgue, 'Tirésias, ou Sainte-Beuve, la critique et le féminin dans les *Portraits de femmes*', *Romantisme*, 115 : 25–39, discusses La Rochefoucauld and the feminine in S.-B.'s work. E. G. Marantz, *'Encore du Sainte-Beuve: Proust, Sainte-Beuve et les salons' *RLMod*, 2001 : 63–74. B. G. Rogers, *'Proust et Barbey d'Aurevilly contre Sainte-Beuve', *ib.*, 167–77. (See also FLAUBERT.)

TAINE. J.-P. Guillerm, 'Le dôme et ses fantasmes. Quelques cathédrales byzantines visitées par Gautier, Taine et Ruskin

(1849–1867)', Prungnaud, *La Cathédrale*, 77–86. P. Seys, *'Le naturalisme esthétique de Taine: entre positivisme et idéalisme', *Dialogue*, 40, 2001:311–42. (See also FLAUBERT.)

VALLÈS. Jules Vallès, *Les Victimes du Livre. Écrits sur la littérature*, ed. and intr. Denis Labouret, La Chasse au Snark, 2001, 338 pp., is a welcome collection of V.'s often polemical literary journalism, containing classics such as the infamous denunciation of Edmond de Goncourt, 'L'Académie des Dix'. Labouret's introduction (7–25) discusses V.'s work in the context of polemical writing.

ZOLA. N. Benhamou et V. Gramfort, 'Quand le jeune Zola monte un canular . . .', *Romantisme*, 116:65–84, is an account of a journalistic hoax in which Z. participated whereby poems written by Paul Alexis were passed off as Baudelaire's. M. N. Richards, '1898: poetry on strike, prose in the papers', Grossman, *Confrontations*, 301–11, contrasts the respectively offensive and defensive modes of writing of Zola and Mallarmé.

5. Theatre

J. A. Simpson, 'Defiant acts: the *Théâtre d'Art*, décor, and the radical Symbolist "total work", Grossman, *Confrontations*, 174–86 (+ 4 pl.). N. White, 'The name of the divorcée: Janvier and Ballot's theatrical critique, *Mon Nom!* (1892)', *RoQ*, 49:215–27, examines J. and B.'s comic trilogy *Les petits côtés du divorce* (1892–95) in relation to the 1884 Loi Naquet. L. Goehr, *'Radical modernism and the failure of style: philosophical reflections on Maeterlinck-Debussy's *Pelléas et Mélisande*', *Representations*, 74, 2001:55–82.

THE TWENTIETH CENTURY 1900–1945

POSTPONED

THE TWENTIETH CENTURY SINCE 1945

POSTPONED

FRENCH CANADIAN LITERATURE

By Christopher Rolfe, *Senior Lecturer in French, University of Leicester*

I. General

So-called 'écriture migrante' is of growing significance in today's Quebec and is attracting more and more critical attention, not least because it reflects a crucial metamorphosis in the Quebec sense of identity. Of course, such a process is not specific to Quebec but, for a variety of reasons, it is perhaps being felt more keenly there. Indeed, S. Harel, 'Entre solitude essentielle et sentiment d'appartenance. Résistances à l'intégration et subversion littéraire', pp. 125–32 of *Définir l'intégration? Perspectives nationales et représentations symboliques*, ed. Yannick Resch, Montreal, XYZ, 2001, 167 pp., makes this very point with some acuity when he refers to Quebec literature's 'démesure à faire de l'écrivain interculturel le porte-parole des impasses identitaires qui traversent une société en mutation'. The same volume includes a second excellent essay on the topic: L. Lequin, 'Les écrivaines migrantes et la troisième solitude' (149–58) which discusses the likes of Nadine Latif, Régine Robin, Bianca Zagolin, and Mona Latif-Ghattas. Harel and Lequin also have contributions in *D'autres rêves. Les écritures migrantes au Québec*, ed. Anne de Vaucher Gravili, Venice, Supernova, 2000, 185 pp., a collection of papers first given at a conference in Venice in 1999. Other contributors include migrant authors of the stamp of Régine Robin, Marco Micone, Abla Farhoud, and Anthony Phelps (a particularly incisive deconstruction of the very concept of 'écriture migrante'). Clément Moisan and Renate Hildebrand, **Ces étrangers du dedans. Une histoire de l'écriture migrante au Québec (1937–1997)*, Quebec, Nota bene, 2001, 364 pp., and D. Chartier, 'Les origines de l'écriture migrante. L'immigration littéraire au Québec au cours des deux derniers siècles', *VI*, 27:303–16, remind us that the contribution to Quebec literary life made by immigrant writers is by no means just a recent phenomenon.

Jules Tessier, *Américanité et francité. Essais critiques sur les littératures d'expression française en Amérique du Nord*, Ottawa, Le Nordir, 2001, 212 pp., brings together nine essays published elsewhere over the past ten years. Pieces on two writers associated with Western Canada — Maurice Constantin-Weyer (117–53) and Ronald Lavallée (193–204) — are particularly worthwhile. *Le Grand Récit des Amériques. Polyphonie des identités culturelles dans le contexte de la continentalisation*, ed. Donald Cuccioletta, Jean-François Côté, and Frédéric Lesemann, Quebec, IQRC–PUL, 2001, 194 pp., makes for good general reading but is recommended especially here for the essay by M. van Schendel,

'Un Québec francopolyphonique: la langue française parmi d'autres'. *Frontières flottantes/Shifting Boundaries. Lieu et espace dans les cultures francophones du Canada*, ed. Jaap Lintvelt and François Paré, Amsterdam, Rodopi, 2001, 260 pp., is a volume whose title is little more than a catch-all under which a variety of themes, approaches and definitions jostle. No matter: many of the 18 essays included are excellent. Marc Lescarbot, Louis Caron, André Langevin, Jacques Godbout, Louis Hamelin, Ying Chen, Jacques Poulin, and Anne Hébert figure among the authors discussed. Especially interesting are the contributions by M. Cardy, 'Place and space in two eighteenth-century French texts' (49–59) and D. Parris, 'Les frontières flottantes du cerveau: bilinguisme et identité dans le roman québécois' (125–33). *Literatura francocanadiense: la literatura quebequesa*, ed. Carmen Fernández Sanchez, Oviedo U.P., 2001, 340 pp., is a multi-authored, nicely detailed overview. Robert Lahaise, *Canada-Québec. Entrouverture au monde 1896–1914*, Outremont, Lanctôt, 258 pp., continues L.'s major historical-literary synthesis. The second chapter (47–61) has some valuable comments on *terroirisme*, *exotisme*, and the Ecole littéraire de Montréal. Gilles Pellerin, *La Mèche courte. Le français, la culture et la littérature*, Quebec, L'Instant même, 141 pp., tackles, amongst other issues, the psychological and sociological aspects of Quebec literature and lambasts what it considers to be the timidity of a certain cultural elite. *Les Cultures du monde au miroir de l'Amérique française*, ed. Monique Moser-Verrey, Quebec, Laval U.P., 234 pp., includes three essays of interest to literature specialists: N. Courcy, 'La culture haïtienne au Québec: interaction ou confrontation? Etude de la réception critique de l'œuvre de Dany Laferrière' (53–66); M. C. Huot, 'Un itinéraire d'affiliations: l'écrivaine francophone Ying Chen' (71–89); and N. Marcoux, 'Le triptyque autobiographique de Michel Tremblay: un peu de soi et des autres' (91–106). T. C. Spear, 'La plume bifide, le cœur québécois. L'usage de l'anglais chez les écrivains québécois francophones', *Globe*, 4, 2001:71–91, is an interesting piece on the implications of the trend amongst many Quebec writers to incorporate English into their texts. H. R. Runte, '"Maudit(e)s étranger(e)s"? Les apatrides de la francophonie nord-américaine', *DFS*, 59:130–43, is a spirited but ultimately rather futile polemic on writers/writing from francophone minorities.

B. T. Freiwald, 'Nation and self-narration: a view from Québec/Quebec', *CanL*, 172:17–38, addresses the political, critical, and autobiographical discourses implicated in the mutual articulation of self and nation. *VI*, 27.2, has a useful dossier on 'La sociabilité littéraire'. Of particular interest are: M. Brunet, 'Prolégomènes à une méthodologie d'analyse des réseaux littéraires. Le cas de la correspondance de Henri-Raymond Casgrain' (216–37), and C. Savoie,

'Des salons aux annales: les réseaux et associations des femmes de lettres à Montréal au tournant du XXe siècle' (238–53), which brings out the value of networks in the development of women's writing. *Doing Gender: Franco-Canadian Women Writers of the 1990s*, ed. Paula Ruth Gilbert and Roseanna L. Dufault, Madison, Fairleigh Dickinson U.P., 2001, 396 pp., is an impressive collection of essays on a wide range of women writers (from Hébert, Brossard, and Théoret to Laberge, Lise Tremblay, and Ying Chen) and the wide range of issues they address (such as ethnic identity, space and gender, death, exile, and loss). Milena Santoro, **Mothers of Invention: Feminist Authors and Experimental Fiction in France and Quebec*, Montreal, McGill–Queen's U.P., xii + 348 pp. M. Rosario Martin Ruano, 'Feminismo, escritura, traducción: la experiencia de lo femenino en la literatura canadiense actual', *L'Erable. Apuntes de civilización y cultura canadiense*, 2, 2001:65–87.

P. Rajotte, 'The Self and the Other: Quebec travellers in the Middle East at the end of the nineteenth century', *CanL*, 174:98–115, provides insight into how Quebec travel accounts of the Holy Land tend to use otherness to reinforce a Catholic and French identity. Yvan Lamonde and Marie-Pierre Turcot, *La Littérature personnelle au Québec (1980–2000)*, Montreal, Bibliothèque nationale, 2000, 100 pp., is a valuable bibliography that supplements L.'s *Je me souviens. La littérature personnelle au Québec (1860–1980)* of 1983. *Bibliography of Comparative Studies in Canadian, Quebec and Foreign Literatures 1930–1995*, ed. Antoine Sirois, Sherbrooke, GGC, 2001, 293 pp., is a useful research tool. Mansour Dramé, *L'Interculturalité au regard du roman sénégalais et québécois*, L'Harmattan, 2001, 303 pp. There is a case to be made for comparing the literatures of such disparate countries but this study does not make it.

Stéphanie Nutting, *Le Tragique dans le théâtre québécois et canadien-français, 1950–1989*, Lewiston, Mellen, 2000, 182 pp., covers works by Marcel Dubé, Michel Tremblay, Jean Marc Dalpé, Pol Pelletier, and Normand Chaurette. Janusz Przychodzen, *Vie et mort du théâtre au Québec. Introduction à une théâtritude*, L'Harmattan, 2001, 431 pp., is a massive, comprehensive survey of what constitutes Quebec theatre (in all the senses of the term). This is a work of intellectual vigour and subtlety, as its final sentence amply demonstrates: 'Car enfin si le théâtre au Québec ne peut s'affirmer qu'aux dépens du théâtre québécois, c'est parce que dans le théâtre au Québec on se heurte irrémédiablement et continuellement au Québec dans le théâtre'. Louis Francœur, **Le Théâtre brèche: essai*, Montreal, Triptique, 231 pp., deals with semiotics and theatre in Quebec. Marc-Aimé Guérin and Réginald Hamel, *Dictionnaire des poètes d'ici de 1606 à nos jours*, Montreal, Guérin, 2001, xiv + 1057 pp., is an invaluable reference book.

Michel Muir, *A l'assaut de la poésie*, Montreal, Varia, 2001, 253 pp., is a lively polemic that targets all poetry, not just French Canadian poetry. Still, M. reserves some of his sharpest judgements for the latter, e.g. 'l'aplaventrisme a succédé au nationalisme et au formalisme. On ne saurait trop mesurer son incidence dans la littérature d'expression française en Amérique.' *Poèmes à dire la francophonie. 38 poètes contemporains*, ed. Nicole Brossard, Bordeaux, Le Castor Astral, 157 pp., is an anthology of francophone poets with French Canadians well represented.

2. Individual Authors

AQUIN. Anthony Soron, *Hubert Aquin ou la révolte impossible*, L'Harmattan, 2001, 316 pp., deliberately sets out to make A. accessible to a non-Québécois readership, one unfamiliar with either the novelist or the recent history of Quebec. However, the study will perhaps still be of value to the initiated. B. Faivre-Duboz, 'Au croisement de la culture et du politique. Pierre Elliot Trudeau et Hubert Aquin face à l'Etat-nation', *Globe*, 4, 2001 : 11–27, examines different aspects of A.'s response, 'La fatigue culturelle du Canada français', to T.'s 1962 'La nouvelle trahison des clercs'. Jean-Christian Pleau, **La Révolution québécoise: Hubert Aquin et Gaston Miron au tournant des années soixante*, Montreal, Fides, 270 pp. Gordon Sheppard and Andrée Yanacopoulo, *Signé Hubert Aquin. Enquête sur le suicide d'un écrivain*, Saint Laurent, Bibliothèque québécoise, 491 pp., is a new edition of the 1985 study that seeks to understand why A. killed himself.

ASSELIN. Hélène Pelletier-Baillargeon, *Olivar Asselin et son temps. Le volontaire*, Montreal, Fides, 2001, 320 pp. This second volume of P.-B.'s splendid biography concentrates on the distinctive (and troubled) role played by A. in the Great War, but does shed light on aspects of his literary career, in particular his passion for Charles Péguy, Léon Bloy, and Nietzsche.

AUBERT DE GASPE. Louis Lasnier, *Les Noces chymiques de Philippe Aubert de Gaspé dans 'L'Influence d'un livre'*, Sainte-Foy, Laval U.P., 328 pp., is at once a fine biography and an insightful study of the novel born of his run-in with the *Patriotes* leaders.

AUBIN. L. Villeneuve, 'Le fantasque de Napoléon Aubin: mutation du genre utopique et jeux de mascarades', pp. 145–71 of *Utopies en Canada (1545–1845)*, ed. Bernard Andrès and Nancy Desjardins, Montreal, UQAM, 2001, 193 pp.

AUDET. *VI*, 28.1, has a dossier on A. Of particular note are essays by J. Allard, 'Pour relire Noël Audet' (45–59), and S. Arsenault, '*La Terre promise, Remember!*: l'odyssée carnavalesque de Noël Audet' (83–97).

BEAUGRAND. L. Choquette, 'Le mythe de la Nouvelle-France en Nouvelle-Angleterre', *QuS*, 33: 129–33, briefly discusses B.'s *Jeanne la fileuse* and Camille Lessard's *Canuck*.

BEAULIEU. *LQu*, 105, has some useful pages on B. (7–12).

BEAUSOLEIL. P. J. Ouellet, 'Le chronotope urbain dans la poésie contemporaine de Clément Marchand et Claude Beausoleil', *Globe*, 5: 89–122, offers a detailed analysis of the urban poetry of these two writers in the light of Bakhtin's concept of the 'chronotope'.

BERNARD. M. Tremblay and G. Gaudreau, 'Le régionalisme littéraire au Canada français. Le point de vue de Harry Bernard', *Globe*, 5: 159–78, examines B.'s attempts to define literary regionalism, as found in his published writings and his extensive correspondence.

CARRIER. V.-L. Tremblay, 'La quête de pouvoir avortée dans *La Guerre, yes sir!*', *QuS*, 34: 59–67, is solid rather than stimulating stuff, though the paragraph on the links between C.'s novel and James Joyce's *Ulysses* is certainly thought-provoking.

CHOQUETTE. E. J. Talbot, 'Choquette's urban fables: questioning a certain modernity', *QuS*, 34: 47–57, revisits C.'s reworkings of La Fontaine's fables. T. argues that C.'s sketches are evidence of the still unresolved tensions between tradition and modernity within Quebec society at the time, a fairly persuasive but ultimately rather restricted/restrictive reading.

CONAN. Laure Conan, *J'ai tant de sujets de désespoir. Correspondance 1878–1924*, ed. Jean-Noël Dion, Montreal, Varia, 2001, 480 pp., will be of significant interest not only to C. specialists but also to all those working on women writers in general.

DES ROSIERS. V. Desroches, 'Un nouveau mythe de la langue déracinée: *Vétiver* de Joël Des Rosiers', *RoN*, 42: 179–85, discusses the immigrant poet's 'poétique de déracinement' and argues that his collection (which won the Grand Prix du livre de Montréal in 1999) is characterized by 'une tension calculée entre l'individuel et le collectif, concerné surtout par l'usage commun de la langue'. *LQu*, 107, has a dossier which would serve as a useful introduction to the poet.

DUCHARME. M.-A. Beaudet, 'Entre mutinerie et désertion. Lecture des épigraphes de *L'Hiver de force* et du *Nez qui voque* comme prises de position exemplaires de l'écrivain périphérique', *VI*, 27, 2001: 103–12. P. Caron, '*L'Hiver de force* de Réjean Ducharme: les enjeux d'une adaption théâtrale', *VI*, 28: 113–25, imaginatively uses Lorraine Pintal's stage adaptation of D.'s novel to assess its aesthetic singularity.

DUMONT. *VI*, 27.1, 2001, has a substantial dossier on the poet and intellectual. Of particular note perhaps is B. Faivre-Duboz and

K. Larose, 'Stylisations de la culture chez Fernand Dumont et Réjean Ducharme' (59–73), which compares D.'s *Le Lieu de l'homme* with Ducharme's *L'Hiver de force*. Both writers, it is argued, share a certain view of culture as foundation, memory, witnessing. J.-P. Warren, 'Anarchism and the French-Canadian intellectual tradition: Fernand Dumont, Marcel Rioux and Pierre Vadeboncœur', *Journal of Indo-Canadian Studies*, 2:112–23, is a slight piece on an intriguing issue.

FERRON. *Jacques Ferron: le palimpseste infini*, ed. Brigitte Faivre-Duboz and Patrick Poirier, Outremont, Lanctôt, 435 pp., presents 26 papers first delivered at a conference of the same name held in 2000. This is a wide-ranging collection of high quality.

GARNEAU, F.-X. L. M. Gasbarrone, 'Narrative, memory and identity in François-Xavier Garneau's *Histoire du Canada*', *QuS*, 34:31–46, argues that G.'s search for an identity for his 'people without a history' leads him away from France and, paradoxically, towards a shared history and destiny with fellow North Americans.

GARNEAU, ST-D. François Charron, *L'Obsession du mal de Saint-Denys Garneau et la crise identitaire au Canada français*, Montreal, Les Herbes rouges, 2001, 590 pp., is a massive biography that sensitively charts the poet's tragic life and deftly contextualizes it in the society and culture of his time. Required reading. Saint-Denys Garneau, *Recueil de poesies: inédit de 1928*, ed. Giselle Huot, Quebec, Nota bene, 184 pp. K. Larose, 'Travers de la modernité; don, culture, et spéculation chez Saint-Denys Garneau', *QuS*, 32:105–17.

GELINAS. J. Pelland, 'La figure du changement dans quatre romans de la Révolution tranquille', *VI*, 28:142–57, identifies a series of morphological traits related to different perspectives on the world in G.'s *Les Vivants, les morts et les autres*, together with Gérard Bessette's *Les Pédagogues*, Yves Thériault's *Le Grand Roman d'un petit homme*, and Richard Joly's *Le Visage de l'attente*.

GODIN. Gérald Godin, *Cantouques & Cie*, ed. André Gervais, Montreal, Typo, 221 pp., is a revised and supplemented version of the 1991 edition.

GRIGNON. Luc Bertrand, *Un peuple et son avare: sources et histoire d'un téléroman*, Outremont, Libre expression, 317 pp., is recommended for its insight into G., his *L'Homme et son péché*, and Quebec literature in general.

GUÈVREMONT. Peter Noble, **Beware the Stranger. The 'Survenant' in the Quebec Novel*, Amsterdam, Rodopi, 121 pp.

HÉBERT. *The Art and Genius of Anne Hébert. Essays on her Works: Night and the Day are One*, ed. Janis L. Pallister, London, Associated U.P., 2001, 399 pp., is a collection of some 26 essays. The volume is divided up into six sections. The first, by far the longest, is devoted to specific novels and short stories. Subsequent sections are on H.'s poetic works (just one essay!), theatre, H. and the cinema, thematic approaches, intertextual studies. Anne Ancrenat, *De mémoire de femmes. 'La mémoire archaïque' dans l'oeuvre romanesque d'Anne Hébert*, Quebec, Nota bene, 320 pp., is a striking, stridently feminist study that seeks to show that the novelist's heroines find their real, autonomous selves in 'une mémoire qui propose non pas le souvenir mais une remontée vers l'émotion initiale avant que ne soit assujettie la subjectivité des femmes'. *CAH*, 3, 2001, focuses on translations of H.'s work. E. M. Furtado, 'Woman's new birth experience: Anne Hébert and Marie-Claire Blais', *Journal of Indo-Canadian Studies*, 2:28–36, rehearses how the two writers have coined new modes of female representation. D. Marcheix, 'Pratique des signes et fascination de l'informe dans les romans d'Anne Hébert', *VI*, 27:317–34, explores the way H.'s characters are threatened 'par la faillite d'un discours miné et brouillé par la violente résurgence de l'indicible'.

HÉMON. Arpád Vigh, *L'Ecriture Maria Chapdelaine. Le style de Louis Hémon et l'explication des québecismes*, Sillery, Septentrion, 250 pp., has little to offer the initiated but might be of use to the newcomer.

HERTEL. P. Guay, 'François Hertel', *Nuit blanche*, 85:14–18, one of the journal's series on 'Ecrivains méconnus du XXe siècle', is a solid introduction.

JACOB. P. Gilbert, 'Discourses of female criminality: Suzanne Jacob's *L'Obéissance*, a novel of infanticide/filicide', *QuS*, 32:37–55.

KATTAN. **Naim Kattan: l'écrivain du passage*, ed. Jacques Allard, Montreal, Hurtubise HMH, 160 pp.

LA FRANCE. Micheline La France, *Le Don d'Auguste*, Montreal, XYZ, 203 pp., is a new edition that includes a useful *dossier d'accompagnement* by Raymond Paul which, amongst other things, draws some interesting parallels between Auguste and Michel Tremblay's Edouard.

LESCARBOT. Eric Thierry, **Marc Lescarbot (vers 1570–1641): un homme de plume au service de la Nouvelle-France*, Champion, 2001, 440 pp.

MIRON. *Miron ou la marche à l'amour. Essais*, ed. Cécile Cloutier, Michel Lord, Ben-Zion Shek, Montreal, L'Hexagone, 293 pp., is a collection of papers (and more besides) from a conference held in Toronto in 1998. The volume is divided into four parts: 'Miron et le langage poétique', 'Miron et l'oralité', 'Miron et l'altérité', and 'Miron, l'amour, le temps, l'espace, la société, le monde . . .'. Contributors include P. C. Malenfant, M. van Schendel, J. Royer, E. Kushner, and C. Tellier (with an effectively detailed account of the creation of *L'Hexagone* in 1953). Y. Resch, 'Le paysage des Laurentides dans l'oeuvre de Gaston Miron' pp. 45–52 of *Lecture(s) du paysage canadien* (see below p. 216).

NELLIGAN. J.-F. Hamel, 'Tombeaux de l'enfance. Pour une prosopopée de la mémoire chez Emile Nelligan, Réjean Ducharme et Gaétan Soucy', *Globe*, 4, 2001 : 93–118, discusses how the 'child–poet' gives expression to a paradoxical historical relationship between Quebec literature and memory. Emile J. Talbot, *Reading Nelligan*, Montreal, McGill–Queen's U.P., 221 pp., is an original, engaging exploration of N.'s poetry. N.'s originality in particular is brought out in a cogent examination of his relationship with the cultural *milieux* of France and Quebec. The nuanced and provocative conclusion on 'Nelligan and decadence' is especially recommended. Paul Wyczynski, *Album Nelligan. Une biographie en images*, Montreal, Fides, 438 pp., is a superb research tool and a delight for all Nelligan lovers. It contains a treasure-trove of over 500 pictures, providing a compelling visual accompaniment to the poet's life and times.

OLLIVIER. Emile Ollivier, *Repérages*, Montreal, Leméac, 2001, 133 pp., provides insight into his own work and into 'l'écriture migrante' in general.

PROULX. M. Cusson, 'La mise en jeu de la ville dans *Les Aurores montréales* de Monique Proulx', *Globe*, 5 : 75–88, discusses the Montreal-inspired act of writing in P.'s book in the light of Hans-Georg Gadamer's concept of play.

RINGUET. B. Faivre-Duboz, 'Seuils de la modernité: *Trente arpents* et *Bonheur d'occasion*', *QuS*, 32 : 71–85, explores how modernity in these novels by R. and Gabrielle Roy largely stems from 'la représentation qu'ils nous livrent d'un moment charnière dans l'histoire du Québec.'

ROBIN. S. Joseph, '"Désormais le temps de l'entre-deux". L'éclatement identitaire dans *La Québécoite* de Régine Robin', *Globe*, 4, 2001 : 29–51, explores how in the novel the migrant oscillates between two identities, the one from before exile and the one born of exile. *Nuit blanche*, 87, has an interview with R. (38–43).

ROY. Gabrielle Roy, *Mon cher grand fou . . . Lettres à Marcel Carbotte 1947–1979*, Montreal, Boréal, 2001, 825 pp., presents the 485 letters that the novelist sent to her doctor husband from the year they met to the year of her first heart attack. Lori Saint-Martin, *La Voyageuse et la prisonnière. Gabrielle Roy et la question des femmes*, Montreal, Boréal, 392 pp. St-M. pursues her feminist agenda. Whilst her study is insightful, the thesis that emerges — that 'de toutes les créatrices québécoises d'avant le féminisme contemporain, c'est sûrement [Roy] qui est allée le plus loin, même si, de son vivant, elle nous l'a soigneusement caché' — is hardly new or challenging. J.-G. Hudon, 'L'actualité de Gabrielle Roy', *Nuit blanche*, 86 : 40–6.

THERIAULT. Eugène Roberto, *L'Hermès québécois*, Ottawa, David, 155 pp., uses the archetypal Hermès representation of three facets of the human personality to reinterpret T.'s *Le Dompteur d'ours*, Germaine

Guèvremont's *Le Survenant*, and Patrice Lacombe's *La Terre paternelle*. A beguiling but rather precious study. Danielle Thaler and Alain Jean-Bart, *Les Enjeux du roman pour adolescents. Roman historique, roman-miroir, roman d'aventures*, L'Harmattan, 330 pp., discusses to good effect issues to do with literature for young people, but is recommended here for its pages on T. whose output was cross-generational in its appeal. F. Lepage, 'Yves Thériault et les Editions Jeunesse', *VI*, 27, 2001: 113–26, explores the correspondence between T. and Réal d'Anjou, director of *Editions Jeunesse*, and sheds further light on T. and on his books for children, especially his *L'Or de la felouque*. **Agora. Revue d'études littéraires*, 2, 2001, has essays on T. and Sergio Kokis.

TREMBLAY. André Brochu, *Rêver la lune. L'Imaginaire de Michel Tremblay dans les 'Chroniques du Plateau Mont-Royal'*, Montreal, Hurtubise HMH, 239 pp., is a lucid exploration of the complex, sophisticated themes in T.'s cycle. Mathilde Dragnat, *Michel Tremblay. Le 'joual' dans 'Les Belles-Soeurs'*, L'Harmattan, 221 pp., is a badly organized stylistic analysis that contains much that is of value and much that is merely flatulent. The posited link between the use of *joual* in literature and in Ti-Pop is ultimately unproductive. P. Riendeau, 'La dramaturgie autobiographique de Michel Tremblay: *Encore une fois si vous permettez*', *QuS*, 34: 69–85. M.-L. Piccione, 'Le paysage lacustre chez Michel Tremblay', pp. 97–102 of *Lecture(s) du paysage canadien. Decoding and Telling the Canadian Landscape*, ed. Michèle Kaltemback and Marcienne Rocard, AFEC, 147 pp.

TURCOTTE. V. Caron, '*Le Bruit des choses vivantes* et *Tableaux*: voix et représentations inédites de la maternité dans la littérature québécoise', *VI*, 28: 126–41, discusses T.'s text in conjunction with D. Kimm's *Tableaux* to show how the present-day assertion of motherhood as a lived experience represents a shift in values and literary innovation.

CARIBBEAN LITERATURE

By Maeve McCusker, *Queen's University, Belfast*

1. General

Mary Gallagher, *Soundings in French Caribbean Writing Since 1950. The Shock of Space and Time*, OUP, 293 pp., is an important study whose basic premise — that French Caribbean writers experience a uniquely intense relationship with the intersecting dimensions of space and time — is amply borne out through assured theoretical insight and deft textual analysis. The first chapter examines the 'theoretical generations' which have accompanied the emergence of the literary tradition; the interrelationship of négritude, Caribbeanness, and créolité is persuasively reinterpreted. Subsequent chapters focus initially on time (the reconstruction of the past in fiction, the 'place' of memory), then, after a bridging chapter on intertextuality, on space (the plantation and the town; the importance of France, Africa, and the broader New World context). The ambitious historical sweep sacrifices neither breadth nor depth, although prose is privileged over drama and poetry. G.'s insights are original and trenchant, and canonical figures (Zobel, Schwarz-Bart, Glissant, and Chamoiseau) are studied alongside neglected writers such as Placoly and Brival. Crucially, too, the anglophone Caribbean context (Derek Walcott, Wilson Harris) is extensively invoked. Jeannie Suk, *Postcolonial Paradoxes in French Caribbean Writing: Césaire, Condé, Glissant*, OUP, 2001, 206 pp., is a welcome addition to the growing corpus of criticism examining Caribbean writing from the perspective of postcolonial theory. An introductory chapter explores key theoretical issues such as paradox, allegory, and return. Subsequent chapters provide theoretically-informed close textual readings of Césaire, Glissant, and, most fully, Condé. Celia Britton, *Race and the Unconcious. Freudianism in French Caribbean Thought*, Oxford, Legenda, 115 pp., is a scrupulously-researched investigation of the complex relationship between psychoanalysis and race in French Caribbean thought. In four succinct chapters B. offers a definitive account of her topic, exploring the initial, surrealist-inspired conceptualization of the unconscious as an authentic repository of blackness, teasing out the ambivalences in Fanon's relationship with the movement and exploring in detail the stance of Glissant and Gracchus. The breadth of the frame of reference, both European and Caribbean, and B.'s unerring insight into, and subtle problematization of, the theories she analyses, make this an important study. Dominique Chancé, *Poétique baroque de la Caraïbe*, Karthala, 2001, 261 pp., situates two francophone Caribbean novelists (Edouard Glissant and Daniel Maximin) and the Cuban Alejo Carpentier in the context of the 'New World' Baroque. While the approach is discrete rather than transversal (one chapter being assigned to each author), a common poetics of hybridity, disorder, excess, and circulation is identified, and C.'s insights are scholarly and original.

C. Kemedjio, 'Founding-ancestors and intertextuality in francophone Caribbean literature and criticism', *Rafl*, 33.2:210–29, explores the dense intertextual networks which characterize Antillean writing, identifies Césaire as 'the tutelary ancestor' of this tradition, and surveys the ongoing intense polemics generated by Caribbean writing in French. M. Munro, '*La discorde antillaise*: contemporary debates in Caribbean criticism', *Paragraph*, 24.3, 2001:117–27, surveys recent synthetic studies of Caribbean identity. His reading, although sympathetic, cautions against the currently dominant reading of the Caribbean as the site of creolization, postmodern play, and exuberance, as such an approach risks 'the perpetuation of the reading of the Caribbean as a place of escape'. S. Haigh, 'L'écriture féminine aux Antilles: une tradition féministe?', *LittéRéalité*, 18.1, 2001:21–38, demonstrates how within the masculinist tradition of French Caribbean literature, the novels of Michèle Lacrosil, Jacqueline Manicom, and Maryse Condé, while not specifically 'feminist', inscribe and explore the sexual difference notoriously neglected by Fanon. J. Khalfa, '*Bords irrémédiables*: vanishing lines in Caribbean poetry in French', Butterworth, *Borders*, 161–85, concentrates on Perse, Césaire, and Glissant, arguing that poetry assumes a privileged position in French Caribbean literature precisely because of its concern with splinter and rupture. S. Crosta, 'History and cultural identity in Haitian literature', *IJFS*, 5:22–38, provides a useful historical and literary introduction to this area, proceeding to a close reading of four contemporary novels.

2. Individual Authors

AIMÉ CÉSAIRE. A. Stafford, 'Travel in the French Black Atlantic: dialoguing and diverging between Aimé Césaire and Edouard Glissant', Forsdick, *Travel*, 15–30, argues that while Césaire's literary heritage remains overshadowed by the political fact of departmentalization, Glissant's postmodern approach risks neglecting the charge of history. E. L. Prieto, 'The poetics of place, the rhetoric of authenticity, and Aimé Césaire's *Cahier d'un retour au pays natal*', *DFS*, 55, 2001:142–51, argues convincingly that despite the *créolistes*' criticism of C.'s political stance, they remain profoundly marked by his conceptualization of the Caribbean landscape as actively constituent of identity. M. Rosello, 'The "Césaire effect," or How to Cultivate One's Nation', *RafL*, 34.2, 2001:77–91, suggests that the metaphor of filiation routinely invoked to describe C.'s heritage takes insufficient account of the chaotic inheritance of any poetic *œuvre*, and has resulted in an overly dogmatic response to his work. With specific reference to the theme of violence, she argues that C. neither endorses nor criticizes, but rather leaves room for the reader's interpretation.

INA CÉSAIRE. S. Haigh, 'Ethnographical fictions/fictional ethnographies: Ina Césaire's *Zonzon Tête Carrée*', *NFS*, 40.1, 2001:75–85, argues that C. is an (unacknowledged) precursor to both the male *créolistes* and to other, higher-profile, female Caribbean authors, and emphasizes the centrality of music and dance in C.'s first novel. V. Bada, 'Slavery and silence in Ina Césaire's *Mémoires d'Isles* and Dennis Scott's *An Echo in the Bone*', *JMMLA*, 33–34, 2001:86–93, outlines thematic convergences between a Martinican and a Jamaican play.

CHAMOISEAU. H. A. Murdoch, 'Postcolonial peripheries revisited: Chamoiseau's rewriting of francophone culture', Bishop, *Prose*, 135–42, shows how C.'s approach expands conventional notions of *francophonie*. L. Milne, 'Sex, gender and the right to write: Patrick Chamoiseau and the erotics of colonialism', *Paragraph*, 24.3, 2001:59–75, nuances the generally negative view of C.'s treatment of gender by focusing on the autonomous female characters of his fiction, but concedes that the absence of literary creativity among these women characters shows C. to be 'still bound to a masculinist aesthetics'. A. D. Curtius, 'La créolité de Chamoiseau: phénomène nouveau ou continuité d'un détour "nègzagonal" ', Henry, *Beginnings*, 181–96, is an unoriginal and insufficiently-focused examination of ethnography and orality in *Chronique des sept misères*. C. Kemedjio, 'De *Ville cruelle* de Mongo Beti à *Texaco* de Patrick Chamoiseau: fortification, ethnicité et globalisation dans la ville postcoloniale' *EsC*, 41.3, 2001:136–50, compares the treatment of city space, and in particular the notion of fortification, by a number of postcolonial authors, notably Chamoiseau and Condé.

CONDÉ. *Maryse Condé: une nomade inconvenante. Mélanges offerts à Maryse Condé*, ed. Madeleine Cottenet-Hage and Lydie Moudileno, Guadeloupe, Ibis Rouge, 190 pp., is a lively collection of short articles. The first half of the volume is composed of 'témoignages' from fellow writers (Daniel Maximin, Myriam Warner-Vieyra, René Depestre) and critics (Antoine Compagnon, Régis Antoine), which only occasionally verges on the hagiographic. The very rich second section, 'Lectures', comprises 14 essays which range across C.'s *œuvre*: G. Spivak argues for a rehabilitation of the now-unfashionable

Heremakhonon; R. Scharfman explores C.'s 'héroïnes péripatétiques et peu sympathiques'. Particularly welcome are a number of contributions on C.'s recent autobiographical work, *Le Cœur à rire et à pleurer*. L. D. Hewitt, 'Transmigrations in Maryse Condé's true tales', Bishop, *Prose*, 75–82, explores the themes of cultural imitation and alienation in this autobiography. Kathleen Gyssels, *Sages Sorcières? Révision de la mauvaise mère dans 'Beloved', 'Praisesong for the Widow' et 'Moi, Tituba, Sorcière noire de Salem'*, Lanham, NY, Univ. Press of America, 2001, 311 pp., usefully situates C. in the wider context of black women's writing (Toni Morrison and the Barbadian Paule Marshall), showing the stereotype of the bad mother/witch to be a patriarchal construct, and exploring the multiple contradictions of motherhood in post-slavery cultures.

GLISSANT. J.-P. Madou, 'Edouard Glissant: Tout-Monde, une poétique de l'archipel (par-delà Faulkner et Saint-John Perse)', Bishop, *Prose*, 1–13, is a rich and wide-ranging exploration of the echoes of two powerful predecessors in G.'s work. J. M. Dash, 'No mad art: the deterritorialized *déparleur* in the work of Edouard Glissant', *Paragraph*, 24.3, 2001 : 105–16, is a sensitive and convincing reading of G.'s relationship with space, in particular his ongoing, often misunderstood, negotiation between the territorial and the relational. C. Kemedjio, 'Glissant's Africas: from departmentalization to the poetics of relation', *RAfL*, 32.4, 2001 : 92–116, shows how the 'pathologization' of post-independence Africa, a discursive construct justifying departmentalization for the Antilles, has been undermined by Glissant and other Antillean authors. Peter Hallward, *Absolutely Postcolonial. Writing between the Singular and the Specific*, MUP, 2001, 433 pp., is a provocative study which argues that, contrary to its usual characterization in terms of plurality and particularity, the postcolonial is best understood as a singular or non-relational category. That G. is one of four authors studied in detail (along with Charles Johnson, Mohammed Dib, and Severo Sarduy) is testament to his growing importance in English-language postcolonial debate. Despite its intensely philosophical perspective, the study offers rewarding literary insights.

JUMINER. R. Little, 'Bertène Juminer, *La Revanche de Bozambo*: clefs pour une lecture', *Interculturel*, 6 : 223–40, is an attentive introductory study of J.'s novel.

MAXIMIN. C. Britton, 'The (de)construction of subjectivity in Daniel Maximin's *L'Ile et une nuit*', *Paragraph*, 24.3, 2001 : 44–59, situates the novel in the context of recent postcolonial and feminist theory, but argues convincingly that its deconstructive thrust positions it (unusually for the postcolonial novel) 'in a closer relation to Lacanian and Derridean poststructuralism'.

SAINT-JOHN PERSE. F. Frégnac-Clave, 'Ligne de fuite: *La Gloire des Rois* de Saint-John Perse', *FR*, 76:358–72, argues for the coherence of this apparently disparate volume. Two articles in Murphy, *Thresholds*, deal with Perse: M. Aquien, 'L'étrangeté de Saint-John Perse' (115–31), is a lexico-semantic study of the relatively infrequent word 'étrange' in S-J.-P.'s *oeuvre*. M. Gallagher, 'Saint-John Perse: another Rimbaud?' (133–50), is a detailed and sensitive reading of the affinities between the French and the Guadeloupean poet.

SCHWARZ-BART. K. Gyssels, 'Du paratexte pictural dans *Un Plat de porc aux bananes vertes* (André et Simone Schwarz-Bart) au paratexte sériel dans *Ecrire en pays dominé* (Patrick Chamoiseau)', Henry, *Beginnings*, 197–213, examines the 'hyperparatextualité' of two works published 30 years apart, arguing that the earlier novel's paratextual density signals a hesitant 'début difficile' to an authentic Antillean novelistic tradition, while Chamoiseau's 'serial paratext' can be read as a defiantly postmodern and postcolonial gesture.

ZOBEL. L. P. Monye and K. A. Swanson, 'Convergences thématiques et narratives dans *La Rue Cases-Nègres* de Joseph Zobel et *L'Enfant noir* de Camara Laye', *CLAJ*, 45, 2001:97–113, is an unoriginal thematic treatment of two much-studied novels. H. Ebrahim, '*Sugar Cane Alley*: re-reading race, class and identity in Zobel's *La Rue Cases-Nègres*', *LFQ*, 30:146–52, is a succinct article which draws interesting comparisons between Z.'s novel and Euzhan Palcy's film.

AFRICAN / MAGHREB LITERATURE

POSTPONED

III. OCCITAN STUDIES

LANGUAGE

By Kathryn Klingebiel, *Professor of French, University of Hawai'i at Mānoa*

1. Bibliographical and General

K. Klingebiel, 'Occitan linguistic bibliography for 2001', *Tenso*, 17:54–70. M. Westmoreland, 'Current studies in Occitan linguistics', *CRLN*, 51:59–71. In *GS*, 84, no. 486:317–19, I. Roqueta presents *Trobadors* (Trimestral d'information de las culturas occitana e catalana), a new journal published by the Région Languedoc-Roussillon that will feature sections on teaching, cultural activities, research, and documentation. M. Mulon, 'Index de la *Nouvelle Revue d'Onomastique* no. 1–2 (1983) à 35–36 (2000)', *NRO*, 37–38, 2001:223–90. M. Assens, **Table des matières de "Lemouzi" ... 5e série, 1ère partie (1961–1986): sous le signe de Ventadour*, Tulle, Lemouzi, 2001, 209 pp., with a foreword by Robert Joudoux.

2. Medieval Period (to 1500)

lexis and lexicology. Kurt Baldinger, with the collaboration of Nicoline Hörsch, has brought out fascicle 8 of his *DAO*, Tübingen, Niemeyer, 2001, 80 pp. M. Meylac characterizes *entreb(r)escar* as a word that is particularly able to encompass a multiplicity of meanings, including its own opposite, in 'Du miel à la poésie: *entreb(r)escar los motz*, la formule méta-poétique des troubadours', *Allières Vol.*, 477–93. X. Ravier, 'Sur le lexique des esprits follets et autres lutins en Languedoc et en Gascogne', *ib.*, 537–47, examines *drac* and *tòrna* 'fantôme, revenant' in the light of Mario Alinei's *étymographie*, a classification of forms and uses. For draco, R. finds: (i) 'dragon aquatique et terrestre'; (ii) 'dragon céleste'; and (iii) une anthropomorphisation du dragon.

particular semantic fields. S. Giralt, *'Nota sobre alguns ictiònims d'origen occità en textos mèdics d'Arnau de Vilanova i d'altres autors medievals', *ER*, 24:103–08.

onomastics. R. Cierbide, 'Los francos de Estella (Navarra): consideraciones onomásticas', *Allières Vol.*, 87–100, examines registers of names from 1102–1150 and 1151–1193, with discussion of first names, family names, trades, and nicknames. P.-H. Billy, *'Souvenirs franciques dans la toponymie de la Gaule méridionale', pp. 532–33 of *Tolosa. Nouvelles recherches sur Toulouse et son territoire dans l'Antiquité*, ed. Jean-Marie Pailler, Rome, École française de Rome, xvi + 601 pp.

X. Ravier, 'Sur la toponymie des cartulaires de Saint-Mont (Gers)', *NRO*, 37–38, 2001 : 57–71, studies the toponymy of the two cartularies of the Cluniac priory of St-Jean-Baptiste de Saint-Mont; handled here are the oldest place and person names, through the Germanic layer; a second part will discuss the Romano-Occitan forms. J.-P. Chambon, *'Note linguistique sur *Cannaco*, nom d'un atelier monétaire mérovingien au *pagus* de Rodez', *Archéologie en Languedoc* [Sète], 24, 2000: 186–99. Id., *'Archéologie et linguistique: aspects toponymiques de la romanisation de la Gaule à la lumière de travaux archéologiques récents concernant la Grande Limagne', *BSLP*, 97:95–122.

DIALECTS

GASCON. J.-P. Chambon and Y. Greub, 'Note sur l'âge du (proto)gascon', *RLiR*, 66:473–95, argue that proto-Gascon must be considered a Romance language in its own right, not as a variant or dialect of a (supposed) linguistic ensemble, i.e. Occitan, that did not yet exist *c.* AD 600. A. Cauhapé concludes his series 'Moulins et meuniers en Béarn' with 'Des baux de locations des moulins à eau', *PG*, 203, 2001 : 7–8 (texts from 1430, 1580, 1384, 1425); and *ib.*, 204, 2001 : 7–8 (texts from 1576, 1775). A new series begins: 'Ces actes qui nous interrogent', Part A, 'Injures, coups et blessures, meurtres et autres délits', *ib.*, 205, 2001 : 7–8 (texts from 1386, 1396, 1369, 1368, 1394); *ib.*, 206, 2001 : 7–8 (texts from 1383, 1405, 1374); *ib.*, 207, 2001 : 7–8 (texts from 1492, 1344); and *ib.*, 208 : 7–9 (texts from 1488, 1600/1601, 1344, 1349, 1427). The new series continues with Part B, 'Curieux, étrange, insolite ou tout simplement . . . amusant!': *ib.*, 209 : 7–8 (texts from 1469, 1465, 1438, 1422, 1545, 1541); *ib.*, 212 : 5–6 (texts from 1418, 1423, 1498, 1396, 1383, 1406, 1413); and *ib.*, 213 : 7–9 (texts from 1468, 1428, 1413, 1548).

LANGUEDOCIEN (INCLUDING S. PÉRIG.). J.-P. Chambon, *'Observations et hypothèses sur la charte de Nizezius (Moissac a. 680): contributions à la protohistoire du galloroman méridional et à la connaissance de la période mérovingienne dans la région toulousaine', *RLaR*, 105, 2001 : 539–605.

PROVENÇAL. L. Duval-Arnould, *'Le coutumier de l'ordre de Chalais', *PrH*, 51, no. 205, 2001 : 283–94. **Cartulaire et chartes de la commanderie de l'hôpital de Saint-Jean de Jérusalem d'Avignon au temps de la Commune (1170–1250)*, ed. Claude-France Hollard, Paris, CNRS, 2001, 303 pp.

LIMOUSIN (INCL N. PÉRIGORD). **Le Cartulaire de l'abbaye de Chancelade*, ed. Louis Grillon and Bernard Reviriego, Périgueux, Archives Départementales de la Dordogne, 2000, 280 pp. J.-L. Lemaître and F. Vielliard, *'La liève de la confrérie des Premières Chandelles à

Limoges (1388)', *BSAHL*, 129, 2001:45–103. M. Toulet, 'Identification de lieux dits d'un acte en langue limousine, mars 1257 (vx. st.)', *ib.*, 333–34.

AUVERGNAT. J.-P. Chambon and C. Lauranson-Rosaz, *'Un nouveau document à attribuer à Étienne II, évêque de Clermont (ca. 950–ca. 960)', *AMid*, 114:351–63. Id., *'Au dossier de la localisation linguistique du *Fierabras* occitan (Brunel Ms 3)', *SCL*, 48, 1997[2002]:83–90.

3. Post-Medieval Period

GENERAL. A. Krispin, 'La reconnaissance de la langue occitane et le débat autour de la *Charte européenne pour les langues régionales*', *Allières Vol.*, 427–36, argues that it is precisely because Occitan is a 'langue de civilisation européenne' that France has such trouble recognizing its legal existence. In an issue edited by Philippe Martel and devoted to the *historique* of the *Revue des Langues Romanes*, several articles involve the Occitan domain: P. Martel, *'Prophète en son pays? La *Revue des Langues Romanes* vue de Montpellier', *RLaR*, 105, 2001:367–83; M. Décimo, *'Un jalon dans l'institutionalisation du romanisme en province: la création de la Société et de la *Revue des langues romanes*, vue à travers divers fragments de la correspondance reçue par Mistral entre 1868 et 1883', *ib.*, 409–27; J.-C. Bouvier, *'Jules Ronjat et la *Revue des Langues Romanes*', *ib.*, 491–502; P. Casado, *'Provas linguisticas del miegjorn occitan', *ib.*, 607–14.

Lengas, 49, 2001, offers P. Martel, *'Lectures de l'ordonnance de Villers-Cotterêts' (7–25); J. Eygun, *'Occitan et Réforme protestante: l'histoire d'une absence' (27–91); G. Bazalgues, *'Letto odressado o Jasmin o soun orribado o Cahors, lou 18 May 1845. Per Victor Carla' (93–99); J. Marty-Bazalgues, *'A propos des lettres du fantassin Marcelin Prosper Floirac. Acte d'écrire d'un paysan quercynois au moment de la Grande Guerre' (101–16); M.-J. Verny, *'Images de la langue et de la littérature occitane dans quelques manuels de littérature française du second cycle des lycées' (117–44). *Lengas*, 50, 2001, includes P. Martel, *'Le mouvement occitan pendant la seconde guerre mondiale ou le temps de la grande tentation' (15–57); A. Viaut, *'Terroir, occitan, patrie et religion chez les prêtres gasconnisants du bordelais (1920–1950)' (59–76).

C. Lagarda, 'Per una critica occitan(ist)a profitosa', *GS*, 84, no. 486:212–15, decries discord between pro- and anti-university factions within the Occitanist community. Jòrdi Escartin, *L' Occitan tout de suite!*, Presses Pocket, 159 pp., promises to have readers *opérationnel* within 2–3 weeks. Jean-Pierre Juge, **Petit Précis: chronologie occitane. Histoire & civilisation: Limousin, Auvergne, Dauphiné, Aquitaine, Languedoc,*

Provence, Portet-sur-Garonne, Loubatières, 2001, 190 pp. T. Field presents *'Occitan', pp. 524–27 of *Facts About the World's Languages: An Encyclopedia of the World's Major Languages, Past and Present*, ed. Jane Garry and Carl Rubino, NY, H. W. Wilson, 2001, 896 pp. In *BIABF*, 191, 2001:48–51, Denis Mallet, director of the CIRDOC, continues his efforts to ensure recognition of this Béziers library and *médiathèque* that is also an active resource for Occitan creativity.

PHONETICS AND PHONOLOGY. P. Sauzet studies 'Assimilations vocaliques en occitan', *Allières Vol.*, 573–92, with two cases of [a] and yod in contact: -ARIU and the imperfect.

MORPHOSYNTAX. J.-L. Fossat and S. Ouanès, 'Prétérit et subjonctif imparfait de l'occitan, en rapport avec les structures de participe passé', *Allières Vol.*, 379–93, demonstrate the alignment of these two series.

LEXIS AND LEXICOLOGY. K. Klingebiel, 'Un basque accouché: culture d'autrefois et lexicographie occitane', *Allières Vol.*, 129–37, studies snippets of cultural information to be found in the Occitan dictionaries of yesteryear. While today's dictionaries no longer serve as encyclopedias, there are alternative sources for culture: collections of regional proverbs, atlases, electronic media, the Internet. J. Lafitte, *ib.*, 153–64, points disconsolately to the 'pauvreté [stupéfiante] de la bibliographie en matière non-languedocienne' in Alibert's dictionary. Renaud Falissard, **Vignes, vins du Pays d'Oc: vocabulaire de la langue d'oc concernant la culture, la vinification, les instruments et la boisson, suivi des dictons et proverbes (avec définitions et explications en français)*, Rodez, Lo Grelh Roergàs, 2001, 301 pp. In the long-running series 'Parlar plan', G. Narièo looks at '*E gai, Papà!*', *PG*, 209:12. *Papagai*, from Arabic, is now pan-European, yielding Occ. *lo gai* 'joie, plaisir' and the exclamation *gai / e gai!* 'trop heureux, bien content' + complement; examples of *gai* are offered in Id., '*Que'm hè gai de'vs véder*', *ib.*, 210:12. N. also says 'yes' to 'Déser òc', *ib.*, 213:10 (*òc, òc-òc, quiò, tiò, òc ben quiò, si*). A. Lagarda, *'Petits mots et gros mots', *GS*, 82, no. 478, 2000:499–501. R. Teulat, *Dorsièr Ventadorn, *Lo Convise*, 36, 2001:2–4.

PARTICULAR SEMANTIC FIELDS. J. Taupiac's series 'L'Occitan blos' continues with 'Dètz èuros', *L'Occitan*, 156:8, and '10 euro, 10 èuros, 10 €, 10 EUR', *ib.*, 157:8. Jean-Yves Bigot, **Vocabulaire français et dialectal des cavités et des phénomènes karstiques*, Spéléo-Club de Paris — Club Alpin Français, 2000, 184 pp.

ONOMASTICS. M. Vaissière, '*Las Parrans*: toponymie et redevance', *NRO*, 37–38, 2001:81–108. Evidence of this toponym, attested in 14 modern-day Occitan-speaking departments, is closely linked to attribution of peasant holdings in the Middle Ages. Michel Tamine has edited *Parlure Champagne-Ardenne. La vigne et les vergers*, Reims,

Reims U.P. — Société Française d'Onomastique, 395 pp., with five articles of interest for Occitan: J. Germain, *'Les noms de famille *Pissavin*, *Pissevin*, *Pisvin*, etc. Vraiment des surnoms d'ivrognes?' (11–20); P.-H. Billy, *'Manger le morceau: le choix du nom' (21–22); C. Marichy, *'La vignasse héraultaise est-elle une "mauvaise vigne"? Et de l'adéquation référentielle des microtoponymes viticoles' (245–59); R. Aymard, *'Cinq mille ans de viticulture dans l'onomastique pyrénéenne' (261–69); and C. Guerrin, *'Toponymie et œnologie. Les noms de terroirs viticoles dans la nomenclature administrative des communes françaises. Evolution depuis 1943' (305–19). See also H. Quesnel-Chalèlh, *'Onomastique bovine', part 5, *Parlèm*, 68, 2001 : 5–6; and part 6, *ib.*, 70, 2001 : 7–8.

SOCIOLINGUISTICS. F. Peter Kirsch, Georg Kremnitz, and Brigitte Schlieben-Lange, *Petite histoire sociale de la langue occitane: usages, images, littérature, grammaires et dictionnaires*, trans. Catherine Chabrant, Canet, Trabucaire, 189 pp. T. Field, *'Literacy and language ideologies in a European situation of language loss', pp. 93–108 of *Sociolinguistic and Psycholinguistic Perspectives on Maintenance and Loss of Minority Languages*, ed. Tom Ammerlaan et al., Münster, Waxmann, 2001, 352 pp.

TEXTS. In the work of the 16th c. Catalan epidemiologist Antoni Girauld, J. Veny finds interferences from Occitan that run the gamut from phonetic through syntactic to lexical: 'La interferència occitana en l'obra epidemiològica d'Antoni Girauld (1587)', *Allières Vol.*, 637–51. Simon Calamel and Dominique Javel, **La Langue d'oc pour étendard: Les Félibres, 1854–2002*, Toulouse, Privat, 238 pp. Jean-Claude Forêt, *7305 jorns: vint ans d'escritura occitana*, Montpeyroux, Jorn, 2001, 139 pp. R. Fruquièra has edited *'Expressions e cançonetas entendudas pel país', *Lo Convise*, 33, 2001 : 14–15.

4. GASCON AND BÉARNAIS

GENERAL. Joan Rigosta and Eric Chaplain, *Que parli gascon. Initiation à la langue gasconne*, Pau, Princi Néguer, 2001, 172 pp. Halip Lartiga, **Las Veas gasconas: identitat culturau, hitas linguisticas / Les Racines gasconnes: identité culturelle, limites linguistiques*, Pau, Princi Néguer, 2001, 56 pp. T. Field, *'Literacy ideologies and the future of Gascon', pp. 85–90 of *Endangered Languages and Literacy*, ed. Nicholas Ostler and Blair Rudes, Bath, Foundation for Endangered Languages, 2000, 150 pp.

Jean Lafitte continues to develop his own approach to modern Gascon. Of general interest are his *'Robèrt Lafont et le gascon', *LDGM*, 17, 2001 : 37–39; *'Las lengas d'ó: 7 o 8 + 1 = 8 o 9', *ib.*, 18, 2001 : 4–8; *'Questions sus las institucions occitanistas', *ib.*, 8–9; *'Un liber de J. Taupiac qui herà data: *L'occitan modèrne*', *ib.*, 10–27; *'Gascon et occitan. Réflexion sur trois publications qui marquent la distance entre ces deux langues', *ib.*, 19: 6–7; 'Compléments au L.-D. 18 (en fait, à l'étude de *L'occitan modèrne* de J. Taupiac)', *ib.*, 18–20.

ORTHOGRAPHY. J. Lafitte, *'Punts de grafia (*hrugle* et *cibót*)', *LDGM*, 17, 2001: 39. Id., *'Tres finaus no gasconas: *-f*, *-l*, *-ón*', *ib.*, 18, 2001: 28–33. Id., *'La grafia de *DiGaM* a la Sta Estela de 1901', *ib.*, 45.

MORPHOSYNTAX. P. Bec provides a 'Note sur le futur du passé en gascon', *Allières Vol.*, 73–80, reviewing the first and second conditional forms and noting in conclusion that he no longer writes *cantère*, but *cantèra*. T. Field, 'La désinence de la personne 5 en gascon pyrénéen', *ib.*, 101–08, argues for reduction of affricate [ts] to explain *cantat* (vs. *cantatz*) rather than early dialect differentiation. M. Haase, 'Basque et gascon en Basse Navarre', *ib.*, 109–17, discusses several examples of Basque structures that developed due to Romance influence and have subsequently disappeared from Basque or been relegated to the spoken register. C. D. Pusch, 'Sur le *dequeismo* en gascon et la pragmatique de la subordination', *ib.*, 259–69, discusses how, unlike French and most Occitan dialects, Gascon allows nominalizations of the type *non crei pas de que sia un dangèr tan gran*; to traditional explanations of *dequeismo* (by analogical transfer), the author adds a pragmatic factor, arguing that this type of subordination functions as a modalizing technique to distance the speaker from full responsibility for what is said.

Claus Dieter Pusch, **Morphosyntax, Informationsstruktur und Pragmatik: Präverbale Marker im gaskognischen Okzitanisch und in anderen Sprachen*, Tübingen, Narr, 2001, x + 304 pp. G. Nariòo, 'Qu'envitis la toa que volem', *PG*, 206, 2001: 13–14, recommends avoiding *que voi plan*, which is nothing more than an unsatisfactory calque of Fr. 'je veux bien'. J. Lafitte, 'Lenga blossa: *tota Gasconha* et *non Gasconha tota*', *LDGM*, 17, 2001: 40. Id., *'Gramatica de *ta*, *tan* e *tant*', *ib.*, 18, 2001: 43–44. Id., *'De la caça aus gallicismes. Ou de l'indispensable mesure qu'il faut montrer en la matière', *ib.*, 19: 9–11. Id., 'Arrevirar "bien"', *ib.*, 21–30. Id., '*Qu'avem a har?*', *ib.*, 31–32. Id., 'De l'advèrbi [(aw)tan] o [(aw)ta]', *ib.*, 33–48.

LEXIS AND LEXICOLOGY. Félix Arnaudin, *Dictionnaire de la Grande-Lande*, vol. 2 (*I–Z*), Bordeaux, Confluences–Parc Naturel Régional des Landes de Gascogne, 714 pp. This seventh volume in the series of A.'s complete works was undertaken by the late Jacques Boisgontier and completed by the team of Bénédicte and Jean-Jacques Fénié, Guy Latry, and Joël Miro; the dictionary itself (pp. 11–377) is followed by A.'s 'Grandes notes' (pp. 388–687) and a number of annexes (pp. 691–710). G. Nariòo, *'*Lo vetèth a la popa* (fr. 'le veau sous la mère')', *PG*, 203, 2001: 10. Id. suggests, *'Au telefòne, digam: *Digatz!*', *ib.*, 208: 10, instead of *allo*. J. Lafitte, *'Vocabulari: *hrugle* (foudre), *piòina* (toupie); *hèra, hèras, hèrs*; traduction de *caoutchouc, emporter, soussigné*; genre de *glucósa* et autres mots en *-ósa*', *LDGM*, 17, 2001: 40–48. Id., *'Vocabulari. Dire en gascon *avec, golfe, canine*', *ib.*, 18, 2001: 34–42.

ONOMASTICS. J. Lafitte, 'Sur un *Dictionnaire de toponymie gasconne* (Toponimes gascons, part 5), *LDGM*, 17, 2001: 2–36.

TEXTS. Roger Touze, **A Biert, village d'Ariège, autrefois, A Bièrt, un bilatgé d'Ariéjo, d'aoutis cops*, E-dite, 2001, 256 pp. A. Viaut, *'La "revue de village": approche d'un genre à partir d'un corpus local en occitan', *Lengas*, 51: 7–82.

5. SOUTHERN OCCITAN

LANGUEDOCIEN (INCLUDING S. PÉRIG.)

LEXIS AND LEXICOLOGY. A. Lagarde, 'Notes relatives aux noms de familles carbonnais', *Allières Vol.*, 165–73, studies the spelling and changes of family names of the 4000 inhabitants of Carbonne, near Toulouse, finding great stability in the makeup of the population. Three review articles praise the late Christian Laux's 2001 *Diccionari occitan-francés (lengadocian)*: S. Granièr, *GS*, 83, no. 484: 214–18, believes it will replace the dictionary of Alibert, which he finds unsuited to practical uses such as teaching or the media; where the GIDILOC led the way by digitizing Alibert, he calls now for a digitized version of Mistral. J. Taupiac, 'Lo diccionari occitan-francés de Cristian Laus', *L'Occitan*, 156: 6, finds it an 'excellent obratge dins l'estat actual de la codificacion de la lenga occitana'. Id. goes further in 'Cò que cal corregir dins lo *Dictionnaire occitan-français* de Cristian Laus', *GS*, 84, no. 487: 358–66, where he offers the following list of suggestions: *adieu-siatz*; *agenda*; *anti-semitisme*; *atac* (m.); *besson*; *cèc(a)*; *dolar*; *epidèrma*; *filme*; *grame*; *inculte*; *paquidèrma*; *pr'aquò*; *prisma*; *vèrbe*. J. Fulhet, *'Pichot bestiari roergas a basa d'expressions idiomaticas', *Oc*, 339, 2001: 40–41, and *ib.*, 340, 2001: 42–43.

PARTICULAR SEMANTIC FIELDS. Lacour have republished Adelin Moulis, *Ariège: les noms de nos oiseaux et autres animaux*, Nîmes, Lacour, 2000, 40 pp., a simple alphabetical listing, without any commentary, but still useful.

ONOMASTICS. Gaston Bazalgues, *Toponymie lotoise: à la découverte des noms de lieux du Quercy et des communes du Lot*, Gourdon, Editions de la Bouriane et du Quercy, 133 pp. Yolanda Guillermina Lopez Franco, **Le Prénom: situation onomastique et attitudes socio-culturelles. L'exemple d'un corpus en Languedoc*, Villeneuve-d'Ascq, Presses Universitaires du Septentrion, 2000, 938 pp. P.-H. Billy, *'Les noms de lieux dans la région de Revel', *Cahiers de l'Histoire de Revel* [Revel], 8: 1–12. J.-L. Veyrac, *'Eis originas de *Montpelhier*, *Oc*, 338, 2001: 40–44. J.-P.

Chambon, 'L'origine de *Montpellier*: à propos d'une contribution récente', *Etudes Héraultaises* [Montpellier], 30–32, 1999–2001 : 319–25, sees two possibilities: MONTE *PESTELĀRIU, MONTE *PISTILLĀRIU.

SUBDIALECTS. Jòrdi Deledar, *L'occitan parlé en Ariège*, Ferrières, Cercle Occitan Prospèr Estieu, 2001, 78 pp. (1st edn 1992).

TEXTS. **La Mandrette: mémoire d'Ariège*, ed. Aimé Lestel, Foix, Maison de retraite de Bellissen, Service d'animation — Nîmes, Lacour, 2001, 241 pp., presents a bilingual collection of stories from residents of a retirement home in the region of Foix.

PAREMIOLOGY . Roger Gabrielle, **Lé nosté patouès, Cadours et alentour: dictons, maximes, proverbes et devinettes*, Paris, Livre d'histoire, 111 pp.

PROVENÇAL

GENERAL. J.-C. Bouvier, *'Place et fonction du dialecte dans les journaux d'opinion au XIXe siècle: Jacquemart et l'*Impartial* de Romans', *BEC*, 159, 2001 : 171–87.

LEXIS AND LEXICOLOGY. Jean-Claude Rey, *Les Mots de chez nous*, vol. III: *Fan de luno*, Marseille, Autres temps, 220 pp. Philippe Blanchet, **Dictionnaire fondamental français-provençal*, Paris, Gisserot, 128 pp.

ONOMASTICS. C. Mariacci, 'Mutations et permanences de la microtoponymie cadastrale depuis le début du XIXe siècle: l'exemple des communes de Mons et de Callian (Var)', *NRO*, 37–38, 2001 : 133–41, is a study of permanence and innovation in the place names of two communes in the Var, by comparison of the *cadastre napoléonien* (1839) and the *cadastre rénové* of 1934–1936. P. Casado, 'Les noms de lieux de la commune de Tresques (département du Gard)', *ib.*, 109–32, provides a balance sheet of losses and gains since the Middle Ages; although there is evidence of renewal, the author concludes that 'la voie de la francisation de la toponymie occitane semble se dessiner'. M. Mulon, *'Noms provençaux', pp. 109–11 of *Origine et histoire des noms de famille: essais d'anthroponymie*, Errance, 196 pp.

The acts of a colloquium held in Aix-en-Provence in December 1998 have been published by Jean-Claude Bouvier and Jean-Marie Guillon as *La Toponymie urbaine. Significations et enjeux*, Paris, L'Harmattan, 256 pp. Articles of interest for Provençal are: X. Ravier, *'Sur la toponymie d'une ville nouvelle, la Bastide de Marciac (1298)' (41–52); R. Bertrand, *'Aux grands hommes, la mairie reconnaissante: hommes illustres et noms de rues à Marseille (vers 1770–1870)' (65–73); C. Martel, *'Aux grands hommes la cité reconnaissante? La patrotoponymie dans les Alpes de Haute-Provence' (75–87); E. Richard, *'Femmes dans la rue ou les "trous de mémoire" de la ville, l'exemple marseillais' (103–10); P. Pasquini examines the rapid growth of street names in Sorgues after WW II (111–22); J.-M. Guillon, *'Batailles de mémoires en Provence' (123–32); M. Ferrières, *'L'Ancien Régime toponymique: le cas d'Avignon' (213–28); J.-C. Bouvier, 'A la Rotonde ou sur le Cours' (239–46).

SOCIOLINGUISTICS. Philippe Blanchet, **Langues, cultures et identités régionales en Provence: la métaphore de l'aïoli*, Paris, L'Harmattan, 248 pp.

SUBDIALECTS. Jacques Chirio, **Pràtica e gramàtica*, Nice, lou Sourgentin, 2000, 95 pp. C.'s articles from *Lou Sourgentin* have been collected and presented by Noël Fiorucci, Jean-Luc Gagliolo, and Roger Rocca. Christine Bovari, **Un périodique populaire en dialecte nissard: 'La Ratapignata': 1900–1912/1934–1936*, Nice, Serre, 181 pp.

TEXTS. M. Ferrières, *'Une enquête sur les statuts de Vaucluse: les Statuts de Gigondas (1592)', *HSR*, 16, 2001 : 177–204.

6. NORTHERN OCCITAN

LIMOUSIN (INCLUDING N. PÉRIG.)

GENERAL. Y. Lavalade, *'De l'Occitan du Limousin au Breton contemporain', *BSLSAC*, 104, 2001 : 351–58.

LEXIS AND LEXICOLOGY. Yves Lavalade and Jacques Peyramaure, **Tournures limousines/Viradas lemosinas*, Saint-Paul, Souny, 2001, 79 pp. Lavalade's *Dictionnaire français-occitan: Limousin-Marche-Périgord*, originally published in 1997, has been revised and enlarged, Saint-Paul, Souny, 2001, 571 pp. His work with less-commonly studied languages continues with *La Langue maltaise et la romanité, lexique maltais roman/arabe et occitan*, Puylaurens, IEO, 2001, 80 pp.

ONOMASTICS. Marcel Villoutreix, **Les Noms de lieux du Limousin, témoins de l'histoire d'une région*, Limoges, Association des antiquités historiques du Limousin, 231 pp. Yves Lavalade, **Guide occitan de la flore: Limousin, Marche, Périgord*, Saint-Paul, Souny, 141 pp. L. Bonnaud, *'L'inscription de l'ancienne porte Manigne à Limoges', *BSAHL*, 129, 2001 : 387–93.

SUBDIALECTS. *Lé Patois dé Chinta Fourtyunada in Courèja/Le Patois de Sainte Fortunade en Corrèze*, ed. André Lagarde, Tulle, Maugein, 2001, iv + 216 pp.

AUVERGNAT (INCLUDING N. PÉRIG.)

MORPHOSYNTAX. R. Teulat, *'Conjugason-tipa de l'auvernhat meridional (nòrd-Cantal, Nauta-Lèira, sud-Puèi-de-Doma)', *Lo Convise*, 35, 2001 : 18–20.

LEXIS AND LEXICOLOGY. Pierre-Gabriel Gonzalez, **Dictionnaire des noms de famille en Auvergne et aux confins du Massif central: origine, fréquence et localisation des patronymes traditionnels les plus répandus dans l'Allier, le Cantal, la Haute-Loire, le Puy-de-Dôme et les départements voisins*, Clermont-Ferrand, Borée, 2001, 286 pp. P. Bonnaud, A.-M. Magot, and S. Soupel, *'Mou pà sen euvarnhàt-français-espanol-english', *Bizà Neirà*, 111, 2001:1–170. K.-H. Reichel, *'L'Auvergne lexicale', *ib.*, 109, 2001:41–44, *ib.*, 110, 2001:21–24, and *ib.*, 112, 2001:33–36. H. Quesnel-Chalèlh, *'Le français local du Puy-en-Velay', *Parlèm*, 71, 2001:3–4.

ONOMASTICS. Véronique Dumas, Florence Guibert, and Sophie d'Orsetti, **Les Noms de famille en Auvergne et Limousin*, Paris, Archives et culture, 384 pp. Pierre-Henri Billy and Marie-Renée Sauvadet, **Dictionnaire historique des noms de famille du Puy-de-Dôme*, vol. 2, Clermont-Ferrand, Assoc. de recherches généalogiques et historiques d'Auvergne, 2001, 285 pp. This second volume is devoted to family names derived from personal names, baptismal names, and from the lexicon; the first volume (1998) handled family names derived from place names, country names, clan names, and ethnic names. P.-H. Billy, 'L'anthroponymie historique. Essai sur la Basse-Auvergne (suite et fin)', *NRO*, 37–38, 2001:151–63, adds observations and a number of methodological principles to a first article in the same journal, 29–30, 1997:19–62. J.-C. Chambon, 'Survivance toponymique de lat. *xenodochium* dans la banlieue de Clermont-Ferrand', *ib.*, 37–38, 2001:73–80, demonstrates that Lat. XENODŎCHIUM 'hospice', e.g., AD 959 *illo Sindocio*, left few toponymic vestiges in Gaule but can be identified with the neighborhood called *les Sandots* in Clermont. H. Quesnel-Chalèlh, *'La toponymie à Ceyssac-la-Roche [43 Haute-Loire]', *Parlèm*, 69, 2001:4–5. C. Hérilier, *'La Vaira = La Veyre (Puy-de-Dôme): hydronyme de désignation latine plutôt qu'occitane', *ib.*, 70, 2001:2–5.

TEXTS. J.-F. Maury, **Contes et légendes de Saint-Vincent de Salers, Cantal: version bilingue, auvergnat-français*, Aurillac, Ostal del libre, 2001, 127 pp.

PAREMIOLOGY. A. Massebeuf, *'Expressions, dictons et proverbes de Brioude et du Brivadois', *Bizà Neirà*, 109, 2001:2–7, and *ib.*, 112, 2001:3–7.

PROVENÇAL ALPIN

ONOMASTICS. Hubert Bessat and Claudette Germi, **Les Noms du paysage alpin. Atlas toponymique: Savoie, Vallée d'Aoste, Dauphiné, Provence*, Grenoble, Univ. Stendhal ELLUG, 2001, 324 pp. Charles Roux, **Noms et sobriquets des Vaudois*, Yens-sur-Morge, Cabédita, 2001, 127 pp.

LITERATURE

MEDIEVAL PERIOD

By Miriam Cabré, *Universitat de Girona*, and Sadurní Martí, *Universitat de Girona*

1. Research Tools and Reference Works

W. Pfeffer, 'Bibliography of Occitan literature for 2000', *Tenso*, 17.1:94–131, lists publications by subject. The bibliographic issue of *CCMe*, 44, 2001, classifies medieval publications under detailed subject-headings and provides several useful indexes. *CrT* regularly includes Occitan research and, in issue 3.3, 2000:1143–60, Occitan reviews. *Arnaut: Rassegna di filologia occitana*, <http://www.arnaut.it> presents new bibliographic sections and M. De Conca's PDF edition of 'Le *albas ses titol* del ms. C (BNF f. fr. 856)'. The prose and verse sections of *Rialto* <http://www.rialto.unina.it> gradually offer newly-edited texts, such as F. Bianchi's Folquet de Lunel, and reproduce existing editions, often with corrections (for instance M. P. Betti's to the *tensos* of Guiraut Riquier published in *SMV*, 44). *Robert Lafont, *La Source sur le chemin: aux origines occitanes de l'Europe littéraire*, L'Harmattan, 581 pp., and Giuseppe Tavani, *Ristauri testuali*, Roma, Bagatto, 2001, 297 pp., gather reprinted articles with some revisions. Lucia Lazzerini, *Letteratura medievale in lingua d'oc*, Modena, Mucchi, 2001, 296 pp., completes her much-needed survey with an annotated bibliography, and a glossary of metrics and rhetoric.

2. Editions and Textual Criticism

Saverio Guida, *Trovatori minori*, Modena, Mucchi, 335 pp., provides archival documentation for the six troubadours edited and translated here. Michael Routledge, *Les Poésies de Bertran Carbonel*, Birmingham, AIEO, 2000, xxxiii + 198 pp., offers a study with special attention to versification, an edition, and a translation into modern French. *La Cort d'amor: A Critical Edition*, ed. Matthew Bardell, EHRC, 169 pp., interprets the *Cort* (re-edited and fully translated into English) as the first vernacular allegorical *roman*, in response to Andreas Capellanus. Marco Piccat, 'La versione occitana dello Pseudo Turpino' (*ZRP*, Beihefte, 308), Tübingen, Niemeyer, 2001, 211 pp., analyses the aims of the text and its features as a translation. Antoine Calvet, *Les Légendes de l'Hôpital de Saint-Jean-de-Jérusalem*, Sorbonne U.P., 2000, 172 pp., discusses several versions of the legends, examining purpose, date, and textual problems, and he includes a previously unpublished

Occitan version. *The Voyage of St Brendan: Representative Versions of the Legend in English Translation*, ed. W. R. J. Barron and Glyn S. Burgess, Exeter U.P., xii + 377 pp., offers M. Burrell's new edition and English translation of the Occitan version (231–47). S. Vatteroni, 'Le poesie di Peire Cardenal, VI', *SMV*, 45, 1999: 89–187, continues his on-going edition (beginning with *SMV*, 36, 1990; see *YWMLS*, 57: 295 and 58: 263). Other articles with full-text editions are P. T. Ricketts, 'Deux textes occitans portant sur la vie de la vierge Marie, une chanson de la Nativité et une plainte', *RLaR*, 105, 2001: 235–46; Id., 'Le roman de Daude de Pradas sur les quatre vertus cardinales', *FL*, 134: 131–83, which corrects Stickney's unavailable edition; and G. Tavani, 'Il sirventese "Al bon rei" di Folquet de Lunel (BdT 154.1): proposta di rivisione testuale e di traduzione', *CrT*, 4, 2001: 347–55. M. Eusebi, 'En abriu s'esclairon il riu', *CN*, 62: 181–92, re-edits Marcabru's poem on the basis of palaeographic data. P. Squillacioti, 'BdT 276,1 *Longa sazon ai estat vas Amor*', *RSTe*, 2, 2000: 185–215, focuses on the complex MS tradition, and proposes a model for multiple-version editions.

TEXTUAL CRITICISM. Pascale Bourgain and Françoise Vielliard, *Conseils pour l'édition des textes médiévaux*, III: *Textes litteraires*, Comité des travaux historiques et scientifiques — École nationale des Chartres, 253 pp., use *vidas* to illustrate editing techniques (134–71). A. Negri, 'Premessa ad una riedizioni delle liriche di Guilhem de la Tor con saggio di edizione critica', *QFRB*, 15, 2001: 407–25, exemplifies her forthcoming work with the edition of *BdT* 236,89. M. De Conca, 'Percorsi testuali ed accidenti di trasmissione nella lirica dei trovatori', *SMV*, 48: 17–32, examines the role of MS C in troubadour transmission. On the ecdotic relationship between different versions: A. P. Fuksas, 'La materia del racconto e le opzioni narrative: ricerche sulla tradizione delle *Novas del papagai*', *QFRB*, 15, 2001: 239–64, and B. Fedi, 'Il canone assente: l'esempio metrico nelle *Leys d'amors* fra citazione e innovazione', *ib.*, 14, 1999: 159–86, who highlights the virtual lack of troubadour quotations in the *Leys*.

MANUSCRIPT TRANSMISSION. S. Asperti, 'La tradizione occitanica', Boitani, *Circolazione*, 521–54, lucidly explores the range of Occitan MS transmission, from local *unica* to the rich international lyrical tradition. *Intavulare. Tavole di Canzonieri romanzi.* I. *Canzonieri provenzali, 2. Bibliothèque nationale de France. I (fr. 854), K (fr. 12473)*, ed. Walter Meliga, Mucchi, Modena, 2001, 381 pp., analyses the codicologic make-up and contents of these closely related MSS. *Tenso*, 17.2: 4–24, publishes a round-table on Elizabeth Poe's *Compilatio*, by W. D.Paden, R. T. Pickens, and P., dealing chiefy with the role of oral and written sources in the making of MS H. Maria Careri et al., *Album de manuscrits français du XIIIe siècle*, Roma, Viella, 2001, xxxvii + 245 pp., includes her description of MS Paris, BNF, fr. 2180 of *Girart de Roussillon* (59–62). I. Zamuner, 'Una sottoscrizione dedicatoria di Carlo I d'Angiò ad Alfonso X di Castiglia', *CrT*, 1, 1998: 919–66, reconstructs a codex offered to the Castilian king, which returned to Italy with additional materials. M. L. Meneghetti, 'La forma-canzoniere fra tradizione mediolatina e tradizioni volgari', *CrT*, 2, 1999: 119–40, discusses author and compilator collections in both traditions. In Zimmermann, *Auctor*, two articles analyse the status of troubadours as *auctores*: L. Kendrick, 'L'image du troubadour comme auteur dans les chansonniers' (507–19), focuses on the iconography of MSS AIK; and F. Vielliard, 'Auteur et autorité dans la littérature occitane médiévale non lyrique' (375–89), highlights this status as a determining factor in MS transmission. F. Zinelli, 'Gustav Gröber e i libri dei trovatori (1877)', *SMV*, 48: 229–74, is an enlightening reappraisal of *chansonnier* theory in German and French scholarship.

3. Cultural and Historical Background

L. Paterson, 'The south', pp. 102–33 of *France in the Central Middle Ages 900–1200*, ed. Marcus Bull (The Short Oxford History of France), OUP, 250 pp., discusses troubadours and courts within her survey of Occitan identity. Jan Rüdiger, *Aristokraten und Poeten, die Grammatik einer Mentalität im tolosanischen Hochmittelalter*, Berlin, Akademie, 2001, 538 pp., includes discussion on Latin and vernacular literature and the emergence of a local Occitan epic. R. Harvey, 'The empress Eudoxia and the troubadours', *MAe*, 70, 2001: 268–77, uses historic evidence to disect this alleged troubadour icon. M. Aurell, 'Le troubadour Gui de Cavaillon (vers 1175–vers 1229): un acteur nobiliaire de la croisade albigeoise', pp. 9–36 of vol. II of *Les Voies de l'hérésie: le groupe aristocratique en Languedoc (XIe–XIIIe siècles)*, Carcassonne, CVPM, 2001, 3 vols, 177, 258, 96 pp., interprets Gui's works in view of his historic context. S. Asperti, 'Testi poetici volgari di propaganda politica (s. XII e XIII)', *Atti* (Todi), 533–59, redefines so-called propagandistic poetry as an ideological vehicle for divulgation within the same court circles. J. A. Abu-Haidar, *Hispano-Arabic Literature and the Early Provençal Lyrics*, Richmond, Curzon, 2001, x + 266 pp., rejects the alleged affinities between both traditions.

4. Poetry

Sarah Kay, *Courtly Contradictions: The Emergence of the Literary Object in the Twelfth Century*, (Figurae: Reading Medieval Culture), Stanford U.P., 2001, xii + 380 pp.,, discusses courtly literature as the result of the interaction of lyric, romance, and hagiography, using 12th-c.

logic and Lacanian theory. Some articles in *Tenso*, 17.1, introduced by S. Kay (1–9), also use converging methodology: K. Brown, 'Bodiless skins binding' (56–74), reads Raimbaut d'Aurenga's 'Car douz' with minute attention to MS variants and Kristevan theory; S. Gaunt, 'Desnaturat son li Frances: language and identity in the twelfth-century Occitan epic' (10–31), applies postcolonial translation theory to disentangle the problem of Occitan epic language. R. Cholakian, 'Saint Francis and the Provençal connection', *Tenso*, 17.2:35–53, suggests psychological and subtextual similarities between troubadour love stories and biographies of the saint. A. Rossich, 'Alternança de llengües en Cerverí de Girona', *EstG*, 22:13–39, discusses the number of languages in Cerverí's *cobla* in terms of their contemporary literary status. Anatole Pierre Fuksas, *Etimologia e geografia nella lirica dei trovatori*, Roma, Bagatto, 258 pp., analyses the range of rhetorical purposes of etymologically-charged place-names, and his 'Il corpo di Blacatz e i quattro angoli della cristianità', *QFRB*, 14, 1999:187–206, discusses three *planhs* with anatomic structuring motifs. P. Canettieri, 'Lo captals', *ib.*, 77–101, is an interesting first approach to the impact of economic changes on troubadour language. Ulf Malm, *Doussor Conina: Lust, the Bawdy, and Obscenity in Medieval Occitan and Galician-Portuguese Troubadour Poetry and Latin Secular Love Song*, Uppsala, AUU, 2001, 296 pp., analyses the language of vernacular obscenity, and the violations of *fin'amors*. L. Rossi, 'Comico e burlesco nelle letterature romanze dei secoli XI-XIII', *SMV*, 47, 2001:33–55, is concerned with the reading of ironic texts. P. G. Beltrami, 'Giraut de Borneil "plan e clus" ', *QFRB*, 14, 1999:7–43, points at a flexible use of styles by Giraut.

ATTRIBUTIONS. Carlo Pulsoni, *Repertorio delle attribuzioni discordanti della lirica trobadorica*, Modena, Mucchi, 509 pp., offers a double classification (by MS and by author) of pieces with plural attributions, sketching the origin of this phenomenon and the clues it provides about MS compilations. F. Gambino, 'Anonimi per caso, anonimi per scelta e nomi censurati: osservazioni sull'assenza del nome d'autore nella tradizione manoscritta trobadorica', Barbieri, *Anonimato*, 11–33, singles out accidents and genre as the reasons for anonymity. S. Vatteroni, 'Un sirventese catalano-occitanico falsamente attribuito a Peire Cardenal', *SMV*, 48:203–28, uses MS transmission to dismiss this attribution. F. Zinelli, 'Attorno al senhal *Gardacor* in Uc de Sant-Circ BdT 456.3: appunti per una storia dei poeti di Savaric de Mauléon', *QFRB*, 14, 1999:245–73, deftly defines this poetic circle identifying the *senhal* with Isabelle d'Angoulême. M. L. Meneghetti, 'Uc e gli altri: sulla paternità delle biografie trobadoriche', *ib.*, 15, 2001:147–62, refutes Uc de Sant Circ's single-handed authorship of the corpus. L. Rossi, 'Ebolo II di Ventadorn,

Cercamon e la nascita della *fin'amor'*, *Liver Vol.*, 539–58, and his 'Du nouveau sur Cercamon: la complainte de Guillaume X d'Aquitaine (BdT 112, 2a): *planh* ou sirventes politique', *Menichetti Vol.*, 87–104, identify Ebles and Cercamon as two stages on the career of the same poet. R. Harvey, 'Textual transmission and courtly communities: the case of Baussan', *Tenso*, 17.1:32–55, reorders a *partimen* and proposes Baussan as a *trobairitz*. M. L. Meneghetti, 'Aldric e Marcabru', *Menichetti Vol.*, 71–86, reinterprets and re-dates the exchange by reordering its sequence.

SOURCES AND GENRES. Alexander Huber, *La Fable dans la littérature provençal du Moyen Age*, Lausanne Univ., Faculté de Lettres, 2001, 235 pp., collects fable references in troubadour literature, and offers a Lachmannian edition of 'Una ciutatz fo, no sai cals' (165–97). B. Barbiellini Amidei, 'Postille intertestuali: Peire Cardenal', *SMV*, 47, 2001:95–127, suggests Odo de Cheriton as Cardenal's direct source. L. Barbieri, '*Vida, amors, mortz*: Jaufré Rudel tra copisti, lettori e interpreti', *Menichetti Vol.*, 56–70, vindicates Ovid's *Heroides* as a source and shows the mystifying impact of the *vida* on all subsequent readers. F. Carapezza, 'Raimbaut travestito da Fedra: sulla genesi del *salut* provenzale', *MR*, 25, 2001:357–95, substantiates Ovid's *Heroides* as the origin of the genre. D. O. Cepraga, 'Sistema dei generi lirici e dinamiche compilative: la posizione della pastorella nei canzonieri occitanici', *CrT*, 3, 2000:827–69, defines the genre both in terms of its evolution and its MS status.

METRICS AND MUSIC. Beggiato, *Vettori*, gathers several articles on these issues: A. Rossell, 'L'intermelodicità come giustificazione delle imitazione metriche nella lirica trobadorica' (33–42), suggests several aims of intermelodicity; A. Menichetti, 'Sul *rinterzo* nella lirica italiana del Duecento e nei trovatori' (75–87), proposes Guiraut de Bornelh as a possible model; and D. Billy, 'Hasard et intertextualité: à propos d'un cas de contrafacture' (95–115), cautions against excessive reliance on metrical aspects to assert intertextual influence, using Arnaut de Maruelh as an example. Id., 'Le flottement de la césure dans le décasyllabe des troubadours', *CrT*, 3, 2000:587–622, defines this procedure as characteristic of Italian troubadours. M. De Conca, 'Approximations métriques et parcours poétiques du troubadour Arnaut Daniel', *RSTe*, 2, 2000:25–79, tests different approaches to order Arnaut's corpus. R. Harvey, 'Rhymes and "rusty words" in Marcabru's songs', *FS*, 56:1–14, outlines Marcabru's trademark versifying style as intentionally idiosyncratic, acting as a signature, and gives a different reading of poem XV based on this previous analysis. P. Gresti, 'La canzone "S'ieu trobes plazer a vendre" di Bartolomeo Zorzi (PC 74.15)', *Liver Vol.*, 521–37, edits and analyses this *contrafactum*. P. Olivella, 'El joc acrobàtic d'Austorc de Galhac i

Joan de Castellnou', Badia, *Literatura*, 385–407, studies *retrogradacio* in treatises and poetic practice. P. Bracken, 'The myth of the medieval ministrel: an interdisciplinary approach to performers and the *chansonnier* repertory', *Viator*, 33: 100–16, surveys different approaches to single out the performers of lyrics. C. Léglu, 'Did women perform satirical poetry? *Trobairitz* and *Soldadeiras* in Medieval Occitan poetry', *FMLS*, 37.1, 2001: 15–25, explores the impact of a feminine performance for satirical pieces. G. Acciai, 'Il testo musicale e le sue esecuzioni', Boitani, *Circolazione*, 341–73, describes the Gregorian origins of troubadour music and highlights the aspects that influenced later schools.

RECEPTION. G. Giannini, 'In margine a *Madonna, dir vo voglio*', *QFRB*, 14, 1999: 305–20, analyses Lentini's MS sources. S. Asperti and M. Passalacqua, 'Quando eu stava in le tu' cathene: note da un seminario', *Contributi di Filologia dell'Italia mediana*, 14, 2000: 5–24, and G. Santini, 'Intertestualità incipitaria fra provenzali e siciliani', *CrT*, 3, 2000: 871–902, propose a wider occurrence of troubadour textual borrowing. Also on the literary reworking of troubadour songs: M. Perugi, '"Verdi piani", non "verdi panni" (la canzone *Er vei vermeilz* di Arnaut Daniel in Dante e in Petrarca', *Menichetti Vol.*, 323–39; and C. Di Girolamo, 'Canti di penitenza da Stroński a Ausiàs March', *CN*, 62: 191–209, who considers Folquet de Marseille and Peire d'Alvernha among March's sources. E. W. Poe, '*Cantairitz* e *trobairitz*: a forgotten attestation of Old Provençal *trobairitz*', *RF*, 114.4: 206–15, analyses the implications of the mention of the term *trobairitz* in the *Doctrina d'acort.* On philological reception: L. Borghi Cedrini, 'Le "traduzioni" dal provenzale di Mario Equicola', pp. 543–59 of *La parola al testo: scritti per Bice Mortara Garavelli*, ed. Gian Luigi Beccaria and Carla Martello, Alessandria, Dell'Orso, 2001, 1034 pp., unveils a widespread use of troubadour lyrics by Equicola. M. De Conca, 'Per una nuova edizione dell'*Arte del rimare* di G. M. Barbieri', *QFRB*, 14, 1999: 103–17, intends to identify Barbieri's troubadour sources in his forthcoming edition. J.-F. Courouau, 'Claude Fauchet et la Chanson de la Sainte-Foy', *RLaR*, 105.2, 2001: 247–61, discusses Fauchet's doubts on the *Chanson*'s language.

5. Narrative Texts

M. G. Capusso, 'Sulla tradizione galloromanza dell'Apollonio di Tiro', *SMV*, 47, 2001: 205–21, explores the reasons for a diverging Occitan version. F. Cigni, 'Il trovatore n'At de Mons di Tolosa', *ib.*, 251–73, focuses on academic patterns in At's non-lyrical pieces. A. Espadaler, 'Sobre la densitat cultural del *Jaufré*', Badia, *Literatura*, 335–53, and C. Lee, 'L'elogio del re d'Aragona nel *Jaufré*', *AHLM 8*,

1051–60, propose dates for *Jaufré* within the reign of James I of Aragon.

6. Scientific, Doctrinal, and other Prose Texts

L. Badia, 'The *Arbor Scientiae*: A "new" encyclopaedia in the thirteenth-century Occitan-Catalan cultural context', Domínguez, *Arbor Scientia,* 1–19, studies the connection of Lull's encyclopaedia with the *Breviari d'Amor* and Cerverí de Girona. P. Canettiere, 'Il tesoro, la misura della torre e la figura del niente', Beggiato, *Vettori,* 117–34, focuses on Peire de Corbiac's *Thezaurs,* interpreted as a *gap,* and on his deep arithmetical knowledge. C. Léglu, 'Vernacular poems and inquisitors in Languedoc and Champagne', *Viator,* 33: 117–32, analyses the context and the persuasion strategies of texts in the inquisitorial orbit, such as the *Novas de l'heretge. The Life of Douceline of Digne, Mother of the Ladies of Roubaud (in Occitan),* trans. Madeleine Jeay et al., Woodbridge, Boydell and Brewer, 2001, 180 pp., complements the English translation with discussion of béguine activity, Douceline's theology, and the purpose of the *Life.*

MODERN PERIOD

By Stanley F. Levine, *University of South Carolina at Aiken*

William Calin, *Minority Literatures and Modernism: Scots, Breton, and Occitan, 1920–1990,* Toronto U.P., 2000, x + 399 pp., examines the modernist literary tradition in Occ. alongside the same tradition in Scots and Breton. C. brings a variety of critical perspectives to a close reading of a series of proof-texts. A highly-respected scholar of medieval literature, C. finds medieval themes and processes reflected in the Occ. modernist tradition: the knight errant and the spiritual/erotic quest of medieval epic, as well as the *fin'amor* of medieval lyric, inform many of the texts discussed. C. also finds elements of the Baroque and of magic realism. His analyses call on contemporary critical approaches including narratology, structuralism, phenomenology, and post-colonial criticism, as well as the techniques of Biblical exegesis. Within each of the three literatures treated, he draws his texts from the three genres of poetry, novel, and theatre. For Occ. (as earlier for Breton) he chooses three poets (Delavouët, Nelli, Manciet), three novelists (Bodon [Boudou], Lafont, Forêt) and three plays by a single playwright (Lafont). Although he traces the beginnings of Occ. modernism to the 1920s, the Occ. proof-texts post-date World War II. In these texts, he often demonstrates the presence of Christian themes. In the penultimate chapter, labelled 'Postmodern', C. surveys literary and social developments following 1968, then focuses on a series of texts by the engaged priest-poet Joan [Jean] Larzac. C.'s work is more than a series of explications. The structure of the book, its 'Introduction' and 'Conclusion', as well as comments throughout the analyses, allow the reader to see this literature in the wider context of international modernism and in comparison with the (strikingly similar) evolution, needs, and purposes of two other minority literatures. Because of his focus on high modernism, C. gives short shrift to significant authors, such as Max and Ives Roqueta [Rouquette]. He tends to neglect the secular, if not anti-clerical, perspective of much Occ. literature. Although C. states elsewhere that he is more interested in the language than the politics of a text, there are a few unfortunate slips. Although he agrees that 'no cause [. . .] can justify [. . .] looking back on the occupation with nostalgia' (117–18), he refers to 'communist thugs in the Resistance' (112), while paraphrasing uncritically the celebration of the *milice* in a Breton text he analyses. Overall, this may be the most important and original book on Occ. literature published in recent years. (See also W. Calin's reviews of Philippe Gardy, *Une écriture en archipel: Cinquante ans de poésie occitane (1940–1990)*, and, Id., *L'Écriture occitane contemporaine: une quête des mots*, in *Tenso*, 14, 1999:251–25, which list some axioms of his approach to modern Occ. literature, as well as discussing two anthologies of recent Occ. writing.)

Giovanni Agresti, *Il segno del desiderio: introduzione alla letteratura occitana contemporanea*, Venasca (Cuneo), Ousitanio vivo, 1999, 241 pp., is, like the first title cited, a survey of modern Occ. literature based on critical readings of individual works. In addition to essays (in Italian) on Bodon, M. Roqueta, Manciet, Lafont, Surre-Garcia, Vernet, Tardif, Forêt, and J. Privat, there are original interviews with Lafont and Roqueta and a bi-lingual (Occ.-Italian) selection of the latter's poetry. An introductory chapter is devoted to theoretical reflections on Occ. literature, space, and poetics. C. Parayre, '*Lo Libre de Catòia* de Jean Boudou: littérature régionale et critique postcoloniale', *EtF*, 16.1, 2001:125–50, applies cultural studies and post-colonial criticism to the situation of 'regionalist literature'. As Calin demonstrates in *Minority Literatures* (see above), Bodon is not just a romantic painter of regional mores, but a modernist dealing with universal themes of world literature. Instead of 'regionalist literature', it might be more accurate to speak of literature in a 'regional language', 'minority language', or 'lenga minorisada'. P. finds the Occ. situation analogous to that of the post-colonial subject in most respects, other than race. Thus, she argues, a 'regionalist' novel such as *Catòia*, because it activates issues vital to contemporary literary criticism, can attain universal significance. P. shows that the underlying conflict in this novel is between essentialism and hybridization. Essentialism (loyalty to the religious as to the linguistic tradition) has led the protagonist (and the Occ. writer) to social isolation and a dead end. Hybridization is the 'ineluctable' future. Yet, as for Fanon, so too for Catòia, *le regard d'autrui* remains unidirectional. There is no example in B.'s novel of a liberating reciprocal, dialogic exchange of *regards*.

J.-C. Forêt, 'Au fil(s) de l'œuf: une traversée de l'espace temps', pp. 189–99 of *Lo Fiu de l'Uòu: Le Fils de l'Œuf* (Occitanas), Anglet, Atlantica — Pau, Institut Occitan, 2001, 199 pp., and R. Lafont, *'A perpaus dau *Libre dels grands nombres* de Joan-Claudi Forêt', *Oc*, 331, 1999: 38–40, each discuss a recent work by the other. Three interesting essays on Max Roqueta [Rouquette] have appeared: S. Björkman, 'Max Rouquette, chantre des paradis perdus et retrouvés', pp. 51–63 of *Langage et référence: mélanges offerts à Kerstin Jonasson à l'occasion de ses soixante ans*, ed. Hans Kronning et al. (SRU, 63), Uppsala, AUU, 2001, 712 pp., after a general discussion of the difficulties facing the Occ. author, outlines R.'s literary biography and discusses three volumes of prose (*Le Corbeau rouge*, *Vert Paradis*, *Vert Paradis II*) and two of poetry (*Bestiari*, *La Pietat dau matin*). R.'s contribution to the Occ. theatre is not discussed. The bibliography provides a useful guide to work on Occ. literature published in Sweden. P. Gardy has written two short but valuable essays on specific works by R.: 'Le miroir des bêtes', pp. 87–92 of Max Rouquette, *Bestiari / Bestiaire* (Occitanas, 00), Biarritz, Atlantica — Pau, Institut Occitan, 2000, 94 pp., and 'L'origine du monde', *Membrança de la vida ordinària*, Max Rouquette (Occitanas, 6), Biarritz, Atlantica — Pau, Insitut Occitan, 2000, 151 pp. The latter essay reviews the major themes in R.'s oeuvre, such as the place of Argilliers and of Biblical inspiration, then looks at the protagonists and at roquetian themes in the two short stories reprinted here: 'Lo gasogèn' and 'La ròsa e las espinhas'.

In poetry, Manciet has received the most critical attention: J.-M. Devesa, *'Le verbe lumineux de Bernard Manciet', *Europe*, 76, 1999: 181–97; C. Lagarde, *'Points de vue sur la Lande: pays et identité chez François Mauriac et Bernat Manciet', *Lengas*, 46, 1999: 167–90; and F. [Ph.] Gardy, *'Bernat Manciet', *Oc*, 333, 1999: 38–41. U. Hahn, 'René [Renat] Nelli — le language à contre courrant', *BAIEO*, 14: 107–13, reads the poet's 'Per Na Gensor' against the theoretical framework of Ricoeur's *La Métaphore vive*. F. Montanhòl, 'Actualitat de Carles Camprós', *GS*, 33, 1999: 352–54, defines C.'s positions on political and ideological issues (capitalism, communism, socialism, (Christian) humanism, imperialism, and federalism (as an alternative structure for the French state)). Gardy has also published articles on two less well-known 20th-c. Occ. poets: 'Pau-Loís Granier, *Òbra poetica occitana*', *Oc*, 342: 38–44, discusses the artistic career of a

Limousin poet, and the themes which mark his works from the first (publ. 1929) to the last (1948): erudition and (Limousine) history, Apocalypse, light as a sign of divine presence, being and destruction, mystery; Id., 'Lei mesuras d'un poeta: Emilo Bonnel', *Oc*, 341 : 33–37, discusses three major collections of poetry (1977–98) by a neglected modernist Félibrige poet who has created a 'univers poetic originau e mai d'un còp estonant'. Louis Moreno, *Ou pastre, r'ange e u seete pecà*, Menton, SAHM, 2000, prints the text in the original and in translation, in addition to M.'s (literary) biography, a bibliography of his published and unpublished works, a brief history of the Occ. pastoral and detailed study of the Mentonesque (dialectal) lyric.

E. Cròs, 'L'uèlh de la font de Pèire Gogaud', *GS*, 33 : 28–31, describes each novel by a bi-lingual author (1912–1988), whose nostalgic and autobiographical writing 'nos pòt far pensar a Joan [Jean] Giono per l'evocacion de la natura e dels païsans'.

I shall review studies on earlier authors chronologically by century. First, two works which span the centuries: Gilles Lades, *Anthologie des poètes du Quercy*, Martel, Laquet, n.d., covers the entire history from the beginning to a few 20th-c. writers (F. Castan, H. Cayre, J.-J. Delmas), supplying background information and a bibliography for each author, as well as bibliographies for poets omitted from the anthology. Gaston Tuaillon, *La Littérature en francoprovençal avant 1700*, Grenoble, ELLUG, 2001, 276 pp., is a bilingual collection of texts, both popular (*noëls* and songs) and literary, concentrating on the 16th and 17th cs. The introduction discusses linguistic, literary, and bibliographical issues. For each chapter, there is a list of works, an introduction and a conclusion, and for each text, there is a biography and a textual history, literary analysis, and extensive footnotes. T. argues that a vast corpus of works in franco-provençal, usually overlooked, coexisted alongside the more prestigious French authors from the region (e.g. Louise Labé). The *querelle des langues* did not occur here, since the two bodies of work addressed themselves to different audiences. Thus, Greco-Roman references, so common in French literature of the time, are nowhere to be found in franco-provençal literature.

The Occ. baroque remains a vital field of study. Robert Lafont, *Baroques occitans: anthologie de la poésie en langue d'oc, 1560–1660*, Montpellier, Lo gat ros — Univ. Montpellier 3, Univ. Paul-Valéry, Centre d'Etudes Occitanes, 325 pp., is an updated and much expanded version of his earlier baroque anthology. Texts are printed bilingually, and annotated. A general introduction describes the stylistic, historical, and sociological background to this literature. There are brief introductions to the seven chapters, and an extensive bibliography, updated to 2002. *Lengas*, 46, 1999, features a special section devoted to one Baroque poet, entitled 'Lecturas de Pèir de Garròs (*ca.*1525–1583)'. It includes P. Escudé, *'Estetica e etica dels personatges dins las Eglògas' (47–65); J.-F. Courouau, * 'Elements per un estudi deu ritme dens las *Eglògas*' (67–85); A. Krispin, *'La guèrra e la patz dins las *Eglògas*' (87–94); and F. Gardy, *'Leis *Eglògas* de Pèir de Garròs: melancolia e melancolia linguistica' (95–112). M. Bizer, ' "Qui a *païs* n'a que faire de *patrie*": Joachim du Bellay's resistance to a French identity', *RR*, 91, 2000:375–95, argues that Du B.'s *Deffense* did not grow out of a dichotomy between Classical languages and French. For Du B., B. argues, French must defend itself against two rivals: the 'superior' languages (Latin, Greek, Italian) with which French must compete, and the 'barbaric tongues' [regional languages] from which French must differentiate itself before it can be illustrated (377). Despite his hostility to non-consecrated languages, Du B. 'may be imitating Italian imitations of Provençal poetry' (388). Furthermore, in *Les Regrets*, Du B.'s nationalism is regional (Anjou), and his enumeration of Angevin pleasures is inspired by the Occ. *Plazer* (389). 'Regional identity plays a rôle even at the level of *imitatio*, since Du B. surreptitiously uses Provençal [as one model] for his most famous sonnet, 'Heureux qui comme Ulysse', commonly (and mistakenly) thought to be a monument to (his) *national* pride' (393–94). On a 16th-century Occ. poet, see J.-Y. Casanova, *'*L'odo a Pierre Paul* de Robert Ruffi', *Lengas*, 46, 1999:113–28.

P. Escudé, 'L'énigme des deux éditions concurrentes du *Ramelet Mondin* de Pèire Godolin (1637–1638): un tournant dans l'histoire littéraire toulousaine', *AMid*, 229, 2000:5–20, argues that a societal shift was responsible for the evolution of the *Ramelet* over the 40 years G. worked on it. Before 1637–38, the local poet was embedded in a social order, within which local rulers could function as both patrons and protagonists of the work. After that time, as power was increasingly concentrated in Paris, the Occ. poet's rôle was either to flatter the new, central authority or to retreat into a fantasy world and linguistic marginality. Christian Bonnet, *François Rempnoux*, 'Les Amours de Colin & Alyson': *La Littérature occitane entre Baroque et Classique*, Gardonne, Fédérop, 2001, 272 pp. An extensively footnoted reprint of R.'s text (pp. 15–56) precedes B.'s well-researched discussion. B.'s stated goal is to contextualize Occ. writing in North Aquitaine during the first half of the 17th c., in order to show that this production does not deserve the disdain with which it has been viewed. He effectively sets the work within the tradition of the Occ. pastoral (defined as 'comédie en patois'), on the one hand, and of 17th-c. Limousine literature on the other. B. thus describes the political and intellectual relations of Montluc, the libertin prince of

Chabanais, protector of Mairet, Regnier, and others, and R.'s relations both with Adrien Montluc and with Godolin and the Toulouse literary revival. He compares *Les Amours . . .* with *Capiote,* the only other known Limousine pastoral from this period (cf. B.'s *Capiote, pastorale limousine [circa 1623]*, Talence, Univ. Michel de Montaigne, Bordeaux III, 1983, and his *Capiote, tragi-comédie limousine (circa 1623): contribution à la littérature dialectale du XVIIe siècle*, Bordeaux, 1984.

(M.) C. Alén Garabato, 'Aperçu des résultats d'une analyse lexico-sémantique et sociopragmatique du texte toulousain de la période révolutionnaire', *BAIEO,* 14:79–90, presents a series of texts, arguing that these are not informational, but rather make a purely emotional appeal for (or against) the Revolution. They were meant to be read aloud to an unalphabetized audience, tending to reduce the antagonism of the Occ.-speaking population towards the local French speaker, who becomes 'one of them' (as well as being their link to the outside world and the world of ideas). A. G. observes that the texts generally portray the Occ. speaker as naïve but endowed with common sense. The article is followed by a comprehensive bibliography. See also R. Merle, *'Quelques remarques sur l'usage de la langue d'oc dans la propagande démocrate-socialiste sous la Seconde République', *Lengas,* 46:33–43; C. Jouval, 'Le légendaire provençal de Gaspard de Besse', *PrH,* 198, 1999:757–69, studies the interplay of historical fact and legend in Provençal texts devoted to this 18th-c. brigand, from the anonymous *complainte* 'Gaspard de Besso, Pouemo en très chants su la priso, la conduito eis prisoun d'Aï et l'execution de G. de B.', through Mistral down to present-day novelists (and guide-book writers).

The Occ. 19th c. is dominated by the Félibrige, Mistral, and the Provençal dialect of Occ. P. Blanchet, 'Littérature, interlocuteur et choix de langues: l'exemple de la littérature provençale de langue française', *LR*, 53, 1999:281–306, despite its title, discusses authors who write in Provençal Occ.: Tronc (16th c.), Coye (18th c.), Mistral (19th c.), d'Arbaud, Féraud, Gièly, and Delavouët (20th c.), as well as authors writing in 'regional Provençal French'. B. uses sociolinguistic analysis, to show that the use of either Occ. or regional French is 'représentatif, voire revendicatif', and thus an assertion of identity. He endorses Delavouët's observation that writing in Prov. permits him to be universal, while writing in Fr. would have 'condemned' him to be a regionalist writer. Although writing in regional French has been scorned by both Fr. and Occ. purists, B. suggests a triple linguistic system, in which Prov. Occ., Prov. Fr., and standard Fr. would receive equal respect and encouragement. D. Cambiès, 'La prose narrative en occitan au XIXe siècle (romans, nouvelles et récits autobiographiques: 1800–1906)', *BAIEO*, 14:91–96, studies the complete corpus of longer (30 + pp.) Occ. prose texts, excluding *contes*. C. identifies 25, which fall into four types: sentimental, historical, realist, and autobiographical. All but two narratives are set in the past or in the countryside. C. concludes that the attachment to rural Occ. virtues (*vs* Parisian decadence) and to outmoded literary modes led to the long paralysis of Occ. prose narrative, finally broken by the publication of *La Vida de Joan Larzinhac* in 1945.

Jean-François Chanet, *Les Félibres cantaliens: aux sources du régionalisme auvergnat (1879–1914)*, Clermont-Ferrand, Adosa, 2000, 349 pp. + 8 pls, describes the socio-political and 'ideological' background of the *Félibrige* in Cantal (*l'escolo oubergnato*), discusses individual writers and their themes. The book's selections from prose and poetry are accompanied by extensive notes. Annexes include biographical notices, membership lists of Félibrige organizations in Cantal, press clippings, and even police reports on Félibrige activities. The bibliography includes reference to unpublished manuscripts. On Mistral, see the special issue of *FL*, 129, 'La poésie de langue d'oc des troubadours à Mistral', ed. Suzanne Thiolier-Méjean, which includes two articles on French translations of Mistral: P. Blanco Garcia, 'La diffusion du provençal par l'autotraduction: Mistral' (251–60), and J.-C. Bouvier, 'Les traductions françaises de Frédéric Mistral' (261–76), as well as C. Mauron, 'Pour en finir avec la strophe de *Mirèio* et de *Calendau*?' (301–16), a study of sources for the structure and rhyme schemes of M.'s epic verse. The volume also includes an article on a contemporary Provençal writer: M. A. Ciprés Palacín, 'La jeune poésie de langue provençale: l'œuvre d'André Resplandin' (277–300). On Mistral's prose see R. Bertrand, 'Frédéric Mistral et les revenants: sur un récit de *Memori e raconti*', *PrH*, 198, 1999:815–25. S. Björkman, 'Tva Nyprovensalsak Diktverk pa Svenska', pp. 43–56 of *Résonances de la recherche: festskrift till Sigbrit Swahn*, ed. Kerstin Jonasson et al. (SRU, 59), Uppsala, Academiae Upsaliensis, 1999, 480 pp., discusses (in Swedish) both Mistral's *Lou pouèmo dóu Rose* and Felix Gras's novel *Li rouge dóu Miejour*. J. Fourié, 'A prepaus d'un centenari', *GS*, 33 [34], 2001:77–82, strives to demonstrate the influence of Aquiles Mir (1822–1901) on Occ. literature of his time, and to explain his popularity over time, as evidenced by late 20th-c. re-editions of *Lutrin de ladèr* and the *Sermon del curat de Cucunhan*. H. Lieutard, *'Aquiles Manavit, felibre contrariat e patriòta convencut', *Lengas*, 46, 1999:143–65, presents a little-known Félibrige author.

Jean-Claude Rixte has been conducting an intense programme of scholarship on Occ. literature of the Drôme. Jean-Claude Rixte, *Textes et auteurs drômois de langue d'oc, des origines à nos jours: essai de bibliographie avec notes et commentaires*, Montélimar, Dauphinat — Provença Terra d'Oc [IEO Dròma], 2000, 311 pp., features approx. 100 authors, with a thumbnail biography of each author and a 1–6 line summary of each text (pp. 39–292 are devoted to the modern period). There is an annotated bibliography of both creative works and critical essays, followed by indices of periodicals, authors, and communes. Continuing his programme, R. has produced an *Anthologie de l'écrit drômois de langue d'oc*, Vol. 1: *XIIe–XVIIIe siècles*, Montélimar–Toulouse, IEO–Daufinat-Provença–Tèrra d'òc, 312 pp., which includes representative works by local troubadours; documents, some literary, from the 12th-18th c. (modern period: pp. 195–245); and anonymous or oral literature derived from 19th-c. collections (pp. 247–85). Many texts are accompanied by a French translation. Each text is preceded by biographical, critical, and bibliographical comments. Jean-Claude Rixte, **Les Noëls de Taulignan en langue d'oc du 17e siècle*, Montélimar–Toulouse, Daufinat-Provença–Tèrra d'òc, Assoc. des Onze Tours, 2000, 69 pp., includes 12 *noëls* written in or before 1673, a few with melodies. He starts from the two 19th-c. editions, both based on a single manuscript which has disappeared; where there are important differences R. publishes both versions. R.'s introduction discusses the textual history and dialectology of the *noëls*, demonstrating that the linguistic traits correspond to those of Taulignan, a village in the Drôme which is mentioned several times in the *noëls*. The book comes with a lively but ultimately haunting CD recording of five of the *noëls*, four sung to guitar accompaniment, and one to traditional pipes and drums. On an author from this same village, see Id., **Amadée Théolas: auteur taulignanais de langue d'oc: aperçu*, Montélimar, Dauphinat-Provença–Terra d'òc, 2000, 31 pp. Another poet from the Drôme, who happens also to be one of the editors of the *Noëls de Taulignan*, is analysed from various perspectives in *Louis Moutier — Félibre drômois — Poète du Rhône*, ed. Jean-Claude Rixte and Jean-Claude Bouvier, Gap, Imprimerie des Alpes, 1999, 205 pp. + vii-lxvii + 5 pls, includes papers presented at a colloquium held in Montélimar, October 1997, dedicated to the author of *Lou Rose* and the founder of *L'escolo doufinalo felibrenca*: P. Martel, 'Le poème du Rhône' (47–69); J.-C. Bouvier, 'Le Rhône et sa batellerie dans les lettres provençales entre 1880 et 1896', traces the growing interest in the Rhône in Fr. and Occ. writing during the years preceding the simultaneous publication of Moutier's and Mistral's poems dedicated to the river; C. Magrini (123–35) discusses the historical, personal, and ethnographic background to Moutier's poem; Jacques Béthemont (137–56) offers a comparative study (in Occ.) of Moutier's Rhône poem and that of Mistral; J.-L. Ramel (173–83) shows how the history of the Rhône, from mythic to historic time, informs

Moutier's text. The publication includes a collection of Moutier's verse.

Finally, for those interested in literary tourism, Daniel Vitaglione, *A Literary Guide to Provence*, Athens, Swallow Press — Ohio U.P., 2001, 259 pp., is a fine, well illustrated, inclusive but 'reader-friendly' survey of sites associated with an author, with emphasis on the Félibrige and provençal authors who wrote in French (Daudet, Giono, Bosco, et al.). V. recommends places to see and to lodge, and sprinkles his book with bi-lingual citations of relevant literary texts. Although it is addressed to a non-specialist audience, the wealth of information on even the least well-known Prov. writer will be useful to scholars as well.

IV. SPANISH STUDIES

LANGUAGE

By Steven Dworkin, *University of Michigan*, and
Miranda Stewart, *University of Strathclyde*

1. General

Ian Mackenzie, *A Linguistic Introduction to Spanish*, 2001, Munich, Lincom Europa, 190 pp., provides a clearly explicated student-orientated introduction to phonetics and phonology, morphology and syntax, illustrated from Spanish which assumes that 'essentially one standard Spanish applies throughout the Spanish-speaking world'. Consequently, later chapters on varieties of Spanish and the sociolinguistics of Spanish sit uneasily with the approach adopted in the earlier part of the work. *Perspectives on Spanish Linguistics 3*, ed. Javier Gutiérrez-Rexach and José del Valle, 1998, Ohio State U.P., 1998, 187 pp., is the proceedings of the first Hispanic Linguistics Symposium. *Advances In Hispanic Linguistics,* ed. Javier Gutiérrez-Rexach and Fernando Martínez Gil, 2 vols, Somerville, Cascadilla, 1999, 547 pp., contains almost 50 papers from the second Hispanic Linguistics Symposium covering the three broad areas of Psycholinguistics and Sociolinguistics; Phonology, Morphology, and Historical Linguistics; and Syntax, Semantics, and Pragmatics. *Hispanic Linguistics at the Turn of the Millennium. Papers from the 3rd Hispanic Linguistics Symposium*, ed. Héctor Campos et al., Somerville, Cascadilla, 2000, 414 pp., is a selection of peer-reviewed articles from this conference grouped into two sections: phonology, phonetics, and historical linguistics; and syntax, semantics, and pragmatics. Together these volumes provide a rich compendium of recent studies into the Spanish language in the U.S.

Lengua y discurso: estudios dedicados al profesor Vidal Lamíquiz, ed. Pedro Carbonero Cano, Manuel Casado Velarde, and Pilar Gómez Manzano, M, Arco, 2000, 1048 pp., is a wide-ranging compilation of some 80 articles principally from Spain but also abroad (for example, H. López Morales (Puerto Rico), M. Sedano (Venezuela)). *Cuestiones de actualidad en la lengua española*, ed. J. Borrego, F. Fernández, L. Santos, and R. Senabre, Salamanca U.P., 2000, 382 pp., is a mixed collection of conference papers. *En torno al sustantivo y adjetivo en el español actual: aspectos cognitivos, semánticos, (morfo)sintácticos y lexicogenéticos*, ed. Gerd Wotjak, Frankfurt, Vervuert, 2000, 487 pp., is a varied collection of articles from the fifth *Coloquio Internacional de Lingüística*

Hispánica, both empirical and theoretical, exemplified from a range of varieties of Spanish.

Actas del I Congreso de la Asociación de Lingüística y Filología de América Latina (ALFAL) Región noroeste de Europa, ed. Bob de Jonge (*Estudios de Linguística Española*, 13) <http://elies.rediris.es/elies13>, 2001, contains the following articles relating to Spanish: E. Arnous and A. Martínez, 'Del oído al ojo: la variación en la producción escrita', H. López Morales, 'Estratificación social del tabú lingüístico: el caso de Puerto Rico', A. Martínez, 'Contacto de lenguas. Discordancias gramaticales y concordancias semánticas: el número', N. M. Montessori, 'Problemas de producción e interpretación del discurso político', D. Soler-Espiauba, 'Mestizaje lingüístico: funciones del español y del inglés en la expresión de los sentimientos en la narrativa hispana femenina de EE.UU.', M. Stewart, 'Los "hedges" y el uso del "yo" en la interacción cara-a-cara', and A. Veiga, ' "Te he pedido que vengas": la forma verbal "cante" y la relación temporal "pos-ante-presente" '.

Research on Spanish in the United States. Linguistic Issues and Challenges, ed. Ana Roca, Somerville, Cascadilla, 2000, 450 pp., is a lively collection of 29 articles primarily focusing on geographical variation in the Spanish spoken in the United States and on language planning issues. *Linguistics* 40.2, devotes an entire volume to 'Quantitative approaches to Spanish linguistics', ed. David Eddington, whose introduction (209–16) precedes the following articles: J. Hualde and M. Prieto, 'On the diphthong/hiatus contrast in Spanish: some experimental results' (217–34); A. Domínguez, J. Segui, and F. Cuetos, 'The time-course of inflectional morphological priming' (235–59); G. Demello, '*Leísmo* in contemporary Spanish American educated speech' (261–83); R. Torres Cacoullo, '*Le:* from pronoun to intensifier' (285–318); 'Spanish evidence for pitch-accent structure' (319–45); E. Willis, 'Is there a Spanish imperative intonation revisited: local considerations' (347–74); Z. Bárkányi, 'A fresh look at quantity sensitivity in Spanish' (375–94); D. Eddington, 'Spanish diminutive formation without rules or constraints' (395–419); E. Alonso Marks, D. Moates, Z. Bond, and V. Stuckmal, 'Word reconstruction and consonant features in English and Spanish' (421–38); K. Geeshin, 'Semantic transparency as a predictor of copula choice in second language acquisition' (439–68).

2. Diachronic Studies

The two thick volumes of *CIHLE 5* contain over 150 of the papers read at the fifth *Congreso Internacional de Historia de la Lengua Española*. In addition to the plenary papers and presentations at various round tables, the papers appear under the following categories: *fonética y fonología, morfosintaxis, historia de la lengua y lingüística histórica, dialectología y onomástica, el español y las lenguas en contacto,* and *lexicografía, lexicología y semántica.* Taken as a whole, these *Actas* offer an overview of the current state of activity in Spanish historical linguistics. Most of the papers focus on quite narrow topics in the history of Spanish, both in Spain and the New World, often without concern for broader issues of language change. Only selected items can be reported in the appropriate sections below.

Students and specialists alike will welcome the second edition of Ralph Penny, *A History of the Spanish Language*, CUP, xix + 398 pp. In addition to changes and updates, especially in the chapters on historical phonology and morphology, the author has added a new final chapter in which he discusses the nature of language history, the concept of world Spanish, processes of convergence and divergence within Spanish, and Spanish-English contact.

Although José María García Martín, *La formación de los tiempos compuestos del verbo en español medieval y clásico. Aspectos fonológicos, morfológicos y sintácticos*, Valencia U.P., 2001, 175 pp., makes no pretensions to originality, it provides a handy summary of work done on the formal and syntactic evolution of compound tenses in Medieval and Early Modern Spanish. G. Colón Doménech, 'Castellano-aragonés en el antiguo reino de Valencia', *CIHLE 5*, 33–51, describes the role of Castilian and Aragonese in the linguistic history of the Kingdom of Valencia. J. Frago Gracia, 'Las lenguas de Aragón en la Edad Media', *BRAE*, 81, 2001:465–78, surveys the historical background to the multilingualism which characterizes the medieval Crown of Aragon. G. Hilty, 'El plurilingüismo en la corte de Alfonso X el Sabio', *CIHLE 5*, 207–20, discusses the role of multilingualism at the court of Alfonso X in the development of the Castilian literary language. D. N. Tuten, '¿Nació el andaluz en el siglo XIII?', *ib.*, 1457–66, critically examines the evidence for J. A. Frago Gracia's hypothesis that Andalusian was constituted as a dialect distinct from Castilian in the 13th century. L. Miniverni, 'La formación de la koiné judeo-española en el siglo XVI', *RLiR*, 66:497–512, describes the social, historical, and cultural background of the formation of the Judeo-Spanish koiné in the 16th-c. Ottoman Empire. The study also offers an outline of the linguistic features of this nascent koiné.

I. Fernández-Ordóñez, 'Hacia una dialectología histórica: reflexiones sobre la historia del leísmo, el laísmo y el loísmo', *BRAE*, 81, 2001:389–464, offers important methodological considerations on the variation of a sociolinguistic marker in the manuscript transmission of a medieval text. Traditional historical grammar has paid insufficient attention to the role of copyists and medieval dialect variation. M. N. Sánchez González de Herrero, 'Rasgos fonéticos y morfológicos de los documentos alfonsíes', *RFE*, 82:139–77, studies formal variation in the documents surveyed for her *Diccionario español de documentos alfonsíes*. She proposes that the variation may reflect the linguistic practices of the different regions to which the documents were being sent.

R. Wright, 'Léxico romance en los glosarios de San Millán', *CIHLE 5*, 2421–26, argues that the glossary preserved in San Millán MS 46 cannot be a Latin-Romance dictionary as the conceptual difference between Latin and Romance had not yet come into being. M. Ariza, 'El habla de Toledo en la Edad Media', *ib.*, 1083–92, discusses the survival of Mozarabic linguistic features. F. González Ollé, 'Hablar bien: Alabanza de la lengua cortesana y menosprecio de la lengua aldeana (II)', *ib.*, 1217–35, continues his meticulous examination of medieval texts that comment on levels of language usage. E. Bustos Gisbert and R. Santiago, 'Para un nuevo planteamiento de la llamada "norma madrileña" (siglos XVI y XVII)', *ib.*, 1123–36, examine methodological issues relevant to the study of the language of Madrid in the early modern period. As indicated in its title, J. Brumme, 'Lingüística variacional e historia de la lengua moderna: una aportación metodológica', *ib.*, 1107–21, offers useful methodological considerations on studying the history of the modern language.

IJSL, 149, 2001, 'Between koineization and standardization: New World Spanish revisited', contains studies which deal with the history of New World Spanish from a sociolinguistics perspective. These essays are important both for the discussion of specific data and broader methodological issues: C. Parodi, 'Contacto de dialectos y lenguas en el Nuevo Mundo: la vernacularización del español en América' (33–53), M. Hidalgo, 'Sociolinguistic stratification in New Spain' (55–78), A. M. Escobar, 'Contact features in colonial Peruvian Spanish' (79–93), and G. de Granda, 'Procesos de *estandardización revertida* en la configuración histórica del español americano: el caso del espacio surandino' (95–118).

3. Diachronic Phonetics and Phonology

Thomas D. Cravens, *Comparative Historical Dialectology: Italo-Romance Clues to Ibero-Romance Sound Change*, Amsterdam, Benjamins, 163 pp., examines the historical motivation for the restructured voicing of Latin /p t k/ and palatalization of initial /l/ and /n/ in varieties of Italo-and Hispano-Romance. These shifts are in the long run attributable to loss of pan-Romance consonant gemination.

K. J. Wireback offers two detailed studies on the workings of consonant + yod metathesis in which he brings into play insights provided by recent work in phonetics and data from non-Romance languages. In 'Consonant + yod metathesis in Hispano-Romance: the interaction of palatalization, perceptual uncertainty, and analogy', *RF*, 114: 133–59, W. concludes that regular /Cj/ metathesis requires a phonetically gradual mechanism of inversion with an intermediate palatalized stage. Analogy and perceptual considerations also play important roles in this process. In 'On the metathesis of labials + /j/ in Hispano-Romance', *HR*, 70: 311–31, W. applies his general findings on consonant + yod metathesis to the specific case of labial + yod metathesis in Spanish and Portuguese. Such metathesis is regular and gradual in Portuguese, whereas the two Spanish cases (CAPIAT > *quepa*, SAPIAT > *sepa*) reflect an abrupt inversion due to analogical influence from other verb stems.

The historical development of sibilants in Spanish continues to attract attention. C. Kauffeld, 'Textual evidence of *seseo* in Andalusian texts (1324–1500)', *Kasten Vol.*, 157–68, reports 67 examples of spelling confusion suggesting *seseo* in 89 non-literary texts from Seville and Córdoba (with three examples from as early as 1398). She concludes that *seseo* was an identifiable phenomenon of the language of those two cities by the end of the 15th century. P. Montero Curiel, 'Confusiones de sibilantes en el manuscrito 20241/13 de la Biblioteca Nacional de Madrid', *RFE*, 82: 45–61, studies sibilant confusions that seem to indicate *seseante* tendencies in an 18th-c. non-literary manuscript from Alburquerque (Extremadura), near the Portuguese border. M. Ariza Viguera, 'En torno a las confusions de sibilantes y otros fenómenos fonéticos', *González Ollé Vol.*, 121–37, discusses once again the importance of the direct consultation of the original manuscripts when studying the sibilant shifts of late medieval and early modern Spanish. P. Sánchez–Prieto Borja, 'Sobre una supuesta evolución circular en español: CAUSA > *cabsa* > *causa* (con reflexiones sobre el concepto de ultracorrección)', *ib.*, 1287–1310, is a contribution to both historical phonology and the history of Spanish spelling. He concludes that in forms such as *abdiencia*, *cabsa*, etc. the graph <ab> represents /au/ and not /ab/ or /ap/. C. Isasi, 'Para un estudio de grafías de palatales en documentos norteños de los siglos XV y XVI', *ib.*, 739–44, examines the representation of palatals in a corpus of 15th-c. and 16th-c. documents from Vizcaya. M. Torreblanca, 'El sistema gráfico-fonológico del castellano primitivo: Las consonantes palatales', *CIHLE 5*, 417–29, studies on the basis of original documents the graphic representations in early Castilian of the palatals derived from Latin /-lj-, -k'l-, -g'l-, -kt-/.

Questions concerning apocope of *–e* continue to be of interest. C. Folgar, 'La apócope de *grande* en la *Primera Crónica General de España*', *CIHLE 5*, 331–40, seeks to explain the dominance in 13th-c.

texts of apocopated *grand/grant* in pre-and post-nominal positions. Post-nominal *grand* reflects an analogical extension of pre-nominal *grand*, which occurs with much higher frequency. M. Torreblanca and R. Blake, 'De morfofonología histórica española: la apócope de *-e* en la época medieval', *ib.*, 431–43, critique Lapesa's external explanation of this phenomenon and stress the role of morphological analogy in this process. R. Penny essays a sociolinguistic approach to the fate of /h/ in Early Modern Spanish in his 'Contacto de variedades y resolución de la variación: aspiración y pérdida de /h/ en el Madrid del s. XVI', *ib.*, 397–406. He specifically applies the insights of work on the role of social networks and koineization on language change in migration contexts.

4. DIACHRONIC MORPHOLOGY

In the category of derivational morphology, pride of place goes to David Pharies, *Diccionario etimológico de los sufijos españoles y de otros elementos finales*, M, Gredos, 769 pp. This monumental work seeks to explain (in alphabetical order) the origin of all Spanish suffixes and suffixoids. Each entry identifies the source(s) of the suffix and describes its semantic evolution and diffusion through the lexicon. P. illustrates the analytical advantage of studying together suffixes that share a common consonantal pillar in his note 'Historia de los sufijos españoles *-ajo, -ejo, -ijo, -ojo- y -ujo*', García-Medall, *Aspectos*, 95–101. The author identifies the various Latin formatives which gave rise to this suffixal series and states that speakers coined *-ujo* to complete the vocalic gamut of suffixes with the consonantal pillar *-j-*. M. M. Renedo Sinovas, 'La sufijación en el léxico científico alfonsí: nombres deadjetivales y denominales', *ib.*, 135–50, studies formal and semantic factors as well as rivalries between competing suffixes observable in deadjectival and denominal nouns found in the Alfonsine *Libro conplido en los iudizios de las estrellas.* The author seems unaware of relevant studies by Penny, Malkiel, and Dworkin. E. Ridruejo, 'El sufijo *-dumbre* en español medieval', *González Ollé Vol.*, 1161–75, examines the conditions which led to a severe reduction, starting in the 14th c., in the productivity and vitality of *-dumbre.*

Adelino Álvarez Rodríguez, *El futuro de subjuntivo del latín al romance* (*Analecta Malacitana*, Anejo 40), Málaga, 2001, 102 pp., argues that the Spanish future subjunctive goes back exclusively to the future perfect, and not to an amalgam of the future perfect with the perfect subjunctive. This hypothesis is supported by the OSp. singular forms in *-o* (e.g. *amaro*) which go back only to the future perfect AMAVERO and not to the perfect subjunctive AMAVERIM. The dominant pattern of *-e* in the first person singular results from analogy. R. Harris-Northall, 'Sources for variation in preterite endings in Old Spanish', *Kasten Vol.*, 135–46, demonstrates how careful study of the Alfonsine textual evidence may throw light on the origins of the variation between diphthongal and non-diphthongal verb suffixes in the OSp. preterite (e.g., *perdiste/perdieste, perdimos/perdiemos, perdistes/perdiestes*). In addition to the long-recognized role of the preterite paradigm of *dar*, the author draws attention to the 'as yet unacknowledged role' of OSp. *dezir* in the variation at issue. R. J. Penny, 'Procesos de clasificación verbal española: polaridad de vocales radicales en los verbos en *-er* e *-ir*', *González Ollé Vol.*, 1053–70, re-examines the factors leading to the association of stem mid-vowels with the *-er* class and high vowels with the *-ir* class. This alignment of vowels may reflect an attempt to differentiate further on the level of form the two classes whose verbal suffixes are almost identical throughout the entire paradigm. He notes the semantic distinction stative/active between the *-er* and *-ir* classes.

R. M. Espinosa Elorza, '¿Alguna vez triunfó el femenino? Revisión de los posesivos en castellano medieval', Veiga, *Historiografía*, 9–18, offers a useful critical review of the historical development of Spanish possessives with some new analytic suggestions. I. Pujol Payet, 'Nuevos enfoques en morfología histórica: derivados en relación al concepto de "cuatro"', *ib.*, 61–74, continues her series of studies of Spanish derivatives based on Latin numerals, in this case some 133 reflexes of QUATTUOR, QUATERNUS, QUATERNI, QUADRUPLEX, QUADRUPLES, and QUADRUS, -A, -UM.

5. Diachronic Syntax

A number of important studies examine syntactic evolution in the wider framework of discourse analysis and text linguistics. Mario Barra Jover's prize-winnning *Propiedades léxicas y evolución sintáctica. El desarrollo de los mecanismos de subordinación en español*, Corunna, Toxosoutos, 421 pp., studies in great detail the evolution throughout the recorded history of Spanish of subordinators whose final element is *que*. J. J. de Bustos Tovar, 'Mecanismos de cohesión discursiva en castellano a fines de la Edad Media', *CIHLE 5*, 53–84, offers methodological considerations on the analysis of discourse markers in doctrinal texts from the first half of the 15th century. Issues of methodology also come to the forefront in A. Narbona Jiménez, 'Sobre evolución sintáctica y escritura-oralidad', *ib.*, 133–58, and E. Ridruejo, 'Para un programa de pragmática histórica del español', *ib.*, 159–77. Both studies contain useful bibliographies. M. Cristobalina Moreno attempts to apply the principles of pragmatics to a concrete issue in 'La cortesía verbal en el Siglo de Oro: los actos de habla directivos, un estudio de pragmática histórica', *ib.*, 1345–59. R. Cano Aguilar, 'La sintaxis del diálogo en Berceo', *Kovacci Vol.*, 113–29, discusses the various syntactic types of intersentence relationships in dialogues.

M. Velando Casanova, 'Algunas consideraciones en torno al adverbio *hy* en castellano medieval', Veiga, *Historiografía*, 35–45, claims that the locative, temporal, and demonstrative uses of *(h)y* and its function as a connector (preceded by *des*) reflect its deictic nature. C. Sánchez Lancis, 'Sobre la pérdida del adverbio medieval *y* en español preclásico', *ib.*, 47–59, identifies several causes for the loss of this element: identity of function with *allí* and *ahí*, and the growing preference for prepositional phrases to express the relations indicated by *y*.

By examining the history of the use of the originally locative preposition *a* as a marker of the direct object (the so-called 'personal *a*'), C. Company, 'Grammaticalization and category weakness', Wischer, *Grammaticalization*, 201–15, wishes to show that there is a close connection between categorical prototypes and diachronic stability on one hand, and category margins and diachronic instability on the other. In her view, grammaticalization processes first affect elements that are on the margins of a given category, items that often exhibit properties belonging to two or more categories. J. L. Girón Alconchel, 'Procesos de gramaticalización del español clásico al moderno', *CIHLE 5*, 103–21, examines several instances of post-medieval grammaticalization which serve to increase the degree of grammatical cohesion.

C. García Gallarín, 'Usos de *haber* y *tener* en textos medievales y clásicos', *Iberoromania*, 55:1–28, examines the syntactic and semantic factors that combined to lead to the replacement of OSp. *aver* by *tener* in the late medieval language as the basic verb indicating possession. In the older language *aver* had an inchoative value while *tener* had a durative value. L. Hartman, '¿De qué provino "de que"? Noun clauses in apposition to nouns in Alfonso el Sabio', *Kasten Vol.*, 147–56, examines noun clauses in apposition in Alfonso and the complementizers that introduce them. H. finds only one example of *de que* rather than *que* in the Alfonsine corpus. The bulk of the article describes the use of *que* and *de que* in Modern Spanish. D. Nieuwenhuisjen, 'Variación de colocación de los pronombres átonos en el español antiguo', *ZRP*, 118:360–75, attempts to explain unstressed pronoun position in Medieval Spanish in terms of hierarchies of functional relevance. In her view the data indicate that communicatively more important unstressed pronouns will occupy preverbal position. M. A. Martín Zorraquino, 'Las construcciones pronominales en los textos del primitivo romance hispánico', *González Ollé Vol.*, 843–84, describes in detail the use of constructions involving reflexive and non-reflexive *se* in the *Glosas Emilianenses* and *Glosas Silenses.*

6. Diachronic Lexicology

Fascicle 22 (pp. 81–160) of the *Diccionario del español medieval* has appeared, bringing this work up to the word *alderredores.* The editors announce that, in order to speed up the pace of publication, fewer examples and no etymological information will be provided in each entry. Two studies by members of the *Diccionario del español medieval* team illustrate how the wealth of lexical data in their files can serve the needs of linguists as well as students of Spanish history and culture. B. Müller, '*Alemán* — zu den soziohistorischen Aspekten der Aufnahme eines Ethnoyms ins Spanische', *Fest. Lüdtke*, 207–15, and E.-M. Güida, '*Indio* und *Indiano* im Spanischen des 13. Jahrhunderts, *ib.*, 217–26, discuss the semantic history of the title words in the medieval language. Specialists in medieval Spanish lexicology will rejoice at the publication of Lloyd A. Kasten and John J. Nitti, *Diccionario de la prosa castellana del rey Alfonso X*, 3 vols, NY, HSMS, 1918 pp. This work records with examples in context all words found in Alfonsine prose texts that have been preserved in manuscripts prepared in Alfonso's Royal Scriptorium. Francisco Gago-Jover, *Vocabulario militar castellano (siglos* XIII–XV), Granada U.P., 398 pp., offers alphabetically arranged lexical vignettes of military terminology found in 50 OSp. texts. Albert Soler and Nuria Mañé have rendered a great service to their fellow scholars by gathering together in *Para la historia del léxico español*, 2 vols, M, Arco–Libro, 823 pp., 32 lexical studies centering on Spanish written over nearly half a century by Germán Colón Doménech. These individual studies would form part of the necessary foundation which Colón has advocated for a thorough history of the Spanish lexicon.

S. N. Dworkin continues his work on the entry and integration of *cultismos* in late medieval Spanish. In 'La introducción e incorporación de latinismos en el español medieval tardío: algunas cuestiones lingüísticas y metodológicas', *González Ollé Vol.*, 421–33, D. raises general issues concerning the introduction of Latinisms and deals specifically with the rivalry between *débil, último, único*, and *útil* and the medieval terms for these notions. In 'Pérdida e integración léxicas: *aína* vs. *rápido* en el español premoderno', *Messner Vol.*, 109–18, he studies the elimination of OSp. *aína* and the entry of *rápido*, which did not gain currency until the 17th century. The demise of *aína* paved the way for the entry of *rápido.*

Issues concerning the formation and content of the late medieval and early modern Spanish medical lexicon are discussed in several papers included in *Herrera Vol.*: G. Colón, 'Diatopismos en el *Diccionario español de términos médicos antiguos (DETEMA)*' (13–19), illustrates the value of this reference work for diachronic lexical research. L. Nieto Jiménez, 'El léxico medicinal en la *Brevis Grammatica* de A. Gutiérrez Cerezo' (143–57), records and comments on the 36 medical terms included by Nebrija's student, Andrés Gutiérrez Cerezo in his *Brevis Grammatica* (Burgos 1485). In like fashion, M. Nieves Sánchez, 'El léxico médico en *El libro de las propiedades de las cosas*' (169–82), discusses selected examples of medical terms found in Books 5 and 7 of the Spanish version (late 15th-c.) of that medieval encyclopedia. Several of the papers in the lexicology section of *CIHLE 5* and in *La historia de los lenguajes iberorrománicos de especialidad: la divulgación de la ciencia. Actas del II Coloquio Internacional, 27–29 de mayo de 1999*, ed. Jenny Brumme, Frankfurt, Vervuert, 2001, 361 pp., deal with the growth over time of the technical and scientific vocabulary of Spanish.

Scholars continue to prepare individual word histories. P. Álvarez de Miranda. 'Una inexistente homonimia: historia de *gitón* (o *getón*) y *guitón*', *ER*, 24: 71–89, traces the history of *gitón* 'token' and *guitón*' vagabond' and the circumstances which led to these Gallicisms being recorded erroneously in the *DRAE* as a set of homonyms under the form *guitón*. Id., 'Para la historia de *americano*', *González Ollé Vol.*, 73–87, offers new documentation of the uses of this ethnonym in the 17th and 18th centuries. F. Bustos Tovar, 'Un problema etimológico y semántico: la palabra *auze*', *CIHLE 5*, 1915–26, supports J. Cornu, R. Menéndez Pidal, and J. Corominas in deriving *auze* from **avicem*. A. García Valle, 'A propósito de *amparanza* y *emparanza* en la documentación notarial medieval', *ib.*, 2063–74, shows a decided preference for *emparanza* in Navarro-Aragonese sources in the meanings 'amparo, protección, tutela' and 'embargo'. P. Montero Curiel traces the intertwined semantic histories of the two adjectives at issue in her '*Enjuto* y *seco*: historia de una confluencia semántica', *ib.*, 2253–63. E. Núñez-Méndez, 'El origen de *trabajar*', *Neophilologus*, 85, 2000: 385–95, adds nothing new to our knowledge of the formal and semantic history of *trabajar* and its Romance cognates.

7. Phonetics and Phonology

C.-E. Piñeros, 'Segment-to-syllable alignment and vocalization in Chilean Spanish', *Lingua*, 111, 2001: 163–88, analyses the vocalization of stop consonants (e.g. *adquirir*). Id., 'Markedness and laziness in Spanish obstruents', *ib.*, 112: 349–413, looks at the processes of devoicing and spirantization of voiced obstruents (e.g. *a<u>b</u>surdo*) and argues that assimilation, rather than accounting for this phenomenon, is merely a side-effect of effort reduction, the 'laziness' of the title.

8. Morphology and Syntax

I. Mackenzie, 'The Spanish subjunctive: the philosophical dimension', *BHS*, 79: 1–13, aims to recast, within a philosophical framework, certain facts about the Spanish subjunctive in restrictive relative clauses. The indicative-subjunctive opposition can be seen as being organized, partly at least, on the bases of the following contrasts: attributive-referential; universal-existential; and notional-relational.

Karen Zagona, *The Syntax of Spanish*, CUP, 286 pp., provides a traditional description of the major characteristics of Spanish grammar within a Chomskyan (principles and parameters and minimalist) framework as part of a series aiming to allow cross-theoretical and cross-linguistic comparison. Alexandre Veiga, *Estudios de morfosintaxis verbal española*, Lugo, Tris Tram, 260 pp., examines issues of morphosyntax such as the 'historic present' using decontextualized, confected examples. While concluding, for example, that the deixis of tense does not necessarily coincide with the moment of utterance, the issues this raises are not tackled and, for example, no pragmatic explanations are sought. Ricardo Maldonado, *A media voz. Problemas conceptuales del clítico 'se'*, Mexico, UNAM, 1999, 480 pp., is also an account based largely on confected examples which could have benefited from testing its hypotheses on naturally-occurring data. Rosario Alonso Raya, *Sintaxis y discurso a propósito de 'las fórmulas perifrásticas de relativo'*, Granada, Granada Lingvistica, 1998, 234 pp., provides a useful framework for the analysis of the discourse function clefts (e.g. *fueron ellos los que . . .*) which remains to be applied to naturally-occurring data. Silvia Beatriz Kaul de Marlangeo, *Los adverbios en -mente del español de hoy y su función semántica y de cuantificación*, Frankfurt, Vervuert, 157 pp., adopts a Coserian (1986) functional structural approach with a pragmatic dimension which nonetheless remains intralinguistic as the use of quantifying adverbs, for instance, is not studied in context. Yolanda González Aranda, *Forma y estructura de un campo semántico (a propósito de la sustancia de contenido 'moverse' en español)*, Almería U.P., 1998, 272 pp., looks at verbs of motion largely in terms of verticality and directionality. Yuko Morimoto, *Los verbos de movimiento*, M, Visor, 2001, 251 pp., investigates the relationship between lexis and syntax in verbs of motion. Maria Kitova-Vasileva, *La 'verosimilitud relativa' y su expresión en español*, Santiago de Compostela U.P., 2000, 190 pp., uses a framework derived from Spanish and Slavic linguistic traditions to investigate modality.

9. Lexicology

Así son los diccionarios, ed. M. Vila Rubio et al., Lleida U.P., 1999, 242 pp., contains the following: M. Bargalló Escrivá, 'La información gramatical en los diccionarios didácticos monolingües en español' (5–42); C. Garriga Escribano, 'Diccionarios didácticos y marcas lexicográficas' (43–75); J. Gutiérrez Cuadrado, 'Notas a propósito de la ejemplificación y la sinonimia en los diccionarios para extranjeros' (77–95); J. Orduña López, 'La función definitoria de los ejemplos: a propósito del léxico filosófico del *Diccionario de autoridades*' (99–119); M. Vila Rubio and M. Casanovas Catalá, 'Lengua especializada y lexicografía: calas en el léxico de la medicina' (121–45); M. A. Calero Fernández, 'Diccionario, pensamiento colectivo e ideología (o los peligros de definir)' (149–201); R. Mateu Serra, '*El DRAE*: algunas consideraciones para un posible enfoque pragmático' (203–19).

Enrique Jiménez Ríos, *Variación lexical y diccionarios: los arcaísmos en el diccionario de la Real Academia*, Frankfurt, Vervuert, 2001, 301 pp., investigates a range of dictionaries of Spanish and principally the 22 editions of the *DRAE* to identify archaisms, the extent to which these are marked as such and in what terms. *RILI*, 1.1, deals with lexicography and contains, amongst others, the following articles: G. de Granda, 'Un caso complejo de *convergencia* morfosintáctica por contacto en el español andino' (35–44), A. Schwegler and T. Morton, 'Vernacular Spanish in a microcosm: *Kayetano* en El Palenque de San Basilio (Colombia)' (45–108), M. Sedano, 'Seudohendidas y oraciones con verbo *ser* focalizador en dos corpus del español hablado de Caracas' (155–84).

10. Sociolinguistics and Dialectology

El lenguaje de los jóvenes, ed. Félix Rodríguez, B, Ariel, 318 pp., contains the following articles on youth language: F. Rodríguez, 'Lengua y contracultura juvenil: anatomía de una generación' (29–56); M. Casado Velarde, 'Aspectos morfológicos y semánticos del lenguaje juvenil' (57–66); G. Herrero, 'Aspectos sintácticos del lenguaje juvenil' (67–96); I. Molina, 'Evolución de las fórmulas de tratamiento en la juventud madrileña a lo largo del siglo xx' (97–121); N. Catalá Torres, 'Consideraciones acerca de la pobreza expresiva de los jóvenes' (123–35); K. Zimmermann, 'La variedad juvenil en la interacción verbal entre jóvenes' (137–63); M. Forment, E. Martinell, and N. Vallero, 'Aproximación al lenguaje gestual de los jóvenes' (165–91); A. Vigara, 'Cultura y estilo de los "niños bien"' (195–240); R. Morant, 'El lenguaje de los estudiantes' (243–63); J. Gómez Capus and F. Rodríguez, 'El lenguaje de los soldados' (265–91).

Tomás Bueso Oliver, *Apuntes de jerga estudiantil en la Universidad de Zaragoza*, Zaragoza, Excma. Diputación de Zaragoza, 1999, 94 pp., contains an up-to-date lexicon which could accompany the above work. Julia Sanmartín Sáez, *Lenguaje y cultura marginal: el argot de la delincuencia*, Valencia U.P., 1998, 272 pp., is a rich sociolinguistic study of 24 informants from Valencia prison stratified by variables such as length of sentence, which looks at issues such as language attitudes and lexical creation (e.g. in the fields of drugs and prostitution).

La lengua y los medios de comunicación. Vol. 1, ed. Joaquín Garrido Medina, M, Univ. Complutense, 1999, 525 pp., contains the proceedings of a conference on this topic. Enrique Alvarez Varó and Brian Hughes, *El español jurídico*, B, Ariel, 352 pp., is aimed principally at students of interpreting and translating, examines current uses of legal Spanish, and, where appropriate, provides English and French equivalents. *Lengua española y comunicación*, ed. María Victoria Romero, B, Ariel, 467 pp., ostensibly provides a guide to Spanish for students of journalism; it contains a number of useful articles based on up-to-date data, e.g. M. Casado Velarde, 'Acortamientos léxicos, formación de siglas y acrónimos' (379–91).

Norma Carricaburo, *El voseo en la literatura argentina*, M, Arco, 1999, 494 pp., discusses *voseo* in America and specifically how it has evolved in Argentina, and then exemplifies and accounts for its use in texts ranging from early Argentinian literature to that of the post-boom. She charts the expansion of *voseo* to the detriment and, ultimately, virtual annihilation of *tú*.

Identidades lingüísticas en la España autonómica, ed. Georg Bossong and Francisco Báez de Aguilar González, Frankfurt, Vervuert, 2000, 192 pp., contains the following: C. Bierbach, 'Cuatro idiomas para un Estado — ¿cuántos para una Región Autónoma? Observaciones acerca del debate sobre plurilingüismo y política lingüística en España' (17–37); M. Strubell, 'La investigación sociolingüística en los Países Catalanes' (39–60); Y. Griley, 'Perspectivas en la política lingüística en Cataluña' (61–67); J. Ariztondo, 'La política lingüística en la Comunidad Autónoma Vasca' (69–80); M. Fernández, 'Entre castellano y portugués: la identidad lingüística del gallego' (81–105); J. Villena, 'Identidad y variación lingüística: prestigio nacional y lealtad vernacular en el español hablado en Andalucía' (107–50); F. Báez, 'Los andaluces en busca de su identidad' (151–86).

Alvaro Arias Cabal, *El morfema de 'neutro de materia' en asturiano*, Santiago de Compostela U.P., 1999, 150 pp., adds to the morphological description of Asturian. Carmen Fernández Juncal, *Variación y prestigio: estudio sociolingüístico en el oriente de Cantabria*, Madrid, CSIC, 1998, 250 pp., also discusses count and non-count nouns, a feature shared with Asturian, and the phenomenon of metaphony (e.g. *añidir* for *añadir*). María Luisa Arnal Purroy, *El habla de la Baja Ribagorza occidental: aspectos fónicos y gramaticales*, Zaragoza, Institución Fernando el Católico, 1998, 489 pp., provides a sociolinguistic description of this variety which has features from Aragonese, Catalan, and Castilian as well as its own distinctive features (e.g. certain palatalizations and forms of *sé* (*ser*)). It is based on a corpus of 88 socially-stratified informants from 24 villages. While this variety is the prime spoken medium for the over 30s, in all but the most conservative localities, it is giving way to Castilian amongst younger speakers. José Luis Aliaga Jiménez, *Aspectos de lexicografía española en el léxico aragonés en las ediciones del diccionario académico*, Zaragoza, Excma. Diputación Provincial de Zaragoza, 2000, 403 pp., traces the inclusion of regional, and specifically Aragonese lexis, in the *DRAE*. While the 15th edition (1925) marks a watershed in attitudes towards regional varieties, the author argues for a more informed debate over what a 'diccionario nacional' should comprise. Antonio Manuel Avila Muñoz, *Léxico de frecuencia del español hablado en Málaga*, Málaga U.P., 1999, 340 pp., uses a varied and carefully designed oral corpus, and discussions about methodology are more interesting than the frequency counts it generates. *Estudios para un corpus del español hablado en Alicante*, ed. Dolores Azorín Fernández, María Antonia Martínez Linares, and Juan Luis Jiménez Ruiz, Alicante U.P., 1999, 213 pp., brings together a series of articles revolving around corpus-building in general and in particular the issues involved in creating the corpus referred to in the title. Manuel A. Esgueva Martínez, *Las plantas silvestres en León: estudio de dialectología lingüística*, M, UNED, 1999, 336 pp., is an immense collaborative study covering some 400 plants. Janick Le Men, *Léxico leonés: estudio bibliográfico, análisis crítico*, León U.P., 1999, 171 pp., provides a critical bibliography of work on the lexis of this variety. Adela Morín Rodríguez, *Las formas pronominales de tratamiento en el español de las Palmas de Gran Canaria: variaciones y actitudes lingüísticas*, Granada, Granada Lingvistica, 2001, 326 pp., is a variationist study of the use of T/V amongst 47 socially-stratified informants, investigating the variables of power, distance, and domain. Sex and status are the least important variables except when status interacts with domain (e.g. professional vs home).

Flora Klein-Andreu, *Variación actual y evolución histórica: los clíticos le/s, la/s, lo/s*, Munich, Lincom, 2000, 167 pp., continues to research what is a rich topic in terms of variationist theory. She concentrates on variables of use, finding that standard syntactic categories such as direct and indirect object are of little help. She proposes variables such as individualization of the referent, number of participants in the event recounted, and hearer reference as being more useful in understanding how each variant functions in context. M. Broce and R. Torres Cacoullos, 'Dialectología urbana rural: la estratificación social de (r) y (l) en Coclé Panamá', *His(US)*, 85:342–53, is a variationist study which extends the variable of social stratification from an urban to a rural setting and finds that the degree of non-standardness of variants does not correlate with the degree of phonetic weakening. A. Wasa, '*A lo mejor* y el subjuntivo', *ib.*, 131–36, investigates why this adverbial phrase does not take the subjunctive unlike other adverbs of possibility such as *tal vez* and argues that, instead of expressing speaker doubt about a proposition, it enables the speaker to choose between competing propositions. D. Ligatto, 'Discourse criteria in the selection of mood in Spanish: concessive clauses', *ib.*, 137–49 suggests that alongside the epistemic value of the subjunctive there is a discursive dimension found in the acts of formulation and reformulation.

The Battle over Spanish between 1800 and 2000. Language Ideologies and Hispanic Intellectuals, ed. José del Valle and Luis Gabriel-Stheeman, London–NY, Routledge, 237 pp., is a fascinating account of how notions of linguistic science are pressed into the service of ideology and contains the following: José del Valle and Luis Gabriel-Stheeman, 'Nationalism, *hispanismo*, and monoglossic culture' (1–13), B. L. Velleman, 'Linguistic academicism and Hispanic community: Sarmiento and Unamuno' (14–41), B. Moré, 'The ideological construction of an empirical base: selection and elaboration in Andrés Bello's grammar' (42–63), J. del Valle, 'Historical linguistics and cultural history: the polemic between Rufino José Cuervo and Juan Valera' (64–77), J. del Valle, 'Menéndez Pidal, national regeneration and the linguistic utopia' (78–105), J. R. Resina, ' "For their own good": the Spanish identity and its Great Inquisitor, Miguel de Unamuno' (106–33), L. Gabriel-Stheeman, 'A nobleman grasps the broom: Ortega y Gasset's verbal hygiene' (134–66), J. Landreau, 'José María Arguedas: Peruvian Spanish as subversive assimilation' (167–92), J. del Valle and L. Gabriel-Stheeman, 'Codo con codo: Hispanic community and the language spectacle' (193–216).

Amílcar Antonio Barreto, *The Politics of Language in Puerto Rico*, Gainesville, Florida U.P., 2001, 221 pp., is written by a political scientist and investigates the 1991 unilingual act and its subsequent reversal two years later within the context of nationalism and the relationship between Puerto Rico and the United States. R. Vann 'Linguistic ideology in Spain's ivory tower: (not) analyzing Catalan Spanish', *Multilingua*, 21:227–46, argues that, due to hegemonic linguistic identities, the Spanish of Catalonia has been overlooked in Spanish dialectology and sociolinguistics, the innovative linguistic forms of this 'illegitimate' variety being dismissed as merely deviance from the norm. A. Pomerantz 'Language ideologies and the production of identities: Spanish as a resource for participation in the multilingual marketplace', *ib.*, 275–302, examines the dichotomy between Spanish simultaneously functioning as an inhibitor to social mobility for its heritage language users and a resource endowing 'competitive edge' to the upwardly mobile US professional. *Multilingualism in Spain: Sociolinguistic and Psycholinguistic Aspects of Linguistic Minority Groups*, ed. María Teresa Turell, Clevedon, Multilingual Matters, 2001, xv + 389 pp., focuses not only on the established minority speech communities in Spain (Catalan, Basque, Galician, Occitan, Asturian, sign language, Gitano, and Jewish) but also on more recently established immigrant communities (Brazilian, Cape Verdean, Chinese, Italian, Maghrebi, Portuguese, UK, US).

R. Torres Cacoullos, 'From lexical to grammatical to social meaning', *LSO*, 30, 2001 : 443–78, compares *estar* + gerund and *andar* + gerund which are subject to conditioning both linguistic (they co-occur with certain classes of verb) and social (variables such as socio-economic group and urban v. rural). She shows how these interact in interesting ways in the evolution of their use.

11. Discourse Analysis and Pragmatics

Cilla Häggkvist, '*Ya hemos pasado deportes y estudios . . .' La gestión temática en el diálogo intercultural*, Stockholm U.P., 169 pp., uses a conversation analytic framework to investigate intercultural interaction between Spaniards and Swedish learners of Spanish, and specifically topic management strategies as a tool to overcoming communicative difficulties arising from the negotiation of identities. S. Murcia Bielsa and J. Delin, 'Expressing the notion of purpose in English and Spanish instructions', *FLang*, 8, 2001 : 79–108, uses a corpus of written instructions in English and Spanish and analyses the factors which influence choice of a particular structure in each language and its placement within the matrix clause.

Actos de habla y cortesía en español, ed. María Elena Placencia and Diana Bravo, Munich, Lincom Europa, 250 pp., contains an introduction to speech act theory and politeness by the editors (1–19), M. Chodorowska-Pilch, 'Las ofertas y la cortesía en español peninsular' (21–36), A. Bolívar, 'Los reclamos como actos de habla en el español de Venezuela' (37–53), C. García, 'La expresión de camaradería y solidaridad: cómo los venezolanos solicitan un servicio y responden a la solicitud de un servicio' (55–88), R. Márquez Reiter, 'Estrategias de cortesía en el español hablado de Montevideo' (89–106), C. Curcó and A. de Fina, 'Modo imperativo y diminutivos en la expresión de cortesía en español: el contraste entre México y

España' (105–40), D. Bravo, 'Actos asertivos y cortesía: imagen de rol en el discurso de académicos argentinos' (141–74), M. Achugar, 'Cambios en la valoración del grado de cortesía de una práctica discursiva' (175–92), M. E. Placencia, 'Desigualdad en el trato en directivas en la atención al público en La Paz' (193–208), J. M. Valeiras Viso, 'Deja tu mensaje después del señal. Despedidas y otros elementos de la sección de cierre en mensajes dejados en contestadores automáticos en Madrid y Londres' (209–32).

12. Language Contact

T. Stolz, 'General linguistic aspects of Spanish-indigenous language contacts with special focus on Austronesia', *BHS*, 79:133–58, examines, as the title suggests, Hispanic contributions to languages such as Cebuano, Tagalog, and Chamorro in the Philippines and the Marianas Islands, languages which are not deeply hispanicized to the degree of becoming varieties of Spanish. S. points to the use of hispanisms in Austronesia as markers of cultural identity as promising to be a fascinating new field for future research. Germán de Granda, *Español y lenguas indoamericanas en hispanoamérica: estructuras, situaciones y transferencias*, Valladolid U.P., 1999, 303 pp., sets within a sociolinguistic frame language contact phenomena such as the Quechua-influenced construction *la dejé pintando* (for *la dejé pintado*) and the Andean double possessive (*su amiga de Juan*). *América negra: panorámica actual de los estudios lingüísticos sobre variedades hispanas, portuguesas y criollas*, ed. Matthias Perl and Armin Schwegler, Frankfurt, Vervuert, 1998, 379 pp., is another welcome addition to the series 'Language and Society in the Hispanic World' and, in addition to the introduction (1–24), contains the following of interest to Hispanists: G. Lorenzo, A. Alvarez, E. Obediente, and G. de Granda, 'El español caribeño: antecedentes socio-históricos y lingüísticos' (25–69); P. Maurer, 'El papiamentu de Carazao' (139–218); A. Schwegler, 'El palenquero' (219–91); J. Lipski, 'Perspectivas sobre el español *bozal*' (293–327).

Sociolingüística: lenguas en contacto, ed. Pieter Muysken, Amsterdam–Atlanta, Rodopi, 1998, 135 pp., contains the following studies on language contact: M. Moyer, 'Entre dos lenguas: contacto de inglés y español en Gibraltar' (9–26); M. Post, 'La situación lingüística del fa d'Ambô' (27–44); E. Hekking and D. Bakker, 'El otomí y el español de Santiago Mexquititlán: dos lenguas en contacto' (45–73); F. Flores Farfán, 'Hablar cuatrapeado: En torno al español de los indígenas mexicanos' (75–86); P. Muysken, 'Contacto lingüística y coherencia grammatical: castellano y quechua en los waynos del Perú' (87–108). Klaus Zimmermann, *Política del lenguaje y planificación para los pueblos amerindios. Ensayos de ecología lingüística*, M, Iberoamericana — Frankfurt, Vervuert, 1999, 198 pp., rejects the notion that the duty of linguists 'is to witness and document the effects of language contact' in the case of endangered languages in Latin America and proposes resistance to language attrition through, amongst other strategies, the modernization of these languages. *La Romania Americana: procesos lingüísticos en situaciones de contacto*, ed. Norma Díaz, Ralph Ludwig, and Stefan Pfänder, Frankfurt, Vervuert, 446 pp., contains sections on the following topics: a multidimensional approach to linguistic variation in contact situations; the historical role of the African languages in the Caribbean; systemic change through contact; Creoles as input and output in language contact; language contact and migration, urbanization and the media; and linguistic processes in contact situations. Luis A. Ortiz López, *Huellas eto-sociolingüísticas bozales y afrocubanas*, Frankfurt, Vervuert, 1998, 203 pp., is a provocative and tightly argued study of the genesis and development of the variety of Spanish spoken in Cuba arguing that semi-creole phenomena have influenced its development not merely lexically but also morpho-syntactically.

Amparo Morales, *Anglicismos puertorriqueños*, San Juan, Plaza Mayor, 2001, 270 pp., provides frequency counts for the most commonly used English borrowings in Puerto Rican Spanish with 'spring mattress' heading the list. Amalia Pedrera González, *Léxico español en el sudoeste de los Estados Unidos*, M, CSIC, 423 pp., uses data from the US linguistic Atlas in order to identify a range of lexical fields (such as the human body, agriculture, clothing), list the variants which occur and detail their frequencies. Milagros Aleza Izquierdo and José María Erguita Utrilla, *El español de América: aproximación sincrónica*, Valencia, Tirant lo Blanch, 335 pp., and Juan Antonio Frago Gracia and Manano Franco Figueroa, *El español de América*, Cádiz U.P., 285 pp., are two more general accounts, the latter raising the issues of language planning and language contact. William Megenny, *Aspectos del lenguaje afronegroide en Venezuela*, Frankfurt, Vervuert, 1999, 311 pp., is a fascinating contribution not only to knowledge about these particular varieties but also to wider issues of the existence of natural language universals and the relationships between Creoles/ pidgins and the national languages, in this case Venezuelan Spanish, with which they are in contact. J. Choi, 'The genesis of *voy en el Mercado*: the preposition *en* with directional verbs in Paraguayan Spanish', *Word*, 52:181–96, argues that while substrate influence from Guaraní is undoubtedly a contributory cause of this syntactic feature, the fact that it occurs in other varieties suggests that the trend towards simplification in the Spanish language is also a contributory factor.

José Luis Blas Arroyo, *Lenguas en contacto. Consecuencias linguísticas del bilinguismo social en las comunidades de habla del este peninsular*, M, Iberomericana — Frankfurt, Vervuert, 1999, 207 pp., initially examines grammatical convergence between two highly cognate languages demonstrating that the evolution of the higher status language (Spanish in the case of Valencia) may also be influenced by the lower status contact variety (here Catalan) as well as vice versa, giving as one example the confusion between *bajo* and *abajo*. He then investigates code-switching between Spanish and Catalan, primarily in a corpus of media discourse, and its value as a rhetorical device in the presentation of self.

MEDIEVAL LITERATURE

POSTPONED

ALJAMIADO LITERATURE

POSTPONED

LITERATURE, 1490–1700 (PROSE AND POETRY)

By Carmen Peraita, *Villanova University*

1. General

Thomas James Dandelet, *Spanish Rome 1500–1700*, New Haven–London, Yale U.P., 2001, 278 pp., uses an innovative perspective and erudite archival research to examine the relationship of Spanish monarchs with the Papacy, paying attention to aspects such as how ritual activity and charitable work helped to create the collective identity of the Spanish empire in Rome, or the crucial role of Spanish ambassadors as nation-builders at a local level. Helen Rawlings, *Church, Religion and Society in Early Modern Spain* (European Studies Series), Basingstoke–NY, Palgrave, 185 pp., studies multicultural influences in Spanish societies. Francisco Loubayssin de Lamarca, *Engaños deste siglo y historia sucedida en nuestros tiempos 1615*, ed. Elisa Rosales Juega, Lewiston, Mellen, 2001, 161 pp., is an edition of a widely disseminated 17th-c. novel by a French author writing in Spanish and publishing in Paris. Juan Márquez, OSA, *Vida de Alonso de Orozco*, ed. Modesto González Velasco, M, FUE, 236 pp., is a hagiographic biography by the author of *El gobernador christiano*, the influential defence of mixed monarchy and an attack on the absolute power of the favourite.

DICTIONARIES. César Hernández Alonso and Beatriz Sanz Alonso, *Diccionario de Germanía*, M, Gredos, 529 pp., and María Inés Chamorro, *Tesoro de Villanos. Diccionario de Germanía. Lengua de jacarandina: rufos, mandiles, galloferos, viltrotonas, zurrapas, carcaveras, murcios, floraineros y otras gentes de carda*, B, Herder, 829 pp., are two relevant lexicographic studies of *germanía* language of marginal classes, profusely used in picaresque, *entremeses*, and *literatura de cordel*. Both works include etymologies (more thoroughly in the latter, a more inclusive volume) and *germanía* bibliography, chronologically organized in the former, which widens the *germanía* period from the second half of the 15th c. to the end of the 18th c. and pays more attention to *germanía* phrases. Manuel Gutiérrez Muñón, *Diccionario de castellano antiguo. Léxico español medieval y del Siglo de Oro*, Cuenca, Alfonsípolis-Alderabán-Diputación, 301 pp., is a useful tool for reading medieval and Renaissance texts.

2. Bibliography, Libraries, Printing, Reading

Jan Lechner, *Repertorio de obras de autores españoles en bibliotecas holandesas hasta comienzos del siglo XVIII*, Utrecht, Hes & De Graaf, 2001, 361 pp., is a seminal contribution to the study of readership patterns and organization of cultural activity. L. lists 5834 books by Spanish authors in Spanish or Latin as well as translations of Spanish texts into any European language and includes excellent indexes that allow searches for printers, places where the books were printed, editors and booksellers, as well as contemporary sales catalogues. The predominant Spanish authors in Dutch libraries were jurists (Juan Gutiérrez, Vázquez de Menchaca, Covarrubias y Leiva), theologians (Luis de Granada, Francisco Suárez, Carranza de Miranda, Domingo de Soto), literary authors (Guevara, Cervantes), humanists (Antonio Agustín, Juan de Quiñones), historians (Mariana, and, conspicuously, translations of Tacitus into Spanish), American *relaciones* and natural history (José de Acosta, fray Bartolomé de las Casas), medicine (Huarte de San Juan, Nicolás Monardes), grammars and dictionaries (Nebrija, Ambrosio de Salazar, Cristóbal de las Casas). Oscar Lilao Franca and Carmen Castrillo González, *Catálogo de manuscritos de la Biblioteca Universitaria de Salamanca,* II, *Manuscritos 1680–2777*, Salamanca U.P., 1455 pp., and *Catálogo de la Real Biblioteca,* vol. XIII: *Correspondencia del Conde de Gondomar,* vol. III, M, Patrimonio Nacional, 834 pp., are much needed essential bibliographical tools. *Biblioteca y epistolario de Hernán Núñez de Guzmán (el Pinciano). Una aproximación al humanismo español del siglo XVI,* ed. Juan Signer Codoñer, Carmen Codoñer Merino, and Aranxa Domingo Malvadi (Nueva Roma, 14), M, CSIC, 2001, 558 pp., examines in detail P.'s library, marginalia, and part of his correspondence, enabling a better grasp of humanist reading methods.

READING. A series of brilliant studies by Antonio Castillo Gómez examine seminal aspects of reading practices: '"No pasando por ello como gato sobre brasas". Leer y anotar en la España del Siglo de Oro', *Lecturas. Revista da Biblioteca Nacional*, 3.9–10:99–121; 'Entre public et privé. Stratégies de l'écrit dans l'Espagne du Siècle d'Or', *Annales,* 4–5, 2001:803–29; 'Leer en comunidad. Libro y espiritualidad en la España del Barroco', *Via Spiritus*, 7, 2000:99–122; 'La escritura representada. Imágenes de lo escrito en la obra de Cervantes', pp. 311–25 of *Volver a Cervantes. Actas del IV Congreso Internacional de la Asociación de Cervantistas*, 2 vols, Palma U.P., 2001, xii + 770, x + 771–1318 pp. C.G. has also edited two collections of studies on the writing and reading practices of the underprivileged classes: *Cultura escrita y clases subalternas: una mirada española,* Oiartzun, Sendoa, 2001, 239 pp., and *La conquista del alfabeto. Escritura y clases populares*, Cenero-Gijón, Trea, 348 pp., which includes J. S. Amelang, 'Clases populares y escritura en la Europa Moderna' (53–70), a study that panoramically explores the problematic status in early modern England and Spain of popular writers in terms of social origin and the public for whom they were aiming to write. Tracing a parallel between the two countries, A. looks at Shakespeare and Lope de Vega, their relationship with audiences, and the role of printing. The volume includes an index that identifies archives containing material on popular writing. *Litterae, Cuadernos de Cultura Escrita*, 1, 2001, is a new journal devoted to the history of reading, the book, and printing; noteworthy is V. Infantes, 'Historia mínima (y desde luego incompleta) de los impresos de una sola hoja', which mimics typographically an *impreso de una sola hoja*. Pedro M. Cátedra, *Invención, difusión y recepción de la literatura popular impresa (siglo* XVI), Mérida, Ed. Regional de Extremadura, 535 pp., contextualizes, through Mateo de Brizuela's inquisitorial process for writing an infamatory *pliego*, the *literatura de cordel* in historical, ideological, editorial, and material frameworks and innovatively charts religious and civil control of *literatura de cordel*, modes of invention, and ways of writing, materials for the *relaciones*, printing, publication, and reception processes. C. examines aspects such as 'La intrahistoria de la literatura de cordel' and 'De la cultura popular, la cultura del ciego y la censura literaria', and includes an 'Apéndice documental' and a chronological catalogue of *literatura de cordel* from the 16th c. to the 19th c. *La cultura del libro en la Edad Moderna: Andalucía y América*, ed. Manuel Peña Díaz, Pedro Ruiz Pérez, and Julián Solana Pujalte, Córdoba U.P., 2001, 297 pp., contains among articles that merit special attention: K. Wagner, 'La imprenta de Gutemberg a las tipografías hispanas en América' (1–20); R. Chartier, 'El manuscrito en la época del impreso. Lectura y reflexiones' (21–36); V. Infantes, 'Los géneros editoriales: entre el texto y el libro' (37–46); M. Peña Díaz, 'El espejo de los libros: lecturas y lectores en la España del Siglo de Oro' (145–58).

PRINTING AND HISTORY OF THE BOOK. Julián Martín Abad and Isabel Moyano Andrés, *Estanislao Polo*, Alcalá de Henares U.P. — Centro Internacional de Estudios Históricos Cisneros, 172 pp., offers an outline of the first 50 years of the printing press, and the Polish printer Polo's workshops in Seville and Alcalá de Henares, where he was the first printer to work. It analyses the typographic and editorial characteristics of P.'s printing and its xylographic features, and presents a comprehensive catalogue of books printed by him. Alonso Víctor de Paredes, *Institución y origen del arte de la imprenta y reglas generales para los componedores*, ed. Jaime Moll, M, Calambur, xxix + 48 ff., presents one of the first treatises printed in Europe (*c.*1680), but which probably did not circulate widely since only two copies were printed.

A series of facsímile reproductions of Gracián's *libros meninos* are eruditely edited by Aurora Egido: *El discreto*, Zaragoza, Institución Fernando el Católico, 2001, xxxvi + 480 pp., is a facsimile of the edition printed in Huesca by Juan Nogués in 1646; and *El Héroe*, Zaragoza, Institución Fernando el Católico, 2001, xxv + 70 ff., is a facsimile of the edition printed in Madrid by Diego Díaz in 1639. *Encuentros en Flandes*, ed. Werner Thomas and Robert A. Verdonk, Louvain U.P., 2000, xii + 376 pp., contains the following of particular note: J. Moll, 'Amberes y el mundo hispano del libro' (30–48); Id., 'Una imprenta para la Biblia Regia' (117–31); M. L. López-Vidriero, '*Non omnis moriar*. Humanismo y saber al servicio de los libros del rey' (311–17); A. Sáenz-Badillos, 'Arias Montano y la Biblia Políglota de Amberes' (327–40); and L. Schwartz, 'Justo Lipsio en Quevedo: neoestoicismo, política y sátira (227–73), a seminal study on the influence on Quevedo of the neo-stoic Lipsius, mainly of his *Politicorum libri sex*. S.'s analysis magisterially recontextualizes Q.'s satirical discourses in ideological and generic frameworks.

3. Humanism and Rhetorical Thought

Bernardo Pérez de Chinchón, *Antialcorano. Diálogos cristianos. Conversión y evangelización de moriscos*, ed. Francisco Pons Fuster, Alicante U.P., 2000, 513 pp., is an excellent edition of two complementary humanist texts, one showing condemnation of Islam (*Antialcorano*), the other a respectful attitude towards the *morisco* interlocutor converted to Christianity (*Diálogos cristianos*), insisting on evangelizing and converting *moriscos* through the use of reason. *Celestina Comentada*, ed. Louise Fothergill-Payne, Enrique Fernández Rivera, and Peter Fothergill-Payne, Salamanca U.P., 508 pp., edits a hitherto unpublished manuscript in Madrid BN, of a commentary written in the second half of the 16th c., which helps us to understand how humanists read *Celestina* with reference to an array of classical authorities. Lorenzo Valla, *Historia de Fernando de Aragón*, ed. Santiago López Moreda, M, Akal, 221 pp., includes an insightful portrait of Ferdinand the Catholic and of nobility factions in Castile and Aragon. Guido Cappelli, *El humanismo romance de Juan de Lucena. Estudios sobre el 'De vita felici'* (Seminario de literatura medieval y humanística), Bellaterra, UAB, 193 pp., broaches the polemical question of Castilian humanism in the 15th c. Francisco Rico, *Estudios de literatura y otras cosas*, B, Destino, 285 pp., gathers previously published articles, adding an irreverent, insightful prologue.

Teresa Jiménez Calvente, *Un siciliano en la España de los Reyes Católicos. Los Epistolarum familiarium libri* XVII *de Lucio Marineo Sículo*, Alcalá de Henares U.P., 2001, 873 pp., presents a short biography, historical and generic frameworks of the correspondence, and an outline of the development of the epistolary genre in Spanish. Each letter includes an explanatory introduction (but not a translation) of the context in which it was penned. Gonzalo Pontón, *Correspondencias. Los orígenes del arte epistolar en España,* M, Biblioteca Nueva, 254 pp., examines from historical and theoretical perspectives the development of the literary epistle, reception processes, *artes dictaminis* regulating epistolary genres, paying attention to the consolatory genre and the output of Fernando del Pulgar. Antonio Castillo Gómez, '"Como o polvo e o camaleão se transformam": modelos e prácticas epistolares na Espanha Moderna', pp. 13–55 of *Destino das letras. História, educação e escrita epistolar,* ed. María Helena Camara Bastos, Maris Teresa Santos Cunha, and Ana Christina Venancio Mignot, Passo Fundo U.P., 140 pp., brings a perspective upon the subject from the point of view of reading and writing practices.

Gonzalo Pontón, *Escrituras históricas. Relaciones, memoriales y crónicas de la guerra de Granada* (Seminario de literatura medieval y humanística), Bellaterra, UAB, 91 pp., examines late 15th-c. Castilian strategies for writing history. Helena Rausell Guillot, *Letras y fe. Erasmo en la Valencia del Renacimiento,* Valencia, Institució Alfons el Magnànim, 2001, 211 pp., studies the influence of Erasmus in 16th-c. Valencian texts. Francisco J. Aranda, *Jerónimo de Ceballos: un hombre grave para la república. Vida y obra de un hidalgo del saber en la España del Siglo de Oro,* Córdoba U.P., 2001, 444 pp., traces C.'s social and professional climb as the Toledo *corregidor,* his production of manuals of jurisprudence, and his relationship as client of the Marquis de Villena's family. Antonio Azaustre Galiana, 'Las obras retóricas de Luciano de Samosata en la literatura española de los siglos XVI y XVII', pp. 35–55 of *Homenaje a Benito Varela Jácome,* ed. Anxo Abuín González, Juan Casas Rigall, and José Manuel González Hebrán, Santiago de Compostela U.P., 2001, 629 pp., examines the influence of Lucian's *encomion paradoxon* and discourses of praise and blame in Spanish rhetorical debates, mainly Jáuregui's *Discurso poético.* A. Blecua, 'Defending neolachmannianism. On the *Palacio* manuscript of La Celestina', *Variants,* 1 : 175–95, determined to show the value of a method that has been the target of some attacks in Spain, convincingly argues that the *Palacio* manuscript transmits an early version of the play and does not rehash (as suggested recently) 'an early text to outdo Rojas'.

4. Cultural Studies

Arte sutilísima, por la cual se enseña a escribir perfectamente. Hecho y experimentado y ahora de nuevo añadido por Juan de Icíar vizcaino, año 1553, ed. Javier Durán Barceló, Valladolid, Junta de Castilla y León — Ayuntamiento, is a facsimile of the influential 16th-c. Spanish calligraphy manual. Juan Velázquez de Azevedo, *Fénix de Minerva o arte de la memoria*, ed. Fernando R. de la Flor, Valencia, Tératos, lviii + 212 pp., presents a 17th-c. manual on artificial memory. Agustín de Horozco, *Historia de la ciudad de Cádiz*, ed. Arturo Morgado García, Cadiz U.P., 2001, xxx + 296 pp., includes a 16th-c. description of the English attack on Cadiz in 1587. *Cuatro tratados médicos renacentistas sobre el mal de ojo*, ed. Jacobo Sanz Hermida, Valladolid, Junta de Castilla y León, 2001, 395 pp., edits and translates the first treatise on *aojo* published by a physician, Diego Álvarez Chanca's *Libro del aojo* (1499) as well as Antonio de Cartagena's *Tratado del aojamiento* (1530), the Portuguese Gaspar de Ribero's *Cuestión sobre el aojo*, and the *Relecciones sobre el aojo* by Tomás Rodríguez da Veiga, professor at the University of Coimbra. A selection of texts (among others from Enrique de Villena, Alfonso Fernández de Madrigal, Pedro Sánchez Ciruelo, Alonso López de Corella, Martín de Castañega, Martín del Río, and Francisco Pérez Cascales) documents Spanish scientific interest in the *mal de ojo*. The Centro de Investigaciones Linguísticas of the University of Salamanca, a lexicographic project on the use of vernacular languages for scientific debates, has produced *Pórtico a la ciencia y a la técnica del Renacimiento*, ed. M. Jesús Mancho Duque, Salamanca U.P. — Junta de Castilla y León, 2001, 524 pp., a collection of prologues to scientific manuals, most of them never before reprinted since the 16th c., dealing with topics such as agriculture and animal husbandry, how to heal animals *(albeitería)*, military arts (Cano's *Arte para fabricar, fortificar y aparejar naos de guerra)*, artillery, astronomy and astrology, cooking, commerce (Saravia de la Calle's *Instrucción de mercaderes muy provechosa)*, construction, distillation, horse riding, geography, cartography, cosmography, natural history, machinery, legislation, mathematics and geometry, medicine, metallurgy and mining, magic, optics (Daça's *Uso de los antojos para todo género de vistas*), and navigation (Besson's *Teatro de todos los instrumentos)*. The volume includes C. Flórez Miguel, 'Otra cara del humanismo' (11–43), and M. J. Mancho Duque, 'La lengua española, vehículo de divulgación científica en el Renacimiento' (45–84). Fernando R. de la Flor, *Barroco. Representación e ideología en el mundo hispánico (1580–1680)*, M, Cátedra, 402 pp., claims to discover a cultural logic of the Baroque as 'anomaly and deviation', widening Maravall's thesis in *La cultura del Barroco* that considers cultural discourse as exclusively hegemonic. Javier Cordero and Ricardo J. Hernández, *Velázquez: un logístico en la Corte de Felipe IV*, Madrid, Centro Español de Logística–Díaz de Santos, 2000, 364 pp., present fascinating documentation about V.'s tasks and responsibilities at the Court.

European Literary Careers. The Author from Antiquity to the Renaissance, ed. Patrick Cheney and Frederick A. de Armas, Toronto U.P., 366 pp., deals with questions such as authors' perceptions of a literary career: 'authorship and agency, genre and genre patterning, imitation and intertextuality, politics and religions, sexuality and gender, all become part of the complex template for defining the idea of a literary career'. It includes M. Vessey, 'From *cursus* to *ductus*: figures of writing in Western Late Antiquity (Augustine, Jerome, Cassiodorus, Bede)' (43–103), which provides a brilliant foundation from which to understand the framework of career criticism. From a Spanish background, articles that merit special attention include A. Cruz, 'Arms versus letters; the poetics of war and the career of the poet in Early Modern Spain' (126–44); F. de Armas, 'Cervantes and the Virgilian wheel: the portrayal of a literary career' (186–205); K. Bollard de Broce, 'Judging a literary career: the case of Antonio de Guevara (1480?–1545)' (165–85).

Barbara Fuchs, *Mimesis and Empire. The New World, Islam, and European Identities*, CUP, xiii + 211 pp., focusing on mimesis, perceived as a powerful rhetorical weapon and cultural phenomenon, examines ways in which the American experience altered European attitudes towards truth in literature. F. convincingly argues that cultural mimesis served to undermine totalizing notions of national identity. José Miguel Morales Folguera, *La construcción de la utopía. El proyecto de Felipe II (1556–1598) para Hispanoamérica*, Málaga U.P. — M, Biblioteca Nueva, 2001, 269 pp., examines the *ordenanzas* that structured the creation of two separated republics for Spaniards and Indians once the utopian project of integrating indigenous people and Spaniards proved a failure, and which influenced the creation, foundation, and forms and evolution of Spanish American societies. The study transcribes significant geographical *relaciones*. Gregorio Bartolomé Martínez, *Don Juan de Palafox y Mendoza. Obispo de Puebla de los Ángeles, y de Osma*, Soria, Diputación, 2000, 116 pp., is a well illustrated biography. Pliegos volanderos del GRISO, Pamplona, has published three *pliegos*: Rafael Zafra, *Las verdaderas imágenes del Alciato de Daza: el caso de la cigüeña*, 13 pp.; Ignacio Arellano, *Un minibestiario poético de Quevedo*, 17 pp., and Gabriela Torres e Ignacio Arellano, *El prodigio de dos mundos, San Francisco Javier, y el Sacro Parnaso de las musas católicas*, 17 pp.

PROTESTANTISM. While Inquisition studies have extensively examined crypto-judaism and heresy, Protestants — mainly a foreign population (of 3000 protestants persecuted by the Inquisition, 2500 were foreigners) — have received less attention. Werner Thomas's following studies are important therefore: *La represión del protestantismo en España 1517–1648*, Louvain U.P., 2001, xv + 448 pp.; *Los protestantes y la Inquisición en España en tiempos de Reforma y Contrarreforma*, Louvain U.P., 2001, xii + 714 pp.

5. Women's Studies

Juan Luis Vives, *The Instruction of a Christen Woman*, ed. Virginia Walcott Beauchamp, Elizabeth H. Hageman, and Margaret Mikesell, Urbana–Chicago, Illinois U.P., 274 pp., edits the complete Tudor English translation. María de San José Salazar, *Book for the Hour of Recreation*, ed. Alison Weber, trans. Amanda Powell, Chicago U.P., 173 pp., is a dialogue by a close collaborator of Teresa of Ávila, defending the discalced nuns' practice of setting aside two hours each day for conversation, music, and staging religious plays. P. Renée Baernstein, *A Convent Tale. A Century of Sisterhood in Spanish Milan*, NY–London, Routledge, xviii + 270 pp., is an historical reconstruction of how the Spanish convent of San Paolo evolved from an evangelical experiment to *clausura*.

Roger Osborne, *The Dreamer of the Calle San Salvador. Visions of Sedition and Sacrilege in Sixteenth-Century Spain*, London, Pimlico, 252 pp., transcribes 35 dreams by the 16th-c. political visionary Lucrecia de León, and comments their historical significance. María Antonia Bel Bravo, *Mujeres españolas en la Historia Moderna*, M, Silex, 308 pp., presents short biographies occasionally complemented with letters. Maria Amparo Vidal Gavidia, *La casa de arrepentidas de Valencia. Origen y trayectoria de una institución para mujeres*, Valencia, Generalitat, 2001, 195 pp.

SOR MARÍA DE ÁGREDA. Several studies on the nun have been published recently; Ricardo Fernández Gracia, *Arte, devoción y política. La promoción de las artes en torno a sor María de Ágreda*, Soria, Diputación, 341 pp. *El papel del sor María Jesús de Ágreda en el Barroco español*, Soria, Univ. Internacional Alfonso VIII, includes: J. I. Tellechea Idígoras, 'La madre Ágreda en la historia de la mística mariana' (11–24); R. Fernández Gracia, 'Patronazgo de las artes en torno a la madre Ágreda. Los legados de una religiosa y de la Casa Ducal de Alburquerque' (25–60), and 'Los primeros retratos de la madre Ágreda. Consideraciones sobre su iconografía hasta fines del siglo XVII' (61–78); P. L. Echevarría Goñi, 'La madre Ágreda y la construcción de su convento' (79–98); M. C. Muñoz Párraga, 'Los monasterios de Clarisas. Un ejemplo de reutilización de espacios' (105–18). *La madre Ágreda, una mujer del siglo XXI*, Soria, Univ. Internacional Alfonso VIII, 2000, 279 pp., includes C. Seco Serrano, 'La madre Ágreda y la política de Felipe IV' (183–94); P. Borges Morán, 'La controvertida presencia de la M. Ágreda en Texas

(1627–1630) (105–54); C. Baranda Leturio, 'La correspondencia de la M. Ágreda y su estilo literario (155–82); M. I. Barbeito Carneiro, 'María de Ágreda fue también arcaduz' (75–104); A. Castillo Gómez, 'La pluma de Dios. María de Ágreda y la escritura autorizada' (61–74).

6. Poetry

Lía Schwartz has published a series of noteworthy studies: 'Herrera, poeta bucólico, y sus predecesores italianos', pp. 475–500 of *Spagna e Italia. Attraverso la letteratura del secondo cinquecento. Atti del colloquio internacional*, ed. Encarnación Sánchez García, Anna Cerbo, Clara Borrelli, Naples, Istituto Universitario Orientale, 2001, 603 pp.; 'Dos poemas en busca de un género: las elegías amorosas de Luis Barahona de Soto', pp. 180–207 of *Analecta Malacitana*, Anejo 43, 432 pp.; 'El *Anacreón* castellano de Quevedo y las *Eróticas* de Villegas: lecturas de la poesía anacreóntica en el siglo XVII', pp. 1171–201 of *El Hispanismo Angloamericano: Aportaciones, problemas y perspectivas sobre Historia, Arte y Literatura españolas (siglo* XVI–XVIII), *Actas de la I Conferencia Internacional 'Hacia un nuevo humanismo' C.I.N.H.U. Cordoba, 9–14 de Septiembre 1997*, 2 vols, 2001, 836, 845–1596 pp.

7. Individual Authors

CERVANTES. *The Cambridge Companion to Cervantes*, ed. Anthony J. Cascardi, CUP, 242 pp., contains the following essays that merit special attention: B. W. Ife, 'The historical and social contexts' (11–31); F. de Armas, 'Cervantes and the Italian Renaissance' (32–57); A. Cascardi, 'Don Quixote and the invention of the novel' (58–79); M. Gaylord, 'Cervantes' other fiction' (100–30); A. Cruz, 'Psyche and gender in Cervantes' (186–205); D. de Armas Wilson, 'Cervantes and the New World' (206–25); and A. Cascardi, 'Appendix: list of electronic resources and scholarly editions' (226–27). María Antonia Garcés, *Cervantes in Algiers. A Captive Tale*, Nashville, Vanderbilt U.P., 349 pp., examines historical and literary episodes of C.'s time in Algiers, applying the insights of 'trauma studies'. Carolyn A. Nadeau, *Women of the Prologue, Imitation, Myth and Magic in Don Quixote 1*, Lewisburg, Bucknell U.P., 188 pp., analyses how Cervantes applied sources cited in the prologue to *DQ*, such as Ovid's Medea or Homer's Calypso, for female characterization.

QUEVEDO. Francisco de Quevedo, *Lince de Italia u zahorí español*, ed. Ignacio Pérez Ibáñez, Pamplona, EUNSA, 157 pp., eruditely edits for the first time Q.'s historical discourse. L. Schwartz has published an outstanding commentary on Q.'s satirical discourse: 'La representación del poder en la sátira áurea: del rey y sus ministros en el Dédalo de B.L. de Argensola y en los *Sueños* de Quevedo', pp. 33–47 of *Le pouvoir au miroir de la littérature en Espagne aux XVIe et XVIIe siécles*, ed. Augustin Redondo, Paris, Sorbonne Nouvelle U.P., 2000, 246 pp., deals with ideological issues, the representation of power, and literary genre perceptions. Antonio Azaustre, 'Algunas influencias de la oratoria sagrada en la prosa de Quevedo', *Criticón*, 84–85 : 189–216, brilliantly analyses the influence of religious rhetoric (Luis de Granada, Diego de Estella, Terrones del Caño) on the *dispositio* of Q.'s political, moral, and religious treatises (*La constancia y paciencia del santo Job*, *Política de Dios*, *Virtud militante*). *La Perinola. Revista de Investigación Quevediana*, 6, is devoted to commentaries on Quevedo's poems; I. Arellano, 'Comentario de un soneto amoroso de Quevedo: "los que ciego me ven de haber llorado" y el arte de la ingeniosa contraposición' (15–27); A. Azaustre, 'Retórica y milicia en un soneto de Quevedo' (29–53), which studies 'No siempre tiene paz las siempre hermosas', poem XXIX from *Musa Clío*; S. Fernández Mosquera, 'Comentario al soneto "No ves Behemoth, cuyas costillas" de Quevedo' (89–107); C. C. García Valdés, 'Bibliografía sobre el comentario de textos' (109–15); A. Martinengo, 'Desterrado Scipión a una rústica casería suya, recuerda consigo la gloria de sus hechos y posteridad' (151–60); V. Nider, 'La Fénix' (161–80); C. Peraita, 'Espectador del naufragio. "Muestra en oportuna alegoría la seguridad del estado pobre y el riesgo del poderoso"' (181–97); F. Plata, 'Comentario de la "Canción a una dama hermosa y borracha"' (225–37). Two articles examine recently discovered marginalia by Q.: L. Schwartz and I. Pérez Cuenca, 'Una notas autógrafas de Quevedo en un libro desconocido de su biblioteca', *BRAE*, 79, 1999 : 77–91, on marginalia in Henri Estienne's edition (1554) of Greek poems attributed to Anacreon of Theos, now at the BN Madrid present a thorough study of Q.'s handwriting; H. Kallendorf and C. Kallendorf, 'Conversation with the dead: Quevedo and Statius, annotation and imitation', *JWCI*, 63, 2000 : 131–68, analyse marginal notes in Q.'s copy of Statius's *Sylvarum libri quinque, Thebaidos libri duodecim, Achilleidos*, Venice 1502, in the Firestone Library in Princeton.

LITERATURE, 1490–1700 (DRAMA)

POSTPONED

LITERATURE, 1700–1823

By Gabriel Sánchez Espinosa, *Reader in Hispanic Studies, The Queen's University of Belfast*

1. Bibliography and Printing

Luis-Miguel Enciso Recio, *Barroco e Ilustración en las bibliotecas privadas españolas del siglo* XVIII, M, Real Academia de la Historia, 216 pp., summarizes previous studies on the most characteristic private libraries of the Spanish 18th c. against the background of regional characterization of book ownership trends and reading habits.

María-Luisa López-Vidriero, *Speculum Principum. Nuevas lecturas curriculares, nuevos usos de la Librería del Príncipe en el Setecientos*, M, Biblioteca Nueva–Instituto de Historia del Libro y de la Lectura, 620 pp., is a study of the private library of Carlos, prince of Asturias and future king Charles IV, based on an inventory written in 1782, which lists 1473 different works in 2833 volumes. This book collection took into account decisive political and cultural contemporary events, such as the expulsion of the Jesuits from Spain in 1767 and the new powerful position of the *manteístas* in the establishment. The Valencian F. Pérez Bayer, who was chosen as head private tutor of the *Infantes* in August 1767, a known anti-jesuit very much influenced by the intellectual ideas of G. Mayans y Siscar, was a decisive figure in the selection of this book collection, that was formed as an educational and political statement, representing the new figure of the enlightened prince.

2. Thought and the Enlightenment

Francisco Sánchez-Blanco, *El Absolutismo y las Luces en el reinado de Carlos III*, M, Marcial Pons, 454 pp., continues the polemic opened with his previous book of 1999, *La mentalidad ilustrada*, which examined the first half of the 18th c. Now focusing on the reign of Charles III, S.B.'s aim is to distinguish between concepts that in the past two decades have been applied indistinctively in the Spanish context, those of *Despotismo ilustrado* and *ilustración*. This has rendered the term *ilustrado* almost without meaning, as it is now applied automatically to every writer, politician, fad or fashion of that century.

3. Literary History

General. J. Álvarez Barrientos, 'Literatura para un cambio de siglo', pp. 185–98 of *1802: España entre dos siglos y la devolución de*

Menorca, ed. J.-J. Luna, M, Sociedad Estatal de Conmemoraciones Culturales, 438 pp., makes a valuable effort to determine the specifics of the new literary trends present at the end of the first decade of the reign of Charles IV.

Juan Antonio Pellicer y Saforcada, *Ensayo de una biblioteca de traductores españoles*, Cáceres, Extremadura U.P., is a superb facsimile edition of this work originally printed in Madrid by A. de Sancha in 1778, to which a somewhat slight presentation has been added. Pellicer's work was intended as a bibliography of Spanish translations of the Bible, and of Greek and Latin authors up to the mid-15th c., which is preceded by three extensive and erudite articles on the lives of the poets L. and B. Leonardo de Argensola and the novelist Cervantes, whose *Don Quixote* he edited in 1797–98.

Russell P. Sebold, *La perduración de la modalidad clásica. Poesía y prosa españolas de los siglos* XVII *a* XIX, Salamanca U.P., 270 pp., is a useful collection of 14 articles previously published in journals and *Festschriften* between the years 1968 and 2000, all of them in support of his widely known thesis on the basic continuity of Classicism in the Spanish poetry and literature written between the 16th and the 19th cs, a continuity which contradicts the traditional critical interpretation of Spanish 18th-c. Neoclassicism as a foreign — French — import, which broke the natural flow of Spanish poetic tradition.

Los jesuitas españoles expulsos. Su imagen y su contribución al saber sobre el mundo hispánico en la Europa del siglo XVIII, ed. Manfred Tietz, M, Iberoamericana — Frankfurt, Vervuert, 2001, 710 pp., gathers together the papers delivered at a conference that took place in Berlin in April 1999. The following articles stand out amongst those included: P. Álvarez de Miranda, 'El padre Terreros, antes y después de la expulsión' (45–75); L. Domergue, 'Les jésuites écrivains et l'appareil d'État (1767–1808)' (265–94); D. T. Gies, 'Unas cartas desconocidas de Juan Clímaco de Salazar a Juan Pablo Forner sobre la tragedia *Mardoqueo*' (323–35); H. C. Jacobs, 'Antonio Eximeno y Pujades (1720–1808) y su novela *Don Lazarillo Vizcardi* en el contexto de sus teorías musicales' (401–12); and M. Tietz, 'Las *Reflexiones imparciales* de Juan Nuix y Perpiñá (1740–1783): el «saber americanista» de los jesuitas y «las trampas de la fe»' (611–46).

NARRATIVE. María José Alonso Seoane, *Narrativa de ficción y público en España: los anuncios en la Gaceta y el Diario de Madrid (1808–1819)*, M, Universitas, 282 pp., registers, transcribes, and comments upon the advertisements of narrative prose works published in this historically eventful decade in the two main Madrid newspapers. This register is not just a useful tool for an initial overview of this scarcely studied narrative, it is also essential to deepen our knowledge of the contemporary book market and reading practices, as the advertisements also include information on printers, bookshops, prices, and subscriptions.

THEATRE. Jesús Pérez Magallón, *El teatro neoclásico*, M, Laberinto, 2001, 317 pp., is a rigorous and solid introduction to the new theatrical practices and theoretical debate brought about by Spanish neo-classicists. P.M. divides his study into four main thematic chapters: 'El discurso teórico-dramático del Neoclasicismo' (13–71), 'Una reflexión sobre el poder y el heroísmo' (73–148), 'Nuevas costumbres en una sociedad nueva' (149–228), and 'La construcción de los modelos humanos ilustrados' (229–94). Very well written, challenging and up-to-date, it deserves to be in every university reading list for courses that include or are specifically devoted to the theatre of this century.

4. Individual Authors

CADALSO. F. Durán López, 'La autobiografía juvenil de José Cadalso', *RLit*, 128:437–72, examines the critical reception of Cadalso's brief autobiographical text, written in the year 1773, concluding that it is an early autobiography in the modern sense, introspective and full of moral and psychological preoccupations.

FERNÁNDEZ DE MORATÍN. P. Deacon, 'Un escritor ante las instituciones: el caso de Nicolás Fernández de Moratín', *CDi*, 2:151–76, outlines the career of the poet N. Fernández de Moratín (1737–1780), demonstrating how he negotiated the complex ways of Spanish *Ancien régime* established institutions, as the literary world was insufficiently developed to allow authors to live by the pen, although the period gave rise to new institutions such as the Royal Academies and the economic societies, or developed new media such as the periodical press.

JUAN Y SANTACILIA. Emilio Soler Pascual, *Viajes de Jorge Juan y Santacilia: ciencia y política en la España del siglo XVIII*, B, Ediciones B, 379 pp., aimed at the general public, is a good introduction to the topic of Spanish 18th-c. scientific expeditions. J. Juan and A. de Ulloa's works deserve to be better known among all interested in the topics of Spanish colonial America and enlightened discussion on colonialism.

MONTENGÓN. Rogelio Blanco Martínez, *Pedro Montengón y Paret (1745–1824): un ilustrado entre la utopía y la realidad*, Valencia, Univ. Politécnica de Valencia, 2001, 414 pp., offers a general perspective on the life and work of the novelist from Alicante, which is undermined by a continuous tendency to construct its text on the basis of listing and quoting the different opinions of previous scholars.

The most original part of the book confronts the issue of the influence of J.-J. Rousseau on Montengón, striving to defend him from being considered a mere follower and imitator of the writer from Geneva. Despite the length of this book, Montengón and his work still await a definitive study. Pedro Montengón, *El Rodrigo*, ed. Guillermo Carnero, M, Cátedra, 324 pp., makes available to the wider reading public another title by the most representative — and by today's tastes most entertaining — novelist of the Spanish Enlightenment. This historical novel set at the dawn of Spain's Middle Ages, a suggestive example of *la cara oscura del siglo de las Luces*, surely deserves a place in any canon of Spanish narrative. Carnero reproduces the text of his 1990 edition, updating the bibliography and slightly extending the orthographic modernization of the text.

SARMIENTO. José Santos Puerto, *Martín Sarmiento: ilustración, educación y utopía en la España del siglo* XVIII, 2 vols, Corunna, Fundación Pedro Barrié de la Maza, 545, 407 pp., contains useful information on the life and works of the erudite Benedictine, although this work would have benefitted significantly from a reduction of its length and a simplification of its literary style. Volume II centres on Sarmiento's ideas on education.

LITERATURE, 1823–1898

POSTPONED

LITERATURE, 1898–1936

By K. M. Sibbald, *McGill University*

1. General

literary and cultural history. 'Hispanic Modernisms', *BSS*, 79.2–3, is a thought-provoking special issue with a preface by editor Nelson R. Orringer (133–48), stressing the plurivalent nature of modernism in five inter-related spheres, namely, a dictionary definition stretching from Darío to the Boom; the still untapped wealth of authors practising modernism in Castilian plus the largely-neglected contributions enriching modernism world-wide of non-Castilian authors from Catalonia and Portugal to Latin America; modernism in different media outside literature; and the various relationships woven between modernism in world cultures with influence on the Hispanic variety. Of particular interest here: M. D'Ors, '"Joyas nuevas de plata vieja" (el Modernismo como tradicionalismo)' (229–45), uses Darío's metaphor to describe specific borrowings from the past where the matter may be traditional but the form is innovative, with examples taken from Juan Ramón, Manuel Machado, Valle-Inclán, and Eduardo Marquina; C. C. Soufas, Jr., 'Julius Petersen and the construction of the Spanish literary generation' (247–62), examines intelligently the paradox whereby Azorín's non-prescriptive call to radicalism in 1913 became, through Salinas's rigid adherence to the Germanic model of the sacrosanct generational paradigm that was taken even further by Dámaso Alonso and Laín Entralgo, a conservative vision of consolidation in a nationalist context, all of which has led to both the paralysis and dysfunction of historical criticism by the severing of vital connections with European traditions, as well as distortion in the national production through confinement to such an exclusive definition; continuing on the same tack, C. A. Longhurst, 'Coming in from the cold: Spain, Modernism and the novel' (263–83), points out how Spanish literature has been wrongly excluded from the concept of high Modernism in Anglo-Saxon historiography because of the meaningless dichotomy of *modernismo* versus Generation of 1898 so fervently foregrounded in Francoist Spain, and instead champions new alignments such as those between Unamuno, Pirandello, and Kafka, or between Ganivet, Italo Svevo, and Robert Musil, or again between Valle-Inclán, Alfred

* I am grateful to the Social Sciences and Humanities Research Council of Canada for support during the preparation of this review.

Jarry, and James Joyce, or between Azorín and Virginia Woolf, or even between Baroja, Conrad, Hesse, Proust, and Valéry Larbaud, all of which highlight coincidence and equality among figures of stature in the European canon; M. S. Collins, 'Orfeo and the Catyline conspiracy in Unamuno's *Niebla*' (286–306), zeroes in on canine loyalties to Saints Hubert, Dominic, and Roch, doggy dialogues ranging from Plato to Cervantes, and Unamuno's speciality of *humorismo confusionista* in Western philosophy and language as subsumed in the oracular pooch of the particular novel; R. A. Cardwell, '*Modernismo, orientalismo, determinismo* and the problematic case of Isaac Muñoz Llorente' (307–29), hispanizes Edward Said to explicate the so-called decadent writer José Esteban Isaac Muñoz Llorente (1881–1925) as a quintessentially modern finisecular artist whose 'collage of reference' typically resists singular wholeness in the constant play between coincidence and divergence; and K. Murphy, 'Subjective vision in *El árbol de la ciencia* and *Jude the Obscure*' (331–53), explicates how both Baroja and Hardy contribute to changes in artistic sensibility at the turn of the century.

Luis T. González del Valle, *La canonización del diablo. Baudelaire y la estética moderna en España*, M, Verbum, 346 pp., takes a long, hard look at the 'colossal' influence of Baudelaire in yet another attempt at breaking down the isolationism that so disadvantages Spanish authors Valle-Inclán, Unamuno, Azorín, and the Machado brothers in any discussion of the literary practice of modernity. A chapter apiece is devoted to a consideration of the treatment of time, as 'tiempo "intemporal"' in *Voces de gesta* and *El embrujado*, as 'tiempo "intrahistórico"' in *Paz en la guerra*, and time and inaction in *Las confesiones de un pequeño filósofo* and *Doña Inés*; the pictorial expressions of modernity and the importance of caricature in relation to *El esperpento de la hija del capitán*; 'autoconciencia artística' and intertextuality in *Las adelfas*; and modernist themes in *Tirano Banderas*. Serious consideration is given throughout to such typical markers of modernity as the metropolis, the figures of the dandy and the *flâneur*, the perception of the circularity of time, art as an agent of fusion, the search for self, the sacred nature of the Word, the reaction against mimesis and realism, the rejection of bourgeois values, and the expression of good and evil, all as found in Spanish sources. F. Beigel, '*España* (1915–1924) y la "conquista cultural" del Perú de Mariátegui', *CA*, 93:194–211, contains useful information about the fruitful connections between the Spanish review and *Nuestra Época*, particularly after 1916 when Luis Araquistain took over as editor from Ortega y Gasset, that came from the up-front affirmation of socialist values, sympathy with the European labour movement, and the diffusion of the work of the literary and artistic Left in news of current events and their protagonists.

Of real interest is Enrique Serrano Asenjo, '*Vidas oblicuas': aspectos teóricos de la 'nueva biografía' en España (1928–1936)*, Zaragoza U.P., 238 pp., which elucidates with some originality the phenomenon first within a European framework of references that include Lytton Strachey, André Maurois, Virginia Woolf, Stefan Zweig, in order to zero in on Antonio Marichalar, Antonio Espina, and Benjamín Jarnés. John Crispin, *Las estéticas de las generaciones de 1925*, V, Pre-Textos–Vanderbilt U.P., 243 pp., jibes innovations in literature, painting, music, and architecture in a common aesthetic endeavour. To be read with Terence McMullan, *The Crystal and the Snake: Aspects of French Influence on Guillén, Lorca and Cernuda*, Anstruther, Fife, La Sirena, 215 pp., who uses detailed textual analysis to illustrate the importance of the visual arts in the shift from residual Symbolism through Cubism to Surrealism; the French influence so anxiously observed in Spain leads to the interpretive acts of poetry well documented here in Guillén's reworking of Valéry and Mallarmé in a 'logique imaginative' that reaches beyond the autonomous text, in Lorca's aesthetics of transition and New York as Le Corbusier's *City of Tomorrow*, and, finally, in the connection between Pierre Reverdy, Cernuda, and the plagiarism of surrealism. I. Navas Ocaña, 'Encuentros y desencuentros: la crítica española y las vanguardias', *ECon*, 14, 2001:95–104, recalls Peter Bürger's distinction between historical vanguards and the neo-vanguard of social commitment in the 'paradójico tradicionalismo' of the Europeanization projects of D'Ors and Ortega y Gasset that weighed so heavily in the critical rejection of surrealism and automatic writing by Pedro Salinas and Dámaso Alonso, and, with *La destrucción o el amor* as a key text, the subsequent favouring of fiercely homophobic and politically conservative parameters to maintain a 'classical' view of art divorced from any politicized social involvement.

¡Agítese bien! A New Look at the Hispanic Avant-Gardes, ed. Mario T. Pao and Rafael Hernández-Rodríguez, Newark, DE, Juan de la Cuesta, 306 pp., is more concerned with vanguard rebelliousness on both sides of the Atlantic and, rightly, stresses the interaction between authors in Spain and Latin America, so that of the 12 essays of special interest here are: A. A. Anderson, 'Herky, jerky: playing fast and loose in Giménez Caballero's *Hercules jugando a los dados*' (1–26), looking at G.C.'s discursive zigzagging and syllogistic legerdemain in an unique blend of social anthropology, arts commentary, and cultural studies *avant la lettre*, all in ludic free association and delirious word-play; N. Dennis, 'The avant-garde oratory of Ramón Gómez de la Serna' (77–117), concentrating on G. de la S.'s attempts to

deflate pompous solemnity and the tired rhetoric of academics and politicians through recourse to absurd costumes, climbing atop an elephant, munching on candles, or performances like the one caught on film in 1928 by Feliciano Vitores, *El orador*, analysed here; W. Bohn, 'Heading West with Rafael Alberti and Buster Keaton' (119–29), reading the poem 'Buster Keaton busca por el bosque a su novia, que es una verdadera vaca' against the film that inspired it, *Go West* (1925); V. Fuentes, 'Transgressive affinities (and one difference) in Buñuel's *La edad de oro* and Lorca's *El público*' (177–87), highlighting how both works extolled the twin allures of Eros and Thanatos, the death and desire combination that permeates most surrealist texts in which normative restrictions of genre and gender give way before the imperative of personal freedom; M. T. Pao, 'A view from the wheel' (213–41), concentrating on texts by Guillermo de Torre, Pedro Salinas, and José María Hinojosa to show how the speeding car not only alters visual perception, but also how such transformations correspond to futurist, cubist, and surrealist modes of viewing external reality (see *YWMLS*, 63:273); J. Highfill, 'An aesthetics of transience: fashion in the Spanish avant-garde' (243–73), reading Salinas's 'París, abril, modelo', to explain that vanguard standards of beauty are not located in classical models but in the changing fashions to be seen on display in store-window mannequins; while S. Larson, 'The commodification of the image of Spain's "new woman" by mass culture and the avant-garde in José Díaz Fernández's *La Venus mecánica*' (275–306), traces well the progression in the novel from prostitute to fashion model, to kept mistress, as well as the vanguard collusion with market forces which eventually annuls most possibilities of emancipation, thus sombrely providing the antidote to any uniperspectival consideration of the avant-garde's presentation of modern life.

Looking well after the seventh art form and the 'woman question' in a suggestive combination, *Women's Narrative and Film in 20th Century Spain*, ed. Kathleen Glenn, London, Routledge, 256 pp., examines the development of the feminine cultural tradition and how this reshaped and nuances the Spanish national identity; with an 'Introduction' by Ofelia Ferran, the chapters focus on representation of autobiography, alienation and exile, marginality, race, eroticism, political activism, and feminism within the changing nationalisms in different regions of modern Spain. *Recovering Spain's Feminist Tradition*, ed. Lisa Vollendorf, NY, MLA, 2001, 407 pp., seeks to rectify the perception of English-speaking colleagues that Spain is little more than bullfights, the Inquisition, Francisco Franco, and a *macho* paradise by historicizing Spanish feminism and illustrating its evolution from an early individual consciousness to collective efforts at social reorganization; of interest here are Maryellen Bieder's examination of Carmen de Burgos, Nancy Vosburgh on María Teresa León, Josebe Martínez-Gutierrez on Margarita Nelken, and María Asunción Gómez on the *Asociación de Mujeres Libres*, all within the critical posture of current cultural convention whereby texts are used to interpret society as the external time frame, and they summarize the biography and concerns of the authors in a veritable wealth of information. *The Feminist Encyclopedia of Spanish Literature*, ed. Janet Perez and Maureen Ihrie, 2 vols, Westport, CT, Greenwood, x + 736 pp., usefully fills an important gap and is a handy work of reference.

2. Poetry

María Victoria Utrera Torremocha, *Historia y teoría del verso libre*, Seville, Padilla, 2001, 337 pp., follows on from her 1999 study of the prose poem (see *YWMLS*, 63:264) with a solid sequel, outlining in some six meaty chapters the vicissitudes of *verso libre* within Spanish irregular versification; she examines the various influences of the French Symbolists, *modernismo*, vanguard practice, and Walt Whitman; the search for new rhythms; she takes account of differences between poetry and prose following Lotman's semantic approach; and, finally, in a review of the historical revisionism of the last 30 years, she signals the move away from really *free* verse to more traditional norms and, particularly, the *silva impar*; all in all, a useful reference tool for browsing. Francisco Javier Díez de Revenga, *Poetas del veintisiete. Cien poemas*, M, Juan Pastor, 183 pp., introduces (7–21) with some bare-bones bio-bibliographical notes (165–77) a minimalist selection of the 'grupo nuclear' for the novel poetry reader. C. G. Bellver, 'Hands, touch and female subjectivity in four Spanish women poets', *ALEC*, 27:317–47, looks at work by Concha Méndez, Josefina de la Torre, Carmen Conde, and Ernestina Champourcin written before postmodern theorizing on gender differences and finds a notable subversion of patriarchal norms, a gynocentric focus on creativity, and an adventuresome celebration of desire present in all four, but particularly in Champourcin and Méndez.

Individual Poets

ALBERTI. **Los bosques que regresan. Antología poética (1924–1988)*, ed. Antonio Colinas, B, Galaxia Gutemberg, 450 pp.; **Historia del soldado*, M, Fundación El Monte, 90 pp., with an introductory study by Eladio Mateos Miera. E. Drumm, 'Rafael Alberti's *Noche de guerra en el Museo del Prado*: the stage enframed', *RHM*, 54, 2001:307–26, examines A.'s use of ekphrasis to find that, although A. calls for proletarian revolution in the play, he undermines such an uprising in the very act of its creation; framed by the incorporation of Goya's captions to the etchings, revolution never moves beyond the boundaries of artistic language. Exile and nostalgia dominate the criticism in one form or another: M. J. Ramos Ortega, 'La España transterrada de Rafael Alberti', *ECon*, 14, 2001 : 105–08, spans the more than 50 years separating the first version published in Argentina (1945) and the latest Seix Barral edition (1999) of *Imagen primera de . . .*, the series of moral portraits written for and in *La España peregrina* in order to recuperate the lost homeland; using modern psychoanalysis, G. Herrmann, 'Nostralgia: María Teresa León, Rafael Alberti, and the memory of absence', *RHM*, 54, 2001 : 327–47, remarks on the curious absence of the self in both autobiographies written by husband and wife in exile, and suggests that, despite very clear differences in the two texts, both are filled with a painful longing for the prior fullness and satisfaction that derived from identification with a nation-based participatory existence, typical of adherence to a political cause in the homeland, and that in exile is no longer available to them; while, in only superficially lighter vein, 'The dogs of war: melancholy and the infinite sadness of Rafael Alberti and María Teresa León', *ALEC*, 27 : 441–63, the same author has recourse to *The Smashing Pumpkins* to highlight the metaphor of traumatic sadness construed in the astonishingly pervasive canine presence of Yemi, Niebla, Tusca, Katy, Guagua, Muk, Alano, Diana, Jazmín, and the never forgotten Centella, all of whom translate the acuity of melancholy for A. and the affective condition of melancholia for María Teresa, his wife and companion in exile. (See also LEÓN below.)

CERNUDA. The centenary junket begins to appear in print: Luis Antonio de Villena, *Rebeldía, clasicismo y crisis: Luis Cernuda. Asedios plurales a un poeta príncipe*, V, Pre-Textos, 141 pp., celebrates a kindred spirit; while, as part of the official homage, *Entre la realidad y el deseo: Luis Cernuda, 1902–1963. Exposición*, ed. James Valender, M, Residencia de Estudiantes, 478 pp., collates material for the catalogue of the exhibition with contributions from Harold Bloom, Nigel Dennis, Guillermo Carnero, Luis Antonio de Villena, et al.; Id., *Luis Cernuda — Album. Biografía*, M, Residencia de Estudiantes, 541 pp., is a nice collector's piece. In comparative vein, Gabriel Insausti Herrero-Velarde, *La presencia del romanticismo inglés en el pensamiento poético de Luis Cernuda*, Pamplona, EUNSA (Anejos de *RILCE*, 34), 2000, 256 pp., deals only with C.'s literary criticism from 'El espíritu lírico' (1932) to *Estudios sobre la poesía española contemporánea* (1957) without any real exegesis of the poetry in order to document how C.'s predisposition towards Romanticism, stemming from his youthful readings of Bécquer and French 19th-c. poetry and complemented after 1930 by knowledge of Hölderlin, Goethe, and Schiller, blossomed in exile in the UK from 1938 to 1946 following his immersion in the work of the English Lake Poets and the critical commentaries of T. S. Eliot, Stephen Spender, and W. H. Auden; such anglophilia led C. to exhibit a pronounced francophobia and, even, a somewhat one-sided vision of Spanish literature that, nevertheless, made him the link between Jorge Manrique, Antonio Machado, and the Generation of 1950 (and, particularly, José Hierro), and informed C.'s personalized view of 'realidad y deseo' in his later work; while M. P. Moreno, 'De poetas y ventrílocuos: el correlativo objetivo y el monólogo dramático en Luis Cernuda, Juan Gil-Albert y Guillermo Carnero', *RHM*, 55:110–22, also goes back to readings in the English Romantics and T. S. Eliot to demonstrate briefly similarities and differences between the two techniques in the three Spanish poets.

GARCÍA LORCA. As usual A. A. Anderson, 'Bibliografía lorquiana reciente (1984–2001)', *BFFGL*, 31:167–96, painstakingly documents new editions, recent articles, and doctoral theses, with some particularly useful information on reviews and audiovisual materials not recorded here. C. de Paepe, 'Federico García Lorca en marcha para su segundo centenario', *ECon*, 14, 2001:109–16, douses the literary fireworks of the first centenary celebrations and provides sage counsel about the limited value of such pyrotechnics by referring to the deplorably *personal* vein of the wrangling over the ownership of the MSS of *Poeta en Nueva York* before the scheduled sale at Christie's, as compared to the *critical* value emphasized in his encomium for Mariano de Paco's edition of *La casa de Bernarda Alba* (1999) highlighting G.L.'s development as a dramatist in the context of the renovation of the Spanish stage (see *YWMLS*, 62:258–59). The death of the poet's sister and sometime custodian of the archives is marked in a special issue, 'Homenaje a Isabel García Lorca (1909–2002)', *BFFGL*, 31, which contains much personal reminiscing, some useful accounts of (family) friendships with women of her generation, and a modicum of information relevant to G.L., and of note here are: 'Juegos de luna y dos lunas de tarde' (15–23), holograph reproductions (18, 20) of the variants of two poems by G.L. dedicated to friends, together with some interesting photographs; M. Hernández, 'Rosas antiguas de Rodas' (25–51), a detailed account of Isabel's post-graduation cruise from 15 June to 1 August 1933 in company with some 190 professors and students, which reproduces a letter of July 1933 written to her parents describing happy memories of Rhodes and disillusion with Crete, a visit to the Jewish quarter, comments on Sephardic Spanish and a version of 'En la siuda de Marselyya' (32–35), that is linked to an interview by G.L. in *Sulem* in

December 1933, his censoring of offensive wording in *La zapatera prodigiosa*, and the (anecdotal) substitution of 'Gerineldo, Gerineldo' for his sister's ethno-musicological discovery earlier that year; Soledad Ortega (56–57) reproduces a letter from Paris dated 1938 that bewails lost contact; Teresa Guillén, 'Recuerdos compartidos' (58), more honestly situates their friendship in later life, first in exile in New York and Middlebury, and then in Madrid, Meco, and Nerja; while Margarita Ucelay, 'El ejemplo de una vida' (59–61), tells of the black, fear-filled days in Madrid just after Federico's death and the different attitudes of sisters Isabel and Conchita; personal reminiscing continues in the theatrical memoirs of A. Bautista, '*Yerma* en Madrid, 1960' (64–65), with details of the pre-*estreno* in Italy in July with Conchita as the Vieja Pagana, and the opening in October at the *Teatro Eslava*; Nuria Espert (67) from her diary of life in Paris in 1982, praise from José Luis Gómez (67), and Lluís Pasqual (68–69), on almost 20 years of friendship, while A. del Hoyo, 'Isabel García Lorca y la primera edición de *Obras completas* de su hermano Federico en España (Aguilar, 1954)' (72–76), comments on the double assassination of the person of the poet and his work by Francoist forces, and how the Aguilar edition was celebrated despite real fears of reprisal; and, finally, jockeying for position, well-known scholars Rodolfo Cardona (77), Gonzalo Sobejano (78), Christopher Maurer (79–80), José García Velasco (81–83), Piero Menarini (84–85), Andrés Soriano (88–89), Luis García Montero (90–91), and Carmen Zulueta (92–94), unanimously praise Isabel's part in amassing and preserving the Lorquian heritage.

Intertextualities abound: **Lorca, Buñuel, Dalí: Art and Theory*, ed. Manuel Delgado Morales and Alice J. Poust, Lewisburg, PA, Bucknell U.P., 2001, 206 pp.; N. R. Orringer, 'García Lorca's *Romancero gitano*: a dialogue with Baudelaire', *ALEC*, 27:507–30, finds an echo of *Les fleurs du Mal* in G.L.'s title and thereupon adduces the substantial input of the French poet in G.L.'s gypsy figures in comparisons between 'Allégorie' and 'Romance de la pena negra', 'La Fontaine de sang' and 'Reyerta', 'Un Martyr. Dessein d'un maître inconnu' and 'El martirio de Santa Olalla', 'La Lune offensée' and 'Romance de la luna, luna', 'La Mauvaise moine' and 'La monja gitana', and, particularly, 'Romancero de la Guardia Civil española' and 'Une charogne', all of which attests G.L.'s affinity with the aesthetics of Modernism (see also Luis González del Valle in LITERARY HISTORY above); while, even more specifically, R. Navarro Durán, 'Inés de Alvarado y "La monja gitana"', *BFFGL*, 31:107–18, claims a direct line to Zorrilla via *Don Juan Tenorio*, *El desafío del Diablo*, and 'El capitán Montoya'; while A. Soria Olmedo, '"Grito hacia Roma": intertextualidad y profecía', *ib.*, 119–32, finds evidence of a pheasant image from Torres Naharro, and echoes of Ángel Ganivet (and Nietzsche) in G.L.'s heterodox rediscovery of his Roman Catholic tradition. M. J. Nandorfy, '*Duende* and apocalypse in Lorca's theory and poetics', *RCEH*, 26:255–70, argues that *Poeta en Nueva York* represents the performative mode of death while G.L.'s essays on *duende* and imagination negate such a conspiracy of silence. C. C. Soufas, Jr., 'Lorca's servants, the audience, and stage authority', *HeT*, 2:81–97, documents well how G.L. uses the servant role to delineate the visual dynamics of play-making, thereby instituting a softer version of Artaud's 'theatre of cruelty' by first ceding enhanced audience vision only to deny it, finally, in order to give greater form, presence, and voice to the invisible forces beyond the margins of the stage.

GUILLÉN. Biographical details loom large. *Correspondencia. Jorge Guillén — José María de Cossío*, ed. Julio Neira and Rafael Gómez de Tudanca, V, Pre-Textos, 202 pp., fleshes out literary history in a useful 'Introduction' (8–44) to the friendship evinced in the 46 letters and cards exchanged between 1921 and 1965 that survived the vicissitudes of war, exile, and politics; most interesting are G.'s early letters of 1921–22 full of literary news from Paris, the revindication of Góngora and his doctoral thesis, and G.'s growing conviction of the value of his own poetic vocation, all complemented by Cossío's plans to 'anthologize' the work of the very special group of friends. Breaking with the family's customary reticence, G. Baquero, 'Entrevista a Teresa Guillén', *BFFGL*, 31 : 133–49, records some spontaneous reminiscing about both her famous father and her mother's important influence, with comments on Carlos Fuentes, Salinas, García Lorca, life in Valladolid and Seville, exile and the return of G. and his family to Spain. Lost for many years and much sought after in the present climate that favours the manoeuvres of literary salvage, *Notas para una edición comentada de Góngora*, ed. Antonio Piedra and Juan Bravo, Valladolid, Fundación Jorge Guillén–Castilla-La Mancha U.P., 250 pp., is the corrected and annotated version of G.'s second attempt at a doctoral thesis (see also *YWMLS*, 52:368), this one successfully defended in the Universidad Central de Madrid in 1925; José María Micó provides a brief prologue, 'El Góngora de Jorge Guillén' (7–13), outlining the innovative nature of G.'s pre-Dámaso critique, while the body of these 'Notas' show G. as a faithful reader of the Baroque, capable of a passionate response to 'el primero de los modernos' that would be reflected well later in *Language and Poetry* (1961).

JIMÉNEZ. Important additions to correct the *corpus* appear: Diego Martínez Torrón compiles, edits, and adds a necessary preliminary study to *La muerte*, B, Seix Barral, 1999 [2000], 176 pp.; *Unidad*, B,

Seix Barral, 128 pp.; and *La realidad invisible*, M, Cátedra, 1999, 269 pp., thereby augmenting Antonio Sánchez Romeralo's pioneer anthologizing (1981–82) by increasing *La muerte* from 32 to 119 texts, and *Unidad* from 31 to 78 texts, citing unedited work and variants from the *obra en marcha*; while a better disposition of the final text of *La realidad invisible* shows clearly how important J.'s writings of the 1920s were in the compilation of the mature work *Dios deseado y deseante*. With a similar preoccupation, J. H. C. Jensen, 'La *Obra* de Juan Ramón Jiménez como elaboración vivida del concepto del absoluto', *RevR*, 37:205–26, reaches the same conclusion about the constant rewriting for the *Obra definitiva o total*, but adduces parallels with Condorcet and the German Romantics, Goethe and Schlegel, about the impossibility of perfection, and uses biography to explain J.'s aspiration to express a subjectivity that might transcend contingency and finitude in a fragmented and fragmentary modern world. Miguel Ángel García, **La poética de lo invisible en Juan Ramón Jiménez*, Granada, Diputación Provincial de Granada, 122 pp.

MACHADO, ANTONIO. Araceli Iravedra, *El poeta rescatado. Antonio Machado y la poesía del 'grupo de "Escorial"'*, M, Biblioteca Nueva, 2001, 251 pp., is dedicated to documenting the reception of M.'s work in postwar Spain by the Generation of 1936, poets centred around the review *Escorial* and including Dionisio Ridruejo, Luis Rosales, Luis Felipe Vivanco, and Leopoldo Panero, who articulated a *rehumanización* of poetry in their nationalist readings of Antonio Machado and the Generation of 1898, and subscribed to a certain discipleship of the older poet despite the fact that he belonged to a very different socio-historical and ideological context from their Francoist reality. Philip G. Johnston, **The Power of Paradox in the Work of Spanish Poet Antonio Machado 1875–1939*, Lewiston, NY, Mellen, 268 pp. Terence McMullan, *Antonio Machado's Monument to Memory: 'A José María Palacio' Revisited* (Occasional Papers, 35), Univ. of Bristol, Department of Hispanic, Portuguese and Latin American Studies, 2001, 22 pp., picks over critical appraisals by Claudio Guillén, Carlos Beceiro, Vicente Gaos, Arthur Terry, and Antonio Sánchez-Barbudo to reread differently the poem's intricate intertextualities and find a discreet but delicately lyrical obituary wherein memories of Leonor are buried for ever beneath the lapidary landscape of Moncayo.

SALINAS. Taking advantage of biographical coincidence, F. Peltzer, 'Homenaje a Pedro Salinas', *BAAL*, 259–60, 2001:69–75, opportunely combines a gloss on S.'s 'Defensa del lenguaje' (1944) with a dual commemoration of the 50th anniversary of the poet's death and 'El día del idioma' in Argentina in order to rally the troops in an attempt to reclaim S.'s 'honor lingüístico' by enriching daily vocabulary; while M. Escartín Gual, 'Pedro Salinas: la letra y la persona', *RLit*, 64:555–66, pays a similar homage in a series of 'instantáneas' from S.'s work denigrating the crass materialism of the American Dream composed of speed, technology, and fast money, and celebrating instead the values of language, friendship, the contemplation of nature and art, and a generally slower pace of life, as befits a son of the *Institución Libre de Enseñanza*. J. Crispin, 'Amor / mundo en peligro: Pedro Salinas ante la sensibilidad posmoderna', *REH*, 36:22–35, draws a line between the 'essentialist' and the 'postmodern' and runs from Saussure to Marshall McLuhan, Alan Wilde, and Mies van der Rohe to conclude rather lamely that S. is neither. Working through all the poetry, Ruth Katz Crispin, *Song of the Self: The Poetry of Pedro Salinas*, Anstruther, Fife, La Sirena, 166 pp., highlights debts to the Romantics and unconscious rivalry with Quevedo as S. resolves the tensions about his own voice and acknowledges his mortality in some of the most haunting love poetry of the 20th century.

3. Prose

Francisco Javier Díez de Revenga, *Las novelas de 1902: espacios murcianos y signos de modernidad*, Murcia, Real Academia Alfonso X el Sabio, 20 pp., notes the curious coincidence in publication date and 'new' style to be found in *Amor y pedagogía*, *Sonata de otoño*, *La voluntad*, and *Camino de perfección*, and documents well the autobiographical commentaries by Azorín and Baroja about Yecla and Yécora, non-religious education as a theme present in the work of all the Generation of 1898, and the literary reality of a new ideology transformed into the new subjectivity of a new novel for the 20th century. Caught up in the shifting ground of objectivity and the novel, Ramón Espejo-Saavedra, *El reto de la novela histórica: narrativa y poder en Galdós, Valle-Inclán y Max Aub*, Newark, DE, Juan de la Cuesta, 172 pp., predictably presses Hayden White, Paul Ricoeur, Georg Lukács, and Linda Hutcheon into service to outline the working of historical imagination in the play between 'official' history and fiction; in separate chapters of interest here, attention is paid to *La lámpara maravillosa* and anti-historical thought (82–124), while treason and complicity are considered the paradox of power in historical representation as depicted in *Campo cerrado* and *Campo del moro* (125–59). *Francisco Ayala, escritor universal*, ed. Antonio Sánchez Trigueros and Manuel Ángel Vázquez Medel, Seville, Alfar, 2001, 234 pp. Juan María Martín prologues and annotates for pedagogical use, Pío Baroja, *Zalacaín el aventurero*, M, Anaya, 2001, 239 pp. Through references to mentor Ortega and contemporary María Zambrano, A. Gómez-Pérez, 'La confesión en la sinrazón de Rosa Chacel',

RHM, 54, 2001:348–53, jibes the theory of confession with its practical realization in Chacel's most ambitious novel. J. McCulloch, '¿El Ramón permeable? Parody and influence in Ramón Gómez de la Serna's *La mujer de ámbar* (1927)', *Hispanófila*, 136:27–38, traces hitherto unsuspected intertextualities from Alessandro Manzoni's *I promessi sposi* in thematic similarities concerning religion and death, the idealization of the female character, and the important roles given national history and landscape, and goes on to claim Gómez de la Serna as a notable vanguard writer deeply rooted in the European literary tradition. Javier Zamora Bonilla, **Ortega y Gasset*, B, Plaza y Janés, 652 pp.; Christian Pierre and Yves Lorvellec, **Ortega y Gasset: l'exigence de la vérité*, Paris, Michalon, 2001, 123 pp. A. A. Ayo, 'Crisis, juego e ilusión en la autobiografía de Ramón Pérez de Ayala', *RHM*, 55:64–78, reads in depth the tetralogy composed of *Tinieblas en las cumbres* (1907), *A.M.D.G.* (1910), *La pata de la raposa* (1912), and *Troteras y danzaderas* (1913), to elucidate how Pérez de Ayala works through the literary crisis of the breakdown of traditional divisions between history and fiction, text and context, author and reader, a crisis that has life and death implications for this writer who tries to regain an (illusionary) authorial presence in the ludic exploration of how art might bring him cause for optimism and some hope for the future. M. Vásquez, '*El lugar de un hombre*: un hito en la narrativa de Sender', *ECon*, 14, 2001:105–12, reviews variants and rewriting over 20 years of this authorial reflection on exile and marginalization in order to highlight a simultaneous portrayal of social outrage at the impotency of the *campesinos* against the power of the Church and the oligarchy, as exemplified in the infamous 'crimen de Cuenca', and Sender's nostalgia for his Aragonese background, exacerbated by his exile in far away Mexico after the Civil War.

INDIVIDUAL WRITERS

AUB. *Hablo como hombre*, ed. Gonzalo Sobejano, Segorbe, Fundación Max Aub, 289 pp., collects the 20 short essays on politics in everyday life written between 1937 and 1964, with a brief but informative introduction (11–29), and copious annotations (247–87); this self-styled 'revoltijo de cartas, artículos y textos inconexos sin más liga que mí mismo' bears poignant witness to A.'s on-going concern in exile for postwar Spain and the Republican cause. Concentrating on those years in exile, S. Faber, 'Un pasado que no fue, un futuro imposible: juegos parahistóricos en los cuentos del exilio de Max Aub', *ETL*, 29, 2000–2001:82–89, uses Paul Ricoeur, Karl Mannheim, and Fredric Jameson to outline A.'s survival strategies in the liberation from any rigid separation of fiction and history in order to invent a parallel, often utopic, history of what might have been if the Republicans had won the war; while Id., 'El exilio mexicano de Max Aub: la relación con el régimen anfitrión', *RCEH*, 26:423–38, describes how, despite a malicious comment in *Excélsior* in June 1953 that caused him specific hardship in tapped phones, censored mail, delays in obtaining his Mexican citizenship, and withdrawal of travel rights, A. never criticized the increasingly conservative government in the country of his exile.

AZORÍN. Comparative criticism ranges over the centuries: T. R. Franz, 'Espronceda, the romantics and Doña Inés', *RHM*, 54, 2000:294–306, identifies A.'s frequent allusions to romantic writers, the romantic period, and, particularly, to Espronceda's work, in order to recreate the dialogue between A. and the realities of the 1920s wherein Primo de Rivera imposed order and A. acknowledged that any restoration of past tradition by the narrator is doomed to failure in mere revivals of trivial stories of troubadours and their ladies; while M. Escartín Gual, 'El diario íntimo, Azorín y la nueva novela', *RLit*, 64:107–20, celebrates the centenary of the publication of *Diario de un enfermo* (1901) by elucidating the connection between the diary as genre and the new sensibility in writing by Azorín (and contemporaries Baroja and Unamuno) in a study of the early work from 1897–1904 that both pinpoints autobiography as a key theme, one used not to record the past out of vanity but as a 'sistema de autoconocimiento irracionalista', and usefully lists A.'s so-called first person writings from 1897–1945. *Journeys in Time and Place. Two Works of Azorín*, trans. Walter Borenstein, Rock Hill, SC, Spanish Literature Publications Co., 204 pp., provides annotated English translations of *Las confesiones de un pequeño filósofo* (1904) and *La ruta de Don Quijote* (1912), together with a very basic introduction to 'Azorín and the Generation of 1898' for the general reader.

JARNÉS. Armando Pego Puigbó provides full critical apparatus for *Teoría del zumbel*, Zaragoza, Institución Fernando el Católico — Excma. Diputación de Zaragoza, 2000, 211 pp., in a corrected update of the Espasa Calpe 1930 edition of 'un proyecto narrativo en ciernes' that was of paramount importance to Spanish vanguard prose, and adds a full and useful bibliography. R. P. Hershberger, 'Tales of seduction on the stage and screen: the beginnings of a cinematic mode in Benjamín Jarnés's *El professor inútil*', *ALEC*, 27:465–505, explicates at length how J. foregrounds cinematic techniques over theatrical representation in his revision of the novelistic convention so that readers might come to grips with modern urban life in the raw rather than merely offering yet another trite and sentimental set piece.

LEÓN. M. M. Bedia, '*Antón Perulero*. Un cuento inédito de María Teresa León', *RLit*, 64:569–85, provides the transcription (576–84) of one short story from an exercise book containing four unfinished short stories, two reviews of work by Jacinto Benavente and Norah Lange, a speech on the *Escuela Hispano-Americana*, and various drafts of essays on the theatre, together with Rafael Alberti's adaptation of *Farsa del licenciado* from the French. Probably written in Argentina in 1939–40, this is a children's tale about the day in the *pueblo* of Mal Abrigo when it rained frogs and Antón Perulero from Peru ran off with Zalamea, and it has many of the same characters as Alberti's *La pájara pinta*, illustrating well how both husband and wife used to good effect the rhymes, refrains, songs, and set phrases of Spanish folklore and children's literature. (See also ALBERTI above.)

UNAMUNO. More correspondence is given wider readership: Pedro Ribas and Fernando Hermida de Blas edit with critical commentary **Cartas de Alemania*, M, Fondo de Cultura Económica, 358 pp.; while Wilfredo Kapsoli Escudero collects the series of texts **Unamuno y el Perú. Epistolario, 1902–1934*, Lima, Univ. Ricardo Palma, 307 pp. According to A. Martínez, 'El paisaje en Unamuno: metáfora de España', *RCEH*, 26:337–49, geographical descriptions are not mimetic transpositions of reality but a linguistic re-elaboration that allows the author in exile to live in the beloved homeland. In some critical pyrotechnics designed to reverse Book x of Plato's *Republic*, F. Larubia-Prado, 'Lethal emotions: the will as imagination in Unamuno's *Abel Sánchez*', *REH*, 36:373–401, prefers Lacan and Kristeva over Hegelian dialectics to elucidate the cultural and linguistic stages in a person's psychological development in order to characterize jealousy, envy, and resentment *apud* René Girard, Georg Simmel, William Davidson, through Deleuze, and thereby champion Abel as the truly active force in his manifestation of the will to power over Joaquín, the master of a warped, defensive hermeneutics of the ultimate narcissist. Filling a perceived lacuna, M. J. Marr, '"Dolor común": autobiographical (in)security in Unamuno's *Rosario de sonetos líricos*', *ECon*, 14, 2001:43–57, finds in verse form a diagnostic assessment of man's ontological condition that anticipates much of U.'s philosophical and religious thinking in the essays and fiction published after this 1911 collection.

VALLE-INCLÁN. A long-awaited edition appears, *Obra completa*, 2 vols, M, Espasa Calpe, xxix + 1990, 2459 pp., put together, although this is not explicitly acknowledged, by Joaquín Valle-Inclán, and that executes a plan first conceived of by V.-I. between 1913–33 in his selective *Opera omnia*, and which surpasses the incomplete Losada *Obras completas* (1938–50), the standard Rúa Nora-Rivadeneyra collection (1944) re-edited by Plenitud (1952, 1954), as well as the selections in 25 vols of Círculo de Lectores or the earlier Colección Austral/Clásicos Castellanos editions. Editorial policy is explained in the prologue, 'Sobre esta edición' (I, ix–xxix), concerning the incorporation of unedited work and a new disposition of the texts; the first volume contains non-dramatic prose, while the theatre and poetry are covered in the second; a comprehensive 'Apéndice' (II, 1839–1945) consists of an extensive glossary of V.-I.'s very rich vocabulary, and an 'Índice alfabético de textos' (II, 1381–2445), gives the publishing history and variants of all material collected here; all in all, if this is not truly a *critical* edition, since all known textual variants are not given, it is a most welcome labour of love that makes V.-I.'s work readily accessible in a pristine and reliable form. In comparative vein: T. R. Franz, 'Valera as icon in the *Sonata de otoño*', *RHM*, 55:39–46, produces some convincing biographical data to indicate the urbane, elegant, and exquisite womanizer, Juan Valera, as the historical embodiment of V.-I.'s literary *tenorio*, Bradomín, and then goes on to show how such refined mimesis becomes a parody in iconic form of the perceived obstacle to a new social sensibility and literary aesthetic in V.-I.'s typical posture of simultaneous, dialogical denigration and admiration; while M. Comellas Aguirrezábal, '*La lámpara maravillosa* de Valle-Inclán y el *Heinrich von Ofterdingen* de Novalis o la poética como "camino de perfección" ', *RLit*, 64:121–50, indicates the seminal nature of a work available in French, Italian, and Spanish at the turn of the century, using Meyer H. Abrams to adduce connections to the Jena Group and attest V.-I.'s own romantic vein, and going on at length about how V.-I. used the *Bildungsroman* to fashion an aesthetic tool of perfection to create a mystical poetics for his Spanish readers. Bringing the criticism up to date, P. Santoro, 'Valle-Inclán on the large screen: *Divinas palabras* and *Luces de Bohemia*', *ALEC*, 27:159–73, documents how the camera lens substitutes for the mirror in the various film versions by Juan Ibáñez (1977), Miguel Ángel Díez (1985), and José Luis García Sánchez (1987); while J. P. Gabriele, 'La vida entre ilusiones: la contextura posmodernista del *Esperpento de los cuernos de Don Friolera*', *La Torre*, 24:127–43, expertly inscribes the *esperpento* in the purest of postmodern interplay between history and fiction, and highlights how V.-I. invents new social, artistic, and ideological discourses in a theatre experience at once pluralist, innovative, and without conventional reference in order to defy, confound, and explode institutional hegemony. *ALEC*, 27, continues into a second year the *Anuario Valle-Inclán* containing news of a *Cátedra Valle-Inclán* (649); P. Cabañas, 'Dos sueños, dos cartas, dos Conchas: *Sonata de otoño* y *El marqués de Bradomín. Coloquios románticos*' (651–75); D. Gambini, '*Sonata de primavera*: itinerarios reales / itinerarios ficticios' (677–716); R. Mascato Rey, 'Valle-Inclán y Berta Singerman: la renovación del arte escénico' (717–37); C. Miguez Vilas, 'Funcionalidad de las acotaciones valleinclanianas en *Divinas palabras*' (739–53); J. M. Pereiro-Otero, 'Los colores del modernismo: *Flor de santidad*' (755–89); M. Tasende, 'La influencia de Ortega y Gasset en la formación del corpus crítico en torno a las *Sonatas*' (791–825); M. P. Veiga Grandal, 'Las ilustraciones de *Voces de gesta*' (827–46); a section devoted to recovering both unedited work and documentation previously published in the Spanish press: A. Gago Rodó, 'El autógrafo como publicación. Un poema de Valle-Inclán' (1922)' (857–63); Á. Gómez Abalo and R. Romero Crego, 'La prensa gallega y el segundo viaje de Valle-Inclán a México' (865–91); L. Schiavo, 'Valle-Inclán y las mujeres itinerantes' (893–908); J. Serrano Alonso, '"De las academias, ¡líbranos, Señor!" Valle-Inclán frente a la Real Academia: una entrevista desconocida (1917)' (909–33); M. P. Veiga Grandal and M. Vidal Maza, '"Dijo la prensa . . ."' (935–39); and, up-dating the bibliography, J. Serrano and A. de Juan Bolufer, 'Bibliografía sobre Ramón Valle-Inclán (2000–2001)' (941–61).

4. Theatre

Critical work on the drama of the period is also noted above under ALBERTI, GARCÍA LORCA, UNAMUNO and VALLE-INCLÁN. José Luis García Barrientos, *Cómo se comenta una obra de teatro*, M, Síntesis, 2001, 367 pp., combines rhetoric and pedagogy by outlining a conceptual model of the interaction of actor, space, time, and public in both dramatic texts and theatrical spectacles with *Luces de Bohemia* and *La casa de Bernarda Alba* as examples, as well as giving an anthology of commentaries on theatrical works by a distinguished list of theoreticians that runs from Marx to Steiner, via Grotowski, Szardi, and Piscator, and includes Spanish authors like Larra, Clarín, and Mihura. Some specific documentation on Spanish theatre space: Nathalie Cañizares Bundorf, *Memoria de un escenario. Teatro María Guerrero 1885–2000*, M, Centro de Documentación Teatral, 2001, 385 pp., is an uneven study of the repertory of the former *Teatro de la Princesa*, with comments on actors Federico Oliver, Carmen Cobeña, María Guerrero, and Fernando Díaz de Mendoza, and on the name change after 1929, together with a useful list of productions put on between 1885–1917, although little information is given on the staging, costumes, or technical details of the theatre's distinguished history; while R. del Cerro Malagón, 'Una arquitectura para el espectáculo. Herencias y cambios del palacio teatral en el cine (1900–1939)', *ALEC*, 27:23–43, notes the inspiration of Charles

Garnier and the Paris *Opéra* in the noble edifices of the *Teatro Real* in Madrid, the *Principal* in Burgos, the *Arriaga* in Bilbao, the *Pérez Galdós* in Las Palmas, the *Victoria Eugenia* in San Sebastián, and the *Lope de Vega* in Seville, and comments on the desecration and decline of such temples of elegance following the advent of the cinema. Juan Antonio Ríos Carratalá, *Cómicos ante el espejo. Los actores españoles y la autobiografía*, Alicante U.P., 2001, 232 pp., is a useful overview of how autobiography keeps faith with the theatre by preserving historical memory of both before and during the Francoist regime; the appraisals of the now standard works of autobiographical reference of actors Enrique Chicote and José Rubio Navajas are of special interest here. K. M. Sibbald, 'Carlos Arniches: política conservadora, sirvientes desclasados y máscaras de lo grotesco', *HeT*, 2:57–80, constructs a theoretical model incorporating socio-linguistic realism, theatrical geography, typology of characters, and scenic creativity in the *sainete* to show how Arniches moves away from an initially comfortable conservatism to foreshadow the dehumanized metalinguistics of the grotesque in his portrayal of the lower classes in a theatrical career that began in 1888 and ended in 1943. The move from theatre to cinema is documented by J. E. Checa Puerta, 'Gregorio Martínez Sierra y el cine: de Madrid a Hollywood', *ALEC*, 27:45–67, who puts into perspective a successful career as playwright (with wife María de la O. Lejárraga), impresario, director of the *Teatro Eslava*, and, finally, in the 'talkies' at Fox in 1931, and later in Argentina in the 1940s; while E. Díez, 'Miguel Mihura: *Yo no soy la Mata-Hari*', *ib.*, 69–87, studies the 1949 film script to find in Mihura's abstract humour and Niní Marshall's parodic acting an 'evasión comprometida' for both Francoist Spain and Peronist Argentina, liked by the general public but panned by the critics.

LITERATURE, 1936 TO THE PRESENT DAY

POSTPONED

V. CATALAN STUDIES

LANGUAGE

POSTPONED

MEDIEVAL LITERATURE

By Lola Badia, *Professor of Catalan Literature at the Universitat de Barcelona* and Miriam Cabré, *Researcher at the Universitat de Girona*

1. General

bibliography and collected essays. *BBAHLM*, 15:1–48, is an annotated list of publications on medieval Catalan for the year 2001. *Qüern*, 4, 2001, covers the years 1999–2000. Tomàs and Joaquim Carreras Artau, *Història de la Filosofia Espanyola. Filosofia cristiana del segle* xiii al xv, 2 vols., IEC, 2001, 661 + 686 pp., is a facsimile of this essential study with new preliminary essays by P. Lluís Font, J. Mensa, J. de Puig, and J. M. Ruiz Simon. J. Romeu i Figueras, *Assaigs de literatura valenciana del Renaixement*, Alacant U.P. — IIFV, 1999, 160 pp., assembles Romeu's published articles on Joan Ferrandis d'Herèdia, songs, and popular forms. Enric Prat and Pep Vila, *Mil anys de llengua i literatura catalanes al Rosselló*, Canet de Rosselló, Trabucaire, 669 pp., is an anthology of Latin, Occitan, and Catalan texts. *Llibre de Consolat de Mar*, ed. Germà Colón and Arcadi Garcia, B, Fundació Noguera, 2001, 1607 pp., revises their 1981–87 edition.

archival research and manuscript transmission. A. Gudayol, 'Inventaris de biblioteques en el món hispànic a l'època tardomedieval i moderna: balanç bibliogràfic (1980–1997)', *Anuari de Filologia*, 21.C, 1998–99: 29–113, offers a classified catalogue. *AHAM*, 20–21.1, 1999–2000, contains relevant archival research on historical background, notably J. Hernando Delgado, 'Escoles i programes acadèmics a la Barcelona del segle xv: l'escola de mestre Ramon Llull i l'ensenyament de disciplines gramaticals i d'arts' (633–62). J. Hernando Delgado, 'Del llibre manuscrit al llibre imprès: la confecció del llibre a Barcelona durant el segle xv: documentació notarial', *ATCA*, 21: 257–603, edits a substantial collection of archival documents on book circulation. F. M. Gimeno Blay, 'Produir llibres manuscrits catalans (segles xii-xv)', Badia, *Literatura*, 115–49, surveys several aspects of book production, from autograph copies to MS circulation. J. N. Hillgarth, 'Documents mallorquins desconeguts dels anys 1356–1359', *Randa*, 49: 9–13, sheds light on civil and religious power structures. G. Colón, 'La llengua a València en l'època del primer Borja', *ib.*, 39–49, analyses some documents published by Rubio Vela. M. Josepa Arnall Juan, *El llibre manuscrit*, B, Servei de Llengua Catalana de la Univ. de Barcelona — Barcelona U.P. — Eumo, 337 pp., is a thorough dictionary, covering all aspects of medieval book-making. A. M. Compagna Perrone Capano, 'La tradizione catalana', Boitani, *Circolazione*, 595–620, provides an overview of Catalan MS sources. *L'edició de textos: història i mètode*, ed. Víctor Martínez-Gil, B, Univ. Oberta de Catalunya — Pòrtic, 2001, 302 pp., contains relevant discussion for medieval editions, notably S. Martí, 'Models i criteris d'edició' (45–102), and J. Pujol, 'L'edició de textos catalans medievals' (149–202).

2. Lyric and Narrative Verse

Lyric Poetry

A. Rossich, 'Alternança de llengües en Cerverí de Girona', *EstG*, 22:13–40, proposes five languages for Cerverí's *cobla*. A. Alberni, 'El *Cançoner Vega-Aguiló*: una proposta de reconstrucció codicològica', Badia, *Literatura*, 151–71, attributes a poem to Melcior de Gualbes thanks to codicological reconstruction. A. Fratta, 'Contributi per una nuova edizione critica delle poesie di Jordi de Sant Jordi', *RSTe*, 2, 2000: 143–62, discusses his forthcoming edition. Two articles in *EstG*, 22, prove the methodological importance of lexical analysis: L. Cabré, 'Dues notes de lèxic medieval: "estremoni" i "ereos"' (51–63); and J. Turró, 'El patró que sorgia en platja i l'*enarratio auctorum*' (353–64). M. Cabré, 'El saber de Joan Ramon Ferrer', Badia, *Literatura*, 228–58, edits and analyses a *sirventes* by the lawyer Ferrer, and in 'Jutges, processos i sentències en la lírica del xv: Joan Ramon Ferrer, mantenidor del gai saber (1475)', *EstG*, 22:409–20, she links Ferrer with vernacular poetic competitions. A. Cobos Fajardo, 'Joan Ramon Ferrer i els humanistes italians del segle xv', Badia, *Literatura*, 259–69, describes Ferrer's access to Italian sources and methodology. F. J. Rodríguez Risquete, 'Del cercle literari del Príncep de Viana i unes poesies satíriques del *Cançoner de Saragossa*', *EstG*, 22:365–91, reinterprets five poems from the Saragossa MS, and his 'Pere Torroella i les corts dels infants d'Aragó al segle xv', *LlLi*, 13:209–22, provides archival evidence of Torroella's presence in several courts. S. Rovira and P. Vila, 'Comentari a dos poemes del *Cançoner de l'Ateneu*, 1', *ELLC*, 44:19–36, link the poems with Francesc Ferrer.

Narrative Poetry

A. Espadaler, 'Sobre la densitat cultural del *Jaufré*', Badia, *Literatura*, 335–53, proposes a 1272–76 date and analyses literary parallels.

A. Carré, 'El *rescrit* de Jaume Roig i les *noves rimades comediades*', *ib.*, 355–72, studies the structure and genre of the *Spill*. A. I. Peirats, 'Una edició desconeguda de l'*Spill* de Jaume Roig?', *ELLC*, 44:65–75, detects contaminations between three 16th-c. editions, and her 'Consilia, disciplina, doctrina: lectura d'un fragment de l'*Spill* de Jaume Roig', *BRABLB*, 48:289–312, discusses ll. 7913–8078 from linguistic, thematic, and rhetorical angles. Marinela Garcia Sempere, *Lo Passi en cobles (1493): edició i estudi*, IIFV–PAM, 537 pp., completes the critical edition and study with a lexical index.

3. Doctrinal and Religious Prose

Ramon Llull and Lullism

Ramon Llull, *Començaments de medicina, Tractat d'astronomia*, ed. Lola Badia (NEORL, 5), Palma de Mallorca, Patronat Ramon Llull, xxi + 379 pp., offers a critical edition of two scientific treatises. Amador Vega, *Ramon Llull y el secreto de la vida*, M, Siruela, 311 pp., discusses L.'s life, his mystical theories and his use of language. Ramon Llull, *Darrer llibre sobre la conquesta de Terra Santa*, trans. P. Llabrés, B, Facultat de Teologia de Catalunya — Fundació Enciclopèdia Catalana, 228 pp., complements the anthology of texts with a useful historic introduction by J. Gayà. Gayà's *Raimondo Lullo. Una teologia per la missione*, Milan, Istem-Jaca, 152 pp., is also an accessible introduction of L.'s missionary project. *Ramon Lull's Book of knighthood and chivalry, and the anonymous Ordene de chevalerie*, trans. William Caxton, revised by Brian R. Price, Union City, CF, Chivalry Bookshelf, 2001, vii + 122 pp., provides a modern English version of Caxton's text. A. Bonner, 'Recent scholarship on Ramon Llull', *RPh*, 54, 2001:377–92, is a thorough discussion of new approches to Llull. Several articles in Domínguez, *Arbor Scientiae*, touch on literary and philologic aspects: L. Badia, 'The *Arbor scientiae*: a "new" encyclopedia in the thirteenth-century Occitan-Catalan cultural context' (1–19), establishes parallels between L.'s work, the *Breviari d'amor*, and Cerverí de Girona; A. Bonner, 'The structure of the *Arbor scientiae*' (21–34), focuses on the structural coherence of the treatise; B. Garí, '"Al despuntar el alba": María y el *Árbol de la madre*' (265–72), has a mariological approach; A. G. Hauf, 'Sobre l'*Arbor exemplificalis*', (303–42), highlights pedagogic techniques and the relationship with John of Capua's *Calila e Dimna*; K. Jacobi, '*De arbore quaestionali:* über den Baum der Fragen' (343–59), analyses different functions of Lullian questions; C. Lohr, '*Arbor scientiae:* the tree of the elements' (79–84), deals with Platonic and Aristotelian aspects of L.'s element theory; M. Pereira, '"Vegetare seu transmutare": the vegetable soul and pseudo-Lullian alchemy' (93–119), discusses Lullian elements in alchemical literature; R. Pring-Mill, 'The role of numbers in the structure of the *Arbor scientia*' (35–63), studies the numerical structure with relation to L.'s art; and J. E. Rubio, 'Sobre l'*Arbor sensualis*' (121–26), is concerned with L.'s views on animal nature. J. Santanach, '*Cové que hom fassa apendre a son fill los XIII articles*: la *Doctrina pueril* com a tractat catequètic', Badia, *Literatura*, 419–30, sets L.'s treatises within the catechetical works for the laity. G. Hägele and F. Pukelsheim, 'Llull's writings on electoral systems', *SLu*, 41, 2001: 3–38, link L.'s system with Dominican electoral treatises. R. Hugues, 'Deification / hominification and the doctrine of intentions: internal christological evidence for re-dating *Cent noms de Déu*', *ib.*, 111–15, gives 1292 as the date on the basis of christological terminology. J. A. Grimalt, 'Notes sobre les fonts del *Llibre de les bèsties* de Ramon Llull', *Randa*, 49: 37–46, is a systematic source analysis. Higuera, *Llull*, offers a spread of articles on L.'s notions of chivalry, morals, and epistemology. Nicolau Eimeric, *Diàleg contra els lul·listes*, ed. Jaume de Puig, B, Quaderns Crema, 162 pp., is an accessible approach (with Catalan translation) to Eimeric's treatise.

ARNAU DE VILANOVA AND OTHER SCIENTIFIC TEXTS

Arnaldi de Villanova Opera Medica Omnia (1975–2000). 25 anys d'un projecte internacional, ed. Jon Arrizabalaga, B, Societat Catalana d'Història de la Ciència i de la Tècnica, 2001, 33 pp., includes articles by J. A. Paniagua, L. García Ballester, and M. McVaugh. S. Thiolier-Méjean, 'Arnaut de Villeneuve comme auctoritas dans l'oeuvre de Bertran Boysset d'Arles', *FL*, 130, 2000: 7–39, edits and translates some poems attributed to Arnau. Lluís Cifuentes Comamala, *La ciència en català a l'Edat Mitjana i el Renaixement*, Barcelona U.P. — Illes Balears U.P., 2001, 410 pp., studies the social environment of science vernacularization and the range of materials in Catalan; and his 'La literatura quirúrgica baixmedieval en romanç a la Corona d'Aragó: escola, pont i mercat', Badia, *Literatura*, 319–33, explores a wide range of aspects involved in vernacularization. *SCHCT 6* contains a number of articles studying Catalan treatises on several scientific disciplines.

FRANCESC EIXIMENIS AND OTHER MORAL TEXTS

X. Renedo, 'Eiximenis i el bon ús del vi', *EstG*, 22: 251–77, discusses E.'s advice within the context of urban society. S. Martí and D. Guixeras, 'Apunts sobre la tradició del *Dotzè* del *Crestià* I', Badia, *Literatura*, 211–23, analyse mobile MS archetypes. D. J. Viera and J. Piqué, 'França a l'obra de Francesc Eiximenis', *ELLC*, 43,

2001:5–16, discuss E.'s disapproval of Valois politics. S. Martí, 'Les cartes autògrafes de Francesc Eiximenis', *EstG*, 22:235–49, edits these documents for further analysis. On the Spanish reception of E.'s works: J. García López, 'Francesc Eiximenis en la Guerra dels Segadors: dos pliegos sueltos de la colección Bonsoms', *ib.*, 421–43; and D. Guixeras, 'Un fragment del capítol 321 del *Dotzè* en castellà', *ib.*, 279–82. P. Evangelisti, 'Un progetto di riconquista e governo della Terrasanta: strategia economica e militare e proposta di un codice etico-politico attraverso il lessico regolativo-sociale', *Atti* (Assisi), 137–99, includes discussion on E. and his 'I *pauperes Christi* e i linguaggi dominativi: i Francescani come protagonisti della costruzione della testualità politica e dell'organizzazione del consenso nel basso medievo (Gilbert de Tournai, Paolino di Venezia, Francesc Eiximenis)', *Atti* (Todi), 315–92, discusses E.'s *Regiment de la cosa pública.* K. Rivers offers a partial English translation of E.'s *Ars Predicandi*, pp. 189–204 of *The Medieval Craft of Memory: An Anthology of Texts and Pictures*, ed. Mary Carruthers and Jan M. Ziolkowski, Philadelphia, Pennsylvania U.P., 311 pp. *Homilies d'Organyà*, ed. Amadeu J. Soberanas, Andreu Rossinyol, and Armand Puig (ENC, B.20), 2001, 338 pp., is an edition (with MS facsimile) and a study of structure and sources. F. Bruni, 'Tra Catalogna e Italia: intorno alla predicazione nella prima metà del XV secolo', *EstG*, 22:283–308, analyses the social role of preaching. Tomàs Martínez Romero, *Aproximació als sermons de sant Vicent Ferrer*, Paiporta, Denes, 187 pp., includes discussion of Ferrer's performance and his views on literature and on marriage. *ATCA*, 21, among other articles on archival material and doctrinal texts, presents some editions by J. Perarnau (123–218, 645–50, and 665–70).

4. Historical and Artistic Prose, Novel

Historiography

J. Bruguera, 'La possible filiació dialectal del *Llibre dels fets* de Jaume I', *ATCA*, 21:605–18, disputes Ferrando's linguistic analysis of the MSS. M. Toldrà, 'Sobre la presència d'algunes cròniques catalanes a l'Arxiu Reial de Barcelona', *ER*, 24:169–88, discusses the use of archival documents in historiography. J. D. Garrido Valls, 'La *Crònica de Sicília* (Chronique de Sicile): traduction catalane médiévale du *Chronicon Siculum*', *Scriptorium*, 55, 2001:93–106, offers a full description of the manuscript.

Bernat Metge

L. Badia, 'Pròleg amb homenatge a *Lo somni*', Badia, *Literatura*, 5–22, outlines the different approches to the study of M. in this volume;

other articles include: L. Cabré, 'De nou sobre Metge, *Laelius* i el *Somnium Scipionis*' (49–62); F. J. Gómez, 'L'ofici del poeta segons Orfeu: una clau hermenèutica per *Lo somni* de Bernat Metge' (63–85); X. Renedo, 'La fe en els pares i la fe en la immortalitat de l'ànima de sant Agustí a Bernat Metge' (87–97); J. M. Ruiz Simon, '*Lo somni* de Bernat Metge: el malson filosòfic d'un epicuri' (25–47); and J. Turró, 'Bernat Metge i Avinyó' (99–111). Stefano Cingolani, *El somni d'una cultura: 'Lo somni' de Bernat Metge*, B, Quaderns Crema, 292 pp., proposes a literary, 'straight', reading, substantiated by his historic interpretation and the Petrarchan model. J. Butinyà, 'Al voltant del final del llibre 1 de *Lo somni* de Bernat Metge i la qüestió de l'ànima dels animals', *BRABLB*, 48:271–88, suggests some sources, and her 'Al voltant de les obres més curtes de Metge', *ELLC*, 43, 2001:17–43, finds parallels between several of M.'s works. *The Dream of Bernat Metge*, ed. Richard Vernier, Aldershot, Ashgate, 87 pp., is a full English translation.

TIRANT LO BLANC AND *CURIAL E GÜELFA*

Josep Pujol, *La memòria literària de Joanot Martorell: models i escriptura en el 'Tirant lo Blanc'* (PAM), 245 pp., analyses Martorell's methodology and maps different types of sources and their distinctive uses; and his 'De Pere el Gran a Tristany de Leonís: models cronístics i novel·lescos per a la mort de *Tirant lo Blanc*', Badia, *Literatura*, 409–18, suggests sources for the final chapters. C. Wittlin, 'L'antiga traducció catalana anònima de la *Letra de reials costums* de Petrarca i el capítol 143 del *Tirant lo Blanc*', *ELLC*, 44:37–64, discusses Martorell's use of a source. J. Turró, 'Joanot Martorell, escrivà de ració', *L'Avenç*, 273:12–18, reads *T.* as a *roman à clef* thanks to new biographical data. A. Varvaro, 'El *Tirant lo Blanch* en la narrativa europea del segle xv', *ER*, 24:149–67, underplays the innovative aspects of *T.* and proposes to rethink the late medieval novel as a whole. J. Moran Ocerinjauregui, 'La família Gualba i el *Tirant lo Blanc*', *LlLi*, 13:7–30, presents new documents, some concerning the *T.* manuscript.

5. Translations and Other Genres and Texts

J. Pujol, 'Expondre, traslladar i reescriure clàssics llatins en la literatura catalana del segle xv', *Quaderns*, 7:9–32, analyses medieval translation methodology and applies his findings to Metge, Martorell, and Corella. L. Cabré, 'Algunes imitacions i traduccions d'Ausiàs March al segle xvi', *ib.*, 59–82, discusses the implicit debate between the Spanish translations of March. On translation in Badia, *Literatura*: J. M. Cacho Blecua, 'Traducciones catalanas y aragonesas en el entorno de Juan Fernández de Heredia' (299–318), discusses sources and methodology in Heredia's workshop; G. Navarro, 'Les *Històries troyanes* dins el compendi historial copiat al ms. 352 de la Biblioteca de Catalunya: un model de ficció per a la història' (371–83), focuses on the translator's method and cultural background; and J. García López, 'El manuscrito de Ripoll del bachiller de la Torre' (173–90), adds a new item, a Catalan translation, to his 1991 *stemma* of the *Visión deleitable*. F. Ziino, 'The Catalan translation of Boethius' *De consolatione*: a new hypothesis', *Carmina Philosophiae*, 10, 2001: 31–38, suggests an indirect witness of Saplana's translation; and her 'Una traduzione latina del *Boezio* catalano', *Romania*, 119, 2001: 465–82, studies some glosses in MSS Harley 4335–39. A. Puig Tàrrech, 'Les traduccions catalanes medievals de la Bíblia', pp. 107–231 of *El text: lectures i història* (PAM, Scripta biblica, 3), 2001, 371 pp., presents the project *Corpus Biblicum Catalanicum* and offers a valuable survey of Catalan MSS of the Latin Bible and Catalan translations. M. Burrell edits and translates one of the two Catalan versions of the *Navigatio*, pp. 249–63 of *The Voyage of St. Brendan: Representative Versions in English Translation*, ed. W. R. J. Barron and Glyn S. Burgess, Exeter U.P., 377 pp. Hernández, *Boccaccio*, contains several articles on translations and reworkings of Boccaccio by Catalan writers. J. Medina, 'Ciceró a les terres catalanes: segles XIII-XVI', *Faventia*, 24.1: 179–221, is concerned with library inventories as well as translations. A. M. Badia Margarit, 'Entorn de Pere Miquel Carbonell: primer comentari sobre les *Regles de esquivar vocables* (edició i estudi de 1999)', *ELLC*, 43, 2001: 83–95, replies to the reviews of his 1999 edition, insisting on Carbonell's authorship. A. Ferrando, 'Sobre l'autoria de les *Regles d'esquivar vocables*, encara', *EMarg*, 70: 67–98, discusses the creation of the *Regles* and proposes Carbonell as compilator. M. Vilallonga, 'Humanisme català', *EstG*, 21, 2001: 475–88, defends the validity of this term, when applied to Latin texts by Catalan writers. On Joan Margarit's works: L. Lucero, 'El *Paralipomenon Hispaniae* de Joan Margarit i els humanistes italians', Badia, *Literatura*, 271–84; Id., 'Joan Margarit, Fidel Fita i Robert B. Tate: la dedicatòria del *Paralipomenon Hispaniae*', *EstG*, 21, 2001: 465–73; and I. Segarra, 'El tractat *Corona regum*: l'humanisme italià i el pensament polític de Joan Margarit', Badia, *Literatura*, 285–96. Ugolino Verino, *De expugnatione Granatae*, ed. Immaculada López Calahorro, Granada U.P., 260 pp., is an edition and Spanish translation of Verino's panegyric.

6. Drama

A number of articles in Rossich, *Teatre*, concern the medieval period, including some surveys of scholarship: notably J. Romeu i Figueras,

'Teatre medieval als Països Catalans' (3–15); an updated bibliography: A. Rossich and P. Vila, 'Bibliografia sobre teatre català antic (s. XIII-XVIII)' (427–508); J. F. Alcina, 'La tragèdia *Galathea* d'Hèrcules Florus i els inicis del teatre neollatí a Barcelona i a València (1485–1527)' (245–59); A. I. Alomar Canyelles, 'El teatre en la festa de l'àngel custodi de Mallorca (s. XV-XVI)' (161–71); J. Castaño, 'Cent trenta anys d'estudi al voltant de la *Festa o Misteri d'Elx*' (235–44); G. Ensenyat and P. Vila, 'Els dos fragments de la Passió mallorquina del s. XIV: estudi, edició i notes' (121–39); M. Gómez Muntané, 'Les arrels del *Cant de la Sibil·la* a la Península Ibèrica' (151–60); G. Llompart, 'Fonts menors i mínimes del teatre medieval mallorquí' (140–50); F. Massip, 'L'infern en escena: presència diabòlica en el teatre medieval europeu' (197–218); J. Solervicens, 'Criats i senyors a la comèdia del Renaixement: *La vesita* de Joan Ferrandis d'Herèdia i *En Coney*' (261–71). A spread of articles on medieval theatre is also to be found in Sirera, *Teatro*, and Sirera, *Actor*. F. Massip and L. Kovàcs, 'La danse macabre dans le royaume d'Aragon: iconographie et spectacle au moyen âge et survivances traditionnelles', *RLaR*, 105, 2001 : 201–28, focus on the Verges dance as well as some iconographic witnesses.

MODERN LITERATURE

POSTPONED

VI. PORTUGUESE STUDIES

LANGUAGE

POSTPONED

MEDIEVAL LITERATURE

POSTPONED

MODERN LITERATURE

POSTPONED

VII. GALICIAN STUDIES

LANGUAGE

By Francisco Dubert García, *Universidade de Santiago de Compostela*,
David Mackenzie, *University College, Cork*, and
Xulio Sousa Fernández, *Universidade de Santiago de Compostela*

1. Bibliographical and General

This is Frei Martín Sarmiento year: the Benedictine was the feted author of the *Día das letras galegas* this year, and the usual mixed bag of publications ensued. These are the best of the bunch. H. Monteagudo Romero, *Martín Sarmiento: sobre a lingua galega. Antoloxía*, Vigo, Galaxia, 424 pp., brings together a selection of S.'s writing, translated into Galician with the aim of giving the reader direct experience of S.'s linguistic theories, and of the work he produced on Galician, all with the benefit of M.R.'s interpretation and commentary. Id., 'Tradición manuscrita e divulgación impresa do *Coloquio en coplas galegas*. Consideración á luz do autógrafo orixinal', *BRAG*, 363:95–122, makes sagacious use of the tools of textual criticism to show that the three recent editions — by Pensado Tomé, Axeitos, and Mariño Paz — of this important work by S. suffer for their omission from consideration of the autograph (for all that the *apparati* of Pensado and Mariño contain excellent material). A. Santamarina Fernández, 'Sarmiento e a lexicografía galega', *ib.*, 189–99, gives an overview of S.'s contributions to Galician lexicography, noting its quality and enduring value. R. Álvarez Blanco, 'O legado lingüístico de Martín Sarmiento', *Sarmiento*, 71–88, takes up and illustrates this theme with a series of examples which show how his work is still useful to linguists today, whether dialectologists, historians of syntax, or lexicographers. She is in turn supported by M. González González, 'Modernidade e actualidade das ideas lingüísticas do padre Sarmiento', *ib.*, 267–86, and S. Varela Pombo, 'Algunhas consideracións sobre a obra lingüística de Sarmiento', *ib.*, 287–300. X. L. Pensado Tomé, 'A formación da conciencia lingüística de Sarmiento', *BRAG*, 363:123–40, was sent to the editors by P.T.'s widow, who discovered it among his papers. In it he suggests what S. must have read in order to have come to his forward-looking position on language.

A. González Guerra, *Miguel de Unamuno e a lingua galega*, Corunna, tresCtres, 319 pp., selects and comments on certain passages in which Unamuno comments on Galician. R. Álvarez Blanco, 'O don da palabra', pp. 201–15 of *Xornadas sobre Otero Pedrayo*, SC, Xunta,

282 pp., examines don Ramón's oratorical style from a syntactic perspective.

2. Historical Linguistics and Dialectology

A. I. Boullón Agrelo, 'Onomástica e dialectoloxía: a propósito de *raposo* e *golpe*', Álvarez, *Dialectoloxía*, 115–36, demonstrates how recourse to the geographical distribution of personal names may help in the elucidation of the evolution of common nouns. A. Seco Orosa, 'Determinación da fronteira lingüística entre o galego e o leonés nas provincias de León e Zamora', *RFR*, 18:73–102, examines seven phonological isoglosses delimiting Leonese and Galician, and discerns areas where the change is abrupt, and others where it is more gradual. A. S. Alonso Núñez, 'Contribución ó estudio da fronteira entre os bloques oriental e central no sueste da provincia de Ourense', Álvarez, *Dialectoloxía*, 223–44, in a similar exercise, though this time intra-Galician, looks at the distribution of certain lexical and morphological features with a view to establishing a more precise frontier between the central and the eastern varieties. B. García Turnes, 'A orixe do galego segundo Francisco Adolfo Varnhagen, editor do *Cancioneiro de Ajuda*', *Madrygal*, 5:53–60, is an interesting critical evaluation of the views of this 19th-c. Portuguese scholar on the relationship between Galician and Portuguese during the Middle Ages. B. Fernández Salgado and X. A. Fernández Salgado, 'Francisco Mirás e a primeira gramática galega', *SEHL 3*, 1, 139–52, examine this first 19th-c. grammar of Galician, and note its influence on later work in the field. C. Valcárcel Riveiro, *Do rural ao urbano*, Pontevedra, Deputación, 261 pp., undertakes a detailed and accurate geolinguistic study of the rural and urban areas within the 'concello' of Pontevedra. C. Silva Domínguez, 'As formas reducidas do paradigma dos posesivos en galego medieval', *Tato Vol.*, 277–90, studies the apocopated possessives *ma*, *ta*, *sa*, and *mia* in the medieval language: she comments on the origin of the forms, and goes on to explain the assymetry of their syntactic distribution, and the changes which gave rise to the modern system. She sticks to her last in 'A perda da serie reducida feminina do posesivo en textos notariais galegos e portugueses da época medieval: cronoloxía e pautas no proceso de difusión da innovación', *Verba*, 29:153–88, examining the different pace of elimination of *ma*, *ta*, *sa* in medieval notarial texts as between Galician and Portuguese, and attempts to develop a hypothesis for the spoken language based on the orthography. E. González Seoane, 'Léxico dialectal e estándar literario', Álvarez, *Dialectoloxía*, 95–113, considers the role of literary texts in the diffusion of lexical items which are poorly represented in the dialects. F. Dubert García and X. Sousa

Fernández, 'Áreas lexicais galegas e portuguesas. A proposta de Cintra aplicada ó galego', *ib.*, 193–222, analyse the dialectal distribution of the names of the eight items used by Lindley Cintra to establish the lexical areas of Portuguese, and show how difficult it would be to attempt to apply the same system to Galician. F. Fernández Rei, 'As estacións do ano en galego: o *inverno*, o *verán* e as *primaveras*', *Tato Vol.*, 129–44, examines the names of the seasons in medieval Galician, and in the modern sub-standard and standard varieties, comparing them with those of other Romance languages, and with those of Basque. Id., 'Do Ortegal ó Douro e de Fisterra ó Navia e ó Padornelo. Notas sobre o léxico moderno da Gallaecia e do seu litoral', Álvarez, *Dialectoloxía*, 147–92, studies the distribution of certain lexical items in coastal areas, and in the interior. G. Navaza Blanco, 'Dialectoloxía e toponimia', *ib.*, 137–46, suggests that historical dialectologists might profitably make greater use of toponymic data. H. Pousa Ortega, 'Léxico fronteirizo no Baixo Miño: a pesca con barco', *ib.*, 245–78, investigates piscatorial terminology on the Galician and Portuguese banks of the R. Miño. H. Monteagudo Romero, 'O contributo de Manuel Curros Enríquez á constitución do galego escrito. Caracterización e evolución dos seus criterios lingüísticos', *Verba*, 29:291–327, situates C.E. in the history of the elaboration of the written code, noting his orthographic and morphological choices, and concluding with a fascinating comparison between the linguistic choices made by writers and the schemes proposed by grammarians. J. Saramago, 'Diferenciação lexical interpontual nos territórios galego e português (estudo dialectométrico aplicado a materiais do ALPI e a materiais galegos do ALGa)', Álvarez, *Dialectoloxía*, 41–68, uses the Galician and Portuguese linguistic atlases in this contrastive areal analysis. M. González González et al., 'El subsistema "arcaico" de las fricativas dentoalveolares del gallego, una reliquia en vías de extinción', *CFE 2*, 215–19, study the disappearance of the strident coronal fricatives of the so-called 'archaic' system, in which the feature [$\pm$ voice] is distinctive; the appearance of non-strident dental fricative segments alongside the stridents allows for a simpler system. M. A. Coelho da Mota, 'O português na fronteira com o galego', *RFR*, 18:103–15, looks at the boundaries between these two languages, with special reference to the phonological links between the verb and the clitic object pronoun and between the verb and the definite article. Ma. González González and B. Varela Vázquez, 'As denominacións da 'chuvia miúda': variedades diatópicas e lingua literaria', Álvarez, *Dialectoloxía*, 329–57, give us the linguist's take on the words for 'drizzle' in Galician, comparing dialect and literary usage: there can be no better place than Galicia — except perhaps Cork — for such a study! M. Romero Triñanes and L. Santos Suárez,

'As denominacións dos dedos da man. Un estudio motivacional', *ib.*, 303–27, is an interesting study of the popular names for the fingers and thumb, though limited, as the authors recognize, because the data are largely derived from the speech of children. R. Lorenzo Vázquez, 'Un documento xurídico de 1430', *Tato Vol.*, 185–200, edits a document dated 13 July 1430, from the *Liuro das posisoes do espital dos pobres* of Muros, with a characteristically thorough linguistic commentary and an exhaustive index of the people cited. R. Mariño Paz, 'A desnasalización vocálica no galego medieval', *Verba*, 29:71–118, basing himself on an analysis of medieval texts and modern studies of Extremaduran dialects of Galician origin, contends that denasalization began before the 13th century. Id., 'O cambio morfolóxico *moiro* > *morro*, *moira* > *morra* e a completa regularización do verbo *morrer*', *Tato Vol.*, 201–10, attempts to determine the chronology of the reanalysis of *morrer*, concluding that the last phase was the regularization of the PP1 of the present indicative and the present subjunctive. R. Aira González and M. Martínez Baleirón, 'As denominacións dos meses do ano: perspectiva lexicográfica', Álvarez, *Dialectoloxía*, 359–82, chart the dialect distribution and the history of the terms used for the first six months of the year. R. Álvarez Blanco and X. L. Rodríguez Montederramo, '*O diálogo de Alberte e Bieito.* Dramaturxia, elites letradas e escrita en galego a fins do século XVI', *BRAG*, 363:241–311, provide an edition and linguistic study of what remains of this interesting early modern text: the excellent colour reproductions show the extent of the damage caused by the fire in the Palacio de Liria. R. Álvarez Blanco, '*El foy a primeira vez*: testemuños antigos de el invariable', *Tato Vol.*, 23–36, brings together data from the medieval language to show the use of the invariable demonstrative pronoun *el*, which would have replaced an earlier *elo*, and, in 'Viño novo en odres vellos: os nomes do millo', Álvarez, *Dialectoloxía*, 69–94, she looks at the introduction of maize into Galicia in the early 16th c. and the lexical field that sprouted as a consequence, noting that a whole series of pre-existing terms was adapted to describe it. S. Alonso Pintos, *Para unha historia do estándar galego. As propostas do período 1966–1980*, Madrid, UNED, 155 pp., is an interesting and informative study of this early stage of the norms debate, particularly relevant now as the Academy moves towards a 'final' resolution. X. Varela Barreiro, 'Ás voltas con *vario(s)*: de novo sobre a súa emerxencia en galego', *Tato Vol.*, 303–19, shows that *varios* is a recent borrowing from Castilian, since it appears in the 19th c. 'fully formed' in terms of its functions, with no evidence of diachronic adaptation; he goes on to describe the grammatical function of *varios* in the modern language. X. H. Costas González, 'Fronteiras lingüísticas no val do río Ellas (Cáceres)', *RFR*, 18:35–50, applies the 'dialectometric' method to certain grammatical and lexical items to demonstrate that the speech of this area of the province of Cáceres is a variety of Galician. Id., 'Léxico e fronteira no val do río Ellas', Álvarez, *Dialectoloxía*, 279–301, is a comparative study between lexical items from this area and the corresponding items in varieties in Galicia. X. Sousa Fernández, 'Graos de gramaticalización de dúas construcións con infinitivo na lingua medieval: *enviar* + infinitivo e *mandar* + infinitivo', *Tato Vol.*, 291–302, sets out to establish the degree of grammaticalization of these constructions. After laying out the theoretical framework and applying the appropriate tests, S concludes that the construction with *enviar* is the more grammaticalized and should therefore be analysed as auxiliary in such contexts.

3. Grammar

R. Álvarez Blanco and X. Xove Ferreiro, *Gramática da lingua galega*, Vigo, Galaxia, 771 pp., is a complete and rigorous descriptive analysis of Galician from an accessibly traditional standpoint, though its authors are clearly aware of modern developments and employ them where appropriate. This is the logical evolution of the earlier work in collaboration with other members of the Instituto da Lingua Galega (R. Álvarez Blanco, H. Monteagudo, and X. L. Regueira, *Gramática galega*, Vigo, Galaxia, 1986), and its sturdy hardbound format will make it the indispensable reference tool for anyone with an interest in the language. C. Silva Domínguez, *Frases nominais con posesivo en galego: estructura e valores referenciais*, SC, Universidade, 227 pp., studies the development of the use of the possessive as a constituent of NPs. F. Cidrás Escáneo, 'Relacións atributivas da FN', *Tato Vol.*, 73–86, examines the semantic and syntactic properties of NPs, distinguishing 'agentive' (*a destrucción da cidade*) from 'non-agentive' (*o neno bonito, o parvo do rapaz, unha marabilla de rapaz*), and going on to determine which element is the semantic nucleus and which the modifier. I. Szijj, 'Desdobramento de morfemas verbais no galego: o sufixo número-persoal na conxugación regular', *ER*, 24:47–69, uses the principles of natural morphology to explain the disambiguation of verbal number morphs found in certain Galician varieties. J. Rivas, 'Complementos directos periféricos', *Tato Vol.*, 255–66, looking at direct object complements not introduced by *a* from a non-discrete typological perspective permitting the inclusion of communicative and cognitive elements, deduces that they mark non-prototypical objects and that they should be designated 'peripherical' direct objects. Cynics might wish to contest their status as direct objects at all, and instead analyse them as prepositional complements.

M. Álvarez de la Granja, 'Ó redor das colocacións e das solidariedades léxicas', *ib.*, 37–48, distinguishes formal cooccurrence (i.e. collocations proper) such as *dar unha volta* and *facer unha viaxe* (**facer unha volta* or **dar unha viaxe* are impossible) from semantic cooccurrence: one says *podar unha árbore* because *podar* is to cut branches, which pertain to trees rather than to aeroplanes, for example. M. M. Rodríguez Añón, 'Verbal idiomatic expressions in English and Galician: a preliminary constrastive analysis', *ICLC 2*, 883–90, compares 100 examples in each language, in respect of syntactic structure and semantic content. R. Álvarez Blanco, 'Gramática contrastiva do portugués e o galego: o diminutivo', *ib.*, 91–101, compares the use and distribution of diminutive suffixes in the two languages, taking into account both the standard and regional varieties.

4. Lexis and semantics

E. González Seoane, 'Sobre as fontes lexicográficas galegas do *DEGC*', *Tato Vol.*, 145–69, assesses Eladio Rodríguez's use of the work of earlier lexicographers in his *Diccionario enciclopédico gallego-castellano* (1958–61), which enables him to go on to distinguish E.R.'s own considerable contribution.

5. Etymology, onomastics and toponymy

A. Santamarina Fernández, 'A journey through Galician onomastics', *ICOS 20*, 3–30, provides an interesting review of the origins and evolution of Galician personal and place names. D. A. Moreira, 'A respecto del hidrónimo ourensano *Arnoia*', *ib.*, 325–28, plausibly wonders whether the roots *Arn-* and *Ar-*, common in non-Hispanic European hydronyms, might lie behind *Arnoia*. E. Bascuas López, *Estudios de hidronimia paleoeuropea gallega*, SC, Universidade, 408 pp. attempts to trace Galician hydronyms to what he supposes to be their Indoeuropean roots. J. A. Ranz Yubero and C. Sáez, 'Nombrar y percibir el agua. Hidrónimos en la documentación de Celanova (842–974)', *ICOS 20*, 1541–52, consider the origin of the hydronyms in the Latin documents of the monastery of Celanova. E. González Seoane, 'Nombres propios, sintagmas fijos y diccionario', *ib.*, 1431–36, looks at the lexicographical treatment accorded to syntagms consisting of proper names. L. Méndez Fernández, 'Questions about the use of articles with toponyms', *ib.*, 503–12, examines the use of the definite article with place names in modern Galician. M. C. García Ares et al., 'La estandarización de los topónimos gallegos: estado de la cuestión', *ib.*, 457–66, examine the criteria used for the adoption and official sanction of Galician toponyms. M. Domínguez García, 'Hagiotoponimia de Galicia', *ib.*, 161–72, is an introduction to the historical study of Saints' names in Galician toponymy. R. Aira González, 'Vitalidad del procedimiento patronímico para la formación de segundos nombres en gallego medieval', *ib.*, 563–72, concludes that the system was still operative between the 13th and the 15th centuries. R. Álvarez Blanco, 'Topónimos en *-edo/-ido*', *ib.*, 87–101, decides that the traditional recourse to metaphony is an inadequate explanation of the origin of toponyms with these suffixes, and proposes another.

6. Phonetics and phonology

X. L. Regueira Fernández, 'A sílaba en galego: lingua, estándar e ideoloxía', *Tato Vol.*, 235–54, considers that the elaboration of 'galego culto' is conditioned by ideological criteria which are more often than not unstated; in order to demonstrate this, he studies the structure of the syllable in both sub-standard and 'culto' Galician, noting that the sub-standard variety incorporates neologisms using alien syllabic structures, and goes on to review the treatment of this area by the creators of normative Galician. Id., 'Acerca de la estructura prosódica del texto: finales de enunciado en gallego', *CFE* 2, 301–06, studies the frequencies of final segments of utterances in order to show that the continuity felicity condition of a text is related to certain tonal elements of its final segments. A. B. Escourido Pernas, 'Contribución ó estudio acústico das vibrantes', *CadL*, 24:111–25, provides an acoustic description of the rhotic segments of a Galician variety, concentrating on frequency and length. E. Rodríguez Banga et al., 'Sistema de conversión texto-voz en lengua gallega basado en la selección combinada de unidades acústicas y prosódicas', *RPLN*, 29:153–58, describe their system, the aim of which is to minimize distortion caused by posterior prosodic modification. E. Fernández Rei, 'Aproximación ó estudio da isocronía en galego', *Tato Vol.*, 115–28, reflects on the well-known problems of objective isochrony, before presenting the preliminary results of her research, which would indicate that Galician is an isochronous language. E. Martínez Celdrán, *Introducción á fonética. O son na comunicación humana*, Vigo, Galaxia, 148 pp., although a basic manual of general phonetics, is useful in that it offers a description of all the phones of Galician. R. Molinos Castro, 'As vocais átonas finais en galego: estudio acústico', *CadL*, 24:55–91, does an acoustic study of the vowels [e], [a], and [o] in phonological word-final position; she concentrates on the first three formants, and on the intensity and length of each vowel, comparing the values obtained for tonic vowels with those from the atonic equivalent.

7. Sociolinguistics and Psycholinguistics

H. Monteagudo Romero and X. M. Bouzada edit *O proceso de normalización do idioma galego 1980–2000*, a projected four-volume study by a team from the Consello da Cultura Galega, whose objective is to ensure that the public is better informed about the level of use of Galician in the public sector, and to provide a means of assessing the efficacy of the language policies of the Regional Governments between 1980 and 2000, with the aim of making recommendations for improvements to the authorities. The first volume is *Política lingüística: análise e perspectivas*, SC, Consello da Cultura Galega, 289 pp., which will be required reading for anyone interested in the state of the Galician language today. A. Iglesias Álvarez, *Falar galego 'No veo por qué'*, Vigo, Xerais, 335 pp., usefully provides a *qualitative* sociolinguistic study, and the result, as one might have predicted, shows that speakers' attitudes towards Galician are much less favourable than the quantitative studies would have us believe. *Política lingüística*, please note! A. M. Fernández Dobao, 'The use of conscious transfer as a communication strategy in the interlanguage of Galician learners of English as foreign language', *ICOS 20*, 391–99, analyses the speech of 23 students of various levels in this promising pilot article on transfer strategies employed by bilingual Galician/Castilian speakers learning English as L2. A. Santamarina Fernández, 'A recuperación e salvagarda da toponimia galega', *ENL 4*, 253–62, looks at the problems involved in the naming of places as a linguist but from a social and practical viewpoint. B. Silva Valdivia, '¿Existe un modelo de fala para a clase de lingua?', *CILM 7*, 233–42; and Id., 'Norma e variación no ensino e aprendizaxe das linguas. O caso do idioma galego', Silva, *Lingua*, 9–36, offers considered and well-documented observations on the problems teachers of the standard language face when the officially-favoured approach is too purist or prescriptivist. More food for thought for the Xunta mandarins. C. Brandín Feijoo, 'Velocidade de procesamento da información de material escrito en escolares bilingües galegos', *CILM 7*, 405–21, looks at the degree of automatism in Castilian and Galician in bilingual Galician children, measures the speed of assimilation of school material in each language, and tests to see whether habitual use of both languages results in balanced processing ability. C. Burban, 'Modèles d'enseignement "bilingüe" et projets politiques dans les "nationalités historiques" d'Espagne', *Leng(M)*, 51:101–18, studies the development of language normalization policies in Spain, and notes the official indifference in this area which sets the Galician case apart from the others. F. Dubert García, 'Os sociolectos galegos', *CadL*, 24:5–27, proposes a classification of Galician sociolects which takes into account its language contact situation: after the usual theoretical excursus, here on language varieties, and a review of the literature, the classification is laid out, based reasonably enough on Creole theory. F. Fernández Rei, 'O galego do Bierzo e a súa situación actual', *BRAG*, 363:327–53, is an informative and disinterested look at the state of Galician in this Leonese region with special reference to legal and political issues. G. Navaza Blanco, 'A galeguización de nomes e apelidos. Estado da cuestión', *ENL 4*, 263–71, examines the 'Galicianing' of personal names, both given and surnames, over the past thirty years, and details the problems that have arisen in this area. H. Boyer, 'O proceso de normalización lingüística visto dende o exterior', *ib.*, 187–98, finds positive things to say about the Galician normalization experience, and highlights the beneficial effect of non-governmental initiatives. M. A. Rodríguez Neira, 'A lingua galega nos comezos do novo milenio', *CILM* 7, 129–47, uses data from the *Mapa Sociolingüístico de Galicia* to provide an overview of the state of the nation's language in various domains. M. Martínez Baleirón et al., 'Política lingüística nos primeiros niveis de ensino: problemas e alternativas', *ATO*, 50:59–72, throw yet another stone at official language policy, this time concentrating on application of the existing law in this area at primary level.

LITERATURE

By Dolores Vilavedra, *Departamento de Filoloxía Galega, Universidade de Santiago de Compostela,* and Derek Flitter, *Senior Lecturer in Modern Spanish Language and Literature, University of Birmingham*

1. General

A further volume has appeared of the encyclopaedic *Galicia. Literatura*, ed. Anxo Tarrío. Vol. xxxiv, *A literatura desde principios do século xxi: narrativa e traducción*, Corunna, Hércules, 567 pp., includes the following: G. Navaza, 'Catro narradores: Fole, Cunqueiro, Blanco-Amor e Neira Vilas' (22–85); C. Noia, 'A narrativa de posguerra' (86–149); S. Gaspar, 'A novela desde 1975' (150–213); and T. Seara and T. Bermúdez, 'A narrativa breve desde 1957' (214–79). C. Armas, *As mulleres escritoras (1860–1879)*, SC, Laiovento, 344 pp., supplies a panoramic overview of women writing for the press. G. Sanmartín, *Os (pre)textos galegos (1863–1936)*, SC, Sotelo, 300 pp., considers key textual components in the configuration of an emerging Galician literary tradition. The same author's *Lendo nas marxes: lingua e compromiso nos paratextos*, Corunna, Espiral Maior, 257 pp., studies the same corpus of material from a linguistic perspective. A. Cortijo, 'Un texto galego descoñecido do século xvi: *a Comedia de la invención de la sortija* da Bancroft Library', *AELG*, 2001 : 17–50, provides transcription with commentary of a Renaissance drama that contains some passages in Galician.

2. Mediaeval Literature

Xosé Ramón Pena, *Historia da literatura medieval galego-portuguesa*, SC, Sotelo, 340 pp., an updating of an earlier study by the same author to embrace recent developments in research and criticism, contains thoroughgoing analysis for the specialist reader. E. Fidalgo, *As 'Cantigas de Santa María'*, Vigo, Xerais, 359 pp., provides exhaustive coverage. S. Gutiérrez and P. Lorenzo, *A literatura artúrica en Galicia e Portugal na Idade Media*, SC, Universidade, 246 pp., examines mediaeval Galician-Portuguese texts with an Arthurian dimension. X. R. Pena, 'De Alcanate a Sta. Mª do Porto. Arredor dun "cancionero" integrado nas *Cantigas de Sta. María*', *AELG*, 2001 : 187–200, discusses the Alfonsine texts generally known as the 'Cancioneiro de Sta. Mª do Porto'. J. Ghanime, 'A tenzón e o partimen: definición dos xéneros a partir das artes poéticas e dos propios textos', *Madrygal*, 5 : 61–72, adopts a fresh approach to questions of definition.

3. Popular Literature

X. R. Mariño and C. L. Bernárdez, *Romanceiro en lingua galega*, Vigo, Xerais, 415 pp., contains in its introduction (pp. 7–22) a wide-ranging introduction to this corpus of ballad material in Galician.

4. Narrative

D. Vilavedra, 'La narrativa gallega en el fin del milenio' (*Cuadernos de Mangana*, 14), Cuenca, Centro de profesores y recursos, 26 pp., is a short critical survey of the prose fiction appearing in the last two decades of the 20th century. X. González, *A novela policial. Unha historia política*, SC, Laiovento, 82 pp., provides a brief history of the development of this novelistic genre in Galician literature.

5. Poetry

T. Seara, 'A voz en espiral. Datos para unha análise da primeira década (1991–2001) de Edicións Espiral Maior', *AELG*, 2001:91–136, is a detailed study of this publishing house's poetry catalogue and its contribution to the development of the genre.

6. Theatre

I. López Silva and D. Vilavedra, *Un Abrente teatral. As Mostras e o Concurso de Teatro de Ribadavia*, Vigo, Galaxia, 306 pp., analyses the impact of a competition that was fundamental in bringing contemporary Galician theatre to both audience and reader. N. Pazó, *A función da traducción no desenvolvemento do mapa teatral galego. Unha achega: 1960–1978*, Madrid, UNED, studies the role of translated material in the development of a distinctive Galician dramatic discourse.

7. Individual Authors

CARBALLO CALERO. The *Actas do Simposio Ricardo Carvalho Calero. Memoria do século*, Corunna U.P., 367 pp., includes the following: E. Torres, 'Como sair do cerco. A legitimaçom galeguista da Literatura Galega por C. Calero e a génese da sua centralidade no campo da crítica literária' (31–66), articulates the canonical role played by C.C.'s critical writing in the configuration of Galician literary history; M. Forcadela, 'A narrativa de C. Calero na encrucillada dos anos cincuenta' (109–18); A Casas, 'A descrición na obra narrativa de C. Calero. Análise retórica e hermenéutica' (119–36); C. P. Martínez, 'Do carácter híbrido na narrativa breve de C. Calero.

(Da ambigua verdade intempestiva de *Aos amores serodios*)' (137–60), a study of the short fiction; X. M. Álvarez, 'O discurso metapoético de R. C. Calero' (163–70); K. March, 'As pegadas de M. Antonio na poesía de R. C. Calero' (171–82) elucidates C.C.'s distinctive attitudes towards avant-garde innovation; P. Pallarés, 'C. Calero. Mitos para un exilio' (183–202), considers the many mythical references in C.C.'s work; J. Guisan, 'C. Calero: o Teatro e a Vida' (205–26); A. Herrero, 'C. Calero no diagrama da comunicación dramática. Carballo, poeta dramático e ironista' (227–48); D. Villanueva, 'C. Calero, novelista' (323–40).

CASTELAO. H. Monteagudo, 'Aínda sobre o ensaísmo castelaiano: a triple significación da iconografía xacobea', *Tato Vol.*, 211–21, sheds light on Risco's influence upon the uses of iconography in C.'s political oratory and essays.

CASTRO. A. Angueira, 'Un poema de Rosalía de Castro', *ATO*, 49:13–38, takes a sociological approach to a piece from *Cantares gallegos* deriving from popular verse.

CONDE. C. Estévez, 'Erotismo y feminidad en tres novelas de A. Conde: *Breixo, Memoria de Noa* e *Xa vai o Griffon no vento*', *Madrygal*, 5:39–46, examines the erotic component of the three cited novels.

CUNQUEIRO. M. X. Nogueira, 'Do vangardismo poético cunqueiroano. Apuntamentos sobre *Soma de craridades*', *Tato Vol.*, 223–34, takes a brief look at some of C.'s least discussed collections of verse. M. X. Lama, 'O mundo artúrico na obra de Álvaro Cunqueiro. Un Merlín compoñedor antes da descrenza e da parodia', *AELG*, 2001:51–90, argues that C.'s work was an attempt to locate Galician literature within a broad European tradition as a force for innovation; R. R. Vega, 'Estraña ave do paraíso. A recepción da obra cunqueiriana na literatura castelá', *ib.*, 201–26, discusses the reception of C.'s work within Spain as a whole.

CURROS. S. Bermúdez, 'La Habana para un exiliado gallego: M. Curros Enríquez, *La Tierra Gallega* y la modernidad nacional transatlántica', *MLN*, 117:331–42, sheds new light on C.'s time spent in Cuba.

MANUEL ANTONIO. See CARBALLO CALERO

MÉNDEZ FERRÍN. *X. L. Méndez Ferrín: o home, o escritor*, ed. X. M. Dobarro and L. Rodríguez, 144 pp., includes M. Forcadela, 'A poesía de X. L. Méndez Ferrín' (87–114), a detailed survey of M.F.'s verse; and X. M. Salgado, 'Arredor da narrativa ferriniana. Notas dun lector de *No ventre do silencio*' (115–44), an evaluation of M.F.'s novelistic production in the light of textual references contained in his own most recent novel.

NOVO. F. Llorca, 'La simbolización de la desnudez según O. Novo', *Madrygal*, 5:85–96, looks at symbols of nakedness in four poems from *Nós nus*.

OTERO PEDRAYO. *Rosalía*, SC, Xunta de Galicia, 206 pp., includes an introductory essay by X. M. Dobarro and L. Rodríguez, 'Otero Pedrayo e Vidal Bolaño arredor de Rosalía' (51–124). The *Xornadas sobre Otero Pedrayo*, SC, Xunta, 282 pp., includes the following studies of O.P.'s creative work: O. Rodríguez, 'Os contos de Otero na revista *Misión*' (111–22); M. C. Ríos, 'Algunhas repercusións da ideoloxía de Otero na súa obra literaria' (217–24); C. Noia, 'Unha nova ollada sobre as innovacións na narrativa de Otero' (225–36), arguing for traces of avant-garde techniques deriving from Ortega y Gasset and Azorín in O.P.'s prose fiction; X. A. Fernández, 'O *Teatro de máscaras*: da prosopopea ó espectáculo' (171–84); C. Paz, 'O *Teatro de máscaras* de Otero. A vangarda teatral en Galicia' (185–90). X. M. Salgado, '"El maniquí": un vieiro cara a *O señorito da Reboraina*', *Tato Vol.*, 267–75, considers the short story as a source for the novel.

PATO. S. González, 'Chus Pato o el hermetismo rupturista', *Madrygal*, 5:73–80, supplies a brief theme-based analysis.

POZO. C. Blanco, *Luz Pozo: a ave do norte*, Ourense, Linteo, 164 pp., is a broad survey centred on two collections: *Códice calixtino* and *Vida secreta de Rosalía*.

RISCO. O. Rodríguez, *V. Risco: escritor, etnógrafo e ideólogo do galeguismo*, Vigo, Ir Indo, 62 pp., appraises R.'s intellectual personality.

SARMIENTO. The Benedictine friar was honorand of the *Día das Letras Galegas 2002*, but the erudite nature of much of his work meant that the number of publications prompted was on this occasion smaller than usual. In *Sarmiento*, those more literary studies include: H. Monteagudo, 'O *Coloquio en mil duascentas coplas galegas* e o seu *Comento*: notas para unha revisión' (11–34), a discussion of issues of transmission and reception of S.'s work; R. Mariño and A. Requeixo, 'Clasicismo e literatura popular no *Coloquio dos 24 gallegos rústicos*' (151–76), an elucidation of this text as an articulation of S.'s ideas on literature, and particularly of his knowledge of popular literature. H. Monteagudo, 'Tradición manuscrita e divulgación impresa do *Coloquio en coplas gallegas*. Consideracións á luz do autógrafo orixinal', *BRAG*, 363: 95–113, establishes the *stemma codicum* of this text. From the collective volume deicated to S., *Día das letras galegas 2002*, SC, Universidade, 221 pp., deserving of mention is H. Monteagudo, 'M. Sarmiento en *El Correo Literario de la Europa* (1782)', which locates S.'s writings for this weekly magazine within the context of his wider output.

TORRES. T. Bermúdez, *Unha lectura de "Adiós, María" de X. Torres*, Vigo, Xerais, 86 pp., is a rigorous short monograph that contextualizes T.'s novel within contemporary Galician narrative.

VIDAL BOLAÑO. See OTERO PEDRAYO.

ZERNADAS Y CASTRO. X. Pardo, *O labor lírico do ilustrado cura de Fruíme*, SC, Laiovento, 375 pp., is an exhaustive philological study of the little-known work of Diego A. de Zernadas, more familiarly known as the 'cura de Fruíme'.

VIII. LATIN AMERICAN STUDIES

SPANISH AMERICAN LITERATURE
THE COLONIAL PERIOD

POSTPONED

THE NINETEENTH CENTURY

By Annella McDermott, *Department of Hispanic, Portuguese and Latin American Studies, University of Bristol*

1. General

BSS, 79, has four articles on Latin American *modernismo*: A. Acereda, 'La modernidad existencial en la poesía de Rubén Darío' (134–69), emphasizes the idea of *modernismo* as existential anguish, referring particularly to four poems from *Cantos de vida y esperanza*; N. Teitler, 'Redefining the female body: Alfonsina Storni and the *modernista* tradition' (171–92), sees Storni surreptitiously undermining the literary canon by incoporating the theme of the female body into her work; C. Canaparo, 'Un mundo modernista para la cultura rioplatense' (193–209), emphasizes *modernismo* as a social, rather than a purely individual impulse, and refers to the works of Echeverría, Darío, Lugones, and Borges. J. E. González, 'Modernismo y capital simbólico' (211–28), applies the ideas of Pierre Bourdieu to the case of *modernismo* in the Río de la Plata region. Oscar A. Díaz, **El ensayo hispanoamericano del siglo* XIX*: discurso hegemónico masculino*, M, Pliegos, 2001, 208 pp. R. Fiddian, 'Under Spanish eyes: late nineteenth-century postcolonial views of Spanish American literature', *MLR*, 97:83–93, reconsiders in the light of modern attitudes late 19th-c. Spanish views on the literature of Latin America, particularly those of Juan Valera in his *Cartas americanas* and *Nuevas cartas americanas*, and of Unamuno in his essay on *Martín Fierro* and in a note on Francisco Grandmontagne's novel *La Maldonada*. A. Gasquet, 'Las dos caras de Jano de la frontera argentina: exploración interna y apropriación de la vieja Europa', *Hispamérica*, 90, 2001:3–22, examines the importance of two directions of travel, west and south to the pampa and Patagonia, and east to Europe, for the formation of a national literature in post-Independence Argentina, citing Echeverría, Sarmiento, and Alberdi. **Las mujeres toman la palabra*, ed. Cristina Arambel-Guinazu and Claire Emilie Martin, 2 vols, Frankfurt, Vervuert–Iberoamericana, 2001, 214, 243 pp., devotes one volume to a study and the other to an anthology of little-known or not easily available women writers. M. R. Rivas Rojas, 'Del criollismo al regionalismo: enunciación y representación en el siglo XIX venezolano', *LARR*, 37:101–28, examines a series of texts, mainly historical, geographical, and journalistic, contributing to the formulation of *criollista* and *regionalista* ideas which subsequently animated literary texts. **Fuera del olvido: los escritores hispanoamericanos frente a 1898*, ed. Lourdes Royano, Santander, Cantabria U.P., 2000, 186 pp.

2. Individual Authors

ALBERDI, JUAN BAUTISTA. L. Demaría, 'Peregrinaciones y palabras de un ausente: los escritos del "traidor" Juan Bautista Alberdi', *RHM*, 54:267–78, focuses on the history of the reception of his *Palabras de un ausente* (1874) and *Escritos póstumos* (1895–1901).

CURROS ENRÍQUEZ, MANUEL. S. Bermúdez, 'La Habana para un exiliado gallego: Manuel Curros Enríquez, *La Tierra Gallega* y la modernidad nacional transatlántica', *MLN*, 117:331–42, examines the important Cuba/Galicia axis at the end of the 19th and beginning of the 20th centuries.

DARÍO, RUBÉN. A. Correa Ramón, 'De niña a mujer en al imaginario de Rubén Darío: el rito de transición a la pubertad en *El palacio del sol*', *JILAS*, 8:29–39, rejects the usual categorization of the story as a fairy tale, and instead interprets it as an account of the awakening to erotic experience, seen in turn as a possibility of redemption from the stifling demands on women of social convention. José María Martínez, **Rubén Darío: Addenda*, Palencia, Cálamo, 2000, 292 pp. Blas Matamoro, **Rubén Darío*, M, Espasa, 2002, 268 pp.

GORRITI, JUANA MANUELA. M. Grzegorcyk, 'Lost space: Juana Manuela Gorriti's postcolonial geography', *JILAS*, 8:55–69, explores the importance for G.'s work of her life as a 'wanderer', a term the author prefers to either 'exile' or 'nomad'.

HEREDIA, JOSÉ MARÍA. Tilmann Altenberg, **Melancolía en la poesía de José María Heredia*, Frankfurt, Vervuert–Iberoamericana, 2001, 325 pp.

MARTÍ, JOSÉ. Octavio R. Costa, **Ser y esencia de Martí*, Miami, Universal, 2000, 253 pp. S. Faber, 'The beautiful, the good and the natural: Martí and the ills of modernity', *JLACS*, 11:173–93, looks critically at M.'s North-American chronicles, arguing that while denouncing the subordination of the Latin peoples to the Anglo-Saxon, M. was using very similar arguments to legitimize the subordination of women and the working classes. I. A. Schulman, 'La modernización de los estudios martianos y el discurso crítico de Roberto Fernández Retamar', *REH*, 36:627–32, insists on the vital importance of the Cuban critic's contribution to a modern vision of M. and of *modernismo*.

MATTO DE TURNER, CLORINDA. F. Schmidt-Welle, *'Harriet Beecher Stowe y Clorinda Matto de Turner: escritura pedagógica, modernización y nación', *Iberoamericana*, 4, 2001 : 133–49.

PALACIOS, PEDRO BONIFACIO. R. Szmetan, 'La crítica a Almafuerte: la recepción de su obra a través del tiempo', *His(US)*, 85:44–53, contrasts the neglect by the critical establishment of this writer, with the continued existence of a loyal readership, to whom he is better known by his pseudonym.

PICÓN FEBRES, GONZALO. C. A. Affigné, 'La patria del amor y la guerra: aproximación a la narrativa de Gonzalo Picón Febres', *Iberoamericana*, 6:45–66, looks at two novels by this Venezuelan author, for the light they shed on the relationship between rural space, the nation, and modernity at the end of the 19th century.

RODÓ, JOSÉ ENRIQUE. *José Enrique Rodó y su tiempo. Cien años de "Ariel"*, ed. Ottmar Ette and Titus Heydenreich, Frankfurt, Lang, 2000, 231 pp. **This America We Dream of: Rodó and 'Ariel' One Hundred Years On*, ed. Gustavo San Román, London, ILAS, 115 pp.

SARMIENTO, DOMINGO FAUSTINO. E. Altuna, *'Sarmiento, lector de *El lazarillo de ciegos caminantes*', *Iberoamericana*, 5:35–36. F. Rodríguez, 'Sarmiento en el desierto', *RevIb*, 58:1111–28, details S.'s reactions to the pampa.

SILVA, JOSÉ ASUNCIÓN. Rodrigo Zuleta, **El sentido actual de José Asunción Silva*, Frankfurt, Lang, 2000, 144 pp.

THE TWENTIETH CENTURY

MEXICO AND CENTRAL AMERICA

By Victoria Carpenter, *University of Derby*

1. History and Literature

In the past two years, there has been a resurgence of non-traditional areas of Latin American literary studies: leaving the familiar bay of the analyses of individual authors, the field now favours intertopical themes, like the influence of history on the formation of particular trends in literature. Recent developments in the study of subalternity in Latin American culture, together with gender and Chicano studies, have opened a new direction, introducing non-traditionalism as a key factor in modern Latin American literature.

The relationship between literature and history is once again a topic of great interest and polemics in Latin American literary studies, in particular within the context of identity/ies. Out of several publications on the topic, the following is definitive if at times controversial: Frederick Nunn, *Collisions with History. Latin American Fiction and Social Science from "el Boom" to the New World Order*, Athens, Ohio Univ. Center for International Studies, 2001, x + 266 pp. N. focuses on the Boom period, as it marks the pinnacle of socio-historical awareness within literary circles. The two outcomes of this interaction, 'fictional histories' and political novels, depict 'cataclysmic history' (as termed by N.), focusing on self-definition by common identity within historical context. As a result, historical figures gradually lose the centre stage to more general issues of social, political, and economic development. N.'s definition of the Boom is perceptibly wider than the traditional framework; rather than following the temporal restrictions of the period, he bases his selection of authors on the commonality of historical themes within the Boom context. The outcome of the study is far from self-evident: the parallel between fiction and social science in Latin America connotes the fluidity of the region's historical identities. Challenges to the existing understanding of the region's past and present provide the Boom historical narratives with a unique perspective on the objectivity of historical representations. Continuing the topic of the interconnection of culture and politics is *El laberinto de la solidaridad. Cultura y política en México (1910–2000)*, ed. Kristine Vanden Berghe and Maarten van

Delden (*Foro Hispánico*, 22), Amsterdam, Rodopi, 189 pp., although the lack of balance in the representation of distinct historical epochs reveals the still existing unfortunate trend of disregarding the post-1968 period in favour of traditionally acceptable (not to say 'safe') topics.

A Twice-told Tale: Reinventing the Encounter in Iberian / Iberian American Literature and Film, ed. Santiago Juan-Navarro and Theodore Robert Young, Newark, Delaware U.P., 2001, 301 pp., has three relevant articles. Victoria Campos, 'Toward a New History: twentieth-century debates in Mexico on narrating the national past' (47–64), continues the analysis of the interaction between Latin American literature and history, focusing on literary narratives as an alternative means of recording history. The examination of the reasons for post-Tlatelolco literature concludes with the analysis of the role of Mexican intellectuals in the revision of history by using 'the writing of history as a mode of critique capable of both demythifying propagandistic images and dismantling Mexico's restrictive social structures'. Unfortunately, Campos does not offer any particular examples of this process in contemporary prose or poetry; indeed, it seems that her knowledge of this period is sketchy at best, as she labels Carlos Monsiváis a 'cultural critic', apparently dismissing his contribution to the Tlatelolco poetry and 'vanguardista' prose. Still, the article posits some valuable and viable conclusions regarding the role of literary revisionism in Mexican history. The themes of marginalization, historical revisionism, and consequent lineality of historical timelines replacing the previously adopted cyclical structure allow for a new dimension in the analysis of post-Boom Mexican narrative. G. Ilarregui, 'Marina: a woman before the mirror of her time in Carlos Fuentes' *Ceremonias del Alba*' (109–22), examines La Malinche's character in connection with the Conquest and the imposition of new cultural and linguistic identity upon Mexico. Starting out rather promisingly with a comparative analysis of the language of Bernardino de Sahagún's *Códice Florentino* and Fuentes's novel, the essay fails to examine the point it claims to be its primary focus — linguistic transgression as a means of cultural re-identification. Fuentes's (meta)narrator is left without attention, as I. concentrates on retelling the plot and restating long-standing conclusions regarding La Malinche's multifaceted cultural significance. The textual analysis is definitely lacking in focus, often ignoring the complexity of Fuentes's language (it would have helped to find the original text alongside the translations): for example, it would have been intriguing to examine the reasons for Fuentes's use of Malintzín's 'European' name over the accepted (albeit derogatory) 'Malinche' or the indigenous 'Malintzín'. A complex language of the novel has been downplayed, thus taking away from the importance of linguistic accuracy in Fuentes's works (a well-established approach, especially after the publication of the now classic *La muerte de Artemio Cruz*). What I. dismisses as an intuitive description of Malinche's fears could be interpreted as Malinche's transcendence of linear time and therefore control of historical time progression, which in itself connotes historical role reversal of Cortés-controller / Marina-controlled. Consequential re-evaluation of these two characters would have added an intriguing perspective to the analysis of literary interpretations of the Conquest; yet I. prefers to follow a well-trodden path of the analysis of Marina-Malinche as a victim figure — a familiar direction of Octavio Paz's *El laberinto de la soledad*, her allegiance to which I. overtly denies. On the whole, this essay does not contribute much novelty to the debate of Marina-Malinche-Malintzin's role in the formation of Mexican national self-perception; moreover, the gender aspect of the debate escapes I.'s analysis. On the other hand, Mary Ann Gosser-Esquilín's comparative analysis of cronista accounts of Puerto Rico's past: 'Ana Lydia Vega's *Falsas crónicas del Sur*: reconstruction and revision of Puerto Rico's past' (193–209), pays particular attention to the language as a primary mechanism of transmitting not only historical information but also the cultural specifics of the Incas. In the analysis of Vega's false chronicle, G.-E. concentrates yet again on the language registers used to multiply the 'I' of the narrative, ultimately multiplying Puerto Rican cultural histories and identities.

Similarly, the role of languages (hence, cultural belonging or lack thereof) is the dominant subject of Roberto Ignacio Díaz, *Unhomely Rooms: Foreign Tongues and Spanish American Literature*, Lewisburg, Bucknell U.P., 248 pp. The evaluation of the role played by untranslated Spanish words within a foreign-language text reveals the conflict between the narrator's (or, in the case of José Martí, the author's) intrinsic connection to the mother culture (mostly through artistic expression or basic physiological factors, such as food) and an overt conscious transplantation of the narrative into a new cultural domain. The subject of exile literature is relatively novel and deserves to be treated in the scholarly and respectful manner demonstrated in D.'s study. However, it is unfortunate that the title betrays a potentially Eurocentric perspective, choosing 'Spanish America' over a less 'colonial' term 'Latin America'.

2. National Identity

A logical extension of the topic of literary revisionism of history is literary (re)interpretations of national identity or nationhood. Among the many contributions in this field one should mention Neil Larsen,

Determinations. Essays on Theory, Narrative and Nation in the Americas, London, Verso, 2001, ix + 214 pp., which continues the contemporary theme of postcolonial readings of Latin American literature, providing (possibly for the first time) a sound and substantiated theoretical background from within the region (Schwartz, Mariátegui) as well as drawing upon the familiar theoretical framework (Marx, Lukács). Hence, it is not surprising that the first five chapters delve into theory in an attempt to clarify the familiar confusion of terminology. The second half of the volume, drawing upon L.'s previous work *Reading North by South*, presents several case studies of reading 'nation' through 'narration', or of analysing literary works in the framework of national identity studies. While, as L. himself posits, this approach is deemed 'commonsensical', it addresses the 'narration' as a subject, thus connoting that there may be certain types of narrative particularly adequate for the expression of the national. Taking the previously defined formula one step further, L. narrows the term 'community' to be concrete rather than pertaining to an abstract concept. He introduces the concept of individual and biographical narration to make the term 'nation' more tangible; henceforth, the relationship between the novel (narration) and community (nation) becomes mutually influenced, as the biographical form of narration changes the abstract nation to the mediator between the individual and its 'life'.

Combining the subjects of nationhood and subalternity in Latin American literature, two works stand out: Alberto Moreiras, *The Exhaustion of Difference: The Politics of Latin American Cultural Studies*, Durham, NC, Duke U.P., 2001, x + 350 pp., and Gareth Williams, *The Other Side of the Popular: Neoliberalism and Subalternity in Latin America*, Durham, NC, Duke U.P., xii + 375 pp. The notion of the subaltern pervades W.'s work, focusing the reader's attention on the underlying factor of the self's commonality with the subaltern Other — a factor which is impossible and therefore sought after. The analysis first addresses transculturation as an influence upon contemporary Latin American discourse within the context of national culture. It then examines the counterhegemonic nature of 1980s discourse. Finally, in this self-questioning and potentially self-contradicting move, the analysis of subalternity revisits the Self/Other theory from the point of view of a Derridean 'perhaps' factor. M.'s study is in the same vein as W.'s, which is not surprising, considering that M. and W. have exchanged ideas on the subject for some time. The two volumes employ Ángel Rama's famous *La ciudad letrada* as a theoretical cornerstone; and both address the notion of friendship through Derridean analysis, as a means of rupture and interruption of the existing pattern of recognition. Yet there is a significant difference in their approaches to the topics addressed. While W. focuses on the hegemonical conflicts and the reacquisition of Self and Other roles, M. is interested in the relationship between literary and cultural studies, and the ensuing theoretical reformulations in light of the redefinition of the two (similar to Larsen's *Determinations*). The term 'subalternity', appearing in both works, nevertheless denotes overtly dissimilar concepts: M. employs it in relation to the position of contemporary literary studies, while W. addresses its intrinsic nature as a reference to cultural 'otherness'. While M.'s study is more region-specific than W.'s, examining the above issues within the South American literary context, both works can be considered 'metaliterary' or 'metacultural' in their approach to contemporary Latin American cultural studies. The change of importance of cultural and literary theories and the shift of cultural focus to deoccidentalization have brought a new focus on the function of the critic's location, first questioning the validity of the analysis from without and then dismissing the unquestionable viability of the analysis from within. The resulting discord between non-Latin American and Latin American scholars of cultural studies fuels M.'s analysis, while at the same time being symbolically dismissed through the very existence of the unity of W.'s and M.'s works. A complement study within this field is *Convergencia de tiempos: Estudios subalternos / contextos latinoamericanos estado, cultura, subalternidad*, ed. Ileana Rodríguez, Amsterdam–Atlanta, Rodopi, 2001, 522 pp.

Ángel Rama's famous novel which W. and M. use as the theoretical background for their studies lends its name to the title of Jean Franco's analysis of Latin American narrative in the Cold War period: Jean Franco, *The Decline and Fall of the Lettered City: Latin America in the Cold War*, Cambridge, MS — London, Harvard U.P., viii + 341 pp. The study concentrates on the changing role of literature under the pressure to conform to some point of view, be it artistic freedom proposed by the United States or the idea of workers' cultural revolution planted in Soviet socialist realism; as a result, the nature of Latin American literature within the conflicting political context of the Cold War is perceived as changing within to resist the change imposed from without. In other words, Latin American literature of the Cold War is the literature of resistance to the imposition of politically determined form and content. The volume is often self-contradictory in its purpose, and to a certain extent self-limiting in its interpretations. The analysis of *La Onda* within the context of rock vs. mainstream culture is refreshingly atypical, appraising rock culture as a means of expression in its own right. Surprisingly, the reading of Diamela Eltit's *El infarto del alma* focuses on the subaltern as the norm within itself. Depolitisation of social discourse has already been admitted by E. herself, yet the mother-centred interpretation presented by F. is somewhat exclusive in comparison to Williams's interpretation of the work as a representation of a community's finitude.

Paul Allatson, *Latino Dreams: Transcultural Traffic and the US National Imaginary*, Amsterdam–NY, Rodopi, 367 pp., continues the subject of conflicting cultural perceptions from a slightly different, yet expected perspective — subalternity of Latin American discourse in the context of US cultural domination. It would appear that this area is still a rather tentative specialism, as A. attempts to establish a theoretical background for his study, often lapsing into the obvious, especially in the discussion of the role of Latin Americanist studies within the region as perceivably secondary to the hegemony of European or North American academe. A. reminds the reader of Ángel Rama's attempt 'to show that local or regional vernacular literary productions could be produced and analysed on local terms without inevitably replicating metropolitan biases, whether these be philosophical discourses, literary genres, or language uses derived from or sanctioned by the Creole national elite or the European imperium'. It is unsettling that A., clearly well-versed in the contemporary trends of discourse analysis, could doubt the above intention enough to launch into a lengthy and often circuitous argument in its defence. In this respect, Moreiras's and Williams's works reinforce the long-standing dichotomy of Latin American discourse analysis from within and from without; A.'s attempt at bridging the two sides suffers from verbosity and confusing terminological rhetoric, ultimately leaving the reader wondering whether the discussion was relevant to the remainder of the study. As a result, this work, overloaded with terminology, is generally unfocused.

The topic of national identity is explored in a more country-specific vein in Anne Doremus, *Culture, Politics and National Identity in Mexican Literature and Film, 1929–1952*, NY–Oxford, Lang, 2001, xi + 206 pp. This study of the portrayal of 'Mexicanness' in film and literature is surprising, at best. Outlining the stark difference between 'high' and 'low' art in the portrayal of Mexican identity, it proceeds to examine its structure from a linear temporal perspective, starting with the works of the 1920s and following on to the early 1950s. D. considers the dichotomy of 'high' and 'low' art a mainspring of Mexican national identity and its intrinsic conflicts. Consequently, the disparity between the two is deemed complementary as the author posits that Mexican national identity is the composite of the two perspectives — a rather disappointingly self-fulfilling (if not obvious) conclusion.

3. Literature and Culture

A more coherent examination of the interconnection between 'high' and 'low' culture is presented in *Latin American Literature and Mass Media*, ed. Edmundo Paz-Soldán and Debra Castillo, NY–London, Garland, 2001, 322 pp. Doremus's extensive analysis of the complementary nature of 'high' and 'low' cultures is rightly reduced in this study to a means of defining a contemporary national character by presenting a survey of inter-influences of mass media and literature. While negating or dismissing neither, it emphasizes the changing nature of the relationship between visual and verbal art, suggesting a revisionist fluid approach over the static juxtaposition of 'high/low culture'.

Continuing the topic of cultural dichotomy, several publications are devoted to literary representations of violence. Aníbal González, *Killer Books: Writing, Violence and Ethics in Modern Spanish American Narrative*, Austin, Texas U.P., 192 pp., offers a study of literary works which represent violence at two distinct stages: physical abuse and writing as a means of abuse, and ethical reflections upon violence. The first section analyses the works of Manuel Gutiérrez Nájera (México), Manuel Zeno Gandía (Puerto Rico), and Teresa de la Parra (Venezuela); the second addresses the writings of Alejo Carpentier (Cuba), Jorge Luis Borges and Julio Cortázar (Argentina). G. cautions against regarding this selection of writers as the dichotomized epitome of the subject; instead, these are examples of the two stages of the portrayal of violence. It is noteworthy that the time scope chosen for the study is the last two centuries, thus precluding the possibility of a conclusion that only the postcolonial period is home to 'la literatura de violencia'. A particularly interesting aspect of this study is the examination of graphophobia as a result of ethical dilemma; the readings of Borges, Carpentier, and Cortázar punctuate the paradox of literary warnings against the evil of writing. The resulting conflict is characteristic of Latin American literary criticism of societal development, often underscored by violence in a struggle for power.

The title of John Wesley Shillington's ambitious study, *Grappling with Atrocity: Guatemalan Theater in the 1990s*, Teaneck, Fairleigh Dickinson U.P., 207 pp., is somewhat misleading, as the volume addresses the works of Guatemalan playwrights from the late 1960s to the present day. Politicized theatre is considered short-lived and therefore not worthy of in-depth analysis, but S. takes on this controversial topic with integrity and dignity befitting a 'high' literature study. The most impressive quality of this study is its structural clarity: with each chapter broken down into interconnected subsections, it reveals a logical link to the contemporary political and social situation in Guatemala. S.'s first-hand experience of the plays adds a much-needed human dimension to the work. The link between the political situation in Guatemala since 1944 and the corresponding stages in the formation of contemporary theatre help the reader follow a rather intricate pattern of the theatre of atrocity and the reason for it, following the path outlined in the three major types of theatre: satiric, didactic, and symbolic. Sometimes the three appear to be assigned rather arbitrarily, since most satiric and didactic plays analysed in this study have a symbolic quality; it might have been more accurate to rename the last type 'abstract' or 'metatheatre'. Unfortunately, the analysis is sometimes superficial, lacking the much needed depth of close readings, especially in the analysis of the fragmented language of *La Crónica fidedigna* by Manuel Corleto. Frequently, the analysis ignores intertextuality: the title of the play 'El General no tiene quien lo inscriba' is an obvious reference to García Márquez's *El Coronel no tiene quien le escriba*, yet S. disregards a potentially significant parallel with 'realismo mágico' and particularly the link between the interpretations of (un)heroic figures. Some interviews interjected into the analysis are left with no further comment or link to the political context of the play to which they supposedly refer; consequently, the objective for the use of these interviews remains unclear, and the focus of the section blurred. An intriguing recurrence of the characters of clowns and insane people is left untraced through the various types of theatre, although it is clear that the notion of clowns/insane people possessing access to the only true view of the world is of paramount importance in the analysis of the symbolic/metaphoric representation of numerous historic truths/untruths/half-truths. A statement, shocking in its simplicity, that 'in Guatemala the truth can only be expressed by people who are mad . . . or fools', is left with no further comment, which is surprising especially since S. returns to the subject of insanity several times in the analysis of other types of theatre. Another symbolism left unexplored is that of names such as 'Pitt' and 'Bouille', 'Don Touch', while 'Vicente Nario' is given a brief mention with no further link to the reason for the mention of 'Bicentennial' in the context of the play (Víctor Hugo Cruz, *'Vicente Nario' — O cómo la Revolución puede ser un juego*). It beggars belief that the author, keen to explore hidden phonetic symbolism, would ignore other, more evident, instances of meaningful names. However, the volume conveys the necessity to study the Guatemalan theatre of atrocity in order to prevent a forgetting of the past during the reconciliation process.

4. Chicano Writing

Within the context of subaltern culture, the subject of Chicano writing has been gaining popularity, as the number of works focusing on Chicano writers grows exponentially: considering the relative youth of this field, in the past two years numerous studies have addressed Chicano literature from a variety of perspectives. However, it appears that the popularity of the subject tends to signify a certain decrease in the quality of work. Helena Grice et al., *Beginning Ethnic American Literatures*, MUP, 2001, vi + 255 pp., is an example of such a superficial approach to Chicano literature. The limitations of the study can be understood as due to the nature of the work as well as to the fact that only one chapter of the volume is set aside for this analysis. It is apparent that the authors recognize the importance of acknowledging the existence of Chicano/a literature elsewhere in the United States; yet, as far as the analysis goes, there is little attempt made to break away from the comfort of familiar territories (Texas) in search of historical antecedents to the movement. While the theoretical basis for the analysis appears sound, one cannot help questioning the equality sign between 'universal', 'dominant', and 'Anglo-American' standard of excellence. Furthermore, the characterization of the US narratives as 'closed texts', arrogantly extolling the virtues of Western European civilization, is annoying at best, considering the extent to which the authors have tried to establish their attention to detail. It is unclear whether they were unsure of what the 'narratives of the United States' mean or whether to them, anything 'US' is immediately associated with white patriarchal supremacy, in which case, black, Beat, and hippy narratives fall into the same category, ultimately negating their own existence. The chapter leaves the impression of an attempt to be nonconformist yet politically correct to a fault.

A considerably more focused study of Chicano/a literature and identity is presented in Paula Moya, *Learning from Experience: Minority Identities, Multicultural Struggle*, Berkeley, California U.P., xii + 235 pp. The approach chosen by M. is not as theoretically restrictive, since she is well aware of the limitations of one particular approach selected against the rest, thus choosing a combination thereof, while recognizing the difference between a political and a theoretical framework. M. goes beyond theorizing about distinct identities by addressing the identity of 'assimilao', a collection of interlinked identity factors. Offering constructive criticism of contemporary theorists, M. posits that Chicano/a (or, as she puts it, Chicana/o) literature remains as yet theoretically undetermined as to the dominance of a particular theory. Although the volume is classified under cultural studies, one might argue that it represents the ever expanding field of metaliterary and metacultural analysis, with the 'meta' factor dominating the study. Nonetheless, chapter 5 is of particular interest to literary specialists, as it applies the theoretical base created throughout the volume to a postpositivist realist reading of Helena Maria Viramonte's novel *Under the Feet of Jesus*, on three levels: metaphorical, structural, and thematic. A metaphorical reading of the power of the word provides a well-argued analysis of the redefined role of barter as 'an ideal form of communicative interaction'. The variable focalization of the structure of the novel is evaluated as a means to gain insight into the characters' inner development as they come into contact with a number of socially designated situations which serve to expand their self-perception and perception of the interactions across (or within) class layers. Finally, as M. discusses the reason behind and the expression of differences in individual identities within the same social stratum, she forewarns activists and academics interested in social change against dismissing the individuality and complexity of the social world.

5. Cross-Cultural Studies

Another familiar subject in Latin American literary studies is the cross-cultural approach. There are some important contributions, focusing on European influences on Latin American narratives: V. Carpenter, '"From yellow to red to black": Tantric reading of "Blanco" by Octavio Paz', *BLAR*, 21:527–44, examines the often neglected impact of non-Western cultural phenomena (in this case, Tantra Yoga) on O.P.'s poetic expression. The article delivers an exhaustive explanation of the nature of Tantra, and analyses 'Blanco' as a poetic/visual representation of Tantric practices, rather than a mostly surrealist work with some Indian overtones (the interpretation presented by the majority of previous analyses).

Foucault and Latin America: Appropriations and Deployments of Discursive Analysis, ed. Benigno Trigo, London, Routledge, xxi + 305 pp., is a significant undertaking in the field of cross-cultural study. The collection presents a number of well-known articles on the subject of Foucaultian reading of Latin America. The four sections of the volume represent the four major themes in Foucault's work: discourse, government, (authorship and) subjectivity, and sexuality. Á. Rama's essay 'The ordered city' (3–16), an excerpt from *La ciudad letrada*, discusses the imposition of a new order upon Latin America as a result of the Conquest. The newly 'ordered' system has to be considered from the point of view of subject/object dichotomy, while the imposition of 'order' and its absorption into reality posits a certain problem in the interpretation of the object. The resulting duality (material vs. symbolic), according to R., is a characteristic of Latin American cities and, by proxy, Latin American societies. It is unfortunate that few modern critics take into consideration the objectifying of Latin America as a result of the Conquest, preferring to focus on the more recent Anglo-American influence as the primary source of objectification. R.'s work (even in as short an excerpt as this) redirects critics' attention back to the starting point of the subject/object relationship which has shaped modern Latin America. D. Sommer, 'Love and country: an allegorical speculation' (103–24), considers the expression of national pride from the point of view of a love affair with the country, asking after Foucault whether sexual desire has indeed become 'an explanation for everything'. Of particular interest is the parallel between government institutions and sexual 'normalcy' as conjugal love. Furthermore, new state systems represent new body constructs, reassigning national and sexual foci according to the need to induce national pride through 'the apparently raw material of erotic love'. Joining in the debate on the nature of Latin American *testimonio* narrative, E. Sklodowska, 'Author (dys)function: rereading *I, Rigoberta Menchú*' (197–210), concentrates on the 'truth of possibility' rather than the 'truth of material events', basing her analysis on Foucault's concept of author-function. From a Foucaultian perspective on authorship, S. attacks what she calls David Stoll's 'self-imposed goal of "separating truth from falsehood"', arguing against the (multiple) authorship of Menchú's testimonial as the key factor in its merits. Instead, S. addresses the 'name-less' nature of testimonial authority as a culture-based (rather than authorship-grounded) phenomenon. B. Sifuentes Jáuregui, 'Sadomasochism in *Paradiso*: bound narratives and pleasure' (263–72), addresses the homosexual character of José Lezama Lima's *Paradiso*, focusing particularly on the factors of exclusion and inclusion of 'normative' sexuality. Reading Farraluque's sexual encounters and sadomasochistic pleasures through Foucault's notion of the link/separation of pleasure and dominance, S.J. raises the question of 'pleasure as form of domination, not just domination as pleasure'.

Herbert E. Craig, *Marcel Proust and Spanish America: From Critical Response to Narrative Dialogue*, Lewisburg, PA, Bucknell U.P., 443 pp., considers the works of a number of Latin American authors within the context of Proust's writings, defining literary relations of the works of Proust and of Latin American authors as those of influence, inspiration, dialogue, and parody. A comparative analysis of these works focuses upon the most characteristic 'Proustian' themes: memory, nature, high society, art, jealousy, and music. The order in which these themes are addressed in the study is rather arbitrary, and it is possible that the integrity of the study would have benefited from a more discerning approach. Unlike *Foucault and Latin America*, whose view of Foucault succeeds in remaining unbiased as a popular 'Foucaultian' view of Latin American culture, this volume lauds P.'s work to such a degree that it soon seems pointless to consider the works of Ricardo Güiraldes, Victoria Ocampo, or Julio Cortázar as original. While C.'s enthusiasm for Proust's talent is understandable, his view of such works as *Don Segundo Sombra* or *Rayuela* as solely possible because of P. is, to put it mildly, unsubstantiated. Furthermore, the Eurocentric and often downrightly chauvinistic language of the study antagonizes its readers by implying that Latin American literature has remained incapable of creative originality and has to rely on Europe for its means of artistic expression. Statements like 'this French writer was able to show many Spanish Americans how they could transcend their simple observation of the world', could have been written in the 19th c. or certainly before Spain's rule of Latin America ended in 1898. C.'s patronizing attitude towards Latin American women writers is even more ignominious than his Eurocentric stance. With one sentence, 'other women writers from Spanish America would also find in Proust a sensitive male author whom they could emulate', he not only establishes Proust's superiority due to his European origin, but also denigrates women writers as mere copycats who need emotional support and artistic guidance from a 'sensitive male'. One cannot disagree that P.'s influence on Latin American literature is significant; however, one cannot agree that P. alone engendered 20th-c. Latin American literature, including post-Boom. The radicalism of C.'s statements, coupled with dated terminology and theoretical background does a definite disservice to this otherwise well-documented and detailed study.

César Augusto Salgado, *From Modernism to Neobaroque: Joyce and Lezama Lima*, Lewisburg, PA, Bucknell U.P., 265 pp., presents a more coherent intertextual study of European influences on Latin American literature, remaining objective in its analysis of Joyce's influence on Latin American literature, thus allowing for original creativity on behalf of Latin American writers: 'Lezama's relation to Joyce is not that of creative dependence, but of recognition'. The study supports its claim of J.'s influence on L.'s writings with a coherent textual analysis, supplemented in the last chapter with cross-examinations of contemporary critiques of both writers' works.

6. Gender

Gender issues in Latin American literature have changed their focus over time, but have not lost their significance for the examination of gender fluidity and changing gender roles. Two studies closely linked to Foucaultian themes are Diane E. Marting, *The Sexual Woman in Latin American Literature: Dangerous Desires*, Gainesville, Florida U.P., 2001, xii + 345 pp., and Ben Sifuentes-Jáuregui, *Transvestism, Masculinity, and Latin American Literature: Genders Share Flesh*, NY–Basingstoke, Palgrave, xi + 240 pp. M. examines the representation of female sexuality in Latin American literature from the early 1960s to the present day. The focus of the volume is on sexuality as a means of women's self-definition as a subject. Interestingly, the three writers selected for the study are not all women: at first glance, the selection of Miguel Ángel Asturias, Clarice Lispector, and Mario Vargas Llosa appears to be as surprising as it seems unsubstantiated. The reason for this selection, as posited by M., is the fact that the three 'stand in for the three decades under consideration [1960s, 1970s, and 1980s] as the rise, apex, and fall of the liberatory stance of an indulgent, radical period in the portrayal of female sexuality'. The positioning of the woman within the novel (as a narrator, protagonist, or recipient) would undoubtedly influence the outcome of the analysis of her sexual role; M.'s study appears to have circumvented (or ignored) this obstruction. The analysis of the three novels chosen concludes that the subjectification of women undermines the traditional gender hierarchy of roles and ultimately reconstructs female sexuality as a means of self-identification and self-assignation of traditional male roles. S.J.'s fascinating work stands out among other gender studies publications because it does not claim to be concerned with the social implications of homosexuality as much as with its literary representations. Although the first two chapters are dedicated to analyses of homoeroticism and transvestism within a broader social context, the majority of research is based upon literary works. As a result, the publication offers a thoughtful insight into the literature of homosexuality (or homosexuality of literature), in particular relating to gender reconstruction through transvestism and role change. Employing the Self/Other dichotomy as a delineation of the subject/object homosexual interaction, S.J. challenges the existing notions of homosexuality and transvestism from within the Latin American literary framework. The role of literature in the (de/re)construction of gender roles becomes, therefore, prevalent over the social context by which the field of gender studies has been dominated. A voyeuristic attitude to language is revealed in the reading of Alejo Carpentier's 'Jacqueline' fashion writing: observing Carpentier 'making up' his Jacqueline, readers are watching the change of Self/Other assignation, questioning the role of the transvestite subject, who 'is as much Other to women as she is to men'. The implications for gender studies are intriguing, since they call for the rethinking of the dominant realm of 'masculinity' determining the validity of 'masculine' tasks performed by women.

7. Individual Authors and Movements

In the past two years, there have been some memorable studies, in particular of modern writers, whose significance in contemporary Latin American literature is downplayed due to an unfortunate pigeonholing as 'narrativa joven'. Merlin H. Forster, *Las vanguardias literarias en México y la América Central: bibliografía y antología crítica*, Frankfurt, Vervuert — Madrid, Iberoamericana, 2001, xxvi + 351 pp., is a comprehensive bibliography of Mexican and Central American 'vanguardia' works, complete with critiques of individual authors, concentrating on works published after 1990. The obvious merit of this work is as an up-to-date exhaustive bibliography, organized by topic (general, Mexico, Central America) and by writers' names. The bibliographical section also includes a list of publications about the movement of Los Contemporáneos, an important yet often under-represented phenomenon of 20th-c. Mexican literature. The critique section presents a series of articles, once again arranged by topic; each article is cross-referenced to the original date and place of publication. A scholar of this literary period would be interested to see the familiar names of Jaime Labastida, Samuel Gordon, and Anthony Stanton among the authors of critiques.

Ronald Friis, *José Emilio Pacheco and the Poets of the Shadows*, Lewisburg, PA, Bucknell U.P., 220 pp., is an overview of P.'s poetic career from *Los elementos de la noche* to the poetry of the 1990s, with the focus of the analysis on intertextuality and its effects on the poet/narrator/reader trichotomy. The subject of intetextuality in modern Mexican literature is far from novel; yet there has been almost no attempt to trace it through the work of P., possibly because the inertia of 'high criticism' ranks him as part of the underestimated 'narrativa joven'. Unfortunately, with the label comes the sense of the 'transitory' nature of their works; as a result, the gap in the analysis of Mexican literature of the 1960s–1990s is growing wider. F.'s book partially fills the gap by addressing P.'s work as poetry in its own right, although there is a disappointing sensation of the author trying to please both camps: on the one hand, the intertextuality of P.'s work is considered a unique feature; on the other hand, the analysis tends to rely too heavily on the backup examination of 'established' writers (Paz, Castellanos) in an apparent attempt to justify addressing P.'s works as part of the accepted canon of 20th-c. Mexican literature. The comparative readings of P.'s poetry and its influences are carried out in a traditional form of close textual analysis, at times overlooking secondary topics in order to support the original primary hypothesis. Consequently, the collection *No me preguntes cómo pasa el tiempo* comes across as little more than a poetic leaflet for an anti-imperialist party. The diversity of historical representations in 'Lectura de los "Cantares mexicanos": manuscrito de Tlatelolco (octubre 1968)' was all but disregarded, thus reducing the subject of the poem to an intertextual linguistic exercise. On the whole, however, the book is solid and valuable as an introduction to the unjustly ignored poetry of P. Surprisingly, there are several mistakes in translation, which undermine the reader's trust in F.'s analysis. Considering the great emphasis F. puts on language accuracy in P.'s works, these mistakes devalue this volume and make the reader question the accuracy of the analysis. Among other unfortunate mistakes, the most glaring is the misspelling of Allen Ginsberg's name as 'Alan', which brings the reader back to the conflict between critics' respect for 'mainstream literature' and disregard of 'narrativa joven' (for the lack of a more accurate term) regardless of its country of origin.

Latin American mainstream literature continues to attract the attention of critics despite general focus shifting towards more unconventional material. One of the most poignant examples is Rubén Darío's work, which was the subject of *Selected Poems of Rubén Darío: A Bilingual Anthology*, ed. and trans. Alberto Acereda and Will Derusha, Lewisburg, PA, Bucknell U.P., 2001, 268 pp. Although Darío has long been a canon of Latin American literature, this collection makes one wonder whether the works of this poet have been consistently overlooked. It appears that, well known as Darío is, publishers in Europe and America are not as quick to reissue his collections as they are to put out yet another 'Obras completas' of Octavio Paz or Pablo Neruda; in fact, the latest re-issue of a complete collection of Darío's poetry is over 50 years old (*Obras poéticas completas*, Florida, El Ateneo, 1953). While the contribution the other two writers have made to world culture is unquestionable, it is unfortunate that in the postmodernist age Darío's poetry and prose have been ignored, considering the significance of his influence on contemporary and modern Spanish and Latin American literature. Consequently, this publication plays a major role in bringing D.'s work back to the public's attention. The bilingual version makes the volume accessible to those who are not fluent enough in Spanish to appreciate D.'s poetic language; several bibliographies and a timeline of D.'s life would please literature specialists and general public alike. However, the introductory sections are harder to praise, mainly because of their rather rambling and defensive nature. Infrequent parallels between D.'s work and life make one wonder whether the reading of 'A Phocas el campesino' as a dedication to D.'s son who died in infancy, is plausible, especially since so much emphasis has been placed upon the dilemma of subjectivity / objectivity as a dominant theme in D.'s poetry. Still, the combination of close textual and phonetic analysis reveals the depth of these works, often dismissed as dated. Indeed, some of D.'s metaphors may appear transparent; nature scenes remind one of the young John Keats, and the didactic air of the later works reduces their psychoanalytic character to a mental hypochondria. However, the juxtaposition of terms such as 'auscultar' and 'linfa' against the backdrop of exquisite images of 'el corazón de la noche' ('Nocturno'), evokes the conflict between the scientific and emotional perception of the world and the individual's place therein. Acereda and Derusha point out the inadequate translation of 'auscultar' as 'hear' which destroys the dual perception of the world, created by the intentional use of two distinct registers. D.'s work should be re-evaluated more closely and accurately than has been done, so that the phenomenon of 1898 (in both hemispheres) can be assessed without putting Latin American culture in the subordinate position to its contemporary Spanish counterpart. Acereda and Derusha's work aims at doing just that, and generally achieves its goal by offering readers a chance to re-discover D. for themselves.

Finally, a rather unfortunate contribution to the field is *Ángeles Mastretta*, ed. Julio Ortega and William Worden, M, Agencia Espanola de Cooperación Internacional — Ediciones de Cultura Hispánica, 2001, 83 pp. As stated in the introduction, M.'s anecdotal approach to *criollista* narrative has long been misunderstood and often discarded as simplistic; as a result, M. has rarely been the focus of serious literary analyses. This collection of papers from the colloquium dedicated to M. (Casa de Américas, Madrid, June 21–23, 1999) does little to dispel this image of her works: often gratuitous mutual praise, occasionally challenged by the audience, adds little of value to the existing body of Latin American literary criticism.

SOUTH AMERICA

By F. J. Mackintosh, *Lecturer in Hispanic Studies in the University of Edinburgh*

1. General

Jorge Ruiz Gusils, **Índice de escritores latinoamericanos*, Mexico, UNAM, 417 pp. Carlos A. Solé and Klaus Müller-Bergh, **Latin American Writers: Supplement* 1, NY, Scribner, 623 pp. Susana Zanetti, **La dorada garra de la lectura : lectoras y lectores de novela en América Latina*, Rosario,

Viterbo, 447 pp. *CLCWeb*, 4.2, is a special issue entitled *Comparative Cultural Studies and Latin America*, ed. Sophia A. McClennen and Earl E. Fitz.

Guadalupe Fernández Ariza, **Literatura hispanoamericana del siglo* XX*: memoria y escritura*, Malaga U.P., 214 pp. Nora Didier de Iungman et al., **Exploración de los rasgos más característicos de la literatura del mundo hispánico de hoy:* XX *Simposio Internacional de Literatura del Mundo Hispánico*, Santa Fe, Argentina, Asociación Santafesina de Escritores, 58 pp., includes essays on globalization and regional literatures. N. Binns, 'Landscapes of hope and destruction: ecological poetry in Spanish America', *Interdisciplinary Studies in Literature and Environment*, 9:105–19. Silviano Santiago and Ana Lucía Gazzola, **The Space In-between: Essays on Latin American Culture*, Durham, Duke U.P., 187 pp. Jorge Carlos Gissi Bustos, **Psicología e identidad latinoamericana: socio-psicoanálisis de cinco premios nobel de literatura*, Santiago, Univ. Católica, 232 pp. John Beverley and Hugo Achugar, **La voz del otro: testimonio, subalternidad y verdad narrativa*, Guatemala, Univ. Rafael Landívar, 257 pp. María Ramírez Ribes, **Las plumas del camaleón: máscaras y testimonios hispanoamericanos*, Caracas, Comala, 221 pp. E. De Costa, 'Voices of conscience: the power of language in the Latin American *testimonio*', pp. 41–57 of **Storytelling: Interdisciplinary and Intercultural Perspectives*, ed. Irene María F. Blayer and Mónica Sánchez, NY, Lang, vi + 175 pp. Amelia Royo et al., **Rosismo y peronismo: de los interrogantes historiográficos a las respuestas ficcionales*, BA, Nueva Generación, 250 pp. J.-V. Saval, 'Carlos Barral's publishing adventure: the cultural opposition to Francoism and the creation of the Latin-American boom', *BHS*, 79:205–11, studies the key role of Barral and his collaborators. *RevIb*, 199, is on 'Literatura y cine en América Latina'. Laura Rosa Loustau, **Cuerpos errantes: literatura latina y latinoamericana en Estados Unidos*, Rosario, Viterbo, 222 pp., includes an essay on Valenzuela. Juan E. de Castro, **Mestizo Nations: Culture, Race and Conformity in Latin American Literature*, Tucson, Arizona U.P., xvi + 161 pp. Marjorie Agosín, **Invisible Dreamer: Memory, Judaism and Human Rights*, Santa Fe, Sherman Asher, 272 pp. T. Halperín-Donghi, 'On Braudel', *JLACS*, 11:107–18, comments on Braudel's surprising lack of influence on Latin American historiography but puts in a reminder to *voir grand*. Francine Masiello, **The Art of Transition: Latin American Culture and Neoliberal Crisis*, Durham, Duke U.P., 2001, 352 pp. Emil Volek, **Latin America Writes Back: Postmodernity in the Periphery*, NY, Routledge, xxviii + 282 pp. Rosa Boldori de Baldussi, **La identidad cultural de Mercosur*, BA, Ciudad Argentina, 343 pp., covers Argentine, Paraguayan, and Uruguayan literature. Jason Weiss, **The Lights of Home: A Century of Latin American Writers in Paris*, NY, Routledge, 272 pp. Daniel Balderston and Marcy

E. Schwartz, **Voice-overs: Translation and Latin American Literature*, Albany, NY, SUNY, 266 pp., is divided into 3 parts: 'Writers on Translation', 'Translating Latin America', and 'Critical Approaches'. R. L. Williams, 'Modernist continuities: the desire to be modern in twentieth-century Spanish-American fiction', *BSS*, 79:369–93. D. L. Shaw, 'When was modernism in Spanish-American fiction?', *ib.*, 395–409. Jorge Schwartz, **Las vanguardias latinoamericanas: textos programáticos y críticos*, Mexico, FCE, 748 pp. + 22 pls. G. Kirkpatrick, 'Romantic poetry in Latin America', pp. 401–16 of **Romantic Poetry*, ed. Angela Esterhammer, Amsterdam, Benjamins, vi + 537 pp. Hermann Herlinghaus, **Narraciones anacrónicas de la modernidad: melodrama e intermedialidad en América Latina*, Santiago, Cuarto Propio, 386 pp. **Do the Americas Have a Common Literary History?*, ed. Barbara Buchenau and Annette Paatz, NY, Lang, 702 pp. Helen Oakley, **The Recontextualization of William Faulkner in Latin American Fiction and Culture*, Lewiston, Mellen, 223 pp., compares him to Bombal, Onetti, and Rulfo.

2. Gendered Writing

**Reflexiones: ensayos sobre escritoras hispanoamericanas contemporáneas*, ed. Priscilla Gac-Artigas, 2 vols, New Jersey, Nuevo Espacio, 408, 392 pp. *Robert Richmond Ellis, *They Dream Not of Angels but of Men: Homoeroticism, Gender and Race in Latin American Autobiography*, Gainesville, Florida U.P., 219 pp. *María Teresa Medeiros-Lichem, *Reading the Feminine Voice in Latin American Women's Fiction: From Teresa de la Parra to Elena Poniatowska and Luisa Valenzuela*, NY, Lang, 240 pp. J. L. Camacho, 'El cirujano y la enferma: la representación de la mujer en la literatura modernista', *RCEH*, 26:351–60, is on Martí, Darío, and Argüello. G. Bellini, 'Recepción de narradoras hispano-americanas en Italia', *QIA*, 91:44–73, includes surveys of S. Ocampo, Peri Rossi, Allende, as well as Central American, Caribbean, and Mexican writers.

3. Individual Countries

Argentina

General. María Teresa Gramuglio, **El imperio realista*, BA, Emecé, 524 pp. Carlos Giordano, **Oficio de viento y sombra: ensayos de historia literaria argentina*, Soveria Mannelli, Rubbettino, 223 pp. C. E. Benzecry, 'Beatriz Sarlo and theories of popular culture', *JLACS*, 11:77–92. C. Canaparo, 'Un mundo modernista para la cultura rioplatense', *BSS*, 79:193–209. I. García, 'Rubén Darío y Francisco Grandmontagne en el Buenos Aires de 1898: la redefinición de los conceptos de hispanismo en América y de Americanismo en España', *RevIb*, 198:49–66, notes a turning point in mutual attitudes with the publication of *Ariel*. Edna Aizenberg, **Books and Bombs in Buenos Aires: Borges, Gerchunoff, and Argentine-Jewish Writing*, Hanover, New England U.P., 195 pp. Paul Verdevoye et al., **Literatura argentina e idiosincrasía*, BA, Corregidor, xxiv + 512 pp. Cristina Iglesia, **La violencia del azar: ensayo sobre literatura argentina*, Mexico, FCE, 153 pp., includes essays on Saer, Piglia, *Sur*.

POETRY. Melanie Nicholson, *Evil, Madness and the Occult in Argentine Poetry*, Gainesville, Florida U.P., 201 pp., is on Orozco, Pizarnik, and Fijman and overlapping forms of esoterism. N. Teitler, 'Redefining the female body: Alfonsina Storni and the *modernista* tradition', *BSS*, 79:171–92, compares her to Darío and Lugones.

THEATRE AND CINEMA. Beatriz Trastoy, **Teatro autobiográfico: los unipersonales de los 80 y 90 en la escena argentina*, BA, Nueva Generación, 356 pp. M. G. Mizraje, 'Morder la tradición: el *Nosferatu* de Griselda Gambaro', *LATR*, 35:79–84, is on vampires. Diana Raznovich, *Actos Desafiantes*, ed. Diana Taylor and Victoria Martínez, Lewisburg, Bucknell U.P., 342 pp., is a bilingual version with an introductory essay. *RCEH*, 26.1, is devoted to the Argentine director María Luisa Bemberg with essays on all her major films.

FICTION. María José Punte, *Rostros de la utopía: la proyección del peronismo en la novela argentina de la década de los 80*, Pamplona, Navarre U.P., 228 pp. A. Osvaldo Gallone, *La ficción de la historia en seis narradores argentinos contemporáneos*, Cordoba, Alción, 201 pp. Andrea Castro, **El encuentro imposible: la conformación del fantástico ambiguo en la narrativa breva argentina (1862–1910)*, Göteborg U.P., 202 pp. Fernando Savater, **Jorge Luis Borges*, Barcelona, Omega, 215 pp. N. Abraham Hall, 'Saving the Gutres: Borges, Sarmiento and Mark', *RCEH*, 26:527–36, is on 'El evangelio según Marcos'. E. Buch, '*Ein deutsches Requiem*: between Borges and Furtwängler', *JLACS*, 11:29–38. A. Pauls, 'Argentine talk', *ib.*, 39–46, is on voice in Borges. K. Jenckes, 'Allegory, ideology, infamy: Borges and the allegorical writing of history', *ib.*, 47–64, sees Borges's historical writing as Benjaminian allegory. J. Prieto, 'La inquietante extrañeza de la autoría: Borges, Macedonio Fernández y el "espectro" de las vanguardias', *LALR*, 59:20–42, discusses the 'mutua impregnación' of their writing. Pablo Rocca and Homero Alsina Thevenet, **El Uruguay de Borges: Borges y los uruguayos (1925–1974)*, Montevideo, Univ. de la República, 220 pp. Julio Prieto, **Desencuadernados: vanguardias ex-céntricas en el Río de la Plata; Macedonio Fernández y Felisberto Hernández*, Rosario, Viterbo, 383 pp. Susanna Regazzoni and René Ceballos, **Homenaje a Adolfo Bioy Casares: una retrospectiva de su obra*, M, Iberoamericana — Frankfurt,

Vervuert, 352 pp. K. Bowsher, 'Eva Perón and Argentine postmodernity reconsidered: Abel Posse's *La pasión según Eva*', *BHS*, 79:225–40, asks whether the post-boom is necessarily post-modern. E. C. Graf, '"Axolotl" de Julio Cortázar: dialéctica entre las mitologías azteca y dantesca', *BSS*, 79:615–36. Gwendolyn Josie Díaz, **Luisa Valenzuela sin máscara*, Buenos Aires, Feminaria, 186 pp. 'Dossier Silvina Ocampo', *CHA*, 622:7–63. J. L. French, '"A geographical inquiry into historical experience": the Misiones stories of Horacio Quiroga', *LALR*, 59:79–99, sees them as literature that addresses the 'Invisible Empire'. Ignacio López-Calvo, **Religión y el militarismo en la obra de Marcos Aguinis*, Lewiston, Mellen, 309 pp. **Luisa Valenzuela: Simetrías / Cambio de armas; Luisa Valenzuela y la crítica*, Caracas, Excultura, 219 pp. Ana Pizarro, **Las grietas del proceso civilizatorio: Marta Traba en los sesenta*, Santiago, LOM, 127 pp. Marta Elena Castellino, **De magia y otras historias: la narrativa breve de Juan Draghi Lucero*, Mendoza, EDIUNC, 223 pp.

BOLIVIA

S. Hart, 'The art of invasion in Jorge Sanjinés's *Para recibir el canto de los pájaros* (1995)', *HRJ*, 3:71–81, discusses the double-consciousness of Aymara culture.

CHILE

Yvonne S. Unnold, **Representing the Unrepresentable: Literature of Trauma Under Pinochet in Chile*, NY, Lang, 202 pp. Alice A. Nelson, **Political Bodies: Gender, History and the Struggle for Narrative Power in Recent Chilean Literature*, Lewisburg, Bucknell U.P. — London, Associated U.P., 307 pp. Stéphanie Decante, **Horizon d'attente et stratégies d'écriture dans le Chili de la transition démocratique: Diamela Eltit, Gonzalo Contreras, Alberto Fuguet, 1988–1997*, Villeneuve-d'Ascq, Septentrion U.P., 449 pp. E. Paz-Soldán, 'Escritura y cultura audiovisual en *Por favor, rebobinar* de Alberto Fuguet', *LALR*, 59:43–54. *LALR*, 60, is a special issue 'Isabel Allende Today', ed. R. G. Feal and Y. E. Miller. Particularly useful are B. E. Jörgensen, '"Un puñado de críticos": navigating the critical readings of Isabel Allende's work' (128–46), which gives a balanced overview; L. Gould Levine, 'Weaving life into fiction' (1–25); and Z. N. Mártinez, 'Isabel Allende's fictional world: roads to freedom' (51–73). Licia Fiol-Matta, **A Queer Mother for the Nation: The State and Gabriela Mistral*, Minneapolis, Minnesota U.P., xxix + 269 pp. I. M. Carrasco, 'Interdisciplinariedad, interculturalidad y canon en la poesía chilena e hispanoamericana actual', *Estudios Filológicos*, 37:199–210. Gisela Norat, **Diamela Eltit and the Subversion of Mainstream Literature in Chile*, Newark, Delaware U.P. — London, Associated U.P., 264 pp.

COLOMBIA

Héctor H. Orjuela, **Historia crítica de la literatura colombiana: Introducción al estudio de las literaturas indígenas*, Bogotá, Guadalupe, 226 pp. J. Noé Herrera, **Bibliografía femenina de Colombia, 1800–2002: guia de monografías*, 3 vols, Bogotá, Libros de Colombia, 1252 pp. G. García Márquez, 'The novel behind the novel', *Review: Latin American Literature and Arts*, 65:48–54. Edison Darío Neira Palacio, *La gran ciudad latinoamericana: Bogotá en la obra de José Antonio Osorio*, NY, Lang, 247 pp. David Jiménez, **Poesía y canon: los poetas como críticos en la formación del canon de la poesía moderna en Colombia, 1920–1950*, Bogotá, Norma, 197 pp. G. Bustamante Zamudio, '*Ekuóreo*: una historia por re-construir; a propósito del minicuento en Colombia', *Cuento en red: estudios sobre la ficción breve*, 5 <http://cuentoenred.org/cer/present/present.html>.

PARAGUAY

O. Araujo-Mendieta, 'La manipulación del discurso a través de su recontextualización en *Yo el supremo*', *RCEH*, 26:123–40.

PERU

James Higgins, **The Literary Representation of Peru*, Lewiston, Mellen, 324 pp. P. Granados, 'Los poetas vivos y más vivos del Perú (y de otras latitudes)', *Crítica: Revista de la Universidad Autónoma de Puebla*, 95:30–42. Kerstin Störl, **Zur Übersetzbarkeit von Sprachkontaktphänomenen in der Literatur: Analyse spanischsprachiger pro-indianischer Prosa aus dem Peru des 20. Jahrhunderts*, Frankfurt, Lang, 197 pp. Three new Peruvian literary journals were launched in 2002: *Libros & artes: revista de cultura de la Biblioteca Nacional del Perú*, Lima, Bib. Nac. del Peru; *Revista hispanoamericana de literatura*, Lima, San Marcos; *Revista peruana de literatura*, Lima, El Centro. S. Castro-Klaren, ' "Como chancho, cuando piensa": el afecto cognitivo en Arguedas y el con-vertir animal', *RCEH*, 26:25–40. J. A. Giménez Micó, 'The deterritorialization of knowledge in *El zorro de arriba y el zorro de abajo*', *ib.*, 83–106. M. Moore, 'Social sciences and the novel in Peru: a study of identity and nomenclature in *Todas las Sangres* by José María Arguedas', *HRJ*, 3:153–66, refers to Arguedas's anthropological work. M. E. Luna Escudero-Alie, 'Cosmovisión andina en el relato "Warma Kuyay" de José María Arguedas', *QIA*, 91:31–43.

URUGUAY

Mario Benedetti, **Subdesarrollo y letras de osadía*, M, Alianza, 249 pp. D. Butler, 'Juan Carlos Onetti: a metaphysics of time', *BSS*, 79:487–512, compares his temporality to Kafka and Beckett. M. L.

Figueredo, 'El eterno retorno entre la poesía y el canto popular: Uruguay, 1960–1985', *RCEH*, 26:299–321. M. Rowinsky, 'Palabras sin aduanas: el escritor y el exilio', *ib.*, 167–78.

VENEZUELA

Belford Moré, **Saberes y autoridades: institución de la literatura venezolana (1890–1910)*, Caracas, La Nave Va, 156 pp. Leonardo Azparren Giménez, **El realismo en el nuevo teatro venezolano*, Caracas, Univ. Central de Venezuela, 111 pp.

BRAZILIAN LITERATURE

By Mark Dinneen, *Spanish, Portuguese and Latin American Studies, University of Southampton*

I. General

Textos de intervenção, ed. Vinicius Dantas, SPo, Duas Cidades–Editora 34, 389 pp., is a collection of 39 articles by Antônio Cândido, previously published in newspapers and journals. Including studies of Brazilian poetry and fiction, discussion of approaches to literary analysis, and articles on various aspects of Brazilian culture and politics, it highlights the extraordinary diversity of C.'s writing. *Bibliografia de Antônio Cândido*, ed. Vinicius Dantas, SPo, Duas Cidades–Editora 34, 269 pp., gives full details of all C.'s published work, and major studies produced of it. Maria Cândida Ferreira de Almeida, *Tornar-se outro: o topos canibal na literatura brasileira*, SPo, Annablume, 295 pp., discusses the different representations of cannibalism in major works of Brazilian literature, with reference to Mário de Andrade, Guimarães Rosa, and José de Alencar, among others. Oswald de Andrade's theory is used to analyse the relationship between cannibalism and perceptions of Brazilian national identity. E. Fitz, 'Internationalizing the literature of the Portuguese-speaking world', *His(US)*, 85:439–48, outlines the new opportunities that exist for literature written in Portuguese to achieve international recognition. M. A. da Costa Vieira, 'Escritura cervantina e mito quixotesco no romance brasileiro', *ib.*, 455–65, analyses the impact of *Don Quijote* on the work of such writers as Machado de Assis, Lima Barreto, and José Lins do Rego. L. Masina, 'Alcides Maya, Cyro Martins y Sergio Faraco: Tradición, transformación y renovación en la literatura de fronteras de Rio Grande do Sul', *RCLL*, 56:129–39, compares the work of the three writers in order to examine the changes regionalist writing has undergone in Rio Grande do Sul, emphasizing its interaction with River Plate cultural currents and practices. Evando Nascimento, *Ângulos: literatura e ensaios*, Chasecó, Argos, 212 pp., includes studies of Guimarães Rosa, Modern Art Week, Machado de Assis, and Lúcio Cardoso in a collection of essays covering diverse aspects of literary criticism and cultural theory. Joaquim Norberto de Sousa e Silva, *História da literatura brasileira e outros ensaios*, R, Ze Mario, 424 pp., claims to be the broadest one-volume collection of S.'s pioneering writing on Brazil's early literary history, mainly of interest for what it reveals about Romantic perceptions of literature and culture. S. L. Prado Bellei, 'Odeandrade @ pindorama.org.br, ou E mail para Oswald', *LBR*, 39.1:43–64, discusses how Oswald de

Andrade's theory of *antropofagia* highlights the uses that Brazilian cultural activity can make of new electronic technology in the context of globalization. Luiz Costa Lima, *Intervenções*, SPo, Edusp, 432 pp., contains 26 of C.L.'s essays of literary analysis, written since the mid 1990s for newspaper publication. Coverage includes major names such as Machado de Assis, da Cunha, and Melo Neto, as well as recent writers like Dora Ribeiro, Bernardo Cavalho, and Milton Hatoum. *Identidades e representações na cultura brasileira*, ed. Rita Olivieri-Godet and Lícia Soares de Souza, João Pessoa, Idéia, 2001, 230 pp., consists of 12 essays on Brazilian artistic production, mainly of the North East. Alencar, Melo Neto, Ramos, and da Cunha are covered in literary studies which emphasize the role of land and memory in the search for Brazilian cultural identity. *Brasil 2001: A Revisionary History of Brazilian Literature and Culture* (*Portuguese Literary and Cultural Studies*, 4–5), Dartmouth, Massachusetts U.P., 2001, 758 pp., contains over 60 essays on Brazilian literature and culture, very varied, but broadly linked by their common concern with issues of national identity. Among the writers studied are Gilberto Freyre, Gonçalves Dias, Machado de Assis, Lins do Rego, Lispector, and Guimarães Rosa. *Personae: grandes personagens da literatura brasileira*, ed. Lourenço Dantas Mota and Benjamin Abdala Junior, SPo, SENAC, 2001, 324 pp., discusses some of the best known protagonists in Brazilian fiction, with studies of 12 novels which contrast their approaches towards characterization. Donaldo Schüler, *Na conquista do Brasil*, Cotia, Ateliê, 2001, 255 pp., discusses the different perceptions of the relationship between centre and periphery that have been presented by Brazilian thinkers and writers. R. Zilberman, 'De *Memórias póstumas de Brás Cubas* a *Grande Sertão: Veredas* — o demônio em viagem', *Veredas*, 3, 2000: 195–215, is a comparative study of the novels by Machado de Assis and Guimarães Rosa, focusing on their treatment of memory and the journey as a theme. E. Finazzi-Agrò, 'Geografias de memória. A literatura brasileira entre história e genealogia', *ib.*, 557–67, reviews how the problem of the origins of Brazilian culture has been debated by various 19th-c. and 20-c. writers. M. K. McNee, 'Alegorizando as periferias: pontos de articulação entre a crítica cultural de Frederic Jameson e Roberto Schwartz', *ib.*, 245–64, highlights similarities in the way in which the two critics reformulate the dichotomy between the local and the universal. João Paulo Coelho de Souza Rodrigues, *A dança das cadeiras: literatura e política na academia brasileira de letras (1896–1913)*, Campinas, Unicamp, 2001, 251 pp., is an informative history of the early years of the Brazilian Academy of Letters, examining growing tensions within it and its relations with the Brazilian government. Of particular interest is its study of contrasting perceptions between major writers of the value and role of literature. David Treece, *Exiles, Allies, Rebels: Brazil's Indianist Movement, Indigenist Politics, and the Imperial Nation-State*, Westport, Greenwood, 2000, 271 pp., seeks new perspectives on Indianism through a detailed re-examination of the movement within its historical context. A wide range of Indianist writers from the colonial period and the 19th c. are analysed, emphasizing the diverse political positions that informed their work.

2. Colonial

Constance Janiga-Perkins, *Immaterial Transcendences: Colonial Subjectivity as Process in Brazil's 'Letter' of Discovery (1500)*, NY, Lang, 2001, 144 pp., is a stimulating and original work of criticism, which offers a detailed analysis of Pêro Vaz de Caminha's letter, drawing particularly on postcolonial theory to suggest new interpretations. The text, it is argued, reveals ambiguities and contradictions that show its representation of the Indian to be considerably more complex than indicated in studies to date. F. Ferreira de Lima, 'Paraíso e inferno na Bahia de Gabriel Soares de Sousa', *Veredas*, 3, 2000:43–53, serves as a good introduction to S.'s *O Tratado descritivo do Brasil em 1587*. J. A. Hansen, 'Ler e ver: pressupostos da representação colonial', *ib.*, 75–90, discusses philosophical aspects of Brazilian art and literature of the 17th century.

3. Nineteenth Century

Silvina Carrizo, *Fronteiras da imaginação. Os românticos brasileiros: mestiçagem e nação*, Niteroí, Eduff, 2001, 174 pp., compares the different ways in which national identity is related to racial identity in seven Romantic novels. Alencar, Macedo, Guimarães, Taunay, and Almeida are the writers studied. Luciano Trigo, *Viajante imóvel: Machado de Assis e o Rio de Janeiro de seu tempo*, R, Record, 2001, 298 pp., discusses how M.'s response to, and participation in, the social and cultural life of late 19th-c. Rio de Janeiro found expression in his writing. Eládio Vilmar Weschenfelder, *A paródia nos contos de Machado de Assis*, Passo Fundo U.P., 2000, 94 pp., examines the creativeness of M.'s parodies of European literary forms and conventions, in studies of 10 of his best known stories. Wagner Luis Madeira, *Machado de Assis, homen lúcido: uma leitura de 'Esaú e Jacó'*, SPo, FAPESP–Annablume, 2001, 134 pp., discusses the methods M. uses in the novel to play with the reader's expectations. Márcia Lígia Guidin, *Armário de vídrio: velhice em Machado de Assis*, SPo, Nova Alexandria, 2000, 189 pp., offers a comparative study of *Memórias póstumas de Brás Cubas* and *Memorial de Aires*. C. Lima Duarte, 'O olhar de uma viajante brasileira: Nílsia

Floresta', *Veredas*, 3, 2000: 141–48, briefly reviews F.'s journeys through Europe and the travel writing she produced as a result. L. Petit, 'Machado de Assis à "Roda da vida": das *Memórias póstumas* as *Memorial de Aires*', *ib.*, 161–70, discusses the reasons underlying M.'s unorthodox approach to novel writing. F. Maciel Silveira, 'O conto machadiano ou "a realidade é boa, o Realismo é que não presta"', *ib.*, 4: 95–103, is a discussion of the particular form of realism evident in M.'s short stories.

4. Twentieth Century

Poetry

Ana Maria Lisboa de Mello, *Poesia e imaginário*, Porto Alegre, Edipucrs, 260 pp., uses theories of the imaginary as a framework for detailed analysis of Cecília Meireles's *Solombra* and Murilo Mendes's *Poesia em pânico*. Joana Matos Frias, **O erro de Hamlet: poesia e dialéctica em Murilo Mendes*, R, Sete Letras, 129 pp. Maria Célia Rua de Almeida Paulillo, *Tradição e modernidade: Afonso Schmidt e a literatura paulista (1906–1928)*, SPo, Annablume–Fapesp–Unifieo, 228 pp., is a carefully researched survey of S.'s early poetry and prose, emphasizing its historical context. The study highlights the diversity of his writing and the contrasting tendencies evident within it. Davi Arrigucci Jr., *Coração partido: uma análise da poesia reflexiva de Drummond*, SPo, Cosac e Naify, 153 pp., discusses a range of Drummond de Andrade's poetry, recognizing different phases but seeking a basic unity in its underlying thought. Marlene de Castro Correia, **Drummond: a magia lúcida*, R, Jorge Zahar, 192 pp. S. Brandellero, 'In between wor(l)ds: the image of the 'entre-lugar' in João Cabral de Melo Neto's *Agrestes*', *PortSt*, 18: 215–29, examines how the poems explore 'in-between spaces' in order to present new perspectives on the issues of major concern to M.N.: literary creation, social deprivation, and his own mortality. M. E. Serra Hügli, 'Escritas de leituras na poética de Drummond', *Veredas*, 3, 2000: 255–63, surveys references to other writers and artists in the poetry of Carlos Drummond de Andrade. Â. M. Dias, 'Topografias poéticas da pós modernidade no Brasil', *ib.*, 4, 2001: 21–44, discusses changing approaches to poetry in Brazil during the second half of the 20th century. M. Ribeiro, 'A produção do signo na escritura de João Cabral de Melo Neto', *ib.*, 233–43, focuses on M.N.'s *Antiode* in a linguistic study of his poetry. M. E. Maciel, 'América Latina en diálogo con oriente: conversación con Haroldo de Campos', *CHA*, 628: 83–94, is an interview in which C. discusses links between Brazilian poetry and poetic traditions elsewhere. Vera Lúcia de Oliveira, *Poesia, mito e historia no modernismo* *brasileiro,* SPo, Edifurb–UNESP, 2001, 342 pp., considers how different modernist poets approached the problem of Brazil's cultural dependency, and attempted to mediate between national concerns and international artistic currents. Oswald de Andrade, Cassiano Ricardo, and Raul Bopp are the poets examined in detail. Italo Moriconi, *Como e por que ler a poesia brasileira do século* XX, R, Objetiva, 153 pp., provides students beginning the study of Brazilian poetry with a useful guide to major movements and poets.

DRAMA

Berenice Raulino, *Ruggero Jacobbi: presença italiana no teatro brasileiro,* SPo, Perspectiva, 305 pp., is a detailed assessment of J.'s contribution to the modern Brazilian theatre, highlighting the creative fusion of European and Brazilian experience. J. C. M. Alves and M. Noe, 'From the street to the stage: the dialectical theatre practice of Grupo Galpão', *LBR*, 39.1 : 79–93, examines the development of the company's work since its foundation in 1983, highlighting its alternation between improvised street performance and formal staged drama. T. Brandão, 'Ora, direis ouvir estrelas: historiografia e história do teatro brasileiro', *LATR*, 35.1 : 67–97, argues that studies of the history of the Brazilian theatre have continued to follow models and concepts established in the 19th c., and urgently need to be revised to take on board changes that have occurred in Brazilian drama during the last 100 years. J. C. M. Alves and M. Noe, 'Myth and madness in Grupo Galpão's expressionistic production of *Álbum de família*, *ib.*, 35.2 : 19–36, studies how the mythic elements and theme of madness in Nelson Rodrigues's play were expressed through innovative techniques in a highly acclaimed 1990 staging of the work. A. L. Vieira de Andrade, '*As moças* de Isabel Câmara: a subversão do drama tradicional', *ib.*, 37–53, examines how C.'s play of 1969 challenges firmly established forms of traditional drama, particularly through its treatment of issues of impotence and passivity. N. Telles, 'O grotesco na dramaturgia de Ariano Suassuna', *ib.*, 35.2 : 57–63, is a brief discussion of the relationship between humour in S.'s plays and forms of comedy common in Brazilian popular culture. Celso de Oliviera, '*Orfeu da Conceição*: variation on a classical theme', *His(US)*, 85 : 449–54, compares the 1953 play by Vinicius de Moraes with the film versions produced in 1959 and 1998. H. Thorau, 'De Arcádia às masmorras — o Teatro de Arena conta Tiradentes', *Veredas*, 4, 2001 : 105–16, focuses particularly on the relationship between the play by Boal and Guarnieri and the theories of Brecht.

PROSE

Closer to the Wild Heart: Essays on Clarice Lispector, ed. Cláudia Pazos Alonso and Claire Williams, Oxford, Legenda, 242 pp., is a valuable contribution to the study of L.'s writing, consisting of 12 thought-provoking essays which offer diverse critical approaches and cover most areas of the author's work. They are thematically grouped into sections on autobiography and identity, issues of gender, class, and race, and on the critical reception of L.'s work. Gabriela Lírio Gurgel, *A procura da palavra no escuro: uma análise da criação de uma linguagem na obra de Clarice Lispector*, R, Sette Letras, 2001, 81 pp., focuses on L.'s original approach towards language in a short survey of her major novels. Edgar Cézar Nolasco, *Clarice Lispector: nas entrelinhas da escritura*, R, Annablume, 269 pp., examines what the newspaper chronicles that L. wrote in the 1960s and 1970s reveal about the creation of her major work. Paulo Germano Barrozo de Albuquerque, **Mulheres claricianas: imagens amorosas*, R, Relume Dumará, 109 pp., studies the links between L.'s work and the philosophy of Gilles Deleuze. Diane E. Marting, *The Sexual Woman in Latin American Literature*, Gainesville, Florida U.P., 2001, 345 pp., includes a chapter on Lispector's *Uma aprendizagem, ou o livro dos prazeres*, in a study of how issues of female sexuality are treated in a series of modern Latin American novels. Alaor Barbosa, *Um cenáculo na paulicéia*, Brasília, Projecto, 294 pp., is a well researched work of literary history, studying the activities and published work of the largely forgotten *Cenáculo* group, of which Monteiro Lobato was the dominant member. Maria Aparecida Lopes Nogueira, *O cabreiro tresmalhado: Ariano Suassuna e a universalidade da cultura*, SPo, Palas Athena, 295 pp., examines S.'s life, work, and aesthetic theories in order to explain how and why his writing seeks to combine the erudite with the popular, and the local with the universal. Luiz Fernando Medeiros de Carvalho, *Literatura e promessa: figuração e paradoxo na literatura brasileira contemporânea*, Niteroi, Eduff, 82 pp., analyses novels of the 1990s by Silviano Santiago, João Gilberto Noll, and Sonia Coutinho. The works are studied in the light of theories of language and speech by Derrida, Austin, and Searle. *Lusosex: Gender and Sexuality in the Portuguese-Speaking World*, ed. Susan Canty-Quinlan and Fernando Arenas, Minneapolis, Minnesota U.P., 320 pp., discusses the writing of Gilberto Freyre, Lispector, Caio Fernando Abreu, and Silviano Santiago, among others, in an exploration of discourses of sexuality in a wide range of cultural expression. Original and provocative, the contributions employ a variety of theoretical approaches. D. R. S. Ferreira, 'Na obra de Carolina Maria de Jesus, um Brasil esquecido', *LBR*, 39.1:103–19, analyses J.'s diary, *Quarto de despejo*, to show how a new and distinct vision of Brazil results from her situation as a marginalized black woman. J. A. Pasta Jr., 'Prodígios de ambivalência: notas sobre *Viva o povo brasileiro*', *NovE*, 64:61–71, is a study of the treatment of history and myth in Ubaldo Ribeiro's novel. Zilá Bernd and Francis Uteza, *O caminho do meio: uma leitura da obra de João Ubaldo Ribeiro*, Porto Alegre U.P.–UFRGS, 2001, 149 pp., contains seven essays on U.R.'s writing, highlighting the relationship between the regional and the universal through an examination of narrative technique, forms, and symbolism. Particular emphasis is given to *Viva o povo brasileiro*. *Civilização e exclusão: visões do Brasil em Érico Veríssimo, Euclides da Cunha, Claude Lévi-Strauss e Darcy Ribeiro*, ed. Flávio Aguiar and Ligia Chiappini, SPo, Boitempo, 2001, 254 pp., brings together scholars from different disciplines in a series of studies of the major work of the four writers. The common objective is to analyse how each responded to different moments of social tension or conflict in 20th-c. Brazil. Raquel Guimarães, **Pedro Nava, leitor de Drummond: a memória, os retratos, a leitura*, Campinas, Pontes, 95 pp. *O clarim e a oração: cem anos de 'Os sertões'*, ed. Rinaldo de Fernandes and Tripoli Gaudenzi, SPo, Gerão, 581 pp., is a mixed assortment of contributions by well-known writers and critics which comment upon the significance of the work for Brazilian cultural history. **'Os sertões' de Euclides da Cunha*, ed. José Leonardo do Nascimento, SPo, Unesp, 206 pp. Deise Dantas Lima, *Encenações do Brasil rural em 'Corpo de baile' de Guimarães Rosa*, Niteroí, Eduff, 2001, 133 pp., examines R.'s recreation of Brazilian rural life through a study of different novellas within the work. Edna Tarabori Calobrezi, *Morte e alteridade em 'Estas estórias'*, SPo, Edusp, 2001, 270 pp., uses a psychoanalytical approach to analyse the work by Guimarães Rosa, emphasizing its treatment of human mortality. B. Zilly, 'A reinvenção do Brasil a partir dos sertões: viagem e literatura em Euclides da Cunha', *Veredas*, 3, 2000: 149–60, discusses the originality of C.'s vision of Brazil, seen as the result of his travels through the interior. C. Pazos Alonso, 'Do centro e da periferia: uma re-leitura de *Laços de família*', *ib.*, 287–99, identifies unifying themes in Lispector's stories, and discusses how they might explain the order in which the stories appear in the collection. R. Silviano Brandão, 'A nau catrineta: velhas receitas, novos sabores', *ib.*, 301–06, analyses a story by Rubem Fonseca in the light of Oswald de Andrade's theory of cultural cannibalism. V. Arêas, 'Além do princípio de superfície: *O filantropo* de Rodrigo Naves', *ib.*, 429–40, analyses the structure, style, and themes of the work. Beatriz Resende, 'Imagens da exclusão', *ib.*, 509–21, discusses the theme of social exclusion in writing by Raduan Nassar, Paulo Lins, and Rubens Figueiredo. R. Cordeiro Gomes, 'Cidade e nação na narrativa brasileira contemporânea; uma guerra de relatos', *ib.*, 609–19, uses critical work by Beatriz Sarlo as the starting point for discussion of the relationship between city and nation in Brazilian prose of the 1980s and 1990s. I. M. Fonseca dos Santos, '*La Pierre du Royaume, version pour Européens et brésiliens de bon sens*: a dupla tradução do romance de Ariano Suassuna', *ib.*, 4. 2001:117–31, discusses problems encountered in producing the French translation of S.'s *A pedra do Reino*. M. C. Villarino Pardo, '40 anos de uma estreia: a entrada de Nélida Piñon no campo literário brasileiro com *Guia-Mapa de Gabriel Arcanjo* (1961)', *ib.*, 233–43, examines the context within which the novel appeared, and its importance for the development of P.'s writing career and for Brazilian fiction as a whole.

IX. ITALIAN STUDIES

LANGUAGE

By Simone Bacchini, *Queen Mary, University of London*, and
Roberta S. Middleton, *University of Bristol*

1. General

La linguistica italiana alle soglie del 2000 (1987–1997 e oltre), ed. Cristina Lavinio, Ro, SLI–Bulzoni, 730 pp., is a useful tool to get an overview of research in all fields of Italian linguistics for the decade. *Multilingualism in Italy Past and Present*, ed. Anna Laura Lepschy and Arturo Tosi, Oxford, Legenda, 230 pp., is a collection of papers presented at the Istituto Italiano di Cultura in London. Consisting of twelve chapters, it deals with various aspects of the linguistic situation of present-day Italy. Multilingualism, the notion of 'standard', sexism and gender issues, and the language of legal texts are some of the topics of this valuable collection. Alfonso Leone, *Conversazioni sulla lingua italiana*, F, Olschki, 159 pp., is an informal but rigorous work, illustrating points of the grammar of Italian, its phonology, and its writing system, together with socio-historical notes. Fabio Rossi, **La lingua in gioco. Da Totò a lezione di retorica*, Ro, Bulzoni, 316 pp., is an exploration of the language used by the famous comedian.

2. History of the Language, Early Texts, and Diachronic Studies

Of particular interest to the historian of the language are Francesco Bruni, **L'italiano nella storia,* Bo, Il Mulino, 228 pp., and Giuseppe Patota, **Lineamenti di grammatica storica dell'italiano*, Bo, Il Mulino, 212 pp. The former is an important tool for the understanding of the creation and development of the literary language from the 14th to the 20th c. revisiting, as it does, some of the most important stages in the process of codification of literary Italian. The latter, on the other hand, is an internal history of the Italian language in which P. traces the major phonetic, morphological, and syntactic changes that took place from Latin into Italian. The book also contains a chapter on the languages of Medieval Italy. The external history of the language is also studied in an original contribution by Luca Serianni, **Viaggiatori, musicisti, poeti*, Mi, Garzanti, 320 pp., which considers, among other aspects, the linguistic impressions of foreign travellers to Italy in the 18th and 19th c. and the language of Verdi's and Puccini's operas. Conference proceedings of interest include **Eteroglossia e* *plurilinguismo letterario*: I. *L'italiano in Europa. Atti del XXI Convegno interuniversitario di Bressanone (2–4 luglio 1993)*. II. *Plurilinguismo e letteratura. Atti del XXVIII Convegno interuniversitario di Bressanone (6–9 luglio 2000)*, ed. Furio Brugnolo and Vincenzo Orioles, 2 vols, Ro, Il Calamo, 248, 585 pp. *L'Accademia della Crusca per Giovanni Nencioni*, pref. Francesco Sabatini, F, Le Lettere, xii + 538 pp., is a very rich and diverse collection of articles in honour of G. Nencioni. Among the studies relevant to this section it contains the following: A. Castellani, 'I più antichi ricordi del primo libro di memorie dei frati di penitenza di Firenze, 1281–7' (3–24), M. Dardano, 'Di *che* nel *Decameron*' (53–64), P. G. Beltrami, 'La voce *azione del* Tesoro della Lingua Italiana delle Origini' (65–76), A. Stussi, 'Una lettera in volgare da Esztergom a Padova verso la fine del Trecento' (77–86). L. Tomasin, 'Perugia 1364', *SLI*, 28:261–71, provides a critical edition of and a linguistic commentary to a text written in *volgare perugino* (British Library Add. MS 23203). A. Ricci, 'Sintassi e testualità dello *Zibaldone di Pensieri* di Giacomo Leopardi', *ib.*, 27, 2001:33–59. E. Stark, 'Indefiniteness and specificity in Old Italian texts', *JSem*, 19:315–32, is an invaluable study of the syntax and semantics of indefinite determiners (*uno, alcuno, certo*) and argues for an intermediate stage in their grammaticalization process as attested in the three Old Tuscan novella collections used as textual evidence. G. Lauta, '"Che cosa", "cosa" nell'italiano antico', *SLI*, 27, 2001:94–96. G. Giusti, 'Possessives in Old Italian', *UVWPL*, 12:83–105, provides an invaluable description of the syntax of possessive adjectives and their pronominal counterparts in Old Italian (Florentine) cast within the Minimalist Program. S. Telve, 'Prescrizione e descrizione nelle grammatiche del Settecento (I)', *ib.*, 3–32, and then continued in 28:197–260, adds an important chapter to the external history of the Italian language by bringing to light obscure and forgotten textual evidence related to 18th-c. grammars. In L. Lindgren, 'Un témoignage de l'italien écrit régional il y a 200 ans: les notes de voyage de Giuseppe Acerbi', pp. 385–92 of *Langage et référence: mélanges offerts à Kerstin Jonasson à l'occasion de ses soixante ans*, ed H. Kronning et al. (Acta Universitatis Upsaliensis, 63), Uppsala, Studia Romanica Upsaliensia, 2001, the author analyses a variety of 18-c. regional Italian written by a merchant who travelled to Lapland and provides a commentary on the spelling, morphology, and some lexical traits, including dialectal and foreign influences.

3. Phonetics and Phonology

In T. Piske et al., *'The production of English vowels by fluent early and late Italian-English bilinguals', *Phonetica*, 59:49–71, the primary aim is to determine if fluent early bilinguals who are highly experienced in their second language (L2) can produce L2 vowels in a way that is indistinguishable from native speakers' vowels. The authors conclude that most of the observed differences between the native English speakers and the early-high groups were for vowels spoken in non-word condition. M. Swerts, E. Krahmer, and C. Avesani, 'Prosodic marking of information status in Dutch and Italian: a comparative analysis', *JPh*, 30:629–54, reports on a comparative analysis of accentuation strategies within Italian and Dutch noun phrases. S. Calamai, 'Vocali d'Italia. Una prima rassegna', *QLLP*, 2, 2001[2002]:83–94, defines the acoustic features of different vocalic systems, focusing in particular on Tuscan varieties. C. Celato, 'Sviluppo storico e acquisizione di categorie fonologiche: le affricate in italiano', *ib.*, 109–19. M. D'Imperio, *'Italian intonation: an overview and some questions', *Probus*, 14:37–69.

4. Morphology

A. Albright, 'Islands of reliability for regular morphology: evidence from Italian', *Language*, 78:684–709, deals with the representation of regular morphological processes. A. presents the results from a non-probe (wug) experiment in Italian, in which speakers rated the acceptability of novel infinitives in various conjugation classes. These results indicate that such subregularities are in fact internalized by speakers even for a regular morphological process. S. C. Sgroi, '"-Uario": un suffisso misconosciuto', *SLI*, 27, 2001:60–74. G. Rovere and J. Schambony, 'Morfologia derivativa del linguaggio giuridico. Il suffisso -ità', *RF*, 114:307–14.

5. Syntax

Caterina Donati, **Sintassi Elementare*, Ro, Carocci, 200 pp., is an introduction to the fundamentals of syntactic theory through the observation and discussion of the syntactic properties of Italian. This textbook also contains practical sections with exercises. M. Squartini, 'The internal structure of evidentiality in Romance', *StLa*, 25, 2001:297–334, discusses the evidential uses of the Future, Conditional, and Indicative Imperfect in various Romance languages (mostly French, Italian, Portuguese, or Spanish) and the semantic factors that underlie the choice between them. C. di Meola, 'Synchronic variation as a result of grammaticalization: concessive subjunctions in German and Italian', *Linguistics*, 39, 2001:133–149, deals with the grammaticalization of German and Italian concessive subjunctions from a primarily synchronic perspective. On the basis of data drawn from contemporary written texts, M. shows that different stages of ongoing grammaticalization can coexist synchronically. M. concludes that morphological, semantic, and synctactic parameters of grammaticalization turn out to be closely interrelated in the two languages, showing considerable similarities. A. Cardinaletti, 'Against optional and null clitics: right dislocation vs. marginalization', *Studia Linguistica*, 56: 29–57, analyses Italian Right Dislocation, which seems to instantiate an optional anticipatory clitic pronoun, from a formal theoretical stance. C. shows that the distribution of the anticipatory clitic pronoun is not free. When the clitic is absent, we do not have an instance of Right Dislocation, but of marginalization. M. A. Depiante, 'On null complement anaphora in Spanish and Italian', *Probus*, 13, 2001 : 193–222, argues for the distinction between deep and surface anaphora on the basis of Spanish and Italian data. By observing that certain verbs in Spanish and Italian allow their infinitival clausal complements to be null, D. proposes that these null clausal complements in Spanish and Italian are instances of Null Complement Anaphora, and not of surface anaphora such as VP ellipsis in English. S. Schneider, 'Beobachtungen zu *il fatto che* in gesprochenen Italienisch', *RF*, 114: 27–34, examines the construction *il fatto che* after verbs expressing factuality: however, the distribution of this item after verbs that do not presuppose the factuality of the dependent clause seems to suggest that *il fatto che* is developing into a semantically empty nominal element in modern Italian. J. Jernej, 'Intorno alle strutture predicative dell'italiano', and A. L. Lepschy, G. Lepschy, and H. Sanson, 'A proposita di *essa*', respectively pp. 387–96 and 397–410 of *L'Accademia della Crusca per Giovanni Nencioni*, cit.

6. Semantics

P. M. Bertinetto, 'Sulle proprietà tempo-aspettuali dell'Infinito in italiano', *QLLP*, 2, 2001[2002]: 9–53, represents a systematic attempt to identify and discuss the temporal-aspectual properties of this verb form. R. Veland, '*Maggiormente* avverbio di comparazione (ma non solo)', *RF*, 114: 35–42, analyses the semantic behaviour of *maggiormente* and argues that in modern Italian this adverb is becoming a synonym of *più*.

7. Pragmatics and Discourse

D. S. Giannoni, 'Worlds of gratitude: a contrastive study of acknowledgement texts in English and Italian research articles', *ApL*, 23: 1–31, brings another contribution to the study of academic texts by looking at the underexplored area of scholarly acknowledgements in English and Italian journals. The indexical meaning of the pronoun *I* in Italian work-meeting conversation, in its marked use, is discussed in A. Fasulo and C. Zucchermaglio, 'My selves and I: identity markers in work-meeting talk', *JP*, 34:1119–44. The authors investigate what motivates marking the first person pronoun through the analysis of a number of *I*-marked utterances. C. Vegaro, ' "Dear Sirs, what would you do if you were in our position?": discourse strategies in Italian and English money-chasing letters', *ib.*, 34:1211–33, looks at a particular type of business letter, the so-called money-chasing letter. The analysis considers both the macro and the micro level, with attention to elements such as mood, modality, reference system, and use of metadiscourse. R. Waltereit, 'Imperatives, interruption in conversation, and the rise of discourse markers: a study of Italian *guarda*', *Linguistics*, 40:987–1010.

8. Lexis

L. Tomasin, *'Schede di lessico marinaresco militare medievale', *SLeI*, 19:11–33. G. Petrolini, *'Necrofili e pipistrelli. Qualche considerazione su "becchino" e "beccamorto" ', *ib.*, 36–57, is a history of the two terms and of the attitudes that have accompanied them. The history of 'ultimamente' and its use is to be found in A. Ricci, *'Ultimamente', *ib.*, 59–66; and a survey of the semantics of the term 'armonia' in C. Luzzi, *'Per la semantica di armonia: in margine a strumenti recenti di lessicologia musicale', *ib.*, 67–107. L. Matt, *'Neologismi e voci rare delle lettere di Giambattista Marino (con uno sguardo all'epistolografia cinquecentesca)', *ib.*, 19:110–82. S. Telve, 'Retrodatazione di voci onomatopeiche e interiettive. Un esempio di applicazione lessicografica degli archivi elettronici', *ib.*, 229–77, is an informative discussion of the way in which the new CD-ROM technology can be used to determine with more precision when a particular term entered the language. P. Cordin and L. Flöss, 'Creature fantastiche nella toponomastica trentina', *RID*, 26:121–44, presents and examines place-names of the Trentino region derived from those of imaginary creatures. J. Hajek, '*Parlaree*: un gergo italianizzante in inglese', *ib.*, 26:167–90, discusses the possible Italian origin of many of the words of the little known English slang *Parlaree* (or *Polari*). M. Fantuzzi, 'Francesismi recenti nella politica italiana', *LN*, 68:34–59, examines recent borrowings from French political lexicon. A history of the word 'scugnizzo' can be found in M. Loporcaro, 'L'etimologia di scugnizzo: un problema di motivazione semantica', *ib.*, 65–72. M. Fanfani, 'Badante e ausiliaria', *ib.*, 121–23, comments on two not-so-new words that seem to have entered the language recently. The world of make-up is investigated in P. D'Achille, 'Rimmel e Mascara', *ib.*, 103–06.

9. Sociolinguistics

Percezione dello spazio, spazio della percezione. La variazione linguistica fra nuovi e vecchi strumenti di analisi, ed. Mari D'Agostino, CSFLS, Palermo, 183 pp., collects the proceedings of a conference, held at Palermo in 2001, whose main theme was perceptual dialectology. General methodological questions are addressed, together with more specific ones, such as language and migration (both internal and external) and more specific topics regarding the linguistic situation in Sicily. Carla Marcato, *Dialetto, dialetti e italiano*, Bo, Il Mulino, 224 pp., is a wide-ranging and accessible work on the relationship between 'dialect' and 'language' both within and outside Italy. It describes the situation of both Italo- and non Italo-Romance idioms in modern Italy with an eye to recent legislation, and in particular that of the dialects (their use, degree of normalization, vitality, etc.) which are placed within the appropriate social and historical context. Notwithstanding the ubiquity of television and, more recently, the advent of the Internet, radio remains a lively medium and offers several possibilities for linguistic study. Enrica Attori, *La parola alla radio. Il linguaggio dell'informazione radiofonica*, F, Cesati, 276 pp., offers a detailed analysis of speech on Italian radio stations. In particular, it focuses on the language of news bulletins and news programmes. The findings are compared and contrasted with the language of the press and that of everyday conversation. The language of the press is scrutinized, and criticized, in M. Arcangeli, 'Se quella dei quotidiani è una lingua. Con esercizi di scrittura', *LN*, 68:107–21. O. Castellani Pollidori, 'Aggiornamento sulla "lingua di plastica"', *SLI*, 28:161–96, is a review of the many clichés and common-places in modern Italian, especially those of the media. F. L. M. Savoia, 'La legge 482 sulle minoranze linguistiche storiche. Le lingue di minoranza e le varietà non standard in Italia', *RID*, 24, 2000[2001]:7–50, takes a close look at the recent law (Nov. 1999) on the protection of the historic linguistic minorities of Italy and compares it with previous legislation, placing it within the wider context of minority language rights. A. Pizzorusso, 'Legislazioni europee sulle lingue minoritarie', *LS*, 36, 2001:211–17, offers a survey of minority-language legislation in Europe, its history, current situation, and future perspectives. The legal status of Italian in Switzerland, as well as that of German, French, and Romansh, is discussed in F. Rash, 'The German-Romance language borders in Switzerland', *JMMD*, 23:112–36. Language-contact phenomena and interference are also discussed, and recent research into language attitudes and linguistic cleavage summarized. L. Eichinger, 'South Tyrol: German and Italian in a changing world', *ib.*, 137–49, presents a picture of the present-day situation of Italian and German in South Tyrol. Historical background and the current legislation with its outcomes are discussed, together with bilingualism, multilingualism, and multiculturalism. Misunderstanding and negotiation of meaning in an intercultural setting within Italy are discussed in A. Boario, 'Fraintendimenti e negoziazione del significato: un'indagine sociolinguistica a Torino', *RID*, 24, 2000[2001]:51–84, where B. looks at verbal exchanges between Italians and non-Italians at such places as a railway information office or a school of Italian for foreigners. Her aim is to show what linguistic strategies are employed by both native and non-native speakers where there is a specific need to obtain and give relevant information. **Comunicare nella torre di Babele. Repertori plurilingui in Italia oggi*, ed. Silvia Dal Negro and Paola Molinelli, Ro, Carocci, 160 pp., looks at the different linguistic repertoires and communicative strategies of different ethnic/linguistic individuals and groups that have been in Italy for centuries, decades, or only months. The situation of Italian as L2, with an outline of the history of its development, can be found in Massimo Vedovelli, **L'italiano degli stranieri. Storia, attualità e prospettive*, Ro, Carocci, 228 pp. L. Ricci, '"Pubblicità": le parole per (non) dirlo. Un caso di eufemismo nell'italiano di oggi', *SLeI*, 19:299–319, deals with the various ways of referring to commercial breaks on Italian television. **Lingue di confine, confini di fenomeni linguistici/Grenzsprachen. Grenzen von linguistischen Phänomenen*, ed. Patrizia Cordin and Rita Franceschini, Ro, Bulzoni, 380 pp., present several papers, from different perspectives, on issues of contact linguistics.

10. Psycholinguistics and Language Acquisition

E. Bascetti and M. S. Bascelli, 'Italian children's understanding of the epistemic and deontic modal verbs *dovere* "must" and *potere* "may"', *JCL*, 29:87–107, an interesting article, presents the result of a study assessing children's understanding of two Italian modal verbs, *dovere* and *potere*, in their double function of qualifications of speaker's belief (epistemic) and behaviour regulation (deontic). The ability of children to use figurative expressions and to create new ones is explored by M. C. Levorato and C. Cacciari, 'The creation of new figurative expressions: psycholinguistic evidence in Italian children, adolescents, and adults', *ib.*, 29:127–50. This article, which shows that the ability to use and create figurative language in a sensible way is a long process spanning many years, will be of interest not only to psycholinguists and linguists in general, but also to teachers. A. Laudanna, M. Voghera, and S. Gazzellini, 'Lexical representations of written nouns and verbs in Italian', *BL*, 81 : 250–63. This article deals with the differences of input representations in the Italian mental lexicon. The authors, basing themselves on visual experimental evidence, conclude that nouns and verbs are represented differently in the orthographic input lexicon. P. Tabossi, S. Collina, and M. Sanz, 'The retrieval of syntactic and semantic information in the production of verbs', *ib.*, 264–75, is an investigation of the syntactic hypothesis, which states that aspectual auxiliary assignment in Italian is a syntactic phenomenon. The authors interpret the findings as suggesting that thematic information is involved. D. Eddington, 'Dissociation in Italian conjugations: a single route account', *ib.*, 291–302, questions a report by Say and Clahsen of an experiment on assignment of past participle suffixes to nonce words in Italian. Their evidence suggests 'a dual-route model that assigns the theme vowel of the first conjugation, while storing it lexically in other conjugations'. L. Colombo and C. Burani, 'The influence of age of acquisition, root frequency, and context availability in processing nouns and verbs', *ib.*, 398–411. Another investigation of both linguistic and pedagogical interest is the article C. Burani, S. Marcolini, and G. Stella, 'How early does morphological reading develop in readers of a shallow orthography?', *ib.*, 568–86, reporting a study of lexical and morpholexical reading in Italian children aged 8–10. The authors came to the interesting conclusion that morpholexical reading is available and efficient in young readers of a shallow orthography, not very differently from adults. Since its inception, the study of language-impaired individuals has always proved useful to shed light on aspects of the functioning of language. In S. Mondini et al., 'Why is "Red Cross" different from "Yellow Cross"? A neuropsychological study of noun–adjective agreement within Italian compounds', *ib.*, 621–34, the researchers investigated the speech of two Italian non-fluent aphasic patients. The focus was on noun–adjective agreement in compounds and noun phrases. The findings led the authors to hypothesize differential processing for compounds as opposed to noun phrases. So-called 'late-talkers' have always been a worry for parents and interesting for linguists. Examining cross-cultural variation in linguistic responsiveness to young children in English- and Italian-speaking dyads of mother and child, L. Girolametto et al., 'Mother-child interactions in Canada and Italy: linguistic responsiveness to late-talking toddlers', *International Journal of Language & Communication Disorders*, 37.2 : 153–71, find that Italian mothers use more utterances, speak more quickly, and use a more diverse vocabulary than their Canadian counterparts, and that this behaviour is mirrored in the children. However, Italian mothers respond to fewer of their children's vocalizations and use a smaller percentage of imitations and interpretations. U. Bortolini et al., 'Specific language impairment in Italian: the first steps in the search for a clinical marker', *ib.*, 77–93, reports on three studies designed to assess the utility of particular language measures to determine specific language impairment in Italian-speaking children. Previous studies have focused exclusively on English and this work tries to redress the imbalance. N. Müller, 'Crosslinguistic influence in early child bilingualism: Italian/German', *EUROSLA Yearbook*, 2:135–54, assumes that early language separation and crosslinguistic influence coexist in the bilingual child during the same developmental stage. The paper aims to show that particular grammatical properties determine how crosslinguistic influence manifests itself. The acquisition of verb and noun morphology in children aged 2–7 is discussed in L. B. Leonard, C. Caselli, and A. Devescovi, 'Italian children's use of verb and noun morphology during the pre-school years', *First Language*, 22.3:287–304, an article presenting the results of a research project designed to assess Italian-speaking children's use of a series of grammatical morphemes, such as present-tense verb inflections and noun plural inflections.

11. Dialectology

Hermann W. Haller, *La festa delle lingue. La letteratura dialettale in Italia*, Ro, Carocci, 360 pp., an important contribution to the study of Italian dialect literature, is divided into two parts: the first offers a linguistic introduction to the different forms of literary production in dialect (poetry, theatre, and prose); the second, comprising 17 chapters, traces the main literary sources for each Italian region and provides useful historical surveys as well as references. C. Lavinio, 'Dialettalismi e regionalismi nella produzione letteraria italiana', *Eudossia*, 1.1:35–45, deals with the unavoidable presence of dialectal and regional terms in literary texts.

PIEDMONT. In C. Goria, 'The complexity of the left periphery: evidence from Piedmontese', *Syntax*, 5:89–115, a central point of contention is the relation in Piedmontese between verb-interrogative clitic inversion and main wh-questions introduced by the complementizer *che* (wh + *che*). By proposing an analysis of Piedmontese interrogatives which separates the features [wh] and [Q], G. claims that interrogative V-to-C movement and matrix wh + *che* questions target different CPs, hence the verbs in C and *che* do not compete for the same position. C. Tortora, 'Romance enclisis, prepositions and aspect', *NLLT*, 20:725–57, provides evidence which supports the view that direct object clitics in Romance are independent syntactic elements adjoined to functional heads. In particular, T. shows that an array of puzzling facts involving potential clitic hosts in the dialect of Borgomanero can be understood once we adopt the view that object clitic hosts must be taken to independently occupy distinct functional heads. T. Hohnerlein-Buchinger, 'Spigolature lessicali in un'area di transizione. Concordanze lessicali dell'Alta Valle Bormida con i dialetti dell'Italia settentrionale', *ZRP*, 118:441–90, offers a lexical study with the aim of identifying and isolating this complex linguistic area.

VENETO. Lorenzo Tomasin, *Il volgare e la legge. Storia linguistica del diritto veneziano*, Padua, Esedra, 2001, 333 pp., provides an illuminating account of Venetian legalese. V. Formentin, 'Antico padovano *gi* da ILLI: condizioni italo-romanze di una forma veneta', *LS*, 37:3–28, offers a very detailed and rich study of the distribution of the forms *li i gi* expressing the masculine plural definite article and identifies *gi* as a conservative Paduan form.

CENTRAL AND SOUTHERN DIALECTS. M. Loporcaro, 'Il pronome *loro* nell'Italia centro-meridionale e la storia del sistema pronominale romanzo', *VR*, 61:48–116, revisits the question of the origin of the central-southern pronominal forms of the type *loro*. He rejects the accepted notion that the forms *loro* in the central-southern varieties of vernacular were not autochthonous but came from the North. In a painstakingly detailed account of the attestations of these forms in texts from central and southern Italy, he demonstrates that, although some examples show external influence, the forms derived from Latin ILLORUM were also continued in these varieties. Id., 'Le consonanti retroflesse nei dialetti meridionali: articolazione e trascrizione', *BCSS*, 19, 2001:206–33, sheds light on some fundamental points about the articulation of retroflex consonants and their phonetic transcription in southern dialects. M. Aprile, 'Fonti per la conoscenza del lessico medievale in Italia meridionale, I: il *Cortulario* del monastero di Santa Maria delle Tremiti', *Contributi di Filologia dell'Italia Mediana*, 15, 2001:5–87.

TUSCANY. L. Gianelli, *Toscana*, Pisa, Pacini, 145 pp. + CD-ROM, is an updated revision of a work, originally published in 1976, describing the varieties of Tuscan. A. Nesi and T. Poggi Salani, 'La Toscana', pp. 413–51 of *I dialetti italiani. Storia, struttura, uso*, ed. Manlio Cortelazzo et al., T, UTET, is an important contribution in two parts: the first part contains a synchronic analysis of the linguistic situation in Tuscany, while the second focuses on the role of Tuscan in the formation of a national language. Silvia Calamai *'Nel gergo nostro brutalissimo'. La parlata di Travalle fra dialetto pratese e dialetto fiorentino.* Prato, Pentalinea, 174 pp., provides an important survey of the linguistic situation of a boundary area. L. Gianelli, M. Magnanini, and B. Pacini, 'Le dinamiche linguistiche al confine tra Toscana e Lazio: conservazione, innovazione e ristrutturazione', *RID*, 26:49–72, probes into the complexities of neighbouring linguistic areas. A very fertile field of research has proved to be the realm of phonetics and phonology: S. Calamai, 'Il vocalismo atono della varietà pisana: prime evidenze sperimentali', *QLLP*, 2, 2001[2002]:64–82. P. Sorianello, 'Per una rappresentazione uditiva dei segmenti vocalici: il caso senese', *ib.*, 159–73. G. Marotta and N. Nocchi, 'La liquida laterale nel livornese', *RID*, 25:285–326. S. Calamai, 'Aspetti qualitativi e quantitativi del vocalismo tonico pisano e livornese', *ib.*, 153–207. **La fonetica acustica come strumento di analisi della variazione linguistica in Italia. Atti delle XII giornate di Studio del Gruppo di Fonetica Sperimentale (AIA) Macerata 13–15 dicembre 2001*, ed. A. Regnicoli, Ro, Il Calamo, includes: P. Sorianello, 'Il vocalismo dell'italiano senese: un'indagine sperimentale' (47–52); S. Brigato and G. Marotta, 'La modalità imperativa nell'italiano di Lucca. Prime linee di tendenza' (111–16); S. Calamai, 'Vocali atone e toniche a Pisa' (39–46); M. Dall'Aglio, P. M. Bertinetto, and M. Agonigi, 'Le durate dei foni vocalici in rapporto al contesto nel parlato di locutori pisani: primi risultati' (53–58); G. Marotta et al., 'Le occlusive sorde dell'italiano parlato a Pisa: varianti aspirate e fricative' (71–76). B. Gili Fivela, 'Tonal alignment in two Pisa Italian peak accents', and G. Marotta, 'L'intonation des énoncées interrogatifs ouverts dans l'italien toscan' (475–78), respectively pp. 339–42 and 475–78 of **Proceedings of Speech Prosody 2002, Aix-en-Provence 11–13 Aprile 2002*, ed. B. Bel and I. Marlien. N. Binazzi, 'Tradizioni del discorso e percezione di identità: riflessioni su alcuni contesti d'uso fiorentino', pp. 247–75 of **'Che cosa ne pensa oggi Chiaffredo Roux?' Percorsi della dialettologia percezionale all'alba del nuovo Millennio. Atti del Convegno internazionale (Bardonecchia, 25–27 maggio 2000)*, ed. M. Cini and R. Regis, Alessandria, Orso. R. Stefanini, 'Su alcuni idronimi tosco-romagnoli (Santerno, Diaterra; Savio, Siave, Savena, Senio)', *LN*, 68:95–100.

CORSICA. Marie-José Dalbera-Stefanaggi, **Essais de linguistique corse*, Ajaccio, Piazzola, 2001, 300 pp., is a collection of articles, some of them already published, on aspects of Corsican phonology and lexis. A. Nesi, 'La Corsica', *I dialetti italiani*, cit., 959–74, brings up to date the linguistic situation of Corsica.

LAZIO. For V. Formentin, 'Tra storia della lingua e filologia: note sulla sintassi della *Cronica* dell'Anonimo romano', *LS*, 37:203–50, an important syntactic analysis conducted for philological ends, see below under 'Duecento and Trecento II', p. 384.

ABRUZZO. R. Hastings, '"Ze sende cchiù fforte". Il rafforzamento fonosintattico nel dialetto abruzzese', *RID*, 25:209–83.

CAMPANIA. M. Cennamo, 'La selezione degli ausiliari perfettivi in napoletano antico: fenomeno sintattico o sintattico semantico?', *AGI*, 87:175–222, illustrates auxiliary selection in a number of Neapolitan texts dating from the 14th–15th c. which show the first signs of change whereby the auxiliary 'have' becomes the only perfective auxiliary. After arguing against two alternative proposals to account for the phenomenon, C. offers an account based on a scalar notion of unaccusativity which allows one to account in a principled way for the variation in the distribution of auxiliary selection in one-argument intransitive verbs in old Neapolitan. M. Russo, 'La categoria neutrale nella diacronia del napoletano: implicazioni morfologiche, lessicali, semantiche', *VR*, 61:117–50, considers the history of the category neutral in Neapolitan and provides a detailed picture of the processes of reanalysis of the morphological forms that signal the neutre genre in the history of Neapolitan. M. Russo, 'Metafonesi opaca e differenzazione vocalica nei dialetti della Campania', *ZRP*, 118:195–223. N. De Blasi, 'Per la storia contemporanea del dialetto nella città di Napoli', *LS*, 37:123–57, offers an important sociolinguistic survey on the complex linguistic situation of modern Naples.

APULIA. Very useful linguistic surveys for Apulia are: M. Aprile et al., *'La Puglia', *I dialetti italiani*, cit., 679–756, and Alberto Sobrero and Immacolata Tempesta, *Puglia*, Ro–Bari, Laterza, 206 pp. A. Miglietta, 'L'infinito in Salento oggi', *RID*, 26:73–93, traces the use of the infinitive, the areas of diffusion, and extralinguistic influences. Of particular interest is **I dialetti dell'Italia meridionale con particolare riferimento a quelli della Calabria. Atti del Convegno di Cassano Ioanio (25–27 ottobre 1996). Linguistica Italiana Meridionale VI-VII, 1998–2000*, ed. Pasquale Caratù, Ro–Bari, Laterza, containing Id., 'Il dialetto di S. Giovanni Rotondo: storia e geografia' (79–96), which, starting from the analysis of vowel and consonant systems as well as morphological traits, shows that the variety spoken in S. Giovanni Rotondo shares many common features with the Adriatic areas of Molise and Abruzzi; Id., 'Saggio di lessico pugliese; il Gargano' (233–40); and M. L. di Biase, 'La lingua delle tavolette votive del Santuario di M. SS. Incoronata di Foggia' (121–232), a morphosyntactic analysis of the language of the *tavolette votive* which concludes that they can be considered genuine evidence of *italiano popolare*. **La dialettologia oltre il 2001. Atti del Convegno di Sappada, 1–5 luglio 2001*, ed. Gianna Marcato, Padua, Unipress, contains Immacolata Tempesta, 'Dal dialetto al repertorio, fra archivi e atlanti. Per un nuovo progetto regionale' (63–72), which proposes a new project aimed at the formation of an 'Archivio Pugliese Linguistico Informatico'; C. Tarantino, 'Inchieste dialettali nella Puglia centro-settentrionale . Prime proposte per un archivio' (325–36); M. Carosella, 'Interferenze di forme o dinamiche di strutture? Influssi bidirezionali fra dialetti e italiano regionale nell'area garganica settentrionale' (299–306), which deals with tonic vowels and their realization in the varieties spoken in northern Apulia. R. Coluccia, 'La grafia dei testi pugliesi', ed. Rosario Coluccia, pp. 85–102 of **Scripta man(n)Ot. Studi sulla grafia dell'italiano*, Congedo, Galatina.

CALABRIA. **Vincenzo Padula. Vocabolario Calabro*, I, *A–E*, ed. John B. Trumper, Ro–Bari, Laterza, 692 pp., is more than a critical edition with commentary of the original work by Padula. In many instances the lexical material is reassessed and revised without losing sight of Padula's aims. S. Zenobi, 'Modelli intonativi dell'interrogazione in una varietà di italiano meridionale (Cosenza)', *RID*, 25:85–108. Francesco Laruffa, **Dizionario calabrese–italiano. Il linguaggio della piana di Gioia Tauro*, Ro, Adnkronos Libri.

SICILY. *BCSS*, 19, 2001, offers a number of outstanding investigations into syntactic, sociolinguistic, and lexical issues in modern and old Sicilian: L. Amenta, 'Costrutti esistenziali e predicazioni locative in siciliano antico' (75–99); D. Bentley, 'Proprietà sintattiche dell'oggetto diretto in siciliano antico: la distribuzione della particella partitiva *(in)di*' (101–19); R. Sardo, 'Le *cronachette* del notaio Li Testi di Paternò (1621–1627): considerazioni di sociolinguistica retrospettiva' (121–42); A. Michel, M. Lehmann, and R. Crinò, 'Le descrizioni del dialetto siciliano: dai viaggiatori stranieri del sette e ottocento fino ai primi romanisti tedeschi' (143–89); G. Alfonzetti, 'Le funzioni di *code switching* italiano–dialetto nel discorso dei giovani' (235–64); A. Leone, 'Terze aggiunte al *Vocabolario siciliano*' (191–206); and M. Napoli, 'Usi particolari e insoliti dei vegetali in Sicilia' (265–91).

12. Sardinian

A. Dettori, *'La Sardegna', *I dialetti italiani*, cit., 898–958, is a very useful survey. F. Floricic, 'La morphologie du vocatif: l'exemple du sarde', *VR*, 61:151–77, examines the morphological and phonological properties of the vocative forms in modern *logudorese*. E. Blasco Ferrer, 'La carta sarda in caratteri greci del secolo XI. Revisione testuale e storico-linguistica', *RLiR*, 66:321–65, provides a new edition of one of the oldest text in Sardianian as well as a textual and linguistic commentary. Pietro Casu, **Vocabolario sardo logudorese–italiano*, ed. Giulio Paulis, Nuoro, Ediz. Ilisso.

DUECENTO AND TRECENTO I
DANTE

By Paola Nasti, *Lecturer in Italian, University of Manchester*

1. General

2002 saw the publication of the much anticipated Hainsworth, *Companion*, which devotes some sixteen entries to D. and his *œuvre*. D.'s presence is, however, all-pervasive in the volume: over 100 entries quote D.'s name and refer to his works and life. The entries on D. are brief and informative, but do not neglect to offer the reader some meaningful insight into the complexity of D. works as well as their *fortuna* and their iconographic renditions. The bibliographical information is up to date and essential. Apart from the more specific entries on Dante, sections on allegory, the Middle Ages, and medieval literary theory devote substantial space to the poet, his works, and his intellectual formation. The volume should prove a useful study tool for English-speaking students of Dante.

Theological, religious, and ecclesiastical aspects of D.'s works continue to attract the attention of D. scholars. Sergio Cristaldi, *Dante di fronte al Gioachimismo*, 1, *Dalla 'Vita Nuova' alla 'Monarchia'*, Caltanissetta, Sciascia, 2000, 418 pp., offers significant insights into the possible influence on D. of the radical *profetismo* of Joachim of Fiore and his followers, Pietro di Giovanni Olivi and Ubertino da Casale. C. urges a reconsideration of the assumptions of modern criticism on the issue and argues that D. had only indirect knowledge of Olivi's ideas. Proceeding mostly by close analysis of passages from *VN*, *Cvio*, and *Mon.*, C. sets out to show that the similarities between D.'s prophetic views and those of Olivi and Ubertino are as fundamental as the differences that divide them. The similarities are said to lie in the common worship of the *usus pauperis*, but C. also subtly suggests that D.'s concerns were chiefly political and judicial, and his perspective mainly secular. The volume is a valuable contribution to the study of D.'s *profetismo* and provides vivid examples of the multiple influences that informed D.'s ideas on the role of the Church, Church poverty, and Church reform. The range of references on these topics extends from Bonaventure to Seneca, which also makes the book a useful journey into the history of medieval ideas. Anna Maria Chiavacci Leonardi, *Dante Alighieri. Invito alla lettura*, Cinisello Balsamo, San Paolo, 2001, 96 pp., is a somewhat 'popularizing' but competent volume, sponsored by the Catholic Church, which focuses on the Christian and ethical dimensions of the *Commedia*. To illustrate her arguments C. presents passages from the *VN*, the *Cvio*, and the *Commedia*. On the same topic but from a more academic perspective, *Dante poeta cristiano*, F, Polistampa, 2001, 232 pp., includes studies by P. Boyde, C. Ossola, A. M. Chiavacci Leonardi, and M. G. Duprè dal Poggetto on the Christian aspects of the *DC* and the relationship between medieval figurative art and D.'s work. The opening and closing essays by P. Boitani and F. Mazzoni respectively address the issue of D.'s Christianity on a more general level and with reference to his *œuvre* as a whole. Based on the belief that D. was a devotee of the Virgin Mary, and devoutly written by Renato Nicodemo, *La Vergine Maria nella Divina Commedia. Aspetti del pensiero teologico di Dante Alighieri*, F, Atheneum, 2001, 77 pp., provides a very brief survey of the presence of Marian themes in the three *cantiche*. N. argues that the Virgin was the muse who inspired the *DC* and maintains that D. believed in the mystery of the Immaculate Conception, but offers insufficient evidence to support his thesis.

A thoughtful and dense meditation on the development of D.'s political thought from the *Cvio* to the *DC* and the *Monarchia* is Gennaro Sasso, *Dante, l'imperatore e Aristotele*, Ro, ISIM, 326 pp. In the substantial section devoted to the *DC*, on the basis of a careful analysis of some of the 'fundamentally' political cantos, S. suggests that little space is given to political theory in the poem: the focus is on lamentation and invective against the Church and secular rulers, and D.'s political thought is mainly developed in the *Cvio* and the *Monarchia*. Presenting a great mass of material and examples, S. reassesses D.'s appropriation of Aristotelian and scholastic ideas and supports D.'s Averroism in those sections of the *Mon.* that deal with the concept of the unity of the intellect.

Several of the 'general' volumes published in 2001–02 are collections of essays by individual scholars. Domenico De Robertis, *Dal primo all'ultimo Dante*, F, Le Lettere, 2001, vii + 216 pp., includes material already published elsewhere since 1971. Recapitulating the achievements of lifelong research into D.'s lyric poetry, the volume anticipated the publication of De R.'s new edition of D.'s *Rime*. The studies cover different areas of D.'s *œuvre* from the *VN* to the *DC*, from the *Fiore* to the *Rime*. Emilio Pasquini, *Dante e le figure del vero. La fabbrica della 'Commedia'*, Mi, Mondadori, 2001, x + 310 pp., is a collection of nine essays on subjects ranging from the phenomenon of intratextuality in D.'s works, to some of the thematic features of the *VN*, from D.'s ambiguous relationship with Cavalcanti to his *imitatio* of the classical *auctores*, from his exile and its impact on D.'s poetry to the use of similes and metaphors in the three *cantiche*. In the last chapter, *Per Dante nel terzo millennio*, P. surveys issues and *cruces* of D.'s *œuvre* that still offer scope for investigation. Luigi Scorrano, *Il Dante 'fascista'.*

Saggi, letture, note dantesche, Ravenna, Longo, 2001, 210 pp., includes *lecturae* of *Inf.* XIII and *Purg.* III and XVI, as well as comparative studies on D., Sereni, and Bevilacqua, but some of these essays, including the one from which the book's title is taken, were already noted in *YWMLS*, 62:343–45 and 63:412. Rather superficial and eclectic is the opening essay in Carmelo Ciccia, *Allegorie e simboli nel Purgatorio e altri studi su Dante*, Cosenza, Pellegrini, 198 pp., a slight treatment of symbols, metaphors, and allegories in *Purgatorio*, and the accompanying studies on the *DC* and D.'s *fortuna* are of a similar standard. Selene Sarteschi, *Per la Commedia e non soltanto per essa*, Ro, Bulzoni, 405 pp., collects some of her latest studies on D.'s *œuvre*, including essays on the *VN*, the *DC*, and the *Epistola a Cangrande*. The final chapter, the only unpublished item in the collection, is an introductory essay on the *DC* written for school and university students. Although lacking a clear structure and wide exemplification, the essay covers the major themes and intellectual concerns of the *DC*, from D.'s choice of title to his exile and *profetismo*. Gabriele Muresu, *Tra gli adepti di Sodoma: saggi di semantica dantesca, terza serie*, Ro, Bulzoni, 345 pp., is a collection of already published writings. Steno Vazzana, **Dante e la bella scola*, Ro, Ateneo, 237 pp., is another volume of collected writings, already published in part. For Giorgio Padoan, **Ultimi studi di filologia dantesca e boccacciana*, ed. A. M. Costantini, Ravenna, Longo, 173 pp., see below under 'Duecento and Trecento II', p. 393.

The last significant 'general' volumes are the collected papers of two conferences to celebrate the seventh centenary of the journey narrated by Dante. Both include essays by leading D. scholars on a variety of issues and set out to trace the current state of D. studies at the turn of the new millennium as well as offer new perspectives for the future. *Atti* (Florence) is divided into four parts: 'Visione/Viaggio', 'Prospettive filologiche', 'Dante e Firenze', and 'Dante e Cavalcanti'. Several articles are discussed in the appropriate sections below. Some studies of a more general scope are worth mentioning here, however. The third section of the volume includes essays on the relation between D. and his native city: G. Mazzotta, 'L'esilio da Firenze: il *De Vulgari eloquentia* e il cerchio della frode' (233–48), investigates the reasons behind the abrupt interruption of the *De Vulgari Eloquentia*. M. argues that they are to be found in D.'s need to merge history and prophecy, the sublime and the humble. To substantiate his thesis, M. shows that traces of the poet's meditation on language are evident in *Inf.* XXXI–XXXIV. A. A. Iannucci, 'Firenze, città infernale' (217–32), outlines the presence of Florence throughout the *DC* and asserts the importance of D.'s exile, 'per lui propedeutico alla sua vera missione di poeta' (228). Providing interesting documentation, S. Noakes, 'Dante e lo sviluppo delle istituzioni bancarie a Firenze: "i subiti guadagni'' '(249–63), suggests the possibility of interpreting D.'s political thought in the light of the development of a sophisticated Florentine financial system. G. Tanturli, 'L'immagine topografica di Firenze nella poesia di Dante' (263–74), reviews Florentine localities mentioned in D.'s works. The last section offers some significant essays on the relationship between D. and Cavalcanti. R. Antonelli, 'Cavalcanti e Dante: al di qua del *Paradiso*' (289–302), reviews the presence of Cavalcanti in the works of D. and competently explores the affinities between the two poets. Proceeding by close reading, A. reveals that D.'s *Donne ch'avete* can be read as a development of themes and meditations first introduced by Cavalcanti, namely 'il valore della parola in sé', and 'il tema della donna "angelicata"' (292). He goes on to argue that in *Purg.* the allusive presence of Cavalcanti is signified by Matelda's reference to the 'possibile intelletto' (*Purg.* xxv, 65). R. M. Durling, '"Mio figlio ov'è" (*Inf.* x, 60)' (303–29), exposes D.'s playful severity against Cavalcanti in the *Vita Nuova*. The study goes on to examine *Inf.* x, 60 and suggests an intertextual relationship between the D. episode and the dialogue between God and Cain in *Genesis* (4. 9–12). According to Durling's ingenious reading D., unlike Cain, did not kill his 'brother' Guido, but 'se Dante uccise o voleva uccidere Guido, non fu col fare ma col dire' (316). L. Leonardi, 'Cavalcanti, Dante e il nuovo stile' (331–54), like Antonelli, invites us to rediscover the similarities between the two poets. To sustain his argument, L. registers for the first time some terms that are common only to Cavalcanti's lyrics and the *VN*, i.e. 'angoscia', 'anima triste', 'sbigottita'. These could be considered the traces of what L. convincingly regards as a continuity of language between the two poets.

Atti (Verona–Ravenna), I, includes four sections. The first, 'Dante uomo, pensatore, poeta', comprises general and informative studies on D., including: M. Miglio, 'Snodi della biografia dantesca' (41–55), on various *cruces* of D.'s biography, and A. A. Iannucci, 'Dante: poeta o profeta?' (93–114) on D.'s prophetic image and his Christianity. The second part, 'L'opera di Dante', includes essays on issues ranging from the influence of Islamic culture to the study of D.'s language, or from Beatrice to cases of intertextuality. C. Bologna, 'Beatrice e il suo *ánghelos* Cavalcanti fra *Vita Nuova* e *Commedia*' (115–41), is another investigation into the presence of Cavalcanti from *VN*, xxv, to *Purg.* xxv–xxx. B. offers a detailed analysis of the echoes of *Donna me prega* in the final cantos of *Purg.* and concludes (140) that 'fino alla fine della *Commedia* questo lessico riemergerà a tratti e a ondate mnemoniche, indicando il carico emotivo e ideologico che il cavalcantismo continua a deporre nell'elaborazione post-lirica' of the *VN* and of the *petrose.* M. Corti, 'Dante e la cultura islamica' (183–203), lucidly examines instances of interdiscursive and intertextual appropriation, as well as cases of actual 'imitation' of Islamic texts in D.'s works. To illustrate the third category of appropriation, C. offers convincing evidence of the presence of various passages of the *Liber Scalae Mahometi* in the *Commedia*. The third and last sections of the volume will be mentioned in the section on D.'s *fortuna*.

Among the article-length studies that deal with earlier as well as later works: E. Malato, 'La bellezza nella poesia di Dante', *Borsellino Vol.*, 97–108, argues that from the *VN* onwards the concept of beauty can be considered synonymous with virtue and purity. To illustrate his argument, M. offers clear close readings of passages taken from *VN*, *Cvio*, and *Commedia*. *AnI*, 20, on 'Exile Literature', gives ample coverage to articles on D.'s experience of exile. G. De Marco, 'L'esperienza di Dante *exul immeritus* quale autobiografia universale' (21–54), explores the way in which D. trasformed his exile into a noble and tragic experience. De M. also gives a survey of the influence of the Dantean model on Italian intellectuals who experienced exile, from Petrarch to Pavese and Levi. In a dense and complex article, G. P. Raffa, 'Dante's poetics of exile' (73–88), considers D.'s exile as an experience that shaped his dialectical hermeneutic, which keeps both past and present in play. D.'s hermeneutic approach is thus opposed to the Pauline-Augustinian model of conversion. R. also traces other medieval representations of exile to understand the specificity of D.'s own discourse. An elegant article by A. Cassell, 'The exiled Dante's hope for reconciliation: *Monarchia* 3:16.16–18' (425–50), asserts that despite the importance granted to the Aristotelian concept of earthly happiness, D. firmly believed in the supremacy of eternal blessedness. The ultimate union with a loving God is the culmination of the poem that D. wrote to attain the unity and order he was denied on earth.

Finally, there are a few items which have lately revitalized study of the cosmological, numerological, and esoteric aspects of D.'s work. G. Bartolozzi, *Exoterismo ed esoterismo nell'opera dantesca*, F, Atheneum, 2001, 74 pp., sympathetically outlines the history of esoteric interpretation of D.'s poetry from Gabriele Rossetti to Luigi Valli. G. Federici Vescovini, 'Dante e l'astronomia del suo tempo', *LIA*, 3:291–309, outlines D.'s astronomical knowledge from the *Cvio* to the *DC* and discusses some of his possibile sources, from Duns Scotus to Alpetragus and Campano of Novara. W. Pötters, '"La spera che più larga gira". Spazio della poesia e disegno del cosmo (*Lectura Dantis Geometrica* II)', *ib.*, 461–506, hypothezises that the number of lines of verse in the *DC* is equal to the diameter of the universal sphere whose rotation D. witnesses at the end of his *itinerarium*. M. Soresina, **Le* *secrete cose: Dante tra induismo ed eresie medievali*, Bergamo, Moretti Honegger, 263 pp.

2. Fortune

Medieval and Renaissance commentaries of the *DC* continue to interest contemporary D. scholars. Franco Quartieri, *Benvenuto da Imola. Un moderno antico commentatore di Dante*, Ravenna, Longo, 2001, 224 pp., considers Benvenuto's textual exposition as a sign of modernity and innovation within an exegetical tradition obsessed by the theological and scientific content of the poem. A. Stefanin, 'Sulle tracce di Pietro Alighieri: note sulla fortuna del *Comentum* in relazione alla fortuna editoriale della *Commedia*', *MR*, 15, 2001 : 177–202, explores at length the presence of Pietro Alighieri's *Comentum* in some modern and contemporary editions of the *Commedia*. A substantial section of *Atti* (Verona–Ravenna), 1, is entirely devoted to the commentary tradition of the *Commedia*. C. Villa, 'Il "secolare commento" alla *Commedia*: problemi storici e di tradizione' (549–68), thoroughly reconstructs the history of the reappropriation of the Medieval and Renaissance commentaries in the 19th and 20th c. Z. G. Barański, 'Lo studio delle fonti e l'esegesi medievale del testo della *Commedia*' (569–600), is a lucid and essential meditation on the appropriateness of different methodological and hermeneutic approaches to the medieval commentary tradition. Offering a number of telling examples, B. shows that the commentaries are useful tools in reconstructing the medieval cultural horizon, as well as D.'s library, but are often ineffective for the study of intertextual phenomena as well as for the understanding of D.'s experimental poetic strategies. Supplemented by a splendid range of illustration, L. Battaglia Ricci, 'Il commento illustrato alla *Commedia*: schede di iconografia trecentesca' (601–41), considers illustrations to have been an integral part of the editorial and exegetic projects that guided the production of the MSS taken into consideration. B. R. conducts two sets of investigations: a comparative analysis of the illustrations to the *DC*'s opening lines and an examination of the MS Riccardiano-Braidense. Highlighting the impact the Italian school system has had on *DC* exegesis, V. Marucci, 'I commenti moderni della *Divina Commedia* in Italia' (641–69), analyses modern and contemporary commentaries from Foscolo's to Chiavacci's. L. Miglio, 'Lettori della *Commedia*: i manoscritti' (295–323), is a fascinating study of the *DC*'s readership based on the traces left by actual readers on various manuscripts of the *Commedia*. M. highlights the distance that separates the image of the ideal reader D. wrote for and projected within his text and the actual readers, often left in their 'picciolettta barca' to make a titanic effort to read and interpret the *poema sacro*. In the same volume, L. Coglievina, 'Lettori della *Commedia*: le stampe' (325–70), offers a substantial analysis of the first printed editions of the *Commedia*. She underlines the importance of these editions for the establishment of the 'libro in volgare' in the humanist centuries and at the same time outlines the evolution of printed editions of the *DC*, from the text printed in Foligno to the philologically more accurate text edited by the *Vocabolario della Crusca*. E. Pasquini, 'Critica e filologia nell'esegesi dantesca' (671–99), sets out to find 'ciò che è vivo e ciò che è morto' in modern and contemporary exegesis of the *Commedia*. P. Stoppelli, 'I commenti danteschi e le nuove tecnologie' (701–09), presents the advantages of the new electronic data-bases of commentaries to the *Commedia*. S. Bellomo, 'Il progetto di censimento e edizione dei commenti danteschi' (711–26), presents the project supported by the Centro Pio Rajna to publish or republish critical editions of all the known commentaries of the *Commedia*. Other studies from *Atti* (Verona–Ravenna), I, describe with admirable clarity the history of D.'s reception among intellectuals and writers throughout the centuries: C. Calenda, 'Dante e i poeti del Tre e Quattrocento' (415–41), brilliantly outlines the substantial influence of the poetry and myth of D. on the Trecento poets and suggests that the humanists' polemical attacks on D. are a clear sign of the endurance of his authority. A. Battistini, 'Il modello e le suggestioni letterarie: Dante nella tradizione della letteratura e nella cultura popolare' (443–84), traces D.'s *fortuna* from the 15th to the 18th c. at both highbrow and 'popular' levels. B. argues that while the attitudes of intellectuals towards D. varied through the centuries, the poet's fame in popular culture withstood the passage of time. Three other studies included in *Atti* (Verona–Ravenna), I, deal with D.'s European fortune and D. studies from the 18th to the 20th c.: B. Basile, 'La scoperta di Dante nella cultura europea del Sette e Ottocento' (485–514), and D. Della Terza, 'Gli studi su Dante fuori d'Italia fra l'Otto e il Novecento' (533–47), and M. Guglielminetti, 'Dante e il Novecento Italiano' (515–31). On the same subject, M. Caesar, '"The central man of all the world": l'esaltazione di Dante nell'Ottocento europeo', *Atti* (Rome), 31–38, traces D.'s Italian and European fortune in the first part of the 19th c. C. argues that the romantic cult of D. was due to the newly perceived unity between past and present and to admiration for the *DC*'s celebration of the individual. In Mario Scotti, **Il Dante di Ozanam e altri saggi*, F, Olschki, 151 pp., the first two essays are 'Dante e i poeti francescani nella prospettiva critica di Frédéric Ozanam' (1–66); and 'Dante nel pensiero del Mazzini' (67–87).

D.'s *fortuna* among living poets and creative writers is the subject of *LC*, 30–31. The first part, 'Poeti d'oggi per Dante', includes writings by contemporary poets such as Elio Fiore, Mario Luzi, Gianni D'Elia, Cesare Viviani, Franco Loi, Luciano Erba, e Vittorio Sermonti. The second, 'Scrittori d'oggi per Dante', collects essays offered by prose writers Roberto Pazzi, Gina Lagorio, Raffaele Crovi, Franco Ferrucci, and Domenico Cofano. L. Gattamorta, 'Stilnovismo e dantismo di Luzi da *La Barca* a *Quaderno critico*', *L'Alighieri*, 19:25–51, sets out to examine Luzi's appropriation of D.'s poetry in his early writings. G. starts from L.'s acknowledgement of the important influence exercized by D. on his own poetic language and imagination, and goes on to provide a series of close readings which unfortunately do not always manage to prove her hypotheses. K. Schödel, 'Intertextueller Dialog: Dantes "Belacqua" in Samuel Becketts Roman *Dream of Fair to middling women*', *DDJ*, 77:149–73.

The influence of D. on classical and contemporary composers is the focus of some interesting studies published in recent years. Maria Ann Roglieri, *Dante and Music. Adaptation of the 'Commedia' from the Sixteenth Century to the Present*, Aldershot, Ashgate, 2001, 318 pp., explores musical adaptations of the *DC* through time. A separate chapter is devoted to each *cantica*, but Francesca da Rimini and the music inspired by her have a whole chapter to themselves. In keeping with her book, M. A. Roglieri, 'Twentieth-century musical interpretations of the "anti-music" of Dante's *Inferno*', *Italica*, 79:149–67, offers an article that analyses the 20th-c. vocal, dance, and multimedia adaptations of *Inferno*. M. Croese, *La Commedia come partitura bachiana. Osservazioni sul cielo del Sole e sul Sanctus della Messa in si minore*, Pisa, ETS, 2001, 126 pp., is a comparative study of *DC*'s rhythmic structure and the music of Bach. Particular attention is devoted to rhythmic forms in *Par.* x.

COMPARATIVE STUDIES. F. Marroni, 'Christina Rossetti dialoga con Dante e Petrarca', *StCrit*, 17:261–82, investigates the web of intertextual references to D. and Petrarch as well as the subversion of their poetry in Christina Rossetti's *Monna Innamorata* (1881). R. Wilson, 'Exile and relegation in Dante and Ovid', *AnI*, 20:55–72, compares and contrasts D.'s rendition of his exile to Ovid's of his confinement. W. highlights the differences between Ovid's relegation to Tomis and D.'s tragic exclusion from Florence, and believes that these fundamental discrepancies may underlie D.'s decision not to refer to Ovid's exile as an archetype for his own experience of exile. R. Imbach, 'Filosofia dell'amore. Un dialogo tra Tommaso d'Aquino e Dante', *SM*, 43:816–32, attempts to glimpse Aquinas's theory of love in D.'s appropriation of the saint's thought. Basing himself on a close reading of *Par.* XXVI and *Purg.* XVII, I. argues that the originality of D.'s thought lies in the emphasis placed on free will. Though interesting, the article is not always original in its conclusions and only touches upon the actual 'influence' of Thomas on D.'s understanding of love. Ferruccio Olivi, **La poesia e la mirabile visione: Dante e Manzoni*, Ro, Studium, 162 pp. I also note: P. Kuon, '"La prima radice del nostro amor". Petrarca zwischen Francesca und Laura', *DDJ*, 77 : 107–36; and T. Leuker, 'Boccaccios *donna Pietra*. Zur Dante-Rezeption in einer Episode des *Filocolo*', *ib.*, 137–47.

3. Textual Tradition

2002 was the year of the much-awaited edition of Dante Alighieri, *Rime*, ed. Domenico De Robertis, 3 vols (in 5 tomes), F, Le Lettere, ix + 991, 1237, 595 pp. De R.'s philological achievement is not without its surprises, such as the completely new ordering adopted for the lyrics. The five volumes collect a vast amount of important documentation, and, as was to be expected, the apparatus is rich and erudite. This is a monumental, albeit difficult and challenging, piece of scholarship. G. Gorni, 'Sulla nuova edizione delle *Rime* di Dante', *LItal*, 54 : 571–98, is a detailed review of De Roberto's work, which weighs the pros and cons of the new edition, but ultimately comes down in favour of what he calls 'questo nuovo modo di leggere Dante' (598). D. De Robertis, 'La tradizione delle *Rime*. Storia/non storia del testo', *Atti* (Florence), 133–48, outlines some of the criteria and conclusions of his edition of the *Rime*. F. Sanguineti, 'Per il testo della *Commedia*', *ib.*, 161–82, reports on the work for his now published new edition of the *DC* based on MS Urbinate latino 366 (cf. *YWMLS*. 63 : 389–80); M. Tavoni, 'Concordanze elettroniche e interpretazioni testuali. Schede per la *Commedia*', *ib.*, 183–201, offers some observations on a number of lexical items collected during the preparation of electronic concordances of the *DC* (http : //cibit.unipi.it) sponsored by the *Biblioteca Italiana Telematica*; E. Cecchini, 'Per un'indagine sistematica su formule e procedimenti argomentativi nelle opere in prosa di Dante', *ib.*, 133–48, starts from an analysis of the use of such terms as *assumpta* and *subsumpta* in the *Mon.*, and suggests the need to look for models other than those proposed by new German and American editors of the treatise. R. Abardo, 'L'edizione critica delle opere di Dante', *ib.*, 281–94, outlines the history of *DC* editing from Petrocchi to the ambitious *Censimento dei manoscritti delle opere di Dante e di interesse dantesco in Italia e nel mondo* planned by the Società Dantesca Italiana. M. Aversano, 'Firenze e il Veltro: prove di filologia dantesca', *CLett*, 30 : 3–10, is a correction to the notes on *Purg.* VI, 151, published in his *Dante daccapo. Il Purgatorio*.

DANTE COMMENTARIES: TEXTUAL TRADITION. Cristoforo Landino, *Comento sopra la Comedia*, ed. Paolo Procaccioli, 4 vols, Ro, Salerno, 2001, 2131 pp., is the first volume of the Edizione Nazionale of Dante commentaries, sponsored by the Centro Pio Rajna. It is an exemplary specimen of learned and meticulous textual scholarship. The first volume consists mainly of a lengthy and substantial interpretative introduction to Landino's work. C. Di Fonzo, 'Per l'edizione dell'ultima redazione inedita dell'Ottimo commento a Dante Alighieri', *L'Alighieri*, 19:5–23, publishes the results of her philological work on the last version of the Ottimo commentary, thoroughly discussing questions of chronology, interpolation, and the text's relationship with its sources. N. Bianchi, 'Brevi note su alcuni postillati danteschi', *StD*, 67:201–18, examines some unknown marginal glosses from MSS in Florentine libraries, which can be studied as important documents for an understanding of the *DC*'s reception. Four unpublished MSS of the *DC* held at the BNCF are described by S. Bertelli, in 'Nuovi testimoni per il censimento dei manoscritti e dei commenti della *Commedia*', *ib.*, 219–24. M. Boschi Rotiroti, 'Un frammento sconosciuto della *Commedia*', *ib.*, 226–33, presents and describes a fragment of *Par.* XIV.16–XV.15, which appeared in Christie's catalogue of 4 June 2002. G. Adini et al., 'Alla ribruscola della *Commedia* e dei suoi interpreti', *MR*, 15, 2001:77–88, gives an account of hitherto unknown commentaries and exegetic material on the *Commedia*.

4. Minor Works

In keeping with its enigmatic and complex nature, the *Cvio* has attracted a good many studies in recent years. E. Fenzi, 'L'esperienza di sé come esperienza dell'allegoria (a proposito di Dante, *Convivio* II i 2)', *StD*, 67:161–200, is a rich and brilliant discussion on one of the most controversial points of the *Cvio*, i.e. D.'s definition of the literal sense. Not all of F.'s conclusions can be considered here, but in line with Barański's latest studies on D.'s presentation of Orpheus, F. believes that 'l'esempio di Orfeo, figura dell'autore del *Convivio*, è [. . .] importante proprio per il modo in cui racchiude il nucleo dell'invenzione dantesca di un soggetto storico che agisce allegoricamente, e di una allegoria che attraverso lui si storicizza' (178). This understanding of the literal and allegorical senses 'authorizes' D. to bridge the distance between secular and sacred texts and transforms secular hermeneutics, which had until that point been based on the notion of *integumentum*: it was upon scripture that D. founded the hermeneutic truth of his writings. On a similar note, though less extensively, F. Ferrucci, 'Allegoria come auto-investitura: osservazioni sul *Convivio* di Dante', *Borsellino Vol.*, 81–96, examines several passages from the *Cvio* and argues that palinodes and the use of allegory were functional to D.'s self-promotion as a providential author. With numerous detailed examples, S. Gentili, 'Due definizioni di "cuore" nel *Convivio* di Dante: "secreto dentro", "parte dell'anima e del corpo" (II, 6, 2)', *LItal*, 54:3–36, analyses D.'s complex understanding of the term 'cuore' in *Cvio* II, vi, 2. The word signifies both the Aristotelian concept of a muscle that promotes the soul's movements as well as the Christian idea of *homo interior*. C. Vasoli, 'Dante filosofo e scienziato', *Atti* (Verona–Ravenna), 71–91, explores D.'s scientific knowledge in the *Cvio* and gives an account of the readings that might have formed his knowledge. On the other treatises: G. C. Alessio, 'Il *De vulgari eloquentia* e la teoria linguistica del medioevo', *ib.*, 203–27, analyses the relationship between D.'s linguistic theory in the *DVE* and medieval discussions on language. Among other things, A. considers the presence/absence in D.'s text of Roger Bacon and of a medieval commentary on Priscian attributed to Robert Kilwardby. A. thinks it not unlikely that 'Dante tenga sullo sfondo della sua intuizione [. . .] il modello che gli offrivano speculazioni linguistiche assimilabili a questa' (226), but ultimately he affirms the originality of D.'s linguistic theory. E. Mozzillo-Howell, '*Monarchia* II.x, and the medieval theory of consequences', *ItS*, 57:20–36, sets out to establish the correct reading of *Mon* II x among those offered by Prue Shaw and Richard Kay in their recent English translations of the treatise. To this end M.-H. examines medieval theories of logical argumentation from Augustine to Walter Burley. On the basis of her study of the *modus tollens* procedure, she accepts Shaw's 'a destructione consequentis' and considers unnecessary 'a positione consequentis'. O. Capitani, 'Dante politico', *Atti* (Verona–Ravenna), 57–79, briefly traces the history of *Mon* interpretation and argues that claims as to D.'s Averroism are not always justifiable or necessary.

On D.'s lyric output: F. Alfie, 'Durante's *Ars Amandi*: a structural reading of the *Fiore*', *FoI*, 36:5–25, analyses the *Fiore* as a parody of the medieval *ars amandi*, which presents a representation of love as sinful and irrational. The subversion of courtly ideology is achieved also through the parody of religious terminology and language. B. Barbiellini Amidei, 'Dante, Arnaut e le metamorfosi del cuore. A proposito di "Sols qui sai lo sobrafan qe.m sortz, vv. 26–28"', *PaT*, 6:91–108, analyses cases of intertextuality between Arnaut Daniel and Dante. In particular, B. A. addresses the occurrence in both poets of the metaphor of the heart as a lake and argues that D. borrowed from Arnaut. P. Allegretti, 'Il Maestro de "Lo bello stile che m'ha fatto onore" (*INF*. 1, 87), ovvero la matrice figurativa della sestina, da Arnaut Daniel a Virgilio', *StD*, 67:11–55, argues that *Inf.* 1, 87, might refer to D.'s works published before the *Commedia*. A. persuasively demonstrates the presence of Virgil's poetry in some of D.'s *sestine* and suggests that Arnaut and Virgil are brought together by D. in such a way that 'la parola rima vive della policromia della parola latina in punta di esametro' (55). Inspired by the work of A. Minnis, A. Ascoli, and many contemporary scholars, T. Levers, 'The image of authorship in the final chapter of the *Vita Nuova*', *ItS*, 57:5–19, carries out a lively and interesting interpretation of D.'s 'bid to appropriate to himself the authority which [. . .] was traditionally reserved for classical and religious non-vernacular authors' (7) in the *VN*. Whereas the rest of the narrative of the *VN* is retrospective, the final chapter blurs the division between narrator, poet, and character, providing 'the first image of Dante as an author figure' (18).

5. Comedy

David Gibbons, *Metaphor in Dante*, Oxford, Legenda, 206 pp., is a fascinating and subtle investigation of D.'s extraordinary experimentation with metaphors in the *DC*. The book is divided into three main sections. The first is mainly methodological. The central section examines D.'s metaphorical language in the three *cantiche*, but focuses primarily on *Paradiso*. G. attributes the high incidence of metaphors in *Par.* to the very religious and spiritual nature of its subject matter. Collecting a number of pertinent references, G. maintains that D. renewed traditional Christian metaphors in ways that are principally structural. He hypothesizes that to rejuvenate his sources D. employed three strategies or techniques: the selection of uncommon words, the extension of a metaphor by means of a grammatical construction based on neologisms, and the pursuit of *rimas caras*. The closing section of the volume concentrates on the reader's response to D.'s metaphors. Three kinds of reader are taken into consideration: the ideal reader, the Trecento commentators, and then Petrarch. Giuseppe Ledda, *La guerra della lingua. Ineffabilità, retorica e narrativa nella 'Commedia'*, Ravenna, Longo, 376 pp., addresses a question of great interest but strangely disregarded by D. scholars: the last monograph on 'ineffabilità' was published almost 70 years ago. L. scrutinizes the ineffability *topos* investigating the system of relations existing between three textual features of the *DC*: the declarations of 'indicibilità', other comments by the poet, and the 'setbacks' of D. poet and character. Drawing on extensive material and sources, from Genette to Aristotle, L. acutely argues that D.'s actualization of the ineffability *topos* contributes to the development of the narrative, as well as to the creation of his authorial self.

As was to be expected, a good number of studies cover a variety of religious and theological aspects of the *DC*. G. Carugati, 'Mistica, ermeneutica, Dante', *MLN*, 117:1–16, thoughtfully returns to the vexed question of D.'s mysticism. After a rather lengthy introduction on methods of reading and interpreting the *DC*, C. focuses on the 'cosa mistica' and discusses its nullifying effects on language. C. then moves on to assess the mystic status of the *DC* and underlines the difference between D.'s experience and that of the mystic: the *DC* should be considered an *itinerarium mentis et litterarum in Deum*. For D., C. argues, salvation and writing correspond: the *DC* is 'nella totalità del gesto di scrittura che la porge, una vigorosa riflessione sul rapporto tra linguaggio-scrittura e verità' (15). N. Cacciaglia, 'Per fede e per opere (una lettura del tema della salvezza nella *Divina Commedia*)', *CLett*, 30:265–74, is an informative study on D.'s idea of salvation in the *Commedia*. Concluding his survey, C. affirms that 'nell'esaltazione della fede, Dante giunge a sfiorare le tesi gianseniste' (274). P. Sabbatino, 'La croce nella *Divina Commedia*', *ib.*, 275–98, reviews the occurrences of the Cross at different points in the poem, from *Inf.* XXXIV and *Purg.* XXXII to *Par.* VI, VII, XII, XVII, XXXIII hinting, only superficially at times, at some of the cultural, religious, and iconographic traditions that may lie behind D.'s figurations to ascertain their significance in the economy of the *Commedia*.

In the past two years, the invention and representation of D.'s providential journey have attracted much attention on the part of D. scholars. L. Battaglia Ricci 'Viaggio e visione: tra immaginario visivo e invenzione letteraria', *Atti* (Florence), 15–73, focuses on the visual nature of the journey narrated by Dante. This rich and remarkable study examines the impact of the visual arts on the imagination and imagery of the *Commedia*. Providing a wide-ranging apparatus of illustrations, B. R. affords telling examples which demonstrate the interdiscursive relationship between the *DC* and the contemporary pictorial tradition. P. Dronke, 'Viaggi al Paradiso terrestre', *ib.*, 93–103, analyses some aspects of D.'s Earthly Paradise against other medieval representations of journeys to Eden. The interesting comparative material includes a variety of documents ranging from classical sources to hagiographical texts. C. Segre, 'Il viaggio di Dante come esperienza totale', *ib.*, 105–16, emphasizes the elements of originality in D.'s account of his journey, namely the centrality of the body and of time. He goes on to underline the poet's ability to employ the whole potential of language to write about his extra-human experience. G. Brugnoli, 'Dante peregrino', *Borsellino Vol.*, 73–80, presents some very interesting cases of intertextuality in *Inf.* I. He compares passages from the Epistle of St James and the *Aeneid* to the prologue of the *DC* in order to substantiate his presentation of James and Aeneas as doubles of D. the pilgrim. Guglielmo Gorni, 'Le "guide" di Dante, o la sibilla negata', *StD*, 67:117–28, speculates on the status of D.'s guides in relation to, and contrast with, the Sybil, Aeneas's guide to the Underworld. Given the importance attributed by D. to the Sybil for the successful realization of Aeneas' *katabasis* in *Cvio* IV, xxvi, 8–9, G. asks what persuaded D. to choose Virgil instead. He questionably asserts that V. was the only choice left to D., who for various reasons could not select Cavalcanti, Guinizelli, or Cacciaguida and feared the ambiguity of the Sybil and her 'foglie levi' (*Par.* XXXIII, 65). A. Tartaro, 'Il Giubileo di Dante', *La Cultura*, 39:395–410, underlines the importance of the Jubilee for the genesis of the *DC* in spite of D.'s hatred of Boniface VIII. T. claims that D.'s intention was in fact to emphasize the event's message of spiritual rebirth and renewal against the backdrop of the condemnation of the corrupt Pope. A. Stussi, 'Gli studi sulla lingua di Dante', *Atti* (Verona–Ravenna), 229–45, is a brief but excellent survey 20th-c. studies on D.'s lexicon and language. Elisa Curti, 'Un esempio di bestiario dantesco: la cicogna o dell'amor moderno', *StD*, 67:129–60, studies the symbolic value of one of the 'animals' populating the *DC*'s metaphorical language: the stork. With examples taken from the classical, biblical, and patristic traditions, C. illustrates the symbolic and learned dimension of D.'s imagery. On the other hand, D.'s appropriation of the stork symbolism demonstrates a personal re-elaboration of existing traditions. D. Scholl, 'Dante und das Groteske', *DDJ*, 77:73–105. F. Mazzoni, 'Epilogo alla introduzione della *Comedìa*', *ib.*, 3–10, is a reprint of the epilogue to *La Commedia di Dante secondo l'antica vulgata*, Alpignano, Tallone Editore, 2000, III, 237–54. Further to work in the same area by G. Gorni, G. Di Pino, and R. Fasani, L. Blasucci, 'Per una tipologia degli esordi nei canti danteschi', *PaT*, 4, 2000: 17–46, makes an incisive contribution to defining the various types of *incipit*. F. Turelli, *'Il ruolo della casualità nelle ripetizioni di rima e note su aritmologia, rima e terza rima nella *Commedia*', *LIA*, 3:507–23.

INFERNO

A. Heil, 'Dantes Staunen und die Scham Vergils. Bemerkungen zu *Inferno* I, 61–87', *DDJ*, 77:27–43. G. Casagrande, '"Accidïoso fummo" (*Inf.* VII 123)', *StD*, 67:56–71, re-examines the meaning of the expression 'accidioso fummo' to offer a convincing explanation of a controversial passage of *Inf.* VII. Analysing classical, biblical, and patristic traditions, C. concludes that the expression refers to a *superabundantia* not a *defectus irae*. A fascinating interpretation of the famous *crux* in *Inf.* X, 63, is M. Ciccuto, 'Il disdegno di San Giacomo. Per una diversa assenza di Cavalcanti dalla *Commedia*', *LIA*, 3, 311–18, which argues that D. may be alluding to a sonnet by Muscia da Siena, *Ecci venuto Guido 'n Campostello*, which presents St James's disdain for Cavalcanti, who had not travelled to Campostela for genuine spiritual reasons. The 'cui' of line 63 could then be St James, later met by D. in *Par.* xxv. Through this strategy, believes C., D. establishes the difference between his pilgrimage and Guido's, and declares his spiritual and poetic superiority. G. Muresu, 'Il bando dell'umana natura (*Inf.* xv 80–81)', *Borsellino Vol.*, 109–14, argues that the expression 'umana natura' is the equivalent of 'life'. The 'bando', then, is to be understood as death itself. T. Cachey Jr, 'Dante's journey between fiction and truth: Gerion revisited', *Atti* (Verona–Ravenna), 74–92, examines the metaliterary connotations of Geryon's presence in *Inferno*. Through the interpretation of the geographical coordinates of the monster in Bks vi and viii of the *Aeneid*, C. argues that the appropriation of Geryon in the *DC* establishes a clear relation between the journeys of Aeneas, Hercules, and the pilgrim. The function of this intertextual strategy would, according to C., be the confirmation of the authenticity of the pilgrim's experience. G. Roellenbleck, 'Lectura Dantis: *Inferno* xvii', *DDJ*, 77:45–60. G. Indizio, 'La profezia di Niccolò e i tempi della stesura del canto xix dell'*Inferno*', *StD*, 67:73–97, analyses canto xix to find convincing elements for the dating of the canto. Having demonstrated the incongruity of the dates favoured by the *communis opinio* (1307), I. claims that the canto was written after 1311–12, the years in which D.'s harsh opinion of Pope Clement V and his policies matured. As for the prophecy regarding the death of the pope, I. cautiously admits that D. might have rewritten lines 79–81 before 1314, the year of publication of the whole *cantica*. M. Bonicatti, '*Inferno*, xxvi', 116–17, *Borsellino Vol.* (61–72), is a convoluted psychological interpretation of the canto.

PURGATORIO

Shrewd observations on fundamental aspects of the *cantica* are made in L. Blasucci, 'Tempo e penitenza nel *Purgatorio*', *Soglie*, 2.2, 2000:33–45. On particular cantos: G. Cavallini, 'Il Canto ii del *Purgatorio* e il rito di riconoscimento', *RLettI*, 20.1:9–24, is a classic *lectura Dantis* which underlines the importance of D. *personaggio*'s recognition of Casella for his process of repentance and cleansing. G. Muresu, 'Casella, il "passaggio negato" e il Giubileo (*Pg.* ii 94–105)', *CLett*, 30:299–320, sensibly discusses the reasons behind Casella's delayed departure for Mount Purgatory and argues that D. did not favour Boniface's Jubilee, considering it to be a simoniac manoeuvre. G. Gorni, 'Il canto viii del *Purgatorio*', *L'Alighieri*, 19:53–67, sets out to promote a new kind of *lectura Dantis* focusing on detailed analysis of *cruces* and problematic issues and avoiding the descriptive and informative elements of the classic *lectura*. He bases his *lectura* on Sanguineti's new edition of the *DC* and praises his textual choices as editor. On the basis of a lucid, though slightly partial, analysis of the influence of Avicenna's theory of dreams on *Purg.* IX, L. Sebastio, 'La mente nostra divina alle visioni (*Pg* IX)', *CLett*, 30:321–42, argues the philosophical nature of the poem, as well as the political interpretation of the pilgrim's dream. A. Tartaro, 'La pedagogia di Virgilio e i segni della superbia (*Purgatorio* XII)', *Borsellino Vol.*, 115–30, offers a *lectura* of the canto highlighting the significant role of Virgil in the moral development and education of Dante. G. Sasso, '"Soleva Roma che il buon mondo feo, / due soli aver" (*Purg.* XVI 106–7)', *La Cultura*, 40:5–23, asks what moment of Roman history Marco Lombardo is referring to in *Purg.* XVI, 106–07. He points out that the Roman Empire was already in decline at the time of the rise of papal authority. To avoid the *impasse* and support his theory of the 'two suns', driven by political passion D. telescoped history in a 'condensazione temporale'. C. and H. Kallendorf, '"Per te poeta fui, per te cristiano" (*Purg.* 22. 73): Statius as Christian, from "fact" to fiction', *DDJ*, 77:61–72, explores the reception of D.'s idea of representing Statius as a Christian among the first interpreters of the *DC*, as well as among medieval exegetes of Statius's works. M. Dell'Aquila, 'Mutazioni di segno e di modelli nella poesia di Dante (*Purg.* XXIV–XXVIII)', Dell'Aquila, *Bello stilo*, 5–35, traces D.'s treatment of other poets in the whole of the *Commedia*, but focuses mainly on *Purg.*, the most metaliterary of the three *cantiche*, and examines D.'s relationship with the vernacular and classical lyric traditions, as well as with his own past as a poet. He suggests that D. surpassed other poets thanks to Virgil, arguably the most important model in the *Comedy*.

PARADISO

This year pride of place goes to the *Lectura Dantis Turicensis. Paradiso*, F, Olschki, 518 pp., which completes the important series of Zurich *lecturae* on the three canticles edited by Michelangelo Picone. U. Eco, 'Lettura del *Paradiso*', pp. 23–29 of his *Sulla letteratura*, Mi, Bompiani, defines *Paradiso* as the apotheosis of virtual reality and celebrates the appeal of its intellectual poetry for the contemporary reader. K. Stierle, '*Paradiso* III', *L'Alighieri*, 19:69–85, highlights the tensions that characterize this canto. S. shows how, after the extraordinary fullness of Cantos I and II, D. *personaggio* becomes aware of the different degrees of beatitude experienced by the blessed souls. G. Arnaldi, 'Il canto di Giustiniano', *La Cultura*, 40:211–20, reflects on the choice of Justinian as speaker for D.'s ideas on the providential nature of the Empire, and concludes that Justinian serves the purpose of underlining the judicial aspects of government. On the basis of the occurrence of similar vocabulary and imagery in *Purg.*, VI, *Par.* VI, and *Cvio* IV, ix, 10, A. believes that the canto was composed at the same time as the *Monarchia.* Id., *'Letture del canto XXVI del *Paradiso*', *RELI*, 19:45–60. P. Boitani, 'Creazione e cadute di *Paradiso* XXIX', *L'Alighieri*, 19:87–103, offers a fascinating analysis of Dante's rewriting of *Genesis* in *Par.* XXIX. B. argues that D. avoids the detailed description of the Bible and offers a very abstract version of the creation based on philosophical (Platonic and Aristotelian) concepts and language. Gone are the seven days of *Genesis*, gone the creatures and the species of the world. In D.'s rendition everything came to life simultaneously and instantaneously, there where only primordial matter and form existed.

DUECENTO AND TRECENTO II (EXCLUDING DANTE)*

By Roberta Capelli and Attilio Motta, *Padua*

1. General

A useful point of departure in defining the socio-cultural context that shaped early literature is afforded by a group of publications methodologically influenced by historiography and material culture studies. Chiara Frugoni, *Medioevo sul naso. Occhiali, bottoni e altre invenzioni medievali*, Ro–Bari, Laterza, 2001, vi + 184 pp., 100 illus., investigates the major innovations (not only in material culture) which the modern world owes to the Middle Ages. S. Pietrini, *Spettacoli e immaginario teatrale nel Medioevo*, Ro, Bulzoni, 2001, 326 pp., 58 illus., is organized in two parts: the first examines various forms of medieval performance (from religious plays to minstrel and other profane shows), while the second analyses the conception of theatre and theatrical experimentation that emerges from the works of the time and from critical scholarship. Glauco Maria Cantarella, *Medioevo. Un filo di parole*, Mi, Garzanti, 216 pp., explores the function of language as expressing the two fundamental forms of dialectic of the age and of medieval society in general: that of human interbreeding and that between the laity and the Church.

2. Duecento and Trecento excluding Boccaccio and Petrarch

Within the general purview of studies on 13th-c. Italian literature it is interesting to note how research into *volgarizzamenti* is assuming an increasingly distinct and substantial place. Alongside valuable data-collection/cataloguing exercises such as C. Delcorno, R. M. Dessì, O. Visani, 'Inventario dei manoscritti di prediche volgari inedite (Roma, Napoli, Città del Vaticano, Francia, Inghilterra)', *LItal*, 54:379–88, based on a survey of the 14th- and 15th-c. vernacular preaching tradition and reporting the first, very substantial results (26 new MSS, chiefly at Naples and in the Vatican), or J. Fohlen, 'Biographies de Sénèque et commentaires des *Epistulae ad Lucilium* (V^e-XVe s.)', *IMU*, 63:1–90, which provides a list of 'textes annexes' to do with the philosopher and his correspondence, and ignored or only superficially mentioned in normal catalogues, there are also

* As in volumes 62 and 63, this section has been translated from Italian by the editor.

numerous contributions arising out of work on critical editions or from investigation of historical-philological problems relating to the transmission and circulation of texts. A. Scolari, 'I volgarizzamenti del *Libellus super ludo scaccorum*. La redazione A: analisi della tradizione e saggio di edizione critica', *SFI*, 59, 2001 : 9–78, concentrates on analysis of the so-called 'Redazione A' of Italian *volgarizzamenti* of Iacopo da Cessole's treatise, a moral allegorization of chess derived from public sermons. This still unpublished draft (preserved in a Genoese monastery), to which 14 of the tradition's 26 MSS and three printed editions belong, appears to be the closest to the much reproduced Latin text (250 known MSS). The author also includes, as an advance specimen, the chapter dealing with the Knight. G. Cura Curà, 'A proposito di Brunetto Latini volgarizzatore: osservazioni sulla *Pro Marcello*', *PaT*, 4 : 27–52, analyses this particular *volgarizzamento* of Cicero in relation to Brunetto's better-known *Rettorica*, *Orationes Caesarianae*, and *Pro Ligario*, in order to highlight both the features it shares with them (i.e. its general stylistic character) and its distinctive features such as the balance struck in it between fidelity to the original and the pursuit of a lively, expressive language. Spanning both philology and history of the language is F. Romanini, 'Tecniche del volgarizzare nella *Pharsalia* antico lombarda di Parma', *LS*, 37 : 29–64, carefully describing and reconstructing the history of the 14th-c. MS (Palatina 2928) containing the first five books of the *Bellum civile*, before going on to analyse the peculiar characteristics of the text — fragmented for teaching purposes into syntagms arranged in vernacular SVO order — of the generic and formulaic translation, and of the Latin glosses, which are grammatical in content. L. C. Rossi, '"Benvenutus de Ymola super Valerio Maximo". Ricerca sull'*expositio*', *Aevum*, 76 : 369–423, analyses the *expositio* of Benvenuto da Imola's commentary in search of useful information relating to the work's dating, sources, and more direct cultural models. G. P. Maggioni, 'La trasmissione dei leggendari abbreviati del XIII secolo', *FilM*, 9 : 87–107, focuses on the so-called *legendae novae* (i.e. handy abridgements of hagiographical works) in their heyday in the 13th c. and down to Iacopo da Varazze's *Legenda Aurea*, and demonstrates 'le caratteristiche del metodo di composizione [e] le conseguenti particolarità nella trasmissione di questi testi' (93). F. Delle Donne, 'Le formule di saluto nella pratica epistolare medievale. La *Summa salutationum* di Milano e Parigi', *ib.*, 249–79, publishes the series of *salutationes* contained in MS E 59 sup. at Milan's Biblioteca Ambrosiana and in MS Lat. 8630 at the Bibliothèque Nationale, describing its characteristics and situating it in a tradition that takes root alongside the more important treatises on the *ars dictaminis*: that of the collections of examples for the use of particular professions, the notaries for example.

In the field of Duecento religious literature, the figure of St Francis of Assisi continues to be the privileged subject of research: Alberto Castaldini, *Il segno del giusto. Francesco d'Assisi e l'ebraismo*, Reggio Emilia, Diabasis, 2001, 105 pp., seeks to identify the marks of the saint's Hebrew sensibility, from spiritual, historiographical, and literary-critical points of view: in this perspective, even the *Cantico delle Creature* is analysed in Hebrew terms. Aldo Menichetti, 'Il *Cantico di frate Sole* e Filippo di Novara', pp. 303–09 of *Italica–Retica–Gallica. Studia linguarum literarium artiumque in honorem Ricarda Liver*, ed. Peter Wunderli et al., Tübingen, Francke, 2001, goes back to the question of meaning of the preposition *per* in the *Cantico*, reinforcing Padre Pozzi's hypothesis (whereby the praiser is neither man nor God's creatures, but God himself) with the help of a passage of Filippo di Novara's *Des quatre tenz d'aage d'ome*, dating from about 1265. Edoardo Fumagalli, *San Francesco, il Cantico, il Pater noster*, Mi, Jaca Book, 112 pp., in the first two chapters addresses the age-old problem of the *Cantico*'s composition (i.e. whether in a single period or otherwise); the third chapter, on the other hand, focuses on the interpretation of the *Cantico*. Lorenzo Maria Ago, 'L'umanità di Maria e il realismo dell'Incarnazione secondo san Francesco di Assisi. Tra Catari e trovatori', pp. 89–109 of *La madre di Dio per una cultura di pace. Atti del X Colloquio Internazionale di Mariologia*, ed. Walter Dall'Aglio and Enrico Vidau, Ro, Ediz. Montefortane, 2001, presents the figure of St Francis as the positive, orthodox 'outcome' of the relationship between Catharism and the troubadours.

To mark the centenary of the Piedmontese scholar's birth, Natalino Sapegno, *Frate Jacopone*, pref. Carlo Ossola, updated bibliography by Giacomo Jori, T, Nino Argano, 2001, xx + 190 pp., republishes a work originally brought out in 1926. Ossola sets Sapegno against the background of his times, underlining his relations with Gobetti and the role of his research on Jacopone in his intellectual development.

Typically historico-critical in approach are contributions centring on the figure of Salimbene de Adam. Pride of place goes to the *Cronaca*, transl. G. Tonna, Reggio Emilia, Diabasis, 2001, 366 pp., a reprint — with a postface added by the scholar's daughter — of the anthologized version edited by Tonna in 1964 for the publisher Garzanti: long out of print, this is still textual scholarship of considerable interest for its pursuit of balance between a modernizing impetus in the direction of philological restoration and the conservative tendency of its choice of linguistic variants (see also R. Greci, 'La *Cronaca* di Salimbene nella traduzione di Giuseppe Tonna', *SUm*, 15.2, 2001:95–102). L. Mascanzoni, 'Salimbene, Riccobaldo e la leggenda di Cola di Pesce', *QMed*, 54:150–62, explores the ancient origins of the legend of Cola di Pesce, which is widely found on the east coast of Sicily, and shows that there is already proof of its diffusion in the 13th and 14th c. thanks to the chronicler Salimbene. G. Cracco, 'Fra Salimbene e la *domus-religio*. Salvare l'Europa cristiana nella cultura del tardo Duecento', *RSLR*, 38:203–33, offers a new interpretation of the personality and writings of the Franciscan. Starting from an analysis of the famous passage: 'Porro ego frater Salimbene et frater Guido de Adam domum nostram destruximus in masculis et feminis religionem intrando, ut eam in celis edificare possemus', C. seeks to show that, for Salimbene, the 'nuova *domus* era la sua *religio*, l'ordine dei Minori' (231) which, through the pages of the *Cronica*, rises to the role of 'guida e arbitro del mondo stesso' (229).

Other chronicle writing is addressed by: L. Capo, 'La cronachistica italiana all'età di Federico II', *RSI*, 114:380–430, and by P. Mula, 'Vérité et impartialité dans la *Cronica* de Dino Compagni', *PaT*, 4:53–89, who examines five specific episodes of the *Cronica*, emphasizing the skilfully pursued ambiguity between the author as directly involved in the events narrated and as their narrator. M. shows that, behind the apparent impartiality of the chronicle genre, the narrative expresses a specifically partisan view of events. Dino Compagni, *Chronique des événements survenant à son époque*, ed. and trans. Patrick Mula, Grenoble, ELLUG, 318 pp., an exemplary French edition, with excellent footnote annotation, introductory material, and historical and lexical 'annexes', amends the Del Lungo text here and there in the light of Davide Cappi's preparatory work for a new critical edition of the original based on Ashburnham 443. V. Formentin, 'Tra storia della lingua e filologia: note sulla sintassi della *Cronica* d'Anonimo romano', *ib.*, 37:203–50, reverts to doubts which a late tradition and a reconstructed archetype full of gaps have always raised over the dating of the Roman dialectal patina of the work attributed by Billanovich to Bartolomeo di Iacovo di Valmontone. To verify them she proceeds to compare a number of syntactic phenomena (the construction 'figlio a', the Tobler-Mussafia law, the position of clitics with restructuring verbs, the order of unstressed pronouns, the use of auxiliaries and subordinating conjunctions) with a vast *corpus* of Roman dialect texts of indisputably early origin, and from this deduces, on the one hand, the archaic character of the language and, on the other, the likely late transcription of the archetype.

Interest in the literature of the Origins gives rise to valuable research tools and constantly occasions debate. With regard to 'technical' publications, we would draw attention to: Adriana Solimena, *Repertorio metrico dei poeti siculo-toscani*, CSFLS, 2000[2001], xxxviii + 840 pp., and *Handschriftenverzeichnis zur Briefsammlung des Petrus de Vinea*, ed. Hans Martin Schaller, Hanover, Monumenta Germaniae Historica, xlvi + 584 pp., a list of the 150-plus MSS containing the so-called 'epistolario' of Pier della Vigna, alphabetically arranged by city of present location and each given a precise material description. Philological discussion, on the other hand, is forthcoming from: R. Gualdo, 'La poesia siciliana e toscana delle Origini. Appunti di lettura da un'edizione in corso', *Per leggere*, 1, 2001: 135–58, and Id., 'L'edizione critica della Scuola poetica siciliana. Una tavola rotonda', *ib.*, 2: 155–60. G. provides an up-to-date account of debates (on lexical, prosodic, and rhymic issues) that have developed within the purview of the CSLFS project (directed by Costanzo di Girolamo and Rosario Coluccia) of an annotated edition and commentary on the texts of the Sicilian poets. Viewing the Sicilian lyric against the background of social, political, and cultural forces within which it flowered, F. Violante, 'Federico II e la fondazione dello *Studium* napoletano', *QMed*, 54: 16–85, first sets the cultural initiative of the Swabian Emperor in the historical situation of the years 1220–24 before going on to analyse the role and importance of Naples university as, on the one hand, an expression of political power and prestige and, on the other, as the place where a whole class of civil servants and state-employed intellectuals was prepared for power. A very well-structured collection of previously published essays (ten in all) which takes the form of an acute critical *excursus* on both Sicilian and Tuscan lyric poetry is Gianfranco Folena, *Textus testis: lingua e cultura poetica delle origini*, T, Bollati Boringhieri, 322 pp. The chapters are thematically arranged in three sections, the first of which reflects on the role of multidisciplinary interaction — especially linguistic and philological — as the methodological presupposition of scientific literary investigation, and comprises: '"Textus testis": caso e necessità nelle origini romanze' (1973), 'Geografia linguistica e testi medievali' (1967), and 'Filologia testuale e storia linguistica' (1960). The second section centres on the tradition of early Italian lyric poetry and includes: 'Cultura e poesia dei Siciliani' (1965) and 'Cultura poetica dei primi Fiorentini (1970)'. The third part applies the principles set out in the preceding sections to the two fundamental poetic personalities of Dante and Petrarch: 'Dante e la teoria degli stili' (1955), 'Dante e i trovatori' (1961), 'Il canto di Guido Guinizzelli' (1977), 'L'orologio del Petrarca' (1979), and 'La canzone del tramonto' (1978). On questions of metre and poetic genres: A. Afribo, 'Sequenze e sistemi di rime nella lirica del secondo Duecento e del Trecento', *SMI*, 2: 3–43, presents a rich array of examples to highlight the scantiness and basic repetitiveness of the rhyme combinations used in *stilnovo* poetry, and shows that, on the contrary, 'la ricerca di tali sequenze smetterà di essere proficua non appena se ne estenda la verifica a due massimi trecenteschi come il Dante comico e in genere post-stilnovista e Petrarca' (4); and Claudio Giunta, *Versi ad un destinatario: saggio sulla poesia italiana del Medioevo*, Bo, Il Mulino, 548 pp., transcends traditional periodization by century in examining a substantial series of poetic texts — roughly extending from the earliest specimens of Italian vernacular verse to Petrarchism — which are addressed to identified historical readers and present different dialogic models and levels. To complement this volume, Id., *Due saggi sulla tenzone*, Ro–Padua, Antenore, xv + 218 pp., analyses 'Le tenzoni nella considerazione dei trattatisti e nella tradizione manoscritta' and 'Metro, forma e stile della tenzone', identifying the basic common features of the *tenzone* as lying in its function as a message addressed in the first instance to a private addressee, and only later, and then indirectly, to a wider readership: G. also, in fact, views the genre in synchronic perspective.

Stilnovo poetry looms large in this survey thanks to numerous studies of individual authors. Guido Guinizzelli, *Rime*, ed. Luciano Rossi, T, Einaudi, lvi + 171 pp., a critical edition, with full commentary, articulated in five sections (*canzoni* and sonnets, and then *canzoni*, sonnets, and fragments of uncertain attribution), plus three appendices respectively comprising the apocryphal *canzoni* attributed to Guinizzelli, the alternative versions, and the reference texts. It should be noted that some details of the 'Nota biografica' are to be rectified in the light of new documentary evidence discovered by Armando Antonelli, whose findings will appear in the forthcoming papers of the Monselice conference *Da Guido Guinizzelli a Dante. Nuove prospettive sulla lirica del Duecento* (May 2002). Rossi's work is also complemented by the valuable list of *addenda* (corrections, integrations, and editorial, linguistic, and exegetic clarifications) in P. V. Mengaldo, 'Noterelle guinizzelliane', *PaT*, 4:215–20. *Intorno a Guido Guinizelli. Atti della Giornata di studi, Università di Zurigo, 16 giugno 2000*, ed. Luciano Rossi and Sara Alloatti Boller, Alessandria, Orso, 214 pp., gather the following contributions: L. Rossi, 'La nuova edizione delle *Rime*' (9–35); F. Brugnolo, 'Spunti per un nuovo commento a Guinizzelli' (37–56); G. Inglese, 'Appunti sulla canzone 'Al cor gentil': *inselva* e altro' (57–67); M. Picone, 'Guittone, Guinizzelli e Dante' (69–84); A. Menichetti, 'Sull'attribuzione a Bonagiunta di *In quanto la natura*' (85–97); A. Cipollone, 'I quattro sensi della scrittura di Bonagiunta. Ancora sulla tenzone con Guinizzelli' (99–135); S. Sarteschi, 'Guinizzelli nella prospettiva dantesca' (137–53); G. Brunetti, 'Guinizzelli, il non più oscuro Maestro Giandino e il Boezio di Dante' (155–91); M. Castoldi, 'Giovanni Pascoli e "La Canzone del cor gentile"' (193–212). Further items on Guinizzelli are: P. Borsa, 'La tenzone tra Guido Guinizzelli e frate Guittone d'Arezzo', *SPCT*, 65:47–88, providing a new key with which to interpret the sonnet 'Caro padre meo, de vostra laude' not as a homage from the youthful Guinizzelli to the Aretine master but as a critique disguised as a eulogy. Pertaining to Cavalcanti: G. Brugnoli, 'Intertesti cavalcantiani', *GIF*, 53, 2001:309–13, traces intertextual links between passages of 'Una figura della Donna mia' and of 'Intelligenza XI', and between ll. 19–20 of C.'s famous *pastorella* and ll. 1736–49 of the *Aeneid*; and C. Giunta, '"Perch'i' no spero di tornar giammai" di Guido Cavalcanti', *Per leggere*, 2:5–16, behind the lexis of this much-discussed text detects codified expressions taken from the technical language of testamentary law and reused in lyric vein. For the output and poetics of Cecco Angiolieri attention is drawn to Fabian Alfie, *Comedy and Culture: Cecco Angiolieri's Poetry and Late Medieval Society*, Leeds, Northern Universities Press, vi + 216 pp., and Id., 'Cast out: the topos of exile in Cecco Angiolieri, Pietro de' Faitinelli, and Pieraccio Tedaldi', *AnI*, 20:113–26. Not to be overlooked is *La Corona di casistica amorosa e le canzoni del cosiddetto 'Amico di Dante'*, ed. Irene Maffia Scariati, Ro–Padua, Salerno, lxxxv + 368 pp., a new fully annotated critical edition of the 66 compositions by the anonymous author which appear at the end of MS Vat. Lat. 3793. The editor aims to demonstrate, through metrical and stylistic analysis, the poet's substantial estraneousness from the *stilnovo* circle, situating him rather in the Siculo-Tuscan sphere. Complementing this volume we also have I. Maffia Scariati, '"Non ha Fiorenza tanti Lapi e Bindi": su un'intricata questione attributiva', *SPCT*, 64:5–62, where she addresses the age-old problem of the identity of the 'Amico di Dante', rejects the candidature of the Florentine Lippo Pasci de' Bardi, and indeed asserts that it is 'un poeta lontano dalla poesia di Guido Cavalcanti e di Dante [. . .] "giovani"' (7). A final item on *stilnovo* poetry is B. Bentivogli, '"Se giovinezza non venisse meno". Per un frammento nel canzoniere Vaticano Latino 3793', *ib.*, 65:5–12, which puts forward the hypothesis that the distich penned by the so-called V13 hand at f. 179*r* (*Segiouneneçça no(n) venisse meno./ aluiuer mai niuporrebbe freno.*) may be a kind of self-contained proverbial expression, subsequently reused in three compositions (the *canzone* stanza at f. 116*v* of MS Riccardiano 818 and two sonnets found, respectively, at f. 96*v* of MS 521 in Holkham Hall Library and at f. 4*r* of BNCF MS Landau 13) which present the first distich as their common *incipit*.

A volume deserving separate mention is *Antichi testi veneti*, ed. Antonio Daniele, Padua, Esedra, 228 pp., with 13 contributions on linguistic, literary, and philological subjects covering the period Due–Cinquecento. The first seven are devoted to the 13th or 14th c.: C. Marcato, 'Grammatica storica e testi antichi volgari: sugli elementi onomastici' (9–15); M. Cortelazzo, 'Lessico marinaresco nel veneziano antico' (17–23); V. Formentin, 'Un caso di geminazione fonosintattica negli antichi volgari e nei moderni dialetti settentrionali' (25–40); A. Stussi, 'Una frottola tra carte d'archivio padovane del Trecento' (40–61); E. M. Duso, 'Echi stilnovistici e classici nelle rime di Giovanni Quirini' (63–79); A. Andreose, 'Fra Veneto e Toscana: vicende di un volgarizzamento trecentesco dell'*Itinerarium* di Odorico da Pordenone' (81–93); and A. Donadello, 'Note sulla lingua del *Lucidario* veneto Laur. Gadd. 115' (95–103). In the same thematic area we note the three articles: M. Schrage, 'Giacomino da Verona: eine Übersicht zur Forschungslage', *LIA*, 3:279–89, which surveys studies and editions devoted to Giacomino over a 150-year period, stressing the prevalence of linguistic and philological over literary-critical analysis; N. Bertoletti, 'Disposizioni per ser Filippo (Verona, verso il 1236)', *LS*, 37:185–202, which publishes with a linguistic commentary a document in 13th-c. Veronese vernacular written on the reverse of a parchment from the Ospedale di S. Giacomo alla Tomba (Verona) containing two notarial deeds of 1229 and 1230; and V. Formentin, 'Antico padovano *gi* da ILLI: condizioni italoromanze di una forma veneta', *ib.*, 3–28, which analyses the characteristics and incidence of the definite article and personal pronoun *gi* (*gli*), underlining its peculiarities in Paduan as compared with the other early Veneto dialects in which the same form occurs.

Finally for the Duecento, we note a group of four miscellaneous items which do not fit into any of the foregoing categories: F. Peruzzo, 'Orrico Scaccabarozzi: un arciprete poeta nella Milano del XIII secolo', *Aevum*, 76:325–68, reconstructing the biography, and suggesting a dating for part of the poetic output, of a Milanese cleric (archpriest from 1261 to 1293) who cultivated the Ambrosian liturgical tradition and composed rhythmic Offices devoted to the Virgin Mary and the Saints, which he collected in MS Milan, Cap. Metrop. II.F.2.1; L. Tosin, 'Jacopo e Bonsignore, mercanti genovesi a Caffa', *QMed*, 53:41–68, documenting from late 13th-c. notarial deeds the presence of Ligurian merchants in the coastal centres of the Black Sea, particularly those on the east coast of the Crimea; A. Ferioli, 'Falchi e falconieri nella letteratura medievale italiana', *ib.*, 6–40, conducting a brief *excursus* on the presence of references to falconry in medieval literature and analysing the symbolic significance and socio-cultural function of this widespread pursuit; Enrico Artifoni, 'Orfeo concionatore. Un passo di Tommaso d'Aquino e l'eloquenza politica nelle città italiane nel secolo XIII', pp. 137–49 of *La musica nel pensiero medievale*, ed. Letterio Cassata, Ravenna, Longo, 2001, 274 pp., investigating the concept of *ars concionandi* down to

Brunetto Latini and Aquinas. (The volume comprises 13 contributions ranging from late Antiquity to the late Middle Ages.)

For the Trecento, we note the appearance of new critical editions. An excellent one of Dante's 'first Venetian imitator' is Giovanni Quirini, *Rime*, ed. Elena Maria Duso, Ro–Padua, Antenore, xciv + 279 pp. Furio Brugnolo's foreword is followed by a weighty introduction bringing together biographical data (Q. was active in overseas trade, is believed to have corresponded with Dante, and dictated a will in 1333) with an account of the MS tradition, which is more extensive (4 + 17) than the albeit fundamental collection in Marciana MS Lat. XIV 223, with its significant twofold division of the 100 poems between the amorous and the religious. The text is also preceded by a classification of the witnesses, an analysis of the poems' language and metrical forms, a bibliography, and a statement of editorial criteria, and is accompanied by a critical apparatus and extremely rich commentary registering not only Q.'s profound yet unostentatious assimilation of Dante, but also his references to the classics and the Bible. The volume concludes with an appendix of poems of uncertain attribution (the three-dialect *tenzone*), a metrical table, and lexical and name indexes. Likewise, Tommaso di Giunta, *Il conciliato d'amore. Rime. Epistole*, ed. Linda Pagnotta, Tavarnuzze, SISMEL-Galluzzo, 2001, cvi + 236 pp., is a valuable critical edition of the prosimetrum (set in 1336), of the stray poems (four in number, assignable to the lost portion of the main work) and the letters (to Fazio degli Uberti, Bindo Altoviti, and Deo Boni), and of the four epistles, complete with critical apparatus and a rich commentary. The dense introduction reconstructs T.'s cultural operation, marked by his post-*stilnovo* recovery of the Medieval Latin (and Dantean) prosimetrum, by the dialogic dramatization typical of the love treatises, and by mingling of styles and heterogeneity of cultural references: the lyric self (archaizing in its metrical forms) is played down and an attempt made to revitalize the courtly code in a didactic and narrative direction. Bio-bibliographical and textual Notes then follow, with a description of the MSS (notably the Marciana's MS It. IX 175, whose 16 miniatures are reproduced) and an analysis of their interrelations and tradition, and a statement of transcription criteria, while the volume closes with a metrical table, rhyme list, glossary, and indexes. Again, *Cantari novellistici dal Tre al Cinquecento*, ed. Elisabetta Benucci, Roberta Manetti, and Franco Zabagli, introd. Domenico De Robertis, 2 vols, Ro, Salerno, li + 1018 pp., is an important edition, carried out by the three young scholars under De Robertis's supervision, of 29 *cantari*, including six from the 14th-c. tradition (*Fiorio e Biancifiore*, *Bel Gherardino*, *Piramo e Tisbe* redaction A, and Antonio Pucci's *Madonna Leonessa*, *Bruto di Bretagna*, and *Gismirante*) and others previously unpublished in modern times. Each has a succinct introductory 'cappello', a set of concise footnotes, and at the end of the second vol. a brief 'nota al testo' and an essential critical apparatus. In the same collection *Il Novellino*, ed. Alberto Conte, pref. Cesare Segre, Ro, Salerno, 2001, xlvi + 499 pp., had already appeared, Segre's presentation underlining the novelty of the stratigraphical results set out by Conte in his introduction. C. distinguishes between the vulgate text, which is the outcome of successive revisions carried out as early as the Trecento (structure) and as late as the early Cinquecento (language), and the Ur-*Novellino* (or *Libro di novelle e di bel parlare gientile*) contained in the earliest manuscript, P[1], which represents the original late-13th-c. project, a less substantial text also different in being interspersed with *sententiae*, in the ordering of the novelle, and in its both pedagogic and artistic purpose. C. gives both redactions with footnote commentary, a 'Nota al testo' going exhaustively into the intricate philological problems, a brief 'Nota sulla lingua di P[1]', a section devoted to sources, a critical apparatus, and lastly indexes.

Output on Trecento religious literature has, as ever, been considerable. In *Il laudario fiorentino del Trecento*, ed. Gilberto Aranci, Montespertoli, Aleph, 206 pp., a note by Silvio Calzolari and a brief introduction by Aranci are followed by a semi-diplomatic transcription of a mid-14th-c. parchment codex in the Florentine Archiepiscopal Archive pointed out by Bettarini (1970) and used by Varanini in his edition of the *Laude cortonesi*. Reproduced in parallel is the only previous edition (complete but with a modified sequence), that of Cecconi (1870). Although the first and last of the 80 compositions are devoted to St Eustace, the *laudario* may have originated in a Marian confraternity in the Pontassieve district. The readings of other MSS are registered in an apparatus. Gabriella Izzi Benedetti, *Il dramma della passione nel Medioevo abruzzese*, Ro, Bulzoni, 169 pp., focuses attention on the *passio Christi* theme in research aiming to reconstruct the forms of sacred drama in the Abruzzo from its liturgical origins via Græco-Byzantine and French influences, the predominance of the vernacular in the *lauda*, the importance of Jacopone and of religious unrest in nearby Umbria for the rise of the dramatic *lauda* alongside *poemetti* on the Passion, and thence to the *Sacre rappresentazioni* of the 15th and 16th c. Interdisciplinary in approach is Lina Bolzoni, *La rete delle immagini: predicazione in volgare dalle origini a Bernardino da Siena*, T, Einaudi, xxx + 250 pp., where the theorist author, after a decade's reflection, analyses the relation between words and images evoked in 14th- and 15th-c. sermons for mnemonic purposes and the typology (*exemplum*, allegory, figure) and chronology of the phenomenon, from the real referents of Giordano da Pisa (Buffalmacco's frescoes of the *Triumph of Death*) to those of Simone da Cascina's *Colloquio Spirituale* which, though only mental, follow patterns that can be found in illuminated MSS, thus demonstrating the vitality of a 'code' already at work in Joachim and Jacopone, which then developed over centuries to attain the vast range of reference of St Bernardino's sermons. G. Auzzas, 'Dalla predica al trattato: lo *Specchio della vera penitenzia* di Iacopo Passavanti', *LItal*, 54:325–42, on a work deriving from a religious methodology widely practised (from Thomas Aquinas to Aldobrandino da Toscanella and Cavalca) in the vernacular dissemination of the mendicant orders' teachings and in *muta praedicatio* for the confraternities, shows how it stands out from the *summe de casibus* by the absence of the examination of conscience and from the *confessorum* manuals by the absence of legal erudition: in A.'s view the work's internal imbalances are not to be attributed to its supposed unfinished state or to the presence of interpolations, but to its being an *in fieri* and at times contradictory experiment in vernacular compilation for the use of the laity.

Turning finally to miscellaneous Trecento articles, we note C. Pelucani, 'Notizia di un antico dizionario padovano', *SFI*, 59, 2001:5–8, which reports on three more MSS containing the compilation of 30,000 headwords carried out in 1324 by Iacopo Dondi dall'Orologio, the eclectic scholar and father of Giovanni. One of them, dating from the 14th c., is extremely close to the original, its *mise en page* shows concern for ease of consultation as compared with both Uguccione's *Magnae Derivationes* and Balbi's alphabetical *Catholicon*, and it can be identified with the copy that belonged to Scardeone whose attestation, until Pesenti's recent finds, was the only proof of the work's existence. F. Alfie, 'A sonnet ascribed to Saint Catherine of Siena: attribution and intertextualities', *ItQ*, 153–54:5–18, discusses the authorship of *Oimé che 'l mondo è tanto discaduto*, which is assigned to the Saint by the sole witness (MS Udine 10) but is an implausible *unicum* in her output. A. reconstructs the reception of the *contemptus mundi* theme from the *Carmina Burana*, via Bindo Bonichi, Cecco Angiolieri, Pietro de' Faitinelli, Pieraccio Tedaldi, and Jacopo da Bologna to its 15th-c. comic *fortuna* (Burchiello). P. Cherchi, '"Il mal passo da spino": *Dittamondo*, III, XIX, 79–94', *SFI*, 59, 2001:79–88, explains the obscure reference to the setting of Tydeus's exploit, which is incomprehensible in the light of Statius's *Thebaid*, by reference to the monster Spins (= Sphynx) found in the universal *Histoire ancienne jusqu'à César* incorporating a prose version of the *Roman de Thèbes*: a source suggested by other details of the 'Theban' passage of Fazio degli Uberti's work, such as the location of the meeting between the Argives and Archemoro's nurse Hypsipyle (the garden, not the wood) and the identity of the dragon-killer (Parthenopeus, not Capaneus).

And on points of detail concerning the prose narrative tradition: M. L. Meneghetti and C. Segre, 'Guilhem, Barral e la cornacchia (per la fonte di *Novellino*, XXXIII)', *Siculorum Gymnasium*, 53.1–2, 2000: 313–23, refute the identification of Imberal del Balzo as the Barral Viscount of Marseille in Jean de Nostredame's *Vies* and see the thematic nucleus of the anecdote as being in a lost *razo* relating to the *tenso* in which Uc de Saint-Circ ironizes on the astrological fanaticism of Guilhem del Baus: it was *his* name, they suggest, that was transformed; M.-J. Heijkant, 'La mésaventure érotique de Burletta della Diserta et le motif de la pucelle esforciée dans la *Tavola Ritonda*', *ZRP*, 118: 182–94, looks at the comic contrasts and scabrous details of the digression on the attempted rape of Burletta with reference to medieval legislation and also to similar episodes in Arthurian texts, in comparison to which significant differences are registered: from speaking names and physical and geographical specifications (the *locus amoenus*), enhanced by internal focalization on the attacker and semantic explicitness, to the doubling of the saviour figure, the culprit's suicide by drowning, and the correspondences with the *Elucidation* (13th c.) in the fairy-like characteristics of the victim; and L. Bartolucci, 'Identità e dissimulazione in *Aiolfo* di Andrea da Barberino', *Siculorum Gymnasium*, 53, 2000: 47–67, underlines the centrality of heraldry and of the colours of garments in the Tuscan version of the OF *Aiol*, from avoidance of the arms of Mayence to the use of disguise in the protagonist's adventures at the court of King Aluigi or in those of his cousin Bosolino, whether for pathos (in combat between kinsmen) or for comic effect.

A new conspectus of the period is A. Varvaro, *'Cultura italiana e cultura europea nel Due-Trecento. Il delinearsi di una identità specifica nel contesto occidentale', *Atti* (Rome), 87–104.

3. Boccaccio

V. Branca, *'Boccaccio protagonista nell'Europa letteraria e artistica fra tardo medioevo e rinascimento', *ib.*, 51–86, through the MS tradition of B.'s works surveys his contribution to European humanism. Of fundamental importance is *Il capolavoro del Boccaccio e due diverse redazioni*, 2 vols, Venice, IV: I, Maurizio Vitale, *La riscrittura del Decameron: i mutamenti linguistici*, x + 572 pp., and II, Vittore Branca, *Variazioni stilistiche e narrative*, 220 pp. Starting from Branca's thesis that the version of the *Decameron* contained in MS Par. It. 482 predates Boccaccio's autograph, Vitale examines the formal variants of the text, first distinguishing features attributable to the scribe Capponi from Boccaccian features via a comparison with the *usus scribendi* and linguistic registers of the time, and then going on to indicate the characteristics of the author's '*ratio* correttoria' (a general background levelling in line with current usage as opposed to formal, idiomatic, expressive colouring of the marked traits). Branca backs up his thesis with an ample selection of variants that can be attributed to the author on critical grounds, followed by an examination of their typology and possible etiology where he concentrates in particular on what would appear to be B.'s growing fondness, in maturity, for parody of linguistic 'municipalisms'. An important exploration is Simonetta Mazzoni Peruzzi, *Medioevo francese nel Corbaccio*, F, Le Lettere, 2001, 350 pp. Starting from Hollander's comic interpretation (and early dating) of the *retractio* modelled on Ovid's *Remedia* (and *Ibis*), the author extends stylistic and textual comparison to similar but neglected works, tracing B.'s combinatory technique back from a possible French ancestor, Gautier le Leu's *La Veuve*, to the medieval Latin *Lamentationes* of Mathieu de Boulogne and the classical *Satyricon*: this with reference not only to the 'Ephesian Matron' episode, which was known to B. at least indirectly through John of Salisbury's *Polycraticus* and taken over via the *Sept sages de Rome* (as in *Decameron* II, 2), but also in the love triangle Encolpius–Ascyltos–Giton, which has come down in the *excerpta longa*. On the basis of her investigation M. P. also reverts inconclusively to the vexed question of the title *Corbaccio*. Her interpretation emphasizes the satirical, comic-transgressive, and ironic-parodic aspects of the text. In the posthumous volume Giorgio Padoan, *Ultimi studi di filologia dantesca e boccacciana*, ed. Aldo Maria Costantini, Ravenna, Longo, 176 pp., after three essays respectively devoted to possible relations between Dante and Mussato, to the dating of the *Epistola a Cangrande*, and to the composition of the *Monarchia*, the Boccaccio section comprises five contributions, four of them already published as articles. The first is a defence of P.'s own editing of the *Corbaccio* from the Codice Mannelli; the second and third are devoted to the textual tradition that leads to the 16th-c. editions by Claricio and Gaetano; the fourth to the composition of the *Epistola consolatoria a Pino de' Rossi*; and the fifth to the presence in B.'s works of the 'kindred' myths of Thyestes and Tereus.

Articles on the *Decameron* are numerous. General in scope, G. Cavallini, 'Postilla sulla geografia del Decameron', *RLettI*, 20.3:91–104, starts from Branca's overall interpretation in a consideration of the function of place: from landscape that sustains a succession of adventures (Landolfo, Andreuccio) or fails to do so (Genoa and Monferrato between France and the Holy Land, I, 5) to the broadening of geographical horizons and human prospects in Day II (Alatiel's 'diversi luoghi', a map of branch offices in the Levant); or from the symbolic topography of Florence (Cisti fornaio and Cavalcanti, VI, 2 and 9) to the mixture of topographical fact and fantasy fed to Calandrino (VIII, 3). Two contributions from the same pen are respectively devoted to the *cornice* and Day I: T. Kircher, 'Anxiety and freedom in Boccaccio's history of the plague of 1348', *LIA*, 3:319–58, compares reactions to the Black Death in Villani's *Cronica* and the *Decameron*. Villani adopts the Dominican view and interprets it as the manifestation of Divine Judgement, whereas the *Decameron* is marked by scepticism as to the possibility of Judgement's historical implementation, an attitude B. shares with the Petrarch of *De viris illustribus* and the *Familiares*: while Villani interprets reality as objective and as symbolic of eschatological truths, B. seems aware of the subjectivity of testimony, and of narrative and its reception, and thus appears to accept its partiality. Id., 'The modality of moral communication in the *Decameron*'s first day, in contrast to the mirror of the exemplum', *RQ*, 54, 2001:1035–73, contrasts the narrative contribution of Cavalca's and Passavanti's *exempla* to B.'s novelle (Delcorno) with the irony they are subjected to right from Day I: this is shown by the way the logical protocol of the ideal 'student' is frustrated in the unexpected outcome of Abram's *perizia* (I, 2), by the reversal of the didactic-moralistic model in the elegant allusion of Bergamino (and Primasso, I, 7), and perhaps also by a retort to Pampinea's moralism in the concluding *ballatella*: all this thanks to the studied, essential collaboration of, respectively, Neifile, Filostrato, and Emilia. Two contributions converge in interpreting the novella of Lisabetta. R. Fenu Barbera, 'La fonte delle lacrime di Elisabetta da Messina: *Decameron* 4–5', *QI*, 22, 2001:103–20, pointing to the need for intertextual knowledge if one is to grasp the parody in a novella which seems dramatic or elegiac, identifies its source in Jacopo da Varagine's *Legenda Aurea* (1288) (or a possible antigraph of the late 14th-c. *volgarizzamento* of the Florentine MS Riccardiano 1254): in ch. 168 of the *Legenda*, which is devoted to St Elizabeth, the beautiful but unmarried Saint, like the protagonist of the novella, weeps abundantly, is consoled with a vision, washes a sick youth's head with her tears, cuts off the hair while resting the head in her lap. The mystical ardour of the Saint's young interlocutor has its metaphorical counterpart in the erotic ardour of Lorenzo, a name metonymically determined, in its turn, by the burning of the homonymous saint, whose dead body moreover was decapitated and translated from Rome's *Agrum Verani* to the *Palatio* in the 6th c.: to a basilica and not a pot of *basilico* (basil). In similar fashion, M. A. Terzoli, 'La testa di Lorenzo: lettura di *Decameron* IV, 5', *NRLI*, 4, 2001[2002]:207–26, proposes extending the theme of concealment and discovery to the same novella. She sees this as justified by signals such as the use of *testo* for the pot and the paronomasia *testo/testa*, and it is highlighted by narrative features not present in the folksong from which it derives: the insistence on the lovers' names (Lisabetta being also the name of St John the Baptist's mother) vs the brothers' anonymity, and the decapitation of the dead lover, which, together with the truthful vision, the perfect preservation of the corpse, and the treatment of the relic, akin to the archetypal cult of Jesus by Mary Magdalen, establishes Lorenzo's affinity to the martyrs in a parodic reversal of that cult: a reversal also suggested by the emblematic name of the Saint, who of course is ironically mentioned in another desecrating novella, the story of Fra' Cipolla. F. Lincio, 'Un capitolo della fortuna della novella di Nastagio degli Onesti (*Decameron* V, 8): l'*Innamoramento di Calisto e Giulia* di Francesco Lancillotti', *LItal*, 54:599–615, describes the one extant copy of the illustrated edition of the *poemetto* in 157 *ottave* published at Florence in 1506, and identifies as its source the novella of Nastagio degli Onesti, whose rather meagre *fortuna* is traced from the *capitolo* 'Nel tempo che riduce il carro d'oro' by Francesco di Bonanno di Malecarni (early 15th c.) to Botticelli's 1483 panels, and then to the twofold 'folk' revival by Lancillotti, who follows it in his construction of the story, crossing it with the myth of Persephone (from the *Morgante*) and formulae typical of the *cantari*, and inserts it into the narrative as a well dramatized *mise en abyme*. S. Benedetti Stow, 'Gli sviluppi del concetto dell'*otium* epicureo: dal *Roman de la Rose* a Dante e Boccaccio', *Testo*, 23:115–26, starting from a reading of Reason as an allegory of neo-Platonic Divine Wisdom (Fleming) interprets 'Oziosa' in relation to the Horatian-Epicurean ideal, as is also demonstrated by the *fortuna* of the mirror motif from the *Fiore* to the *Commedia* and in the mystical interpretation of the meeting with Matelda, of the 'fiamma di doppiero', and, in B., of sensual pleasure and the *ballata* 'Io son sì vaga' in the conclusion to Day I, recited by Emilia as is its negative counterpart, novella 8 of Day VI, which again closes with the *locus amoenus* of the *Valle delle Donne*. G. Gorni, 'Invenzione e scrittura nel Boccaccio. Il caso di Guido Cavalcanti', *LIA*, 3:359–74, reads the celebrated novella as a parable *de recta verborum interpretatione*, in which understanding is the first and true subject. Betto Brunelleschi's interpretation is faulty: for his wittiness (here taken over from Dino Del Garbo in Petrarch's *Rerum memorandarum*) there is some historical basis notwithstanding Cino's judgement in 'Qua' son le cose vostre', which the novella seeks to rectify, as there is also for the character of Guido, which is similar in Compagni's *Cronica*. Cavalcanti is indeed a philosopher, as his sonnet against Guittone and an academician's dedication to him of the *Questio de felicitate* confirm, but an Averroist and not an Epicurean, as is borne out by his metaphorical death in 'L'anima mia vilment'è sbigotita', a tendentious reading of 'Una figura della Donna mia', his broken-off pilgrimage, the 'cui [. . .] ebbe a disdegno' of the *Commedia*, and the traditional dichotomy Dante–Guido. The company of storytellers, on the other hand, *are* Epicurean, at home amid tombs like those of *Inf.* 10: the novella, whose source is seen by Gorni to lie in the sonnet 'Se mia laude scusasse te sovente' sent by Compagni to Guido, would therefore be the story of a misunderstanding: the story of Cavalcanti's unbelief. Lastly, G. Lalomia, '*Decameron* X 6: rapporti intertestuali con il *Perceval* di Chrétien de Troyes?', *Siculorum Gymnasium*, 53, 2000: 237–59, posits a common model for the first appearance of the daughters of Neri degli Uberti to King Charles and for the episode of the Castle of the Grail in the motif of the procession that enigmatically interrupts a peaceful conversation and triggers the protagonist's maturing process, with religious symbols (the fish) which B., as in other references to texts by Chrétien, parodies despite his homage to the chivalric virtues of the Arthurian world.

4. Petrarca

The approach of the eighth centenary of P.'s birth has given a marked boost to Petrarch studies. We open the section by noting Klaus Ley, *Die Drucke von Petrarcas 'Rime' 1470–2000. Synoptische Bibliographie der Editionen und Kommentare, Bibliotheksnachweise*, Hildesheim, Olms, lx + 704 pp., an impressive work conducted in collaboration with Christine Mundt-Espìn and Charlotte Krauss. Lists of sources, both traditional (catalogues and bibliographies) and computerized, and of libraries, are followed by a compendium of all the printed editions of P.'s vernacular works (*RVF* and/or the *Trionfi*), from a *princeps* possibly earlier than 1470 (but not extant) to the latest English translation of the millennium and amounting altogether to 1254 bibliographical entries. In the most important cases (mainly, but not solely, incunables and *cinquecentine*) the entries are usefully accompanied with substantial quotations from the chief commentaries and catalogues. Indexes of names and places complete the volume. Devoted to P.'s *fortuna* in European culture, *Dynamique d'une expansion culturelle: Pétrarque en Europe XIVe-XXe siècle. Actes du XXVIe congrès international du CEFI, Turin et Chambéry, 11–15 décembre 1995*, ed. and introd. Pierre Blanc, Paris, Champion, 2001, 767 pp., gathers almost 50 contributions grouped in four sections. The first two are devoted to the defining problems of literary Petrarchism (Hepfer, Kennedy, De Rentiis, Guglielminetti) and extraliterary Petrarchism (Balsamo, Rieger, Bonnifet), the third to illustrating direct cultural influences, plurilingual or translational, projective and interdisciplinary (literature and music), and the last to a differential history of P.'s influence in Europe, from the Low Countries to Camoens's Portugal, and from Poland to Moravia,

Bohemia, and Estonia. Mario Quinto Lupinetti, *Francesco Petrarca e il diritto*, Alessandria, Orso, 1999, 142 pp., expands a study, already published in 1995, which reconstructs P.'s education from his lessons as a four-year-old with Convenevole da Prato at Carpentras to his enforced law studies at Montpellier and Bologna (where he also attended the literary lectures of Giovanni del Virgilio). L. underlines the importance of the law studies notwithstanding their interruption and P.'s return to Provence on the death of his father (1326), the unknown fate of his legal volumes and his rejection of a career in law (possibly practised, however, in Mastino's lawsuit), and his disapproval of the sclerotic academic world with its lack of historical sense. F. Rico, *'Petrarca e il Medioevo', *Atti* (Rome), 39–50.

For the *Canzoniere* pride of place goes to Adelia Noferi, *Frammenti per i fragmenta di Petrarca*, ed. Luigi Tassoni, Ro, Bulzoni, 2001, 248 pp., a collection of studies partly published as articles and comprising three sections respectively devoted to the introductory function of sonnets 1–3, to 'costruzioni di lettura' on other poems in the *Canzoniere* (sonnets 74, 46, 151, 143, 188, 192, 198, and 338, and canzone 127), and to freer 'costruzioni e decostruzioni di senso' which involve other Petrarch texts (*Seniles* IV, 5). In particular, P.'s own fragmentary commentary on *RVF* is traversed following two guiding ideas: the *canzoniere* as self-portrait and P.'s discourse as labyrinthine and (unlike Dante's) unending desire, ever renewed by the *voluptas* of writing. Luca Marcozzi, *La biblioteca di Febo. Mitologia e allegoria in Petrarca*, F, Franco Cesati, 314 pp., aims at a precise definition of the importance in P.'s culture, and especially in *RVF*, of mythology and allegory understood as interpretation based on biblical exegesis and applied, under Augustine's guidance, to non-sacred classical texts (Virgil and Horace). From the definition of allegory the study proceeds via P.'s relations with the mythographic tradition (Isidore of Seville, Fulgentius, Lactantius Placidus, Albrico) to a survey of mythological presences in the *Fragmenta*. Maria Cecilia Bertolani, *Il corpo glorioso. Studi sui 'Trionfi' del Petrarca*, Ro, Carocci, 2001, ix + 96 pp., in the light of the speculative structure of Christian culture proposes a rereading of the *Trionfi* in five essays respectively devoted to P.'s relations with medieval onirology, the symbolic potential of the *visio* in *TM* II, the passage 'Dal sonno alla resurrezione', the changes in the symbology of snow from Cavalcanti's *plazer*, via Dante, to *TM* I 160, and lastly an interpretation of the *Triumphus Aeternitatis* in a profoundly theological perspective.

Still on the *RVF* but in article form: D. De Robertis, 'Di una possibile "pre-forma" petrarchesca', *SFI*, 59, 2001: 89–116, provides a meticulous description and index of a late-14th- or early-15th-c. MS with Umbrian patina preserved at the Laurenziana (Acq. e Doni

831). Its poor physical condition belies its exceptional textual coherence, bringing together as it does not only the partial collections of Dante's *canzoni* but also, and especially, 150 of the *RVF* in a sequence which, with losses that can be reconstructed, does not go beyond the 'forma-Chigi' *corpus* but affords a partly different image of it: 'uno schieramento di materiali in preparazione di una "forma" ancora da mettere a fuoco'. The proceedings of the Paduan Academy carry four *lecturae Petrarcae*: G. Regn, 'L'altra via: umanesimo, filosofia e poesia nel *Canzoniere* di Petrarca (su *Rerum vulgarium fragmenta*, n. 7)', *AMAGP*, 113, 2001: 191–211, analyses the humanistic instance in P.'s vernacular writing, starting from 'La gola e 'l somno et l'otïose piume', his first non-amorous text, perhaps addressed to the monk Giovanni Colonna, a *figura* of the poet, whose 'magnanima impresa' (the *De viris illustribus*?) is contrasted with sensual pleasures and money-making (the context of Avignon is hinted at here), which make solitary the path of a moral philosophy that is not scholastic nor divorced from 'vaghezza di lauro', love of Laura and at the same time love of poetry, which is at the centre of P.'s programme of humanist renewal; G. Ferroni, 'La fenice (*RVF* CLXXXV e altri testi)', *ib.*, 213–29, points out that in P.'s sonnet the mythical creature loses the features (later reverted to in 'Qual più diversa et nova') that it typically has in bestiaries and the Romance lyric: in particular, there is no reference to death (but this re-emerges *in morte* with *RVF* 318 and 321), and what prevails is the phoenix's uniqueness, nobility, and, following Pliny's *Naturalis historia*, its refined and dignified beauty marked by rich details (such as gold round the neck); M. Bianco, 'Fortuna metrica del Petrarca nel Cinquecento: la canzone CCVI', *ib.*, 114: 185–213, looks into the 16th-c. reception of P.'s *escondit*, a homage to Bertran de Born, the specific metrical scheme (*retrogradatio* and *coblas unissonans* and *doblas*) and rhetorical devices (the anaphoric formula 'S'il dissi') of which are taken over by Pietro Barignano ('S'altro amor seguo, i' prego il ciel che mai'), Giulio Poggio ('Se mai più l'amoroso e cieco ardore'), Giacomo Zane ('S'i' 'l dissi mai, che 'l cielo empio e rubello'), Lodovico Paterno ('S'i' 'l dissi mai, che m'arda sempre amore'), and Luigi Groto ('S'io amo altra che voi, che 'l mio morire'); M. Praloran, 'La canzone CXXV', *ib.*, 215–30, reverts to the apparent contrast between *dulcedo* (prevalence of *settenari*, metrical and thematic links with the *suavis* of *RVF* 126) and *gravitas* (the rhymes and *rusticitas* of the *envoi*), underlining the way structural analogies with 'Chiare fresche e dolci acque' (metre–syntax relations, the clear-cut bipartite tonal division, the powerful forward movement) overcome the initial *obscuritas* and a sense of the obsessive harshness of the thought of Love (whereby 'Se 'l pensier' comes to resemble the *petrosa* 'Così nel mio parlar') only when the *impasse* is resolved in the fetishistic conversation with the 'verde riva' and the ensuing contemplation of the imagined beloved.

Turning to P.'s correspondence: E. Fenzi, 'L'ermeneutica petrarchesca tra libertà e verità (a proposito di *Sen.* IV 5)', *LItal*, 54: 170–209, analyses the theory of interpretation evolved by P. in relation to the allegories of the *Aeneid* while grappling (from the *Secretum* to the letter to Federico d'Arezzo) with the fundamental problems raised by Augustine (*Confessions* XI-XII) as to the morality of the biblical exegete and the plurality of interpretations deriving from the notion of truth as being related to the *notitia Dei in interiore homine*; the distinction between *veritas* and *voluntas auctoris* (unknowable) would seem to authorize exegetic freedom (Bernardo Silvestre, William of Conches, Abelard), with a consequent shift, from the sacred to the profane, of the prevalence of the *littera* over the *intentio*. Finally, V. Pacca, 'Un ignoto corrispondente di Petrarca: Francesco Vergiolesi', *NRLI*, 4, 2001[2002]: 151–206, reverts to the variant and the gloss to *TC* 16–18 contained in three of the 16th-c. MS compilations from P. autographs and clarifies the allusion to the addressee of the lost letter of 4 November 1358: not the duped protagonist of *Decameron* III, 5, a presumed Pistoiese *podestà* of Milan in 1326, but a relative of Cino's Selvaggia (banished repeatedly from Pistoia, her family took refuge in such Ghibelline and anti-Florentine cities as Pisa, Lucca, and Milan) who in 1364 was Giudice delle Acque under the Visconti and addressee of sonnet LXXV, 'Io te domando da che nasce el vento', by Antonio Beccari, himself one of P.'s friends and correspondents.

HUMANISM AND THE RENAISSANCE

POSTPONED

SEICENTO

POSTPONED

SETTECENTO

By G. W. Slowey, *Senior Lecturer in Italian, University of Birmingham*

1. General

Hainsworth, *Companion*, covers the 18th c. with a mix of articles on topics (notably Arcadia, the Enlightenment, Literary Theory 1690–1800), of substantial contributions on major writers such as Alfieri, Goldoni, Parini, and the Verri brothers, and well over 100 shorter entries on lesser figures. A. Fabrizi, 'Tra le discussioni sulla lingua nel secondo Settecento (I)', *LN*, 63:1–17, outlines some aspects of the debate on language in the Settecento in relation to position vis-à-vis the Trecento–Cinquecento tradition and attitude towards the growing influence of French in the work of writers such as Algarotti, the Verri brothers, and Beccaria. Id., 'Tra le discussioni sulla lingua nel secondo Settecento (II)', *LN*, 63:72–88, continues the analysis by looking at Alfieri and Parini in particular and at a reforming and innovative tendency in the language linked to changes in the political and social climate. This is contrasted with Carlo Gozzi's opposition not only to such influences on language but also, and even more, to Enlightenment ideas in general. R. Cairo, 'La cultura italiana a Vienna all'epoca di Metastasio', *CLett*, 30:465–83, traces the influence of Italian culture from the time of Eugene of Savoy and deals with various impresarios, musicians and writers, including many who simply passed through, but with whom Metastasio remained in contact. Metastasio's death in 1782 is seen as signalling the decline of Italian cultural influence in Vienna.

AAL, 14:42–183, with the title 'Saggi preparativi per *Settecento riformatore*', contains the text of material prepared by Franco Venturi for his unfinished fifth volume of *Settecento riformatore*, most of which has not previously appeared. The first part deals with Genoa, the second with Tuscany, both in the second half of the 18th century. P. Vitali, 'Lettere d'arte del secolo XVIII. Luigi Crespi ad Innocenzio Ansaldi (1768–1776)', *AAC*, 40, 2000[2001]:47–75, deals with correspondence concerning Ansaldi's book, edited by Crespi, on art in Pescia, though the letters touch on many other cultural aspects of the two men's lives. Luise Flavia, *Librai editori a Napoli nel XVIII secolo. Michele e Gabriele Stasi e il circolo filangeriano*, Na, Liguori, 2001, 276 pp., sets the production of the Stasi family in the context of their links with important figures in 18th-c. Naples, such as Filangieri, Salfi, and Alfonso de' Liguori, and demonstrates the Jansenist aspect of many of Michele's publications, which reflect the anti-Curia stance of Michele and his friends; his activities were carried on by his son,

Gabriele, whose Masonic sympathies led him to support republican ideas, for which he was imprisoned after the fall of the republic in 1799. Again on bookshops as focuses of radical thought we find F. Barbierato, 'La bottega del cappellaio: libri proibiti, libertinismo e suggestioni massoniche nel '700 veneto', *SV*, 44:327–60, which looks at Bortolo Zorzi's shop, known in the 1730s as a meeting point for discussion by various members of Venice's intellectual community, including figures such as Antonio Dolfin and Vittore Molin, until Zorzi was denounced to the Inquisition. The article goes on to examine Zorzi's extensive library, a list of which figures in an appendix. Arianna Grossi, *Annali della tipografia goriziana del Settecento*, Gorizia, Biblioteca Statale Isontina, 2001, lxxv + 298 pp., after an introduction to the work of printers in the city, offers a catalogue of all works published in Gorizia between 1754 and 1800. On the printing of texts in non-roman characters, we have *La stampa e l'illustrazione del libro greco a Venezia tra il Settecento e l'Ottocento. Atti della Giornata di studio, Venezia, 28 ottobre 2000*, Venice, Istituto Ellenico di Studi Bizantini e Postbizantini di Venezia, 2001, 608 pp. In addition, there is Giorgio Vercellin, *Venezia e l'origine della stampa in caratteri arabi*, Padua, Il Poligrafo, 2001, 126 pp., which accompanied an exhibition, held at the Marciana in 2000, on the printing of sacred texts in Venice from the 15th to the 18th c. **Biblioteche nobiliari e circolazione del libro tra Settecento e Ottocento. Atti del Convegno nazionale di studio: Perugia, Palazzo Sorbello, 29–30 giugno 2001*, ed. Gianfranco Tortorelli, Bo, Pendragon, 430 pp. **Editori e tipografi a Varese: l'editoria nel circondario di Varese dal Settecento alla metà del Novecento. Atti del Convegno di studi, 17 novembre 2000, Palazzo Estense, Varese, dedicati a Ernesto Redaelli*, ed. Giorgio Montecchi, Varese, Lativa, 2001, 343 pp.

The whole of *RMC*, 9, 2001[2002], is devoted to *Roma repubblicana, 1798–99, 1849*, and for the Settecento it contains the following: M. P. Donato, 'Costituzione, sovranità, democrazia. La lotta politica nella repubblica del 1798–99' (29–45), which includes in an appendix Damaso Morini's speech of 1799; M. Caffiero, 'La costruzione della religione repubblicana a Roma nel 1798–99: l'uso politico della storia antica' (47–86); C. Canonici, 'Una politica condivisa. Influenze romane e dinamiche locali nella "democratizzazione" del territorio (1798–99)' (87–112); D. Armando, 'Antonio Francesco e la politica religiosa della prima repubblica romana' (113–47); M. Cattaneo, 'Eresia e libertinismo nella Roma di fine Settecento. Il caso Chinard-Rater' (149–92); P. P. Racioppi, 'La repubblica romana e le belle arti (1798–99). Dispersione e conservazione del patrimonio artistico' (193–215). The first fascicule of *RMC*, 10, is on the subject *La città degli artisti nell'età di Pio VI*, ed. Liliana Barroero and Stefano Susinno, and contains the following articles: S. Ferrari, 'L'eredità culturale di

Winckelmann: Carlo Fea e la seconda edizione della *Storia delle arti del disegno presso gli antichi*' (15–48), which discusses Fea's Rome edition of 1783–86, previously considered one of the best versions of Winckelmann's work, but which, in the eyes of the author, is full of 'contradittorie sfaccettature' due to the difficult cultural transition into Italian; S. Rolfi, 'Roma 1793: gli studi degli artisti nel *Giornale* di viaggio di Sofia Albertina di Svezia' (49–89); S. A. Meyer, '"Una gara lodevole". Il sistema espositivo a Roma al tempo di Pio VI' (91–112); D. Wronikowska, 'Gli artisti romani e la corte polacca al tempo di Stanislao Augusto Poniatowski (1764–1795)' (113–29); F. Leone, 'Temi antiquari e letterari come allegoria politica. La decorazione pittorica della Sala delle Muse del Museo pio-clementino' (131–52); P. Coen, 'L'attività di mercante d'arte e il profilo culturale di James Byres of Tonley (1737–1817)' (151–78); S. Grandesso, 'La vicenda esemplare di un pittore "neo-classico": Gaspare Landi, Canova e l'ambiente erudito romano' (179–203); M. Tatti, 'La "dolce tristezza" dell'esplorazione dell'antico: l'ambiguo disincanto di Alessandro Verri' (205–30), which claims that V. is interested in the classical because it touches on his own identity and is his way to 'interagire con il presente storico': she points out that almost all his Roman output is based on, or set in, the classical world; G. Buttazzi, 'Moda e lumi. Il ritratto della Marchesa Margherita Gentili Sparapani Boccapaduli di Laurent Pécheux' (231–39); S. A. Meyer and S. Rolfi, 'L'"Elenco dei più noti artisti viventi a Roma" di Alois Hirt' (242–61). G. Ricuperati, 'La scrittura di un ministro: a proposito della relazione sulle negoziazioni con la corte di Roma di Carlo Vincenzo Ferrero, Marchese d'Ormea', *RSI*, 114:538–76, refers to material in the Turin State Archive detailing the complex relations between Savoy and the Church, and discusses problems relating to Sardinia as well as to the mainland. R. Rugolo, 'Troppe feste! Francesco Maria Preti nella Venezia dei lumi', *SV*, 43:263–97, discusses Preti's *Memorie ed osservazioni intorno alle feste* of 1747 (published in an appendix), which recommend reducing the number of celebrated feast days as being detrimental to the economy; the report is placed in the context of moves to promote more advanced *illuminismo* in Venice, even as late as the 1770s. M. Mamiani, 'The map of knowledge in the age of Alessandro Volta', *StSet*, 21, 2001 [2002]: 159–69, examines the different ways in which 18th-c. encyclopaedists attempted to subdivide and classify the various branches of knowledge according to the distinction between the natural and the artificial, and goes on to show how Volta's defence of man-made electricity helped enhance the intellectual prestige of physics. A. Laguzzi, 'Carlo Barletti e la Società Italiana detta dei XL', *ib.*, 171–215, explores the correspondence and debate between Barletti and Anton Maria Lorgna, as the latter sought to set up a kind of national scientific academy, and also dwells on Barletti's disputes with Gregorio Fontana. A. Bassani, 'Gli scienziati veneti e le ceneri di Roscano: gli studi di Marco Carburi, Pietro e Giovanni Arduino e Anton Maria Lorgna', *SV*, 44:157–240, details technical experimentation in glass production, and sets it against a background of Enlightenment interest which the Venetian state proved incapable of developing; appendices contain aide-memoires by Marco Carburi, Giovanni Arduino, and Anton Maria Lorgna.

Analecta Romana Instituti Danici, 28, has a number of items on the Settecento. G. Salmeri, 'La Sicilia nei libri di viaggio del Settecento tra letteratura e riscoperta della grecità' (65–82), discusses 18th-c. writing on Sicily (notably by Patrick Brydone and Johann Hermann von Riedesel) which served as a model for later writers; particular attention is paid to Goethe. P. Persiani, ' "Vedere biblioteche e vedere il mondo": Frederick Münter ricercatore di manoscritti ed i suoi *Fragmenta Patrum Graecorum*' (83–100), is on the influence of Sicily on Münter's later works, describing his visits to libraries in Naples and Sicily, where he was especially interested in Greek works. In the same issue, there are two items from a conference on Scandinavian travellers in Italy held in Rome in January 2000: M. G. Maiorini, 'I danesi a Napoli nel Settecento: il corpo diplomatico attraverso documenti dell'Archivio di Stato di Napoli' (125–33); and S. Ferrari, 'Libri, storia e *Altertumswissenschaft*. Amadeo Svaier e gli eruditi danesi a Venezia sul finire del Settecento' (135–52). Salvatore Zarcone, **Settecento siciliano*, Palermo, Porta Felice, 123 pp.

**Istituzione, riti e cerimonie dell'ordine de' Franc-Maçons, ossia Liberi muratori: colla descrizione e disegno in rame della loro loggia e insieme un preciso dettaglio delle funeste loro peripezie*, ed. Vittorio Vanni, F, Libreria Chiari–Firenze Libri, 133 pp., is a facsimile reprint of the work first published in 1785. **Antonino Baldovinetti e il riformismo religioso toscano del Settecento*, ed. Daniele Menozzi, Ro, ESL, 266 pp.

Sandra Casellato and Luciana Sitran Rea, **Professori e scienziati a Padova nel Settecento*, Padua, Antilia, xxi + 779 pp. **Periodici toscani del Settecento. Studi e ricerche*, ed. Giuseppe Nicoletti, F, Cadmo, 448 pp. Girolamo Addeo,**Il giornalismo napoletano tra Settecento e Ottocento*, Na, Loffredo, 2001, 248 pp. Anna Lisa Sannino, **L'altro 1799: cultura antidemocratica e pratica politica controrivoluzionaria nel tardo Settecento napoletano*, Na, ESI, 244 pp.

2. Poetry, Prose, Drama

Cristina Bracchi, *Le carte socratiche della poesia. L''otium' critico settecentesco e il canone oraziano*, T, Thélème, 2001, 165 pp., collects and revises a number of studies concerned with 18th-c. interest in Horace on the part of writers such as Volpi, Algarotti, Galiani, and Cesarotti. There is one new item: 'Dalla *Ragion poetica* di Gian Vincenzo Gravina' (9–22), examining Gravina's conception of a 'scienza poetica' which elevates poetry to a level where universal laws of poetry can be established, and identifying Gravina, through his study of poetry, and of Horace in particular, as a promoter of the notion that the form gives pleasure and the content gives profit, along the lines of Horace's 'utile dulci'. A. Di Ricco, 'Fortuna del genere satirico nella Toscana del Settecento', *RLI*, 106:32–59, draws on Giuseppe Bianchini's *Trattato della satira italiana* (1714) to introduce a discussion which also relates to Masi's publication of the Italian satirists (Livorno, 1786–88) under the editorship of Gaetano Poggiali. The writer also looks at the contribution made by Anton Maria Salvini's *Discorsi accademici* of 1712, the *Satire* of Benedetto Menzini (1718) and the satires of Anton Filippo Adami (1757). C. E. Roggia, 'Sulla lingua della poesia nell'età dell'illuminismo', *LS*, 37:251–85, traces the process of language specialization which has been identified as a feature of poetic language in the Settecento, drawing on Parini's *Giorno* and *Discorso sopra la poesia* as well as on contributors to *Il Caffè*, on Cesarotti's *Saggio sulla filosofia della lingua*, and on Beccaria's writings. *Antologia della poesia italiana*, ed. Cesare Segre and Carlo Ossola, VI: *Il Settecento*, T, Einaudi, xxiii + 356 pp., is a reprint of the Pléiade edition published in 1977.

Tatiana Crivelli, *Né Arturo né Turpino né la Tavola rotonda: romanzi del secondo Settecento italiano*, Ro, Salerno, 339 pp., discusses elements such as pseudo-autobiography and the presentation of female protagonists to show the contemporary nature of late-18th-c. Italian novel writing. C. examines the models used by Italian writers, looks at the public, authors, and publishers, points out the educative intent of some of the writing, and in the last part analyses in detail the typology of the *romanzo* with much reference to Antonio Piazza and Pietro Chiari. She concludes with an extremely useful catalogue of Italian novels of the period. P. Rambelli, 'La funzione della pseudotraduzione nella ridefinizione dell'intellettuale nel secondo Settecento', *AIV*, 160, 2001–02:195–262, a lengthy case-study of the Italian version of a French pseudo-translation, Jacques Cazotte, *Le Lord Impromptu*, highlights the function of pseudo-translations as aiming to promote and legitimize a new 'authorial profile' founded on the principle of authorship, as opposed to authority.

Franco Arato, *La storiografia letteraria nel Settecento italiano*, Pisa, ETS, 507 pp., is an excellent work, most of it entirely new, which ranges widely over aspects of literary analysis and debate in the Settecento, from analysis of *La Biblioteca* of Giusto Fontanini, and Apostolo Zeno's criticisms of it, through discussion of *buon gusto* and the perennial literary debates on the relative value of French and Italian literature by writers such as Giacinto Gimma and Francesco Saverio Quadrio. There are sections on biography and theatre history, and extensive discussion of such figures as Girolamo Tiraboschi, Saverio Bettinelli, and Carlo Denina; there is also an interesting chapter on the Spanish Jesuit exile Juan Andrés and his *Dell'origine, progressi e stato attuale d'ogni letteratura*, published in Parma between 1782 and 1799. Enrico Tiozzo, **La trama avventurosa nelle autobiografie italiane del Settecento*, Göteborg, Hovidius Forlag, 321 pp. *Annali della Biblioteca Statale e Libreria Civica di Cremona*, 54, 263 pp., is devoted to Enzo Rangognini, 'L'istitutore aragonese. Lettere di Ramón Ximénez de Cenarbe a Fabio Ala (1787–1815)', an edition of Italian correspondence from an exiled Spanish Jesuit who became tutor to the sons of the Ala family and frequented Enlightenment and Masonic circles in Cremona.

Legge, poesia e mito. Giannone, Metastasio e Vico fra 'tradizione' e 'trasgressione' nella Napoli degli anni Venti del Settecento, ed. Mario Valente, Ro, Aracne, 2001, lxxvii + 530 pp., the proceedings of a conference held in Naples, 3–5 March 1998, contains five main sections: I. *Gli intellettuali e la vita civile*, comprises R. Ajello, 'Una cultura "trasgressiva" nella formazione di Metastasio. Aspetti del dibattito epistemologico a Napoli negli anni Venti del Settecento' (3–30); G. Ricuperati, 'Pietro Giannone da Napoli a Vienna, alle prigioni piemontesi: per una rilettura critica' (31–78); S. Gensini, 'G. B. Vico e la tradizione della retorica civile e dell'ingegno: tra Napoli e l'Europa' (79–98); G. Giarrizzo, 'Da Napoli a Vienna: il circolo meridionale della filosofia del Metastasio' (99–126); II. *Metastasio e la tradizione*: M. Valente, 'Pietro Metastasio e il senso del "tradere" ' (127–64); F. Lomonaco, 'Tra "Ragion poetica" e vita civile: Metastasio discepolo di Gravina e Caloprese' (165–202); G. Ferroni, 'Il Metastasio napoletano tra l'*Istoria civile* e la *Scienza nuova*' (203–22); III. *Metastasio tra teoria e pratica teatrale*: M. T. Marcialis, ' "Un'imperfetta tragedia che non può avere applauso fuori delle note e del canto." Il melodramma fra bizzaria e illusione' (225–46); E. Sala di Felice, 'Non solo i classici: Metastasio lettore delle *Réflexions critiques sur la poësie et sur la peinture* di Jean-Baptiste Du Bos' (247–80); F. Cotticella and P. Maione, 'Funzioni e prestigio del modello metastasiano a Napoli: Saverio Mattei e le proposte di una nuova drammaturgia' (281–322); F. Coscia, 'La scena del mito nel teatro di Metastasio' (323–33); IV. *Metastasio e la musica*: T. M. Gialdroni and A. Ziino, ' "Quella grazia che non nasce dalla stravaganza." Osservazioni sul gusto musicale di Metastasio' (337–62); C. Campa, 'Metastasio, Napoli e l'Europa: omologazione del melodramma tra estetica dell'imitazione e modelli riformistici' (363–96); P. Cinque, 'La declamazione tra parlato e canto nel secondo Settecento e Pietro

Metastasio' (397–416); R. Meyer, 'Die Rezeption der Dramen Metastasios im 18. Jahrhundert' (417–51); v. *Metastasio e Napoli 'instruita' e costruita*: M. A. Pavone, 'Riflessi del teatro metastasiano sulla pittura napoletana della prima metà del Settecento' (455–78); L. Di Mauro, 'Architettura e urbanistica a Napoli al tempo di Pietro Metastasio' (479–95). An appendix contains three autograph letters from Metastasio to Anna de Amicis.

R. Rabboni, 'Il carteggio fra Antonio Conti e Cornelio Bentivoglio (con lettere inedite)', *AMAGP*, 113, 2000–01 : 81–138, considers the two writers' discussion of tragedy, which concentrated in particular on Conti's *Giulio Cesare* and *Druso*; their exchange of letters is given in an appendix. **La maschera e il volto: il teatro in Italia*, ed. Francesco Bruni, Venice, Marsilio, ix + 498 pp. Francesca Bascialli, **Opera comica e opéra comique al Teatro Arciducale di Monza, 1778–1795*, Lucca, Libreria Musicale Italiana, 172 pp. **I teatri di Ferrara: commedia, opera e ballo nel Sei e Settecento*, ed. Paolo Fabbri, Lucca, Libreria Musicale Italiana, 2 vols, xlvii + 538, xvii + 542–740 pp.

3. Individual Authors

ALFIERI. *Alfieri in Toscana. Atti del Convegno internazionale di studi, Firenze, 19–20–21 ottobre 2000*, ed. Gino Tellini and Roberta Turchi, F, Olschki, 2 vols, vii + 1–426, 427–833, is divided into four sections: I. *Introduzione*: A. Di Benedetto, '"Arrivammo a Firenze...". La Toscana di Vittorio Alfieri tra mito ed esperienza' (3–20); G. Ricuperati, 'Alfieri politico e testimone critico del suo tempo' (21–49); II. *Edizioni e Lettori*: R. Turchi, 'Dalla Pazzini Carli alla Didot' (51–86); R. Pasta, 'Guglielmo Piatti editore di Alfieri' (87–120); C. Doni, 'Le tragedie nella recensione del *Corriere europeo*' (121–30); F. Arduini, 'Vicende della biblioteca di Alfieri: un dono "munifico" di François-Xavier Fabre alla Palatina di Ferdinando III' (131–66); L. Melosi, 'Agli inizi della critica alfieriana: la polemica Carmignani–De Coureil' (167–201); III. *Le opere degli anni toscani*: G. Tellini, 'Storia e romanzo dell'io nella "bizzarra mistura" della *Vita*' (203–20); G. Nicoletti, 'Dalla "fonte delle rime" alfieriane: i sonetti fiorentini della *Parte seconda*' (221–39); M. Biondi, '"Saette dell'ira scrivana". Temi e stile del discorso politico alfieriano' (239–62); S. Costa, 'Per una poetica del "riso": Alfieri comico' (263–82); A. Bruni, 'Presenza di Shakespeare in Alfieri' (283–306); P. Luciani, 'Alfieri e le poetiche settecentesche del comico' (307–22); M. Sterpos, 'Il misogallismo alfieriano e gli avvenimenti toscani dell'anno 1799' (323–42); C. Barbolani, 'Suggestioni dantesche nella *Congiura de' Pazzi*' (343–68); E. De Troja, 'Vita e scrittura nelle lettere agli amici di Toscana'

(369–84); B. Anglani, 'Il personaggio della *Vita*' (385–410); E. Mattioda, 'Machiavelli nei trattati politici' (411–24); F. Fido, 'Il circolo tirannide/tirannicidio nella saga medicea: *L'Etruria vendicata*' (427–36); G. A. Camerino, ' "Sublimi verità in sublime stile notate". Un dialogo "toscano" e la poetica dell'Alfieri tragico' (437–50); C. Domenici, 'Seneca nel giudizio di Alfieri: "poeta magnus" o "declamator"?' (451–90); C. Del Vento, ' "Io dunque ridomando alla plebe francese i miei libri, carte ed effetti qualunque". Alfieri "émigré" a Firenze' (491–578); V. Colombo, 'Episodi inediti dell'Alfieri spiemontizzato' (579–602); M. Danzi, 'Un ritrovamento alfieriano: l'idiografo D.II del *Misogallo* (e una lettera di François-Xavier Fabre a Giovanni degli Alessandri)' (603–45); IV. *Soggiorni toscani, cultura figurativa e musicale*: A. Fabrizi, 'Alfieri e i letterati toscani' (647–732); G. Santato, 'Alfieri e Firenze: dai viaggi letterari alla fuga nella classicità' (737–56); C. Sisi, 'Temi figurativi intorno ad Alfieri' (757–66); P.-C. Buffaria, 'Illusioni ottiche e silenzi autobiografici: François-Xavier Fabre pittore della "fiorentinità" secondo Alfieri' (767–80); A. Sacchetti, 'L'arte musicale intorno ad Alfieri: realtà del suo tempo e riflessi creativi' (781–804).

The supplement to the *Italianist*, 21, 2001–02, ed. John Lindon, is entitled *Alfieri Revisited* and contains the following items: V. Branca, 'Alfieri fra tragedia mitico-orrorosa e dramma realistico borghese' (7–18), which discusses A.'s move from psychological tragedy in *Oreste* and *Agamennone* and the theatre of passions towards an expression of individual personality in plays such as *Mirra* and *Saul*, with parallel linguistic development thanks to an 'ostinata ricerca di linguaggio piano e domestico'; P. Trivero, 'Solitudini alfieriane' (19–30), which begins with an examination of sonnet 173 and moves through the *Vita* and *Rime*, as well as the plays, to illustrate the concept of solitude in A.'s personal as well as artistic life; A. Di Benedetto, 'Le occasioni di un anniversario: Vittorio Alfieri tra Parini e Goethe' (31–47), which draws on Parini's comments and much-valued suggestions to A. on his style and then goes on to A.'s exact contemporary Goethe, never mentioned by A. but who took an interest in A.'s work while expressing reservations about its grandiose aspirations and some of its structural elements; A. Fabrizi, 'Da Alfieri a Gobetti' (48–57), which deals with Gobetti's use of the Alfierian motto τί μοι σὺν δούλοισιν (che ci ho a fare coi schiavi) for his publishing ventures, including the first edition of Montale's *Ossi di seppia*; M. Cerruti, 'Alfieri e la cultura inglese' (58–65), which contrasts A.'s enthusiasm for England in his first two visits with his lack of sparkle in describing the other two, ascribing this to political as well as literary factors; J. Lindon, 'Ancora su "l'amore londinese di Vittorio Alfieri" ' (66–78), which uses court documents alongside the draft and definitive versions of the *Vita* to illustrate the process of *riscrittura* in A.'s account of his affair with Lady Penelope Ligonier and of the subsequent divorce — in which the husband was awarded a massive sum in damages — and thus to explain A.'s thirteen-year absence from England after the second visit.

Vittorio Cian, *Vittorio Alfieri a Pisa*, ed. Alessandra Panajia, Pisa, ETS, 84 pp., which includes an essay by L. Veronesi Pesciolini, is a reprint of an item which first appeared in *Nuova Antologia* in 1903. F. Longoni, '"Ecco il tiranno". Quale testo della *Merope* maffeiana lesse l'Alfieri?', *StSet*, 21, 2001[2002]: 111–40, comments on Scipione Maffei's lack of interest, for many years, in editions of his own work, and attempts to identify which of two probable editions (1730 and 1745) was the text Alfieri used the most, discussing the textual differences between them, and concluding from the evidence that A. was using the 1730 edition rather than the 1745, Maffei's own revision of the work. L. Scotto D'Aniello, 'Considerazioni sull'*Andria* di Terenzio tradotta da Vittorio Alfieri', *AION(SR)*, 44:155–73, discusses how Terence's universality attracted A. in his self-imposed task of translating, in 1790, the plays of Terence in order to discover his own comic style. C. Leri, '"All'orlo della vita". Il tempo nelle *Rime* di Vittorio Alfieri', *LItal*, 54:210–41, links composition of some of A.'s verse with specific episodes of the *Vita*, emphasizing the 'illusoria fantasmatica' of Fortune in order to highlight the notion of 'saggio'. The article also asserts that A.'s idea of interiority is a kind of refuge. P. Rambelli, 'La scoperta dell'Io e la (ri)costruzione della figura del letterato nelle prose e nelle tragedie di Alfieri', *CLett*, 30:35–69, draws on early works such as *Esquisse du jugement universel* (1773) as well as on the *Vita* to examine A.'s re-creation and repositioning of himself in his partly autobiographical works as well as in the *Giornale*; in the analysis of the tragedies, the tyrant is seen as A.'s authorial 'doppio', while points are made about the interior dramatization of the *Io* in works such as *Saul* and *Mirra*, claiming that A. worked hard to keep this figure of the intellectual above changes in late-18th-c. society and in particular away from bourgeois notions of the market. A. Fabrizi, 'Qualche novità su Alfieri e "Aillaud"', *ib.*, 30:495–506, concerns Jean-Antoine Ailliaud and writing on him and Alfieri by Auguste Hus in his book on famous men of Piedmont and France: some of the references from Hus are given in an appendix. Id., 'Alfieri da Gobetti a Fubini', *ib.*, 30: 71–77, analyses the contribution to A. studies made by 20th-c. writers. *'Per far di bianca carta nera'. Prime edizioni e cimeli alfieriani*, ed. Vittorio Colombo et al., Savigliano, L'Artistica Savigliano, 2001, 152 pp., is the catalogue of an exhibition (Biblioteca Reale, Turin, 2001), but its value goes beyond the exhibition in that it reproduces letters, prints, manuscripts, and other interesting documents with useful description and comment by the editors.

BANDINI. Rosario Pintaudi, **Un erudito del Settecento: Angelo Maria Bandini*, Messina, Sicania, 224 pp.

BENTIVOGLIO D'ARAGONA. R. Rabboni, '"Riflessioni sopra la divina traduzione del libro X della Tebaide di Stazio", di anonimo bolognese', pp. 67–109 of *Testi e linguaggi per Paolo Zolli*, ed. Giampaolo Borghello, Modena, Mucchi, 2001, 206 pp., is a follow-up to Rabboni's 2000 edition of B.'s translation of Statius (*YWMLS*, 63:494) and looks at a paper with various comments and suggestions which were probably made by an old acquaintance of B.'s in Bologna.

BERTOLA. Aurelio de' Giorgi Bertola, *Della filosofia della storia*, ed. Fabrizio Lomonaco, Na, Liguori, lxxvi + 185 pp., a welcome addition to modern editions of Bertola, follows the 1787 text but reproduces marginalia from B.'s own 'working copy' preserved at Rimini. An illuminating introduction traces the tract's genesis and 'philosophic' sources, notably Montesquieu and Hume.

BETTINELLI. Saverio Bettinelli, *Tiranni a teatro: 'Demetrio Poliorcete' e 'Serse re di Persia'*, ed. Francesco Saverio Minervini, Bari, Palomar, 319 pp.

BIANCHINI. L. Zaniboni, 'Francesco Bianchini a Londra nel 1713', *QLL*, 26, 2001:71–86, discusses B.'s journeys on behalf of the Pope in his official capacity as superintendent of Rome's antiquities, and gives the text of his report to the papal authorities, *Cose più cospicue di Londra*.

CAMINER TURRA. C. M. Sama, 'Becoming visible: a biography of Elisabetta Caminer Turra (1751–1796) during her formative years', *SV*, 43:349–88, looks at the attacks of such as Carlo Gozzi on a woman not content to remain on the fringes of culture and learned society, and at her differences of opinion with Cristoforo Venier in 1770 in the context of what the author describes as her ability 'to successfully manipulate the system of male patronage'.

CASANOVA. *Casanova, fin de siècle. Actes du Colloque, Grenoble 8–10 Octobre 1998*, ed. Marie-Françoise Luna, Paris, Champion, 384 pp., contains the following items: I. *Casanova et l'Europe fin de siècle*: M.-F. Luna and J. Oudart, 'La maison de Casanova à Grenoble' (13–26); J. Polišenský, 'Les trois dernières années de la vie de Casanova' (27–30); S. Ostrovská, 'Casanova et la société de Bohême' (31–36); H. Watzlawick, 'Casanova et la Vienne de Joseph II à Franz II' (37–54); A. Stroev, 'Les frères Casanova et le prince Alexandre Belosselski' (55–72); M.-F. Viallon-Schoneveld, 'Casanova avocat de Venise' (73–92); G. Luciani, 'Les lettres du patricien Pietro Zaguri à Casanova e la chute de Venise' (93–104); J. Solé, 'Casanova et la

Révolution française' (105–13); II. *Le mémorialiste*: G. Coppel, 'L'argent de Casanova' (117–40); G. Nerdrum, 'Casanova, inspirateur de la doctrine juridique en Norvège?' (141–44); M.-O. Laflamme, 'Le monde et l'experience: esthétique de la connaissance dans les *Mémoires* de Casanova' (145–56); A. Leroy, 'Casanova ou l'instinct de conversation' (157–64); H. A. Glaser, 'I viaggi di Casanova o "le beau moment de partir"' (165–78); I. Kovács, 'Casanova e Marivaux' (179–92); R. Bombosch, 'Casanova et la pensée politique de Voltaire' (193–202); H. Scheible, 'Les *Mémoires* de Casanova et la littérature allemande' (203–32); A. Sebbah, 'De Casanova à Luis Buñuel' (223–55); III. *Le 'philosophe'*: B. Didier, 'Les couleurs dans l'*Icosaméron*' (259–66); M.-F. Bosquet, 'Le féminin dans l'empire mégamicre de l'*Icosaméron*' (267–82); M. Stefani, 'Casanova et la culture des Lumières; l'*Icosaméron*' (283–302); P. Mengal, 'Autour de *Lana Caprina*: la controverse de l'"utero pensante"' (303–10); E. Straub, 'L'article "chimie" dans l'*Essai de critique sur les mœurs, sur les sciences et sur les arts*' (311–22); G. Lahouati, 'Testament écrit sur du vent: la lettre *A Leonard Snetlage*, autoportrait au dictionnaire' (323–37); in appendix there is a transcription by Federico Di Trocchio of *Delle passioni*.

Francesco Serra, *Casanova autobiografo*, Venice, Marsilio, 2001, x + 156 pp., is more concerned with C.'s writings than with the bare, well-known facts of his life, and bases itself primarily on the *Mémoires*, presenting his intellectual side as fully part of the Enlightened world of the 18th c.

Alberto Boatto, **Casanova e Venezia*, Ro–Bari, Laterza, 180 pp. Giacomo Casanova, **Il mio apprendistato a Parigi*, F, Passigli, 144 pp. **Passioni e teatri di Casanova*, ed. Giuseppe Gargiulo, F, Cadmo, 126 pp. Marcello Vannucci, **Casanova*, F, Polistampa, 190 pp.

CASTI. M. I. Palazzolo, 'Le vicissitudini di un libertino. Fortuna editoriale e sfortuna critica delle opere di Giambattista Casti', *NRLI*, 4:383–413, discusses the banning in Italy of works by C. such as *Gli animali parlanti* as well as the *Novelle galanti* and the *Poema tartaro*, both published after his death. The author notes the institutional censorship, but also the broadly negative response to these works in the early 19th c.

CESAROTTI. *Aspetti dell'opera e della fortuna di Melchiorre Cesarotti: Gargano del Garda, 4–6 ottobre 2001*, ed. Gennaro Barbarisi and Giulio Carnazzi, Mi, Cisalpino, 2 vols, xxi + 437, 476 pp., contains the following articles: F. Biasutti, 'Tra ragione ed esperienza. Melchiorre Cesarotti nella cultura filosofica del suo tempo' (1–17); A. Battistini, 'Un "critico di sagacissima audacia": il Vico di Cesarotti' (19–70); G. Pizzamiglio and M. Fantato, 'Per l'*Epistolario* di Melchiorre Cesarotti' (71–114); L. Lehnus, 'Cesarotti e la questione omerica' (115–32); F. Fedi, 'Aspetti neoclassici della traduzione omerica'

(133–54); F. Favaro, '*La Morte di Ettore* dall'epica al dramma' (157–81); G. Benedetto, 'Cesarotti e gli oratori attici' (183–204); F. Lo Monaco, 'Il Demostene di Cesarotti' (205–20); M. Mari, 'L'incerto Giovenale dell'ultimo Cesarotti' (221–38); W. Spaggiari, 'Le satire di Giovenale fra Sette e Ottocento' (239–82); R. Zucco, 'Il polimetro di Ossian' (283–342); D. Goldin Folena, 'Cesarotti, la traduzione e il melodramma' (343–68); G. Melli, ' "Gareggiare con il mio originale". Il "personaggio" del traduttore nel pensiero di Melchiorre Cesarotti' (369–89); T. Matarrese, 'Le traduzioni da Voltaire e il linguaggio del teatro tragico' (391–402); P. Ranzini, 'Dalla traduzione alla critica e alla poetica. L'importanza del dibattito sulla tragedia e sul tragico nell'opera di Cesarotti' (403–35); G. Carnazzi, 'Alfieri, Cesarotti e il "verso di dialogo" ' (437–68); A. Beniscelli, 'Cesarotti e Alfieri: ai confini di una nuova drammaturgia' (469–95); A. Nacinovich, 'Cesarotti e l'Arcadia. Il *Saggio sulla Filosofia del gusto*' (497–517); L. Frassineti, 'Ricezione del soprannaturale in Cesarotti traduttore di Voltaire' (519–37); F. Brioschi, 'Cesarotti e il sensismo' (539–48); G. Venturi, 'La selva di Giano: Cesarotti e il Genius Loci' (549–67); D. Tongiorgi, ' "Rozze rime e disadatte forme": (pre)storia di una traduzione elegiaca' (569–95); E. Farina, 'Aspetti dell'ossianismo ortisiano' (597–617); A. Terzoli, 'Cesarotti e Foscolo' (619–47); C. Del Vento, 'Foscolo, Cesarotti e i "poeti primitivi" ' (649–59); A. Bruni, 'Cesarotti nell'*Iliade* di Vincenzo Monti' (661–724); A. Colombo, 'L' eredità dantesca di Cesarotti. Quirico Viviani editore della *Commedia* in un postillato di Vincenzo Monti' (725–84); L. Blasucci, 'Sull'ossianismo leopardiano' (785–816); L. Danzi, 'Cesarotti e Manzoni' (817–33); F. Mazzocca, 'La fortuna figurativa di Ossian in Italia negli anni della restaurazione' (835–55).

CHIARI. M. Saulini, 'Le eroine tragiche dell'abate Chiari', *Angelini Vol.*, 139–62, looks at C.'s four historical tragedies, discussing the secondary role played by women, yet showing women as characters who can stand up to misfortune, being equal to men in courage and determination.

COMPAGNONI. Giuseppe Compagnoni, *Lettere varie (1776–1832)*, introd. and ann. Marcello Savini, Ravenna, Longo, 2001, 224 pp., in addition to matters political and social, discusses cultural and literary topics, especially in C.'s correspondence with Francesco Albergati Capacelli, where he writes of Alfieri and the theatre, and his lack of sympathy with the post-1815 restauration is also clear.

CORILLA OLIMPICA. *Corilla Olimpica e la poesia del Settecento europeo. Atti del convegno tenuto in occasione delle celebrazioni del secondo centenario della morte di Maria Maddalena Morelli, Pistoia, 21–22 ottobre 2000*, ed. Moreno Fabbri, Pistoia, Artout, 190 pp., useful for its analysis of Corilla

Olimpica's improvisation and attesting to her influence well outside Tuscany and Italy, contains the following articles: R. Risaliti, 'La poesia in Russia nel secondo Settecento' (17–30)'; F. Finotti, 'Il canto delle Muse: improvvisazione e poetica della voce' (31–42); E. Biagini, 'Corilla, Corinne e *L'Improvisation poétique en Italie*' (43–54); A. Di Ricco, 'L'improvvisazione poetica nel Settecento' (55–58); L. Morelli, 'Fascino, genio, mistero e "affari di Stato": il successo italiano e europeo di Corilla Olimpica' (59–64); S. Merendoni, 'Il carteggio fra Corilla Olimpica e l'abate Giovanni Cristofano Amaduzzi' (65–68); G. Cantarutti, '"Doctus Italus, Amadutius", con documenti su Corilla e gli "Oltramontani"' (69–86); I. Amaduzzi, 'Corilla Olimpica e il mio avo Giovanni Cristofano Amaduzzi' (87–90); M. Feo, 'Il *canzoniere* di Corilla' (91–116); A. Cipriani, 'Corilla Olimpica e Pistoia nel Settecento' (117–22); M. Battignani, 'Il ritorno di Corilla' (123–34); F. Savi, 'Catalogo. Mostra di manoscritti, libri, stampe' (135–52); and P. Giuli, 'Corilla Olimpica improvvisatrice: a reappraisal' (155–72).

CUOCO. Fulvio Tessitore, *Filosofia, storia e politica in Vincenzo Cuoco*, Cosenza, Marco, 366 pp., collects both already-published essays and some C. texts published for the first time. Id., 'Vincenzo Cuoco e la rivoluzione napoletana del 1799', *AISS*, 17, 2000[2001]: 669–87, looks at C.'s distinction between active and passive revolution (and refusal to distinguish between the good and the bad) and also at his unwillingness to argue that there is a perfect form of government. D. Morlino, 'Il pensiero economico di Vincenzo Cuoco: agricoltura, demani ed usi civici', *RSR*, 89: 483–502, deals with various writings by C. on economic matters, seeing them as part of the context in which an interpretation of his political thought can be attempted, but characterizes him as having a 'scarsa conoscenza della realtà del Regno' because he is too closely concerned with a 'concezione illuministica' of economic problems. **Vincenzo Cuoco nella cultura di due secoli. Atti del Convegno internazionale, Campobasso, 20–22 gennaio 2000*, ed. Luigi Biscardi and Antonino De Francesco, Ro–Bari, Laterza, vi + 287 pp.

DA PONTE. G. Nicastro, 'La commedia dell'amore e della seduzione nei libretti viennesi di Da Ponte', *RLettI*, 20.2: 41–67, traces the influence of Goldoni and Beaumarchais, not only on the three libretti for Mozart, but also on *Il ricco di un giorno* for Salieri and *Una cosa rara* for Martín y Soler as well as *Il demogorgone* for Vincenzo Righini and other works which illustrate Da P.'s constant themes of love and seduction. N. also looks at other libretti written for Salieri before Da P. left Vienna after the death of Joseph II. Lorenzo Da Ponte, **Saggio di traduzione libera di Gil Blas*, Mi, Il Polifilo, 94 pp.

DI LORENA CARIGNANO. L. Ricaldone, 'Una letterata a corte: Giuseppina di Lorena Carignano', Bracchi, *Alterità*, 47–63, presents one born into French nobility but who spent nearly all her life in Piedmont, where she wrote novels and travel accounts in which the ideal woman with moral strength, self-confidence, and cultural intelligence is able to make her own way in life.

GAGLIARDI. M. Toscano, 'Gaetano Maria Gagliardi (1758–1814): una testimonianza intellettuale a Napoli tra Settecento e Ottocento', *AISS*, 17, 2000[2001]: 609–68, examines G.'s participation in literary academies and his poetic production whose results are described as 'molto diseguali'. In later life he cultivated antiquarian pursuits, became involved in Masonic circles, and participated in the Neapolitan republic of 1799; after which he wrote verse for the restored Bourbons and took charge of the Accademia di Belle Arti and various museum projects.

GALDI. A. Granese, 'La rivoluzione culturale di Matteo Angelo Galdi', *CLett*, 30: 507–26, begins by examining G.'s *Necessità di stabilire una repubblica in Italia* (1796), then traces through his other writings (those, for example, in the *Giornale de' patrioti d'Italia*) his vision of history, which drew inspiration from Filangieri and Pagano, in support of rights which had been won by Italian democrats and Jacobins.

GENOVESI. M. T. Marcialis, 'Scienza e filosofia nella *Dissertatio physico-historica de rerum origine et constitutione* di Antonio Genovesi', *RSF*, 57: 601–12, examines G.'s theory that scientific thinking develops around notions of chaos and order in three stages: poetic, metaphysical, physical.

GIANNONE. Giuseppe Ricuperati, *La città terrena di Pietro Giannone: un itinerario tra crisi della coscienza europea e illuminismo radicale*, F, Olschki, 2001, xvi + 196 pp., is part of a series on toleration in Europe. The first chapter examines questions of tolerance as presented in the *Istoria civile* and also, in the *Triregno*, touches on the treatment of Jews and Muslims, covering G.'s attack on unjust persecution; chapter two looks at an incomplete MS of the *Triregno* in the archives of the Inquisition in Rome, linking it with the necessity for a properly researched edition; chapter three deals with, in particular, the *Ape ingegnosa* as an example of G.'s interest in the links between man and nature, in what R. calls his 'antropologia religiosa'; chapter four looks at questions of historiography in relation to G. and his autobiography. Michele Dell'Aquila, **Pietro Giannone: il pensatore, il perseguitato, l'esule*, Fasano, Schena, 104 pp.

GIULIANI. Veronica Giuliani, *Pagine autobiografiche*, ed. Luisa Ricaldone, Balerna, Ulivo, 2001, 48 pp., offers selections from G.'s diary.

GOLDONI. Giuseppina Scognamiglio, *Ritratti di donna nel teatro di Carlo Goldoni*, Na, ESI, 158 pp., argues that G. is openly in favour of women and that he fights with them in the name of justice and freedom: while he presents noblewomen in a largely negative light, he shows the positive side of those from lower levels of society. Mirandolina is extensively discussed and defined as a woman through comparison with figures in a number of other plays. Also on G.'s presentation of women, but from a different angle is G. Da Pozzo, 'Coerenza e sperimentalità goldoniana nella *Dalmatina*', *RLI*, 106:13–31, which examines *La Dalmatina* (1758) alongside other plays, emphasizing G.'s development of the link between *virtù* and *coraggio* and of some notion of *patria*. P. Trivero, 'Una soap-opera settecentesca: la trilogia persiana di Carlo Goldoni', *Angelini Vol.*, 93–105, considers the presentation of young versus old in the trilogy, linking the argument with the disputes, or difficulties, at the S. Luca theatre, where G. wanted to give good parts to the young Caterina Bresciani as well as to the older Teresa Gandini, who also just happened to be the wife of the *capocomico*. L. Squartana, 'Due *Ventagli*', *Borsellino Vol.*, 473–77, discusses the background to the Italian and French versions of *Il ventaglio*, and points out the element of melancholy to be found in the play. P. Del Negro, 'Carlo Goldoni e la massoneria veneziana', *StS*, 43:411–19, draws on *Le donne curiose* to present G.'s stage Masonic lodge, set in Bologna, which is shown to be no threat to the Church or the established state, but on the contrary to be innocuous, dedicated to 'onoratissima conversazion'. F. Angelini, 'Nei dintorni della villeggiatura', *Borsellino Vol.*, 467–71, links G.'s own experiences on his travels, where he saw different kinds of theatre in places such as Rome and Parma, with the general circumstances of the composition of the trilogy of the *Villeggiatura*, asserting that the plays reflect G.'s increasing concern at the inability of people to achieve social solidarity or true freedom. C. Alberto, 'Maschere raggelate. Lettura de *Le massere* di Carlo Goldoni. Esercizio di drammaturgia: dal testo al copione', *Angelini Vol.*, 107–37, presents the four different characters of the *massere* in their domestic and carnival setting, interpreting the play in the context of a 'decadimento che investe ogni categoria sociale' and emphasizing the presence throughout the play of 'un soffio di morte'. Ginette Herry, **Goldoni à Venise. La Passion du poète*, Paris, Champion, 264 pp. New volumes have appeared in the national edition of G.'s comedies: Carlo Goldoni, *Gl'innamorati*, ed. Siro Ferrone, Venice, Marsilio, 194 pp.; Id., *La cameriera brillante*, ed. Roberto Cuppone, Venice, Marsilio, 278 pp.; and Id., *Il ventaglio*, ed. Paola Ranzini, Venice, Marsilio, 291 pp. Other editions include Carlo Goldoni, *Gli innamorati, I rusteghi, La casa nova, Le smanie per la villeggiatura*, ed. Guido Davico Bonino, Mi,

Garzanti, lxviii + 306 pp. Id., *Il servitore di due padroni, La famiglia dell'antiquario, La bottega del caffè*, ed. Guido Davico Bonino, Mi, Garzanti, lxviii + 258 pp. Id., *Sior Todero brontolon, Le baruffe chiozzotte, Una delle ultime sere del carnevale*, ed. Guido Davico Bonino, Mi, Garzanti, lxviii + 259 pp. Id., *I pettegolezzi delle donne, La locandiera, Il campiello*, ed. Guido Davico Bonino, Mi, Garzanti, lxviii + 245 pp. Id., *Il servitore di due* padroni, ed. Guido Davico Bonino, T, Einaudi, xvi + 150 pp. Id., *Arlecchino servitore di due padroni, La bottega del caffè*, ed. Giuliana Cislagh, Mi, Mondadori, 270 pp. Id., *La locandiera*, ed. Ettore Caccia, Brescia, La Scuola, 319 pp.

GOZZI. Gérard Luciani, *Carlo Gozzi ou l'enchanteur désenchanté*, Grenoble U.P., 2001, 310 pp., first looks at the autobiographical elements represented by the *Memorie inutili*, then goes on to consider G.'s literary output, emphasizing the 'ironia gozziana' but stressing that he definitely has nothing to do with Romanticism. **Carlo Gozzi*, ed. Ferdinando Taviani, Ro, IPZS, 2000[2001], xxviii + 1351 pp.

GRIMALDI. C. Chiodo, 'Un illuminista calabrese: Domenico Grimaldi', *Archivio Storico per la Calabria e la Lucania*, 2000[2001], 67:85–146, examines the work of a disciple of Genovesi, whose activity as an economist was directed towards improving the conditions of the peasants.

GRISELINI. Francesco Griselini, *I liberi muratori. Commedia*, ed. Edoardo Ghiotto, Vicenza, Menin–Schio, 2000, 87 pp., was written by Griselini under an almost anagrammatic pseudonym, Ferling' Isac Crens, and dedicated to another pseudonymous and anagrammatic playwright, Aldinoro Clog, who is, of course, Carlo Goldoni. As with Goldoni's *Le donne curiose*, for which see above, the play was intended to dispel suspicions about freemasonry, but the work, written around 1753, was never performed and only published in 1785.

LUNELLI SPINOZA. A. Alacevich, 'Benedetta Clotilde Lunelli Spinoza: un'erudita eclettica', Bracchi, *Alterità*, 23–44, outlines the activities of one of the first women to be awarded the title of *doctor* (1714), who was linked with various academies in Piedmont, and who was the object of sonnets and other literary offerings from admirers of her intellectual capabilities.

MARMI. L. Guerrini, 'Anton Francesco Marmi e la vita filosofica italiana di inizio Settecento', *StSet*, 21, 2001[2002]:9–34, highlights, through M.'s correspondence with Uberto Benvoglienti, the varied discussions of thinkers such as Galileo, or Alessandro Marchetti who had translated Lucretius's *De rerum natura*, or writers like Paolo Mattia Doria, whose *Vita civile*, was much admired. In appendix there are the previously unpublished letters from Marmi to Benvoglienti.

MASCHERONI. Alberto Gigli Berzolari, *Lorenzo Mascheroni: abate, insigne matematico, leggiadro poeta, ottimo cittadino*, Bo, Cisalpino, 2001, xviii + 204 pp., examines M.'s formative years in the philosophical and scientific atmosphere of Bergamo and Pavia, and develops the theme of the increasing cultural awareness of Lombardy under the Hapsburgs. The book examines, of course, the importance of M. as a mathematician (and concerned citizen), but also devotes many pages to his poetry, reproducing the *Invito a Lesbia Cidonia* of 1793.

METASTASIO. *Il melodramma di Pietro Metastasio: la poesia, la musica, la messa in scena e l'opera italiana nel Settecento*, ed. Elena Sala di Felice and Rossana Caira Lumetti, Ro, Aracne, 2001, xvii + 928 pp., the proceedings of a conference held in Rome, contains more than 30 articles divided into the seven sections: I. *Teoria e poetica del melodramma*, II. *Le strutture del melodramma*, III. *Le ragioni della scena*, IV. *I modi della musica*, V. *Le arti per Metastasio*, VI. *Metastasio e la critica*, VII. *Fortuna ed echi poetici metastasiani*. E. Benzi, '"Un esteriore maestoso, ma senza fasto": strutture logiche e sintattiche dell'aria metastasiana. Parte prima: la sintassi', *SMI*, 2:117–59, argues that M.'s reforming intentions are shown in his arias, especially from the point of view of metrical structure when compared to predecessors such as Zeno and Rolli. The article carries out a detailed textual analysis, looking at effects such as parataxis and scansion variants. Pietro Metastasio, *Drammi per musica*, I: *Il periodo italiano 1724–1730*, ed. Anna Laura Bellina, Venice, Marsilio, 621 pp., contains *Didone abbandonata, Siroe, Catone in Utica, Ezio, Semiramide, Alessandro nell'Indie*, and *Artaserse*.

MONTI. I. di Leva, 'I *Pittagorici* di Vincenzo Monti: tra genesi storica e cultura massonica', *CLett*, 30:123–51, analyses a play of 1799, set to music by Paisiello, as an allegory in which the 'pittagorici' are the martyrs of the Neapolitan republic, where treacherous Carthage is England, Archita Napoleon, and the cult of the 'pittagorici' the allegorical depiction of the Masonic organization to which M. himself belonged. The work is intended as an encomium of Napoleon and, in a second stage, of Joseph Bonaparte who became Masonic Grand Master after his elevation to the throne of Naples. L. Tomasin, 'Nuovi autografi montiani relativi alla *Proposta*', *LS*, 37:75–99, deals with various autograph papers in the Marciana which relate mainly to corrections and alterations to the *Proposta di alcune correzioni ed aggiunte al vocabolario della Crusca*. N. Costa-Zalessow, 'Teresa Carniani Malvezzi and Vincenzo Monti', *RStI*, 19.2:48–64, concludes that the friendship between Monti and Malvezzi was not sentimental, but based, via correspondence, on mutual interests, especially her desire to be accepted in her own right as a poet and literary figure. **Vincenzo Monti fra Roma e Milano*, ed. Gennaro Barbarisi, F, Il Ponte Vecchio, 2001, 270 pp. Vincenzo Monti, **Lezioni di eloquenza e prolusioni accademiche*, ed. Duccio Tongiorgi and Luca Frassineti, Bo, CLUEB, 391 pp.

MORPURGO-TAGLIABUE. Guido Morpurgo-Tagliabue, **Il gusto nell'estetica del Settecento: Guido Morpurgo-Tagliabue*, ed. Luigi Russo and Giuseppe Sertoli, Palermo, Centro Internazionale Studi di Estetica, 254 pp.

MURATORI. *I difetti della giurisprudenza ieri e oggi. Atti della Giornata di studi L. A. Muratori, 2 dicembre 2000, Vignola*, ed. Guido Alpa, Mi, Giuffrè, 211 pp., is particularly concerned to place M. within the cultural context of his day and to look at the importance of his thought for future generations. Divided into two parts, it contains the following items: I. U. Petronio, 'Una critica arcadica di Ludovico Antonio Muratori ai difetti della giurisprudenza' (3–81); R. Villata, 'Ludovico Antonio Muratori e la scienza giuridica della sua epoca tra conservazione e suggestioni di riforma' (83–119); A. Spaggiari, 'Considerazioni in merito allo spunto occasionale per la stesura de *I difetti della giurisprudenza*' (121–29); C. E. Tavilla, 'L'influenza di Ludovico Antonio Muratori sul diritto e sulla cultura giuridica estense' (131–52); II. G. Alpa, '"Impossibil cosa è il guarir da' suoi mali la giurisprudenza". Attualità del programma riformatore di L. A. Muratori' (155–66); O. Diliberto, 'I difetti della giurisprudenza nella prospettiva di uno *ius commune* europeo' (167–73); F. Capelli, 'Riflessioni sulle prospettive di unificazione del diritto europeo' (175–92); A. Cavarra, 'Spunti di attualità della giurisprudenza di Ludovico Antonio Muratori. I "difetti esterni" della giurisprudenza (deontologia giudiziaria)' (193–203); U. Petronio, 'Muratori, il codice, il processo' (205–11). Lodovico Antonio Muratori, *Dei difetti della giurisprudenza*, introd. Carmelo Elio Tavilla, Sala Bolognese, Forni, 2001, 184 pp., is a facsimile reprint of the 1742 edition.

PAOLINI MASSIMI. Michela Volante, *Petronilla Paolini Massimi. Una donna che visse 'd'arte e di fede'*, T, Trauben, 2001, 46 pp., contains some unpublished poetry by P. M. under the pseudonym of Fidalma Partenide.

PARINI. V. Placella, 'Gli epiteti di ascendenza omerica nel *Giorno* e l'impegno civile del Parini', *RLettI*, 20.1:26–46, examines P.'s parodistic use of Homeric reference for the purposes of anti-aristocratic satire, while at the same time recognizing a certain admiration on P.'s part for the world of nobility. G. Biancardi, 'Gli *Scherzi* pariniani (*Il parafuoco, La ventola, Il ventaglio*)', *Acme*, 55.3: 83–125, discusses the circumstances of these brief compositions for Teresa Mussi, tracing the editorial and MS tradition of these and other pieces, including *Stava un giorno Citerea*, with a critical rereading of all of them.

PERUZZI. *Le Antellesi. Il Decamerone di Bindo Simone Peruzzi*, ed. Massimo Casprini, F, Olschki, 111 pp., presents a work by a founder member of the Società Colombaria which takes as its starting point the great Arno flood of 1740. The stories, like those of the *Decameron*, are based on real stories of love and passion and current events, and also on comic challenges to authority. The work remained incomplete after P. was caught up in the persecution of freemasons such as his friend Tommaso Crudeli, whose poetry was put on the Index (cf. *YWMLS*, 63 : 504–05).

PIAZZA. Aldo Maria Morace, *Il prisma dell'apparenza. La narrativa di Antonio Piazza*, Na, Liguori, 326 pp., traces P.'s activities as novelist from *L'omicida irreprensibile* of 1762 through more than 30 novels plus poetry and writings for the theatre, noting P.'s eye for characters and places and his ability to develop the character of his protagonists, as well as his lively depiction of local colour, all with an occasional tinge of satire.

RAMAZZINI. R. Turchi, 'Bernardo Ramazzini: medico-letterato', *RLI*, 106 : 453–59, is a review of studies on Ramazzini.

ROBERTI. Giovanni Battista Sandonà, *Ragione e carità: per un ritratto di Giambattista Roberti (1719–1786)*, Venice, IV, viii + 299 pp., presents an extensive biography of R. — drawing widely on his own words in his letters to illustrate his close friendship with Bettinelli and the Remondini publishing family — before going on to explore R.'s early writing, especially his poetry, and trace his activities as a Jesuit until the suppression of the Society and his return to Bassano at the moment of the publication of his poetic reworking of Aesop's fables. The final section is an analysis of his writings on religious, philosophical, and social topics.

ROLLI. C. Bendi and P. Rambelli, 'Il mito della vittoria di Roma sugli Etruschi nel *Porsenna* di Domenico Rolli', *StSet*, 21, 2001[2002] : 43–51, interprets R.'s *Porsenna* of 1731 as intended to celebrate the renewed importance of the Papal States under the dynamic control of the newly-elected Clement XII, but concedes that the work has little artistic merit.

VERRI, A. Alessandro Verri, *Saggio sulla storia d'Italia*, ed. Barbara Scalvini, Ro, ESL, 2001, xlvi + 388 pp., is the first edition of the *Saggio*, which V. himself did not wish to publish, although parts of it have been used by scholars in the past. T. Scappaticci, 'Irrazionale pubblico e privato nei "tentativi drammatici" di Alessandro Verri', *Campi Immaginabili*, 1, 2001 : 121–39, examines V.'s plays *Pantea* and *La congiura di Milano* of 1779, tracing the influence of Shakespeare and classical models.

VERRI, P. Carlo Capra, *I progressi della ragione. Vita di Pietro Verri*, Bo, Il Mulino, 631 pp., is an exhaustive study, based extensively on the Archivio Verri, tracing V.'s deep involvement in movements for reform, both literary and social, and detailing the enormous impact his thinking and participation had on his time. The book is an invaluable tool for the study of the Settecento in Italy.

Pietro Verri, *Memorie*, ed. Enrica Agnesi, Modena, Mucchi, 2001, 271 pp., collects various writings from the period 1771–89, omitting the early works. Other editions include Id., *Discorsi sulla felicità e sull'indole del piacere e del dolore*, ed. Antonio A. Santucci, Ro, Ed. Riuniti, xxi + 137 pp., and Id., *Discorso sull'indole del piacere e del dolore*, ed. Silvia Contarini, Ro, Carocci, 2001, 170 pp.

VIALE. L. Ricaldone, 'Una maestra novelliera: Lucia Cattarina Viale', Bracchi, *Alterità*, 67–85, presents aspects of V.'s work, especially her *Lettere critiche e morali* (1777) and *Biblioteca di campagna* (1792), which were intended to demonstrate to the daughters of noble families that education and interest in culture, provided that the legitimate constraints of religion and family were not ignored, could only produce positive results.

VICO. Robert C. Miner, *Vico, genealogist of modernity*, Notre Dame U.P., xvi + 215 pp., is a reading of Vico which aims to understand his critique of secular modernity and is divided into three parts: an analysis of V.'s early thought, followed by a section on the *Diritto universale* as articulating an 'historical view of human culture' and by an examination of the *Scienza nuova*. Maurizio Martirano, *Giuseppe Ferrari editore e interprete di Vico*, Na, Guida, 2001, 171 pp., deals with the diffusion and analysis of V.'s thought, especially in the early 19th c. in the work of Giuseppe Ferrari, who was the first editor of V.'s complete works. Nicola Perullo, *Bestie e bestioni: il problema dell'animale in Vico*, Na, Guida, 254 pp., looks at questions connected with V.'s ideas on the link between man and animal. The first chapter introduces the parameters of the argument, drawing on the *Vici vindiciae* to focus on the themes of *bestialità* and *animalità*; this is followed by chapters analysing the *De antiquissima* and *Diritto universale* before moving on to the *Scienza nuova*, where the author illustrates the theme of the origin of the human race through examples drawn from 'bestie, primitivi, selvaggi e fanciulli'. In conclusion, the author touches on V.'s use in the *Scienza nuova* of mythological examples of monsters and hybrids, and discusses the origin of religion. G. Costa, 'Il Vico desanctisiano alla luce dei documenti del S. Uffizio', *Borsellino Vol.*, 479–98, discusses De Sanctis's positive opinion of V.'s work, in particular his categorization of the *Scienza nuova* as an essentially poetic work, but the author takes issue with De Sanctis's idea that V. created very little disturbance of faith and doctrine by showing how some members of the Inquisition were critical of the first edition of the *Scienza nuova*. A. Martone, 'Giambattista Vico e il senso comune. Note di lettura e qualche proposta in discussione', pp. 91–104 of *L'idea di cosmologia*, ed. Lorenzo Bianchi, Na, Liguori,

488 pp., discusses V.'s main 'stazioni' on the route of *senso comune* — divine providence, matrimony, and burying the dead — through which man's humanity can be recognized and which show the conditions under which individuals become aware of the *senso comune*. E. Nuzzo, 'Cittadini della storia. La "gran città del gener'umano" in Giambattista Vico', *ib.*, 71–89, identifies V.'s notion in the *Scienza nuova* that all nations are part of a historical process of civilization, and links it also with the idea of a religious and Christian universality, stressing V.'s idea of 'eroi contadini', the 'Hercules' figures who first cultivated the earth and gave rise to basic legal and political institutions.

Antonio Verri, **Con Vico nel secolo dei lumi*, Galatina, Congedo, viii + 287 pp. **Studi sul 'De antiquissima Italorum sapientia' di Vico*, ed. Giovanni Matteucci, Macerata, Quodlibet, 219 pp. Giuseppe Cospito, **Il gran Vico: presenza, immagini e suggestioni vichiane nei testi della cultura italiana pre-risorgimentale: 1799–1839*, Genoa, Name, 259 pp. Maurizio Martirano, **Sesto contributo alla bibliografia vichiana*, Na, Guida, 224 pp. Monica Riccio, **Governo dei molti e riflessione collettiva: Vico e il rapporto tra filosofia e democrazia*, Na, Guida, 80 pp. Paolo Fabiani, **La filosofia dell'immaginazione in Vico e Malebranche*, Florence U.P., 368 pp. **Giambattista Vico: i segni della storia*, ed. Stephan Otto et al., Na, ESI, 112 pp. Giambattista Vico, *Principj d'una scienza nuova d'intorno alla comune natura delle nazioni. Napoli, 1730, con postille autografe, ms 13. H 59*, ed. Fabrizio Lomonaco and Fulvio Tessitore, Na, Liguori, 528 pp., is a facsimile reprint of the 1730 edition with autograph corrections by the author. Id., *The First New Science*, ed. and trans. Leon Pompa, CUP, lxiv + 302 pp.

OTTOCENTO

By John M. A. Lindon, *Professor of Italian Studies, University College London*

(This survey covers the years 2000, 2001, and 2002)

1. General

Hainsworth, *Companion*, covers the Ottocento with a combination of entries ranging from 1000- to 2000-word articles on the canonical authors and shorter, yet substantial, pieces on the major topics — Romanticism, Risorgimento, Nationalism, Positivism, Darwinism, Verismo, Scapigliatura, Decadentismo — to a host of brief entries on lesser phenomena or on figures of secondary importance from a literary perspective. It will be of value as a work of rapid reference, particularly to those unable to consult more authoritative works in Italian. Franco Restaino, *La rivoluzione moderna: vicende della cultura tra Otto e Novecento*, Ro, Salerno, 2001, 601 pp., is a revised and expanded version of material published in Salerno's *Storia della letteratura italiana*.

Other reference items include, in a valuable series of surveys of recent Italian studies, A. Ciccarelli, 'L'italianistica negli Stati Uniti: vent'anni di studi sul Sette-Ottocento', *EL*, 25.3–4:247–62, while *Donne: due secoli di scrittura femminile in Sardegna, 1775–1950. Repertorio bibliografico*, ed. Franca Ferraris Cornaglia et al., introd. Laura Pisano, Cagliari, CUEC, 2001, 355 pp., extends to women's writing in all disciplines.

Relating to intellectual and literary movements: P. Fasano, 'Geografia e storia del "romantico". La parola e la cosa', *Borsellino Vol.*, 623–45; 'La deriva romantica', Palandri, *Deriva*, 97–115; G. Cogoi, 'Le diverse anime del Risorgimento: Gioberti e Mazzini', in *Italianistica debreceniensis*, 6, 1999:119–34; *Daniele Manin e Niccolò Tommaseo: cultura e società nella Venezia del 1848*, ed. Tiziana Agostini, Ravenna, Longo, 2000, 442 pp., gathering the proceedings of a 1999 conference in a double issue of *QVen*; Paola Villani, *Carlo Del Balzo tra letteratura e politica: contributi al dibattito sul realismo*, ESI, 2001, 354 pp; U. Dotti, 'La questione meridionale e i problemi del realismo (Verga–De Roberto–Pirandello)', *GSLI*, 178, 2001 : 1–46; P. Bettella, 'The debate on beauty and ugliness in Italian scapigliatura and Baudelaire', *RStI*, 18.1, 2000:68–85; Giuliano Ladolfi, *Per un'interpretazione del decadentismo*, introd. Elio Gioanola, Novara, Interlinea, 2001, 58 pp. More circumscribed in scope are: M. Vitale, 'Ruggero Bonghi e la questione della lingua italiana', *Archivio di storia della cultura*, 12, 1999:21–32; N. Longo, 'Il problema del Canone Cinquecentesco prima e dopo la *Storia della letteratura italiana* di Francesco de Sanctis', *CLett*, 30:527–43.

There are many collections of essays ranging across parts of the Ottocento, or concerning more than one 19th-c. author: Massimo Riva, *Malinconie del moderno. Critica dell'incivilimento e disagio della nazionalità nella letteratura italiana del XIX secolo*, Ravenna, Longo, 178 pp., on Romantic melancholy from Alfieri and Foscolo to Manzoni, Leopardi, and D'Annunzio; Giorgio Manacorda, *Materialismo e masochismo: il Werther, Foscolo e Leopardi*, Ro, Artemide, 2001, 190 pp., a welcome revised edn of the seminal 1973 volume; Giorgio Luti, *Letteratura e rivoluzioni: saggi su Alfieri, Foscolo, Leopardi*, F, Pagliai Polistampa, 2002, 123 pp., usefully gathering already published writings; Gérard Genot, *La fiction poétique: Foscolo, Leopardi, Ungaretti*, Paris, Sorbonne, 1998, 152 pp.; Emilio Pasquini, *Ottocento letterario: dalla periferia al centro*, Ro, Carocci, 2001, 196 pp.; Grazia Melli, *Un pubblico giudicante: saggi sulla letteratura italiana del primo Ottocento*, Pisa, ETS, 193 pp.; Dell'Aquila, *Nominanza*, mainly on the 19th-c. authors Manzoni, Cantù, Leopardi, Boito; Dell'Aquila, *Bello stile*, gathering, for the 19th-c., contributions on Tarchetti, Verga, and Borgese's *Storia della critica romantica in Italia*; Giuseppe Catanzaro, *Bonghi, Rosmini, Manzoni*, ed. Peppino Pellegrino, Milazzo, SPES, 2001, 142 pp.; Giuseppe Leone, *Nuove note di critica letteraria: Della Casa, Leopardi, Nievo, Capuana...*, Cava de' Tirreni, Avagliano, 2000, 117 pp.; Campailla, *Controcodice*, with contributions, for the 19th c., on Verga, Capuana, De Roberto; Moretti, *Da Dante*, including, among much else, pieces on Compagnoni, Monti, Leopardi, Manzoni, and Verga; Alberto Granese, *Le occasioni del Sud: civiltà letteraria dall'Ottocento al Novecento*, Salerno, Edisud, 230 pp.

For 19th-c. verse: *La poesia italiana da Leopardi a Montale*, ed. Lucio Izzo, Salerno, Oedipus, 2000, 101 pp., are the papers of a conference held in 1999. Anna Bellio, *Cigni, Leopardi e altri poeti: percorsi di letteratura tra Sette e Novecento*, Mi, ISU Univ. Cattolica, 267 pp., ranges from Parini to Leopardi and beyond. F. di Brazzà, 'Pindemonte, Vittorelli, Antonio di Brazzà: nuove testimonianze', *QVen*, 33, 2001:127–36. Important contributions on the influence of Ossian in 19th-c. Italy are to be found in the *atti* (noted in the previous section under CESAROTTI) *Aspetti dell'opera e della fortuna di Melchiorre Cesarotti*, notably by Antonietta Terzoli on Foscolo and Luigi Blasucci on Leopardi. 'L'ultimo viaggio di Ulisse o l'azione impossibile', Boggione, *Poesia*, 163–73, traces the motif of Ulysses' last voyage from Graf to Pascoli and Gozzano. The original (1997) of the valuable *Antologia della poesia italiana*, VII: *Ottocento*, ed. Cesare Segre and Carlo Ossola, T, Einaudi, xix + 741 pp., was not noted at the time. *Poeti del Risorgimento*, ed. Valerio Marucci, Ro, Salerno, 2001, 389 pp., is a substantial anthology with copious notes (pp. 307–76). *Dagli scapigliati ai crepuscolari*, ed. Gabriella Palli Baroni, Ro, IPZS, 2000, x + 1075 pp., is an anthology selected by the recently deceased Attilio Bertolucci.

On the 19th-c. novel and short-story: Alberto Cadioli, *La storia finta: il romanzo e i suoi lettori nei dibattiti di primo Ottocento*, Mi, Il Saggiatore, 2001, 318 pp., is a revised and expanded version of *Il romanzo adescatore*, published in 1988. G. Pinna, '"Il romanzo è un libro romantico". Teoria del romanzo e classici italiani nei *Frammenti* di Friedrich Schlegel', *RELI*, 15, 2000: 129–36. A. Zangrandi, 'Figure storiche, eroi e altri personaggi nel romanzo storico italiano: funzioni e ruoli narrativi', *AARA*, ser. 8, 2001: 187–217, concentrates on historical personages who became characters in novels published in the period 1827–38. N. Del Corno, 'I Paridi della letteratura. Romanzi e reazionari nell'Italia preunitaria', *Belfagor*, 55, 2000: 37–54. T. Iermano, 'L'intraducibilità del reale. *L'eredità Ferramonti* nella Roma Bizantina', *CLett*, 26, 1998: 55–72. Caterina Verbaro, *Il castello di carta: l'impotenza sperimentale della narrazione scapigliata*, Rende (Cosenza), Calabria University Centro Editoriale e Librario, 2001, 201 pp. Enrico Cesaretti, *Castelli di carta: retorica della dimora tra Scapigliatura e surrealismo*, Ravenna, Longo, 2001, 158 pp., is a collection of writings most of which unpublished hitherto. Andrea Rondini, *Cose da pazzi: Cesare Lombroso e la letteratura*, Pisa, IEPI, 2001, 215 pp. Giacomo L. Vaccarino, *La follia rappresentata: matti, degenerati, e idioti nella letteratura e nell'arte figurativa dell'Ottocento*, F, Athenaeum, 2001, 151 pp. Mario Tropea, *Nomi, ethos, follia negli scrittori siciliani tra Ottocento e Novecento*, Caltanissetta, Lussografica, 2000, 127 pp., comprises six essays, two of them previously unpublished. A. Olivi, 'Hystérie et névrose. Capuana, Tarchetti, Pirandello', *REI*, 47, 2001: 247–64. G. Oliva, 'Vigo, Capuana, Guastella, Verga: cultura e società in Sicilia nell'Ottocento', *CLett*, 30: 545–60. Maria Cassano, *Visioni di folla: scienze nuove e nuove tipologie di romanzo fra Ottocento e Novecento*, Lecce, Pensa multimedia, 2000, 294 pp. C. Mazzoni, 'Pregnant bodies of knowledge: Italian narratives of fetal movement (1880's-1920's)', *RStI*, 17.1, 1999: 222–41. Tra letti e salotti: norma e trasgressione nella narrativa femminile tra Otto e Novecento, ed. Gisella Padovani and Rita Verdirame, Palermo, Sellerio, 2001, 269 pp., is an anthology of short stories. Antonio Illiano, *Invito al romanzo d'autrice '800–'900: da Luisa Saredo a Laudomia Bonanni*, Fiesole, Cadmo, 2001, 192 pp. A. Caesar, 'Women readers and the novel in nineteenth century Italy', *ItS*, 56, 2001: 80–97. W. Sahlfeld, 'Literarische Milieus im italienischen Roman vom späten 19. Jahrhundert bis zur Nachkriegszeit', *ItStudien*, 21, 2000: 213–32. Federica Merlanti, *Genova tra le righe: la città nelle pagine di narratori italiani fra '800 e '900*, pref. Franco Contorbia, Genoa, Marietti, 2000, viii + 430 pp. M. Colin, 'La naissance de la littérature romanesque pour la jeunesse au XIXe siècle en Italie; entre l'Europe et la nation', *RLC*, 76:507–18. *Scrivere lettere: tipologie epistolari nell'Ottocento italiano*, ed. Gino Tellini, Ro, Bulzoni, 428 pp., explores the forms taken by the art of epistolography in the Ottocento.

Turning to the theatre and opera, G. M. Tosi, '*L'inutile precauzione* di Rossini o dell'agio della civiltà', *Italica*, 78, 2001:326–36, reflects on the modernity of content of the young R.'s opera in relation to the fiasco of its Roman première (1816) and his prior attempt to ingratiate himself with the aged Paisiello, who in 1782 had staged his own *Barber of Seville* in Rome. S. Ragni, 'Rossini: la musica e la zona del male oscuro', *Cenobio*, 49, 2000:113–28. G. Nicastro, '*Beatrice di Tenda* di Vincenzo Bellini: dalla "Tragedia istorica" di Carlo Tebaldi-Flores al libretto di Felice Romani', *Siculorum gymnasium*, 52, 1999[2001]:687–94. The *Anno verdiano* has been marked by some of the literary journals. G. Regn, '"Con una voce soffocata". Verdis *Macbeth*, das romantische Musikdrama und die Erneuerung des italienischen Sprachtheaters um 1850', *Italienisch*, 46, 2001:2–20, shows how Italian Romanticism, initially opposed to opera, eventually adopted the new Romantic opera with its anti-declamatory emotionality and its Shakespearean mingling of genres. L. K. Gerhartz, 'Zwischen Wunschbild und Wirklichkeit. Entwurf für eine musik- und theaterhistorische Standortbestimmung des Verdischen Operntyps', *ib* ., 22–33, emphasizes V.'s links with Schiller and Shakespeare, and the importance of French influences coming from Hugo and his Spanish followers. N. Abels, 'Ein Buckliger, der singt? Motivgeschichtliche Aspekte su einem Topos der Abweichung', *ib.*, 34–43, discusses the image of the hunchback in V.'s *Rigoletto* and Hugo's *Le roi s'amuse.* K. Ley, 'Zur Affektregie in Verdis *Aida.* Musikdrama und historischer Roman', *ib.*, 44–60, draws attention to the importance of the historical novel (in particular, Flaubert's *Salammbô*) for both librettist (A. Mariette) and composer. P. Dini, 'Una visita di Giuseppe de Nittis a Giuseppe Verdi', *NA*, 2219, 2001:155–59. A. Bassi, 'Giuseppe Verdi attraverso le sue lettere', *ib.*, 2216, 2000:208–15. P. Petrobelli, 'Dall'alessandrino all'anapesto. Struttura poetica e composizione musicale in un *Ballo in maschera*', *ParL*, 594–98, 1999:164–74. Id., 'Le théâtre en musique entre France et l'Italie à la fin du XIXe siècle', *REI*, 47, 2001:99–102. D. Bini, '*Cavalleria rusticana* from Verga to Mascagni to Zeffirelli', *FoI*, 33, 1999:95–106. A. Bassi, 'Cento anni fa, la *Tosca*', *NA*, 2214, 2000:228–32. L. Hutcheon and M. Hutcheon, '"Beve, beve con me": an operatic brindisi — for and to Gian-Paolo Biasin', *FoI*, 33, 1999:73–94. *Francesca da Rimini, da Napoli: tre esilaranti farse napoletane dell'Ottocento*, ed. Gordon Poole, Na, Filema, 1999, 79 pp., comprises plays by Antonio Petito, Salvatore De Angelis, and Eduardo Scarpetta, this last previously unpublished. D. Fedele, 'La Divina e il Dottor mistico. Lettere di Eleonora Duse ad Angelo Conti', *CLett*, 28, 2000: 297–334.

On journalism and publishing: Cimino, *Evasione*, opens with well-documented chapters on 'Il giornalismo illuministico-romantico in Abruzzo' (15–45) and 'Profilo storico del giornalismo vastese dall'Unità al secondo dopoguerra' (47–79); G. Morelli, 'Presenze abruzzesi nei periodici napoletani dell' '800 (1832–1847)', *Bullettino della Deputazione Abruzzese Storia Patria*, 89, 1999[2001]: 359–78. L. Montobbio, 'Notizie sull'Abate Antonio Meneghelli primo direttore del *Giornale Euganeo*', *AMAP*, 111, 1998–99: 101–18. P. Vignoli, 'Editoria a Pisa nell'età della Restaurazione: Giuseppe Rossi e l'*Indicatore Pisano*', *BSP*, 68, 1999: 45–62. *Il Vieusseux: storia di un Gabinetto di lettura, 1819–2000. Cronologia, saggi, testimonianze*, ed. Laura Desideri, F, Polistampa, 2001, 299 pp. *Carteggio Manno–Vieusseux (1830–1846)*, ed. Narciso Nada, F, Le Monnier – Fond. Spadolini Nuova Antologia, 2000, vi + 55 pp., publishes (in part for the first time) V.'s correspondence with Giuseppe Manno (1786–1868). A. Volpi, 'Medici versus Machiavelli: temi rinascimentali nell'*Antologia* di Giovan Pietro Vieusseux', *RSI*, 113, 2001: 195–218. L. Perini, 'Il Rinascimento al Vieusseux', *ASI*, 159, 2001: 171–90. G. Cultrera, 'Editori e giornali nella Firenze di metà Ottocento', *NA*, 2213, 2000: 271–80. G. Lucchini, 'Dalla corrispondenza di Eugenio Camerini: tra editoria ed Accademia (1855–1873)', *ASL*, 6, 2000[2001]: 379–434. Cimini, *Evasione* gathers already published essays and articles, some noted separately elsewhere in these pages. Miriam Stival, *I dilemmi di Cordelia: tra tradizione e innovazione. Frammenti d'epoca*, Padua, CLEUP, 2001, 90 pp., looks at the women's journal *Cordelia* published from 1881 to 1911.

On cultural institutions and miscellaneous aspects of 19th-c. Italian culture: *Esortazioni alle storie. Atti del Convegno 'Parlano un suon che attenta Europa ascolta': poeti, scienziati, cittadini nell'Ateneo pavese tra riforme e rivoluzione, Università di Pavia, 13–15 dicembre 2000*, ed. Angelo Stella and Gianfranco Lavezzi, Mi, Cisalpino, 2001, xvi + 818 pp. *Leopoldo Cicognara ad Antonio Canova: lettere inedite della Fondazione Canova di Possagno*, ed. Paolo Mariuz, Cittadella, Bertoncello, 2000, 137 pp. M. Ceppi and C. Giambonini, 'Pietro Giordani e un catalogo delle opere di Antonio Canova (un inedito in Laurenziana)', *ASI*, 159, 2001: 591–620. M. Braga, 'Un collezionista e mercante d'arte nella Piacenza dell'Ottocento: il conte Giacomo Costa e la sua quadreria', *BSPia*, 94, 1999: 79–114. F. Barsotti, 'Una mostra di arte sacra (1897). L'ambiente culturale e politico a Pisa alla fine dell'Ottocento',

BSP, 68, 1999: 63–88. S. Morgana, 'Volta e la lingua della comunicazione scientifica', *Acme*, 54.3, 2001: 205–26.

The impact and reception of others cultures is variously examined in: A. Conti, 'Le grammatiche per l'insegnamento del francese pubblicate a Milano nel periodo napoleonico (1796–1814)', *ib.*, 54.2, 2001: 227–44; R. Bellei, 'I manuali di Carlo Maselli per insegnare il francese (Modena: 1808 e 1809)', *ib.*, 275–93; L. Elda Funaro, '"Mes deux patries". Minime aggiunte all'epistolario del Sismondi', *ASI*, 160: 555–88; P. Grossi, 'Un témoin indélicat: un témoignage inédit de Pierre-Louis Ginguené sur Simonde de Sismondi', *REI*, 47, 2001: 223–42; V. Furno, 'Bernard Mandeville nella cultura italiana dei secoli XVIII e XIX', *FoI*, 34, 2000: 206–18; M. Curreli, 'Postille romantiche degli archivi pisani, con inediti byroniani', *BSP*, 68, 1999: 89–112. N. Costa-Zalessow, 'Teresa Carniani Malvezzi as a translator from English and Latin', *Italica*, 76, 1999: 497–511; F. Belski Crespi, 'Lettori e traduttori italiani del *Faust* nell'Ottocento', *Testo*, 37, 1999: 37–70; A. Di Benedetto, 'Traduttori italiani di Heine nell'Ottocento: Del Re, Nievo, Zendrini, Carducci', *GSLI*, 179: 361–88. E. Pierobon, 'Realismo, inettitudine e filosofia schopenaueriana nelle *Mediocrità* di Emma', *ItQ*, 149–50, 2000: 27–40.

On Italian abroad I note *Brand Vol.* which, further to the Dante items noted in *YWMLS*, 62: 342–43, includes: D. Mack Smith, 'Britain and the Italian Risorgimento' (13–31); D. Kimbell, 'The performance of Italian opera in early Victorian England' (45–66); H. Fraser, 'Ruskin, Italy, and the past' (87–106); and I. Campbell, 'Carlyle and Italy' (107–20); to conclude with a posthumous piece straddling two centuries: U. Limentani, 'Leone and Arthur Serena and the Cambridge chair of Italian (1919–1934)' (154–77), where (158–62) the remarkable figure of Thomas Okey, the chair's first incumbent, is affectionately evoked. S. Antonelli, 'La riscoperta dell'America: Carpentier e Pascarella', *Il Veltro*, 44, 2000: 25–36. *Italoamericana: storia e letteratura degli Italiani negli Stati Uniti, 1776–1880*, ed. Francesco Durante, Mi, Mondadori, 2001, 844 pp., accompanied by lengthy introductory and bibliographical material, is the first volume of an anthology of Italo-American writing, comprising texts by 50 18th–19th c. authors.

On Italians abroad and travellers to Italy: Caterina De Caprio, *Inaffidabili e pellegrini: viaggiatori italiani tra Ottocento e Novecento*, Na, Libreria Dante & Descartes, 2000, 124 pp. A. Zimbone, 'Un illuminista italiano in Grecia: l'abate G. B. Casti', *Siculorum gymnasium*, 52, 1999[2001]: 1189–97. R. P. Coppini, 'Diario inedito di Cosimo Ridolfi: viaggio in Svizzera e Francia (1820)', *NA*, 2220, 2001: 337–43. On the Anglophile author of the first biography of Ugo Foscolo: V. Gabrieli, 'Giuseppe Pecchio (1785–1835): illuminista lombardo anglicizzato', *La Cultura*, 38, 2000:39–58. M. M. Dell'Aquila, 'L'Ofanto nelle relazioni dei viaggiatori stranieri in Puglia tra Sette e Ottocento', *RLettI*, 19.2–3, 2001:133–42, also in Dell'Aquila, *Nominanza*, 113–22, and focusing particularly on Edward Lear. C. di Donna Prencipe, 'L'Ofanto nelle prose di viaggio di Giustino Fortunato', *RLettI*, 20.3:171–86.

2. Individual Authors

BELLI. From the Centro Studi Giuseppe Gioachino Belli come two volumes: Stefania Luttazzi, *Belli e l'Ottocento europeo: romanzo storico e racconto fantastico nello Zibaldone*, pref. Giulio Ferroni, Ro, Bulzoni, 2001, 309 pp., a new monograph; and Muzio Mazzocchi Alemanni, *Saggi belliani*, ed. Leonardo Lattarulo and Franco Onorati, Ro, Colombo, 2001, 223 pp., gathering already published writings. *Muscetta Vol.* has a group of three Belli contributions: M. T. Lanza, 'Giuseppe Gioachino Belli e alcune (certe o probabili) "occasioni"' (143–63), N. Merola, 'Belli e le stelle di Roma' (165–85), and M. Teodonio, 'Il Centro studi Giuseppe Gioachino Belli' (187–95). Other items include R. Marsico, 'Grafia semicolta nei *Sonetti semidialettali* di Giuseppe Gioacchino Belli', *RStI*, 18.2, 2000:117–37; 'La carità romana in un sonetto del Belli', Cerboni, *Letture*, 205–211, concerning a sonnet indirectly related to strophes in Byron's *Childe Harold*; M. Beer, '"Loghi scampaggnati" e "polvere di deserti": comicità dialettale e ironia romantica. Lettura del sonetto *Er deserto* di G. G. Belli', *Borsellino Vol.*, 555–76, and the very substantial M. Mancini, 'Il teatro di parola nei *Sonetti* del Belli: intonazione, pronuncia, prosodia', *ib.*, 577–622; and Giuseppe Renzi, *Aforismi, latinismi e preziosismi linguistici in Belli*, Ro, EdUP, 2000.

BERCHET. I. Bertelli, 'L'ultimo tempo della poesia berchettiana: la traduzione delle *Vecchie romanze spagnole*', *RLettI*, 20.1:47–64

BERSEZIO. To mark the centenary of his death the Centro Studi Piemontesi has published: Vittorio Bersezio, *I miei tempi*, ed. Pier Massimo Prosio, T, 2001, 283 pp., B.'s memoirs; Id., *La commedia piemontese: appendici a 'La gazzetta del popolo', 1898*, ed. Gualtiero Rizzi, T, 2001, 94 pp.; Id., *Le novelle di Travet: antologia di racconti*, ed. Vincenzo Jacomuzzi, T, 2001, 260 pp.; and Id., *Le miserie 'd monsù Travet*, ed. Gualtiero Rizzi and Albina Malerba, T, 2001, xxx + 353 pp., a reprint of the 1980 critical edition.

BOITO, A. A. Fornasetti, 'Inventario metrico dell'*Amleto* di Arrigo Boito', *Acme*, 54.3, 2001:227–72. Arrigo Boito, *Opere letterarie*, ed. Angela Ida Villa, Mi, Otto/Novecento, 2001, 714 pp., is an anthology of poems, short stories, and other writings, some in French, already published by IPL in 1996 but not noted in *YWMLS*.

BOITO, C. Camillo Boito, *Senso. Racconto interpretato da Clotilde Bertoni*, Lecce, Manni, 166 pp., provides a critical edn of the short story.

CAPUANA. E. Fusaro, 'Intuizioni pre-freudiane nelle prime opere di Luigi Capuana (1879–1890)', *Versants*, 39, 2001 : 123–34. P. Barnaby, '*Il marchese di Roccaverdina*: myth, history, and hagiography in post-Risorgimento Sicily', *ItS*, 55, 2000 : 99–120, returns to the apparent conflict between the Marchese's uncultivated feudal upbringing and his subsequent transformation with a view to reconciling naturalist and neo-idealist interpretations. F. Brancaleoni, 'Le origini del tema della maschera: da Verga a Capuana. Linee di un percorso', *CLett*, 26, 1998 : 551–82. Luigi Capuana, *Teatro italiano*, ed. Gianni Oliva and Luciana Pasquini, 2 vols, Palermo, Sellerio, 1999, lix + 656, viii + 313 pp., is the first complete edn of C.'s writings for the theatre. Vol. 1 comprises texts published between 1886 and 1915 and *Garibaldi* (1861), vol. 2 the libretti and the puppet and children's theatre. Luigi Capuana, *Lettere inedite a Lionardo Vigo, 1857–1875*, ed. Luciana Pasquini, Ro, Bulzoni, 211 pp.

CARDUCCI. Giosuè Carducci, *Confessioni e battaglie*, ed. Mario Saccenti, Modena, Mucchi, 2001, 408 pp. Umberto Panozzo, *Carducci di Carducci*, Rimini, Panozzo, 2000, 143 pp. L. Pete, '*La leggenda di Teodorico* del Carducci', *Italianistica debreceniensis*, 6, 1999 : 135–46. G. P. Maragoni, 'Aspetti stilistici del Carducci interprete degli Arcadi', *Testo*, 37, 1999 : 71–86. S. Cavazzuti, 'Carducci e i collaboratori modenesi', *Italianistica*, 29, 2000 : 83–92. A. Donnini, 'Due note a Carducci: *OB* II 4 [XXIX] 33–34, *RN* LVIII 1–4', *SPCT*, 61, 2000 : 131–42. M. Saccenti, 'La poesia di Carducci nella poesia delle rovine', *NA*, 2214, 2000 : 181–202. A. Di Benedetto, '"E uno due e tre . . .". Brevissima divagazione da Alfieri a Carducci', *GSLI*, 179 : 272–73. F. Audisio, 'Carducci, la *Poesia barbara* e gli umanisti dell'area meridionale', *RLI*, 105, 2001 : 423–58. P. Arpaia, 'Constructing a national identity from a created literary past: Giosuè Carducci and the development of a national literature', *JMIS*, 7 : 192–214. Elena Candela, *Carducci lettore europeo*, Na, L'Orientale, 2000, 155 pp. *Carducci e Roma*, Ro, Istituto Nazionale di Studi Romani, 2001, 367 pp. Antonino Carbone, *Carducci e la Sicilia: gli incontri storico-letterari*, Ro, Armando, 1125 pp., has an appendix which includes five hitherto unpublished letters. The publisher Mucchi of Modena has brought out several more vols of the Edizione Nazionale: Giosuè Carducci, *Carteggio Giosuè Carducci – Mario Menghini (ottobre 1888–aprile 1904)*, ed. Torquato Barbieri, 2000, 195 pp., a hitherto unpubl. correspondence; *Carteggio Paola Pes di Villamarina – Giosuè Carducci (agosto 1887–febbraio 1906)*, ed. Anna Maria Giorgetti Vichi, 105 pp., partly publ. for the first time; Giosuè Carducci, *Carteggio*

Giosuè Carducci – Isidoro Del Lungo (ottobre 1858–dicembre 1906), ed. Marco Sterpos, 376 pp. I also note Luciano Bezzini, *Sparate al Carducci: biografia di Michele Carducci, padre, medico, rivoluzionario. I Carducci a Bolgheri tra cipressetti e fucilate*, Pontedera, Bandecchi & Vivaldi, 1999, 249 pp.

CARRER. M. Giachino, 'In "ignorata stanza": appunti sulla formazione del corpus testuale nelle raccolte in versi di Luigi Carrer', *RLI*, 104, 2000: 420–31.

CASTIGLIONE. F. Labombarda, 'Storie di fanciulle: la *Cingallegra* di Giuseppe Castiglione', *CLett*, 28, 2000: 163–78

CATTANEO. Carlo Cattaneo, *Lettere*, I: *1820–15 marzo 1848*, ed. Margarita Cancarini Petroboni and Mariachiara Fugazza, F, Le Monnier — Bellinzona, Casagrande, 2001, lxxvi + 724 pp., the first vol. of letters in the Edizionale Nazionale of C.'s works, includes some published for the first time. L. Ambrosoli, 'Molte notizie di Carlo Cattaneo', *Belfagor*, 56, 2001: 708–18.

CAVALLOTTI. *Felice Cavallotti. Atti del Convegno, Arona, 7 marzo 1998*, ed. Luigi Polo Friz, Novara, Istituto per la Storia del Risorgimento – Alberti libraio, 2000, 93 pp., gathers the papers of a 1998 conference marking the centenary of the birth of the politician, journalist, and man of letters.

CHIARINI. Raffaele Gaetano, *L'autore mio prediletto: in margine al leopardismo di Giuseppe Chiarini*, Soveria Mannelli, Rubbettino, 2001, 124 pp.

COFFA. N. Bellucci, 'La triste storia di Marianna Coffa da Noto', *Muscetta Vol.*, 213–35, discusses the autobiographical *Lettere ad Ascenzo*, edited by Gino Raya in 1957.

COLLODI. *Pinocchio nella letteratura per l'infanzia*, ed. Carlo Marini, Urbino, Quattro Venti, 2000, 295 pp., assembles a useful anthology of critical writing, mainly from introductions to editions of *Le avventure di Pinocchio. Ipotesi su Pinocchio*, ed. Alessandro Gnocchi and Mario Palmaro, Mi, Ancora, 2001, 152 pp., draws parallels between Collodi and the New Testament. *Le avventure di Pinocchio: tra un linguaggio e l'altro*, ed. Isabella Pezzini and Paolo Fabbri, Ro, Meltemi, 310 pp., contains a revised selection of the papers presented at a conference held at Urbino in 2001. Rossana Dedola, *Pinocchio e Collodi*, B. Mondadori, 249 pp.

COLOMBI. *La marchesa Colombi: una scrittrice e il suo tempo. Atti del Convegno internazionale, Novara, 26 maggio 2000*, ed. Silvia Benatti and Roberto Cicala, introd. Antonia Arslan, Novara, Interlinea, 2001, 285 pp. Clotilde Barbarulli, *L'arma di cristallo: sui discorsi trionfanti. L'ironia della Marchesa Colombi*, Ferrara, Tufani, 1998, 93 pp. E. Pierobon, 'La marchesa Colombi (1840–1920): profilo bio-bibliografico', *RStI*, 17.2, 1999: 68–88.

COMPAGNONI. Giuseppe Compagnoni, *Lettere varie (1754–1833)*, introd. and ann. Marcello Savini, Ravenna, Longo, 2001, 219 pp., brings to light many hitherto unpublished letters by the many-sided literary *abate*. R. Fedi, 'Le *Veglie*, Tasso e Compagnoni', *FC*, 25, 2000: 442–56, traces the composition of the *Veglie* in relation to T.'s *fortuna* in the French literary tradition and to their wider literary-historical genealogy, which includes T.'s *Rime* and *Liberata* (and more generally the Romantic stereotype of T.), Alfieri, Goethe's *Werther* and *Torquato Tasso*, and Foscolo's 1798 *Ortis*, to conclude that the fake, or hypertext, was 'un'operazione intelligente... proprio perché saldava la tradizione con una rilettura in linea con i tempi: astraeva dal suo contesto storico un personaggio celeberrimo e lo ricostruiva, lanciandolo nel teatro delle traduzioni europee', where it was to be noted by such as Byron and Leopardi.

CUOCO. *Platone in Italia: sette possibili itinerari*, ed. Rosario Diana, pref. Fulvio Tessitore, Na, Pagano, 2000, xxiv + 136 pp. Tommaso Possumato, *Vincenzo Cuoco e il giovane Manzoni: saggio storico-letterario*, Campobasso, Enne, 1999, 123 pp. *Contributo alla bibliografia cuochiana*, ed. Giorgio Palmieri, introd. Luigi Biscardi, Campobasso, Enne, 2000, 61 pp. F. Tessitore, 'Cuoco lungo due secoli', *Archivio di storia della cultura*, 13, 2000: 53–74.

D'ANNUNZIO. Two collections of miscellaneous essays are Cosimo Cucinotta, **Il cavaliere e la sua ombra. Studi dannunziani*, Messina, Sicania, 2001, 358 pp. Alida D'Aquino, **L'alchimia del verbo: studi dannunziani*, Catania, CUECM, 2000, 171 pp. On D'A. as poet the most substantial item has been *Da Foscarina a Ermione. Alcyone: prodromi, officina, poesia, fortuna. 27. Convegno di studio, 25–27 maggio 2000, Francavilla al Mare*, Pescara, Ediars, 2000, 281 pp. Otherwise, I note the critical edn Gabriele D'Annunzio, *Elegie romane*, ed. Maria Giovanna Sanjust, Mi, Mondadori, 2001, lix + 85 pp., which belongs to the Edizione Nazionale of D'A.'s works, and a handful of other items: A. Girardi, 'Appunti sulla lingua del D'Annunzio lirico', *ParL*, 594–98, 1999, 194–205; V. Giannantonio, 'Il primo d'Annunzio tra musicalità e mito', *CLett*, 28, 2000: 531–46; P. Gibellini, 'Un autografo veneziano di D'Annunzio e i *Sogni di terre lontane*', *QVen*, 35: 77–88; Marco Santagata, *Per l'opposta balza: la cavalla storna e il Commiato dell'Alcyone*, Mi, Garzanti, 155 pp.; T. Amos, 'Die Anrufung des Lorbeers. Poetisch-poetologische konzeptionen bei D'Annunzio und George', *Italienisch*, 46, 2001: 74–81. More generally on his aestheticizing bent as a writer: A. Andreoli, 'Per una ridefinizione dell'estetismo di D'Annunzio', *ParL*, 600–04, 2000, 38–65; and Valeria Giannantonio, *L'universo dei sensi: letteratura e artificio in D'Annunzio*, Ro, Bulzoni, 2001, 346 pp. More specifically on his narratives: a section of 'Dannunziana' in Cimini, *Evasione*, comprising 'Archetipi culturali e primitivismo sociale nella novella *Bestiame*' (157–71), 'Note su quattro romanzi dannunziani' (173–201), and 'Un caso di "dannunzite": il viaggio "alla scoperta dell'Abruzzo" nel 1909' (203–41); Ennio Saffi, *Narrativa dannunziana e critica coeva*, Pasian di Prato (Udine), Campanotto, 1998, 216 pp.; A. Panicali, 'L'idea di bellezza nelle cronache, nelle *Favole mondane*, nel *Piacere* di Gabriele d'Annunzio', *RLettI*, 20.3: 127–50; and R. Castagnola, 'Una riscrittura dannunziana di Boccaccio', *RELI*, 19: 61–71. The ten conference papers gathered in *D'Annunzio e il teatro in Italia fra Ottocento e Novecento*, ed. E. Tiboni, Pescara, Ediars, 1999, 152 pp., cover D.'A.'s catalytic theatre from many angles, but for his Parisian years (1910–15) we also have P. Martinuzzi, 'D'Annunzio allo Châtelet', *Ariel*, 41, 1999: 113–26.

The bulk of published work continues to centre on the life, exploits, or relationships of D'A. the man. A useful survey of biographies was E. Albertelli, 'Il vivere inesplicabile. Rassegna delle biografie dannunziane', *Testo*, 41, 2001: 115–34. The latest, Annamaria Andreoli, *Il vivere inimitabile: vita di Gabriele D'Annunzio*, Mi, Mondadori, 2000, 670 pp., already had a second edition the following year, which also saw, from the same pen, *D'Annunzio e l'Abruzzo*, Ro, De Luca, 2001, 63 pp. *D'Annunzio: l'uomo, l'eroe, il poeta*, ed. Anna Maria Andreoli, Ro, De Luca, 2001, 206 pp., the catalogue of a Roman exhibition, also included essays by Andreoli. Luigi De Vendittis, *L'altro D'Annunzio*, Alessandria, Orso, 2000, 158 pp., comprises mainly new material (5 out of 9 essays). Attilio Mazza, *D'Annunzio sciamano*, Mi, Bietti, 2001, 197 pp. The title of Vittorio Martinelli, *La guerra di D'Annunzio: da poeta a dandy a eroe di guerra e comandante*, Udine, Gaspari, 2001, 343 pp., speaks for itself. *Interviste a D'Annunzio: 1895–1938*, ed. Gianni Oliva, in collaboration with Maria Paolucci, Lanciano, Carabba, 669 pp.

On his relations with the Treves family, his publishers for 47 years: hard on the heels of Gabriele D'Annunzio, *Lettere ai Treves*, ed. Gianni Oliva, Mi, Garzanti, 2000, 837 pp., to which he contributed an appendix of letters from Emilio Treves, Ilvano Caliaro, *L'amorosa guerra: aspetti e momenti del rapporto Gabriele D'Annunzio – Emilio Treves*, Venice, IV, 2001, ix + 193 pp., has brought out his study of the relationship; and this has been followed by R. Bertacchini, 'D'Annunzio e i Treves', *NA*, 2213, 2000: 253–63. On D'A.'s relations with the painter Francesco Paolo Michetti: Franco Di Tizio, *D'Annunzio e Michetti: la verità sui loro rapporti*, Casoli, Ianieri, 404 pp. For his relations with women: *Il Camarlingo e la Camarlenga: carteggio inedito Gabriele D'Annunzio – Marietta Camerlengo*, ed. Franco Di Tizio, Pescara, Ediars, 2000, 127 pp., his correspondence with his mother's housemaid; Gabriele D'Annunzio, *'Infiniti auguri alla nomade': carteggio con Luisa Casati Stampa*, ed. Raffaella Castagnola, Mi, Archinto, 2000

[2001], 209 pp.; Gabriele D'Annunzio, *Lettere a Fiammadoro*, ed. Vito Salierno, Ro, Salerno, 2001, 175 pp., presenting D.'s almost entirely unpublished letters to Margherita Besozzi di Castelbarco; Gabriele D'Annunzio, *Lettere d'amore*, ed. Annamaria Andreoli, Mi, Mondadori, 219 pp., likewise largely consisting of hitherto unpublished material; *Sono dieci anni che vi giro intorno: carteggio Gabriele D'Annunzio – Vinca Sorge Delfico*, ed. Paola Sorge, Ro, Le Impronte degli Uccelli, 2001, 55 pp.; Gabriele D'Annunzio, *Buona sera, cara notte: lettere, messaggi e una fotografia a Marie de Régnier*, ed. Nicola Muschitiello, Na, Filema, 2001, 63 pp. J. R. Woodhouse, '"Il gran Pan non è morto": the vitality of D'Annunzio's irrepressible critics', *MLR*, 97:850–62, a review article by D'A.'s English biographer (cf. *YWMLS* 61:476), examines seven recent items, mainly of biographical import, a few of which are mentioned above. Enrico Di Carlo, *Luigi Savorini e il fondo dannunziano della Biblioteca provinciale M. Delfico di Teramo*, pref. Elena Ledda, L'Aquila, Libreria Colacchi, 1999, ix + 323 pp.

DE AMICIS. Bianca Danna, *Dal taccuino alla lanterna magica. De Amicis 'reporter' e scrittore di viaggi*, F, Olschki, 2000, 188 pp. Flavia Bacchetta, *I viaggi en touriste di De Amicis: raccontare ai borghesi*, Tirrenia, Cerro, 2001, 186 pp. E. Tosto, 'De Amicis: la lingua si studia', *RLI*, 104, 2000:91–106. E. Genevois, 'Le Paris de Edmondo De Amicis', *ChrI*, 69–70:65–82. F. Millefiorini, 'Quattro lettere inedite di Paolo Mantegazza a Edmondo De Amicis', *RLettI*, 19.2–3, 2001:173–87. G. Gorni, 'L'invenzione del *Cuore*', *StIt*, 24, 2000:85–93, argues that the work's structure, far from being 'fragile ed elementare', is 'studiatissima' and 's'iscrive . . . nella tradizione alta delle patrie lettere'.

DE MARCHI. G. P. Marchi, 'Apici, iota, esse alte: minuzie tipografico-testuali a proposito della recente edizione del *Demetrio Pianelli* di Emilio de Marchi', *SPCT*, 63, 2001:133–42. *Emilio De Marchi (1851–1901): documenti, immagini, manuscritti*, ed. Nicoletta Trotta, pref. Maria Corti, Mi, Comune di Milano – Biblioteca Trivulziana, 79 pp. Angelo Lacchini, *Rileggendo il Demetrio: il laboratorio narrativo di Emilio De Marchi*, Pesaro, Metauro, 141 pp.

DE ROBERTO. A. Pagliaro, 'Federico De Roberto's *L'illusione*: theory and fiction in constructing the female character', *RStI*, 17.1, 1999:203–21.

DE SANCTIS. Francesco Bruno, *De Sanctis e il realismo*, Na, ESI, 2000, 102 pp. Francesco De Sanctis, *Lezioni di scrittura: lettere a Virginia Basco (1855–83)*, ed. Fabiana Cacciapuoti, Ro, Donzelli, 2001, xxx + 145 pp. Toni Iermano, *La scienza e la vita: i manoscritti di Francesco De Sanctis presso la Biblioteca provinciale Scipione e Giulio Capone di Avellino*, Cava de' Tirreni, Avagliano, 2001, 132 pp. G. Muscardini, 'Antiretorica e spontaneità in Francesco De Sanctis', *NA*, 2219,

2001 : 277–81. D. Tanteri, 'De Sanctis e il naturalismo', *Siculorum gymnasium*, 52, 1999[2001]: 1051–76. A. Di Benedetto, 'Francesco De Sanctis e le feste ariostee del 1875', *GSLI*, 179: 95–98.

DI GIACOMO. A. Benvenuto, 'Di Giacomo novelliere', *CLett*, 28, 2000: 129–50. Id., 'Le *Cronache* di Salvatore di Giacomo', *ib.*, 345–60. N. De Blasi, 'Note sulla lingua e sulla letteratura di Salvatore di Giacomo, *Italica*, 76, 1999: 480–96. L. Russo, 'Salvatore di Giacomo poeta grande del reame di Napoli', *Belfagor*, 56, 2001 : 257–68.

DOSSI. Francesca Caputo, *Sintassi e dialogo nella narrativa di Carlo Dossi*, F, Crusca, 2000, 236 pp. D. Isella, 'Dossiana', *StCrit*, 15, 2000: 399–426. P.-C. Buffaria, 'Dossi e la politique: espoirs et désillusions d'un lecteur marginal', *REI*, 47, 2001 : 193–208.

FARINA. L. Ricaldone, 'Il silenzio delle Penelopi e la voce delle Sirene: figure femminili ricorrenti nella narrativa di Salvatore Farina tra il 1870 e il 1880', *ItStudien*, 21, 2000: 201–12. *Salvatore Farina: la figura e il ruolo a 150 anni dalla nascita. Atti del Convegno, Sassari–Sorso, 5–8 dicembre 1996*, ed. Dino Manca, 2 vols, Sassari, EDES, 2001, 256, 257–514 pp.

FOGAZZARO. Raffaele Cavaluzzo, *Fogazzaro: i romanzi. Contraddizioni e forma di una passione azzurra*, Bari, Graphis, 2000, 160 pp. Giorgio Cavallini, *Fogazzaro: ieri e oggi*, Na, Loffredo, 2000, 115 pp. *Carteggio Antonio Fogazzaro – Henri Brémond: un dialogo sulla santità e il peccato (1903–1910)*, ed. Federica Ranzato Santin, Vicenza, Accademia Olimpica – Esca, 2000, 200 pp., publishes a correspondence for the most part not hitherto available. *Testo*, 41, 2001, a special issue on F., includes: E. N. Girardi, 'La terza fase della narrativa fogazzariana' (7–12); R. Cavaluzzi, 'L'ultimo Fogazzaro: parabola della dimensione religiosa' (13–30); P. A. Sequeri, 'L'ordine degli affetti. Moderno e anti-moderno nella poetica religiosa di A. Fogazzaro' (31–42); G. Cavallini, 'Intorno a *Piccolo mondo moderno*' (43–56); C. A. Madrignani, 'Persuasione e misticismo' (57–66); and F. Finotti, 'Pensiero e poesia: per una lettura "metastorica" del *Santo*' (67–86).

FOSCOLO. Maria Antonietta Terzoli, *Foscolo*, Ro–Bari, Laterza, 2000, 227 pp., is a valuable monograph which combines coherence in its account of F.'s career as a writer with considerable skill in presenting biography and politics through his writings. The author carries over and extends the emphasis on scriptural intertextuality that marked her *Il libro di Jacopo* (cf. *YWMLS*, 51 : 509). Ettore Catalano, *Foscolo tragico: dal Tieste alle Ultime lettere di Jacopo Ortis*, Bari, Laterza, 2001, 159 pp. Ugo Foscolo, *Tieste*, ed. Ettore Catalano, Bari, Adda, 2000, 115 pp. Ugo Foscolo, *Orazione a Bonaparte pel Congresso di Lione*, ed. Lauro Rossi, introd. Umberto Carpi, Ro, Carocci, 145 pp. E. Neppi, 'Edonismo e elegia nella prima raccolta foscoliana', *RLI*, 105, 2001 : 57–71. R. A. Rushing, 'Traveling by metonymy: Foscolo's

A Zacinto', *AnI*, 20:201–16. S. Carrai, 'Per un dittico foscoliano: le odi maggiori', *StIt*, 23, 2000:59–73. R. Cotrone, 'Ugo Foscolo: *immanenza* e *rappresentazione* del "sacro" nel commento alla *Chioma di Berenice*', *CLett*, 29, 2001:761–74. M. Palumbo, 'Note su Foscolo traduttore dei classici', *EL*, 27.3:39–54. V. Di Benedetto, 'Discutendo di Foscolo', *RCCM*, 43, 2001:323–32. F. Longoni, 'Foscolo e Milton', *FC*, 24, 1999:337–74. Id., 'Alcune note e riflessioni sull'*Ars Commemorandi* foscoliana', *StIt*, 23, 2000: 49–83. G. Da Pozzo, 'Una redazione inedita dell'epigramma foscoliano "Tombe siam noi di tre fratelli"', *GSLI*, 179:212–23. J. Lindon, 'Foscolo 1825', *ib.*, 177, 2000:385–400, with the help of documents from Hendon, Hertford, and Livorno sheds light on the obscurest year of Foscolo's adult life, when he was in hiding outside London. C. Gaudenzi, 'Exile, translation, and return: Ugo Foscolo in England', *AnI*, 20:217–34.

'Dossier Foscolo', *ChrI*, 61, 2000, included: P. Abbrugiati, 'Pour une analyse comparative de la structure des *Sepolcri* et des *Grazie*' (59–77); P.-C. Buffaria, 'Apories autobiographiques chez Ugo Foscolo' (79–84); C. Del Vento, 'Quelques considérations sur la fortune historiographique de Foscolo' (85–102); E. Neppi, 'Foscolo et l'énergie: la poétique des *Ultime lettere di Jacopo Ortis*' (103–26); X. Tabet, 'Ugo Foscolo, des désillusions italiennes à la Venise retrouvée' (127–46); and M. A. Terzoli, 'Déracinement et nostalgie d'appartenance: la choix d'une identité culturelle chez Foscolo et Ungaretti' (147–73). Francesco D'Episcopo, *Ugo Foscolo: le metamorfosi della memoria. Salvatore Quasimodo e Alfonso Gatto*, Na, Eurocomp 2000 – Graus, 77 pp.

GALLINA. Giacinto Gallina, *Tutto il teatro*, ed. Piermario Vescovo, Venice, Marsilio – Regione del Veneto, II, *1874–1877*, III, *1878–1884*, 2000, 437, 517 pp., comprise plays mostly written in Venetian: one, in vol. III, by Gallina and R. Selvatico, appears in print for the first time.

GIORDANI. Laura Melosi, *In toga e in camicia: scritti e carteggi di Pietro Giordani*, Lucca, Pacini Fazzi, 242 pp., gathers already publ. writings, partly in revised form.

GIUSTI. N. Mineo, 'Teatralità implicita negli *scherzi* di Giuseppe Giusti', *Moderna*, 3.1, 2001[2002]:81–96.

GRAF. A. S. Defendi, 'Arturo Graf's *Medusa*: toward a demystification of myth', *Italica*, 77, 2000:26–44. F. Romboli, 'Arturo Graf, la scienza positiva, il darwinismo sociale', *CLett*, 28, 2000:361–78. S. Miccolis, 'Antonio Labriola intermediario per Arturo Graf', *Belfagor*, 55, 2000:74–78. Arturo Graf, *Confessioni di un maestro: scritti su cultura e insegnamento con lettere inedite*, ed. Stefania Signorini, Novara, Interlinea, 199 pp.

GROSSI. E. Gennaro, 'La discussa paternità di un sonetto adespoto attribuito a Tommaso Grossi e ad altri autori e forse opera di Padre Giacomo Manetta di Treviglio', *GSLI*, 179:420–30.

GUERRINI. Olindo Guerrini, *Postuma*, ed. Claudio Mariotti and Mario Martelli, Ro, Salerno, 2001, 209 pp., complements the biography noted in *YWMLS*, 59:570, with a timely critical edition of G.'s poetry.

IMBRIANI. L. Sasso, 'Vittorio Imbriani e le forme della citazione', *Italianistica*, 2001, 30:85–94, shows how I. overcomes the Romantic dilemma imitation vs originality in a neo-baroque contamination of quotation and narrative discourse. M. Mola, 'La corrispondenza inedita di Vittorio Imbriani', *AAPN*, 50, 2001[2002]:75–90.

LARA. Contessa Lara, *Tutte le novelle*, ed. Carlotta Moreni, Ro, Bulzoni, 711 pp.

LEOPARDI. As predicted in *YWMLS*, 69:480, the spate of celebratory publications has continued well past the 1998 bicentenary of L.'s birth: an impressive but inflated output, and such as to impose summary report if only to keep a three-year survey within reasonable limits.

Collections of conference papers include: *I diletti del vero: lezioni leopardiane*, ed. Alberto Folin, Padua, Il Poligrafo, 2001, 250 pp., the *acta* of the 1998 Paduan conference *Leopardi: poesia e filosofia a confronto. Leopardi e la filosofia*, ed. Gaspare Polizzi, F, Polistampa, 231 pp.; *Ripensando Leopardi: l'eredità del poeta e del filosofo alle soglie del millennio*, ed. Alberto Frattini, Giancarlo Galeazzi, and Sergio Conocchia, Ro, Studium, 2001, 456 pp., the proceedings of a conference held at Ancona; *'Quei monti azzurri': le Marche di Leopardi*, ed. Ermanno Carini, Paola Magnarelli, and Sergio Sconocchia, Venice, Marsilio, 870 pp., the proceedings of another Ancona conference; *Leopardi e lo spettacolo della natura. Atti del Convegno internazionale, Napoli 17–19 dicembre 1998*, ed. Vincenzo Placella, Na, L'Orientale, 2000, xv + 612 pp.; *Leopardi e l'astronomia. Atti del Convegno nazionale di studi*, ed. Luciano Romeo, Gianfranco Abate, and F. Walter Lupi, Cosenza, Progetto 2000, 2000, 252 pp., the papers of a conference held at the Accademia degli Inculti, Montalto Uffugo (Cosenza); *Giacomo Leopardi e il pensiero scientifico*, ed. Giorgio Stabile, Ro, Fahrenheit 451, 2001, 223 pp., the *acta* of a Roman bicentenary conference; *Lo Zibaldone cento anni dopo: composizione, edizioni, temi. Atti del 10. Convegno internazionale di studi leopardiani (Recanati, Portorecanati, 14–19 settembre 1998)*, ed. Rolando Garbiglia, 2 vols, F, Olschki, 2001, xii + 902 pp.; *Microcosmi leopardiani: biografie, cultura, società*, ed. Alfredo Luzi, 2 vols, Fossombrone, Metauro, 2001, xxix + 870 pp., the proceedings of a conference held at Recanati in 1998, including letters published for the first time; *Leopardi oggi. Incontri per il bicentenario della nascita del poeta, Brescia, Salò,*

Orzinuovi, 21 aprile-23 maggio 1998, ed. Bortolo Martinelli, Mi, Vita e Pensiero, 2000, x + 189 pp.; *Leopardi a Firenze. Atti del Convegno, Firenze, 3–6 giugno 1998*, ed. Laura Melosi, F, Olschki, xii + 514 pp., the papers of a Gabinetto Vieusseux conference; *Leopardi e l'Oriente. Atti del Convegno internazionale, Recanati, 1998*, ed. Filippo Mignini, Macerata, Provincia di Macerata, 2001, 239 pp. *Leopardi e la parola simbolica*, ed. Lia Fava Guzzetti, Fossombrone, Metauro, 2001, 175 pp., contains the *acta* of a seminar. *Omaggio a Giacomo Leopardi nel bicentenario della nascita*, ed. Nicola Calabria, Messina, Calabria, 1998, 111 pp., comprises a set of five essays marking the 1998 centenary. *Giacomo Leopardi e Bologna: libri, immagini e documenti*, ed. Cristina Bersani and Valeria Roncuzzi Roversi Monaco, Bo, Pàtron, 2001, 415 pp., is an interesting exhibition catalogue.

Further special issues of journals have been given over to Leopardi articles (which in some cases are conference papers). Indeed, one case, 'Leopardi philosophe et poète', extends to two annual volumes. *REI*, 45, 1999, contains: F. Livi, 'Présentation' (163–64); M. Luzi, 'Giacomo Leopardi' (165–66); Y. Bonnefoy, 'Giacomo Leopardi' (167–71); 'Cinq poèmes de Giacomo Leopardi traduits par Yves Bonnefoy' (172–83); G. Luti, 'Leopardi e la Toscana' (185–88); M. A. Bazzocchi, 'Un poeta, l'ozio e la città (Leopardi a Bologna)' (189–206); N. Bellucci, 'Roma per Leopardi' (207–12); P. Landi, 'Leopardi e Milano – Milano per Leopardi' (213–18); F. Cacciapuoti, 'Leopardi filosofo della differenza (Napoli)' (219–26); F. Ceragioli, 'Lo Zibaldone pisano' (277–34); N. Jonard, 'Une idée du bonheur: Leopardi et l'apologétique francaise' (235–50); G. Savoca, 'Leopardi e Pascal: tra (auto)ritratto e infinito' (251–64); B. Toppan, 'Leopardi en France. Parcours parmi les études léopardiennes au XXe siècle' (265–76); G. Genot, 'Le francais, langue sans illusions' (277–87). The sequel in *REI*, 46, comprises: L. Quartermaine, 'Giacomo Leopardi: il punto di vista britannico (1830–1998)' (3–20); M. Mandolini Pesaresi, ' "Tra le vaste californie selve". (Leopardi negli Stati Uniti)' (21–26); J. C. Barnes, 'Un decennio della fortuna di Leopardi in Irlanda' (27–38); G. Berréby, 'Antiqua edere, novo modo' (39–42); S. Neumeister, 'Leopardi nei paesi di lingua tedesca' (43–48); M. Engelhard, 'La traduzione poetica delle poesie di Giacomo Leopardi' (49–56); D. Sabolová, 'Il pensiero leopardiano tradotto nella lingua slovacca' (63–74); D. Gelli Mureddu, 'L'opera di Leopardi in Russia' (63–74); S. Valle, 'Leopardi, Buffon et l'idéal du savant philosophe' (75–100); N. Jonard, 'Leopardi, matérialiste athée?' (101–14); E. Ghidetti, ' "Quel caro immaginar mio primo" ' (115–24); E. Cantavenera, 'Un usage du mythe et de la mémoire dans le *Operette morali*' (125–34); and F. Livi, 'Leopardi in Francia. Il silenzio dei poeti?' (135–46).

Testo, 38, 1999, an issue devoted to the papers of 'Giacomo Leopardi tra negazione e rapporti con l'infinito' (Milan, 1998), ed. Elena Landoni, includes: E. Landoni, 'Introduzione al convegno' (5–10); E. N. Girardi, 'La componente biblica nei *Canti* e nelle *Operette morali*' (11–20); G. Cavallini, 'Su alcuni modi, aspetti ed esiti della tensione dialettica leopardiana' (21–36); L. Blasucci, 'L'amore, l'infinito. Lettura del *Pensiero dominante*' (37–48); E. Gioanola, 'Infinito e ricordanza: *Alla luna*' (49–58); S. Cristaldi, 'Splendore e fragilità del segno: *Sopra il ritratto di una bella donna*' (59–104); E. Landoni, 'Il realismo nella ricerca della verità: annotazioni di metodo nel *Frammento apocrifo di Stratone di Lampsaco*' (105–18); I. Vaccarini, 'L'antitesi tra coscienza lirica e coscienza tragica negli opposti atteggiamenti esistenziali di Leopardi e di Pascal' (119–36); B. Martinelli, 'Leopardi e Leibniz' (137–206). After the weighty issue (16.2) already devoted to L. in the centenary year, *RStI*, 17.1, 1999, carried: E. Giordano, 'Ranieri e Leopardi, non senza Monaldo' (1–19); A. Luzi, 'Idillio e patema nell'*Infinito* leopardiano' (20–31); R. M. Monastra, '"Fuggitivo Consalvo", o della felicità infelice' (32–44); G. Tini, 'L'*Appressamento della morte* tra modelli letterari e novità' (45–58); and P. Zanni Ulisse, 'Il manifesto leopardiano: l'epistola *Al conte Carlo Pepoli*' (55–88).

General monographs or collections of essays include: Antonino Sole, *I due pastori di Leopardi e altri scritti*, Palermo, Palumbo, 303 pp.; G. Cesare Galimberti, *Cose che non sono cose: saggi su Leopardi*, Venice, Marsilio, 2001, 277 pp.; Alberto Folin, *Leopardi e l'imperfetto nulla*, Venice, Marsilio, 2001, 147 pp., including two essays published for the first time; Elena Landoni, *Questo deserto, quell'infinità felicità. La lingua poetica leopardiana oltre materialismo e nichilismo*, Ro, Studium, 2000, 194 pp.; Winfried Wehle, *Leopardis Unendlichkeiten. Zur Pathogenese einer 'poesia non poesia'* (Schriften und Vorträge des Petrarca-Instituts Köln, n.s., 2), Tübingen, Narr, 2000, 116 pp.; Gaetano Raffaele, *Giacomo Leopardi e il sublime: archeologia e percorsi di una idea estetica*, pref. Giovanni Lombardo, Soveria Mannelli, Rubbettino, 502 pp.; Anna Bellio, *Cigni: Leopardi e altri poeti. Percorsi di letteratura tra Sette e Novecento*, Mi, ISU Università cattolica, 2000, 267 pp.

Miscellaneous writing on L.'s thought and prose works includes: E. Ördögh, 'Alle origini del pensiero leopardiano: materialismo e religione', *Italianistica debreceniensis*, 6, 1999: 106–19; M. A. Rigoni, 'Leopardi, Schelling, Madama de Staël e la scienza romantica della natura', *LItal*, 53, 2001: 247–56, which finds an anticipation of L.'s conception of nature (an *unicum* in early 19th-c. Italy) in Mme de Staël's references, in *De l'Allemagne*, to Schelling's notion of the gnoseological primacy of artistic imagination; R. Bonavita, 'Classicismo sperimentale. La prosa del *Discorso di un italiano intorno alla poesia romantica* e gli itinerari creativi di Leopardi', *CLett*, 26, 1998:483–524; Id., 'L'autenticità è apocrifa. Lingua e stile nel *Discorso di un italiano intorno alla poesia romantica* di Giacomo Leopardi', *StCrit*, 16, 2001:297–324; D. Fornesi, 'Alcune considerazioni sul classicismo di Leopardi', *ib.*, 135–58; Loretta Marcon, *Vita ed esistenza nello Zibaldone di Giacomo Leopardi*, pres. Giovanni Casoli, Ro, Stango, 2001, 174 pp.; A. Marinotti, 'Heidegger, Leopardi e la poetica dell'immaginare–rimembrare', *RLI*, 104, 2000:76–84; M. Lollini, 'La scrittura dell'inizio. Leopardi e il problema della genesi', *FoI*, 34, 2000:30–48; L. Marcon, '"Incontro" sul limite: Kant e Leopardi', *RLettI*, 20.1:201–16; S. Randino, 'Leopardi e la teoria del tradurre', *LItal*, 54:616–37; F. Curi, 'Leopardi, utopie estetiche e pensiero paradossale', *Intersezioni*, 22:395–418; G. Cesaro, 'Giacomo Leopardi: "curriculum mortis"', *NA*, 2218, 2001:310–17; P. Moreno, 'Leopardi lettore di Francesco Guicciardini', *SPCT*, 62, 2001:155–72; E. Cesaretti, 'La parola e l'immagine. Alcune riflessioni su G. Leopardi e C. D. Friedrich', *Testo*, 40, 2000:77–92; D. Van den Berghe, 'Osservazioni sull'"omerismo leopardiano"', *Italianistica*, 30, 2001:341–61; G. Savarese, 'Il figurativo e Leopardi', *RLI*, 106:411–18; A. Del Gatto, 'Leopardi e "il coraggio di ridere"', *Cenobio*, 50, 2001:195–205. For the *Operette* : Antonella Del Gatto, *Uno specchio d'acqua diaccia. Sulla struttura dialogico-umoristica del testo leopardiano: dalle Operette morali ai Canti pisano-recanatesi*, F, Cesati, 2001, 321 pp.; Giuseppe Sangirardi, *Il libro dell'esperienza e il libro della sventura: forme della mitografia filosofica nelle 'Operette morali'*, Ro, Bulzoni, 2000, 294 pp.; A. Sole, 'Verso l'*Islandese* : la traduzione leopardiana di due frammenti di Simonide di Amorgo', *GSLI*, 178, 2001:321–50; P. Abbrugiati, 'Quelques savants léopardiens: le Physicien, Ruysch, Copernic et les autres', *ChrI*, 63–64, 2000:321–46; G. Gronda, 'Una vita per due: il *Dialogo di Torquato Tasso e del suo genio familiare*', *Borsellino Vol.*, 515–35. Giuliana Benvenuti, *Un cervello fuori di moda: saggio sul comico nelle Operette morali*, Bo, Pendragon, 2001. Giacomo Leopardi, *Il passero e la ginestra: in libertà tra le Operette morali di Giacomo Leopardi*, ed. Nino Giordano, F, Cesati, 223 pp., presents modernized texts of the *Operette*. Antonio Negri, *Lenta ginestra: saggio sull'ontologia di Giacomo Leopardi*, Mi, Mimesis, 2001, 241 pp., is a new edition of a work first published in 1987.

On the *Canti* in general: pride of place is deserved by Francesco De Rosa, *Dalla canzone al canto: studi sulla metrica e lo stile dei Canti leopardiani*, Lucca, Pacini Fazzi, 2001, 225 pp., which gathers and partially revises already published essays in metrical analysis; and to P. Rambelli, 'Il ripristino del concerto interrotto, ovvero la mitologia della vitalità nei *Canti* di Leopardi', *LS*, 36, 2001:169–88, which investigates the linguistic-rhetorical solutions whereby L. achieves a revival of the late

18th-c. 'interrupted concert' (E. Raimondi) between man and nature: the 'melodramaticization' of the self in a natural setting and a mythology of despairing vitality. I also note: Francesco Paolo Botti, *Leopardi e il destino della poesia: dalla crisi del classicismo alla Ginestra*, Na, Dante & Descartes, 155 pp. On an important monograph noted in *YWMLS*, 61:485, L. Blasucci, '*Decrifrare Leopardi*: su un libro postumo di Cesare Luporini', *AION(SR)*, 44:727–37, while voicing some dissent, notes approvingly how the deceased critic's interpretation of L. had moved from the political formula 'Leopardi progressivo' (the title of his celebrated 1949 volume) to a more extensive ethical and existential 'positivo' and an emphasis on heroic intensity. Id., 'Leopardi e Pindemonte', pp. 247–63 of *Leopardi e l'età romantica*, ed. Mario Andrea Rigoni, Venice, Marsilio, 1999, shows that L. appreciated P., but that it was not his poetry, but the *Prose campestri* (and particularly the fifth, in praise of country life) that left their mark on L.'s *Idilli*. Id., 'Sugli antroponimi (e qualcosa sui toponimi) nei *Canti* leopardiani', *ASNP*, 28, 1998[2000]: 181–94. Id., 'Lo stormire del vento tra le piante: parabola di un'immagine leopardiana', *SMI*, 1, 2001: 259–76. C. Milanini, 'Leopardi, l'ordine dei *Canti* ', *Belfagor*, 57:307–30. A. Sorella, 'Spunti di stile tragico nella lirica leopardiana', *ItS*, 56, 2001: 57–65, highlights the presence of tragic imperatives and other devices characteristic of Italian tragic style (with clear signs of Della Valle's specific influence): in a poem like *A se stesso* 'Il poeta parla [. . .] come un personaggio tragico e il suo è, per l'appunto, stilisticamente, un monologo tragico [. . .] gli stilemi tragici servono a delineare il ruolo del lirico come quello di un tragedo che si rivolge ad un interlocutore assente, il divino, appellato qui con il nome di Natura o di fato'. D. Colussi, 'Segni di Della Casa in Leopardi: postilla a *L'infinito* 10–11', *FC*, 25, 2000: 476–91, explores echoes of Della Casa (especially *Rime* LXIII) in *L'infinito*, *Alla luna*, *Canto notturno* (first draft, ll. 84–90), and *La ginestra*. V. Zaccaria, 'Nota sul "Petrarchismo leopardiano" ', *AMAPG*, 111, 1998–99: 75–88. G. Güntert, ' "Di te mi dolse e duol . . ." Leopardi im Dialog mit Petrarca und Tasso', *ItStudien*, 21, 2000: 65–80. N. J. Perella, 'Translating Leopardi?', *Italica*, 77, 2000: 357–85. M. Morreale, 'I *Canti* di Giacomo Leopardi in una suggestiva traduzione spagnola recente', *RANL*, 10, 1999: 335–86, relates to the excellent Giacomo Leopardi, *Cantos*, trans. Maria de las Nieves Muñiz Muñiz, for which see *YWMLS*, 61: 481.

For particular *canti* or groups of *canti*: P. Palmieri, 'Monti e Leopardi: la dedicatoria delle *Canzoni* del '18', *SPCT*, 63, 2001: 107–26. M. Gigante, 'Leopardi *All'Italia*, v. 16 s.', *GSLI*, 177, 2000: 594. N. Borsellino, 'Storia e cronistoria nella canzone *Ad Angelo*

Mai ', *RLMC*, 44, 2001 : 17–26. M. Palumbo, 'Il *Bruto minore* e l'antifoscolismo di Leopardi', *Borsellino Vol.*, 527–35. L. Felici, 'Lettura della *Saffo* leopardiana', *GSLI*, 179 : 321–60. J. Gutiérrez Carou, '*L'infinito* di Leopardi: un "sonetto libero"?', *FC*, 24, 1999 : 300–13. Francesco Giardinazzo, *La voce e il vento: variazioni su L'infinito di Leopardi*, F, Aletheia, 2001, 109 pp. *Interminati spazi, sovrumani silenzi, un infinito commento: critici, filosofi e scrittori alla ricerca dell'Infinito di Leopardi*, ed. and introd. Vincenzo Guarracino, Grottamare (Ascoli Piceno), Arancio, 2001, 415 pp., anthologizes writing on the poem, some of it hitherto unpublished. L. Blasucci, '*Alla luna* di Giacomo Leopardi', *Per leggere*, 2.2 : 63–70. R. Pestarino, 'Di un antico modulo retorico negli sciolti leopardiani al Pepoli', *ParL*, 594–98, 1999 : 107–24. *ItQ*, 143–46, 2000, a special issue for Vittore Branca, includes: F. Fido, 'Dall'*Epistola al Pepoli* alla *Palinodia*, per una lettura non idillica dei *Canti*' (253–66). Fiorenza Ceragioli, *La stagione di Silvia*, Ro, Sossella, 2001, 61 pp. L. Blasucci, 'Due noterelle testuali sul paesaggio nei canti pisani', *Leopardi e lo spettacolo della natura* (noted above), 585–90, on the interpretation of *Il risorgimento*, ll. 53–54, and *A Silvia*, l. 24. Id., 'Breve introduzione al *Canto notturno* ', *Poetiche*, 2, 2001 : 149–64. G. Aquilecchia, '"Indi ti posi": un tassello poetico bruniano nel *Canto notturno* di Leopardi?', *BrC*, 7, 2001 : 11–15. P. Fasano, 'Rileggendo il *Sabato del villaggio*. Un finale per i *Canti* del '31', *Muscetta Vol.*, 93–123. M. Nieves Muñiz, 'La funzione di "Aspasia" nei Canti. "Fabula quanta fui"', *Belfagor*, 56, 2001 : 411–28. L. Blasucci, 'Sui canti fiorentini', *Leopardi a Firenze* (noted above), 251–69. Id., 'L'amore, l'infinito. Lettura del *Pensiero dominante* ', *Testo*, 38, 1999 : 37–47. H. Poehlmann, 'Il percorso odoroso della memoria leopardiana in Aspasia', *LetP*, 110–11, 2001 : 27–32. M. Marti, 'Sulla datazione della prima sepolcrale leopardiana (*Canti*, xxx)', *GSLI*, 178, 2001 : 108–13. L. Blasucci, 'Precisazioni sulla prima "sepolcrale"', *Moderna*, 1.2, 1999 : 75–84.

For L.'s biography: Francesco Paolo Maulucci Vivolo, *Casa Leopardi: la vita quotidiana e le vicende familiari*, Foggia, Bastogi, 2001, 133 pp.; Sandro Scarrocchia, *Leopardi e la Recanati analoga*, Mi, UNICOPLI, 2001, 153 pp.; Rolando Damiani, *All'apparir del vero. Vita di Giacomo Leopardi*, Mi, Mondadori, 529 pp., a reprint of the 1998 revised edn of a work first published in 1992. For his correspondence: G. Nencioni, 'Studio linguistico sull'epistolario di Leopardi', *Il Veltro*, 44, 2000 : 551–73. L. Blasucci, 'Una nuova edizione dell'epistolario leopardiano', *Italianistica*, 28, 1999 [2000] : 455–60. E. Benucci, 'Un autografo leopardiano ritrovato: la lettera a Carlo del 30 aprile 1827', *RLI*, 106 : 67–75. C. Genetelli, 'I "frammenti monaldiani dati da Resnati". Su una lettera di Pietro Giordani a Antonio Gussalli', *FC*, 24, 1999[2000] : 291–99.

On aspects of L.'s *fortuna*: *Leopardi nel carteggio Vieusseux: opinioni e giudizi dei contemporanei, 1823–1837*, ed. Elisabetta Benucci, Laura Melosi, and Daniela Pulci, 2 vols, F, Olschki, 2001, lxxxii + 735 pp., draws on letters, in part published for the first time, from and to Giovan Pietro Vieusseux. M. Mustè, 'Gioberti e Leopardi', *La Cultura*, 38:59–112. L. Felici, 'Schopenhauer lettore di Leopardi e il *dialogo* desanctisiano', *Borsellino Vol.*, 537–54, returns to the vexed question of Schopenhauer's reception of Leopardi's writings and De Sanctis's role in it. A. Barbuto, 'Alcuni dati per una storia della sfortuna critica della *Palinodia*', *Borsellino Vol.*, 499–513. *La musica in Leopardi nella lettura di Clemente Rebora*, ed. Gualtiero De Santi and Enrico Grandesso, Venice, Marsilio, 2001, 127 pp. *Composizioni per Leopardi: la raccolta musicale del Centro nazionale di studi leopardiani*, ed. Paola Ciarlantini and Ermanno Carini, introd. Franco Foschi, Recanati, CNSL, 2000, 367 pp. Rossana Caira Lumetti et al., *Prosa e poesia: modelli intertestuali tra Leopardi e Primo Levi*, Fossombrone, Metauro, 2001, 142 pp.

New editions of L.'s works include: Giacomo Leopardi, *Teorica delle arti, lettere, ec., parte pratica, storica ec.: edizione tematica dello Zibaldone di pensieri stabilita sugli Indici leopardiani*, ed. Fabiana Cacciapuoti, pref. Antonio Prete, Ro, Donzelli, xciv + 528 pp.; Giacomo Leopardi, *Appressamento della morte*, ed. crit. Sabina Delcò-Toschini, introd. and comm. Christian Genetelli, Ro–Padua, Antenore, lxxvii + 130 pp.; Giacomo Leopardi, *I nuovi credenti*, ed. Elio Fiore, introd. Mario Luzi, Recanati, CNSL, 16 pp.; and Giacomo Leopardi, *Paralipomeni della Batracomiomachia*, ed. Marco Antonio Bazzocchi and Riccardo Bonavita, Ro, Carocci, 291 pp.

Finally, three past students of L. have been honoured with editions of their writings on him: Francesco De Sanctis, *Studi su Giacomo Leopardi*, ed. Enrico Ghidetti, Venosa, Osanna Venosa, xxxii + 391 pp., a revised critical edn.; Giovanni Mestica, *Studi leopardiani*, ed. Franco Foschi, Ancona, Il Lavoro Editoriale, 2000, 557 pp., the first collected edn of M.'s work; and Giulio Natali, *Viaggio col Leopardi nell'Italia letteraria*, ed. Marcello Verdenelli, Ancona, Il Lavoro Editoriale, 2000, 273 pp., an edn of lectures with notes, indexes, and an introduction.

LEOPARDI, P. Paolina Leopardi, *Viaggio notturno intorno alla mia camera e altri scritti*, ed. Elisabetta Benucci, Venosa, Osanna Venosa, 2000, xvii + 198 pp., includes Paolina's translation of De Maistre from the French, with introductory texts by Franco Foschi and Lucio Felici.

LUPO. Luigi Marrella and Luigi Scorrano, *Un inno e un sospiro: Adele Lupo di Casarano*, Manduria, Barbieri, 2001, 143 pp., marks the 150th anniversary of the Apulian poetess's birth.

MANZONI. A reprint like Ezio Raimondi, *Il romanzo senza idillio: saggio sui Promessi sposi*, T, Einaudi, 2000, 340 pp., first publ. 1974, only highlights the dearth of new book-length criticism: works such as Michele Dell'Aquila, *Invito alla lettura di Manzoni*, Bari, Palomar, 223 pp., hardly count, while collections of essays usually contain much already-published material. Volumes which, however, do seem worth noting are Clara Leri, *Manzoni et la littérature universelle*, pref. Ezio Raimondi, Mi, CNSM, xxi + 177 pp.; Piero Alberti, *I porcellini d'India e il pastorello: personaggi dei Promessi sposi di Manzoni. Fine di un messaggio cattolico*, Ro, Armando, 2001, 287 pp.; Remo Fasani, *Non solo quel ramo. . .: cinque saggi su I promessi sposi e uno sul canto 5. dell'Eneide*, F, Cesati, 184 pp. (and also, on M.'s early verse translation from Virgil, Id., 'Il Manzoni e la corsa a piedi. Sul canto v dell'*Eneide*', *Versants*, 40, 2001 : 229–36); and Boggione, *Poesia*, containing original work on *Il cinque maggio* (also published as an article, for which see below), *L'Ira d'Apollo*, and the text of the lines *A Maria Dandolo* .

For a three-year survey, even articles are not overabundant. On M.'s mature poetry I note only: G. Brugnoli, 'Nota a Manzoni, *Il Natale*, vv. 71–91', *RCCM*, 44 : 163–65. V. Boggione, ' "Ei si nomò" : Napoleone, Adamo e l'Anticristo. Per una lettura biblica del *Cinque maggio* ', *LItal*, 54 : 262–85. G. Cavallini, 'Postilla sul *Cinque Maggio* ', *SPCT*, 63, 2001 : 127–31. R. Morabito, 'Il *Cinque Maggio* e un'ode di Ignazio Ciaia', *ib*., 64 : 125–32. D. Isella, 'Delle manzoniane *Strofe per una Prima Comunione* (e di una ritrovata)', *StCrit*, 17 : 375–78. E. Aschieri, 'Il modulo manzoniano nella traduzione poetica dell'Ottocento: Pietro Bernabò Silorata traduce Lamartine', *LItal*, 54 : 431–59, highlighting the influence of M.'s verse. On the historical dramas I note only: F. Brunori, 'Il re e la vittima. Un modello shakespeariano per l'*Adelchi* di Alessandro Manzoni', *FC*, 25, 2000 : 457–75, who finds in *Adelchi* echoes and analogies of Shakespeare's historical tetralogy, especially *Henry V*; and P. Italia, 'La nuova edizione critica dell'*Adelchi*', *Italianistica*, 29, 2000[2001] : 463–78. A new edition of the verse and plays is Alessandro Manzoni, *Poesie e tragedie*, ed. Valter Boggione, T, UTET, 1013 pp.

For the first version of the historical novel: Alessandro Manzoni, *Fermo e Lucia*, introd. and ed. Salvatore Silvano Nigro, Mi, Mondadori, cxlv + 1402 pp., revises the established critical text; while on the figure of Geltrude in it we have F. Sberlati, 'Tra retorica e giurisprudenza. Geltrude nel *Fermo e Lucia* ', *Intersezioni*, 22 : 33–60. On *I promessi sposi* itself articles range widely. More general in scope are: G. Palen Pierce, 'I *Promessi sposi* between Enlightenment and Romanticism: Alessandro Manzoni as economic libertarian and environmentalist', *ItQ*, 151–52 : 5–26; P. Barlera, 'Figurazioni teologiche nel paesaggio morale dei *Promessi sposi* ', *FC*, 25, 2000 : 114–35;

D. Ferraris, 'Lisander in fabula', *ChrI*, 17.1, 2001:49–76; F. De Cristofaro, '"Un animale selvaggio addomesticato". Il bestiario manzoniano in movimento', *Intersezioni*, 21, 2001:37–78; L. Parisi, 'L'umorismo di Manzoni', *ItS*, 57:75–96; R. J. Lokaj, 'Manzoni, lettore di Dante in chiave comica', *RCCM*, 44:89–150. Other articles relate to specific episodes. P. A. Perotti, '"Siés baraòs trapolorum" (*I promessi sposi*, cap. XIV)', *GSLI*, 178, 2001:258–69, in the wake of L. Russo, G. Bézzola, and others, reinterprets the drunken Renzo's reference to Ferrer's alleged mystificatory abuse of Latin as devoid of overall sense but deriving from the Spaniard's *Asì es* and *guardaos* and, under Church Latin influence, the Italian *trappole*: G. Petrocchi's more coherent gloss 'siete barattieri da trappola' is thus decisively rejected. A. Pallotta, 'Manzoni's conte zio', *FoI*, 35, 2001:48–57, studying *I promessi sposi*, XIX, concludes that M. 'uses a strategy of incompleteness' (by denying the Conte Zio and the Padre Provinciale 'a face and a name') in order 'to convey a distinct disdain for both'. E. Ardissino, 'L'orazione funebre per il cardinal Federico e la manzoniana "vita"', *Testo*, 40, 2000:93–106. M. Boaglio, 'Manzoni: il *romanzo* dell'Innominato come modello di conversione', *CLett*, 28, 2000:263–96. On Don Ferrante, also in relation to Cervantes: M. Arnaudo, 'Biblioteche, bibliofilia e alienazione letteraria nel *Don Quijote* e nei *Promessi sposi*', *StCrit*, 17:75–106. Id., 'Le correzioni minime dei *Promessi Sposi*', *Cenobio*, 50, 2001:45–50. U. Zuccarelli, 'In margine alla lingua dei *Promessi Sposi*. (Note sugli avverbi *allora, ancora, tuttavia, tuttora*)', *CLett*, 30:97–108.

Manzoni's 'anti-*Promessi sposi*' has now appeared as vol. 14 of his 'Edizione nazionale e europea': Alessandro Manzoni, *Del romanzo storico e, in genere, de' componimenti misti di storia e d'invenzione*, ed. Silvia De Laude, pref. Giovanni Macchia, Mi, CNSM, 2000, lxxxvii + 286 pp. On the edition as a whole: M. Mancini, 'L'edizione nazionale delle opere di Manzoni', *RLI*, 106:60–67.

Miscellaneous articles include: C. M. Fiorentino, 'Gli ultimi momenti di Alessandro Manzoni', *NA*, 2217, 2001:259–67; N. Cacciaglia, 'Alessandro Manzoni e l'impresa familiare', *FoI*, 33, 1999:61–72; F. Abodi, 'Machiavelli in Alessandro Manzoni', *EL*, 27.3:55–72; G. Langella, 'Manzoni e il "bello morale"', *Testo*, 42:5–38, on the *Morale cattolica*; A. Cottonaro, 'Manzoni in Purgatorio, l'inordinato amore', *Belfagor*, 56, 2001:531–44; L. Baldini Confalonieri, '"Testimonium animae": per un tema manzoniano', *GSLI*, 178, 2001:481–92. E. Raimondi, 'Un colloquio europeo. Newman e Manzoni', *LItal*, 53, 2001:347–53, focuses on N.'s response to M.'s writings.

On his wider critical reception: 'Gli scrittori e Manzoni' and 'Manzoni e il pubblico', Dell'Aquila, *Nominanza*, 44–53 and 54–66 respectively; Alfredo Cottignoli, *Manzoni fra i critici dell'Ottocento: studi e ricerche*, Bo, CLUEB, 147 pp., a revised and expanded second edition of a work first published in 1978; L. Parisi, 'Manzoni e la modernità: un dialogo con Ezio Raimondi', *FoI*, 35, 2001 : 332–50, which reviews R.'s writings on M. to test R.'s thesis that M. is 'one of the most important representatives of modernity in European literature'. Reflecting (à propos the recent Gallimard edition of *Les Fiancés*) on Manzoni's 'difficult' reception in a country where he defies all expectations, J. Risset, 'Tra Sade e *Les Annales*: Manzoni in Francia', *Muscetta Vol.*, 125–30, suggests that perhaps 'la maggior modernità di Manzoni risiede proprio nella sua coscienza del male. Più che Stendhal o Balzac, Manzoni ricorda Dostoevskij'. F. Zabagli, 'Geno Pampaloni e i *Promessi Sposi*', *ParL*, 618–22, 2001 : 117–24. *Rivisitazione manzoniana nella prospettiva del vero e nell'attualità del messaggio. Seminario CEISLO, Santa Maria La Vite, Olginate 12–15 settembre 1998*, Olginate, CEISLO, xi + 305 pp.

For convenience we note under Manzoni: Giulia Beccaria, *Col core sulla penna: lettere 1791–1841*, ed. Grazia Maria Griffini Rosnati, pref. Carlo Carena, Mi, CNSM, 2001, xliv + 366 pp.

MONTI. Vincenzo Monti, *Il Prometeo: edizione critica, storia, interpretazione*, ed. Luca Frassineti, Pisa, ETS, 2001, 470 pp., goes back to the MSS, including autograph annotations, and also brings to light unpublished letters and documents relevant to the poem's editorial history. V. Giannetti, 'Il *Sermone sulla mitologia* di Vincenzo Monti', *LItal*, 53, 2001 : 509–24, relates the editorially successful *Sermone* of 1825 (four editions in as many months) to its historical moment and explores its subsequent reception and influence. F. Favaro, 'Politica e varianti in due poemetti di Vincenzo Monti: la *Musogonia* e la *Feroniade*', *LItal*, 54 : 96–118.

NIEVO. *Ippolito Nievo e il Mantovano. Atti del Convegno nazionale*, ed. Gabriele Grimaldi, introd. P. V. Mengaldo, Venice, Marsilio, 2001, 553 pp., contains the proceedings of a conference held at Rodigo. G. Paolini, 'Ippolito Nievo: letteratura e rivoluzione', *NA*, 2219, 2001 : 88–96. M. Colummi Camerino, 'Vivere il tempo, guardare il mondo: tragitti spaziali e temporali nelle *Confessioni* di Nievo', *QVen*, 35 : 29–48. T. Zanato, 'Su e per un'edizione critica della *Confessioni d'un Italiano*', *ib.*, 49–77. V. Giannetti, 'Nievo e la "religione dantesca"', *LItal*, 54 : 343–62. 'Il progetto di Nievo', Palandri, *Deriva*, 87–96. Carla Gaiba, *Il tempo delle passioni: saggio su 'Le confessioni d'un italiano' di Ippolito Nievo*, Bo, Il Mulino, 2001, 302 pp.

NOTA. Albarosa Camaldo, *Alberto Nota drammaturgo*, Ro, Bulzoni, 2001, 638 pp., includes eight plays published for the first time.

PADULA. M. Dondero, 'La data di composizione dell'*Antonello* di Vincenzo Padula', *RLI*, 104, 2000 : 85–90. Id., 'Lettura di *Antonello*, dramma in prosa di Vincenzo Padula', *GSLI*, 178, 2001 : 553–78. Id., 'Calabria "contro": Vincenzo Padula. Saggio di edizione critica e annotata dell'*Antonello*', *Muscetta Vol.*, 197–212. Vincenzo Padula, *Critica letteraria e linguistica*, Ro, GLF, 2001, 219 pp., is the second in the three-volume edition of P.'s *Scritti di estetica, linguistica e critica letteraria*, ed. Pasquale Tuscano and promoted by the Fondazione Vincenzo Padula di Acri.

PASCOLI. *ParL*, 588–92, 1999[2000], a special issue on the theme 'Giovanni Pascoli. Sconosciuto? Incompreso? Reticente?', included: M. Santagata, '*Alcyone*: un "congedo" fra Pascoli e Petrarca' (3–26); G. Nava, 'Commento a *Psyche*' (27–52); C. Garboli, 'Da Massa a a Livorno. Dall'*Ultima passeggiata* alle *Ballate piccole e spiritali*' (53–111); A. Oldcorn, 'Ὦ τὸν Ἄδωνιν' (111–22); G. Capovilla, 'Per un ordinamento cronologico della poesia pascoliana. Le prime edizioni dei testi pubblicati in vita' (123–40); F. Zabagli, 'Note da una lettura di Pascoli latino' (141–55); E. Salibra, 'Folclore, mito, ritorno. Lettura dell'*Ultimo viaggio*' (156–97); F. Nassi, 'Il pellegrino e l'ebreo errante' (198–221); B. Cordati, 'Pascoli e Barga' (222–26); F. Nassi, 'Pascoli e Psyche' (227–32); E. Salibra, 'Caproni e Pascoli' (232–35); C. Garboli, 'Da un alloro divelto a un altro reciso' (235–38).

M. Castoldi, '"Io non credo che Matelda cessi di danzare!" Materiali per una lezione di metrica pascoliana', *ib.*, 606–10, 2000 : 61–98, pending publication of G. Moroni's projected manual on the subject, provides a useful summary of P.'s metrical experimentation, which consistently creates 'nel solco della tradizione . . . un ritmo complesso e molteplice e in costante metamorfosi'. Id., 'Giovanni Pascoli, la "miscellanea tassoniana" e la genesi del ciclo di re Enzio', *ib.*, 600–04, 60–97. 'Nei dintorni di *Myricae*: come muore una lingua poetica?', Girardi, *Prosa*, 27–50. G. Genco, 'Il Leopardi del Pascoli', *Testo*, 42, 2001 : 39–66. 'L'agonia di un nume. Il Manzoni sfruttato e tradito di Pascoli', Boggione, *Poesia*, 175–83, discusses P.'s adaptation of lines from Manzoni's *Pentecoste* in his own *X Agosto*. L. Alboreto, 'Approssimazioni ai *Poemata christiana* di Giovanni Pascoli, *AIV*, 158, 2000 : 95–120. W. Hirdt, 'I *Poemi conviviali* fra mitografia e filosofia', *StIt*, 23, 2000: 75–97. C. Damiani, 'Pascoli dopo il '900', *NArg*, 8, 1999 : 110–19. 'Pascoli secondo Pasolini', Girardi, *Prosa*, 199–209.

Recent volumes include: Pier Luigi Cerisola, *Giovanni Pascoli: tra estetica ed ermeneutica*, F, La Nuova Italia, 2000, xii + 205 pp., collected writings, some previously unpublished; Enrico Elli, *Pascoli e l'antico: dalle liriche giovanili ai Poemi conviviali*, Novara, Interlinea, 195 pp., all but one hitherto unpublished; and Mario Pazzaglia, *Pascoli*, Ro, Salerno, 356 pp., also published in the Salerno *Storia della Letteratura*

Italiana. Among recent editions of P.'s verse the more important are Giovanni Pascoli, *Poesie: Myricae, Canti di Castelvecchio*, ed. Ivano Ciani and Francesca Latini, introd. Giorgio Bárberi Squarotti, T, UTET, 2002, 1038 pp.; Giovanni Pascoli, *Canti di Castelvecchio*, ed. Nadia Ebani, 2 vols, Scandicci, La Nuova Italia, 2001, xxxii + 1256 pp., a critical edition in the Edizione Nazionale of P.'s works. I also note *Carteggio Giovanni Pascoli – Augusto Guido Bianchi*, ed. Manuela Montibelli, Mi, La Nuova Italia, 2001, 199 pp., and '*Lettere agli amici urbinati* di Giovanni Pascoli', Cerboni, *Letture*, 213–31, including the texts letters to Tommaso Ricciarelli and Giovanni Marchigiani,

PINDEMONTE. *I Sepolcri di Ippolito Pindemonte: storia dell'elaborazione e testo critico*, ed. Nadia Ebani, Verona, Fiorini, 103 pp., usefully (for wider circulation) reproduced in volume from *BSLV* 1982, would not appear to have been noted at that time.

PITRÉ. Giuseppe Pitré, *Carteggio*, I, *1861–1869*, ed. Gian Luigi Bruzzoni, Palermo, ILA Palma — Ragusa, Documenta, 2000, 529 pp., is the first vol. published in the Edizione Nazionale of P.'s works.

PORTA. F. Capoferri, 'L'oscenità del Porta', *FoI*, 34, 2000: 444–67. Carlo Porta, *Poesie edite e inedite*, ed. Angelo Ottolini, Mi, Hoepli, 1999, lxxxi + 570 pp., usefully reproduces the important 1946 edition.

PUCCINI. *Niccolò Puccini: un intellettuale pistoiese nell'Europa del primo Ottocento. Atti del Convegno di studio, Pistoia, 3–4 dicembre 1999*, ed. Elena Boretti, Chiara D'Afflitto, and Carlo Vivoli, F, Edifir, 2001, 270 pp., illus., gathers the proceedings of a conference marking the bicentenary of P.'s birth.

ROVANI. Giuseppe Rovani, *Cento anni*, ed. Silvana Tamiozzo Goldmann, 2 vols, Mi, Rizzoli, 2001, 1358 pp. L. A. Biglione di Viarigi, 'Autografi inediti dei *Cento Anni* di Rovani rinvenuti nel fondo De' Rosmini-Valotti presso l'Archivio Lechi in Brescia', *Testo*, 42, 2001: 129–42. *Testo*, 44, is given over to a set of six *Rovaniana*: S. T. Goldmann, 'Ragioni di un'edizione: i *Cento anni* di Giuseppe Rovani' (7–16); A. M. Mutterle, 'Glossa sul gondoliere poeta' (17–21); M. Giachino, 'I *Cento anni* in *Gazzetta*' (23–43); L. A. Biglione di Viarigi, 'L'officina di Rovani: da manoscritti e appunti inediti al testo della *Giovinezza di Giulio Cesare*' (45–53); E. N. Girardi, 'Teoria e critica letteraria di Giuseppe Rovani' (55–74); and A. Carli, 'Storia di una salma. Giuseppe Rovani, Carlo Dossi e Paolo Gorini' (75–86).

SALGARI. Ann Lawson Lucas, *La ricerca dell'ignoto. I romanzi d'avventura di Emilio Salgari*, F, Olschki, 2000, xvi + 206 pp. Gian Paolo Marchi, *La spada di sambuco: cinque percorsi salgariani*, Verona, Florini, xii + 128 pp. Felice Pozzo, *Emilio Salgari e dintorni*, pref.

Antonio Palermo, Na, Liguori, 2000, xiv + 339 pp. There have also been a number of serious editions: Emilio Salgari, *Romanzi di giungla e di mare: Le tigri di Mompracem, I misteri della giungla nera, Un dramma nell'Oceano Pacifico*, ed. Ann Lawson Lucas, T, Einaudi, 2001, lxxvi + 772 pp., also including an essay by Michele Mari; Id., *Il mistero della foresta e altri racconti*, introd. Emanuele Trevi and with an essay by Luciano Tamburini, T, Einaudi, xxii + 272 pp.; Id., *Storie di montagna*, ed. Felice Pozzo, T, Centro Documentazione Alpina, 2001, 154 pp., with an introductory essay.

SERAO. L. Palma, 'Matilde Serao tra riedizioni di testi e studi critici: una rassegna (1996–2002)', *EL*, 27.3:111–16. M. Serao, 'Lettere inedite a Enrico Nencioni (1881–1891)', *NA*, 2223:304–13.

SESTINI. A. M. Morace, 'L'incanto e la sofferenza: gli *Amori campestri* di Bartolomeo Sestini', *SPCT*, 60, 2001:115–44.

SETTEMBRINI. Luigi Settembrini, *I neoplatonici*, Palermo, Sellerio, 2001, 67 pp., republishes the short story with an editorial note by Beppe Benvenuto.

TARCHETTI. E. Coda, 'La cultura medica ottocentesca nella *Fosca* di Igino Ugo Tarchetti', *LItal*, 52, 2000:438–54.

TOMMASEO. P. Pepe, 'Niccolò Tommaseo: antiromanzo fra dialogo, diario e confessione', *NA*, 2220, 2001:327–39. E. Sormani, 'Tommaseo poeta', *Muscetta Vol.*, 131–42. Also on T.'s verse: '"Le opposte cose": Tommaseo, lo specchio e san Paolo', Boggione, *Poesia*, 151–61. G. Paolini, 'Niccolò Tommaseo e il Risorgimento "contestato"', *NA*, 2213, 2000:291–303. V. Zaccaria, 'L'accademico Giuseppe Barbieri e il Tommaseo', *AMAGP*, 113, 2001:21–50.

VERGA. In volume I note several new monographs or collections of essays: Antonio Di Silvestro, *Le intermittenze del cuore: Verga e il linguaggio dell'interiorità*, Catania, Fond. Verga, 2000, 248 pp.; Mariella Muscariello, *Gli inganni della scienza: percorsi verghiani*, Na, Liguori, 2001, 135 pp., revising and expanding already published writings; Giuseppe Lo Castro, *Giovanni Verga: una lettura critica*, Soveria Mannelli, Rubbettino, 2001, 243 pp.; Natalia Vacante, *L'estremo realismo di Verga: un percorso genetico bloccato*, introd. Vitilio Masiello, Bari, Graphis, 2000, viii + 172 pp.; Vittorio Roda, *Verga e le patologie della casa*, Bo, CLUEB, 2001, 221 pp., gathering five essays, one unpublished, two noted below; and Maria Gabriella Riccobono, *Dai suoni al simbolo: memoria poetica, relazioni analoghe, fonosimbolismo in Giovanni Verga*, Pisa, IEPI, 481 pp.

For 1874, a decisive year in V.'s development: V. Roda, 'Il fantasma della pluralità: *Tigre reale* di Giovanni Verga', *SPCT*, 61, 2000:99–130; P. Pellini, 'Verga e i "cavoli" di Flaubert. Una lettera del 1874 e la logica del naturalismo', *RLettI*, 20.3:151–70; and D. Conrieri, 'Lettura di *Nedda* ', *GSLI*, 178, 2001:161–91, quoting

L. Sozzi's words 'Il est vain et erroné d'étudier la littérature dans un cadre strictement national' and showing how *Nedda* conforms to the international short-story code of its time, particularly in the distancing of the unfortunate protagonist through, among other things, the presence of a reassuring middleman narrator, and the coexistence of 'miserabilismo' and emotion.

Italianistica, 30, 2001, devoted a special number to 'Da *Rosso Malpelo* a *Ciàula scopre la luna*', which contained: P. Clemente, 'Lettura folklorica' (515–34); F. Fido, 'Lettura narratologica' (535–42); R. Luperini, 'Lettura storico sociologica' (543–52); M. Picone, 'Lettura simbolica' (553–62); B. Porcelli, 'Lettura onomastica' (563–78); A. Stussi, 'Lettura linguistica' (579–608); D. De Camilli, 'Note di storia della critica' (609–22). Other work on V.'s short stories included P. Garofalo, 'Once upon a time . . . Narrative strategies in Verga's *Jeli il pastore* and *Rosso Malpelo*', *MLN*, 117:84–105; E. Saccone, 'I mondi di Verga: l'ossimoro di *Cavalleria Rusticana*', *ib.*, 106–14; and R. Zagari-Marinzoli, 'Sicilia mitica e reale in *La lupa* di Giovanni Verga', *FoI*, 36:130–39. For *I Malavoglia*: A. Illiano, 'Questionario sulla narrativa malavogliesca', *ib.*, 33, 1999:107–30; P. Galignani, 'Due forme narrative a confronto: *I Malavoglia* e le *Fiabe fantastiche*. Le novelle della nonna di Emma Perodi', *ib.*, 36:140–64. F. De Cristofaro, 'Le segnature dei corpi. Effetti di reale e paradigmi fisiognomici in Verga', *Intersezioni*, 20, 2000:87–114. V. Roda, 'Patologie della casa: l'abitare "in fondo" di Giovanni Verga', *SPCT*, 64:133–54. Id., 'La casa violata: note su un tema verghiano', *StIt*, 25, 2001:23–74. Giovanni Verga, *Dal tuo al mio: dramma e romanzo*, ed. Giuseppe Lo Castro, Rende (Cosenza), Centro Editoriale e Librario, 1999, xxx + 196 pp., includes V.'s last work in its Rome 1904 stage version (for the first time), together with the 1906 novel adaptation and the original third act of the Milan 1903 production. B. Alfonzetti, 'Verga fra critica e filologia', *Mazzacurati Vol.*, 101–05, is a brief appraisal of M.'s work on Verga. *Giovanni Verga*, ed. Simona Cigliana, introd. Roberto Fedi, Ro, IPZS, xxvii + 1227 pp.

VERRI, A. In a comparative study which also discusses works in French on the same subject by Henri-Auguste Barbier and the Polish-born Russian diplomat Ksawery Łabeński, J. Lindon, 'Attualità di Erostrato fra istanze illuministiche, rivolta prometeica, e democrazia borghese', *ItS*, 56, 2001:66–79, discusses Alessandro Verri's multilayered novel *La vita di Erostrato* (1782–1815) with its (possibly anti-Napoleonic) anti-heroic thrust and a prometheic dimension which reflects the influence of *Ultime lettere di Jacopo Ortis* but moves beyond Foscolo towards Leopardi.

VISCONTI. G. Lupo, 'Alcuni documenti inediti intorno agli anni giovanili di Ermes Visconti (1797–1814)', *RIL*, 133, 1999[2000]: 3–28.

NOVECENTO

By Roberto Bertoni, *Senior Lecturer in Italian, Trinity College Dublin* and Catherine O'Brien, *Professor of Italian, National University of Ireland, Galway*

1. General

Hainsworth, *Companion*, besides entries on many individual 20th-c. authors includes a range of general entries such as Contemporary Italy, Modernism, Post-modernism, Versification, Women Writers, and Science Fiction. *Dizionario degli autori del secondo Novecento*, pref. Ferruccio Ulivi, introd. Neuro Bonifazi, Arezzo, Helicon, 282 pp. For Novecento literary history we note: Massimiliano Capati, *Storia letteraria del Novecento italiano*, Venice, Marsilio, 239 pp.; *Il secondo Novecento dal 1956 ad oggi: la poesia e la narrativa. Atti del Seminario di studi diretto da Romano Luperini, Forte dei Marmi, 16–17–18 aprile 1999*, ed. Valeria Nicodemi, Palermo, Palumbo, 165 pp.; Luigi Reina, *Lo specchio di Narciso: verifiche e sondaggi novecenteschi: scrittori, editori e critici del '900*, Ro, Libreria Croce, 246 pp.

On literature and war: L. Ceva, 'Scrittori e poeti della Grande Guerra', *NA*, 2223: 100–16, includes writers of various nationalities, and, with regard to Italian literature on the First World War, shows that, although it was ideologically influenced by Fascism, some freer voices penetrated the barrier of conformism, for example Emilio Lussu, Ernesto Rossi, and Neri Pozza. R. Turci, 'Renato Serra e la Grande Guerra', *LetP*, 113–14: 135–39, examines Serra's notes on Romain Rolland and the First World War. On Italian intellectuals and ideology (see also the paragraph on writers and politics below under Narrative): N. Borsellino, 'Maschere del dissenso nella letteratura del Ventennio', *NA*, 2220, 2001: 330–36. Arcangelo Leone De Castris, *Intellettuali del Novecento tra scienza e coscienza*, Venice, Marsilio, 2001, 174 pp., observes that Crocean ideology determined Italian intellectuals' tendency to disregard social and economic factors, so that, while cultural history, in Gramscian terms, ought to have a materialistic basis, even in recent times such a history has not been fully written in Italy: one chapter is devoted to an analysis of Galvano della Volpe's theories (121–28), another to 'Pirandello e la civiltà europea' (155–68). Mirella Serri, *Il breve viaggio. Giaime Pintor nella Weimar nazista*, Venice, Marsilio, 250 pp., reconstructs P.'s life and ideology, dates to 1943 his decisive transition to anti-Fascism, and shows how, for ideological reasons, P. was seen by Valentino Gerratana and others as an exemplary anti-Fascist from an earlier date. Also illustrated are P.'s reactions to Fascism up to 1943 as characterized by a position which was neither supportive of Mussolini, nor conspiratorially anti-Fascist. P.'s participation in the 1942 Weimar conference of intellectuals is discussed, and proof given, that P., like Enrico Fermi and Attilio Momigliano, discovered the totalitarian nature of Fascism when it affected him personally in 1943, at which point he made a clear choice in favour of anti-Fascism before his tragic death in the Resistance.

On early 20th-c. avant-garde movements: M. Calvesi, 'Marinetti e le avanguardie europee', *Atti* (Rome), 351–58, includes comparisons of Futurism with André Breton's Surrealism and Tristan Tzara's Dadaism. G. Angeli, 'De Chirico, Savinio e il surrealismo', *ib.*, 359–89. Simona Cigliana, *Futurismo esoterico: contributi per una storia dell'irrazionalismo italiano tra Otto e Novecento*, Na, Liguori, viii + 364 pp. Antonio Saccone, *'La trincea avanzata' e 'la città dei conquistatori'. Futurismo e modernità*, Na, Liguori, 2000, 172 pp., offers a series of essays on different aspects of Futurism and modernity. Antonio Lucio Giannone, *L'avventura futurista: Pugliesi all'avanguardia, 1909–1943*, Fasano, Schena, 124 pp. *Il dizionario del futurismo*, ed. Ezio Godoli, 2 vols, F, Vallecchi, 2001, xxx + 1276 pp. B. Guarnieri, 'Umberto Boccioni e i futuristi fiorentini. Sodalizio e rottura: testimonianze inedite', *LetP*, 113–14: 125–34, focuses on the relationship between Boccioni (and the Milanese Futurists in general) and the Florentine intellectuals led by Papini and Soffici, which ended when Boccioni and Marinetti supported war in 1914. P. Sica, 'Maria Giannini: Futurist woman and visual writer', *Italica*, 79: 339–52, is about G.'s poetics and ideology. On post-modernism: Monica Jensen, *Il dibattito sul postmoderno in Italia: in bilico tra dialettica e ambiguità*, F, Cesati, 354 pp. See also *Da Calvino agli ipertesti* below under NARRATIVE.

The following entries are on poetics and criticism in general. Carla Benedetti, *Il tradimento dei critici*, T, Bollati Boringhieri, 229 pp., includes previously published articles, partly revised, and an introduction (7–25) where the expression 'treason of the critics' is used to indicate those set interpretations which confine literature within formulae such as the end of the novel or the end of history, whereas criticism should be more dynamic, and concerned with social conflict and truth. In addition, a number of writers, namely Carlo Emilio Gadda, Pier Paolo Pasolini, and more recently Antonio Moresco, are seen as representative of positive and complex literary values thanks to their constant testing of literary forms and established ideas. Alberto Cadioli, *Il silenzio della parola: scritti di poetica del Novecento*, Mi, Unucopli, 135 pp., is a revised version of already published texts. Umberto Eco, *Sulla letteratura*, Mi, Bompiani, 364 pp., includes previously published essays on symbol (152–71), style (172–90), hypotyposis ('Le sporcizie della forma', 215–26), and the functions of criticism to practise language as a collective heritage and to be both faithful to the text and free in interpretation (7–22). It also includes statements on Eco's own work as a novelist: 'Borges e la mia angoscia dell'influenza' (128–46), 'Ironia intertestuale e livelli di lettura' (227–52), and 'Come scrivo' (324–59). Romano Luperini, *Breviario di critica*, introd. Ciro Vitiello, Na, Guida, 136 pp., reflects on the contemporary crisis of literary criticism in Italy due to post-modern eclecticism, changes in the literary market, and the fragmentation of militant intellectual circles. It proposes to restore the objectivity of philology, integrated with value judgements and interpretation based on history, close reading of texts, and Marxist hermeneutics. Ciro Vitiello, *Idetica*, Naples, Guida, 56 pp., seeks to promote a kind of literary criticism which he calls *idetica*, a science based on the interplay of intrinsic features of literary works, their relation to history and society, and the critic's personal views. Also taken into consideration are the theories of critics such as Francesco De Sanctis, Benedetto Croce, and Luciano Anceschi.

Many essays focus on individual literary critics. Issue 44 of *Autografo* is devoted to Maria Corti, and includes some of her letters to Benvenuto Terracini (101–13), abstracts (ed. C. Nesi) from the novel *La leggenda di domani* (81–99) and 'Appunti di diario 1942–1970' (35–79), letters by various authors to Corti (115–93), and texts on Corti by B. Mortara Garavelli, G. Nencioni, F. Pusterla, and E. Raimondi. A section of *RLettI*, 20.3: 13–88, is devoted to Bruno Maier's critical output and includes essays by G. Baroni, C. Benussi, I. Bertelli, M. Cecovini, M. Coretti, M. Dell'Aquila, G. Semacchi Gliubich, E. Guagni, R. Ponis, R. Scrivano, and G. Criscione Stuparich. B. Casagrande, 'La critica di Alberto Frattini dagli anni Quaranta a oggi', *ib*, 20.1: 129–81. V. Branca, 'Carlo Bo o della letteratura come verità e vita', *NA*, 2220, 2001: 283–99, reconstructs Bo's itinerary as a critic, and reflects on the duty and responsibility of committed attitudes on the part of intellectuals. A. Cortellessa, 'A lezione dell'elzeviro. Cauto omaggio a Pampaloni', *NArg*, 16, 2001: 314–27, highlights some aspects of Geno Pampaloni's criticism, mentions his interpretation of Carlo Emilio Gadda's discontent with society as personally rather than politically motivated, and his view that Tommaso Landolfi's poetics of play disguised existential *angst*. B. Manetti, 'L'orologio del padre e l'angelo della storia: un ritratto di Geno Pampaloni', *ParL*, 36–38, 2001: 103–16, reflects on the collapse of values in the generation of critics previous to Pampaloni and on his recovery of the ethical and existential significance of literature. It underlines Pampaloni's sympathy for writers such as Corrado Alvaro, which was due to the latter's interest both in history and style, and concludes that Pampaloni's legacy does not consist of a specific literary canon, but rather in his interrogation of literature seen as the field where the malaise of the individual is expressed in relation to history. L. Ghidetti, 'Cecchi critico d'arte e la *Fiera letteraria* (1925–1926). Il carteggio inedito con Umberto Fracchia (con un'appendice di scritti dispersi)', *RLI*, 106: 113–74. D. Della Terza, 'Binni critico e storico della letteratura', *ib.*, 106: 5–12, reviews and reconsiders Walter Binni's work. A. Di Benedetto, 'Mario Fubini: la critica come rivelazione e professione di umanità', *GSLI*, 178, 2001: 493–508. P. V. Mengaldo, 'La teoria del romanzo di Giacomo Debenedetti', *StCrit*, 17: 1–17, observes that D. built a history of the novel based more on individual authors than on literary theory and prefers his work on Tozzi to his comments on Pirandello. Also noted is the fact that D.'s concern for novels was motivated by his psychological interests, his tendency to highlight the relationship between texts and their authors, and his view that the novel was the leading modern genre and able to espress the notion of crisis. D.'s concept of the post-naturalist 'personaggio-uomo' is described and interwoven with the concept of destiny and autobiography, to conclude that what is missing from D.'s complex network of critical reflexions is a full treatment of the historical dimension. Id., 'La critica militante di Gianfranco Contini', *ib.*, 191–206, highlights the link between Contini's philology and his militant position on modern writers. D. De Martino, 'Gianfranco Contini è sicuramente un giovane di largo avvenire', *Belfagor*, 57: 177–86, is about letters exchanged by Luigi Russo and Contini in March 1943. A section of *L'ospite ingrato. Annuario del Centro Studi Franco Fortini*, 4–5: 15–56, devoted to Sebastiano Timpanaro, includes P. Anderson, 'Sebastiano Timpanaro' (17–40), and R. Luperini, 'Il dibattito sul materialismo e altre questioni degli anni Sessanta e Settanta' (41–56). In his essay Luperini sees Timpanaro and Franco Fortini as the masters of his generation who, despite their differences, were similar in intellectual and political coherence. He appreciates T.'s interest in nature and science and identifies his materialist sense of history by contrast to recurrent types of Crocean idealist historicism. *Allegoria*, 39, 2001, likewise devoted to T., included U. Carpi, 'Appunti sull'antimoderatismo di Timpanaro' (7–30), on T.'s politics and philosophy; R. Castellana, 'Timpanaro o l'etica del saggio (40–51); G. Corlito on T. and psychoanalysis (52–72); C. Cristofolini on the Leopardian component in T.'s materialism (73–84); A. G. Drago on T.'s work *La filologia di Giacomo Leopardi* (105–21); A. T. Drago and P. Totaro on T.'s philology (85–104); R. Dombrowski on the impact of *Il lapsus freudiano* and *Sul materialismo* in the English speaking world (122–31); and R. Luperini on T.'s legacy as a critic (31–39). Also devoted to T. is the 388-page issue *Il Ponte*, 57.10–11, entitled 'Per Sebastiano

Timpanaro', with a 76-page supplement, 'L'opera di Sebastiano Timpanaro: la bibliografia', comprising essays by a range of authors on T.'s various activities including, for T. as a critic, contributions from M. Buiatti, U. Carpi, S. Landucci, C. A. Madrignani, G. Panello, and G. Tellini. C. Segre, 'Avalle: la filologia travolgente', *NA*, 2221 : 131–33, briefly illustrates Silvio D'Arco Avalle's contribution to semiotics.

On miscellaneous topics: 'L'inchiesta: cinque domande sulla letteratura', *Testo*, 43:9–113, publishes the replies of almost four dozen Italianists to a questionaire asking whether marginalization of humanistic studies in schools and universities is irresistible, whether study of 20th-c. literature should replace the classical canon, whether literary studies should re-establish links with the moral and human sciences, whether literature should resist commercialization and reconsider its aesthetic function, whether it can still help to preserve the cultural identity it has powerfully contributed to form. Romano Luperini, *Insegnare la letteratura*, Lecce, Manni, 215 pp., stresses the importance of literature in the educational curriculum, relates the teaching of literature to the formation of literary canons, and defends textual hermeneutics accompanied by historical interpretation. M. Farnetti, *'Il doppio nel testo', *AARA*, ser. 8, 1, 2001:273–84. Marziano Guglielminetti, *Dalla parte dell'io: modi e forme della scrittura autobiografica nel Novecento*, Na, ESI, 362 pp. *AIPI 14* has some essays on individual 20th-c. writers in vol. 1, while the three sections of vol. 2 are entirely devoted to the 20th century: VI, 'Percorsi marini nella letteratura: la poesia del Novecento' (11–88); VII, 'Percorsi marini nella letteratura: la narrativa del primo Novecento' (89–226); and VIII, 'Percorsi marini nella letteratura: la narrativa del secondo Novecento' (227–493). Luigi Malerba, *La composizione del sogno*, T, Einaudi, 111 pp., explores the processes of dreaming, partly relates them to narrative discourse, and shows how even though the logic of dreams and narrative is similar they differ because creative writers adopt an intentional perspective and reconstruct reality. *Intersezioni di forme letterarie e artistiche*, ed. Elena Sala Di Felice, Laura Sannia Nowé, and Roberto Puggioni, Ro, Bulzoni, 2001, 452 pp. *Letteratura siciliana del Novecento: le domande radicali*, ed. Massimo Naro, Caltanissetta, Sciascia, 333 pp. *Bilancio della letteratura del Novecento in Liguria. Atti del Convegno, Genova 4–5 maggio 2001*, ed. Giovanni Ponte, Genoa, Accademia Ligure di Scienze e Lettere, 233 pp., includes, among others, essays by P. Zovoli, S. Verdino, and L. Surdich on Ligurian poetry and its developments from Camillo Sbarbaro to Eugenio Montale and thence to Giorgio Caproni and Edoardo Sanguineti, and studies on Ligurian narrative including authors such as Italo

Calvino and Alberto Biamonti (by F. De Nicola) and on theatre (by G. Corsinovi and E. Bonaccorsi).

On periodicals: Paolo Casini, *Alle origini del Novecento. Leonardo, 1903–1907*, Bo, Il Mulino, 187 pp., confronts the ideology of the three series of the Italian journal *Leonardo*, illustrates Papini's and Prezzolini's attitudes to idealist philosophy (as in their discussion with Croce and Gentile), to politics (their rejection of socialism), to psychology (the influence of, in particular, William James). C. notes the pragmatism of the journal and sets its theories in its context of contemporary journalism (with special reference to *Il Regno* and *Lacerba*) and discusses the views of a number of intellectuals such as Enrico Corradini and Giovanni Vailati. S. Gentili, '*Lacerba*: una nobile follia?', *NA*, 2221:259–68. A. R. Pupino, ' "Modernità" della *Ronda*', *GSLI*, 179:403–10, discusses the autonomy of literature from politics advocated by the *Rondisti*, and situates them against the background of *frammentismo* and *lirismo puro*, but objects to considering the journal as an exercise in restoration of order, and sees its classicism as modern rather than conservative since it was not distant from contemporary foreign poetics of the void, nothingness, and existential *angst*. On publishing: G. Turi, 'Ricordo di Tristano Codignola. Tristano Codignola e La Nuova Italia', *AnVi*, 22:115–26, notes continuity between Codignola and his predecessors at La Nuova Italia, and his role in promoting connections between culture and politics.

2. Poetry

V. Fossati, 'Su alcune antologie dell'ultimo Novecento', *Atelier*, 25:46–63, outlines the confusing and often contradictory images that emerge from certain anthologies. The author also outlines four points of reference used to judge writers, viz. tradition, the canon, what is new, what is historical. L. Ceva, 'Scrittori e poeti della Grande Guerra', *NA*, 2223:100–16. Edoardo Sanguineti, *Atlante del Novecento italiano. La cultura letteraria*, Lecce, Marini, 2001, 128 pp., ed. Erminio Risso, records a lengthy discussion between S. and Risso on the concept and chronology of the Italian literary *Novecento* together with a discussion on the main figures and movements that dominated the century. Id., 'La poesia italiana del secondo Novecento', *Comunicare. Letterature, Lingue*, 1, 2001:27–58, sees the poetry of the later Novecento as diametrically opposed to that of the previous half century and characterized by avantgarde movements which S. strongly endorses. Gaia De Pascale, *Scrittori in viaggio: narratori e poeti italiani del Novecento in giro per il mondo*, T, Bollati Boringhieri, 2001, 247 pp. *Poesia 2001: Annuario*, ed. Giorgio Manacorda, Ro, Cooper &

Castelvecchi, 270 pp., details important publications and events in the field of poetry for 2001. *Annuario di poesia 2002*, ed. Guido Oldani, Mi, Crocetti, 208 pp., performs a similar function for 2002. Stefano Giovanuzzi, *Tempo di raccontare. Tramonto del canone lirico e ricerca narrativa (1936–1956)*, Alessandria, Orso, 216 pp., examines the borders between prose and poetry, the links that bind them, and the dominance of the poetic tradition in Italy. It pays particular attention to the 'avvicinamento' of poetry to prose between the 1930s and the 1950s, and assesses the ensuing consequences in the work of Caproni, Gatto, Luzi, Saba, Quasimodo, Penna, Montale, and Bertolucci. It also looks at the position adopted by poets and critics during this crucial period of transition that is characterized by the meeting and clash between these two models of literary production. Alberto Frattini, *Avventure di Parnaso nell'Italia del Novecento*, 2 vols, Viareggio, Baroni, 612 pp., brings together material previously published elsewhere. Maria Antonietta Grignani, *La costanza della ragione: soggetto, oggetto e testualità nella poesia del Novecento*, Novara, Interlinea, 185 pp., includes some Montale letters published for the first time. D. Piccini, 'I poeti e l'automobile', *Poesia*, 163: 2–14, comments on the way such poets as Apollinaire, Bassani, Brecht, Heaney, Luzi, Marinetti, Penna, Ramat, Zanzotto, Tranströmer, and others used the car as a subject of individual poems.

G. L. Beccaria, *Le forme della lontananza. Poesia del Novecento, fiaba, canto, romanzo*, Mi, Garzanti, 2001, 381 pp. P. G. Beltrami, *Gli strumenti della poesia*, Bo, Il Mulino, 243 pp., is a new edition of an earlier publication. Boggione, *Poesia*, chiefly concerns Gozzano. Mario Luzi, *Vero e verso. Scritti sui poeti e sulla letteratura*, Mi, Garzanti, 250 pp. Claudio Pezzin, *Letteratura italiana del Novecento*, I: *Poesia*, Sommacampagna, Cierre, 225 pp., defines the characteristics of 20th-c. poetic language as it changed through the decades. Stefano Guglielmi, *Scritti nomadi. Spaesamento ed erranza nella letteratura del Novecento*, Verona, Anterem, 2001, 149 pp., on the themes of 'erranza' and 'spaesamento' ranges widely (Beckett, Ionesco, Fenoglio, Viganò, Calvino, Volponi, Sanguineti, Giuliani, Poeta, Balestrini, Campana, Conte, Trake, Zanzotto, and Ermini) and ends with a redefinition of post-modern literature.

Poesia del Novecento italiano. Dalle avanguardie storiche alla seconda guerra mondiale, ed. Niva Lorenzini, Ro, Carocci, 294 pp., *Poesia del Novecento italiano. Dal secondo dopoguerra a oggi*, ed. Niva Lorenzini, Ro, Carocci, 324 pp., and Niva Lorenzini, *Le parole esposte: fotostorie della poesia italiana del Novecento*, Mi, Crocetti, 233 pp., chart the development of 20th-c. poetry within the time-frames indicated in the titles. *Genealogia della poesia nel secondo Novecento*, ed. Maria Antonietta Grignani, Pisa, IEPI, 251 pp., is a monographic issue of conference proceedings previously published in *Moderna* (3.2). Oreste Macrì, *La vita della parola: da Betocchi a Tentori*, ed. Anna Dolfi, Ro, Bulzoni, 852 pp., includes several articles by M. on poets, critics, and translators mainly in the second half of the 20th-c. as far as the arrival of the poetry of Francesco Tentori. This is the final part of a trilogy, the previous sections being *Studi su Ungaretti e poeti coevi* (1998) and *Studi montaliani* (1996), and all the material is preserved in the M. papers in Florence. *La poesia italiana da Leopardi a Montale*, ed. Lucio Izzo, Salerno, Oedipus, 2000, 101 pp., is a collection of conference proceedings. Ramat, *Passi*, gathers nineteen previously published essays on 20th-c. poetry, noted below under individual authors, which illustrate the changing poetic idiom of the century. *Autobiografia in versi: sei poeti allo specchio*, ed. Marco Bazzocchi, Bo, Pendragon, 180 pp., is a collection of essays on Caproni, Sereni, Pasolini, Sbarbaro, Rosselli, and Sanguineti. G. Guglielmi, 'Poesia della prosa', *Poetiche*, 3:337–52, considers the changed relationship between prose and poetry in the 19th- and 20th- c., thanks especially to the departure from poetic conventions in the work of Mallarmé, Govoni, Ungaretti, and Baudelaire, while also discussing the absence of 'obblighi ritmico-metrici' in the *Novecento* in the work of Rebora, Cardarelli, Montale, Zanzotto, Magrelli, Sanguineti, Luzi, and Gabriele Frasca. The same area is the subject of 'Prosa in versi', the opening essay (7–26) of Girardi, *Prosa*, and is illustrated in 'Poeti allo specchio: Corazzini, Sbarbaro', *ib.* 65–74, both previously unpublished. G. Mesa, 'Il verso libero e il verso necessario', *Il Verri*, 20:135–48, outlines the use of traditional metrical schemes, new closed verse forms, and forms not governed by any type of metre, in the work of Biagio Cepollaro, Gabriele Frasca, Florinda Fusco, and Massimo Sannelli. Yet another general manual is G. Lavezzi, *I numeri della poesia: guida alla metrica italiana*, Ro, Carocci, 266 pp. C. Calabrò, 'Il poeta alla griglia', *Poesia*, 157:57–62, questions the stance adopted by certain poets with regard to the use of language in poetry and concludes that the best poetry comes from metaphor which takes us beyond the confines of feeling, experience, and expression. *AIPI 14*, as well as papers on individual poets, includes T. Heydenreich, 'Infiniti adriatici: Marin, Michelstaedter, Saba, Slataper, Magris' (II, 61–65), which examines the way in which these Adriatic authors have used the sea as background to other themes in their work. *Vent'anni di poesia (1982–2002)*, pref. Maria Luisa Spaziani, F, Passigli, 152 pp., is an anthology of work by poets awarded the *Premio Montale* over the years, brought out to mark the 20th anniversary of the Centro Internazionale Eugenio Montale in Rome.

For Futurism and the avant-garde in the field of poetry: A. Contò, 'Una rivista del futurismo veronese: *Magazzino*', *AARA*, ser. 8, 1,

2001:253–71, discusses a Veronese journal published in 1934–35 and containing work by the 'Boccioni' futurist group, including the poet Lionello Fiumi; G. E. Viola, '"Il Futurismo non è più una audacia". Ancora sul distacco di Lucini dal movimento: qualche inedito', *Avanguardia*, 19:23–34, examines the exchange of letters and cards between Gian Pietro Lucini and Marinetti from 1909 to 1912; P. Sica, 'Maria Ginanni: Futurist woman and visual writer', *Italica*, 79:339–52, examines the contribution of M. G. to Florentine Futurism, her promotion of cultural debates, her attempts to promote the new lyric forms together with her production of works that had a strong visual component; Fausto Curi, *La poesia italiana d'avanguardia: modi e tecniche*, Na, Liguori, 2001, viii + 276 pp., has an appendix of documents and texts, some hitherto unpublished.

Nos x–xviii in the ongoing series G. Langella, 'La parabola delle avanguardie (1895–1923)' comprise: x, 'Parole in libertà', *Poesia*, 157:49–51, which deals with the freedom accorded to language by Futurists in Florence and Milan; xi, 'Lo strapaese futurista', *ib.*, 159:51–54, discussing the impact of Futurism throughout the peninsula; xii, 'La koinè periferica', *ib.*, 161:59–61, which details the nationalistic fervour of several journals during the years 1915–18; xiii, 'I nodi al pettine', *ib.*, 162:63–67, outlining the policy and themes adopted by the Neapolitan journal *Diana* from 1915 to 1918; xiv, '"Brigatisti" in crisi', *ib.*, 163:53–55, which discusses the impact of the war and the ensuing crisis of conscience of those associated with the journal *Brigata* (founded in Bologna in 1916); xv, 'Una nuova parola d'ordine', *ib.*, 164:65–67, looking at the way in which journals such as *Cronache letterarie*, *La Scalata*, and *Avanscoperta* carried out their literary reform during the war years; xvi, 'Il ritorno del figliol prodigo', *ib.*, 165:63–65, showing how the Bolognese journal *La Raccolta* reflected a new literary climate no longer tolerant of pre-war literary transgressions; xvii, 'La vittoria mutilata', *ib.*, 166:53–54, pointing to the way journals such as *Il nuovo contadino* (founded by P. Jahier in 1919) and *L'Astico* (named after a river which saw heavy fighting during the War) responded to the demand for social justice by those survivors who had fought for the Italian cause; xviii, 'Le porte orientali d'Italia', *ib.*, 167:51–54, which examines the levels of intercultural exchange and leadership projects in Trieste and the surrounding Carnaro area. Nanni Balestrini and Alfredo Giuliani, *Gruppo 63 – L'Antologia*, T, Testo e Immagine, 320 pp., includes debates and articles on prose, poetry, and theatre by various people occasionally associated with the Gruppo 63 from 1964 to 1969. L. Leonardo, 'To eff the ineffable: can metasemantic poetry be translated?', *FoI*, 36:69–83, discusses metasemantic poetry (created by Fosco Maraini) together with its neologisms and phonic substratum and argues that it is 'squisitamente tangenziale' and 'fortemente bipolare'.

Dialect poetry is the subject of several studies. *Autografo*, 43, has a number of essays on modern dialect poetry: A. Zanzotto, 'Appunti e abbozzi per un'ecloga in dialetto sulla fine del dialetto (1969–1971)' (9–17), presents the poem with an Italian translation; M. Bordin, 'Morte e rinascita del *vecio parlar*: gli inediti. Appunti e abbozzi per un'ecloga in dialetto' (19–48), looks at variants of the above and at the language used, providing a glossary and useful indications to understand the text; F. Santi, 'Dialettali novissimi' (49–63), examines characteristics of the work of Edoardo Zuccato, Gian Maria Villalta, and Giovanni Nadiani; V. Bagnoli, 'La lingua dell'altro. La recente poesia in dialetto dell'Emilia Romagna' (65–77), looks in particular at the dialect forms used by Cesare Zavattini, Tonino Guerra, Raffaello Baldini, Emilio Rentocchini, and Giovanni Nadiani; L. Benini Sforza, 'Il microreale e la parola. Continuità e sviluppi nella poesia di Giuseppe Bellosi' (79–91); and M. Bignamini, ' "Si seri estrus . . .". Sull'espressionismo dialettale di Franco Loi' (93–118). J. Vitiello, 'Translating the contemporaneity of neodialect Italian poetry', *FoI*, 35, 2001 : 498–506. Vittoriano Esposito, *Panorama della poesia dialettale*, Foggia, Bastogi, 258 pp., is an anthology of dialect poetry and the sixth vol. of *L'altro Novecento*, a series launched in 1995. A series of anthologies present varied selections of the dialect poetry of individual areas of Italy. These include: *Voci nella nebbia: antologia di poeti in dialetto cremonese*, ed. Gian Luca Barbieri, Venice, Marsilio, 108 pp.; *Poeti a Como*, ed. Vincenzo Guerracino, Olgiate Comasco, Dialogo, 262 pp.; *L'orizzonte di bruma: luoghi del Novecento poetico in Emilia: Modena, Reggio Emilia, Parma, Piacenza*, ed. Carlo Alberto Sitta, Modena, Laboratorio, 297 pp.; *Poeti triestini contemporanei*, ed. Roberto Dedenaro, Trieste, LINT, 126 pp.; and Ernesto Calzavara, *Ombre sui veri: poesie in lingua e in dialetto trevigiano (1946–1987)*, Mi, Garzanti, 2001, xxiv + 409 pp., which includes an appendix with Fra Enselmino's 14th-c. *El pianto de la Verzen Maria*. Emilio Rentocchini, *Ottave*, Mi, Garzanti, 2001, 160 pp., presents R.'s work in the dialect of Sassuolo with a parallel Italian translation.

Some attention has also been paid to regional poetry. M. Merlin, 'Di alcuni caratteri della poesia romana', *Atelier*, 25 : 36–45, examines the theme of the family in the work of Giselda Pontesilli, Annelisa Alleva, Edoardo Albinati, and Emanuele Trevi, and linguistic euphoria in the work of Paolo Del Colle. D. Valli, 'Per un recupero di senso della poesia meridionale del Novecento', *CLett*, 30 : 725–46, while looking at Quasimodo, Sinisgalli, and Gatto as the 20th-c. Southern poets generally accepted as best, makes a case for inclusion of Girolamo Comi and Luigi Fallacara from Puglia and others such as Cattafi, V. Bodini, Penna, Libero De Libero, Di Giacomo, Pierro, and Carrieri. He particularly challenges the anthologists Giovanardi and Cucchi who excluded the entire South (with the exception of Basilicata) from their recent anthology of poetry in Italy.

P. Valesio, 'Parole e poesia nella diaspora italiana', *Poesia*, 167:73–76, details some of the peculiarities of Italian as used by Italian poets resident in the United States. P. M. Filippi, 'Perché insegnare a tradurre letteratura', *Comunicare. Letterature, Lingue*, 1, 2001:155–69, makes a good case for the need to teach how to translate correctly and well between different languages. C. Gentile, 'La traduzione come atto ermeneutico. Tradurre e "comprendere diversamente"', *Poetiche*, 2:293–311. F. Nasi, 'Sussurri cinesi e le squale mobili: sulla traduzione di poesie per bambini', *LetP*, 113–14:27–48.

3. Narrative, Theatre

Il romanzo, II. *Le forme*, ed. Franco Moretti, T, Einaudi, 748 pp., follows I, *La cultura del romanzo*, and includes several essays on foreign and Italian topics, and on past and modern themes, subdivided into four sections: 1. 'I generi letterari' where various essays address the status of the novel as a literary genre in relation to the epic and other genres; 2. 'La scrittura romanzesca', including inter alia F. Fido, 'Dialogo / monologo' (251–69), which examines the title concepts from Cervantes on; E. Testa, 'Stile, discorso e intreccio' (272–99), on language and its context in the modern novel; and M. Barenghi, 'Manifesti di poetica' (301–38); 3. 'Alto e basso', on the dialectics of popular and learned novels, comedy and tragedy, and expression of feeling; and 4. 'Incerti confini', on the uncertain boundaries of the novel form, which interweaves reality, fantasy, narrative, and poetry: here we single out P. Colaiacomo, 'La tentazione lirica' (537–66); and A. Quayson, 'Realismo magico, narrativa e storia' (615–35). M. Siracusa, 'Dialogo tra l'innamorato della trama e il romanziere', *ParL*, 39–41:166–72, is a theatrical dialogue whose characters discuss plot as a coherent sequence of events but also a labyrinth, on the flux of experience in relation to the representation of reality, and on how truth can be expressed through fiction.

Items on a plurality of novelists include: U. Dotti, 'Romanzo e società. D'Annunzio, Pirandello, Svevo', *GSLI*, 179:1–42, where against the background of social history at the turn of the 19th–20th c. modern aspects of texts by Gabriele D'Annunzio, Luigi Pirandello, and Italo Svevo are analysed; Nicola Longo, *Letture novecentesche: Zeno, Agilulfo, Carlo Levi*, Ro, Bulzoni, 2001 [printed 2002], 182 pp.; Alessandro Lattanzio, *Nichilismo, esistenzialismo e letteratura. Forme e attualità della crisi*, Melegnano, Montedit, 103 pp., which reflects on the crisis of moral and religious values, philosophical persuasions, and the concept of totality in the 20th c. as voiced philosophically by Kierkegaard, Nietzsche, Heidegger, and Sartre and as expressed in the form of subjectivity and fragmentation of thought and language in a number of works by writers of different nationalities including Luigi Pirandello and his *Uno, nessuno e centomila*; Giorgio Luti, *Memoria del Novecento*, F, Cesati, 124 pp., with essays on Romano Bilenchi, Beppe Fenoglio, and Ignazio Silone.

On the Italian short story: A. Asor Rosa, 'Un'Italia di racconti', and A. Berardinelli, 'Forma e identità del racconto italiano', *NArg*, 17:248–60, reflect on *Racconti italiani del Novecento* (ed. Enzo Siciliano, three volumes, Mi, Mondadori, 2001). Asor Rosa observes that in early 20th-c. Italian short stories, peripheral aspects prevail over cultural, psychological, and political centralization, and rural realities feature prominently, whereas in the last two decades of the century, representation of what is marginal vanishes and Italian social identities are portrayed by storytellers as being undefined. Berardinelli argues that extravagant and paradoxical short stories prevail in 20th-c. Italy and that they are often anecdotes close in style and content to novellas.

On neorealism: R. Luperini, 'Riflettendo sulle date: alcuni appunti sul neorealismo in letteratura', *Allegoria*, 37, 2001:125–32, sees neorealism as a complex narrative movement subdivided into three phases: political realism in the 1930s, mythical and symbolic realism 1940–1948, and socialist realism 1949–1955.

A substantial body of work concerns Italian fiction in the last three decades. A topical issue of *Il Verri*, 19, 143 pp., under the title *Il libro di narrativa*, includes the answers given by a number of writers (Alberto Arbasino, Ermanno Cavazzoni, Franco Cordelli, Giuliano Gramigna, and Giuseppe Pontiggia) to a questionnaire on the style and reasons behind storytelling in relation to the contemporary world of the mass media. It includes interviews with Gianni Celati, Gabriella Frasca, and Daniele Del Giudice, essays by Niva Lorenzini on Giovanni Arbasino (110–17), and by Guido Guglielmi, 'Ragiono per (non) essere ottimista' (9–20) on the 'crisi espressiva' from which Italian contemporary literature seems to suffer. Giuseppe Amoroso, *Le sviste dell'ombra: narrativa italiana 1999–2000*, Soveria Mannelli, Rubbettino, 436 pp., is a revised collection of published articles and reviews. Franco Cordelli, *Lontano dal romanzo*, F, Le Lettere, 352 pp., among a number of reviews and articles, includes a short essay entitled 'Romanzo e politica', where a contemporary crisis in novel-writing is identified and the proposed solution is an appropriate choice of both content and form. Lidia De Federicis, *E tu fingi?*

Cronache dell'immagine narrativa in sette anni (1995–2002), T, Trauben, 176 pp., includes texts previously published in the journal *L'Indice*. Angiola Ferraris, *Una vita maleducata. La narrativa italiana (1981–1999) e la musica popolare dal rock all'hip hop*, Na, Liguori, 40 pp., is about writers such as Andrea De Carlo and Enrico Brizzi and their narratives on contemporary society interlinked with motifs which they draw from contemporary music. Raffaele La Capria, *Letteratura e salti mortali*, Mi, Mondadori, 210 pp., with a number of texts published in the 1980s in *Il Corriere della sera* includes a longer essay, 'Il sentimento della letteratura' (101–202), which questions the commercial character of much literature in the age of the mass media and offers a concept of good literature based on skilful writing, authenticity, the ability of writers to provide ethical and social images of reality, to revitalize individual and collective memory, to create links with the literary tradition, portray the truth, and adopt a communicative language. Antonio Moresco, *L'invasione*, Mi, Rizzoli, 240 pp., laments the superficiality of contemporary discussion on literature and proposes that the writer should break free from the cultural market, promote deeper and more original ways of thinking and writing, imitate the complexity of life, reflect seriously on literature, and express the difficulty of existence in the contemporary world. Andrea Rondini, 'Il Novecento', pp. 93–203 of *Sociologia della letteratura*, Mi, B. Mondadori, 213 pp., confronts 20th-c. debate on the reading public, the mass media, and more in general on the sociology of literature. He briefly summarizes and comments on a number of theories, including Antonio Gramsci's analysis of science fiction and serial novels, Umberto Eco's discussion of 'apocalittici' and 'integrati', Giuseppe Petronio's studies of detective stories, Vittorio Spinazzola's approach to democratization of literature, Giancarlo Ferretti's concept of best-selling quality novels and Alberto Cadioli's views on samples of fiction which could be both aesthetically good and written for a large audience. *Da Calvino agli ipertesti: prospettive della postmodernità nella letteratura italiana*, ed. Laura Rorato and Simona Storchi, F, Cesati, 232 pp., presents the proceedings of the London conference, *Postmodernist Discourse and Contemporary Italian Fiction* (27–28 October 2000) and includes E. Palandri, 'Il postmodernismo tra libertà e storia' (17–26); M. Francioso, 'Il discorso sul postmoderno in Italia' (27–36), noting reluctance in the use of the term *postmodernismo* among some Italian critics, unlike their American counterparts, but also highlighting explicit definitions of the same term by Italians such as R. Ceserani, M. Ganeri, and G. Patella (27–36); M. Jansen, 'Il postmoderno in Italia, una mutazione antropologica? Da Pasolini a *Gli sfiorati* di Sandro Veronesi' (37–52), ascribing the origins of Italian post-modernism to Pier Paolo Pasolini's concept of anthropological mutation in the framework of mass society and concluding with an analysis of Veronesi's novel *Gli sfiorati*; R. Glynn, 'La *Verwindung* di un genere letterario: Vattimo e il romanzo storico nell'età postmoderna' (141–56). Essays on orality in relation to post-modern writing include M. Codebò on Gianni Celati's *Narratori delle pianure* (93–102) and M. Spunta on Antonio Tabucchi, Claudio Magris, Francesca Duranti, and Erri De Luca. There are also essays by U. Musarra Schroeder on listening perceptions in postmodern fiction and especially in works by Italo Calvino, Claudio Magris, Roberto Pazzi, and Andrea Camilleri (103–16); by S. Matthiassen on recent trends in Italian fiction after the so-called *cannibali* and in particular on works by Guido Conti, Stefano Massaron, and Paolo Nori (205–20); and on individual writers or works: B. Van den Bossche on Calvino (53–64); A. Spadaro on Tondelli (65–78); L. Rorato on Palandri's *Boccalone* (79–92); S. Storchi on Tabucchi's *Sogni di sogni* (157–68); N. Di Ciolla McGowan on Rossana Campo (169–76); D. De Ferra on Francesca Duranti's *La casa sul lago della luna* (177–92); H. Serkowska on Paola Capriolo's *Con i miei mille occhi* (193–204); and G. Gargiulo on Lorenzo Miglioli (221–32). Fulvio Senardi, *Gli specchi di Narciso: aspetti della narrativa italiana di fine millennio*, Manziana, Vecchiarelli, 283 pp. Id., 'Narrativa di fine millennio: "la sintassi dei casi"', *Problemi*, 119–20, 2001 : 101–24, examines Italian post-modernism in the 1980s (Umberto Eco, Andrea de Carlo, Vittorio Tondelli, and Italo Calvino) and quality works by best-selling authors in the 1990s (including Susanna Tamaro, *Va' dove ti porta il cuore*). It notes a tendency in recent novels to portray intimate life rather than major events and intellectual rather than ordinary characters, and concludes with the question whether new works will succumb to, or win over, the current commercialization of literature. Alessandro Tamburini, *La narrativa italiana di fine secolo nella retrospettiva di un osservatore partecipe, 1979–1999*, Trento, Giunta della Provincia Autonoma, 2000, 61 pp.

A number of essays focus on writers and politics. Marino Biondi, *Scrittori e miti totalitari. Malaparte, Pratolini, Silone*, F, Polistampa, 357 pp., devotes sections to each of the three writers, highlighting the war themes in their work and their attitudes to Fascism, and in particular Malaparte's 'caporettismo', Pratolini's interpretation of Fascism in *Lo scialo* as a metaphor for illusion, loss, and death, and Silone's social concerns interwoven with reference to Niccolò Machiavelli's thought. G. Lombardi, 'Parigi o cara: terrorism, exile, and escape in contemporary cinema and fiction', *AnI*, 20 : 403–24, examines memoirs as well as fiction by and on Italian terrorists living in France. A. Menetti, 'Il partigiano allo specchio. Variazioni girardiane tra storia e letteratura', *Intersezioni*, 22 : 109–25, reflects on the human as opposed to the political dimension of the Resistance movement — on memory and scapegoats — partly on the basis of René Girard's theories and with examples taken from Carlo Cassola's *La ragazza di Bube* and Alberto Bevilacqua's *La polvere sull'erba*. Arising out of a conference of Italian writers in Milan on 24 September 2001, *Scrivere sul fronte occidentale*, ed. Antonio Moresco and Dario Voltolini, Mi, Feltrinelli, 255 pp., includes reflection on the consequences, for individuals, society, and literature, of the collapse of the Twin Towers. Antonio Moresco questions whether we really live in a virtual world (7–8); Piersandro Pallavicini (54–64) suggests that fiction has been crushed by the reality of the New York catastrophe; Marco Senaldi (124–37) argues that the symbolic network of reality has fallen apart with the destruction of the Twin Towers; Giuseppe Genna (153–62) reflects upon the osmosis of fiction and reality; Marosia Castaldi (98–111) sees the Twin Towers as a symbol linked to the Tower of Babel, as both crash of Western civilization and clash of cultures, but also as a myth of harmony that could not die; Federico Nobili (216–31) advocates the importance of logic in an irrational world; and Marina Mander (166–76) proposes that Western authors should write about marginal and obscure people. Other contributors are Andrea Bajani, Carla Benedetti, Mauro Covacich, Marco Drago, Ivano Ferrari, Donata Feroldi, Federica Fracassi, Andrea Inglese, Elena Janeczek, Renzo Martinelli, Giorgio Mascitelli, Giuliano Mesa, Raul Montanari, Giulio Mozzi, Paolo Nori, Antonio Piotti, Christian Raimo, Tiziano Scarpa, and Gian Mario Villalta.

On a specific aspect of intertextuality, viz. the influence of Proust, we note A. Macrì Tronei, 'Uno sguardo al proustismo fiorentino. Specularità e rifrazioni in Vittorini, Bilenchi, Pratolini', *EL*, 27.1 : 87–100; on the influence of Spanish culture, Mercedes Gonzáles De Sande, *La cultura española en Papini, Prezzolini, Puccini y Boine*, Ro, Bulzoni, 2001, 271 pp.

On women's writing: A. Contini, '"Archivio per la memoria e la scrittura delle donne": un cantiere aperto', *ASI*, 160 : 769–87. *La fama e il silenzio: scrittrici dimenticate del primo Novecento*, ed. Francesco De Nicola and Pier Antonio Zannoni, Venice, Marsilio, 85 pp., after an introduction, C. Marabini, 'Scrittrici dimenticate' (7–12), on the paradox that, when women's consciousness has developed, the creative works written by Italian women authors in the first half of the 20th c. are forgotten, includes the following essays on individual writers whose work is reappraised and seen as characterized both by traditional motifs (in certain cases also by novelette traits) and by representation of important social problems: M. Serri, 'Annie Vivanti, ragazza sventata' (13–18); F. De Nicola, 'Willy Dias e Flavia Steno, scritttrici a Genova' (19–30); E. Guagnini, 'Paola Drigo' (31–40);

M. Guglielminetti, 'Amalia Guglielminetti: "Vergine folle" o "Femminista"?' (41–50); M. Cedrola, 'Marise Ferro' (51–58); G. Manacorda, 'Paola Masino' (59–64); and F. Merlanti, ' "L'armonia bianca e perduta". Testimonianza ed esorcismo della scrittura nell'opera di Irene Brin' (65–82). Monica Farnetti, *Il centro della cattedrale: i ricordi d'infanzia nella scrittura femminile. Dolores Prato, Fabrizia Ramondino, Anna Maria Ortese, Cristina Campo, Ginevra Bompiani*, Mantua, Tre Lune, 152 pp. F. Rigotti, 'Fare la spola tra le sponde dell'essere. Filosofia e condizione femminile in Edith Stein, Maria Zambrano, Hannah Arendt, Carla Lonzi', *Intersezioni*, 22 : 289–303, argues that the writers indicated in the title have two aspects in common: on the one hand, an individual human tone in their style and, on the other, transitions from one to other types of existential situations. The author then reflects on the different ways in which female consciousness is portrayed: more explicitely by Stein and Lonzi, less directly by Zambrano, and only implicitely by Arendt.

On narrative and territorial identity: N. Borsellino, 'Da Sciascia a Camilleri', *NA*, 2222 : 223–27, discusses the link between S.'s literary output and his intellectual consciousness and involvement with Sicilian folklore and history. He also finds connections between history and literature in Stefano D'Arrigo's *Horcynus Orca* (seen as a major work on Sicilian identity) and in this context goes on to mention Giuseppe Bonaviri, Andrea Camilleri, and Vincenzo Consolo. R. Damiani, 'Sommario novecentesco di letteratura del Nord-Est', *QVen*, 35 : 129–46. Wolfgang Sahlfeld, 'Gli ambienti letterari nel romanzo italiano del primo Novecento', *Versants*, 39, 2001 : 135–60, argues that the high number of Southern Italian writers at the turn of the 19th and 20th centuries was not due to chance but to their encounter with united Italy, to the influence of non-Southern intellectual circles and to the formation of a new type of readership. He then examines the representation of literary milieux and salons by Luigi Pirandello, Pier Maria Rosso di San Secondo, Vitaliano Brancati, Ercole Patti, Corrado Alvaro, and Margherita Scarfatti. *La Ciociaria tra letteratura e cinema*, ed. Franco Zangrilli, Pesaro, Metauro, 385 pp., includes essays on the represention of Ciociaria in the works of a number of writers: F. Zangrilli and B. Hernández on Giuseppe Bonaviri, M. Carlino and N. De Giovanni on Tommaso Landolfi, R. Pellecchia on Giuseppe Neri, and G. Faustini on Alberto Moravia. On stories of migration: J. Burns, 'Exile within Italy: interactions between past and present "homes" in texts in Italian by migrant writers', *AnI*, 20 : 369–84, examines three novels written by migrants living in Italy: Salah Methani's *Immigrato* (co-written with Mario Fortunato in 1990), Mohsen Melliti's *Pantanella* (1992), and Ron Kubati's *Va e non torna* (2000), seen from the angle of exile literature but also as samples of minority literature within the Italian literary canon. Carmine Chiellino, *Parole erranti: emigrazione, letteratura e interculturalità: saggi 1995–2000*, Isernia, Iannone, 2001, 118 pp. See also *Bilancio della letteratura del Novecento in Liguria*, above.

On fiction and landscape: Giorgio Bertone, *Letteratura e paesaggio. Liguri e no*, Lecce, Manni, 2001, 261 pp., includes one previously published essay, a reworked essay on Ligurian literature and landscape (7–86), and two hitherto unpublished essays. In 'La lente di Anna Maria Ortese' (173–98), the eye conveys a sense of unfulfilled desire for what is seen; the spectator converts his sensual observation into a visionary and oblique type of writing which includes description of emotions and even of the invisible, and perception of an opaque world and of suffering. In 'Il paesaggio diviso di Francesco Biamonti' (199–224), on a number of contradictory but coexisting concepts in B.'s fiction, landscape can be read as a metaphor for the frontier or border; it embodies a sense of catastrophe, includes the sacred nature of places, but excludes redemption, is often symbolic, and explores the various dimensions of light.

On fiction and the city: Gianni Puglisi and Paolo Proietti, *Le città di carta*, Palermo, Sellerio, 132 pp., comprises Puglisi's 'La città e il cittadino: immagini di uno specchio' (13–52), where the relationship between the city, the citizen-writer, and the literary text is highlighted through examples from a number of authors, amongst them Luigi Malerba and Parma, Italo Calvino and the ideal models of *Le città invisibili*, and Pier Paolo Pasolini in relation to his realistic representation of Rome; Proietti's 'Le parole e le immagini: la città' (53–96), where Italian cities as seen by foreign writers are examined; and Puglisi's 'Immagini letterarie di Milano' (97–124), where, among other intellectuals concerned with Milan, we find Alberto Savinio, Dino Buzzati, and Alberto Arbasino.

On detective fiction: R. Pagetto, '*La Domenica del Corriere* e il giallo 1920–1940', *Problemi*, 119–20, 2001:67–100, is on structure, commercial success, and serialization of translated foreign detective stories in the Italian magazine.

On theatre: R. Alonge and F. Malaria, 'Il teatro italiano di tradizione', pp. 567–701 of *Storia del teatro moderno e contemporaneo*, ed. Roberto Alonge and Guido Davico Bonino, T, Einaudi, 2001, 1404 pp., sees substantial continuity in 20th-c. theatre from the previous century, and a predominance of actor over director, but indicates Luigi Pirandello, Eduardo De Filippo, and Dario Fo as substantial innovators. The work also includes S. Sinisi, 'Neoavanguardia e postavanguardia in Italia' (703–36), where a change in recent Italian theatre is seen as starting in 1959 with Carmelo Bene's work, from which an unfolding experimental line leads to the avant-garde of the late 1960s and thence to a number of forms of innovative work in the 1970s. P. Quarenghi, 'Il copione, lo spettacolo, il testo. Riflessioni sulla drammaturgia d'attore', *Ariel*, 15.3, 2001:83–119. *Italian Grotesque Theatre*, ed. Michel Vena, Cranbury, Associated University Presses, 2001, 194 pp., includes plays by Luigi Antonelli, Luigi Cavicchioli, and Luigi Chiarelli, and an introduction (11–42) by the editor. Issue 3 of *Scena aperta*, devoted to Neapolitan theatre, includes texts by Manlio Santanelli (157–219), essays by M. P. Granisso and W. Zidaric on Eduardo De Filippo, and essays by S. Contarini, E. Donnarel, and J. Nimis on Manlio Santanelli.

4. Individual Authors

ADORNO. E. Pellegrini, 'Le piccole prospettive di Luisa Adorno', *LetP*, 113–14:115–24, highlights A.'s interest in minor events and repeated situations, but also her insight into social and anthropological history obtained by combining autobiography and fiction. It also indicates her debt towards Giuseppe De Roberto and Vitaliano Brancati.

ALERAMO. S. Kolski, 'Changing places: space in Sibilla Aleramo's *Una donna*', *ItQ*, 152–53:57–66, discusses women's space individually and socially, and especially the dichotomies private–public, house–workplace, imprisonment–liberation confronted by the protagonist in her breaking of norms and development towards a freer identity. Also discussed are some Dantean echoes.

ALVARO. *Corrado Alvaro. Atti del Convegno letterario di Mappano Torinese, 16–17 marzo 2001*, ed. Alda Maria Morace and Antonio Zappia, Reggio Calabria, Falzea, 206 pp. Giuseppe Fontanelli, *L'ultimo Alvaro*, Messina, Sicania, 2000, 337 pp. Corrado Alvaro, *Colore di Berlino: viaggio in Germania*, ed. Anne Christine Faitrop-Porta, Reggio Calabria, Falzea, 2001, 340 pp.

BACCHELLI. M. Donadoni Omodeo, 'Riccardo Bacchelli e *L'infedele innocente*', *NA*, 2221:114–20, describes the origin and content of B.'s opera libretto based on Cervantes. 'Consuntivo per Bacchelli', in Saccenti, *Scrittoio*, 183–201, reviews 1985–1991 critical work on B.

BANDINI. A. Afribo, 'È primavera, Bandini. Sulla poesia di Fernando Bandini', *ParL*, 39–41:121–33, details the various key roles assigned to the theme of 'primavera' in B.'s poetry, particularly that of catalyst and 'provocatore di eventi'. The essay also looks at his use of trauma, rupture, and revolt, and analyses his 'lessico dell'alterazione, dello strappo, della lacerazione'. 'Bandini e la lingua della poesia', Ramat, *Passi*, 221–27.

BASSANI. Andrea Guiati, *L'invenzione poetica. Ferrara e l'opera di Giorgio Bassani*, Pesaro, Metauro, 215 pp., offers a reappraisal of B.'s poetry (mostly written in the 1940s), taking issue with critics who dismissed it and showing how important it is for an understanding of his subsequent prose writings. L. Kroha, 'The same and/or different: narcissism and exile in Bassani's work', *AnI*, 20: 307–24, adopts some Oedipal Freudian theory and examines a number of texts on the experience of the ghetto.

BECK. G. Landolfi, 'Il realismo cristiano nella poesia di Marco Beck', *ON*, 26.1: 133–53, examines the constant religious dimension in the work of this poet (born Milan 1946).

BELLEZZA. Dario Bellezza, *Poesie: 1971–1996*, ed. Elio Pecora, Mi, Mondadori, xv + 229 pp.

BETOCCHI. *Anniversario per Carlo Betocchi*, ed. Anna Dolfi, Ro, Bulzoni, 2001, 336 pp., has a selection of papers presented at a 2000 Betocchi conference in Florence. ' "Qualcosa che sa di leggenda". La madre (e il figlio) nella poesia di Betocchi', Ramat, *Passi*, 137–52.

BIGONGIARI. Piero Bigongiari, *Un pensiero che seguita a pensare*, ed. Paolo Fabrizio Iacuzzi, T, Aragno, 2001, 378 pp., a posthumous diary, records B.'s thoughts on poetry, cinema, the arts, daily and intellectual life, and historical and personal events.

BOINE 'La polemica Boine-Croce (con due testi in appendice)', Ramat, *Passi*, 29–46.

BONTEMPELLI. F. Genovesi, 'Rassegna di studi su Bontempelli (1978–2000)', *GSLI*, 179: 108–22. F. Airoldi Namer, 'Insularité et utopie dans l'œuvre de Massimo Bontempelli', *REI*, 47, 2001: 265–84, on the myth and utopia of insularity, starts with a short analysis of Carlo Dossi's *La colonia felice* and Luigi Pirandello's *La nuova colonia*, and continues with a study of retreat from the city in an apartment defined as 'l'isola di Irene' in B.'s *La vita operosa*, on the island of Leucoteria in *Terzo viaggio*, and in other works (such as *Viaggio d'Europa*) where shelter from time and trouble is found; a comparison is also made between B.'s insularity and Gabriele Salvatores's 1992 film *Mediterraneo*.

BORGESE. G. Baldi, 'Il caso e l'inconscio. Sulla costruzione narrativa del *Rubé* di Borgese', *LItal*, 54: 548–70, investigates Freudian aspects of the novel and its relationship to the worldview of contemporary authors, including Pirandello.

BUZZATI. V. Caratozzolo, 'Miti, letterature e filosofie nel *Deserto dei tartari*', *Testo*, 43: 137–66, detects ancient Egyptian motifs, especially the myth of Osiris, connected with death and resurrection, religion and the supernatural, in *Il deserto dei tartari* (confirmed by B.'s interest in Egyptology in his youth). Drogo's story is interpreted not only as a *Bildungsroman* but as a process of initiation. C. finds allusions to cyclical time, metempsycosis, *anima mundi*, and Plato's myth of the cave, and examines B.'s treatment of sight and vision. I. Gallinaro, 'Fonti pascoliane nel *Deserto dei Tartari*', *REI*, 47, 2001: 291–98, sees relations between *Il deserto* and Giovanni Pascoli's contamination of the story of Gog and Magog with the life of Alexander in *Poemi conviviali*, and shows textual similarities by comparing passages from both authors.

CALABRÒ. D. Piccini, 'Corrado Calabrò: intermittenze e richiami', *Poesia*, 166: 14–19, discusses the way in which C.'s poetry reflects the dynamism of natural elements and is often marked by the work of Quasimodo, Montale, Spaziani, and Luzi.

CALVINO. *Italo Calvino newyorkese. Atti del Colloquio internazionale 'Future Perfect: Italo Calvino and the Reinvention of Literature', New York University, 12–13 aprile 1999*, ed. Anna Botta and Domenico Scarpa, Cava de' Tirreni, Avagliano, 224 pp., comprises an introduction by A. Botta (8–11); 'I quaderni degli esercizi', a 1985 interview with C. by P. Fournel where, among other things, he reveals that the structure of *Palomar*, based on the number three, is related to Dante's *Commedia*, and compares *Le cosmicomiche* to *Palomar*, the latter being still self-ironic but pessimistic by contrast with the former (15–26); and numerous essays. M. Barenghi, 'La forma dei desideri' (27–40), also published as a prologue to *Mondo scritto e mondo non scritto* (see below), highlights C.'s epistemological view of literature, or the relationship between the real and literary worlds, sees *Le città invisibili* as an encyclopedia and notes C.'s renunciation of totality, his choice of limitations and partiality; M. McLaughlin, 'Calvino saggista: anglofilia letteraria e creatività' (41–66), shows how literature written in English, and in particular work by Conrad and Stevenson, influenced C.'s creative writing as well as his essays; M. Bénabou, 'Se una notte d'inverno un oulipiano' (67–76), already published in 1990, illustrates some of C.'s work based on oulipien-like constraints; L. Re, 'Calvino e il cinema: la voce, lo sguardo e la distanza' (77–91); A. Botta, 'Italo Calvino, San Girolamo e i nodi gordiani della modernità' (92–116), includes reference to paintings with St Jerome as their subject, and compares C.'s approach to modernity to Bruno Latour's essay *Nous n'avons jamais été modernes*; M. Riva, 'Le frecce della mente: Calvino, Arakawa e l'iper-romanzo' (117–46); A. Ricciardi, 'Destini incrociati. Calvino, Pynchon e il paesaggio post-metafisico' (147–62), examines *Le città invisibili* and Thomas Pynchon's *Mason & Dixon* inside the framework of post-modernism; F. La Porta, 'Il Calvino dimezzato' (163–76), notes similarities but above all differences between C. and more recent Italian writers with regard to the relationship between author and reader, the function of objects, and the experience of life and the outside world; D. Scarpa, 'Dieci lemmi calviniani' (177–204), includes ten entries ('Torino', 'New York', 'Roma', 'Parigi', 'Paesaggio', 'Fumetti e vignette', 'Disegni e quadri' and 'Palomar dei suoni') not included in Domenico Scarpa's *Italo Calvino*, published in 1999. M. Corti, 'Calvino "per le vie del mondo"', *Atti* (Rome), 391–99, highlights C.'s intertextual relations with Jorge Luis Borges and his interest in formal logic detectable especially in *Se una notte d'inverno un viaggiatore*. R. Donnarumma, 'Calvino verso il postmoderno: dalla "Sfida al labirinto" alla "Memoria del mondo"', *Allegoria*, 40–41: 80–109, shows how C.'s concept of modernism differs from the neo-avantgarde but may be linked to post-modernism. J. Francese, 'Lo scrittore che non venne dal freddo, ovvero il primo viaggio di Calvino negli USA', *ib.*, 37: 38–61, notes that while C. maintained a left-wing ideology and did not write an apology of American society as a result of his journey to the U.S.A., his work gained in popularity in the English-speaking world thanks to that same journey. M. Longobardi, 'Parlar coperto: le scritture segrete e il poliziesco oulipiano', *LetP*, 113–14: 3–26, includes a few paragraphs on 'Calvino poliziesco' (21–23) which focus on 'L'incendio della casa abominevole'. M. McLaughlin and A. Scientella, 'Calvino e Conrad: dalla tesi di laurea alle *Lezioni americane*', *ISt*, 57: 113–32, examines the political context which motivated C. to choose Conrad for his university dissertation, the independent contribution C. made to criticism on Conrad, and the re-emergence of some Conrad in C. texts after 1964–65.

On individual works. *La visione dell'invisibile. Saggi e materiali su 'Le città invisibili' di Italo Calvino*, ed. Mario Barenghi, Gianni Canova, and Bruno Falcetto, Mi, Mondadori, 247 pp., published on the occasion of the Milan Triennale exhibition *La memoria e il futuro* (held from 5 November 2002 to 9 March 2003), includes passages from C.'s works; an iconographic section; some previously published reviews by G. Pampaloni, G. Piovene, P. Milano, and G. Almansi (11–29); two unpublished reviews by G. Manganelli and G. Celati, originally broadcast on the radio in 1972 (105–10); and the following essays: M. Barenghi, 'Gli abbozzi dell'indice. Quattro fogli dall'archivio Calvino' (74–95), on the genesis of the novel; G. Canova, 'All'ombra delle nostre palpebre abbassate. Il paradosso del non-visibile in Calvino e nel cinema contemporaneo' (131–39); B. Falcetto, 'Le cose e le ombre. *Marco Polo*: Calvino scrittore per il cinema' (62–73), on a work written and conceived in 1960 for a film on Marco Polo; A. Ferlenga, 'Invisibili profondità' (140–48), on architectural representation of the city in the novel; F. Gambaro, 'Illustrare l'invisibile. Le copertine delle *Città invisibili*' (96–103); P. Kuon, 'Critica e progetto dell'utopia: *Le città invisibili* di Italo Calvino' (24–41), on C.'s interrogation of the positive and negative sides of the concept of

Utopia (24–41); M. McLaughlin, 'Le città invisibili di Calvino' (42–61), on the representation of cities in C.'s work prior to *Le città invisibili*; and U. Volli, 'Il testo urbano: visibilità e complessità' (149–59), on the city as a semiotic text. A. Petrella, 'Psicoanalisi della luna. Un confronto tra Italo Calvino e Tommaso Landolfi', *LetP*, 112, 2001:3–8, compares C.'s cosmicomic story 'La molle luna' to Landolfi's 'Il racconto del lupo mannaro', adopting the Junghian concept of subconscious content emerging to consciousness, and interpreting the image of the moon as a feminine symbol and an indication of a reaction of the irrational against the excesses of scientific rationalizations. Adriano Piacentini, *Tra il cristallo e la fiamma: le Lezioni Americane di Italo Calvino*, F, Athenaeum, 128 pp.

CAMILLERI. S. Filipponi (ed.), 'Il laboratorio del *cantastorie*. Intervista ad Andrea Camilleri', *Acme*, 55.2:201–20. C. A. Madrignani, 'Camilleri voluttuoso', *Belfagor*, 57:217–22, notes C.'s affable relationship with his readers, sees him as a realist 'artista-artigiano' whose detective novels are non-conformist because they avoid spectacular clichés, and highlights the importance of his Sicilian background.

CAMPANA. *I portici della poesia; Dino Campana a Bologna (1912–1914)* ed. Marco Antonio Bazzocchi and Gabriel Cacho Millet, Bo, Pàtron, 198 pp., presents a miscellany of papers and writings relating to C.'s time in Bologna. G. Crini, '"Au devant on vois": la polvere spolverata di Rimbaud in Campana', *GSLI*, 179:224–58, addresses the much-discussed question of R.'s influence on C. and argues that there are sufficient traces in C.'s poetry to justify further research on the topic. Rather than a 'polvere spolverata' the author concludes that it is more like a 'sabbia impalpabile' or 'un mobile fondale nei mari interiori e poetici di Campana'. A. Castronuovo, 'Un'ignota cartolina di Dino Campana', *RLI*, 106:503–06, discusses a postcard of Marradi sent by C. in 1917 to Luigi Orsini in Imola. A. Camps, 'Viaggio e esilio in Dino Campana: per un'ermeneutica della sua opera', *AnI*, 20:259–74. A. Parronchi, 'Ancora su Dino Campana', *RLI*, 105, 2001:416–22. Federico Ravagli, *Dino Campana e i goliardi del suo tempo, 1911–1914: autografi e documenti, confessioni e memorie*, Bo, CLUEB, 151 pp., a new edn of a work first published in 1941, includes fresh introductory material. '*La chimera* di Campana', Ramat, *Passi*, 15–28.

CAMPO. *Cristina Campo in immagini e parole*, ed. Domenico Brancale, Salerno, Ripostes, 98 pp., includes C.'s memoirs and writings by Simone Weil which C. translated into Italian. *Andrea Emo: lettere a Cristina Campo*, ed. Giovanna Fozzer, Città di Castello, In Forma di parole, 2001, 80 pp.

CAPRONI. Angela Barbagallo, *La poesia dei luoghi non giurisdizionali di Giorgio Caproni*, Foggia, Bastogi, 118 pp. 'Giorgio Caproni, "poeta del fil di voce" ', Ramat, *Passi*, 189–92. '*Il Congedo* in breve', Girardi, *Prosa*, 211–21, is a new item on Caproni in a volume also containing several already published.

CARDARELLI. P. E. Leuschner, 'Vincenzo Cardarelli: Settembre a Venezia / September in Venedig', *Italienisch*, 48:66–69, analyses C.'s poem on Venice and shows how he turned a negative situation into something positive through selected vocabulary, syntax, and metre. L. Badini Confalonieri, 'Cardarelli et le soleil des matins d'été: pour une lecture de "A Omar Kayyâm" ', *REI*, 47:285–89, centres on a poem, written in 1914 but published in 1942, which reinterprets lines of the Persian poet in terms of a 'superamento dell'umano' as detailed in Nietzsche's *Zarathustra*.

CARRÀ. *Il carteggio Carrà–Papini. Da 'Lacerba' al tempo di 'Valori Plastici'*, ed. Massimo Carrà, Geneva–Mi, Skira, 2001, 149 pp., covers four decades from the post-war period to P.'s death in 1956, documenting a friendship dating from 1913, when C. was persuaded to abandon his Futurist leanings and collaborate with the journal *Lacerba*.

CARRERI. 'Un pugliese a Milano. Ricordo di Raffaele Carreri', Dell'Aquila, *Bello stilo*, 171–83 (previously published in 1998).

CATTAFI. 'Bartolo Cattafi: qualcosa di preciso?', Ramat, *Passi*, 195–201.

CELATI. F. Marchiori, 'Tra cinema e scrittura: lo spazio narrativo nel *Cinema naturale* di Celati', *Nuova corrente*, 48:315–21.

COMISSO. I. Crotti, 'La "memoria terribile": Comisso interprete del Settecento', *QVen*, 35:89–120.

CONSOLO. Giuseppe Traina, *Vincenzo Consolo*, Fiesole, Cadmo, 140 pp., charts C.'s work down to *Spasimo di Palermo* and includes an interview with him. T. Pagano, 'A world of ruins: the allegorical vision in Fabrizio Clerici, Vincenzo Consolo and Luigi Malerba', *Italica*, 79:204–23, assesses the influence of Clerici on C.'s and M.'s work, which was due especially to the painter's allegorical vision.

CORDELLI. A. Berardinelli, 'Cordelli e lo spirito del romanzo', *NArg*, 20:294–308, underlines the importance of literary theory for C. the narrator, his aversion for rhetoric in fiction, his interest in a number of writers, and his appreciation of Ennio Flaiano's work.

CORTI. 'Maria Corti: tra il romanzo e il "romanzo per dire" ', Scorrano, *Carte*, 7–42, explores C.'s attempt to write 'storie' where a free-flowing imagination and a rigorous structure created a new and intriguing mode of narration.

CREMASCHI. Luigi Picchi, *A un uomo del futuro: la poesia di Inìsero Cremaschi*, F, Gazebo, 2001, 62 pp.

CURTO. Carmine Chiodo, *Sulla poesia di Francesco Curto*, Perugia, Guerra, 1999, 91 pp.

D'ARZO. Silvio D'Arzo, *Luci e penombre: liriche*, ed. Gabriele Pedullà, Reggio Emilia, Diabasis, 57 pp. Roberto Carnero, *Silvio D'Arzo: un bilancio critico*, Novara, Interlinea, 157 pp.

DE ANGELIS. *La poesia di Vincenzo De Angelis: pioniere del socialismo in Calabria*, ed. Vincenzo De Angelis Jr, Reggio Calabria, Laruffa, 2001, 160 pp.

DE FILIPPO. V. Reda, '*La tempesta* di Eduardo', *AAPN*, 50, 2001[2002]: 283–308. F. Angelini, '"Se ne care 'o teatro!": Eduardo e il pubblico', *Ariel*, 15.3, 2001: 73–81. A. Barsotti, 'Grandi giocolieri e giullari contro la macchina che pialla i teatranti: Eduardo e Fo', *ib.*, 83–119.

DE LIBERO. Giuseppe Lupo, *Poesia come pittura. De Libero e la cultura romana (1930–1940)*, Mi, Vita e Pensiero, 264 pp., offers a timely assessment of the impact of prevailing trends in Roman culture on De L.'s work in those years.

DE LUCA. Attilio Scuderi, *Erri De Luca*, Fiesole, Cadmo, 144 pp., considers the style of both autobiographical and creative texts seen against the background of politics and religion.

DE PALCHI. Alfredo De Palchi, *In cao del me paese: poesie in italiano*, Verona, West Press, 2001, 109 pp., has accompanying English and Veronese dialect translations, the former by Sonia Raiziss, the latter by Giampaolo Feriani and Enzo Franchini.

DEL SERRA. R. Bertoldo, 'Le mani e il cuore di Maura Del Serra', *Hebenon*, 7.9–10: 57–63.

D'ERAMO. C. Lucas-Fiorato, 'Des colonnes d'Hercule à Nnoberavez: l'art du déplacement dans l'œuvre de Luce d'Eramo', *ChrI*, 69–70: 129–38.

DESSÌ. *Giuseppe Dessì: storia e catalogo di un archivio*, ed. Agnese Landini, Florence U.P., 372 pp., has been produced at the 'Biblioteca digitale' of the University's Italian Department and in the context of a project (coordinated by Anna Dolfi) to catalogue a number of contemporary texts including D.'s published and unpublished writings held by the Gabinetto Vieusseux.

DI GIACOMO. E. Vecchione, 'Rassegna di studi su Salvatore Di Giacomo', *CLett*, 30: 153–61, outlines recent studies and new critical opinions on contrasting interpretations of Di G.'s literary and poetic writings.

ECO. *Eco in fabula . . .*, ed. Franco Musarra et al., Leuven U.P. — F, Cesati, 452 pp. D. W. Landrum, 'The unwoman in *The Name of the Rose*', *ItQ*, 151–52: 33–34, examines the narrative functions of the only female character in the novel, a peasant girl, and concludes that 'the semiotic feminine' is in opposition to the 'male symbolic'. K. R. West, 'Pascalian quixotism in Umberto Eco's *L'isola del giorno prima*', *Italica*, 79: 224–39, defines Cervantes's influence on E. on the basis of

Miguel de Unamuno's definition of quixotism as 'a total hope in the rationally absurd'.

ERBA. *Poesia*, 165, marked E.'s 80th birthday with S. Ramat, 'Luciano Erba: svagato e metafisico' (24–26), and S. Verdino, '"I deserti della disattenzione" – Intervista con Luciano Erba' (26–31).

FAUSTINI. Liliana Porro Andriuoli, *La ricerca del trascendente nella poesia di Margherita Faustini*, Recco, Le Mani, 1999[2002], 86 pp.

FENOGLIO. Attilio C. Milanini, 'Beppe Fenoglio, lettere ritrovate e carte neglette', *Belfagor*, 57:619–22, is on the Einaudi edition of F.'s letters, 1940–62.

FO. See DE FILIPPO, above.

FORTINI. S. Montalto and A. Napoli, 'Franco Fortini: "scrittore sempre politico?"' *Atelier*, 25:5–7. G. Landolfi, 'Franco Fortini: "Di maniera e dal vero"', *ib.*, 25:8–28, outlines F.'s lifelong intellectual, critical, and political activities.

FRUTTERO and LUCENTINI. G. Cenati, 'Le prospettive di Fruttero–Lucentini e le donne della domenica', *Problemi*, 119–20, 2001:47–66, examines multiple narrative perspectives, diversity of the two authors' viewpoints, free indirect speech and sociological discourse, the relationship between provincial and metropolitan forms of life, and the interaction between detective and sentimental themes in Carlo Fruttero's and Franco Lucentini's novel *La donna della domenica*.

GADDA. N. Bouchard, '(Re)considering Gadda and Futurism', *Italica*, 79:23–43, while noting that G. explicitly distanced himself from Futurism, argues that Futurist poetics play a role in his complex intertextuality as a 'space of recorded memory'. Giuseppe Bonifacino, *Il groviglio delle parvenze: studio su Carlo Emilio Gadda*, Bari, Palomar, 444 pp. K. Fagioli, 'Una "chiave antilirica" di interpretazione. La poesia "Autunno" nella *Cognizione del dolore*', *Allegoria*, 40–41:21–52, conducts a genetic and textual analysis on the insertion of 'Autunno' in the novel. Franco Gàbici, *Gadda: il dolore della cognizione: una lettura scientifica dell'opera gaddiana con una sua riflessione dimenticata sull'amore*, Mi, Simonelli, 121 pp. G. Pedriali, 'La Bibbia illustrata dell'ingegnere. Osservazioni per un bestiario gaddiano', *MLN*, 17:194–206. Rinaldo Rinaldi, *L'indescrivibile arsenale: ricerche intorno alle fonti della 'Cognizione del dolore'*, Mi, UNICOPLI, 2001, 153 pp.

GATTO. Alfonso Gatto, *La pecora nera*, ed. Francesco D'Episcopo, Na, ESI, 2001, 126 pp., comes with a useful editorial introduction to G.'s work.

GELLI. Licio Gelli, *Poesie 1959–1999*, Bari, Laterza, 2001, 431 pp.

GIGLI. R. Rabboni, 'Piero Gigli post-futurista: due racconti da *Storie di una cittadina di provincia*', *FC*, 26, 2001[2002]:423–39, includes the texts of two stories by G. and examines the influence of his

Futurism on his subsequent non-rhetorical style where humour combines with crepuscular and surreal aspects.

GINZBURG. Clara Borrelli, *Notizie di Natalia Ginzburg*, Na, L'Orientale, 185 pp.

GIUDICI. Simona Morando, *Vita con le parole: la poesia di Giovanni Giudici*, Pasian di Prato, Campanotto, 2001, 257 pp. Alberto Bertoni, *Una distratta venerazione: la poesia metrica di Giudici*, Bo, Book, 2001, 157 pp. 'Giudici rifà Caproni', Girardi, *Prosa*, 223–40. 'Giovanni Giudici, i versi della vita', Ramat, *Passi*, 215–20.

GIULIOTTI. M. Biondi, 'Abitare la battaglia. Lo stile belva di Domenico Giuliotti', *Il Cristallo* (Supplement), 44.1 : 71–89.

GOVONI. Fornaretto Vieri, *Intorno alle Fiale. Incunaboli del protonovecento govoniano*, F, Le Lettere, 2001, 111 pp., considers Govoni's 'anticrepuscolarismo' and the poet's movement from the 'poesia gioiello' to the 'poesia giocattolo'.

GOZZANO. E. Citro, 'Gozzano: l'esotismo mancato', *ON*, 26.1 : 67–102, demonstrates how the 'ideale' and the 'reale' seldom coincide in G.'s work, thereby ensuring that his descriptions of the exotic lack conviction. For G., Boggione, *Poesia*, includes: 'Poesia come citazione: Gozzano attraverso D'Annunzio' (75–89); 'Ancora sulla preistoria di Felicita: la Signorina e Silvia' (91–101); 'Contro la tentazione della nudità. Abiti e acconciature nella poesia di Gozzano' (103–22); and 'Il rito della letteratura: la morte esorcizzata' (123–47).

GRASSO. S. Wood, 'Sicily and *Sicilitudine* in the novels of Silvana Grasso', *RoS*, 20 : 89–99.

GUARNIERI. A. Colasanti, 'Tenebre d'Inferno e Paradiso in Luigi Guarnieri', *NArg*, 17 : 261–76, concerns G.'s novel *Tenebre sul Congo*, its debt to Conrad, and its poetics of mystification.

GUIDACCI. R. Taioli, 'Lettere di Margherita Guidacci a Grazia Maggi', *CV*, 52 : 145–50, publishes three unpublished letters to G. M. (daughter of the poet Luigi Fallacara) that offer details of a friendship (which began in 1937) previously unknown to G.'s biographers. *Margherita Guidacci – La voce dell'acqua*, ed. Giancarlo Battaglia and Ilaria Rabatti, Pistoia, CRT, 150 pp., illustrates the *modus operandi* of G. as translator, particularly her Italian version of Emily Dickinson, in relation to which, in an article on poetic translation, she discusses the dilemma of the 'brutta fedele' or the 'bella infedele' version in translation and explains why she opts for the latter.

JAHIER. G. Benvenuti, 'Discorsività e coralità nella poesia di Piero Jahier', *Poetiche*, 3 : 371–90. Piero Jahier, *Ragazzo: il paese morale*, ed. Antonio Di Grado, T, Claudiana, 228 pp., comprises an autobiographical novel, some critical material, and a collection of articles from *La voce* on Jahier. '"Qui siamo *uniforme*" (*Con me e con gli alpini* di Jahier)', Ramat, *Passi*, 67–79.

JESI. E. Zignai, 'La notte, il vampiro, il ritorno nella narrativa di Furio Jesi', *StN*, 27, 2000: 279–327, relates J.'s narrative to his essays on myth.

LA CAPRIA. M. Onofri, 'Sull'ultimo La Capria', *NArg*, 16, 2001: 284–96, defines the concept of *candore* (derived from Voltaire's *Candide* and used in La C.'s 1974 text *False partenze*) as critical reflection on received ideas and rejection of clichés, interest in clarity and common sense, a philosophy of harmony and aversion from resentment.

LANDOLFI. P. Trama, 'Dalla bestemmia al bestiario: una lettura di *La pietra lunare* di Tommaso Landolfi', *RLettI*, 20.2: 153–79, highlights the relationship between the sacred and the profane, and between the highbrow and the lowbrow literature in L.'s work.

LEVI. C. Imberty, 'Le mot juste dans *Se questo è un uomo* de Primo Levi', *ChrI*, 69–70: 83–100. J. C. Vegliante, 'Primo Levi et la traduction radicale', *ib.*, 69–70: 181–208. A. Rondini, '"Dare un nome a una cosa è gratificante come dare il nome a un'isola". Onomastica e letteratura nell'*Altrui mestiere* di Primo Levi', *Il nome nel testo*, 4: 189–202, clarifies the use of certain names in L.'s work. G. Tosi, 'Dall'attesa alla storia-esilio. La memoria e l'identità in *Se non ora, quando?* di Primo Levi', *AnI*, 20: 285–306, includes a section on identity threatened and recreated under the impact of historical events.

LINGUAGLOSSA. R. Bertoldo, 'La poesia metafisica: teoria e pratica poetica in Giorgio Linguaglossa', *Hebenon*, 7.9–10: 144–46.

LORIA. U. Fracassa, '"La lezione di anatomia". Un esercizio intertestuale', *LetP*, 112, 2001: 91–98, finds reference to Tommaso Campanella's 'Canzone in dispregio della morte' in Arturo Loria's short story 'Lezione di anatomia'.

LUZI. Maria Sabrina Tritone, *Cantiche del Novecento. Dante nell'opera di Luzi e Pasolini*, F, Olschki, 2001, xxxi + 226 pp. Lorenza Gattamorta, *La memoria delle parole: Luzi tra Eliot e Dante*, Bo, Il Mulino, 310 pp. *Gli intellettuali italiani e la poesia di Mario Luzi*, ed. Roberto Cardini and Mariangela Regoliosi, Ro, Bulzoni, 2001, xiv + 118 pp. L. Gattamorta, 'Il platonismo del primo Luzi', *StCrit*, 17: 239–59. F. Ricci, 'Sulle tracce del *tu*. Percorsi intertestuali nella poesia di Luzi e Montale', *SPTC*, 63, 2001: 165–86. G. Bonacchi Gazzarrini, 'L'opera poetica di Mario Luzi', *Cenobio*, 51: 362–64, examines the dramatic impact found in two of L.'s essays on theatre, viz. 'Ceneri e ardori' and 'Il fiore del dolore'. M. Modesti, 'Sul teatro di Mario Luzi', *NA*, 2222: 333–40. G. Cavallini, 'L'ultimo Luzi: *Sotto specie umana*', *GSLI*, 179: 389–402, provides an analysis of L.'s latest poetry collection. Details of recently discovered poems and papers on Luzi's early work are given in: S. Verdino, 'Mario Luzi. Gli inediti giovanili ritrovati', *Poesia*, 159:2–7, and D. Piccini, 'La vita è più grande delle sue mortificazioni', *ib.*, 8–15, which records a lengthy interview with L. on his life and work. A. Luzi, '"Il mare, sai, mi associa al suo tormento": il topos marino nella poesia di Mario Luzi', *AIPI 14*, II, 65–72. 'Nel "grande codice" di Mario Luzi', Ramat, *Passi*, 181–87.

LUZZI. F. Pappalardo La Rosa, 'Intervista a Giorgio Luzzi (con poesie inedite dell'autore', *Hebenon*, 7.9–10:9–21.

MACRÌ. 'Oreste Macrì, un seminario ininterrotto', Ramat, *Passi*, 173–79.

MAGRIS. C. Magris and D. Del Giudice, 'A colloquio su *La mostra*', *NA*, 2223:171–95, is a dialogue on M.'s theatrical text *La mostra*. E. Golino, 'Claudio Magris e il naufragio dell'Io', *NArg*, 19:288–98, ascribes the origin of M.'s narrative to some of his essays (in particular *Danubio*), highlights the persistence of the motif of the sea in his fiction, and views him as a socially committed, though politically independent, intellectual.

MALERBA. See *La composizione del sogno* in GENERAL, above. R. Glynn, 'Fiction as imprisonment in Luigi Malerba's *Il fuoco greco*', *MLR*, 97:72–82.

MANGANELLI. Mariarosa Bricchi, *Manganelli e la menzogna. Notizie su Hilarotragoedia con testi inediti*, Novara, Interlinea, 211 pp., reconstructs the genesis of *Hilarotragœdia* (in particular its relation to Jung's psychoanalysis), examines in detail its lexis, figures of speech, and syntax, identifies a number of echoes from Italian literary models, and includes some of M.'s previously unpublished letters and some variants of his first text. L. Lastilla, 'Manganelliana: i percorsi della letteratura', *FoI*, 36:84–108, analyses M.'s complexity of language, dissolution of literary genres, intertextuality, self-referential aesthetics, and literary space as defined from different perspectives. M. Manotta, 'Ipotesi sul testo di *Nuovo commento*', *Il Verri*, 20:73–84, focuses on structural instability, interrogation of language, and the disintegration of the self through intellectual peregrination in multiple territories of the mind. Grazia Menechella, *Il felice vanverare. Ironia e parodia nell'opera narrativa di Giorgio Manganelli*, Ravenna, Longo, 258 pp., even though not specifically focusing on irony and parody, discusses a number of works by M.; she devotes a chapter to 'Manganelli neobarocco', identifying his style of 'chiacchiera' or 'vanverare', textual relations with Pontormo and Daniello Bartoli, and the baroque motifs of love, death, disease, the macabre, nothingness, miracles, and *meraviglia* (77–90); she sees M.'s work as a linguistic network unconcerned with society. The same author, '*Centuria*. Manganelli aspirante sonettiere', *MLN*, 117:207–26, shows how the micronovels included in *Centuria* are related to other works by M. and to his views on the sonnet. She ascribes the texts included in *Centuria* to a narrative form which stands between the short story and the novel, notes the fragmentation of the narrative 'I' in these texts, and concludes that *Centuria* aspires to be a Borgesian library comprising all books that can be imagined and therefore belonging to all fictional genres. Marco Paolone, *Il cavaliere immaginale. Saggi su Giorgio Manganelli*, F, Carocci, 176 pp., reads M.'s work with the aid of Carl Gustav Jung's and James Hillman's psychoanalysis, thus highlighting a number of symbolic aspects based on M.'s suggestion that reality is unreal and verisimilitude therefore subject to fantasy. V. Papetti, 'Manganelli anglomane, non anglista', pp. ix–xvi of Giorgio Manganelli, *Incorporei felini*, 1: *Poeti inglesi degli anni Cinquanta*, Ro, Storia e Letteratura, 224 pp. G. Isotti Rosowsky, '"As I have heard from the Hell". Manganelli, la scrittura dell'eccesso', *Allegoria*, 40–41 : 110–31, deals with *Dall'inferno*, and especially its Junghian aspects, its visionary writing, and its subjective language.

MARAINI. S. Amatangelo, 'Coming to her senses: the journey of the mother in *La lunga vita di Marianna Ucrìa*', *Italica*, 79:240–56. T. Gabriele, 'From prostitution to transexuality: gender, identity and subversive sexuality in Dacia Maraini', *MLN*, 117:241–56. I. Marchegiani Jones, 'La dualità tra individuo e storia: per una lettura di *La lunga vita di Marianna Ucrìa* di Dacia Maraini', *ItQ*, 151–52:45–60, notes the protagonist's development from passivity to activity, the importance of recounting history from a woman's viewpoint, and the dualities of body–soul, thought–sentiment.

MARIN. Pericle Camuffo, *Biagio Marin, la poesia, i filosofi: tracce per una interpretazione*, Monfalcone, Laguna, 173 pp.

MARINETTI. Simona Bertini, *Marinetti e le 'eroiche serate'*, Novara, Interlinea, 202 pp., details the famous 'serate futuriste' and their subsequent impact on poetry, prose, and theatre. The author gives a history of Futurism during the years 1909–13 when, following a performance of *Trieste in giù*, Marinetti and his followers provoked audience reaction to their 'proposta poetica'. *Nei proiettori del futurismo: carteggio inedito 1917–1940 Filippo Tommaso Marinetti – Primo Conti*, ed. Gabriel Cacho Millet, Palermo, Novecento, 2001, 215 pp., provides a first edition of this correspondence.

MARNITI. 'Risolutezza di Biagia Marniti', Scorrano, *Carte*, 43–85, traces the resolute nature of M.'s poetry.

MASTRONARDI. A. Menetti, 'Al dio sconosciuto: storia e confessione in Lucio Mastronardi', *StN*, 27, 2000:399–421.

MENEGHELLO. C. D'Alessio, 'Un maladense a Reading: il dispatrio e i cocci della memoria. Nota su Luigi Meneghello', *FC*, 26, 2001[2002]:440–61, shows how M.'s experience in both Reading and Malo influenced his work, especially his use of dialect, his concept of time, and his realistic and, at the same time, dreamlike attitude to places. Ernestina Pellegrino, *Luigi Meneghello*, Fiesole, Cadmo, 154 pp., examines the autobiographical nature of M.'s work and narrative style.

MERINI. E. Biagini, 'Nella prigione della carne: appunti sul corpo nella poesia di Alda Merini', *FoI*, 35:442–56. Alda Merini, *Il meglio del poeta*, pref. Giorgio Patrizi, Lecce, Manni, 62 pp., has some previously unpublished 'inediti'.

MICHELSTAEDTER. A. Perli, 'L'essere e il nulla nella poesia di Michelstaedter', *EL*, 27.2:3–28.

MONICELLI. S. Fancello, 'I romanzi di Furio Monicelli', *Belfagor*, 57:484–86.

MONTALE. Eugenio Montale, *Giorni di libeccio: lettere ad Angelo Barile (1920–1957)*, ed. Domenico Astengo and Giampiero Costa, Mi, Archinto, 145 pp., offers stimulating insights into the long friendship between M. and B. Two months before his death in 1981 Montale approved the suggestion that these letters be published. Luigi Blasucci, *Gli oggetti di Montale*, Bo, Il Mulino, 234 pp., outlines certain peculiarities of M.'s language, especially his use of objects and their precise function in poetry. Gianluigi Simonetti, *Dopo Montale. 'Le Occasioni' e la poesia italiana del Novecento*, Lucca, Pacini Fazzi, 423 pp., details the lasting impact of M.'s poetry on 20th-c. literature. Clodagh Brook, *The Expression of the Inexpressible in Montale's Poetry*, Oxford, Clarendon, 196 pp., determines what constitutes the inexpressible for M. She questions the stylistic choices M. makes when dealing with the limits of language and emphasizes the way in which certain elements of his style, such as negation and silence, brought the inexpressible into language in the earlier collections *Ossi di seppia, Le occasioni*, and *La bufera e altro*. Gianfranco Contini, *Una lunga fedeltà: scritti su Eugenio Montale*, T, Einaudi, ix + 115 pp. Francesca Ricci, *Il prisma di Arsenio. Montale tra Luzi e Sereni*, Bo, Gedit, 192 pp. Giovanna Ioli, *Montale*, Ro, Salerno, 315 pp., provides an overall critical survey of M.'s work. Tiziano Arvigo, *Guida alla lettura di Montale. Ossi di seppia*, Ro, Carocci, 246 pp. Rosita Tordi Castria, *Montale europeo. Ascendenze culturali nel percorso montaliano da 'Accordi' a 'Finisterre' (1922–1943)*, Ro, Bulzoni, 217 pp., assesses M.'s debt to the 'area mitteleuropea', particularly to Michelstaedter and Roberto Bazlen. Pietro Cataldi, *Parafrasi e commento: nove letture di poesia da Francesco D'Assisi a Montale*, Palermo, Palumbi, 199 pp. P. Sica, 'Il femminile nell'opera giovanile di Eugenio Montale. Sensi e fantasmi di una adolescente', *RStI*, 18.2:236–46, shows how in M.'s early work a feminine matrix leads to a poetic experimentation opposed to the most traditional Italian literary models and to a critique of official accounts of history. 'Appunti sulla trama dei *Mottetti*', Ramat, *Passi*, 103–19. J. Butcher, 'Contributo allo studio delle fonti del Sabià montaliano', *Allegoria*

40–41 : 159–63. Id., 'A "lauro risecchito?" The poet Montale and self-deprecation from *Satura* to *Altri versi*', *The Italianist*, 21–22 : 82–102. A. Zollino, 'Il riferimento dannunziano nell'ultimo Montale (da *Satura* ad *Altri versi*)', *NRLI*, 4 : 269–92. I. Melis, ' "La tua pagina rombante": il mare come referente poetico nel primo Montale', *AIPI 14*, 49–63.

MORAVIA. L. Russo, 'Alberto Moravia, scrittore senza storia. Con postille di Geno Pampaloni e Luigi Russo dal *Conformista* al *Disprezzo*', *Belfagor*, 57 : 55–63.

MORAZZONI. M. Heyer-Caput, 'Il concetto di "verità" nella narrazione "al passato" di Marta Morazzoni', *Italica*, 79 : 62–79.

MORETTI. *Marini Moretti a Giuseppe Ravegnani. Lettere 1914–21 / 1952–63*, ed. Lucia Benedini and Clelia Martignoni, introd. C. Martignoni, Pavia, Nuova Tipografia Popolare, 2000, 208 pp., drawn from the Ravegnani papers in the Biblioteca Civica, Pavia, is an anthology of 117 letters sent by Moretti to the Ferrarese critic Ravegnani. *Carteggio Marino Moretti – Aldo Palazzeschi*, II: 1926–1939, ed. Alessandro Panchieri, Ro, Storia e Letteratura — F, Università degli Studi, 2001, xxxi + 453 pp., completes an edn of unpublished correspondence.

MORSELLI. Maria Fiorentino, *Guido Morselli tra critica e narrativa*, Na, Eurocomp, 187 pp. *Guido Morselli: immagini di una vita*, ed. Valentina Fortichiari with a memoir by Giuseppe Pontiggia, Mi, Rizzoli, 2001, 142 pp.

ONGARO. B. Maier, 'Itinerario narrativo di Vinicio Ongaro', *RLettI*, 20.1 : 115–26, considers O.'s psychological detective novels.

ONOFRI. The correspondence *Carteggi Cecchi – Onofri – Papini*, ed. Carlo D'Alessio, Mi, Bompiani, 2000, 221 pp., details O.'s involvement in literary journals and his contact with Cecchi (one of the founders of *La Ronda*) and Papini who co-founded *Leonardo* with Prezzolini.

ORELLI. P. Pellini, 'Il san buco e i sentieri da capre. Sulla poesia di Giorgio Orelli', *EL*, 26.3 : 93–106. Pietro De Marchi, *Dove portano le parole: sulla poesia di Giorgio Orelli e altro Novecento*, Lecce, Manni, 260 pp., includes one hitherto unpublished piece by Orelli.

ORENGO. M. Actis-Grosso, 'Nico Orengo, un Francis Ponge italiano? Cartoline di mare vecchie e nuove (1984–1999)', *AIPI 14*, II, 13–20.

ORTESE. F. Amigoni, 'I rottami del niente: il fantastico nell'opera di Anna Maria Ortese', *StCrit*, 17 : 207–37. Luca Clerici, *Apparizione e visione: vita e opera di Anna Maria Ortese*, Mi, Mondadori, 732 pp., provides a lengthy biography of this writer. Gabriella Fiori, *Anna Maria Ortese, o dell'indipendenza poetica*, T, Bollati Boringhieri, 143 pp., focuses on O.'s style as a woman writer, her vision of life in relation to her views on love, and her self-effacing concepts of 'poco' and 'nulla'. G. Iannaccone, 'Anna Maria Ortese: il "Monaciello" e la nostalgia del perduto', *CLett*, 30: 109–21, identifies an intuitive aspect of reality behind the ordinary experience of the outside world in O.'s story 'Il monaciello di Napoli'.

PALAZZESCHI. *Aldo Palazzeschi: il palio dei buffi*, ed. Rita Guerricchio, Mi, Mondadori, 290 pp., provides a useful analysis of P.'s *novelle* published by Vallecchi in 1937. *L'opera di Aldo Palazzeschi. Atti del Convegno internazionale, Firenze, 22–24 febbraio 2001*, ed. Gino Tellini, F, Olschki, xvi + 466 pp. Aldo Palazzeschi, *Tutte le poesie*, ed. Adele Dei, Mi, Mondadori, lxxxix + 1310 pp., updates the corpus of P.'s poetry. P. Pieri, 'Il *Codice* della poesia nelle maschere di Palazzeschi', *Poetiche*, 2: 193–218, outlines various modes of representation in P.'s work. G. Adamo, 'Osservazioni sull'iter variantistico delle poesie giovanili di Aldo Palazzeschi, *StCrit*, 17: 19–44, analyses variants in morphology, lexis, metre, and structure of P.'s early poems over four and a half decades until the 1958 anthology considered definitive by the author, and comments upon his free and non-traditional poetics of ambiguity. *Atti del Colloquio internazionale, Istituto Italiano di Cultura, Parigi, 17 novembre 2000*, ed. Gino Tellini, F, Soc. Ed. Fiorentina, x + 142 pp.

PAPINI. *Giovanni Papini – Ardengo Soffici: carteggio*, III. *1916–1918. La grande guerra*, ed. Mario Richter, Ro, Storia e Letteratura, 271 pp., and *Giovanni Papini – Ardengo Soffici: carteggio*, IV. *1919–1956*, ed. Mario Richter, Ro, Storia e Letteratura, 335 pp. Further Papini letters are published in *Carteggio Mario Novara – Giovanni Papini 1906–1943*, ed. Andrea Aveto, Ro, Storia e Letteratura, lxxxvi + 272 pp. See also ONOFRI, above.

PARISE. A. Daniele, 'Goffredo Parise e Giuseppe Faggin. Tracce di un'amicizia', *GSLI*, 179: 99–102, includes a letter written by P., in November or December 1974, to his former Liceo teacher, Faggin.

PARRONCHI. S. Ramat, 'Alessandro Parronchi: tre poesie inedite', *FoI*, 36: 165–68. M. Biondi, 'Nei mari estremi. 'Paura di vivere' e altri versi di Alessandro Parronchi', *Il Cristallo* (Supplement), 44.1: 103–17. *Conversando con Alessandro Parronchi*, F, Polistampa, 2001, 118 pp., records an interview with Renzo Cassigoli and Parronchi.

PASOLINI. Pier Paolo Pasolini, *La nuova gioventù: poesie friulane 1941–1974*, T, Einaudi, 334 pp., includes an essay on P.'s Friulan poetry by Furio Brugnolo. Issue 1 (2001) of *Quaderni del Novecento* is devoted to P. and includes S. D'Ortenzi's 'Bibliografia della critica' (103–25); essays by R. Cortella (5–20) on P.'s poetry, F. Crispino (21–30) on P.'s cinema and psychoanalysis, F. Ferri (31–46) on P.'s language and committed ideology, together with other essays by S. Giovanardi, C. Graziano, S. Petrocchi, T. Morosetti, and L. Vitali.

Filippo La Porta, *Pasolini. Uno gnostico innamorato della realtà*, F, Le Lettere, 100 pp., focuses on P.'s importance as an essayist, his sense of reality, and his politics, and also examines *Petrolio* as a text in progress. *Contributi per Pasolini*, ed. Giuseppe Savoca, F, Olschki, 222 pp., consists chiefly of papers read at a Catania seminar. Fabio Vighi, *Le ragioni dell'altro: la formazione intellettuale di Pasolini tra saggistica, letteratura e cinema*, Ravenna, Longo, 2001, 286 pp. Carlo A. Augieri, *Sul senso affabulante: Pasolini, la letteratura e la ri-simbolizzazione orizzontale della storia*, Lecce, Milella, 2001, 203 pp., comprises writings, some hitherto unpublished. *Pier Paolo Pasolini: generi e figure*, ed. Neil Novello, Ancona, Mediateca delle Marche, 2001, 229 pp. Vincenzina Levato, *Lo sperimentalismo tra Pasolini e la neoavanguardia, 1955–1965*, Soveria Mannelli, Rubbettino, 243 pp. Antonia Mazza, *Fortuna critica e successo di Pier Paolo Pasolini*, Pisa–Ro, IEPI, 175 pp., reconstructs the various phases of P.'s critical reception as a creative writer, film director, and committed intellectual.

PAVESE. *La scrittura*, 14–15, 2001, includes P. Perilli, 'Cesare Pavese al vaglio delle generazioni' (4–10), on P.'s legacy as seen in literature, ideology, and songs; A. F. Colonna, 'Un uomo da nulla. Pavese e il cinema' (14–18); and L. Sisti, 'La notte e la coscienza. Pavese, Cioran e lo sguardo interiore' (19–22). *Narrativa*, 22, includes essays on P. by C. Imberty on the fantastic (5–25); M. Masoero on the genesis of P.'s novels from *Il carcere* to *il compagno* (39–56); A. Salpietro on myth and symbols in *Paesi tuoi* (57–71); A. M. Mutterle, on a comparison between *La casa in collina* and *Il carcere* (73–88); V. Binetti on *La casa in collina* in relation to the Resistance and the dilemmas of its protagonist (83–103); G. Isotti Rosowsky on *La luna e i falò* (105–18); D. Ferraris on P.'s narrative modernity (119–34); B. Van den Bossche on a typology of P.'s narrative voices (135–49); A. Bianchi, on the concepts of 'dialogo oscuro' and 'scrittura dialogica' (150–61). A. Bianchi, 'L'avventura della solitudine: il mare nella poesia di Cesare Pavese', *AIPI 14*, 21–29. A. Battistini, 'Ancora su Pavese e il "grande laboratorio" della letteratura americana', *CLett*, 30:831–56. Roberto Gigliucci, *Cesare Pavese*, Mi, Bruno Mondadori, 114 pp., is a volume in the series 'Biblioteca degli scrittori' comprising biography, bibliography, and a dictionary of significant entries varying from description of works to other relevant items: cf. in particular the entries in this vol. on symbols such as *belva*, *gorgo*, *roccia*, *rupe*, *sacrificio*, *terra*, and *vigna*.

PENNA. M. E. Debenedetti, 'Il fanciullo lontano', *RLettI*, 20.1:185–96, shows that P.'s poetry overcomes the prejudice whereby it is often seen it simply as a variation on Saba but demonstrates the clear poetic vocation that runs through his work, where the experience of love has its own harsh and incandescent dimension. *Trasparenze*, 14, contains the following articles on Penna: P. Febbraro, 'Una giornata con Penna' (25–27); E. Pecora, 'L'ultima giornata con Sandro Penna' (29–33); B. Corà, 'Nella casa – magazzino di Penna per un inventario' (35–38); I. Pizzetti, 'Sandro Penna e l'immediatezza' (39–40); P. Lagazzi, 'Penna e l'Oriente' (41–50); D. Marcheschi, 'Leggendo Penna. Alcune considerazioni sulla poesia "Il vegetale"' (51–57); G. Leonelli, 'Letture penniane' (59–66); and R. Deidier, 'L'ultima poesia' (67–71). Sandro Penna, *Il viaggiatore insonne*, ed. Roberto Deidier, Genoa, San Marco dei Giustiniani, 71 pp., includes a critical introduction by Natalia Ginzburg and Giovanni Raboni.

PENNATI. *Hebenon*, 7.9–10, has a supplement entirely devoted to the poetry of P. It includes the following: S. Quasimodo, '*Landscapes* di Camillo Pennati' (9–10); V. Sereni, 'Notizia su Camillo Pennati' (11–13); G. Luzzi, 'Sull'opera di Camillo Pennati' (14–25); E. Krumm, 'Camillo Pennati' (26–27); R. Bertoldo, 'Camillo Pennati, *Una distanza inseparabile*' (28–29); Id., 'Intervista a Camillo Pennati' (30–33); G. Gramigna, 'Nota critica su Camillo Pennati' (34–36); P. Lezziero, 'Camillo Pennati, *De sideree vicende*' (37–38); P. Flecchia, 'La stessa sua risconvolgente immagine (una nota su Camillo Pennati)' (39–45); S. Montalto, 'Camillo Pennati, una tralucente lucentezza' (46–55); E. Salvaneschi, 'Ritmo e aritmia: Camillo Pennati *et ceteri*' (56–90); M. Marchisio, 'Arcana immanenza' (91–95); P. Lezziero, 'Note su *Una distanza inseparabile* di Camillo Pennati' (96–98); G. Fantato, 'Verso una geografia della gioia (note su *Sotteso blu* di Camillo Pennati)' (99–103).

PIOTTI. E. N. Girardi, 'Lettura critica de "Il labirinto" di Pier Luigi Piotti', *ON*, 25.3:85–106, presents a critical analysis of a wide number of themes used by P. in this work, such as his overall view of humanity, national politics, and episodes in the history of Brescia, his love for his wife, his friendship with Ungaretti and Alda Merini, and with friends real and imaginary.

PIOVENE. *Guido Piovene: tra realtà e visione*, ed. Massimo Rizzante, Trieste, Dipartimento di Scienze filologiche e storiche, 156 pp.

PIRANDELLO. *Luigi Pirandello: biografia per immagini*, Cavallermaggiore, Gribaudo, 2001, 157 pp., includes texts by Andrea Gareffi et al. *Luoghi e paesaggi nella narrativa di Pirandello. Atti del Convegno di Roma, 19–21 dicembre 2001*, ed. Gianvito Resta, Ro, Salerno, 256 pp. A. Barbina, 'La grande (e piccola) "conversazione" Pirandello–Cesareo', *Ariel*, 16.1:29–35. N. Borsellino, 'Pirandello: creatività e sperimentazione', *Atti* (Rome), 331–39, reclaims the field of creativity for P., rejects accusations of intellectual artificiality, and reappraises P.'s simplicity by reference to the critical views of Massimo Bontempelli, Alberto Savinio, and Corrado Alvaro. Paola Casella, *L'umorismo di Pirandello: ragioni intra e intertestuali*, Fiesole, Cadmo, 342 pp. C. Chiummo, '"Nel vuoto di un tempo senza vicende": natura e storia ne *I vecchi e i giovani*', *SPCT*, 62, 2001 : 173–97, examines the relationship between nature and history, the former interpreted as perennial, the latter defined as a 'sogno inquieto', where events that took place in recently united Italy are deconstructed, and disillusion, parody, and the grotesque prevail, so that P.'s view would appear to be anti-historical. The author also compares *I vecchi e i giovani* to Giuseppe Verga's short story 'Libertà' and sees Zola's *Germinal* as the common origin of both texts. I. Crotti, 'In viaggio con Mattia Pascal: da Miragno a Roma, andata e ritorno', *RLI*, 106 : 76–95, on the logic of travel and the search for meaning in P.'s novel. A. De Crescenzo, 'Pirandello e il cristianesimo', *EL*, 27.3 : 117–34, is a bibliographical review on the theme indicated by the title of the article. M. Fazio, 'Reinhardt: sulla ripresa dei *Sei personaggi*', *Ariel*, 16.1 : 157–62. E. Ghidetti, 'I luoghi di Mattia Pascal', *RLI*, 106 : 419–30, argues that even though *Il fu Mattia Pascal* is an imaginary story it is based on documentary evidence and is therefore partly linked to naturalism, but that it moves away from *verismo* because it questions deterministic cause–effect relations. S. Giannini, 'La passionale genesi di *Come tu mi vuoi*', *RLettI*, 20.2 : 217–34, is on the letters exchanged between P. and Marta Abba, and their relation to P.'s work. P. Langella, 'Teatro illustrativo e teatro dialettico', pp. 409–40 of *La maschera e il volto*, ed. Francesco Bruni, Venice, Fondazione Cini–Marsilio, 502 pp., discusses the theatrical nature of *Sei personaggi in cerca d'autore*. E. Licastro, 'Pirandello's chauvinism, obsessions, characters and his muse Marta Abba', *FoI*, 36 : 190–95. Umberto Mariani, *La creazione del vero: il maggior teatro di Pirandello*, Fiesole, Cadmo, 2001, 191 pp., illustrates P.'s major works and sees him as the source of subsequent modern drama. E. Providenti, 'Formiggini editore di Pirandello', *Belfagor*, 57 : 73–86. A. R. Pupino, 'Lo sguardo della natura. Un'idea di paesaggio in Pirandello', *RLI*, 106 : 431–52, interprets P.'s countryside as a *locus amoenus* vs his urban landscape characterized by a sense of constraint. *Interviste a Pirandello: parole da dire, uomo, agli altri uomini*, ed. Ivan Pupo, pref. Nino Borsellino, Soveria Mannelli, Rubbettino, iv + 651 pp. *Agenda letteraria Luigi Pirandello 2002*, ed. Gianni Rizzoni con la collaborazione di Silvia Nicoletta Tesè, Mi, Mondadori, 2001, 159 pp. Franco Zangrilli, *Pirandello*, Padua, Messaggero, 240 pp., explores the theme of religion in P.'s work. G. Taviani, 'Dalla parola al silenzio: le *Novelle per un anno* di Luigi Pirandello', *Allegoria*, 37, 2001 : 14–37, argues in favour of unity, rather than fragmentation in the *Novelle*, and conducts a thematic and structural analysis of this text.

PORTA. D. Piccini, 'Antonio Porta. "Preferisco del linguaggio quel che ha di divino" ', *Poesia*, 166:60–6, looks at P.'s opposition to the destruction of life in death in his later works, particularly in *Giardiniere contro il becchino* (1988).

POZZI. Alessandra Cenni, *In riva alla vita. Storia di Antonia Pozzi poetessa*, Mi, Rizzoli, 300 pp., offers a timely biography of the poet. Antonia Pozzi, *Parole*, ed. Alessandra Cenni and Onorina Dino, Mi, Garzanti, 2001, xv + 424 pp., is an updated edn of P.'s poetry. 'Memorietta su Antonia Pozzi', Scorrano, *Carte*, 87–126, notes the link between the spontaneity of adolescence and lyrical expression in P.'s poetry.

PREZZOLINI. Roberto Salek, *Giuseppe Prezzolini: una biografia intellettuale*, introd. Marino Biondi, F, Le Lettere, xxv + 162 pp., defines P. as a social man motivated by his sense of history, and concentrates in particular on his early years as a writer.

QUASIMODO. Salvatore Quasimodo, *Autobiografia per immagini*, ed. Giovanna Musolino, Pistoia, Via del Vento, 2001, 32 pp. E. Gioanola, 'Quasimodo: la passione del figlio', *EL*, 27.1:21–44, penetrates the roots of Q.'s poetry and pays particular attention to the lines of 'Ed è subito sera'. At the core of Q.'s poetry lies a node of pain and a craving for the absolute: the saint and the poet are dominated by the same totalitarian passion. Such observations brush aside the supposed paganism ascribed to him. *ON*, 26.1, has the following articles on Quasimodo: G. Baroni, 'Elementi primordiali nella lirica di Salvatore Quasimodo' (5–15), assessing primordial features such as the return to the maternal womb and a return to nature in 'Terra e acqua'; P. Paolini, 'Quasimodo traduttore di Catullo, carme 65 (con Foscolo e Cetrangolo)' (17–26), arguing that Q.'s translation is very close to the original: he compares it to Foscolo's 1803 translation of the same poem (which deviates considerably from the original) and with Cetrangolo's 1950 translation and concludes that Q.'s is the most graceful and sensitive of these three translations; A. Bellio, '. . . e i giorni una maceria' (27–38), detailing the role of time in Q.'s lyrics and his constant effort to escape the 'naufragio'; E. Mezzetta, 'Quasimodo critico di Messina poeta' (39–48), recording how Q. defined the link between sculpture and poetry in Messina as 'sfuocato', and also how Q. compared M.'s sculpture with his poetry and found that the latter pulsates with the vital themes of past and present and with memories of Sicily, which was also M.'s native land; and F. D'Alessandrio, 'Quasimodo, Sereni e la lirica' (49–63), making specific reference to the influence of Q. on S.'s poetry in the mid 1930s. Francesco D'Episcopo, *Ugo Foscolo: le metamorfosi della memoria. Salvatore Quasimodo e Alfonso Gatto*, Na, Eurocamp 2000–Graus, 77 pp. F. Santi, 'La vera storia di Quasimodo', *ParL*, 33–35:84–102, offers a reappraisal of Q.'s poetry. Natale Tedesco, *L'isola impareggiabile. Significati e forme del mito di Quasimodo*, Palermo, Flaccovio, 158 pp. Salvatore Quasimodo, *Senza di te, la morte. Lettere a Curzia Ferrari (1963–1968)*, ed. Giovanna Musolino, Mi, Archinto, 2001, 79 pp., consists of 30 letters written by Q. to Ferrari, the last flame of his life, which detail his 'amore tenero e violento' for this woman thirty years his junior. *Salvatore Quasimodo nel vento del Mediterraneo. Atti del Convegno internazionale, Princeton, 6–7 aprile 2001*, ed. Pietro Frassica, Novara, Interlinea, 155 pp.

RABONI. M. Forti, 'Raboni poematico e scenico: la Croce e i Vangeli in versi', *NA*, 2221 : 134–55. G. Luzzi, 'Giovanni Raboni. Nel cielo di Mozart', *Poesia*, 159:32–37, examines the range of musical intertextual links in R.'s poetry, particularly in *Versi guerrieri e amorosi* (1990). A. Cortellessa, 'Giovanni Raboni. Lo stopper della morte', *ib.*, 38–43, assesses the 'pulsione di morte' in R.'s work and concludes that his verse successfully blocks off the onset of death and decline.

RAMAT. 'La poesia di Silvio Ramat con quattro poesie inedite dell'autore', *Hebenon*, 7.9–10, includes essays on R.'s poetry by C. Marchesini, 'A un passo dal buio' (48–50), G. Leto, 'Due libri' (50–52), and F. Vitelli, 'La "poesia colta"' (52–56). Silvio Ramat, *Mia madre un secolo: Racconto in versi*, introd. Luigi Baldacci, Venice, Marsilio, 130 pp., details in hendecasyllables the family life and vicissitudes of the poet's mother (a centenarian in 2002) and has been acclaimed as one of the best poetry collections of the year.

RANCHETTI M. Pacioni, 'Limite e apertura nella poesia di Ranchetti', *Allegoria*, 40–41 : 174–84, shows how R.'s language tends to gravitate towards facts, not 'parole', and that he considers poetry to be 'esecuzione, interpretazione (nel senso musicale del termine) del linguaggio'. Michele Ranchetti, *Verbale–Minutes–Tuairisc*, ed. Cormac Ó Cuilleanáin, Eiléan Ní Cuilleanáin, and Gabriel Rosenstock, Dublin, Istituto Italiano di Cultura, 176 pp., is a trilingual anthology with English and Irish translations of R.'s poetry.

REBORA G. Rella, 'Annotazioni in margine ai *Frammenti lirici* di Clemente Rebora o del tempo come inquietudine', *AFLLSB*, 15, 2001 : 573–81. Attilio Bettinzoli, *La coscienza spietata: studi sulla cultura e la poesia di Clemente Rebora: 1913–1920*, Venice, Marsilio, 197 pp., includes two previously unpublished texts. Clemente Rebora, *Curriculum vitae*, ed. Roberto Cicala and Gianni Mussini, Novara, Interlinea, 2001, 195 pp., provides the first comprehensive commentary on R.'s poems and also refers to some previously unpublished drafts presented here for the first time. 'La poesia di Rebora nel giudizio dei suoi primi lettori (con tre testi in appendice)', Ramat, *Passi*, 47–65.

RECALCATI. A. Mari, 'La poesia di Claudio Recalcati', *Hebenon*, 7.9–10 : 134–36.

RIGONI STERN. L. Polato, 'La "memoria" di Rigoni Stern', *StN*, 27, 2000: 384–98, highlights individual and collective memory seen as 'coralità epica' and 'totalità oggettiva'.

RIPELLINO. F. Roana, '"Teatralizzazione dell'esistenza" nella poesia di Angelo Maria Ripellino', *ON*, 26.1: 103–32, outlines the border between laughter and tears used by R. to cope with the highs and lows of life.

ROMANO. *Poesie, forse, utili: con autografi e disegni inediti*, ed. Antonio Ria, Novara, Interlinea, 98 pp., discusses R.'s poetry including some hitherto unpublished poems.

ROSSELLI. P. Bagnoli, 'Amelia Rosselli: la dolcezza e il ricordo', *NA*, 2222: 143–50, provides an interesting image of the mother of Carlo, Aldo, Nello, paternal grandmother of Amelia Rosselli. G. Russo, 'Ricordo di Amelia Rosselli', *ib.*, 2224: 85–87, recalls the human and psychological drama of the poet's life.

RUFFATO. R. Bertoldo, 'Il procedimento analogico sinsemico in Cesare Ruffato', *Hebenon*, 7.9–10: 147–48. E. Ó Ceallacháin, 'Preface: su *Saccade* di Cesare Ruffato', *ib.*, 149–51. Elettra Bedon, *Al di là della veste: per Scribendi licentia di Ruffato – una proposta di lettura*, Mi, Hebenon, 2000, 90 pp., provides an analysis of R.'s *Scribendi licentia.*

RUFFILLI. G. E. Ligotti, '*La gioia e il lutto* di Paolo Ruffilli', *LetP*, 113–14: 83–93, looks at the use of the oxymoron in R.'s most recent work (pub. in 2001) and suggests that it represents the writer's 'geografia dell'anima'.

SABA. C. Gavagnin, 'Lirica e narrativa nei *Versi militari* di Saba', *FC*, 26, 2001[2002]: 350–95. On the same poems: 'Saba e la guerra', Dell'Aquila, *Nominanza*, 146–56. 'Il lessico del primo *Canzoniere*', 'Diminutivi e altre parole leggere e vaganti', and 'I *Lieder* di Saba', Girardi, *Prosa*, 75–93, 95–102, and 147–60 respectively, are rewritings of published articles. P. Frandini, 'Umberto Saba. La casa delle *Scorciatoie*', *NArg*, 17: 310–22, examines S.'s prose writing and its connection with his life and poetry. It pays particular attention to S.'s *Scorciatoie e Raccontini* (1946) which he dedicated to Giacomo Debenedetti who had sheltered him in Rome for several months in 1944. S. Ramat, 'Umberto Saba prosatore: una vocazione molteplice', *Poesia*, 159: 56–61. F. Chiara, 'Poesia in cucina. Lina e il mondo femminile nella rappresentazione di Umberto Saba', *MLN*, 117: 174–93, examines the progressive change of the image of Lina and women generally in S.'s poetry. Silvana Ghiazza, *Carlo Levi e Umberto Saba. Storia di un'amicizia*, Bari, Dedalo, 380 pp., traces the relationship between Saba, Levi, and S.'s daughter Linuccia, L.'s lifelong companion. S. Ritrovato, 'Un "dattiloscritto sogno mediterraneo" nella poesia di Umberto Saba', *AIPI 14*, II, 73–88.

SALARI. A. Curcetti, 'L'infrascritta divisione: su *Il Pellegrino Babelico* di Tiziano Salari', *Hebenon*, 7.9–10:137–9.

SANGUINETI. E. Sanguineti, 'La mia poesia', *Comunicare. Letterature, Lingue*, 1, 2001:59–90, consists of a discussion by S. on his own poetry (59–76) and a question and answer session (77–90) between S. and those attending a poetry course held by the Istituto Trentino di Cultura in 2000. Elisabetta Baccarini, *La poesia nel labirinto. Razionalismo e istanza 'antiletteraria' nell'opera e nella cultura di Edoardo Sanguineti*, Bo, Il Mulino, 340 pp., shows how in *Laborintus* S. explored the psychology of the subconscious and irrational philosophies from a rational angle through the adoption of significant images (in particular the bog and the moon) and in relation to authors such as Jung and Heidegger, and subsequently moved towards increasingly rational convictions. His poetics, though characterized by different phases, is consistently opposed to classicism, but his aversion for traditional literature and preference for literary experiment is based on a deep knowledge of a number of classical authors such as Dante, Benvenuto da Imola, and St Ambrose. L. Weber, 'Dal *Capitale* ai *Quaderni*: per una storia della critica sanguinetiana', *Poetiche*, 2:219–49.

SATTA. Vanna Gazzola Stacchini, *Come in un giudizio: vita di Salvatore Satta*, Ro, Donzelli, vi + 170 pp.

SAVINIO. A. Castronuovo, 'Alberto Savinio e il cristianesimo', *Belfagor* 57:37–42.

SCIALOJA. Toti Scialoja, *Poesie 1961–1998*, pref. G. Raboni, Mi, Garzanti, 552 pp.

SCIASCIA. M. Belpoliti, '*L'affaire Moro*: un'idea di letteratura', *NArg*, 18:228–36, sees *L'affaire Moro* as a literary work where an inversion of the customary roles of reality and literature occurs, and an intriguing interplay between literary narrative and essay writing takes place. Matteo Collura, *Alfabeto eretico. Da Abbondio a zolfo: 58 voci dall'opera di Sciascia per capire la Sicilia e il mondo d'oggi*, Mi, Longanesi, 192 pp., includes, among the alphabetical entries, Bellodi, Borges, Calvino, Irredimibile (on S.'s unredeemable Palermo), Moro, and Pirandello. Pietro Milone, *L'udienza: Sciascia scrittore e critico pirandelliano*, Manziana, Vecchiarelli, 271 pp. I. R. Morrison, 'Leonardo Sciascia's *Candido* and Voltaire's *Candide*', *MLR*, 97:59–71, is an intertextual comparison between the two texts. J.-C. Rebejkov, '*Candido*, ou quand Sciascia réécrit Voltaire', *Versants*, 39, 2001:231–49, sees *Candido* as a variation on Voltaire's *Candide*, closely associated to its model even though the ending of S.'s novel is optimistic and direct allusions to the French predecessor are few. A. Motta, 'Leonardo Sciascia e i *peintres et acqua-fortistes*', *NA*, 2221:326–32, is about S.'s interest in prints and paintings, and on his friendship with certain artists. Id., 'Laterza nella storia di Sciascia', *ib.*, 2224:257–64. Erika Monforte, *I teatri di Leonardo Sciascia*, Caltanissetta, Sciascia, 2001, 240 pp., studies S.'s texts for the theatre and examines his work in relation to Pirandello and the theatrical aspects on his narrative.

SCOTELLARO. A. L. Giannone, 'Profilo di Rocco Scotellaro', *CLett*, 30:867–88, outlines the 'caso Scotellaro' and looks at the new image of S. that emerges following the publication of previously unpublished work. This new work means that S. is no longer viewed in a political-ideological dimension and shows the links that he had with trends and writers of his time. Such re-evaluation moves S. to a broader, less isolated position in 20th-c. Italian poetry. F. Vitelli, 'La rivolta del 1942 a Tricarico', *FoI*, 36:169–78.

SERENI. Vittorio Sereni, *Poesie*, ed. Dante Isella and Clelia Martignoni, T, Einaudi, xvi + 220 pp., provides a timely critical ed. of C.'s poetry. *Vittorio Sereni: un percorso poetico: poesie, studi, testimonianze*, ed. Stefano Raimondi, Mi, CUEM, 153 pp., includes among other things a collection of already-published items on Sereni. Stefano Sasso, *Vittorio Sereni tra canzoniere e diario. Alla riscoperta di un percorso poetico (1935–1952)*, Hamburg, Kovać Wissenschaftsverlag, 362 pp. Stefano Cipriani, *Il libro della prosa di Vittorio Sereni*, F, Ed. Fiorentina, 242 pp. A. Cortellessa, 'Tracce di un'"altra" guerra tra le "materie prime" di Vittorio Sereni', *Allegoria*, 40–41:53–79, discusses how war is seen as 'l'attesa di un evento risolutore' throughout *Diario d'Algeria*, *Frontiera* and *Gli strumenti umani* and then contrasts it with the palpable disappointment experienced by S. in the post-war period. L. Wittmann, 'Vittorio Sereni o "L'istinto della gioia"', *FoI*, 35, 2001:403–31. M. Ciccuto, 'Vittorio Sereni: le occasioni più vive della scrittura', *ParL*, 33–35:87–102. '*Pin-up girl* e dintorni (con testi di Vittorio Sereni in appendice)', Ramat, *Passi*, 161–72.

SILONE. Ignazio Silone, *Il fascismo. Origini e sviluppo*, ed. M. Franzinelli, Mi, Mondadori, xlvii + 310 pp., has an introduction reconstructing the genesis of the work, originally published in German as *Der Fascismus* (1934) and dealing with the subject from a socialist perspective. G. Marrone, 'Il segno culinario come campo di tensione nella narrativa di Ignazio Silone', *Italica*, 79:353–62, examines food as a material object and metaphor in writing.

SINISGALLI. *Sinisgalli a Milano. Poesia, pittura, architettura e industria dagli anni Trenta agli anni Sessanta*, ed. Giuseppe Lupo, Novara, Interlinea, 270 pp., includes a number of essays dealing with the impact of Milan on S.'s work in the 1960s. L. Sinisgalli, *I martedì colorati. Un poeta alle mostre*, Genoa, Graphos, 195 pp., is a collection of articles and reviews by S. originally published in 1967 in the weekly paper *Tempi illustrati*. Leonardo Sinisgalli, *Furor geometricus*, ed. Giuseppe Lupo, T, Aragno, 2001, 136 pp., consists of articles, reviews, and autobiographical memoirs previously published in journals and now gathered for the first time. They cover the years 1934–39 when S. lived in Milan, an ideal city which acted as a foil for his poetry and his passion for mathematics. F. Vitelli, 'Sinisgalli. Storia di Via Velasca e dintorni', *CLett*, 30:795–830, looks at the importance of location, in this case Via Velasca, and the 'poetica dell'indizio' in S.'s poetry. A. Ottieri, '"Il corpo si vendica dell'intelletto": Sinisgalli e Valéry', *FC*, 26, 2001[2002]:396–422, analyses the impact of V.'s *Charmes* on S. from 1930 onwards. S. met the French poet in Rome in 1937, and O. suggests that S. was initially seduced by V.'s 'mito della precisione'. 'Sinisgalli / 20 anni', Dell'Aquila, *Bello stilo*, 159–70, highlights the meditative nature of S.'s poetry, his interest in mathematics and the *logos*, his interwoven dimensions of 'meridionalismo di memorie e di affetti' and 'tensione sperimentale e gnomico-epigrammatica', and his relation to a number of painters and to Giacomo Leopardi.

SLATAPER. E. Coda, 'The representation of the metropolis in Scipio Slataper's *Il mio Carso*', *MLN*, 117:153–73, argues that S. is unable to accept Trieste's intrinsic contradictions while he observes its complex reality and portrays the alienation of the individual searching for a unifying meaning amid a sense of fragmented existence and the variety of aspects he observes in the urban environment, with the result that *Il mio Carso* is a literary text open to a number of different interpretations.

SOFFICI. 'Un incunabolo di Soffici poeta', Ramat, *Passi*, 9–11, sees S.'s 1896 poem "Dai campi" as the earliest example of S.'s poetry and a suitable forerunner of the new century. See also PAPINI, above.

SOLMI. A. Di Benedetto, 'Alain nelle interpretazioni di Solmi e Bonora', *Intersezioni*, 22:155–63. 'Da Solmi a Montale a Solmi', Ramat, *Passi*, 121–36.

SVEVO. *Aghios. Quaderni di studi sveviani*, 3, includes S. Crise, 'La pudica attrazione per la musica del dilettante Ettore Schmitz' (11–44); N. Danieli, 'Italo Svevo e il suo educatore Samuel Spier' (45–62); S. Buglione, 'Malattia individuale e malattia sociale nel finale della *Coscienza di Zeno*. Considerazioni di Svevo e Freud sulla malattia' (63–70); S. Adamo, 'Il "caso" Svevo nell'ex Unione Sovietica' (71–92); C. Verani, 'Svevo e Joyce: bibliografia ragionata (fino al 1940)' (93–101); and 'Un "Waste Book" di Italo Svevo' with an introduction by B. Moloney (105–10). V. Brombert, 'Svevo's European dimensions', *Atti* (Rome), 340–50, highlights the formative cosmopolitan nature of Trieste, Jewishness, relations with James Joyce, and more in general S.'s European horizon, and shows how his novels draw on 19th-c. fiction but are essentially modern, especially at the level of language and of his debt towards Sigmund Freud. S. Lazzarini, 'Alfonso Nitti e la *Questione del Costume*. Note su *Una vita* e la tradizione del Bildungsroman', *RLettI*, 20.2: 125–52.

TABUCCHI. B. Ferraro, 'Antonio Tabucchi: da un "Sogno in forma di lettera" ai sogni di una "Lettera da scrivere"', *Il Ponte*, 57.12, 2001: 109–25, highlights the increasing and multifaceted presence of oneiric elements in Tabucchi's works from *Donna di Porto Pim* (1983) to his last collection of short stories in letter form, *Si sta facendo sempre più tardi* (2001). L. Surdich, 'Antonio Tabucchi: storie, nomi, storie di nomi', *Il nome nel testo*, 4: 203–26, is about puzzling aspects and games implicit in T.'s choice of fictional names for his characters. Id., 'Il "porto secco" di Pereira e altri vini nella narrativa di Antonio Tabucchi', *Nuova corrente*, 48: 287–314.

TAROZZI. S. Tamiozzo Goldmann, 'Il canto della buranella. Note sulla poesia di Bianca Tarozzi', *QVen*, 35: 147–66, provides a useful analysis of the work of T., born in Rome and now living in Venice.

TESSA. G. Anceschi, 'Bibliografia degli scritti su Delio Tessa. Integrazioni e aggiunte', *ON*, 26.2: 171–86, offers useful bibliographical and critical information on T.'s work. Mauro Novelli, *I 'saggi lirici' di Delio Tessa*, Mi, LED, 2001, pays particular attention to the dialect base and intertextual links of T.'s poetry.

TESTA. A. Cortellessa, 'Enrico Testa. Sé come un altro', *Poesia*, 159: 63–67, offers a short critical overview of T.'s poetry.

TOMASI DI LAMPEDUSA. Alessandro Carrera, *Il principe e il giurista: Giuseppe Tomasi di Lampedusa e Salvatore Satta*, pref. Allen Mandelbaum, Ro, Pieraldo, 2001, 123 pp. R. Donnarumma, 'Le contraddizioni conciliate. Narratore, personaggio e punto di vista nel *Gattopardo*', *StN*, 27, 2000: 369–83. Nunzio La Fauci, *Lo spettro di Lampedusa*, Pisa, ETS, 2001, 110 pp. Gioacchino Lanza Tomasi and Margareta Dumitrescu, *Sulla parte sesta del Gattopardo: la fortuna di Lampedusa in Romania*, Bucharest, Fundatiei Culturale Române — Catania, Maimone, 2001, 165 pp. G. M. Tosi, 'Gli scritti critici di Tomasi di Lampedusa o della letteratura come modello di esistenza', *ItQ*, 153–54: 55–56.

TOMIZZA. In N. Milani and E. Deghenghi Olujić, 'Due voci per Fulvio Tomizza', *RLettI*, 20.1: 66–112, Milani discusses T.'s engagement with history and its failures (66–69), Olujić the relationship between literature and history in T.'s work where both representation of historical events and personal interpretation are present. In this connection a comparison is made with Sciascia's exploration of collective history in order to avoid oblivion of important events. C. Perrus, 'À la frontière de l'histoire: *La miglior vita* de Fulvio Tomizza', *ChrI*, 69–70: 139–50.

TONDELLI. R. Carnero, 'Tondelli: classico o no?', *NArg*, 17:294–309.

TOZZI. R. Castellana, 'Il punto su Tozzi: 1990–2000', *Moderna*, 3.1:97–190, is a useful survey of T. criticism. Id., *Tozzi*, Palermo, Palumbo, 292 pp., is a brief biography, bibliography, and anthology of criticism. 'La Toscana povera e aspra nella narrativa di Federigo Tozzi', Dell'Aquila, *Bello stilo*, 135–58, shows how the title theme, at the geographical and social levels, is expressed in a number of stories including 'Il podere' and *Tre croci*. *Federigo Tozzi fra tradizione e modernità*, ed. Marco Marchi, Assisi, Cittadella, 2001, 234 pp., are the proceedings of a conference held at Assisi in 2001. F. Petroni, 'Ciclicità e linearità nella narrativa di Federico Tozzi. Analisi della novella "Il cieco"', *Allegoria*, 37:5–13, is about Christianity and other ideologies in T.'s work. Marina Fratnik, *Paysages: essai sur la description de Federigo Tozzi*, F, Olschki, xv + 180 pp. P. Ureni, 'Filigrane psicologiche nell'opera di Tozzi: da Binet a Bergson', *NA*, 2223:249–71, highlights the psychological dimension of T.'s work, relates it to pre-Freudian French theory (Janet, Bergson, Binet) and shows how literary aspects are combined with scientific interests, especially in some of T.'s imagery.

TUSIANI. E. Bandiera, 'L'emigrazione come esilio nella poesia latina di Joseph Tusiani', *Italiana*, 10, 2001:17–42. *Two languages, two lands: l'opera letteraria di Joseph Tusiani. Atti della Giornata di studi, San Marco in Lamis, 15 maggio 1999*, ed. Cosma Siani, San Marco in Lamis, Quaderni del Sud, 2000, 183 pp.

UNGARETTI. Emerico e Noemi Giachery, *Ungaretti verticale*, Ro, Bulzoni, 2000, 168 pp., defines 'verticale' as something suspended between space and silence, examines its ability to transform words and verses into sensations and shows how it offers a 'lettura emozionata eppure non emotiva' of U.'s work. S. Ghiazza, 'Diacronia di *Levante* di Giuseppe Ungaretti', *CLett*, 30:757–77, outlines the various re-writings of 'Levante', one of the most important poems in *Allegria*, which offer superb examples of the early U.'s 'modo di fare poesia'. Such rewritings go from 1914 to the final 1942 version. R. Gennaro, 'Giuseppe Ungaretti tra fiumi, mari e naufragi', *AIPI 14*, II, 39–47. W. Mauro, 'Memore innocenza e radicata memoria. Da Dante a Ungaretti', *Pagine della Dante*, 75.2:48–52, shows how U. owes much to D. in his treatment of the theme of the journey. N. Lorenzini, 'Ungaretti, Petrarca, Góngora: per una rilettura', *Poetiche*, 3:353–69, discusses the well-known impact of P. on U. and shows how U.'s interest in G. centres on the cult of language and the poetics of memory. Giuseppe Ungaretti, *Vita d'un uomo. Viaggi e lezioni*, ed. Paola Montefoschi, Mi, Mondadori, 2000, 1647 pp., completes the edition of U.'s œuvre with his travel writings and university lectures.

M. Dell'Aquila, 'Ungaretti e Leopardi all'università di Roma', *CLett*, 30:747–56, discusses U.'s lectures on Leopardi in his years as Rome's first professor of modern and contemporary literature. E. Conti, 'Ungaretti, mediatore culturale di *Commerce*', *Intersezioni*, 22:89–108, discusses U.'s relationship with and contribution to this Parisian literary journal from 1925 to 1929. While favouring prose, following U.'s suggestion *Commerce* published texts by Bacchelli, Barilli, Cardarelli, and Cecchi: U. felt that all valid Italian literature should experience the French avant-garde. G. Bevilacqua, 'Ungaretti in Germania', *RLI*, 106:499–502, addresses U.'s success in Germany.

VALDUGA. A. Schneider Soltanianzadeh, 'Patrizia Valduga – Formen der Liebe und des Gebets', *Italienisch*, 47:101–07, analyses the exclusive use of the imperative form in the poem 'Vieni, entra e coglimi . . .' from the collection *Cento quartine a altre storie d'amore* (1997).

VALERI. G. Burrini, 'Modi e tempi del giovane Valeri', *LetP*, 113–14:95–103, documents echoes of Leopardi, Manzoni, and Pascoli, and traces of *crepuscolarismo*, in V.'s early poems. A. Cinquina Pari, 'Il valore della leggerezza nelle liriche di Diego Valeri', *AIPI 14*, II, 31–38. 'Città di Valeri', Ramat, *Passi*, 83–101.

VIGOLO. Giorgio Vigolo, *Poesie religiose e altre inedite*, ed. Giuliana Rigobello, Ro, Aracne, 2001, 140 pp., presents previously unpublished poems written between 1960 and 1968.

VIVANTI. C. Caporossi, 'Per rileggere Annie Vivanti a sessant'anni dalla morte', *NA*, 2221:269–92, provides a reappraisal of a prose-writer and poet whose experience as a victim of the racial laws, was aggravated by the fact that she was a British citizen. In particular, it explores her statement that 'la Realtà è terribile Romanziera', examines the main themes of her novels, and observes that their literary value does not consist in raising feminist issues but rather in the vitality of her protagonists and the emotional intensity of the fictional world she projects.

VITTORINI. Gianpiero Chirico, *Elio Vittorini. Epistolario americano*, pref. A. Crovi, Palermo, Siracusa, xxxix + 290 pp., includes an introduction consisting of the letters exchanged by V. and his American publisher, James Laughlin. Chirico also illustrates V.'s affinity for the American writers he was in contact with and detects the influence of Hemingway, Steinbeck, and Gertrude Stein on his style based on repetition.

VIVIANI. Stefano Verdino, *La distanza del nome: saggio sulla poesia di Cesare Viviani*, Pasian di Prato, Campanotto, 2001, 206 pp.

VOLPONI. D. Piccini, 'Paolo Volponi. L'antica moneta e il Capitale', *Poesia*, 161:40–49, discusses some of the tensions that exist in V.'s poetry between the ever-expanding tentacles of the capital,

Rome, and the rest of the country. G. L. Picconi, '"Un corpo che doveva essere enorme": la cicatrice di *Corporale*', *Nuova corrente*, 48:243–86, includes a comparison between *Corporale* and Pier Paolo Pasolini's *Petrolio*.

ZANZOTTO. Luigi Tassoni, *Caosmos. La poesia di Andrea Zanzotto*, Ro, Carocci, 171 pp., searches for the real meaning and significance of Z.'s poetry. *Omaggio a Zanzotto per i suoi ottanta anni*, ed. Raffaele Manica, Manziana, Vecchiarelli, 2001, 129 pp., includes articles by various literary critics on Zanzotto. N. Gardini, 'Linguistic dilemma and intertextuality in contemporary Italian poetry: the case of Andrea Zanzotto', *FoI*, 35:432–41. G. Cordibella, 'L'hölderlinismo di Andrea Zanzotto: un percorso interpretativo dai *Versi giovanili* a *Sovrimpressioni*. Parte I', *Poetiche*, 3:391–414. Andrea Zanzotto, *Scritti sulla letteratura*, ed. Gian Maria Villalta, 2 vols, Mi, Mondadori, 2001, 399, 495 pp., includes the whole corpus of Z.'s author criticism from *Fantasie di avvicinamento* (1991) to *Aure e disincanti del Novecento letterario* (1994), plus some unpublished articles.

Poetiche, 1, is entirely devoted to Zanzotto's work. It includes the following: S. Agosti, 'Luoghi e posizioni del linguaggio di Andrea Zanzotto. Nuove precisazioni in forma di appunti' (3–9); N. Lorenzini, '"Citazione" e "mise en abîme" nella poesia di Andrea Zanzotto' (11–28); A. Noferi, 'Per Andrea Zanzotto: *Sovrimpressioni*' (29–38); A. Battistini, 'L'intelligenza geologica di Zanzotto tra poesia e scienza' (39–44); L. Tassoni, 'Il silenzio del commentatore e altri silenzi per Zanzotto' (45–51); S. Dal Bianco, 'Margini, scampoli e babau' (53–59); G. M. Villalta, 'Sul maestro' (61–67); M. Manotta, 'La semantica come *felix culpa* della poesia' (69–87); F. Carbognin, 'Percorsi percettivi e "finzione" tra *Dietro il paesaggio* e *Vocativo* (89–110); S. Colangelo, 'Il giardino dei semplici: una traccia tematica' (111–17); M. A. Bazzocchi, 'Zanzotto: nutrimenti terrestri' (119–25); G. M. Annoni, 'A faccia a faccia (natura morta con canarino e specchio)' (127–41); E. Rónaky, 'Zanzotto: immaginario e critica' (143–48); A. Cortellessa, 'Geiger nell'erba. Prospezioni su Zanzotto critico' (149–75); R. Stracuzzi, 'La casa, il paesaggio: in margine a *Premesse all'abitazione* di Andrea Zanzotto' (177–92). 'Andrea Zanzotto in "avvicinamento"', Ramat, *Passi*, 203–13.

ROMANIAN STUDIES*

LANGUAGE

By Martin Maiden, *Professor of the Romance Languages, University of Oxford*
(This survey covers the years 2001–2002)

1. General

A major new reference book, important both for Romanian and general Romance linguistics, is *Enciclopedia limbii române*, ed. Marius Sala, Univers Enciclopedic, 2001, 634 pp. The 638 entries — presented in an admirably concise and clear fashion — cover all aspects of the structure and history both of Romanian and of Romanian dialects; there is also a select bibliography. Michael Metzeltin, *România: Stat, Naţiune, Limbă*, Univers Enciclopedic, 149 pp., is an extremely useful (if sometimes prolix) introduction to the country, the culture and the language. Of particular interest is the account it offers of the earliest grammars of Romanian for foreigners. It is to be hoped that the book will soon be translated into other languages (preferably with the addition of an index). G. Mihăilă, *Langue et culture roumaines dans l'espace sud-est européen*, Editura Academiei, 2001, 714 pp., gathers together 50 studies published by the author over the past four decades (a number of them in Russian), many dealing with aspects of Romanian philology and history of the language.

Obligatory reading for Romanists should be L. Ionescu-Ruxăndoiu, 'Românesc şi romanic', *LiR*, 48, 1999[2001]:83–87, which attacks, with some justification, the relative ignorance of Romanian among many Romance scholars. Her critique of what she regards as a widespread tendency to treat Romanian as little more than a 'muzeu al curiozităţilor' may however be slightly misplaced: for many Romanists it is more a 'muzeu al minunilor', and their fault lies in regarding the language too much as a 'museum', rather than a living language whose remarkable properties can be directly observed. Those seeking a more accurate knowledge of Romanian may be helped to some extent by Laura Daniliuc and Radu Daniliuc, *Descriptive Romanian Grammar. An Outline*, Munich, Lincom Europa, 2000, xviii + 411 pp., but the grammar — although a very commendable and useful undertaking — is not entirely satisfactory. The authors recognize that a more thorough study would require a much

* The place of publication of books is Bucharest unless otherwise stated.

longer work, but one still feels that some of the more intriguing and demanding complexities of Romanian grammar deserved a more explicit treatment than they get here. One has the sensation that because both authors are native speakers they have not always succeeded in getting a 'foreigner's-eye-view' of the language, taking some rather complex issues for granted. For example, the treatment of the so-called 'possessive-genitival article' (*al, ai, a, ale*) is too cursory. There are also occasional misleading slips and misprints, e.g. the claim that feminine nouns have a distinct genitive-dative case-form in the *plural* (34).

The life and works of individual linguists continue to receive the attention which seems typical of the Romanian academic world. *Marius Sala. Contemporanul lor. Contemporanii lui*, ed. Aurora Peţan, Univers Enciclopedic, 350 pp., offers an intriguing and affectionate insight into the professional life and times of one of Romania's most distinguished linguists. As the title suggests, the volume contains both a series of appreciations of other linguists by Sala and appreciations of Sala by his contemporaries. Regrettably, the book has an extremely limited print-run: one hopes that it will become more widely available. *LiR(M)*, 11, 2001:46–94, has a series of appreciations by various scholars of the life and work of Eugeniu Coşeriu. Originally intended as a eulogistic account of Coşeriu's work, on the occasion of his 80th birthday, M. Borcilă, 'Eugeniu Coşeriu', *LiL*, 47.3–4:5–11, appears, alas, as an obituary. Historians of Romanian linguistics will be entertained by *Alexandru Rosetti & Alf Lombard. Corespondenţă (1934–1990)*, I: *(1934–1964)*, ed. Nicolae Mocanu, Ioana Anghel, and Heinz Hoffmann, Cluj, Clusium, 2000, 397 pp., where even the most routine correspondence between the two scholars is presented with minute attention to philological detail (e.g. colour of ink, crossings out, size of postcard and illustration it bears!). **Alexandru Graur. Centenarul naşterii (Omagiul foştilor elevi şi colaboratori)*, ed. Ion Fischer, Lucia Wald, and Constantin Dominte, Editura Academiei, 2000, 295 pp. A. Avram, 'Academicianul Emanuel Vasiliu la 70 de ani', *FD*, 18, 1999[2002]:5–16, includes a list of the subject's publications as does N. Saramandu for 'Grigore Brâncuş – 70', *ib.*, 17–23. V. Zagaevschi, 'Profesorul Valeriu Rusu dialectolog', *LiR(M)*, 11, 2001:102–04. *Sextil Puşcariu. Biobibliografie*, ed. Elisabeta Faiciuc, Cluj, Clusium, 2000, xvii + 293 pp., in addition to comprehensive bibliography of works by and about P., provides 75 pages of 'iconografie'.

Ioan Oprea, *Curs de filozofia limbii*, Suceava, Editura Universităţii, 2001, 256 pp., is a general introductory book that deals particularly with the theories of Romanian scholars such as E. Coşeriu, A. Philippide, and G. Ivănescu, and has a section on linguistic philosophy with special reference to Romanian. E. Munteanu, 'Câteva reflecţii asupra statului actual al cercetării filologice româneşti', Ichim, *Identitatea*, 113–18, deals with the author's concerns about the transfer of knowledge and techniques from the older to the younger generation of Romanian philologists.

Gheorghe Chivu and Lucia Wald, *Institutiones Linguae Valahicae. Prima gramatică a limbii române scrisă în limba latină*, Editura Academiei, 2001, 163 pp., offers a philological commentary on this 18th-c. grammar and a translation and revision of the original Latin text.

Passion and polemic is mixed with much useful factual information about the situation of Romanian in the Republic of Moldova/ Bessarabia in A. Ciobanu, 'Limba română şi politica lingvistică în Republica Moldova', Ichim, *Identitatea*, 41–52, and S. Berejan, 'Despre cauzele pierderii identităţii lingvistice şi etnice într-o regiune ruptă din întreg', *ib.*, 53–60.

2. History of the Language

A. Poruciuc, 'Observaţii asupra modelului confluenţial şi asupra genezei limbii române', Ichim, *Identitatea*, 80–91, calls for a reconsideration of the force of non-Latin influences on the genesis of the language. W. Dietrich, 'Individualitatea limbii române întemeiată pe influenţa morfosintactică a limbii greceşti vechi şi bizantine asupra latinei vulgare balcanice', *ib.*, 103–12. Ion Oprea and Rodica Nagy, *Istoria limbii române literare. Epoca modernă*, Suceava, Editura Universităţii, 370 pp., traces the development of Romanian since the 19th c. in the light of then prevailing linguistic ideologies. Alexandru Gafton, *Elemente de istorie a limbii române*, Iaşi, Restitutio, 2001, 181 pp. + 4 maps, in fact offers an overview of the *early* attested history of Romanian. Ion Gheţie and Alexandru Mareş, *De când se scrie româneşte?*, Univers Enciclopedic, 2001, 224 pp., develop their view of the emergence of Romanian writing as a gradual and geographically diffuse process. N. Ursu, 'Trecut, prezent şi perspective în cercetarea filologică românească', *Prelegeri Academice*, 1, 37–56, in a general overview of the Romanian philological tradition pays particular attention to the problems of the origins of writing in Romanian. Alexandru Gafton, *Evoluţia limbii române prin traduceri biblice din secolul al XVI-lea*, Editura Universităţii A. I. Cuza, Iaşi, 2001, 387 pp., offers a detailed linguistic analysis of *Codicele Bratul* in comparison with *Codicele Voroneţean, Praxiul Coresian* and *Apostolul Iorga. Contribuţii la studiul limbii române literare. Secolul al XVIII-lea (1688–1780)*, ed. Ion Gheţie and Gheorghe Chivu, Cluj, Clusium, 2000, 333 pp., is concerned with a neglected century in the history of the language, and contains: M. Georgescu, 'Cultura lingvistică în secolul al XVIII-lea' (21–90), which offers among other things a survey of grammars, manuals, and dictionaries of the period; I. Gheţie. 'Secolul al XVIII-lea şi unificarea limbii române literare' (91–111), which further develops his argument, first expressed some thirty years ago, that the literary language begins to emerge in the mid 18th c. through the acceptance of Muntenian models in texts used in religious services; F. Zgraon, 'Normele limbi române literare la jumătatea secolului al XVIII-lea (tipărituri religioase de lectură, tipărituri laice, manuscrise)' (112–52); E. Suciu, 'Influenţa turcă' (153–98), reviews Turkish influence on vocabulary, while other sources of loans (and the nature of their structural adaptation) are examined in A. Moraru, 'Influenţa occidentală în limba română în secolul al XVIII-lea (1688–1780). Împrumuturi de origine latino-romanică' (190–226), and F. Vârban, 'Influenţa rusă asupra limbii române între 1688 şi 1780' (227–87); G. Chivu, 'Evoluţia stilurilor limbii literare' (288–330), shows how styles associated with literary, judicial-administrative, and technical writing acquired their definitive characteristics at different rates during the 18th c.

M. Avram, 'Unificarea limbii noastre literare şi cultivarea limbii în România interbelică', *LiR*, 47, 1998[2000]: 293–303. M. Anton, 'Schooling in Romanian language in the eighteenth century: attempts at its systematization', *Synthesis*, 26, 1999[2001]: 113–37.

A problem of historical phonology is addressed in C. Vătăşescu, 'Diftongul lat. *au* în română şi albaneză', *FD*, 18, 1999[2002]: 117–25, dealing with the historical significance of the fricativization of the final element of the diphthong.

A valuable survey of synthetic and analytic verb structures based on texts written between 1521 and 1780 is Ana-Maria Minuţ, *Morfosintaxa verbului în limba română veche*, Iaşi, Editura Universităţii 'Alexandru I. Cuza', 258 pp. An aspect of the history of the lexicon is studied in Aurelia Bălan-Mihailovici, **Poarta spre 'sanctuarul' limbii române: lingvistică şi istorie în studiul lexicului medieval românesc: terminologia socială*, Minerva, 448 pp. C. Vătăşescu, 'Alb. *-ullë*, rom. *-ură* în cuvinte de origine latină', *LiR*, 48, 1999[2001]: 173–78.

3. Texts

Eugen Pavel, *Carte şi tipar la Bălgrad (1567–1702)*, Cluj, Clusium, 2001, 380 pp. + 21 pls, traces the history, and linguistic and cultural significance, of a major centre for printing Romanian books in the 17th c. A. Mareş, 'Texte din nord-vestul Transilvaniei atribuite greşit secolului al XVI-lea', *LiR*, 47, 1998[2000]: 345–50, attributes 'Fragmentele de la Hălmagiu' and 'Miscelaneu de la Chişlaz' both to the second half of the 17th c. G. Mihăilă, 'Un experiment (în legătură cu transcrierea *Tetraevanghelui* de la Sibiu, 1551–1553)', *ib.*, 48, 1999[2001]: 107–16. The manuscript of an 18th-c. translation of an Italian original is the subject of Galaction Verebceanu, *Viaţa lui Bertoldo. Un vechi manuscris românesc*, Chişinău, Museum, 256 pp. The book includes an index of words (with morphological variants).

4. Orthography and Phonology

Ioana Chitoran [sic], *The Phonology of Romanian: A Constraint-Based Approach*, Berlin–New York, Mouton de Gruyter, 277 pp., is a major overview of Romanian phonology (and 'morphophonology') which caters both for readers interested in the data and for those concerned with the implications of those data from an Optimality Theoretic perspective. The work pays particular attention to the role of the syllable in Romanian phonology especially where vowel alternations, and what the author describes as its characteristic 'glide-happiness', are concerned. Laurenţia Dascălu-Jinga, *Melodia vorbirii în limba română*, Univers Enciclopedic, 2001, 184 pp., addresses the largely neglected area of Romanian intonation patterns and their associated functions and meanings, and includes observations on dialectal intonations. By the same author is *Specificul limbii române în intonaţia vorbită*, Editura Academiei Române, 26 pp. M. Mărdărescu-Teoderescu and A. Lăzăroiu, 'Consoanele fricative din limba română literară. Analiza computerizată a parametrilor acustici: *durata* şi *nivelul*', *FD*, 18, 1999[2002]: 63–92. A. Avram, 'Observaţii asupra consoanelor vibrante în română şi în albaneză', *LiR*, 48, 1999[2001]: 47–49. E. Timotin, 'Regulile ortografice din 1932. Îndreptarele din epocă', *LiL*, 47.1–2: 13–29.

5. Morphology and Syntax

Corneliu Dumitru, **Tratat de gramatică a limbii române. Sintaxa*, Iaşi, Institutul European, 749 pp. G. Pană Dindelegan, 'Formaţii substantivale recente şi rolul "clasificatorilor" în actualizarea lor contextuală', *LiR*, 48, 1999[2001]: 117–27, deals with inflectional peculiarities of recent loans.

M. Avram, 'Variante regionale ale pronumelui demonstrativ de apropiere la feminin-neutru plural', *ib.*, 15–18. I. Mărgărit, 'Pronume personale cu funcţie verbală. Noi atestări', *ib.*, 93–99, examines constructions of the type 'mi foame', 'ne bine', etc. C. Dominte, 'Pronumele negative *nimic* (studiu micromonografic)', *ib.*, 59–67.

Constantin Frâncu, *Conjunctivul românesc şi raporturile lui cu alte moduri*, Iaşi, Demiurg, 2000, 235 pp., examines in detail both historical development and modern uses of the Romanian subjunctive, paying particular attention to the relation between the subjunctive and the infinitive.

M. Maiden, 'Unicitatea structurală a limbilor romanice şi rolul limbii române în determinarea ei', Ichim, *Identitatea*, 95–102, identifies highly abstract and distinctive paradigmatic patterning which the Romanian verb shares with other Romance languages. E. Vasiliu, '[ə/e] analogic în flexiunea verbală', *LiR*, 48, 1999[2001]:171. T. Cotelnic, 'Despre verbele cu sau fără sufixele gramaticale *-ez*, *-esc*', *ib.*, 43–46, examines the intriguing problem of the lexical distribution of these 'suffixes'. S. Drincu, '"Sînt" şi "sunt"', *ib.*, 46.3–4, 2001:10–12, attributes the variant 'sunt' to Latinizing influence.

Nicolae Felecan, **Sintaxa limbii române. Teorie. Sistem. Construcţie*, Cluj, Dacia Educaţional, 313 pp. F. Dîrul, 'Legătura subordonatoare dintre cuvintele ce ţin de aceeaşi clasă categorială', *LiR*, 48, 1999[2001]:51–57. V. Ciobanu, 'Exprimarea complementului direct prin acuzativul numelor cu prepoziţia *pe* (în diacronie)', *LiR(M)*, 11, 2001:131–35, concludes that prepositional object marking predates the 16th c., but does not become the norm until the 18th. V. Motapanyane, 'Object-to-subject raising in *tough*-constructions', *RRL*, 43, 1998[2000]:35–72, relates strategies for complement object deletion to the parametric setting for structural operators, and argues that *tough*-construction effects may involve other syntactic constraints than empty operator raising. Romanian *tough*-constructions (involving supine complements with complementizer *de*) display NP-movement to object position in configurations which avoid quantification. V. Hill, 'The gray area of supine clauses', *Linguistics*, 40:495–517, analyses the Romanian supine as a [+ N] [+ V] category lacking phi-features, which makes it valid only in DP and CP constructions, and the optimal form for use in *tough*-constructions. D. Craşoveanu, 'Completiva directă introdusă prin locuţiunea conjuncţională *pentru că*', *LiL*, 46.1–2, 2001:31–38, explores, from a prescriptive perspective, the use of the type 'vă mulţumesc pentru că . . .' rather than 'vă mulţumesc că . . .'. I. Crăiniceanu, 'The semantics of English and Romanian habituals and iteratives', *RRL*, 43, 1998[2000]:56–63. L. Avram, 'Romanian *have*', *ib.*, 65–92, presents a unified analysis of *a avea* (lexical verb and auxiliary) from a minimalist perspective, arguing that its different values result from the different structural positions it occupies. *The Expression of Possession in Romance and Germanic Languages*, ed. Liliane Tasmowski, Cluj, Clusium, 2000, 226 pp., contains a number of studies dealing wholly or partly with Romanian: S. Reinheimer Rîpeanu, 'Les verbes de la possession' (1–12), reaches the surprising conclusion that in Romanian and other languages "have" is rather rarely used as a verb of possession; A. Cornilescu, 'Some "have" curiosities in Romanian' (13–27), deals with structures of the type 'Are cine pleca'; L. Avram, 'From possessive clitics to object clitics: a unifying analysis' (83–100); A. Şerbănescu, 'Dative possessive revisited' (133–47), seeks to identify the possessive dative with the Experiencer; M. van Peteghem, 'Datif possessif et inaliénabilité en français, roumain et russe' (149–62), argues that differences in the range of inalienability structures have a grammatical rather than a cognitive basis; T. Cristea, 'Structures possessives complexes en roumain et en français' (163–70), examines cases where more than one possessor and more than one 'possessee' are copresent, arguing that double-binding is expressed through strategies which obviate ambiguity; and A. Cuniţă, 'Les dictionnaires bilingues et l'expression de la possession: de quelques *métonymies intégrées*' (171–81), discusses constructions of the type 'un câine scurt de coadă'. I. Ştefănescu, 'The syntax of possessive phrases in Romanian', *RRL*, 43, 1998[2000]: 93–120, argues that possessive DPs in Romanian show AGRP recursion, and express different syntactic properties of pronominal and common/proper noun possessors. Pronominal possessors are argued to have characteristics of postnominal adjectives. N. Corver, 'Predicate displacement within the adjectival system. Evidence from degree modification in Romanian', pp. 139–56 of *Adverbial Modification*, ed. Reineke Bok-Bennema et al., Amsterdam–Atlanta, Rodopi, 2001, 208 pp., deals with the 'extrem de înaltă' type. Mihaela Secrieru, *Cumulul de funcţii sintactice în limba română ('elementul predicativ suplimentar')*, Iaşi, Editura Universităţii A. I. Cuza, 2001, 234 pp., analyses (from a diachronic as well as a synchronic perspective), the status of apparent double syntactic complements in Romanian. C. Uşurelu, 'Semantica şi sintaxa construcţiilor cauzative/factitive', *AUBLLR*, 170, 2001: 61–66, looks at Romanian causative constructions (which reveal considerably more syntactic autonomy than the French *faire* + infinitive type). A specifically Romanian thematization strategy is explored in G. Pană Dindelegan, 'Un tipar sintactic de "tematizare forte": *De văzut, am văzut destule*', *LiL*, 46.1–2, 2001: 5–14. S. Krieb, 'Poziţiile sintactice ale interjecţiilor în vorbirea populară', *ib.*, 20–30.

6. Lexicon, Phraseology, and Onomastics

Andrei Cornea, *Cuvintelnic fără frontiere*, Polirom, 197 pp., offers an entertaining and ironic perspective on the etymological significance of certain key terms in everyday political and social discourse such as 'ministru', 'crima', 'revoluţia'. M. Avram, 'Comentarii lingvistice despre *politică* şi probleme conexe', *LiR*, 48, 1999[2001]: 181–92.

Laura Manea and Elena Dănilă, *Mic dicţionar de locuţiuni ale limbii române*, Iaşi, Universitas XXI, 187 pp., is aimed at a student readership but constitutes a useful and well-referenced list of the most commonly used idioms and expressions. G. Coltun, **Frazeologia limbii române*, Chişinău, Arc, 2000, 208 pp. Raluca-Felicia Toma, *Locuţiunile. Marcă a tiparului gândirii analitice*, Târgovişte, Editura Bibliotheca, 100 pp., addresses the analysis and interpretation, from a logical-semantic perspective, of set phrases in Romanian.

D. Tufiş, 'Balkanet — tezaur lingvistic multilingv pentru limbile din Balcani', Ichim, *Identitatea*, 177–92. D. Cristea and D. Tufiş, 'Resurse lingvistice romaneşti şi tehnologii informatice aplicate limbii române', *ib.*, 193–210. Originally published in Spanish (1958–61) as a consequence of the author's exile abroad, a major (and perhaps the best) etymological dictionary of Romanian now appears in a translated and revised version in Alexandru Ciorănescu, *Dicţionarul etimologic al limbii române*, ed. Tudora Şandru Mehedinţi and Magdalena Popescu Marin, Saeculum I. O., 1055 pp. Most of the (relatively minor) revisions were made in consultation with the author, but it is a pity that a constant (if petty) irritation of the original, namely the use of an apparently Spanish rather than a Romanian alphabetical order, could not be fully revised. G. Mihăilă, *Contribuţii la etimologia limbii române*, Univers Enciclopedic, 199 pp., is divided into three sections dealing respectively with the earliest attestations of Romanian words; the etymology of some indigenous (substrate) words; the main types of southern Slav loans in Romanian. Iulia Mărgărit, *Probleme de etimologie dialectală*, Univers Enciclopedic, 179 pp., is a collection of largely unpublished notes on etymological problems principally in southern Romanian dialects, which takes a semasiological as well as an onomasiological perspective. M. Purdela Sitaru and L. Vasiluţă, *Cercetări etimologice*, Univers Enciclopedic, 179 pp., deals particularly with loans originating in varieties of German, and the role of German in conferring a 'Western' air on parts of Romanian vocabulary. A special section deals with phonological and morphological aspects of German loans in the dialect of the Banat, as an essential element in the identification of German loans in Romanian. Vasile Arvinte, *Raporturi lingvistice româno-germane. Contribuţii etimologice*, Bacău, Editura Egal, 329 pp., contains, among other things, a discussion of Germanisms in the 1688 Bucharest Bible, and constitutes an excellent overview of German influences on the Romanian lexicon. Emil Vrabie, *Etimologii româneşti şi străine*, Univers Enciclopedic, 2001, 153 pp., brings together about 160 Daco-Romanian and 150 Aromanian etymological explanations published by the author in various journals over the past forty years. Mihai Mitu, *Studii de etimologie româno-slavă*, Univers Enciclopedic, 2001, 239 pp.

G. Tohăneanu, '"E chestiune de traducere"', *LiL*, 47.3–4: 12–17, traces the history of Romanian expressions meaning 'translate', and the meanings associated with 'a traduce' as used by Caragiale. A survey of the semantics of Romanian colour terminology is F. Dimitrescu, 'Despre culori şi nu numai. Din cromatica actuală (I)', *ib.*, 21–23.

E. Buchi, 'Convergences et divergences entre les russismes du roumain et ceux des autres langues romanes', Ichim, *Identitatea*, 151–76, reaches the surprising conclusion that the stock of Russianisms distinctive of Romanian (among the Romance languages) is largely attributable to the czarist, rather than the Soviet, era.

G. Chivu, 'Neologisme latino-romanice în *glosarul* primului dicţionar academic românesc', *LiR*, 48, 1999[2001]: 35–41. Z. Mihail, 'Lat. *ARCA* "Panroman sauf roumain", şi unele concordanţe semantice sud-est europene', *ib.*, 101–06. Alexander Pele, **Perenitatea elementelor lexicale dacoromâne*, Oradea, Adsumus, 2001, 208 pp. A. Enache, 'Banca de inovaţii lingvistice', *LiR*, 48, 1999[2001]: 192–96, describes the data base of neologisms set up at the Iorgu Iordan institute. M. Popescu, 'Argument pentru o a treia ediţie a *Dicţionarului explicativ al limbii române*', *ib.*, 405–17.

Remus Creţan, **Toponimie geografică*, Timişoara, Mirton, 2000, 130 pp. Ion Nicolae and Bogdan Suditu, **Toponimia României*, Eurogena Exim, viii + 100 pp. Dumitru Loşonţi, *Toponime româneşti care descriu forme de relief*, Cluj, Clusium, 2000, 256 pp., concerns itself with names denoting raised, depressed, and level terrain. Gerhardt Hochstrasser, **Untersuchungen des Ortsnamens: Castrum de Tymes – Castrum Temesiensis – Temeschburg – Temesvár (Temeswar) – Temisvar – Tamişvar – Timişoara)*, Timişoara, Eurobit, 72 pp. Gabriela Macovei, *Tezaurul toponimic al Vrancei*, I, Domino, n.d., 473 pp., is a detailed examination of the linguistic and ethnological status of placenames of Vrancea. A. Rezeanu, 'Structuri sintactice în toponimia urbană', *LiR*, 48, 1999[2001]: 197–204. Id., 'Valori stilistice în toponimia urbană', *LiL*, 45.1–2, 2000: 18–24.

Domniţa Tomescu, *Gramatica numelor proprii în limba română*, Editura ALL, 1999, 252 pp. Aspasia Reguş, *Numele de persoană române. Perspectivă istorică*, Univers Enciclopedic, 2001, 160 pp. Corneliu Reguş, *Numele de femei în vechi acte istorice (sec. XIV-XVI)*, Mustang, 1999, 226 pp. Dumitru Loşonţi, *Soluţii şi sugestii etimologice*, Univers Eniclopedic, 2001, 219 pp., offers new interpretation of a large number of etymological problems. Simona Goicu, *Termeni creştini în onomastica românească*, Timişoara, Amphora, 1999, 234 pp.

S. Găitănaru, 'Din istoria numeralului cardinal', *LiR*, 48, 1999[2001]: 77–80. M. Saramandu, 'Numeralul – parte de vorbire eterogenă', *ib.*, 129–36. N. Ursu, 'Note etimologice: *cârneleagă* (şi it.

carnevale), *câşlegi*', *ib.*, 163–69. I. Mărgărit, 'Contribuţii etimologice pe baza textelor dialectale: *boală, gutuie*', *ib.*, 427–32. V. Ioniţă, 'Contribuţii etimologice: *senin2, seninare2*', *ib.*, 47, 1998[2000]: 337–44, disputes the claim made in *DLR* that (in the relevant senses) these two terms do not share a common etymology. I. Mărgărit, 'DR Garagánele', *ib.*, 245–50, suggests that this regional term is related to 'Cana galilei'. V. Arvinte, 'Expresia "a-i trage checocuri apilpisite" ', *LiL*, 47.1–2: 5–7, elucidates this peculiar expression, used by Caragiale, as meaning 'drink cocktails desperately/like mad', 'checocuri' deriving from a presumed French 'queue de coq' = 'cocktail'! Ivan Evseev, *Componenta mitologică a vocabularului românesc*, Editura Academiei Române, 1999, 20 pp. S. Goicu, 'Termeni pentru sărbătoarea "înalţarea domnului" ', *FD*, 18, 1999[2002]: 55–62. F. Dimitrescu, 'Materialele artificiale textile şi limba română', *LiR*, 48, 1999[2001]: 9–13. P. Zugun, 'Etimologie multiplă inclusiv românească', Ichim, *Identitatea*, 119–24, deals with the interesting problem of native Romanian lexical influences on words 'borrowed' from other languages. C. Florescu, 'Elemente lexicale ale limbajului familar românesc în context romanic', Ichim, *Identitatea*, 125–34.

The problems faced by translators in the terminological integration of Anglicisms are the subject of R. Albu, S. Spinaru, and L. C. Albu, 'Limba română, limba engleză şi integrarea europeană, perspectivă terminologică', Ichim, *Identitatea*, 69–80.

F. Dimitrescu, 'Un sufix nou şi rar: *-şima*', *LiL*, 45.1–2, 2000: 25–27, explores a new suffix, derived from 'Hiroshima'!

7. Discourse analysis, Stylistics, and Pragmatics

Vasile Arvinte, *Normele limbii literare în opera lui Ion Creangă*, Iaşi, Editura Universităţii A. I. Cuza, 292 pp., offers a wide-ranging survey of Creangă's use of Romanian. Adriana Stoichiţu-Ichim, *Vocabularul limbii române actuale. Dinamică, influenţe, creativitate*, All Educational, 2001, 158 pp., examines innovations (especially the influence of foreign languages) on Romanian since 1989. A. Şerbănescu, 'Funcţia întrebărilor în argumentaţie', *LiR*, 48, 1999[2001]: 151–61. A. Bidu-Vrănceanu, 'Mărcile stilistice (diastratice) ale lexicului specializat în Dex2', *ib.*, 19–23. C. Mărănduc, 'Mesajul-text ca macroact intenţional multiplu sau indirect', *ib.*, 393–403. V. Năstase, 'Afirmaţia sigură întărită în limba română', *ib.*, 419–25, deals also with paralinguistic means of affirmation, such as head gestures. Georgeta Ghiga, *Elemente fatice de vorbire în româna vorbită*, Alcris-M94, 1999, 256 pp. Dorin Uriţescu, *Greşeli de exprimare*, Steaua Procion, 1999,

296 pp. Anna Barbély, **Nyelvcsere. Szociolingvisztikai kutatások a magyarországi románok közösségében*, Budapest, MTA Nyelvtudományi Intézetének, 2001, 306 pp., is a sociolinguistic study of the bilingual Romanian-speaking communities of Hungary. By the same author is 'Schimbarea de cod la Românii din Ungaria —o strategie de comunicare în discursul bilingv', *LiR*, 47, 1998[2000]: 316–24. S. Găitănaru, 'Structurile prezumtive în limba română', *ib.*, 325–35, examines the type 'să fi având', 'să fi avut', etc. M. Ciolac, '*Competenţa comunicativă* în perspectivă sociolingvistică (II Componenta psiho-sociolingvistică), *FD*, 18, 1999[2002]: 39–53. M. Tiugan, 'Comportamentul verbal între libertate şi necesitate', *ib.*, 93–105, basing herself on *Texte dialectale: Muntenia III*, examines how freedom of linguistic choice and the necessity of giving a culturally correct answer conditions the individual's linguistic behaviour in the direction of a supradialectal norm. S. Dumistrăcel, 'Textul jurnalistic: un teren experimental de ambiguitate', Ichim, *Identitatea*, 135–50. V. Guţu Romalo, 'Forme ale politeţei verbale', *LiL*, 45.1–2, 2000: 5–10, deals with the range of address pronouns in Romanian.

8. Dialects

Ion Mării, *Harta lexicală semantică*, Cluj, Clusium, 189 pp., offers semasiological and onomasiological perspectives on a number of terms in the major linguistic atlases of Romania; the significance of gestures is also considered. I. A. Florea et al., 'Editarea asistată a atlaselor lingvistice şi a textelor dialectale', Ichim, *Identitatea*, 211–32. V. Neagoe, 'Din arhiva de scrisori şi documente dialectale. Texte scrise de Pătru Vlad din com. Cerbăl, jud. Hunedoara (ţinutul Pădurenilor)', *FD*, 18, 1999[2002]: 179–210, which includes a glossary of dialect terms. *Cercetări asupra graiurilor româneşti de peste hotare,* ed. Maria Marin et al., Bucureşti Noi, 2000, 144 pp., contains studies on Romanian dialects spoken in Bulgaria, Russia, Moldova, and the Ukraine. These have been previously published in other journals in the last decade, but since many of them have been relatively inaccessible in the West, it is worth mentioning some of the contents here: M. Marin, 'Iotacizarea verbelor. Reflexe şi consecinţe în unele graiuri româneşti vorbite în medii alogene' (5–9), deals with analogical reformations affecting allomorphy in the first person singular present and the subjunctive; I. Mărgărit and V. Neagoe, 'Cercetări asupra graiurilor romànşsti vorbite în nord-estul Bulgariei (regiunea Loveci)' (10–29), show that these dialects share archaizing affinities with south-east Oltenia and south-west Wallachia; V. Neagoe, 'Consideraţii asupra graiului din Apşa de Jos, raionul Teceav, regiunea transcarpatică (Ucraina)' (30–41); M. Marin, I. Mărgărit, and V. Neagoe, 'Graiuri româneşti din Ucraină şi Republica Moldova' (42–121), is a substantial overview of these varieties; V. Pavel, 'Graiuri româneşti în medii aloglote. Consideraţii sociolingvistice' (122–33); and I. Mărgărit, 'Miteluţ, miticuţ, mâţicuţ' (132–36), examines the origins of these terms, common in the Republic of Moldova and the Ukraine. Maria Marin et al., *Graiuri româneşti din Basarabia, Transnistria, Nordul Bucovinei şi nordul Maramureşului. Texte dialectale şi glosar*, 2000, xxxix + 531 pp., is of value not only for its linguistic content (much information on linguistic structures can be garnered from the glossary), but also for its sociological and ethnological information. V. Pavel, 'Graiurile româneşti de la est de Bug', Ichim, *Identitatea*, 61–68. G. Vasiliu, 'Cercetări dialectale din Sălaj – surse bibliografice pentru redactarea dicţionarului tezaur al limbii române', *Acta Musei Porolissensis*, 24:585–88. A welcome addition to the impressive body of Romanian linguistic atlases is *Atlasul Lingvistic Român pe Regiuni. Transilvania 3*, ed. Grigore Rusu, Viorel Bidian, and Dumitru Loşonţi, Editura Academiei, xxxvi + 312 pp. Adrian Turculeţ, *Graiul din zona Câmpulungului Moldovenesc. Fonetica*, Iaşi, Editura Universităţii A. I. Cuza, 497 pp. + map. Ion-Horia Bîrleanu, *Graiurile din Valea Şomuzului Mare*: I, *Formarea numelor de sate*; II, *Fonetică*, Iaşi, Sedcom Libris, 1999–2000, 202, 296 pp. The second volume includes an interesting discussion of root-stressed participles of the type 'văst' for 'văzut', for which the author proposes a phonological rather than a morphological origin. M. Vulpe (coord.), 'Noul Atlas Lingvistic Român pe Regiuni. Oltenia. Indice general', *FD*, 18, 1999[2002]:243–418, is a lexical index of the atlas. I. Mărgărit, 'Pe marginea glosarului dialectal. Muntenia', *ib.*, 153–58, deals with the terms 'Burtucală', 'Crai slozuiesc', 'Trecut'. Id. 'Consideraţii în legătură cu expresia *mii şi firimii*', *ib.*, 159–66. T. Teaha, '"Panroumain, sauf Roumain"? (Rom. dial. *gâmfá, mursecá*)', *ib.*, 167–77. A. Ulivi, 'Consoane lungi şi consoane duble în graurile dacoromâne', *ib.*, 107–16. A. Avram, 'Probleme de cronologie în legătură cu apariţia şi de evoluţia oclusivelor prepalatale în graiurile dacromâne', *ib.*, 25–38, dates prepalatal occlusives arising from palatalization of dentals to the 15th c. I. Mărgărit, 'Numeralul colectiv în graiurile din Muntenia', *LiR*, 47, 1998[2000]:330–35. T. Oancă, 'Arii dialectale ş antroponimice', *ib.*, 351–57.

P. Neiescu, 'Texte istroromâne din Jeiăn şi Suşnieviţa', *FD*, 18, 1999[2002]:211–18, has parallel Romanian translations. Petar Atanasov, *Meglenoromâna astăzi*, Editura Academiei, xii + 407 pp., is a translation and enlargement of a study published in 1989, which now includes an overview of Megleno-Romanian syntax.

LITERATURE

By Mircea Anghelescu, *Professor of Romanian Literature in the University of Bucharest*

1. Works of reference and of general interest

Dicționarul Scriitorilor Români, iv: *R–Z*, Albatros, xxxiii + 947 pp., completes the most comprehensive general dictionary of writers of Romanian literature; the volume comprises 431 entries, and each entry offers, apart from a general presentation of the works, extensive biographical and bibliographical information. There are, however, some minor omissions: for I. D. Sîrbu the year of birth, for Leonida Teodorescu the year of death, is missing; for Teodor Scorţescu there is no mention in the bibliography of a volume he published while in exile; the bibliography of the article on the writer Radu Rosetti (103) cites a study on C. A. Rosetti, etc. The dictionary was in preparation from as early as the 1970s by three university professors from Cluj, Mircea Zaciu, Marian Papahagi, and Aurel Sasu (the first two now deceased), with the co-operation of over forty specialists, mainly academics, but before 1989 was banned by state censorship. It now comprises information up to the year 1990 on over 1,600 Romanian writers, from the earliest to the contemporary, including Romanian authors from neighbouring countries and in exile. This is the most complete and best documented work of reference so far produced in the area. Also useful for a researcher of Romanian literature is *Bibliografia generală a etnografiei şi folclorului românesc*, ii, ed. Adrian Fochi et al., Saeculum I.O., 703 p., which records contributions to ethnography and folklore published in books and newspapers between 1892 and 1904. Among writers of this period active in the field are I. L. Caragiale, G. Coşbuc, B. Delavrancea, P. Dulfu, and A. Odobescu. One may also note Iordan Datcu's *Dicționarul etnologilor români*, iii, Saeculum I.O., 2001, which includes articles concerning ethnographers also known as writers such as C. Amăriuței, I. P. Culianu, D. H. Mazilu, C. Mircea, A. Popescu-Telega, I. D. Sîrbu, and others.

A dictionary of another kind is that of Doina Ruşti, *Dicționar de teme şi simboluri din literatura română*, Univers enciclopedic, 391 pp., which comprises an inventory of situations (themes such as *craving*, *love*, *hunting*, types such as *the ascetic*, *the old woman*, *the village schoolmaster*, motifs or symbols such as *the rain*, *the poplar*, *the bridge*, and so on) in approximately 300 entries that make reference to approximately 600 works of Romanian literature, inventoried in a list of titles where, strangely enough, what is missing is the authors: the list begins with

Caragiale's *Abu Hasan* (which is, however, a mere adaptation) and ends with Sadoveanu's *Zodia cancerului.*

Andrei Oişteanu, **Das Bild des Juden in der rumänischen Volkskultur ; zum Problem scheinbar positiver Vorurteile*, aus dem Englischen von Marie-Elisabeth Rehn, Konstanz, Hartung-Gorre Verlag, 66 pp. *Din istoria feminismului românesc. Antologie şi studiu (1838–1929)*, ed. Ştefania Mihăilescu, Iaşi, Polirom, 371 pp., includes texts by I. Heliade Rădulescu, Sofia Cocea, Maria Flechtenmacher, Adela Xenopol, et al.

Victor Corcheş, Gelu Culicea, and Cătălina Grideanu, *Revista Fundaţiilor Regale. Caleidoscop*, Constanţa, Europolis, 467 pp., is a bibliography of the well-known journal published in Bucharest between 1934 and 1947, with a 'chrestomathy' (37–158) of texts published in it, a selection of the papers establishing the Royal Foundation and the journal itself, a section of addenda (159–84), and an index of names (441–66).

2. Collected works, literary monographs, and criticism

Mircea Muthu, *Balcanologie*, I, Cluj-Napoca, Dacia, 192 pp., in its first part, is devoted to an inventory of themes in contemporary Romanian literature, in authors such as Eugen Barbu, Z. Stancu, Ştefan Bănulescu, Ştefan Agopian et al., and then to comparative inquiries into neighbouring literatures, in Kazantsákis, Kadare, etc. The subject comes up again, and the topic of Balkanism in Romanian literature is also investigated, in Id., *Balcanismul literar românesc*, 3 vols, Cluj-Napoca, Dacia, 283, 178, 180 pp., comprising studies grouped by category: *Etapele istorice ale conceptului* in vol. 1 , *Permanenţe literare* in vol. 2 and *Balcanitate şi balcanism* in vol. 3.

Old Romanian literature

In this field several editions of early texts or studies of old translations or adaptations which circulated in manuscript ('popular books') have been published. Among them, in a series entitled 'the oldest books in Romanian literature', came out *Texte uitate – texte regăsite*, Fundaţia Naţională pentru Ştiinţă şi Artă, 220 pp., comprising editions of and studies on some anonymous manuscripts of the 17th c. such as *Viaţa sfântului Hristofor, Pentru fulgere şi pentru tunete.* Another volume of previously unpublished texts, *Scrieri eshatologice post-bizantine*, ed., introd., and ann. Andrei Timotin and Emanuela Timotin, Fundaţia Naţională pentru Ştiinţă şi Artă, 176 pp., includes texts such as *Vedenia Sofianei, Viaţa lui Atanasie*, and *Vedenia lui chir Daniil.*

Ovidiu Moceanu, *Literatura română veche*, Braşov, Universităţii Transilvania, 206 pp., covers the 14th–16th centuries. P. Guran, 'Aspects et rôle du saint dans les nouveaux états du "commonwealth byzantin" ', pp. 45–69 of *Pouvoirs et mentalités. Textes réunis par Laurenţiu Vlad à la mémoire du Pr. Alexandru Duţu*, Babel, 1999, 476 pp., concerns the isychastic movement and the circulation of specific texts in the so-called (after the syntagm coined by D. Obolensky) 'Byzantine commonwealth' (Southern Slavs, Russians, Romanians, and the Orthodox countries of the Caucasus). Liviu Onu, *Tradiţia manuscrisă a unei sinteze europene la români: 'Mântuirea păcătoşilor'*, Academiei, 329 pp., focuses on the first translation from Greek of this text, by N. Spătarul, at the end of the 17th c., also the anonymous 1696 translation, and the one from Paleoslavonic executed at the beginning of the following century; the annexes reproduce the titles of the chapters and fragments from all versions, for better comparison. Dan Buciumeanu, *Dosoftei. O hermeneutică a 'Psaltirii în versuri'*, Viitorul românesc, n.d., 439 pp., includes chapters such as: 'Psaltirea în versuri' ca operă simbolică', 'Geneza stilului poetic', 'Imaginarul "Psaltirii în versuri" ', 'Posteritatea operei poetice a lui Dosoftei', etc.. Cristina Dobre-Bogdan, *'Imago mortis' în cultura română veche (sec. XVII-XIX)*, pref. Dan Horia Mazilu, Universităţii din Bucureşti, 232 pp., draws on funeral orations, Church orders, memorials, funeral poems, chronicles etc., to trace her theme. Her Romanian text is accompanied by a summary in French. D. H. Mazilu, 'Despre *Viaţa sfinţilor Varlaam şi Ioasaf*', pp. 391–95 of *Omagiu. Virgil Cândea la 75 de ani*, ed. Paul H. Stahl, IV, gives a brief synthesis of studies concerning the originals from which the legend was translated and adapted on Romanian soil. C. Velculescu, 'Über Blitz-Donner-Blitzschlag in Rumänischen Handschriften', *ib.*, II, 371–84. F. Zgraon, 'Direcţii de difuzare a *Alexandriei* şi cele mai vechi redacţii care au circulat în spaţiul dacoromanic', *ib.*, II, 415–29. Dragoş Şesan, *Noul Testament de la Bălgrad (1648)*, Braşov, Pentru Viaţă, 274 pp., comprises chapters on bishop Simion Ştefan, on the prefaces to previous translations of the New Testament, on marginal glosses of the text. D. Zamfirescu, 'Neagoe Basarab şi Niccolò Machiavelli', pp. 266–71 of *Cultura română – sinteză europeană*, Bucureşti–Chişinău, Litera internaţional.

EIGHTEENTH CENTURY

This year has seen a considerable crop of items relating to Dimitrie Cantemir. Gabriel Mihăilescu, *Universul baroc al 'Istoriei ieroglifice'. Între retorică şi imaginar*, Fundaţia Naţională pentru Ştiinţă şi Artă, 271 pp., originally a Ph.D. thesis, provides an analysis of the relation between the imaginary and rhetoric in Cantemir's novel. Dragoş Moldovan,

Dimitrie Cantemir între umanism şi baroc, Iaşi, Universităţii 'A. I. Cuza', 300 pp., studies the typology of Cantemir's style from the perspective of the dominant rhetorical figure. E. Sorohan, 'Dimitrie Cantemir, imaginarul anti-utopic', pp. 245–56 of *Omagiu. Virgil Cândea la 75 de ani*, cit., II. V. P. Stancu, 'Paratext şi alegorie la Dimitrie Cantemir şi Ion Budai-Deleanu', *ib.*, 267–80. S. Ştefănescu, 'Dimitrie Cantemir şi metoda în istorie', *ib.*, 313–20. P. Cernovodeanu, 'Dimitrie Cantemir la Constantinopol (1700–1710). Activitatea politică şi culturală', *ib.*, I, 143–52. M. Mitu, 'Dimitrie Cantemir în context cultural româno-polon (date şi interpretări noi)', *ib.*, II, 17–30, covering 'Limba polonă în cultura lingvistică a lui Cantemir', 'Sursele de informare poloneze', and 'Cantemir în posteritatea poloneză)'. G. Mihăilă, 'Antioche Cantemir, biographe de son père, Démètre Cantemir', *ib.*, I, 431–47.

NINETEENTH CENTURY

Two general studies relating to Romanticism are: M. Anghelescu, 'Le brave d'autrefois, héros des romantiques roumains', pp. 260–69 of *Mythes et symboles politiques en Europe Centrale*, ed. Chantal Delsol, Michel Maslowski, and Joanna Nowicki, Paris, PUF; and I. Bot, 'Le modèle français dans la poésie patriotique roumaine de 1848. Le cas de Lamartine', pp. 251–61 of *La révolution de 1848. La France et l'identité nationale roumaine*, ed. Ramona Bordei-Boca, Dijon U.P.

ARICESCU. Constantin D. Aricescu, *Memoriile mele*, ed., ann., and pref. Liviu Petreanu, Profile Publishing, 214 pp.

CARAGIALE. Ion Luca Caragiale, *Opere*, IV, ed. and ann. Stancu Ilin and Constantin Hârlav, Univers enciclopedic, 1189 pp., containing the correspondence, is the last volume in this edition of the author's complete works. *Dicţionarul personajelor din opera lui Caragiale*, ed. C. Cubleşan, Cluj-Napoca, Dacia, 313 pp., is rich in references to the stage history of the plays. Ioan Derşidan, *Nordul caragialian. Periplul versiunilor*, Univers enciclopedic, 220 pp. Dorina Grăsoiu, *Caragiale în presa vremii*, Jurnalul literar, 175 pp. Ieronim Tătaru, *Conexiuni şi confluenţe*, Ploieşti, Premier, 312 pp., for Caragiale has the chapters 'Traduceri caragialiene din E. A. Poe' and 'Caragiale şi Emil Cioran', while Constantin Trandafir, *Efectul Caragiale*, Vestala, 207 pp., includes among others chapters on '"Un om cît o lume"', 'Atitudinea Caragiale', 'Delicate lucruri vechi şi noi', 'Lumea ca spectacol', 'Modelul şi strategiile'. Ion Vartic, *Clanul Caragiale*, Cluj-Napoca, Biblioteca Apostrof, 212 pp., is an analysis of C.'s works through his biography: special attention is paid to the relation of the writer to Transylvania and Transylvanian writers, especially those from Cluj.

CREANGĂ. Mircea A. Diaconu, *Ion Creangă. Nonconformism şi gratuitate*, Cluj-Napoca, Dacia, 203 pp. Dan Grădinaru, *Creangă. Monografie*, Allfa, 476 pp., contains chapters on the art of dissimulation, on the epic cycles of the 'mother' (1874–78) and 'father' (1880–88), on the writer's art, his relation to Caragiale, etc. D. Zamfirescu, 'Universalitatea lui Creangă', pp. 216–64 of the cit. vol. *Cultura română – sinteză europeană*.

EMINESCU. Constantin Cubleşan, *Eminescu în oglinzile criticii*, I, Cluj-Napoca, Dacia, 2001, 230 pp., presents a selection of texts by Romanian and foreign critics. *Detractorii lui Eminescu*, I, ed. and pref. Alexandru Dobrescu, Iaşi, Junimea, xliv + 337 pp., includes texts by P. Grădişteanu, A. Grama, G. Gellianu, A. Densusianu, and A. Demetriescu. *Corpusul receptării critice a operei lui M. Eminescu. Secolul XIX*, ed. Ionel Oprişan and Theodor Vârgolici, 3 vols, Saeculum I.O., 399, 431, 447 pp., is probably comprehensive in its coverage of the 19th-c. reception of Eminescu's poetry, including the uncomprehending and the negative as well as the positive response. *Mihai Eminescu, poet naţional român. Istoria şi anatomia unui mit cultural*, ed. Ioana Bot, Cluj-Napoca, Dacia, 319 pp., includes the studies ' "Eminescu" – arheologia unui mit cultural', 'Nebunia – dimensiune esenţială a mitului eminescian', and 'Eminescu în manualele şcolare' presenting Eminescu as interpreted by Eliade, Culianu, Vitner, and others. George Gană, *Melancolia lui Eminescu*, Fundaţiei Culturale Române, 335 pp., is an important study of E.'s work from the perspective of the dominant feeling, comprising nine chapters whose titles are so many quotations: ' "Dar eu sunt melancolic . . ." ', ' "Căci ce-i poetu-n lume şi astăzi ce-i poetul?" ', "Alte măşti . . .", etc. Ilina Gregori, 'Eminescu la Berlin', pp. 1–132 of her *Studii literare*, pref. M. Martin, Fundaţiei Culturale Române. George Lateş, *Eminescu, orfism şi gnomism*, Junimea, Iaşi, 2001, 284 pp. Leca Morariu, *Eminescu. Note pentru o monografie*, ed. Liviu Papuc with pref. and bibliography, Iaşi, Timpul, 2001, 238 pp., contains articles published by the author in journals between the wars: 'Obîrşia lui Eminescu', 'Mărturii noi despre studentul Eminescu', 'Eminescu şi Veronica Micle', 'Eminescu în nemţeşte', etc. Vasile Voia, *Aspectele ale comparatismului românesc*, Cluj-Napoca, Dacia, 239 pp., inappropriately entitled, comprises studies on Romanian authors seen from a comparatist perspective, but most are focused on Eminescu: Eminescu and the myth of Ondine, Kant and Eminescu, the reception of Eminescu by German readers: 'floare albastră', etc. I. Bot, 'Mihai Eminescu, un mythe culturel', pp. 269–81 of *Mythes et symboles politiques en Europe Centrale*, cit.

HASDEU. Bogdan Petriceicu Hasdeu, *Studii şi articole de economie politică*, ed. Ionel Oprişan, Saeculum I.O., 303 pp., is an addendum to his *Publicistica politică*.

HELIADE RĂDULESCU. Ion Heliade Rădulescu, *Opere*, ed., ann., pref. Mircea Anghelescu, 2 vols, Univers enciclopedic, lxiv + 1301, 1078 pp., includes (vol. 1) the works H. published in French during his exile in Paris: *Le Protectorat du Czar ou la Roumanie et la Russie*, *Souvenirs et impressions d'un proscrit*, and *Mémoires sur l'histoire de la regénération roumaine ou sur les événements de 1848*.

MACEDONSKI. C. M. Spiridon, 'Macedonski, adversarul lui Eminescu', pp. 244–54 of *Atitudini literare*, Cartea românească, II.

MAIORESCU. Constantin Popescu-Cadem, *Titu Maiorescu. Date biografice*, Caritas, xxvi + 326 pp. + 8 pls.

POP. Pavel Ţugui, 'Vasile Gr. Pop, istoric literar', pp. 226–40 of his *Bucovina. Istorie şi cultură*, Albatros.

PUMNUL. Ilie Rad, *Aron Pumnul. 1818–1866*, Cluj-Napoca, Centrul de Studii Transilvane, 280 pp.

SBIERA. Pavel Ţugui, 'I. G. Sbiera, animator cultural, profesor şi istoric literar' and 'Cîteva observaţii asupra scrierilor lui I. G. Sbiera', respectively pp. 151–215 and 216–25 of his *Bucovina. Istorie şi cultură*, cit.

VĂCĂRESCU. Victor Petrescu, *Iancu Văcărescu*, Ager, 152 pp.

VULCAN. Iosif Vulcan, *Însemnări de călătorie*, II, ed. and ann. L. Drimba, Fundaţia Naţională pentru Ştiinţă şi Artă, 356 pp.

TWENTIETH CENTURY

SYNTHESES. Ion Bogdan Lefter, *Anii '60–'90. Critica literară*, Piteşti, Paralela 45, 504 pp., is the sketch of a projected history of literary criticism in the second half of the 20th century, containing chapters on critics in exile, literary historians, literary critics, and essayists. Florin Mihăilescu, *De la proletcultism la postmodernism*, Constanţa, Pontica, 327 pp., groups the studies it contains in three sections: *Fundamentele proletcultismului*, *Între sincronism şi protocronism* (the two tendencies manifest in Romanian literature in the second half of the 20th century: the pro-and anti-Western, respectively inspired by E. Lovinescu and E. Papu), and *Fundamentele postmodernismului*. Eugen Negrici, *Literatura română sub comunism. Proza*, Editura Fundaţiei Pro, 407 pp., without truly being a history of literature between 1946 and 1989, analyses its evolution in relation to official ideology and its pressures: censorship, indirect forms of manipulation, party propaganda, etc. Nicolae Creţu, *Timpul lecturii. Selecţie de cronicar*, Cluj-Napoca, Dacia, 361 pp., groups literary reviews according to the reviewers' generation: 'the war generation', 'the generation of the '60s-'70s', etc. Luca Piţu, *Temele deocheate ale timpului nostru*, Piteşti, Paralela 45, 286 pp., gathers poems and pamphlets on contemporary authors. Gabriela Groza, *Presa arădană post-decembristă (1989–2001)*,

Arad, Fundaţia Culturală Ioan Slavici, 98 pp., with a preface by Emil Şimăndan.

ROMANIAN EXILES. *Caiete de dor*, II, ed. and ann. Mihaela Constantinescu-Podocea and Nicolae Florescu, Jurnalul literar, 200 pp., contains 1952 issues 5 and 6 of the journal of Romanian exiles in Paris, ed. V. Ierunca and C. Amăriuţei). Florin Ţurcanu, 'Une correspondance inédite autour de la revue *Luceafărul* (1948–1949)', pp. 191–216 of *Pouvoirs et mentalités*, cit. above, draws on correspondence between Mircea Eliade, Vintilă Horia, and Alessandru Busuioceanu preserved among the Busuioceanu Papers at the Bucharest State Archive and relating to a journal published by a group of exiled Romanian writers. Georgeta Adam and Ioan Adam, *Proba exilului*, Viitorul românesc, 315 pp., consists of interviews with various Romanian writers in exile: Vona, Stolojan, Balotă, Mariana Şora, et al. Eva Behring, *Rumänische Schriftsteller im Exil, 1945–1989*, Stuttgart, Steiner, 209 pp., an overview of the rich literature of post-WW2 Romanian exile, combines a historical outline of the three 'waves' of emigration with analytical forays into the works of five representative authors: Mircea Eliade, Paul Goma, Ion Caraion, Norman Manea and Dumitru Þepeneag. (A slightly different Romanian version was published by the Romanian Cultural Foundation in 2001.) Theodor Cazaban, *Eseuri şi cronici literare*, Jurnalul literar, 173 pp., contains essays and articles published in exile journals. Titu Popescu, *Din perspectiva exilului*, Cluj-Napoca, Dacia, 186 pp., includes studies of, among others, Horia Stamatu and Ioan Petru Culianu.

BESSARABIA. *Lumini modelatoare. Legături literar-spirituale între Moldova (Basarabia) şi Ardeal*, ed. Institute for Literature and Folklore of the Academy of Moldavia, Fundaţiei Culturale Române, 179 pp., includes, inter alia, A. Ciobanu-Tofan, 'Atitudini regionaliste în literatura română din Basarabia interbelică'; A. Burlacu, 'Liviu Rebreanu şi începuturile romanului basarabean'; and M. Cimpoi, 'Lumini modelatoare: Lucian Blaga şi Basarabia'. On Bessarabian literature between the wars is A. Burlacu, 'Poezia basarabeană: Arcadia în negativ', *Metaliteratură. Analele Facultăţii de filologie, Universitatea de Stat 'Ion Creangă' din Chişinău*, 2, 2001 : 62–69.

On memorial literature and, more generally, on writing in the field of biographical documents I note Eugen Simion, *Genurile biograficului*, Univers enciclopedic, 288 pp.

A fi conservator, ed. Ioan Stanomir and Laurenţiu Vlad, Universitatea din Bucureşti, 525 pp., an anthology with commentary and bibliography, is the first collection of classic texts of Romanian conservative ideology, including excerpts from Maiorescu, Heliade Rădulescu, Eminescu, Iorga, Caragiale, et al.

ADAMEŞTEANU. Nicolas Popa, 'Masque et totalitarisme dans *Matinée perdue* de Gabriela Adameşteano', pp. 103–10 of *Masque et carnaval dans la littérature européenne*, ed. Edward Welch, Paris, L'Harmattan, papers delivered at a colloquium in Ljubljana, July 2000.

ARGHEZI. C. M. Spiridon, 'Testamentul artistic arghezian', pp. 114–24 of *Atitudini literare*, II, cited above.

BACOVIA. Five hitherto unpublished texts by George Bacovia (†1957), 'Sunt', 'Dialog', 'Tăcere de savant', 'Oameni civilizaţi', and 'Consideraţii finale', *Manuscriptum*, 31, 2001 : 17–21, are introduced by M. Coloşenco.

BĂNULESCU. In Georgeta Horodincă, *Ştefan Bănulescu sau ipotezele scrisului*, Du Style, 301 pp., the author (who has lived in Paris for thirty years) starts from her experience as a translator of Bănulescu's books into French and reads his prose from the perspective of one who must grasp all the hints and nuances of the text. An important chapter is devoted to presenting Bănulescu within an autochtonous tradition going back to the early 19th c.: Negruzzi, Filimon, Odobescu, among others.

BIBESCU. Dumitru Hîncu, *Martha Bibescu. Intrigă fără iubire*, Vivaldi, 154 pp., is about the accusations brought against the writer concerning her activities before and during WW I. The book opens with an unfortunate blunder: the title of the newspaper article, *Vingt ans avant*, given in facsimile, is translated as 'După douăzeci de ani . . .' – 'After twenty years'.

CARAGIALE. Ion Iovănel, *Mateiu Caragiale. Portretul unui dandy român*, Compania, 171 pp., is a documented biography drawing on a large number of MS sources and attempting to identify the originals of characters in the writer's work.

CĂLINESCU. George Călinescu, *Opere*, III-IV, ed. and ann. N. Mecu, textual apparatus by Laurentiu Hanganu and Nicolae Mecu, Fundaţia Naţională pentru Ştiinţă şi Artă, vii + 401, 430 pp., include the novel *Bietul Ioanide* (published 1953) in the original version, as it was prior to censorship). E. Simion, 'Portretul lui Maiorescu desenat de G. Călinescu' and 'Călinescu şi ideea de biografie', pp. 177–85 and 186–96 of the cit. vol. *Genurile biograficului*. Larisa Casangiu and Marin Iancu, *Dicţionar de personaje călinesciene*, Sigma, 2001, 126 pp., contains a study and brief records of 149 characters in the writer's fictional work, some of them present in several of his novels.

COTRUŞ. Aron Cotruş, *Opere*, II, ed. and ann. Alexandru Ruja, Fundaţia Naţională pentru Ştiinţă şi Artă, x + 303 pp., contains verse from the volumes *Neguri albe* (1920), *Versuri* (1925), *În robia lor* (1926), *Cuvinte către ţăran* (1928).

ELIADE. Matei Călinescu, *Despre Ioan P. Culianu şi Mircea Eliade. Amintiri, lecturi reflecţii*, Iaşi, Polirom, 231 pp., has chapters on Ionesco and Eliade, Eliade and Sebastian, Eliade and Jung, the fantastic in the works of Eliade, etc. Mircea Handoca, *Eliade şi Noica*, Cluj-Napoca, Dacia, 261 pp., contains 19 essays including studies of his relations with L. Rebreanu and Haig Acterian, as well as C. Noica, of the reception of his work in Romania and Italy, of his posthumous writings, etc. I. Gregori, 'Mircea Eliade: trei analize', pp. 135–207 of *Studii literare*, Fundaţiei Culturale Române, comprises the chapters 'Fantasticul în proza lui M. Eliade', 'M. Eliade: fantasticul şi metaforica exilului' and 'Intimităţi şi intimitate: diaristica lui M. Eliade'. Alexandra Laignel-Lavastine, *Cioran, Eliade, Ionesco: l'oubli du fascisme. Trois intellectuels roumains dans la tourmente du siècle*, Paris, PUF, 553 pp., addresses inter alia 'Aspects d'un mythe. Les années trente', 'Anatomie d'un engagement: un historien de la religion au service de la révolution nationale', and 'Eugène Ionesco face aux rhinocéros'.

FUNDOIANU. *Cahiers Benjamin Fondane*, 5, 2001–2002, Paris–Jerusalem, contains texts translated into French for the first time ('Une nouvelle idole logique: la relativité', 'Théophile Gautier', etc.); letters to his family edited by Leon Volovici from originals in a private collection in Romania; papers delivered at the colloquium *De la Fundoianu spre Fondane*, held at Peyresq between 19 and 25 August 2001; a study by Xavier Accart on Fundoianu and René Guénon; and notes, reviews, bibliography. Ramona Fotiade, **Conceptions of the Absurd. From Surrealism to the Existential Thought of Chestov and Fondane*, OUP, 2001, 259 pp. M. Cârneci, 'Fondane şi Celan', pp. 119–26 of *Poetrix. Texte despre poezie poezie şi alte eseuri*, Piteşti, Paralela 45; E. Moangă, 'B. Fundoianu: privelişti şi lumini', *Caietele Institutului Catolic*, 1.1 : 134–39.

GALACTION. Gala Galaction, *Opere*, VII, ed. and ann. Theodor Vârgolici, Fundaţia Naţională pentru Ştiinţă şi Artă, 334 pp., contains the writer's articles and essays published between 1896 and 1918.

GOMA. Eugen Simion, 'Ficţiunea autobiografică: "Din calidor" ', in his *Genurile biograficului*, cited above, pp. 122–27.

IONESCU, E. Laura Pavel, *Ionesco. Anti-lumea unui sceptic*, Piteşti, Paralela 45, 312 pp., has chapters on Judaic ethics, representation and Don-Quixotism, neo-Gothic theatre, the parody of tragedy, etc. Alexandra Laignel-Lavastine, *Eliade, Cioran, Ionesco: l'oubli du fascisme*, cited under ELIADE above.

IONESCU, N. Dora Mezdrea, *Nae Ionescu. Biografia*, II, Acvila, 618 pp., completes a biography of the right-wing ideologist of the interwar years (the first part of which was published in 2000) with chapters on his activity as Conta's publisher, as editor of the journal

Ideea europeană and as mentor of the influential newspaper *Cuvîntul*, etc.

ISOPESCU. Pavel Ţugui, 'Claudiu Isopescu animatorul traducerii în italiană a literaturii române', pp. 364–402 of *Bucovina* cited above, brings many previously unpublished documents to light.

LOVINESCU. Eugen Lovinescu, *Sburătorul. Agende literare*, VI, ed. Monica Lovinescu and Gabriela Omăt, ann. Alexandru George, Margareta Feraru, and Gabriela Omăt, postface by Gabriela Omăt, Fundaţia Naţională pentru Ştiinţă şi Artă, 707 pp., completes the edition with the critic's notes from 1940 to 12 July 1943, less than a week before his death.

MANOLESCU. Nicolae Manolescu, *Cititul şi scrisul*, Iaşi, Polirom, 347 pp., is a volume of memoirs focusing on childhood and childhood reading.

ORNEA. *Zigu Ornea — permanenţa cărturarului*, ed. Geo Şerban, Hasefer, 432 pp., a tribute to the deceased literary critic and historian, comprises texts by A. Marino, A. Buzura, L. Ciocârlie, N. Manolescu, M. Anghelescu, R. Cosaşu, and others.

PALEOLOGU. Alexandru Paleologu, *Sfidarea memoriei. Convorbiri cu Stelian Tănase*, Cluj-Napoca, Dacia, 232 pp.

PAPADAT-BENGESCU. Eugenia Tudor-Anton, *Hortensia Papadat-Bengescu, marea europeană*, Naţional, 2001, 112 pp.

PETRESCU. Radu Petrescu, *Prizonier al provizoratului. Jurnal 1957–1970*, ed. Ruxandra Mihăilă, ann. Adela Petrescu, Piteşti, Paralela 45, 448 pp.

PHILIPPIDE. Ioana Lipovanu, *Eseistica lui Alexandru A. Philippide. Critica ideilor în context românesc şi universal*, Ars Docendi, 406 pp.

POPA. R. Zăstroiu, 'Portretul unui necunoscut. N. I. Popa, publicist', *Anuar de lingvistică şi istorie literară* (Iaşi), 34–38, 1994–98 : 57–64, looks at the journalism of N. I. Popa (professor of French and Comparative Literature at the University of Iaşi).

PREDA. In Marin Preda, *Opere*, ed. and ann. Victor Crăciun, pref. Eugen Simion, 3 vols, Univers enciclopedic, cxiv + 1358, 1733, 1660 pp., the first volume contains short stories and the first part of the novel *Moromeţii*, the second volume the second part of *Moromeţii*, and *Risipitorii*, *Intrusul*, *Marele singuratic*), the third volume the novels *Delirul* and *Cel mai iubit dintre pământeni*.

REBREANU. Liviu Rebreanu, *Opere*, XXI, ed. and ann. Niculae Gheran, Fundaţia Naţională pentru Ştiinţă şi Artă, xvii + 463 pp., contains the writer's correspondence with his family.

SADOVEANU, I. Izabela Sadoveanu, *Cărţi şi idei. Pagini de critică literară*, II, ed. Margareta Feraru, Fundaţia Naţională pentru Ştiinţă şi Artă, 358 pp.

SADOVANEAU, M. P. Şeicaru, 'Mihail Sadoveanu', pp. 159–99 of *Scrieri din exil*, II, cited below. L. Maniu, ' "Fenomenul Sadoveanu" în viziunea lui C. Ciopraga', *Anuar de lingvistică şi istorie literară*, 39–38, 1944–98: 13–22.

SEBASTIAN. Mihail Sebastian, *Jurnal de epocă. Publicistică*, ed. Cornelia Ştefănescu, Fundaţia Naţională pentru Ştiinţă şi Artă, 665 pp., reproduces texts published in the magazines *Rampa, Tiparniţa literară, Reporter, Revista Fundaţiilor Regale*, etc. Mihail Sebastian, *Convorbiri cu ...*, Universal Dalsi, 120 pp., ed. Geo Şerban, collects interviews given to Sebastian in 1935 by such writers as Arghezi, Rebreanu, or Stere. Two letters, from 1942 and 1943, are published with an introd. in A. Goci, 'Epistolar: M. Sebastian către Martha Bibescu', *Manuscriptum*, 31, 2001: 164–67.

SORESCU. Marin Sorescu, *Opere*, I-II: *Poezii*, ed. and ann. (with a chronology) Mihaela Constantinescu-Podocea, pref. Eugen Simion, Univers enciclopedic, lxxix + 1816, 1830 pp., contain the entire corpus of S.'s poetry, including one section of verse from periodicals and another of posthumous texts. H. Fassel, 'West-östliche Clownerien. Marin Sorescu und die deutsche Sorescu-Rezeption', *Anuar de linguistică şi istorie literară*, 39–38, 1944–98: 147–61.

STAMATU. T. Popescu, 'Poetul Horia Stamatu', pp. 522–120 of *Din perspectiva exilului*, cit. above.

STĂNESCU. Nichita Stănescu, *Opere*, ed. and ann. M. Coloşenco, pref. Eugen Simion, 3 vols, Univers Enciclopedic, xci + 1320, 1280, 1384 pp. Horia Avrămuţ, *Nichita Stănescu în Sinele tragic*, Universitatea 'Al. I. Cuza' din Iaşi, Iaşi, 181 pp., includes inter alia chapters on 'Raportarea la canon', 'Visul din vis', 'Intrarea în labirint', 'Magia gnozei', and 'Estetica imperfecţiei'.

ŞEICARU. In Pamfil Şeicaru, *Scrieri din exil*, ed. Ion Opraşan, 2 vols, Saeculum I.O., 537, 415 pp., I: *Figuri din lumea literară*, comprises memoirs and pamphlets on Arghezi, Sadoveanu, Lovinescu, Karnabatt, Panait Istrati, Busuiceanu, and others, while II, *Portrete politice*, also includes a number of texts devoted to such figures as Argetoianu, Ralea, Stere, and Iorga.

VIANU. Ion Ianoşi, ' "Ultimul" Vianu', pp. 421–59 of *Prejudecăţi şi judecăţi*, Hasefer.

XI. RHETO-ROMANCE STUDIES

By Ingmar Söhrman, *Göteborg University*

1. Bibliographical and General

Of interest, as ever, although published relatively late, is the overview: Mark Janse and Sijmen Tol, *Bibliographie linguistique / Linguistic Bibliography. Année 1997 et compléments des années précédentes / Year 1997 and supplements for Previous Years*, Dordrecht–Boston–Lancaster, 2001, pp. 552–57. At an 'inter-Ladin' conference held at Villa Manin, Passariano, delegates representing the three Rheto-Romance linguistic groups signed a declaration of unity calling for recognition and respect based on the European Charter on regional and minority languages. Attention was focused particularly on the linguistic situation in Friuli. See 'Document finâl dai partecipants al Congrès inter-ladin 2001 ai 23, 24, 25 di november, a Vile Manin di Passarian (Friûl)', *Ladinia*, 24–25, 2000–2001[2002]:447–49. H. Goebl, 'Externe Sprachgeschichte des Rätoromanischen (Bündnerromanisch, Dolomitenladinisch, Friaulisch). Ein Überblick', *ib.*, 199–249, provides a very good overview of the linguistic situation in the three Rheto-Romance regions. All three varieties are presented from the same perspectives: geography, political history, sociolinguistics, language contacts, oldest texts, and standardization, as well as lexicography and the history of grammars. The article includes maps and an extensive bibliography. Joachim Grzega, *Romanica Gallica Cisalpina. Etymologisch-Geolinguistische Studien zur Oberitalienisch-Rätoromanischen Keltizismen* (ZRP Beih. 311), Tübingen, Niemeyer, 2001, viii + 342 pp., offers a wide-ranging and thorough account of Celtic influence on the Rheto-Romance languages and northern Italian dialects. The present situation of Ladin and Friulan is also discussed in D. Kattenbusch, 'Zum Stand der Kodifizierung von Regional- und Minderheitssprachen in Spanien, Frankreich und Italien', pp. 207–25 of *Linguistica romanica et indiana. Festschrift für Wolf Dietrich zum 60. Geburtstag*, ed. Bruno Staib, Tübingen, Narr, 2000. Short bibliographies are to be found in the *MLA International Bibliography of Books and Articles on the Modern Languages and Literatures*, III: *Linguistics*, 242–44, and in K. H. Rogers, 'Current studies in Rhaeto-Romance linguistics', *CRLN*, 49, 2000:63–66. P. Videsott, 'La palatalizzazione di CA e GA nell'arco alpino centrale. Un contributo alla delimitazione dei confini dell'Italia linguistica dell'anno 1000', *VR*, 60, 2001:25–50, discusses the intriguing problem of palatalization in Italy's Rheto-Romance varieties.

2. Ladin

BIBLIOGRAPHICAL AND GENERAL. A number of interesting contributions are gathered in *Pellegrini Vol.* In H. Dorsch, 'Ein Hochzeitsgedicht von Antoine Agreiter aus dem Jahre 1838', *Ladinia*, 24–25, 2000–2001[2002]: 145–55, folk poetry provides testimony of early attempts to write a language and archaic orthography, phonology, and vocabulary are commented upon. L. Craffonara, 'Die Studentenverbindung "Ladinia" (1910–1920), ihr Wappen und ihre Zeitschrift', *ib.*, 157–98, presents a student society and its work in promoting Ladin and Ladin culture at the beginning of the 20th c. A very useful short summary of the present situation of standard Ladin is Erwin Valenti, *Ladin Standard. N lingaz scrit unitar per i ladins dles Dolomites*, Vich, ICLMF — San Martin de Tor, ICLMR, 24 pp. He also discusses future prospects in the light of the present availability of linguistic resources in standard Ladin. An updated and very full bibliography of what has been written on Ladin of late is P. Videsott, 'Dolomitenladinische linguistische Bibliographie 1999 – 2000 – 2001', *Ladinia*, 24–25, 2000–2001[2002]: 452–67.

MORPHOSYNTAX. An interesting syntactic problem is put in focus in S. Thiele, 'Die Gadertalischen und Grödnerischen Personalpronomina', *Ladinia*, 24–25, 2000–01[2002]: 251–86, discussing the position and possible doubling of clitics in two varieties of Ladin. In a short space she gives many variants and compares the situation with other Romance languages, showing that these systems are far more complex than those of Spanish or Italian. The use of subject pronouns is also discussed, as is the non-existence of congruence between a verb and a post-positioned nominal syntagm as a subject. Thiele's interest in the pronominal system goes much further than the former article might lead the reader to believe. She has also published an in-depth study of the topic: *Gadertalische und grödnerische Pronominalsyntax*, Münster, Münsterische Beiträge zur Romanischen Philologie, 2001, 150 pp. Cecilia Poletto, *The Higher Functional Field: Evidence from Northern Italian Dialects*, NY, OUP, 207 pp., also discusses some aspects of Ladin syntax.

ONOMASTICS AND LEXIS. P. Anreiter, *'Der Ostalpenraum im Spiegel vordeutscher Namen', *Namenkundliche Informationen*, 79–80, 2001: 89–123. An interesting aspect of the production of linguistic atlases today is the handy use of computer technology, which is discussed in R. Bauer and H. Goebl, 'Utilisation nouvelle de l'informatique dans les atlas linguistiques en Europe (1980–2000)', *Verbum*, 22, 2000: 169–86. Bauer and Goebl, together with Edgar Haimerl, have put their ideas into practice in the computerized version of the first volume of their Ladin linguistic atlas (see *YWMLS*,

63:563), **ALD I – CD-ROM I: CARD, IRS, Atlante Sonoro (cartine 439–844)*, Salzburg, Institut für Romanistik, 1999–2000. M. Besse, 'Artifizielle und genuine toponomische Namenpaare in Südtirol', *BNF*, 36, 2001:299–334, furnishes us with an interesting analysis of toponomic creativity. C. Cima, 'Una particolare toponomastica dolomitica: alcune considerazioni', *AAA*, 93–94:89–95, makes some interesting remarks on mountain toponyms. A substantial dictionary of Val Gardena Ladin is published by Marco Forni, *Wörterbuch Deutsch–Grödner-Ladinisch / Vocabuler Tudësch–Ladin de Gherdëina*, San Martin de Tor, ICLMR, 672 pp. It gives more than 18,000 German entries and some 55,000 Val Gardena forms. It not only provides Gardena Ladin with an extensive standard work of reference but is also a valuable tool for the normalization of Ladin. It is easy to use and lives up to its declared aims. The SPELL project (Servisc de Planificazion y colaborazion dl Lingaz Ladin) has now started to produce some serious and useful tools for Ladin speakers and linguists dealing with this language and its varieties. F. Ghetta, 'Vial dal pan o Troi pagan', *Mondo Ladino*, 24, 2000:169–76, discusses the possible origin of the word *pan* in the flower name *Vial dal pan* <PAGUS. Aspects of the elaboration of his magnum opus, the Ladin linguistic atlas, are presented by H. Goebl, 'Introductio ALD-I revisionato da Roland Bauer', *Europa Ethnica*, 57, 2000:64–73. L. Guglielmi, *'Il problema dei confini della Marmolada. L'apporto della linguistica', *Pellegrini Vol.*, 161–67. The very name of the journal is discussed in C. Kollmann, *'Der Name "Schlern"', *Der Schlern*, 75, 2001:974–91. A facsimile edition of a 1953 MS now in the custody of Dr Edgar Moroder is *Wörterbuch Deutsch–Grödnerisch v. Gottfried Moroder Diss*, 2 vols, San Martin de Tor, ICLMR, 212, 338 pp. The original text has been slightly modified as to size and in the use of black and white photography. The pages are not numbered, but that is of little or no importance for the usefulness of the dictionary: a valuable tool for the researcher but not suitable for general consultation since the handwriting, though neat, may be liable to misreading. Marco Forni has used the text as a source for his dictionary. Two lexical variations are confronted in V. Palabazzer, 'Vicende di parole: *bolgia* e *bolga*', *Pellegrini Vol.*, 175–78. G. A. Plangg, *'Nomi ladini e toponimi nelle leggende dolomitiche', *ib.*, 53–64. In another study P. focuses on the toponyms of Mazzin: Id., *'Ladinische Ortnamenbildungen in Mazzin (Fassa)', *AAA*, 93–94, 1999–2000:341–51. The vocabulary of Cortina d'Ampezzo is briefly looked at in G. B. Pellegrini and E. Croatto, *'Sul lessico dialettale di Cortina d'Ampezzo', *ib*, 1999–2000:331–40. A critical analysis of the development of lawgiving in Ladin is provided by Eva Ploner, *Ladinisch – Deutsch – Italienisch Gesetzetexte. Eine Übersetzungskritik mit Verbesserungsvorschlägen*,

Innsbruck, Institut für Romanistik — San Martin de Tor, ICLMR, 141 pp. By using a comparative corpus P. focuses on interference by loan words, as well as the role of Italian and German in the process of opening a new semantic field, i.e. legal texts to Ladin vocabulary. Under the coordination of Erwin Valenti the SPELL project has produced a dictionary comprising 13,500 lexemes of Ladin dolomitan: *Dizionar dl Ladin Standard*, Urtijei, UGLD — Vich, ICLMF — San Martin de Tor, ICLMR — Bolzano, IsPL, xxxi + 408 pp., which completes the normalizing process initiated in 1988 and complements Id. et al., *Gramatica dl ladin standard*, 2001, reviewed in *YWMLS*, 63:564. However, as indicated on the cover of the volume, the project is still to be seen as work in progress: a sequel to the two provisional versions of *Dizionar dl ladin dolomitan* published in 1987 and 1999. In this new dictionary the forms are given not only in the new standard but also in the Ampezzan, unified Budiot, Fascian, Fodom, and Gardena varieties of Ladin. Together with the above-discussed dictionary of Marco Forni and with Giovanni Mischì, *Wörterbuch Deutsch–Gadertalisch / Vocabolari Todësch–Ladin (Val Badia)*, 2001 (noted in *YWMLS*, 63:564), as well as forthcoming works on the other varieties, it provides a solid and ample linguistic instrument, thereby considerably improving the possibility of using Ladin in most fields. Its weak point is clearly the rather limited number of lexemes included, but this will hopefully be expanded in the future. Standardization and toponomastics are discussed in P. Videsott, 'Zur Standardisierung der ladinischen Ortsnamen in Südtirol', *Onoma*, 35, 2000:289–317, and in Id., 'Zur ladinischen Toponomastikin Südtirol', *Südtirol in Wort und Bild*, 44.4, 2000:4–7. The potential of ALD-I as a corpus for toponomastic studies is shown in Id., 'Gli italianismi nel ladino brissino-tirolese: alcuni aspetti quantitativi e cronologici in base all'ALD-I', *Linguistica*, 41, 2001:129–58. He also discusses the etymology of certain toponyms and patronyms in Id., 'Deutsch oder Romanisch? Zur Etymologie einige Gadertaler Orts- und Familiennamen', pp. 251–63 of *Sprache und Name in Mitteleuropa. Festschrift für Maria Hornung*, ed. Hans Dieter Pohl, Wien, Praesens, 2000. L. Craffonara, 'Ortsnamen und Siedlungsgeschichte am Beispiel des Gadertals', pp. 219–31 of *Ortsnamen und Siedlungsgeschichte. Akten des Symposiums in Wien vom 28.–30. September 2000*, ed. Peter Ernst and Isolde Hausner, Heidelberg, Winter. Finally, M. T. Vigolo and P. Barbierato *'Il lessico dei laudi Cadorini', *Pellegrini Vol.*, 99–147.

SOCIOLINGUISTICS AND LANGUAGES IN CONTACT. A short overview of the present situation of Ladin at schools in Val Badia is given in *Sas dla Crusc 2001. Cronica dla val Badia*, pp. 344–47. A thorough description of the linguistic reality of the Ladin-speaking region is given in Kurt Egger, *Sprachlandschaft im Wandel. Südtirol auf dem Weg zur Mehrsprachigkeit*, Bolzano, Athesia / Europeische Akademie, 2001, 256 pp. A special study is devoted to the sociolinguistic situation of Val Gardena in Id. and Margaret McLean, *Dreisprachig werden in Gröden. Eine Studie zum Spracherwerb in der frühen Kindzeit*, Bolzano, IPL, 2001, 160 pp. Continuing his research into the linguistic situation in Northern Italy, J. Kramer, 'Sprachen im Südtirol vor den Römer', *Der Schlern*, 74, 2000: 831–42; Id., 'Il problema storico-linguistico del ladino', pp. 35–50 of *Saggi dialettologici in area italo romanza*, ed. Alberto Zamboni et al., Padua, Istituto di Fonetica e Dialettologia, 2000, and Id., 'Wie das Lateinische nach Südtirol kam', *Der Schlern*, 75, 2001: 675–86. Giampaolo Salvi, 'Il ladino. Schizzo linguistico', *Verbum. Analecta neolatina*, 2000.1: 151–69. The process of implementation of Ladin Dolomitan is presented in P. Videsott, *'Teorie e implementazione della pianificazione linguistica: il caso del ladino dolomitico (con un epilogo storico)', pp. 263–75 of *Simposi Pompeu Fabra. Jornades científiques de l'Institut d'Estudis Catalans*, ed. J. A. Argenter, Barcelona, Institut d'Estudis Catalans.

3. Swiss Romansh

BIBLIOGRAPHICAL AND GENERAL. The question whether the dialect of Val Müstair should be counted as a sixth Romansh dialect is controversial. That it should is argued with passion at a general level in M. Gross, 'La schuorz da zoppa do ün salzer. Reflexiuns davart il dialect da la Val Müstair al cunfin linguistic tranter il Vnuost, la Vuclina e l'Engiadina', *ASR*, 115: 7–50. The elaboration and implementation of a new standard is summed up in C. Solèr, 'Rumantsch Grischun, eine 200-jährige Vision wird Wahr', *Bündner Jahrbuch*, 44: 94–102. Id., *'Sprachwahl in bilingualen Kleingemeinschaften', pp. 295–302 of *Comunicare in ambiente professionale plurilingue. Atti del Convegno tenuto a Lugano dal 14 al 16 settembre 2000*, ed. S. Cigada et al., Lugano, Università della Svizzera Italiana, 2000, deals with bilingualism and language choice in the Grischun.

PHONOLOGY AND MORPHOLOGY. D. Gaudenz, *'Quist bel romantsch jauer. Bos-cha, frus-chaglia e pomma-raida in Val Müstair. Las quatter conjugaziuns. Specialitats pro'ls substantivs. Quei char be ret', *Chalender Ladin*, 92: 58–64. Gerhold Hilty, **Gallus und die Sprachgeschichte der Nordostschweiz*, St. Gallen, Verlagsgemeinschaft St. Gallen, 2001, 238 pp. Dialectal plurals are dealt with in M. Picenoni, 'Note sul plurale femminile nel bregagliotto e sul suo uso', *Almanacco del Grigioni Italiano*, 84: 116–21.

MORPHOSYNTAX. A syntactic model is developed in D. Varga, 'La subordination en vallader, rhéto-roman de la Basse Engadine', *RLiR*,

65:169–96. Màrio Eduardo Viaro, **A construção verbo + advérbo de lugar no romanche. Herença latina ou decalque germânico?*, 2 vols, SPo, Viaro 2001, 258, 360 pp.

ONOMASTICS AND LEXIS. Three more fascicles of *Dicziunari Rumantsch Grischun*, ed. Felix Giger et al. have been published by the Rheto-Romansh Society of Chur: 141–42, *LE–LEVGIAMENT* in 2001, and in 2002 143–44, *LEVGIAMENT–LIMITAZIUN*, and 145–46, *LIMITAZIUN–LOCAL*. New bilingual dictionaries are Alexi Decurtins, *Niev vocabolari Romontsch sursilvan–Tudestg*, Chur, Cadonau, 2001, xxv + 1243 pp., and Jean-Jacques Furer, **Vocabolari Romontsch sursilvan–Franzos / Dictionnaire Romanche sursilvan–Français*, Laax, Fundaziun Retoromana, 2001, 632 pp. A good introduction to a recently-discovered bilingual dictionary of the Val Müstair dialect dating from the mid 18th-c. is given in G. Hoyer, 'Un dictionnaire bilingue de Müstair (1759)', *ASR*, 115:51–79. This document will be a rich source for anyone interested in the history the Rheto-Romance. A meticulous description of flower names in Samnaun is provided by Karl Jenal-Ruffner, *Die Orts- und Flurnamen der Gemeinde Samnaun*, Chur, Kommissionsverlag Desertina, 472 pp. + map. E. Gabriel, *'Lautnachahmende Wörter im Gebiet *Vorarlberger sprachatlas* (VALTS)', *Montfort*, 53, 2001:278–97. H. Klausmann, *'Die wortgeographischen Besonderheiten Vorarlbergs (II). Der Bregenzerwald', *ib.*, 298–312. S. M. Berchthold and T. A. Hammer, *'Siedlungsgeschichte im deutsch-romanischen Grenzraum des St. Gallen und Vorarlberger Rheintales', pp. 69–82 of *Ortsnamen und Siedlungsgeschichte. Akten des Symposiums in Wien vom 28.–30. September 2000*, ed. Peter Ernst and Isolde Hausner, Heidelberg, Winter. A. Garovi, *'Die Besiedlung der vier Waldstätte im Spiegel der Toponomastik und Archäologie', *ib.*, 27–38. A short description and analysis of toponyms in two villages is given by Natalia Arpagaus and Irena Caduff, *Nums locals e da funs dallas vischnauncas Cumbel e Murissen*, Chur, Jäger, 2000, 76 pp + map. P. Barandun, *'Pazen – Farden, sieus nums funsils', *Per Mintga Gi*, 80:136–45. Toponymic survivals of pre-Roman languages are discussed in D. Schürr, 'Weiteres zu Burgeis: vorrömischen Ortsnamen und ihrer Herkunft. Das Problem, diese Namen einer Sprache zuzuordnen', *Der Schlern*, 76:39–49.

SOCIOLINGUISTICS AND LANGUAGES IN CONTACT. A good overview of the present situation of Romansh is to be found in R. Bauer, 'Rumantsch, romontsch (Bündnerromanisch)', pp. 231–36 of *Sprachkulturen in Europa: Ein internationales Handbuch*, ed. Nina Janich and Albert Greule, Tübingen, Narr. A possible connection between two varieties is described in M. Picenoni, 'Tra bregagliotto e il romancio', *Almanacco del Grigioni Italiano*, 83, 2001:279–81.

3

CELTIC LANGUAGES

I. WELSH STUDIES

LANGUAGE

By David Thorne, *Professor of Welsh Language and Literature, University of Wales, Lampeter*

1. General

Patrick Sims-Williams, *The Celtic Inscriptions of Britain: Phonology and Chronology, c. 400–1200*, 464 pp., Oxford, The Philological Society, is a comprehensive linguistic study of the stones from Western Britain and Brittany inscribed in the Roman and Irish Ogam alphabets which attempts to reassess the chronology of the inscriptions. Pierre-Yves Lambert, *Recueil des Inscriptiones Gauloises*, volume 2, section 2, Paris, CNRS 432 pp., continues the detailed work already begun on Gallic inscriptions. This volume in the series focuses on Gallo-Latin inscriptions found on movable goods such as pottery, glassware, tiles, and metal objects.

2. Grammar

G. R. Isaac, 'Perfectivity, transitivity, egrativity: the grammar of case in Welsh non-finite clauses', *JCLin*, 7:39–61, is a case study of the interaction of various formally distinct grammatical subsystems maintaining that in non-finite clauses Welsh realizes the same basic pattern of structural case marking as appears, with differing details, in ergative and active languages. H. Pilch, 'L'Accentuation comparée des langues celtiques', *ib.*, 103–27, challenges the traditional reconstruction of stress syllables basing his theories wholly on evidence gleaned from the surviving Celtic languages. A. Price, 'An analysis of the errors of adult learners in Welsh', *ib.*, 149–58, presents the results of an innovative and important study of the syntactic errors made by a modest sample of adult learners of Welsh. G. R. Isaac, 'Colli sillafau mewn Brythoneg', *SC*, 34:105–18, revisits Jackson's discussion of the loss of final syllables in Brythonic, arguing that it is perfectly feasible to reinterpret the relevant facts. The chronology of change, however, is not discussed.

3. Etymology and Lexicography

Parts 59, 60, 61 of GPC (ed. G. A. Bevan and P. J. Donovan) cover TWRW-WAGNERAIDD, WAGON-YMLIDIAF, YMLIDIAF-ZWINGLÏAIDD respectively. These three parts complete the final volume of Geiriadur Prifysgol Cymru, A Dictionary of the Welsh Language, the first part of which appeared in 1950. Sabine Heinz, *Welsh Dictionaries in the Twentieth Century: A Critical Analysis*, 536 pp., Munich, Lincom Europa, presents an investigation of modern Welsh dictionaries in their socio-historical context. The work focuses primarily on the analysis of the grammatical information contained in modern general-purpose dictionaries. Whilst appreciative of the lexicographical work produced thus far in Wales, H. argues convincingly for the inclusion of comprehensive morphological information in dictionary entries as well as phonetic transcriptions. G. R. Isaac, *SC*, 34, has notes on *Leubrit, Loubrit*, in the Book of Llandâf (271–72), *uca trintaut, beaut ri-d-ent* in the Juvencus stanzas (272–73), *crees, oet re ereint* in the Black Book of Carmarthen (274). E. Poppe, *ib.*, 275–78, has notes on *y gadw, paratoi llong idaw, ac a neidyawd y neill hanner idi*, from Buchedd Dewi. J. L. García Alonso, 'The place names of ancient Hispania and its linguistic layers', *SC*, 35:213–44, outlines the methodology of a comprehensive toponomic survey, offering a comment on every single name, a linguistic affiliation of the name, the historic and linguistic data on each ethnic group as well as a tentative classification of the relevant place names. G. R. Isaac, *ib.*, has notes on several awdlau in the Gododdin (271–83), on the fourth century Gaulish inscription of Séraucourt a Bourgres (350–53), and on Middle Welsh *gwant* (354–59). Lowri Williams and Delyth Prys, *Anabledd ac Iaith: Defnyddio Terminoleg Anabledd/Disability and Language: Guidelines for the use of Disability Terms*, Bangor, Y Ganolfan Safoni Termau, 64 pp., offers constructive advice on the phraseology that should be selected or avoided when discussing disability and disabled persons.

4. Sociolinguistics

Dylan Phillips and Catrin Thomas, *Effeithiau Twristiaeth ar yr Iaith Gymraeg yng Ngogledd-Orllewin Cymru, The Effects of Tourism on the Welsh Language in North-East Wales*, Aberystwyth, CAWCS, 217 pp., is a bilingual study sampling public opinion and assembling useful evidence on the relationship between tourism and in-migration and language use in a popular tourist region which is also one of the heartlands of the Welsh language. Gwenfair Parry, *'Nid Iaith Fain Mohoni': Y Gymraeg ym Mangor a Chaernarfon yn ystod y Bedwaredd Ganrif ar Bymtheg'*, Aberystwyth, CAWCS, 54 pp., investigates the situation of the Welsh language in Bangor and Caernarfon during the course of the 19th c.

EARLY AND MEDIEVAL LITERATURE

By OWEN THOMAS,, *Lecturer in Welsh, University of Wales, Lampeter*

A further three volumes of poetry have appeared this year in the UWCASWC series, *Cyfres Beirdd yr Uchelwyr*, under the general editorship of Ann Parry Owen, two of which are germane to this section of the critical bibliography. *Gwaith Dafydd y Coed a Beirdd Eraill o Lyfr Coch Hergest*, ed. R. Iestyn Daniel, Aberystwyth, UWCASWC, xviii + 213 pp., is an edition of the poetry of Dafydd y Coed, Ieuan Llwyd ab y Gargam, Meurig ab Iorwerth, Y Proll, Y Mab Cryg, Tudur ap Gwyn Hagr and Tudur Ddall. Despite the traditional form of his extant output Dafydd y Coed, who is associated with the patron Hopgyn ap Tomas of Ynysforgan, the content and tone of his *awdlau* and *englynion* are less intricate and complex than the fare traditionally associated with the work of the *Gogynfeirdd*. The editor suggests that the influence of the newly-emerging *cywydd* might explain the relaxed and personal tone of Dafydd y Coed's eleven poems. Also associated with Hopgyn ap Tomas are the 14th-c. poets, Ieuan Llwyd ab y Gargam, possibly from Anglesey, Meurig ab Iorwerth from Breconshire, and a poet curiously named Y Proll. Only three of Y Mab Cryg's poems survive but their satirical levity and narrative dynamic, according to the editor, manifests the influence of the *clêr*. A plaintive poem by Tudur ap Gwyn Hagr contains references to some of the hardships caused by the Black Death and Tudur Ddall's solitary poem subverts the conventions of medieval Welsh praise poetry to a patron's new house.

Gwaith Dafydd Epynt, ed. Owen Thomas, Aberystwyth, UWCASWC, xx + 214 pp., provides an annotated edition of all 24 of the 15th-c. Breconshire bard's complete poems. His poetry, some of which is incomprehensible, connects him with the area surrounding Brecon and Abergavenny and the major patrons of the day, including the Havards and the Herberts. He also sang to Saint Cynog, patron saint of Merthyr Cynog, and Saint Cathen, pleading for some respite from his recurring malaria. An important aspect of Dafydd Epynt's poetry is his literacy, and almost all of his poetry has been recorded in his own hand in Peniarth 54, 55, and 60.

D. F. Evans, '"Gwlad y Gwn"?: Cymru, y canon a'r dryll hyd at ddiwedd oes Elisabeth I', *Cof Cenedl* 17 : 1–32 discusses the impact of ordinance on Welsh military history from its first appearance in medieval Welsh poetry (in an eulogy by Iolo Goch to Rhys ap Gruffydd (Sir)) to the end of the Elizabethan era, concluding that Welshmen, at least in the eyes of the poets, generally regarded killing at distance as dishonourable and incompatible with the ideals of the *uchelwr* class. J. Cartwright, 'Dead Virgins: Feminine sanctity in medieval Wales', *MAe* 71:1–28, synthesizes the source material (namely Welsh and Latin Lives, genealogies, calendars, prayers, *Cywyddwyr* poetry, law texts, and place names) available for the female saints of Wales in order to shed new light on the medieval traditions associated with Welsh holy women. The pattern present within their biographies and issues of feminine sanctity in relation to Welsh hagiography are also explored. J. Morgan-Guy, *What* ***Did*** *the Poets See? A Theological and Philosophical Reflection*, Aberystwyth, UWCASWC, 24 pp., cogently argues that post-Reformation man still dwells under the illusion that medieval art and thought were suffused with the dichotomies of the sacred and the secular, and mingled Christian beliefs with pagan customs. This illusion must be shattered, posits Morgan-Guy, if we are to make sense, for example, of the creatures from the bestiaries and the scatological figures which adorn the tower at Llywel in Breconshire and if we are to appreciate medieval man's 'unified reality', in which 'pagan survivals' in art and poetry, for instance, were regarded not as debasements of Christianity but as essential facets 'of God' which were given a perfect direction by the Scriptures and by their incorporation into the world of the text. H. M. Evans, 'Lewys Glyn Cothi (*c.* 1425–*c.* 1489), *Y Traethodydd* 157:15–37, provides an overview of Carmarthenshire's most famous poet but offers little in the way of new insight. P. Sims-Williams, 'The Five Languages of Wales in the Pre-Norman Inscriptions, *CMCS*, 44:1–36, gives a comprehensive survey of the evidence for the presence of Latin, Irish, Norse, English, and Welsh in early Wales (but mainly concentrates on the Irish and Welsh evidence) and, in the process, clears the path of many misinterpreations, paying close attention to the phonological divergences between Irish and Welsh, and assenting with R. Geraint Gruffydd's view that had the Irish grip on Wales not been loosened Wales would have developed into a second Scotia. G. R. Isaac, '*Gwarchan Maeldderw*: A 'lost' medieval Welsh classic?', *ib.*, 73–96, demonstrates the flaws of Kathryn Klar and Eve Sweetser's 'unusual reading' of the notoriously impenetrable 'Gwarchan Maeldderw' by giving a few examples of their misinterpre-ations and linguistic shortcomings. Isaac does not presume to offer an elaborate theory to replace that offered by the Californian scholars but confines himself to offering a few general introductory remarks, which confute the view of Klar and Sweetser and which show 'Gwarchan Maeldderw' to have been a single 'heroic praise-poem of the familiar medieval type', before producing an edition of the text accompanied by a translation with textual and linguistic notes. E. Poppe, ' "Beues of Hamtoun" in Welsh bardic poetry', *ib.*, 49–57 examines the use made by the poets of this literary figure and concludes that their interest in him was part of the internationalization undergone by Welsh poets from the 14th c. onwards. N. Jacobs, '*Lledwag kronffair*: What kind of fair and why so little frequented?', *ib.*, 97–101, discusses the sixth line of the July stanza of 'Englynion y Misoedd', namely *llwm ydlan lledwag kronffair* and, in particular, the disputed meaning and significance of *kronffair*. Jacobs offers a brief account of the nature of petty hiring-fairs in late medieval Wales based on evidence from later periods, although he does not entirely dismiss the possibility of metathesis, which would cause *kronffair* to become *kornffair* (a corn fair). Pierre-Yves Lambert, 'Two Middle Welsh epithets for horses: *trybelid* and *ffraeth* (Breton *fraez*)', *ib.*, 103–6 concludes that *trybelid* and *ffraeth* have followed the same semantic development, first used of a manufactured implement, then of a trained horse and finally of a fit person.

N. Jacobs, '"Englynion" y misoedd: Testun C neu fersiwn Nyffryn', *LlC* 25:1–11, discusses the MS traditions associated with 'Englynion y Misoedd' and produces a fully annotated variant text. G. R. Isaac, '"Ymddiddan Taliesin ac Ugnach": propaganda Cymreig yn oes y croesgadau?', *ib.*, 12–20, offers a new and compelling interpretation of the poem's context, paying particular attention to B. F. Roberts's suggestion that the white dogs mentioned in the poem represent the dogs of the Otherworld. G. R. Isaac concludes that Ugnach represents the hunter from the Otherworld, that there is indeed a reference to ancient Greece and to Zionism in the poem and that these allusions provide a context for the poem and help to date it. D. Huws, 'Llyfr Melangell: ail-greu Llyfr Defosiynol', *ib.*, 21–7, discusses MSS Peniarth 191, Bangor 1, and Llanstephan 200, which make up a book of hours, entitled 'Llyfr Melangell' by D. Huws, and which, he argues, were closely connected to Pennant Melangell in Montgomeryshire. G. A. Williams, 'Nodiadau', *ib.*, 155–57, conclusively confirms, with the aid of an ultraviolet lamp, that the subject of Dafydd Nanmor's *awdl*, beginning with '*Dewis wyd, ŵr llwyd, ar holl wŷr Brytaen*', is indeed Dafydd ab Ieuan ab Einion of Harlech castle fame, and not Dafydd Llwyd ap Dafydd of Gogerddan. A. Brooke, 'Golwg ar "Pedair Cainc y Mabinogi"', *Y Traethodydd*, 157:209–21, argues tendentiously for a central meaning to the Four Branches of the Mabinogi, namely the theme of the lost child in a lost kingdom in an eternal struggle, frequently fought against the Otherworld.

G. A. Williams, 'The Literary Traditions to *c.* 1560', pp. 507–628 of *History of Merioneth: Volume II: The Middle Ages*, ed. J. Beverley Smith and Llinos Beverley Smith, Cardiff, Univ. of Wales Press, xxiv + 751 pp., gives an in-depth survey, grouped according to the principal families and homes of the county, of literature associated with Merioneth, from the early saga poetry, the Mabinogi, the legend of Gwion Bach, the tale of Maelgwn Gwynedd's Chair, the age of the Gogynfeirdd, the poetry of the 14th c., and from the Owain Glyndŵr revolt to *c.* 1560 and includes some discussion of the work of lesser-known poets, such as Rhisart ap Hywel ap Dafydd ab Einion, as well as the pre-eminent poets of the age. The final section of this sweeping overview deals with poets from outside Merioneth and reinforces the view that Merioneth's literary life — like that of many other counties in Wales — did not exist in isolation. K. Chandler, 'The humour in *Breuddwyd Rhonabwy*', *SC*, 36:59–71, argues that too many critics have attempted in vain to establish an authoritative meaning for this medieval text. Chandler stresses the role of its humour and how that humour operates within the narrative to produce a destabilizing effect. N. Jacobs, 'Englynion Calan Gaeaf a'r Misoedd o "Englynion Duad"', *ib.*, 73–87, offers a new fully annotated edition of the gnomic 'Calan Gaeaf' *englynion* together with a series of *englynion* on the subject of each month of the year. G. R. Isaac, 'Cymraeg *rhyngu, rhanc*, Hen Wyddeleg *ro-icc*; *Dadl y Corff a'r Enaid* ll. 128 *dinag*', *ib.*, 141–45, argues that the line *Ny llettaud lle dinag* from the Black Book of Carmarthen does not require emendation, as previous editors have assumed, but can be understood as *dinang*. A. Falileyev, 'Canu Llywarch Hen 11. 46: *eglwysseu Bassa ynt ffraeth heno*', *ib.*, 150–52, believes that the meaning of *ffraeth* in this instance is the result of an early semantic development and that its metaphorical connotation in Middle Welsh was obscure to early modern Welsh scribes. K. M. Wickham-Crowley, *Writing the Future: Lazamon's Prophetic History*, Cardiff, Univ. of Wales Press, viii + 182 pp., uses the theoretical work of Mikhail Bakhtin to demonstrate the use of prophecy in Lazamon's *Brut*, in which the Arthurian legends first appear in English. Of particular interest is Wickham-Crowley's discussion of the role which Merlin plays in the prophecy and also the short exposition on the role of oral and Welsh traditions on Lazamon's *Brut*.

H. M. Edwards, 'Ymgodymu â Dafydd', *Taliesin*, 114:133–46, discusses the translations of Dafydd ap Gwilym's poetry in a review article on Gwyn Thomas, *Dafydd ap Gwilym: His Poems* and offers notes and suggestions. A. Breeze, 'The kingdom and name of Elmet', *Northern History* 39:157–71, in the second part of this article, uses Celtic philology to suggest what the name of Elmet means, in the course of which he translates two of Taliesin's poems to Gwallog, king of Elmet in the 580s. The poems, argues Breeze, provide important clues to the group identity, cultural perspectives, social activity, and even world pictures of Celtic Elmet. *Id.*, 'Welsh tradition and the baker's daughter in *Hamlet*', *NQ* 247 : 199–200 provides an illuminating account of the background to one of Ophelia's remarks in *Hamlet*, 'They say the owl was a baker's daughter', and links it with the legion of Blodeuwedd in the Mabinogi. R. G. Gruffydd, '"Edmyg Dinbych": Cerdd Lys Gynnar o Ddyfed', Aberystwyth, UWCASWC, 30 pp., is an insightful lecture discussing the earliest recorded court poem from south Wales and a poem which belongs to a period, little researched, straddling the *Cynfeirdd* and *Gogynfeirdd* and producing a modern Welsh translation. The poem, argues Gruffydd, demonstrates that Dyfed, as well as Gwynedd and Powys, contributed to the literary tradition of Celtic eulogy between 600 and 1100. Secondly, the poem is evidence of the Wales-wide focus of the bard. It also contains a reference to the symbolic union or marriage between the poet and his patron and, finally, according to Gruffydd, the poem demonstrates the Celtic and Indo-European belief that the praise of man ultimately derives from the praise of God. B. Lewis, 'Trafod barddoniaeth yn yr Oesoedd Canol: Y traddodiad mawl a chrefydd', *Dwned*, 8 : 9–34, argues that Welsh poetry in the Middle Ages was the ground for ideological struggles between the bardic order and the clerics and provides insights into their relationship. E. Miles, 'Y darlun o blant yn y canu mawl', *ib.*, 35–57, explains how Lewys Glyn Cothi's poetry, to a far greater degree than the work of his contemporaries, reflects the turning-point at the end of the Middle Ages in society's attitude towards children. Penrhyn Castle has long been a symbol of oppressive landlordism, dating back to the revolt of Owain Glyndŵr and in D. J. Bowen, 'Y Canu i Gwilym ap Gruffydd (died 1431) o'r Penrhyn a'i fab Gwilym Fychan (died 1483)', *ib.*, 59–78, the poetry associated with Gwilym ap Gruffudd, the founder of the large estate at Penrhyn, is discussed with particular attention given to Rhys Goch Eryri's work and its historical and political context. G. R. Isaac, 'Dewiniaeth yn *Manawydan fab Llŷr*', *ib.*, 79–86, emphasizes the realism of *Pedeir Keinc y Mabinogi* and argues that Llwyd fab Cil Coed would not have been interpretated by medieval audiences as a mythical, incorporeal or ethereal character belonging to a Celtic otherworld but as an example of a dangerously ambitious cleric gaining privilege and position through witchcraft. A. C. Lake, 'Y Tri Hael: Rhai ystadegau', *ib.*, 87–98, uses statistics in the poetry of Hywel Cilan, Hywel Swrdwal, Lewys Glyn Cothi, Tudur Penllyn, Tudur Aled, Lewys Môn, Lewys Daron, Siôn Ceri, Mathau Brwmffild and Gruffudd Hiraethog to establish the extent to which the poets used allusions to The Three Generous Men of the Island of Britain triad in their eulogies and concludes that the bards did not use this technique uncritically and when a group of bards singled out the generosity of a patron, for instance in the cases of the paterfamilias of Plasiolyn, it can be assumed that it was not mere flattery.

An indispensable electronic database of all Welsh prose texts in 13th-c. MSS, dated as such by D. Huws, have appeared in G. R. Isaac and S. Rodway, *Rhyddiaith Gymraeg o Lawysgrifau'r 13eg Ganrif: Testun Cyflawn*, Aberystwyth, University of Wales, CD-ROM.

Chwileniwm: Technoleg a Llenyddiaeth, ed. Angharad Price, Cardiff, University of Wales Press, xi + 222 pp., includes H. Fulton, 'Orality and Literacy in Early Welsh Literature', 17–35, which discusses the extent to which the technology of book production moulded the nature of medieval MSS., paying particular attention to the Red Book of Hergest and drawing on the work of Sioned Davies on the Four Branches of the Mabinogi. Fulton also draws attention to the distinct clerical and secular traditions associated with medieval book production and finds the mingling of oral and literary styles most prevalent in books associated with the clergy. M. Lamb and P. Middleboe, 'Addasu y Mabinogi yn ffilm animeiddiedig', *ib.*, 139–56, reveals the background to the adaptation of the Mabinogi for television. M. van Rootseler, 'Fersiynau electronig o'r Mabinogion', *ib.*, 170–88, details the advantages of using XML (eXtensible Mark-up Language) as a mark-up language for producing comprehensive digital versions of the Mabinogion texts and also explains the process of preparing the texts, which can then be readily transferred to a website or easily converted for word-processing applications or desktop publishing programmes on various platforms. S. Higley has produced a text with accompanying sound files and a translation of 'Preiddiau Annwfn' which can be viewed on the internet at http://www.library.rochester.edu/camelot/annwn.htm

LITERATURE SINCE 1500

By A. Cynfael Lake, *Lecturer in Welsh, University of Wales Swansea*

Gwaith Mathau Brwmffild, ed. A. Cynfael Lake, Aberystwyth, UWCAWCS, 129 pp., contains the extant works of a minor poet who flourished between 1530–45. One interesting aspect of his work concerns the geographic distribution of his patrons. *Y Canu Mawl i Deulu'r Chwaen Uchaf*, ed. Dafydd Wyn Wiliam, Llangefni, p.p., 52 pp., is an edited collection of the poetry addressed to the Chwaen Uchaf family in Llantrisant parish, Anglesey, between the days of Gruffudd Hiraethog and Huw Huws. P. Williams, 'Arlliw y Diwygiad Protestannaidd ar destun pabyddol honedig', *LlC*, 25:28–42, shows that the Welsh translation of Gesta Romanorum copied by Llywelyn Siôn was based on two versions, the first, published by Wynkyn de Worde, Catholic in tenor, the second, by Richard Robinson, Protestant. *Treigl y Marchog Crwydrad*, ed. D. Mark Smith, Cardiff, Univ. of Wales Press, 212 pp., is the first edited version of the Welsh translation of William Goodyear's *Voyage of the Wandering Knight*. The introduction focuses upon the translator and target audience and the text is considered in the light of other allegoric material. The relationship between the five extant MS copies is also considered in detail. Id., 'Llawysgrifau rhyddiaith Morgannwg yr unfed ganrif ar bymtheg cynnyrch ysgol o gyfieithwyr? Pum cyfieithiad', *NLWJ*, 32:205–23, sees common features in five prose works translated by a group of 16th-c. Glamorganshire scribes. J. G. Jones, 'Cyfieithiad Rowland Vaughan, Caer-gai, o *Eikon Basilike* (1650)', *SC*, 36:99–138, provides the text of a Welsh rendering of *Eikon Basilike* translated and copied by Rowland Vaughan.

A. R. Jones, 'Adaptations by a "proud hot Welshman"', *NLWJ*, 32:61–72, describes four short Welsh prose works by Lewis Morris based on English models. G. H. Jenkins, 'Lewis Morris: "The fat man of Cardiganshire"', *Ceredigion*, 14:1–23, surveys Morris's various interests and focuses on his prose and poetry which 'reveal his delight in smutty lavatorial humour and lusty brawdiness'. Tegwyn Jones, *Fy annwyl nai, Siôn Owen*, Ebbw Vale, Cymdeithas Lyfrau Ceredigion, 200 pp., contains an interesting biographical portrayal of Lewis Morris's nephew together with an edited and annotated version of 29 letters written by him. His caustic comments show his uncle in a less than favourable light. J. B. Edwards, 'John Jones (Jac Glan-y-Gors): Tom Paine's Denbighshire henchman', *Transactions of the Denbighshire Historical Society*, 51:95–112, lists parallels between J.J.'s two essays and *Rights of Man*. Tegwyn Jones, 'Brasolwg ar y faled newyddiadurol',

Canu Gwerin, 25:3–25, describes those ballads which recounted contemporary event such as the Gunpowder Plot and the translating of the Scriptures into Welsh prior to the advent of the printing press. G. M. Awbery, 'Cofia ddyn wrth fyned heibio', *LlC*, 25:46–73, compares 70 versions of a popular verse recorded on gravestones in south east Wales. M. G. Thomas, 'Gŵyl a galar: golwg ar faledi Benjamin Benjamin (Bardd Coch), Maesteg, a rhai o'i gyfoeswyr', *Taliesin*, 114:37–51, sheds light on the three extant ballads of Benjamin Benjamin. E. W. James, 'A'r byd i gyd yn bapur. . .', *Canu Gwerin*, 25:48–58, discusses a popular Eastern motif found in hymns by Dafydd William and Hywel Gruffydd. Mari Ellis, 'Detholiad o lythyrau John Jones ('Tegid'; 1792–1825)', *JMHRS*, 14:40–54, transcribes 15 letters which attest to Tegid's literary interests. Hywel Teifi Edwards, 'Ar drywydd y 'magnitudes barddol'', *YB*, 26: 52–74, shows that not all commentators commended the poetry composed during the 19th c., and that occasional voices were to be heard deploring the dearth of a meaningful literary debate. Id. and E. G. Millward both draw heavily on poetic evidence in their essays on Victoria's silver and diamond jubilee celebrations of 1887 and 1897 in *Jiwbilî y Fam Wen Fawr*, Llandysul, Gomer, 47 pp. D. Ben Rees, *Y Polymath o Gymro*, Oxford, Cyhoeddiadau Modern Cymraeg, 20 pp., offers a summary of Gwilym Hiraethog's career and literary achievements. A. Cynfael Lake, 'Dirgelwch yr ewyllys', *Y Traethodydd*, 157: 108–18, suggests a possible answer to one of the several mysteries in Daniel Owen's *Gwen Tomos*. Rh. Ifans, 'Beriah Gwynfe Evans: mab y dyn od', *LlC*, 25:74–93, assesses the dramatic quality of B.G.E.'s first and last plays, composed between 1879 and 1904. E. W. James, ' "Nes na'r hanesydd. . ."; Glyndŵr a llenyddiaeth Gymraeg y cyfnod modern', *Taliesin*, 110:59–86, *ib.*, 111:117–31, *ib.*, 112:96–106, *ib.*, 113:93–100, *ib.*, 114:116–25, *ib.*, 115:72–88, examines the portrayal of Owain Glyndŵr in modern literature. He accounts for the paucity of references until the latter decades of the 18th c. and for the prominent place afforded to him during the following century not least as a result of Beriah Gwynfe Evans's plays. Rh. Llwyd, 'Llên y Mynydd Bach', *Ceredigion*, 14:61–78, sketches the activities of poets from the Mynydd Bach area in central Ceredigion, and mentions three relatively unknown mid 19th-c. figures styled Manod Wyllt, Llinos Wyre, and Myfenydd.

Gorau Cyfarwydd, ed. Gerwyn Williams, Caernarfon, Barddas, 381 pp., is a most valuable compilation of previously published essays by Bedwyr Lewis Jones on 18–20c. literary figures. R. M. Jones, *Mawl a Gelynion ei Elynion*, Llandybïe, Barddas, 414 pp., the sequel to *Mawl a'i Gyfeillion* and the second part of the triology which explores praise as a fundamental stimulus, focuses on the 19th and 20th centuries. *Chwileniwm Technoleg a Llenyddiaeth*, ed. Angharad Price, Cardiff, Univ. of Wales Press, 222 pp., contains 13 essays on literature and technology. Of particular interest will be J. Hunter, 'Cyfrinachau ar dafod leferydd: ideoleg technoleg yn ail hanner yr unfed ganrif ar bymtheg', *ib.*, 36–53, who questions the long-held notion that the poets, when pressed by the humanistic scholars to put their learning into print, spurned their advances because of their antagonism towards the new medium. E. W. James, 'Ann Griffiths: o lafar i lyfr', *ib.*, 54–85, describes the environment in which A.G. composed her hymns and explains the differences between the earliest printed versions and original oral version. Alan Llwyd, 'Yr awdlau i Dŷ Ddewi', *Barddas*, 268: 6–13, discusses three strict-metre odes inspired by St David. The piece by Waldo is seen as a turning point in his poetic career. D. Densil Morgan, 'Incarnate glory: the spirituality of D. Gwenallt Jones', *Celts and Christians*, ed. Mark Atherton, Cardiff, Univ. of Wales Press, 146–68, plots the spiritual and poetic pilgrimage of Gwenallt and the central themes of sin and salvation in his published collections of poems. Manon Rhys and M. Wynn Thomas, *James Kitchener Davies Detholiad o'i Waith*, Cardiff, Univ. of Wales Press, 263 pp., provide the text of Kitchener's three most important works together with a selection of critical, political, and biographical essays. The preface warns that the familiar image of the author is a misleading one and calls for a critical reassesment of the texts. M. Wynn Thomas duly does this in *James Kitchener Davies*, Cardiff, Univ. of Wales Press, 108 pp., a study which looks in detail not only at Kitchener's three pivotal and controversial works but also at his poems, plays, essays, and letters both private and published, and all are analysed in the light of the author's era and his personal tribulations and political activity. Alan Llwyd, 'Cofio "Cwm Glo", Cofio Kitch', *Barddas*, 270: 6–11, reiterates the themes of Kitchener Davies's contentious play and reactions to it. *Rhydwen Williams*, ed. Emyr Edwards, Llandybïe, Barddas, 124 pp., is an interesting and balanced compilation in the *Bro a Bywyd* series. Alan Llwyd, 'Gwallgofrwydd arglwyddes hardd', *Taliesin*, 109: 22–37, *ib.*, 110: 87–98, *ib.*, 111: 106–116, *ib.*, 112: 72–91, *ib.*, 113: 80–92, *ib.*, 114, 93–115, contemplates aspects of Caradog Prichard's personal life and traces the themes of insanity, guilt, and suicide in his work before offering an in-depth analysis of three prose poems, 'Y Briodas', 'Penyd', and 'Y gân ni chanwyd'. Menna Baines, 'Tafwys a Chil y Cwm: Caradog Prichard yr alltud', *THSC*, 2001[2002], 213–25, describes the nature of C.P.'s exile and its effect on his creative works. *Ffydd a gwreiddiau John Saunders Lewis*, ed. D. Ben Rees, Liverpool, Cyhoeddiadau Modern Cymreig, 104 pp., contains three discussions on religion in Lewis's poetry, plays, and prose works. Ifor ap Dafydd,

'Beirniadaeth gynnar a llythyrau Saunders Lewis: teithio, iaith a chenedligrwydd', *YB*, 26:75–95, suggests that S.L.'s letters to Margaret Gilcriest together with his study *A School of Welsh Augustans* represent his journey of selfdiscovery as a Welshman and as a literary critic. Gerwyn Williams, 'Rhyddiaith rhyfel y pedwardegau', *Y Traethodydd*, 157:133–156, outlines four works concerned with the Second World War. Of the four only one, the last to be composed, conveys the effects of that catastrophic event. Id., '"Cymry ar wasgar": tair o nofelau'r ail ryfel byd', *YB*, 26:115–23, refers to three novels which reveal an alternative reaction to the Second World War. Gwyn Thomas, *Ystyr Hud a Ffantasi* (no publication details), 21 pp., discusses the use made of magic and fantasy in literature. Two novels by G. E. Thomas are singled out for praise. M. P. Bryant-Quinn, 'Golwg ar *Tywyll Heno*', *YB*, 26:124–29, implies that Kate Roberts had first-hand experience of the symptoms which Bet in *Tywyll Heno* describes. G. A. Jones, '"Beirdd ac athronwyr a diwinyddion i gyd": y gymdeithas chwarelyddol ddiwylliedig yng ngwaith Kate Roberts a T. Rowland Hughes', *LlC*, 25:94–104, suggests that the portrayal of the quarrymen and their values in the works of K.R. and T.R.H. was tempered by the changes which were evident by the 1930s and 40s. Gwenan Mared, 'Llwgu a llais y ferch? ailddehongli *Sal*, Gwenlyn Parry', *Taliesin*, 116:15–29, sees in the play *Sal* a manifestation of female self-expression and sexuality. John Rowlands, 'Nofelwyr Cymraeg a'r "Gymru Americanaidd"', *LlC*, 25:130–54, reflects on the reluctance of Welsh novelists, in contrast with their English-medium compatriots, to portray the industrial life of Wales and the hardship of the Depression years. He proceeds to analyse Rhydwen Williams's triology *Cwm Hiraeth* which at least attempts to readdress the balance. Angharad Price, *Rhwng Gwyn a Du*, Cardiff, Univ. of Wales Press, 175 pp., explores the relationship between author, reader, and society, with particular reference to the works of Robin Llywelyn, and builds upon the ideas initially presented in her brief study *Robin Llywelyn* (2000). M. Wynn Thomas, 'Gwlad o bosibiliadau: golwg ar lên Cymru ac America', *Y Traethodydd*, 157:38–52, infers provoking American influences on early 20th-c. Welsh literature.

Mari Ellis, 'Merched y bedwaredd ganrif ar bymtheg a'r Eisteddfod', *Taliesin*, 116:111–22, outlines the role played by women in the provincial Cambrian *eisteddfodau* of the 1820–30s, and mentions Angharad Llwyd's literary pursuits. Herbert Hughes, 'Thomas Price (Carnhuanawc) of Cwmdu, 1787–1848, 'the lovable patriot", *Brycheiniog*, 34:133–52, describes Price's work and involvement with the Eisteddfod movement in the early 19th c. Hywel Teifi Edwards, 'Y môr a'r morwyr yn ein Prifwyl', *Maritime Wales*, 23:20–9, considers the attention given by the National Eisteddfod through its poetry and essay competitions during the past two centuries to seafaring. Gerwyn Williams, 'Daniel, y fedal a'r nofel', *Taliesin*, 116:78–110, underlines the importance of the two most prestigious prose competitions at the National Eisteddfod and the way both have promoted the medium between 1977–2002, but also senses tension between the two. Cath Filmer-Davies, *Eisteddfod A Welsh Tradition in Australia*, Brisbane, Seren Press, 2001, 196 pp., describes the first *eisteddfod* held in Australia in 1855, and shows that although events which are termed *eisteddfodau* are still held in many parts, the Welsh origins have long disappeared.

II. BRETON AND CORNISH STUDIES

POSTPONED

III. IRISH STUDIES

EARLY IRISH

By Kevin Murray, *Department of Early and Medieval Irish, University College, Cork*

1. Language

J. Borsje, 'The meaning of *túathcháech* in early Irish texts', *CMCS*, 43: 1–24, suggests translating 'the compound as "with a sinister eye", which covers the general meaning of *cáech* as "one-eyed" and hints at the range of meanings of *túath-*'. P. Mac Cana, 'The *ingen moel*', *Ériu*, 52: 217–27, investigates this not uncommon phrase in medieval Irish, conceding, however, that 'it is still difficult to give it a precise, inclusive definition'. Elsewhere in *Ériu* 52 there are short notes by R. Ó hUiginn, on 'Embedded imperative clauses' (231–34) and by A. Willi on 'Old Irish *(h)uisse* "just, right, fitting"' (235–40). N. Nikolaeva, 'The drink of death', *SC*, 35: 299–306, investigates the phrase *deog tonnaid*, a formulation which occurs in various medieval Irish texts. In *Peritia* 16 (in honour of Gearóid Mac Niocaill), C. Bourke, 'Cairrecan Tempuill Solman' (474–77), suggests that the *carracán* here named, stolen from the church of Clonmacnoise in 1129, was not a model of Soloman's temple but was rather 'a stone believed to derive from Solomon's temple'.

A. Falileyev, *Éigse* 33: 71–74, 'Early Irish *céir* "bee's wax"', proposes that *céir* is a 5th- or 6th-c. borrowing from British Latin. D. Ó Cróinín, *ib.*, 75–76, 'A new Old Irish gloss in a Munich manuscript', draws attention to a hitherto unnoticed Old Irish gloss on fo. 225va6 of MS Munich Clm 14429 where Latin *serum* 'whey' is glossed *medc* (this may be added to the five other Old Irish glosses from this MS printed in *Thesaurus palaeohibernicus* ii, 43). C. Bruy, *Études Irlandaises*, 27.2: 77–105, '*Tánaise ríg*: an alternative interpretation', suggests that 'during the period from the beginning of the seventh century until the end of the tenth century, there were no heir-designates in Irish society'; C. Ó Dochartaigh, *ib.*, 119–31, 'Language and identity in early medieval Ireland', analyses the Irish 'pride and . . . interest in their native language which was unique in western Europe'.

2. Literature

J. Carey, 'Werewolves in medieval Ireland', *CMCS*, 44: 37–72, is a detailed study of the Irish evidence for lycanthropy, most of which is to be dated after 1000 AD with much of the material relating to Ossory. However, he believes that 'the reasons for this association of werewolves with Ossory may not be retrievable'. S. Arbuthnot, 'The manuscript tradition of *Cóir anmann*', *SC*, 35 : 285–98, discusses aspects of the late Middle Irish tract 'The fitness of names'. In *Éigse* 33, T. Ó Cathasaigh discusses the early Irish saga "The destruction of Dind Ríg" in 'The oldest story of the Laigin: observations on *Orgain Denna Ríg*' (1–18), D. Dumville, '*Félire Óengusso*: problems of dating a monument of Old Irish' (19–48), does not commit himself to a date for "The Martyrology of Óengus" other than the Old Irish period after 797, while K. Murray compares two texts designated *baili* in '*Baile in scáil* and *Baile Bricín*' (49–56).

J. Borsje, 'Fate in early Irish texts' *Peritia* 16 : 214–31, notes that the passive notion of fate, rather than the active notion, 'is almost omnipresent in early Irish literature'. D. Ó hAodha, 'The first Middle-Irish metrical tract: two notes', *ib.*, 232–41, shows in note 1 that 'there are four different versions of the first of Thurneysen's *Mittelirische Verslehren*' and in note 2 draws attention once again to a better translation than has otherwise been offered of a problem line in the first Middle-Irish metrical tract. D. Ó Corráin,, *ib.*, 335–43, 'Synodus II Patricii and vernacular law', traces 'a legal sentence from Synodus II Patricii through its subsequent development and expansion as contract law in Irish vernacular law texts', N. McLeod, *ib.*, 344–59, 'Compensation for fingers and teeth in early Irish law', uses evidence about 'bandage wounds' to show that compensation for 'mutilating people's fingers and knocking out their teeth' was not as small as may first appears in the legal texts. T. Mohr, *ib.*, 360–95, 'Salmon of knowledge', investigates the use made of brehon law in cases involving fishing rights in the 1930s and 1940s.

M. Ní Mhaonaigh, 'Tales of three Gormlaiths in medieval Irish literature', *Ériu*, 52 : 1–24, examines a body of material relating to three historical royal women named Gormlaith 'to shed light on the process whereby an historical figure is transformed into a complex literary character'. J. Carey, *ib.*, 53–88, 'The Lough Foyle colloquy texts: *Immacaldam Choluim Chille ⁊ ind óclaig oc Carraic Eolairg* and *Immacaldam in druad Brain ⁊ inna banfhátho Febuil ó Loch Fhebuil*', presents editions with translations and notes 'of two texts associated with the legendary origin of Lough Foyle'. N. McLeod, *ib.*, 123–216, '*Di ércib fola*', presents editions, translations, and analysis of the medieval Irish legal materials concerned with mild injuries.

C. Maignont, *Études Irlandaises* 27.2: 9–28, 'Traces de la tradition païenne dans la première Irlande chrétienne', argues that 'the "nativist" and "anti-nativist" theories are not mutually exclusive, but complementary'. P. Guelpa, *ib.*, 139–60 re-examines the question of

Gaelic influence on scaldic poetry in 'L'influence gaélique sur la poésie scaldique'. D. Edel, 'Nineteenth century national and gender determinism and the reception of early Irish literature', *ib.*, 161–79, offers 'a historical survey of the use of early mediaeval Gaelic literature as an instrument of political rhetoric and national assertiveness'.

3. Other (Onomastics, Festschriften etc.)

In *Téada dúchais: aistí in ómós don Ollamh Breandán Ó Madagáin*, ed. M. Ó Briain and P. Ó Héalaí, Cló Iar-Chonnachta, 580 pp., P. Mac Cana analyses and contextualizes a very well-known Old Irish poem in 'Techt do Róim' (71–90); L. Mac Mathúna, 'Go Duiblind rissa ráiter Áth Clíath: ainmneacha Gaeilge na príomhchathrach' (121–48), focuses on the Irish names of Dublin. In other matters onomastic, D. Ó Murchadha, 'Carman, site of Óenach Carmain: a proposed location', *Éigse*, 33:57–70, suggests locating the important site of Carman at or near the townland of Siliothill, parish of Carnalway, barony of Naas South, county Kildare. Id., *Peritia*, 16, offers a contribution titled 'Belach Conglais: one or two?' (435–43), arguing that 'Baltinglass in Co Wicklow is the only genuine Belach Conglais', M. Ní Dhonnchadha, 'Inis Teimle, between Uí Chennselaig and the Déissi' (451–58), identifies Inis Teimle with Great Island in the estuary of the Suir, the Barrow and the Nore, and E. Ó Mórdha, 'On Loch Uachtair (Lough Oughter, Co Cavan)' (477–48), suggests that 'at the beginning of the eighth century the lake that is today known as Lough Oughter was known as Loch Erne'.

Beatha Aodha Ruaidh: The Life of Red Hugh O'Donnell, Historical and Literary Contexts', ed. P. Ó Riain, Irish Texts Society, London, viii + 164 pp., the result of the annual ITS seminar, contains six new studies of this important text. These are: H. Morgan 'The real Red Hugh' (1–35); M. Mac Craith, 'The *Beatha* in the context of the literature of the Renaissance' (36–53); D. McManus, 'The language of the *Beatha*' (54–73); M. Caball, 'Politics and religion in the poetry of Fearghal Óg Mac an Bhaird and Eoghan Ruadh Mac an Bhaird' (74–97); N. Ó Muraíle, 'Paul Walsh as editor and explicator of *Beatha Aodha Ruaidh*' (98–123) and P.A. Breatnach, 'Irish records of the Nine Years' War: a brief survey with particular notice of the relationship between *Beatha Aodha Ruaidh Uí Dhomhnaill* and the Annals of the Four Masters' (124–47).

In the second volume of the CSANA yearbook, *Identifying the 'Celtic'*, ed. J. F. Nagy, Dublin, Four Courts Press, 144 pp., M. Tymoczko attempts 'to stand back and consider the framework and premises of the discipline of Celtic studies' ('What questions should we ask in

Celtic studies in the new millennium?') (10–29); P. McQuillan, '*Gaoidhealg* as the pragmatic mode in Irish' (30–48), argues that 'the analysis of verb categories in the Irish grammatical tracts can best be accounted for in terms of discourse structure and, in particular, in terms of the opposition between a "pragmatic" or communicative mode (*gaoidhealg*) and a "syntactic" or regulated mode (*suidhioghadh*)'; T. O'Loughlin turns his attention once more to the theme of 'Celtic Christianity', in '"A Celtic theology": some awkward questions and observations' (49–65); C. McKenna investigates 'the extent to which the seventh- and eighth-century authors of the earliest extant lives of Brigit may have been aware of traditions associated with . . . a pre-Christian goddess of the same name', in 'Between two worlds: Saint Brigit and pre-Christian religion in the *Vita Prima*' (66–74); J. Borsje studies the motif of being one-eyed 'adding "ominous sign" to the range of the already proposed meanings', in 'Approaching danger: *Togail bruidne Da Derga* and the motif of being one-eyed', (75–99) and P. Ford investigates Irish familiarity with classical traditions about the Amazons , in 'Amazon dot choin' (100–10).

P. Ó Riain, *Four Irish Martyrologies: Drummond, Turin, Cashel, York*, Henry Bradshaw Society, vol. 115, Woodbridge, xiv + 260 pp., presents editions of four late 12th-c. martyrologies, all of which are descended at some remove from *Félire Óengusso*. Although written in Latin, the texts also contain much Irish language material, particularly personal names and place names. Id., 'A Northumbrian phase in the formation of the Hieronymian martyrology: the evidence of the martyrology of Tallaght', *AB*, 120:311–63, further scrutinizes the martyrological traditions, concluding that 'all principal versions of the Hieronymian Martyrology can be shown, simply by comparison with the text of the Martyrology of Tallaght, to have gone through what may be described as a Northumbrian phase'. J. Carey presents an article on 'Nodons, Lugus, Windos' (99–126) in *Dieux des Celtes / Götter der Kelten / Gods of the Celts*, ed. C.M. Ternes and H. Zinser, Luxembourg xiv + 284 pp. Id., writes on 'Ideal Kingship in Medieval Ireland' (45–65), in *Monarchy*, London, Temenos Academy.

In *Corpvs Christianorvm: Series Apocryphorum*, 2 vols (13 and 14) of great importance to Irish scholars have recently been published. These are the vols titled *Apocrypha Hiberniae: I Evangelia Infantiae*, ed. M. McNamara et al., Brepols, xvi + 1203 pp. These vols include editions, translations and analysis of the Irish infancy narratives from Liber Flavus Fergusiorum and Leabhar Breac, of a versified narrative of the childhood deeds of Jesus, of short texts relating to the nativity of Christ along with a detailed study of the Latin infancy gospels as found in certain manuscripts. The volumes are beautifully produced and meticulously indexed.

In matters hagiographical, P. Ó Riain, 'Hagiography without frontiers: borrowing of saints across the Irish Sea' (41–48), contributes an article on the borrowing of Irish saints and churches into Welsh hagiography in *Scripturus Vitam, Lateinische Biographie von der Antike bis in die Gegenwart: Festgabe für Walter Berschin zum 65. Geburtstag*, Heidelberg, while the same author, in a piece titled 'Irish saints' cults and ecclesiastical families' (291–302), in *Local Saints*, ed. R. Sharpe and A. Thacker, O.U.P., emphasizes the importance of the hereditary ecclesiastical families in the spread of saints' cults.

The mammoth publication, *The Field Day Anthology of Irish Writing*, vol. iv: Irish Women's Writings and Traditions, Cork U.P., lii + 1490 pp., contains important material for scholars of medieval Ireland. Of particular interest are the first 457 pp., 'Medieval to Modern, 600–1900' under the general editorship of M. Ní Dhonnchadha which comprises the following sections: D. Ó Corráin, 'Early medieval law, *c.* 700–1200' (6–44); M. Ní Dhonnchadha, 'Mary, Eve and the church, *c.* 600–1800' (45–165); M. Ní Dhonnchadha, 'Gormlaith and her sisters, *c.* 750–1800' (166–249); M. Herbert, 'Society and myth, *c.* 700–1300' (250–72); M. Nic Eoin, 'Sovereignty and politics, *c.* 1300–1900' (273–92); M. Ní Dhonnchadha, 'Courts and coteries I, 900–1600' (293–340); A. Nic Dhonnchadha, 'Irish medical writing' (341–57); and M. Ní Dhonnchadha, 'Courts and coteries II, *c.* 1500–1800' (358–457). As well as commentary and analysis, this tome contains many new or re-worked translations from medieval and modern Irish. It is to be hoped that it will prove possible to publish this opening section as a volume in its own right.

MODERN IRISH

POSTPONED

SCOTTISH GAELIC STUDIES

POSTPONED

4

GERMANIC LANGUAGES

I. GERMAN STUDIES

LANGUAGE

By Charles V. J. Russ, *Reader in the Department of Language and Linguistic Science, University of York*

1. General

Surveys, collections, bibliographies. A major work is *Kleine Enzyklopädie Deutsche Sprache*, ed. W. Fleischer et al., Frankfurt, Lang, 2001, 845 pp. This volume, initiated by the publishers, contains 11 chapters and covers both the sociolinguistic aspect of German as well as the structure and history of German: 'The German language in the present-day world'; 'Recent linguistic concepts in German linguistics'; 'Lexicology'; 'Word formation'; 'Grammar', which includes syntax, 'Phonology and Orthography'; 'Linguistic variation', which includes variation in general, variation according to medium, territorial differentiation, e.g. dialects, stylistic variation, and technical languages; 'Text linguistics'; 'History of German'; 'Onomastics', both place and family names; and finally 'Cultivation of the language' (*Sprachkultur*). Each chapter contains numerous sub-sections, clearly headed. There are also copious diagrams and maps, particularly good for the dialect section. The large bibliography comes at the end of the book rather than after each chapter. Finally an index of terms closes the book. The detailed sub-headings and the index enable the volume to be used successfully as a reference work. The authors come from a variety of traditions, although the majority are from Eastern Germany and of an older generation, indeed several had passed away even before the publication of the book. The chapters give a clear overview of research, definition of terms, and are illustrated by copious, well-chosen examples. Space forbids detailed discussion of each chapter but a few comments can be made. The syntax in the grammar chapter steers clear of Chomskyan syntax and uses a valency approach. The treatment of dialects is very well illustated and is to be found in the section 'Territoriale Differenzierung'. Perhaps an unusual usage is *literal* for 'written' in the treatment of the history of German although its first occurrence is in brackets after *schriftlich*. All in all, this book is a mine of information, well set out and clearly presented. It is certainly a must for all libraries.

The history of the study of German as a foreign language through the centuries is a new and very fruitful field of study. H. Glück, *Deutsch als Fremdsprache in Europa vom Mittelalter bis zur Barockzeit*, Berlin, de Gruyter, viii + 606 pp., is a pioneering work. G.'s goal is to show that in the Middle Ages and early modern times there was a need for learning German as a foreign language. The term 'German' is used in an anachronistic and pre-modern sense which includes all varieties of German, Low German, and Dutch. G. has amassed a great deal of evidence with reports dating back to the ninth century. Quotations in Latin and other foreign languages are always glossed in German. There was a wide range of motives for learning German, ranging from the needs of merchants and traders, craftsmen who went on journeys, exchanges between young nobles and skilled workers, marriage, foreign travel, students visiting different universities, nobles on a Grand Tour, migration (willing or unwilling) and other reasons. German was learned in most parts of Europe but in the Romance countries and Great Britain it did not obtain a high status. In eastern Europe there was a continuing tradition of learning German. A large number of grammars, language, and vocabulary books exist and G. presents these in a special source bibliography. He has drawn on an amazing amount of general historical evidence to back up his exposition. He also freely admits where he has to resort to speculation. There are three indexes, one of topics, one of personal names, and one of geographical names. G. points to the gap in the story that there needs to be a detailed account of how in the 18th and 19th cs German came to be a truly world language. On the evidence of this carefully researched book G. himself should continue this work. The continuing research on this theme is represented by *Die Volkssprachen als Lerngegenstand im Mittelalter und in der frühen Neuzeit. Akten des Bamberger Symposions am 18. und 19. Mai 2001*, ed. H. Glück (Die Geschichte des Deutschen als Fremdsprache, 3), Berlin, de Gruyter, xv + 143 pp., which contains the following contributions: A. Rossebastiano, 'Deutsch-italienische Vokabulare des 15. Jahrhunderts: Inhalt, Struktur, Zielgruppe' (1–19); O. Pausch, 'Lateinisch-deutsch-tschechische Vokabulare für Habsburger Regenten im 15. Jahrhundert' (21–35); B. Bruzzone, 'Fremdsprachen in der Adelserziehung des 17. Jahrhunderts: die Sprachbücher von Juan Angel de Sumarán' (37–45); S. Miehling, 'Matthias Kramer als Deutschlehrer' (47–55); Z. Opava, 'Bestseller in der frühen Neuzeit. Die verschiedenen Ausgaben des Gesprächsbüchleins von Ondrej Klatovsky (1540)' (57–76); A. Simecková, 'Zum Dialog im tschechisch-deutschen Gesprächsbuch von Ondrej Klatovsky' (67–76); H. Klatte,

'Fremdsprachen in der Schule. Die Lehrbuchtradition des Sebald Heyden' (77–86); L. Spácilová, 'Deutsch-tschechische Lehrbuchtraditionen in den böhmischen Ländern von 1740 bis 1918' (87–101); V. Winge, 'Wann wurde Deutsch eine Fremdsprache? Die Anfänge des Deutschunterrichts in Dänemark' (103–11); H. Glück, 'Mittelalterliche Zeugnisse für den Erwerb des Deutschen als Fremdsprache' (113–24). The volume concludes with a full bibliography of the source works and the secondary literature as well as an index of names. This collection of papers shows particularly the strength of German learning in Eastern Europe (Pausch, Opava, Simecková, Spácilová). Even a 16th-c. Latin conversation book was printed with German, Czech, and Polish versions soon after its initial publication (Klatte). Rossebastiano, on the other hand, shows in a detailed philological study how in the 15th c. in Northern Italy bilingual Italian-German teaching aids were being developed. Although the learning of languages was undertaken by the nobility (Pausch, Bruzzone) it was not restricted to this class. Miehling shows how M. Kramer used his great linguistic ability to develop innovations in his grammars and dictionaries. Winge demonstrates the fact that medieval Denmark was a multilingual state. Glück reviews some of the Old and Middle High German evidence for the acquisition of German as a foreign language. It is pleasing that such active research in this area is being pursued with international cooperation.

The study of the German language in the Far East finds treatment in I. Eijirô, 'Studien zur deutschen Sprache in Japan. Eine skizzenhafte Beschreibung ihrer Geschichte', *LiLi*, 127:7–18; Z. Jianhua, 'Germanistische Linguistik in China', *ib.*, 58–77; and S. Seongho, 'Die Geschichte der germanistischen Sprachwissenschaft in Korea', *ib.*, 78–96.

The general situation of German with regard to English and in a European context is illustrated by the articles in *Deutsch — Englisch — Europäisch*, ed. R. Hoberg (Duden Thema Deutsch, 3), Mannheim, Duden, 384 pp., which contains the following contributions: H. D. Haarmann, 'Sprachenvielfalt im Globalisierungsprozess' (9–29); H. Weinrich, 'Europa — Linguafrancaland?' (30–43); K. Ehlich, 'Die Zukunft des Deutschen und anderer Sprachen — außer der Englischen — in der wissenschaftlichen Kommunikation' (44–53); A. Greule, 'Deutsch am Scheideweg: National- oder Internationalsprache? Neue Aspekte der Sprachkultivierung', (54–66); J.-F. Leonhard, 'Deutsch in einem vielsprachigen Europa' (67–73); J. Nida-Rfimelin, 'Die Verantwortung der Politik: ein Plädoyer für Mehrsprachigkeit' (74–82); E. Barthel, 'Deutsche Sprache als politisches Thema' (83–86); A. Burkhardt, ' "Weitschweifig" — "wälderhaft", "Antimusikalisch". Die "schreckliche" deutsche Sprache im

Spiegel Literarischer (Vor-)Urteile' (87–104); U. Busse and H.-J. Solms, 'Englisch und Deutsch: die Geschichte zweier ungleicher "Schwestern"' (105–38); U. Ammon, 'Deutsch unter Druck von Englisch in Wissenschaft und Politik' (139–51); H. Haarmann, 'Englisch, NetWork Society und europäische Identität: eine sprachökologische Standortbestimmung' (152–70); R. Hoberg, 'English rules the World. Was wird aus Deutsch?' (171–83); K. Heller, 'Was ist ein Fremdwort? Sprachwissenschaftliche Aspekte seiner Definition' (184–98); A. Kirkness and M. Woolford, 'Zur Herkunft der Anglizismen im Deutschen: Beobachtungen und Vorschläge anhand des Anglizismen-Wörterbuchs' (199–219); R. Glahn, 'Englisches im gesprochenen Deutsch: Einfluss und Bewertung' (220–35); D. Hofmann, 'Do you understand Denglisch? Eine Umfrage zum Anglizismenverständnis' (236–46); J. Spitzmüller, 'Selbstfindung durch Ausgrenzung Eine kritische Analyse des gegenwärtigen Diskurses zu angloamerikanischen Entlehnungen' (247–65); J. Eichhoff, 'Deutsche Einflüsse auf das Englische' (266–85); M. Durrell, 'Die Sprachenpolitik der Europäischen Union aus britischer Sicht' (286–97); P. Braselmann, 'Englisch in der Romania' (298–332); A. T. Salon, 'Die Sprachenfrage in der EU aus französischer Sicht. Eine sprachpolitisch-praktische Perspektive' (333–40); C. Földes, 'Deutsch und Englisch: ein Sprachnotstand? Befunde und Anmerkungen aus einer ostmitteleuropäischen Perspektive' (341–67); and I. Zint-Dyhr, 'Deutsch und Englisch in Skandinavien' (368–81).

The pluricentric and regional nature of German features in E. Piirainen, '"Landschaftlich", "norddeutsch" oder "berlinisch"', *DaF*, 39:36–46, and H. Löffler, 'Austriazismen, Helvetismen, Teutonismen. Zu einem trinationalem deutschen Wörterbuch', *NMi*, 103:147–59. German in Switzerland is represented by F. Rash, 'The German-Romance language borders in Switzerland', *JMMD*, 23:112–36; P. Dalcher, 'Über Anglizismen im Schweizerdeutschen', *Sprachspiegel*, 56, 2000:197–204; I. Hove, 'Wie sollen die Deutschschweizer/Deutschschweizerinnen Hochdeutsch sprechen?', *ib.*, 57, 2001:90–100, and J. Stefanakova, 'Helvetismen in deutschschweizerischen Tageszeitungen', *ib.*, 196–203. Items on German in Austria include P. Eisenberg, 'Es gibt Gerüchte über eine Rettung Österreichs. Zur Rekonstruktion der Grammatik von Karl Kraus', *Fest. Stickel*, 55–87, and S.-J. Lee, **Heimito von Doderer's 'Die Wasserfälle von Slunj'. Eine sprachwissenschaftliche Untersuchung zum österreichischen Deutsch* (Schriften zur deutschen Sprache in Österreich, 29), Frankfurt, Lang, 311 pp. More general contributions to aspects of the role and function of German in different linguistic situations are represented by the following contributions from *Akten (Wien)*, III: G. Hogan-Brun, 'Deutsch in seiner nationalen Vielfalt in Europa:

Momentaufnahme und Zukunftsperspektiven' (403–09); S. Stanescu, 'Das Rumäniendeutsche nach 1989 im Spiegel der ADZ' (411–16); R. S. Baur and T. Ostermann, 'Die Rolle der deutschen Sprache im Rahmen europaweiter Kontakte zwischen Schulen und Hochschulen' (417–24); G. Stickel, 'Einstellungen der Deutschen zur innerdeutschen und zur europäischen Mehrsprachigkeit' (425–35); A. Greule, 'Sprachloyalität als Aufgabe der Sprachkultivierung' (437–43). Also noted: M. Clyne, 'Die Rolle des Deutschen bei interkulturellen Erscheinungen unter Dreisprachigen', *Fest. Stickel*, 325–46; C. Földes, 'Kontaktsprache Deutsch: das Deutsche im Sprachen- und Kulturenkontakt', *ib.*, 347–70; S. Grosse, 'Zur sprachlichen Situation in der Euroregion Neiße (D)/ Nisa (CZ)/Nysa (PL)', *ib.*,, 371–86; K. Ehlich, 'Was wird aus den Hochsprachen?', *ib.*, 387–418; A. Almeida, 'Die terminologische Datenbank der Europäischen Union', *Fest. Göschel*, 392–405; C. Földes, 'Deutsch als Sprache mit mehrfacher Regionalität. Die diatopische Variationsbreite', *Muttersprache*, 112:225–39; and L. M. Eichinger, 'South Tyrol: German and Italian in a changing world', *JMMD*, 23:137–49.

The language of the old GDR lives on in K.-D. Ludwig, 'Markierungen DDR-spezifischen Wortschatzes im Wandel', *Fest. Cherubim*, 349–56. Also noted: J. Gessinger, 'Deutsche reden deutsch', *Fest. Cherubim*, 243–56, and **Regionale Standards. Sprachvariationen in den deutschsprachigen Ländern*, ed. E. Knipf-Komlósi and N. Berend, Budapest–Pécs, Dialóg Campus Kliadó, 2001, 162 pp. Luxemburgish features in P. Gilles, 'Die Konstruktion einer Standardsprache. Zur Koinédebatte in der luxemburgischen Linguistik', Stellmacher, *Dialektologie*, 200–12.

Items on Yiddish include M. Aptroot and H. Nath, **Einführung in die jiddische Sprache und Kultur*, Hamburg, Buske, xlv + 465 pp.; S. Neuberg, **Pragmatische Aspekte der jiddischen Sprachgeschichte am Beispiel der Zenere* (Jiddische Schtudies, 7), Hamburg, Buske, 1999, viii + 214 pp.; S.-H. Chang, **Der Rückgang des Präteritums im Jiddischen kontrastiv zum Deutschen* (Jiddische Schtudies, 9), Hamburg, Buske, x + 205 pp.; **Jüdische Sprache in deutscher Umwelt. Hebräisch und Deutsch von der Aufklärung bis ins 20. Jahrhundert*, ed. M. Brenner, Göttingen, Vandenhoeck & Ruprecht, 134 pp.; and J. A. Fishman, 'The holiness of Yiddish: who says Yiddish is holy and why?', *Language Policy*, 1:123–41.

INTERDISCIPLINES. Language used in the public domain is the subject of the following contributions to *Akten (Wien)* III: W. Holly, 'Einleitung zu "Sprache in der Öffentlichkeit"' (323–27); F. Liedtke, 'Sprache — Denken — Politik' (329–36); I. Bartoszewicz, 'Topoi der deutsch-polnischen Versöhnung' (337–42); I. Hudabiunigg, 'Nationale Stereotypen in Europa' (343–48); J. Klein, 'Plenardebatte und

Fraktionsdebatte. Zwei Modi parlamentarischer Auseinandersetzung' (349–53); L. Gautier, 'Verfassungen aus linguistischer Sicht: semantische Analyse eines österreichischen Korpus' (355–60); G. Gréciano, 'Amtlichkeit und Bürgernähe im Europakorpus' (361–66); F. Kanatli, 'Politische Argumentation' (367–73); S. M. Meireles, 'Der Tanz in der Distanz: *Face-work* in Diskussionen' (375–80); E. Forgács, 'Deutsche Printwerbung als multimediale Kommunikation. Verbale und nonverbale Strategien' (381–88); C. Thim-Mabrey, 'Sprachberatung für die Kommunikation im Internet' (389–94); and E. W. B. Hess-Lüttich, 'Angewandte Mediensemiotik. Kommunikationswandel in der Informationsgesellschaft' (395–402).

Technical communications and languages feature in T. Roelcke, 'Zusammenhänge zwischen typologischen und funktionalen Charakteristika der deutschen Fachsprachen — eine systematische Annäherung', *Sprachwissenschaft*, 27:37–53; S. Arend, 'Sprachliches zur Pflegeversicherung. Der Einfluss des Sozialgesetzbuches XI auf die deutsche Sprache', *Muttersprache*, 112:253–60; F. Menz et al., 'Geschlechtsspezifische Unterschiede bei der Beschreibung von Brustschmerzen: Ergebnisse einer medizinisch-linguistischen transdisziplinären Studie', *LBer*, 191:343–66; C. Schultze, 'Dialogtypen im familientherapeutischen Erstgespräch', *Fest. Cherubim*, 331–40; S. Wichter, 'Besetzungstypen', *ib.*, 341–48; A. Busch, 'Kommunikative Spannungsfelder in der technischen Dokumentation', *ib.*, 357–66; S. Goes, 'Manufactum: der Mythos vom genialen Handwerker als Strategie im Direktmarketing', *ib.*, 367–76; and R. Knirsch, '"Eine Art Magie" — Essayistisches zur Abweichungsbewältigung in der Anrufbeantworter-Kommunikation', *ib.*, 377–86.

Computers and language are the subject of S. Rabanus, 'Befehl oder Dateiname nicht gefunden. Möglichkeiten und Grenzen der Kommunikation mit dem Computer', *Muttersprache*, 112:193–207.

The treatment of political language surfaces in M. Wengeler, '"1968", öffentliche Sprachsensibiltät und political correctness. Sprachgeschichtliche und sprachkritische Anmerkungen', *Muttersprache*, 112:1–24; R. Geier and G. Schuppener, '"Bestürzt und schmerzlich berührt." Reden von Bundeskanzler Schröder und Bundespräsident Rau zum 11. September 2001', *ib.*, 15–24; and K. S. Roth, '"Man nimmt die Sprache immer nur dann wahr, wenn man ein Problem hat . . ." Thesen zum Sprachbewusstsein von Politikern', *ZGL*, 30:73–99.

Both first and second language acquisition are treated in W. Reinecke, 'Spracherwerbsforschung. Prämissen — Daten — Perspektiven' *DaF*, 39:9–18; S. Traoré, 'Gedächtnis, Gehirnsysteme und Wissenserwerb. Ein integrierter Ansatz zum Erlernen fremder

Sprachen', *ib.*, 19–25; K. Kleppin, 'Motivation. Nur ein Mythos? (II)', *ib.*, 31–35; J. Iluk, 'Probleme der Befähigung zum Ausdruck von Emotionen in der Fremdsprache aus curricularer Sicht', *ib.*, 96–102; A. Wittek and M. Tomasello, 'German children's productivity with tense morphology: the Perfekt (present perfect)', *JCL*, 29:567–89; T. F. H. Smits, 'Referentielle und Kommunikationsstrategien bei deutschsprachigen Lernern des Niederländischen', *LBer*, 189:59–88; N. Müller et al., 'Zum Spracheinfluss im bilingualen Erstspracheneerwerb: Italienisch-Deutsch', *ib.*, 190:157–206; and D. Stellmacher, 'Muttersprachenunterricht und Sprachwissenschaft. Ein Fallbeispiel dialektologisch betrachtet', *Fest. Cherubim*, 257–62.

Treatment of language and gender appear in E. Demey, 'Leser und Leserinnen gesucht! Zum generischen Gebrauch von Personenbezeichnungen in deutschen Stellenanzeigen und Zeitungsartikeln', *DSp*, 30:28–49; K. Sobatta, 'Sprachpraxis und feministische Sprachkritik. Zu einer Sonderentwicklung in Ostdeutschland', *ZGL*, 30:147–68; and A. Betten, 'Männermonolog vs. Frauenmonolog oder der Umgang mit Unterbrechungen. Weiteres Material zu einer provokanten These', *Fest. Cherubim*, 291–302.

The teaching of German as a foreign language features in: H. Bassler and H. Spiekermann, 'Regionale Varietäten des Deutschen im Unterricht Deutsch als Fremdsprache', *DaF*, 39:31–35; S. Jahr, 'Die Vermittlung des sprachlichen Ausdrucks von Emotionen im DaF-Unterricht', *ib.*, 88–95; D. Rösler and E. Tschirner, 'Neue Medien und Deutsch als Fremdsprache. Viele Fragen und ein Aufruf zur Diskussion', *ib.*, 156–66; E. Kwakernaak, 'Nicht alles für die Katz. Kasusmarkierung und Erwerbssequenzen im DaF-Unterricht', *ib.*, 156–66; F. Grucza, 'Theoretische Voraussetzungen einer holistischen Fremdsprachenpolitik', *Fest. Stickel*, 439–61; M. Townson, 'Kannst du Deutsch, was kannst du?', *ib.*, 463–75; and K. Beyer, 'Gibt es eine spezifisch pädagogische Kommunikation?', *Fest. Cherubim*, 317–30.

Language and literature features in M. Siguan, 'Über Sprache und ihre Grenzen: einige Beispiele zur Bewältigung von Sprachlosigkeit in der Literatur (Jean Améry, Primo Levi, Jorge Semprún)', *Fest. Stickel*, 605–22; R. Freudenberg, 'Thomas Mann auf Englisch. Zu einer Fehlertypologie beim Übersetzen literarischer Texte', *Fest. Göschel*, 366–91; M. Luukkainen, 'Der Satztyp im literarischen Text', *Fest. Cherubim*, 171–80; C. Perels, 'Sprache der Wissenschaft und Sprache der Dichtung. Zu Gottfried Benns Sprachkritik zwischen 1914 und 1920', *ib.*, 223–32; and H. Kämper, 'Bertolt Brecht, der Nationalsozialismus und die Sprachkritik', *ib.*, 233–42.

General Linguistics, Pragmatics, and Textlinguistics. The general question of cultivating language is the subject of J. A. Bär,

'Darf man als Sprachwissenschaftler die Sprache pflegen wollen?', *ZGL*, 30:222–51, and B. Döring, '"Die Pflege und Reinhaltung unserer Muttersprache scheint mir eine Aufgabe zu sein, die unserer Akademie gemeinnütziger Wissenschaften wohl ansteht." — Sprachkritik im Umfeld der Erfurter Akademie gemeinnütziger Wissenschaften', *Fest. Cherubim*, 215–22. On varieties of language, see M. Hoffmann, 'Werbesprache — Gesamtsprache — Sprachsystem. Eine varietätenlinguistische Betrachtung', *Muttersprache*, 112:208–24, and V. Ülkü, 'Sprachnationalismus und Sprachpolitik. Deutsche und türkische Modelle', *Fest. Stickel*, 419–38. The history of linguistics is treated in H. J. Dingeldein, 'Karl Bernhardi und die Sprachgrenzen im Deutschen. Ein Beitrag zur Geschichte der deutschen Sprachwissenschaft im 19. Jahrhundert', *Fest. Göschel*, 161–75. Studies of texts include I. Zhokov and N. Gafurova, 'Der Tschetschenien-Krieg im internationalen Pressediskurs', *Muttersprache*, 112:42–54; L. Häusler, 'Flexibilität und Rigidität in "Elterninterviews". Sprachliche Manifestation und Gesprächsfunktion', *DSp*, 30:66–90; K. Petrus, 'Was sind illokutionäre Akte?', *LBer*, 190:131–56; and P. Auer, 'Schreiben in der Hypotaxe — Sprechen in der Parataxe? Kritische Bemerkungen zu einem Gemeinplatz', *DaF*, 39:131–38. The spoken language finds treatment in M. Thurmair, 'Standardnorm und Abweichungen. Entwicklungstendenzen unter dem Einfluss der gesprochenen Sprache', *DaF*, 39:3–8; T. Weber, 'Reparaturen: Routinen, die Gespräche zur Routine machen', *LBer*, 192:417–56; R. Fiehler and R. Schmitt, 'Das Potenzial der angewandten Gesprächsforschung für Unternehmenskommunikation: das Beispiel: "Kundenorientierung"', *Fest. Stickel*, 501–27; and W. Kallmeyer and T. Spranz Fogasy, 'Führung im Gespräch — am Beispiel von "Eingreifen zur grundsätzlichen Voraussetzungserklärung"', *Fest. Stickel*, 529–54. Contrastive studies feature M.-L. Piiliilainen and L. Tiittula, 'Absatzstruktur als Organisationsmittel in deutschen und finnischen Texten', *Fest. Stickel*, 251–70, and S. Yoshijima, 'Erzählerperspektive. Eine pragmatisch-kontrastive Untersuchung mit einer Bildgeschichte', *ib.*, 271–304. Also noted: R. Wimmer, 'Noch Mal zu "Leitkultur"', *Fest. Stickel*, 653–69; N. R. Wolf, 'Wie spricht ein Populist? Anhand eines Beispiels', *ib.*, 671–85.

2. History of the Language

Neue deutsche Sprachgeschichte. Mentalitäts-, kultur und sozialgeschichtliche Zusammenhänge, ed. D. Cherubim et al. (SLG, 64), x + 415 pp., deals with 18th-c. to 20th-c. history of German. The contributions concentrate on three different areas. The first discusses methods and theory: P. von Polenz, 'Sprachgeschichte und Gesellschaftsgeschichte von Adelung bis heute' (1–23), who shows how the approaches of Adelung and J. Grimm were not adequate but since the 1980s new innovative connections between the history of language and society have developed; O. Reichmann, 'Nationale und europäische Sprachgeschichtsschreibung' (25–42), who wants to get away from the nationalistic, individual language focus and embed the history of German more in a European context; M. Wengeler, '"Bedeutung" und "Sprache" in der Geschichtsschreibung. Ein Blick auf Nachbardisziplinen der germanistischen Sprachwissenschaft' (43–64), who shows how helpful it would be to consider new ways of looking at aspects of linguistic history from neighbouring disciplines; F. Hermanns, 'Attitüde, Einstellung, Haltung. Empfehlung eines psychologischen Begriffs zu linguistischer Verwendung' (65–89), who emphasizes the importance of ascertaining the meaning of words, including the attitudes of speakers. The second group of articles focuses on the application of methods to different sets of data: F. Steiner, '"Die Maske mit dem Gesicht verwechseln." Autorschaftsfiguren in naturwissenschaftlichen Texten um 1800' (91–110), who shows how changes in authorship of scientific texts around 1800 lead to a discussion of results rather than simply making authoritative pronouncements; E. Ziegler, 'Die Band-Metapher im nationalsprachlichen Diskurs des 19. Jahrhunderts' (111–38), who outlines the rise and fall of the 'bond of language' metaphor; J. Kilian, 'Scherbengericht. Zu Quellenkunde und Quellenkritik der Sprachgeschichte' (139–65), who uses Bismarck's socialist law to argue for a systematic review and classification of linguistic text sources; J. Klein, 'Topik und Frametheorie als argumentations- und begriffsgeschichtliche Instrumente, dargestellt am Kolonialdiskurs' (167–81), who describes in detail with diagrams how his approach can deal with topics such as the discussion of colonial policy; A. Lobenstein-Reichmann, 'Liberalismus — Demokratie Konservatismus. Moeller van den Bruck, das Begriffssystem eines Konservativen zu Beginn der Weimarer Republik' (183–206), which is a detailed philological analysis of a seminal work from the Weimar period, A. Moeller van den Bruck's *Das dritte Reich* (1923), showing the system of values developed in it; H. Schmidt, 'Anfänge der Moderne. Nietzsches Wortbildungstechniken und Formulierungsvariationen' (207–38), who emphasizes the experimental and creative use of Nietsche's language using a wide range of examples; H. Kämper, 'Sigmund Freuds Sprachdenken. Ein Beitrag zur Sprachbewusstseinsgeschichte' (239–51), who flags up Freud's positive attitude to language; and S. Grosse, 'Zur deutschen Sprache zwischen 1918 und 1933' (253–68), who gives some interesting illustrations of new words and stylistic changes and shows how some new text types arose. The third area to be treated is that of the relations with Eastern Europe. The contributions illustrate how interwined and complicated such relations could be: D. Bering, 'Juden und die deutsche Sprache. Fundierung eines Forschungsprojekts' (269–91); D. Zakharine, 'Konversations- und Bewegungskultur in Russland. Von der "Sprachdiachronie" zur historischen Kommunikationswissenschaft' (293–315); E. Liphardt, 'Politische Rede der extremen Linken in Deutschland und Russland in den Jahren 1914 bis 1919' (317–36); J. F. Wiktorowicz, 'Die deutsch-polnische Nachbarschaft und ihre Widerspiegelung in der polnischen Sprache' (337–48); W. Holly, '"Tschechen" und "Deutsche" in den Böhmen-Debatten der Paulskirche. Ein frame-analytischer Beitrag zur Geschichte der sprachlichen Konstruktion deutsch-tschechischer Beziehungen' (349–78); and M. Nekula, 'Deutsch und Tschechisch in der Familie Kafka' (379–415). This is a thought-provoking volume which broadens the approach to the recent history of German in many illuminating ways.

Akten (*Wien*), III contains the following contributions on the historical development of German: N. R. Wolf, 'Einleitung zu "Aufgaben einer zukünftigen Sprachgeschichtsforschung' (13–14); N. Babenko, 'Deutsche Sprachgeschichtsschreibung im Umfeld der modernen linguistischen Theorien' (15–20); M. Durrell, 'Sprachgeschichte als Nationalgeschichte. Zur Historiographie der deutschen Sprache im 19. Jahrhundert' (21–26); J. West, 'Vorwärts durch Neodarwinismus' (27–32); D. Busse, 'Sprachgeschichte als Teil der Kultur- und Wissensgeschichte. Zum Beitrag einer historischen Diskurssemantik' (33–38); M. L. Kotin, 'Die deutsche Sprache *in statu viae*: Erbgut und eigene Wege' (39–46); G. Brandt, 'Gleichbehandlung der Geschlechter — notwendige Voraussetzung für die Optimierung soziolinguistisch orientierter Sprachgeschichtsforschung und Sprachgeschichtsschreibung' (47–52); A. Ziegler, 'Möglichkeiten einer korpusorientierten Sprachgeschichtsforschung. Zum Konzept einer quantitativ-linguistisch fundierten Textsortenklassifikation' (53–59); T. Czarnecki, 'Die ältesten deutsch-polnischen Sprachkontakte' (61–65); W. Hoffmann, 'Regionale rheinische Sprachgeschichte: Projekte und Desiderate' (67–72); M. Hundt, 'Das Sprachspiel als Gegenstand der Sprachgeschichtsschreibung' (119–29); and A. Schwarz, Metakommunikationsgeschichte' (147–53).

A unique work witnesses to the history of the language in one town. *Regensburger Deutsch. Zwölfhundert Jahre Deutschsprachigkeit in Regensburg*, ed. S. Nässl (RBDSL, 80), 331 pp., contains the following articles: H. Tiefenbach, 'Die Anfänge der deutschen Schriftlichkeit in Regensburg' (13–48); M. Prinz, 'Geographische Namen in und um Regensburg' (49–81); R. and V. Kohlheim, 'Personennamen im mittelalterlichen Regensburg' (81–126); E. Eggers, 'Die Rolle

Regensburgs bei der Entstehung des Jiddischen' (127–38); H.-U. Schmid, 'Die deutschen Inschriften des Mittelalters und der Frühen Neuzeit in Regensburg' (139–52); E. Skála, 'Das Regensburger und das Prager Deutsch' (153–70); R. Harnisch, 'Der Stadtschreiber Ulrich Saller und die Anfänge des frühneuhochdeutschen Schreibdialekts in Regensburg' (171–200); I. Reiffenstein, 'Zur Schreibsprache des Runtingerbuches (1383–1407)' (201–24); S. Nässl, 'Regensburger Schreibsprache in Rechnungsbüchern des 15. Jahrhunderts' (225–48); A. Greule, 'Die Peinliche Gerichtsordnung Karls V. Regensburg 1532. Perspektiven der sprachwissenschaftlichen Erforschung' (249–58); T. Herrnleben, 'Untersuchungen zum Vokalismus in den gedruckten Regensburger Ratsdekreten des 16. Jahrhunderts' (259–82); U. Götz, 'Hochsprache und Mundart im 17. Jahrhundert. Das Zeugnis des Regensburgers Johann Ludwig Prasch' (283–302); H. Grill, 'Mundart in Regensburg. Gedichte' (303–06); and L. Zehetner, 'Der Dialekt der Stadt Regensburg' (307–31).

Also noted: Z. Muljacic, 'Auf der Suche nach einer wahrscheinlich nicht fertiggestellten historischen Grammatik', *Fest. Göschel*, 76–79; P. Seidensticker, 'Kräuterbücher und Sprachwissenschaft. Ein Forschungsbericht', *ib.*, 80–94; J. Riecke, 'Deutsche Sprache und deutschsprachige Zeitungen in Lodz. Aspekte einer Geschichte des Neuhochdeutschen in Ostmitteleuropa', *ib.*, 95–118; and **Rheinisch-westfälische Sprachgeschichte*, ed. J. Macha et al. (NdS, 46), 2000, xii + 409 pp.

Germanic is represented by K. Düwel, 'Kämme mit Runeninschriften', *Fest. Cherubim*, 11–22; J. Goossens, '*r*-Metathese vor Dental im Westen der kontinentalen Germania', *Splett Vol.*, 10–22; D. H. Green, 'Zu den germanischen Wochentagsnamen in ihren europäischen Beziehungen', *Fest. Ruberg*, 223–36; A. Bammesberger, 'Urgermanisch **ajuk-* und altenglisch *ēcel/Ǫce* "ewig": Wortbildung und Phonologie', *Fest. Seebold*, 23–32; F. Heidermanns, 'Die germanischen Adjektive auf *-i-/-ja* und ihr indogermanischer Hintergrund', *ib.*, 145–76; and W. Hock, 'Zur Suppletion beim Adjektiv im Altgriechischen und Germanischen', *ib.*, 207–24. Gothic is represented by N. Wagner, 'Gotisch *weinnas*', *HSp*, 115:90–92; D. Kölligan, 'Gotisch hunsl "Opfer"', *ib.*, 99–111; and H. Fromm, 'Über Wahrscheinlichkeit und Unwahrscheinlichkeit gotischer Lehnwörter im Ostseefinnischen', *Fest. Seebold*, 93–104.

A detailed description of OHG is found in E. Meinecke and J. Schwerdt, *Einführung in das Althochdeutsche*, Paderborn, Schöningh, 2001, 350 pp. This goes all the way back to Indo-European, and then follows with an account of Germanic. The story really begins in Chapter 3 where there is a very detailed account of OHG texts with copious textual and historical notes containing references to secondary literature. Then comes the sound system and its development, inflectional morphology (very much like that in W. Braune's OHG grammar), word formation and syntax. In the chapter on the sound system there is an exceedingly long and involved discussion of the Second Sound Shift. After discussing the various theories it is then concluded that there is really no such thing as the Second Sound Shift! This whole section could be made more concise and enlivened with diagrams. One very curious point is why the authors use the terms *tenues* and *mediae*, which are certainly not state-of-the-art. The chapter on word formation, on the other hand, is very much to be welcomed. There is a detailed description of the suffixes and their functions but only hints as to their productivity. The syntax chapter deals primarily with sentence patterns and word order. The volume contains many maps and diagrams and an extensive bibliography which, however, is typographically unclear. It seems to have been squeezed into two columns on each page because it is rather long. This is rather a mixed work. Parts of it are very stimulating while other parts rather frustrating.

The vocabulary of OHG is the subject of *Chronologisches Wörterbuch des deutschen Wortschatzes. Der Wortschatz des 8. Jahrhunderts (und früherer Quellen)*, ed. E. Seebold et al., Berlin, de Gruyter, 2001, 532 pp. This is a comprehensive work dealing with the OHG vocabulary of the 8th c. and before. The term OHG includes Old Low German and the neologism *düdisch* is used for this larger variety. Its material derives from *Isidor* and other smaller texts, dictionaries, and glossaries such as *Abrogans*, and glosses. There is also a special section which lists the words quoted in Latin texts. After preliminary remarks the main part of the dictionary forms two sections, one dealing with all the vocabulary and another one listing those NHG words which date from the 8th c. or earlier. These are listed alphabetically and then chronologically. Among the earliest words are *hier* and *tun*. The section dealing with the whole vocabulary is a word-family dictionary. The head word is normalized according to *Tatian* and all the other related words listed. The nominal compounds occur in fact twice, once under the first component and secondly under the second component. Prefixes and some suffixes are listed so that it is clear what compound verbs exist so this a very useful work for the history of word formation. One hopes that a further volume will take the history of German vocabulary further. OHG also features in: N. B. Pimenova, 'Die funktional-semantische Verteilung der Eigenschaftsnomina auf *-î(n)* und *-ida* im Althochdeutschen und die Subjekt-Objekt-Relation', *ZDP*, 121:89–120; Id., 'Die Semantik der althochdeutschen Nomina aus zweiten Partizipien', *Sprachwissenschaft*,

27 : 1–24; A. Bammesberger, 'Althochdeutsch tiurlîh and altenglisch dêorlic', *ib.*, 25–29; P. W. Tax, 'Das Längezeichen *e* im Fränkischen und Alemannischen schon um 1000? Eine neue Hypothese', *ib.*, 129–42; R. Gusmani, 'Althochdeutsch *(hari)sliz*, lateinisch *(st)lis*', *HSp*, 115 : 111–16; W. Sanders, 'Zu ahd. *lenka* 'die Linke' im "Abrogans" ', *Splett Vol.*, 243–54; S. Sonderegger, 'Erneuerungstendenzen bei den althochdeutschen Personennamen auf *-wolf*', *ib.*, 290–97; V. Harm, 'Zur Genese der verallgemeinernden Relativsätze des Althochdeutschen', *IF*, 106, 2001 : 241–61; A. Greule, 'Semantische Relationen im althochdeutschen Verblexikon', *Fest. Ruberg*, 237–46; B. Bulitta, 'Ein Phantomwort im Althochdeutschen: *alapi*', *Fest. Seebold*, 33–40; V. Harm, 'Behauchung, Affrizierung, Frikativierung. Überlegungen zum Ausgangsstadium der althochdeutschen Tenuesverschiebung', *Fest. Göschel*, 17–30; Id., 'Neue Wege in der Lautverschiebungdiskussion?', *ZDL*, 69 : 56–68; and A. Mikeilitis-Winter, **Der Bereich Nahrungszubereitung im althochdeutschen Wortschatz. Onomasiologisch-semasiologische Untersuchungen* (Althochdeutsches Wörterbuch, Beiband), Berlin, Akademie, 2001, 386 pp.

Middle Low German items include R. Peters, '*Sust — Sost — Saust.* Zur Schreibung von mnd. ô' in Soest', *Splett Vol.*, 213–32, and C. Wanzeck, 'Zu Phraseologismen und Sprichwörtern in Dyl Vlenspiegel', *Fest. Seebold*, 373–90. Middle High German is represented by E. Meineke, 'Theorie und Praxis — Empirie und Rekonstruktion. Zum Projekt des neuen mittelhochdeutschen Wörterbuchs', *ZDA*, 131 : 143–71; K. Gärtner and R. Plate, 'Zur aktuellen Situation der Lexikographie des Mittelhochdeutschen', *Fest. Ruberg*, 247–56; R. Schmidt-Wiegand, 'Schweigen vor Gericht im Sachsenspiegel Eikes von Repgow', *ib.*, 257–62; N. R. Wagner, 'Zur Zeit des Zusammenfalls von mhd. *z* and *s*', *Sprachwissenschaft*, 27 : 143–47; R. Schmidt-Wiegand, '*Mit Finger und Zunge.* Formen des Schwörens in Text und Bild des Sachsenspiegels', *Splett Vol.*, 255–62; H.-J. Spitz, 'Zur Bedeutung von "Andacht" im St. Trudperter Hohenlied', *Splett Vol.*, 317–32; R. Bentzinger, 'Sprachschichtungen im spätmittelalterlichen Thüringisch', *Fest. Göschel*, 31–47; and E. Skála, 'Frühneuhochdeutsche Fachprosa in Böhmen: die Egerer Forstordnung von 1379', *ib.*, 48–57.

Early NHG studies include P. O. Müller, 'Usus und Varianz in der spätmittelalterlichen und frühneuzeitlichen Schreibsprache Nürnbergs', *ZGL*, 30 : 56–72; R. Bentzinger, 'Deutsch bei Ulrich von Hutten. Eine Betrachtung anhand syntaktischer Erscheinungen in seinen Dialogen', *Splett Vol.*, 1–9; I. Rösler, 'Sprachenwechsel in Norddeutschland (am Beispiel Mecklenburg)', *Akten* (*Wien*) III, 73–78; I. T. Piirainen, 'Zentrum und Peripherie in der frühneuhochdeutschen Schriftlichkeit in Schlesien und in der Slowakei', *ib.*,

79–85; U. Möllmann, 'Lexikalische Variation im Ostoberdeutschen des 15./16. Jahrhunderts', *ib.*, 97–105; J. Meier, 'Kommunikation im Spätmittelalter und in der frühen Neuzeit. Zur Textsortenklassifikation des Frühneuhochdeutschen', *ib.*, 107–12; M. Peters, 'Das 16. Jahrhundert als sprachtheoretische Epochenschwelle. Theodor Bibliander und Conrad Gessner', *ib.*, 113–18; W. Schindler, 'Bindestrich-Komposita im Frühneuhochdeutschen', *Fest. Seebold*, 313–30; M. Habermann, **Deutsche Fachtexte der frühen Neuzeit. Naturkundlich-medizinische Wissensvermittlung im Spannungsfeld von Latein und Volkssprache* (SLG, 61), 2001, xvii + 583 pp.; and A. Mihm, 'Ausgleichssprachen und frühneuzeitliche Standardisierung', *RVB*, 65, 2001: 315–59. Items on Luther noted: G. Hindelang, 'Denn von dieser Secten ist vns kund. Zur Übersetzung von *airesis* bei Luther und in den Revisionen der Lutherbibel', *Splett Vol.*, 99–116, and H. Wolf, 'Luthers Umgang mit Anthroponymen', *Fest. Göschel*, 58–75.

Acquisition of German in the 17th c. is the subject of H. Glück, 'Wie haben die Hugenotten Deutsch gelernt?', *DaF*, 39: 172–77. Also noted E. Papp, 'Deutsche Etymologie im 17. Jahrhundert. Johann Clauberg "Ars Etymologica Teutonum"(1663)', *Fest. Cherubim*, 81–96.

The 18th c. is represented by N. Semenjuk, 'Sozial-stilistische Schichtung der mündlichen Kommunikation nach den deutschen Sprachführern des 18. Jahrhunderts', *Akten* (*Wien*), III, 299–304; C. V. J. Russ, 'Mundart und Schriftsprache in den Briefen von Schillers Mutter', *ib.*, 305–11; G. Objartel, 'Sprachreflexivität bei Goethe: sogenannt. Mit vergleichenden Ausblicken', *Fest. Cherubim*, 97–104; and G. Lerchner, '"Nach den Mustern der besten Schriftsteller ..." Zu Gottscheds Konzept literaler Vorbilder in der standardsprachlichen Entwicklung des Deutschen', *Fest. Richter*, 21–29. Items on the 19th c. include G. Lerchner, 'Lebenserinnerungen eines sächsischen Gardereiters. Sprachgeschichtliche Beobachtungen an einem regionalsprachlichen Alltagstext um 1900', *Fest. Göschel*, 128–34; S. Elspass, 'Standardsprachliche Orientierung und regionale Variation im 19. Jahrhundert', *Akten* (*Wien*), III, 131–37; N. Nail, '*Go-in/Go-out*: Kontinuität und Wandel in der deutschen Studentensprache des 19. und 20. Jahrhunderts — ein Versuch', *ib.*, 135–53; W. Brandt, '"Turner üben, Sportler trainieren." Zur Turn- und Sportsprache im 19. Jahrhundert', *ib.*, 308–34; D. Stellmacher, 'Fußballberichterstattung im Vergleich. Auch ein Beitrag zur Geschichte des Deutschen im 20. Jahrhundert', *ib.*, 335–43; U. Püschel, '"Soft News" 1810. Wie die Zeitung über Unglücke berichtet', *Fest. Cherubim*, 35–44; W. Holly, 'Die Geschäftsordnung der Paulskirche als Text. Anmerkungen zur Geschichte einer Textsorte', *ib.*, 45–56; A. Burkhardt, '*Wühler*, *wühlen*, *Wühlerei*. Anmerkungen zu einer

"Schreckwort"-Familie der 48er Revolution', *ib.*, 57–68; I. Schikorsky, '"Dein in den Tod" — Zur Sprache der Liebe unter den Bedingungen des Krieges', *ib.*, 69–80; H. Blume, 'Städtisches und ländliches Hochdeutsch in Ostfalen um 1900', *ib.*, 105–14.

Items on the 20th c. are A. Lobenstein-Reichmann, 'Die Dolchstoßlegende. Zur Konstruktion eines sprachlichen Mythos', *Muttersprache*, 25–41, and A. Betten, '"1945 oder die 'Neue Sprache"'? Überprüfung einer Zäsur nach 50 Jahren', *Akten* (*Wien*), III, 139–46.

3. Orthography

Different aspects of orthography feature in S. Johnson, 'On the origin of linguistic norms: orthography, ideology and the first constitutional challenge to the 1996 reform of German', *JMMD*, 23:549–76; R. Hildebrandt, 'Zur unbewältigten Orthographie der neuhochdeutschen Dehnung', *Splett Vol.*, 92–98; W. P. Klein, 'Der Apostroph in der deutschen Gegenwartssprache. Logographische Gebrauchserweiterungen auf phonographischer Basis', *ZGL*, 30:169–97; and R. E. von Studnitz and D. W. Green, 'Interlingual homograph interference in German-English bilinguals: its modulation and locus of control', *Language and Cognition*, 5:1–24.

4. Phonology

A wide range of items was noted: M. Schnabel, 'Nochmals zum Problem der deutschen "r-Diphthonge"', *Sprachwissenschaft*, 27:105–22; U. Hirschfeld, 'Phonetik in Deutsch als Fremdsprache. Situation — Arbeits- und Forschungsschwerpunkte — Perspektiven', *DaF*, 39:82–87; T. A. Hall, 'Against extrasyllabic consonants in German and English', *Phonology*, 19:33–75; S. Mossmüller, 'The influence of creaky voice on formant frequency changes', *Forensic Linguistics*, 8:100–12; T. Wesener, 'Some non-sequential phenomena in German function words', *JIPA*, 31:17–27; A. P. Simpson, 'Does articulatory reduction miss more patterns than it accounts for?', *ib.*, 29–39; M. Grice and S. Baumann, 'Deutsche Intonation und GToBI', *LBer*, 191:267–98; R. Lauf, 'Aspekte der Sprechatmung: zur Verteilung, Dauer und Struktur von Atemgeräuschen in abgelesenen Texten', *Fest. Göschel*, 406–20; H. J. Künzel and J. E. Schmidt, 'Phonetische Probleme bei Tonakzent 1. Eine Pilotstudie', *ib.*, 421–39; W. H. Vieregge and A. P. A. Broeders, 'Ein Ansatz zur Bestimmung der Aussprachevariation aufgrund phonetischer Transkriptionen', *ib.*, 440–52; A. Braun, 'Sprechstimmlage und regionale Umgangssprache', *ib.*, 453–62; R. Meyer-Kalkus, **Stimme und Sprechkünste im 20. Jahrhundert*, Berlin, Akademie, 2001, vii + 508 pp.;

B. Alber, 'Regional variation and edges: glottal stop epenthesis and dissimilation in standard and southern varieties of German', *ZS*, 20, 2001 : 3–41; S. Moosmüller and R. Vollmann, '"Natürliches Driften" im Lautwandel: die Monophthongierung im österreichischen Deutsch', *ib.*, 42–65; M. Selting, 'Berlinische Intonationskonturen: "Die Treppe aufwärts"', *ib.*, 66–116; H.-H. Lieb, 'Was ist Wortakzent? Eine Untersuchung am Beispiel des Deutschen', *Fest. Seebold*, 225–62; and G. Debon, **Die Leistung der Sprachlaute. Zum Klangwort im Westen und Osten*, Ubstadt-Weiher, Guderjahn im Vlg Regionalkultur, 2001, 216 pp.

5. Morphology

A very important work is *Historische Wortbildung des Deutschen*, ed. M. Habermann et al. (RGL, 232), Tübingen, Niemeyer, ix + 474 pp., which gives a state-of-the-art account of historical word formation and its application to German. The following articles focus on the renaissance of historical word formation and discuss the paradigm switch to a historical/synchronic study: P. O. Müller, 'Historische Wortbildung im Wandel' (1–11); E. Seebold, 'Was ist synchronische Wortbildungslehre? Was ist diachronische Wortbildungslehre?' (13–22); H. H. Munske, 'Wortbildungswandel' (23–40), which sets out a whole programme; M. Habermann, 'Sprachwandel im Licht diachroner und synchroner Wortbildung' (41–57); O. Panagl, 'Verbal-abstrakta. Onomasiologische Vielfalt und semantischer Wandel' (59–74); F. Simmler, 'Pseudomorpheme. Ermittlungsmethoden, Typologie und Sprachgeschichte' (75–103); E. Ronneberger-Sibold, 'Volksetymologie und Paronomasie als lautnachahmende Wortschöpfung' (105–27), which deals with puns. The following treat aspects of the historical development of word formation in German and range from OHG to Early NHG: A. Bammesberger, 'Zur Vorgeschichte der althochdeutschen *lih*-Bildungen' (129–35); N. Pimenova, 'Die semantische Stellung von deverbalen *i(n)*-Nomina im althochdeutschen Wortbildungssystem' (137–58); K.-P. Wegera and H.-J. Solms, 'Wortbildung des Mittelhochdeutschen. Zur Methode und zum Stand ihrer Erforschung, dargestellt am Beispiel der Diminutive' (159–69); T. Klein and H. Sieburg, 'Basensuche und Bestimmung der Motivationsdichte in historischen Textkorpora. Theoretische Überlegungen und praktische Umsetzung' (171–91); K. Kronenberger, 'Die Substantivableitung mit *-e*, *-ede* und *-heit* in der Urkundensprache des 13. Jahrhunderts' (193–209); H. Sieburg, 'Zur Substantivableitung des Ripuarischen aus historischer Sicht' (211–25); V. Pavlov, 'Deverbale Nominalisierung im Frühneuhochdeutschen im Vergleich mit dem Neuhochdeutschen' (227–44);

O. Reichmann, 'Wortbildungsfelder des Frühneuhochdeutschen. Aufbau, Probleme ihrer lexikographischen Behandlung, sprachgeschichtliche Perspektiven' (245–67); M. Schulz, 'Wortbildung in Wörterbüchern und Texten des 17. Jahrhunderts' (269–87); M. Hundt, 'Die Instrumentalisierung der "Wortforschung" im Sprachpatriotismus des 17. Jahrhunderts' (289–313); S. Stricker, 'Konkurrenzen im Wortbildungssystem um 1800. Aufgezeigt an der Wortbildung Goethes' (315–39); L. M. Eichinger, 'Nominale Wortbildung in Sachtexten des 18. Jahrhunderts' (341–63); R. Bergmann, 'Wortbildung in einem historischen Neuhochdeutschen Wörterbuch' (365–79). The role and influence of borrowing in word formation are evidenced by: K. Dietz, 'Lexikalischer Transfer und Wortbildung am Beispiel des französischen Lehngutes im Mittelenglischen' (381–405); A. Lutz, 'Sprachmischung in der deutschen und englischen Wortbildung' (407–37); D. Kastovsky, 'Einheimische und entlehnte Morphophonemik in der deutschen Wortbildung synchron/diachron' (439–54). Finally, I. Barz, 'Phraseologisch gebundene Wortbildungen' (455–57), and P. von Polenz, 'Historische Wortbildung und Sprachbewußtseinsgeschichte' (459–63), draw some of the threads together. This is a very stimulating work and one hopes that research in this area will continue to flourish.

A detailed exemplification of historical word formation in action is found in B. Thomas, *Adjektivderivation im Nürnberger Frühneuhochdeutsch um 1500. Eine historisch-synchrone Analyse anhand von Texten Albrecht Dürers, Veit Dietrichs und Heinrich Deichslers* (Wortbildung des Nürnberger Frühneuhochdeutsch, 3), Berlin, de Gruyter, xvi + 593 pp., which completes this word formation project at the university of Erlangen. The corpus on which the work is based is largely that of Albrecht Dürer but there are two smaller corpora from Veit Dietrich and Heinrich Deichsler. The volume falls into three parts: a theoretical discussion and review of literature, the morphological analysis, and then a detailed synthesis of the material with a global comparison with NHG. The morphological analysis comprises a complete listing of all the 726 lexemes, their morphological and semantic analysis. All the material is made available so that linguists can easily make comparisons with their own lists. Of the three morphological formations, suffixation, prefixation, and circumfixation, suffixation is the most frequent. The top suffixes are *-lich* and *-ig* which represent over 50% of the recorded forms. In NHG this has changed and *-ig* has become the most frequent suffix in written NHG followed by *-isch* with *-lich* in third place. Among the prefixes *un-* is the most frequent. This is very carefully researched work which is a major contribution to the history of German word formation. An important feature of the volume is the clear type.

A theoretically challenging work is H. Baeskow, *Abgeleitete Personenbezeichnungen im Deutschen und Englischen. Kontrastive Wortbildungsanalysen im Rahmen des minimalistischen Programms und unter Berücksichtigung sprachhistorischer Aspekte* (SLG, 62), 769 pp., which, for the first time, undertakes a comparative study of word formation in two languages. The theoretical framework is Chomsky's minimalist program and there is a detailed chapter outlining how it can be applied to word formation. 15 suffixes in German and English are dealt with and subdivided into *nomina agentis*, *nomina patientis*, *nomina qualitatis*, and *nomina originis*. Loan suffixes predominate, particularly in English. There is a detailed account of the modern functions of each suffix as well as a good historical account of their development. This volume is good on theory and on many aspects of word formation but one or two sections, e.g. on English loans in modern German, are rather thin. The historical insights of this book will probably outlive its theoretical usefulness. The originality of comparing word formation systems is very much to be welcomed.

A practical work on word formation is I. Barz et al., *Wortbildung — praktisch und integrativ. Ein Arbeitsbuch* (Leipziger Skripten, 2), Frankfurt, Lang, 187 pp., which would be very handy for a course on word formation. The first chapter is concerned with the analysis of word derivations, their semantic motivation, and types of word formation. The remainder of the book deals with word formation and different linguistic levels: grammar, lexicology, textlinguistics/stylistics, orthography, lexicography, and finally with diachronic aspect of word formation. The definitions given in the book are clear and supported by the glossary. Quite a large amount of the text is taken up by *Aufgaben*, over 100 of them, bristling with examples, some in texts to which answers are given. This is a really useful book in this supremely creative area of language.

Also noted: W. Motsch, 'Wortbildungsregeln', *Fest. Stickel*, 39–54; A. Pounder, 'Adverb-marking in German and English: system and standardization', *Diachronica*, 18, 2001 : 301–58; A. Seiffert, 'Probleme synchroner Fremdwortbildungsforschung', *NMi*, 103 : 161–78; B. Kaltz, 'Zur Entwicklung der Wortbildungstheorie in der deutschen Grammatikographie 1750–1800', *BGS*, 12 : 27–48; N. Döring, '"Kurz. wird gesendet." Abkürzungen und Akronyme in der SMS-Kommunkiation', *Muttersprache*, 112 : 97–14; M. Aronoff and N. Fuhrhop, 'Restricting suffix combinations in German and English: closing suffixes and the monosuffix constraint', *NLLT*, 20 : 451–90; T. Savolainen, 'Zur Produktivität des Wortbildungsmodells *herum* + Verb', *Fest. Cherubim*, 187–94; and E. Fobbe, 'Präfigierte Indefinitpronomina', *ib.*, 195–206.

Inflectional morphology includes the historical article: L. Gaeta, 'Umlaut extension in German modals as natural change', *Diachronica*, 19:1–41; B. Forssman, '*schworen, schwur, geschworen*', *Fest. Seebold*, 77–92; R. Harnisch, **Grundform- und Stamm-Prinzip in der Substantivmorphologie des Deutschen. Synchronische und diachronische Untersuchung eines typologischen Parameters* (Germanistische Bibliothek, 10), Heidelberg, Winter, 2001, xii + 306 pp.; and G. Bellmann, 'Standardisierung und Umstandardisierung: der siebente/der siebte', *ZDL*, 69:1–37.

6. Syntax

A general item is R. Lühr, 'Konzeptionierungen des Prädikativums in der Indogermania', *ZS*, 21:4–24. Items on the noun phrase and its members include: N. Fries, 'Ist Deutsch eine schwere Sprache? Am Beispiel des Genus-Systems', *Fest. Cherubim*, 131–46; G. Müller, 'Syntaktisch determinierter Kasuswegfall in der deutschen NP', *LBer*, 189:89–114; P. Baerentzen, 'Deren oder derer? Versuch einer Richtigstellung', *BGDSL*, 124:44–48; C. Dürscheid, '"Polemik satt und Wahlkampf pur" — Das postnominale Adjektiv im Deutschen', *ZS*, 21:57–81; P. Bassola, 'Adjektive mit passivischen Infinitivkonstruktionen und konjunktional eingeleitete passivische Infinitivkonstruktionen in einem historischen Korpus', *Fest. Stickel*, 1–19; and L. M. Eichinger, 'Adjektive Postmodern: wo die Lebensstile blühen', *ib.*, 579–604.

Items on the verb phrase and its members include: H.-W. Eroms, 'Kontrollverben und Korrelate', *Fest. Stickel*, 21–38; J. Sabel, 'Die Doppelobjekt-Konstruktion im Deutschen', *LBer*, 190:229–44; S. Featherston, 'Coreferential objects in German: experimental evidence on reflexivity', *LBer*, 192:457–84; A. Heine, 'Funktionsverbgefüge im Lernerwörterbuch am Beispiel von Langenscheidts Großwörterbuch Deutsch als Fremdsprache (LGWDaF)', *NMi*, 103:51–62; J. van Pottelberge, **Verbonominale Konstruktionen, Funktionsverbgefüge. Vom Sinn und Unsinn eines Untersuchungsgegenstandes* (Germanistische Bibliothek, 12), Heidelberg, Winter, 2001, xii + 482 pp.; A. Golato, 'Grammar and interaction: reported discourse and subjunctive in German', *ZS*, 21:25–56; U. Bredel and H. Lohnstein, 'Zur Ableitung von Tempus und Modus in der deutschen Verbflexion', *ib.*, 20, 2001:218–50; O. Leirbukt, 'Über temporale Perspektivierung und modale Differenzierungen in Konstruktionen mit vergangenheitsbezogenen Formen des Konjunktivs', *Fest. Cherubim*, 161–70; B. Sieberg, 'Analytische Imperfektbildungen in der gesprochenen Sprache', *Muttersprache*, 112:240–52; A. Lipsky, 'Eine semantische und pragmatische Darstellung der Konstruktion *werden* + Infinitiv', *DaF*, 39:103–07.

Word order surfaces in J. P. Zitterbart, 'Zur Mittelfeldfähigkeit des Korrelats *es* in Verbindung mit Subjektsätzen', *Sprachwissenschaft*, 27: 149–95, and R. Musan, 'Informationsstrukturelle Dimensionen im Deutschen', *ZGL*, 30: 198–221.

Subordinate clauses feature in K. Rohs, 'Zum Begriffsverständnis des modalen Nebensatzes', *DaF*, 39: 167–71; K. K. Grohmann, 'Anti-locality and clause types', *TL*, 28: 43–72; H. Rehbock, 'Exzitative W-Sätze', *Fest. Cherubim*, 147–60. Adverbs are the subject of W. P. Schmid, 'Adverb und Adverbiale im Deutschen', *Fest. Cherubim*, 181–86. Particles and conjunctions feature in S. Günther, 'Konnektoren im gesprochenen Deutsch — Normverstoß oder funktionale Differenzierung?' *DaF*, 39: 67–74; M. Egbert, 'Sytaktische Merkmale von übrigens in seiner Hauptposition: im Mittelfeld des Verb-Zweit-Satzes', *ZGL*, 30: 1–22; and B. Strecker, 'Ja doch, eigentlich schon noch. Alltagsroutinen des Kommunikationsmanagements', *Fest. Stickel*, 555–77.

Historical studies are represented by K. Axel, 'Zur diachronen Entwicklung der syntaktischen Integration linksperipherer Adverbialsätze im Deutschen: ein Beispiel für syntaktischen Wandel?', *BGDSL*, 124: 1–43; S. de Groodt, 'Reanalysis and the five problems of language change: a case study on the rise of the concessive subordinating conjunctions with *ob-* in Early Modern German', *STUF*, 55: 277–88; and F. Simmler, 'Zur Geschichte prä- und postnuklearer Adjektivattribute vom 9. bis 16. Jahrhundert', *Akten* (*Wien*), III, 87–96.

Also noted: M. Schlesewsky et al., 'Das Problem mit syntaktischen Funktionsambiguitäten. Eine kritische Betrachtung zu einem Überblick von Bader/Meng/Bayer/Hopf', *ZS*, 20, 2001: 251–65, and M. Bader et al., 'Syntaktische Funktionsambiguitäten im Deutschen — eine Klarstellung', *ib.*, 266–79.

7. Semantics

The concept of the word has always been controversial and much discussed but in *Fest. Reichmann* it has a whole volume devoted to it. The first, and larger half, consists of contributions which concentrate on the systematic and present-day aspects of the word: V. Ágel and R. Kehrein, 'Das Wort: Sprech- und/oder Schreibzeichen? Ein empirischer Beitrag zum latenten Gegenstand der Linguistik' (3–28), argue that the word is a written sign with internal speech sign divisions for literate language users; D. Geeraerts, 'The scope of diachronic onomasiology' (29–43), examines the notion of onomasiology and how the word is useful at the level of *parole*; U. Hass-Zumkehr, 'Das Wort in der Korpuslinguistik. Chancen und Probleme empirischer Lexikologie' (45–70), shows how a theoretical lexicology which uses corpus linguistics has to answer anew the question of what a word is; A. Lobenstein-Reichmann, 'Die Syntagmenangabe, ein Stiefkind der Bedeutungslexikographie' (71–88), exemplifies from the Early NHG dictionary how the study and choice of syntagms can reveal the attitudes and 'world view' of the people of that time; H. Speer, 'Deutsches Rechtswörterbuch' (89–110), asks how changes in medium, e.g. from oral to written, can influence the meaning of legal terms and whether digital dictionaries can provide the necessary links between words to study their historical development; A. Gardt, 'Wort, Text und Bedeutung. Aspekte der semantischen Erschließung von Texten' (111–32), argues that the meaning of individual words must be put into a wider context in the ascertaining of their meaning; J. A. Bär, 'Das Wort im Spiegel der Sprachkritik' (133–58), sketches the historical development of word criticism and shows that it chiefly arises when there is a perceived mismatch between the word and its meaning; P. Wiesinger, 'Austriazismen als Politikum. Zur Sprachpolitik in Österreich' (159–82), gives a survey of language policy in Austria since 1945, pointing out that there is no coherent internal language policy and that young people face a barrage of German, as opposed to Austrian, usage from the print and electronic media; A. Betten and P. Mauser, 'Deutsche Wörter im Exil' (183–200), find that Jewish speakers of German who have lived in Israel since the 1930s still maintain a high fluency in literary standard German; they show some interference word formation from English and Hebrew and, if they have been back in Germany, have some difficulty in understanding some forms of present-day German, especially prefixed verbs; S. Sonderegger, 'Philologische Probleme der deutschen Bibelübersetzung: der Prolog des Lukas-Evangeliums' (201–16), in a detailed analysis shows how Luke 1 : 1–4, which is one elegant period in older versions, has only really become simplified into two or more sentences in the 20th c. when new translations have converged more than in the past; and G. Rau, 'Zur Funktionalität einer Wort -Gottes-Theologie im 20. Jahrhundert' (217–26), gives an account of theological traditions of the word of God, emphasizing how the word of God theology is enjoying a renaissance at the present time. The smaller second section deals with historical themes: K.-P. Wegera, '*Mich enhabe diu âventiure betrogen.* Ein Beitrag zur Wort- und Begriffsgeschichte von *âventiure* im Mittelhochdeutschen' (229–44), uses a broad range of sources to ascertain the different meanings of *âventiure*; W. Kühlmann, 'Rätsel der Wörter: Zur Diskussion von "Fachsprache" und Lexikographie im Umkreis der Paracelsisten des 16. Jahrhunderts' (245–62), turns the spotlight on a 16th-c. discussion of technical terms, illustrated by a letter to the Fugger family; J. Telle,

'Fachschriftsteller als "Rhätersschreiber". Rätselreime aus deutschen Alchemica der frühen Neuzeit' (263–77), introduces the riddles that alchemists used in the 16th and 17th cs and presents a collection of them; W. Besch, 'Lexikalischer Wandel in der Zürcher Bibel. Eine Längsschnittstudie' (279–96), using Matthew's Gospel, shows how there was an independent trend in the Swiss Bible tradition although eventually the Luther forms win through but not until the 19th c. and in other cases both the Zurich and Lutheran version choose a neutral term; J. Schildt, 'Präfigierung von Simplexverben. Beobachtungen zur semantischen Entwicklung frühneuhochdeutscher Verben' (197–302), describes how prefixed verbs take over some of the meanings of unprefixed verbs, with the consequence that the latter's meaning becomes restricted; T. Roelcke, 'Das Niederländische in der deutschen Sprachreflexion des Barock und der Aufklärung' (303–19), reviews German opinions about Dutch in the 17th and 18th cs: the preferred term for Dutch in the 17th c. is *Niederländisch* and it is regarded mostly as a dialect of German, but in the 18th c. the preferred name is *Holländisch* and it is regarded more as an independent language; and H. Schmidt, 'Frühneuhochdeutsche Zustände im Spätneuhochdeutschen?' (321–42), reveals how there is a variety of actual linguistic usage which lurks beneath the veneer of the modern standard. He flags up many unnoticed tendencies of changes towards weak declension, uncertainty with regard to the cases after verbs, adjectives and prepositions with exact documentation. Some of the examples would hearten any undergraduate class! This stimulating volume contains a wide range of examples and theoretical approaches, mostly semantic but in some instances grammatical.

General items on semantics are: F. Hundsnurscher, 'Pragmatische Wortsemantik. Zum pragmatischen Hintergrund einer gebrauchstheoretisch orientierten lexikalischen Semantik', *Splett Vol.*, 128–42; E. Weigand, 'Wortfamilien und Semantik', *ib.*, 342–50; S. Wichter, 'Zur vergleichenden Analyse varietätenspezifischer Bedeutungen', *ib.*, 351–61; T. Kaneko, 'Wo die Semantik anfängt', *Fest. Stickel*, 89–122; K. Ehlich, 'Wissen, Sprache. Thesen zu einer Pragmatischen Fundierung von Semantik', *Fest. Cherubim*, 207–14; and G. Bellmann, 'Biographie und Lexik: der Konspekt', *Fest. Göschel*, 154–60.

Contrastive studies feature R. Safina, 'Komponentenanalyse der Phraseologismen. Kontrastive Untersuchung deutsch-russisch', *Sprachwissenschaft*, 27:55–77; H. Schottmann, 'Deutsche und schwedische Phraseologie', *Splett Vol.*, 263–80; and H. Liedtke, 'Zum Anredesystem im Deutschen und Dänischen', *Fest. Cherubim*, 303–15.

The study of individual words occurs in W. Scholze-Stubenrecht, '"Die Auswahl der Einträge ist äußerst beliebig." Warum Jagdherr und Pokémon nicht im Duden stehen', *Sprachwissenschaft*, 27:225–48; W. Zillig, '*Ähnlich, gleich* und *identisch*. Einige Probleme der Bestimmung von Adjektivbedeutungen, dargestellt an drei "schwierigen" Adjektiven', *Splett Vol.*, 362–76; P.-A. Mumm, Deutsch *Kamm*, *Kimme* und die Bedeutung von idg. **gombho-*, **gembh-*', *Fest. Seebold*, 295–312; G. A. M. Sigl, 'Die Entstehung der Bedeutung "Erkältungskrankheit" beim Wort *Grippe*', *ib.*, 331–48; T. Vennemann gen. Nierfeld, 'Zur Etymologie von Senne. Mit einem Anhang zur Etymologie von lat. *câseus* "Käse"', *ib.*, 359–72; and J. Udolph, **Ostern. Geschichte eines Wortes* (Indogermanische Bibliothek, 3, Untersuchungen, 20), Heidelberg, Winter, 2001, 125 pp.

Also noted: C. S. Borneto, 'Was im Deutschen *steht* und *liegt*. Überlegungen zur Raumsemantik', *Fest. Stickel*, 123–47; H. Günther, 'Stolz darauf, ein (z.B.) Germanist zu sein', *ib.*, 149–63; G. Strauss and G. Zifonun, 'Auf der Suche nach Identität', *ib.*, 165–213; K. Steyer, 'Wenn der Schwanz mit dem Hund wedelt. Zum linguistischen Erklärungspotenzial der korpusbasierten Kookkurrenzanalyse', *ib.*, 215–36; and H. Altmann, 'Zur Semantik der Farbadjektiva im Deutschen', *Fest. Seebold*, 1–22.

Loan words feature in K.-H. Best, 'Ein Beitrag zur Fremdwortdiskussion', *Fest. Cherubim*, 263–70; C. Krause-Braun, '"Aliens in der deutschen Pressesprache." Anglizismen im heutigen Pressedeutsch — ein Vergleich der *Badischen Zeitung* von 1949 und 1999', *Muttersprache*, 112:155–73; W. Schäfer, 'Von Handys und Erbex. Zur Diskussion um Anglizismen im heutigen Deutsch', *DaF*, 39:75–81; K. Baumann, 'Entwicklungen beim Gebrauch von Anglizismen in Werbetexten aus Ost- und Westdeutschland', *ib.*, 138–43; E. O'Halloran, 'Gallizismen und Anglizismen in der deutschen Mode- und Gemeinsprache im 20. Jahrhundert', *DSp*, 30:50–65; E. Morlicchio, 'Germanismen im Wortschatz des Italienischen', *Splett Vol.*, 185–97; G. Gréciano, 'Europaphraseologie. Zur Findung und Verbreitung der Begriffe über Bilder', *Fest. Stickel*, 305–23; and W. Sarcher, **Das deutsche Lehngut im Französischen als Zeugnis für den Wissenstransfer im 20. Jahrhundert* (Philologia, 49), Hamburg, Kovac, 2001, 699 pp.

Youth language is dealt with by H. Elsen, 'Neologismen in der Jugendsprache', *Muttersprache*, 112:136–54.

Lexicographical studies are represented by H. Schmidt, 'Lieblingsrenommierwörter und Verbalmissgeburten oder Sprach-Fülldrang von Lesepudding bis Wortschleim. Über die Aufgaben allgemeinsprachlicher und autorenspezifischer Wörterbücher', *Fest. Cherubim*, 271–78, and G. Kolde, 'Zur Geschichte der lexikographischen Definition im allgemeinen einsprachigen Wörterbuch des Deutschen', *ib.*, 279–90.

Hermann Paul, *Deutsches Wörterbuch. Bedeutungsgeschichte und Aufbau unseres Wortschatzes*, ed. H. Henne, 10th edn, Tübingen, Niemeyer, xxi + 1243 pp., has undergone a make-over. It is now concerned both with the history and the structure of German vocabulary. The main player in this is the *Sachregister* which comprises two parts: a two-page summary with headings such as *Adelung, Anglizimus*, some of which have cross-references, the latter to *Amerikanisches Englisch* and *Englisch*, and a more detailed index with examples of head-words. Word formation, for instance, has about 20 cross-references. Thus *Amerikanisches Englisch* refers to: *ausflippen*, *clever*, *Yankee*, *Vamp*, whereas *Englisch* refers to more examples, from *Adresse*, *Analyst* to *Video*, *Waggon*, and *Zoo*. It is perhaps rather pedantic to ask whether the authors distinguish exactly between the two types of English. One can easily criticize the choice of categories but in general the expansion is very positive. The volume could easily be used for a course on German vocabulary. The omission of a separate category on Luther is however a loss. He appears in the summary headings but with cross references to several other more general categories such as *Wortschöpfung*. The structure of the vocabulary is illustrated with the treatment of 13 word fields, e.g. *klug*. There is also a category of antonyms and homonyms. The main area of interest, however, remains the historical domain and this has been brought up to date by using categories such as *DDR*, *Nachkriegszeit*, and *Wende*. The dictionary is based on quotations, whose sources are listed in the final section. The inside covers show how the *Sachregister* and dictionary intertwine and how to read the dictionary entries. All in all a fascinating book for anyone interested in words.

The *Deutsches Wörterbuch*, Stuttgart–Leipzig, Hirzel, continues on its way with vol. 3, fasc. 2, 2000, *appelliere-Arzneiglas*, cols 161–320, fasc. 3, 2001, *Arzneiglas-auffassen*, cols 321–480, fasc. 4, *auffassen-aufpfeifen*, cols 481–640, and vol. 9, fascs 1–2, 2001, *F-Feldprediger*, cols 1–320. Also noted: D. Herberg, 'Der lange Weg zur Stichwortliste. Aspekte der Stichwortselektion für ein allgemeinsprachliches Neologismenwörterbuch', *Fest. Stickel*, 237–250; C.-P. Herbermann, 'Benennungsprinzipien und Benennungssituationen. Zu einigen Grundbegriffen der Etymologie', *Splett Vol.*, 70–91; and B. Paraschkewow, Zur lexikographischen Darstellung des Phänomens etymologischer Duplizität', *ZGL*, 30:23–55.

8. Dialects

Some general aspects of dialectal and regional linguistic differences are dealt with in the following contributions from *Akten* (*Wien*), III: H. Löffler, 'Einleitung zu "Gesprochene Sprache in regionaler und sozialer Differenzierung"' (157–64); E. Werlén, '"Dichte Beschreibung" in der Erforschung sprachlicher Variation' (165–72); L. M. Eichinger, 'Alltagssprache zwischen regionaler Bindung und sozialer Wahl' (173–79); E. Neuland, 'Stilbildung und Substandardisierung — am Beispiel von Jugendsprachen' (181–86); D. Tophinke and E. Ziegler, 'Plädoyer für eine kontextsensitive Modellierung von Spracheinstellungen' (187–93); D. Hartmann, 'Bewertungen der regionalen Umgangssprache des Ruhrgebiets. Zum Forschungsstand heute' (195–204); A. Vierhufe, 'Berliner Schnauze. Sprach- und Stilbewertung einer Stadtmundart im Feuilleton des 19. und 20. Jahrhunderts' (205–10); A. Häcki-Buhofer, 'Der Zusammenhang von Dialektbewusstsein und Charakteristik der gesprochenen Sprache' (211–16); H. Christen, '"Swissdate" — Aspekte dialektalen Sprechens im Schweizer Privatfernsehen' (217–25); G. Schunk, 'Wo bitte geht's zum Regiolekt? Wege dialektaler Regionalisierung' (227–33); H. Tatzreiter, 'Gleichklänge und Hemmschwellen im Sprung vom Dialekt zur Standardsprache — anhand von Beispielen fallender Diphthonge im Mittelbairischen' (235–41); F. Patocka, 'Die Großstadt als syntaktisches Spannungsfeld' (243–48); P. Gilles, 'Untersuchungen zur regionalen Färbung der Intonation des Standarddeutschen. Diskussion eines methodischen Zugangs' (249–55); J. K. Androutspoulos, 'Ethnolektale Entwicklungen im Sprachgebrauch Jugendlicher' (257–62); K. Siewert, 'Sondersprachenforschung in Deutschland' (263–71); S. Krämer-Neubert, 'Reliktgebiete in Unterfranken im 21. Jahrhundert' (281–86). H. Löffler, 'Stadtsprachen-Projekte im Vergleich: Basel und Mannheim', *Fest. Stickel*, 477–500. Also noted: R. Harnisch, 'Sprachwissenschaft im Epochenumbruch von der Spätaufklärung zur Romantik. Zum 150. Todestag von Johann Andreas Schmeller (1785–1852)', *ZDL*, 69:257–74; P. Wagener, 'Gesprochenes Deutsch online. Zur Modernisierung des Deutschen Spracharchivs', *ib.*, 314–35; P. Wiesinger, 'Die deutsche Dialektologie zwischen Tradition und Neuansätzen', Stellmacher, *Dialektologie*, 15–30; E. Ziegler, '"Wir reden so und nicht so und das bleibt auch so." Sprachgebrauch und Spracheinstellung im Familienkontext', *ib.*, 65–77; J. Ruge, 'Generationsspezifische Untersuchungen am mundartlichen Fachwortschatz', *ib.*, 136–42; P. Auer et al., 'Intonation regionaler Varietäten des Deutschen. Vorstellung eines Forschungsprojekts', *ib.*, 222–39; E. Eggers, 'Überlegungen zur Entwicklung der Phonologie aus der Sicht der Allgemeinen und Indogermanischen Sprachwissenschaft und ihre Implikationen für die Dialektologie', *ib.*, 240–48; E. Glaser, 'Erhebungsmethoden dialektaler Syntax', *ib.*, 258–76; D. B. Burry, 'Deutsche Dialekte in der formalsyntaktischen Forschung', *ib.*, 277–84; K. Rein, 'Dringend anstehende Aufgaben der internationalen germanistischen Dialektologie', *ib.*, 285–87; H. Scheuringer, 'Mit den Methoden des 19. Jahrhunderts auf dem Weg ins 21. Jahrhundert? Vorschläge zur Standortbestimmung in der deutschen Dialektologie', *ib.*, 431–39. General items on dialect lexicography are G. Koch, 'Das Dialektwörterbuch zwischen ein- und zweisprachigem Wörterbuch: wie wichtig ist der Zugriff auf grammatische Angaben?', *Sprachwissenschaft*, 27:79–103, and H. Weber, '"Wenn das Wörtchen *wenn* nicht wär ..." Konjunktionen im Mundartwörterbuch', *Fest. Göschel*, 213–17. Berlin and Brandenburg are discussed by J. Wiese, *Kleines Brandenburg-Berliner Wörterbuch*, Leipzig, Reclam, 1996, 139 pp., which is based on larger works and gives the regional distribution of the words it treats.

Low German features in H. Menke, 'Niederdeutsch: eigenständige Sprache oder Varietät einer Sprache?', *Fest. Splett*, 171–84; P. Siemund, 'Mass versus count. Pronominal gender in regional varieties', *STUF*, 55:213–33; J. Peters, 'Intonation und Fokus im Hamburgischen', *LBer*, 189:27–58; P. Martens, 'Zur Schreibung des Niederdeutschen. Eine Kritik der "Bremer Schreibung" in der "Niederdeutschen Grammatik" von 1998', *ZDL*, 69:146–62; G. Reershemius, 'Bilingualismus oder Sprachverlust? Zur Lage und zur aktiven Verwendung des Niederdeutschen in Ostfriesland am Beispiel einer Dorfgemeinschaft', *ib.*, 163–81; H.-W. Appel, 'Vom Zettelkasten zur elektronischen Datenbank. Probleme einer synchronen Phonologie niederdeutscher Dialekte und computergestützte Lösungsansätze', Stellmacher, *Dialektologie*, 399–416; U. Föllner, 'Beobachtungen zur Rolle der Vertriebenen beim Wandel im Gebrauch des Ostfälischen nach dem Zweiten Weltkrieg', *ib.*, 166–71; and B. Kellermeier, 'Gibt es in Duisburg auch (noch) eine Sprachbarriere?', *ib.*, 126–35.

Bavarian features F. Patocka, 'Aspekte der Syntax des Bairischen', Stellmacher, *Dialektologie*, 249–57; K. Hohensinner, 'Zur Datierung des mittelbairischen -ch- Schwundes anhand der urkundlichen Überlieferung der Siedlungsnamen auf mhd. -ach in Oberösterreich', *ZDL*, 69:129–45; **Sprachatlas von Oberösterreich* (SAO), fasc. 4, 32 maps, fasc. 5, maps 127–58, ed. S. Gaisbauer and H. Scheuringer, Linz, Adalbert-Stifter-Institut des Landes Oberösterreich, 2001; and A. Wildfeuer, **Der Dialekt im Kirchdorfer Land. Stand und Tendenzen eines zentralmittelbairischen Subdialekts* (RBDSL, Reihe B, Untersuchungen, 76), 2001, 226 pp.

East Franconian studies include S. Krämer-Nebert, 'Was also ist des Pudels Keil? Zu Sprachräumen in Unterfranken', Stellmacher, *Dialektologie*, 172–87, and B. Dürrschmidt, **Dialektwandel im fränkisch-bairischen Kontaktraum* (Schriften zum Bayerischen Sprachatlas, 5), Heidelberg, Winter, 2001, 41 pp. + 71 maps.

Low Alemannic is represented by M. Philipp and E. Weider, *Sein und haben im elsass-lothringischen Mundartraum. Ein organisiertes Chaos* (*ZDL*, Beihefte, 122), Stuttgart, Steiner, 107 pp. + 28 maps; and A. Bothorel-Witz and D. Huck, 'Die Dialekte im Elsaß zwischen Tradition und Modernität', Stellmacher, *Dialektologie*, 143–55. The development of language in the Upper Rhine area is dealt with in W. Kleiber, 'Otfrids liber evangeliorum (863/871) — HSS: Historischer Südwestdeutscher Sprachatlas (1280–1430) — SSA: Südwestdeutscher Sprachatlas (1984ff.) 1100 Jahre Sprachgeschichte am Oberrhein in diatopischer Sicht (Mit vier Karten)', *Fest. Ruberg*, 263–84.

Swabian is covered by D. Berroth, **Altersbedingter Mundartgebrauch. Wandel und Kontinuität in einem mittelschwäbischen Dialekt* (ZDL, Beihefte, 116), Stuttgart, Steiner, 2001, 220 pp.

Aspects of Swiss German feature in P. Dalcher, 'Innerschweizer Dialekt-Spezialitäten', *Der Geschichtsfreund*, 154, 2001: 63–74; H. Christen, '*Wo chiemte mer hi*: zum Überleben eines sprachhistorischen Fossils', *Fest. Seebold*, 55–76; W. Haas, 'Sprachwandel in *apparent time* und in *real time*', *ib.*, 125–44; H. Christen, 'Chamäleons und Fossilien. Forschungsperspektiven für die konsolidierte schweizerisch-alemannische Dialektologie', Stellmacher, *Dialektologie*, 31–47; and B. Siebenhaar, 'Variation und Einstellung in einer dialektologischen Labilitätszone', *ib.*, 99–125.

One of the isolated Alpine dialects of highest Alemannic is described by C. V. J. Russ, *Die Mundart von Bosco Gurin. Eine synchronische und diachronische Untersuchung* (*ZDL*, Beihefte, 120), Stuttgart, Steiner, 211 pp. + 8 maps. R. documents this dialect in a very detailed way, his study deriving both from field work and the use of secondary sources. The study covers phonetics/phonology, grammar, and vocabulary. The latter comprises a treatment of word formation and loans, and then the rest of the vocabulary is presented according to lexical areas. The historical dimension is also included, particularly with regard to the phonology. Chapter 5 gives a useful summary of both the synchronic and the diachronic. The research on this dialect goes back over a century but this is the first time that a complete description has been presented. R. gives a survey of what has already been undertaken as well as setting Bosco Gurin in its geographical and historical setting. Appendices provide a collection of quotations on Bosco Gurin, a collection of writing texts, and transcriptions of tape-recordings. Also noted: O. Holzapfel, 'Die Entstehung des alpenländischen Mundartliedes nach 1800 als Spiegelbild einer neuen Wertschätzung des Dialekts', *ZDL*, 69: 38–57, and P. Zürrer, 'Kontaktlinguistische Variation in Sprachinseldialekten', *Europa Ethnica*, 57, 2000: 148–65.

The dialect areas of Vorarlberg and Liechtenstein are treated in a number of items by H. Klausmann: **Wortgeographie der Sprachlandschaften Vorarlbergs und Liechtensteins. Umgrenzung, Innengliederung und äußere Einflüsse in der Wortgeographie zwischen Alpenrhein und Arlberg* (DDG, 94), Marburg, Elwert, 190 pp. + 100 maps; Id., 'Wortgeographische Besonderheiten Vorarlbergs I: der Nordrand', *Montfort*, 52, 2000: 250–63; Id., 'Wortgeographische Besonderheiten Vorarlbergs II: der Bregenzerwald', *ib.*, 53, 2001 : 298–312. Also noted: E. Gabriel, 'Die Ebniter Mundart', pp. 48–57 of *650 Jahre Walsersiedlung*, ed. W. Matt et al. (Dornbirner Schriften. Beiträge zur Stadtkunde, 28), Dornbirn; Id., 'Lautnachahmende Wörter im Gebiet des "Vorarlberger Sprachatlas" (VALTS)', *Montfort*, 53, 2001 : 278–97.

West Central German is splendidly represented by the two latest volumes of *Mittelrheinischer Sprachatlas*, ed. G. Bellmann et al., vol. 4: *Konsonantismus*. Tübingen, Niemeyer, 1999, x + maps 314–478, and vol. 5: *Formenlehre*, Tübingen, Niemeyer, xi + maps 479a-683. Vol. 4 uses West Germanic as a reference system for the development of the consonants. At the beginning of the volume is a map showing dialect deviation from the standard. The trend seems to be towards more standard forms. Many of the maps shed interesting light on the Second Sound Shift, showing more relic forms and a shift of intervocalic *ck* in *gebacken* to [x] in the Ahr valley. There are many isoglosses which cross the region and this work would repay hours of detailed study. Many of the famous north/south lines run through the area: *us/uns*, final *nk*/ŋ and *st/scht*. Through the use of the two series of data, changes can be seen taking place: [r] is on the increase as is [s] for *ch* after front vowels. Similar symbols are used for the same phenomena in different maps. One difficulty is that the category 'Ausfall des Konsonanten' is used in a very general way and only a careful examination of the samples of actual responses can help to elucidate its exact meaning. Vol. 5 is very important since it deals with inflectional and derivational morphology, both rather neglected aspects of dialectology. All aspects of noun and verb morphology are covered. The regularization of the vowel in the past participle or the presence of *rückumlaut* features to a large extent. Again as in vol. 4 several important isoglosses cross the region: demonstrative *der/dere*, relative pronoun *der/vo*, *wenn* vs *wann/wann* (for both functions), *-sche/-in* for the morpheme to designate female forms.This a very important brick in the edifice of German dialectology.

Also noted: H. Schmidt, 'Austrasien — ein Pfälzischer Landschreiber entwirft einen Staat, einen Friedensvertrag und eine deutsche Verfassung. Text und Wortgebrauch', *Fest. Stickel*, 623–52; J. Herrgen, 'Dialektgeographie und Dialektwandel. Zu rezenten konsonantischen Entwicklungstendenzen im Westmitteldeutschen',

Stellmacher, *Dialektologie*, 48–64; K.-H. Bausch, 'Dialektologie und interpretative Soziolinguistik am Beispiel des Sprachwandels im Rhein-Neckar-Raum', *ib.*, 78–98; and G. Cornelissen, 'Muster regionaler Umgangssprache. Ergebnisse einer Fragebogenaktion im Rheinland', *ZDL*, 69:275–313.

East Central German studies include R. Grosse, 'Phonetisch-phonologische Anmerkungen zum Westmeißnischen um Borna und Geithain', *Fest. Göschel*, 176–87; K.-D. Ludwig, 'Mundartliches aus *Grimorch* im Meißnischen', *ib.*, 188–205; G. Bergmann, ' "Märt nicht so lange an dem Wörterbuch rum!" Der Typ *herummären* im Sächsischen', *ib.*, 206–12; and W. Lösch, 'Zur Dialektsituation im Grenzraum zwischen Südthüringen und Nordbayern', Stellmacher, *Dialektologie*, 156–65.

The following dialect dictionaries are proceeding on their way: *Schweizerisches Idiotikon*, vol. 16, fasc. 205, *Wan-wun, ge-winnend — Fëder-Ge-wand*, Frauenfeld, Huber, 2001, cols 257–384, fasc. 206, *Fëder-Ge-wand — Ober-wind*, cols 385–512; *Niedersächsisches Wörterbuch*, fasc. 46, *Hundeknust — in*, Neumünster, Wachholtz, 2001, cols 641–768, fascs 49 and 50, *Kä — Kisker*, Neumünster, Wachholtz, 2001, cols 1–256; *Preußisches Wörterbuch*, vol. 1, fasc. 2, *Adebarbein — anteigen*, Neumünster, Wachholtz, 2001, cols 129–256, fasc. 3, *Anteil — aufstutzen*, cols 257–384, fasc. 4, *aufsuchen — Backe*, cols 385–512; *Hamburgisches Wörterbuch*, vol. 3, fasc. 19, *laabsalven — livisch*, Neumünster, Wachholtz, 2001, cols 1–128, fasc. 20, *Lo — möten*, Neumünster, Wachholtz, cols 129–384; Wörterbuch der bairischen Mundarten in Österreich, fasc. 35, *treiben — (Dach)tropfen*, Vienna, Österreichische Akademie der Wissenschaften, cols 385–576; K.-H. Weidemeier, **Oberharzer Wörterbuch. Die Mundart der Oberharzer Sprachinsel*, vol. 6, *S-T*, Clausthal-Zellerfeld, Schriftenreihe des Oberharzer Geschichts- und Museumsvereins, 2001, 400 pp.

Speech islands feature in W. Oschlies, ' "Die ánunk der svigrmutr aus Brynel . . ." Germanismen in Regiolekten Mährens', *Muttersprache*, 112:55–66; H. Gehl, 'Erfahrungen aus der donauschwäbischen Wörterbucharbeit', *Fest. Göschel*, 218–41; L. Naiditsch, 'Die Entwicklung des Vokalismus im Mennonitenplatt', *ib.*, 242–56; K. Kehr, '*Ramps* (Allium tricoccum) als Wiedervereinigung in Wort und Sache. Zum Hintergrund der Wildknoblauchfeste in den amerikanischen Alleghenies', *ib.*, 344–65; W. Schabus, 'Die emblematische Funktion der Landlerdialekte in Siebenbürgen', *Akten (Wien)*, III, 287–92; E. Knipf-Komlósi, 'Zur Funktion und zum Status der Varietäten im Sprachgebrauch der Ungarndeutschen', *ib.*, 293–98; A. Rowley, ' "Mocheno e Cimbro". Von Dialekten zu Sprache(n)?', Stellmacher, *Dialektologie*, 213–21; H. Gehl, 'Aktuelle Erkenntnisse in der donauschwäbischen Dialektologie', *ib.*, 288–333; A. F. Toma, 'Deutsch als makrosoziolinguistische Fallstudie am Beispiel des heutigen rumänischen Banats', *ib.*, 334–46; C.-A. Szabó, 'Aspekte des heutigen Gebrauchs der deutschen Sprache im Sathmarer Gebiet, Nordwestrumänien', *ib.*, 347–61; J. Meier, 'Die deutschen Dialekte in der Zips/Spis. Anmerkungen zur Sprachinsel- und Sprachkontaktforschung', *ib.*, 362–86; A. Domascnew, 'Die Marburger Schule und die Entwicklung der deutschen Sprachinselforschung in Rußland', *ib.*, 387–98; and M. Muzikant, 'Sprachatlanten und die deutsch-tschechischen Sprachkontakte auf lexikalischer Ebene', *ZDL*, 69 : 182–88.

9. Onomastics

General items are A. Klosa, 'Eigennamen und Appellativa von A-Z. Anmerkungen zu ihrer Verteilung auf das Alphabet', *Sprachwissenschaft*, 27 : 197–223; J. Macha, 'Diskontinuität durch Auswanderung: der Umgang mit Eigennamen', *Splett Vol.*, 161–70; E. Neuss, 'Über usuelle und aktuelle Eigennamen', *ib.*, 198–212; M. Thurmair, 'Der Harald Juhnke der Sprachwissenschaft. Metaphorische Eigennamenverwendungen', *DSp*, 30 : 1–27; and I. Frank, 'Namen im Internet — zwischen Spiel und Kommerz', *Namenkundliche Informationen*, 79–80, 2001 : 37–55.

Names in Switzerland are represented by K. Jenal-Ruffner, **Die Orts- und Flurnamen der Gemeinde Samnaun*, Chur, Desertina, 474 pp.; H. Stricker, 'Namenforschung im Wandel. Von Robert von Planta und Andrea Schorta bis zum Liechtensteiner Namenbuch', *Bündner Monatsblatt. Zeitschrift für bündnerische Geschichte und Landeskunde*, 3 : 171–200; P. Masüger, 'Das St. Galler Rheintal wird toponomastisch erschlossen. In Wartau entsteht das Werdenberger Namenbuch', *ib.*, 201–05; E. Nyffenegger, 'Das Thurgauer Namenbuch', *ib.*, 206–15; S. Davatz, 'Meine Erfahrungen beim Sammeln der Fanaser Flurnamen', *ib.*, 216–20; R. Hartmann, 'Vom blanken Zettel zum Bilderatlas. Arbeitstechniken eines lokalen Flur- und Ortnamensammlers', *ib.*, 221–27; W. Haas, 'Liechtensteiner Namenbuch: zum Nutzen der Ortsnamenforschung', *ib.*, 228–35; and K. Kunze, 'Familiennamen am Bodensee', *Badische Heimat*, 80, 2000 : 538–47.

Names in Austria are covered by *Österreichische Namenforschung*, 28, 2000, which contains the following: P. Ernst, '"Echte" und und "unechte" Siedlungsnamen' (5–16); A. Gruber, 'Siedlungsgeschichte von Axams im Licht der Namenkunde' (17–37); K. Hohensinner, 'Siedlungsnamentypen im Bezirk Freistadt, OÖ' (39–55); H. Krawarik, 'Die Siedlungsnamen im Altsiedelland des Lungau' (57–66); J. Kuhn, 'Romanische Orts- und Flurnamen der Ortsgemeinde Quarten/St. Gallen' (67–84); T. Ogris, 'Hisna imena na Radisah/

Hausnamen auf dem Radsberg' (85–96); E. Windberger-Heidenkummer, 'Pflanzennamen eine pseudo-onymische Kategorie' (97–114); W. Wirkner, 'Der Schnapsgenzian (Gentiana lutea) in Natur, Kultur und Sprache' (115–20); and P. Zigo, 'Das onymische Objekt, der Eigenname und die Kategorie der Zeit' (121–27). Also noted: C. Antenhofer, **Flurnamenbuch der Gemeinde Pfalzen. Eine historische Landschaft im Spiegel ihrer Namen* (Schlern-Schriften, 316), Innsbruck, Wagner, 2001, 165 pp.; K. Hohensinner et al., **Die Ortsnamen der politischen Bezirke Kirchdorf an der Krems, Steyr-Land und Steyr-Stadt (Südöstliches Traunviertel)* (Ortsnamenbuch des Landes Oberösterreich, 7), Vienna, Österreichische Akademie der Wissenschaften, 2001, xi + 241 pp. + 32 maps; **Altdeutsches Namenbuch. Die Überlieferung der Ortsnamen in Österreich und Südtirol von den Anfängen bis 1200*, ed. H. Bito et al., fasc. 13, *Salzburg — Sittendorf*, Vienna, Österreichische Akademie der Wissenschaften, 2000, 857–936 pp.; and E. Windberger-Heidenkummer, **Mikrotoponyme im sozialen und kommunikaten Kontext. Flurnamen im Gerichtsbezirk Neumarkt in der Steiermark* (Schriften zur deutschen Sprache in Österreich, 30), Frankfurt, Lang, 2001, 387 pp.

Also noted: N. Nail, 'Die Marburger *Sorge* — oder: Warum der "Gasthof zum Schützenpfuhl", vulgo "Wirtshaus an der Lahn", nicht unbedingt auf "Fürsorge" gegründet ist', *Fest. Cherubim*, 23–34, and L. Reichardt, **Ortsnamenbuch des Kreises Böblingen* (Veröffentlichungen der Kommission für geschichtliche Landeskunde in Baden-Württemberg. Reihe B, Forschungen, 149), Stuttgart, Kohlhammer, 2001, vii + 309 pp.

A wide-ranging volume is *Stadtbücher als namenkundliche Quelle. Vorträge des Kolloquiums vom 18.–20. September 1998*, ed. F. Debus (Akademie der Wissenschaften und der Literatur, Mainz: Abhandlungen der Geistes- und sozialwissenschaftlichen Klasse, Einzelveröffentlichung, 7), Stuttgart, Steiner, 2000, 518 pp., whose contributions cover virtually the whole of the German-speaking area: F. Debus, 'Einführung in die Thematik' (11–15); D. Geunich, 'Was sind eigentlich "Stadtbücher"? Versuch einer Definition' (17–29); R. Kluge, 'Das Stadtbuch als onomastische Quelle. Entstehung, Funktion und Stand der Erfassung in den neuen Bundesländern' (31–43); W. Laur, 'Stadtbücher in Schleswig-Holstein. Eine Übersicht' (45–55); U. Scheuermann, ' "Stadtbücher" in südniedersächsischen Kommunalarchiven. Ein Exemplum für ihre namenkundliche Auswertung: Familiennamen aus Toponymen' (57–75); S. Luther, 'Zu den mittelniederdeutschen Stadtbüchern in Haldensleben und den Möglichkeiten ihrer namenkundlichen Auswertung' (77–86); I. Rösler, 'Das DFG-Projekt "Atlas frühmittelniederdeutscher Schreibsprachen": Möglichkeiten der namenkundlichen Auswertung des Quellenkorpus' (87–105); W. Hoffmann,

'Namenkundlich auswertbare Bestände der stadtkölnischen Quellenüberlieferung' (107–18); E. Neuss, 'Zu personennamenkundlichen Quellen kleinerer Städte in der Nordeifel und im vorgelagerten Tiefland' (119–38); U. Braasch-Schwesmann and H. Ramge, 'Stadtbücher und vergleichbare Quellen in Hessen. Eine Übersicht und Beispiele unter besonderer Berücksichtigung von Marburg und Frankfurt am Main' (139–76); V. Hellfritzsch, 'Stadtbücher in Sachsen und die Herausbildung des Systems der Personennamen. Mit besonderer Berücksichtigung der Städte Chemnitz, Zwickau und Plauen' (177–90); D. Krüger, 'Leipziger Stadtbücher als namenkundliche Quelle' (191–204); F. Reinhold, 'Ein dörfliches Gerichts- und Handelsbuch (Rittergut Waltersdorf/Neumühle — Kreis Greiz) aus der Mitte des 16. Jahrhunderts als namenkundliche Quelle' (205–24); F.-P. Scherf, 'Zur namenkundlichen Erschließung der Zwickauer Reihenakten des 15. bis 17. Jahrhunderts. Ein Erfahrungsbericht' (225–35); E. Skála, 'Die Stadtbücher in Böhmen bis 1526 und die beteiligten Sprachen' (237–45); R. Srámek, 'Rechnungsbücher der Stadt Brünn aus den Jahren 1343–1365 als namenkundliche Quelle' (247–60); H. Protze, 'Stadtbücher der Zips als namenkundliche Quelle' (261–81); S. Krämer-Neubert, 'Städtische Amtsbücher in Unterfranken' (283–96); G. Koss, 'Die Stadtbücher des Stadt- und Landkreises Coburg als namenkundliche Quellen' (297–305); Id., 'Familiennamen in fränkischen Stadtbüchern' (307–13); R. and V. Kohlheim, 'Namenkundliche Quellen aus dem Raum Bayreuth — Kulmbach (1250–1550)' (315–24); V. Kohlheim, 'Die Rufnamen der beiden ersten Bayreuther Stadtbücher (1430–1472)' (325–39); R. Kohlheim, 'Zur Bei-/ Familiennamenführung in Bayreuth um die Mitte des 15. Jahrhunderts' (341–67); R. Schuh, 'Amtsbücher der Reichsstadt Nürnberg als personennamenkundliche Quelle' (369–86); A. Greule, 'Das "Gelbe Stadtbuch" von Regensburg. Zur Problematik der Stadtbücher von Regensburg und ihrer onomastischen Auswertbarkeit' (387–93); L. Reichardt, 'Übersicht über namenkundlich relevante Amtsbuchgattungen in Stadtarchiven Württembergs' (395–401); T. Steiner, 'Stadtbücher im Allgäu und ihr namenkundlicher Aussagewert. Eine Übersicht' (403–07); W. Kleiber, 'Urbare als namenkundliche Quellen' (409–24); A. Hug, 'Archivlandschaft Innerschweiz und der namenkundliche Wert von Verwaltungsschriftgut und Rechtsaufzeichnungen' (425–49); V. Weibel, 'Die Schwyzer Ratsprotokolle und das Landbuch von Schwyz als namenkundliche Quelle' (451–59); E. Waser, 'Stadtbuchähnliche Quellen von Luzern und ihr Wert für die Namenforschung' (461–74); C. Grolimund, 'Die Stadtbücher Basels als Quellen für die Namenkunde' (475–92); W. Müller, 'Die mittelalterlichen Amtsbücher von Fribourg als namenkundliche Quellen' (493–500); and P. Ernst,

'Stadtbücher und verwandte Quellen in Österreich, exemplarisch dargestellt' (501–16).

Also noted: L. Reichardt, '*Mücke*, *Linsengericht*, *Grafenau* und *Neulingen*. Ortsnamen der Gebietsreform der 1970er Jahre in Hessen und Baden-Württemberg', *Fest. Göschel*, 257–61; U. Scheuermann, '*In der Klappe*. Zu einem vornehmlich ostfälischen Mikrotoponym', *ib.*, 262–82; R. and V. Kohlheim, 'Von *Hartmann* bis *Janzen*. Die Patronymika unter den 1000 häufigsten Familiennamen in Deutschland', *ib.*, 283–307; H. Freytag, ' "God heft vorseen, dat se worden is en crone unde en hovet aller Hansestede." Über Interpretationen des Stadtnamens Lübeck als polnisch liubice — "Krone" ', *Fest. Ruberg*, 45–60; U. Ernst, 'Der Name als Kostüm. Spielarten literarischer Onomastik im Werk Grimmelshausens', *ib.*, 75–98; A. Krause and J. Sternkopf, 'Zur Akzeptanz von mundartlichen Elementen in Gaststätten-Namen', Stellmacher, *Dialektologie*, 188–99; **Beiträge zur slavisch-deutschen Sprachkontaktforschung*, 1: *Siedlungsnamen im oberfränkischen Stadt- und Landkreis Bamberg*, ed. E. Eichler et al. (Sprache — Literatur und Geschichte, 20), Heidelberg, Winter, 2001, 256 pp.; J. Udolph, 'Gewässernamen in Deutschland', *Namenkundliche Informationen*, 77–78, 2000:41–52; and **Historisches Ortsnamenbuch von Sachsen*, ed. E. Eichler and H. Walther (Quellen und Forschungen zur sächsischen Geschichte, 21), Berlin, Akademie, 2001, vol. 1, *A-L*, 634 pp., vol. 2, *M-Z*, vol. 3, *Apparat und Register*, 395 pp.

MEDIEVAL LITERATURE

By Nigel W. Harris, *University of Birmingham*

1. General

Lexikon Literatur des Mittelalters. Vol. I: *Themen und Gattungen*, vol. II: *Autoren und Werke*, 2 vols, Stuttgart, Metzler, xxxviii + 530, xxxviii + 467 pp., contains articles taken unchanged from the *Lexikon des Mittelalters*. Given that these were composed between 1980 and 1998, some are more up to date than others; but together they constitute an extremely useful resource for readers interested in medieval literature of any kind or in any language. Of the four categories listed, themes are, perhaps inevitably, the least adequately covered; but all the really important genres, authors, and anonymous works are included. *Die deutsche Literatur des Mittelalters. Verfasserlexikon*, ed. Kurt Ruh et al., Berlin, de Gruyter, vol. 11, 621–959 cols, is the third fascicle of this additional volume, stretching alphabetically from 'Heliand' to 'Maler- und Färberbücher'. Along with addenda and corrigenda, entirely new articles are allotted to such figures as John Chrysostom (V. Honemann), Isidore of Seville (F. J. Worstbrock), and Johannes Klimakos (N. F. Palmer), and to the vernacular reception of Hildegard von Bingen (M. Embach). Late medieval authors treated for the first time include Johannes Hug and Konrad von Soltau (Worstbrock), Johannes von St. Lambrecht (W. Stelzer), and Konrad Koler von Soest (W. Eberhard); and anonymous works new to the *Verfasserlexikon* include the *Iatromathematisches Corpus* (L. Welker), *Der Herr von Brauschweig* (H.-J. Ziegeler), the *Indulgentia ecclesiarum urbis Romae* (N. Miedema), and *Von der juden jrrsal* (M. Niesner).

Helmut Birkhan, *Geschichte der altdeutschen Literatur im Licht ausgewählter Texte*. Part I: *Althochdeutsche und altsächsische Literatur;* Part II: *Mittelhochdeutsche vor- und frühhöfische Literatur* (Studienbücher, 6–7), 2 vols, Vienna, Praesens, 230, 281 pp., contains the texts of introductory lectures given by B. in 2001–02. Both volumes proceed more or less chronologically, the first covering literature from the earliest runic inscriptions up to the *St. Trudperter Hohelied*, and the second reaching as far as the *Rolandslied*, *Herzog Ernst*, and the *Spielmannsepen*. B.'s work is extremely well informed, his style approachable, and his use of philological and historical background material (and of illustrations) judicious — though perhaps he does not always fully exploit the many excerpts from texts which he prints and translates.

In *MDG*, 49, U. Schulze (248–62) and C. Kiening (264–77) problematize conventional attempts at periodizing medieval German literary history, and B. Quast (240–47) re-assesses E. R. Curtius's conception of literary epochs. Meanwhile *Kleine literarische Formen in Einzeldarstellungen* (UB, 18187), 278 pp., contains several essays which deal entirely or in part with medieval literature: F.-J. Holznagel on the *bîspel* (54–70), A. Suerbaum on the fable (89–110), V. Schupp on the riddle (191–210), W. Mieder on the proverb (211–40), and J. Schulz-Grobert on the verse narrative (241–58).

Das Mittelalter in Daten. Literatur, Kunst, Geschichte 750–1520, ed. Joachim Heinzle (UB, 17040), 408 pp., is a welcome and handy reference book which, whilst useful for students and scholars of many disciplines, will probably be valued especially by Germanists — by and for whom it was primarily conceived. The period covered is divided into sections of five years; within each section major historical events are listed first, and then works of pictorial art, music, and literature. Each segment dealing with literature is sub-divided according to language. No commentary or bibliography is given, but there are good indexes.

Ulrich Knefelkamp, *Das Mittelalter* (UTB, 2105), Paderborn, Schöningh, 411 pp., is an excellent new introduction to medieval history for the student or general reader. In many ways it is refreshingly old-fashioned: one author covers the entire period between 391 and 1519, and presents an unashamedly chronological, politically-orientated, reign-by-reign narrative bristling with facts and dates (the latter, indeed, are printed in the margins for ease of reference). K.'s focus is firmly on the Holy Roman Empire; but he is consistently mindful of his target audience, making for example inventive use of maps and other images, and providing a helpful glossary. Corinna Dörrich, *Poetik des Rituals. Konstruktion und Funktion politischen Handelns in mittelalterlicher Literatur*, WBG, viii + 222 pp., fruitfully combines insights from historical and literary research. Following a series of theoretical chapters in which the various aspects of medieval ritual are defined and illustrated, D. turns to the presentation of political rituals in medieval literature. She emphasizes that these can both reflect extra-textual realities and serve important inner-literary functions, and provides illuminating analyses of relevant passages from *Willehalm*, and from the *Herzog Ernst* tradition.

Rüdiger Schnell, *Sexualität und Emotionalität in der vormodernen Ehe*, Cologne, Böhlau, x + 595 pp., is a masterly study of the complex views on marriage expressed in texts of various kinds from the 10th up until the 17th centuries. S. makes extensive use of Foucault's model of discourse analysis, an approach which works well given the high level of social conditioning that informs many of the perspectives discussed. Whilst his conclusions are manifold, an over-arching theme is that the sexual and emotional aspects of marriage were more closely linked in the Middle Ages than is commonly assumed. In Bennewitz, *Genderdiskurse*, I. Bennewitz (1–10) considers the applicability to medieval literature of the gender theories of Judith Butler and Thomas Laqueur; and B. Spreitzer (11–28) examines their relevance to our understanding of heterosexual discourses on homosexuality. Elsewhere C. Winter, *Fest. Röll*, 153–64, discusses the education of girls as thematized in medieval literature.

Claudia Spanily, *Autorschaft und Geschlechterrolle. Möglichkeiten weiblichen Literatentums im Mittelalter* (Tradition–Reform–Innovation, 5), Frankfurt, Lang, 417 pp., is a persuasive study which shows a scrupulous awareness of both the possibilities and the limitations of feminist theory for the interpretation of medieval literature by women. S. discusses ways in which numerous female writers (from Hugeburc von Heidenheim to Caritas Pirckheimer) present themselves and their role as authors, demonstrating clearly that, not least in their copious use of humility formulae, they remained highly indebted to male-dominated literary traditions. Nevertheless they used these formulae somewhat differently from their male counterparts — with greater frequency and intensity, using certain gender-specific images and, above all, emphasizing strongly their dependence on divine commission and inspiration. Indeed, S. argues that female authors tended increasingly to legitimize their participation in medieval literary culture by styling themselves as visionary prophets, whose personal experience of God lent authority to their writings. Katrin Graf, *Bildnisse schreibender Frauen im Mittelalter. 9. bis Anfang 13. Jahrhundert*, Basle, Schwabe, 297 pp. + 85 pls, studies depictions of women involved in the production of illustrated MSS, whether as authors, scribes, illustrators, patronesses — or indeed Sibylline oracles. G.'s extremely well illustrated volume, which takes full account of both iconographical and literary traditions, is notable not least for its detailed treatment of images depicting Hildegard von Bingen. The role of Admont nuns in the production of MS illustrations is meanwhile examined by Stefanie Seeberg, *Die Illustrationen im Admonter Nonnenbrevier von 1180* (IMA, 8), xii + 233 pp. + 37 pls. S.'s assiduous study, based especially on her examination of a breviary, clarifies not only the extent of the nuns' involvement in illustrating 12th-c. Admont books, but also the innovative nature of this involvement. Many of the illustrations she analyses feature new motifs, reflecting in particular the nuns' interest in Mary, in the Song of Songs, and in mystical union.

Ursula Frühe, *Das Paradies ein Garten — der Garten ein Paradies. Studien zur Literatur des Mittelalters unter Berücksichtigung der bildenden Kunst und Architektur* (EH, XVIII, 103), xiv + 409 pp., is a genuinely multidisciplinary study of medieval conceptions of the garden as paradise, which takes account of changing perspectives on nature, space, work, and leisure. F. begins by surveying the relevant Classical and biblical traditions, and then covers images of paradise as a garden of delights in relation to both the beginning and the end of time. Further sections deal with attempts to re-establish paradise on earth, with perceptions of the garden as a *locus amoenus* in courtly poetry, and with contrasts drawn between gardens and labyrinths or forests.

Articles dealing with connections between literature and the pictorial arts include N. H. Ott's survey and discussion (Lutz, *Wandmalerei*, 153–97) of the surviving illustrations of German narrative works, and J. Thali's description, in the same volume (595–605), of a Fribourg database documenting medieval wall paintings and sculptures. Moreover T. Cramer, Poag, *Construction*, 9–30, sees medieval literature and art alike as characterized by surface, ornamental variation of unchanging, authoritative patterns; and A. Classen, *SM*, 43:503–34, argues that a medieval monastery and its various artistic activities constituted a 'Gesamtkunstwerk' dedicated to God's glory. Meanwhile H. Wandhoff, *Akten* (Wien), v, 81–88, considers the role played by heraldry in the visualization of literature between the 12th and 14th centuries.

Albrecht Classen, *Verzweiflung und Hoffnung. Die Suche nach der kommunikativen Gemeinschaft in der deutschen Literatur des Mittelalters* (Beihefte zur *Mediävistik*, 1), Frankfurt, Lang, xxvii + 499 pp., is a broad-based study of the problem of social communication as presented in medieval literature. C. concentrates especially on linguistic communication, but also deals with actions that either reinforce or negate it. Certain of the works studied emerge as presenting an optimistic view of the possibilities of appropriate communication: these include *Erec*, Walther L58,35, *Parzival*, and *Tristan*. The *Hildebrandslied*, *Helmbrecht*, and Wittenwiler's *Ring*, however, are interpreted as illustrating the socially destructive consequences of communicative failures. Particular strengths of C.'s book are his careful and appropriate use of Habermas's and Luhmann's theories of communication, and his appreciation of his subject's striking relevance to contemporary problems. In Classen, *Meeting* (xi–lxxiii), C. surveys constructions of identity and alterity, as well as xenological perspectives, in various medieval works. In the same volume, A. Sager (27–44) examines the use of Hungarians as examples of the foreign; and D. F. Tinsley (45–70) discusses the tension between foreignness and courtliness in *Parzival* and the *Nibelungenlied*.

Andreas Scheidgen, *Die Gestalt des Pontius Pilatus in Legende, Bibelauslegung und Geschichtsdichtung vom Mittelalter bis in die frühe Neuzeit* (Mikrokosmos, 68), Frankfurt, Lang, 343 pp., is an impressive study which begins by examining the images of Pilate in ancient Christian and Jewish literature, and in the standard medieval exegetical and historiographical compendia. These chapters show clearly that the fundamental ambivalence surrounding Pilate in the biblical narrative continued throughout the Latin Middle Ages. S. then turns to a substantial corpus of vernacular literature, including the MHG *Vers-Pilatus*, Jans Enikel's *Weltchronik*, Johannes Rothe's *Thüringische Weltchronik* and *Passion*, Johannes von Frankenstein's *Der Kreuziger*, and writings by various mystics. In these also, perspectives on Pilate vary enormously; but S. nevertheless discerns a tendency to use Pilate to thematize contemporary political and social problems (often at the expense of spiritual questions), and in so doing to portray him in an unequivocally negative light.

In Schiewer, *Präsenz*, 5–17, K. Grubmüller discusses various aspects of the role of manuscripts in medieval literary culture; H. Bansa (19–39) describes restoration work done on the St Emmeram *Codex Aureus* in the 10th, 17th, and 20th centuries; T. Brandis (303–35) surveys MS purchases made by the Staatsbibliothek zu Berlin — Preußischer Kulturbesitz since 1973; and H.-J. Schiewer (337–49) describes the notable private MS collection of Dr Hans-Jörg Leuchte (Berlin). Elsewhere J. Klinger, *Akten* (Wien), v, 255–60, considers the historicity of the texts transmitted in the *Ambraser Heldenbuch*; A. Mentzel-Reuters, *DAEM*, 57, 2001[2002]:555–601, assesses a number of MS catalogues published between 1995 and 2000; and I. T. Piirainen, Simmler, *Textsorten*, 407–20, essays a typology of the German MSS housed in Slovakian archives. M. Springeth and M. E. Dorninger's ongoing bibliography of work on the editing of MHG texts (*Editio*, 16:213–22) reaches the years 1998–99; and in *Akten* (Wien), v, the effects of 'New Philology' on editorial work are discussed by T. Bein (309–15), who speculates on some of their consequences for literary historians, and by J. Wolf (317–22), who stresses the importance of taking appropriate account of textual stability, as well as variability.

Other general articles include J. Voloj's survey (Domrös, *Judentum*, 15–30), of the contribution made by Jewish authors to the medieval literature of Germany; K. Grubmüller's deliberations (*MDG*, 49:116–26) on the indispensability of literary interpretation for the adequate understanding of medieval texts; W. Beutin's exploration (*JOWG*, 13:195–217) of apocalyptic and utopian fantasies from a literary-psychological perspective; and S. Hartmann's reflections (*ib.*, 219–38) on the possible functions of medieval studies in the new millennium. Meanwhile H. Kôzô, *LiLi*, 127:19–37, discusses the history and current position of medieval German studies in Japan; and C. Händl (Bein, *Walther*, 329–41) and A. A. Bragança Júnior

(*Akten* (Wien), v, 203–09) consider the teaching of MHG literature (especially Walther) at Italian and Brazilian universities respectively.

ELECTRONIC MEDIA. *Mittelhochdeustche Wörterbücher im Verbund*, ed. T. Burch et al., Stuttgart, Hirzel, 1 CD-ROM with booklet, is an invaluable research tool, for which those who have grappled for years with the multi-volume dictionaries of Lexer and of Benecke, Müller and Zarncke will be infinitely grateful — not least because the CD includes, along with these two venerable works, E. Timm's *Findebuch zum mittelhochdeutschen Wortschatz* (see *YWMLS*, 54:665–66), and E. Nellmann's *Quellenverzeichnis zu den mittelhochdeutschen Wörterbüchern* (see *YWMLS*, 59:676). The database is easy to understand and use, and even those less confident in the use of electronic media will find the accompanying booklet informative and user-friendly. Another remarkable achievement which demonstrates the potential of the CD-ROM medium is David N. Yeandle and Carol Magner, *Stellenbibliographie zum 'Parzival' Wolframs von Eschenbach für die Jahrgänge 1984–1996*, Tübingen, Niemeyer, 1 CD-ROM with booklet. At the centre of this project stands Lachmann's 1891 text of *Parzival*, with, in respect of each line, a list of themes discussed and scholars who have discussed them. All of this material has hyperlinks to indexes of themes (ordered both hierarchically and alphabetically) and to full bibliographical details; and there are further convenient links to indexes of authors, and the titles, types, languages, and dates of their work. The accompanying booklet explains all of these features in both German and English. This is a priceless aid to bibliographical and interpretative work on *Parzival*, and one is delighted to read that updates are planned.

Reclam (Stuttgart) have issued two separate CD-ROMs which contain an enormous amount of introductory reference material, not least on medieval topics. Volker Meid, *Reclams elektronisches Lexikon der deutschen Literatur*, bases its articles on already published material, not always of the most recent vintage. It is nevertheless a very useful database, which has two searchable alphabetical indexes, one listing some 900 authors and the other about 1000 other lemmata. The first of these contains, along with the usual suspects, a number of medieval names one would not necessarily expect to find (for example Heinrich Kaufringer, Ulrich von Etzenbach, or Hadamar von Laber); and the second ranges very widely indeed (encompassing, for example, 'Deutschordensdichtung', 'Dirigierrolle', 'Didaktische Literatur', and 'Dialogizität'). *Reclams elektronisches Roman-Lexikon*, ed. Frank Rainer Max and Christine Ruhrberg, is a digitized version of the encyclopaedia discussed in *YWMLS*, 62:723. Its entries are somewhat fuller than those of Meid's CD, and are individually attributed to named scholars. Again it has two alphabetical indexes, one listing authors and the other titles; and again the Middle Ages are well represented. One is surprised but gratified, for example, to find articles on Herrand von Wildonie's *Der nackte Kaiser* (A. Mühlherr), Ruprecht von Würzburg's *Treueprobe*, and Sibote's *Frauenerziehung* (both J. Theisen), as well as (somewhat puzzlingly) on the *Narrenschiff* and Albrecht von Eyb's *Ehebüchlein* (both U. Rautenberg).

ZDA's estimable series *Mittelalter-Philologie im Internet* continues in vol. 131. Most of the websites and databases it discusses concern manuscripts. J. Wolf (577–80) describes the electronic archive of some 19,000 MS descriptions originally prepared between 1902 and 1944 for the Prussian Academy of Sciences <http://www.bbaw.de/forschung/dtm/HSA/startseite-handschriftenarchiv.htm>. Additionally, B. Koll (139–41) presents a catalogue of MS fragments from the University Library in Salzburg <http://www.ubs.sbg.ac.at/sosa/fragmente/handschriftenfragmente.htm>, and C. Glassner (405–07) a catalogue of the manuscripts from the Benedictine monastery of St Paul im Lavanttal <http://www.oeaw.ac.at/ksbm/stpaul/inv/>. M. Effinger and E. Pietzsch (137–39) introduce *Palatina digital*, a project which has digitized some 27 illustrated 15th-c. MSS from Heidelberg <http://palatina-digital.uni-hd.de>, and M. Baldzuhn (272–73) an analytical database of German *Cato* MSS <http://www.rrz.uni-hamburg.de/SFB538/a7/>. J. Heinzle and S. Hein (274–75) describe an inventory of Freidank MSS which forms part of the *Marburger Repertorien* (<http://www.marburger-repertorien.de>) — whose database of 13th-c. German MSS is also described by Heinzle in Schiewer, *Präsenz*, 40–48, and used fruitfully by C. Bertelsmeier-Kierst in her assessment, in the same volume (49–63), of the importance of writing in 13th-c. literary culture. M. Stolz (*ZDA*, 131:407–08, and also *Akten* (Wien), v, 293–99) discusses the electronic edition of *Parzival* being produced in Basle. Elsewhere T. Schassan, *GLM*, 40:45–50, describes a remarkable project which seeks to make available via the internet the entire MS collection of the Erzbischöfliche Diözesan- und Dombibliothek in Cologne <http://www.ceec.uni-koeln.de>.

Other work on electronic media includes T. Bein et al.'s survey (Bein, *Walther*, 277–304), of the many websites containing material on Walther von der Vogelweide; and H. Jurzik's reflections, in the same volume (305–28), on the advantages and problems of digital editions (with special reference to Walther's *Palästinalied*).

2. Germanic and Old High German

Klaus Rosen, *Die Völkerwanderung*, Munich, Beck, 128 pp., is a readable but reliable account for non-specialists of the Germanic invasions of the Roman Empire and their consequences. The period covered is 378–585 A.D.; but R. considers interpretations of the events in question from various centuries, including that of Paulus Diaconus (*c.* 795). Moreover he discusses in detail the political instrumentalization of the *Völkerwanderung* in Germany since the French Revolution.

Cyril Edwards, *The Beginnings of German Literature. Comparative and Interdisciplinary Approaches to Old High German*, Columbia SC, Camden House, xviii + 197 pp., is a distinguished set of essays examining aspects of the breakthrough of German as a literary language between about 750 and 950. E. concentrates on shorter poetic texts: two essays each are devoted to the *Wessobrunner Gebet* and the *Merseburger Zaubersprüche*, whilst a further chapter investigates the oldest traces of the German love lyric. These are framed by a survey of the MS transmission of the earliest German texts, and by a fascinating discussion of the so-called 'OHG Lullaby', almost certainly forged by Georg Zappert in the mid-19th century. E.'s analysis is based throughout on careful consideration of the relevant MS evidence (an approach which pays dividends not least in his discussion of the application of acid reagents to the *Hildebrandslied* and *Muspilli* MSS); and he makes fruitful use of analogues and motif parallels in other medieval literatures, notably Latin and OE. *Die Sprache*, 41, 1999[2002], contains four further essays on the *Merseburger Zaubersprüche*: W. Beck (89–103) interprets the textual crux 'birenkict' as meaning 'eingerenkt'; A. H. Feulner (104–52) assesses the metre of both *Sprüche* against the background of other OHG, OS, and OE verse forms; S. Schaffner (153–205) discusses the names of the gods and goddesses referred to in the second *Spruch*; and R. Schuhmann (206–18) adduces parallels in OE poetry that suggest the first *Spruch* may not be of German provenance. Elsewhere, H.-J. Behr, *Henne Vol.*, 335–49, problematizes the accepted classifications of OHG and OS charms and blessings.

Elke Krotz, *Auf den Spuren des althochdeutschen Isidor. Studien zur Pariser Handschrift, den Monseer Fragmenten und zum Codex Junius 25*, Heidelberg, Winter, 744 pp., is an immensely meticulous study of the OHG translations and glosses of Isidore of Seville (especially his *De fide catholica*) in these three MSS. K. describes and evaluates their contents, establishes a close connection between the Latin texts of the Paris MS and those found in MSS from St. Gallen and Reichenau, supplies a new edition of the Oxford MS Junius 25, reconstructs the original form of the Monsee fragments (now in Vienna), and assesses the precise nature of the influence of the Paris and Vienna MSS on the Oxford one.

Achim Masser, *Kommentar zur lateinisch-althochdeutschen Benediktinerregel des Cod. 916 der Stiftsbibliothek St. Gallen. Untersuchungen, philologische Anmerkungen, Stellennachweis, Register und Anhang* (SA, 42), 443 pp., is the final volume of three that M. has devoted to this work (see *YWMLS*, 59:674–75, 62:603). The bulk of this volume consists of a commentary dealing with a wide range of philological questions. This is followed by indexes, and by a somewhat more user-friendly edition of the Latin Rule than the one M. printed in 1997. A substantial introduction discusses the origins and purpose of the MS, and the methods and achievement of its glossator and scribes.

Prisca Augustyn, *The Semiotics of Fate, Death and the Soul in Germanic Culture. The Christianization of Old Saxon* (Berkeley Insights in Linguistics and Semiotics, 50), NY, Lang, xvi + 198 pp., is basically a study of the *Heliand*, perceived as standing at the interface between paganism and Christianity. A. examines the work's use of terms signifying fate, death, the self, and the immortal soul, and interprets these, using the semiotic theories of Charles Sanders Peirce and others, as perpetuating aspects of ancient belief in a newly Christianized context — and indeed as forming part of a cultural continuum of habitual belief in fate and destiny that remains relevant today. Some readers will no doubt find A.'s analysis fresh and illuminating; others may regard it as opaque and a trifle pretentious. Also on the *Heliand*, Y. Kawasaki, *DB*, 108:59–68, analyses its language, with particular reference to graphemic problems raised by its MSS; and H. Haferland contributes two articles (*GRM*, 52:237–59 and *ZDA*, 131:20–48) centering on its techniques of oral narration and the light these might shed on its genesis. On Otfrid von Weissenburg's *Evangelienbuch*, C. Staiti, *Fest. Berschin*, 755–68, assesses its dedicatory prologue; and U. Ernst, *Akten* (Wien), v, 51–56, points to its important position in the history of literary media.

Mathias Herweg, *'Ludwigslied', 'De Heinrico', 'Annolied'. Die deutschen Zeitdichtungen des frühen Mittelalters im Spiegel ihrer wissenschaftlichen Rezeption und Erforschung* (IMA, 13), xiv + 584 pp., is a thorough and perceptive discussion of research into these three much debated texts, which also suggests avenues of future research — most involving detailed intertextual comparison, both between the three works on which H. concentrates, and between them and the Latin historiographical tradition. H. himself takes certain steps in this direction, especially in the introductory sections of his three main chapters, in which he assesses the representation of history in the work under discussion. Elsewhere J. Schneider, *AKG*, 84:1–39, re-evaluates the date and historical context of *De Heinrico*.

Christine Hehle, *Boethius in St. Gallen. Die Bearbeitung der 'Consolatio Philosophiae' durch Notker Teutonicus zwischen Tradition und Innovation*

(MTU, 122), xii + 400 pp., analyses Notker's work in considerable detail, and also situates it within the context both of the early-medieval tradition of Boethius reception and of the intellectual trends of his own time. It emerges as a substantial achievement, showing a profound knowledge both of Boethius's text and of earlier interpretations of it, but also a notable degree of innovation. Notker restructures the *De consolatione* into chapters and sub-chapters; and he arranges each sub-chapter systematically, with a re-ordering of its Latin words preceding grammatical and lexicographical elucidations, a translation into OHG, and an interpretative commentary (also mainly in OHG) which stresses the importance of rhetoric and dialectic. Of these features, H. regards the quantity and quality of the OHG used as perhaps the most remarkable. Notker Teutonicus's Latin works are meanwhile surveyed by P. W. Tax, *BGDSL*, 124:411–41.

Other articles include K. Düwel's study (*Birkhan Vol.*, 23–35) of runes definitely or possibly written by women, and M. Harmat's examination (*Akten* (Wien), v, 195–201) of the notion of heroic honour in the *Hildebrandslied* and in Russian epics.

3. Middle High German

GENERAL. Thordis Hennings, *Einführung in das Mittelhochdeutsche*, Berlin, de Gruyter, 2001, x + 251 pp., is a clear survey of MHG, both based on and intended for use in the German undergraduate classroom. As such, it includes exercises and a key to these. More than half of its pages are devoted to phonology and morphology, but there are also sections on metre and syntax, as well as a brief one on semantics. It also has a helpful opening chapter which introduces some basic philological concepts, and surveys the historical development of German. Beat Wolf, *Vademecum medievale. Glossar zur höfischen Literatur des deutschsprachigen Mittelalters*, Berne, Lang, 174 pp., constitutes an ideal pendant to Hennings's volume, in that it discusses, in a lucid and well organized way, some 110 items of MHG vocabulary that were of particular importance in courtly literature. The etymology and semantic development of each term are analysed; and a few concepts (*herre*, *hulde*, *saelde*, *tjoste*, *triuwe*, *tugent*, *turnei*, *vrowe* and *wîp*, and *wunne*) are dealt with in greater detail, with the aid of pictures from illustrated MSS.

Cora Dietl, *Minimalgrammatik Mittelniederdeutsch* (GAG, 699), 30 pp., will also be of great value to students. It is admirably clear and concise, and as such reminiscent of Gärtner and Steinhoff's MHG *Minimalgrammatik* (see *YWMLS*, 38:574–75). After a general introduction, D. discusses the phonology, morphology, and syntax of a normalized MLG based on the language of later 15th-c. Lübeck; and she makes constructive use of relevant examples from MHG, NHG, and English.

C. Stephen Jaeger, *Scholars and Courtiers: Intellectuals and Society in the Medieval West* (Variorum Collected Studies Series, 753), Aldershot, Ashgate, xii + 312 pp., includes twelve of J.'s contributions to journals and collective volumes published between 1980 and 2001 (the last item being his chapter in Poag, *Construction*, 75–90, in which he examines the tendency of some 12th-c. authors to regard the written text as a sign of decadence). Together they amount to a distinguished and cohesive summation of a career that has been concerned above all with medieval humanism, and with the related influence of clerical on secular culture. Elsewhere Jaeger's thesis of the impact of *curialitas* is problematized by W. Haug, *ICLS 10*, 52–75, but largely supported by H. Wenzel, Poag, *Construction*, 49–74. In *Fest. Mertens*, 853–70, the latter also argues that metaphors of the sword, the pen, and the fiddle suggest a closer link between the *vita activa* and *vita contemplativa* than is generally recognized.

A stimulating new view of courtliness is proposed by Will Hasty, *Art of Arms. Studies of Aggression and Dominance in Medieval German Court Poetry*, Heidelberg, Winter, 154 pp. For H., courtly culture did not so much sublimate, transfigure, or overcome aggression, but rather controlled and channelled it more effectively in the interests of military, religious, or socio-political dominance. Moreover courtly literature of the *Blütezeit* both reflected such new perceptions of violence and suggested a variety of sometimes contradictory strategies for achieving and maintaining dominance. On the basis of these considerations, H. deals in turn with *Minnesang*, Arthurian romances, *Tristan*, *Gregorius*, *Der arme Heinrich*, the *Nibelungenlied*, and *Willehalm*. Inevitably, his paradigm works better with some of these texts than others; but much of his analysis is persuasive, and certainly this important work will encourage many readers to re-consider their understanding of the canonical courtly works.

In *JOWG*, 13, H. Brall-Tuchel (61–76) comments on research by MHG scholars into questions surrounding the apocalypse; H. Freytag (45–60) examines constructions of paradise in the German *Summa Theologiae*, the *Ezzolied*, and *Reynke de vos*; and T. Tomasek (178–93) investigates utopian visions presented in high- and late-medieval texts. In Lieb, *Situationen*, L. Lieb (41–67) discusses the connection, in epic and romance, between story-telling and eating, and A. Lasch and B. Liebig (69–88) that between story-telling and riding. Other studies include B. Hasebrink's analysis (*BGDSL*, 124:442–65) of the language of lovers' union in both secular and mystical literature; J. Margetts' treatment (*Fest. Mertens*, 535–49) of cases in which characters and/or narrators behave in surprising ways towards women; A. Classen's discussion (*GQ*, 75:71–87) of idealized mother-daughter relationships; B. Haupt's examination (*Akten* (Wien), v, 163–73), of the dreams of female characters; and E. and D. Kartschoke's consideration (*Fest. Mertens*, 309–33), of role play in 12th-c. and 13th-c. narratives.

EARLY MIDDLE HIGH GERMAN

Markus Stock, *Kombinationssinn. Narrative Strukturexperimente im 'Straßburger Alexander', im 'Herzog Ernst B' und im 'König Rother'* (MTU, 123), viii + 335 pp., is a successful attempt to demonstrate that the bipartite structural patterns, based on the principles of combination, repetition, variation, and contrast, which are used to construct meaning in courtly romances, were employed also in earlier vernacular narratives such as those mentioned in S.'s title and the *Kaiserchronik.* S.'s analysis is distinguished by close attention to textual detail, by a sharp eye for differences between the works studied (*König Rother*, for example, is shown to engage in markedly less structural experimentation than do the others), and by the appropriate and productive use of modern theory (especially the structural-semiotic method of Yuri Lotman). V. Milde, Schulze, *Juden*, 13–34, discusses the dispute between Christianity and Judaism in the Silvester legend of the *Kaiserchronik*; and D. Buschinger, Mölk, *Alexanderdichtungen*, 162–77, studies the Tyre episode in the *Vorauer Alexander* and in 12th-c. French analogues. S. Schmitz, Lieb, *Situationen*, 167–90, analyses the narrative technique of *König Rother*, arguing that the narrator's taciturnity is a deliberate didactic device; and S. Müller, *Akten* (Wien), v, 333–34, interprets a marginal addition to the Heidelberg MS of *König Rother* as a form of travel charm. More generally on *Spielmannsepik*, A. Schulz, *BGDSL*, 124:233–49, argues that the 'Brautwerbungsschema' is deconstructed from within through the use of hagiographical motifs; and M. Schulz, *ZDP*, 121:1–20, claims that the works posit as a prerequisite for successful rule a Christian marriage based on a mutual *nudus consensus*.

Jasmin Schahram Rühl, *Welfisch? Staufisch? Babenbergisch? Zur Datierung, Lokalisierung und Interpretation der mittelalterlichen Herzog-Ernst-Fassungen seit König Konrad III auf der Grundlage der Wortgeschichte von 'Burg' und 'Stadt'*, Vienna, Praesens, xiv + 408 pp., is a highly original study of the *Herzog Ernst* tradition. Its novelty is manifest in its attempts to date and locate the work's various versions on the basis of their use of certain specific terms (mainly those designating 'town'); in its treatment of the Latin and German versions as parts of one textual tradition; and, not least, in its striking and controversial conclusions.

These include very early datings for *Herzog Ernst A* and *B* (to *c.* 1140 and 1175–80 respectively); the claim that all three surviving Latin versions are dependent on one lost Latin text, based in turn on German version *A*; and the attribution of the genesis of version *A* not to the Welf court of Henry the Lion, but to the Hohenstaufen court of Emperor Conrad III. Meanwhile I. Kasten, *Akten* (Wien), v, 149–55, discusses political and Oedipal subtexts in *Herzog Ernst B.*

'Brandan'. Die mitteldeutsche 'Reise-Fassung', ed. Reinhard Hahn and Christoph Fasbender (Jenaer Germanistische Forschungen, 14), Heidelberg, Winter, xxxviii + 231 pp., is a welcome new edition of this account of Brendan's travels (1934 lines of rhyming couplets), based on the sole surviving MS (Berlin, Mgo 56). The edition is supported by a useful commentary and glossary, and by an afterword situating this version within the literary tradition surrounding Brendan. The language of Mgo 56 is discussed both in the introduction and (by F.) in *ABäG*, 56: 103–22, in which he also accounts for the work's popularity amongst Carthusians. In *ZDA*, 131: 277–89, C. Strijbosch discusses the source and nature of truth as presented in the Brendan tradition.

On the *Rolandslied*, A. Gerok-Reiter, *ICLS 10*, 77–92, points to the congruence in it of religious and secular ideals; and B. Bastert, *ib.*, 195–210, discusses aspects of its historical context, on the basis of which he dates it to the later 1180s.

MIDDLE HIGH GERMAN HEROIC LITERATURE

The Nibelungen Tradition. An Encyclopaedia, ed. Francis G. Gentry et al., NY, Routledge, xxvii + 375 pp., is a major new reference work. The quality of its contributions (from some 58 predominantly but far from exclusively American scholars) is high, and it casts its net very wide: many Scandinavian works are included, for example, and there are numerous articles on the *Nibelungenlied's* modern reception, as well as on such topics as compact discs, postage stamps, and the Siegfried Line. One's only reservation concerns the abandoning of strict alphabetical order in favour of ten thematically discrete sections. The inconvenience of this is mitigated by the provision of an index, but one is at least initially disconcerted to find, say, Dietrich epics under 'primary texts', Rudolf von Ems and Bligger von Steinach under 'scholarship', and Wittenwiler's *Ring* under 'literary reception'.

Otfrid Ehrismann, *'Nibelungenlied'. Epoche — Werk — Wirkung*, 2nd edn, Munich, Beck, 221 pp., is a commendably conscientious revision of this time-honoured handbook (see *YWMLS*, 49: 632). It has been abbreviated by some 100 pages, diligently updated, and almost entirely re-written. The basic structure of the original work has survived, though its opening section on the epic's social context and mythic origins has been pruned with particular vigour. In its radically new form, E.'s book can be recommended even to those who possess the 1987 edition.

There are also two entirely new introductory guides to the *Nibelungenlied*. Fritz R. Glunk, *Das Nibelungenlied*, Munich, Piper, 144 pp., is aimed squarely at the general reader. She may well feel adequately served by G.'s fluent if brief summary of the work's plot, precursors, possible authors, and versions, but will perhaps be disconcerted to discover that more that half of the volume is devoted to the epic's post-medieval reception. Of far greater value to the serious student is Jan-Dirk Müller, *Das Nibelungenlied* (Klassiker-Lektüren, 5), Berlin, Schmidt, 176 pp. M.'s is a slightly unorthodox introductory volume, in that it does not seek to synthesize the findings of previous research so much as to offer its own reading of the epic, the contours of which are broadly familiar from M.'s remarkable *Spielregeln für den Untergang* (see *YWMLS*, 60:588). Given that this involves insights from various schools of modern literary interpretation, M.'s book is at times a challenging read for the novice medievalist; but it is lucidly written, and certainly stimulating. Moreover it covers an exceptionally wide range of topics, including the epic's historical background, literary precursors, style, structure, politics, psychology, and mythic dimensions. M. also deals convincingly with the tensions it adumbrates between courtly and pre-courtly, individual and collective, and public and private; and he includes a chapter on *Die Klage*. Elsewhere he contributes an article to Greenfield, *Nibelungenlied* (50–77), discussing contamination in the work's textual (and indeed oral) transmission. In the same volume W. Haug (27–49) challenges M.'s view of the *Nibelungenlied*'s author and the unity or otherwise of his conception; and in *Euphorion*, 96:273–86, T. Gubatz contends that the seventh *âventiure* is more coherently motivated than M. (and others) have allowed.

Greenfield, *Nibelungenlied*, also includes essays by M. Wynn (9–25), who suggests that its 'meaning' is to be found in its portrayal of culture giving way to barbarity; and by H. Haferland (79–94), who places the epic in the tradition of oral literature intended to be memorized for performance (he argues similarly in Lieb, *Situationen*, 245–82). Further, J. Greenfield (95–114) examines the relationship between death and femininity in the *Nibelungenlied*; R. Krüger (115–44) interprets its references to travel in the light of contemporary cosmological, astronomical, and geographical literature; N. Voorwinden (145–67) observes parallels between the *Nibelungenlied* and Ovid's *Metamorphoses*; and U. Wyss (169–83) assesses various attempts made by Germanists to situate it within MHG literary history.

Elsewhere B. Quast, *Euphorion*, 96:287–302, discusses the treatment of knowledge and power in Part 1 of the *Nibelungenlied*; U. Schulze, *Fest. Mertens*, 669–89, examines the nature (and literary precursors) of Siegfried's heroism; B. Schmitz, *ABäG*, 56:123–54, argues that the figures of the *Nibelungenlied* change their behaviour and identity as they interact with the circumstances they face; S. Müller, Lieb, *Situationen*, 89–120, examines the narratives of messengers and minstrels in *Das Nibelungenlied* and *Die Klage*; and K. Klein, *ZDA*, 131:61–65, describes and prints a 14th-c. fragment of the *Klage* from Amberg. Also noted: Tanja Weiss, **Reimverzeichnis zum 'Nibelungenlied'* (*ZDA*, Beihefte, 4), Stuttgart, Hirzel, ix + 65 pp.

Kerstin Schmitt, *Poetik der Montage. Figurenkonzeption und Intertextualität in der 'Kudrun'* (PSQ, 174), 326 pp., is a penetrating study which argues that, far from merely constituting an 'answer' to the *Nibelungenlied*, *Kudrun* constructs a montage of motifs and narrative structures from many sources, which are combined, varied, or re-configured in such a way as to suggest responses to several of the central questions raised by courtly literature. These include the nature of both femininity and masculinity, the problematic relationship between the individual and the collective, and, above all, approaches to the consolidation and extension of political power. S.'s work is distinguished in particular by her judicious use of various modern theoretical perspectives, her stress on the experimental nature of many of *Kudrun*'s innovations, and her allotment of appropriate weight to the narrative strands involving Hagen and Hilde, as well as Kudrun herself.

Michael Mecklenburg, *Parodie und Pathos. Heldensagenrezeption in der historischen Dietrichepik* (FGÄDL, 27), 235 pp., is the first detailed study of the diverse ways in which five 13th-c. epics (*Dietrichs Flucht*, *Die Rabenschlacht*, *Alpharts Tod*, *Biterolf und Dietlieb*, and the fragmentary *Dietrich und Wenezlan*) adapt material from earlier epics or sagas. Three forms of response are singled out: the arguably unsuccessful attempt, in *Alpharts Tod*, to combine a pre-courtly heroic ethos with elements of courtly culture; the transformation, in *Dietrichs Flucht* and the *Rabenschlacht*, of heroic pathos into a more individualistic, sentimental emotionality; and the comically parodistic use, in *Biterolf und Dietlieb* and *Dietrich und Wenezlan*, of material from the Nibelungen tradition. Underlying the emphasis on both pathos and parody is, in M.'s view, a new form of individual subjectivity that also manifests itself elsewhere in 12th-c. and 13th-c. literature. A. Schulz, *ZDP*, 121:390–407, examines aspects of the narrative technique of *Dietrichs Flucht*; G. Beck, *ZDA*, 131:172–80, describes a forthcoming edition of that epic being prepared in Bremen; S. Müller, Hellgardt, *Thüringen*, 1–30, analyses the material concerning Iring and Irmfried in the *Nibelungenlied*, the *Klage*, and *Biterolf und Dietrich*; and L. Miklautsch, *Neophilologus*, 86:87–99, discusses the thematization of orality and oral sources in the prologue of *Wolfdietrich D*. Moreover C. Händl, *SM*, 43:165–202, comments on the relationship between text and pictures in the illustrated MSS of the *Jüngerer Sigenot*; U. Störmer-Caysa, *ZGer*, 12:7–24, studies motifs in the Heidelberg *Virginal* which imply it was a unified epic intended for oral performance; and S. Kerth, *ib.*, no.2:262–74, examines constructions of warlike masculinity in several later heroic epics.

Ute von Bloh, *Ausgerenkte Ordnung. Vier Prosaepen aus dem Umkreis der Gräfin Elisabeth von Nassau-Saarbrücken: 'Herzog Herpin', 'Loher und Maller', 'Huge Scheppel', 'Königin Sibille'* (MTU, 119), x + 473 pp. + 30 pls, considerably enhances our understanding of these four early 15th-c. adaptations of *chansons de geste*. B. begins by examining the little studied MS tradition of *Herpin* and *Loher* (*Huge* and *Sibille* are both preserved only in one MS), establishing the relative chronology of the four works, and discussing the extent to which they constitute a cycle. A second major section is devoted to the tensions within them between historicity, fictionality, and imagination; a third to their construction of love, marriage, kinship, and friendship; and a shorter fourth to their MS illustrations. Overall, the epics emerge as works in which both accepted social norms and established narrative models are reflected, played with, and at times subverted.

Ogier von Dänemark. Nach der Heidelberger Handschrift Cpg 363, ed. Hilkert Weddige et al. (DTM, 83), lxxxii + 697 pp., follows on from the *DTM* edition of the German *Malagis* in 2000 (see *YWMLS*,62:611) in providing the text of a Heidelberg verse adaptation of a Middle Dutch epic. The *Ogier*, which weighs in at some 23,731 lines, is preserved only in Cpg 363 (dated 1479). W.'s edition of it is predictably meticulous, and is supported by a comprehensive index of names and a glossary. His introduction describes the MS and its language, the contents of the work, and its relationship to its Dutch source and French precursors (including the *Chanson de Roland*).

THE COURTLY ROMANCE

D. H. Green, *The Beginnings of Medieval Romance. Fact and Fiction, 1150–1220* (Cambridge Studies in Medieval Literature, 47), CUP, xiv + 292 pp., is a highly erudite study of the emergence of romance as a form of fictionality, with reference primarily to German, but also to works in Latin and French. G. begins by defining 12th-c. fictionality, and then surveys its Classical and earlier medieval predecessors, before explaining the difficulty encountered in finding a place for fiction within the established literary genres. Subsequent chapters discuss the connections between fictionality and literacy, history, and narrative structure; and there is a discrete chapter on aspects of fiction in *Parzival*. Overall G.'s book is not only a substantial contribution to the current debate surrounding the problem of fictionality in MHG literature, but also establishes a sounder basis than we have had hitherto for discussions of the nature of fiction in other genres, periods, or languages. Much of Green's first chapter appears (in German) in *LJb*, 43:25–37. Meanwhile the tensions between fictionality, orality, and literacy are discussed also by K. Ridder, in *Poetica*, 34:29–40, and *Akten* (Wien), v, 261–63. W. Haug, Knapp, *Erzählen*, 115–31, explains and evaluates various conceptions of medieval fictionality; and, in Poag, *Construction*, 31–48, he associates its development with a re-evaluation of divine inspiration.

Alexandra Sterling-Hellenbrand, *Topographies of Gender in the Middle High German Arthurian Romance*, NY, Garland, 2001, xviii + 244 pp., is a reading of *Erec*, *Iwein*, *Parzival*, and *Tristan* inspired by contemporary theories of spatialization and of the mobility and negotiability of gender. These come together to form S.-H.'s (and Sigrid Weigel's) concept of 'gender topology', according to which poets construct identities and ideas through their characters' encounters with others in and through various narrative spaces. S.-H.'s analysis shows how this enables courtly poets (especially Gottfried, to whom her approach is perhaps best suited) to offer their audiences several possibilities for 'being' and 'becoming', not least in relation to their gender. Some of these, of course, question or subvert courtly norms.

D. Kartschoke, Lieb, *Situationen*, 21–39, and M. Kern, *Fest. Mertens*, 385–414, discuss examples of 'literary experiences' and narratives-within-narratives in various *Blütezeit* romances; and H. Wandhoff, Lieb, *Situationen*, 123–42, considers the consequences for a knight's honour of telling stories about himself. Both M. Schnyder, *Euphorion*, 96:257–72, and E. Schmid, *Akten* (Wien), v, 141–47, discuss the concept of *âventiure* in high-medieval romance, the latter with particular reference to monsters. A. Ebenbauer, *Fest. Mertens*, 105–31, ascribes to the Keie figure of French and German romances a mythical character and function analogous to those of the Norse god Loki; and W. Haug, *Fest. Mertens*, 247–67, studies the presentation and problematization of 'mythic' gender roles in *Erec*, *Iwein*, and *Parzival*.

HARTMANN VON AUE

Scott E. Pincikowski, *Suffering in the Works of Hartmann von Aue* (SMHC, 11), xxvii + 196 pp., is a thoughtful and persuasive study of the complex role of pain in Hartmann's narratives. On the basis of a solid theoretical undergirding that takes account of both medieval and modern perspectives on pain, P. points to its ubiquity in Hartmann's works, to its essential physicality, and to its frequently ambiguous moral and theological connotations. Above all, he shows how H. instrumentalizes both the infliction and the suffering of pain in his construction of individual identity, gender roles, and social norms — using its enigmatic nature as an important part of his strategy of simultaneously propagating and criticizing courtly values. Elsewhere R. K. Weigand, *Fest. Mertens*, 829–52, examines Hartmann's thematization of legal questions in all four of his narratives; B. Quast, *Akten* (Wien), v, 133–39, discusses Victor Turner's theories of liminality and ritual in relation to *Erec* and *Iwein*; and J. Mühlemann, Lutz, *Wandmalerei*, 199–254, describes the *Krakauer Kronenkreuz* depicting scenes from *Erec*, and compares it with the Rodenegg frescoes of *Iwein*. Specifically on *Erec*, I. Bennewitz, *Fest. Mertens*, 1–17, assesses the role of horses in Hartmann's construction of masculinity, femininity, and power relationships; D. Klein, *Fest. Mertens*, 435–63, examines the role of violence in developing masculine identity; C. J. Steppich, *MDLK*, 94:165–88, argues that certain of the knights' names listed in lines 1665–93 imply that Hartmann used Geoffrey of Monmouth and Wace as secondary sources; and M. Schnyder, *Akten* (Wien), v, 301–07, discusses the work's MS fragments, and their evaluation by numerous scholars. On *Iwein*, F. Wenzel, *Akten* (Wien), v, 95–102, uses Kalogrenant's narrative to illustrate aspects of narrative art at high-medieval courts.

Ulrich Ernst, *Der 'Gregorius' Hartmanns von Aue. Theologische Grundlagen — legendarische Strukturen — Überlieferung im geistlichen Schrifttum* (Ordo, 7), Cologne, Böhlau, xiv + 285 pp., contains revised versions of three long essays first published in *Euphorion*: E.'s 1978 and 1979 studies of the antagonism between the *vita carnalis* and the *vita spiritualis* (see *YWMLS*, 40:644, 41:702), and his 1996 article on the MS transmission of *Gregorius* and the *Vie du pape Saint Grégoire* (*YWMLS*, 58:733). Elsewhere W. Röcke, *Fest. Mertens*, 627–47, discusses the mythological, theological, courtly, and narratorial discourses of *Gregorius*; and K. Schmitt, Bennewitz, *Genderdiskurse*, 135–55, examines the work's construction of masculinity. H.-J. Schiewer, *Fest. Mertens*, 649–67, considers the role of the *meier*'s daughter in the standard editions of *Der arme Heinrich* and in its 'B' MSS; K. Gärtner, *Fest. Röll*, 79–93, edits and discusses the work's Benediktbeuern fragments; and R. Kroll, Bennewitz, *Genderdiskurse*, 77–95, analyses the effect on men of the combination of female nakedness and dignity in *Der arme Heinrich* and in OF texts.

WOLFRAM VON ESCHENBACH

Hermann Reichert, *Wolfram von Eschenbach 'Parzival' für Anfänger* (Studienbücher, 4), Vienna, Praesens, 206 pp., is a readable and appealing introduction to *Parzival.* Following an introduction dealing with Wolfram's biography and issues such as the Kyot problem and the work's date and MSS, R. interprets the romance book-by-book, with the aid of copious quotations and parallel NHG translations. His closing synthesis admits that *Parzival* poses many complex problems which it does not solve, but argues also that it is pervaded by a conservatively-inclined religiosity that lays particular stress on trust in God, humility, and loyalty.

Andreas Urscheler, *Kommunikation in Wolframs 'Parzival'. Eine Untersuchung zur Form und Funktion der Dialoge* (DLA, 38), 315 pp., rectifies a perhaps surprising omission in *Parzival* scholarship by providing a meticulous study of the work's dialogues which employs techniques of both literary and linguistic analysis. Following a substantial theoretical introduction, U. constructs a typology of the dialogues which divides them into eight main categories. He concludes from these that Wolfram uses dialogues to fulfil a variety of functions: to create comedy or suspense, to convey information, to structure his romance, or to suggest mutually complementary or contradictory interpretations. Above all, however, they are an important means of characterization, not least in the case of Parzival himself, whose victory over *tumpheit* is interpreted by U. as a gradual acquisition of communicative competence.

Cornelia Schu, *Vom erzählten Abenteuer zum 'Abenteuer des Erzählens'. Überlegungen zur Romanhaftigkeit von Wolframs 'Parzival'* (Kultur, Wissenschaft, Literatur, 2), Frankfurt, Lang, 483 pp., argues that *Parzival* has many aspects in common with a humorously ironic, 'dialogic' modern novel (Cervantes, Sterne, and Fielding are named as standing broadly in the same tradition). These include a range of different perspectives and values, an emphasis on the limitations of human perception, an elusive and unpredictable narrator, and complex and ambivalent characters. Taken together, S. argues, such elements challenge the reader to develop her own opinions on the events narrated, and promote humanity and tolerance. S. offers much detailed and intelligent textual analysis (notably of the *Vorgeschichte* and of the links between the Parzival and Gawain books); and, though by no means all readers will find her conclusions convincing, many will find her arguments thought-provoking.

Groos, *Perceval*, reprints five distinguished essays on *Parzival*: G. himself on the narrative styles of Chrétien and Wolfram (119–36), W. Mohr on Parzival's knightly guilt (137–53), D. H. Green on his failure (155–74), M. Wynn on Parzival and Gawain (175–98), and L. P. Johnson on the Grail question (199–218). Other essays on *Parzival* include S. Keppler's investigation (*ASNS*, 239:241–67) of evidence suggesting that parts of the romance might have been composed under the joint patronage of the Wertheim, Abenberg, and Durne families; J. Greenfield's analysis (*Fest. Mertens*, 159–73) of Herzeloyde's status and role as a widow; E. Parra Membrives's exploration (*GSR*, 25:25–35) of the function of Herzeloyde, Belakane, and Cundrie as 'alternative' female characters; L. Lieb's evaluation (Hellgardt, *Thüringen*, 109–25) of the role of stories told by characters; and J. A. Schultz's assessment (*ZDP*, 121:342–64), of the consequences for men of Wolfram's conception of love service. Further, M. Baisch, *Akten* (Wien), v, 243–48, comments on *Parzival*'s textual variability; M. Schnyder, *ZDA*, 131:308–25, discusses the work's dice metaphors and their role in constructing a 'Poetik der Kontingenz'; L. E. Saurma-Jeltsch, Lutz, *Wandmalerei*, 283–327, studies the cycle of early 14th-c. *Parzival* frescoes in the 'Haus zur Kunkel' in Constance; and I. Karg, *JIG*, 33:63–81, problematizes the perception of the family as a metaphor for humankind in *Parzival* and *Willehalm*.

Wolfram-Studien, 17, begins with studies by F. P. Knapp (10–29) on the relationship between the narrator's subjectivity and his story's fictionality, and by D. H. Green (30–45), who argues that Wolfram sought and found 'blank spots' in Hartmann's narratives which he then filled with his own material and perspectives. Thereafter P. Kern (46–62) interprets the *Bogengleichnis* as reflecting on general aspects of romance narrative style; B. Schirok (63–94) discusses Wolfram's theory of literature, stressing *Parzival*'s fundamental ambivalence; and C. Schmid (95–113) argues that the narrator's criticism of Chrétien reveals a certain 'anxiety of influence'. Both S. Coxon (114–35) and K. Ridder (136–56) consider comedy in *Parzival*, the former concentrating especially on the use of *fabliau* or *Schwank* motifs, and the latter on tensions between the sacred and the profane. Further, E. Lienert (223–45) examines violence against women in *Parzival*; M. Stolz (294–321) pleads for an electronic edition of *Parzival* that would take full account of its textual instability; E. Brüggen and D. Lindemann (377–86) report on a forthcoming new Reclam translation of the romance; and D. Oltrogge and M. J. Schubert (347–76) describe and evaluate an examination of the so-called *Rappoltsteiner Parzival* using reflectography and image processing. Both *Parzival* and *Willehalm* are discussed by H. Hartmann (157–81), who lists and interprets their heraldic motifs, and by U. Ernst (182–222), who examines their 'semantics of the body'. C. Kiening (246–75) elucidates *Willehalm*'s political anthropology; and R. Decke-Cornill (387–414) extends her Wolfram bibliography to cover work published in 1999 and 2000.

Jones, *Willehalm*, combines several essays that explore the connections between *Willehalm* and aspects of its literary context. P. E. Bennett (1–19) examines heroism and sanctity in the *Cycle de Guillaume*, with their many implications for the composition of *Willehalm*; J. Ashcroft (21–41) explores the close intertextual relationship between Wolfram's work and the *Rolandslied*; F. Shaw (291–306) discusses the reception of *Willehalm* (as an historical source) in Heinrich von München's *Weltchronik*; and D. A. Wells (145–65) investigates the relationship between *Willehalm* and Latin religious disputation literature. Moreover A. Volfing (45–59) examines aspects of narrative continuity between *Parzival* and *Willehalm*, a perspective which also informs N. Harris's essay (211–29) on Wolfram's (and his source's) presentation of natural phenomena. Meanwhile J. Greenfield (61–76) explores the complex theme of *triuwe* in *Willehalm*; D. N. Yeandle (167–90) illuminates the characterization of Rennewart by means of a careful study of the concept of *schame*; and M. Chinca (77–94) studies Willehalm's behaviour at Laon, with special reference to his use of expressive public gestures. Giburc is the focus of contributions by M. H. Jones (97–120) and by T. McFarland (121–42), the former analysing especially the events surrounding the siege of Orange, and the latter the tension Giburc faces between the calls of consanguineous and spiritual kinship. Further, M. E. Gibbs (191–209) discusses Wolfram's use of imagery as an aspect of his narrative art; A. Suerbaum (231–47) considers structures of dialogue in *Willehalm*; C. Young (249–69) studies the work's construction of gender (within a still essentially patriarchal framework); and S. M. Johnson (271–89) discusses passages from Book I in the light of Bakhtin's theory of dialogicity.

Also on *Willehalm*, K. Starkey, *GQ*, 75:20–34, discusses the relevance of the work's multilingualism to its themes of tolerance and alterity; and in *ZDP*, 121:321–41, she re-evaluates the Laon scene, arguing that it is dominated by Willehalm's threat to withdraw his fealty. Elsewhere, C. Brinker-Von der Heyde, *Akten* (Wien), v, 89–94, assesses Wolfram's image and understanding of the world as these are revealed in *Willehalm*; C. Fasbender, *ZDP*, 121:21–33, proposes a new interpretation of 2,16f.; and D. Kartschoke, *ib.*, 424–32, re-examines 377,4–6, interpreting the image of the duck as a joke by the narrator against himself.

Wolfram von Eschenbach, *Titurel*, ed. and trans. Helmut Brackert and Stephan Fuchs-Jolie, Berlin, de Gruyter, x + 514 pp., fills in exemplary fashion one of the most yawning gaps in MHG research. It contains a long overdue new edition of the *Titurel* fragments, based where possible on MS 'M' (Cgm 19), and transcribed in a faithful but readable way. This is accompanied by a designedly literal modern

German translation; and a substantial introduction deals with the *Titurel* MSS, their verse form, and their relationship both to each other and to Albrecht's *Jüngerer Titurel*. Perhaps the most remarkable aspect of the volume is, however, its 265-page commentary, which succeeds in being not just exhaustive but also genuinely helpful — avoiding, for example, otiose repetition of ground covered in J. Heinzle's 1972 commentary (see *YWMLS*, 34:511–12).

GOTTFRIED VON STRASSBURG

Kristine K. Sneeringer, *Honor, Love, and Isolde in Gottfried's 'Tristan'* (STML, 61), viii + 252 pp., examines various notions of honour adumbrated in *Tristan*. She begins with a survey of the ethical evolution of honour that culminates in Gottfried's perception of it as closely linked with love and *saelde*. A second chapter, focusing especially on the literary excursus, sees honour as a gift of wisdom bestowed on the poet by God; and a third examines the relationship between honour and female sexuality, especially as articulated in the *huote* excursus. Finally S. reads the *Minnegrotte* episode as legitimizing both female sexuality and the poet's creativity through divinely bestowed honour.

In Huber, *Tristan*, I. Bennewitz (9–22) explores the work's MSS and editions, and makes suggestions for a future edition; E. Brüggen and H.-J. Ziegeler (23–74) discuss the Cologne *Tristan* MS and its illustrations; and T. Tomasek (75–85) analyses the little known Lower Franconian *Tristan* fragment. Analogues and contrasts with other works are explored by E. Hellgardt (167–98), who considers the presentation of love as passion in *Tristan* and the *Volsunga Saga*; by G. Dicke (199–220), who re-interprets Gottfried's description of the tryst in the orchard in the light of comparable scenes in both Western and Eastern texts; and by D. Rocher (87–96), who examines the differing conceptions of love which inform the romances of Béroul, Thomas, and Gottfried. The latter's indebtedness to the themes and techniques of *Minnesang* is considered by U. Wyss (327–38), and by C. Huber (339–56), who studies in particular the motif of yearning. Meanwhile S. Köbele (97–115) studies the techniques of repetition in Gottfried's romance, and its implications for our understanding of narrative time, a topic which is dealt with also by J.-D. Müller (379–87), who concentrates especially on the 'mythic' time of the *Minnegrotte*. N. Zotz (117–29) examines the use of French in Gottfried's dialogues, seen as a means of establishing distance between the characters; K. Kellermann (131–52) contrasts Gottfried's presentation of conflict with his construction of courtly display and physical love; and E. Schmid (153–66) discusses the confrontation of nature and culture in the hunting scene and prologue. Gottfried's religious motifs are treated by H. Lähnemann (221–42), who argues that the allusions to the Fall do not point to any coherent theological message, and by B. Wachinger (243–55), who stresses the metaphorical nature of Gottfried's religious references and their role in constructing a secular discourse. Further, C. Young (257–79) sees Gottfried's narration of events surrounding the consumption of the love potion as part of a process of literarization; W. Haug (281–94) interprets the narrator's commentaries and excursuses as literary-theoretical reflections which reinforce the message of the prologue; E. C. Lutz (295–315) argues that Gottfried's own reading of his source was informed by the scholastic model of the meditative *lectio*; A. Mühlherr (317–26) shows that, in Gottfried's 'literary excursus', his praise and criticism alike are differentiated, equivocal, and self-referential; and V. Millet (357–77) contends that Tristan's love for Isolde of Ireland is maintained in the realm of memory throughout the episode with Isolde of the White Hands.

Elsewhere A. Gerok-Reiter, *ZDP*, 121:365–89, argues that, in *Tristan*, love and honour are closely linked, but that *minne* acquires a new primacy; A. Keck, *Poetica*, 34:41–72, compares the 'Carlisle Fragment' of Thomas's *Tristan* with relevant passages from Gottfried, Eilhart, and Brother Robert's *Tristrams-Saga*; E. C. Lutz, Lutz, *Wandmalerei*, 365–403, examines the 14th-c. paintings of scenes based on *Tristan* in the 'Haus zur Mageren Magd' in Zürich; and in the same volume A. Gottdang (435–60) considers the cycle of *Tristan* paintings at Burg Runkelstein. On Eilhart's *Tristrant*, M. Backes, *LJb*, 43:373–80, suggests that the author might be the Hildesheim Canon 'Eilardus' mentioned in documents from between 1146 and 1166; and in *Akten* (Wien), v, H. Popper (157–62) examines Eilhart's conception of the heart against the background of Classical and patristic psychology, and D. Buschinger (235–41) discusses the 'H' redaction of *Tristrant*.

OTHER ROMANCES AND SHORTER NARRATIVES

The recent renewal of interest in Heinrich von dem Türlin's *Diu Crône* continues with the publication of two English-language monographs. Neil Thomas, *'Diu Crône' and the Medieval Arthurian Cycle* (Arthurian Studies, 50), Cambridge, Brewer, x + 152 pp., should appeal to English-speaking medievalists of various disciplines, partly because it provides translations of quotations and summaries of analogues, but above all because of its own solidly interdisciplinary approach. T. characterizes Heinrich as a creative re-writer of motifs culled from a wide range of works, but especially from French and German

Arthurian material. Specific examples of elements renewed by Heinrich's re-interpretation of them include the Arthur–Guinevere–Lancelot love triangle, and the Grail Quest; above all, however, T. shows how Heinrich reconstructs Gawain as a form of secular saviour who rescues the Arthurian court and its values by a combination of loyalty and chivalric prowess. Gary C. Shockey, *Homo Viator, Katabasis, and Landscapes. A Comparison of Wolfram von Eschenbach's 'Parzival' and Heinrich von dem Türlin's 'Diu Crône'* (GAG, 674), vi + 455 pp., is also a study of intertextuality, focusing as it does on Heinrich's presentation of the individuation and development of Gawain in the light of the comparable processes undergone by Parzival. S.'s at times opaque analysis makes particular use of the concepts listed in its title, as well as the roles of predestination and of mentors, and the two knights' eventual *ascensus* — a stage which, perhaps surprisingly, is interpreted as being less equivocal in the case of Gawain, who, having himself been revitalized, is able at the romance's end to reconstruct both the Arthurian and the Grail domains.

On Konrad Fleck's *Flore und Blanscheflur*, M. Egidi, *Fest. Mertens*, 133–58, studies the characterization of Flore, and J. Eming, *Akten* (Wien), v, 335–40, examines the relationship the work posits between reading and the expression of emotion. C. Dietl, *TeK*, 24:98–112, analyses the Namur episode of *Wigalois*; and H. Brunner, *Fest. Mertens*, 55–65, considers the role of the hero's wife in *Wigalois*, *Wigamur*, and *Daniel von dem blühenden Tal*. M. Nix, *ib.*, 619–25, argues that the judge in Der Stricker's *Der Richter und der Teufel* is punished for his curiosity about the Devil; and J. Mohr, *ASNS*, 239:366–75, studies the metaphors of *Die Gäuhühner* and assesses their importance for the *bîspel*'s structure.

Katharina-Silke Philipowski, *Minne und Kiusche im deutschen Prosa-Lancelot* (EH, 1, 1842), iv + 224 pp., discusses the monastic criticism of *minne* as articulated in the *Prosa-Lancelot* in such a way as to clarify what exactly, in this work at least, the term entails. P. argues that *minne* denotes much more than romantic or sexual love, but rather, along with honour, is central to the whole notion of courtliness and to the expression of courtly identity. It is also by nature destructive, a point that is vividly confirmed by the events of the *Prosa-Lancelot*, from which all (including the Grail and the entire Arthurian world) emerge as damaged losers. The victory of the spiritual over the worldly which this interpretation implies is also, P. thinks, symbolized by the work's use of prose, conforming to a Christian ideal of simplicity as against the poetic complexity and artificiality of earlier romances. Elsewhere R. Voss, *ZDA*, 131:195–212, argues that Ulrich Füetrer used the

Prosa-Lancelot as a source for both his prose and his verse re-tellings of the Lancelot story.

On Rudolf von Ems, F. Wenzel, Lieb, *Situationen*, 219–43, analyses the narrator's comments on literary communication in *Willehalm von Orlens*; S. Schmidt, Mölk, *Alexanderdichtungen*, 290–331, examines Rudolf's apparently largely independent perspectives on the history of salvation and on Alexander's empire; and in the same volume J. Cölln (332–57) postulates a comparable level of independence in his construction of *werdekeit*. Elsewhere in Mölk, *Alexanderdichtungen*, R. Finkch (358–411) discusses the theme of power in Ulrich von Etzenbach's *Alexander-Anhang*, and R. Schlechtweg-Jahn (267–89) examines power and its limits as constructed in several Alexander romances. In Kooper, *Chronicle*, 223–37, S.-J. points to the combination of romance style and hagiographical techniques in the Alexander texts of Rudolf, Seifrit, and Johannes Hartlieb.

There are several articles on Konrad von Würzburg. On *Engelhard*, D. Peschel, *JIG*, 33:8–27, traces what he sees as the psychological and sexual maturation process of the protagonist; but in the same volume (28–40), E. Schmid argues that his eventual sacrifice of his children to save his friend constitutes a regression into adolescent latency. On *Partonopier und Meliur*, A. Classen, Classen, *Meeting*, 226–48, discusses Konrad's remarkably open-minded portrayal of the Saracens; E. R. Hintz, *MDLK*, 94:153–64, defines the 'psychology of paradox', and illustrates Konrad's use of it as a rhetorical device; C. Huber, *Fest. Mertens*, 283–308, interprets Partonopier's behaviour as ambivalent and inconsistent; and J. Eming, Bennewitz, *Genderdiskurse*, 29–48, analyses the work (and *Mai und Beaflor*) in the light of Freud's and Lévi-Strauss's theories of incest, and of recent revisions of these. On the *Trojanerkrieg*, B. Hasebrink, *Fest. Mertens*, 209–30, studies the characterization of Medea, Jason, and the Argonauts; I. Scherbaum, *ZDA*, 131:326–34, discusses and contextualizes the narrator's preference for unaccompanied vocal music; and both L. Miklautsch (*Fest. Mertens*, 575–96) and A. Sieber (Bennewitz, *Genderdiskurse*, 49–76) examine the implications of Achilles's cross-dressing (with reference also to Jans Enikel's *Weltchronik*). Referring to the prologues of *Partonopier* and the *Trojanerkrieg*, M. Unzeitig, Plachta, *Edition*, 55–69, discusses the inadequacy of modern conceptions of the roles of author and translator. In the same volume (45–54), H. Kliege-Biller attempts to reconstruct the Latin source of Konrad's *Silvester*, and discusses his approach to adaptation; and in *Fest. Mertens* (361–84), B. Kellner argues that, in *Heinrich von Kempten*, Konrad thematizes the ambivalent role of violence within courtly constructions of knighthood. Meanwhile W. Achnitz, *Euphorion*, 96:349–68, discerns the influence of Konrad's conception of art in

Peter Suchenwirt's *Von der mynn slaff.* M. Meyer, *Fest. Mertens*, 551–73, discusses the female characters and their function in Berthold von Holle's *Demantin.*

Andrea Lorenz, *Der 'jüngere Titurel' als Wolfram-Fortsetzung. Eine Reise zum Mittelpunkt des Werks* (DLA, 36), 381 pp., pays Albrecht's romance the unusual compliment of taking seriously its narrator's claims to be both continuing and elucidating *Parzival* and *Titurel.* This approach necessitates a re-definition of what 'continuing' a medieval romance really entailed. L. argues that the process could involve fundamentally re-interpreting the original work, resolving the questions it had left open-ended, and developing or expanding the narrative motifs it had introduced or implied. Moreover she contends that Albrecht does all of these things, and that the apparent long-windedness, heterogeneity, and inconsistency of his work often result from his trying to exploit all of the possibilities Wolfram has offered — and/or from clashes between his twin strategies of providing alternative and contrasting material.

Wolfgang Achnitz, *Babylon und Jerusalem. Sinnkonstituierung im 'Reinfried von Brauschweig' und im 'Apollonius von Tyrland' Heinrichs von Neustadt* (Hermaea, 98), Tübingen, Niemeyer, viii + 482 pp., brings fresh clarity not only to the issue of the relationship between these two romances, but also to the question of what constitutes the genre of 'Minne- und Abenteuerromane' to which they are generally assigned. In spite of many similarities, A. shows that the two works employ quite different strategies with regard to their themes, structure, characterization, narrator, and audience: above all, *Apollonius* interprets its material within an explicitly religious framework which is largely absent in *Reinfried,* and adopts a pro-Habsburg position as against *Reinfried*'s anti-Habsburg stance. All this suggests that *Apollonius* (here dated before 1298) was composed in conscious reaction to the then very new *Reinfried* (after 1291). Both, however, share with other 'Minne- und Abenteuerromane' from *König Rother* through to *Friedrich von Schwaben* a profound interest in the exercise and legitimation of political power. C. Kiening, *Fest. Mertens*, 415–31, argues that the descriptions of monsters in *Apollonius* form part of a discussion of the tension between nature and culture; and W. G. Rohr, *Akten* (Wien), v, 249–54, assesses the abbreviated Stuttgart version of Johann von Würzburg's *Wilhelm von Österreich.*

Michaela Willers, *Heinrich Kaufringer als Märenautor. Das Oeuvre des cgm 270*, Berlin, Logos, vi + 319 pp., examines, as a coherent oeuvre, the thirteen *Mären* and four framing stories attributed to Kaufringer in this Munich MS (1464, from Augsburg or Landsberg). The central thesis of this oeuvre, according to W., is that the world is characterized by various forms of wrongdoing, which, however, can be successfully combated if people of goodwill possess the wisdom to develop appropriate strategies for dealing with them. W. claims further that many of Kaufringer's literary techniques are designed specifically to promote this thesis, including the apparent discrepancies between his stories and their prologues and epilogues. These arguments are perhaps suspiciously elegant, and at times forced; and one wonders how different W.'s conclusions would have been if she had accorded equal weight to the Kaufringer texts found in Berlin, Mgf 564. Nevertheless this is a painstaking and often persuasive study which should give new impetus to Kaufringer research. Elsewhere K. Grubmüller, *Fest. Mertens*, 193–207, studies the role and characterization of knights in *Mären*, and especially in Kaufringer's *Der zurückgegebene Minnelohn*; K. O. Seidel, *Fest. Mertens*, 691–711, examines the relationship between book learning and sexual naivety in several *Mären*; and G. Dicke, *BGDSL*, 124:261–301, analyses the principal obscene motifs of *Das Nonnenturnier*.

LYRIC POETRY

Poetische Sprachspiele. Vom Mittelalter bis zur Gegenwart, ed. Klaus Peter Dencker (UB, 18238), 428 pp., contains texts of poems by Walther von der Vogelweide (*Nieman kan mit gerten*), Konrad von Würzburg and Dürinc, and from the *Liederbuch der Clara Hätzlerin*. R. Luff, *BGDSL*, 124:250–60, discusses the difficulty of establishing the influence of Romance lyrics on German *Minnesang*; R. W. Fisher, *AUMLA*, 98:29–44, reflects on some consequences for the interpretation of *Minnesang* of our increasing awareness of the instability of medieval texts; V. Mertens, *Wolfram-Studien*, 17:276–93 interprets several high-medieval dawn songs with reference to their literary register and complexity in performance; and U. von Bloh, Bein, *Walther*, 117–44, discusses songs by various poets in which the themes of love and old age are combined. In *Neophilologus*, 86, M. Kern (567–86) analyses the textual hybridity and grotesque motifs of several 'falcon songs', whilst M. Meyer (417–35) sees these songs as exemplifying a 'poetics of evocation'. In *Fest. Mertens*, both T. Cramer (79–104) and U. Müller (597–617) challenge modern orthodoxies, the former by arguing that there is no medieval evidence of *Minnesänger* performing their songs in public at court, and the latter by suggesting that *Minnesang* might after all reflect the personal experience of its authors.

M. Schnyder, *MDG*, 49:142–54, reads the anonymous song 'Dû bist mîn' in the light of modern theories of literary communication. H. Fischer, *Euphorion*, 96:321–47, discusses the textual crux 'sumer von triere' in Hausen 47,9. On Heinrich von Morungen, J. Dewhurst,

FMLS, 38 : 24–36, examines the relationship between the presentation of the *vrouwe* and the poet's own self-projection in several songs; A. Groos, *Fest. Mertens*, 175–91, re-assesses the *Preislied* (122,1), pointing especially to the overlap between the roles of singer and author; T. Neukirchen, *Euphorion*, 96 : 303–20, discusses editorial problems associated with 123,10; and M. Egidi, *Akten* (Wien), v, 219–27, comments on the relationship between textual *mouvance* and performance in 131,25.

Two major collections of essays are devoted to Walther von der Vogelweide. In *Fest. Schulze*, E. Hilscher (1–14) and F. V. Spechtler (227–34) discuss difficulties of translating Walther's songs into modern German; T. Nolte (15–37) examines L 102,29, referring especially to its combination of *Lied* and *Spruch* elements; M. G. Scholz (39–50) considers the *Staete-Lied* L 96,29, pointing to close parallels between it and Hartmann 211,27; P. Strohschneider (59–81) discusses L 69,1, emphasizing the extent of its departures from tradition; G. Hahn (83–92) looks at L 49,25, dwelling particularly on the phrase 'und hâst genuoc'; and I. Bennewitz (93–103) contributes an interpretation of the *Sumerlatenlied* L 72,31 which takes particular account of MS 'E'. Further, V. Mertens (105–32) argues that Walther's reflections on Reinmar's death (L 82,24 and 83,1) constitute an attempt to put himself forward as the latter's natural successor; T. Cramer (133–43) interprets Reinmar's 'Herre, wer hât sie begozzen' as a parody of Walther; D. Kartschoke (147–66) suggests that, in L 100,24, the singer expresses a desire to liberate himself from courtly life; R. Bauschke (167–94) sees in L 27,17 and 27,27 parallels with contemporary Sicilian poetry; and T. Bein (195–214) discusses the authorship of the song 'Werder gruoz von frowen munde'. Moreover H. Brunner (215–25) investigates the possibility that Eberhard von Cersne may have borrowed the melody of L 92,9; U. Müller and M. Springeth (235–53) discuss the difficulty of deciding on a base MS for an edition of the *Reichston*, and present a sample edition that prints the readings of all the MSS; and S. Schmidt (255–77) assesses the images of Walther and his poetry offered to teenagers via schools, museums, and youth literature.

Bein, *Walther*, begins (11–26) with I. Gephart's analysis of the poet's conception of *schame*. Thereafter H. Haferland (27–58) argues that the lady in Walther's love poetry is a literary fiction, based, however, on the convention that she and the poet are real; W. Hofmeister (59–91) examines his use of proverbs as a technique of political agitation; M. Unzeitig (93–110) discusses the complex meanings and connotations of his phrase 'wîbes gruoz'; and P. Göhler (111–16) interprets his use of the term 'ze hove und an der strazen' in 105,36. Meanwhile T. Bein (145–50) discusses proposed changes to the

Lachmann/Cormeau edition of Walther; P. Kern (151–63) suggests a textual emendation to L 12,8; R. Luff (165–98) introduces a project which will re-assess the MS transmission, genres, and reception of Walther's oeuvre; M. Schiendorfer (199–218) argues that a Walther edition which reproduced the readings of all the MSS would aid our understanding of his metrical structures; E. Willemsen (219–23) outlines his plans to study the use of MS variance to construct particular images of Walther; and H.-J. Schiewer (249–76) investigates ways in which 13th-c. *Minnesänger* viewed themselves in relation to earlier poets, especially Walther. Finally F. Ringeler (343–54) suggests ways of teaching Walther in schools, using a 'production-oriented' method. Elsewhere A. M. Rasmussen, Klinck, *Woman's Song*, 168–86, examines the tension between reason and female honour in Walther's love songs; R. W. Fisher, *Akten* (Wien), v, 228–34, discusses and interprets the textual variability of his *Testamentstrophe* L 60,34; P. Strohschneider, Hellgardt, *Thüringen*, 85–107, comments on L 20,4 in relation to the 'communication systems' of medieval courts; and R. Voss, *Fest. Röll*, 51–77, argues that a paradigm shift might, after all, have taken place in the course of Walther's career as a love poet.

Reinhard Bleck, *Neidhart. Leben und Lieder* (GAG, 700), vi + 200 pp., flies in the face of much recent scholarship by reconstructing a detailed biography of Neidhart based on references found in his poems — roughly half of which B. prints, in modern German translation and in a putative chronological order. In some ways, B.'s approach is refreshing, but many of his judgments are decidedly suspect, not least the basic one that Neidhart came from Reinthal near Landshut. Meanwhile R. Böhmer, Lutz, *Wandmalerei*, 329–64, discusses the Neidhart-inspired frescoes (*c.* 1330) of the house 'Zum Brunnenhof' in Zürich; A. Hausmann, *Akten* (Wien), v, 287–92, suggests a method of editing Otto von Botenlauben's lyrics that would take account of the tension between corpus and oeuvre; and M. E. Amtstätter, *BGDSL*, 124:466–83, examines the relationship between text and melody in *Minnelieder* by Wizlav von Rügen.

Repertorium der Sangsprüche und Meisterlieder des 12. bis 18. Jahrhunderts, ed. Horst Brunner et al., Tübingen, Niemeyer, has arrived at its 15th volume (xii + 660 pp.). This consists of an index of *Stichwörter* found in the titles, sub-titles, and summaries of songs given in earlier volumes. Some of these are very general (e.g. 'Bibel', 'Tier'), others more specific (e.g. individual biblical figures or animal species); and concepts which constitute the main theme of a poem are helpfully differentiated by asterisks from secondary or incidental motifs. Like the *Repertorium* as a whole, this is a splendid research tool for which many will be grateful.

Margreth Egidi, *Höfische Liebe: Entwürfe der Sangspruchdichtung. Literarische Verfahrensweisen von Reinmar von Zweter bis Frauenlob* (*GRM*, Beihefte, 17), Heidelberg, Winter, 415 pp., seeks to revise certain deficient or misguided notions she sees as permeating previous research: the concept of courtly love as a fixed system of ideas, the clear dividing line often drawn between *Minnesang* and *Sangspruchdichtung*, an emphasis on the latter's didactic content at the expense of its aesthetic qualities, and, more specifically, a tendency to regard Frauenlob as more indebted to learned Latin, rather than vernacular German, traditions. E. successfully relativizes all of these positions through a painstaking examination of three types of *Sangspruch* dealing with love (songs urging lovers to behave in particular ways, songs praising women, and songs describing the process of love). Throughout she emphasizes not so much the obvious 'content' of the poems studied, but rather their structure, techniques of literary communication, and linguistic organization.

Michael Baldzuhn, *Vom Sangspruch zum Meisterlied. Untersuchungen zu einem literarischen Traditionszusammenhang auf der Grundlage der Kolmarer Liederhandschrift* (MTU, 120), xii + 551 pp., begins where Egidi leaves off. His is an extensive and innovative investigation of the didactic lyric roughly between the time of Frauenlob and of Hans Sachs, which focuses particularly on the gradual development from the single-stanza *Sangspruch* to the often much lengthier *Meisterlied*. He wisely concentrates mainly on the Colmar MS of *c.* 1460 ('k'), a remarkably revealing witness to this trend. B.'s central thesis is that the older stanzas transmitted in 'k' functioned as building blocks from which *Meisterlieder* were constructed, and that the latter should therefore be seen primarily as institutionalized combinations of existing stanzas, rather than as entirely new creations. Among his many other conclusions is the important one that the process just described accompanied a shift away from oral and towards written communication. In *FCS*, 27:21–43, M. Derron discusses the use of the motif of the sad king in a *Meisterlied* from 'k', and in the *Predigtmärlein*.

Karl Stackmann, *Frauenlob, Heinrich von Mügeln und ihre Nachfolger*, ed. Jens Haustein, Göttingen, Wallstein, 237 pp., is the third collection of reprints of S.'s essays (see *YWMLS* 59:664, 60:570–71), assembling ten pieces from between 1992 and 2000. The range of topics is somewhat narrower than in the earlier volumes, reflecting S.'s preoccupation in recent years with Frauenlob and Mügeln, though two articles deal with general questions relating to *Meisterlieder*. Many readers will welcome in particular the inclusion of S.'s important but hitherto rather inaccessible 'Frauenlob — Eine Bilanz' (34–89). *Fest. Stackmann* is similarly devoted to studies of Frauenlob and Mügeln: U. Kühne (1–14) discusses the relationship of the former's *Marienleich* to the Latin translation of it, and C. März (15–30) refutes the received wisdom that the *Marienleich* was used as a source by the author of the Old Czech *Otep myry*. The *Minneleich* is considered by C. Huber (31–50), who uses it as the basis of his discussion of Frauenlob's imagery, and by M. Schiendorfer (51–59), who discusses the notoriously opaque phrase 'Sit wip der süze ir süze vürbaz reichet'. H. Brunner (61–79) describes and assesses the structure of Frauenlob's *Spruchtöne*; M. Baldzuhn (81–102) examines the thematization of the singer as performer in several of his songs; and M. Egidi (103–23) points to similarities of structure between selected *Minnelieder* and *Minnesprüche*, to which she appends a discussion of *Lied 3*. Finally C. Fasbender (125–44) investigates a rubric appended in various MSS to Frauenlob's so-called *Sterbegebet*. On Mügeln, M. Stolz (175–209) discusses the presentation of the Seven Liberal Arts in both *Der meide kranz* and several *Sangprüche*; A. Volfing (211–29) discerns an artistic unity (centred on the common theme of metamorphosis) in Book x of the Göttingen Mügeln MS; and B. Kellner (231–51) examines Mügeln's conception of love in Book xvi of that MS. Meanwhile J. Rettelbach (145–74) surveys developments in *Sangspruchdichtung* from the period between Frauenlob and Mügeln.

Other work on *Sangspruchdichtung* includes I. Bennewitz's comments (*Birkhan Vol.*, 55–74) on the construction of Mary as virgin, mother, and queen in several songs; A. Krass's assessment (Hellgardt, *Thüringen*, 127–41) of the songs of Der Tugendhafte Schreiber; F. Löser's reflections (*Fest. Mertens*, 507–33) on the role of the literary opponent; W. Achnitz's interpretation (*ZDP*, 121:34–53) of Der Wilde Alexander's strophes ii,1–3; H. Brunner's analysis (*Fest. Röll*, 95–106), of Konrad von Würzburg's *Töne*; and F. Wenzel's discussion (Hellgardt, *Thüringen*, 143–63) of the strategies and limits of the communication of knowledge as thematized in the *Hort von der Astronomie*.

On Oswald von Wolkenstein, C. Wand-Wittkowski, *WW*, 52:178–91, examines the interplay of autobiographical accuracy and literary stylization in Kl. 1. In *Fest. Röll*, A. Robertshaw (107–35) discusses methods of dating Oswald's songs, and suggests dates specifically for Kl. 88 and 103; and A. and U. M. Schwob (137–51) examine the literary and documentary evidence suggesting that Oswald was emotionally attached to his property. In *JOWG*, 13, M. J. Schubert (261–68) discusses new recordings of Oswald's songs; R. Böhm (269–78) shows that the melody of Kl. 100 is taken from the tenor line of Gilles Binchois's *Triste plaisir*; P. Schulze-Belli (279–96) examines the interplay between religious and secular elements in Oswald's Marian verse (especially Kl. 12); and S. Hartmann and

E. Vavra (297–332) suggest, remarkably, that he might be one of the figures shown on a 15th-c. *Schutzmantelmadonna* from Le Puy-en-Velay. The congruence of Mary and the secular beloved is explored also in F. P. Knapp's discussion (*ZDA*, 131:181–94) of Oswald's ideal of female beauty.

Martin Kirnbauer, *Hartmann Schedel und sein 'Liederbuch'. Studien zu einer spätmittelalterlichen Musikhandschrift (Bayerische Staatsbibliothek München, Cgm 810) und ihrem Kontext* (Publikationen der Schweizerischen Musikforschenden Gesellschaft, 42), Berne, Lang, 417 pp., is the first really thorough description and investigation of this MS from *c.* 1460 that contains some 154 secular polyphonic songs, not all of which appear in full: over 40 Romance songs, for example, have little or no text, whereas 25 German songs appear with texts and no music. The codex is of great value to the musicologist partly because few comparable MSS have survived (some 70 songs are transmitted only in it), but also because of its multi-lingual character; it has, however, been somewhat neglected because it was plainly not designed for use in performance. Rather, it was copied by the Nuremberg humanist Hartmut Schedel for preservation in his library. K.'s book is of interest to the literary historian not least for its central section, which sheds new light on Schedel's life, library, musical interests, and copying techniques. Elsewhere M. Staehelin, Schiewer, *Präsenz*, 651–81 describes a Göttingen project to catalogue and interpret fragmentary MSS of polyphonic songs from before 1550; V. Mertens, *Akten* (Wien), v, 114–23, examines the effects of printing on the transmission and reception of several late 15th-c. songs; A. Roeleveld and E. Langbroek, *ABäG*, 56:179–97, print a MLG version of *Vnser leuen frowen rozenkrantz* and discuss the work's MS tradition; and A. Rapp Buri, Lutz, *Wandmalerei*, 491–506, considers the Basle tapestries of 1475–80 based on *Der Graf von Savoyen.*

DIDACTIC, DEVOTIONAL, AND RELIGIOUS LITERATURE

Marlies Hamm, *Der deutsche 'Lucidarius'*. Vol. 3: *Kommentar* (TTG, 37), viii + 36* + 603 pp., is the long-awaited companion volume to D. Gottschall and G. Steer's 1994 edition of the work (see *YWMLS*, 56:755). H.'s assiduous commentary is concerned to situate the *Lucidarius* as precisely as possible within the theological, philosophical, scientific, and literary landscape of the 12th century. To this end it combines with the elucidation of linguistic and interpretative difficulties an enormous amount of material on the work's sources (where possible quoted verbatim), motif parallels, and techniques of adaptation. It becomes plain that the author used many sources in addition to Honorius Augustodunensis's *Elucidarium*, that he was particularly indebted to the insights of Hugh of St Victor and his school, and, not least, that the skill and originality of his adaptation qualify him to be regarded as more than merely a translator. In *ZDA*, 131:290–307, H. discusses the 'A' prologue of the *Lucidarius*.

Wenzel, *Beweglichkeit*, contains 12 papers on the texts and images of the illustrated MSS of *Der welsche Gast*. C. Brinker-Von der Heyde (9–32) discusses Thomasin's theory and practice of (verbal) imagery; N. H. Ott (33–64) compares the *mise en page* of the earlier (12th-c. and 13th-c.) and later (14th-c. and 15th-c.) MSS; and K. Lerchner (65–81) demonstrates that the pictures cover a wide spectrum between abstract and narrative styles. H. Wenzel (82–103) examines the illustrations of Thomasin's prologue, showing that they vary much more than does its text; H. Wandhoff (104–20) analyses the illustrations and mnemonic function of the 'Lektürekatalog' of Book I; and K. Starkey (121–42) sees in the illustrations of Thomasin's passages on the vices of the tongue a progression from symbolic to scenic representation. C. Lechtermann (143–55) comments on Thomasin's instrumentalization of the courtly romance; S. Romeyke (156–73) examines picture 41 (in Kries's edition), its accompanying text, and the links it implies to the court of Wolfger of Aquileia; A. Klare (174–99) discusses Thomasin's concept of *unstete* in his text and in pictures 32 to 38; C. Kühn (200–16) examines the illustrated fables and animal images, especially in the Dresden MS ('D'); and G. Blaschitz (216–37) considers the depiction and symbolic meanings of women's clothing in various MSS. Finally M. Schumacher (238–55) compares Thomasin's use of the metaphor of imprisonment with that of authors as diverse as Boethius and Nabokov. Images from *Welsche Gast* MSS also feature in M. Curschmann's article on the correlation between the vernacular and pictorial language (Lutz, *Wandmalerei*, 9–46); and the work's construction of masculine identity and behaviour is studied by R. Weichselbaumer in Bennewitz, *Genderdiskurse*, 157–77.

Die Minnelehre des Johann von Konstanz, ed. Dietrich Huschenbett, Wiesbaden, Reichert, xxxii + 138 pp., is the first new edition of the work since 1934. It differs from previous editions in being based on the (incomplete) text of the *Weingartner Liederhandschrift*, but also taking full account of the other five MSS. Hence, H.'s text is completed using MS 'E' (Prague), and features an alternative ending from MS 'C' (Heidelberg). It also supplies the so-called *Minneklage* which follows the *Minnelehre* in the Weingarten MS. H.'s concise introduction stresses Johann's learning, and suggests that he himself composed the *Minnelehre*'s 24 Latin hexameters. Meanwhile A. M. Rasmussen, *Speculum*, 77:1168–94, discusses the eavesdropping male narrator who appears in some 25 late-medieval *Minnereden*; O. Neudeck,

BGDSL, 124:74–91, comments on metaphor and allegory in Hermann von Sachsenheim's *Die Unminne*; R. Schlechtweg-Jahn, *Akten* (Wien), v, 347–54, examines Hermann's parodistic deconstruction of contemporary legal processes in his *Mörin*; and C. Brinker-Von der Heyde, *JIG*, 33:41–62, surveys some 31 MHG *Lehrgespräche* featuring representatives of different generations.

Das 'Solsequium' des Hugo von Trimberg. Eine kritische Edition, ed. Angelika Strauss (WM, 39), xvi + 385 pp., is the first critical edition of Hugo's Latin exemplum collection, and a highly impressive one at that. The edition is supplemented by an introduction discussing issues such as the work's date, title, sources, structure, and didactic purpose, by full descriptions of its MSS, and by a particularly well conceived set of indexes. R. K. Weigand, Schiewer, *Präsenz*, 83–105, discusses the characterization of knights in the text and illustrations of Hugo's *Renner*.

Doreen Fischer, *'Witwe' als weiblicher Lebensentwurf in deutschen Texten des 13. bis 16. Jahrhunderts* (EH, 1, 1820), 296 pp., is a lucid and valuable study of a subject hitherto little researched. F. begins by discussing biblical and patristic perspectives on widowhood, with their emphasis on widows as 'brides of Christ' who should not remarry, but rather devote themselves to religious observance and good works. She then shows how this message was both reinforced and modified (in order to make it more relevant and palatable for a lay audience) in a number of vernacular didactic works, by authors such as Pseudo-Berthold von Regensburg, Erhard Gross, Heinrich der Teichner, Michael Beheim, and Albrecht von Eyb. Subsequent chapters deal with 16th-c. narratives, medical texts, and the writings of Protestant reformers.

Thomas Kock, *Die Buchkultur der Devotio moderna. Handschriftenproduktion, Literaturversorgung und Bibliotheksaufbau im Zeitalter des Medienwechsels* (Tradition–Reform–Innovation, 2), Frankfurt, Lang, 471 pp., is a remarkable study which demonstrates afresh the central importance of the written word for all the branches and activities of the *Devotio Moderna*. K. shows that, far from producing MSS to be sold to as wide a lay audience as possible, adherents of the *Devotio* copied books mainly for their own use and/or to be stored in their community's libraries — which often, indeed, bought books from outside sources. Moreover books in *Devotio* libraries were mainly in Latin, and access to them was strictly controlled. K. is also able to account for the movement's reluctance to embrace the invention of printing: the combination of reading, meditation, and physical labour involved in the prayerful copying of a MS made this activity, for them, an important element of Christian training and development. In Schiewer, *Präsenz*, F. Heinzer (107–29) re-examines the relationship between book production and religious reform in the Middle Ages; and F. Löser (177–208) uses examples of MSS from the lay brothers' library at Melk to demonstrate the potential of 'material philology'. Elsewhere F.-J. Holznagel, *ZDP*, 121:121–27, lists and discusses the didactic poems by Der Stricker found in MSS belonging to the Teutonic Order; and P. Hörner, *ZDP*, 121:408–23, refutes the traditional attribution of *Der Sünden Widerstreit* to that Order. E. Haberkern, *Mediaevistik*, 13, 2000[2002]:15–38, describes and evaluates the 23 vernacular MSS known to have been written for the Austin Canons house at Indersdorf.

Jeffrey F. Hamburger, *St. John the Divine. The Deified Evangelist in Medieval Art and Theology*, Berkeley, California U.P., xiv + 323 pp., contains brief discussions of numerous vernacular German presentations of the Evangelist, including those of Eckhart, Seuse, Mechthild von Magdeburg, and Katharina Tucher. Moreover its appendices feature editions of a German sermon for St John's Day and a German translation of the sequence *Verbum Dei Deo Natum*, both taken from a Basle MS. A shortened German version of chapter 5 of H.'s book, dealing with the St. Katharinenthal Gradual, appears in Schiewer, *Präsenz*, 131–75.

Peter Dinzelbacher, *Himmel — Hölle — Heilige. Visionen und Kunst im Mittelalter*, Darmstadt, Primus, 175 pp., looks like a coffee-table book, but is very much more than that. It is a fascinating study of the complex interaction between art and visionary experience in the Middle Ages. D.'s proven combination of erudition and lucidity makes him an ideal guide to this intricate subject. He furnishes a stimulating general introduction, and then presents, invariably on two facing pages, texts and images relating to some 54 visionaries or reporters of visions. Each of these short chapters includes biographical details, a brief text (in modern German translation) describing a vision, and a relevant picture, whose iconography is briefly elucidated. Among the German figures discussed are the Mönch von Werden, Hildegard von Bingen, Agnes Blannbekin, Elisabeth von Schönau, Heinrich Seuse, and Nikolaus von Flüe.

Köpf, *Theologen*, includes a piece on Eckhart by O. Langer (149–67), which emphasises the unity of theology, philosophy, and spirituality in his writings. G. Steer, Schiewer, *Präsenz*, 209–301, surveys critically the MS transmission of Eckhart's Latin and German works and previous research into it; and in *Fest. Mertens*, 713–53, he demonstrates that neither Eckhart himself nor his contemporaries saw him as a mystic, but rather as a teacher and preacher of religion. S. Köbele, *BGDSL*, 124:48–73, examines the structure and techniques of Eckhart's argumentation in his *Rechtfertigungslehre*; and K. H. Witte, *ZDA*, 131:454:87, identifies Johannes Hiltalingen von Basel as the author of the anti-Eckhart *Traktat von der Minne*. H. Stadler, Bennewitz, *Genderdiskurse*, 233–54, discusses the re-evaluation of the body in the works of several female mystics; B. Kratz, *ABäG*, 56:155–78, argues that Elisabeth von Schönau's *Liber visionum* was the principal source of the 15th-c. Assumption tapestries in Donaueschingen and Cologne; and M. Hubrath, *Akten* (Wien), v, 281–86, assesses the Latin and German MS tradition of Mechthild von Hackeborn's *Liber specialis gratiae*. Elsewhere R. D. Schiewer, *ZDA*, 131:436–53, describes and interprets a newly identified German translation of Wichmann von Arnstein's *Miraculum primum*; U. Störmer-Caysa, *Fest. Mertens*, 755–80, suggests a textual emendation to the editions of Seuse's *Büchlein der Weisheit*; and S. Altrock and H.-J. Ziegeler, *Akten* (Wien), v, 323–32, trace the increasing importance attached to the person of the author in the MS tradition of his *Exemplar*. Blumenfeld-Kosinski, *Spirit*, includes articles by U. Wiethaus (209–38), on the autobiographical writings of Seuse and Margarete Ebner, and by W. Williams-Krapp (239–59), who surveys the whole field of 15th-c. religious literature in German. C. Wand-Wittkowski, *Mediaevistik*, 13, 2000[2002]:117–34, discusses Rulman Merswin's *Fünfmannenbuch* and his lives of the nuns Margarete and Katharina; and in Simmler, *Textsorten*, 139–47, A. Rings examines the prose style of his *Neunfelsenbuch*.

Jutta Meindl-Weiss, *Eine vergessene Heilige. Studien zur 'Martina' Hugos von Langenstein* (EH, I, 1844), 207 pp., is an admirable attempt to rehabilitate Hugo's massive poem, seldom read and generally disapproved of by generations of Germanists. M.-W. meets its detractors head-on: their charges of indisciplined verbosity, narrative discontinuity, and thematic incoherence are answered by arguments which stress the appropriateness of the work's collage-like structure, its carefully planned and didactically effective use of rhetorical devices (notably metaphor and allegory), and its over-arching theme of the need to overcome the world, the flesh, and the Devil. D. Steeb, Bennewitz, *Genderdiskurse*, 221–31, interprets *Martina* as a soteriological compendium that explores the boundaries between subject and object. Meanwhile B. K. Vollmann, Knapp, *Erzählen*, 63–72, discusses truth and fiction in hagiographical literature; I. Kasten, Bennewitz, *Genderdiskurse*, 199–219, claims that a distinction between sex and gender is drawn in some medieval saints' lives; and U. Küsters, *Akten* (Wien), v, 57–61, examines perceptions of the saint's body in MHG legends of St Francis. C. Gutscher-Schmid, Lutz, *Wandmalerei*, 563–94, interprets wall paintings in Berne depicting the life of St Anthony in the light of literary accounts of his life; P. Strohschneider, *Fest. Mertens*, 781–811, discusses the functions and representations of sanctity in Reinbot von Durne's *Georg*; J. Jungmayr, Simmler,

Textsorten, 89–104, investigates the 15th-c. *Geistlicher Rosengarten*, and its reception of Raymond of Capua's *Legenda maior*; and C. Hennig von Lange, Schulze, *Juden*, 135–62, examines the characterization of Jews in Christian legends, especially *Das Jüdel*.

On sermons, R. Schnell, Poag, *Construction*, 91–134, considers the construction of authority in written and orally delivered sermons; H.-J. Schiewer, Simmler, *Textsorten*, 275–87, comments on the relationship between sermons and other 13th-c. mendicant prose; D. Neuendorff, *Akten* (Wien), v, 273–79, evaluates the fact that, in several MSS, Berthold von Regensburg's sermons are transmitted alongside catechetical texts; and C. Bendick, Domrös, *Judentum*, 31–59, examines anti-Jewish perspectives in Berthold's sermons. In Schulze, *Juden*, U. Schulze (109–33) surveys the attitudes towards Jews evinced in various sermons from between the 12th and 16th centuries. Meanwhile J. Klingner, *MSS*, 46:42–56, examines the German sermons of Felix Fabri, dealing particularly with his efforts to promote observantist reforms amongst Swabian nuns; and V. Mertens, *Editio*, 16:70–85, discusses problems of editing Johannes Geiler von Kaysersberg's sermons.

Das Münchener Gedicht von den 15 Zeichen vor dem Jüngsten Gericht. Nach der Handschrift der Bayerischen Staatsbibliothek Cgm 717. Edition und Kommentar, ed. Christoph Gerhardt and Nigel F. Palmer (TSM, 41), 172 pp., is a remarkably well documented edition of this 317-line poem, dated by earlier scholars to the 12th c., but here convincingly ascribed to the 14th. Almost half of the volume is devoted to an extensive commentary dealing with linguistic, theological, and literary-historical problems; but it also contains a thoroughgoing analysis of Cgm 717 (1347–8, Augsburg, conceivably from the Franciscan monastery there) which culminates in an account of the sense of crisis prevalent at the time and place of its origins. The volume also contains lists of works structured around the number 15, and of vernacular texts dealing with the 15 signs of the Last Judgment. The latter list is based on a much more detailed catalogue, accessible online at <http://users.ox.ac.uk/~npalmer/ signa.htm>.

Peter Lõkös, '*Das Puch von menschlicher aigenschafft.*' *Untersuchungen zu einem spätmittelalterlichen Textzeugen der Laienandacht aus der Steiermark* (GAG, 703), 102 pp., is a clear, concise, and scholarly introduction to Petrus von Ainstetten's almost entirely unknown adaptation of Innocent III's *De miseria humanae condicionis*, made *c.* 1433 and transmitted only in Budapest, Széchényi National Library, Cod. Germ. 10. L. summarizes what little is known about Petrus and his work's dedicatee (almost certainly the Göss Canoness Barbara Teuffenbacherin), describes his source and its vernacular reception, and investigates his techniques of translation and expansion. He also situates the *Puch* in the context of the *contemptus mundi* tradition, and of late-medieval religious literature in German.

Other articles on religious works include S. Shitanda's examination (*Akten* (Wien), v, 265–71) of aspects of the German reception of the Latin *Physiologus*; F. Simmler's analysis (Simmler, *Textsorten*, 289–367) of the German representatives of the *Diatessaron* tradition; E. Ukena-Best's study (*Fest. Berschin*, 185–206) of Konrad von Fussesbrunnen's adaptation of his sources in the robber episode of his *Kindheit Jesu*; C. Virchow's discussion (*MAe*, 71:269–85) of the *Basler Dialog zwischen Seele und Leib* in the context of late-medieval Dominican literature; R. Hanamann and H. Tiefenbach's consideration (*Sprachwissenschaft*, 27:295–319) of the German sections of the trilingual (Latin, Polish, and German) *St. Florian Psalter*; M. J. Schubert's reflections (Plachta, *Edition*, 219–34) on problems of editing the anonymous German verse translation of the *Speculum humanae salvationis*; and U. Möllmann's treatment (Simmler, *Textsorten*, 257–73) of the reception of a late 15th-c. Memmingen print of a German version of the Rule of St Benedict.

DRAMA

Alsfelder Passionsspiel. Frankfurter Dirigierrolle mit den Paralleltexten. Weitere Spielzeugnisse. Alsfelder Passionsspiel mit den Paralleltexten, ed. Johannes Janota (Die Hessische Passionsspielgruppe: Edition in Paralleldruck, 2), Tübingen, Niemeyer, xvi + 921 pp., continues the three-volume project intended to present this group of plays in reliable modern editions which document and clarify the relationships between them (see *YWMLS*, 59:703–04). The current volume begins with a synoptic edition in which the *Frankfurter Dirigierrolle* forms the leading text alongside the parallels found in the *Frankfurter*, *Alsfelder*, and *Heidelberger Passionsspiele*, and concludes with a comparable edition in which the leading text is the Alsfeld play. This also encompasses the first edition of the so-called *Trierer Marienklage*; and between the two parallel editions J. provides texts of other, shorter representatives of the Alsfeld tradition, namely the *Fritzlarer Passionsspielfragment*, the *Friedberger* and *Alsfelder Dirigierrollen*, the *Alsfelder Spielerverzeichnis*, and the various *Alsfelder Einzelrollen*. The entire enterprise maintains the highest scholarly standards. It has also spawned Klaus Wolf, *Kommentar zur 'Frankfurter Dirigierrolle' und zum 'Frankfurter Passionsspiel'* (Die Hessische Passionsspielgruppe: Edition in Paralleldruck, Ergänzungsband, 1), Tübingen, Niemeyer, vi + 914 pp. This too is work of excellent quality, which greatly increases our knowledge of these plays, and does so in a systematic and user-friendly way. W.'s material on each play begins with a substantial introduction dealing with issues relating to its performance and function within the cultural and socio-political life of Frankfurt. This is followed by a scene-by-scene commentary, based on Janota's edition, which focuses initially on linguistic problems but goes on to cover sources, parallels, references to local events or issues, and the scene's theatrical and/or literary qualities. W. is further concerned to define the complex links between the plays and the religious epic *Die Erlösung*.

The 'rheinfränkisch-hessische Spielgruppe' is also discussed in detail in Dorothea Freise, *Geistliche Spiele in der Stadt des ausgehenden Mittelalters. Frankfurt — Friedberg — Alsfeld* (Veröffentlichungen des Max-Planck-Instituts für Geschichte, 178), Göttingen, Vandenhoeck & Ruprecht, 624 pp., a study by a social historian which seeks to establish not only who participated in the composition and performance of religious plays in late-medieval towns, but also why and to what effect they did so. The Frankfurt, Friedberg, and Alsfeld plays prove very appropriate subjects for such a study. Elements common to all the towns include a concern both to glorify God and to edify participants and audience, a wide and socially heterogeneous spectrum of performers, and a somewhat aggressive and potentially exclusive *Passionsfrömmigkeit.* Major differences emerge, however, especially between Frankfurt and the other towns, with regard to the precise social composition of participants, the role of the clergy and the ruling classes, and the extent of the Council's involvement.

Much work has been published on anti-Jewish motifs in late-medieval drama. In Schulze, *Juden*, F. Rommel (183–207) studies these in relation to various Passion plays, and M. Wolf (35–58) examines the dispute between Church and Synagogue in the Donaueschingen and Alsfeld plays. The *Donaueschinger Passionsspiel* is also the main example used by T. Bartoldus (Domrös, *Judentum*, 121–46) in his discussion of anti-Jewish themes in religious plays, and by I. Kasten (*Fest. Mertens*, 335–60) in her study of their potentially intimidating use of ritual. Moreover in *FCS*, 27:149–60, M. Z. Heintzelmann discusses the hatred for Christians expressed by Jewish characters. The alleged anti-Semitism of Hans Folz is also discussed: by R. Schiel (Domrös, *Judentum*, 147–77) in relation to his *Fastnachtspiele*, by M. Schönleber (Schulze, *Juden*, 163–82) in relation to these and some *Schwänke*, and by W. Frey (Classen, *Meeting*, 249–67), who considers the dialogue ('krieg') between a Christian and a Jew. Meanwhile H. Ragotzky, *ZDP*, 121:54–71, examines the function of the Antichrist figure in Folz's *Der Entkrist vasnacht* and *Der Herzog von Burgund.*

Elsewhere C. Kubé, *ZDA*, 131:346–54, edits and assesses the *Lübener Osterspielfragment*; B. Stuplich, *Fest. Röll*, 165–85, examines the political *Fastnachtspiele* of Hans Rosenplüt; and J. Keller, *Akten* (Wien), v, 103–08, discusses obscenity in the 15th-c. *Fastnachtspiel.*

SCIENTIFIC AND SPECIALIZED LITERATURE

Deutsche Rechtsregeln und Rechtssprichwörter. Ein Lexikon, ed. Ruth Schmidt-Wiegand (BsR, 1470), 402 pp., is a fascinating volume which lists, alphabetically by *Stichwort*, some 1800 aphorisms or maxims with a legal theme, or simply with legal origins. Meanings are discussed with reference to their historical development, and relevant etymological and bibliographical information is given.

There is a new translation of *Der Sachsenspiegel*, by Paul Kaller, Munich, Beck, xvi + 179 pp. K.'s rendering, based on the Quedlinburg MS, is well turned and sensible, and he also provides a glossary, an index, and an introduction which together supply all the basic information a newcomer to the work will need to know. Harald Rainer Derschka, *'Der Schwabenspiegel', übertragen in heutiges Deutsch mit Illustrationen aus alten Handschriften*, Munich, Beck, x + 503 pp., is an articulate translation of the relatively neglected *Schwabenspiegel*, based on the flawed Lassberg edition of 1840, but also incorporating variant readings from a range of MSS. This is supported by admirably full indexes and, not least, by excellent black-and-white reproductions of all the known illustrations from *Schwabenspiegel* MSS, notably the 69 found in Brussels, Bibliothèque Royale, Ms. 14689–91 (from the workshop of Diebolt Lauber). The pictures are analysed in detail, but the introductory discussion of the actual text is a little thin. In *ZDA*, 131:66–78, C. Fasbender makes a critical survey of research into Lauber and his work. A. Schmidt, Schulze, *Juden*, 87–105, examines the oaths prepared for Jews to swear in court, as these are recorded in the *Sachsenspiegel* and in documents from Erfurt and Heidelberg; and U. Bruchhold, Hellgardt, *Thüringen*, 31–44, concentrates particularly on the *Erfurter Judeneid*. Meanwhile N. Spengler, Simmler, *Textsorten*, 459–73, surveys common characteristics of legal documents written in 13th-c. Constance.

Reiner Leng, *'Ars belli.' Deutsche taktische und kriegstechnische Bilderhandschriften und Traktate im 15. und 16. Jahrhundert*, vol. 1: *Entstehung und Entwicklung*, vol. 2: *Beschreibung der Handschriften*, 2 vols (IMA, 12), xii + 493 pp. + 34 pls, vi + 514 pp., offers a monumentally thorough introduction to a little-known late-medieval genre — consisting of works, often illustrated, which deal in generally applicable terms with the technology, organization, and tactics of warfare. H.'s history of these works stresses that they developed primarily in reaction to new inventions (notably of firearms) and the concomitant changes in the composition of armies. By the end of the 15th c. they were already numerous and varied, and often copiously illustrated. The 15th-c. texts dealt with in greatest detail are the *Bellifortis* of Konrad Kyeser, and the *Feuerwehrbuch von 1420*; but less frequently transmitted works are also given full coverage, not least in the exhaustive collection of MS descriptions that constitutes L.'s second volume. Also on warfare, F. Fürbeth, *BGDSL*, 124:302–38, presents a previously unknown 15th-c. translation of Vegetius's *Epitoma rei militaris* found in Seitenstetten Ms. LXV.

Reiner Bach, *'der ritterschaft in eren.' Das Bild des Krieges in den historiographischen Schriften niederadliger Autoren des 15. und frühen 16. Jahrhunderts* (IMA, 10), xii + 244 pp., studies in detail three works about war (in the term's broadest sense) written by members of the lower nobility in Franconia between roughly 1430 and 1516: Heinrich Steinrück's *Aufzeichnungen*, Michel von Ehenheim's *Familienchronik*, and Ludwig von Eyb the Elder's *Denkwürdigkeiten*. His discussion of each focuses particularly on the author's biography, his conception of war, and his likely motives for writing. Significant differences between the three works emerge, of course, but B. points also to certain common elements: a marked (auto)biographical impulse and consequent relative independence of written sources; a tendency to perceive war as still an essentially aristocratic pursuit; a concentration on specific incidents within the description of combat; and a relative reluctance to discuss the enemy, the reasons for fighting them, and the deaths and injuries suffered in the process. Meanwhile Ludwig von Eyb the Younger's *Geschichten und Taten Wilwolts von Schaumberg* is discussed by H. Ulmschneider in *Fest. Berschin*, 1077–99.

Also on historiography, P. Johanek, Knapp, *Erzählen*, 9–25, examines the concept of truth as understood by various medieval historians and their audiences; K. Kellermann, *Akten* (Wien), v, 63–68, studies aspects of the representation of rulers; T. Scharff, *LiLi*, 126:8–26, discusses treatments of public acts of confession and/or penance performed by rulers; J. Sarnowsky, *AKG*, 84:66–91, assesses accounts of conflicts between Popes and Emperors in the works of several late-medieval historians; V. Bok, *Fest. Mertens*, 33–54, comments on the portrayal of Přemysl Otakar II, King of Bohemia, in Ottokar's *Steirische Reimchronik*; and W. Haubrichs, *ib.*, 231–45, discusses that work's conception of the role of the artist. With reference especially to the verse prologue of the *Sächsische Weltchronik*, G. von Olberg, Simmler, *Textsorten*, 385–406, points to characteristic aspects of the *Weltchronik* tradition; R. Wetzel, Lutz, *Wandmalerei*, 405–33, examines the Runkelstein MS of Heinrich von München's *Weltchronik* in the light of other art works from the castle; and in *Akten* (Wien), v, 75–80, he interprets the Runkelstein wall paintings as polyvalent cultural documents. Moreover, P. Zahn, *GJ*, 77:124–44, evaluates Albrecht Dürer's contribution to the woodcuts of Koberger's 1493 edition of Hartmann Schedel's *Weltchronik*; and R. Klein, *ib.*, 145–58, considers this work's treatment of Constantine the Great.

Randall Herz, *Die 'Reise ins Gelobte Land' Hans Tuchers des Älteren (1479–1480). Untersuchungen zur Überlieferung und kritische Edition eines spätmittelalterlichen Reiseberichts* (WM, 38), xviii + 792 pp. + 28 pls, provides the first modern edition of Tucher's pilgrimage report, but also much more. H.'s painstaking analysis of the work's MSS and early prints enables him not only to produce detailed descriptions and assessments of these, but also to reconstruct the stages of production that the text underwent: from an announcement of it in a letter from Tucher to his brother, through two MS redactions, a printer's copy (the Nuremberg MS on which this edition is based), and finally the printed text that Tucher had always envisaged. H. also considers the extent of the work's originality and aspects of its reception, and prints some fascinating related documents, such as Tucher's letter to his brother, his will, and medicinal recipes prepared for him by Hermann Schedel. Elsewhere W. G. Rohr, Plachta, *Edition*, 359–65, discusses problems of editing numerals in the Lower Rhenish adaptation of Mandeville's *Travels*.

Gesundheits- und Haushaltslehren des Mittelalters. Edition des 8° Ms 875 der Universitätsbibliothek Greifswald, ed. Christa Baufeld (Kultur, Wissenschaft, Literatur, 1), Frankfurt, Lang, lxxiii + 216 pp., is a meticulous edition, with codicological description, introduction, and glossary, of this 15th-c. MS, most of which was probably written in Nuremberg in the 1430s. It transmits a wide variety of texts intended for the everyday use of a doctor. Along with practical medical treatises, these include two herbals, a lapidary, a work on the four seasons, a letter purportedly sent by Aristotle to Alexander the Great, and even a treatise on love (written from a medical perspective). Also on medicine, K. Zimmermann, *ZDA*, 131:343–45, identifies a fascicle of Heidelberg, Cpg 280, as containing texts of Johannes Hartlieb's translations of *Trotula* and the *Secreta mulierum*; and H. E. Keller, *Akten* (Wien), v, 175–81, explores forms of visualization in gynaecological texts from around 1500. Moreover, M. Weiss Adamson, *Birkhan Vol.*, 105–24, examines the motif of male pregnancy in works from Jans Enikel to Hans Sachs.

Rhetorica deutsch. Rhetorikhandschriften des 15. Jahrhunderts, ed. Joachim Knape and Bernhard Roll (Gratia, 40), Wiesbaden, Harrassowitz, 337 pp., fills a significant gap in our knowledge of 15th-c. rhetoric by providing texts of some 11 previously unedited works in German prose, dating mainly from the century's second half. Six of these stand broadly in the tradition of the *ars epistolandi*: the so-called *Nördlinger Rhetorik*, Friedrich von Nürnberg's *Deutsche Rhetorik*, Magister

Friedrich's *Wie man gute Briefe machen soll*, Johann Senff's *Formularrhetorik*, the *Ingolstädter Rhetorik*, and the *Stadtschreibers Examen*. These are followed by Niclas von Wyle's *Unterweisung* and *Figurenlehre*, and by three somewhat more sophisticated and specialized treatises in *Die Räte von der Rede* (adapted from Albertanus Brixensis), an *Ars oratoria deutsch*, and a *Gerichtsrhetorik*. In Kooper, *Chronicle*, 117–29, Knape examines rhetorical gestures characteristic of historiographical texts.

Other articles include G. Steer's discussion (Meier, *Enzyklopädie*, 181–88) of Konrad von Megenberg's *Buch der Natur* in relation to its Latin source; T. Gloning's analysis (Simmler, *Textsorten*, 517–50) of characteristic structures and functions of vernacular cooking recipes; and M. Habermann's study (Simmler, *Textsorten*, 551–71) of ways in which herbals organize their material.

OTHER LATER MEDIEVAL LITERATURE

Corinna Laude, *'Daz in swindelt in den sinnen . . .' Die Poetik der Perspektive bei Heinrich Wittenwiler und Giovanni Boccaccio* (PSQ, 173), 363 pp., is an original and interesting, if controversial study, whose point of departure is that the theory of perspective adumbrated by 14th-c. Italian artists had an impact also on late-medieval literature — not least on so apparently unlikely a work as Wittenwiler's *Ring*. Wittenwiler's poetic premise (and for that matter Boccaccio's) is, according to L., that the perception of reality depends on the perspective from which it is viewed. On this basis he deconstructs accepted social norms and narrative strategies, and instead opens up new horizons for both author and audience to exercise a new freedom to create and construct their own relationships to reality. The methods he uses include the use of multiple narrative perspectives, the apparently haphazard combination of disparate didactic messages and of epic and discursive elements, and an insistence on the imaginative and artistic character of his own work.

Bea Lundt, *Weiser und Weib. Weisheit und Geschlecht am Beispiel der Erzähltradition von den 'Sieben Weisen Meistern' (12.–15. Jahrhundert)*, Munich, Fink, 561 pp., analyses in detail four representatives of this tradition: Johannes de Alta Silva's *Dolopathos* (Latin, later 12th c.), Johannes Gobi Junior's *Scala Coeli* (Latin, 1320s), Hans von Bühel's *Dyoclecianus' Leben* (German, 1412), and the anonymous printed *Sieben Weisen Meister* (German, 1473). L. is interested above all in the different ways in which these texts construct the nature of a wise man, his masculinity and that of his aristocratic pupil, and their attitudes and behaviour towards women. For all their structural and thematic similarities, no consensus on these issues emerges between the four works; rather, they are very much products of particular times, places, and authorial perspectives. As such they demonstrate also that the exempla on which all are based are themselves more flexible, open constructs than is generally imagined.

In Wilhelmi, *Brant*, T. Wilhelmi contributes an introductory account of Brant's life and works (7–35), and a study of his collaboration with Dürer both on the *Narrenschiff* and on a planned, but never published, edition of Terence (103–24). Three additional contributions focus on the *Narrenschiff*. In a richly illustrated piece, J. Hartau (125–69) examines Brant's use of the ship metaphor in the light of earlier and later parallels; P. Habicht (171–85) assesses the work's local allusions to Basle; and J. Uebelhart (187–241) analyses in detail Brant's use of biblical references (a full list of which is appended to the article). Other aspects of Brant's career are covered by S. Schünicke (37–81), who analyses anti-Turkish motifs in several of his works, and by J. Geiss (83–102), who investigates the nature and extent of his contribution to Amerbach's Petrarch edition of 1496. Elsewhere H. Thomke, Plachta, *Edition*, 309–16, discusses methods of elucidating linguistic difficulties in editions of the *Narrenschiff*.

Following N. Hartl's book on Jakob Locher's *Stultifera Navis* (see *YWMLS*, 63:656), we now have a still more comprehensive study of the relationship between his adaptation and Brant's *Narrenschiff*: Michael Rupp, *'Narrenschiff' und 'Stultifera Navis'. Deutsche und lateinische Moralsatire von Sebastian Brant und Jakob Locher in Basel 1494–1498* (STMFN, 3), 263 pp. R. begins by establishing both the closeness of the personal association between Brant and Locher, and the differences in their conceptions of poetry and theology. He then analyses Brant and Locher's introductory material, and five chapters of the *Narrenschiff* which thematize the relationship between Latin and German culture. R. shows that Locher places less emphasis on Brant's moral-theological message, often replaces proverbs and references to everyday German life with allusions to Classical literature, and in general favours a smoother, sharper form of argumentation. In short, his adaptation is plainly directed at an international *res publica litterarum*, whose expectations he meets at the expense of a certain textual openness.

Gabriele Jancke, *Autobiographie als soziale Praxis. Beziehungskonzepte in Selbstzeugnissen des 15. und 16. Jahrhunderts im deutschsprachigen Raum* (Selbstzeugnisse der Neuzeit, 10), Cologne, Böhlau, viii + 264 pp., studies a wide range of both Latin and vernacular autobiographical writings, paying particular attention to ways in which the authors define and position themselves vis-à-vis their social contexts. Of the 234 works considered, however, only 15 date from before 1500 (though there is interesting material about Nicolaus Cusanus's perspectives on patronage). Similarly Wilfried Kettler, *Trewlich ins Teütsch gebracht. Lateinisch-deutsches Übersetzungsschrifttum im Umkreis des schweizerischen Humanismus*, Berne, Lang, 416 pp., is concerned mainly with 16th-c. translations, but also has chapters on late 15th-c. work by Albrecht von Bonstetten and Johannes Geiler von Kaysersberg. The former's translations are characterized by a word-for-word technique that reveals the influence of Niclas von Wyle, whereas the latter, seeking to appeal to a wider audience, adopts a markedly freer approach.

Anti-Jewish perspectives in late-medieval texts are examined by B. Berghausen (Schulze, *Juden*, 233–53) and M. Willeke (Domrös, *Judentum*, 61–83), who study the pogrom in Deggendorf in 1338, and the 15th-c. *Lied von Deggendorf* which seeks to justify it; and by N. Spengler (Schulze, *Juden*, 211–31) and S. Olgemann (Domrös, *Judentum*, 85–119), who consider accounts of alleged ritual murders of children by Jews.

Elsewhere C. Huber, Hellgardt, *Thüringen*, 165–77, studies Johannes Rothe's descriptions of Landgrave Ludwig IV's knighting ceremony in his chronicles, *Ritterspiegel*, and *Elisabeth-Leben*; and in the same volume H. Lähnemann (179–90) analyses the didactic techniques of the *Ritterspiegel*. In *GJ*, 77, S. Obermaier (63–75) examines the relationship between the title woodcuts and texts of printed fable collections by Heinrich Steinhöwel, Anton von Pforr, and Ulrich von Pottenstein; and F. Eisermann (77–83) discusses a single-leaf print in which Maximilian I appeals for troops. W. Wunderlich, *Fest. Berschin*, 125–38, addresses the use of biographical fiction in various lives of Aesop; R. Schlusemann, *FCS*, 217–37, considers violence in the text and illustrations of *Reynke de vos*; and M. Schilling, Lieb, *Situationen*, 191–216, assesses the roles of the work's narrator and glossator. A. Classen, *ABäG*, 56:199–222, summarizes the evidence of women's activities as poets, collectors of poems, scribes, and editors in 15th-c. and 16th-c. Germany; Id., Simmler, *Textsorten*, 65–88, discusses the polyvalence and 'multivocality' of the *Volksbuch* as a genre; and N. Knischewski, Bennewitz, *Genderdiskurse*, 179–98, examines the construction of masculine identity in *Fortunatus*. D. Hempen, *GNR*, 33:13–17, evaluates Marquard von Stein's attempts, in *Der Ritter vom Turn*, to warn his female readers against gluttony; H. Kokott, *DUS*, 54.1:9–15, explores the late-medieval 'Dance of Death' tradition; and W. Hofmeister, *ZDA*, 131:335–42, describes a newly discovered late-medieval MS fragment from Admont which contains blessings, prayers, and a recipe for ink.

THE SIXTEENTH CENTURY

By Mark Taplin

1. General

Wahrnehmungsgeschichte und Wissensdiskurs im illustrierten Flugblatt der Frühen Neuzeit (1450–1700), ed. Wolfgang Harms and Alfred Messerli, Basle, Schwabe, 512 pp., presents papers from a conference held to mark the publication of the first volume of broadsheets from the Zurich *Wickiana*. In their introductory essays, the editors highlight the *Flugblatt's* ability to combine a variety of genres and forms of representation, and stress the interdependence of illustration and text in early modern broadsheets. Relevant contributions include M. Schilling, 'Flugblatt und Krise in der Frühen Neuzeit' (33–59); H. Irler (85–108), which applies Erwin Panofsky's 'iconological method' to depictions of *Landsknechte* in two Augsburg *Flugblätter* published around 1560; P. Kaenel (113–41), on the role of 16th-c. broadsheets in the prehistory of caricature; B. Bauer, 'Die Krise der Reformation. Johann Jacob Wicks Chronik außergewöhnlicher Natur- und Himmelserscheinungen' (193–236), which relates Wick's interest in prodigies to uncertainty about the future of Protestantism following the massacre of St Bartholomew's Eve; T. Gutwald (239–61), which compares descriptions of the aurora borealis in *Wickiana* broadsheets and in Conrad Gessner's *Historia et interpretatio prodigii* (1561); U.-B. Kuechen (265–303), on providentialist interpretations of abnormal plant forms in *Flugblätter*; F. Mauelshagen (309–38), on techniques employed by the authors of *Flugblätter* to authenticate the events that they describe; W. Adam, 'Textelemente des Briefes auf illustrierten Flugblättern der frühen Neuzeit' (341–67); K. Stegbauer (371–414), on the propagandistic use of the murder of Juan Diaz in anti-Catholic texts; S. S. Tschopp (415–42), on the development of a Swiss national consciousness and its exploitation for confessional purposes in broadsheets of the late 16th and early 17th cs; and D. Peil, 'Strafe und Ritual. Zur Darstellung von Straftaten und Bestrafungen im illustrierten Flugblatt' (465–86). The volume includes numerous illustrations, along with summaries of the conference discussions of each paper.

Res et verba in der Renaissance, ed. Eckhard Kessler and Ian Maclean (Wolfenbütteler Abhandlungen zur Renaissanceforschung, 21), Wiesbaden, Harrassowitz, 398 pp., examines the way in which the Classical and medieval distinction between words, concepts, and things was received and reformulated by writers in a variety of disciplines (linguistic philosophy, mathematics, theology, law, medicine, and ethics) during the period 1450–1650. The following articles are of particular interest: M. L. Bianchi, 'Signs, *signaturae* and *Natursprache* in Paracelsus and Böhme' (197–215); N. G. Siraisi (217–40), on interpretations of the Galenic concepts of cause, disease, and symptom by 16th-c. writers on medicine, including Leonhart Fuchs; J. Rohls (241–72), on the significance of the distinction between *res* and *verba* for the early Protestant doctrine of scripture (among the writers considered are Luther, Melanchthon, and Flacius); and B. Vickers, '"Words and things" — or "Words, concepts, and things"? Rhetorical and linguistic categories in the Renaissance' (288–335), which notes the variability in meaning of the terms *res* and *verba*, depending on whether they refer to the tradition of Classical rhetoric or to that of Aristotelian linguistics.

Festivals and Ceremonies: A Bibliography of Works Relating to Court, Civic and Religious Festivals in Europe 1500–1800, ed. Helen Watanabe-O'Kelly and Anne Simon, London, Mansell, 2000, xix + 533 pp., catalogues almost 3,000 works in 13 languages from the British Library, the Herzog August Bibliothek Wolfenbüttel, the British National Art Library, and the Rondel Collection of the Bibliothèque de l'Arsenal. Watanabe-O'Kelly, *Court Culture*, focuses on the artistic patronage of the Albertine Electors of Saxony during the period 1553–1733. Of particular relevance to the 16th c. are the first two chapters, on the Lutheran legacy (church music, biblical drama etc.) and on the reception of Italian culture under the Electors Maurice and Augustus I. W. highlights the role of Giovanni Maria Nossini, originally from Lugano, who in the late 16th c. transformed court tournaments at Dresden through the use of Italian theatrical technology. Other chapters discuss the electors' support for alchemy (a by-product of their mining interests), and the formation of the Dresden collections. W. shows that the early contents of the *Kunstkammer* closely reflected Augustus I's intellectual preoccupations (mapmaking, ivory turning, gardening, surgery, geology, architecture, and gunnery).

Elisheva Carlebach, *Divided Souls: Converts from Judaism in Germany 1500–1750*, New Haven, Yale U.P., 2001, xii + 324 pp., argues that from the 16th c. onwards converts such as Victor von Calven, Johannes Pfefferkorn, and Antonius Margaritha played a crucial role in shaping the Christian image of Jews and in mediating knowledge of Jewish belief and ceremonial to society at large. Peter Nusser, *Deutsche Literatur von 1500 bis 1800. Lebensformen, Wertvorstellungen und literarische Entwicklungen*, Stuttgart, Kröner, xv + 511 pp., is the second of a projected three volumes in N.'s history of German literature. The work is organized into chapters on humanism, the Baroque, and the 18th c. Chapter 1, which deals primarily with the 16th c., offers a useful introduction to intellectual and literary developments during the period for the non-specialist reader. There are sections on each of the principal genres, and brief synopses of some works (the *Epistolae virorum obscurorum*, Reuchlin's *Henno*, Fischart's *Flöh Hatz Weiber Tratz* and *Geschichtklitterung*) are provided. Klaus Garber, *Imperiled Heritage: Tradition, History, and Utopia in Early Modern German Literature* (Studies in European Cultural Transition, 5), Aldershot, Ashgate, 2000, xxx + 268 pp., contains English translations of eight essays by the literary historian. W. Harms, *MDG*, 49:278–93, emphasizes the heterogeneity of early modern literary production.

2. Humanism and the Reformation

Wilfried Kettler, *Trewlich ins Teütsch gebracht: Lateinisch-deutsches Übersetzungsschrifttum im Umkreis des schweizerischen Humanismus*, Berne, Lang, 416 pp., following his recent study of the Zurich German Bible, examines translations by nine writers from Switzerland and south-western Germany (Albrecht von Bonstetten, Johannes Geiler von Kaysersberg, Leo Jud, Huldrych Zwingli, Jacob Ceporin, Georg Binder, Johannes Fries, Johannes Stumpf, and Johann Fischart) covering the period 1477–1578. The works chosen represent three different approaches to translation: word-for-word translation, literal translation, and free translation. K. compares the style, syntax, and vocabulary of selected passages from each text with those of the Latin originals to which they refer. Special attention is given to the works of Leo Jud, whom K. regards as the most important Swiss translator of the 16th c. According to K., Jud's chosen method reflects his background as a preacher and biblical exegete. Like Luther, Jud proceeds from the premise that vernacular translations should be comprehensible to the 'common man'; to that end, he systematically replaces Latin constructions with more idiomatic German equivalents. Subsequent writers such as Stumpf (in his translation of Ludwig Lavater's history of the Eucharistic controversy) and Fischart (in his *Philosophisches Ehezuchtbüchlein*) take even greater liberties with the Latin text, modifying and expanding it in the light of their own concerns. K. associates the drift from literal towards free translation with the growing acceptance of German as a literary language, to be used alongside (although not yet instead of) Latin. Joachim Hamm, *Servilia bella. Bilder vom deutschen Bauernkrieg in neulateinischen Dichtungen des 16. Jahrhunderts* (Imagines medii aevi, 7), Wiesbaden, Reichert, 2001, ix + 373 pp., analyses 18 texts from a variety of genres, including plays, prose dialogues, and occasional, epic, and bucolic poems. According to H., the authors' treatment of their subject matter is shaped by three main influences: the historical events of the

Peasants War, as related in contemporary chronicles; the humanist ideals of *aemulatio* and *imitatio*; and their own religious stance. He further distinguishes between 'confessional', 'historical-panegyrical', and 'humanist' perspectives, associating each approach with particular genres. In most cases, the texts considered endorse the prevailing Catholic or Protestant interpretations of the Peasants War (which is seen either as an inevitable consequence of the Reformation, or as having been engineered by Thomas Müntzer). However, according to H., forms such as the elegy, the eclogue, and the school drama permit writers greater independence of outlook: for example, Joachim Camerarius's eclogues 'Thyrsis' and 'Lycidas' contain veiled criticisms of the authorities in Bamberg for their conduct following the war. In an appendix, H. publishes the full text of one of the works discussed, Johannes Atrocianus's *Elegia de bello rustico*, with a German translation and commentary. K. Lambrecht, 'Communicating Europe to the region: Breslau in the age of the Renaissance', *German History*, 20: 1–19, seeks explanations for the emergence of Breslau as a cultural centre within the east-central European triangle of Cracow, Prague, and Vienna. L. focuses on the contribution of the early-16th-c. bishop John Thurzó and the role of poliographic works such as Bartholomäus Stein's *Descripcio Vratislavie* in projecting the city's image as a 'cultural metropolis'.

Anne T. Thayer, *Penitence, Preaching and the Coming of the Reformation*, Aldershot, Ashgate, xiv + 226 pp., posits a link between the appeal of the Reformation in different parts of Europe and regional variations in late medieval teaching on penitence. T. identifies three distinct approaches to penitence in collections of model sermons published between 1450 and 1520: 'rigorist', which emphasized the individual responsibility of the penitent for contrition and satisfaction; 'moderate', which stressed the importance of both confession and contrition; and 'absolutionist', which highlighted the sacramental role of the priest. On this basis, she offers a fresh interpretation of Luther's doctrine of penitence, as a reaction against key elements of rigorist teaching. More contentiously, she argues that the Protestant message of forgiveness freely given through Christ was most likely to be perceived as liberating (and hence, that the Reformation was most likely to be successful) in areas with a strong rigorist tradition, such as Germany. Rebecca Wagner Oettinger, *Music as Propaganda in the German Reformation*, Aldershot, Ashgate, 2001, xv + 435 pp., examines the role of popular song as a vehicle for the dissemination of Protestantism during the period 1517–55, drawing on collections held at the Staatsbibliothek zu Berlin, Preußischer Kulturbesitz, and the Bayerische Staatsbibliothek. O. suggests that polemical song was the medium best equipped for spreading the Lutheran message because it did not require a literate audience, was less complex than many woodcut images, and could be transmitted orally. In addition, the use by Protestant authors of familiar melodies ensured that their songs had broad social appeal and were easily memorized. Topics considered include Luther's contribution as a songwriter, the Protestant use of contrafacta (for example, Hans Sachs's adaptation of Marian hymns, and anti-papal versions of the *Judaslied*) and the role of music in the opposition to the Augsburg Interim. O. sees Reformation songs as characterized by a series of bipolar oppositions (Christ versus Antichrist, truth versus falsehood) which helped foster a confessional mindset in populations newly converted to Lutheranism. Song, in the form of chorales, went on to become a marker of Lutheran identity, setting it apart from both Catholicism and Reformed Protestantism. A catalogue appended to the text provides bibliographical information on 230 songs, many of which are reproduced in full with accompanying English translations. M. Stähli, *Zwa*, 29:95–116, discusses an unpublished defence of the visual arts by a member of the Zurich Heidegger family. I. Backus, 'Prière en latin au 16e siècle et son rôle dans les églises issues de la réforme', *AR*, 93:43–71, includes consideration of collections by Brunfels, Capito, and Melanchthon. Angela Baumann-Koch, **Frühe lutherische Gebetsliteratur bei Andreas Musculus und Daniel Cramer*, Frankfurt, Lang, 2001, 672 pp.

3. Genres

DRAMA AND DIALOGUE. Glenn Ehrstine, *Theater, Culture, and Community in Reformation Bern, 1523–1555* (SMRT, 85), xviii + 346 pp., is a major new study of the plays of Niklaus Manuel and Hans von Rüte. E. argues that theatre helped forge a new cultural identity for the Bernese population following the introduction of religious reforms. In their writings on drama, Protestant theologians showed a keen awareness of the genre's didactic potential; because of the theatre's impact on the viewer, they regarded it as a particularly effective form of preaching. In Berne, theatrical performances were also encouraged by the city council, in the belief that they provided a focus for the expression of communal unity. Over the course of the period examined by E., Bernese drama evolved to meet the demands imposed on it by both ecclesiastical and civic authorities. During the 1520s, the dominant form was the carnival play, but after the abolition of the Mass in January 1528 the violent and licentious elements of carnival came to be seen as incompatible with Protestant values. In its place emerged a rich tradition of biblical drama, influenced both by humanist school drama and by the passion plays of neighbouring Lucerne. Works such as Rüte's *Joseph* and *Gedeon* served to promote the new Reformed morality and to uphold the authority of the state against dissenters, both Catholic and Anabaptist. In a city that had banished images from its churches, plays also functioned as a substitute for the visual image; E. highlights the use by Manuel and Rüte of deictic devices such as 'pointing' figures and heralds, who interpret events on stage for the audience much as the text in a Protestant broadsheet interprets the accompanying image for the reader. Despite the Zwinglian ban on congregational singing, Rüte also included choral interludes in his plays, which helped sustain Berne's tradition of devotional music and may even have paved the way for its reintroduction to formal worship in the 1570s. E. concludes that the 'multimediality' of theatre in Berne was crucial to the success of efforts to construct a new religious identity for the city: 'In uniting the media of reform, Bern's Protestant theatre became the mediator of reform.'

Trivmphvs Divi Michaelis Archangelis Bavarii/Triumph des Heiligen Michael, Patron Bayerns (München 1597), ed. Barbara Bauer and Jürgen Leonhardt (Jesuitica, 2), Regensburg, Schnell & Steiner, 2000, 440 pp., presents a critical edition of the *Trivmphvs*. The editors' introduction provides details of the historical background to the play (performed in July 1597 to celebrate the consecration of the Jesuit church of St Michael in Munich), discusses its music, language, versification, staging, and characters, and explores the significance of its apocalyptic subject matter. B. and L. interpret the *Trivmphvs* as a response to the Protestant vision of church history and the end times set out in the Magdeburg Centuries. The Latin text of the work is accompanied by a German prose translation and detailed commentary. E. Borza, *NJb*, 3:29–45, reviews 16th-c. Latin editions of Sophocles, including the translations of Veit Winsheim (1549), Joachim Camerarius (1556), and Thomas Naogeorg (1558).

PROSE AND VERSE. Erica Bastress-Dukehart, *The Zimmern Chronicle: Nobility, Memory, and Self-Representation in Sixteenth-Century Germany*, Aldershot, Ashgate, viii + 223 pp., identifies Wilhelm Werner von Zimmern and his nephew Froben Christoph as the co-authors of the Zimmern Chronicle, and examines the chronicle's interpretation of Zimmern family history with reference to other sources. B.-D. sees the chronicle as a work of conscious artistry, inspired by humanist historiography and incorporating fictional elements such as ribald stories for the amusement, as well as the edification, of the reader. The primary purpose of the chronicle, however, is didactic: by recording their ancestors' mistakes, which had brought the family close to extinction, the Zimmerns hoped to caution future generations against repeating them. According to B.-D., the work articulates the values not just of the Zimmerns, but of the Swabian nobility as whole during this period, as well as illustrating the reasons for its decline. Ki-Hyang Lee, *Armut als neue Qualität der Helden im Fortunatus und im Goldfaden* (WBDP, 23), 144 pp., relates changes in the portrayal of poverty in the early modern novel to the decline of feudal values. Whereas in medieval literature status is determined by birth, in *Fortunatus* the only criterion for social advancement is the acquisition of wealth and property. In *Der Goldfaden* class distinctions are similarly fluid, although here Lewfrid's rise from humble origins is attributed not to money but to his possession of Christian virtues such as courage, loyalty, and nobility of character. P. Fuss, *WW*, 52:333–60, contrasts Paracelsus's *Signaturenlehre* with the more 'modern' semiology of Johann Fischart. Whereas Paracelsus continues to posit an intrinsic connection between signs or words and the things that they represent, Fischart views language as a closed system. T. Althaus, 'Kurzweil. Überlegungen zum Verhältnis von Darstellungsintention und geringem Textumfang in der Kleinen Prosa des 16. Jahrhunderts', Simmler, *Textsorten*, 23–38. A. Classen, *ib.*, 65–88, finds in the early modern *Volksbuch* an openness to influence from other sources, both literary and non-literary. J. Jungmayr, 'Der geistliche Rosengarten (*Legenda Maior* des Raimund von Capua, deutsch) im Deutschland des 15. und 16. Jahrhunderts', *ib.*, 89–104. A. Schwarz, 'Eulenspiegeleien zwischen Prosaroman und Schwankroman', *ib.*, 171–79. U. Möllmann, *ib.*, 257–73, compares a 15th-c. published translation of the Benedictine rule with a Würzburg manuscript copy dated 1517. B. Stolt, *ib.*, 631–42, situates the 16th-c. consolatory letter in a late medieval pastoral tradition that combines *consolatio* with *admonitio*. J. Meier, 'Briefwechseltypologien der Frühen Neuzeit. Die Kommunikationsform "Brief" im 16. Jahrhundert', *ib.*, 369–84.

A. Classen, *Daphnis*, 30, 2001:665–89, discusses major contributors, both Protestant and Catholic, to the development of the German *Kirchengesangbuch* during the 16th c., with particular reference to the involvement of women (Elisabeth Cruciger, Mary of Hungary, Elisabeth of Braunschweig-Calenberg). J. Robert, *GRM*, 52:437–61, considers the use of Ovid's *Tristia* and *Epistulae ex Ponto* as models for the treatment of exile in 16th-c. neo-Latin verse.

4. Other Work

Arndt Weber, *Affektive Liebe als 'rechte eheliche Liebe' in der ehedidaktischen Literatur der Frühen Neuzeit: Eine Studie unter besonderer Berücksichtigung der Exempla zum 'locus Amor Coniugalis'*, Frankfurt, Lang, 2001, 230 pp., aims to demonstrate that the 'moraldidaktische Literatur' of the 16th and 17th cs was not uniformly critical of passionate love. According to W., early modern writers on marriage distinguish between two types of love: orderly love, informed by reason and confined to marriage, and disorderly love, based solely on passion. However, in practice they do not always observe this distinction. Some authors, such as Cyriakus Spangenberg and Johann Mathesius, regard emotional and physical attachment as preconditions for a successful marriage, while nearly all of them accept that young people should be permitted to choose their own partners. W. concludes that, well before 1600, the traditional opposition between romantic love and 'Vernunftliebe' had begun to break down, as writers sought to harmonize the two within the framework of Christian marriage. Christiane Schwarz, *Studien zur Stammbuchpraxis der Frühen Neuzeit: Gestaltung und Nutzung des Album amicorum am Beispiel eines Hofbeamten und Dichters, eines Politikers und eines Goldschmieds (etwa 1550 bis 1650)* (Mikrokosmos, 66), Frankfurt, Lang, 379 pp., compares the *Stammbücher* of Daniel Hermann, Nicolaus von Vicken, and Hanns Strich (chosen because of their authors' shared regional origins and links to the Habsburg court). On the basis of this analysis, S. identifies features of the early modern *Stammbuch* that distinguish it from related genres, such as the journal and the autobiography. She also discusses the influence of the printed book on the format and content of *Stammbücher*. Of particular importance for S. is the degree to which *Stammbuch* owners exercise control over their albums' development, through the selection of contributors and the insertion of illustrations, documents, and prefatory material.

J. Geiss, *Zentren der Petrarca-Rezeption in Deutschland (um 1470–1525). Rezeptionsgeschichtliche Studien und Katalog der lateinischen Drucküberlieferung*, Wiesbaden, Reichert, xi + 281 pp., dates the first significant reception of Petrarch north of the Alps to the middle decades of the 15th c. (just as his popularity in Italy was waning), and links it to the spread of humanist thought more generally. Through an analysis of surviving copies, G. is able to reconstruct both the 'Druckgeschichte' and the 'Gebrauchsgeschichte' of Petrarch's works in the Empire. Five major centres for their production are identified: Strasbourg, Ulm, the north-west (Cologne, Deventer), Leipzig, and Basle. G. notes the significance of the 1496 Basle edition (whose genesis is particularly well documented) for the subsequent reception of Petrarch's works: not only was it widely distributed, but it served as the basis for two Venetian editions (1501 and 1503) destined mainly for the German market. During the 1510s and 1520s, however, interest in Petrarch declined, partly because of humanist objections to his Latin style and partly in response to changes in the German book market caused by the Reformation. The catalogue section of the volume lists Latin, German, and Dutch-language editions of

Petrarch's works by title, with bibliographical information and descriptions of copies inspected.

Mechthild Habermann, *Deutsche Fachtexte der Frühen Neuzeit. Naturkundlich-medizinische Wissensvermittlung im Spannungsfeld von Latein und Volkssprache* (SLG, 61), 2001, xvii + 583 pp., compares the structure, language, and style of early modern botanical and medical texts in German with those of equivalent Latin works. H. argues that, because vernacular texts were targeted at the 'gemeiner man' rather than the educated élite, they tend to be more 'pragmatic' in orientation. This explains some of the more striking differences between German and Latin editions of the same work (for example, in the content and layout of title pages). Stylistically, however, vernacular writers continued to draw inspiration from Latin models. H. suggests that this influence was largely positive, as it expanded the repertoire of German and caused the rhetorical requirements of the Latin *genus subtile* to be applied to the vernacular, thus helping to overcome the perception of German as an 'inferior' language. H.'s research is summarized in Simmler, *Textsorten*, 551–71.

Romualda Poljakov, *'Mit aufrichtiger Feder meist gegenwärtig aufgezeichnet': Rußlandberichte deutscher Reisender vom 16. bis zum 19. Jahrhundert* (Deutsch-Russische Literaturbeziehungen, Forschungen und Materialien, 10), Frankfurt, Lang, 1999, 218 pp., has chapters on Sigmund von Herberstein's *Rerum Moscoviticarum Commentarii* (1549), and its 16th-c. and 17th-c. reception. Sabine Rahmsdorf, *Stadt und Architektur in der literarischen Utopie der frühen Neuzeit* (BNL, 168), 1999, 345 pp., includes a consideration of Kaspar Stiblin's *Commentariolus de Eudaemonensium Republica* (1555). R. sees Eudaemon as embodying the twin ideals of Renaissance town planning and aristocratic government. D. N. Hasse, 'Die humanistische Polemik gegen arabische Autoritäten. Grundsätzliches zum Forschungsstand', *NJb*, 3, 2001:65–79, focuses on Leonhart Fuchs's *Errata recentiorum medicorum* (1530). H. argues that the work formed part of a campaign by Fuchs to establish his humanist credentials. K. Crowther-Heyek, *RQ*, 55:904–35, highlights the religious significance attached to procreation and childbirth in medical and devotional texts of the period.

N. Hayes, 'Negativizing nurture and demonizing domesticity: the witch construct in Early Modern Germany', pp. 179–200 of *Maternal Measures: Figuring Caregiving in the Early Modern Period*, ed. Naomi J. Miller and Naomi Yavneh, Aldershot, Ashgate, 2000, xvi + 374 pp., discusses the characterization of witches as 'anti-mothers' in late-15th-c. and early-16th-c. texts. M. Schwegler, *ZDP*, 121:72–88, examines the techniques used by authors of early modern *Wunderzeichenberichte* to authenticate the events that they describe. A. F. Creasman, *SCJ*, 33:963–80, investigates the connections between anti-Jewish violence and Marian devotion in the early 16th c., as evidenced by polemical works on the pilgrimage to the shrine of the Schöne Maria in Regensburg. U. Friedrich, 'Grenzen des Ordo im enzyklopädischen Schrifttum des 16. Jahrhunderts', Meier, *Enzyklopädie*, 391–408, compares approaches to classification in Theodor Zwinger's *Theatrum vitae humanae*, and Conrad Gessner's *Bibliotheca universalis* and *Historia animalium*. F. argues that 16th-c. encylopaedists had difficulty reconciling the humanist ideal of universal learning with the increasing specialization of knowledge. U. Ernst, *ib.*, 451–94, includes a discussion of theories on the origin of writing in Gregor Reisch's *Margarita philosophica* (1517) and Heinrich Cornelius Agrippa von Nettesheim's *De incertitudine et vanitate scientiarum atque artium* (1530). K. Heck, 'Genealogie als dynastische Sphärenbildung. Herzog Ulrich zu Mecklenburg in Güstrow', pp. 137–44 of *Genealogie als Denkform in Mittelalter und Früher Neuzeit*, ed. Kilian Heck and Bernhard Jahn (STSL, 80), 2000, 265 pp. J. Leonhardt, 'Eine Leipziger Vorlesung über Ciceros *De legibus* aus dem Jahre 1514', *WRM*, 26:26–40. T. Brooks, '"Alletagsworte" und "Fey'rtagswandl". Anmerkungen zu Stil und Syntax in der Predigt der Frühen Neuzeit', Simmler, *Textsorten*, 217–28. P. Roessler, 'Machtrituale-Textrituale. Zu habsburgischen Krönungsbeschreibungen im 16. und 17. Jahrhundert', *ib.*, 421–36. H. Günther, 'Das Projekt Kaiser Maximilians für sein Grabmal', *SFDES* 12, 77–111.

5. Individual Authors

BODENSTEIN VON KARLSTADT, ANDREAS. **Querdenker der Reformation — Andreas Bodenstein von Karlstadt und seine frühe Wirkung*, ed. Ulrich Bubenheimer and Stefan Oehming, Würzburg, Religion & Kultur Vlg, 2001, 297 pp.

BUCER, MARTIN. Martin Bucer, *Briefwechsel — Correspondance*. Vol. IV *(Januar-September 1530)* (Studies in Medieval and Reformation Thought, 78), Leiden, Brill, 2000, lxvi + 324 pp. *Martini Buceri Opera Latina* continues with vol. 5, *Defensio Adversus Axioma Catholicum id est Criminationem R.P. Roberti Episcopi Abrincensis (1534)*, ed. William Ian P. Hazlett, Leiden, Brill, 2000, xlvii + 224 pp. *Martin Bucer (1491–1551): Auf der Suche nach Wiederherstellung der Einheit. Begleitbuch zur Ausstellung im Universitätsmuseum Heidelberg 9. November 2001–24. Januar 2002*, ed. Albert De Lange and Thomas Wilhelmi (Archiv und Museum der Universität Heidelberg, Schriften, 5), Ubstadt-Weiher, Vlg Regionalkultur, 2001, 79 pp., provides an overview of B.'s career and contains information on the critical editions of his works and correspondence.

BUGENHAGEN, JOHANNES. Hans-Günter Leder, *Johannes Bugenhagen Pomeranus — Vom Reformer zum Reformator: Studien zur Biographie*, ed. Volker Gummelt (Greifswalder theologische Forschungen, 4), Frankfurt, Lang, 438 pp., brings together 12 essays by the author, four of them new. L. is particularly strong on B.'s education and early career (for example, he is able to substantiate the tradition that links B.'s conversion to Protestantism with his reading of Luther's *De captivitate Babylonica* in October 1520). Other essays highlight B.'s role as organizer of new Lutheran territorial churches in north Germany (Braunschweig, Hamburg, Pomerania) and Denmark. The main deficiency of the volume is a lack of studies covering the troubled later phase of B.'s life, especially his involvement in conflicts arising from the Interim.

BULLINGER, HEINRICH. The publication of B.'s correspondence continues with vol. 9, *Briefe des Jahres 1539*, ed. Hans Ulrich Bächtold and Rainer Henrich, Zurich, Theologischer Vlg, 295 pp. B. Gordon, '"Welcher nit gloubt der ist schon verdampt": Heinrich Bullinger and the spirituality of the Last Judgement', *Zwingliana*, 29:29–53, discusses B.'s *Das Jüngste Gericht* (1555). A. Mühling, 'Welchen Tod sterben wir? Heinrich Bullingers "Bericht der Kranken" (1535)', *ib.*, 29:55–68, contrasts B.'s Christocentric theology of death with the medieval *Ars Moriendi* tradition. R. Jörg, 'Heinrich Bullinger kontra Johannes Salat. Ein Historikerstreit im 16. Jahrhundert', pp. 9–28 of *Von Cyprian zur Walzenprägung. Streiflichter auf Zürcher Geist und Kultur der Bullingerzeit*, ed. Hans Ulrich Bächtold (Studien und Texte zur Bullingerzeit, 2), Zug, Achius, 2001, 247 pp. W. P. Stephens, 'Bullinger's sermons on the Apocalypse', pp. 261–80 of *Die Zürcher Reformation: Ausstrahlung und Rückwirkungen*, ed. Alfred Schindler and Hans Stickelberger (Zürcher Beiträge zur Reformationsgeschichte, 18), Berne, Lang, 2001, 552 pp.

CAMERARIUS, JOACHIM. Stephan Kunkler, **Zwischen Humanismus und Reformation. Der Humanist Joachim Camerarius (1500–1574) im Wechselspiel von pädagogischem Pathos und theologischem Ethos* (Theologische Texte und Studien, 8), Hildesheim, Olms, 2001, 259 pp.

CELTIS, CONRAD. J. Blänsdorf, *Gutenberg-Jb.*, 77:57–62, notes references to Mainz, the invention of printing, and the need for women's education in C.'s *Amores*. J. Robert, *BGDSL*, 124:92–121, discusses C.'s self-stylization as the harbinger of a new Augustan age under Emperor Maximilian I.

CINCINNIUS, JOHANNES. Andreas Freitäger, *Johannes Cincinnius von Lipstadt (ca.1485–1555). Bibliothek und Geisteswelt eines westfälischen Humanisten* (Westfälische Biographien, 10), Münster, Aschendorff, 2000, 438 pp., seeks to define the characteristics of 'Lower Rhine humanism' through an examination of C.'s career and writings.

F. notes the influence of Erasmus on C.'s intellectual development, but also his continued devotion to medieval authors such as the 12th-c. Benedictine Rupert of Deutz. C.'s reception of the new learning is seen to involve not a break with Catholic tradition (as it did for many humanists on the Upper Rhine) but 'eine Erweiterung der scholastischen Gelehrsamkeit'. The volume includes a catalogue of C.'s library, listing more than 150 titles, and documents relevant to his biography.

DÜRER, ALBRECHT. Heike Sahm, *Dürers kleinere Texte: Konventionen als Spielraum für Individualität* (Hermaea, n.F., 97), Tübingen, Niemeyer, viii + 215 pp., examines D.'s shorter works (the *Familienchronik*, the *Bruchstück aus Dürers Gedenkbuch*, the *Tagebuch der Reise in die Niederlande*, rhyming couplets, letters, and dedications) in the light of early modern stylistic and genre conventions. S. proposes that these texts are valuable less for the insights that they afford into D.'s personality and artistic subjectivity (the traditional view) than for what they tell us about the literary culture of Nuremberg during this period. Although the variety of D.'s output sets him apart from his contemporaries, in the main he works within established and readily identifiable literary traditions. Rather than using his writings to project his identity as an artist, D. tends to present himself differently in different texts, depending on their function. According to S., the apparent contradictions to which this approach gives rise reflect D.'s background as an 'Aufsteiger' and autodidact, and the corresponding insecurity of his position within the upper echelons of Nuremberg society.

EULENSPIEGELBUCH. T. Weber, Simmler, *Textsorten*, 203–16, compares the first German and French editions of *Till Eulenspiegel.*

FLACIUS ILLYRICUS, MATTHIAS. Oliver K. Olson, *Matthias Flacius and the Survival of Luther's Reform* (Wolfenbütteler Abhandlungen zur Renaissance-Forschung, 20), Wiesbaden, Harrassowitz, 428 pp., is the first volume of a planned two-part biography of the Croatian reformer, covering the period up to the colloquy of Worms in August-September 1557. O. emphasizes the breadth of F.'s intellectual achievement: not only was he the 'Father' of church history and hermeneutics, but he made important contributions as a collector and editor of manuscripts and as a rhetorician, polemicist, and theologian. As one would expect, the main focus of the book is on F.'s role in co-ordinating Protestant opposition to the Augsburg and Leipzig Interims, first in Wittenberg and then in Magdeburg. According to O., the fundamental issue in dispute between F. and the 'adiaphorists' was the nature of the relationship between ecclesiastical and secular authority, with F. insisting that it was ministers' duty to resist magisterial interference in the affairs of the church. Although

O. is sometimes less than even-handed when discussing his subject's opponents, this richly illustrated volume provides a sound basis for future work on F.

FREDER, JOHANNES. Martin Bausen, *Lob und Unschuld der Ehefrauen: Analytische Betrachtungen zu Leben und Werk des Johannes Freder. Ein Beitrag zur Querelle des femmes des 16. Jahrhundert*, Frankfurt, Lang, 383 pp., examines F.'s dialogue *Lob und Unschuld der Ehefrauen* (1543) in the context of early modern views on the position of women. B. regards F.'s mode of argument, which is based largely on the use of *exempla*, as typical of contributors to the *Querelle des femmes*. Like Luther, F. is principally concerned to defend the utility of marriage against the misogynistic ideas of writers such as Sebastian Franck, whose *Sprichwörter* are specifically refuted in the dialogue. However, his praise of women's positive qualities (which includes support for female education) is set within a traditional Christian understanding of gender roles that emphasizes the natural inferiority of women to men. A modernized edition of F.'s dialogue, based on Andreas Hondorff's expanded version of 1569 rather than the original Low German text, is appended, with notes on the authorities and *exempla* cited.

GWALTHER, RUDOLF. K. J. Rüetschi, 'Bildgedichte Rudolf Gwalthers: Eine Quelle für Nachweis und Datierung von Zürcher Kunstwerken', pp. 145–229 of Bächtold, *Von Cyprian zur Walzenprägung* (see p. 000 above).

HEUSSLER, LEONHARD. Irmgard Bezzel, *Leonhard Heußler (1548–1597): Ein vielseitiger Nürnberger Drucker und geschickter Verbreiter von Neuigkeitsberichten* (Buchwissenschaftliche Beiträge aus dem Deutschen Bucharchiv München, 62), Wiesbaden, Harrassowitz, 1999, 199 pp., provides details of H.'s career and published works.

HUTTEN, ULRICH VON. W. Ludwig, *NJb*, 3, 2001 : 103–16, sees H.'s invectives against Ulrich of Württemberg as modelled on Cicero's orations 'In Catilinam'.

LUTHER, MARTIN. V. Leppin, *AR*, 93 : 7–25, argues that the understanding of penitence reflected in L.'s first two theses against indulgences owes much to the influence of Tauler. T. Bell, *Luther*, 72, 2001 : 124–36, discusses L.'s commentary on the Magnificat. V. Mertens, Simmler, *Textsorten*, 243–56, compares one Latin and three German versions of L.'s sermon *Von dem ehelichen Stand* for evidence of a shift 'vom Autor- zum Inhaltszentrischen'.

MANUEL, NIKLAUS. **Niklaus Manuel. Werke und Briefe*, ed. Paul Zinsli and Thomas Hengartner, Berne, Stämpfli, 1999, 784 pp.

MELANCHTHON, PHILIPP. Nicole Kuropka, *Philipp Melanchthon: Wissenschaft und Gesellschaft. Ein Gelehrter im Dienst der Kirche (1526–1532)* (Spätmittelalter und Reformation, n.s., 21), Tübingen, Mohr Siebeck, xii + 324 pp. This revised doctoral dissertation places M.'s work as a teacher at the universities of Wittenberg and Jena in the context of his political activities during the first decade of the Reformation. The principal texts examined are M.'s manuals on rhetoric and dialectics, and his commentaries on Colossians, Romans, Proverbs, and Aristotle's *Ethics* and *Politics*. K. argues that, for M., the reform of education is a precondition for the reform of church and society. Conversely, it is the duty of academics, through their writings, to seek solutions to concrete political problems. According to K., the limitations of this approach became apparent at the Diet of Augsburg, with the failure of M.'s attempts to restore church unity through dialogue. The confused publishing history of M.'s works for the period 1526–32 is clarified in an appendix. *Melanchthon und Europa. 2. Westeuropa*, ed. Günter Franck and Kees Meerhoff, Stuttgart, Thorbecke, 364 pp., publishes proceedings of a 1999 conference at the Melanchthonhaus Bretten. The 17 essays contained in the volume assess the impact of M.'s works in Italy, Spain, France, the Netherlands, England, and the United States, with an emphasis on the reception of his commentaries and handbooks of rhetoric and dialectic. L. D. Green, 'Melanchthon, rhetoric and the soul', *ib.*, 11–27. P. Mack, *ib.*, 29–52, divides M.'s commentaries on Latin literature into five classes: grammatical/rhetorical commentaries, logical commentaries, paraphrases, gloss commentaries, and arguments. R. Pozzo, *ib.*, 53–65, discusses the reception of M.'s logic by the Paduan Aristotelians Francesco Piccolomini, Francesco Patrizi, and Jacopo Zabarella, and attempts by later Protestant scholars to produce a synthesis of humanist (M.) and traditional (Zabarella) approaches. P. Walter, *ib.*, 67–84, and O. Millet, *ib.*, 85–96, compare M.'s *Loci communes* with the theological systems of Melchor Cano and John Calvin. I. Pantin, 'La reception française des "Initia doctrinae physicae"', *ib.*, 97–116. J.-C. Moisan and M.-C. Malenfant, *ib.*, 117–37, compares commentaries on Ovid's *Metamorphoses* by M.'s son-in-law Georg Sabinus and by Barthélemy Aneau. M.-L. Demonet, *ib.*, 139–62, examines the reception of three aspects of M.'s logic in works by the French Calvinists Claude Aubery and Philippe Canaye: the treatment of method, the distinction between the necessary and the probable, and the notion of scripture as a dialectical text. K. Meerhoff, *ib.*, 163–92, includes a consideration of Melanchthonian elements in the thought of Pierre Ramus. I. Maclean, *ib.*, 211–32, discusses conflicts arising from the posthumous publication of M.'s works. S. Kusukawa, *ib.*, 233–54, provides evidence for more intensive reception of M. in Cambridge than in Oxford during the period 1535–76. A. Moss, *ib.*, 255–68, assesses M.'s contribution to the process of conceptual change in Renaissance Europe, with specific reference to techniques of argument and the use of allegory. G. Weng, *ib.*, 269–86, discusses M.'s role in the appointment of the English exile John Rogers to the post of superintendent in Dithmarschen. H. J. Selderhuis, *ib.*, 303–24, gives examples of M.'s influence in the 16th-c. and 17th-c. Netherlands. M. Plathow, *Luther*, 73:140–53, contrasts M.'s eirenical attitude towards the Jews with his intolerance of Islam. K. J. Rüetschi, 'Fünf "Conciones" Melanchthons. Rudolf Gwalther's Nachschrift am Regensburger Reichstag 1541', pp. 53–107 of Hans Ulrich Bächtold, Rainer Henrich, and Kurt Jacob Rüetschi, *Vom Beten, vom Verketzern, vom Predigen: Beiträge zum Zeitalter Heinrich Bullingers und Rudolf Gwalthers* (Studien und Texte zur Bullingerzeit, 1), Zug, Achius, 1999, 120 pp.

MUSCULUS, WOLFGANG. Reinhard Bodenmann, *Wolfgang Musculus (1497–1563): Destin d'un autodidacte lorrain au siècle des Réformes* (THR, 343), 2000, 724 pp., includes a critical edition of Abraham Musculus's biography of M., as well as studies of the reformer's family, correspondence, writings, and thought. Although the work contains much valuable material, it is poorly organized and lacks focus.

PIRCKHEIMER, WILLIBALD. **Willibald Pirckheimers Briefwechsel*, vol. 5, ed. Helga Scheible, Munich, Beck, 2001, 530 pp. Ulrich Winter, *Willibald Pirckheimer: 'Apologia seu Podagrae Laus.' Ein Kommentar* (Beihefte zum Euphorion, 43), Heidelberg, Winter, 118 pp., is the companion volume to W.'s critical edition of the *Apologia*, which is reproduced here. The commentary provides details of Classical allusions in the text, and highlights stylistic and grammatical peculiarities of P.'s Latin.

PLATTER, THOMAS. *Platteriana. Beiträge zum 500. Geburtstag des Thomas Platter (1499?–1582)* (Basler Beiträge zur Geschichtswissenschaft, 175), Basle, Schwabe, 182 pp., reassesses P.'s contribution to the cultural and intellectual life of 16th-c. Basle. W. Meyer, *ib.*, 17–57, approaches P.'s autobiography as a source of information about economic and social conditions in early modern Switzerland. K. von Greyerz and F. Brändle, 'Basler Selbstzeugnisse des 16./17. Jahrhunderts und die neue historische Forschung', *ib.*, 59–75. B. R. Jenny, *ib.*, 77–121, gives an account of the development of Basle's Latin schools during the 16th c. J. concludes that the printing industry, rather than political patronage or formal educational institutions, was mainly responsible for the city's emergence as a centre of humanist learning. M. Vogel, *ib.*, 123–55, considers the relationship between illustration and text in publications by P.'s contemporary Sebastian Münster. D. Sasse, *ib.*, 157–69, discusses P.'s achievements as a schoolmaster and his interest in medicine. R. Günthart, *MJ*, 37:83–101, examines the curriculum devised by P. for the Basle Latin school 'auf Burg'. P.'s choice of works by contemporary grammarians as textbooks for his pupils is seen to constitute an important break with medieval pedagogical tradition.

REUCHLIN, JOHANNES. H.-G. Roloff, Simmler, *Textsorten*, 149–58, discusses the structure of R.'s German prose.

RINCK, MELCHIOR. W. Breul-Kunkel, *AR*, 93:26–42, provides details of R.'s studies in Leipzig and early engagement with humanism.

RÜTE, HANS VON. G. Ehrstine, 'Motherhood and Protestant polemics: stillbirth in Hans von Rüte's *Abgötterei* (1531)', pp. 121–34 of Miller and Yavneh, *Maternal Measures* (see p. 629 above), links R.'s portrayal of the characters Dichtli Schnabelräss and Cordili Syman to attempts to combat Marian devotion among Bernese women.

SACHS, HANS. Julia-Maria Heinzmann, *Die Buhllieder des Hans Sachs: Form, Gehalt, Funktion und sozialhistorischer Ort* (Gratia, 38), Wiesbaden, Harrassowitz, 2001, 229 pp., edits and analyses S.'s 19 surviving courtship songs. H. interprets the *Buhllieder* as occasional poems, in which the didactic element is consequently much less pronounced than in S.'s other works (from archival sources, she is able to identify some of the individuals to whom the songs are addressed). Although S. is influenced by the *Minnesang* tradition, his poems reflect 16th-c. bourgeois expectations of women rather than courtly ideals, and the Protestant notion of love as a basis for partnership in daily life.

SPANGENBERG, CYRIAKUS. B. Jahn, 'Genealogie und Kritik. Theologie und Philologie als Korrektive genealogischen Denkens in Cyriakus Spangenbergs historiographischen Werken', pp. 69–85 of Heck and Jahn, *Genealogie als Denkform* (see p. 630 above).

TRITHEMIUS, JOHANNES. T. Ernst, *Daphnis*, 30, 2001:513–95, discusses a counterfeit manuscript of T.'s *Steganographia.* G. P. Marchal, 'Bundschuh und schweizerische Eidgenossenschaft: des Johannes Trithemius Bericht über den Untergrombacher Bundschuh und seine wundersamen Folgen', *Schweizerische Zeitschrift für Geschichte*, 52:341–51, associates T.'s *Annales Hirsaugienses* with a south German humanist tradition of anti-Swiss polemic.

VADIAN, JOACHIM. K. Fetrenheuer, '*Disertus* oder *durus*? Zur Argumentationsstruktur in Joachim Vadians Urteil über Persius', *NJb*, 3, 2001:47–63.

ZWINGLI, HULDRYCH. O. Tache, 'Koordination und Subordination in Huldrich Zwinglis "Glaubensbekenntnis"', Simmler, *Textsorten*, 181–201.

THE SEVENTEENTH CENTURY

By Anna Carrdus, *University of Bristol*

(This survey covers work published in 2001 and 2002)

I. General

Laufhütte, *Künste*, contains papers delivered at the ninth 'Kongress des Wolfenbütteler Arbeitskreises für Barockforschung' at the Herzog August Bibliothek in 1997. It is introduced by a number of plenary papers, five of which are closely related to the literary arts: W. Barner, 'Spielräume. Was Poetik und Rhetorik nicht lehren' (33–67); B. Bauer, 'Naturverständnis und Subjektkonstitution aus der Perspektive der frühneuzeitlichen Rhetorik' (69–132); W. Schmidt-Biggemann, 'Welche Natur wird nachgeahmt? Beobachtungen zur Erscheinung der Natur in der barocken Literatur' (133–56); A. K. Varga, 'Alte und neue Formen der Multimedialität' (241–62); B. M. Stafford, 'Analogy in an age of difference' (263–74). Many essays dealing with specific aspects of the relationship between art and nature, particularly in the field of drama, appear in the sections below. Further more general essays in the collection are: A. M. Cordie, 'Mimesis bei Aristoteles und in der Frühen Neuzeit' (277–88); D. Niefanger, 'Galanterie. Gründzüge eines ästhetischen Konzepts um 1700' (459–72); G. S. Johnston, 'Lamentation to consolation: aspects of music and rhetoric in funerary compositions of the German Baroque' (913–35); A. Keller, 'Spaziergang und Lektüre: Analogien zwischen fiktionaler Bewegung und faktischem Rezeptionsverhalten als hermeneutische Hilfestellung für Textkonzeptionen des 17. Jahrhunderts' (951–76); L. Auteri, 'Die Kunst der Verstellung bei Virgilio Malvezzi, Johann Moscherosch und Johann Sebastian Mitternacht' (969–83); P. Hess, ' "Nachäffin der Natur" oder "aller Völker Sprachen"? Zur Rolle visueller Bildlichkeit in Poetik und Rhetorik der Barockzeit' (1047–62).

Court culture is the topic of two important monographs, one focusing on Darmstadt, one on Dresden. Both draw widely on material held in the respective court archives and both contain substantial sections on the 17th c. which place it in the context of longer-term cultural developments. Helga Meise, *Das archivierte Ich. Schreibkalender und höfische Repräsentation in Hessen-Darmstadt 1624–1790* (Arbeiten der Hessischen Historischen Kommission, n.F., 21), Darmstadt, Hessische Historische Kommission, 644 pp., concentrates on the uses made of 'Schreibkalender' by a series of princes and their consorts, relating this personal form of record-keeping in fascinating detail both to courtly ceremonial and other modes of writing practised by the same individuals. Watanabe-O'Kelly, *Court Culture*, traces the evolution of court culture from the beginning of Elector August's reign (1553) to the end of August the Strong's (1733), showing how religious, political, economic and scientific influences from within the Empire and outside it were reflected in the cultural organization of the court, not only in its festivals and building programmes, but also — for example — in its archives, libraries, and other great collections. A number of articles also deal with aspects of court culture: M. R. Wade, 'Georg Engelhard Loehneyss' *Della Cavalleria* als höfische Kunstlehre', Laufhütte, *Künste*, 577–85, discusses a treatise on training horses, first published in 1588, which in the later editions of 1609/10 and 1624 came to represent a compendium of information on Protestant court festivals around 1600; H. Meise, 'Schreibkalender und Autobiographik in der Frühen Neuzeit', *ib.*, 707–17, outlines the changing functions of 'Schreibkalender' in the lives of three generations of princely couples at the Darmstadt court; J. Bepler, ' "Im dritten Gradu ungleicher Linie Seitwarts verwandt." Frauen und dynastisches Bewußtsein in den Funeralwerken der Frühen Neuzeit', *Zeitschrift für Historische Forschung*, Beiheft 28:135–60, is complemented by a further article on princesses' roles in a court context: J. Bepler, 'Die Fürstin als Betsäule — Anleitung und Praxis der Erbauung am Hof', *Morgenglantz*, 12:249–64.

Didacticism is the theme of two articles on 17th-c. media: W. W. Schnabel, ' "Kurtz=Sinn=reiche Sprüche." Barocke Mustersammlungen für Albuminskriptionen', *Morgenglantz*, 12:101–33; and I. Timmermann, 'Didaktische Implikationen der deutschen Zeitungsdebatte von Mitte des 17. bis Mitte des 18. Jahrhunderts: Comenius, Weise, Fritsch, Stieler, Ludewig und Schumann', *ib.*, 135–166.

Ingen, *Gebetsliteratur*, is a collection of papers delivered at a colloquium held at the Herzog August Bibliothek, Wolfenbüttel, in 1998. Of general interest are: J. Wallmann, 'Zwischen Herzenssgebet und Gebetbuch: zur protestantischen deutschen Gebetsliteratur im 17. Jahrhundert' (13–46); J. Bepler, 'The use of prayer books at court: the example of Wolfenbüttel' (47–62); G. van Gemert, 'Zur katholischen Gebetsliteratur der Barockzeit. Stellenwert und Funktion der Verseinlagen in Nakatenus' *Himmlisch Palm-Gärtlein*' (77–92); C. Niekus Moore, 'Lutheran prayer books for children as usage literature in the sixteenth and seventeenth centuries' (113–29); P. Veit, 'Die Hausandacht im deutschen Luthertum: Anweisungen und Praktiken' (193–206); A. de Reuver, 'Stellung und Funktion des Gebets in Calvins Theologie. Eine Skizze' (259–90).

Literary responses to war with the Turks are examined in M. Disselkamp, 'Discordia, Concordia. Zerfallsbewußtsein und Einheitsappelle in Türkenkriegsprojekten des ausgehenden 16. und 17. Jahrhunderts', *Daphnis*, 31:187–213.

The exceptionally handsome volume *Rosenkreuz* contains a collection of papers delivered at a symposium held in 1994 under the auspices of the Herzog August Bibliothek, Wolfenbüttel, and the University Library, Amsterdam: C. Gilly, 'Die Rosenkreuzer als europäisches Phänomen im 17. Jahrhundert und die verschlungenen Pfade der Forschung' (19–58); J. R. Ritman, 'Die Geburt der Rosenkreuzerbruderschaft in Tübingen' (59–76); R. Edighoffer, 'Die Manifeste der Rosenkreuzer' (161–75); C. Gilly, 'Der "Löwe von Mitternacht", der "Adler" und der "Endchrist": die politische, religiöse und chiliastische Publizistik in den Flugschriften, illustrierten Flugblättern und Volksliedern des Dreissigjährigen Krieges' (249–70).

Two publications make significant contributions to the study of 17th-c. women's writing: Charlotte Woodford, *Nuns as Historians in Early Modern Germany*, Oxford, Clarendon, 229 pp.; and J. L. Flood, 'Neglected heroines? Women poets laureate in the Holy Roman Empire', *BJR*, 84.3:25–47.

2. Poetry

Individual Authors

FLEMING. Two articles analyse Stoic influences on poems by F.: J. Schmidt, '"Du selbst bist dir die Welt." Die Reise nach Utopia als Fahrt zum stoisch verfaßten Ich. Paul Fleming's Gedicht "In grooß Neugart der Reussen"', *Daphnis*, 31:215–33; and B. Meymeyr, 'Das autonome Subjekt in der Auseinandersetzung mit Fatum und Fortuna. Zum stoischen Ethos in Paul Flemings Sonett "An sich"', *ib.*, 234–54.

GREIFFENBERG. C. M. Pumplun, '"Die freyheit des geistes/ gehet in die Unendlichkeit." Catharina Regina von Greiffenbergs Kompositmetaphern und die ars combinatoria', Laufhütte, *Künste*, 1063–71.

OPITZ. S. S. Tschopp, 'Imitatio und renovatio. Martin Opitz' *Schäfferey von der Nimfen Hercinie* als Modell der Aneignung literarischer Tradition', Laufhütte, *Künste*, 673–85. G. Dunphy, 'Martin Opitz und die mittelalterlichen Alexandergeschichten. Wissenschaft und Polemik in der editio princeps des *Annoliedes*', *Daphnis*, 31:299–316.

SCHERFFER. *Daphnis*, 30, 2001, contains a collection of essays on Scherffer (1598/9–1674), a Silesian court musician and poet: T. Althaus, 'Scherffers Versbau' (391–415); E. Pietrzak, 'Ein schlesisches carmen heroicum. Wencel Scherffers von Scherffensstein *Pitschnische Schlacht* im Vergleich mit ihrer wiedergefundenen lateinischen Quelle' (417–40); M. Schilling, 'Literatur und Malerei. Ein Namenstagsgedicht Wencel Scherffers von Scherffenstein als Kabinettstück für den Brieger Hofmaler Ezechiel Paritius' (441–64); J. Bomers, '"Du göttliches Geschenk/ des Herzens wehrte Lust." Weltanschauung und Kunsterfahrung in Wencel Scherffers *Der music Lob*' (465–89); B. Jahn, 'Encomium musicae und Musica historica. Zur Konzeption von Musikgeschichte im 17. Jahrhundert an Beispielen aus dem schlesisch-sächsischen Raum (Scherffer, Kleinwechter und Printz)' (491–511).

SCHOTTELIUS. M. Cottone, 'Die Bedeutung des Gartens in der Barockzeit: Gartenkunst und Gartenmetaphorik bei J. G. Schottelius', Laufhütte, *Künste*, 985–98. I. Höpel, 'Beziehungen zwischen Sprichwort und Emblem. Justus Georg Schottelius und die *Dreiständigen Sinnbilder* (1643)', *ib.*, 999–1017.

SCHWABE VON DER HEYDE. A. Aurnhammer, 'Neues vom alten Ernst Schwabe von der Heyde. Drei Sonette auf die Krönung des Kaisers Matthias (1612)', *Daphnis*, 31 : 279–98, examines three newly rediscovered Alexandrine sonnets by a poet whose interest in poetic reform pre-dated that of Opitz.

SCHWARZBURG-RUDOLSTADT. Two publications by the same author on this hitherto neglected woman writer promise two more in the near future and an eventual monograph: J. P. Aikin, 'Die Letzte ihres Geschlechts. Aemilie Juliane von Schwarzburg-Rudolstadt als letzte Gräfin von Barby', *Blätter der Gesellschaft für Buchkultur und Geschichte*, 5, 2001 : 9–37; and 'Der Weg zur Mündigkeit in einem Frauenleben aus dem 17. Jahrhundert. Genesis und Publikationsgeschichte der geistlichen Lieder der Gräfin Aemilie Juliane von Schwarzburg-Rudolstadt', *WBN*, 9 : 33–59.

SPEE. R. Häfner, '"Ars apparet ubique miranda." Friedrich Spees *Güldenes Tugend-Buch* und der apologetische Hintergrund der jesuitischen theologia naturalis', Laufhütte, *Künste*, 1033–45.

STIELER. J. P. Aikin, 'The "Vaterunser" in all shapes and sizes: a poetical-musical-devotional exercise in the works of Johann Franck and Caspar Stieler', Ingen, *Gebetsliteratur*, 207–26. Id., 'The devotional songs of Caspar Stieler', *Daphnis*, 30, 2001 : 97–158, is a companion piece to an equally substantial article in *Daphnis*, 29: 221–79, on the four collections of songs compiled by S.; it attempts to identify his own anonymously published songs from among those in these compilations and gives a *catalogue raisonné* of the successfully identified songs.

OTHER WORK

D. Schubart, '"Weil immer eine Kunst die ander' liebt und ehrt." Der Beitrag des Leipziger Dichterkreises zur Herausbildung einer deutschsprachigen Kunstdichtung', Laufhütte, *Künste*, 635–44, examines the relationship between music and poetry in the work of e.g. Johann Hermann Schein and Paul Fleming and its importance in the development of vernacular poetry by figures such as Christian Brehm and David Schirmer.

3. Prose

Individual Authors

ANDREAE. *Theophilus*, ed. Jana Matlová and Jirí Beneš, trans. Viktor Friedrich Oehler and Frank Böhling with commentary and introduction by Jirí Beneš, Stuttgart–Bad Cannstatt, Frommann-Holzboog, 469 pp., represents vol. 16 in A.'s *Gesammelte Schriften*, ed. Wilhelm Schmidt-Biggemann. Other work on A. includes: M. Brecht, 'Der alte Johann Valentin Andreae und sein Werk — eine Anzeige', *Rosenkreuz*, 77–83; W.-D. Otte, 'Der Nachlaß Johann Valentin Andreaes in der Herzog August Bibliothek', *ib.*, 85–100; W. Schmidt-Biggemann, 'Von Damcar nach Christianopolis. Andreaes 'Christianopolis' als Verwirklichingskonzept der Rosenkreuzerideen', *ib.*, 102–32.

ARNOLD. B. Hoffmann, '"Das ganze leben und wandel war vor dem angesicht Gottes ein gebet." Die Rezeption von Gottfried Arnolds *Erste Liebe* in radikalpietistischen Gruppen', Ingen, *Gebetsliteratur*, 167–78.

BEER. Handsome new editions of five of B.'s novels have appeared in two volumes: Johann Beer, *Sämtliche Werke*, ed. Ferdinand van Ingen und Hans-Gert Roloff, vol. 8: *Die kurtzweiligen Sommer-Täge* (Mittlere Deutsche Literatur in Neu- und Nachdrucken, 8), Berne, Lang, 2000, 347 pp.; vol. 10: *Der verliebte Europäer, Der verkehrte Staatsmann, Bruder Blaumantel, Der verliebte Österreicher* (Mittlere Deutsche Literatur in Neu- und Nachdrucken, 10), Berne, Lang, 349 pp.

BIRKEN. H. Laufhütte, 'Ein frühneuzeitliches Briefarchiv — editorische Perspektiven und Probleme', Bauer, *Edition*, 47–62, describes the uniquely extensive remains of B.'s correspondence archive, problems arising from editing it and — tantalizingly — the new light publication will throw on the life and work of B. and many of his correspondents, including Catharina Regina von Greiffenberg. His correspondence with her will be the first part of the archive to be published.

FRANCKENBERG. C. Gilly, 'Abraham von Franckenberg und die Rosenkreuzer. Zur Datierung der Tabula Universalis Theosophica Mystica et Cabalistica von 1623', *Rosenkreuz*, 217–32.

GREIFFENBERG. C. M. Pumplun, '"Eine offentliche Bekenntnis vor aller Welt." Form und Funktion der Andächtigen Betrachtungen der Catharina Regina von Greiffenberg (1633–1694)', Ingen, *Gebetsliteratur*, 63–75.

GRIMMELSHAUSEN. D. Breuer, 'Irenik — Bestrebungen zur Überwindung des Konfessionsstreits im Barockzeitalter', *Morgenglantz*, 11, 2001:229–50, re-examines the historical background to the still-disputed question of G.'s confessional beliefs. I. M. Battafarano, '1941 — ein glückliches Barockjahr! André Gide's Lob von Grimmelshausens *Simplicissimus*', *ib.*, 317–25, discusses an aspect of G.'s reception, as does the article by I. M. Battafarano and H. Eilert, '"Es ist ein Bild aus Grimmelshausen." *Simplicissimus* als Kriegsroman bei Stefan Zweig, Arthur Schnitzler, Rosa Luxemburg', *ib.*, 12:523–48. In '*Anhang* und *Extract* (1667): Überlegungen zur Autorschaft Grimmelshausens angesichts der *Spezification* (1665). Mit dem ersten Neudruck der *Spezification*', *ib.*, 11, 2001:333–59, the same two critics reconsider the ascription of three brief texts to G.'s authorship. *Simpliciana*, 23, 2001, contains articles on the theme 'Grimmelshausen und die Moderne': F. Gaede, 'Vom göttlichen zum tödlichen Licht. Grimmelshausen — Grass — Jünger' (13–28); R. G. Czapla, 'Ringelnatz, Mühsam, Böll und andere. Kathi Kobus' "Simplicissimus" — Künstlerkneipe als Treffpunkt der Münchener Moderne' (29–52); B. Kasties, 'Ein Barockdichter als Mittler zwischen Stalinismus und Nationalsozialismus. Zu J. R. Bechers Grimmelshausen' (53–74); P. Hesselmann, 'Ein "wiedergebor Simpel-zisch-i-muß." Hubert Konrad Franks Sprachexperimentierkunst im Roman *Baden-Dubel. Simplicius neu* (1992)' (75–85); D. Breuer, 'Bärenhäuter des 20. Jahrhunderts: vom Soldatenspiel Hans Baumanns (1942) zum Heimkehrerstück von Paul Willems (1953)' (87–99); H. Eilert, 'Mehr Demokratie mit der Landstörtzerin? Grimmelshausens *Courasche*-Editionen im 20. Jahrhundert' (101–26); I. M. Battafarano, 'Brechts Maternisierung von Grimmelshausens *Courasche*' (127–58); T. Strässle, 'George Taboris Drama *Mutters Courage* — ein Text in der Tradition Grimmelshausens?' (159–76); R. Uhrig, 'Illustration als Rezeptionsanleitung: die Illustrationen des zwanzigsten Jahrhunderts zu Grimmelshausens *Courasche*' (177–205); E. Mannack, 'Der *Simplicissimus Teutsch* — ein Bestseller im 20. Jahrhundert' (207–20); R. Zeller, 'Ein Simplicissimus für die Jugend. Ludwig Harigs Hörspiel *Simplicius Simplizissimus*' (221–34); H. Schanze, 'Grimmelshausen im großen Fernsehen. Anmerkungen zum *Simplicissimus* in vier Teilen von Leopold Ahlsen und Fritz Umgelter (ZDF/ORF 1975)' (235–45); K. W. Niemöller, 'Die Oper *Simplicius Simplicissimus*. Karl Amadeus Hartmanns Beitrag zur Grimmelshausen-Rezeption in Entstehung (1934/35), Uraufführung (1949) und Neufassung (1956)' (247–61). The topic of the manipulative narrator and his attempts to recall Springinsfeld to the paths of virtue is the focus of M. Bozza,

'"Feingesponnen und grobgewirkt." Zu Grimmelshausens *Springinsfeld*', *Daphnis*, 31:254–78. *Simpliciana*, 24, contains papers delivered at a colloquium entitled 'Kontroversen um Grimmelshausens *Courasche*': V. Meid, 'Von der *Pícara Justina* zu Grimmelshausens *Courasche*' (15–26); P. Hesselmann, 'Ein "Spiegel böser Art"? Grimmelshausens *Courasche* in den Kommentaren der posthumen Gesamtausgaben' (27–46); R. Hillenbrand, 'Courasche als negatives Exempel' (47–65); S. Streller, 'Ambivalentes Frauenbild in Grimmelshausens *Courasche*' (67–77); N. Kaminski, '*Reine des Bohémiens*. Politische Utopie und "zigeunernde" Textur in Grimmelshausens *Courasche*' (79–121); K. Haberkamm, '"Sebel unter dem Schenkel." Zur Funktion des Hermaphroditischen in Grimmelshausens *Courasche*' (123–40); A. Solbach, 'Grimmelshausens *Courasche* als unzuverlässige Erzählerin' (141–64); H. Eilert, 'Courasche, von anderen Figuren erzählt' (165–86); I. M. Battafarano, 'Courasches sich legitimierende Literarizität' (187–212); C. Kalkuhl and W. Solms, 'Unter den Zigeunern. Grimmelshausens Darstellung einer verachteten Minderheit' (213–27); D. Breuer, 'Courasches Unbußfertigkeit. Das religiöse Problem in Grimmelshausens Roman' (229–42). This same volume also includes J. J. Berns, 'Simplicius bei Hofe. Eigenart und Funktion der Hofdarstellung im Simplicissimus-Roman' (243–64).

GUARINONIUS. G. van Gemert, 'Medizinisches Naturverständnis und gegenreformatorisches Literaturprogramm. Zum Stellenwert des erzählerischen Moments in Hippolytus Guarinonius' *Grewel der Verwüstung Menschlichen Geschlechts*', Laufhütte, *Künste*, 1123–37, focuses on the many instances where G. narrates incidents and experiences from his own life in the text of an otherwise scholarly work.

KNORR. Numerous articles on the diverse literary and scientific activities of K. (1636–89) and his associates in Sulzbach and elsewhere appear in *Morgenglantz*, the journal of the 'Christian Knorr von Rosenroth-Gesellschaft': R. Zeller, 'Naturmagie, Kabbala, Millennium. Das Sulzbacher Projekt um Christian Knorr von Rosenroth und der Cambridger Platoniker Henry More', *ib.*, 11, 2001:13–75; G. van den Heuvel, 'Leibniz und die Sulzbacher Protagonisten Christian Knorr von Rosenroth und Franciscus Mercurius van Helmont', *ib.*, 77–104; K. Jaitner, 'Der Sulzbacher Rat Johann Abraham Poemer (1604–1687) und die Sozietätsbewegung bis zum Ausgang des Dreißigjährigen Krieges', *ib.*, 125–39; V. Wappmann, 'Johann Leonhard Frisch (1666–1723) als Sprach- und Naturforscher in der Tradition Knorrs von Rosenroth', *ib.*, 183–203; G. van Gemert, 'Christian Knorr von Rosenroth und Petrus Serrarius. Die Apokalypsekommentare im Deutungszusammenhang', *ib.*, 205–27; M. Lommer, 'Geistiges Leben in der Residenzstadt Sulzbach in der zweiten Hälfte des 17. Jahrhunderts. Ausgewählte Personen und

Institutionen von Kirche und Schule, Hof und Stadtregiment vor dem Hintergrund der Bevölkerungssituation', *ib.*, 251–87. Other essays look at the role of translation in K.'s work: L. Balbiani, 'Die Übersetzung der *Magia Naturalis* von Giovan Battista Della Porta. Christian Knorr von Rosenroth als Vermittler naturwissenschaftlicher Kenntnisse', *ib.*, 105–23; I. M. Battafarano, 'Didaxe in der Übersetzung. Meyfarts, Seiferts und Schmidts Verdeutschungen von Spees *Cautio Criminalis* und Knorrs von Rosenroth Übersetzung von Della Portas *Magia Naturalis*', *ib.*, 12:279–340. K. Burmistrov, 'Die hebräischen Quellen der *Kabbala Denudata*', *ib.*, 341–76, concentrates on an aspect of K.'s greatest single work.

MUSCULUS. A. Baumann, 'Zur Rezeption patristischer Texte in den Gebetbüchern des Andreas Musculus', Ingen, *Gebetsliteratur*, 227–58.

RIST. T. Mast, 'Patriotism and the promotion of German language and culture: Johann Rist's *Rettung der Edlen Teutschen Hauptsprache* (1642) and the language movement of the seventeenth century', *Daphnis*, 30, 2001:71–96.

ZESEN. F. van Ingen, 'Form- und Stilfragen der Gebetsliteratur in der Frühen Neuzeit. Am Beispiel von Philipp von Zesens *Frauenzimmers Gebeht-Buch* (1657)', Ingen, *Gebetsliteratur*, 131–46. J. Breyl, 'Assenat und Isis — eine poetologische Kontroverse in Bild und Text. Zum Verhältnis von Kunst und Natur bei Philipp von Zesen', Laufhütte, *Künste*, 719–39, takes Z.'s novel *Assenat* (1670) as its starting-point.

OTHER WORK

Several articles on the 17th-c. novel have appeared, including two on 'Musiker-Romane': A. Wicke, 'Gelehrte Autorschaft und Politischer Roman — zu ausgewählten Paratexten von Weise, Riemer, Ettner und anderen Autoren', *Morgenglantz*, 12:481–522; A. Martino, 'Der deutsche *Buscón* (1671) und der literatursoziologische Mythos von der Verbürgerlichung des Pikaro', *Daphnis*, 30, 2001:219–32; A. Anglet, '"Ich bin kein Spiel-Mann." Die Verteidigung des bürgerlichen Status und das künstlerische Selbstbewußtsein der Hauptfiguren in der Musiker-Romanen von Wolfgang Caspar Printz', *ib.*, 333–54; H. Thomke, 'Leben, Beruf und Kunstauffassung im Spiegel der barocken Musikerromane', Laufhütte, *Künste*, 741–54.

4. DRAMA

INDIVIDUAL AUTHORS

GRYPHIUS. H. J. Drügh, '"Was mag wol klärer seyn?" — Zur Ambivalenz des Allegorischen in Andreas Gryphius' Trauerspiel *Leo Armenius*', Laufhütte, *Künste*, 1019–31.

HARSDÖRFFER. S. Bauer-Roesch, 'Gesangspiel und Gesprächspiel — Georg Philipp Harsdörffers *Seelewig* als erste Operntheorie in deutscher Sprache', Laufhütte, *Künste*, 645–64.

KNORR. Christian Knorr von Rosenroth, *Conjugium Phoebi et Palladis. Oder die erfundene Fortpflanzung des Goldes / Chymische Allegorie*, ed. I. M. Battafarano (Iris, 16; FEK), 2000, 89 pp., is the first modern edition of K.'s 'Singspiel' in celebration of the 1676 wedding of Leopold I. to Eleonora Magdalena Theresia von Pfalz-Neuburg.

LEMIUS. A. Kollatz, 'Ästhetik der katholischen Reform am Beispiel der Dramen des Gottfried Lemius SJ (1562–1632)', Laufhütte, *Künste*, 851–70.

LOHENSTEIN. H. Esselborn, 'Von Sodom zum Phlogiston. Der Schwefel im Spannungsfeld von Naturwissenschaft und Mythologie in Lohensteins Dramen', Laufhütte, *Künste*, 1159–70.

OTHER WORK

Judith P. Aikin, *A Language for German Opera. The Development of Forms and Formulas for Recitative and Aria in Seventeenth-Century German Libretti* (WAB, 37), 347 pp., is a detailed and important interdisciplinary study of the word/music relationship as it developed in opera in 17th-c. Germany up to 1683. G. Ehrstine, 'Vom Zeichen zum (leeren) Abbild. Das Drama der Frühen Neuzeit als visuelles Medium', Laufhütte, *Künste*, 407–17; H. Loos, 'Die Kritik an Senecas Tragödie bei Vossius, Heinsius und Grotius', *ib.*, 419–31; M.-T. Mourey, 'Die Kunst des Balletts. Rhetorik und Grammatik einer neuen Sprache', *ib.*, 561–76, examines both the physical language of dance and how it was recorded; it is complemented by A. Traninger, '"Wie die Buchstabwechsel zu den Dantzspielen oder Balleten zugebrauchen?" Zur Bedeutung der *ars combinatoria* für den frühneuzeitlichen Tanz und seine Beschreibung', *ib.*, 1095–1106. Different aspects of improvised performance are dealt with by V. Mergenthaler, 'Imitatio und ingenium in der Commedia dell'arte. Spuren des Ciceronianismusstreits im Stegreiftheater', *ib.*, 591–602; and M. A. Katritzky, 'Carnival and comedy in Georg Straub of St. Gallen's printed *album amicorum* of 1600', *ib.*, 603–33 (with many illustrations). Very different dramatic genres are the topic of C. Caemmerer, 'Normierung des Neuen. Die deutschen Schäferspiele des 17. Jahrhunderts und ihr Platz in den poetischen Schriften', *ib.*, 665–72; and S. Krump, 'Sinnenhafte Seelenführung. Das Theater der Jesuiten im Spannungsfeld von Rhetorik, Pädagogik und ignatianischer Spiritualität', *ib.*, 937–50. On Jesuit theatre see also D. Breuer, 'Geschichtsdidaktik auf dem Theater der Jesuiten', *Morgenglantz*, 12:231–47. Three articles in this journal focus on the didactic potential of court theatre:

A. Beise, 'Hofbühne als pädagogische Anstalt: Stieler, Anton Ulrich, Knorr von Rosenroth', *ib.*, 167–87; B. Jahn, 'Gelingende und scheiternde Didaxe im Musiktheater oder: ist die Oper ein didaktisches Medium?', *ib.*, 189–205; H. Meise, '"Tantzen den gantzen Tag." Der höfische Tanz als Didaxe und Botschaft', *ib.*, 207–30. Another essay looks at drama at court in Vienna: A. Noe, 'Die Rezeption spanischer Dramen am Wiener Kaiserhof des 17. Jahrhunderts. Versuch einer Bilanz', *Daphnis*, 30, 2001 : 159–218.

THE CLASSICAL ERA

POSTPONED

THE ROMANTIC ERA

By Carol Tully, *University of Wales, Bangor*

1. General Studies

There has been a degree of interest in the relationship of Goethe to the Romantic School with the publication of two major volumes. The first, *Goethe und das Zeitalter der Romantik*, ed. Walter Hinderer (Stiftung für Romantikforschung, 21), Würzburg, Königshausen & Neumann, 524 pp. + 8 pls, contains a variety of essays with sections relating to philosophy, art, music, and history. Of particular interest is the section examining the *Klassik-Romantik* axis. Worthy of note here are D. Borchmeyer, 'Zur Typologie des Klassischen und Romantischen' (19–29), which highlights G.'s ambivalence towards Romanticism. B. sees G. attempt to reconcile the two perspectives in order to achieve a level of synthesis. He then goes on to show how the Schlegel brothers are in search of a similar synthesis, albeit from a different starting point, which is then found in G.'s work, and which they describe as 'progressiv'. The emphasis is on a dialectic rather than the creation of ideological boundaries; G. Neumann, ' "Mannigfache Wege gehen die Menschen." Romananfänge bei Goethe und Novalis' (71–90), is a fascinating study which examines the responses of G. and N. to the problems of narrating individual experience in the context of Enlightenment redefinitions of the self, driven by *Naturgesetze*, rather than the guiding hand of God. Neumann identifies a tendency towards 'Lebenswissenschaft' which seeks to understand life as a series of elements and phases, recorded according to the scientific principles of observation. G. and N.'s novels, or novel fragments, employ a variety of strategies to give voice to individuality within the context of Enlightenment encyclopaedism, including the letter, the puppet theatre, vocalization, and dreams; A. von Bormann, ' "Sie grüßen den alten Held." Zur Goetherezeption in der Hochromantik' (133–48), uses the work of Eichendorff to construct a case study of the reception of G. by late Romantic writers. Other essays included in this section are: J. Le Rider, 'War die Klassik farbenfeindlich und die Romantik farbengläubig? Von Lessings *Laokoon* zu Goethes *Farbenlehre* und deren Nachwirkung' (31–49); G. Oesterle, 'Das Faszinosum der Arabeske um 1800' (51–70); I. Oesterle, ' "Es ist an der Zeit!" Zur kulturellen Konstruktionsveränderung von Zeit gegen 1800' (91–119); W. Vosskamp, ' "Jeder sey auf seine Art ein Grieche! Aber er sey's." Zu Goethes Romantikkritik in der Zeitschrift *Ueber Kunst und Alterthum*' (121–31). Amongst the wide range of essays included elsewhere in this volume are: D. E. Wellbery, 'Goethes Lyrik und das frühromantische Kunstprogramm' (175–92); P. Chiarini, '"Alte Meister" in klassisch-romantischem Kontext. Goethe, Friedrich Schlegel und die "Deutsche Renaissance"' (245–63); D. Ottmann, 'Gebändigte Natur. Garten und Wildnis in Goethes *Wahlverwandtschaften* und Eichendorffs *Ahnung und Gegenwart*' (345–95); C. Lubkoll, '"Neue Mythologie" und musikalische Poetologie. Goethes Annäherungen an die Romantik' (399–412); M.-C. Hoock-Demarle, 'Europa, die Frühromantik und der "europäische" Goethe' (475–87).

The second major study is Hartmut Fröschle, *Goethes Verhältnis zur Romantik,* Würzburg, Königshausen & Neumann, 564 pp., which provides a detailed study of G.'s relations with all the major figures of the period, as well as his approach to the key fields of Romantic scholarship, including Germanist, Romanist, and Orientalist studies. The volume is structured in such a way as to be of optimum use to those with an interest in the individual writers and issues discussed, and constitutes an excellent source book for scholars of the period. Also noted: Gretchen L. Hachmeister, **Italy in the German Literary Imagination. Goethe's 'Italian Journey' and its Reception by Eichendorff, Platen and Heine*, NY, Camden House, 230 pp.

Feminine tropes are discussed in two valuable contributions: A. Geisenhanslüke, 'Aspekte der Marienlyrik um 1800: Schlegel — Novalis — Hölderlin', *ZDP*, 21:510–28, examines the upsurge in interest in Marianism around 1800, which can be traced back to Herder, in a move away from the Protestant rejection of the cult of the Virgin Mary. There is a particular focus on attempts to re-evaluate the feminine in the context of a Romantic understanding of faith and the representation of the Trinity. P. Meyer, 'Melusine: the Romantic appropriation of a medieval tale', *GRM*, 52:289–302, examines how Romantic writers reinvented myth rather than restoring it and traces the development of M. from a tragic heroine to a sub- or superhuman representation of the power of nature, thus becoming a modern abstract construct, not a purely mythological figure.

Also noted: **Wo das philosophische Gespräch ganz in Dichtung übergeht. Platos Symposium und seine Wirkung in der Renaissance, Romantik und Moderne*, ed. Stefan Matuschek (Jenaer germanistische Forschungen, n.F., 13), Heidelberg, Winter, iv + 232 pp.; U. Hentschel, '. . .da wallfahrte ich hin, oft mit der neuen Héloise in der Tasche . . . Zur deutschen Rousseau-Rezeption im 18. und beginnendem 19. Jahrhundert', *Euphorion*, 96:47–74; M. Caspari, 'The critical potential of German Romanticism re-examined in Morgner's "Gauklerlegende"', *GN*, 33:3–13.

THEMES. Jutta Schlich, *Literarische Authentizität. Prinzip und Geschichte* (Konzepte der Sprach- und Literaturwissenschaft, 62), Tübingen, Niemeyer, 186 pp., is an introductory study which attempts to guide the reader to an understanding of the notion of authenticity as an 'Effekt der Darstellung'. S. examines the concept through a number of writers ranging from the 18th to the 20th cs. She pays particular attention to women writers, including Bettina von Arnim and Karoline von Günderrode, and also explores key Romantic sociological and cultural ideals. Sabine Haupt, *'Es kehrt alles wieder.' Zur Poetik literarischer Wiederholungen in der deutschen Romantik und Restaurationszeit: Tieck, Hoffmann, Eichendorff* (Studien zur Literatur- und Kulturgeschichte, 17), Würzburg, Königshausen & Neumann, 759 pp., provides a detailed examination of repetition as a narrative strategy, tracing the development of cyclical concepts in the Romantic understanding of philosophy and history, before examining the use of the strategy in the work of individual authors. Of particular interest is the final section of the study which focuses on theories of genre, highlighting the contrast between the uses of a repetitive, cyclical narrative as opposed to a linear, progressive approach. The study of the individual authors is detailed and well-structured.

Laurie Ruth Johnson, *The Art of Recollection in Jena Romanticism. Memory, History, Fiction, and Fragmentation in Texts by Friedrich Schlegel and Novalis* (SDL, 164), 196 pp., is a well-argued and informative study of the early Romantic perception of memory as an 'unstable but indispensable' historical source. J. examines the manifestation of this perception in the fragment form, arguing that the Romantic recourse to the fragment is 'symptomatic of a crisis of memory, identity, and representation still present today'. Her discussion of the nature of memory and its relation to the depiction and perception of the past is followed by a chronological analysis of memory in aesthetic theory from Herder and Schiller to the Jena Romantics.

Volker Gastreich, *Kindheit und absolute Musik. Eine literaturwissenschaftliche Untersuchung romantischer Ideale* (Medien und Fiktionen, 3), Berne, Lang, 232 pp., evaluates the representation and association of the twin Romantic ideals of childhood and music in the portrayal of the protagonists of key Romantic novels by Tieck, Novalis, Wackenroder, Heinse, and Hoffmann. The study examines the relationship of music and literature in the quest for the utopian notion of a Golden Age and traces the development of concepts of childhood and music from the *Aufklärung* to the Romantic period. Ruth Pouvreau, *Schöpferische Weltbetrachtung. Zum Verhältnis von Einbildung und Erkenntnis in Texten der deutschen Romantik* (Fichte-Studien-Supplementa, 15), Amsterdam–NY, Rodopi, 208 pp., examines the literary representation of the Fichtean notion of a cyclical dialectic relating to the individual's imaginative experience of an inner and an outer world. Selecting examples from works by a number of writers, including Fichte, Tieck, Eichendorff, Arnim, and Hoffmann, P. focuses firstly on the fusion of self and the outer world in the *Naturdichtung* of the 18th c. and then turns her attention the Romantic treatment of imagination as a means to create the self in relation to the outside world.

Wissen in Literatur im 19. Jahrhundert, ed. Lutz Danneberg and Friedrich Vollhardt, Tübingen, Niemeyer, 385 pp., takes as its point of departure the question whether literature can be seen to stand in 'Deutungskonkurrenz' with science since the 19th c. Of particular interest is M. Titzmann, 'Die "Bildungs-"/Initiationsgeschichte der Goethe-Zeit und das System der Altersklassen im anthropologischen Diskurs der Epoche' (7–64), which provides a detailed sociological analysis of the contemporary understanding of human development in terms of behaviour and character traits, focusing on phases of initiation and transition and their literary representation in the work of a number of Romantic writers, including Novalis, Hoffmann, and Eichendorff; M. Engel, 'Naturphilosophisches Wissen und romantische Literatur — am Beispiel von Traumtheorie und Traumdichtung der Romantik'(65–91), examines the dream theories of Romantic anthropology and their impact upon the literature of the period, making particular reference to Novalis's *Heinrich von Ofterdingen* and Hoffmann's *Die Bergwerke zu Falun*. Peter-André Alt, *Der Schlaf der Vernunft. Literatur und Traum in der Kulturgeschichte der Neuzeit*, Munich, Beck, 464 pp., also concentrates on the role of dreams in literature. The volume contains studies of Jean Paul and Hoffmann, as well as a section focusing on the relationship between dreams, desire, and the soul in the work of Novalis, Tieck, Brentano, and Kleist. A. argues that, for writers of the period, the dream constitutes 'ein poetisches Modell', closely associated with issues of content and form, which enables representation of individuality on an intimate level. This study is notable for the detailed contextualization of cultural notions of dreams from the Classical age to the 20th century.

Alexandra Hildebrandt, *'Lebewohl, du heiterer Schein!'. Blindheit im Kontext der Romantik* (Ep, 406), 276 pp., provides an overview of the 17th-c. and 18th-c. understanding of the human senses, tracing its development from the Classical age, before focusing on the motif of blindness in the Romantic period. The study, which centres mainly on the work of Brentano, Hoffmann, and Chamisso, identifies blindness as a key motif in Idealist and Romantic discourse. Therefore, whilst playing a key role in a number of central Romantic themes, such as darkness, shadow, and death, the notion of blindness is not seen to be a solely Romantic motif. The reading of *Peter Schlemihl* is particularly thought-provoking, as is the dual theological interpretation of blindness as either a path to Salvation or a path away from God. Also noted: **Erinnern und Vergessen in der europäischen Romantik*, ed. Günter Oesterle (Stiftung für Romantikforschung, 20), Würzburg, Königshausen & Neumann, 278 pp.

GENRES. Nicola Kaminski, *Kreuz-Gänge. Romanexperimente der deutschen Romantik*, Paderborn, Schöningh, 2001, 446 pp., refutes the thesis that the novelists of the Romantic period were in any way 'genialische Pfuscher und Schlamper', unable to reach the creative heights required by the genre. K.'s methodology favours instead a hermeneutic analysis of the texts as experimental pieces which challenge contemporary, and indeed current, notions surrounding the interaction between author, reader, and structure in the development of meaning. The challenge to meaning is reflected in the multi-layered significance of the title chosen for the study. The volume borrows its title in the first instance from the figure of Kreuzgang from the *Nachtwachen*. The word itself denotes a favoured setting for Romantic writers, the cloister, but is rendered here in modified plural form — *Kreuz-Gänge* — to suggest a crossing of ways or a crossover. These experimental texts are shown to represent just such a crossover, simultaneously testing the boundaries of theoretical speculation and creative exploration. By concentrating on such shifts in meaning, K. succeeds in bringing out the richness of these texts, both as examples of developing Romantic theory in practice, and inspired, and indeed inspirational, poetic texts. Whilst furnishing the reader with a discussion of the genre as a whole, the author focuses on six key texts: *Nachtwachen. Von Bonaventura*, Friedrich Schlegel's *Lucinde*, Brentano's *Godwi*, Arnim's *Gräfin Dolores*, Hoffmann's *Die Elixiere des Teufels*, and Eichendorff's *Ahnung und Gegenwart*.

Anna Cullhed, *The Language of Passion. The Order of Poetics and the Construction of a Lyric Genre 1746–1806* (EH, XVIII, 104), 337 pp., is a lucid examination of the integration of the lyric genre into poetics in the late 18th and early 19th cs. C. identifies this period as the point where the lyric finally establishes a place alongside the epic and the drama in the literary canon. The study takes its title from Blair's definition of all poetry as the language of passion, one which seems particularly suited to the lyric genre. However, C.'s study challenges the notion that the Romantic and the lyric are intertwined, questioning the view of the Romantic period as the age of lyric poetry and also the notion of the lyric as an expression of sincere emotion. The study focuses on the theoretical works of the period, including those by A. W. Schlegel, Schelling, Sulzer, and Bouterwek.

Edgar Pankow, *Brieflichkeit. Revolutionen eines Sprachbildes*, Munich, Fink, 222 pp., traces a radical redefinition of the literary usage of letters as 'Sprachbilder' from 1789 onwards. The volume includes a detailed study of Hölderlin's quest for a meaningful interpretation of the relationship between the writing of a letter and the fate of a given entity, the response to which is the epistolary novel *Hyperion*. Issues of genre are also discussed in relation to Jean Paul's *Hesperus* which is seen as an attempt to revolutionize the *Briefroman* and to create a narrative which presents the novel itself as a letter.

H. Brown, 'German women writers in English short story anthologies of the 1820s', *MLR*, 97:620–31, provides an insight into the publishing world of the early 19th c. and looks in detail at the reception of writers such as Benedikte Naubert, Caroline Pilcher, and Caroline de la Motte Fouqué. B. shows how these women writers were accorded the same level of interest as male contemporaries including Tieck as part of the vogue for short fiction, especially the fairy tale. Such success was, however, subject to limitation: the short format was deemed suitable for women writers and the translations provided were often of poor quality.

2. Individual Authors

BÖHL VON FABER, JOHANN NIKOLAS. C. Tully, 'How German Romanticism travelled to Spain: the intellectual journey of Johann Nikolas Böhl von Faber', *PEGS(NS)*, 71:78–90, examines the development of critic and Hispanophile B., from his youth in Hamburg as a pupil of the Enlightenment pedagogue, Joachim Heinrich Campe, to his subsequent 'Bekehrung zur Romantik', a personal and ideological journey which culminated in his dissemination of Schlegelian thought in Spain in 1814.

BRENTANO, CLEMENS. H. Härtl, 'Eine Buchbinderrechnung für den jungen Brentano', *Euphorion*, 96:157–70.

FICHTE, JOHANN GOTTLIEB. *Fichte und die Literatur — Beiträge des vierten Kongresses der Internationalen Johann Gottlieb Fichte Gesellschaft, Berlin 03.–08. Oktober 2000, und Ergänzungen*, ed. Helmut Girndt and Klaus Hammacher (Fichte-Studien, 19), Amsterdam–NY, Rodopi, 269 pp., highlights the centrality of F.'s thought to contemporary letters. Two studies examine the relation between F. and Goethe: S. Iovino, '"Ich ist Nicht-Ich" = "Alles ist Alles". Goethe als Leser der *Wissenschaftslehre*. Ein Beitrag zur Geschichte des Verhältnisses Fichte-Goethe' (55–94); M. Da Veiga, 'Selbstdenken und Stil bei J. G. Fichte und Goethe' (95–108). F.'s seminal role in early Romanticism is also discussed: B. Loheide, 'Artistisches Fichtisieren: zur Höheren Wissenschaftslehre bei Novalis' (109–23); M. Goetze, 'Das praktische Ich in der *Wissenschaftslehre* und in der frühromantischen Philosophie des Lebens' (137–47). J. Kreuzer, 'Vom Ich zur Sprache' Fichte und

Hölderlin' (185–98), provides an interesting discussion of H.'s response to the *WL* in relation to issues of memory, identity, and language. Also noted: C. Cesa, 'Sensibilité et conscience. Remarques sur la théorie des Triebe chez Fichte', *RGI*, 18:121–32; L. Fonnesu, 'Entre Aufklärung et idéalisme: l'anthropologie de Fichte', *ib.*, 133–47; J.-M. Vayase, 'Dynamique et subjectivité selon Fichte: effort, pulsion, aspiration', *ib.*, 149–60; J.-F. Goubet, 'L'impératif catégorique fichtéen comme tendence et décision', *ib.*, 161–76.

GRIMM, JACOB AND WILHELM. Richard Faber, *'Sagen lassen sich die Menschen nichts, aber erzählen lassen sie sich alles.' Über Grimm-Hebelsche Erzählung, Moral und Utopie in Benjaminischer Perspektive*, Würzburg, Königshausen & Neumann, 192 pp., seeks to provide an alternative assessment of the *KHM* by reappraising parallels with H.'s narrative. The study provides some thought-provoking material and deals with a broad range of topics ranging from the concept of 'Volksdichtung' to the Anti-*Märchen*. Appended are three excursus, the first of which, perhaps controversially, juxtaposes the Grimms' nationalism and antisemitism with H.'s cosmopolitanism and pro-Semitism. The 1998 *Jahrbuch der Brüder Grimm-Gesellschaft* appeared this year. It contains three studies: I. Murayama, 'Ein Stamm und zwei Äste. Wilhelm Grimm und der Norden' (23–39), examines the role of W.G.'s reception of Nordic culture in the establishment of his notion of a German cultural identity; B. Gobrecht, 'Hexen im Märchen' (41–57), examines the image of the witch figure in folk narrative and explores the definition and characteristics found in relation to the Grimms' stylization of such figures; C. Tully, 'Zur Rezeption der Brüder Grimm in Spanien im 19. Jahrhundert' (59–77), documents the reception of the *KHM* in Spain from the first attempt to publish some of the tales in Spanish translation in 1846 to their established canonical status by the end of the 19th century. T. uncovers the development of a dual *Grimm-Mythos* which saw the brothers revered as philological role models but also rendered quasi-fictional folk heroes. J. E. Sennewald, '"Es war einmal mitten im Winter" — die poetischen Konstruktionen der *Kinder- und Hausmärchen* durch die Brüder Grimm', *EG*, 57:689–708, examines the possible poetological function of threat in the *KHM*, focusing on the central Winter topos which underpins the poetic structure of key tales. Issues of self-referentiality within the collection are also discussed as is the Grimms' use of Romantic theory and literary discourse. Also noted: G.-L. Fink, 'Du discours de Rousseau aux contes des frères Grimm. Le mythe du peuple et le miroir de la bourgeoisie', *EG*, 57:233–66; H. Rölleke, 'Die Brüder Grimm als Bühnenfigur', *Euphorion*, 96:93–100; L. Blum, '"Wir scheinen überhaupt bestimmt, an einander zu rennen." Anmerkungen zum Briefwechsel der Brüder

Grimm mit Ludwig Hassenpflug und zum Streit um die "Kasseler Ausgabe"', *WW*, 52:458–65.

HAUFF, WILHELM. Two volumes dealing with H.'s life and work have appeared this year, the bicentenary of his birth. Stefan Neuhaus, *Das Spiel mit dem Leser. Wilhelm Hauff: Werk und Wirkung*, Göttingen, Vandenhoeck & Ruprecht, 240 pp., presents an enthusiastic revaluation of H. which provides a well-structured overview of his work along genre lines in which individual texts are studied in detail. N. defends H.'s work against accusations of imitation, highlighting instead the subtle use of parody and irony which often leads to problems of categorization, with certain texts functioning as both an example and a parody of the same genre. This study is to be recommended to anyone seeking a comprehensive discussion of H.'s work. *Wilhelm Hauff. Aufsätze zu seinem poetischen Werk*, ed. Ulrich Kittstein (Mannheimer Studien zur Literatur- und Kulturwissenschaft, 28), St Ingbert, Röhrig, 183 pp., also aims to reassess H.'s work in its entirety, stressing the variety of H.'s literary output which stretches far beyond the popular *Märchen*. U. Kittstein, 'Das literarische Werk Wilhelm Hauffs im Kontext seiner Epoche' (9–43), highlights H.'s awareness of market forces and his firm grounding in the *Biedermeier Weltanschauung*. Two essays focus specifically on the *Märchen*: R. Wild, 'Wer ist der Räuber Orbasan? Überlegungen zu Wilhelm Hauffs Märchen' (45–61), and also D. L. Smith, 'Zeit- und Gesellschaftskritik in Wilhelm Hauffs *Das kalte Herz*' (63–81), who asks whether H.'s tale can be seen as a means of implicit social criticism, the subtlety of which avoids a direct, more aggressive approach. F. Vögele, '"Hie gut Württemburg allezeit." Eine Untersuchung zum politischen Gehalt von Wilhelm Hauffs Roman *Lichtenstein*' (83–111), discusses the contemporary socio-critical significance of the political, religious, and dynastic issues found in H.'s novel. Finally, two studies focus on H.'s *Novellen*: J. Landwehr, '*Jud Süß* — Hauffs Novelle als literarische Legitimation eines Justizmords und als Symptom und (Mit-) Erfindung eines kollektiven Wahns' (113–45), and U. Kittstein, '"Vive l'Empereur!" Napoleon und Württemberg in Wilhelm Hauffs Novelle *Das Bild des Kaisers*' (147–67), which assesses H.'s text as a reflection on the historical process by examining the depiction and contemporary reception of the Napoleonic era.

HEBEL, JOHANN PETER. G. Oesterle, 'Beobachten und Erinnern. Johann Peter Hebels *Rheinländischer Hausfreund*', *DVLG*, 76:229–49, looks at the relationship between the reader and the calendar writer and examines the strategies used to create intimacy, discussing simulated orality as a means to explore the historical, as well as the distancing strategies of satire and camouflage. See also GRIMM, JACOB AND WILHELM.

HEGEL, GEORG WILHELM FRIEDRICH. Noted: Paul Cobben, **Das Gesetz der multikulturellen Gesellschaft. Eine Aktualisierung von Hegels 'Grundlinien der Philosophie des Rechts'*, Würzburg, Königshausen & Neumann, 256 pp.; Peter Trawny, **Die Zeit der Dreieinigkeit. Untersuchungen zur Trinität bei Hegel und Schelling*, Würzburg, Königshausen & Neumann, 220 pp.; R. Gagan, 'Hegel beside himself: unworking the intellectual community', *ERR*, 13: 139–45; K. Mueller-Vollmer, 'Das Besondere des Allgemeinen: vom Zu-Wort-Kommen der Sprache in Hegels *Phänomenologie des Geistes*', *Athenäum*, 12: 69–90.

HIPPEL, THEODOR GOTTLIEB VON. J. Kohnen, 'Neues zur Hippel-Forschung. Zu Anke Lindemann-Starks *Leben und Lebensläufe des Theodor Gottlieb von Hippel*', *E. T. A. Hoffmann-Jahrbuch*, 10: 130–34.

HOFFMANN, E. T. A.. *E. T. A. Hoffmann. Der goldene Topf. Ein Märchen aus der neuen Zeit, Text und Kommentar* (BasisBibliothek, 31), Frankfurt, Suhrkamp, 157 pp., includes a useful new commentary by Peter Braun. *Das Land der Sehnsucht. E. T. A. Hoffmann und Italien*, ed. Sandro M. Moraldo, Heidelberg, Winter, 201 pp., discusses the role of Italy in various aspects of H.'s work ranging from theatre and music to aesthetics and the uncanny. Of particular note are F. Loquai, 'Die Bösewichte aus dem Süden. Imagologische Überlegungen zu E. T. A. Hoffmanns Italienbild in *Ignaz Denner* und anderen Erzählungen' (35–53), which examines H.'s use of cliché and stereotype in depicting numerous evil characters, many of whom hail from Italy; also D. Kremer, '"Das Land der Kunst" — Italien als Spiegel einer klassizistischen und einer manieristischen Ästhetik (Goethe — Arnim — Hoffmann)' (91–104), which examines the aesthetic function of images of Italy around 1800, defining the country as a topological and allegorical location, a phenomenon common to Goethe's classical and Arnim and H.'s Romantic representations; also H. Steinecke, '"Ein Spiel zum Spiel." E. T. A. Hoffmanns Annäherungen an die Commedia dell'arte' (127–43), which looks at the reception of the *commedia* around 1800. H. is drawn to the genre through his musical work and also via Brentano. S. highlights the influence of Gozzi and Callot in underpinning H.'s view of the *commedia* as a Romantic art form 'in seinem Sinne'. Also included in this volume: W. Segebrecht, 'Hoffmanns imaginäre Bibliothek italienischer Literatur' (9–23); C. Giacobazzi, 'Die Rezeption E. T. A. Hoffmanns in Italien im kritischen Diskurs' (25–34); M. E. D'Agostini, 'Bis an die Grenzen des Alltäglichen: das Unheimliche und die Ironie bei E. T. A. Hoffmann und Pirandello' (55–67); S. M. Moraldo, 'Zur Semantik der *femme fragile* bei E. T. A. Hoffmann, Gabriele D'Annunzio und Tennessee Williams oder Geburt, Blüte und Niedergang einer italienischen Frauengestalt (69–89); M. Cometa, 'Hoffmann und die italienische Kunst' (105–26); L. Pikulik, 'Die Hieroglyphenschrift von Gebärde, Maske, Spiel. E. T. A. Hoffmann, Jacques Callot und die Commedia dell'arte' (145–57); P. Collini, '*Die Fermate*: Zeit der Musik, Zeit der Liebe' (159–65); M. Galli, ' "Die Schrecken der entsetzlichen Zeit": *Signor Formica*' (167–77); A. Destro, 'Das Romanhafte bei E. T. A. Hoffmann' (179–89); F. Cercignani, 'E. T. A. Hoffmann, Italien und die romantische Auffassung der Musik' (191–201).

Melanie Klier, *Kunstsehen — Literarische Konstruktion und Reflexion von Gemälden in E. T. A. Hoffmanns Serapions-Brüdern mit Blick auf die Prosa Georg Heyms* (MSLKD, 35), 297 pp., provides a discussion of the dialectic between text and image from the point of view of the adaptation and restructuring of specific images within H.'s work. K. points to a gap in research on H. in this area which is puzzling given the acknowledged breadth of H.'s talents. The integration of paintings into literary texts is discussed primarily in relation to H.'s *Doge und Dogaresse* with comparisons drawn with Heym's *Der Dieb*. This area is also discussed by E. Pankow, 'Medienwechsel. Zur Konstellation von Literatur und Malerei in einigen Arbeiten E. T. A. Hoffmanns', *E. T. A. Hoffmann-Jahrbuch*, 10:42–57. Other notable contributions to the *Jahrbuch* include C. Lieb, 'Und hinter tausend Gläsern keine Welt. Raum, Körper und Schrift in E. T. A. Hoffmanns *Das öde Haus*' (58–75), who provides an insightful study of distorted perception, effected by means of a number of glass-related motifs, and the representation of woman as 'Kunstprodukt' as the object perceived. L. shows how these merge into self-perception; C. Weder, 'Ein medezinisch-literarisches Symptom: zum Schwindel bei E. T. A. Hoffmann und im Kontext des medezinischen Diskurses der Zeit' (76–95), which examines the prevalence of dizziness in H.'s work and discusses the phenomenon in relation to the theories of Marcus Herz, a member of Karl Philip Moritz's Berlin circle; K. Volobeuf, 'E. T. A. Hoffmann: "Urheber" einer der ersten brasilianischen Kurzgeschichten' (120–29), who reveals the unexpectedly significant role played by H.'s *Das Fräulein von Scuderi* in the establishment of the modern Brazilian narrative tradition. Also included in this volume: B. Schemmel, 'Neue Hoffmanniana der Staatsbibliothek Bamberg' (10–30); F. Auhuber, 'Der Autor und sein Leser. E. T. A. Hoffmanns Briefe an Hippel (1794–1813)' (31–41); T. Strässle, 'Johannes Kreisler im Dialog mit einem "geistreichen Physiker". Zu E. T. A. Hoffmanns Auseinandersetzung mit Johann Wilhelm Ritter' (96–119).

B. Röder, ' "Denn sie lebt nur, wenn sie singt!" The idealization of art and femininity in E. T. A. Hoffmann's *Künstlernovellen*', Kohl, *Words*, 41–53, discusses the role of woman as muse and Romantic ideal in H.'s work. R. focuses on the depiction of woman as an enabling figure whose existence is defined in terms of the needs of the Romantic artist. The feminine is often presented as a synthesis of art and love yet the search for the ideal this represents invariably descends from euphoria into despair as reality supercedes imagination. A. Dunker, 'Die schöne Insulanerin. Kolonialismus in E. T. A. Hoffmanns Südsee-Erzählung *Haimatochere*', *DVLG*, 76:386–402, takes a post-colonial approach to the text, based on Said, to show how H. involves contemporary discourse and cultural expectation but also subverts these through the structure of the narrative. J. Simpson, 'Canny allusions: Der Sandmann as Kontrafaktur', *PEGS(NS)*, 71:37–49, identifies allusions to the work of Goethe, especially *Werther*, with reference to the concept of contrafactur and Harold Bloom's 'anxiety of influence'. S. Haupt, 'Erzählrythmus im Zeichen von Wiederholung, Analogie und "idée fixe". E. T. A. Hoffmann und seine Nachfolger in der französischen, russischen und angloamerikanischen Literatur des 19. Jahrhunderts', *Colloquium Helveticum*, 32:91–121, provides a study of the use of repetition in *Der Sandmann* via Genette and early 19th-c. notions of the 'idée fixe', going on to discuss similar strategies employed by other writers including Poe. E. Horn, 'Die Versuchung des heiligen Serapion. Wirklichkeitsbegriff und Wahnsinn bei E. T. A. Hoffmann', *DVLG*, 76:214–28, looks at H.'s depiction of madness via isolation and its relation to the literary imagination. Issues of madness, perception, and self-invention are discussed in relation to Blumenberg and Foucault.

C. N. Brooks and R. G. Whitinger, 'Olivier's jewel box: a reassessment of the "usual suspects" in Hoffmann's *Das Fräulein von Scuderi*' *JEGP*, 101:68–89, examines the text in the context of the development of the modern murder mystery with the jewel box as the central symbol. The study proposes a series of unreliable narrative strategies and questions previous interpretations which find closure in the text. M. Wigbers, 'Von Paris über "Bramme" in die Eifel. Orte und Schauplätze in kriminalliterarischen Texten von der Romantik bis in die Gegenwart', *WW*, 52:276–92, includes a discussion of the use of location in *Das Fräulein von Scuderi*. Also noted: F. Degler, 'Aisthetische Subversionen des Wissens. Analysen zur Phantastik zwischen *Der goldene Topf* und *Matrix*', *Athenäum*, 12:155–73.

HÖLDERLIN, FRIEDRICH. *Hölderlin Handbuch. Leben — Werk — Wirkung*, ed. Johann Kreuzer, Stuttgart, Metzler, 558 pp., provides a detailed, thematic analysis of H.'s life and work which underlines the centrality of the writer in the context of German and European literature. Various aspects of H. studies are addressed, ranging from the individual editions of his work to recent developments in reception. Individual works are given careful attention with clear contextualization of H.'s development as a thinker and a writer. Particularly valuable is the detailed section on the reception of H.'s work which focuses on individuals such as Heidegger, Benjamin, Adorno, and Szondi, as well as juxtaposing responses in National Socialist and Exile literature, and also West German and GDR approaches to his work. The chronology and bibliography are worthy of praise for their attention to detail. This volume is to be recommended to all scholars of H.'s work but would also provide a valuable resource for anyone with an interest in the history of ideas.

Hans-Georg Pott, *Schiller und Hölderlin. Studien zur Ästhetik und Poetik* (Oppelner Beiträge zur Germanistik, 4), Berne, Lang, 151 pp., brings together a number of essays by the author. H. Bay, '"De revolutionibus." Bahnen und Bahnungen im Werk Hölderlins', *MLN*, 117:599–633, is a fascinating discussion of H.'s notion of the 'exzentrische Bahn' as a means of describing the 'Bildungprozeß'. H.'s work is not seen as a comment on revolution but as result of it, reflecting a desire for a centred existence and closely linked to the poet's experiences during his Tübingen years. M. Behne, 'Kanonisierung, Lebensstil und Selbstdarstellung: Friedrich Hölderlin und der Kanon literarischer Eliten und Avantgarden, mit besonderem Blick auf Oskar Pastior', *TK* (Sonderband 'Literarische Kanonbildung'), 9.2:129–55, is a wide-ranging but rather disjointed essay which examines H.'s place within the canon and the impact of his reception and the exploitation and reappropriation of his work in modern discourse. There is also a discussion of the depiction of H. himself as an outsider figure, as well as an examination of Pastior's reading of H. as language. J. Suglia, 'On the nationalist reconstruction of Hölderlin in the George circle,' *GLL*, 55:387–97, looks at the reception of H. in the early 20th c., especially in relation to Stefan George himself. H. is seen as a prophetic figure who embodies the conditions of modernity in national, sacrificial terms.

Also noted: Fabian Stoermer, **Hermeneutik und Dekonstruktion der Erinnerung. Über Gadamer, Derrida und Hölderlin*, Munich, Fink, 400 pp.; Elena Polledri, *'*. . . immer bestehet ein Maas.' Der Begriff des Maßes in Hölderlins Werk* (Ep, 418), 308 pp.; Silke-Maria Weineck, **The Abyss Above. Philosophy and Poetic Madness in Plato, Hölderlin, and Nietzsche*, NY, SUNY, 224 pp.; Karin Schutjer, **Narrating Community after Kant. Schiller, Goethe, and Hölderlin*, Detroit, Wayne State U.P., 288 pp.; L. Reitani, 'Face to face. Hölderlin in a new Italian bilingual edition', *MLN*, 117:590–98. G. Stiening, 'Entre Fichte et Schiller. La notion de Trieb dans le *Hyperion* de Hölderlin', *RGI*, 18:87–103; F. Breithaupt, 'Warum das Ich Eigentum braucht (Locke, Rousseau, Moritz, Hölderlin)', *Athenäum*, 12:33–68.

KLEIST, HEINRICH VON. Klaus Müller-Salget, *Heinrich von Kleist*, Stuttgart, Reclam, 357 pp., provides a wide-ranging introductory study with a biographical section and thematic discussion of K.'s works with some reference to modern reception on stage and screen. Barbara Gribnitz, *Schwarzes Mädchen, weißer Fremder. Studien zur Konstruktion von 'Rasse' und Geschlecht in Heinrich von Kleists Erzählung Die Verlobung von St. Domingo* (Ep, 408), 222 pp., is described by the author as belonging in the field of Gender Studies but would clearly also fit into the post-colonial debate. After placing K.'s work in the context of contemporary notions of gender and race, G. provides an insightful textual analysis which examines the narrative from female and male perspectives. This is followed by an attempt at contextualization which draws on the work of Sigrid Weigel and Susanne Zantop, referring, amongst others, to *Othello* and the colonial love story. Urs Strässle, *Heinrich von Kleist. Die keilförmige Vernunft* (Ep, 392), 313 pp., focuses on what the author refers to as the modernity of K.'s 'Welthaltung' which, he claims, is manifested in a specifically Kleistian materialism and for which the focal point is K.'s *Kant-Krise*. S. bases his argument on three key interpretative levels. The first of these is biography, where he sees parallels between K.'s *Krise* and the rise of the subjective around the turn of the 18th and 19th cs. The second level is textual, centering on the prevalence of coincidence, metaphor, and physiognomy. The third level is the metalevel of written symbols which are used to create K.'s own universe and which the author links to Foucault.

Kleists Erzählungen und Dramen. Neue Studien, ed. Paul Michael Lützeler and David Pan, Würzburg, Königshausen & Neumann, 263 pp., offers a reassessment of K.'s work and is divided on genre lines. The section devoted to K.'s narrative prose opens with L. Weissberg, '*Michael Kohlhaas* or, the monstrous disorder of the world' (15–23), a somewhat unexpected comparison of M.K.'s life with that of Germanist Benno von Wiese, focusing on the latter's Nazi past. Perhaps more edifying is David Pan, 'The aesthetic foundation of morality in *Das Erdbeben in Chili*' (49–59), which provides a fascinating discussion of the dual perspectives which shadow the moral judgements of both characters and reader. P. juxtaposes the perception of the earthquake as voiced by the narrator and then the *Chorherr*, and also the perception of the protagonists' sexual act and the outcome thereof as voiced again by the narrator and then by the townspeople. In each case, the narrator is seen to sympathize with the young couple whereas the others uphold the established value system which the couple have violated. P. then highlights how events, even the actions of the authorities, are determined by the townspeople's aesthetic interpretation of certain supposedly outrageous occurrences. A further juxtaposition, that of self-sacrifice with self-preservation highlights the fusion of aesthetic and ethical found in Kant's notion of the sublime which P. relates to the sacred in order to show how K. develops Kantian concepts to demonstrate the culture-specific nature of the sacred; L. Raihala, 'Who has control of her life? *Die Marquise von O . . .*' (93–106), discusses notions of displacement, patriarchy, and power, whilst drawing biographical parallels with the 'gender constraints' placed by K. on his own sister. There is also a discussion of Rohmer's film version of the *Novelle*; L. R. Johnson, 'Psychic, corporeal, and temporal displacement in *Die Familie Schroffenstein*' (121–33), referring to Foucault, centres on the problem of displacement via disembodiment and misrecognition and examines issues of knowledge and identity. Also included in the volume are A. Seyhan, 'Moral agency and the play of chance: the ethics of irony in *Der Zweikampf*' (25–34); P. M. Lützeler, 'Verführung und Missionierung. Zu den Exempeln in *Die Verlobung in St. Domingo*' (35–48); L. Tatlock and J. Loewenstein, 'Wer da? The displaced *Bettelweib von Locarno*' (61–76); A. Stephens, 'Stimmengewebe: Antithetik und Verschiebung in *Die heilige Cäcilie oder Die Gewalt der Musik*' (77–92); C. Niekerk, 'Men in pain: disease and displacement in *Der Findling*'(107–20); B. Greiner, ' "Die große Lücke in unserer dermaligen Literatur auszufüllen": Kleists unausführbare Tragödie *Robert Guiskard*' (135–50); E. Fischer-Lichte, 'Mißlingende Inkorporation? Zur rituellen Struktur des *Prinz Friedrich von Homburg*' (151–64); B. Fischer, 'Fremdbestimmung und Identitätspolitik in *Der Hermannschlacht*' (165–78); H.-J. Kreutzer, '*Amphitryon*: Mythos und Drama' (179–90); S. K. Schindler, 'Die blutende Brust der Amazone: bedrohliche weibliche Sexualität in *Penthesilea*' (191–202); H. D. Zimmermann, 'Der Sinn im Wahn: der Wahnsinn. Das "große historische Ritterschauspiel" *Das Käthchen von Heilbronn*'(203–14); N. Müller, ' "Du hast mir deines Angesichtes Züge bewährt." *Der zerbrochene Krug* und die Probe auf den Augenblick' (215–40); T. Hennig and M. Rüsel, 'Kleists virtuelle Welten — ein intermediales Projekt' (241–60).

BKF, 15, 2001, contains a number of studies of individual texts, including M. Hetzner, 'Der Kaufmann als Held. Das Problem der bürgerlichen Identität in Kleists *Michael Kohlhaas*' (69–98); J. Harnischfeger, 'Liebe und Vertrauen in Kleists *Verlobung in St. Domingo*' (99–127); H. Häker, 'Wessen Recht und Ehre? Parabolische Hinweise in Heinrich von Kleists Erzählung *Der Zweikampf*' (129–48); D. Jürgens, ' "...und nach Zusammenraffung einiger Sachen". Kleists *Bettelweib von Locarno*' (149–62). Other contributions include R. Görner, ' "Der einsame Mittelpunkt im einsamen Kreise." Über Kleists Ästhetik' (11–25), which examines the development of K.'s aesthetics from music to the written word, paying particular attention to the relationship between the poetic and the scientific and K.'s troubled relationship with art; A. Steinhilber, ' "O der Verstand! Der unglückselige Verstand!" Zu Heinrich von Kleists Verhältnis zur Musik' (27–45), which explores K.'s understanding of and relationship with music via his letters and his text *Die heilige Cäcilie*, and questions K.'s reputation as a musician. The role of music in religious ritual is discussed and S. points to flaws in K.'s references to music; A. Weigel, ' "Warte zehen Jahre u Du wirst mich nicht ohne Stolz umarmen." Einige Gedanken zu Kleists Würzburger Reise' (47–67), reassesses K.'s Würzburg experience and places his first attempts at drama in this period. W. sees the journey as both a flight and a process of self-discovery which enabled K.'s dramatic talent to develop. This year's *BKF*, 16, contains the proceedings of the 2001 *Frankfurter Kleist-Colloquium*, on the theme 'Kleist — Musik und Literatur in der Romantik'. The interaction of language and music is discussed in M. Durzak, 'Die Wahrheit des Gefühls in der Musik und die Unzulänglichkeit der Sprache bei Kleist' (75–87), and H. Häker, 'Mit der Musik der Rede: zum Wortschatz der Klänge und Töne in Kleists Werken' (89–102). Issues concerning the senses and the body are dealt with in B. Choluj, 'Auf den Körper schauen und hören. Zur Körperproblematik in Heinrich von Kleists *Penthesilea* und *Die Marquise von O...*' (103–16); F. Stoermer, 'Laut und Sinn in der Poetik Heinrich von Kleists' (117–38); S.-M. Weineck, 'Jenseits von Oedipus: Vaterkörper und Vaterschaft in Kleists Erzählungen' (139–54); H. C. Seeba, 'Paukenschlag der Wahrheit: Hören und Sehen in Kleists epistemologischer Poetik' (155–73). Other essays included in the volume are J. Endres, ' "Bonum durch Malum"? Kleist, die Welt und das Übel' (205–18), which focuses on K.'s narrative prose. The issue of misplaced retribution is discussed and K.'s work is seen to reflect the Leibnizian notion of good resulting from and, thus, mollifying evil. E. does not suggest that K.'s thought is wholly in line with Enlightenment ideology; W. G. Schmidt, ' ". . .wie losgelassene Gewitterstürm', am Himmelsplane brausend." Aspekte der Übertretung in Heinrich von Kleists Ossianrezeption' (219–37), is a first attempt to uncover the presence of *Ossian* in K., and incorporates a philological study, including examples such as K.'s use of the 'Eichenbild' and the concepts of 'joy in grief' and the sublime. S. also examines the significance of *O* for K. which represents part of a change in the nature of German literary reception in the period following the *Sturm und Drang*. There are also studies of individual texts: C. S. Grassau, 'Recht und Rache. Eine Betrachtung der inneren Wendepunkte in Kleists *Michael Kohlhaas*' (239–58); T. Friedrich, ' "Ein Scandalum durch Anspielung auf das Mysterium

. . . erklären" — Zur Mariensymbolik in Heinrich von Kleists *Die Marquise von O . . .*' (259–82).

G. Müller, 'Aus eigener Erfahrung hinzugetan: zu Kleists Konzept von Intertextualität "avant la lettre"', *SN*, 74:98–112, looks at the development of K.'s intertextual approach, placing the notion of 'Erfindung' in a literary-historical context. It is claimed, perhaps rather contentiously, that his use of other texts, including classical and scientific works, is before its time. P. Staengle, '"noch ein Blättchen Papier für Dich." Zu Heinrich v. Kleists Brief an Wilhelmine v. Zenge vom 20/21 August 1800', *MLN*, 117:576–83, highlights the problem of the 'letter' as a literary text and a means of communication, when the publication of private material blurs the boundaries between literature and correspondence. This is particularly problematic when it is assumed that private manuscript material is automatically intended for print. K. Ebisch-Burton, '"Wie über alles Gedachte und zu Erdenende lieb ich Dich": Kleist's and Henriette Vogel's *Todeslitanei* as poetic figuration of the beloved — a reassessment of Kleist's feminine credentials', *GLL*, 55:235–47, also focuses on K.'s correspondence, discussing the pre-suicide *Todeslitanei* and its poetic representation of the beloved. V. is seen as the co-author of K.'s last work, which is described as a work of two halves. Reading the text via Cixous, E.-B. argues that V.'s contribution exceeds that of K.

Also noted: Claudia Brors, **Anspruch und Abbruch. Untersuchungen zu Heinrich von Kleists Ästhetik des Rätselhaften* (Ep, 404), 204 pp.; Rüdiger Campe, **Spiel der Wahrscheinlichkeit. Literatur und Berechnung zwischen Pascal und Kleist*, Göttingen, Wallstein, 472 pp.; P. Niebaum, 'Die lateinische Syntax in Heinrich von Kleists Novellenprosa', *Euphorion*, 96:75–92.

MOTTE FOUQUÉ, CAROLINE DE LA. K. Baumgartner, 'Defining national identity: Caroline de la Motte Fouqué responds to Madame de Staël's *De l'Allemagne*', *ColGer*, 35:59–73, discusses F.'s argument for the central role of women in the renewal of the German nation in response to the Napoleonic occupation, in particular within the culture of the salon. B. shows how F. both exploits and takes issue with de S.'s work, using similar strategies of nation-building but questioning the breadth of de S.'s knowledge.

NOVALIS. Martin Schierbaum, *Friedrich von Hardenbergs poetisierte Rhetorik. Politische Ästhetik der Frühromantik*, Paderborn, Schöningh, 594 pp., is a major study which addresses N.'s responses to the failure of the French Revolution and the need for alternative political paradigms. Introducing the notion of 'poetisierte Rhetorik', S. explores N.'s contribution to the contemporary debate surrounding the role of art as a means to overcome political instabilities.

S. provides detailed contextualization of the debate from a number of perspectives including hermeneutic and deconstructionist approaches, before centring his study on key areas of N.'s poetological and philosophical work, in particular, N.'s fragments (including *Allgemeines Brouillion*), the collection *Glauben und Liebe*, and *Die Christenheit oder Europa*. Discussion of the latter text is particularly interesting, highlighting the relationship of anarchy and religion. The study draws together aspects of N.'s work which show a continuous interaction between philosophy, aesthetics, and the artistic process.

T. Wilke, 'Poetiken der idealen und der möglichen Sprache. Zu den intertextuellen Bezügen zwischen Novalis "Monolog" und Hofmannsthals "Chandos-Brief"', *ZDP*, 121:248–64, looks, via detailed textual analysis, at the relationship between language and reality, the subject and poetry, and argues that H.'s text is based on a transformation of N.'s concept of language and poetry.

J. M. Baker, Jr., 'Bipolarity in Novalis' critique of the Christian religion', *ERR*, 13:215–22, discusses the religiosity of N.'s work, juxtaposing the interpretations of Karl Barth and William O'Brien. According to B., N.'s work needs to be seen in the context of 'negative theology'. The underlying dynamic juxtaposes the bipolarity of totality with a concentrated centre. Also noted: H. J. Hahn, ' "Einem gelang es . . ." Die Grammatik der Natur in Novalis' *Die Lehrlinge zu Sais*', *Words*, 55–68.

RICHTER, JEAN PAUL. Ralf Berhorst, *Anamorphosen der Zeit. Jean Pauls Romanästhetik und Geschichtsphilosophie* (SDL, 162), 430 pp., discusses the interaction of literature and history in R.'s work, focusing on three texts, *Hesperus*, *Titan*, and *Die Flegeljahre*. B. argues that these texts are not lacking structure, as has often been suggested, but are, rather, indicative of R.'s notion of history as an 'unvollendeter Roman'. The study discusses issues of progress and completion and highlights the perpetual nature of art, the soul, and history. There is also an interesting discussion of R.'s reception and critique of contemporary thought, especially Herder.

Schrift- und Schreibspiele. Jean Pauls Arbeit am Text, ed. Geneviève Espagne and Christian Helmreich, Würzburg, Königshausen & Neumann, 123 pp., contains essays which discuss R.'s creative *modus operandi*. The development of individual texts is examined in J. Golz, 'Die Fassungen der *Unsichtbaren Loge*. Blicke in die Werkstatt' (11–27), and E. Dangel-Pelloquin, 'Proliferation und Verdichtung. Zwei Fassungen des *Siebenkäs*' (29–41). Intra- and intertextual methods are examined in G. Espagne, 'Jean Pauls *Palingenesien*, oder: Hat das Schreibspiel ein Ende?' (43–58), and H. Esselborn, 'Intertextualität und Selbstbehauptung des Autors in Jean Pauls Werken' (59–79). Other studies included are: E. Spedicato, 'Jean Pauls und Carlo

Emilio Gaddas Werkstatt des humoristisch-witzigen Stils' (81–98), and C. Helmreich, '"Einschiebeessen in meinen biographischen petits soupers." Jean Pauls Exkurse und ihre handschriftlichen Vorformen' (99–122).

C. J. Minter, 'Jean Paul and women's anthropology', *FMLS*, 38:315–25, places R.'s view of women in its contemporary context and identifies a dual emphasis which juxtaposes a negative satirical depiction with the more positive characterization found in his sentimental writings. This is particularly marked in the novel *Titan* and the central female character Princess Idione. B. Menke, 'Jean Pauls Witz. Kraft und Formel', *DVLG*, 76:201–13, looks at R.'s definition of wit as a witticism. Also noted: D. Peyrache-Leborgne, 'Paradis mélancoliques de Jean Paul à Edgar Poe', *Romantisme*, 117.3:13–29.; R. Luckscheiter, *'Die Sprache des Chaos und der Geist der Emanzipation. Jean Paul und Joseph Görres in der französischen Rezeption zwischen 1830 und 1860', *JDSG*, 184–98.

RUNGE, PHILLIP OTTO. Noted: J. J. K. Reusch, 'Child advocacy and pedagogical theories in the works of Phillip Otto Runge', *GSR*, 25:79–100.

SCHELLING, FRIEDRICH WILHELM JOSEPH VON. *Clara or, On Nature's Connection to the Spirit World*, ed. and trans. Fiona Steinkamp, NY, SUNY, 116 pp., provides a detailed introduction and the first English translation of S.'s philosophical novel fragment. Steinkamp provides evidence to revise the dating of the text to 1810 and elaborates upon a number of biographical issues which feed into the work. The identity of Clara is also discussed and parallels are drawn with examples from S.'s personal correspondence. Id., 'Schelling's *Clara* — editor's obscurity', *JEGP*, 101:478–96, looks at the editorial and publication history of S.'s text and the difficulties in assessing the order and content of a fragmentary work.

SCHLEGEL, AUGUST WILHELM. Dorota Masiakowska, *Vielfalt und Einheit im Europabild August Wilhelm Schlegels* (EH, 1, 1846), 276 pp., discusses S.'s approach to the notion of Europe as part of a reaction to French hegemony. M. examines his work on the cultures of the so-called 'Hauptnationen' or peoples of Europe: the Germans, French, Italians, Spanish, and Portuguese. The variety this suggests is then juxtaposed with S.'s notion of European unity, centred on an apotheosis of the culture and thought of the Middle Ages, the French contribution to which being notably underplayed. M. also examines S.'s subsequent turn towards oriental studies. Also noted: C. Couturier-Heinrich, '"Tendence naturelle au rythme" et "observation instinctive de la mesure": l'inscription du rythme dans le domaine du spontané chez Johann Georg Sulzer et August Wilhelm Schlegel', *RGI*, 18:53–70.

SCHLEGEL, DOROTHEA. S. Worley, 'Ethical aesthetics and the immutable model in Friedrich Schiller's *On the Aesthetic Education of Man* and Dorothea Schlegel's *Florentin*', *NGR*, 17: 107–38, looks at how D.S.'s work parallels S.'s text in advocating the role of art as a mediating force between reason and emotion, thus ensuring a stable social structure.

SCHLEGEL, FRIEDRICH. There are two major studies of the role of irony in S.'s work. Ute Maack, *Ironie und Autorschaft. Zu Friedrich Schlegels Charakteristiken*, Paderborn, Schöningh, 251 pp., explores the notion of incomprehensibility in the work of the *Frühromantiker* and discusses the role which irony plays in achieving this as a central element in all forms of verbal communication and comprehension. M. examines the interplay between opposites used to create uncertainty and irony in S.'s work, focusing on his essay 'Über die Unverständlichkeit' and the three 'Charakteristiken': 'Georg Forster', 'Über Lessing', and 'Über Goethes Meister'. M. suggests the 'Meister' essay as the scenario for S.'s 'Abschied von der Ironie'. The argument is taken up by Matthias Schöning, *Ironieverzicht. Friedrich Schlegels theoretische Konzepte zwischen Athenäum und Philosophie des Lebens*, Paderborn, Schöningh, 362 pp., which examines the development of S.'s approaches to irony from the Jena years through to his later works. He is seen to turn away from irony as a theoretical concept, only to return to it from a different angle in later life. Whereas the irony of the *Frühromantik* tends towards the notion of an abstract absolute, the later 'Ironie der Liebe' bears a direct relation to God, the former is seen to be horizontal and symmetrical in structure, whereas the latter is vertical and asymmetrical. S.'s work is also discussed in the context of the current debate on irony. B. Rehme-Iffert, 'Friedrich Schlegel über Emanzipation, Liebe und Ehe', *Athenäum*, 12: 111–32, highlights S.'s progressive views relating to women's abilities, rights, and education which contrast with those espoused by many other writers of the period. S. sees the need for women to achieve a level of completeness and promotes a vision of marriage which encapsulates the seemingly incongruous notions of idealization and emancipation.

SCHOPENHAUER, JOHANNA. C. Brewer, 'Resignation and rebellion: the dual narrative of Johanna Schopenhauer's *Gabriele*', *GQ*, 75: 181–195, identifies two levels of narrative in S.'s text, one seeming to depict social resignation, the other subverting social structures. The latter is carried by a series of contradictions and inconsistencies which show G. in defiance of patriarchy. Her rebellion is, however, quashed by the demands of social propriety.

TIECK, LUDWIG. Martina Schwarz, *Die bürgerliche Familie im Spätwerk Ludwig Tiecks. 'Familie' als Medium der Zeitkritik* (Ep, 403), 315 pp., examines T.'s often neglected later works, *Der Aufruhr in den*

Cevennen, *Der junge Tischlermeister*, and *Vittoria Accorombona*, and relates his depiction of the family to changes in the function and perception of the family unit through the 19th century. The interaction of individual and family in T.'s texts is seen to reflect and comment upon wider sociological trends and parallels are drawn between the family as microcosm and the state as macrocosm. The emerging bourgeois ideal is confirmed as an aspirational goal. H. R. Brittnacher, 'Die Zeit des Zauberschlafs. Ein Motiv romantischer Erzählkunst bei Ludwig Tieck und Washington Irving', *Athenäum*, 12:133–54, focuses on T.'s *Die Elfen* and I.'s *Rip van Winkle*, both of which employ the motif of enchanted sleep. B. then examines the ideal of childhood in Romantic literature, especially the *Kunstmärchen* and discusses T.'s rather pessimistic depiction of society.

VARNHAGEN, RAHEL LEVIN. Luisa Callejón Callejón, *Briefliche Momentbilder. Lektüren zur Korrespondenz zwischen Rahel Levin Varnhagen und Pauline Wiesel* (Berliner Beiträge zur Germanistik, 2), Berlin, Saint Albin, 234 pp., seeks to interpret the correspondence, described in terms of Heine's notion of 'Hieroglyphen', as texts bound by the concepts of their time but nevertheless imbued with a degree of modernity. Certain leitmotifs and metaphors are identified. The sensuality of sight as a cipher for happiness and love is discussed in relation to Kierkegaard and Goethe, whereas the recurrence of conceptual references to the colour green emerge as a metaphor for freedom and are linked to townscape and nature alike. Finally the relation between human behaviour and emotion and the weather is explored. Also noted: Claudia Christophersen, *'. . .*es ist mit dem Leben etwas gemeint'. Hannah Arendt über Rahel Varnhagen*, Königstein/Ts, Ulrike Helmer, 300 pp.

LITERATURE, 1830–1880

By BARBARA BURNS, *Lecturer in German, University of Strathclyde*

I. GENERAL

REFERENCE WORKS AND GENERAL STUDIES. *Handbuch österreichischer Autorinnen und Autoren jüdischer Herkunft 18. bis 20. Jahrhundert*, ed. Susanne Blumesberger et al., 3 vols, Munich, Saur, 1818 pp., contains some 8,000 compact but informative entries on authors and other figures from the world of journalism, science, and culture. Each biography is supplemented by a useful section containing abbreviated references to source materials, thus facilitating further research. The work is a considerable achievement which will be welcomed by scholars from a range of disciplines. *Harmony in Discord. German Women Writers in the Eighteenth and Nineteenth Centuries*, ed. Laura Martin, Oxford–Berne, Lang, 266 pp., offers fresh insights into the works of 11 women writers, all non-canonical with the exception of Droste-Hülshoff, and is a stimulating contribution to the ongoing reassessment of the literary achievement of women. Of particular interest for our period are: S. Colvin, '"Ein Bildungsmittel ohnegleichen": Marie von Ebner-Eschenbach and the theatre' (161–82); A. Webber, 'Traumatic identities: race and gender in Annette von Droste-Hülshoff's *Die Judenbuche* and Freud's *Der Mann Moses*' (185–205); C. Tully, 'Droste on the Costa? Cecilia Böhl von Faber: a parallel life' (239–60).

THEMES. Elke Richlick, *Zwerge und Kleingestaltige in der Kinder- und Jugendliteratur vom Beginn des 19. Jahrhunderts bis zur Gegenwart*, Frankfurt–Berlin, Lang, 295 pp., is a Bielefeld dissertation which makes reference to an impressive range of some 1000 primary texts. The disadvantage of such a broad base, however, is that individual works are not examined in any detail. Moreover the absence of an index, combined with the fact that the sections are arranged thematically rather than chronologically, makes it difficult to locate specifically 19th-c. material. After an opening chapter tracing the descent of the dwarf-figure through a range of genres from myth to *Märchen*, the remainder of the book is devoted to an analysis of over 50 different 'roles' of dwarfs in literature from 'smith' to 'environmentalist'. Gabrielle Gross, *Der Neid der Mutter auf die Tochter. Ein weibliches Konfliktfeld bei Fontane, Schnitzler, Keyserling und Thomas Mann*, Berne–Berlin, Lang, 245 pp., is a Zurich dissertation which approaches the topic from the perspective of psychoanalysis. The lengthy theoretical introduction, reinforced by a bibliography containing 48 different publications by Freud alone, leave the reader in no doubt as to the line of the investigation. A solid section on Fontane is divided into separate chapters on *Effi Briest*, *Mathilde Möhring*, and *Schach von Wuthenow*, in which the analysis is at times predictable and heavy-handed, but can also be thought-provoking. One wonders, however, whether the consistent mis-spelling of the important name 'Innstetten' is indicative of a more general carelessness with respect to the primary texts. Dorothee Kimmich, *Wirklichkeit als Konstruktion: Studien zu Geschichte und Geschichtlichkeit bei Heine, Büchner, Immermann, Stendhal, Keller und Flaubert*, Munich, Fink, 345 pp., is a Giessen 'Habilitationsschrift'. This is a scholarly and innovative study which draws on the work of a range of English, French, and German writers in an exploration of the complex and controversial relationship between history and literature. An impressive bibliography testifies to the prodigious research underlying this volume which, in addition to the writers listed in the title, also refers to Burckhardt, Gutzkow, Laube, and Nietzsche, among others. Volker Mergenthaler, *Sehen schreiben — Schreiben sehen: Literatur und visuelle Wahrnehmung im Zusammenspiel*, Tübingen, Niemeyer, vi + 438 pp., is a Tübingen dissertation which includes analysis of Büchner's *Leonce und Lena* and Raabe's *Die Chronik der Sperlingsgasse*. Ursula Hassel, *Familie als Drama. Studien zu einer Thematik im bürgerlichen Trauerspiel, Wiener Volkstheater und kritischen Volksstück*, Bielefeld, Aisthesis, 403 pp., is a Bonn dissertation which refers to works by Wagner and Hebbel and includes a central section on Raimund and Nestroy. Ingrid Spörk, *Liebe und Verfall. Familiengeschichten und Liebesdiskurse in Realismus und Spätrealismus*, Würzburg, Königshausen & Neumann, 2000, 271 pp., is a Graz dissertation which examines works by A. Christen, M. von Ebner-Eschenbach, K. E. Franzos, F. Kürnberger, and L. and W. von Sacher-Masoch among others. Thomas C. Müller, **Der Schmuggel politischer Schriften. Bedingungen exilliterarischer Öffentlichkeit in der Schweiz und im Deutschen Bund (1830–1848)*, Tübingen, Niemeyer, 2001, ix + 471 pp., is a Zurich dissertation. Berit Pleitner, *Die 'vernünftige' Nation. Zur Funktion von Stereotypen über Polen und Franzosen im deutschen nationalen Diskurs 1850 bis 1871*, Frankfurt–Berlin, Lang, 472 pp., is an Oldenburg dissertation. Anne-Rose Meyer, *Jenseits der Norm. Aspekte der Bohèmedarstellung in der französischen und deutschen Literatur 1830–1910*, Bielefeld, Aisthesis, 379 pp., is a Bonn dissertation. Uwe Hentschel, *Mythos Schweiz: Zum deutschen literarischen Philhelvetismus zwischen 1700 und 1850*, Tübingen, Niemeyer, 424 pp., draws on over 500 literary and journalistic texts in a comprehensive and illuminating investigation of German enthusiasm for Switzerland. Much of the study falls outside our period, but the chapter entitled 'Apotheosen und neue Klischees nach 1815' (275–328) is substantial in its own right and examines the 19th-c. image of the Alps as a wholesome and restorative travel destination, and the function of narrative fiction in shaping this stereotype. Jefferson Chase, *Inciting Laughter. The Development of 'Jewish Humour' in 19th-century German Culture*, Berlin, de Gruyter, 2000, viii + 330 pp., investigates Moritz Gottlieb Saphir, Ludwig Börne, and Heinrich Heine.

K. Tebben, 'Selbstmörderinnen in der deutschen Literatur des 19. und 20. Jahrhunderts: zur poetologischen Signifikanz ihrer Todesarten', *CGS*, 35:1–25, discusses Hebbel's *Maria Magdalena*, Storm's *Auf der Universität* and Fontane's *Cécile* among others. A. Linke, 'Sich das Leben erschreiben: zur sprachlichen Rolleninszenierung bürgerlicher Frauen des 19. Jahrhunderts im Medium des Tagebuchs', Davies, *Autobiography*, 105–29. S. Simon, '"Fern-Sehen" und "Fern-Hören". Zur Wahrnehmung von musikbegleiteten Bilderreisen im 19. Jahrhundert', pp. 255–69 of *Wahrnehmung und Medialität*, ed. Erika Fischer-Lichte, Tübingen, Francke, 2001, 431 pp. T. Stöber, 'Die Ostentation des Todes. Epistemologisches Apriori und kulturelles Gedächtnis in Todesrepräsentationen des 19. Jahrhunderts', pp. 131–48 of *Topographie der Erinnerung. Mythos im strukturellen Wandel*, ed. Bettina von Jagow, Würzburg, Königshausen & Neumann, 2000, 264 pp. J. Skolnik, 'Writing Jewish history in the margins of the Weimar classics: minority culture and national identity in Germany, 1837–1873', Vazsonyi, *Searching*, 227–38. I. Schikorsky, 'Briefe aus dem Krieg. Zur Schreibpraxis kleiner Leute im 19. Jahrhundert', pp. 451–65 of *Lesen und Schreiben in Europa 1500–1900. Vergleichende Perspektiven*, ed. Alfred Messerli and Roger Chartier, Basle, Schwabe, 2000, 652 pp. K. Eibl, 'Darwin, Haeckel, Nietzsche. Der idealistisch gefilterte Darwin in der deutschen Dichtung und Poetologie des 19. Jahrhunderts. Mit einer Hypothese zum biologischen Ursprung der Kunst', pp. 87–108 of *Fritz Mauthner — Sprache, Literatur, Kritik. Festakt und Symposion zu seinem 150. Geburtstag*, ed. Helmut Henne and Christine Kaiser, Tübingen, Niemeyer, 2000, viii + 185 pp. G. Frank, '*Crime and sex*. Zur Vor- und Frühgeschichte der "Sexualität"', *FVF*, 5, 1999:11–35. H. Krah, 'Freundschaft oder Männerliebe? Heinrich Hösslis *Eros. Die Männerliebe der Griechen; ihre Beziehungen zur Geschichte, Erziehung, Literatur und Gesetzgebung aller Zeiten* (1836/38) im diskursgeschichtlichen Kontext', *ib.*, 185–221.

LYRIC. U. Gaier, 'Die historischen Balladen der schwäbischen Schule', Woesler, *Ballade*, 35–62. W. Hinck, 'Geschichte im Gegenlicht. Zur historischen Ballade der Droste, Heines und Fontanes', *ib.*, 82–99. E. Mai, 'Bild-Geschichten und Balladen. Die literarische Historienmalerei der Düsseldorfer und Hermann F. Plüddemanns', *ib.*, 156–79.

NARRATIVE PROSE. Hiltrud Gnüg, *Der erotische Roman: von der Renaissance bis zur Gegenwart*, Stuttgart, Reclam, 422 pp., includes analysis of Fontane's *L'Adultera* and *Effi Briest*, examining them alongside Flaubert's *Madame Bovary* and Tolstoy's *Anna Karenina* in the context of the late-19th-c. novel of adultery. The book serves a useful purpose in contextualizing these important works, but the treatment of individual texts is rather pedestrian. M. P. Davies, 'Laughing their heads off: nineteenth-century comic versions of the Bluebeard tale', *GLL*, 55:329–47, examines texts by Franz von Pocci, Alexander von Sternberg, F. W. Hackländer, and Roderich Benedix. K. Guthke, 'Der Kanon und die weite Welt. Das außereuropäisch Fremde in der deutschsprachigen erzählenden Literatur des 19. Jahrhunderts', *JDF*, 27, 2001:15–70. H. Hillmann, 'Romantische Erweiterung und realistische Reduktion der Künstlervita in Deutschland', pp. 135–52 of *Der europäische Entwicklungsroman in Europa und Übersee. Literarische Lebensentwürfe der Neuzeit*, ed. Heina Hillmann and Peter Hühn, Darmstadt, WBG, 2001, 301 pp., includes material on Keller. W. Lukas, '"Weiblicher" Bürger vs. "männliche" Aristokratin. Der Konflikt der Geschlechter und der Stände in der Erzählliteratur des Vor- und Nachmärz', *FVF*, 5, 1999:223–60.

DRAMA. Hutchinson, *Landmarks*, offers 14 compact and well written analyses by British scholars of seminal German dramas from the 18th to the 20th c. The collection will be of value to students and academics alike, for the individual contributions combine an informative digest of received knowledge on the texts with thought-provoking fresh perspectives. Two chapters fall within our period: A. Webber, 'Büchner, *Woyzeck*' (95–110), and W. E. Yates, 'Grillparzer, *Die Jüdin von Toledo*' (111–25). *From Perinet to Jelinek. Viennese Theatre in its Political and Intellectual Context*, ed. W. E. Yates et al., Oxford–Berne, Lang, 290 pp., is another welcome addition to academic libraries, consisting of 20 very readable articles prefaced by a historical introduction. The various contributions explore aspects of the political and intellectual developments that influenced the last 200 years of theatre in Vienna. The following are relevant to our period: I. F. Roe, 'The reception of Raimund's *Moisasurs Zauberfluch*' (35–49); H. Höller, 'Zur Rhetorik des Sensualismus in Grillparzers Dramen' (51–62); B. Pargner, 'Charlotte Birch-Pfeiffer und das kommerzielle Theater im Wien des 19. Jahrhunderts' (63–78); F. J. Lamport, 'History, myth and psychology in *Libussa* and *Die Nibelungen*' (79–90); R. Vilain, 'The sublime and the ridiculous: dramatic Wagner parodies' (103–14); W. E. Yates, 'The rise and fall of the one-act play' (115–26). *Theaterverhältnisse im Vormärz*, ed. Maria Porrmann and Florian Vassen, Bielefeld, Aisthesis, 383 pp., has: M. Porrmann and F. Vassen, 'Vorwort — "Doch die Verhältnisse, sie sind nicht so!" Theaterverhältnisse im Vormärz' (13–24); J. Wiesel, 'Zum Verhältnis von Theater und Staat im Vormärz. Heinrich Theodor Rötscher und der Chor' (25–41); H. Zielske, 'Zwischen monarchischer Idee und Urbanität. Hoftheater und Stadttheater im Vormärz' (43–69); B. Pargner, 'Das Münchner Theater im Vormärz' (71–97); M. Giesing, 'Das Ritterschloß auf der Westseite, oder: Der Hamburger Theaterstreit' (99–137); H.-P. Bayerdörfer, '"Lokalformel" und "Bürgerpatent". Ausgrenzung und Zugehörigkeit in der Posse zwischen 1815 und 1860' (139–73); E. Pluta, 'Komödienstoffe zu vermieten. Vom Vaudeville zur Gesellschaftssatire: Metamorphosen eines französischen Sing-Spiels im deutschen Theater des Vormärz' (175–96); B. Kortländer, '". . . was gut ist in der deutschen Literatur, das ist langweilig und das Kurzweilige ist schlecht." Adaptionen französischer Lustspiele im Vormärz. Anmerkungen zu einem unübersichtlichen Thema' (197–211); W. Beutin, '"Der Weg führt vom Leben zur Bühne." Ludwig Börnes *Dramaturgische Blätter* (1829)' (213–41); P. Hartmann, 'Das "dramatische" Ende des Jungen Deutschland' (243–68); F. Reininghaus, 'Die Opern im Vormärz — Vormärz in den Opern. Das deutsche Musiktheater 1830–1848' (269–301).

MOVEMENTS AND PERIODS. *Zwischen Goethezeit und Realismus. Wandel und Spezifik in der Phase des Biedermeier*, ed. Michael Titzmann, Tübingen, Niemeyer, 505 pp., is a valuable contribution to scholarship on the Biedermeier period, covering a wide range of authors and providing an important dimension of historical and cultural context. The individual articles are of a high standard and offer much to interest the 19th-c. specialist. The volume contains: M. Titzmann, 'Zur Einleitung: "Biedermeier" — ein literarhistorischer Problemfall' (1–7); H. Thomé, 'Platens *Venedig-Sonette* im Hinblick auf die *Römischen Elegien* Goethes. Überlegungen zum historischen Ort des "Biedermeier-Ästhetizismus"' (11–38); M. Lindner, '"Noch einmal": das tiefenpsychologische und künstlerische Konservieren der Erinnerung an den "Liebesfrühling" in Liebeslyrik-Zyklen 1820 bis 1860' (39–77); C. Begemann, 'Kunst und Liebe. Ein ästhetisches Produktionsmythologem zwischen Klassik und Realismus' (79–112); W. Lukas, '"Entsagung" — Konstanz und Wandel eines Motivs in der Erzählliteratur von der späten Goethezeit zum frühen Realismus' (113–49); H. Krah, 'Zur Neustrukturierung bestehender Kategorien im Drama: Temporalisierung, Mediatisierung und Pathologisierung von "Wissen" am Ende der Goethezeit' (151–82), which deals with Grabbe and Grillparzer; J. Osinski, 'Katholische Restauration und "Biedermeier": Ästhetik, Religion und Politik in spätromantischen Harmoniemodellen. Sieben Thesen' (183–95), which has reference to Droste, Stifter, and Grillparzer; J. Link, 'Zum Anteil der Normalität an der Bifurkation Romantik vs "Biedermeier"' (197–211); U. Köster, 'Marktorientierung und Wertkonservatismus' (215–36), which examines Hauff, Gutzkow, and Heine; I. Sagmo, 'Nach Norwegen! Zur politischen Reiseberichterstattung und Publizistik der Biedermeierepoche' (237–47); D. Volkert, '"Wenn ich von meiner Freundin schriftliche Ergüsse ihrer Liebe erhalte." Konstruktionsmechanismen von Briefen und ihre Funktionalisierung für Brieftexte um 1830' (249–68); M. Wünsch, 'Struktur der "dargestellten Welt" und narrativer Prozeß in erzählenden "Metatexten" des "Biedermeier"' (269–82), which has analysis of Gutzkow, Immermann, and Stifter; H. Laufhütte, 'Annette von Droste-Hülshoffs Novelle *Die Judenbuche* als Werk des Realismus' (285–303); H.-P. Ecker, 'Versicherungsdiskurse. Zivilisationstheoretisch motivierte Institutionsanalysen zur Dorfliteratur des 19. Jahrhunderts' (305–30); J. Schönert, 'Berthold Auerbachs *Schwarzwälder Dorfgeschichten* der 40er und der 50er Jahre als Beispiel eines "literarischen Wandels"?' (331–45); C.-M. Ort, 'Roman des "Nebeneinander" — Roman des "Nacheinander". Kohärenzprobleme im Geschichtsroman des 19. Jahrhunderts und ihr Funktionswandel' (347–75), which focuses mainly on Freytag's *Die Ahnen*; V. Hoffmann, 'Der Konflikt zwischen anthropologischer Extremisierung und Harmonisierung in der Literatur vor und nach 1848' (377–91); T. Anz, 'Das Poetische und das Pathologische. Umwertungskriterien im programmatischen Realismus' (393–407); G. Frank, 'Der "Mythos vom Matriarchat" als realistische Reaktion auf Experimente des Biedermeier bei Bachofen, Gutzkow, Hebbel, Wagner und anderen' (409–39); M. Titzmann, '"Natur" vs "Kultur": Kellers *Romeo und Julia auf dem Dorfe* im Kontext der Konstituierung des frühen Realismus' (441–80); R. Baasner, 'Der Blick auf die Väter. Literarische Traditionsbildung und Abgrenzung aus der Perspektive des realistischen Paradigmas' (481–95).

Briefkultur im Vormärz, ed. Bernd Füllner, Bielefeld, Aisthesis, 2001, 266 pp., has: G. Werth, '"Gedanken über das Briefeschreiben." Ein Fragment' (11–15); O. Briese, 'Auf Leben und Tod. *Briefwelt* als Gegenwelt' (19–39); W. Bunzel, 'Ver-Öffentlichung des Privaten. Typen und Funktionen epistolarischen Schreibens bei Bettine von Arnim' (41–96); J. Nickel, 'Zur Figur biblischen Sprechens in Heinrich Heines *Briefen aus Helgoland*' (97–122); B. Füllner, "An den Früchten sollt ihr sie erkennen." Literarische Dialoge in Georg Weerths Briefwechsel mit der Mutter (1843–1846)' (123–52); M. Friedrich, 'Der Briefwechsel zwischen Friedrich Wilhelm IV von Preußen und Christian Carl Joaias von Bunsen' (153–62); J. A. Kruse, 'Heines Briefe. Literarische Qualität und historisch-biographische Quelle' (165–77); B. Kortländer, 'Probleme einer Edition der Briefe des Jungdeutschen Heinrich Laube' (179–94); U. Promies, 'Probleme einer Gutzkow-Briefedition' (195–218);

I. Pepperle, 'Probleme und Proben einer Herwegh-Briefedition' (219–44); V. Giel, 'Ferdinand Freiligraths Korrespondenzen. Bestandsaufnahme und Plädoyer für eine Neuedition des Briefwerks in einer Kombination von Print- und Online-Ausgabe' (245–66).

W. Albrecht, 'Wegweiser zu neuer Poesie? Ästhetische Kriterien politisierter deutscher Literaturkritik um 1850', *FVF*, 6, 2000: 23–47. F. Foerster, 'Der Gesandte Bunsen — zum Briefnachlaß eines Vormärz-Politikers. Forschungsbericht über eine Biographie', *ib.*, 291–302. M. Friedrich, 'Sozialer Protestantismus im Vormärz', *ib.*, 303–07. L. Vanchena, 'The Rhine crisis of 1840: *Rheinlieder*, German nationalism, and the masses', Vazsonyi, *Searching*, 239–51. S. Herrenkind, 'Die Frankfurter Oberpostamtszeitung im Revolutionsjahr 1848', *AGB*, 54, 2001: 171–218.

LITERARY LIFE, JOURNALS, AND SOCIETIES. Angela Koch, *Druckbilder. Stereotype und Geschlechtercodes in den antipolnischen Diskursen der 'Gartenlaube' (1870–1930)*, Cologne–Weimar, Böhlau, 367 pp., is a thorough and revealing study of the anti-Polish attitudes, couched in sexually-coded stereotypes, which were promulgated by this influential middle-class periodical. A useful introduction traces the history of German relations with Poland in the 19th c. and documents the developing political ideology of the *Gartenlaube*. Of primary interest to readers of this section is the first of four main chapters, entitled 'Die Sprache der Dominanz im Deutschen Kaiserreich' (49–136), which examines the pejorative use of 'feminine' characteristics in representations both of the people and the land itself. Randall P. Donaldson, *The Literary Legacy of a 'Poor Devil'. The Life and Work of Robert Reitzel (1849–1898)*, NY–Washington, Lang, 244 pp., focuses on the editor of *Der arme Teufel*, which was a weekly journal in Detroit, Michigan. Although the style of this work is not rigorously academic, it nonetheless offers an engaging account of the aesthetic purpose and achievement of this charismatic writer, orator, and literary critic as well as recalling a vibrant aspect of German culture in late 19th-c. America. The study highlights Reitzel's wit and idiosyncrasy, his use of the journal to express his own unorthodox views on diverse social and political issues, and his attempts to popularize great works of German literature. An appendix contains five of his own prose compositions published in the journal. C. A. Bernd, 'Politik, Religion und Ästhetik in der deutschsprachigen Welt des 19. Jahrhunderts. Zum literaturkritischen Programm Julian Schmidts', *Fest. Bender*, 295–306. G. Mosl, 'Politisches Zeitgeschehen im "Börsenblatt" (1866 bis 1890)', *Buchhandelsgeschichte*, 2000: 17–27.

REGIONAL LITERATURE. M. Rajch, 'Preußische Zensurpolitik und Zensurpraxis in der Provinz Posen 1848/49 bis 1918', *AGB*, 56: 1–77. R. Charbon, 'Kein "Rückzug in die Innerlichkeit". Demokratische

Tendenzen in der deutschsprachigen Literatur nach 1848', *IASL*, 26, 2001 : 158–72. *Literatur in Westfalen*, ed. Walter Gödden (Beiträge der Forschung 6), Bielefeld, Aisthesis, 428 pp., includes material on Droste-Hülshoff, Grabbe, and Weerth.

2. Individual Authors

AUERBACH. K. R. Sazaki, 'B. A.'s *Deutscher Volks-Kalender*: editing as political agenda', *GLL*, 55 : 41–60.

BÜCHNER. *Georg Büchner und die Moderne. Texte, Analysen, Kommentar*, ed. Dietmar Goltschnigg, Berlin, Schmidt, has added vol. 2, *1945–1980*, 647 pp., an impressive study documenting the range of approaches to B. in East and West Germany after the war. A third volume is to follow. *'Friede den Hütten! Krieg den Palästen!' G. B.*, ed. Hanjo Kesting, Hamburg, Nautilus, 126 pp., is a commentary on B.'s letters and *Der hessische Landbote. G. B.: Woyzeck*, ed. Georg Patzer (Lektüre easy), Stuttgart–Düsseldorf, Klett, 64 pp. *G. B.: Leonce und Lena*, ed. Wilhelm Grosse (Reclams U.-B., Lektüreschlüssel für Schüler, 15319), Stuttgart, Reclam, 94 pp. *Erläuterungen zu G. B.: Leonce und Lena*, ed. Rüdiger Bernhardt, Hollfeld, Bange, 104 pp. Konrad Kirsch, **Vom Autor zum Autosalvator: G. Bs 'Lenz'*, Sulzbach, Kirsch, 2001, 68 pp. B. Faber, 'B. und Kierkegaard — eine Wahlverwandtschaft?', *DVLG*, 76 : 403–45. H. Müller, 'Geschichte, Allegorie, historisches Drama. Sieben Notizen zu G. B., Peter Weiss und Heiner Müller', *GR*, 77 : 117–27, has analysis of *Dantons Tod*. W. C. Reeve, 'G. B. as a Huxleyan negative visionary', *Fest. Gaede*, 187–200.

BURCKHARDT. J. B., *Werke. Kritische Gesamtausgabe*, ed. J.-B.-Stiftung, Munich, Beck — Basle, Schwabe, has added vol. 2, *Der Cicerone: Eine Anleitung zum Genuss der Kunstwerke Italiens. Architektur und Sculptur*, ed. Bernd Roeck et al., 2001, 827 pp.; vol. 3, *Der Cicerone: Eine Anleitung zum Genuss der Kunstwerke Italiens. Malerei*, ed. Bernd Roeck et al., 2001, 504 pp.; vol. 5, *Die Baukunst der Renaissance in Italien: nach der Erstausgabe der 'Geschichte der Renaissance in Italien'*, ed. Maurizio Ghelardi, 2000, 532 pp.; vol. 19, *Griechische Culturgeschichte* I: *Die Griechen und ihr Mythus — Die Polis*, ed. Leonhard Burckhardt et al., 636 pp.; vol. 21, *Griechische Culturgeschichte* III: *Die bildende Kunst — Die Poesie — Zur Philosophie und Wissenschaft*, ed. Leonhard Burckhardt et al., 897 pp. Stefan Bauer, *Polisbild und Demokratieverständnis in J. Bs 'Griechischer Kulturgeschichte'*, Basle, Schwabe, 2001, 271 pp. I. Eltink, 'Der Sulzbacher J. B. und die *Respublica Litteraria*. Ein Gelehrtenleben zwischen Ideal und Wirklichkeit', *Morgen-Glantz*, 11, 2001 : 289–315.

BUSCH. S. Grosse, 'Interdialektale Beobachtungen an deutschen Mundartübersetzungen von W. Bs "Max und Moritz" ', pp. 133–46 of *Sprachgeschichte, Dialektologie, Onomastik, Volkskunde*, ed. Rudolf Bentzinger, Stuttgart, Steiner, 2001, 358 pp.

DAHN, FELIX. S. Lodato, 'Problems in song cycle analysis and the case of *Mädchenblumen*', Bernhart, *Song Cycle*, 103–20.

DROSTE-HÜLSHOFF. *Transformationen. Texte und Kontexte zum Abschluss der Historisch-kritischen D.-Ausgabe*, ed. Ortrun Niethammer, Bielefeld, Aisthesis, 263 pp., presents the proceedings of a conference in Münster in 2001 to celebrate the completion of the HKA of A. v. D.-H.'s *Werke, Briefwechsel*, 14 vols in 28, ed. Winfried Woesler, Tübingen, Niemeyer, 1978–2000. The contributors include a number of the compilers of the edition as well as other D.-H. experts who reflect on the change in D.-H.'s image that has been effected by the edition's fresh contribution to scholarship. The volume contains: A. Hülsenbeck and R. Kuhlmann, '"Nun rührt sich's — die Lebendige spüret": Stigma und Berührung. *Das Fräulein von Rodenschild.* Videoskript einer Installation' (17–31); M. Wagner-Egelhaaf, '"Stigma und Berührung" — D. anders lesen' (33–48); M. Schneider, 'Das Amt der Dichterin' (51–68); W. Jaeschke, 'Das *Geistliche Jahr* — ein Zeugnis der Frömmigkeitsgeschichte des Vormärz' (69–85); G. Oesterle, 'A. v. D.-H.: *Bei uns zu Lande auf dem Lande.* Dekonstruktion von Detailrealismus und Übertreibung jungdeutscher Schreibmanier' (87–101); E. Ribbat, 'Ein Moortopf, der sich selbst kocht. Bemerkungen zum *Joseph*' (103–07); U. Heeke, '"Sie sehen schärfer als ich, stehn dort die Schriften der Jane Baillie?" Transformationen von Theorie und Praxis oder der Einfluss der englischen Schriftstellerin Joanna Baillie auf A. v. D.-H.' (109–40); O. Niethammer, 'Die D. als Romantikerin? A. v. D. und Joseph von Eichendorff vor dem Hintergrund der katholischen Spätromantik' (141–63); R. von Heydebrand, 'A. v. D.-H.: der Weg einer Frau in den literarischen Kanon' (165–82); B. Hahn, '"Anders wie ich mir gedacht" — oder wie baut man ein Denkmal für A. v. D.-H.?' (185–97); R. Nutt-Kofoth, '"Ich fand des Dichtens und Corrigierens gar kein Ende." Über A. v. D.-Hs dichterisches Schreiben — mit einem besonderen Blick auf das *Geistliche Jahr*' (199–217); L. Köhn, 'Edierter und interpretierter Text. Im Blick auf eine Briefstelle der D.' (219–24); B. Kortländer, 'Vom Exotismus der Provinz' (227–40). *A. v. D.-H.: Die Judenbuche,* ed. Manfred Eisenbeis (Lektüre easy), Stuttgart–Düsseldorf, Klett, 71 pp.

R. von Heydebrand, 'Interferenzen zwischen Geschlechterdifferenz und Poetik. A. v. D.-H. und Levin Schücking als schreibendes Paar', *IASL*, 26, 2001: 121–57. L. Kolago, 'Die Musik in A. v. D.-Hs Leben und Werk', *Studniem*, 23: 79–127. T. Pittrof, '"Bertuchs Naturgeschichte"; les't ihr das? A. v. D.-H: "Die Mergelgrube". Naturgeschichte, Poesie, Apokalypse', *LJb*, 42, 2001: 145–73. M. E.

Gibbs, 'A. v. D.-H. (1797–1848): the poet of the ever-open wounds', Harper, *Sappho*, 223–62. O. Niethammer, 'Kanonisierung als patriachalischer Selektionszwang? Das Beispiel A. v. D.-H.', Arnold, *Kanonbildung*, 181–93. P. G. Klussmann, 'Poetische Konzepte der historischen Westfalen-Balladen im Werk der A. v. D.-H.', Woesler, *Ballade*, 100–15. E. Ribbat, 'Waldromanze statt Geschichtsrhetorik: Eichendorffs "Kaiser Alberts I. Tod". Mit einem Ausblick auf D.-Hs "Der Graf von Thal"', *ib.*, 234–45. T. Schneider, 'A. v. D.-H.: der Tod des Erzbischofs Engelbert von Cöln. Quellenkommentar der D. als eigene Positionsbestimmung', *ib.*, 263–79. H.-J. Jakob, 'Vom Marktwert des Schönen. Literatur und literarischer Markt in A. v. D.-Hs Lustspiel *Perdu! oder Dichter, Verleger und Blaustrümpfe*', *Fest. Bender*, 281–93.

FELDER, FRANZ MICHAEL. Michaela Neumann, *F. M. F. als Volkserzieher. Eine Analyse der Schriften des Bauerndichters unter pädagogischen Gesichtspunkten*, Frankfurt–Berlin, Lang, 2001, 217 pp., is an Augsburg dissertation. J. Thaler, 'Unbekannte Briefe von F. M. F. an Engelbert Kessler', *JFA*, 1999: 9–18.

FONTANE. *T. F.: Frühe Erzählungen*, ed. Tobias Witt, Berlin, Aufbau, 218 pp. *T. F.: Hundert Gedichte*, ed. Gotthard Erler, Berlin, Aufbau, 167 pp. T. F.: *Unterm Birnbaum: eine Kriminalgeschichte*, ed. Otto Drude, Frankfurt–Leipzig, Insel, 190 pp. T. F.: *Unterm Birnbaum*, ed. Georg Patzer (Lektüre easy), Stuttgart–Düsseldorf, Klett, 59 pp. T. F. : *Unterm Birnbaum (1885)*, ed. Klaus Lüderssen and Hugo Aust, Baden-Baden, Nomos, 2001, 171 pp., has some 40 pages of interesting commentary on the criminological aspects of the story. T. F.: *Effi Briest*, ed. Georg Patzer (Lektüre easy), Stuttgart–Düsseldorf, Klett, 58 pp. *Theodor Fontane und Martha Fontane — ein Familienbriefnetz*, ed. Regina Dieterle, Berlin–NY, de Gruyter, xvi + 971 pp., has appeared just a year after Erler's similar edition of correspondence between F. and his daughter (see *YWMLS*, 63: 708), but Dieterle's is the more significant of the two, containing, in addition to the 331 letters dating from 1867 to 1915, over 450 pages of critical annotation and other information, as well as a selection of portraits and photographs of some original manuscripts. Included are a number of letters from the broader circle of family and friends, as well as some from the period between 1902 and 1915 which reveal tensions concerning the publication of F.'s papers after his death. The volume facilitates an improved understanding of relationships in the F. family and will be a valuable tool for scholars, albeit one which may be rather expensive for purchase by individuals. Gotthard Erler, *Das Herz bleibt immer jung: Emilie Fontane; Biographie*, Berlin, Aufbau, 460 pp., is a beautifully executed biography of F.'s wife Emilie. Containing previously unpublished material, the work affords a fascinating insight into the life of this remarkable woman who began life as an illegitimate child and endured an unsettled upbringing, only to find that marriage to F., whom she loved dearly, did not bring the security for which she longed, but instead for many years a difficult existence on the verge of poverty. The work portrays the courage and integrity, as well as the fears and vulnerability of a woman who lost four of her seven children and contended with long periods of separation from her husband. Published to coincide with the 100th anniversary of her death, the volume is a fitting tribute to a cultured, much-admired woman who was a cohesive and inspirational force not only in her own family, but also in the wider circle of literary figures with whom they engaged. The extensive index of names is indicative of her sphere of acquaintance and influence.

F. und die Fremde, F. und Europa, ed. Konrad Ehlich, Würzburg, Königshausen & Neumann, 320 pp., contains: K. Ehlich, 'Preußische Alterität — Statt einer Einleitung' (8–22); E. Ziegler, 'Fremd auf dieser Welt. Das Aparte an Fs literarischen Heldinnen' (23–35); H. Reinhardt, 'Die Rache der Puritanerin. Zur Psychologie des Selbstmords in Fs Roman *Unwiederbringlich*' (36–56); G. Neumann, ' "Invalide ist ja doch eigentlich jeder." Fs "fremde" Helden' (57–69); H. Nürnberger, 'Ein fremder Kontinent: F. und der Katholizismus' (70–87); N. Mecklenburg, ' "Alle Portugiesen sind eigentlich Juden." Zur Logik und Poetik der Präsentation von Fremden bei F.' (88–102); F. Jannidis and G. Lauer, ' "Bei meinem alten Baruch ist der Pferdefuß rausgekommen." Antisemitismus und Figurenzeichnung in *Der Stechlin*' (103–19); W. Müller-Seidel, 'Fremde Herkunft. Zu Fs erzähltem Personal und zu Problemen heutiger Antisemitismusforschung' (120–56); G. Häntzschel, 'Die Inszenierung von Heimat und Fremde in T. Fs Roman *Der Stechlin*' (157–66); M. Ewert, 'Heimat und Welt. Fs Wanderungen durch die Mark' (167–77); W. van Peer, ' "Erst die Fremde lehrt uns, was wir an der Heimat besitzen." Fs Schottlandreise und die interkulturellen Unterschiede zwischen Reise-Gründen' (178–91); K. Koszyk, 'Fs journalistischer Blick nach draußen' (192–211); R. Parr, 'Kongobecken, Lombok und der Chinese im Hause Briest. Das "Wissen um die Kolonien" und das "Wissen aus den Kolonien" bei T. F.' (212–28); K. Feilchenfeldt, 'Leutnant Greeley — ein amerikanisches Vorbild für Europa? Zu Fs *Der Stechlin* (Achtunddreißigstes Kapitel)' (229–47); A. Heitmann, ' "Alles war Abkommen auf Zeit." Nördliche Grenzen und Grenzübertritte im Werk T. Fs' (248–61); H. Fischer, 'Polnische Verwicklungen' (262–75); C. Grawe, ' "Italian Hours." T. F. und Henry James in Italien in den 1870er Jahren' (276–94); R. Warning, ' "Causerie" bei F.' (295–306); H. Häntzschel, 'F. im Gepäck der Emigranten' (307–20).

Wolfgang Feyerabend, *Spaziergänge durch Fs Berlin*, Zurich–Hamburg, Arche, 188 pp., is a well-illustrated book for F.-enthusiasts with short entries on numerous locations in Berlin associated with the writer. The index of almost 400 names of contemporary artists and public figures connected with F. is evidence of the work's informative nature and attention to detail. Gabriele Radecke, *Vom Schreiben zum Erzählen: Eine textgenetische Studie zu T. Fs 'L'Adultera'*, Würzburg, Königshausen & Neumann, 345 pp., is a Mainz dissertation offering a meticulously executed, albeit highly specialized, investigation of a single literary work. A detailed study of the manuscripts of F.'s *L'Adultera* is employed to reconstruct the writing process behind the finished novel. The first half of the volume analyses F.'s working methods from the early stages of collecting material up to the final revision of the text; it also has a section examining the changes to the work's title and one devoted to the 12th chapter of the novel, 'Unter Palmen'. The second half reproduces in printed format manuscript excerpts with their original deletions and alterations. *'Die Décadence ist da': T. F. und die Literatur der Jahrhundertwende*, ed. Gabriele Radecke, Würzburg, Königshausen & Neumann, 149 pp., seeks to redefine the concept of decadence in the literary work of a number of authors at the end of the century, and explores connections in this context with F.'s novels, essays, and lyric. The volume includes: D. Kafitz, 'T. Fs Roman *Der Stechlin* aus der Perspektive des Décadence der 90er Jahre des 19. Jahrhunderts' (9–32); R. Selbmann, 'Die Décadence unterwandert die Gründerzeit — Epochengeschichtliche Überlegungen zu einigen Figuren aus T. Fs Romanen' (33–45); M. Ewert, 'T. F. als Essayist' (47–59); G. Radecke, 'Das Motiv des Duells bei T. F. und Eduard von Keyserling' (61–77); W. Hettche, 'Großstadtlyrik um 1890' (79–93); S. Janson, '"Einsame Wege" und "weites Feld" : zum Todesmotiv bei Arthur Schnitzler und T. F.' (95–108); Y.-G. Mix, 'Der Untertan, der Oberlehrer und der Mythos unverbildeter Natürlichkeit und Dekadenzthematik im Schulroman der frühen Moderne' (125–42).

Karen Bauer, *Fs Frauenfiguren. Zur literarischen Gestaltung weiblicher Charaktere im 19. Jahrhundert*, Frankfurt–Berlin, Lang, 288 pp., analyses the presentation of female characters in 16 novels by F. in a range of thematic groupings including the witch-figure, the temptress, the fallen woman, the sick woman, the stage artiste, and the bluestocking. Although the writer identifies recurring types, she seeks to illustrate the individual complexity of F.'s protagonists and thereby refute the notion of stereotypes. The study traces the wider European influences on F.'s thought and includes examination of works by Flaubert, Sand, Ibsen, Tolstoy, Brontë, and Clarín as well as taking account of the portrayal of women in 19th-c. painting. Hans

Blumenberg, *Vor allem F.: Glossen zu einem Klassiker*, Frankfurt–Leipzig, Insel, 188 pp., is a posthumous collection of over 60 brief reflections on aspects of F.'s poetry, prose, and correspondence. The pieces are well written and reflect the writer's appreciation of F.'s import and style, but the volume lacks any critical apparatus and would be valued more by the intelligent general reader than by the student of literature. Christian Grawe, **'Der Zauber steckt immer im Detail': Studien zu T. F. und seinem Werk 1976–2002*, Dunedin, Otago U.P., 431 pp. Humbert Settler, **'Effi Briest' — Fs Versteckspiel mittels Sprachgestaltung und Mätressenspuk*, Flensburg, Baltica, 1999, 145 pp.

Fontane-Blätter, 73, contains K.-P. Möller, '"Sehr gute Kenntniße der Chemie Pharmacie Botanik und Latinität." Fs Zeugnisse aus seiner Ausbildungszeit zum Apoktheker als biographische Quellen' (8–41); M. Neuhaus, 'Eine zweilichtige Angelegenheit: Fs *Unterm Birnbaum*' (44–70); C. Hehle, 'Von Krotoschin nach Kessin. Zu Landschaft und Mythos der Ostsee in T. Fs Roman *Effi Briest*' (71–87); U. Röper, 'F. und die Bethanischen Schwestern' (88–104); C. von Braun, 'Fs Melusine-Gestalten' (116–22); G. Wolpert, '"Der Schlei" oder "die Schleie"? Die ersten Buchausgaben des vierten Wanderungsbandes *Spreeland*. Fragen zur Edition' (123–33). *Fontane-Blätter*, 74, has: '*Reisen* — Die Erstfassung von *Modernes Reisen* aus dem Jahr 1873', ed. W. Rasch (10–27); 'T. Fs und Bernhard von Lepels Tenzone *Röschen oder Rose*', ed. R. Steinnkrauss (48–57); P. Wruck, 'Wie F. die Mark Brandenburg entdeckte' (60–77); H. Fischer, '*Unser Fritz*: F. im Dreikaiserjahr' (78–98); H. D. von Wolzogen, '"Mein lieber Wolfsohn aus Odessa . . ." Briefe Fs an Wilhelm Wolfsohn im F.-Archiv' (132–33); K.-P. Möller, '"Ein sehr mäßiges Kauf-Publikum in Deutschland." Zu Fs Beziehung mit dem Verlag Julius Springer' (138–40).

C. Benne, 'Orientalismus? F., Nietzsche und die "gelbe Gefahr"', *Arcadia*, 37:216–46, has treatment of Chinese motifs in *Effi Briest* and *Der Stechlin*. P. J. Bowman, 'F's *Der Stechlin*: A fragile utopia', *MLR*, 97:877–91. B. Earle, 'Negotiating the "weites Feld": realism and discursive performance in Nietzsche and *Effi Briest*', *GR*, 77:233–53. K. Tebben, '"Der Roman dahinter": zum autobiographischen Hintergrund von T. Fs *L'Adultera*', *GLL*, 55:348–62. M. Grimberg, 'Louise, un modèle pour la protagoniste *d'Effi Briest?*', *Germanica*, 30:9–22. S. Becker, '"Wer ist Cécile?" Der "Roman einer Phantasie": T. Fs *Cécile*', *Raabe-Jb.*, 43:130–54. B. Plachta, 'Ein preußischer Alkibiades. T. Fs "Prinz Louis Ferdinand"-Ballade', Woesler, *Ballade*, 208–33. H. Ester, 'T. F. und der Berliner Roman', pp. 7–16 of *Das Jahrhundert Berlins: eine Stadt in der Literatur*, ed. Jattie Enklaar and Hans Ester (Duitse Kroniek, 50), Amsterdam, Rodopi, 2000, 298 pp. W. Rieck, 'Die Hohenzollern auf dem Königsthron im Urteil T. Fs',

Studniem, 19, 2000: 349–68. N. Mecklenburg, 'Zur Poetik, Narratologie und Ethik der Gänsefüßchen: T. F. nach der Postmoderne', pp. 165–85 of *Instrument Zitat. Über die Literarhistorischen und instutionellen Nutzen von Zitaten und Zitieren*, ed. Klaus Beekman and Ralf Grüttemeier, Amsterdam, Rodopi, 2000, 443 pp. H. Nürnberger, 'T. F. und Theodor Mommsen. Mit ungedruckten Briefen', *Fest. Mittenzwei*, 125–47. R. Berbig, 'T. Fs Akte der Deutschen Schiller-Stiftung. Mit einem unveröffentlichten Gutachten Fs für Karl Weise', *ib.*, 149–66. B. Plett, 'Aufbruch ins Eisenbahnzeitalter. Fs frühe Erzählung "Zwei Post-Stationen"', *ib.*, 167–77. H. Aust, 'Fs "Fein Gespinnst" in der Gartenlaube des Realismus: *Unterm Birnbaum*', *ib.*, 179–92. E. Sagarra, 'Berliner Göre und brave Mädchen in der deutschsprachigen Erzählliteratur des Realismus: zum Beispiel Olga Pittelkow', *ib.*, 193–202. C. Jolles, 'Unwiederbringlich — der Irrweg des Grafen Holk', *ib.*, 203–18. C. Hehle, 'Venus und Elisabeth. Beobachtungen zu einigen Bildfeldern in T. Fs Roman *Unwiederbringlich*', *ib.*, 219–33. W. Müller-Seidel, 'Alterskunst. Fs autobiographischer Roman *Meine Kinderjahre* an der Epochenschwelle zur Moderne', *ib.*, 235–62. H. H. H. Remak, 'Ehe und Kinder im Leben T. Fs und Thomas Manns', *ib.*, 269–81. L. Köhn, '"Bei dem Fritzen-Denkmal stehen sie wieder." Fs Preußen-Balladen als Schlüssel zu seinem Werk', Jürgens, *Exchanges*, 342–59. D. Schilling, 'T. F.: *L'Adultera*', *ib.*, 360–69.

FRANKL, LUDWIG AUGUST. C. Walker, 'Two Jewish poetry anthologies: L. A. F.'s *Libanon* (1855) and Siegmund Kaznelson's *Jüdisches Schicksal in deutschen Gedichten* (1959)', pp. 21–34 of *Jews in German Literature since 1945. German-Jewish Literature?*, ed. Pól O'Dochartaigh, Amsterdam, Rodopi, 2000, x + 673 pp.

FRANZOS. A. Corbea, 'Bürger F.', *Arcadia*, 35, 2000: 295–317. G. v. Essen, '"Im Zwielicht" — Die kulturhistorischen Studien von K. E. F. über Halb-Asien', Holzner, *Wechselwirkungen*, 57–84.

FREILIGRATH. H. Rösch, 'Kunst und Revolution. Gottfried Kinkel und F. F. — Stationen einer schwierigen Freundschaft', *Grabbe Jb.*, 19–20, 2000–01: 260–83. E. Bourke, 'Hermann von Pückler-Muskau und F. F. zum irischen Zehntensystem', *ib.*, 284–301. W. Büttner, 'F. und Marx, 1848 und später — eine Freundschaft auf Zeit', *ib.*, 302–14. G. Schmitz, 'Zwischen Romantik und Revolution: F. Fs Übersetzungen während des ersten Londoner Exils (1846–1848)', *ib.*, 315–23. V. Giel, 'Dichtung und Revolution. Die Lyrik F. Fs und Georg Herweghs in der Revolution von 1848/49. Ein analytischer Vergleich', *ib.*, 324–50. I. Hufnagel and K. Roessler, 'Die Krone Assmannshausen in der Revolution und im Nachmärz', *ib.*, 351–57. K. Nellner and J. Hiller von Gaertringen, 'F.-Bibliographie 1998–2000. Mit Nachträgen', *ib.*, 460–67.

FREYTAG. H. Ridley, 'Zwischen Anstand und Ästhetik: zu sozialen und literarischen Codes in Fs *Soll und Haben*', *ZGer*, 11, 2001 : 105–16. M. Hollender, '"Zeitgemäßgekürzt." Eine Pressepolemik um Streichungen in G. Fs *Soll und Haben*', *Buchhandelsgeschichte*, 2001 : 82–91. I. Surynt, 'G. F. und der oberschlesische Annaberg. Überlegungen zu G. Fs Beziehungen zu Oberschlesien', *Convivium*, 2001 : 67–97. L. Stockinger, 'Polen als "grüne Stelle"? Ästhetische und politische Implikationen des Polenbildes bei G. F.', *ib.*, 99–127. L. Tatlock, 'Regional histories as national history: G. F's *Bilder aus der deutschen Vergangenheit*', Vazsonyi, *Searching*, 223–51.

FRÖHLICH, ABRAHAM EMANUEL. B. Plachta, '*Flüchtend aus der Weltverwirrung*. Die Wiederentdeckung des Schweizer Fabulisten A. E. F. und seines Illustrators Martin Disteli', *Euphorion*, 95, 2001 : 123–26.

GRABBE. *Grabbes Welttheater. Christian Dietrich Grabbe zum 200. Geburtstag*, ed. Detlev Kopp and Michael Vogt, Bielefeld, Aisthesis, 2001, 324 pp., contains: B. Budde, 'Bestien unter sich. Die "dramatische" Welt- und Menschenkunde in Gs Tragödie *Herzog Theodor von Gothland*' (13–35); H. Krah, '". . . nun werd ich lebendig abgehäutet." Zur Rhetorik des Sterbens/Todes in Gs Dramen' (37–70); N. O. Eke, '"Alle Ehre deiner Narbe." Die Spur des Körpers im Werk Gs' (71–101); M. Vogt, '"Nicht diese breiten Gleichnisse, wo es richtige Gedanken gilt." Zur Rhetorik des Erhabenen im Drama Gs' (103–17); J. Fohrmann, 'Die Ellipse des Helden (mit Bezug auf C. D. Gs *Napoleon oder die Hundert Tage*)' (119–35); H. Oehm, 'Gemeinschaft und Gesellschaft in Gs Geschichtsdramen' (137–62); K. Jauslin, 'Das ausgelesene Buch der Welt. Gs groteske "Vieh=(loso=)Vieh" der Geschichte' (163–92); E. Bartsch, 'Schöpfung und Fall. Überlegungen zu dem Bühnenfragment *Marius und Sulla*' (193–204); D. Kopp, '"Toll will ich eintreten und vernünftig enden." Gs forcierter Eintritt in die Literatur' (205–25); K. Lindemann and R. Zons, '"Dies glückliche Unglück." Geld und Glück in C. D. Gs Briefen und Dramen' (227–62); F. Vassen, 'Theatralität und szenisches Lesen. Gs Theatertexte im Theatralitätsgefüge seiner Zeit' (263–81); M. Porrmann, '"Mit dem Cid haben Sie sich geirrt."' (283–313); O. Kutzmutz, 'Auf dramatischen Routen. Schöner reisen mit G.' (315–24).

Grabbe-Jb., 19–20, 2000–01, has: F. Bratvogel, 'C. D. G. — Theaterdichter, Schauspieler und Dramaturg' (18–25); F. U. Krause, 'Zur Ästhetik von Werk und Gestalt C. D. Gs' (26–31); Id., 'Erfahrung oder Idee als Prinzipien für dramaturgische Entscheidungen (Schiller, Goethe, Grabbe und Wittgenstein)' (32–47); P. Schütze, 'Echte Tränen? Lachen und Weinen im Theater' (48–67); F. Kragl, 'Kohäsion und Kohärenz in Gs Lustspiel *Scherz, Satire, Ironie und tiefere*

Bedeutung' (71–94); R. Béhar, 'Gs "tiefere Bedeutung" aus der Sicht König Ubus. Alfred Jarrys Übersetzung von Gs Lustspiel: ein Beitrag zu dessen Wirkungsgeschichte' (96–115); J. Huerkamp, '"Die finsteren Chorgenossen" — C. D. G. und Arno Schmidt' (122–39); K. Zehnder-Tischendorf, 'Gs Oper *Der Cid*. Neue Erkenntnisse zur Vertonung von Norbert Burgmüller' (140–46); E. Möller, 'Ein verunglücktes Leben? Zum G.-Bild in der deutschen Lyrik der 1970er und 1980er Jahre' (169–81); P. Schütze, 'G.-Gesichter und -Gesichte von Rainer Nummer' (183–91); K. Nellner and J. Hiller von Gaertringen, 'G.-Bibliographie 1998–2000. Mit Nachträgen' (445–59). See also under FREILIGRATH, HEINE, and WEERTH.

N. O. Eke, '"Wir spielen um's Höchste." C. D. G. als Stratege des Literaturmarkts und eine Ausstellung zu seinem 200. Geburtstag in der Lippischen Landesbibliothek Detmold', *ZDP*, 121:607–13. M. Vogt, '"... die Kunst hat kein Heil, als das Leben!" Zum literarischen Paradigmenwechsel um 1830', *FVF*, 6, 2000:49–81.

GRILLPARZER. *F. G.: Gegen den Zeitgeist*, ed. Ekkehart Krippendorff, Frankfurt–Leipzig, Insel, 85 pp., is a collection of excerpts from G.'s works and letters, with a 'Nachwort' by the editor. E. Sagarra, 'G. the Catholic?', *MLR*, 97:108–22, examines G.'s relationship with Roman Catholic culture and mentality. M. B. Helfer, 'Framing the Jew: G.'s *Die Jüdin von Toledo*', *GQ*, 75:160–80. M. G. Ward, 'G.'s dreams', Castein, *Images*, 79–90. U. H. Gerlach, 'Helferin oder Hindernis? Die Frau in Gs *König Ottokars Glück und Ende*', Gerlach, *Einwände*, 26–45. Id., 'Rudolf, der kritisierte Kaiser: Bemerkungen zu Gs *König Ottokars Glück und Ende*', *ib.*, 46–61. I. M. Battafarano, 'Epilog 2001. Juden in der Prager Judenstadt anno 1826. Hätte G. doch Christian von Rosenroth (oder zumindest Goethe) gelesen ...', *Morgen-Glantz*, 11, 2001:367–73. H. Kuzmics, 'Bürgerliche Individualisierung im vormärzlichen Österreich: G., *Der arme Spielmann*', Beutner, *Literatur*, 104–17. M. Scheffel, 'Beschränktes Biedermeier? F. Gs *Der Traum ein Leben* oder: Die Geburt der Moral aus dem Geist der Psychologie', *Fest. Mittenzwei*, 65–77. E. Tobler, 'Misslungene Identitätsfindung. Zur Symbolik der Musik in F. Gs *Der arme Spielmann*', pp. 237–49 of *Symbole im Dienste der Darstellung von Identität*, ed. Paul Michel, Berne–Berlin, Lang, 2000, xxv + 371 pp. B. Hoffmann, 'Opfer der Humanität. Ideologiekritik und Diskursanalyse bei F. G.', pp. 131–38 of *Österreichische Sprache, Literatur und Gesellschaft*, ed. Kurt Bäckström, Münster, Nodus, 2000, 164 pp. S. P. Scheichl, 'Zum "Anti-Revolutions"-Monolog Kaiser Rudolfs II. in Gs *Bruderzwist*', pp. 159–75 of *Noch einmal Dichtung und Politik. Vom Text zum politisch-sozialen Kontext und zurück*, ed. Oswald Panagl and Walter Weiss, Vienna–Cologne, Böhlau, 2000, 462 pp. S. P. Scheichl '"Kaum schön, von schwachem Geist und dürft'gen Gaben." Was können wir über Erny in Gs "Treuem Diener seines Herrn" wissen?', pp. 183–99 of *Käthchen und seine Schwestern. Frauenfiguren im Drama um 1800*, ed. Günther Emig and Anton Philipp Knittel, Heilbronn, Kleist-Archiv Sembdner, 2000, 198 pp.

GRIMM, HERMAN. K. Grzywka, '"Meine Tage vergehen mir in gleichermäßigem Vergnügen und wunschlos." Zu H. Gs Tagebuch von 1847', *Studniem*, 22, 2001 : 149–66.

GROTH. U. Bichel and I. Bichel, 'Zwei Gedichte K. Gs auf dem Weg zu seinem *Quickborn*', *Fest. Menke*, 57–69. *Jahresgabe der K.G.-Gesellschaft*, 44, contains: U. Bichel and I. Bichel, 'Vor 150 Jahren. K.G. im Jahre 1852' (9–60); R. Hansen, 'Hermann Claudius' Gedicht "Klaus Groth" zur Hundertjahrfeier des *Quickborn* 1952. Eine Wiederentdeckung' (61–80); R. Goltz, 'Kontrastgedanken zum Thema: Literaturmuseen, Andacht und Event' (105–12) concerns the K.-G.-Museum.

GUTZKOW. *G. lesen! Beiträge zur Internationalen Konferenz des Forum Vormärz Forschung vom 18. bis 20. September 2000 in Berlin*, ed. Gustav Frank and Deltev Kopp, Bielefeld, Aisthesis, 2001, 416 pp., contains: G. Frank, 'G. lesen! G. edieren! — G. liest! Einleitende Bemerkungen zu diesem Band' (9–17); G. Vonhoff, 'Gegenlektüren in Gs *Wally, die Zweiflerin*' (19–50); H. Brandes, '"Seine Feder in den Strom des Lebens tauchen." Über Gs frühe Journalkritik' (51–64); W. Lukas, 'Experimentelles Schreiben und neue Sprachästhetik in den 30er Jahren. Zu Gs *Seraphine*' (65–97); U. Promies, 'Ihrer Zeit voraus: Gs Bildungskritik' (99–121); W. Rasch, '"Zuviel Krieg ist gefährlich." Aus dem Briefwechsel zwischen K. G. und Ludwig Wihl 1838–40' (123–59); H. Krah, 'Bühne und Lektüre. Zur Mediendiskussion in Gs Drama *Patkul*' (161–88); M. Wünsch, 'Religionsthematik und die Strategien der Selbstverhinderung in Erzähltexten Gs der 1830er bis 50er Jahre' (189–205); T. Bremer, 'Gs Briefe aus Paris, die Wahrnehmung intellektueller Öffentlichkeitserfahrung' (207–26); S. Landshuter, 'Von "Gottfried" zu "Ottfried" und zurück. Wertewandel im Werk K. Gs am Beispiel von *Die Selbsttaufe* und *Ottfried*' (227–61); O. Briese, '"Das Auge der Polizei." Großstadtoptik um 1850' (263–97); P. Hasubek, '"Rückblicke" auf die "Knabenzeit". Zur Autobiographie K. Gs' (299–324); G. Frank, 'Der "Krystallseher" und "des unsterblichen Alciati Emblemata": Literatur, Geschichte und die Macht der Bilder in Gs *Hohenschwangau* (1867/68)' (325–61); K. Jauslin, 'Ansichten "realistischen" Erzählens. Gs *Die neuen Serapionsbrüder* im Vergleich mit Spielhagens *Sturmflut*' (363–84); C. Haug, "Populäres auch populär vertreiben [. . .]" — K. Gs Vorschläge zur Reform des Buchhandels und zur Beschleunigung des Buchabsatzes. Ein Beitrag zur Geschichte der Buchdistribution und Buchwerbung im 19. Jahrhundert' (385–416).

G. Frank, '*G. lesen!* Bericht über die Konferenz des Forum Vormärz Forschung in Berlin', *FVF*, 6, 2000: 233–36. M. Lauster, 'K. Gs Werke und Briefe im Internet: gutzkow.de. Vorstellung des Editionsprojekts und Aufruf zur Mitarbeit', *ib.*, 237–41. D. Naumann, 'Zeitungsroman und Zeitroman. Zu Gs *Die Ritter vom Geiste*', *Fest. Mittenzwei*, 91–108.

HEBBEL. E. Brüns, 'Vater Staat und die weibliche Leiche: Hs *Agnes Bernauer*', *IJBAG*, 13–14, 2001–02: 129–40. U. H. Gerlach, '"Wenn nichts als Trotz mich triebe ...": Betrachtungen zum Todeswunsch von Hs Mariamne', Gerlach, *Einwände*, 62–80. Id., '"Schattenrisse der Seele" — Die Briefe F. Hs', *ib.*, 81–101. Id., '"Ende gut, alles gut": Dramenschlüsse bei Schiller und H.', *ib.*, 102–23. *H.Jb.*, 57, has: M. Ritzer, '75 Jahre H.-Gesellschaft. Zur Geschichte einer literarischen Vereinigung' (7–24); X. Wu, 'Zur Rezeption F. Hs in China: Ansätze und Aspekte' (25–49); R. Görner, '"Aber ich will Ich werden." Hs Spuren im Werk Benns, Borchardts und Thomas Manns' (51–64); S. Thielking, 'Lektionen vom Trauerspieler. Der Schul-Hebbel des 20. Jahrhunderts' (65–80); J. Strobel, 'Ent-stellungen: Zum Briefwechsel zwischen F. H. und Friedrich von Uechtritz und seiner Edition durch Felix Bamberg. Mit einem ungedruckten Brief von Uechtritz an H.' (81–105); H. Reinhardt, '"Ich treib' die Sünde bis zum Aeußersten." Die Golo-Tragödie in F. Hs *Genoveva*' (107–37); J. Wang, 'Das Tragische bei H. — eine textimmanente Kategorie? Zur Inszenierung des Tragischen in *Maria Magdalena*' (139–63); V. Nölle, 'Die patrenale Zeichensprache in Hansgünther Heymes Inszenierung der *Maria Magdalena* (am Beispiel der Szene I.6)' (165–85); U. H. Gerlach, 'H. und die G7' (187–98); H. Knebel, 'Zwei ungedruckte H.-Breife' (199–205); H. Thomsen, 'Theaterbericht' (207–23).

HEINE. H.-specialists will welcome the return after a ten-year hiatus of *H. Hs Werk im Urteil seiner Zeitgenossen*, ed. Christoph auf der Horst and Sikander Singh (formerly Hoffmann und Campe). The project has been taken on by Metzler and maintains the high standard of this important series with the publication of two new vols, both ed. Sikander Singh: vol. 7, *Rezensionen und Notizen zu H. Hs Werken aus den Jahren November 1841 bis Dezember 1843*, xxii + 423 pp., and vol. 8, *Rezensionen und Notizen zu H. Hs Werken aus den Jahren 1844 bis 1845*, xxv + 524 pp. Each volume has an introduction documenting the background to the respective period covered, and has separate indexes of authors, periodicals, and works. *H. H.: Hundert Gedichte*, ed. Jan-Christoph Hauschild, Berlin, Aufbau, 186 pp. *H. H.: Der Rabbi von Bacherach: Ein Fragment*, ed. Joseph A. Kruse, Frankfurt–Leipzig, Insel, 117 pp. Karl-Josef Kuschel, *Gottes grausamer Spass?: H. Hs Leben* *mit der Katastrophe*, Düsseldorf, Patmos, 359 pp., examines H.'s experience of suffering and his relationship with God. Gerhart Hoffmeister, *H. in der Romania*, Berlin, Schmidt, 208 pp., is a successful attempt to present in a single volume a concise and readable overview of H.'s influence across a range of Romance languages and cultures. There are individual chapters on the translation and reception of H.'s work in France, Italy, Spain, and Latin America, with additional shorter sections on Romania and Portugal, revealing the divided perception of H. on the one hand as a writer of sentimental and escapist love poetry, and on the other as a controversial satirical commentator on the cultural and political issues of the day. The broad scope of the study highlights H.'s position as an international literary figure, but a potential disadvantage is that its usefulness depends on a good reading knowledge of French, Italian, and Spanish as well as German, as there are no translations of the numerous quotations. Madleen Podewski, *Kunsttheorie als Experiment: Untersuchungen zum ästhetischen Diskurs H. Hs*, Frankfurt–Berlin, Lang, 241 pp., is a dissertation from the Freie Univ. Berlin which examines H.'s aesthetic conception of the function of art and literature during the 1830s in the light of Foucault's discourse analysis. Adam Smykowski, *Heinrich Heines 'Lyrisches Intermezzo' in Vertonungen von Robert Schumann und Robert Franz*, Frankfurt–Berlin, Lang, 293 pp. Jan-Christoph Hauschild and Michael Werner, *H. H.*, Munich, DTV, 159 pp. Helmut Landwehr, **Der Schlüssel zu Hs 'Romanzero'*, Hamburg, Kovač, 2001, 282 pp. Constanze Wachsmann, **Der sowjetische H. Die H.-Rezeption in russischsprachigen Rezeptionstexten der Sowjetunion (1717–1953)*, Berlin, Weissensee, 2001, 311 pp. **Das Jerusalemer H.-Symposium. Gedächtnis, Mythos, Modernität*, ed. Klaus Briegleb and Itta Shedletzky, Hamburg, Dölling & Galitz, 2001, 218 pp.

H.-Jb, 41, contains: S. Neuhaus, 'Dekonstruktion nationaler Mythologeme: H. H. und Deutschland' (1–17); J. Pizer, 'H.'s unique relationship to Goethe's *Weltliteratur* Paradigm' (18–36); S. Ferguson, 'H. Hs "Die Bäder von Lukka" als perverse Ethopoetik: die Ästhetik der Sexualabweichung und/oder die Rhetorik homophobischer Verunglimpfung' (37–53); C. Mielke, 'Der Tod und das novellistische Erzählen. H. Hs "Florentinische Nächte"' (54–82); R. Schnell, 'H. H. und Bertolt Brecht. Das Exil als poetische Lebensform' (83–105); K. Fingerhut, '"Manchmal nur, in dunkeln Zeiten." H., Kafka, Celan. Schreibweisen jüdischer Sellbstreflexion' (106–29); L. Min, 'Hs Lyrik in China — vom Anfang bis 1949' (130–60); I. Rippmann, 'Emanzipation und Akkulturation. Ein nicht ganz typisches Beispiel: Ludwig Börne' (161–87); C. Wachsmann, '"Ein mutiger Trommler der Revolution." Zur H. H.-Rezeption in der Sowjetunion (1917–1953)' (188–204); U. Broicher, 'Der legislatorische Sonderweg des Rheinlandes oder H. und der Fonk-Prozess' (205–20); H. Heidermann, '1847: ein "Anti-Musik-Verein" im Wohnhaus der Familie H.' (221–26). B. Morawe, 'Der Lazarus-Prolog. Kontrafaktur und Kollektivwerk', *DVLG*, 76:446–63. Id., 'Hs *Weltlauf*. Der Lazarus-Prolog und das Recht zu leben', *IJBAG*, 13–14, 2001–02:141–92. S. Bierwirth, 'Hs Naturästhetik', *FVF*, 6, 2000:125–36. I. Brendel-Perpina, 'Zur Ambivalenz in Hs Kunstauffassung. Versuch einer ästhetischen Standortbestimmung der publizistischen Prosa der Pariser Jahre', *ib.*, 137–45. G. Emig, 'H. Hs Verhaftung auf dem Wartberg am 16, November 1827', *JSFG*, 34, 2001:217–28. K. Fingerhut, 'Kanonisierung als Vereinnahmung. Hs "Buch der Lieder" und "Deutschland. Ein Wintermärchen" als Schullektüren', Arnold, *Kanonbildung*, 156–80. W. Gössmann, 'Revolution oder Geschlechterfolge. Zur Vermittlung der Balladen "Karl I." von H. H. und "Vorgeschichte (Second sight)" von Annette von Droste-Hülshoff', Woesler, *Ballade*, 63–81. J. A. Kruse, '"Da reist' ich nach Deutschland hinüber." H. unterwegs in Europa — Beweglichkeit als Vorform der Revolution', *Grabbe Jb.*, 19–20, 2000–01:197–213. Id., 'H. H. spricht über Heinrich von Kleist', *BKF*, 2001:261–68. Id., 'H. Hs "Der Dichter Firdusi": fremde Historie als eigene Situation', Woesler, *Ballade*, 116–34. T. Neumann, '". . . beim H. aber könnte uns der Rahm von der Milch geschöpft werden." Oskar Walzels H.-Ausgabe im Insel-Verlag', *AGB*, 54, 2001:219–70. R. F. Cook, 'The tyrannical "knout" of world history. Russia in the writings of H. H.', Barabtarlo, *Fusion*, 102–12. G. A. Goldschmidt, 'H. H. und die deutsche Sprache', pp. 69–94 of *Die Deutschen und ihre Sprache. Reflexionen über ein unsicheres Verhältnis*, ed. Volker Michael Strocka, Bremen, Hempen, 2000, 156 pp. S. Bierwirth, 'Die Erotik der "Gesundheitsliebe" — H. und seine Mouche', *FVF*, 5, 1999:317–26.

HENSEL, LUISE. A. J. Harper, 'L. H. (1798–1876): a little bird sits captive within its narrow cell', Harper, *Sappho*, 189–222.

HERWEGH, GEORG. I. Pepperle, 'G. H. im Briefwechsel mit Marie d'Agoult über Bettina von Arnim (1844)', *IJBAG*, 13–14, 2001–02:23–33.

HEYSE. B. Mullan, '"Auf 'Stücke mit nackete Füß' wartet in Deutschland kein Mensch." P. H.'s classical tragedy *Alkibiades* (1881)', *ASNS*, 154:21–45.

HOFFMANN VON FALLERSLEBEN. M. Halub, 'H. v. F. und Johann Gustav Gottlieb Büsching. Zur Geschichte einer Fehde zwischen einem "Zwecklosen" und einem "Philister"', *Studniem*, 21, 2001:381–98. E. Rohse, '"Frankfurt nicht Betlehem" — Pauluskirchenparlament und 48er Revolution im Spiegel literarischer Texte', pp. 40–67 of *Die Sprache des deutschen Parlamentarismus. Studien zu 150 Jahren parlamentarischer Kommunikation*, ed. Armin Burkhardt and

Kornelia Pape, Wiesbaden, Westdeutscher Vlg, 2000, 494 pp. E. Rohse, 'Im Vorfeld der Bote-Forschung: *Van veleme rade* als "Findling" des Germanisten H. v. F.', *Fest. Menke*, 603–23.

HOLTEI. P. J. Brenner, 'Behaglichkeit. Konservatives Erzählen in Hs Romanen', *Raabe Jb.*, 43:111–29. S. P. Scheichl, 'Berichte aus einem "dissoluten Leben." Liebesaffären in Hs Autobiographie', *FVF*, 5, 1999:341–54.

IMMERMANN. *Immermann Jahrbuch*, 3, contains: K. Immermann, ' "De la peinture en Allemagne au XIXe siècle." Herausgegeben von H. Karge' (9–33); H. Karge, 'K. Is Zeitgeschichte der deutschen Malerei. Kommentar' (34–50); K. Hirakawa, '*Die Epigonen* als Geschichte des Herzen' (51–69); G. Kluge, 'Der Philister auf dem Musenberg — der Poet bei Philistern. Is Reise in die Niederlande und Mijnheer van Streef in *Münchhausen*' (71–84); T. Althaus, 'Sich etwas in den Kopf setzen. Is Roman *Münchhausen* und die Richtungssuche des partikulären Subjekts' (85–112); S. Itoda, 'Is *Oberhof* als "Bote des Deutschtums" in Fernost' (113–24); P. Hasubek, 'Drei unbekannte Briefe Is' (125–31).

JENSEN, WILHELM. G. Leisten, 'Marmor und Mnemosyne. Romantische Bildnisbewegung und animatorische Erinnerung in W. Js *Gradiva*', *Raabe Jb.*, 43:155–71.

KELLER. The HKA of K.'s *Sämtliche Werke*, ed. Walter Morgenthaler, Basle–Frankfurt, Stroemfeld, has added vols 4 and 5, *Die Leute von Seldwyla 1* and *Die Leute von Seldwyla 2*, ed. Peter Villwock, 2000, 315, 361 pp.; vol. 6, *Züricher Novellen*, ed. Walter Morgenthaler, 1999, 415 pp.; vols 16.1 and 16.2, *Studienbücher* and *Notizbücher*, ed. Walter Morgenthaler, 2001, 443, 408 pp.; vol. 21, *Die Leute von Seldwyla. Apparat zu Band 4 und 5*, ed. Peter Villwock, 2000, 657 pp.; vol. 22, *Züricher Novellen. Apparat zu Band 6*, ed. Walter Morgenthaler, 1999, 631 pp. Walburga Freund-Spork, *G. K.: 'Kleider machen Leute'* (Reclams U.-B., Lektüreschlüssel für Schüler, 15313), Stuttgart, Reclam, 85 pp. Daniel Rothenbühler, *Der grüne Heinrich 1854/55: Gottfried Kellers Romankunst des 'Unbekannt-bekannten'*, Berne–Berlin, Lang, 404 pp., is a Berne dissertation offering detailed examination of the first version of K.'s novel. The volume includes analysis of the work's intertextual relationships, its geographical and historical settings, the 'Jugendgeschichte' and the Meretlein-story, as well as the mother-son theme. H. Hildebrandt, 'Die Erleuchtung des Naturwissenschaftlers. Beobachtungen zur Gestaltung von G. Ks *Sinngedicht*: Stufungs- und Erzählprinzipien', *Fest. Brandt*, 98–116. H. Reinhardt, 'Die Kunst des Sehens. Goethe und das Realismus-Credo in G. Ks *Der grüne Heinrich*', Beutler, *Spuren*, 285–310.

LENAU. *N. L. Liebesgedichte*, ed. Wilfrid Lutz, Frankfurt–Leipzig, Insel, 132 pp. Michael Ritter, **Zeit des Herbstes. N.-L.-Biografie*, Vienna–Frankfurt, Deuticke, 381 pp. N. O. Eke, 'Faustisches im Schatten Goethes. N. Ls vormärzlicher *Faust* — eine Erinnerung', *FVF*, 6, 2000: 243–60. *Lenau Jb.*, 27, 2001, has: H. Steinecke, '"Mit L." Person und Werk im Spiegel der Literatur 1850–2000' (9–28); I. Gombocz, 'Die Verlobung mit Karoline Unger. Ein gescheiterter Fluchtversuch Ls' (29–38); E. W. Partsch, 'Zu den L.-Vertonungen von Benedict Randhartinger' (39–50); A. Huber, 'Nachdichtung oder Gegendarstellung? Fanny Hensels *Lied für das Pianoforte* op. 8/3 "Lenau"' (51–74); A. Tschense, 'Im Herzen den Tod. N. Ls Gedicht "Der schwere Abend" in den Vertonungen von Robert Schumann, Robert Franz und Othmar Schoeck' (104–20); H. Lengauer, 'Post mortem erst wird die Figur Gestalt. Zur L.-Rezeption in der österreichischen Literatur' (121–49); S. Thürmer, 'Levin Schücking und N. L.' (151–78).

LEWALD. B. Sapala, 'Zur Position der Frau in der Königsberger bürgerlichen Gesellschaft in der ersten Hälfte des 19. Jahrhunderts. F. L.: *Meine Lebensgeschichte*', *Studniem*, 23: 311–26. G. Schneider, 'Zwischen Reflexion und Realismus: F. L. und der "Roman des Lebens"', *FVF*, 6, 2000: 209–29. C. Ujma, 'Life as a journey: F. L.'s autobiographical travel writing', Davies, *Autobiography:* 131–47. D. Pinfold, R. Whittle, and C. Schönfeld, 'Representing 1848: autobiography and fiction in F. L.', *ColGer*, 33, 2000: 239–54. A. Kley, 'F. Ls *Meine Lebensgeschichte*: eine Autobiographie zwischen bürgerlicher Anpassung und emanzipatorischem Aufbruch', Loster-Schneider, *Geschlecht*, 129–50.

LINDAU, RUDOLF. R. Hillenbrand, 'Skeptischer Realismus in der Erzählkunst R. Ls', *GLL*, 55: 363–86.

MEYER. D. Kimpel, '"Meine Gedanken verklagten und entschuldigten sich unter einander." Zur Bedeutung des Gewissens in C. F. Ms Novelle *Das Amulett*', *Fest. Mittenzwei*, 109–24. B. Wanning, 'Der Gewalt begegnen Aktualität und Geschichtlichkeit in C. F. Ms Ballade "Die Füße im Feuer"', Woesler, *Ballade*, 280–98. R. Zeller, 'Wandlungen der Ballade im Werk C. F. Ms', *ib.*, 299–315. U. H. Gerlach, '*Gustav Adolfs Page* — der unzulänglich verkappte Feigling? Eine Neuinterpretation von C. F. Ms Novelle', Gerlach, *Einwände*, 124–44. Id., 'Doppelkreuz und Doppelspiel in C. F. Ms *Plautus im Nonnenkloster*', *ib.*, 145–60. P. Sprengel, 'Antiautoritäres Theater als Bekräftigung von Autorität?', pp. 760–81 of *Autorität der/in der Sprache, Literatur, neuen Medien*, ed. Jürgen Fohrmann et al., 2 vols, Bielefeld, Aisthesis, 1999, 410, 416–837 pp.

MÖRIKE. The Stuttgart (Klett Cotta) edition of M.'s *Werke und Briefe*, ed. Hubert Arbogast et al., has added vol. 17, *Briefe 1857–1863*, ed. Regina Cerfontaine et al., 1086 pp. *E. M.: Sämtliche Gedichte in einem Band*, ed. Bernhard Zeller, Frankfurt–Leipzig, Insel, 2001, 511 pp. M. Hahn, 'Doppelte und dreifache Mißverständnisse. Subjektive Befangenheit und "trügerische Zeichen" in E. Ms *Maler Nolten*', *Fest. Mittenzwei*, 33–64. W. J. A. Bender, 'Ingenium animum humanum iuvat. Gedanken zum Inspirationsgeschehen in Ms *Mozart auf der Reise nach Prag*', *Fest. Bender*, 381–92. F. Lösel, 'E. M.: *Einer Reisenden*. Das Problem der Umkehr im Gedichtwerk', Kavanagh, *Exchanges*, 152–66.

MUNDT, THEODOR. I. Rippmann, 'Die ersäuften Liebhaber. Zu einem Motiv zweier Werke aus dem Jahr 1835', *FVF*, 5, 1999: 37–65, refers also to Büchner.

NESTROY. The HKA of N.'s *Sämtliche Werke*, ed. Jürgen Hein et al., Vienna, Deuticke, has added *Stücke*, 37: *Lohengrin*, *Zeitvertreib*, ed. Peter Branscombe, 2001, xvii + 229 pp. Herbert Zeman, **Johann Nepomuk Nestroy*, Vienna, Holzhausen, 2001, v + 353 pp. *J. N., 'Reserve' und andere Notizen. Eine Veröffentlichung der International N.-Gesellschaft und des Deutschen Theatermuseums München*, ed. W. Edgar Yates, Vienna, Lehner, 2000, 112 pp. D. Horvat, 'N. unter den Burgenländischen Kroaten', *ZGB*, 6, 2001 : 76–84. *Nestroyana*, 22, has: F. Walla, 'Der zusammengestoppelte Dampfwagen: neu aufgetauchte Manuskripte zu N.-Stücken. *Die Fahrt mit dem Dampfwagen — Die zusammengestoppelte Komödie*' (13–28); H. Aust, 'Faktoren, Freunde und Finanzen: N. und Balzac' (29–42); M. Stern, 'N. und Horváth oder Happy-End für Staatenlose. Zu Text und Uraufführung von Horváths *Hin und Her* in Zürich' (43–53); F. Walla, 'Von der Urfassung zur (Ur-)Aufführung oder: Wie echt sind Ns Texte? 1. Teil' (101–20); J. Danielczyk and W. E. Yates, 'Zwei N.-Handschriften. Nachtrag zu den Bänden *Stücke 16/I* und *Stücke 18/I* der HKA' (121–29); J. Hein, '*Eisenbahnheirathen*-Miszelle: Nachtrag zu HKA *Stücke 20*' (130–31); M. Bobinac, 'N. auf kroatisch' (132–55).

NIETZSCHE. This year has seen the completion of the huge project undertaken by the Stiftung Weimarer Klassik (Stuttgart–Weimar, Metzler) to document all the literature in any language on N. between 1867 and 1998. The result is an impressive 5-vol. publication which will greatly benefit N.-specialists. This year's volumes, all ed. Susanne Jung et al., are: vol 2, *Sekundärliteratur 1867–1998: Allgemeine Grundlagen und Hilfsmittel; Leben und Werk im Allgemeinen; Biographische Einzelheiten*, x + 500 pp.; vol. 3, *Sekundärliteratur 1867–1998: Ns geistige und geschichtlich-kulturelle Lebensbezeihungen, sein Denken und Schaffen*, viii + 1013 pp.; vol. 4, *Sekundärliteratur 1867–1998: Zu Ns philosophisch-literarischem Werk insgesamt. Zu einzelnen Werken.*, vi + 254 pp.; vol. 5, *Sekundärliteratur 1867–1998: Wirkungs- und Forschungsgeschichte. Register zu den Bänden 2–5*, viii + 805 pp. *Nietzsche*, ed. Richard White, Aldershot, Ashgate, xxiv + 561 pp. Philip Pothen, *N. and the Fate of Art*, Aldershot, Ashgate, 208 pp. *N. und die Kultur – ein Beitrag zu Europa?*, ed. Georges Goedert and Uschi Nussbaumer-Benz, Hildesheim–Zurich, Olms, 309 pp. Rüdiger Safranski, *N.: Biographie seines Denkens*, Frankfurt, Fischer, 398 pp. Ingo Christians, *Reiz und Sporn des Gegensatzes: zu F. Ns Konzeption der Kraft*, Würzburg, Königshausen & Neumann, 398 pp. *Natur und Kunst in Ns Denken*, ed. Harald Seubert, Cologne–Weimar, Böhlau, xii + 207 pp. Brian Leiter, *Routledge Philosophy Guidebook to N. on Morality*, London–NY, Routledge, xxii + 323 pp. Eugen Biser, *N.: Zerstörer oder Erneuerer des Christentums?*, WBG, 178 pp., is a highly original contribution to the theological and philosophical debate on N. that will doubtless prove controversial. The writer, a professor of theology with a lifelong interest in the meaning of N.'s announcement of the 'death of God', contends that N.'s statements on Christianity are ambivalent, occasionally even paradoxical, and that his later work in part exhibits affirmative gestures towards the Christian faith which have been obscured by critical discussion. Based on the tentative framework he identifies in N.'s writing, Biser postulates a reconstruction of Christianity which fundamentally challenges the received wisdom of N. scholarship. Sybe Schaap, *Die Unfähigkeit zu vergessen: Ns Umwertung der Wahrheitsfrage*, Würzburg, Königshausen & Neumann, 316 pp., is a translation of the Dutch original. Susanne Dieminger, *Musik im Denken Ns*, Essen, Die blaue Eule, 68 pp. Daniel Havemann, *Der 'Apostel der Rache': Ns Paulusdeutung*, Berlin–NY, de Gruyter, x + 312 pp., is a Greifswald dissertation. Ansgar M. Hof, *Das Poetische der Philosophie: Friedrich Schlegel, F. N., Martin Heidegger, Jacques Derrida*, Bonn, DenkMal, 364 pp., is a Bonn dissertation. Johann Prossliner, *Ns Zarathustra*, Munich–Zurich, Piper, 122 pp. Stephan Günzel, *Geophilosophie: Ns philosophische Geographie*, Berlin, Akademie, 2001, 337 pp., is a Jena dissertation. Wolf G. Zachriat, *Die Ambivalenz des Fortschritts: F. Ns Kulturkritik*, Berlin, Akademie, 2001, 230 pp., is a dissertation from the Freie Univ. Berlin. Robert Gooding-Williams, *Zarathustra's Dionysian Modernism*, Stanford U.P., 2001, 440 pp. Joachim Köhler, *Zarathustra's Secret: The Interior Life of F. N.*, trans. Ronald Taylor, New Haven–London, Yale U.P., 336 pp. Chiu-yee Cheung, **Lu Xun: The Chinese 'Gentle' N.*, Frankfurt–Berlin, Lang, xx + 197 pp., is a comparative study of N. and the Chinese left-wing intellectual leader Lu Xun. Michael Hinz, **Verfallsanalyse und Utopie. N.-Rezeption in Thomas Manns 'Zauberberg' und in Robert Musils 'Der Mann ohne Eigenschaften'*, St. Ingbert, Röhrig, 2000, 213 pp. Andrea Bollinger and Franziska Trenkle, **N. in Basel*, Basle, Schwabe, 2000, 98 pp. Klaus Goch, **Ns Vater oder die Katastrophe des deutschen Protestantismus. Eine Biographie*, Berlin, Akademie, 2000, 408 pp. Marc Crépon, **Le Malin Génie des langues: N., Heidegger, Rosenzweig*, Paris,

Vrin, 2000, 224 pp. Ulrich Claesges, **Der maskierte Gedanke. Ns Aphorismenreihe 'Von den ersten und letzten Dingen.' Text und Rekonstruktion*, Würzburg, Königshausen & Neumann, 1999, 168 pp.

C. Dawidowski, 'N. und das vielbeschworene Seilläufertum. Das Prinzip des Ikarischen als Denkbild der Epochenschwelle', *WB*, 48:531–47. C. J. Emden, 'Sprache, Musik und Rhythmus. N. über die Ursprünge von Literatur, 1869–1879', *ZDP*, 121:203–30. H. Birus, 'Das imaginierte Als Ob. Ns *Also sprach Zarathustra. Ein Buch für Alle und Keinen*', *Neumann Vol.*, 21–42. M. Mayer, 'Die Rhetorik der Lüge. Beobachtungen zu N. und Hofmannsthal', *ib.*, 43–63. M. Mayer, 'Deutsche Verhängnisse. N.-Spiegelungen', *NRu*, 111, 2000:11–29. K. P. Liessmann, 'Der verstorbene Freund. F. N. und Ferdinando Galiani', *ib.*, 30–36. G. Falke, 'Dekadenter Klassizismus. Wohin Brahms gehört?', *ib.*, 37–42, concerns N.'s reception of Brahms. U. J. Wenzel, 'Unter Null. Simmel, N., Schopenhauer, Kant und die "ewige Wiederkehr"', *ib.*, 43–46. K. Fischer, 'Ein Geruch von Grausamkeit. N. als Avantgardist der Rationalisierungskritik', *ib.*, 58–76. M. Stingelin, 'Kriegerische und kämpferische Lektüre. F. N., Michel Foucault und Gilles Deleuze', *ib.*, 77–81. E. Behler, 'Die frühromantische Sprachtheorie und ihre Auswirkung auf N. und Foucault', *Athenäum*, 11, 2001:193–214. D. Bering, 'Ns Rettung der Sprache aus dem Geiste der Musik', *JDASD*, 2001:44–70. Á. Bernáth, 'Über Ns Begriff der Metapher in seinem Essay "Über Wahrheit und Lüge im aussermoralischen Sinne"', *JUG*, 2001:15–32. J. Villwock, 'Die Geschichte als Labyrinth. Zonen des Paradoxen im Werk F. Ns', *Fest. Wuthenow*, 225–42. M. Zayani, 'The Nietzschean temptation: Gilles Deleuze and the exuberance of philosophy', *CLS*, 36, 1999:320–40. E. Matala de Mazza, 'Wahrheitsrituale. Ur-Szenen einer tragischen Philosophie bei F. N.', pp. 219–52 of *Szenographien. Theatralität als Kategorie der Literaturwissenschaft*, ed. Gerhard Neumann, Freiburg, Rombach, 2000, 471 pp. H. Müller-Sievers, '"Eine ungeheure Kluft." N., die Geburt der Tragödie und das Maß der Dichtung', pp. 271–91 of *Kunst — Zeugung — Geburt. Theorien und Metaphern ästhetischer Produktion in der Neuzeit*, ed. Christian Begemann and David E. Wellbery, Freiburg, Rombach, 423 pp. G. Martens, 'Schon zu Beginn der Moderne "postmodern"? Zur poetologischen Konzeption in Ns Frühwerk', pp. 73–97 of *'In die Höhe fallen.' Grenzgänge zwischen Literatur und Philosophie*, ed. Anja Lemke and Martin Schierbaum, Würzburg, Königshausen & Neumann, 2000, 320 pp. R. Doran, 'N.: utility, aesthetics, history', *CLS*, 37, 2000:321–43. B. Glatzer Rosenthal, 'N.'s hidden voice in Socialist Realism', Barabtarlo, *Fusion*, 197–211. S. Dietzsch, 'N. und die *Gesänge des Maldoror*', pp. 193–207 of *Genuß und Egoismus. Zur Kritik ihrer geschichtlichen Verknüpfung*, ed. Wolfgang Klein and Ernst Müller,

Berlin, Akademie, xx + 364 pp. H. Decuble, 'Faulheit und Fragmentarismus. Zum fragmentarischen Stil F. Ns', pp. 280–94 of *Zum Thema Mitteleuropa. Sprache und Literatur im Kontext*, ed. Markus Bauer, Constance, Hartung-Gorre, 2000, 372 pp.

N.-Studien, 31, has: M. Skowron, 'Ns weltliche Religiosität und ihre Paradoxien' (1–39); D. Hillard, 'History as a dual process: N. on exchange and power' (40–56); L. Simonis, 'Der Stil als Verführer. N. und die Sprache des Performativen' (57–74); U. Tietz, 'Musik und Tanz als symbolische Formen: Ns ästhetische Intersubjektivität des Performativen' (75–90); P. S. Loeb, 'The dwarf, the dragon, and the ring of eternal recurrence: a Wagnerian key to the riddle of N.'s *Zarathustra*' (91–113); C. Landerer and M.-O. Schuster, 'Ns Vorstudien zur *Geburt der Tragödie* in ihrer Beziehung zur Musikästhetik Eduard Hanslicks' (114–33); E. Müller, '"Aesthetische Lust" und "dionysische Weisheit". Ns Deutung der griechischen Tragödie' (134–53); G. Gödde, 'Ns Perspektivierung des Unbewußten' (154–94); W. Stegmaier, 'Ein Mathematiker in der Landschft Zarathustras. Felix Hausdorff als Philosoph' (195–240).

Nietzscheforschung, 9, includes: P. Stekeler-Weithofer, 'Stolz und Würde der Person: Grundprobleme der (Bio)Ethik in einer mit N. entwickelten Perspektive' (15–29); K. Joisten, 'Der Weg Zarathustras als der Weg über den Menschen: Ns Überwindung der Anthropozentrität als philosophische Herausforderung unserer Zeit' (31–46); U. Tietz, 'Das *animal rational* und die Grundlagen der wissenschaftlichen Vernunft: zur anthropologischen Transformation der Erkenntnnistheorie bei F. N.' (47–66); K. Jauslin, 'Als-ob gegen An-sich: etwas über den Zusammenhang von Ästhetik und Kontingenz im Denken F. Ns' (69–81); H. J. Schmidt, '"Ich würde nur an einen Gott glauben, der" oder Lebensleidfäden und Denkperspektiven Ns in ihrer Verflechtung (1845–1888/89)' (83–104); V. Ebersbach, 'Ein versprengter Satyr: N. und das "Elitäre"' (105–29); E. Marsal, 'Wen löst Dionysos ab? Der "Gekreuzigte" im Facettenreichtum der männlichen N.-Dynastie: Friedrich August Ludwig Nietzsche, Carl Ludwig Nietzsche und F. N.' (131–46); J. Figl, '"Dionysos und der Gekreuzigte": Ns Identifikation und Konfrontation mit zentralen religiösen "Figuren"' (147–61); E. Hufnagel, 'Dionysos: Metaphysik, Mythos und Moderne' (163–88); P. D. Volz, '"Der Begriff des Dionysos noch einmal." Psychologische Betrachtungen zum Dionysischen als Herkunftsmythos' (189–205); M. Meyer, 'The tragic nature of Zarathustra' (209–18); T. Hoyer, '"[. . .] ich bedarf der Hände, die sich ausstrecken." Zarathustras pädagogisches Scheitern' (219–31); M. Liebscher, 'Zarathustra —

Der Archetypus des "Alten Weisen"' (233–45); H.-J. Pieper, 'Zarathustra — Sisyphos. Zur N.-Rezeption Albert Camus" (247–61); H.-G. von Seggern, 'Allen Tinten-Fischen feind. Metaphern der Melancholie in Ns *Also sprach Zarathustra*' (263–76); D. Solies, 'Die Naturwissenschaften des 19. Jahrhunderts und der Lebensbegriff des *Zarathustra*' (277–87); C. Zittel, 'Sprüche, Brüche, Widersprüche. Irritationen und Deutungsprobleme beobachtet am Erzählverhalten und an der Erzählperspektive in Ns *Also sprach Zarathustra*' (289–300); R. Heinen, 'Zum "Spiel auf der Grenze des Ästhetischen und des Moralischen." Ns Vorlesungen über Rhetorik' (303–23); S. Seyfi, 'Das hundertköpfige Hunds-Ungetüm, das ich liebe. F. N. und das Meer' (325–41); A. Schneider, 'Ns ökonomisch-philosophisches Manuskript Metaphysik, Ökonomie und Zeitlichkeit in der zweiten Abhandlung der *Genealogie der Moral*' (343–62); A. Becke, 'Askese und Ekstase. Über Weltflucht und Weltablehnung bei N. und Sloterdijk' (363–80); A. Venturelli, 'Die Wiederentdeckung des Negativen. N. und der Neomarzismus in Italien' (381–89).

OTTO-PETERS, LOUISE. Carol Diethe, *The Life and Work of Germany's Founding Feminist, L. O.-P. (1819–1895)*, Lewiston–Queenston, Mellen, 212 pp., is an informative and carefully researched study of this influential woman who, as well as being a popular novelist, was an ardent proponent of women's rights. One chapter is devoted to major themes in O.-P.'s novels from 1850–67, but this literary analysis is only one aspect of a broader approach. The strength of the work as a whole lies in its skillful presentation of the social, political, and cultural context of O.-P.'s bold thinking on a variety of topics concerning women's issues, religious extremism, and urban and rural poverty. There is an examination of O.-P.'s response to the events of 1848, expressed in her newspaper the *Frauen-Zeitung* (1849–52), and of her subsequent activity as president of the 'Allgemeiner deutscher Frauenverein' and contributor to its bi-monthly publication *Neue Bahnen*. The book represents a valuable contribution to research on this prolific writer and significant, if 'moderate', feminist figure whose work has still to be fully explored.

PÜCKLER-MUSKAU, HERMANN VON. I. Rippmann, 'Das Schöne und das Nützliche', *FVF*, 6, 2000: 183–207. B. Wolf, '*Ma petite folle!* Zu den Französismen in den Briefen von Hermann Fürst von P.-M.', *ASNS*, 154: 70–103.

RAABE. O. Neudeck, '"Der wahrhaffte Dietrich und Hauptschlüssel aller Heldenthaten." Zur Rezeption der deutschen Heldenepik in W. Rs *Das Odfeld*', *ZDP*, 121: 231–47. S. Thielking, 'Sonderbare Aktenstücke. Inszenierte Verschriftlichung bei W. R.', *ZGer*, 12: 25–35. *Raabe-Jb.*, 43, contains H. V. Geppert, 'R. und Faulkner' (1–20); A. Solbach, 'Die gekränkte Seele. Unzuverlässiges Erzählen in W. Rs *Drei Federn* (1865)' (21–49); S. Stockhorst, 'Zwischen Mimesis und magischem Realismus. Dimensionen der Wirklichkeitsdarstellung in Kriminalnovellen von Droste-Hülshoff, Fontane und R.' (50–81); C. Müller, 'Subjektkonstituierung in einer kontingenten Welt. Erfahrungen zweier Afrika-Heimkehrer — Gottfried Kellers *Pankratz, der Schmoller* und W. Rs *Abu Telfan*' (82–110). A. Rüttiger, 'Frauenfiguren im Bildungsroman. Zur Darstellung "der Frau" in W. Rs *Die Leute aus dem Walde* und *Prinzessin Fisch*', Loster-Schneider, *Geschlecht*, 105–27.

RAIMUND, FERDINAND. *Der Barometermacher auf der Zauberinsel: Zauberposse in zwei Aufzügen*, ed. Jürgen Hein, Vienna, Lehner, 72 pp.

REUTER. *F. R. — Leben, Werk und Wirkung. '. . .ich bin das geworden, was ich immer sehnlichst gewünscht habe . . .'*, ed. Cornelia Nenz, Rostock, Hinstorff, 2001, 104 pp., is the catalogue for the permanent exhibition in the F.-R.-Literaturmuseum. **F. R. im Werk von Schriftstellern des späten 19. Jahrhunderts*, ed. Christian Bunners (Beiträge der F.-R.-Gesellschaft, 10), Rostock, Hinstorff, 2001, 199 pp.

RÜCKERT. The HKA of R.'s works, ed. Rudolf Kreutner and Hans Wollschläger, Göttingen, Wallstein, has added vols 3–4, *Liedertagebuch. Werke der Jahre 1848–1849*, ed. Rudolf Kreutner et al., 560 pp.

SACHER-MASOCH. K. Kaufmann, 'Slavische Exotik und Habsburger Mythos. L. v. S.-Ms Galizische Erzählungen', *GRM*, 52:175–90. P.-H. Kucher, 'Drehscheibe Galizien — Zu L. v. S.-M.', Holzner, *Wechselwirkungen*, 37–56. B. Hyams, 'Casual connections: the case of S.-M.', pp. 139–54 of *One Hundred Years of Masochism. Literary Texts, Social and Cultural Contexts*, ed. Michael C. Finke and Carl Niekerk, Amsterdam, Rodopi, 2000, viii + 215 pp.

SCHOPENHAUER. A. Schmidt, 'Paradoxie als Wahrheit im Denken Ss', *Fest. Wuthenow*, 19–25. C. Kaminsky, 'Ausgerechnet S! Der (vermeintliche) Frauenhasser und die feministische Ethik', pp. 95–105 of *FrauenKulturStudien. Weiblichkeitsdiskurse in Literatur, Philosophie und Sprache*, ed. Astrid Böger and Herwig Friedl, Tübingen, Francke, 2000, 335 pp.

SEALSFIELD. C. S., *Sämtliche Werke*, ed. Karl J. R. Arndt, Hildesheim, Olms, has added another volume to the multi-volumed vol. 31: *Supplementreihe Materialien und Dokumente*, ed. Alexander Ritter, vol. 7: *Dokumente zur Rezeptionsgeschichte.* Part 1: *Die zeitgenössische Rezeption in Europa*, ed. Primus-Heinz Kucher, 476 pp. It contains: P.-H. Kucher, 'Die Rezeption des Werkes von C. S./Karl Postl in Europa. Forschungsstand, Thesen und neue Materialien' (10–47); H. Chambers, 'Die S.-Rezeption in Großbritannien seit 1840' (48–79); S. Gödicke, 'Die Rezeption Ss in der französischen periodischen Presse im 19. Jahrhundert' (80–106); A. Ritter, 'C. S. als Autor der

Verleger Cota (Stuttgart) und Murray (London). Zu Publizitätsanspruch wie Wirkungsrealität in der Vormärzzeit und dem Publizitätsverlust nach 1848' (107–51); 'C. Ss Werke im Spiegel der literarischen Kritik. Eine Sammlung zeitgenössischer Rezensionen mit einer Einleitung herausgegeben von Reinhard F. Spiess' (155–374); 'Dokumente zur Rezeption von C. Ss Werk in Großbritannien. Zusammengestellt von Helen Chambers' (375–430); 'Die S.-Rezeption in französischen Zeitschriften des 19. Jahrhunderts. Eine Auswahl, zusammengestellt von Stéphane Gödicke und Primus-Heinz Kucher' (431–54). C. S., *Lebensbilder aus der westlichen Hemisphäre in fünf Teilen.* Part 5: *Nathan, der Squatter-Regulator, oder, Der erste Amerikaner in Texas*, ed. Waldemar Fromm and Andreas Geyer (Schriftenreihe der C.-S.-Gesellschaft, 13), Munich, 2001, 217 pp., reprints the original text and has a 'Nachwort' by Günter Schnitzler.

SPYRI. *Johanna Spyri: verklärt, vergessen, neu entdeckt*, ed. Georg Escher and Marie-Louise Strauss, Zurich, Neue Zürcher Zeitung, 2001, 127 pp., is an exhibition catalogue.

STIFTER. The HKA of S.'s *Werke und Briefe*, ed. Alfred Doppler et al., Stuttgart, Kohlhammer, has added vol. 3.1: *Erzählungen* 1, ed. Johannes John et al., 281 pp. **A. S.: Tra filologia e studi culturali*, ed. Maria L. Roli, Milan, CUEM, 2001, 255 pp., has 17 articles, 8 of which are in German, on individual works by S., some from an interdisciplinary perspective. **Stiftersphäre. Annäherungen aus Literatur und Gegenwartskunst. Publikation zur Ausstellung in der Galerie im S.-Haus, 1 Dezember 2000 bis 31 Jänner 2001*, ed. Karl-Heinz Klopf and Sigrid Kurz, Linz, A.-S.-Institut, 2000, 150 pp. K. Jeziorkowski, 'Die verschwiegene Mitte. Zu A. Ss *Turmalin*', *Fest. Mittenzwei*, 79–89. H. Ragg-Kirkby, '"Warum nun dieses?": *Verblendung* and *Verschulden* in the stories of A. S.', *GLL*, 55:24–40. J. Metz, 'The Jew as sign in S.'s *Abdias*', *GR*, 77:219–32. M. Ritzer, 'Von Suppenwürfeln, Induktionsstrom und der Äquivalenz der Kräfte. Zum Kulturwert der Naturwissenschaft am Beispiel von A. Ss Novelle *Abdias*', *Kulturpoetik*, 2:44–67. T. Meurer, 'Stein-Strukturen. Zur Ästhetik der literarischen Komposition in A. Ss Erzählung *Granit*', *Fest. Bender*, 353–80. H. Höller, 'Ss indianische Seele', Beutner, *Literatur*, 118–27. M. Saar, 'Die Kunst des Lebens. Nietzsche und S.', *NRu*, 111, 2000:47–57. S. Schmidt, 'A. Ss *Nachsommer*: subjektive Idealität. Heinrich Drendorfs Subjektkonstitution im Spiegel seiner Selbstdefinition', Loster-Schneider, *Geschlecht*, 81–104. C. Begemann, 'Metaphysik und Empire. Konkurrierende Naturkonzepte im Werk A. Ss', Danneberg, *Wissen*, 92–126. L. Weissberg, 'Das starre Subjekt, das bewegliche Auge. Zur Geburt des "realistischen" Blicks', *ib.*, 127–46, is on *Bunte Steine*. G. von Graevenitz, 'Wissen und Sehen. Anthropologie und Perspektivismus in der Zeitschriftenpresse des 19. Jahrhunderts und in realistischen Texten. Zu Ss *Bunten Steinen* und Kellers *Sinngedicht*', *ib.*, 147–89.

STORM. *T. S. Sämtliche Gedichte in einem Band*, ed. Dieter Lohmeier, Frankfurt–Leipzig, Insel, 573 pp. Winfried Freund, *T. S.: 'Der Schimmelreiter'* (Reclams U.-B., Lektüreschlüssel für Schüler, 15315), Stuttgart, Reclam, 90 pp. *T. S. — Constanze Esmarch: Briefwechsel (1844–1846)*, ed. Regina Fasold, 2 vols, Berlin, Schmidt, 484, 592 pp. S. scholars will be delighted to see this long-awaited edition which publishes C.'s letters to her fiancé during their engagement (1844–46) for the first time, and S.'s correspondence with C. during this period now in its entirety. These unabridged and intimate texts allow the personalities of both figures to emerge more fully than before, and the volume will prove a valuable resource for research. The format is the same as for the others in this now extensive series, with thorough critical annotation of the letters and a comprehensive index. David Jackson, *T. S.: Dichter und demokratischer Humanist; eine Biographie*, Berlin, Schmidt, 2001, 358 pp., is an updated German translation of the English original which won the S. prize in 1998. Karl Ernst Laage, *Unterwegs mit T. S.*, Boyens, Heide, 136 pp., documents well over 100 locations visited by S. throughout Germany and beyond. Although not strictly-speaking a work for an academic library, the book displays the quality and attention to detail one associates with Laage, and its references to some 80 poems and novellas, together with numerous photographs and illustrations, provide both students and general readers with intriguing background information and explanations of the models for many geographical and architectural features described in the primary texts. Christian Neumann, **Zwischen Paradies und ödem Ort: Unbewußte Bedeutungsstrukturen in T. Ss novellistischem Spätwerk*, Würzburg, Königshausen & Neumann, 200 pp., is a Berlin dissertation.

STSG, 51, has: R. Morrien, 'Der dunkle "Garten der Vergangenheit" — historisches Erzählen als Lizenz zur Ausschweifung in den Chroniknovellen T. Ss' (9–25); D. Jackson, 'Leiden und Freuden des Biografen' (27–35); G. Eversberg, 'Ein modernes S.-Bild. 50 Jahre "Schriften der T.-S.-Gesellschaft"' (37–42); K. E. Laage, 'T. Ss Bekanntschaft mit Wilhelm Tolberg und seiner Ehefrau Agnes (mit unveröffentlichten Briefen)' (43–51); H. Detering, 'Kinderpsychologie und Erzählung. Ss *Der kleine Häwelmann*' (53–68); H. Rölleke, '*Hans Bär*. T. Ss früheste Märchendichtung intertextuell' (69–72); J. Lefebvre, 'Von der Identifikation mit Tierbräutigam-Märchen zur autonomen Existenz. Gedanken zu Ss Novelle *Eine Malerarbeit*' (73–85); T. Baltensweiler, 'Die Aphorie in der bürgerlichen Familie.

Zur Funktion des Erwerbsinns in *Hans und Heinz Kirch* und *Der Schimmelreiter*' (87–100); P. Goldammer, 'T. S. zwischen Philosemitismus und Antisemitismus' (101–15); R. Bouillon, 'Blumen im Werk T. Ss' (117–25); W. Zimorski, 'Das schärfere Auge des Dichters. Ein neu entdecktes Portrait von T. S.' (127–28); E. Jacobsen, 'S.-Bibliographie' (129–36); G. Eversberg, 'S.-Forschung und S.-Gesellschaft' (137–44). H. G. Peters, '*Der Schimmelreiter* als überlesene Ethnographie', Jürgens, *Exchanges*, 136–47. U. H. Gerlach, 'Aber "Glaube" in Ss *Schimmelreiter*?', Gerlach, *Einwände*, 161–81.

WAGNER. Ulrich Müller and Oswald Panagl, *Ring und Gral. Texte, Kommentare und Interpretationen zu den Musikdramen R. Ws: 'Der Ring des Nibelungen', 'Tristan und Isolde', 'Die Meistersinger von Nürnberg' und 'Parsifal'*, Würzburg, Königshausen & Neumann, 345 pp., is a substantial collection of contributions written by the two authors for Bayreuth Festival programmes between 1988 and 2001. The introduction defends the suitability of these pieces for inclusion in an academic work, given that programmes have traditionally been aimed at a discerning audience and the interpretations have not been performance-specific. The volume includes a commentary on the medieval sources for the *Ring des Nibelungen* and examinations of W.'s treatment of themes from Classical antiquity, Germanic mythology, and Indian thought. Overall this is a stimulating and informative work, marred only by the lack of a general bibliography and index. **'Alles ist nach seiner Art.' Figuren in R. Ws 'Der Ring des Nibelungen'*, ed. Udo Bermbach, Stuttgart, Metzler, 2001, viii + 253 pp. Morten Bartnaes, **R. Ws 'Tristan und Isolde'. Literarische Alleinswerdung als literaturwissenschaftliches Problem*, Hanover, Wehrhahn, 2001, 143 pp. Bernd Zegowitz, **R. Ws unvertonte Opern*, Frankfurt–Berlin, Lang, 2000, 305 pp., is a Heidelberg dissertation. P. Jost, 'Les écrits de R. W. publiés en traduction française du vivant du compositeur', *EG*, 57:689–707. W. G. Schmidt, 'Der ungenannte Quellentext. Zur Wirkung von Fouqués *Held des Nordens* auf Ws *Ring*-Tetralogie', *Athenäum*, 11, 2001:159–91. G. Brandstetter, 'Wunden der Liebe. Körperdarstellung im dekadenten Musiktheater nach W.: *Le Martyre de Saint-Sébastien*', *Neumann Vol.*, 135–69. M. Breatnach, 'Writing about music. Baudelaire and Tannhäuser in Paris', Bernhart, *Song Cycle*, 49–63. R. Company and J. Miguel, 'Una epifanía wagneriana monserratina: *Parsifal* (Daniel Mangrané/Carlos Serrano de Osma, 1951)', pp. 215–17 of *Parzival. Reescritura y transformación*, ed. Karen Andresen, Valencia U.P., 2000, 281 pp. A. Janés, 'El *Parsifal* de W.', *ib.*, 203–14.

WEERTH. B. Füllner, 'G. Ws *Leben und Thaten des berühmten Ritters Schnapphahnski.* Nachbemerkungen zur illustrierten Teilausgabe von 1848', *FVF*, 6, 2000:309–10. Id., 'G. Ws *Leben und Thaten des berühmten Ritters Schnapphahnski.* Von der Journal- zur Buchfassung', *ib.*, 147–81.

Id., '"Der Handel ist für mich das weiteste Leben, die höchste Poesie." G. W. und die 1848er Revolution', *Grabbe Jb.*, 19–20, 2000–01: 358–72. K. Nellner and J. Hiller von Gaertringen, 'W.-Bibliographie 1998–2000. Mit Nachträgen', *ib.*, 468–73. F. Melis, '"Ja, das ist er, wie er liebte und lebte; wie er auf der Rheinischen Zeitung am Redactionstisch neben mir saß . . ." Eine andere Sicht aud G. Ws Wirken für die *Neue Rheinische Zeitung*', *ib.*, 373–94. F. Takaki, 'G. W. und Paris', *ib.*, 413–18. G. Vonhoff, '"Eine frische Literatur." G. Ws *Skizzen aus dem sozialen und politischen Leben der Briten*', Kavanagh, *Exchanges*, 80–95.

LITERATURE, 1880–1945

By Malcolm Humble, *formerly Lecturer in German, University of Saint Andrews*

1. General

Bengt Algot Sørensen, **Geschichte der deutschen Literatur, 2: Vom 19. Jahrhundert bis zur Gegenwart* (Becksche Reihe, 1217), 2nd rev. edn, Munich, Beck, 468 pp. Gerald Bartl, **Spuren und Narben. Die Fleischwerdung der Literatur im zwanzigsten Jahrhundert*, Würzburg, Königshausen & Neumann, 380 pp. Vera Jost, **Fliegen oder Fallen. Prostitution als Thema in Literatur von Frauen im 20. Jahrhundert* (Frankfurter feministische Texte, Literatur und Philosophie, 6), Königstein/Ts., Hellmer, 280 pp. Theo Buck, **Vorschein der Apokalypse: Das Thema des Ersten Weltkriegs bei Georg Trakl, Robert Musil und Karl Kraus*, Tübingen, Stauffenberg, 2001, 84 pp. Gundula M. Sharman, *Twentieth-Century Reworkings of German Literature* (SGLLC), 210 pp., deals in part with the treatment of Joan of Arc by Schiller and Brecht, and with Thomas Mann's *Der Tod in Venedig* and Koeppen's *Der Tod in Rom*. **Le milieu intellectuel de gauche en Allemagne, sa presse et ses réseaux (1890–1960). Das linke Intellektuellenmilieu in Deutschland, seine Presse und seine Netzwerke (1890–1960)*, ed. Michel Grunwald and Hans Manfred Bock (Convergences, 24), xii + 708 pp. G. R. Kaiser, 'Parisbilder in der nichtfiktionalen deutschsprachigen Literatur zwischen den späten achtziger Jahren des 19. und den dreißiger Jahren des 20. Jahrhunderts', Kaiser, *Paris*, 1–60. L. Dietz, 'Verfasserangaben Franz Bleis für Artikel seiner Zeitschrift der Anonymen "Der Lose Vogel". Zu Attributionen an Robert Musil und Rudolf Borchardt', *Hofmannsthal-Jb.*, 10:7–36. A. Graf, 'Feuilleton-Korrespondenzen (1871–1939). Publizistische Anfänge des literarischen Vermittlungswesens in Deutschland', *Buchhandelsgeschichte*: 55–63.

2. Drama

Alan Menhennet, *The Historical Experience in German Drama. From Gryphius to Brecht* (SGLLC), 224 pp., includes a chapter on Schnitzler and Brecht. K. Leydecker, 'The drama of divorce: marriage crises and their resolution in German drama around 1900', *Neophilologus*, 86:101–17. B. Besslich, 'L'Empereur zwischen Expressionismus und Exil. Napoleon-Dramen von Hermann Essig, Fritz von Unruh, Walter Hasenclever und Georg Kaiser', *JDSG*, 46:250–78. B. Weyand, 'Gesichtslosigkeit. Konzeptualisierungen von Photographie und Theater im neusachlichen Jahrzehnt', *ZGer*, 12:70–82, is on Kracauer, Ernst Jünger, Benjamin, Kaiser, and Brecht. G. Fischer,

'Engagierte Literatur als historisch-kritische Darstellung der Gesellschaft. Zum Zeitstück der Weimarer Republik', Neuhaus, *Literatur*, 116–30. C. Jung-Hofmann, 'Engagagierte Literatur und rhetorischer Realismus. "Panamaskandal" und Weimarer Republik bei Wilhelm Herzog und Eberhard Wolfgang Möller', *ib.*, 219–37. F.-J. Deiters, 'Revolution als Arbeit am Text. Die Kolonisierung der Lebenswelt durch die Literatur im "politischen" Theater', *ib.*, 207–18. B. Haas, '"Wirrwarr" oder "Medizin"? Erwin Piscators theatertechnische Neuerungen der zwanziger Jahre', *ib.*, 238–50. K. Reimers, 'Das Drama als Tribunal — Justizkritik auf den Bühnen der Weimarer Republik', *ib.*, 251–60. G. Brandstetter, 'Die Szene des Virtuosen. Zu einem Topos von Theatralität', *Hofmannsthal-Jb.*, 10:213–44. *JKLWR*, 7, is devoted to the theatre, and includes: T. Röber, 'Aspekte des sachlichen Theaters der zwanziger Jahre' (9–44); E. Djomo, 'Afrika-Dramen der Weimarer Republik zwischen Erinnern und Mahnen. Anmerkungen zu Heinz Lewarks *Unvergessene, ferne Heimat!* und Paul Kedings *Deutsch-Südwest*' (45–68); and articles on operetta and opera of the 1920s.

3. Narrative

Johannes Sabel, *Text und Zeit. Versuche zu einer Verhältnisbestimmung, ausgehend von Carl Einsteins Roman Bebuquin oder die Dilettanten des Wunders* (HKADL, 31), 213 pp., also deals with Beer-Hofmann, *Der Tod Georgs*, Andrian, *Der Garten der Erkenntnis*, Rilke, *Malte*, Robert Müller, *Tropen*. Bettina Plett, **Problematische Naturen? Heldenkonzept und Heroismusdiskurs in deutschsprachiger Erzählliteratur 1860–1898*, Paderborn, Schöningh, 450 pp. Heinz J. Galle, *Populäre Lesestoffe. Groschenhefte, Dime Novels and Penny Dreadfuls aus den Jahren 1850 bis 1950* (Kleine Schriften der Universitäts- und Stadtbibliothek Köln, 120), Cologne, Universitäts- und Stadtbibliothek Köln, 112 pp., is a richly illustrated catalogue of an exhibition held in Cologne. Anja C. Schmidt-Ott, *Young Love — Negotiations of the Self and Society in Selected German Novels of the 1930s* (EH, I, 1835), xii + 300 pp., concerns Fallada, Aloys Schenzinger, Maria Leitner, Irmgard Keun, Marie Luise Kaschnitz, Anna Gmeyner, and Horváth.

4. Lyric

Georg Philipp Rehage, **'Wo sind Worte für das Erleben.' Die lyrische Darstellung des Ersten Weltkrieges in der französischen und deutschen Avantgarde (G. Apollinaire, J. Cocteau; A. Stramm, W. Klemm)* (Studia Romanica, 111), Heidelberg, Winter, xviii + 293 pp.

5. Movements and Periods

R. Robertson, 'Modernism and the self 1890–1924', Saul, *Philosophy*, 150–96. G. Hübinger, 'Politik mit Büchern und kulturelle Fragmentierung im Deutschen Kaiserreich', *Buchhandelsgeschichte*: 42–48. **Kolonialismus als Kultur. Literatur, Medien, Wissenschaft in der deutschen Gründerzeit des Fremden*, ed. Alexander Honold and Oliver Simons (Kultur — Herrschaft — Differenz, 2), Tübingen, Francke, 291 pp. Carola von Edlinger, **Kosmogonische und mythische Weltentwürfe aus interdiskursiver Sicht. Untersuchungen zu Phantasus (Arno Holz), Das Nordlicht (Theodor Däubler) und Die Kugel (Otto zur Linde)* (SDLNZ, 46), 329 pp. Gabrielle Gross, **Der Neid der Männer auf die Töchter. Ein weibliches Konfliktfeld bei Fontane, Schnitzler, Keyserling und Thomas Mann* (EH, 1, 1822), 245 pp. A. Aurnhammer, 'Wiederholte Spiegelung. Zur Interdependenz gemalter und gedichteter Antikebilder bei Georg Ebers und Lawrence Alma-Tadema. Mit einem Ausblick auf Hugo von Hofmannsthal', Aurnhammer, *Antike-Rezeption*, 273–98. T. Fitzon, 'Pompejanische Schatten. Die Rezeption Pompejis in der Literatur um 1900', *ib.*, 299–332. W. Kühlmann, 'Der Mythos des ganze Lebens. Zum Pan-Kult in der Versdichtung des Fin de Siècle', *ib.*, 363–400. Ariane Wild, *Poetologie und Decadence in der Lyrik Baudelaires, Verlaines, Trakls und Rilkes* (Ep, 340), 344 pp., brings out the similarities and differences between these poets, especially in relation to the felt need to define their roles in fresh terms, as decadence offers new themes and encourages the view that it is no longer possible to convey them according to classical models. Y.-G. Mix, 'Bildungskritik und Décadence in der Literatur des Fin de Siècle', Radecke, *Fontane*, 125–42; W. Hettche, 'Großstadtlyrik um 1890', *ib.*, 79–94. *Fin de Siècle*, ed. Rainer Warning and Winfried Wehle (Romanistisches Kolloquium, 10), Munich, Fink, 355 pp., includes contributions on Hofmannsthal, Thomas Mann, Rilke, and Musil in dialogue with artists and writers of other countries. *Neumann Vol.* includes contributions on Nietzsche, 'Lebensphilosophie', illustrations for the *Nibelungenlied*, and the work of Debussy and Mahler. W. Erhart, 'Die Wissenschaft vom Geschlecht und die Literatur der décadence', Danneberg, *Wissen*, 256–84. R. Bauer, 'Décadence und Dekadenz', *Euphorion*, 96: 117–26. B. Dahlke, 'Der müde Jüngling. Eine Denkfigur der vergeschlechtlichen Moderne', *ZGer*, 12: 287–95. R. A. Berman, 'The subjects of community: aspiration, memory, resistance 1918–1945', Saul, *Philosophy*, 197–244. Thomas Anz, *Literatur des Expressionismus* (SM, 329), viii + 258 pp., relates Expressionism to modernism by means of an examination of groups, media, key concepts, representative fictional figures, modern phenomena (the metropolitan milieu, science and technology, war and revolution), and aesthetics. A. Larcati, 'Zolas Erbe im Expressionismus. Ein Beitrag zur Rekonstruktion der Revolutionsdebatte im expressionistischen Jahrzehnt', *WB*, 48:181–201. A. Kramer, 'Goethe and the cultural project of German Modernism: Steiner, Kandinsky, Friedlaender, Schwitters and Benjamin', *PEGS*, 71, 2001:18–36. S. Simmons, 'Chaplin smiles on the wall: Berlin-Dada and wish-images of popular culture', *NGC*, 84, 2001:3–36. Neuhaus, *Literatur*, provides not only a thorough survey of its subject in the form of essays on individual writers, but considers the controversial question of definition and the shifting proportion of political and aesthetic elements in their work. Richard McCormick, **Gender and Sexuality in Weimar Modernity. Film, Literatur and New Objectivity*, Houndmills, Palgrave, 2001, 256 pp. Johannes Roskothen, *Verkehr. Zu einer poetischen Theorie der Moderne*, Munich, Fink, 320 pp., includes a chapter on Berlin novels of *Neue Sachlichkeit.*

Klein, *Literatur*, is concerned with the cultural disjunctions which define the Weimar Republik in relation to the Kaiserreich and later historical phases and includes: M. Beyer, 'Weimar: Anspruch und Wirklichkeit der Provinz' (15–28); P. Sprengel, 'Vorschau im Rückblick — Epochenbewußtsein um 1918, dargestellt an der verzögerten Rezeption von Heinrich Manns *Der Untertan*, Sternheims *1913*, Hesses *Demian* und anderen Nachzüglern aus dem Kaiserreich in der Frühphase der Weimarer Republik' (29–44). The contributions by Sprengel and Pütz on Thomas Mann, and Doppler on Musil are particularly noteworthy for the quality of their engagement with the volume's main issue (see below). E. Schütz, 'Romantik der Sachlichkeit. Die Marke Remarque, Ernst Jüngers Lehren und die rechten Konsequenzen daraus', *Fest. Orłowski*, 283–302. P. Davies, S. Parker, and M. Philpotts, 'The modern Restoration? revisiting the periodization of German literature 1930–1960', Kohl, *Words*, 111–33. J. McNally, '"Die Moorsoldaten": from circus-cum-cabaret to international anthem', *ib.*, 215–300. D. Sevin, 'The German literary diaspora: return and reception in post-war Germany', Knight, *Frontiers*, 25–34. E. Schneider Handschin, '"For him exile always meant the escape into his true homeland, into the spirit of humanity": on the cultural identity of Hermann Broch and Stefan Zweig', *ib.*, 65–76. W. Schopf, 'Das Freie Deutsche Buch im Porträt. Josef Breitenbachs Photodokumentation der ersten Buchmesse des Exils (Paris 1936)', Neuhaus, *Literatur*, 367–77. **Fluchtziel Paris. Die deutschsprachige Emigration 1933–1940*, ed. Anne Saint Sauveur-Henn (Dokumente, Texte, Materialien, 48), Berlin, Metropol, 336 pp. **Rechts und links der Seine. Pariser Tageblatt und Pariser Tageszeitung 1933–1940*, ed. Hélène Roussel and Lutz Winckler (STSL, 89), x + 373 pp. Klaus Grosse Kracht, **Zwischen Berlin und Paris: Bernhard Groethuysen*

(1880–1946) (STSL, 91), ix + 336 pp. *Gender — Exil — Schreiben*, ed. Julia Schöll and Martin Stern, Würzburg, Königshausen & Neumann, 250 pp., consists of essays on Maria Gleit, Ruth Landshoff-Yorck, Horváth, Maria Leitner, Anna Gmeyner, Irmgard Keun, Heinrich Mann, Thomas Mann, and Döblin. Sabine Rohlf, *Exil als Praxis — Heimatlosigkeit als Perspektive? Lektüre ausgewählter Exilromane von Frauen*, Munich, Text + Kritik, 350 pp., deals with novels by Irmgard Keun, Alice Rühle-Gerstel, Adrienne Thomas, Christa Winsloe, and Annemarie Schwarzenbach. *Deutschsprachige Schriftsteller im Schweizer Exil 1933–1950: eine Ausstellung des Deutschen Exilarchivs 1933–1945 der Deutschen Bibliothek. Ausstellung und Begleitbuch: Frank Wende* (Gesellschaft für das Buch, 8), Wiesbaden, Harrassowitz, 344 pp. C. Linsmayer, '"...die von uns geforderte Bewährungsprobe nicht bestanden ..." Die Situation emigrierter Schriftsteller in der Schweiz der Jahre 1933 bis 1950', *Exil*, 11–22. S. Schlawin, 'Die Anthologie "Heart of Europe" — ein Exilprojekt von Hermann Kesten und Klaus Mann für den L. B. Fischer Verlag (New York)', *AGB*, 54, 2001 : 1–110.

Changing Countries: The Experience and the Achievement of German-Speaking Exiles from Hitler in Britain from 1933 to Today, ed. Marian Malet and Anthony Grenville, London, Libris, xx + 240 pp., provides memoirs of exiles whose activities have not been confined to writing. *Exilforschung*, 20: 'Metropole des Exils', ed. Claus-Dieter Krohn et al., Munich, Text + Kritik, 308 pp., includes: C.-D. Krohn, 'Migrationen und Metropolenkultur in Berlin vor 1933' (14–35); S. Becker, 'Die literarische Moderne im Exil. Kontinuitäten und Brüche der Stadtwahrnehmung' (36–52); I. Schaber, '"Die Kamera ist ein Instrument der Entdeckung ..." Die Großstadtfotografie der fotografischen Emigration der NS-Zeit in Paris, London und New York' (53–73); C. Kambas, 'Exil des Intellekuellen und Großstadt. Zu Walter Benjamin' (74–96); H. Roussel and L. Winckler, 'Zur Topographie des literarischen und publizistischen Exils in Paris' (131–58); P. Becher, 'Metropole des Exils — Prag 1933–1939' (159–77); M. Winkler, 'Metropole New York' (178–98); E. Bahr, 'Los Angeles als Zentrum der Exilkultur und die Krise des Modernismus' (199–212); M. G. Patka, 'Wildes Paradies mit Ablaufzeit. Struktur und Leistung deutschsprachiger Exilanten in México Ciudad' (213–41); A. Saint Sauveur-Henn, 'Exotische Zuflucht? Buenos Aires, eine unbekannte und vielseitige Exilmetropole (1933–1945)' (242–68); A. Freyeisen, 'Shanghai: Rettung am "schlechtest möglichen Ort" der Welt?' (269–93).

Christian Klösch and Regina Thumser, *'From Vienna.' Exilkabarett in New York 1938 bis 1950* (Österreichische Exilbibliothek), Vienna, Pincus, 176 pp., accompanies the exhibition with the same title mounted by the Österreichische Exilbibliothek in the Vienna Literaturhaus. Winfried Halder, **Exilrufe nach Deutschland: die Rundfunkreden von Thomas Mann, Paul Tillich und Johannes R. Becher 1940–1945: Analyse, Wirkung, Bedeutung* (Tillich-Studien: Beihefte), Münster, Literatur Vlg, 101 pp. J.-P. Barbian, 'Verordneter Kanon. Literarische Kanonbildung während der NS-Diktatur 1933–1945', Arnold, *Kanonbildung*, 212–32.

6. German-Jewish Studies

Handbuch zur deutsch-jüdischen Literatur des 20. Jahrhunderts, ed. Daniel Hoffmann, Paderborn, Schöningh, 488 pp., includes: C. Blasberg, 'Der Meister und die Juden. Das Phänomen des George-Kreises' (81–102), which concentrates on Wolfskehl; M. Voigts, 'Die Dichter des Neuen Clubs: Jakob van Hoddis, Ernst Blass, Kurt Hiller, Erwin Loewenson, Erich Unger und Oskar Goldberg' (103–29); R. Kauffeldt, 'Jüdische Tradition und revolutionärer Geist. Gustav Landauer zum Beispiel' (131–50); G. Cepl-Kaufmann, 'Der Expressionismus. Zur Strukturhomologie von Epochenprofil und jüdischer Geisteswelt' (151–84); E. Reichmann, 'Übernationale kosmopolitische Europäer — die jüdischen Romanciers Lion Feuchtwanger, Georg Hermann, Joseph Roth, Jakob Wassermann, Franz Werfel, Arnold und Stefan Zweig' (185–218); H.-P. Bayerdörfer, '"Die Advokaten sind alle Juden" — Justizdebatte und Zeitstück auf der Bühne der Weimarer Republik' (219–34), which considers plays by Bruckner, Mehring, and Rehfisch-Herzog; D. Hoffman, 'Die Masken des Lebens — Die Wiener Moderne im Lichte jüdischer Hermeneutik' (235–70), which concerns Hofmannsthal, Beer-Hofmann, Andrian, and Schnitzler; W.-D. Hartwich, 'Die Verzweiflung war ihre Inspiration. Der Prager Kreis und die deutsch-jüdische Literatur' (271–98), which concentrates on Brod, Kafka, and Oskar Baum in relation to other cultures, the impact of Wagner, and theological issues; D. Hoffman, 'Essayismus und jüdische Diasporaexistenz' (299–322), dealing with Benjamin, Kracauer, Wolfenstein, Brod, Susmann, Simmel, Efraim Frisch, Heimann, Broch, and Theodor Lessing; H. Kiesel and S. Kluwe, 'Großstadtliteratur: Franz Hessel, Walter Benjamin, Alfred Döblin' (323–62); W. Strickhausen, 'Exil: Berthold Viertel, Ernst Waldinger, Anna Seghers, Albert Drach, Hans Sahl' (363–97). Readers will find here as much information on lives and works as in a reference work with entries in alphabetical order. The arrangement in a series of essays proves to be a bold strategy, revealing the importance of groups and networks and other developments in the German-Jewish symbiosis. Particularly valuable are pieces on groups, topics, trends, and genres, which have not previously had the attention they deserve in this context. e.g. the Neue Club and Expressionism, plays on miscarriages of justice, and the cultivation of the essay. The problematics of assimilation and the search for cultural identity — of Germans and Jews — are central to the contributions.

**German Literature, Jewish critics, The Brandeis Symposium*, ed. Stephen D. Dowden and Meicke C. G. Werner, Columbia, Camden House, 268 pp. Elisabeth Albanis, **German-Jewish Cultural Identity from 1900 to the Aftermath of the First World War: A Comparative Study of Moritz Goldstein, Julius Bab and Ernst Lissauer* (CJ, 37), viii + 310 pp. *Jüdische Identitäten in Mitteleuropa. Literarische Modelle der Identitätskonstruktion*, ed. Armin A. Wallas et al. (CJ, 38), vi + 325 pp., includes: A. Herzog, 'Ludwig Strauß und Ernst Sommer als Vertreter der Jüdischen Renaissance. Ein Beitrag zur Buber-Rezeption' (47–60); A. A. Wallas, 'Kulturzionismus, Expressionismus und jüdische Identität. Die Zeitschriften *Jerubbaal* (1918/19) und *Esra* (1919/20) als Sprachrohr und Diskussionsforum der zionistischen Jugendbewegung in Österreich' (61–99); H. Mittelmann, 'Jüdische Autobiographien und ihre Subtexte. Am Beispiel von Stefan Zweig und Albert Ehrenstein' (101–10); P. Rychlo, 'Jüdische Identitätssuche im Werk von Alfred Gong' (171–86); H. O. Horch, '"Messianische Zuversicht." Aspekte jüdischen Geschichtsdenkens im Werk von Manès Sperber' (187–213).

Jüdische Intellektuelle im 20. Jahrhundert. Literatur- und kulturgeschichtliche Studien, ed. Ariane Huml and Monika Rappenecker, Würzburg, Königshausen & Neumann, 230 pp., has contributions on Theodor Lessing, Karl Kraus, Selma Stern, Hannah Arendt and Susan Taubes, Käthe and Werner Vordtriede, Jenny Rosenbaum, Anna Seghers, Aharon Appelfeld, and Jean Améry. *Saskia Schreuder, *Würde im Widerstand. Jüdische Erzählliteratur im nationalsozialistischen Deutschland 1933–1938* (CJ, 39), 330 pp. Annegret Völpel, Zohar Shavit, and Ran HaCohen, *Deutsch-jüdische Kinder- und Jugendliteratur. Ein literaturgeschichtlicher Grundriß*, Stuttgart, Metzler, xii + 465 pp.

7. Austria and Switzerland

Literature in Vienna at the Turn of the Centuries. Continuities and Discontinuities around 1900 and 2000, ed. Ernst Grabovszki and James Hardin (SGLLC), 220 pp., includes, after an introduction by E. Grabovszki (1–23): J. Stewart, 'The written city: Vienna 1900 and 2000 (27–47); R. Görner, 'Notes from the counter-world' (51–66); D. C. G. Lorenz, 'Austrian women and the public: women's writing at the turn of the centuries' (67–88); T. P. Benfiglio, 'Dreams of interpretation: psychoanalysis and the literature of Vienna' (89–115); J. Pfizer, 'Venice as mediator between province and Viennese metropolis: themes in Rilke, Hofmannsthal, Gerhard Roth and Kolleritsch' (117–31); G. C. Howes, 'Critical observers of their times: Karl Kraus and Robert Menasse' (133–51); D. Crow, 'Art and architecture 1900 and 2000' (155–74); W. Riemer, 'Literature and cinema culture at the turn of the centuries' (179–204); H. H. Herzog and T. Herzog, '"Wien bleibt Wien": Austrian-Jewish culture at two *Fins de Siècles*' (205–20).

A. Anglet, 'Das frühexpressionistische "Gesamtkunstwerk" als Traumspiel bei Kokoschka, Pappenheim und Schönberg', *Arcadia*, 37:269–88. **Erfolg und Verfolgung. Österreichische Schriftstellerinnen 1918–1945*, ed. Christa Gürtler and Sigrid Schmid-Bortenschläger, Salzburg, Residenz, 320 pp. **Handbuch österreichischer Autorinnen und Autoren jüdischer Herkunft vom 18. bis zum 20. Jahrhundert*, ed. Österreichische Nationalbibliothek, 3 vols, Munich, Saur, 1742 pp. *Aug' um Ohr: Medienkämpfe in der österreichischen Literatur des 20. Jahrhunderts*, ed. Bernard Banoun, Lydia Andrea Hartl, and Yasmin Hoffmann (PSQ, 171), 2001, 248 pp., includes contributions on Canetti, Kafka, and Rilke. Hermann Dorowin, **'Mit dem scharfen Gehör für den Fall.' Aufsätze zur österreichischen Literatur im 20. Jahrhundert*, Vienna, Praesens, 184 pp. Wendelin Schmidt-Dengler, *Ohne Nostalgie. Zur österreichischen Literatur der Zwischenkriegszeit* (Literaturgeschichte in Studien und Quellen, 7), Vienna, Böhlau, 216 pp., contains previously published essays on authors (Broch, Nabl, Brunngraber, Schnitzler, Horváth), themes (the military, 1918), music (Krenek), and genres (the historical novel and lyric poetry). C. Benne, '*Also sprach Confusius*. Ein vergessenes Kapitel aus Nietzsches Wiener Früh-Rezeption', *OL*, 57:370–402. C. Leitgeb and R. Reichensperger, 'Von Textanalysen zur Literaturgeschichte. Studien zu einer Sprachstilgeschichte österreichischer Literatur: Grillparzer, Musil', Böhler, *Kulturtopographie*, 87–96. G. Streim, 'Literarische Moderne und nationale Identität. Zur Differenzierung von deutscher und österreichischer Moderne in der Publizistik um 1900', *ib.*, 231–43. Hartmut Steinecke, **Von Lenau bis Broch. Studien zur österreichischen Literatur — von außen betrachtet* (Patmos, 7), Tübingen, Francke, 215 pp. Stefan Simonek, *Distanzierte Nähe. Die slawische Moderne der Donaumonarchie und die Wiener Moderne*, ed. Leopold R. G. Decloedt und Stefan Simonek (Wechselwirkungen, 5), Berne, Lang, 242 pp., is not primarily concerned with German-speaking writers.

U. Amrein, 'Nationale Identität und Erinnerungspolitik. Die deutschsprachige Schweizerliteratur in der Vor- und Nachgeschichte des Nationalsozialismus', Böhler, *Kulturtopographie*, 245–68.

8. Individual Authors

ANDREAS-SALOME, LOU. Michaela Wiesner-Bangard and Ursula Welsch, *'. . .*wie ich Dich liebe, Rätselleben': Lou Andreas-Salomé. Eine Biographie*, Leipzig, Reclam, 296 pp. S. Michaud, '"Im Strudel der einzigschönen Stadt." Das Parisbild L. A.-Ss', Kaiser, *Paris*, 97–116.

BAB, JULIUS. J. B., *Leben und Tod des Judentums: Essay, Briefe und 'vita emigrationis'*, ed. Klaus Siebenhaar, Berlin, Bostelmann & Siebenhaar, 174 pp.

BAHR, HERMANN. Donald G. Daviau, *Understanding Hermann Bahr* (Österreichische und internationale Literaturprozesse, 14), St. Ingbert, Röhrig, 500 pp., brings together previously published work. N. Bachleitner, 'Im Feenland der Moderne. H. Bs Parisbild in den Jahren 1888/9', Kaiser, *Paris*, 61–74.

BARLACH, ERNST. R. Schnell, 'E. B. und das "Dritte Reich". Konfigurationen der Inneren Emigration', Schütz, *Reflexe*, 311–23.

BAUM, VICKI. Nicole Nottelmann, **Strategien des Erfolgs. Narratologische Analysen exemplarischer Romane Vicki Baums* (Ep, 405), 405 pp.

BECHER, JOHANNES R. P. Davies, 'Die Überwindung der Sprache. J.R. Bs Weg in die Partei', Neuhaus, *Literatur*, 277–85.

BEER-HOFMANN, RICHARD. R. B.-H., *Der Briefwechsel mit Paula 1896–1937*, ed. with commentary and postscript by Richard M. Scheirich and Peter Michael Braunwarth, Oldenburg, Igel, 511 pp., is the second supplementary volume following the six-volume edition. Elke Surmann, *'*Ein dichtes Gitter dunkler Herzen'. Tod und Liebe bei Richard Beer-Hofmann und Arthur Schnitzler*, Oldenburg, Igel, 116 pp. G. Vassiliev, 'R. B.-Hs "Der Tod Georgs." Zum Problem Ästhetizismus und Judentum', *ÖGL*, 46:120–33.

BENJAMIN, WALTER. **Walter Benjamin and Romanticism*, ed. Andrew Benjamin and Beatrice Hassen (Walter Benjamin Studies), NY, Continuum, vii + 246 pp. Susanne Kaufmann, **Mit Walter Benjamin im Théâtre Moderne oder: Die unheimliche Moderne* (Ep, 377), 332 pp. *NGC*, 83, 2001, includes: G. Markus, 'W.B. or: the commodity as phantasmagoria' (3–42); U. Steiner, 'The true politician: W.B.'s concept of the political' (43–88); C. P. Long, 'Art's fateful hour: B., Heidegger, art and politics' (89–118); N. Isenberg, 'The work of W.B. in the age of information' (119–50); D. Kaufmann, 'Beyond use, within reason: Adorno, B. and the question of theology' (151–76); M. Löwy, 'Messianism in the early work of Gershom Sholem' (177–91). D. Giuriato, 'Löschblatt. Vom Umgang mit W. Bs Handschriften', *MLN*, 117:560–75. S. Knaller, 'A theory of allegory beyond W. B. and Paul de Man', *GR*, 77:83–101. U. Steiner, '"Das Höchste wäre zu begreifen, dass alles Factische schon Theorie ist." W. B. liest

Goethe', *ZDP*, 121:265–84. B. Mertens, 'The anxiety of influence: B., Scholem and Molitor', Berghahn, *Essays*, 127–41.

BENN, GOTTFRIED. H. Esselborn, 'Atavismus und Modernität in G. Bs Gedichten der zwanziger Jahre', *WW*, 52:398–16. T. Pittrof, 'G. Bs Antikerezeption bis 1934', Aurnhammer, *Antike-Rezeption*, 471–502. R. Dressel, 'G. Bs "Paris". Eine Stadt als poetologisches Prinzip', Kaiser, *Paris*, 217–52.

BLOCH, ERNST. D. C. Durst, 'E. B's theory of nonsimultaneity', *GR*, 77:171–94.

BÖHLAU, HELENE. A. Richards, '"Halb Tier, halb Engel": women, animals and vegetarianism in the fiction of H. B. (1856–1940) and Hedwig Dohm (1831–1919)', Berghahn, *Essays*, 111–25.

BORCHARDT, RUDOLF. *Gesammelte Briefe*, ed. Gerhard Schuster and Hans Zimmermann, part II, vol. 8: *Briefe 1936–1945*, Munich, Hanser, 740 pp. *Rudolf Borchardt. Verzeichnis seiner Schriften*, ed. Ingrid Grüninger and Reinhard Tgahrt (Deutsches Literaturarchiv. Verzeichnisse, Berichte, Informationen, 28), Marbach, Deutsche Schillergesellschaft, 429 pp. *Akzente*, 49.2, is a special issue devoted to 'Unbekannte Texte von Rudolf Borchardt'. *Dichterische Politik. Studien zu Rudolf Borchardt*, ed. Kai Kauffmann (Publikationen zur *ZGer*, n.F., 4), Berne, Lang, 214 pp., after the editor's foreword consists of: W. Schuller, 'Nation und Nationen bei R.B.' (11–25); K. Kauffmann, 'R. Bs Rhetorik der "Politischen Geographie"' (27–61); B. Petzinna, 'Wilhelminische Intellektuelle. R. B. und die Anliegen des Ring-Kreises' (63–79); R. Herzinger, 'Kulturautorismus. Von Novalis über Borchardt bis Botho Strauß: zyklische Wiederkehr des deutschen Antimodernimus?' (81–95); G. Streim, 'Evolution, Kosmogonie und Eschatologie in R. Bs "Theorie des Konservatismus", mit besonderer Berücksichtigung von *Der Fürst*' (97–113); M. Bernauer, 'R. B. und Ezra Pound im faschistischen Italien' (115–45); U. Ott, 'Die *Jamben* als politische Dichtung' (147–61); A. Kissler, '"Alles, was nicht unrein ist, ist Garten." Politische Hygiene, politisierte Liebe und botanische Politik bei R. B.' (163–81); F. Hofmann, 'Literarische Annexion? Bs Übersetzung zwischen Politik und Phantasma' (183–203).

BRAUNE, RUDOLF. T. Unger, 'Klassenkampf mit einer Portion Erotik. R. Bs *Junge Leute in der Stadt*', Neuhaus, *Literatur*, 104–15.

BRECHT, BERTOLT. *Brecht-Handbuch*, ed. Jan Knopf, vol. 3: *Prosa, Filme, Drehbücher*, Stuttgart, Metzler, xii + 500 pp. Hiltrud Häntzschel, *Brechts Frauen*, Reinbek, Rowohlt, 317 pp. *Brecht-Jahrbuch*, 27. *Begegnung der Extreme. Brecht und Beckett — Eine Re-Interpretation / Where Extremes Meet. Rereading Brecht and Beckett*, ed. Antony Tatlow, Madison, Wisconsin U.P., x + 232 pp., contains A. Tatlow, 'Saying yes and saying no: Schopenhauer and Nietzsche as educators' (9–42); H. Blau, 'Among the deepening shades: the Beckettian moment(um) and the Brechtian arrest' (65–82); J. Kalb, 'Through the lens of Heiner Müller: Brecht and Beckett — three points of plausible convergences for the future' (95–120); S.-E. Chase, 'Time and time again: playing Brecht and Beckett's real time in the digital age' (163–77); E. Sakellaridou, 'Feminist theater and the Brechtian tradition: a retrospect and a prospect' (179–98).

**Der Mond über Soho: 66 Gedichte mit Interpretationen*, ed. Marcel Reich-Ranicki, Frankfurt, Insel, 279 pp. *Empedocles' Shoe: Essays on Brecht's Poetry*, ed. Tom Kuhn and Karen Leeder with a Foreword by David Constantine, London, Methuen, 256 pp., contains, after an introduction by T. Kuhn: R. Speirs, ' "Of poor B.B." — and others' (37–52); H.-H. Müller, T. Kindt, and R. Habeck, 'Love — not — memory. An interpretation of "Erinnerung an die Marie A." ' (53–71); D. Midgley, 'The poet in Berlin: B.'s city poetry of the 1920s' (89–106); E. Boa, 'The eulogistic mode in B.s poetry' (107–30); A. Phelan, 'Returning generals. B.'s "The Manifesto" and its contexts' (131–50); D. Constantine, 'B.'s sonnets' (151–74); R. Ockenden, 'Empedocles in Buckow: a sketch-map of misreading in B.'s poetry' (175–206); E. Wizisla, ' "May it seem to us our dearest . . .": B.'s "Children's Anthem" ' (207–20); K. Leeder, ' "After Brecht": the reception of B.'s poetry in English' (221–56). All the authors combine close readings of single poems with overviews of forms and show a wide cultural awareness of past and present, fulfilling the editor's promise of a productive re-reading of Brecht's poetry in another century. Aimed at a readership beyond the Brecht research community, the collection pays throughout particular attention to problems of translation and to the changing political context of the *oeuvre* both in its creation and reception.

Hans-Harald Müller and Tom Kindt, **Brechts frühe Lyrik: Brecht, Gott, die Natur und die Liebe*, Munich, Fink, 160 pp. J. Hermand, 'Bs Hitler-Satiren', Neuhaus, *Literatur*, 153–68. E. Wizisla, 'Allons Enfants. Brechts "Kinderhymne" ', *SuF*, 54:273–78. N. Oellers, 'Das ernste Spiel mit der Kunst. Bs *Die heilige Johanna der Schlachthöfe*', Klein, *Literatur*, 109–26. K. Kanzog, 'Bertolt Brecht *Die Maßnahme*. Über das angemessene Verstehen eines schwierigen Textes. Ein literaturwissenschaftlicher Kompaß', *Fest. Gaede*, 201–16. P. Hutchinson, 'Brecht, *Die Dreigroschenoper*', Hutchinson, *Landmarks*, 177–92. R. Speirs, 'Brecht, *Mutter Courage und ihre Kinder*', *ib.*, 193–208. H. Loeper, 'Noch einmal "Anderweis". Ein Gedicht von Margarete Steffin im Nachlaß Bertolt Brechts und ein Stück von Bertolt Brecht (?) im Nachlaß Ruth Berlaus', *NDL*, 50.5:161–62. E. Wizisla, 'Verzicht auf Traumproduktion? Politischer Messianismus bei Benjamin und B.', *SuF*, 54:559–64. S. Kebir, ' "Der große

Vergnügungspark." Ein Kafkaesker Albtraum von Brecht, inspiriert von Ruth Berlau', *NDL*, 50.5: 154–60.

BRITTING, GEORG. *Georg Britting als Theaterkritiker in Regensburg, 1912–1914 und 1918–1921. Eine Dokumentation*, ed. Ingeborg Schuldt-Britting and M. Herrschel (RBDSL, A 12) 205 pp.

BROD, MAX. H. Holzkamp, 'B. und Kafka in Paris', Kaiser, *Paris*, 171–98.

CANETTI, ELIAS. S. Bub, 'E. C., Cesare Pavese und die Buschmänner. Ein Beitrag zur Rezeption ethnologischer Stoffe in der modernen Literatur', *GRM*, 52: 303–12.

CANETTI, VEZA. *V.C.* (TK, 156), 111 pp., has, besides three texts by her: H. Göbel, 'Zur Wiederentdeckung V. Cs als Schriftstellerin. Einige persönliche Anmerkungen (3–10); B. Bannrasch, 'Zittern als eine Bewegung des Widerstands. V. Cs frühe Erzählungen "Geduld bringt Rosen" und der Roman "Die Gelbe Straße"' (30–47); R. Robertson, 'Häusliche Gewalt in der Wiener Moderne. Zu V. Cs Erzählung "Der Oger"' (48–64); I. van der Lühe, '"Zum Andenken an die fröhlichste Stadt Zentraleuropas." V. Cs "Die Schildkröten" im Kontext der deutschsprachigen Exilliteratur' (65–81); A. Schedel, '"Bitte das über seine Frau *nicht* auslassen." Briefe an Erich Fried, eine "gefälschte" Autorenschaft und Frauen im Hintergrund — ein Beitrag zu V. Cs Jahren im Londoner Exil' (82–94). Angelika Schedel, *Sozialismus und Psychoanalyse. Quellen von Veza Canettis literarischen Utopien* (Ep, 378), 222 pp.

DAHN, FELIX. Hans Rudolf Wahl, *Die Religion des deutschen Nationalismus. Eine mentalitätsgeschichtliche Studie zur Literatur des Kaiserreichs: Felix Dahn, Ernst von Wildenbruch, Walter Flex* (Neue Bremer Beiträge, 12), Heidelberg, Winter, 404 pp., traces the evolution of nationalism in the Kaiserreich with reference to Dahn's *Ein Kampf um Rom*, Wildenbruch's poems on Bismarck and his Festspiel *Willehalm*, and Flex's *Der Wanderer zwischen beiden Welten*, showing the breakdown of its fusion with monarchical adulation.

DÖBLIN, ALFRED. Wulf Koepke, *The Critical Reception of Alfred Döblin's Major Novels*, Columbia, SC, Camden House — Woodbridge, Boydell and Brewer, 218 pp. *Internationales Alfred Döblin-Kolloquium Bergamo 1999*, ed. Torsten Hahn (*JIG*, A 51), 314 pp. Seonja Gong, **Studien zu Alfred Döblins Erzählkunst am Beispiel seiner Berliner Romane: 'Wadzeks Kampf mit der Dampfturbine' und 'Berlin Alexanderplatz'* (EH, 1, 1823), 250 pp. Christian Schärf, **A. Ds 'Berlin Alexanderplatz' — Roman und Film. Zu einer intermedialen Poetik der moderne Literatur*, Stuttgart, Steiner, 2001, 46 pp. M. Boussart, 'Die Aktualisierung des Bibeltextes in A. Ds Montageroman *Berlin Alexanderplatz. Die Geschichte vom Franz Biberkopf*', *Germanica*, 31: 99–127. T. Jentsch, 'Modelle der Erlösung — Jesus, Raskolnikow, Biberkopf', *WB*, 48: 399–419.

A. Detken, 'Zum Politischen in Ds *Berlin Alexanderplatz* und *Die Ehe* — Versuch einer Revision', Neuhaus, *Literatur*, 69–88. A. W. Riley, '"Der Satz der Griechen": zu einem unveröffentlichten essayistischen Fragment A. Ds', *Fest. Gaede*, 235–43. R. E. Sackett, 'D.'s destiny: the author of *Schicksalsreise* as Christian, Jew and German', *Neophilologus*, 86:587–608. S. Trappen, 'Grass, D. und der Futurismus. Zu den futuristischen Grundlagen des Simultaneitätskonzepts der Vergegenkunft', *Euphorion*, 96:1–26. D. Schiller, 'A. D., Hans Siemsen und der Bund Neues Deutschland 1938/1939', *Exil*, no. 1:44–61.

EINSTEIN, CARL. Johannes Sabel, **Text und Zeit: Versuche zu einer Verhältnisbestimmung, ausgehend von Carl Einsteins Roman Bebuquin oder Die Dilettanten des Wunders* (Historisch-kritische Arbeiten zur deutschen Literatur, 31), Frankfurt, Lang, 213 pp.

ELBOGEN, PAUL. G. Rinke, 'Vom alten Österreich nach Kalifornien — Der Schriftsteller und Herausgeber P. E.', *Exil*, no. 1:62–71.

ERNST, PAUL. Hildegard Châtellier, **Verwerfung der Bürgerlichkeit. Wandlungen des Konservatismus am Beispiel Paul Ernst (1866–1933)*, Würzburg, Königshausen & Neumann, 222 pp. *Paul Ernst. Außenseiter und Zeitgenosse*, ed. Horst Thomé, Würzburg, Königshausen & Neumann, 220 pp. contains: V. Žmegač, 'Text und Kontext in der Gattungspoetik von P. E.' (11–24); H. Aust, 'Novellenform und Sprachlogik. Überlegungen zu einigen Novellen von P. E.' (25–36); H. Thomé, 'Ariadne bei P. E. und Hugo von Hofmannsthal. Konzepte der Metatragik nach 1900' (37–60); G. Hartung, 'P. Es *Kassandra*' (61–78); H. Steiger, 'P. Es Aufsatz *Die Zerstörung der Ehe* von 1917 oder die Angst vor Veränderung' (79–88); G. Häntzschel, 'P. Es Epos *Das Kaiserbuch*' (89–100); H. Dainat, 'Die Herrscher, das Reich, die Dichter. Vorstellungen sozialer Ordnung eines konzervativen Revolutionärs: *Das Kaiserbuch* von P.E.' (101–32); C. Groppe, 'Die Welt des Geldes. P. E. und die Intellektuellen seiner Zeit: Georg Simmel, Rudolf Borchardt' (133–58); V. Žmegač, 'P. E. und das Judentum' (159–68); K. Ifkovits, 'P. E. und die Anfänge des Insel-Verlages. Mit zwei unveröffentlichten Briefen P. Es an Rudolf von Poellnitz' (169–88); A. Rammstedt, 'P. Es Freundschaft mit Georg und Gertrud Simmel im Spiegel der überlieferten Korrespondenz' (187–204); A. Reinthal, '"Aber Paul Ernst kann man schätzen." Zur Rezeption P. Es bei Ernst Blass' (205–16); H. Châtellier, 'P. E. und Werner Sombart' (217–30).

FALLADA, HANS. Jenny Williams, **Mehr Leben als eins. Hans Fallada, Biographie*, Berlin, Aufbau, 391 pp. Michael Grisko, *Erläuterungen und Dokumente: Hans Fallada, 'Kleiner Mann — was nun?'* (UB, 16024), 184 pp.

FLEISSER, MARIELUISE. S. Doering, 'Schauplatz Andorra. Die Inszenierung der Fremde in M. Fs Reiseprosa', Klein, *Literatur*, 127–44.

FÖRSTER-NIETZSCHE, ELISABETH. K. Bauer, 'Domesticating Nietzsche: toward a genealogy of E. F.-N.'s "Novellen-Eierchen"', *OL*, 57:343–69.

GEORGE, STEFAN. Robert E. Norton, *Secret Germany: Stefan George and his Circle*, Ithaca, Cornell U.P., 847 pp., is a major biography, which in range and thoroughness has no equal in English. Readers familiar with George and well aware of his lack of political correctness may nevertheless be surprised at the negative portrait of his personality as reflected in his work and his relationships. However, the documentation, drawn from every relevant source, including the memoirs of members of the circle, supports the author's case. Chapters are devoted to the individual volumes of the poetic *oeuvre*, and extensive translations of poems and prose by George and the circle are provided. J. Suglia, 'On the Nationalist recontruction of Hölderlin in the George Circle', *GLL*, 55:387–97. H. Hudde, '"Getreue Nachbildung" und "Deutsches Denkmal" zugleich. Eine Verlaine-Umdichtung Gs', *CP*, 253–54:21–27. W. Deinert, 'Am Urquell des Augenblicks. Gs verkannte Gründung', *ib.*, 28–36. K. Landfried, '"Ich liess mich von den schulen krönen"', *ib.*, 37–39. A. Rink, 'Algabal — Elagabal. Herrschertum beim frühen S. G.', *WB*, 48:548–67. W. Braungart, 'Hymne, Ode, Elegie. Oder: von den Schwierigkeiten mit antiken Formen der Lyrik (Mörike, G., G.-Kreis)', Aurnhammer, *Antike-Rezeption*, 245–72.

GLAUSER, FRIEDRICH. Patrick Bühler, **Die Leiche in der Bibliothek: Friedrich Glauser und der Detektivroman* (Probleme der Dichtung, 31), Heidelberg, Winter, 177 pp.

GOLL, YVAN. Y. G., *Die Eurokokke: Roman*, Göttingen, Wallstein, 176 pp., presents a facsimile of the first edition, with an afterword by Barbara Glauert-Hesse and drawings by Georges Annenkoff.

GONG, ALFRED. A. G., *Gnadenfrist. Gedichte*, ed. Joachim Herrmann (Texte aus der Bukowina, 16), Aachen, Rimbaud, 96 pp.

GRIMM, HANS. S. Neuhaus, '"Radikaler Ethnozentrismus." H. Gs *Volk ohne Raum* (1926)', pp. 244–60 of Stefan Neuhaus, *Literatur und nationale Einheit in Deutschland*, Tübingen, Francke, 587 pp.

HALBE, MAX. Andreas Lothar Günter, **Präfaschistische Weltanschauung im Werk Max Halbes* (EH, 1, 1841), 171 pp.

HARTLAUB, FELIX. *'*In den eigenen Umriss gebannt*'*: Kriegsaufzeichnungen, literarische Fragmente und Briefe aus den Jahren 1939 bis 1945*, ed. Gabriele Lieselotte Ewenz, 2 vols, Frankfurt, Suhrkamp, 1200 pp.

HASENCLEVER, WALTER. A. Anglet, '"Heimat [..] in einer leichteren, klareren Atmosphäre." W. H. in Paris', Kaiser, *Paris*, 371–406.

HAUPTMANN, CARL. C.H., *Sämtliche Werke, Erzählungen und epische Fragmente aus dem Nachlaß*, IX.1, ed. Eberhard Berger and Elfriede Berger, Stuttgart, Frommann-Holzboog, 500 pp.

HAUPTMANN, GERHART. Sigfrid Hoefert, *Internationale Bibliographie zum Werk G. Hs*, vol. III (Veröff. der G.-.H.-Gesellschaft, 12), Berlin, Schmidt, 180 pp. P. Hofmann, 'Versuch über das Scheitern. Zu G. Hs Geburt der Tragödie aus dem Geist des (Selbst-)Opfers', *DVLG*, 76:138–62. P. Sprengel, 'Der Dionysos-Mythos im Werk G. Hs: Kunstreligion, Vitalismus und Totenkult', Aurnhammer, *Antike-Rezeption*, 401–20. F. Schössler, 'Wahrnehmungsprozesse und Sehertum in Hs frühen Dramen', *MK*, 46.3–4: 131–50. M. Stewart, 'Hauptmann, *Vor Sonnenaufgang*', Hutchinson, *Landmarks*, 127–42. E. Weber, 'Naturalismuskritik in G. Hs frühen Dramen *Das Friedensfest* und *Einsame Menschen*', *LitL*, 25: 168–88.

HAUSMANN, RAOUL. B. Stiegler, 'R. Hs Theorie der Optophonetik und die Erneuerung der menschlichen Wahrnehmung durch die Kunst', *Hofmannsthal-Jb.*, 10:327–56. H. Korte, 'Am Anfang war die Bühne Dada. R. Hs Auftritts- und Bewegungskunst', *JKLWR*, 7:69–90.

HERZL, THEODOR. T. R. Kuhnle, 'L'émulation du monde ancien: *Altneuland* de T. H.', *Germanica*, 31: 143–57.

HESSE, HERMANN. Birgit Lahann, **Hermann Hesse: Dichter für die Jugend der Welt. Ein Lebensbild* (ST, 3478), 160 pp. Hans-Jürgen Schmelzer, *Auf der Fährte des Steppenwolfs: Hermann Hesses Herkunft, Leben und Werk*, Stuttgart, Hohenheim, 450 pp. G. Decke, 'Ansichten zu Hermann Hesse', *SuF*, 54:248–63. M. Schickling, 'H. Hs Literaturkritik für "Bonniers Litterära Magasin"', *Buchhandelsgeschichte*: 2–9. B. Urban, '"Schüler des Heiligen Thomas." Archivalische Anmerkungen zu Hermann Hesses Thomas Aquin-Rezeption', *JDSG*, 46:23–40. *Hermann Hesse — Diesseits des 'Glasperlenspiels'*, ed. Heike Gfereis (*MaM*, 98), 120 pp., is a thorough documentation of the novel's gestation from 1932 until its publication in 1943. **'Der Dichter sucht Verständnis und Erkanntwerden.' Neue Arbeiten zu Hermann Hesse und seinem Roman 'Das Glasperlenspiel'*, ed. Eva Zimmermann, Berne, Lang, 216 pp. L. Müller, 'Leises Schaudern. Beim Lesen des "Glasperlenspiels"', *JDSG*, 46:427–37.

HESSEL, FRANZ. A. Corbineau-Hoffman, 'Bilder und Stimmen der Stadt. F. H. und Léon-Paul Fargue als "Flaneurs" in Paris', Kaiser, *Paris*, 441–68.

HOFMANNSTHAL, HUGO VON. *Sämtliche Werke. Kritische Ausgabe*, ed. Rudolf Hirsch et al., vol. 27: *Ballette, Pantomimen, Filmszenarien*, Frankfurt, Fischer, 600 pp. Martin E. Schmid, *Hofmannsthal Brief-Chronik. Regest-Ausgabe*, 3 vols, Heidelberg, Winter, 1800 pp. *A Companion to the Works of Hugo von Hofmannsthal*, ed. Thomas A. Kovach (SGLLC),

286 pp. consists, after an introduction by the editors, of H. C. Seeba, 'H. and *Wiener Moderne*: the cultural context' (25–46); A. Thomasberger, 'H's poems and lyrical dramas' (47–64); E. Ritter, 'H.'s narrative prose: the problem of individuation' (65–84); T. Kovach, 'H.'s "Ein Brief": Chandos and his crisis' (85–96); B. J. Bennett, 'H.'s theatre of adaptation' (97–116); J. Bottenberg, 'The H.-Strauß correspondence' (117–38); W. E. Yates, 'H.'s comedies' (139–58); J. Beniston, 'H. and the Salzburg Festival' (159–80); K. Arens, 'H.'s essays: conservation as revolution' (181–204); N. Berman, 'H. v. H.'s political vision (205–26); D. A. Joyce, 'H. reception in the twentieth century' (227–50). As in the other volumes of this series (see KAFKA below), most of the authors succeed in conveying their expertise and summarizing previous research in a way that makes their topics accessible to readers only slightly acquainted with the subject. Philip Ward, *Hofmannsthal and Greek Myth: Expression and Performance* (British and Irish Studies in German Language and Literature, 24), Oxford, Lang, 295 pp., covers work in drama, opera, and the dance in relation to contemporary debates on psychoanalysis, feminism, and the crisis of language and performance practice in a case-study of the reception of the Classics in *fin-de-siècle* Vienna. **'Lieber Lord Chandos': Antworten auf einen Brief*, ed. Hubert Spiegel et al., Frankfurt, Fischer, 256 pp. M. Mayer, 'Die Rhetorik der Lüge. Beobachtungen zu Nietzsche und H.', *Neumann Vol.*, 43–63. H. Hiebler, '"...mit Worten (Farben) ausdrücken, was sich im Leben in tausend anderen Medien komplex äußert ..." H. und die Medienkultur der Moderne', *Hofmannsthal-Jb.*, 10:89–182. B. Neuhoff, 'Ritual und Trauma. Eine Konstellation der Moderne bei Benjamin, Freud und H.', *ib.*, 183–212. A.-M. Baranowski, 'De l'histoire étrange au récit fantastique. L'aventure du maréchal de Bassompierre chez Goethe et H.', *Germanica*, 31:59–69. R. Helmstetter, 'Erlebnis und Dichtung. Beobachtung der Form in Hs *Erlebnis des Marschalls von Bassompierre*', *DVLG*, 76:250–60. P. Matussek, 'Intertextueller Totentanz. Die Reanimation des Gedächtnisraums in Hs Drama "Der Tor und der Tod"', Danneberg, *Wissen*, 313–37. D. Martin, '"Bruder Kreon." Zu Hs *Ödipus und die Sphinx*. Mythisierung und Remythisierung der Antike', Aurnhammer, *Antike-Rezeption*, 333–62. E. Dangel-Pelloquin, '"Das kleine Falsificat." Ein Spiel von Original und Fälschung in Hs "Die Lästigen. Komödie in einem Akt nach Molière"', *Hofmannsthal-Jb.*, 10:59–88. R. Simon, 'Paradoxien der Interpretation (ausgehend von Hs "Der Schwierige")', *JDSG*, 46:199–218. W. G. Schmidt, '"...wie nahe beisammen das weit Auseinanderliegende ist." Das Prinzip der *Metamorphose* in der Oper *Die Ägyptische Helene* von H. v. H. und Richard Strauß', *JKLWR*, 7:169–223. K. Rossbacher, 'Sucherin und

Sucher. H. von Hs Tragödienfragment *Ascanio und Gioconda* (1892)', Radecke, *Fontane*, 109–24.

HOLITSCHER, ARTHUR. C. Grubitz, 'Die Wirklichkeit der großen Stadt, 1924. Hs und Masereels "Narrenbaedeker": ein Denkbild', Kaiser, *Paris*, 199–216.

HORVÁTH, ÖDÖN VON. Y. May, 'Zwischen Konformismus und Engagement. Ö. von H. als kritischer Autor', Neuhaus, *Literatur*, 326–37. M. Truwant, 'Hs Exilliteratur aus einer anderen Sicht betrachtet: *Figaro läßt sich scheiden* als neuartiges Stationendrama', *MK*, 46.3–4:77–92. K. Bartsch, '"Nicht gerade besonders vornehm." Zu Ö. von Hs Hörspielversuchen. Mit einer persönlichen Anmerkung und marginalen Beobachtungen zur Aktualität des Autors', *Fest. Orłowski*, 497–508.

JAHNN, HANS HENNY. Reiner Niehoff, **Hans Henny Jahn. Die Kunst der Überschreitung*, Munich, Matthes & Seitz, 2001, 525 pp. M. Gasser, 'Der Griff in die Eingeweide. H. H. Js *Perrudja*', Klein, *Literatur*, 69–108.

JÜNGER, ERNST. Ulrich Prill, **'Mir ward Alles Spiel.' Ernst Jünger als homo ludens*, Würzburg, Königshausen & Neumann, 160 pp. H. R. Brittnacher, 'Von Kriegern und Duldern, Schindern und Mönchen. Bilder vom Mann bei Hanns Heinz Ewers und E. J.', *ZGer*, 12:308–23. C. Öhlschläger, '"Der Kampf ist nicht nur eine Vernichtung, sondern auch die männliche Form der Zeugung." E. J. und das "radikale Geschlecht" des Kriegers', Begemann, *Kunst*, 325–52. M. Tauss, 'Der halluziatorische Rausch als archaische Initiation. Zum hermetischen Drogenheroismus in E. Js Erzählung "Besuch auf Godenholm" (1952)', *WW*, 52:441–57. H. Mottel, '"Vor Actium". E. J. im Kontext des Diskurses der prophetischen Literatur nach 1918', *Fest. Orłowski*, 563–97.

KÄSTNER, ERICH. *Erich Kästners weltweite Wirkung als Kinderschriftsteller. Studien zur internationalen Rezeption des kinderliterarischen Werks. Unter Mitarbeit von Ute Dettmar*, ed. Bernd Dolle-Weinkauff and Hans-Heino Ewers (Kinder- und Jugendkultur, -literatur und -medien. Theorie–Geschichte–Didaktik, 18), Frankfurt, Lang, 366 pp. Patricia Brons, **Erich Kästner, un écrivain journaliste* (Convergences, 19), Berne, Lang, x + 451 pp. M. Klein, 'E. K.: einige Überlegungen zu den Schwierigkeiten der Germanistik mit dem Schriftsteller und seinem Werk', Klein, *Literatur*, 173–88.

KAFKA, FRANZ. *Amtliche Schriften: Text- und Materialienband*, ed. Klaus Hermsdorf and Benno Wagner (Kritische Ausgabe der Werke), Frankfurt, Fischer, 1150 pp. Reiner Stach, *Kafka: Die Jahre der Entscheidungen*, Frankfurt, Fischer, 673 pp., despite being a blockbuster biography which has had a mixed reception, because it is restricted to the years 1910 to 1915 and has novelistic features, deserves attention. These crucial years are marked by the breakthrough which began with *Das Urteil* and by the entire course of the relationship with Felice Bauer, which is traced by the author with remarkable empathy. The author has also much to say about the literary scene in Prague and other centres, the First World War and Kafka's family and friends and his professional activity. The book's main value lies in the links established between Kafka's psychological lability and the works, which are nevertheless given their literary due. Because Stach deliberately distances himself from the various academic approaches to interpretation of the texts, a refreshing view emerges of an author inspired more by personal crises than by theories. Peter Demetz, *Die Flugschau von Brescia. Kafka, d'Annunzio und die Männer, die vom Himmel fielen*, Vienna, Zsolnay, 252 pp. F. Bacaud, 'De l'éducation corruptrice ou: les années de déformation du jeune Kafka', *Germanica*, 30:23–40. M. Harman, 'Dr. Kaesbohrer und die Puppenbriefe. Zwei kleine Rätsel um Kafkas Aufenthalt in Berlin', *SuF*, 54:845–52.

The Cambridge Companion to Kafka, ed. Julian Preece, CUP, 254 pp., contains: J. Preece, 'Kafka's Europe' (1–8); D. Constantine, 'Kafka's writing and our reading' (9–24); A. Fuchs, 'A psychoanalytic reading of *The Man who Disappeared*' (25–41); R. J. Goebel, 'The exploration of the modern city in *The Trial*' (42–60); E. Boa, '*The Castle*' (61–79); R. V. Gross, 'Kafka's short fiction' (80–94); S. Corngold, 'Kafka's later stories and aphorisms' (95–110); J. Preece, 'The letters and diaries' (111–30); B. Dodd, 'The case for a political reading' (131–49); I. Bruce, 'Kafka and Jewish folklore' (150–68); D. C. G. Lorenz, 'Kafka and gender' (169–88); A. Northey, 'Myths and realities in Kafka biography' (189–205); O. Durrani, 'Editions, translations, adaptations' (206–25); M. Brady and H. Hughes, 'Kafka adapted to film' (226–41); I. Bruce, 'Kafka and popular culture' (242–46). The authors demonstrate Kafka's quintessential modernity, as they apply the latest or reapply in original terms older critical paradigms (feminism, decontruction, Marxism, psychoanalysis, and Jewish studies) to the whole range of his work. The last pieces on the reception and adaptation in later writing and other media indicate how Kafka has entered the blood-stream of contemporary culture.

A Companion to the Works of Franz Kafka, ed. James Rolleston (SGLLC), 388 pp., contains: J. R. Rolleston, 'Introduction: Kafka begins' (1–19); Id., 'Critical editions I: the 1994 paperback edition' (21–25); C. Koelb, 'Critical editions II: will the real Franz Kafka please stand up?' (27–31); W. H. Sokel, 'Beyond self-assertion: a life of reading Kafka' (33–59); J. L. Ryan, 'Kafka before Kafka: the early stories' (61–83); R. A. Berman, 'Tradition and betrayal in "Das Urteil"' (85–99); R. Robertson, 'Kafka as anti-Christian: "Das

Urteil", "Die Verwandlung" and the aphorisms' (101–22); H. Sussman, 'Kafka's aesthetics: a primer. From the fragments to the novels' (123–48); S. Corngold, 'Medial allusions at the outset of *Der Process*; or, *res in media*' (149–70); B. Theisen, 'Kafka's circus turns: "Auf der Galerie" and "Erstes Leid"' (171–86); R. J. Goebel, 'Kafka and postcolonial critique: "Der Verschollene", "In der Strafkolonie", "Beim Bau der chinesischen Mauer"' (187–212); R. T. Gray, 'Disjunctive signs: semiotics, aesthetics and failed mediation in "In der Strafkolonie"' (213–45); R. V. Gross, 'Hunting Kafka out of season: enigmatics in the short stories' (247–62); S. L. Gilman, 'A dream of Jewishness denied: Kafka's tumor and "Ein Landarzt"' (263–79); J. Zilcosky, 'Surveying the castle: Kafka's colonial visions' (281–324); M. Harman, 'Making everything "a little uncanny": Kafka's deletions in the manuscripts of *Das Schloß* and what they can tell us about his writing process' (325–46); C. Koelb, 'Kafka imagines his readers: the rhetoric of "Josefine die Sängerin" and "Der Bau"' (347–59). While in comparison with its Cambridge counterpart the interpretations in some of the contributions can be idiosyncratic or obfuscating, Sokel's magisterial retrospect of the decades of his own engagement with Kafka is a suitable beginning to a collection which includes interesting new readings based on post-colonial and other recently developed critical approaches.

**Franz Kafka. Zur ethischen und ästhetischen Rechtfertigung*, ed. Beatrice Sandberg and Jakob Lothe (Rombach Wissenschaften, Reihe Litterae, 85), Freiburg, Rombach, 2001, 304 pp. Bertram Rohde, **'Und blätterte ein wenig in der Bibel.' Studien zu Franz Kafkas Bibellektüre und ihren Auswirkungen auf sein Werk* (Ep, 390), 262 pp. Weidong Ren, **Kafka in China. Rezeptionsgeschichte eines Klassikers der Moderne* (EH, 1, 1824), 184 pp. *Kafkas Fabriken*, ed. Hans-Gerd Koch et al. (*MaM*, 100), Marbach, Deutsche Schillergesellschaft, 159 pp., contains: K. Wagenbach, 'Kafkas Fabriken' (3–40); K. Hermsdorf, 'Franz Kafka und die Arbeiter-Unfall Versicherungsanstalt' (41–78); P. U. Lehner, 'Die moderne Unfallversicherung in Österreich. Ein geschichtlicher Rückblick' (97–108); B. Wagner, 'Poseidons Gehilfe. Kafka und die Statistik' (109–30); H.-G. Koch, 'Dichtung und Arbeit. Interferenzen in den Texten Kafkas' (139–56). Gerhard Rieck, **Franz Kafka und die Literaturwissenschaft. Aufsätze zu einem kafkaesken Verhältnis*, Würzburg, Königshausen & Neumann, 136 pp. G. Neumann, '"Wie eine regelrechte Geburt mit Schmutz und Schleim bedeckt." Die Vorstellung von der Entbindung des Textes aus dem Körper in Ks Poetologie', Begemann, *Kunst*, 293–324. I. W. Holm, 'Verkörperlichung der Symbole. F. Ks Metaphern zwischen Poetik und Stilistik', *Hofmannsthal-Jb.*, 10:303–26. H. Kraft, 'Ein Mensch wie K. Die Romane Kafkas', *LWU*, 35:3–14. Simela Delianidou, **Frauen, Bilder* *und Projektionen von Weiblichkeit und das männliche Ich des Protagonisten in Franz Kafkas Romanfragmenten. Unter besonderer Berücksichtigung der Schuldfrage im Proceß* (EH, 1, 1826), 233 pp. S. Gebert, 'Ks "Grammatik" im *Proceß*', *WB*, 48:364–79. M. Neuhaus, 'Entgründung. Auch ein Kommentar zu Ks "Das Urteil" ', *WB*, 48:344–63.

Kafkas 'Urteil' und die Literaturtheorie. Zehn Modellanalysen, ed. Oliver Jahraus and Stefan Neuhaus, (UB, 17636), 271 pp., contains an introductory piece by the editors, 'Die Methodologie der Literaturwissenschaft und die Kafka-Interpretation' (23–34); R. Selbmann, 'K. als Hermeneutiker. *Das Urteil* im Zirkel der Interpretation' (36–58); M. Scheffel, '*Das Urteil*. Eine Erzählung ohne "geraden, zusammenhängenden, verfolgbaren Sinn"?' (59–77); S. Neuhaus, 'Im Namen des Lesers. Ks *Das Urteil* aus rezeptionsästhetischer Sicht' (78–100); C.-M. Ott, 'Sozialgeschichte der Literatur und die Probleme textbezogener Literatursoziologie — anlässlich von Ks *Das Urteil*' (101–25); T. Anz, 'Praktiken und Probleme psychoanalytischer Literaturinterpretation — am Beispiel von Ks Erzählung *Das Urteil*' (126–51); C. Kanz, 'Differente Männlichkeiten. Ks *Das Urteil* aus gendertheoretischer Perspektive' (152–75); L. Bluhm, ' "ein Sohn nach meinem Herzen." Ks *Das Urteil* im Diskursfeld der zeitgenösssichen Goethe-Nachfolge' (176–96); N. Ort, 'Zum Gelingen und Scheitern von Kommunikation. Ks *Urteil* — aus systemtheoretischer Perspektive' (197–219); S. Schedel, 'Literatur ist Zitat — "Korrespondenzverhältnisse" in Ks *Das Urteil*' (220–40); and O. Jahraus, 'Zeichen-Verschiebungen: vom Brief zum Urteil, von Georg zum Freund. Kafkas *Das Urteil* aus poststrukturalistischer dekonstrukivistischer Sicht' (241–62).

Rainer J. Kaus, **Eine kleine Frau — Kafkas Erzählung in literaturpsychologischer Sicht* (BNL 189), 97 pp. W. Berentelg, 'Ks Parabel *Der Kreisel*', *LitL*, 25:91–100. H. Rudloff, 'King Kong und Kafka. Katastrophenfilme und F. Ks "Das Stadtwappen" ', *DUS*, 55:26–29. A. Disselkötter and C. Albert, ' "Grotesk und erhaben in einem Atemzug" — Kafkas Affe', *Euphorion*, 96:127–44. P. Avenel-Cohen, 'Et s'il n'était pas mort à Prague? de Marco Bacci: une réécriture de *La Métamorphose* de F. K.', *Germanica*, 31:11–22. F. Bancaud, 'La réécriture de Bouvard et Pécuchet dans *Un célibataire entre deux ages* (1915), *Recherches d'un chien* (1922) de F. K. et dans *Toute une histoire* (1995) de Günter Grass', *Germanica*, 31:39–58. S. Corngold, 'Adorno's "Notes on Kafka": a critical reconstruction', *MDLK*, 94:24–42.

StZ, 40, contains: A. Wagnerová, 'Ein überraschendes Zeugnis über Hermann Kafka' (373–78); H.-G. Koch, 'Teuflisch in aller Unschuld' (379–91); M. Voigts, 'F. Ks Freund Felix Weltsch' (393–410); H. D. Zimmermann, 'Joseph Schwejk und Josef K.' (411–23).

KAISER, GEORG. Seán Allan, 'Kaiser, *Von morgens bis mitternachts*', Hutchinson, *Landmarks*, 159–76.

KANDINSKY, WASSILI. M. Eto, 'Die Idee und Geschichte des Gedicht- und Holzschnittbuches "Klänge" ', *DB*, 108: 151–61.

KESSLER, HARRY GRAF. Tamara Barzantny, **Harry Graf Kessler und das Theater. Autor — Mäzen — Initiator 1900–1933*, Cologne, Böhlau, 368 pp.

KEYSERLING, EDUARD VON. G. Radecke, 'Das Motiv des Duells bei Theodor Fontane und Eduard von Keyserling', Radecke, *Fontane*, 61–78.

KLABUND. *Werke. In acht Bänden.* ed. Christian von Zimmermann with Ralf Georg Bogner, Heidelberg, Elfenbein, vol. 6: *Dramen und Bearbeitungen.* 1. *Dramen und dramatische Szenen*, ed. Christian von Zimmermann, 2001, 400 pp.; 2. *Bearbeitungen und Nachdichtungen*, ed. Christian von Zimmermann, 2001, 423 pp.; vol. 7. *Übersetzungen und Nachdichtungen*, ed. Christian von Zimmermann, 288 pp.

KOENIG, ALMA JOHANNA. D. Hempen, 'Und alles lauschte dem Liede Horands: Kunst und Humanität in A.J.Ks *Gudrun*', *Neophilologus*, 86: 273–85.

KOLB, ANNETTE. Armin Strohmeyr, **Annette Kolb. Dichterin zwischen Zeiten* (DTV Sachbuch, 30868), 333 pp.

KOLMAR, GERTRUD. Annegret Schumann, **Bilderrätsel statt Heimatlyrik. Bild und Identität in Gertrud Kolmars Gedichtsammlung 'Das Preußische Wappen'*, Munich, Judicium, 290 pp.

KOMMERELL, MAX. E. Geulen, 'Wiederholte Spiegelungen. Formgeschichte und Moderne bei K. und Preisendanz', *DVLG*, 76: 271–84.

KRAUS, KARL. **Feinde in Scharen: Ein wahres Vergnügen da zu sein. Karl Kraus — Herwarth Walden: Briefwechsel 1909–1912*, ed. George C. Avery, Göttingen, Wallstein, 675 pp. Irina Djassemy, **Der 'Produktivgehalt kritischer Zerstörerarbeit'. Kulturkritik bei Karl Kraus und Theodor W. Adorno* (Ep, 399), 446 pp. D. Winkelmann, 'Die Verschmelzung zweier Gelächter — K. K. und Jacques Offenbach', *Fest. Michel*, 195–209. D. Goltschnigg, 'Parodie und Satire bei K. K. und Johann Nestroy', *LitL*, 25: 129–42.

KRENEK, ERNST. F. Trapp, 'E. K. im Spiegel seiner Autobiographie', *Exil*, no. 1: 30–43.

KUBIN, ALFRED. L. Simonis, 'Bildende Kunst als Movens der literarischen Avantgarde. Text-Bild-Beziehungen im Werk A.Ks', Kircher, *Avantgarden*, 249–70.

LANDAUER, GUSTAV. S. Wolf, ' ". . .der Geist ist die Gemeinschaft, die Idee ist der Bund." Gustav Landauers Judentum', *Schriften der Erich Mühsam-Gesellschaft*, 2: 85–116.

LASKER-SCHÜLER, ELSE. *Werke und Briefe, kritische Ausgabe*, ed. Norbert Oellers, vol. 5: *Das Hebräerland*, Frankfurt, Jüdischer Vlg, 550 pp. Uta Grossman, **Fremdheit im Leben und in der Prosa E. L.-Ss* (Literatur und Medienwissenschaft, 82), Oldenburg, Igel, 2001, 266 pp. A. Meier, '"am liebsten unter Arbeitern": Inszenierungen einer kulturellen Schlüsselfigur bei E. L.-S.und Ernst Toller', Neuhaus, *Literatur*, 298–311. A. Krauss, 'Schnittstellen im Text. Zur Poetologie des Dramas "Ichundich" von E. L.-S.', *JDSG*, 46: 219–49.

LEIP, HANS. Rüdiger Schütt, **Dichter gibt es nur im Himmel. Leben und Werk von Hans Leip. Biographie und Briefedition 1893–1948*, Hamburg, Dölling & Galitz, 2001, 499 pp.

LINDAU, RUDOLF. R. Hillenbrand, 'Skeptischer Realismus in der Erzählkunst R. Ls', *GLL*, 55: 363–86.

LISSAUER, ERNST. Rainer Brändle, *Am wilden Zeitenpaß. Motive und Themen im Werk des deutsch-jüdischen Dichters Ernst Lissauer*, pref. Guy Stern (AD, 46), 286 pp.

MANN, HEINRICH. H. M. and Félix Bertaux, *Briefwechsel 1922–1948*, Frankfurt, Fischer, 799 pp. Peter Stein, *Heinrich Mann* (SM, 340), x + 208 pp. Karin Verena Gunnemann, *Heinrich Mann's Novels and Essays. The Artist as Political Educator* (SGLLC), 200 pp., examines Heinrich Mann's entire literary career in terms of an education of his compatriots to democracy, while taking account of the changes made to his aesthetic inspired by the need both to adapt to new readership expectations and to experiment with new forms. Special attention is given to the reception of the novels in Germany. G. von Essen, 'Engagierte Literatur im Exil: H. Ms *Es kommt der Tag*', Neuhaus, *Literatur*, 286–97. S. Ireton, 'Heinrich Manns Auseinandersetzung mit dem Haß: Analyse der *Henri Quatre*-Romane im Rahmen der exilbedingten Haßliteratur', *OL*, 57: 204–21. S. Hirsch, 'Bildwelten eines Königs — Zur Verwendung und Funktion der Bildquellen in den *Henri-Quatre*-Romanen H. Ms', *Exil*, no. 1: 92–98. M. Joch, 'Nüchternes Pathos. Ein Vorzug Heinrich Manns als Romancier und Publizist', *ZGer*, 12: 36–50. W. Gast, 'Rosa Lola oder Was hat Rainer Werner Fassbinders Film "Lola" mit Heinrich Manns Roman "Professor Unrat" zu tun?', *DUS*, 55: 20–25.

MANN, KLAUS. Peter Schröder, *Klaus Mann zur Einführung* (Zur Einführung, 253), Hamburg, Junius, 192 pp. Alexa-Désirée Casaretto, **Heimatsuche, Todessehnsucht und Narzißmus in Leben und Werk Klaus Manns* (EH, I, 1845), xix + 261 pp. S. Lamb, '"Als Ästhet beginnen und als Sozialist enden" — ein Paradox? Überlegungen zur Problematik "Literatur und Engagement" am Beispiel K. Ms', Neuhaus, *Literatur*, 89–103. M.-S. Benoit, '"À la recherche d'une voie". Les écrits de jeunesse de Klaus Mann', *Germanica*, 30: 61–76. C. von

Zimmermann, 'Sommergeschichte — Reiseerzählung — Exilroman. Klaus Manns Roman *Flucht in den Norden*', *LitL*, 2001, 24:230–50.

MANN, THOMAS. *Buddenbrooks: Verfall einer Familie*, ed. with commentary by Eckhart Heftrich (Große kommentierte Frankfurter Ausgabe), Frankfurt, Fischer, 1280 pp. (Text and commentary also available in separate volumes). *Der Zauberberg: Text*, ed. Michael Neumann (Große kommentierte Frankfurter Ausgabe), Frankfurt, Fischer, 1120 pp. (with commentary volume). *Essays* II: *1914–1926*, ed. Hermann Kurzke (Große kommentierte Frankfurter Ausgabe), Frankfurt, Fischer, 1120 pp. (with commentary volume). Theodor W. Adorno und T. M. *Briefwechsel*, ed. Christoph Gödde and Thomas Sprecher (Theodor W. Adorno, *Briefe und Briefwechsel*, 3), Frankfurt, Suhrkamp, 179 pp.

The Cambridge Companion to Thomas Mann, ed. Ritchie Robertson, CUP, 257 pp., contains: T. J. Reed, 'M. and history' (1–21); P. Bishop, 'The intellectual world of T.M.' (22–41); M. Minden, 'M.'s literary techniques' (43–63); A. J. Webber, 'M.'s man's world: gender and sexuality' (64–84); M. M. Anderson, 'M.'s early novellas', (84–94); R. Robertson, 'Classicism and its outfalls: *Death in Venice*' (95–106); A. Bance, 'The political becomes personal: *Disorder and Early Sorrow* and *Mario and the Magician*' (107–18); J. L. Ryan, '*Buddenbrooks*: between realism and aetheticism' (119–36); M. Beddow, '*The Magic Mountain*' (137–50); W.-D. Hartwich, 'Religion and culture: *Joseph and his Brothers*' (151–67); S. von R. Scaff, '*Doktor Faustus*' (168–84); Y. Elsaghe, '*Lotte in Weimar*' (185–98); F. A. Lubich, '*The Confessions of Felix Krull, Confidence Man*' (199–212); H. Siefken, 'M. as essayist' (213–25); T. J. Reed, 'M. as diarist' (226–34); T. J. Buck, 'M. in English' (235–48). The titles of these contributions do not in all cases give an idea of their range and depth. For example, Bishop relates Mann to Schopenhauer, Nietzsche, and Wagner, Romanticism, psychoanalysis, and Weimar Classicism; Anderson relates the early stories to melodrama; Reed and Bance show the depth of his political engagement beneath the surface of his art. Myth is central not only to Hartwich on the Joseph novels, but also to Lubich on Felix Krull, sexuality not only to Webber's contribution but also to Reed on the diaries. The incisive and succinct argumentation does justice to a writer whose classic status remains assured and whose work continues to be open to new insights.

Astrid Roffmann, **'Keine freie Note mehr.' Natur im Werk Thomas Manns* (Ep, 420), 250 pp. Friedhelm Marx, *'Ich aber sage Ihnen . . .' Christusfigurationen im Werk Thomas Manns* (TMS, 25), 364 pp., provides much more than a documentation of all direct and indirect references to Christ from the earliest short stories to *Der Erwählte* and *Die Betrogene*; it also places this life-long preoccupation in the context of Mann's developing view of myth and the growing concern with the relation between religious and sacrificial imagery and the irrational in fascist political movements. G. Peter McMullin, **Childhood and Children in Thomas Mann's Fiction* (SGLL, 29), iv + 123 pp.

Literatur und Krankheit im Fin-de-siècle (1890–1914). Thomas Mann im europäischen Kontext. Die Davoser Literaturtage 2000, ed. Thomas Sprecher (TMS, 26), 284 pp., contains: J. Eigler, 'T. M. — Ärzte der Familie und Medizin in München — Spuren in Leben und Werk (1894–1925)' (13–34); T. Sprecher, 'Die Krankenschwesterfiguren im frühen Werk T. Ms unter besonderer Berücksichtigung von Adriatica von Mylendonk' (35–72); R. Böschenstein, 'Analyse als Kunst. T. M. und Sigmund Freud im Kontext der Jahrhundertwende' (73–94); V. Roelcke, 'Psychiatrische Kulturkritik um 1900 und Umrisse ihrer Rezeption im Frühwerk T. Ms' (95–114); H. Koopmann, 'Krankheiten der Jahrhundertwende im Frühwerk T. Ms' (115–30); T. Rütten, 'Krankheit und Genie. Annäherungen an Frühformen einer Mannschen Denkfigur' (131–70); C. Virchow, 'Das Sanatorium als Lebensform. Über einschlägige Erfahrungen T. Ms' (171–98); P. Pütz, 'Das Sanatorium als Purgatorium' (199–212); D. von Engelhardt, 'Neurose und Psychose in der Medizin um 1900' (213–32); I. Jens, 'T. M. Auszeichnung durch Krankheit' (233–52); H. Koopmann, 'Als Nachrede ein Interview' (253–58). The collection is particularly valuable for placing Mann's preoccupation with illness in the context of the medical, especially psychiatric and psychoanalytical, diagnoses and advances of his early life and his personal experience of sanatoria.

Jochen Bertheau, **Eine komplizierte Bewandtnis. Der junge Thomas Mann und die französische Literatur* (Heidelberger Beiträge zur deutschen Literatur, 11), Frankfurt, Lang, 133 pp. Stefan Pegatzky, *Das poröse Ich. Leiblichkeit und Ästhetik von Arthur Schopenhauer bis Thomas Mann* (Studien zur Literatur- und Kulturwissenschaft, 16), Würzburg, Königshausen & Neumann, 500 pp., is a major dissertation which can be placed in the context of recent attempts to examine the literature of the turn of the 19th c. in relation to a paradigm shift evident in the impact of Darwinism, monism, and Nietzsche, in which an affirmation of life seeks to overcome the pessimism of Schopenhauer and the prevalence of 'Geist' in German idealist philosophy. Pegatzky traces Mann's changing position towards these developments exemplified in his early work (up to *Der Tod in Venedig*) and in his response to brother Heinrich, the 'Lex Heinze', Mereshkovsky, the *Lebensreform* movement, and the theatre. The conflict between 'Geist' and 'Leben' gives way to an accommodation and the promise of an art marked by 'Einheit von Leiblichkeit und Geistigkeit.'

Thomas Klugkist, *Der pessimistische Humanismus. Thomas Manns lebensphilosophische Adaption der Schopenhauerschen Mitleidsethik*, Würzburg, Königshausen & Neumann, 114 pp. T. Körber, 'Thomas Manns lebenslange Nietzsche-Rezeption', *WW*, 52:417–40. Barbara Besslich, *Faszination des Verfalls: Thomas Mann und Oswald Spengler*, Berlin, Akademie, 170 pp., traces Mann's initial enthusiasm for Spengler after the first reading in 1919–20 as reflected in his diaries and correspondence, then the later response in essays and the influence on *Der Zauberberg* (especially Naphta) and *Doktor Faustus* (Breisacher), with the assistance of recent theories of intertextuality. The study provides the first detailed examination of his marginal comments on *Der Untergang des Abendlandes*. Meike Schlutt, **Der repräsentative Außenseiter. Thomas Mann und sein Werk im Spiegel der deutschen Presse 1898 bis 1933* (Frankfurter Forschungen zur Kultur- und Sprachwissenschaft, 5), Frankfurt, Lang, 320 pp. T. Klugkist, 'Die Welt als Makanthropos. Zur Poetik und Selbstverwirklichung am Beispiel T. Ms', *TeK*, 24:41–61. S. Thielking, 'Vom Kanon als Lebensform zur öffentlichen Didaktik geformten Lebens. Der Fall Thomas Mann', Arnold, *Kanonbildung*, 194–211. Y. Elsaghe, 'Kalamographie und gemalte Schrift. Zur Graphologie und ihren ideologischen Implikationen in Thomas Manns Frühwerk', *ZGer*, 12:51–69. P. Pütz, 'Thomas Manns Wandlung vom "Unpolitischen" zum Demokraten', Klein, *Literatur*, 45–58.

C. Gremler, '"Doch lockt es einen auf die Berge hinauf." Georg Brandes in T. Ms "Zauberberg"', *TeK*, 24:25–40. M. Dierks, '"Ein schöner Unsinn." Hans Castorps Träume im Zauberberg', Castein, *Dream Images*, 112–27. H. Eilert, '"[. . .] das lichtschleudernde, reklameflammende Paris." T. Ms "Pariser Rechenschaft" im Kontext zeitgenössischer Großstadtwahrnehmung', Kaiser, *Paris*, 293–308. Angelika Abel, **Thomas Mann im Exil. Zum zeitgeschichtlichen Hintergrund der Emigration*, Munich, Fink, 256 pp. Id., **Musikästhetik der Klassischen Moderne. Thomas Mann — Theodor W. Adorno — Arnold Schönberg*, Munich, Fink, 400 pp.

Bernd-Jürgen Fischer, *Handbuch zu Thomas Manns 'Josephsromanen'*, Tübingen, Francke, xxvii + 893 pp. The main value of this massive compendium lies in the detailed exposition in the commentary of Mann's debt to all his primary and secondary sources. It also provides form and content summaries of each section of the tetralogy, full documentation on gestation, publication, and reception, the elucidation of myths and symbols, an examination of language, style and structure, comparisons with other works by Mann, a full history of earlier treatments of Joseph in the Bible, literature, and theology, and a bibliography with summary comments. It also offers an original interpretation based on the notion that Joseph is presented as a mature socially integrated individual. Wolfram Ette, *Freiheit zum Ursprung. Mythos und Mythoskritik in Thomas Manns Josephtetralogie* (Ep, 372), 226 pp. is an investigation of the philosophical issues raised by the tetralogy with reference to Derrida, Ricoeur, Freud, gnosticism, etc. It criticizes the tendency of recent approaches to the work to associate it with a conservative theory of myth, preferring instead to link it to Adorno and Horkheimer, *Dialektik der Aufklärung*. V. Tumanov, 'Jacob as Job in T.Ms *Joseph und seine Brüder*', *Neophilologus*, 86: 287–302. Walter Schomers, *Serenus Zeitblom und die Ideen von 1914. Essays*, Würzburg, Königshausen & Neumann, 129 pp.

Kirsten Grimstad, **The Modern Revival of Gnosticism in Thomas Mann's Doctor Faustus* (SGLLC), 256 pp. Y. Elsaghe, 'Serenus Zeitbloms Katholizismus. Zum Spätwerkscharakter des "Doktor Faustus"', *WB*, 48:226–41. R. Wimmer, 'T. Ms Zeitroman "Doktor Faustus": Aburteilung Deutschlands oder "Gerichtstag über das eigene Ich"?', *Fest. Gaede*, 217–34. M. Neumann, 'Zwölftontechnik? Adrian Leverkühn zwischen Schönberg und Wagner', *LJb*, 43:193–212. Evelyn Cobley, *Temptations of Faust. The Logic of Fascism and Postmodern Archaeologies of Modernity*, Toronto U.P., 305 pp., is an ambitious study which re-examines the debt of *Doktor Faustus* to Adorno's *Philosophie der Neuen Musik* in order to claim that aesthetic modernism is in a sense complicit with fascism (as Mann himself implied in the parallel between Leverkühn and Germany's political development), but also that postmodernist fragmentation cannot ultimately challenge the totalitarianisms they seek to disrupt. The author thus extends the parameters of what has become a familiar debate. Id., 'Avant-garde aesthetics and Fascist politics: T. Ms 'Doktor Faustus' and Theodor W. Adorno's *Philosophy of Modern Music*', *NGC*, 86:43–70. J. Joachimsthaler, 'Politisierter Ästhetizismus. Zu T. Ms *Mario und der Zauberer* und *Doktor Faustus*', *Fest. Orłowski*, 303–32. Heike Weidenhaupt, **Gegenpropaganda aus dem Exil: Thomas Manns Radioansprachen für deutsche Hörer 1940 bis 1945* (Journalismus und Geschichte, 5), Konstanz, UVK, 2001, 173 pp. M. Herwig, '"Liebhabereien und szientifische Nebendinge": T. M.'s playful imitation of Goethe's science', *PEGS*, 71, 2001:1–17. B. von Consbruch and J. Michelfeit, 'Von Wunderkindern und Menchenkindlein. Hommage an hundert Jahre Liebes- und Schaffensbund Thomas und Katia Mann', *GRM*, 52:230–48.

Neue Rundschau, 112.3, 2001, is a special issue devoted to 'Buddenbrooks nach 100 Jahren' with 10 articles. *TMJb*, 15, contains: K. E. Laage, 'Theodor Storm — ein literarischer Vorfahre von T. Ms *Buddenbrooks*' (15–34); H. Lehnert, 'Tony Buddenbrook und ihre literarischen Schwestern' (35–54); K. Bohnen, 'Bild-Netze. Zur "Quellenmixtur" in den *Buddenbrooks*' (55–68); H.-J. Sandberg, 'Gesegnete Mahlzeit(en) — Tischgespräche im Norden' (69–88);

E. Heftrich, 'Die *Große kommentierte Frankfurter Ausgabe* — das Beispiel *Buddenbrooks*' (89–102); R. Wimmer, '*Buddenbrooks* und *Jörn Uhl* — zwei norddeutsche Erfolgsromane des Jahres 1901' (117–34); M. Dierks, '*Buddenbrooks* als europäischer Nervenroman' (135–52); H.-J. Gerigk, 'Epen des Niedergangs. *Buddenbrooks*, Belyjs *Petersburg* und Faulkners *Absalom, Absalom!*' (153–74); J. Hillesheim, 'Über die Verführung Adrian Leverkühns. Bertolt Brechts "pornographisches Sonett" und Thomas Manns *Faustus*-Roman' (175–89); W. Schomers, 'Thomas Mann und Paul Bourget' (193–99); A. Schirnding, ' ". . .die unlitterarische Stadt par excellence." Thomas Mann und das München der Familie Pringsheim' (201–08).

MORGENSTERN, SOMA. *Soma Morgensterns verlorene Welt. Kritische Beiträge zu seinem Werk*, ed. Robert G. Weigel (New Yorker Beiträge zur Literaturwissenschaft, 4), Frankfurt, Lang, 190 pp., consists of the proceedings of a conference held at the University of Auburn, Alabama in 2001.

MÜHSAM, ERICH. *Erich Mühsam und das Judentum: Zwölfte Erich-Mühsam Tagung in der Gustav-Heinemann-Bildugsstätte in Malente, 25.–27. Mai 2001*, ed. Jürgen-Wolfgang Goette (Schriften der Erich-Mühsam-Gesellschaft, 21), Lübeck, Erich-Mühsam-Gesellschaft, 184 pp., includes: C. Hirte, 'E. M. und das Judentum' (52–70); L. Baron, 'E. Ms jüdische Identität' (157–70); R. Kauffeldt, 'Zur jüdischen Tradition im romantisch-anarchistischen Denken E. Ms und Gustav Landauers' (171–94).

MÜNCHHAUSEN, BÖRRIES VON. T. F. Schneider, ' "Heldisches Geschehen" und "reiner blaublonder Stamm". Die "Erneuerung" der Ballade und ihre Instrumentalisierung durch B. von M. (1874–1945) seit 1898', *Fest. Orłowski*, 541–61.

MUSIL, ROBERT. Hans-Joachim Pieper, *Musils Philosophie: Essayismus und Dichtung im Spannungsfeld der Theorien Nietzsches und Machs*, Würzburg, Königshausen und Neumann, 164 pp. Musil's philosophical interests are well known, yet he rejected systematic philosophy. His reading of Nietzsche and Mach influences the essayistic approach to life of the title figure of *Der Mann ohne Eigenschaften* and the experimental nature of its narrative technique. By an examination of M.'s essays, P. demonstrates how by means of an amalgam of philosophy and 'Dichtung' he takes account of the criticisms of cognition and causality provided by his philosophical mentors. Villö Huszai, *Ekel am Erzählen: Metafiktionalität im Werk Robert Musils, gewonnen am Kriminalfall 'Tonka'* (Musil-Studien, 31), Munich, Fink, 285 pp. Fred Lönker, *Poetische Anthropologie: Robert Musils Erzählungen 'Vereinigungen'* (Musil-Studien, 30), Munich, Fink, 211 pp. Loredana Marini, *Der Dichter als Fragmentist. Geschichte und Geschichten in Robert Musils Roman 'Der Mann ohne Eigenschaften'* (Musiliana, 8), Berne, Lang,

268 pp. A. Doppler, '"Seinesgleichen führt zum Krieg." R. Ms Auseinandersetzung mit dem Krieg', Klein, *Literatur*, 59–68. T. Borgard, 'R. Ms früher Beitrag zur Wissenschaftsgeschichte im Einflußbereich Lotzes und Fechners', Danneberg, *Wissen*, 285–312.

NADHERNY, SIDONIE. *'Sei ich ihr, sei mein Bote.' Der Briefwechsel zwischen Sidonie Nadherny und Albert Bloch*, ed. Elke Lorenz, Munich, Iudicium, 358 pp.

PAASCHE, HANS. U.-K. Ketelsen, 'Ein Blick von der Cheopspyramide. H. Ps Bild vom kolonialen Afrika', *Fest. Orłowski*, 61–85.

PAPPENHEIM, MARIE. L. A. McLary, 'The dead lover's body and the woman's rage: M. P.'s *Erwartung*', *CGer*, 34, 2001: 257–70.

POLITZER, HEINZ. H. C. Seeba, 'Autorität des Wortes. H.P. und die Heimat der Sprache im Exil', *Fest. Michel*, 245–58.

RASCHKE, MARTIN. *Martin Raschke (1905–1943). Leben und Werk*, ed. Wilhelm Haefs, Dresden, web-Vlg, 336 pp. W. Haefs, 'Ahnenkult und Lebenspädagogik. Der Programmatiker der "Kolonne", M. R., als Erzähler im Dritten Reich', *TeK*, 24: 62–97.

REGLER, GUSTAV. G. R., *Ruhrtiger, Locarno-Engel und rote Matrosen. Seine Beiträge als Journalist in Nürnberg, 1926–1928/30*, ed. Günter Scholdt (Schriften der Universitätsbibliothek Eichstätt, 50), St. Ingbert, Röhrig, 204 pp.

REMARQUE, ERICH MARIA. *Remarque-Jb.*, 12, contains: G. Nyada, 'Gewalt und Freiheit bei E.M.R' (7–24); K. Hohler, 'E.M.Rs Exilzeit im Spiegel seiner Tagebücher' (25–60); H. Placke, 'Rs Denkschrift *Practical educational work in Germany after the war* (1944) im Kontext zweitgenössischer Konzeptionen für das nahende Nachkriegsdeutschland (Denkschrift und Tagebuch als kontrastierende Gebrauchstextsorten)' (61–96); C. Gellunek, 'R. und Grass als deutsche Dichter der Weltbürgerlichkeit' (97–101); M.-H. Ahn, 'Ein ewiger Liebhaber. Das Bild E.M.Rs in Korea' (112–33).

RILKE, RAINER MARIA. R.M.R., *Briefwechsel mit Rolf von Ungern-Sternberg und weitere Dokumente zur Übertragung der Stances von Paul Moréas*, ed. Konrad Kratzsch and Vera Hauschild, Leipzig, Insel, 157 pp. R.M.R. and Claire Goll, *'Ich sehne mich sehr nach Deinen blauen Briefen': Briefwechsel*, ed. Barbara Glauert-Hesse (IT, 2868), 215 pp. Erich Unglaub, *Rilke-Arbeiten*, Frankfurt, Lang, 308 pp. Silke Pasewalck, *'Die fünffingrige Hand': Die Bedeutung der sinnlichen Wahrnehmung beim späten Rilke* (QFLK), x + 331 pp. Ruth Hermann, *Im Zwischenraum zwischen Welt und Spielzeug. Eine Poetik der Kindheit bei Rilke* (Ep, 373), 168 pp., while admitting that the child is a marginal figure in Rilke's work, traces the theme in his poems and letters as a reflection of his attitude to his own childhood, which involved the desire to repress it. This repression paradoxically ensures its potential as poetic inspiration, and makes possible the examination of the relation of childhood to poetry which the author undertakes. Martine Wegener-Stratmann, **Über die 'unerschöpfliche Schichtung unserer Natur.' Totalitätsvorstellungen der Jahrhundertwende. Die Weltbilder von Rainer Maria Rilke und C. G. Jung im Vergleich* (GANDLL, 22), 244 pp. Roswitha M. Kant, **Visualität in Rainer Maria Rilkes Die Aufzeichnungen des Malte Laurids Brigge. Eine Untersuchung zum psychoanalytischen Symbolbegriff* (AD, 45), 276 pp. Martine Carré, *Les Elégies de Duino. Essais de lecture* (Convergences, 25), 2 vols, Berne, Lang, xviii + 416 pp. C. Breger, 'Hieroglyphen der Männlichkeit. Echnaton-Phantasien und ägyptologische Szenarien bei R. und Thomas Mann', *ZGer*, 12:296–307. S. Arndal, ' "Ohne alle Kenntnis und Perspektive"? Zur Raumperzeption in R. M. Rs *Aufzeichnungen des Malte Laurids Brigge*', *DVLG*, 76:105–37. R. Warning, 'Der Zeitungsverkäufer am Luxemburg', *ib.*, 261–70, concerns an episode in *Die Aufzeichnungen des Malte Laurids Brigge*. G. Schmitt, 'Rs *Lied vom Meer* — ein Ding aus Angst', *GRM*, 52:218–29. S. Löwenstein, 'Apotheose der Dichtkunst. Ästhetische und poetologische Betrachtungen in Rs Stundenbuch', *LitL*, 24, 2001:216–29. T. Kotrikadze, 'Die Gestalt des Engels in R.M.Rs Werk', *ÖGL*, 46:309–15. C. Louth, 'R. on Capri', Kohl, *Words*, 83–92. *Blätter der Rilke-Gesellschaft*, 24, ed. Rudi Schweikert, 320 pp., is entitled: ' "Die Welt ist in die Hände der Menschen gefallen": Rilke und das moderne Selbstverständnis'.

ROTH, JOSEPH. Eva Raffel, **Vertraute Fremde: Das östliche Judentum im Werk von Joseph Roth und Arnold Zweig* (MBSL, 54), 330 pp. Valérie Chevassus-Marchioni, **Le roman original de Joseph Roth. Analyse des stratégies de la création littéraire dans l'oeuvre de Joseph Roth* (Convergences, 21), Berne, Lang, xvi + 372 pp. J. Hughes, ' "Ein neuer Weg des Film": J. R.'s reviews of documentary films', Berghahn, *Essays*, 11–22. J. Bel, ' "Ich zeichne das Gesicht der Zeit." J. R. in den Jahren 1925–1939: Berichterstattung aus Paris', Kaiser, *Paris*, 407–18. D. Schlenstedt, 'Feuilletons: Annäherungen an eine poetische Prosa. R., Kracauer, Kisch und andere', *WB*, 48:420–33. E. K. Dzikowska, 'Das Merkwürdige ist das Selbstverständliche. Die Völkertafeln J. Rs', *Fest. Orłowski*, 727–38. M. Kłańska, 'Kreuz contra Hakenkreuz. Zu Deutungen des Kreuzes im Werk von J. R.', *ib.*, 739–57.

SALTEN, FELIX. Jürgen Ehness, **Felix Saltens erzählerisches Werk* (RBDSL, B 81), 344 pp.

SCHICKELE, RENÉ. E. Nährlich-Slatewa, 'Das Paris-Zeitbuch von R. S. "Schreie auf dem Boulevard" ', Kaiser, *Paris*, 117–70.

SCHMITZ, OSCAR A. H. O.A.H.S., *Haschisch: Erzählungen*, ed. Wilhelm W. Hemecker (Bibliothek Gutenberg, 1), Graz, Gutenberg, 134 pp., has 13 drawings by Alfred Kubin included.

SCHNITZLER, ARTHUR. Bettina Riedmann, *'Ich bin Jude, Österreicher, Deutscher.' Judentum in Arthur Schnitzlers Tagebüchern und Briefen* (CJ, 36), 477 pp. Wolfgang Sabler, *Arthur Schnitzler. Ecriture dramatique et conventions théâtrales* (Contacts, 1; Theatrica, 21), Berne, Lang, xvi + 418 pp.

Arthur Schnitzler: Zeitgenossenschaften / Contemporaneities, ed. Ian Foster and Florian Krobb (Wechselwirkungen. Österreichische Literatur im internationalen Kontext, 4), Berne, Lang, 412 pp., includes: M. Swales, 'S. revisited' (19–32); K. Fliedl, 'O du mein Österreich': Ss schwierige Heimat' (33–42); M. V. Lazarescu, 'Zur Rezeption Ss in Rumänien — Ss Beziehungen zur rumänischen Literatur' (43–54); L. R. G. Decloedt, 'Eine mühsame Reise ins Unbekannte. A. S. und Belgien' (55–70); C. Brinson and M. Malet, '"Die sonderbarste Stadt, die man sich denken kann"? A. S. in London' (71–88); J. F. Berlin, 'A. S.'s views on intellectual property, illustrated by the trials and tribulations of *Casanova's Homecoming*' (89–112); H. Scheible, 'Sublata lucerna nullum discrimen inter mulieres? Individualität und Identität in Ss Komödie "Die Schwestern" oder Casanova in Spa' (113–40); A. Gillman, '"Ich suche ein Asyl für meine Vergangenheit." S.'s poetics of memory' (141–56); C. Künzel, 'Gendered perspectives: über das Zusammenspiel von "männlicher" und "weiblicher" Erzählung in Ss "Kleine Komödie" (1895)' (157–72); E. E. Smith, 'Dawning self-awareness: female characters between submission and dominance in S.'s "Komödie der Verführung"' (173–84); I. Foster, 'Leutnant Gustl: the military, the press and prose fiction' (185–98); F. Krobb, '"Der Weg ins Freie" im Kontext des deutsch-jüdischen Zeitromans' (199–216); J. Beniston, 'S. in Red Vienna' (217–32); F. W. Tweraser, 'S.'s "Reigen" and the freedom of the artist: the first Austrian republic in constitutional crisis' (233–44); W. E. Yates, 'S.'s theatre-going' (245–58); J. Stewart, 'The world of the waltz: dance and non-contemporaniety in S.'s texts' (259–74); K. Leydecker, 'Marital crisis, open marriage, separation and divorce in S.'s dramas' (275–88); M. Ritzer, '"Weltschmerz? Nein, Weltironie." Zur Funktion von Ss Komödien' (289–306); G. J. Weinberger, 'The "Unbekannte" in Arthur S.'s *Zum großen Wurstel*' (307–14); G. K. Schneider, 'Zur künstlerischen Rezeption von A. Ss *Reigen*' (315–28); D. G. Daviau, 'A. S.'s *Liebelei* and Max Ophuls's film adaptation' (329–48); T. Rothschild, 'Charmante Egozentriker, egozentrische Charmeure. Ein Interpretationsvergleich' (349–58); K. Kanzog, 'A. S. *Fräulein Else*. Der innere Monolog in der Novelle in der filmischen Transformation' (359–72); C. Spencer, 'Translating S. for the stage: losing *Liebelei*?' (373–90); G. S. Daviau, 'Stanley Kubricks *Eyes Wide Shut*. Eine neue Dimension für Ss Traumnovelle' (391–405). Most of the contributions concern Schnitzler's difficulties with his environment, as reflected in scandals, court cases, and political upheavals but also in the interest in his work taken by the Austrian left, but the collection is also important for its wide-ranging attention to S.'s personal contacts with other countries and his international reception, both during his own lifetime and later.

J. M. Fischer, 'Moralist in Moll: Ss Tagebücher', *Merkur*, 56:333–37. A. Koschorke, '"Blick und Macht." Das Imaginäre der Geschlechter im neunzehnten Jahrhundert und bei A. S.', *Neumann Vol.*, 313–35. K. Grätz, 'Die Macht der Fiktion und die Kunst des Fingierens. Eine Analyse von A. Ss Erzählung "Das Tagebuch der Redegonda" auf der Grundlage erzähltheoretischer Überlegungen', *WW*, 53:385–97. M. Vorbrugg, 'Imagination des Begehrens. A. Ss *Traumnovelle* und Stanley Kubricks *Eyes Wide Shut*', *LitL*, 25:143–67. C. Kretschmann, 'Bauformen in Schnitzlers Schauspiel "Der einsame Weg"', *JFDH*, 296–316. S. Janson, '"Einsame Wege" und "weites Feld". Zum Todesmotiv bei A. S. und T. F.', Radecke, *Fontane*, 95–108. A. Lange-Kirchheim, 'Zwei frühe Rezensionen zu Arthur Schnitzlers Spätwerken "Fräulein Else" und "Therese"', *Hofmannsthal-Jb.*, 10:37–58. C. Pross, 'Das Gesetz der Reihe. Zum Verhältnis von Literatur, Wissen und Anthropologie in Ss "Reigen"', *ib.*, 245–66. O. Neudeck and G. Scheidt, 'Prekäre Identität zwischen romantischer und galanter Liebe. Zu Zerfall und Restitutierung des Subjekts im dramatischen Werk A. Ss', *ib.*, 267–302.

SCHULER, ALFRED. J. M. Fischer, 'A. S. — Antike als Kostümfest', Aurnhammer, *Antike-Rezeption*, 421–44.

SEGHERS, ANNA. Nicole Suhl, **Anna Seghers: Grubetsch und Aufstand der Fischer von St. Barbara. Literarische Konstrukte im Spannungsfeld von Phänomenologie und Existenzphilosophie* (HBG, 36), 342 pp. Helen Fehervary, *Anna Seghers. The Mythic Dimension*, Ann Arbor, Michigan U.P., 2001, xi + 275 pp., is a critical reassessment based on recently available archival materials which situates S.'s legacy within the context of Central European intellectual history (her husband László Radványi, Budapest Sunday Circle, Lukács, Benjamin, Brecht), interviews with friends, and a study of her library, including the Hungarian texts. *Argonautenschiff*, 11, has a large number of articles on the author's exile in France and Mexico and the works it inspired (*Transit*, *Das wirkliche Blau*, *Überfahrt*, *Ausflug der toten Mädchen*). The volume also includes 'Der Briefwechsel zwischen A. S. und den Redakteuren der Moskauer Zeitschriften "Das Wort" und "Internationale Literatur" zwischen 1933 und 1945' (261–304).

SIEBURG, FRIEDRICH. D. Bousch, 'Gott in Paris? F. Ss ambivalentes Parisbild in "Gott in Frankreich" (1929)', Kaiser, *Paris*, 351–70.

SONNENSCHEIN, HUGO. Dieter Wilde, **Der Aspekt des Politischen in der frühen Lyrik Hugo Sonnenscheins* (LU, 34), 324 pp.

STERNHEIM, CARL. H. Macher, 'Zum Parisbild in C. Ss "Lutetia. Berichte über europäische Politik Kunst und Volksleben 1926"', Kaiser, *Paris*, 309–50.

STERNHEIM, THEA. T.S., *Tagebücher 1903–1971*, ed. Thomas Ehrsam and Regula Wyss, 5 vols, Göttingen, Wallstein, 3568 pp.

SUSMAN, MARGARETE. E. Pöder, 'Lebendige Dialektik: Sprache und (jüdische) Identität bei M.S. Zur Charakteristik ihrer Essays der Weimarer Republik', Klein, *Literatur*, 145–72.

TOLLER, ERNST. V. Ladenthin, 'Engagierte Literatur — wozu? Aussage oder Sinn: Aporien in Ts Literaturästhetik', Neuhaus, *Literatur*, 53–65. S. Neuhaus, 'Strategien der Entmythologisierung in E. Ts *Der entfesselte Wotan* und *Nie wieder Friede*', Neuhaus, *Literatur*, 169–83. G.-D. Grozdanic, 'Der entfesselte Dichter: E. Ts *Der entfesselte Wotan* als satirische Selbstbespiegelung', Neuhaus, *Literatur*, 184–91. E. Jäger, 'Engagierte Literatur? Untersuchungen zum Erfolg von Ts Dramen in den dreißiger Jahren am Beispeil des Stückes *Feuer aus den Kesseln*', Neuhaus, *Literatur*, 261–67. C. Davies, 'E. Ts Dramen als "Engagierte Literatur" betrachtet', Neuhaus, *Literatur*, 268–74. J. Jordan, 'Objektivität, Engagement und Literatur: die Darstellung politisch motivierter Verbrechen bei E. J. Gumbel und E. T.', Neuhaus, *Literatur*, 312–25. R. G. Czapla, 'Verismus als Expressionismuskritik. Otto Dix' Streichholzhändler I, E. Ts Hinkemann und George Grosz' Brockenbrow-Illustrationen in Kontext zeitgenössischer Kunstdebatten', Neuhaus, *Literatur*, 338–66.

TRAKL, GEORG. B. Neymeyr, 'Ts lyrische Quintessenz. Poetologische Décadence-Reflexion und Hermetik in seinem Gedicht "Helian"', *ZDP*, 121:529–47. A. Stillmark, 'Interpreting T.'s dreams with the help of Edgar A. Poe', Castein, *Dream Images*, 99–111.

TRAVEN, BEN. *Der Feuerstuhl und die Fahrtensucher Rolf Recknagel, Erich Wollenberg, Anna Seghers auf den Spuren B. Travens*, ed. Bernd Kramer and Christoph Ludszuweit, Berlin, Kramer, 192 pp.

TUCHOLSKY, KURT. K.T., *Texte 1925*, ed. Bärbel Boldt and Andrea Spingler, Reinbek, Rowohlt, 965 pp., is vol. 7 of the *Gesamtausgabe*, ed. Antje Bonitz. K.T., *Das literarische und publizistische Werk*, ed. Sabina Becker and Ute Maack (WBG), 288 pp., has an introduction and 12 contributions, which together provide a survey of T.'s work in the novel, travel writing, and poetry and as a critic and correspondent against the background of the cultural history of the Weimar Republic. R. Selbmann, 'Zwischen Max Hölz und Adolf Hitler. K.T., Ernst Toller und *Die Weltbühne*', Neuhaus, *Literatur*, 131–40. I. King, 'Ts Konzept der Gebrauchslyrik', *ib.*, 141–49. S. Neuhaus, 'Wider die innere Teilung. K. Ts *Deutschlandbuch* (1929)', pp. 261–74 of Stefan Neuhaus, *Literatur und nationale Einheit in Deutschland*, Tübingen, Francke, 587 pp.

UNGAR, HERMANN. H.U., *Sämtliche Werke in 3 Bänden*, ed. Dieter Sudhof, Oldenburg, Igel, vol. 2: *Erzählungen*, 2001, 266 pp.; vol. 3: *Gedichte, Dramen, Feuilletons, Briefe*, 475 pp.

UNRUH, FRITZ VON. F. Szász, '"Der einzelne muß in sich den Geist des Krieges töten." Über F. v Us "Flügel der Nike"', Kaiser, *Paris*, 253–92.

WALSER, ROBERT. **Gedankenspaziergänge mit Robert Walser*, ed. C. Arthur M. Noble, Berne, Lang, 341 pp. Kil-Pyo Hong, **Selbstreflexion von Modernität in Robert Walsers Romanen 'Geschwister Tanner', 'Der Gehülfe' und 'Jacob von Gunten'* (Ep, 394), 212 pp. Peter Rippman, **Robert Walsers politisches Schreiben* (Aisthesis Studien-Bücher, 14), Bielefeld, Aisthesis, 82 pp. Markus Schwahl, *Die Wirklichkeit und ihre Schwestern. Epistemologische Ideologiekritik und ihre ethischen Implikationen im Werk Robert Walsers* (EH, 1, 1816), 268 pp. W. Groddeck, 'Schrift und Textkritik. Vorläufige Überlegungen zu einem Editionsproblem in R. Ws Mikrogrammen am Modell der "Bleistiftskizze"', *MLN*, 117:544–59. A. Wittwer, 'Das inszenierte Scheitern. R. Ws Tagebuch-Fragment von 1926', *Fest. Michel*, 175–94. **Entdeckungen. Über Jean Paul, Robert Walser, Konrad Bayer und anderes*, ed. Klaus Bonn, Edit Kovàcs, and Csaba Szabó (Debrecener Studien zur Literatur 9), Frankfurt, Lang, 149 pp., includes: W. Droste, 'Zehn Gründe, Walser zu lieben'; K. Bonn, 'R. Ws Entdeckung als Schaf'; E. Kiràly, '"Vom Podium der Landstraße herab." Zur Rhetorik des Zu-Fuß-Gehens in Ws *Bleistiftgebiet*'; M. Horvàth, 'Der Weg des Wanderers. Wahrnehmung in R. Ws Mikrogrammen'.

WASSERMANN, JAKOB. P. Avenel-Cohen, 'En quête du jeune homme idéal: *L'affaire Maurizius* de J. W. et ses premiers critiques', *Germanica*, 30:41–59.

WEDEKIND, FRANK. Fred Whalley, *The Elusive Transcendent. The Role of Religion in the Plays of Frank Wedekind* (British and Irish Studies in German Language and Literature 23), Oxford, Lang, 204 pp., follows Wedekind's ultimately doomed efforts to find a form of transcendence alternative to that reflected in bourgeois morality and claims that throughout his work he shows the artist, as exemplified by his pseudo-autobiographical protagonists, testing the limits of the acceptable and embracing the roles of both sinner and sacrifice in such a way that that his audience shares the experience without discomfort. U. H. Gerlach, 'Wer ist der "vermummte Herr" in Ws Frühlings Erwachen?', in U. H. Gerlach, *Einwände und Einsichten. Revidierte Deutungen deutschsprachiger Literatur des 19. und 20. Jahrhunderts*, Munich, Iudicium, 302 pp. R. Florack, 'Kaufhaus Babylon. F. W. und Paris', Kaiser, *Paris*, 75–96. J. Bel, '*Der Marquis von Keith* de Frank Wedekind et *Die Ehe des Herrn Mississippi* de Friedrich Dürrenmatt: réappropriation subjective et déplacement de sens', *Germanica*, 31 : 71–83. D. Midgley, 'W., *Erdgeist*', Hutchinson, *Landmarks*, 43–58.

WERFEL, FRANZ. B. Bloch, 'F. W.: *Jeremias. Höret die Stimme*, roman de la protestation ou le courage de la confiance', *Germanica*, 31 : 23–38.

WITTLIN, JOZEF. M. Klanska, 'Paris und Frankreich in Leben und Werk des polnischen Dichters J. W. Mit vergleichbarem Blick auf Joseph Roth', Kaiser, *Paris*, 419–40.

WOLFSKEHL, KARL. C. Blasberg, 'Weißer Mythos und schwarze Feste. K. Ws Antikerezeption', Aurnhammer, *Antike-Rezeption*, 445–70.

ZUCKMAYER, CARL. C. Z., *Geheimreport*, ed. Gunther Nickel and Johanna Schrön (Zuckmayer-Schriften), Göttingen, Wallstein, 528 pp. *Zur Diskussion: Zuckmayers 'Geheimreport' und andere Beiträge zur Zuckmayer-Forschung*, ed. Ulrike Weiss (*Zuckmayer-Jb.*, 5), Göttingen, Wallstein, 589 pp.

ZUR MÜHLEN, HERMYNIA. H.Z.M., *Vierzehn Nothelfer und andere Romane aus dem Exil*, ed. Deborah J. Vietor-Engländer, Eckart Früh, and Ursula Seeber (Exil-Dokumente, verboten, verbrannt, vergessen, 5), Berne, Lang, 436 pp. H.Z.M., *Nebenglück. Ausgewählte Erzählungen und Feuilletons aus dem Exil*, ed. Deborah J. Vietor-Engländer, Eckart Früh, and Ursula Seeber (Exil-Dokumente, verboten, verbrannt, vergessen, 6), Berne, Lang, 279 pp. A. Hammel, 'Politisches Schreiben als Frau. H.Z.M. als proletarisch-revolutionäre Schriftstellerin', Neuhaus, *Literatur*, 192–204.

ZWEIG, MAX. M. Z. *Autobiographisches und verstreute Schriften aus dem Nachlaß. Werke in Einzelbänden*, 6, ed. Eva Reichmann, Paderborn, Igel, 456 pp.

ZWEIG, STEFAN. S. Fraiman, 'Das tragende Symbol: Ambivalenz jüdischer Identität in S. Zs Werk', *GLL*, 55 : 248–65.

LITERATURE FROM 1945 TO THE PRESENT DAY

By Joanne Leal, *Lecturer in German, Birkbeck College, University of London*

1. General

German Culture and the Uncomfortable Past. Representations of National Socialism in Contemporary Germanic Literature, ed. Helmut Schmitz (Warwick Studies in the Humanities), Aldershot, Ashgate, 2001, 184 pp., is a stimulating collection of essays focusing on the substantial body of texts produced in the 1990s which concern themselves with Germany's Nazi past and, in many cases, its relationship to the post-unification present. The volume goes quite some way towards addressing the diversity and plurality of this writing, beginning with B. Niven's useful survey article, 'Literary portrayals of National Socialism in post-unification German literature' (11–28). Further articles on specific authors and works serve to highlight shifts in the way different generations have approached this theme. Three chapters focus on older writers. J. Preece (29–43) and S. Taberner (45–64) explore respectively developments in Günter Grass's and Martin Walser's positions on 'Vergangenheitsbewältigung', while A. Williams examines W. G. Sebald's 'postmodern aesthetics of memory' (65–86). Responses of the second post-war generation form the subject of S. Parkes's contribution on Bernhard Schlink's *Der Vorleser* and Klaus Modick's *Der Flügel* (87–101), as well as J. Wigmore's assessment of Elisabeth Reichart's *Nachtmär* (103–18). Further contributions relate to works by a third generation for whom the experience of the Third Reich is no longer authentic but rather 'secondary and mediated'. H. Schmitz analyses Marcel Beyer's portrayal of a 'Mitläufer' in *Flughunde* (119–41), A. Parkinson examines both the book and film of *Aimée und Jaguar* (143–63), particularly in relation to their reception by the lesbian and Jewish communities, and finally S. Tebutt offers a thought-provoking contribution on transgressions in Gudrun Pausewang's children's novel about the Holocaust, *Reise im August* (165–80). C. Blasberg, 'Geschichte als Palimpsest. Schreiben und Lesen über die "Kinder der Täter"', *DVLG*, 76:464–95, analyses memories of National Socialism and the Holocaust as they form the subject of Wolfgang Koeppen's *Tod in Rom*, Ingeborg Bachmann's *Der Fall Franza*, Christoph Meckel's *Suchbild*, Anne Duden's *Das Judasschaf*, and Bernhard Schlink's *Der Vorleser*. **Kulturelle Repräsentation des Holocaust in Deutschland und in den Vereinigten Staaten*, ed. Klaus L. Berghahn, Jürgen Fohrmann, and Helmut J. Schneider (GLC, 38), 264 pp. K. Schubert,

'Auschwitz als europäische Erfahrung. Zum komparitistischen Arbeiten über die Shoah anhand literarischer Texte jüdischer Autorinnen in Deutschland und Frankreich', *ZGer*, 12:83–98. Stephan Braese, **Die andere Erinnerung. Jüdische Autoren in der westdeutschen Nachkriegsliteratur*, Berlin–Vienna, Philo, 2001, 596 pp. **Deutsch-jüdische Literatur der neunziger Jahre. Die Generation nach der Shoa*, ed. Sander L. Gilman and Hartmut Steinecke (Beihefte zur *ZDP*, 11), Berlin, Schmidt, 272 pp. R. C. Holub, 'Coming to terms with the past in postwar literature and philosophy', Saul, *Philosophy*, 245–90.

U. Breuer, 'Autobiographisches Schreiben der 70er Jahre: Aspekte der Forschung', *JIG*, 33.2, 2001:9–25. **Mythen in nachmythischer Zeit. Die Antike in der deutschsprachigen Literatur der Gegenwart*, ed. Bernd Seidensticker and Martin Vöhler, Berlin–New York, de Gruyter, xii + 378 pp. **Schreiben nach der Wende. Ein Jahrzehnt deutscher Gegenwartsliteratur 1989–1999*, ed. Gerhard Fischer and David Roberts (Studien zur deutschsprachigen Gegenwartsliteratur, 14), Tübingen, Stauffenburg, x + 332 pp. **Legacies and Identity. East and West German Literary Responses to Unification*, ed. Martin Kane (British and Irish Studies in German Language and Literature, 31), Oxford, Lang, 209 pp. Moritz Bassler, **Der deutsche Pop-Roman. Die neuen Archivisten*, Munich, Beck, 222 pp. **Alles nur Pop? Anmerkungen zur populären und Pop-Literatur seit 1990*, ed. Thomas Jung (Osloer Beiträge zur Germanistik, 32), Frankfurt, Lang, 240 pp. H.-P. Schwander, '"Dein Leben ist eine Reise mit dem Ziel Tod . . ." Tod in der neuen Pop-Literatur', *DUS*, 54.1:72–84. H. Spittler, 'Die Dichter der "Generation Golf"', *LitL*, 25:189–96, on Florian Illies, Benjamin von Stuckrad-Barre, Joachim Bessing, Christian Kracht, and Alexander von Schönberg. **Zwischen Trivialität und Postmoderne. Literatur von Frauen in den 90er Jahren*, ed. Ilse Nagelschmidt et al., Frankfurt, Lang, vi + 249 pp. **Erfahrung nach dem Krieg. Autorinnen im Literaturbetrieb 1945–1950. BRD, DDR, Österreich, Schweiz*, ed. Christiane Caemmerer et al., Frankfurt, Lang, 304 pp. Vera Jost, **Fliegen oder Fallen. Prostitution als Thema in Literatur von Frauen im 20. Jahrhundert* (Frankfurter Feministische Texte, 6), Königstein/Ts., Helmer, 280 pp. Sabine Puhlfürst, *'Mehr als bloße Schwärmerei.' Die Darstellung von Liebesbeziehungen zwischen Mädchen / jungen Frauen im Spiegel der deutschsprachigen Frauenliteratur des 20. Jahrhunderts*, Essen, Die blaue Eule, 366 pp. E. Jeremiah, 'The hand that rocks the cradle: maternity, agency and community in women's writing in German of the 1970s and 1980s', *GLL*, 55:75–90. A. B. Willeke, '"Father wants to tear out my tongue": daughters confront incestuous fathers in postwar German literature', *ib.*, 100–16. C. Kanz, 'Familiendesaster. Töchter in deutschsprachigen literarischen Texten der siebziger, achtziger und neunziger Jahre', *JIG*, 33.2, 2001:145–63. T. Tholen, 'Vater-und-Sohn-Verhältnisse in der Literatur der Moderne. Von Goethe bis zur Gegenwart', *WB*, 48:325–43. Monika Spielmann, *Aus den Augen des Kindes. Die Kinderperspektive in deutschsprachiger Romanen seit 1945* (IBKG, 65), 242 pp., examines six novels, some intended for adults, others for children, which have in common their narrative perspective: all are written from the point of view of a child. The study begins with a brief historical overview of changes in social perceptions of childhood and corresponding shifts in the way the child has been depicted in literature and sets out its literary theoretical basis (a combination of the narrative theories of Jürgen H. Petersen and Franz K. Stanzel), before continuing with close readings of the chosen texts — Leo Katz's *Brennende Dörfe* and *Tamar*, Erwin Strittmatter's *Tinko*, Helga Novak's *Die Eisheiligen*, Gabriele Wohmann's *Paulinchen war allein zu Haus*, and Diana Kempff's *Fettfleck* — in an attempt to explore the variety of narrative consequences this particular perspective brings with it. Frederick Alfred Lubich, **Wendewelten: Paradigmenwechsel in der deutschen Literatur- und Kulturgeschichte nach* 1945, Würzburg, Königshausen & Neumann, 206 pp.

Roxana Nubert, *Paradigmenwechsel moderner deutschsprachiger Literatur*, Timişoara, Mirton, 257 pp., combines chapters on Kafka, Mann's *Der Zauberberg* and Musil's *Der Mann ohne Eigenschaften* with sections on Thomas Bernhard's dramas and Christoph Ransmayr's *Die letzte Welt* with the intention of exploring 'der Übergang von der Moderne zur Spät- und Postmoderne'. In the final chapters the developments identified in German literature are juxtaposed with those discernible in the Rumanian-German literature of the inter-war years (with a focus on Oskar Walter Cisek) and in the post-war period (with reference to Herta Müller, Richard Wagner, and the writers associated with the 'Aktionsgruppe Banat'). Bertram Salzmann, **Schreiben im Angesicht des Schreckens. Globale Verantwortung als Thema und Herausforderung deutschsprachiger Literatur nach 1945*, Munich, Fink, 262 pp. K. Bullivant, 'Endzeitszenarien: die nukleare Apokalypse und die deutsche Literatur der 80er Jahre', *LitL*, 25:101–12. S. C. Anderson, 'Outsiders, foreigners, and aliens in cinematic or literary narratives by Bohm, Dische, Dörrie, and Ören', *GQ*, 75:144–59, explores understandings of the concepts 'German' and 'foreigners' in four works of the 1980s and 1990s: Irene Dische's 'The Jewess', Aras Ören's *Bitte nix Polizei*, Hark Bohm's film *Yasemin*, and Doris Dörrie's film *Keiner liebt mich*. **Migration und Interkulturalität in neueren literarischen Texten*, ed. Aglaia Blioumi, Munich, Iudicium, 162 pp. Also by A. Blioumi, *Interkulturalität als Dynamik: ein Beitrag zur deutsch-griechischen Migrationsliteratur seit den siebziger Jahren*, Tübingen, Stauffenburg,

2001, vii + 276 pp. Olivia Spiridon, *Untersuchungen zur rumäniendeutschen Erzählliteratur der Nachkriegszeit* (Literatur und Medienwissenschaft, 86), Oldenburg, Igel, 356 pp. L. A. Adelson, 'The Turkish turn in contemporary German literature and memory work', *GR*, 77:326–38. T. Cheesman, 'Akçam — Zaimoğlu — "Kanak Attak": Turkish lives and letters in German', *GLL*, 55:180–95. Wioletta Knütel, **Verlorene Heimat als literarische Provinz. Stolp und seine pommersche Umgebung in der deutschen Literatur nach 1945* (Danziger Beiträge zur Germanistik, 3), Frankfurt, Lang, 259 pp. Hans Bergel, **Bukowiner Spuren. Von Dichtern und bildenden Künstlern* (Studien zur Literaturgeschichte, 3), Aachen, Rimbaud, 96 pp. M. Wigbers, 'Von Paris über "Bramme" in die Eifel. Orte und Schauplätze in kriminalliterarischen Texten von der Romantik bis in die Gegenwart', *WW*, 52:276–92. A. Blühdorn, '"Der Enkel aus Berlin": Udo Lindenberg and the German cabaret tradition', *GLL*, 55:416–33. Michaela Monschein, *Des Kaisers neue Kleider. Literaturbeilage der 'Welt' 1964 bis 1971* (Innsbrucker Veröffentlichungen zur Alltagsrezeption, 6), Innsbrucker Zeitungsarchiv, 210 pp.

Berghahn, *Essays*, contains a number of papers focusing on post-war film, including J. Gregson's examination of representations of masculinity and constructions of national identity in Wolfgang Kohlhaase's and Gerhard Klein's *Berlin-Ecke Schönhauser* (63–77), and G. Müller's exploration of the representation of teenage identity in Helmut Dziuba's *Jana und Jan* (79–91), as well as P. Graves's informative survey of literary developments in the 1990s (143–57). Kohl, *Words*, includes a number of contributions relating wholly or in part to the post-war period, including S. Meacher on Peter Härtling's *Das Windrad* (93–110), P. Davies, S. Parker, and M. Philpotts on the periodization of German literature between 1930 and 1960 (111–33), S. Tebutt on images of the gypsy in 20th-c. art (135–51), and A.-E. Kurth on Jochen Hick's 1990 film *Via Appia* (199–214).

AUSTRIA. *Modern Austrian Prose. Interpretations and Insights*, ed. Paul F. Dvorak (Studies in Austrian Literature, Culture, and Thought), Riverside, CA, Ariadne, 2001, 386 pp., is a collection of essays on Austrian prose writing from the 1970s to the 1990s. Each chapter focuses on an individual work by a particular author, often one that might be considered his or her 'major' piece of writing, in an attempt to bring together a set of texts representative of the period in question, particularly in relation to 'uniquely Austrian forms of expression as they unfolded during the last three decades of the twentieth century', and with a view to demonstrating the 'wide range and deep richness of modern Austrian literature'. It is certainly the case that recurrent themes, focal points, and characteristics emerge in a number of the individual contributions. For instance, the influence of Wittgenstein on Ingeborg Bachmann's *Malina* (R. Duffaut, 16–40), and Thomas Bernhard's *Beton* (K. E. Webb, 218–46); the anti-Heimat thrust of Elfriede Jelinek's *Die Liebhaberinnen* (R. S. Thomas, 59–85), and Gerhard Roth's *Der stille Ozean* (R. S. Thomas, 174–99); the exploration of the relationship between fiction and autobiography in Peter Henisch's *Die kleine Figur meines Vaters* (T. C. Hanlin, 86–106), and Elias Canetti's *Die gerettete Zunge* (R. L. Burt, 129–49); or the development of postmodern literary strategies in Friederike Mayröcker's *Reise durch die Nacht* (B. Bjorklund, 247–68), Christoph Ransmayr's *Die Schrecken des Eises und der Finsternis* (M. Lamb-Faffelberger, 269–85), Robert Menasse's *Schubumkehr* (R. S. Posthofen, 325–46), and Michael Köhlmeier's *Telemach* (G. Ulm Sandford, 347–66). Hermann Dorowin, **'Mit dem scharfen Gehör für den Fall.' Aufsätze zur österreichischen Literatur im 20. Jahrhundert*, Vienna, Praesens, 184 pp. **Österreich (1945–2000). Das Land der Satire*, ed. Jeanne Benay and Gerald Stieg (Convergences, 23), Berne, Lang, xiv + 388 pp. Monika Shafi, **Balancing Acts. Intercultural Encounters in Contemporary German and Austrian Literature* (Studien zur deutschsprachigen Gegenwartsliteratur, 17), Tübingen, Stauffenburg, 2001, xxvi + 277 pp. Gerhard Fuchs, **Literatur und Kleinformat. Österreichische Gegenwartsautoren in der "Neuen Kronenzeitung" 1972–1981*, Vienna, Residenz, 240 pp. W. Straub, 'Richtige Menschen und unmögliche Bauwerke. Das Kraftwerk: ein Seitenstrang österreichischer Literatur zwischen Mythos und touristischem Topos', *ÖGL*, 46:26–39. J. Stewart, '"Nicht die Kunst darf sich vereinnahmen lassen": Franzobel, literature and politics in the "New Austria"', *GLL*, 55:219–33.

SWITZERLAND. Patrick Heller, *'Ich bin der, der das schreibt.' Gestaltete Mittelbarkeit in fünf Romanen der deutschen Schweiz, 1988–1993* (EH, I, 1827), 367 pp., concerns itself with the question 'wie Romane ihre Mittelbarkeit gestalten' in relation to Swiss literature of the late 1980s and early 1990s, that is, with questions of narrative perspective and technique and with novels' metanarrative reflection on the process of narration. These issues are explored in relation to Swiss literature, the 'Grundton' of which, it is claimed, has been provided at least in part since the late 1960s by a continual problematization of the act of narration. The novels considered in the study have been chosen for the degree of self-consciousness with which they treat the act of narration and for their concern with the relationship between fiction and reality. The first part of the study sets out the theoretical basis for the analysis of the individual novels, looking particularly at the narrative theory of Käte Hamburger and Franz K. Stanzel. In the second part five novels are explored individually before the study concludes with a comparative analysis of them: Hermann Burger's *Brenner*, Lukas Hartmann's *Die Seuche*, Otto F. Walter's *Zeit des Fasans*,

Eveline Hasler's *Die Wachsflügelfrau*, and Adolf Muschg's *Der Rote Ritter*. Irena Šebestová, *Frauenliteratur der 70er Jahre in der Schweiz* (EH, I, 1821), 167 pp, details initially the socio-political and literary factors which allowed for the emergence and development of a body of women's writing in Switzerland in the 1970s. An exploration of the particular characteristics and the most commonly explored themes of this literature forms the main body of the study, with interpretations of works by Gertrud Leutenegger, Hanna Johansen, and Laure Wyss providing illustrations. Particular attention is paid to the reasons for the development of an interest in the theme of 'Hexenverfolgung' and the study's final chapter offers an extended reading of Eveline Hasler's *Anna Göldin. Letzte Hexe*. G. Stocker, 'Traumen des Aufwachsens. Drei Variationen aus der schweizer Literatur der neunziger Jahre', *WB*, 48:380–98, explores the theme of childhood in Zoë Jenny's *Das Blütenstaubzimmer*, Ruth Schweikert's *Erdnüsse. Totschlagen*, and Silvio Huonder's *Adalina*.

EAST GERMANY. Helen Bridge, *Women's Writing and Historiography in the GDR*, Oxford, Clarendon, vii + 280 pp., explores 'the complex relationships between literature and other discourses in the GDR' with a view to demonstrating that literature's peculiar properties allowed it, unlike historiography, to emancipate itself from, and provide a critical alternative to, official state discourses in a way which could in turn transform other cultural and intellectual spheres. In order to show this, the study focuses in particular on 'the development of critical approaches to history in narrative fiction by women' from the late 1960s onwards, in the light of the fact that feminism represents 'one of the most significant and fundamental challenges to the orthodox model of history voiced by GDR literature'. While the initial chapters explore broad developments in literature and historiography from the 1970s onwards, subsequent sections home in on the critical potential of those areas which were of particular concern to women writers: the female experience of fascism (with reference to Helga Schütz's Jette/Julia novels, Christa Wolf's *Kindheitsmuster*, as well as later treatments of this theme); women's place in history (focusing on works by Wolf, Sigrid Damm, Renate Feyl, and Brigitte Struzyk); and fantasy and myth (with analyses of Irmtraud Morgner's *Trobadora Beatriz* and *Amanda*, Helga Königsdorf's *Respektloser Umgang* and Wolf's *Kassandra*). A. Gilleir, '"Was zu erstreiten wir nicht aufgegeben haben: das menschenwürdige Leben." Dissidente weibliche Literatur aus der DDR', *GM*, 55:25–38. Verena Kirchner, *Im Bann der Utopie. Ernst Blochs Hoffnungsphilosophie in der DDR-Literatur* (NL, 187), 272 pp., explores the influence of Bloch's philosophy above all on writers who remained 'kritisch-loyal' to the GDR until 1989, examining the extent to which these writers' reception of Bloch's work helped to promote an ambivalent attitude to the state, not least because 'der Bezug auf sein Denken dazu beigetragen [hat], einen Bruch mit dem System zu verhindern'. The study shows that writers continued to search for a realizable socialist utopia beyond the real-existing oppression of the SED régime right up until the end of the GDR, with the individual textual readings demonstrating the extent to which 'die Hoffnungsphilosophie [. . .] als Kompensat für den Sozialismus in der Krise deutlich wird'. The study's first chapter explores Bloch's philosophy while subsequent sections are devoted to Bloch's influence on a range of writers, including Irmtraud Morgner, Uwe Johnson, and Christa Wolf. Central to the study are readings of Fritz Rudolf Fries's *Das Luft-Schiff* and *Alexanders neue Welten*, and Volker Braun's *Guevara oder Der Sonnenstaat*, *Hinze-Kunze-Roman*, and *Das Nichtgelebte*. Y.-G. Mix, 'Des Kaisers nackte Kleider oder die Negation der Literaturvermittlung. Zur Praxis, Rezeption und Kritik inoffiziellen Schreibens in der DDR (1979–1989)', *Euphorion*, 96:27–45. C. Gansel, 'Für "Vielfalt und Reichtum" und gegen "Einbrüche bürgerlicher Ideologie". Zur Kanon und Kanonisierung in der DDR', Arnold, *Kanonbildung*, 233–58. R. Stott, 'Continuity and change in GDR cinema programming policy 1979–1989: the case of the American science fiction import', *GLL*, 55:91–99.

2. Lyric Poetry

Winfried Woesler, **Deutsche Gegenwartsliteratur: Lyrik (1968–2000). Darstellung und Textbeispiele. Ein literaturwissenschaftliches Arbeitsbuch* (Bochumer Germanistik, 3), Bochumer U.P., 153 pp. Gregory Divers, **The Image and Influence of America in German Poetry since 1945*, Rochester, NY, Camden House, 296 pp. M. Schmitz-Emans, 'Rhythmisierung als Musikalisierung: zu Selbstbeschreibungen und ästhetischer Praxis in der experimentellen Dichtung des 20. Jahrhunderts', *ColH*, 32, 2001:243–87.

3. Drama

Klaus von Schilling, *Die Gegenwart der Vergangenheit auf dem Theater. Die Kultur der Bewältigung und ihr Scheitern im politischen Drama von Max Frisch bis Thomas Bernhard* (FMT, 29), Tübingen, Narr, 2001, 204 pp., is an exploration of developments in forms of political drama from the 1960s to the 1980s in relation to their attempts to participate in, or explore the consequences of, processes of 'Vergangenheitsbewältigung' in the Federal Republic of Germany. Individual chapters focus initially on four examples of the 'Aufklärungstheater' of the 1960s,

Max Frisch's *Andorra*, Rolf Hochhuth's *Der Stellvertreter*, Peter Weiss's *Die Ermittlung*, and Martin Walser's *Der Schwarze Schwan*, as early attempts to explore the consequences of the Third Reich for German self-definition in the present. Attention then turns to plays of the late 1970s and early 1980s, a moment in the history of the Federal Republic at which there was a renewed focus on the Third Reich but under the influence of changed social conditions and a transformed — postmodern — historical consciousness. The study demonstrates that in plays from this period the interest is no longer in the process of 'Vergangenheitsbewältigung' itself but in the consequences of the failure of this process for a sense of German identity. Heinar Kipphardt's *Bruder Eichmann*, George Tabori's *Die Kannibalen*, *Jubiläum*, and *Mein Kampf*, and Thomas Bernhard's *Vor dem Ruhestand* and *Heldenplatz* are examined in the light of this changed relationship to history, as well as in relation to a shift in developments in drama away from the Brechtian influenced 'Parabelstück' and documentary drama to 'das artifizielle, sich selbst thematisierende Spiel auf der Bühne'.

Branka Schaller, **Der Atridenstoff in der Literatur der 1940er Jahre. Unter besonderer Berücksichtigung der Nachkriegsdramatik* (BBNDL, 24), x + 206 pp. Karin Uecker, **Hat das Lachen ein Geschlecht? Zur Charakteristik von komischen weiblichen Figuren in Theaterstücken zeitgenössischer Autorinnen*, Bielefeld, Aisthesis, 216 pp. **From Perinet to Jelinek. Viennese Theatre in its Political and Intellectual Context*, ed. W. E. Yates, Allyson Fiddler, and John Warren (British and Irish Studies in German Language and Literature, 28), Oxford, Lang, 290 pp. K. Brzović and C. Decker, 'Geschichtstheater — Theatergeschichte: Szenen aus der Zweiten Republik', *ÖGL*, 46:17–25. Gerhard Fischer, **GRIPS. Geschichte eines populären Theaters (1966–2000)*, Munich, Iudicium, 488 pp.

4. Prose

Irmgard Scheitler, **Deutschsprachige Gegenwartsprosa seit 1970*, Tübingen, Francke, 2001, 386 pp. Joachim Garbe, *Deutsche Geschichte in deutschen Geschichten der neunziger Jahre*, Würzburg, Königshausen & Neumann, 284 pp., explores the contribution of literary works to a process of 'Neuorientierung' and 'Neudeutung der Geschichte' in the wake of the events of 1989–90. The study analyses a number of novels written between 1990 and 1998, some of which are autobiographically based and many of which are the work of writers who until 1990 had lived in the GDR, chosen because they thematize German history and because 'das Historische im Werk dem Interesse einer Deutung oder Orientierung im gesellschaftlichen Prozess folgt.' Readings of individual novels, grouped together under such headings as 'Vom Umgang mit der Geschichte', 'Familiengeschichten', 'Vom Umgang mit der Schuld', and 'Deutsch-jüdische Geschichten', contribute to the study's attempt to explore ways in which literature participates in the development of 'das öffentliche Bewusstsein' through its exploration of history. The study also attempts to identify the chief characteristics of German literature of the 1990s and to address the question of whether it can still be described as a 'Literatur der Nachkriegszeit' or whether in this decade a literary 'Paradigmenwechsel' has taken place. Ursula Knapp, **Der Roman der fünfziger Jahre. Zur Entwicklung der Romanästhetik in Westdeutschland*, Würzburg, Königshausen & Neumann, 160 pp. Michael Zimmermann, **Suicide in the German Novel 1945–89* (GSC, 12), 186 pp. I. Scheitler, 'Reisebeschreibung — Metafiktionale Verwendung in der Gegenwartsprosa', *LJb*, 43:277–92.

5. Individual Authors

ALIOTH, GABRIELLE. S. R. Falkner, 'Sinnkonstitution durch Wahrheitsvielfalt: G. As polyphoner Roman *Die stumme Reiterin*', *Seminar*, 38:364–82.

AMANSHAUSER, GERHARD. G. Stocker, 'Aufzeichnungen aus der Distanz. Über das "Terassenbuch" und das "Mansardenbuch" von G. A.', *Sprachkunst*, 32, 2001:257–77.

BACHMANN, INGEBORG. **Bachmann-Handbuch: Leben, Werk, Wirkung*, ed. Monika Albrecht and Dirk Göttsche, Stuttgart, Metzler, ix + 330 pp. Joachim Eberhardt, **Es gibt für mich keine Zitate. Intertextualität im dichterischen Werk I. Bs* (SDL, 165), ix + 505 pp. Leslie Morris, **'Ich suche ein unschuldiges Land': Reading History in the Poetry of I. B.* (Studien zur deutschsprachigen Gegenwartsliteratur, 9), Tübingen, Stauffenburg, 2001, 124 pp. M. Dufresne, 'I. B.: *Undine geht.* À la recherche d'un nouveau langage', *Germanica*, 31:113–27. J. McVeigh, 'I. B. as radio scriptwriter', *GQ*, 75:35–50. I. Dusar, 'Die Mythologie der Wienerin. I. Bs Arbeit am habsburgischen Mythos im Zeichen poetischer Gerechtigkeit', *GM*, 55:39–66. L. Friedberg, '"Verbrechen, die ich meine . . .": *Manners of Death* as a thickly descriptive translation of *Todesarten*', *MDLK*, 94:189–208. S. Kogler, 'Gegenwartsliteratur und zeitgenössische Musik: *Der junge Lord* von I. B. und Hans Werner Henze', *Seminar*, 38:261–76. Z. Gluscevic, 'I. B.'s sentimental journey through the "Haus Österreich" and (post)colonial discourse in "Drei Wege zum See"', *ib.*, 344–63.

BAUM, VICKI. Nicole Nottelmann, **Strategien des Erfolgs. Narratologische Analysen exemplarischer Romane V. Bs* (Ep, 405), 405 pp.

BAYER, KONRAD. **Entdeckungen. Über Jean Paul, Robert Walser, K. B. und anderes*, ed. Klaus Bonn, Edit Kovács, and Csaba Szabó (Debrecener Studien zur Literatur, 9), Frankfurt, Lang, 149 pp. C. K. Stepina, 'K. B. und die Wiener Gruppe', *NGR*, 17:28–46.

BECKER, JUREK. Anna P. Enslin and Wolfgang Gast, **J. B. Schriftsteller und Drehbuchautor*, Stuttgart, Klett, 47 pp.

BERNHARD, THOMAS. *A Companion to the Works of T. B.* ed. Matthias Konzett (SGLLC), 351 pp., is a collection of essays which grew out of a symposium at Yale University held in 1999 to commemorate the author's work on the tenth anniversary of his death. The tone of this volume, 'its balance between critical and reconstructive readings', is set by M. Konzett's stimulating introductory essay in which T. B.'s location within the tradition of the Austrian avant-garde and the nature and effectiveness of his own iconoclasm are explored (1–21). The volume contains a further 13 wide-ranging contributions ordered into thematic sections covering 'Bernhard in the public', 'Bernhard's poetics', 'Bernhard and drama', and 'Bernhard's social worlds', and includes two literary pieces by Marlene Streeruwitz evaluating B.'s legacy in the period immediately after his death and again ten years later. Gitta Honegger, **T. B.: The Making of an Austrian*, New Haven–London, Yale U.P., 2001, 341 pp. Steffen Vogt, **Ortsbegegnungen. Topographische Erinnerungsverfahren und politisches Gedächtnis in T. Bs 'Der Italiener' und 'Auslöschung'* (PSQ, 172), 340 pp. Radoslava Minkova, **Zur Problematik des Fremdseins in T. Bs und Christoph Heins Erzählwerken. Eine vergleichende Untersuchung* (EH, I, 1818), 2001, 192 pp. **T. B. und seine Lebensmenschen: Der Nachlass*, ed. Martin Huber, Manfred Mittermeyer, and Peter Karlhuber, Frankfurt, Suhrkamp, 206 pp. **Politik und Medien bei T. B.*, ed. Franziska Schössler and Ingeborg Villinger, Würzburg, Königshausen & Neumann, 265 pp.

BOBROWSKI, JOHANNES. M. Rankl, 'Sarmatien — Arkadien des Ostens. Strukturen des Idyllischen im Werk J. Bs', *LWU*, 35:115–30.

BÖLL, HEINRICH. Christine Hummel, **Intertextualität im Werk H. Bs* (Schriftenreihe Literaturwissenschaft, 59), Trier, Wissenschaftlicher Vlg, 396 pp. Viktor Böll, Markus Schäfer, and Jochen Schubert, **H. B.* Munich, dtv, 192 pp. **30 Jahre Nobelpreis H. B. Zur literarisch-theologischen Wirkkraft H. Bs*, ed. Georg Langenhorst, Münster, Lit, 256 pp. W. Bellmann, 'Textkritische Anmerkungen zu H. Bs *Gruppenbild mit Dame* nebst einem Hinweis zu *Das Brot der frühen Jahre*', *WW*, 52:249–56. R. E. Sackett, 'Germans, guilt, and the second threshold of H. B.: a study of three non-fictional works', *MLR*, 97:336–52.

BORN, NICOLAS. Jörg Eggerts, **Langsam kehrten die Farben zurück. Zur Subjektivität im Romanwerk, im lyrischen und literaturtheoretischen Werk N. Bs*, Frankfurt, Lang, 350 pp.

BRAUN, VOLKER. K. Weder, 'Geschichte als Mythos. Zu V. Bs *Iphigenie in Freiheit*', *Sprachkunst*, 32, 2001 : 241–55.

BRINKMANN, ROLF DIETER. C. Zeller, 'Unmittelbarkeit als Stil. R. D. Bs *Rom. Blicke*', *JIG*, 33.2, 2001 : 43–62.

BRUSSIG, THOMAS. F. Weinmann, 'La jeunesse chez trois jeunes auteurs des années 90: T. B., B. von Stuckrad-Barre et B. Lebert', *Germanica*, 30 : 117–27.

CELAN, PAUL. **Interpretationen: Gedichte von P. C.*, ed. Hans Michael Speier, Stuttgart, Reclam, 214 pp. *P. C.*, ed. Heinz Ludwig Arnold (TK, 53–54), 3rd rev. edn, 185 pp. *Celan-Jahrbuch*, vol. 8, ed. Hans Michael Speier (BNL, 190), 378 pp. Roland Reuss, *Im Zeithof. Celan-Provokationen*, Frankfurt, Stroemfeld, 2001, 181 pp. Anja Lemke, **Konstellation ohne Sterne. Zur poetischen und geschichtlichen Zäsur bei Martin Heidegger und P. C.*, Munich, Fink, 596 pp. Myeongsoon Jeong, *Hoffen auf das kommende Wort. Annäherung an P. Cs Dichtung anhand eines Vergleichs mit R. M. Rilke*, Göttingen, Zohab, 2001, 199 pp. F. Pennone, 'Césure du temps. Valéry, Rilke, C.: différences de rythme', *ColH*, 32, 2001 : 201–27. Martin Hainz, *Masken der Mehrdeutigkeit. Celan-Lektüren mit Adorno, Szondi und Derrida* (Untersuchungen zur österreichischen Literatur des 20. Jahrhunderts, 15), Vienna, Braumüller, xi + 188 pp. U. Seiderer, 'Körper unter Wasser. Die illegitime Geste der Fiktion — Flussleichen des 20. Jahrhunderts: Georg Heym, P. C., Peter Szondi', *RG*, 32 : 145–85. Michael Braun, *'*Hörreste, Sehreste.' Das literarische Fragment bei Büchner, Kafka, Benn und C.*, Cologne, Bölau, xi + 311 pp. A. Geisenhanslüke, 'Energie der Zeichen. Zur Tradition artistischer Lyrik bei Gottfried Benn, P. C., Thomas Kling und Marcel Beyer', *LitL*, 25 : 2–16. Theo Buck, **Celan und Frankreich. Darstellung mit Interpretationen* (Celan-Studien, 5), Aachen, Rimbaud, 112 pp. M. Lackey, 'Poetry as overt critique of theology: a reading of P. C.'s "Es war Erde in ihnen"', *MDLK*, 94 : 433–46.

DELIUS, FRIEDRICH CHRISTIAN. A. Cozic, 'Pour en finir avec les pères? La nouvelle de F. C. D. *Amerikahaus und der Tanz um die Frauen*', *Germanica*, 30 : 101–16.

DÜRRENMATT, FRIEDRICH. J. Bel, '*Der Marquis von Keith* de Frank Wedekind et *Die Ehe des Herrn Mississippi* de F. D.: réappropriation subjective et déplacement de sens', *Germanica*, 31 : 71–83. S. Ringel, 'Der stumme Hiob. Parodie in Ds Dramentheorie und in seinem frühen Stück *Der Blinde*', *MDLK*, 94 : 346–67. S. G. Donald, 'D.'s dogs: intimations of evil, death and spirituality', *FMLS*, 38 : 63–74.

DUVE, KAREN. 'K. D., Kathrin Schmidt, Judith Hermann: "Ein literarisches Fräuleinwunder"?', *GLL*, 55 : 196–207.

EDEL, PETER. Manfred F. Schenke, * . . . *und nächstes Jahr in Jerusalem? Darstellung von Juden und Judentum in Texten von P. E., Stephan*

Hermlin und Jurek Becker (Studien zur Reiseliteratur und Imagologieforschung, 6), Frankfurt, Lang, 504 pp.

ENZENSBERGER, HANS MAGNUS. E. Grimm, 'The disappearance of fury: H. M. E.'s diplomatic poetry of the 1990s', *GR*, 77:7–33. H.-J. Heise, 'Poesie und Putsch im Labor. H. M. E. blickt den Wissenschaftlern über die Schulter', *Die Horen*, 47.2:191–94.

FASSBINDER, RAINER WERNER. Michael Töteberg, **R. W. F.*, Reinbek, Rowohlt, 158 pp. Joanna Firaza, **Die Ästhetik des Dramenwerks von R. W. F. Die Struktur der Doppelheit* (GANDLL, 23), 233 pp. Sabine Pott, **Film als Geschichtsschreibung bei R. W. Fs Darstellung der Bundesrepublik Deutschland anhand ausgewählter Frauenfiguren in seiner 'BRD-Trilogie': 'Die Ehe der Maria Braun' (1978), 'Lola' (1981) und 'Die Sehnsucht der Veronika Voss' (1982)*, Frankfurt, Lang, 260 pp.

FICHTE, HUBERT. Ulrich Carp, **Rio Bahia Amazonas. Untersuchungen zu H. Fs Roman der Ethnologie. Mit einer lexikalischen Zusammenstellung zur Forschung der Religionen Brasiliens* (Ep, 400), 238 pp. Hanna Köllhofer, **Akustische Imitationen. Einführung in das Hörspiel 'Ich würde ein . . .' von H. F.*, St. Ingbert, Röhrig, 266 pp. R. Kamath Rajan, 'Die Welt ist ich — Ich bin die Welt. H. F. im autobiographischen Diskurs der 70er Jahre', *JIG*, 33.2, 2001:27–42. S. Bub, 'Die Begegnung mit dem Numinosen im fremden Ritus. Zu einem ethnologischen Motiv am Beispiel von Michel Leiris, H. F. und anderen', *KulturPoetik*, 2:213–35.

FRISCH, MAX. Heinz Ludwig Arnold, *'Was bin ich?' Über M. F.* (Göttinger Sudelblätter), Göttingen, Wallstein, 72 pp.

FRITSCH, GERHARD. A. P. Dierick, 'Politics, the elegiac, and the carnivalesque: G. F.'s *Moos auf den Steinen* and *Fasching*', *Seminar*, 38:46–58.

FRITSCH, WERNER. Anna Opel, **Sprachkörper. Zur Relation von Sprache und Körper in der zeitgenössischen Dramatik — W. F., Rainald Goetz, Sarah Kane*, Bielefeld, Aisthesis, 194 pp.

FÜHMANN, FRANZ. A. Pinkert, 'Excessive conversions: antifascism, Holocaust, and state dissidence in F. F.'s *Das Judenauto* (1962)', *Seminar*, 38:142–53.

GRASS, GÜNTER. Claudia Mayer-Iswandy, **G. G.*, Munich, dtv, 248 pp. Sabine Moser, **'Dieses Volk, unter dem es zu leiden galt.' Die deutsche Frage bei G. G.* (KSL, 13), 306 pp. Klaus von Schilling, **Schuldmotoren. Artistisches Erzählen in G. Gs 'Danziger Trilogie'*, Bielefeld, Aisthesis, 127 pp. Anika Davidson, **Advocata Aesthetica. Studien zum Marienmotiv in der modernen Literatur am Beispiel von Rainer Maria Rilke und G. G.* (Literatura, 12), Würzburg, Ergon, 2001, 429 pp. Jin-Sok Chong, **Offenheit und Hermetik. Zur Möglichkeit des Schreibens nach Auschwitz: Ein Vergleich zwischen G. Gs Lyrik, der 'Blechtrommel' und dem Spätwerk Paul Celans* (EH, 1, 1830), 399 pp. *My Broken Love. G. G. in*

India and Bangladesh, ed. Martin Kämpchen, New Delhi, Viking–Penguin Books India, 2001, 303 pp., is a collection of interviews, documents, articles and lectures relating to G.'s three trips to India, with the focus particularly on his prolonged stay in Calcutta in 1986–87. H. Kinefuchi, 'Zahnarzt, Ratte, Monitor. Zur Bildkommunikation bei G. G.', *DB*, 108: 186–98. S. Trappen, 'G., Döblin und der Futurismus. Zu den futuristischen Grundlagen des Simultaneitätskonzepts der *Vergegenkunft*', *Euphorion*, 96: 1–26. F. Bancaud, 'La réécriture de *Bouvard et Pécuchet* dans *Un célibataire entre deux âges* (1915), *Recherches d'un chien* (1922) de Franz Kafka et dans *Toute une histoire* (1995) de G. G', *Germanica*, 31: 39–58. M.-S. Benoît, 'Réécriture et déconstruction. *Ein weites Feld* de G. G.', *ib.*, 85–97. S. Kiefer, 'Frühe Polemik und späte Differenzierung. Das Heidegger-Bild von G. G. in *Hundejahre* (1963) und *Mein Jahrhundert* (1999)', *WB*, 48: 242–59. H. Beyersdorf, 'Von der *Blechtrommel* bis zum *Krebsgang*. G. G. als Schriftsteller der Vertreibung', *ib.*, 568–93. M. Caspari, '*Im Krebsgang* gegen den Strich: Das schwierige Geschäft des Erinnerns bei G. G.', *GN*, 33: 106–09. L. Wille, 'Die Übersetzung im Polysystem der Gastkultur. Zur polnischen und englischen Übersetzung ausgewählter Prosa von G. G.', *LitL*, 25: 113–26.

GRÜN, MAX VON DER. Wozan Urbain N'Dakon, **Kinder lesen 'Vorstadtkrokodile'. Eine empirische Studie zur Rezeption des Kinderromans M. v. d. Gs* (BBL, 23), 2001, 268 pp.

GRÜNBEIN, DURS. *D. G.*, ed. Heinz Ludwig Arnold (TK, 153), 93 pp. M. Eskin, 'Body language. D. G.'s aesthetics', *Arcadia*, 37: 42–66. M. Eskin, ' "Stimmengewirr vieler Zeiten": G.'s dialogue with Dante, Baudelaire, and Mandel'shtam', *GR*, 77: 34–50.

HACKS, PETER. E. Szymani, 'Ausbruch aus der Konvention: Frauenfiguren in P. Hs *Margarete in Aix* und Heiner Müllers *Anatomie Titus Fall of Rome. Ein Shakespearekommentar*', *FMT*, 17: 53–64.

HANDKE, PETER. Wolfram Frietsch, **P. H. — C. G. Jung. Selbstsuche — Selbstfindung — Selbstwerdung. Der Individuationsprozess in der modernen Literatur am Beispiel von P. Hs Texten*, Gaggenau, Scientia Nova, 256 pp. Rhea Thönges-Stringaris, *'*Je länger aber das Ereignis sich entfernt . . .' Zu Joseph Beuys und P. H.*, Wangen, FIU, 110 pp.

HARIG, LUDWIG. Werner Jung, *'*Du fragst, was Wahrheit sei?' L. Hs Spiel mit Möglichkeiten*, Bielefeld, Aisthesis, 300 pp. Werner Jung and Marianne Sitter, *Bibliographie L. H.* (Bibliographien zur deutschen Literaturgeschichte, 12), Bielefeld, Aisthesis, 339 pp.

HENISCH, PETER. C. Parry, 'Von den Vorzügen der Fiktionalisierung. P. Hs und Peter Handkes Elternbiographien und die Suche nach einer adäquaten literarischen Form der Wahrheitsfindung', *JIG*, 33.2, 2001: 81–100.

HERMLIN, STEPHAN. Annie Lamblin, **S. H. et la France. Un poète allemand à contre-courant ou l'éternel exilé*, Berne, Lang, x + 205 pp.

HEYM, STEFAN. Hermann Gellermann, **S. H. — Judentum und Sozialismus. Zusammenhänge und Probleme in Literatur und Gesellschaft*, Berlin, Wissenschafts Vlg, 172 pp. Doris Lindner, **Schreiben für ein besseres Deutschland. Nationenkonzepte in der deutschen Geschichte und ihre literarischen Gestaltung in den Werken S. H.* (Ep, 398), 190 pp.

HILBIG, WOLFGANG. Markus Symmank, *Karnevaleske Konfigurationen in der deutschen Gegenwartsliteratur: Untersuchungen anhand ausgewählter Texte von W. H., Stephan Krawczyk, Katja Lange-Müller, Ingo Schulze und Stefan Schütz* (Ep, 370), 196 pp., offers close readings of a number of contemporary texts in an attempt to explore the relevance of Bakhtin's notion of a 'Karnivalisierung von Literatur in Phasen epochalen Paradigmenwechesels' for German literature of the last 15 years. G. Laschen, '". . . diese langen Traditionen der Dämmerung am Ende der Neuzeit": zum Gedicht W. Hs', *Die Horen*, 47.2: 173–81. J. Hell, '*Wendebilder*: Neo Rauch and W. H.', *GR*, 77: 279–303. M.-L. Botl, 'Odyssee 2001. Zu W. Hs Gedichtband *Bilder vom Erzählen*', *Die Horen*, 47.3: 40–64.

HILDESHEIMER, WOLFGANG. A. Knafl, 'Monologpartitur. Musikalische Erzählstrukturen in W. Hs *Tynset*', *Sprachkunst*, 32, 2001: 213–39.

HOFMANN, GERT. '"Als Hitler und der Tonfilm kamen": cinematic, technological, and historical narratives in G. H.'s *Der Kinoerzähler*', *MLR*, 97: 632–52.

HONIGMANN, BARBARA. B. Rossbacher, 'The topography of mourning in B. H.'s *Eine liebe aus nichts*', *Seminar*, 38: 154–67.

HÜRLIMANN, THOMAS. G. Kaiser, 'Nomina antes res. Das Stigma des Namens in T. Hs Novelle *Fräulein Stark*', *DeutB*, 32: 18–28.

INNERHOFER, FRANZ. Johannes Birgfeld, **F. I. als Erzähler. Eine Studie zu seiner Poetik* (Helicon. Beiträge zur deutschen Literatur, 28), Berlin, Lang, 251 pp.

JELINEK, ELFRIEDE. Alexandra Heberger, *Der Mythos Mann in ausgewählten Prosawerken von E. J.*, Osnabrück, Andere, 185 pp. Bärbel Lücke, *Semiotik und Dissemination: Von A. J. Greimas zu Jacques Derrida. Eine erzähltheoretische Analyse anhand von E. Js 'Prosa' 'Oh Wildnis, oh Schutz vor ihr'* (Ep, 409), 452 pp. C. Klein, '*Ce qui arriva après que Nora eut quitté son mari ou les soutiens des sociétés* (1977). Une récriture d'Ibsen par E. J.', *Germanica*, 31: 129–42. A. Fiddler, 'Staging Jörg Haider: protest and resignation in E. J.'s *Das Lebewohl* and other recent texts for the theatre', *MLR*, 97: 353–64. B. Morgan, 'J., *Krankheit oder moderne Frauen*', Hutchinson, *Landmarks*, 225–42.

JOHNSON, UWE. Christian Elben, **'Ausgeschriebene Schrift.' U. Js 'Jahrestage': Erinnern und Erzählen im Zeichen des Traumas* (Aporemata, 5),

Göttingen, Vandenhoeck & Ruprecht, 284 pp. *Johnson-Jb.*, vol. 9, ed. Holgar Helbig, Ulrich Fries, and Irmgard Müller, Göttingen, Vandenhoeck & Ruprecht, 398 pp. T. Buck, 'Verhinderte Innovation. Die in der DDR ungedruckt gebliebenen Bücher von U. J. und Hans Joachim Schädlich', *EG*, 57 : 287–319. J. Hell, 'The melodrama of illegal identifications, or, post-Holocaust authorship in U. J.'s *Jahrestage. Aus dem Leben von Gesine Cresspahl*', *MDLK*, 94 : 209–29.

JÜNGER, ERNST. M. Tauss, 'Der halluzinatorische Rausch als archaische Initiation. Zum hermetischen Drogenheroismus in E. Js Erzählung *Besuch auf Godenholm* (1952)', *WW*, 52 : 441–57.

KLEIN, GEORG. S. Willer, 'Rohrpostsendungen. Zeichen und Medien in der Prosa G. Ks', *WB*, 48 : 113–26. S. Taberner, 'A new modernism or "neue Lesbarkeit"?: hybridity in G. K.'s *Libidissi*', *GLL*, 55 : 137–48.

KLUGE, ALEXANDER. B. Wolf, 'Sichtverhältnisse im Krieg. Zur historischen Dokumentation und Spurensicherung bei A. K.', *WB*, 48 : 5–23.

KLÜGER, RUTH. A. Reiter, '"Ich wollte, es wäre ein Roman." R. K.'s feminist survival report', *FMLS*, 38 : 326–40.

KOEPPEN, WOLFGANG. Lothar Veit, **Einsam in der Menge. Der Schriftsteller in W. Ks Nachkriegsromanen*, Marburg, Tectum, 97 pp. Jörg Döring, *' *. . . ich stellte mich unter, ich machte mich klein . . .' W. K. 1933–1948*, Frankfurt, Stroemfeld, 2001, 358 pp. Sahbi Thabet, **Das Reisemotiv im neueren deutschsprachigen Roman. Untersuchungen zu W. K., Alfred Andersch und Max Frisch*, Marburg, Tectum, 180 pp.

KÖHLMEIER, MICHAEL. A. Strasser, 'M. Ks Sicht der Antike am Beispiel des Romans *Kalypso*', *Germanica*, 31 : 175–86.

KRACHT, CHRISTIAN. A. S. Biendarra, 'Der Erzähler als "popmoderner Flaneur" in C. Ks Roman *Faserland*', *GLL*, 55 : 164–79.

KRÜGER, MICHAEL. M. Braun, 'Schiffbruch mit Zuschauer. M. Ks philosophische Liebesromane', *Merkur*, 56 : 519–23.

KUNERT, GÜNTER. C. A. Costabile-Heming, 'Offizielle und inoffizielle Zensurverfahren in der DDR: eine Fallstudie zu G. K.', *LitL*, 25 : 33–46.

KUNZE, REINER. B. Lermen, '"So viele antworten gibt's, doch wir wissen nicht zu fragen." Zur Poetik R. Ks', *LWU*, 35 : 47–53.

LANGE, HARTMUT. S. Kleinschmidt, 'Gewissheit der Ungewissheit. H. Ls Poetik der Irritation', *SuF*, 54 : 224–34.

LANGE-MÜLLER, KATJA. C. D. Conter, 'Eine kleine Einführung in Werk und Leben der Berliner Schriftstellerin K. L.-M.', *DeutB*, 32 : 121–27.

LENZ, SIEGFRIED. D. Merchiers, '"Wie sie uns mit Heimatsinn düngten!": le témoignage de Zygmunt Rogalla dans *Heimatmuseum*', *Germanica*, 30 : 77–89.

LIND, JAKOV. Ulrike Schneider, **Die Dekonstruktion des bürgerlichen Subjekts am Beispiel ausgewählter Werke J. Ls* (Deutsche Hochschuledition, 126), Neuried, Ars Una, 290 pp.

MARON, MONIKA. *M. M. in Perspective. 'Dialogische' Einblicke in zeitgeschichtliche, intertextuelle und rezeptionsbezogene Aspekte ihres Werkes*, ed. Elke Gilson (*GMon*, 55), Amsterdam–Atlanta, Rodopi, 341 pp., is a collection of essays which grew out of a conference held at the University of Ghent to celebrate the author's 60th birthday. The collection's literary theoretical points of departure are Bakhtinian notions of the multi-referentiality of language and intertextuality and in keeping with this it contains a series of contributions 'in denen die Grenzen des Textes mit je eigenem Akzent nach außen hin überschritten wurden'. A number of essays focus on individual works: A. Bolterauer's reading of the story *Das Mißverständnis* and its examination of 'die Kontingenz und unhintergehbare [. . .] Konstruiertheit einer jeden Weltsicht' (21–33), S. Klötzer's exploration of the themes of 'Erinnerung und Identität' in *Flugasche* and *Pawels Briefe* (35–56), H. Lee's location of *Stille Zeile Sechs* within autobiographical discourses after 1989 (57–73), A. Geier's analysis of 'biographisches Erzählen' in *Animal triste* (93–122), and G. Leisten's examination of the themes of 'Schrift und Körper' in *Stille Zeile Sechs* (139–56). Others trace themes which run through the whole of M.'s *oeuvre*, such as A. Lewis's paper on 'Engagement und weibliche Identitätsstiftung' in M.'s novels (57–73), or H. Habers's on the theme of 'gefährliche Freiheit' (123–37). A number of contributions read M.'s work in the light of that of her contemporaries: F. Eigler explores the theme of memory in Martin Walser's *Ein springender Brunnen* and M.'s *Pawels Briefe* (157–80), B. Konze considers the depiction of a childhood in the GDR in works by M., Uwe Johnson, Irmtraud Morgner, and Thomas Brussig (181–203), and J. P. Wieczorek compares M. and Judith Kuckart (225–54). In the final contribution W. Sievers looks at English and French translations of M.'s work (225–54). Katharina Boll, *Erinnerung und Reflexion: Retrospektive Lebenskonstruktionen im Prosawerk M. Ms* (Ep, 410), 112 pp.

MAYRÖCKER, FRIEDERIKE. **F. M. oder 'das Innere des Sehens'. Studien zu Lyrik, Hörspiel und Prosa*, ed. Renate Kühn, Bielefeld, Aisthesis, 289 pp. *'*Rupfen in fremden Gärten.' Intertextualität im Schreiben F. Ms*, ed. Inge Arteel and Margrit Heidy Müller, Bielefeld, Aistheisis, 174 pp. E. A. Kunz, ' "Der Rhythmus muß nur wachgeküßt werden . . ." Zur Prosa F. Ms', *ColH*, 32, 2001:229–41. I. Arteel, 'Stirb und Werde. Der Subjektbegriff in F. Ms *Das Herzerreißende der Dinge*', *GM*, 55:67–78.

MORGNER, IRMTRAUD. Geoffrey Westgate, *Strategies under Surveillance. Reading I. M. as a GDR Writer* (APSL, 148), viii + 276 pp., is concerned above all to demonstrate the importance for an understanding of M.'s work of the GDR context in which it was written and to establish her status as 'a central and aesthetically radical GDR phenomenon'. The study explores the influence of the SED's 'Autorenpolitik' on M.'s work during three decades and focuses on her 'associative textual strategies' as a response to state control, offering readings not only of the much discussed later works but also of the often overlooked works from the late 1960s. M. Caspari, 'The critical potential of German Romanticism re-examined in M.'s *Gauklerlegende*', *GN*, 33:3–13.

MÜLLER, HEINER. Yasmine Inauen, *Dramaturgie der Erinnerung. Geschichte, Gedächtnis, Körper bei H. M.* (Studien zur deutschsprachigen Gegenwartsliteratur, 16), Tübingen, Stauffenburg, 2001, 226 pp. Michael Ostheimer, *Mythologische Genauigkeit. H. Ms Poetik und Geschichtsphilosophie der Tragödie* (Ep, 391), 212 pp. Yo-Sung Suh, **Das Opfer des Individuums und die Geschichte in den Stücken Bertolt Brechts und H. Ms*, Aachen, Shaker, 332 pp. Katharina Ebrecht, *H. Ms Lyrik. Quellen und Vorbilder* (Ep, 359), 2001, 242 pp. B. Sascha Löscher, *Geschichte als persönliches Drama. H. M. im Spiegel seiner Interviews und Gespräche*, Frankfurt, Lang, 270 pp. H. Philipsen, 'Hinkend zwischen Ich und Ich. Bekenntnisse oder: der Vater-Topos in H. Ms später autobiographischer Prosa', *GM*, 55:7–24. A. Beise, 'Geburt eines Vampirs. Auto(r)reflexion H. Ms vor und nach 1989', *WB*, 48:165–80.

MÜLLER, HERTA. *H. M.*, ed. Heinz Ludwig Arnold (TK, 155), 105 pp. Carmen Wagner, *Sprache und Identität. Literaturwissenschaftliche und fachdidaktische Aspekte der Prosa von H. M.* (Literatur und Medienwissenschaft, 87), Oldenburg, Igel, 305 pp. B. Haines, '"The unforgettable forgotten": the traces of trauma in H. M.'s *Reisende auf einem Bein*', *GLL*, 55:266–81.

PLENZDORF, ULRICH. P. Vaydat, '*Les nouvelles souffrances du jeune W.* de U. P.: négation contestataire et littérature', *Germanica*, 30:91–99.

RANSMAYR, CHRISTOPH. Monica Fröhlich, *Literarische Strategien der Entsubjektivierung. Das Verschwinden des Subjekts als Provokation des Lesers in C. Rs Erzählwerk* (Literatura, 13), Würzburg, Ergon, 2001, 201 pp., establishes evidence in its introductory section for the development of a marked trend in German literature since the 1960s, 'das Verschwinden von Figuren, von literarischen Subjekten'. The quite literal disappearance of protagonists in literary works is seen to reflect writers' awareness of the subject's endangerment by political and social realities. A brief overview of developments in the philosophical discourse on 'das verschwindende Subjekt' (Foucault, Horkheimer/Adorno, Derrida, and Lyotard), is followed by a demonstration of a shift in the way literature has explored the subject's dissolution. While the 1960s are characterized by a melancholic sense of a crisis of subjectivity (evident in works by Thomas Bernhard, Wolfgang Hildesheimer, and Max Frisch), in the 1980s a (postmodern) sense of freedom and a positive potential for reconstruction accompanies depictions of disappearing subjects, as seen in texts by Markus Werner and Hartmut Lange. The main body of the study follows the development of this theme in four novels by C. R., exploring the literary strategies this writer uses to problematize the notion of subjectivity and his depiction of the relationship between the subject and his environment, before exploring the works' potential to suggest positive new ways in which subjectivity can be constituted. N. Kaminski, 'Ovid und seine Brüder. C. Rs *Letzte Welt* im Spannungsfeld von "Tod des Autors" und pythagoreischer Seelenwanderung', *Arcadia*, 37:155–72. T. Neukirchen, '"Aller Aufsicht entzogen." Nasos Selbstentleibung und Metamorphose. Bemerkungen zum (Frei)Tod des Autors in C. Rs Roman *Der letzte Welt*', *GRM*, 52:191–209.

REZZORI, GREGOR VON. A. Corbea-Hoisie, '"Maghrebinien" — Ein Gedächtnisort ex negativo', *Austriaca*, 54:11–24. C. Schlicht, 'Epochenverschleppung im Kontext des Weiblichen', *ib.*, 25–40. G. Ravy, 'R. et la France', *ib.*, 41–58. A. Landolfi, '"In italiano è meglio." G. v. Rs italienische Sendung', *ib.*, 59–71. S. P. Scheichl, '"Das Leben spielt sich in Satiren ab." Satirisches in G. v. Rs *Hermelin in Tschernopol*', *ib.*, 73–90. K. Jaśtal, 'Bukowiner nationale Spielarten und G. v. R', *ib.*, 91–105. J. Le Rider, 'Mémoires d'un antisémite et *Neiges d'antan* de G. v. R. ou la démystification du mythe habsbourgeois', *ib.*, 107–15. G. Schmid, 'Der Multiplexcharakter der Kultureindrücke bei R.', *ib.*, 117–25. H. Schumacher, 'G. v. Rs Erzählung *Skuktschno* — Ein Lehrstück über die Mechanismen antisemitischer Gewalt', *ib.*, 127–45. B. Westphal, 'Czernowitz ou les limites de l'autobiographie. *Neiges d'antan* de G. v. R.', *ib.*, 147–61. J. Lajarrige, 'R. face à l'histoire. Vienne, mars 1938', *ib.*, 163–83. G. Stieg, 'Der "Tschusch" R. oder Name und Identitätssuche', *ib.*, 185–99. F. Rinner, 'Ein Mitteleuropäer auf Wanderschaft: G. v. Rs Autobiographie *Mir auf der Spur* im mitteleuropäischen Kontext', *ib.*, 201–12. K. W. Vowe, 'Film, Literatur und Traum: G. v. Rs Kain, Mord und Todschlag', *ib.*, 213–26. É. Dopont, 'G. v. R. Repères bibliographiques', *ib.*, 227–40.

ROES, MICHAEL. R. Tobin, 'Postmoderne Männlichkeit: M. R. und Matthias Politycki', *ZGer*, 12:324–33.

SCHALLÜCK, PAUL. *'*Wenn man aufhören könnte zu lügen . . .' Der Schriftsteller P. S., 1922–1976*, ed. Walter Gödden and Jochen Grywatsch, Bielefeld, Aisthesis, 412 pp.

SCHLINK, BERNHARD. B. M. Dreike, 'Was wäre denn Gerechtigkeit? Zur Rechtsskepsis in B. Ss *Der Vorleser*', *GLL*, 55:117–29.

H. Schmitz, 'Malen nach Zahlen? B. Ss *Der Vorleser* und die Unfähigkeit zu trauern', *ib.*, 296–311.

SCHMIDT, ARNO. Doris Plöschberger, **SilbmKünste & BuchstabmSchurkereien! Zur Ästhetik der Maskierung und Verwandlung in A. Ss 'Zettel's Traum'*, (BNL, 191), 191 pp. **Der Prosapionier als letzter Dichter. Acht Vorträge zu A. S.*, ed. Timm Menke and Robert Weninger (Hefte zur Forschung, 6), Bargfeld, Arno Schmidt Stiftung, 2001, 163 pp. F. Rathjen, 'Die drei Buchruinen. Zur Relevanz von Grillparzer, Stettinius und Thorne Smith für *Brand's Haide* und *Schwarze Spiegel*', *BaB*, 261–62:3–19. L. Harig, 'Unter dem papierenen Mond. Die Entdeckung der Kunst des Schreibens von A. S.', *ib.*, 263–64:3–27. W. Brandes, 'Der "niedersächsische Diderot" und der "Idiot" der "Stahlgewitter". Mutmaßungen über A. S., Alfred Andersch und Ernst Jünger', *ib.*, 265:3–20.

SCHNEIDER, PETER. C. A. Costabile-Heming, 'P. S.'s *Eduards Heimkehr* and the image of the "new Berlin"', *GSR*, 25:497–510.

SCHROTT, RAOUL. K. Leeder, 'The *poeta doctus* and the new German poetry: R. S.'s *Tropen*', *GR*, 77:51–67. K. Leeder, '"Erkenntnistheoretische Maschinen": questions about the sublime in the work of R. S.', *GLL*, 55:149–63.

SEBALD, W. G. J. Ceuppens, 'Im zerschundenen Papier herumgeisternde Gesichter. Fragen der Repräsentation bei W. G. S.', *GM*, 55:79–98. G. Kochhar-Lindgren, 'Charcoal: the phantom traces of W. G. S.'s novel-memoirs', *MDLK*, 94:368–80.

SEGHERS, ANNA. Nicole Suhl, **A. S.: 'Grubetsch' und 'Aufstand der Fischer von St. Barbara'. Literarische Konstrukte im Spannungsfeld von Phänomenologie und Existenzphilosophie* (HBG, 36), 301 pp. Birgit Schmidt, **Wenn die Partei das Volk entdeckt A. S., Bodo Uhse, Ludwig Renn und andere. Ein kritischer Beitrag zur Volksfrontideologie und ihrer Literatur*, Münster, Unrast, 340 pp.

ŞENOCAKS, ZAFER. R. Dollinger, 'Hybride Identitäten: Z. Şs Roman *Gefährliche Verwandschaften*', *Seminar*, 38:59–73.

SPÄTH, GEROLD. Charlotte E. Aske, *G. S. und die Rapperswiler Texte. Untersuchungen zu Intertextualität und kultureller Identität* (Texte und Studien zur Literatur der deutschen Schweiz, 9), Berne, Lang, 408 pp.

STRAUSS, BOTHO. C. Menke, '"Niemals." Märchen und Komödie in Ithaka', *DVLG*, 76:306–12. S. Otsuka, 'Der junge B. S. und sein Programm des kommenden Theaters', *DB*, 108:172–85. T. Oberender, 'Das Sehen sehen. Über B. S. und Gerhard Richter', *SuF*, 54:32–41.

STREERUWITZ, MARLENE. Nele Hempel, *M. S. — Gewalt und Humor im dramatischen Werk* (Studien zur deutschsprachigen Gegenwartsliteratur, 13), Tübingen, Stauffenburg, 2001, viii + 223 pp, offers a comprehensive critical interpretation of M. S.'s dramatic work, focusing particularly, but not exclusively, on the five-play cycle consisting of *New York. New York, Waikiki Beach, Sloane Square, Ocean Drive,* and *Elysian Park.* The first chapter contextualizes S.'s work, providing biographical information, an assessment of the influence of the 'Literaturstandort Österreich' on her plays and an overview of their reception. A further section explores some of the characteristic elements of S.'s drama, including her use of fragmentary language and her interest in the deconstruction of myths. The focus of the analysis then shifts in the study's two main chapters to the subversive potential of 'Gewalt' and 'Humor' in the five plays.

SÜSKIND, PATRICK. Maria C. Barbetta, **Poetik des Neo-Phantastischen. P. Ss Roman 'Das Parfum'* (Ep, 354), 252 pp.

TREICHEL, HANS-ULRICH. R. W. Williams, '"Mein Unbewusstes kannte . . . den Fall der Mauer und die deutsche Wiedervereinigung nicht": the writer H.-U. T.', *GLL*, 55:208–18. S. Taberner, 'H.-U. T.'s *Der Verlorene* and the problem of German wartime suffering', *MLR*, 97:123–34.

VANDERBEKE, BIRGIT. M. Uecker, 'Missverständnisse, Rollenspiele, Double Binds: Kommunikation und Bewusstsein im Werk B. Vs', *GLL*, 55:312–27.

WALSER, MARTIN. Joanna Jablkowska, *Zwischen Heimat und Nation. Das deutsche Paradigma? Zu M. W.* (Studien zur deutschsprachigen Gegenwartsliteratur, 15), Tübingen, Stauffenburg, 2001, 306 pp. Martin Reinhold Engler, *Identitäts- und Rollenproblematik in M. Ws Romanen und Novellen* (Cursus, 16), Munich, Iudicium, 2001, 309 pp. Hyun-Seung Yuk, *Das Prinzip 'Ironie' bei M. W. Zu den Poetik-Vorlesungen und den Erzählwerken der mittleren Phase* (Zeit und Text, Münstersche Studien zur neueren Literatur, 18), Münster, Lit, 2001, 197 pp. D. Jürgens, '"Geschichte will er abstoßen." M. Ws *Zimmerschlacht*', *LitL*, 25:17–32. G. Dommes, 'Kein Fall für sich. M. Ws "Tassilo"-Hörspiele', *LWU*, 35:199–217. *Der Streit um M. W. Beiträge und Interviews von Eckard Henscheid, Joachim Kaiser, Heimo Schwilk, Martin Walser, Günter Zehm u. a.*, Berlin, Junge Freiheit, 114 pp. Alexander Krisch, **Auschwitz. Und damit hat sich's verwirkt. M. W. und die Reaktionen auf seine Friedenspreisrede*, Marburg, Tectum, 174 pp. A. Mathäs, 'The presence of the past: M. W. on memoirs and memorials', *GSR*, 25:1–22. S. Brockmann, 'M. W. and the presence of the German past', *GQ*, 75:127–43. A. Fuchs, 'Towards an ethics of remembering: the Walser-Bubis debate and the other of discourse', *ib.*, 235–46. A. Takeda, 'Bildung des Ichbewusstseins: Zu M. Ws *Ein springender Brunnen.* (Versuch, den Roman vom Kontext der Friedenspreisrede zu befreien)', *GM*, 56:27–47. W. Böhme, 'Suche nach Halt in Zeit der Haltlosigkeit. Zu M. Ws umstrittenen Buch *Tod eines Kritikers*',

Zeitwende, 73.3:44–45. Matthias N. Lorenz, *M. W. in Kritik und Forschung. Eine Bibliographie*, Bielefeld, Aisthesis, 258 pp.

WEISS, PETER. Arnd Beise, **P. W.*, Stuttgart, Reclam, 296 pp. H. Müller, 'Geschichte, Allegorie, historisches Drama. Sieben Notizen zu Georg Büchner, P. W. und Heiner Müller', *GR*, 77:117–27. M. Minden, 'W., *Marat/Sade*', Hutchinson, *Landmarks*, 209–24.

WELLERSHOFF, DIETER. G. Laudin, '"La vérité de la littérature." Intertextualités littéraires et mythiques chez D. W.', *Germanica*, 31:159–73.

WOLF, CHRISTA. Hajo Drees, *A Comprehensive Interpretation of the Life and Work of C. W., Twentieth-Century German Writer*, Lewiston, NY, Mellen, vi + 170 pp. Irmgard Nickel-Bacon, *Schmerz der Subjektwerdung. Ambivalenzen und Widersprüche in C. Ws utopischer Novellistik* (Studien zur deutschsprachigen Gegenwartsliteratur, 18), Tübingen, Stauffenburg, 2001, 320 pp. Karin B. Büch, **Spiegelungen. Mythosrezeption bei C. W. 'Kassandra' und 'Medea. Stimmen'*, Marburg, Tectum, 106 pp. M. Tabah, 'Unschuldig, selbstbewußt — und doch Opfer. Entmythologisierung und Re-Mythisierung in C. Ws *Medea*', *EG*, 57:111–25. Evy Varsamopoulou, *The Poetics of the 'Künstlerinroman' and the Aesthetics of the Sublime* (Studies in European Cultural Transition, 11), Aldershot, Ashgate, xxvi + 268 pp., contains an introductory section defining the relationship between the 'Künstlerinromane' which this study explores and the German Romantic tradition. The novels examined in detail include French, German, and English-language examples of the genre from the 19th c. to the contemporary period. The study includes a lengthy and illuminating chapter on W.'s *Nachdenken über Christa T.* (138–95) which reads the novel in relation to Hélène Cixous's 'La Venue à l'Écriture' and examines it from a number of perspectives, including what is described as its metafictional discourse on the sublime, especially as it relates to writing, its exploration of the themes of subjectivity, death, and authorship, and its relationship to postmodernism in the light of its interaction with a Romantic, a modernist, and a social realist inheritance. Elwira Pachura, *Polen — Die verlorene Heimat. Zur Heimatproblematik bei Horst Bienek, Leonie Ossowski, C. W., Christine Brückner*, Stuttgart, Ibidem, 306 pp. C. Scribner, 'August 1961: C. W. and the politics of disavowal', *GLL*, 55:61–74.

WÜHR, PAUL. **Die poetische Republik. Annäherungen an P. Ws 'Salve res publica poetica'*, ed. Sabine Kyora (Bielefelder Schriften zu Linguistik und Literaturwissenschaft, 17), Bielefeld, Aisthesis, 175 pp.

ZÜRN, UNICA. C. Hilmes, 'Zeigen und erzählen: Texte, Bilder und wie sie zusammengehören. Überlegungen zu den Arbeiten von U. Z.', *Arcadia*, 37:67–84.

II. DUTCH STUDIES

LANGUAGE

POSTPONED

LITERATURE

POSTPONED

III. DANISH STUDIES*

LANGUAGE

By Tom Lundskær-Nielsen, *Senior Lecturer in Danish, Department of Scandinavian Studies, University College London*

1. General

**M/K — mod og kvindehjerte. Festskrift til Mette Kunøe 5. november 2002*, ed. Jens Cramer, Ole Togeby, and Peter Widell, Kolding, Institut for Erhvervssproglig Informatik og Kommunikation, University of Southern Denmark, 112 pp., is a *Festschrift* for Mette Kunøe at Aarhus University. Nina Møller Andersen, *I en verden af fremmede ord. Bachtin som sprogbrugsteoretiker*, Akademisk, 194 pp., argues that Bakhtin's works, as well as being a powerful influence on literary and philosophical theories, also contain the germs of a communication model. Erik W. Hansen, *The Synchronic Fallacy. Historical Investigations with a Theory of History*, Odense U.P., 2001, 481 pp., is a doctoral thesis which delivers a strong critique of the synchronic view of language. I. L. Pedersen, *'European standard languages and multilingual Europe — The Nordic Language Council', pp. 73–84 of *Europäische Hochsprachen und mehrsprachiges Europa*, ed. Gerhard Stickel, Mannheim, Institut für Deutsche Sprache, 260 pp. Kirsten Rask, *Rasmus Rask. Store tanker i et lille land*, Gad, 255 pp., is a biography of the famous Danish linguist, tracing his life and work and showing his later influence on both the Danish and the international linguistic community. Ebbe Spang-Hanssen, *Sprogets verden og din. Om menneskets mærkelige evne for sprog*, Gyldendal, 219 pp., deals with the influence of language on cultures and explores the extraordinary human ability for learning and using language. Its three main sections outline: (i) signs, words, and categories; (ii) the combination of words and phrases (grammar); (iii) communication, rhetoric, and strategies (pragmatics), all in a universal context.

Sprog i Norden, ed. Henrik Holmberg, Novus, 238 pp., has the following articles on inter-Scandinavian language co-operation: O. Josephson, 'Språknämndernas roll, framtid och uppgifter. En självrannsakande språkvårdarenkät' (7–22); O. Grønvik, 'Det nordiske språksamarbeidet — eit mønster til etterlikning?' (23–46); N. Davidsen-Nielsen, 'Statusplanlægning som et nyt arbejdsområde for Dansk Sprognævn' (47–57); H. Møller, 'Hvordan går det egentlig

* The place of publication of books is Copenhagen unless otherwise stated.

med nabosprogsundervisningen?' (59–72); H. Sandøy, 'Moderne importord i Norden. Ei gransking av bruk, normer og språkholdningar' (73–100); L.-O. Delsing, 'Bron och språket — en undersökning av dansk-svensk språkförståelse' (101–14); A. Karker, 'Et blad af leksikografiens glemmebog' (143–51); and H. Holmberg, 'Sprogsamarbejde i Norden 2001' (153–59). D. Duncker, 'Dynamikken i sproget', *Studier i Nordisk*, 15–29, is a critical discussion of the structuralist view of language. Inspired by a project started by the Ministry of Education in 2001, two articles (with the same title as the project) discuss the subject of Danish in the future: O. Ravnholt, 'Fremtidens danskfag', *Nyt fra Sprognævnet*, no. 1 : 1–4; and C. Tilling, 'Fremtidens danskfag', *Sprog & Samfund*, no. 1 : 8–9. The latter author also looks at the role of the 'Sprog & Samfund Society' on the Danish Language Council: Id., 'Selskabets rolle i Dansk Sprognævn', *ib.*, no. 2 : 10–11. H. Jørgensen, 'Der *føres* sprogpolitik i Danmark!', *Vandfanget*, Institut for Sprog og Litteratur, Århus, no. 2 : 10–13. E. V. Larsen, 'Den kognitive trend i lingvistikken', *ib.*, 30–33. **Elektroniske tekster*, ed. Søren Peter Sørensen, Århus, Systime, 187 pp., reflects the ever more frequent and widespread use of electronic texts and presents a variety of them in different types of media.

2. History of the Language, Phonology, Morphology, Lexis, Syntax, Semantics, and Pragmatics

M. Thelander, 'Utvecklingen av de nordiska språken 1550–1800', *Studier i Nordisk*, 83–84. I. L. Pedersen, 'Sociolingvistiske strukturer i Danmark i perioden 1550–1800', *ib.*, 85–98. U. Teleman, 'Språkplanering och språkhistoria i Sverige under 16– och 1700–talen', *ib.*, 99–103. H. Ruus, 'Danske sprogholdninger fra reformationen til romantikken', *ib.*, 105–14. B. Holmberg, *'Research in Danish language history 1850–1950. An overview, the Nordic languages', pp. 68–75 of *An International Handbook of the History of the North Germanic Languages*, ed. Oskar Bandle et al., 1, Berlin–NY, de Gruyter, 1057 pp. Mads Julius Elf, *Apropos smagen. Repræsentation, mad, danskpædagogik og andre problemer omkring Ludvig Holbergs Peder Pårs*, Dansklærerforeningen, 136 pp. M. Kunøe, 'Trendy sproghistorie', *Vandfanget*, Institut for Sprog og Litteratur, Århus, no. 2 : 27–29.

Jens Rasmussen, *Dansk fonetik i teori og praksis*, Special-pædagogisk forlag, 107 pp., presents a clear overview of the rules for the pronunciation of Danish sounds in simple words and derivations, including the use of the glottal stop, and also deals with stress in words and word combinations. **Sætningsskemaet i generativ grammatik*, ed. Per Anker Jensen and Peter Rossen Skadhauge, Kolding, Institut for

Erhvervssproglig Informatik og Kommunikation, University of Southern Denmark, 112 pp. There are several shorter contributions in *Nyt fra Sprognævnet*: A. Duekilde, 'Om lydord', no. 3:7–9; A. Hamburger, 'Kavalergang', no. 4:5–7; E. Hansen, 'Længer og længere', no. 2:9–10; J. N. Jensen, 'Om ordet forhøring', no. 2:8–9; O. Ravnholt, 'Ordet portfolio — er det nødvendigt?', no. 4:1–5; V. Sandersen, 'Om bogstavet å', no. 3:1–7; plus a general article with information about the new comma: 'Nyt om nyt komma', no. 4:7–10.

Sprint, 2, includes the following three articles: V. Smith, 'Nydansker — eller mener vi danlænder? Ord, egenbetydning og national identitet' (37–46); J. Gustavsson, 'Tegn — kategori — ideologi. Om "nydansker", "andengenerationsindvandrer" og andre kategorier' (47–59); and J. Kornbech and C. Weyers, 'Om eurotegnets placering — før eller efter tallet' (60–66). E. Hansen, 'Forandring fryder ikke', *Sprog & Samfund*, no. 3:6–7; and Id., 'Lave priser', *ib.*, no. 4:11. E. S. Jensen, 'Hvordan bliver et sætningsadverbial til et sætningsadverbial?', *Studier i Nordisk*, 31–50. M. F. Nielsen, 'Nå! En skiftemarkør med mange funktioner', *ib.*, 51–67. K. Rifbjerg, 'Livskvalitet', *Sprog & Samfund*, no. 2:12. V. Engerer, 'Faseverbernes tidsbetingelse. Grundtræk af den semantiske beskrivelse af faseverbkonstruktioner', *Hermes*, 29:53–71. O. Togeby, 'Hvad er betydning?', *ib.*, 33–52.

3. Dialectology, Contrastive Linguistics, Bilingualism, and Applied Linguistics

**Ømålsordbogen. En sproglig-saglig ordbog over dialekterne på Sjælland, Lolland-Falster, Fyn og omliggende øer*, vol. 6 (Institut for Dansk Dialektforskning, Universitets-Jubilæets danske Samfunds skrifter, 550), C. A. Reitzel, 473 pp. *Dialekter — sidste udkald?*, Modersmål-Selskabets årbog 2002, C.A. Reitzel, 196 pp., has Danish dialects as its theme and contains the following articles: G. Søndergaard, 'Sproget på Lars Tyndskids marker — om rigsmål og dialekt' (15–37); I. L. Pedersen, 'Hovedtrækkene i de danske dialekter' (39–80); Id., 'Sociolingvisternes dialekter' (81–93); P. Zinckernagel, 'DR Dialekt — et personligt synspunkt fra en chef i DR' (95–99); P. Quist, 'Nye danskere, nye dialekter' (101–07); K. Touborg (in a conversation with G. T. Leffers), 'Ingen tvivl om det: dialekten er bevaringsværdig' (109–18); K. Sørensen, 'Hjemstavnen og dens sprog' (119–23); I. Carlsen, 'We' wi wæ' we' wi er wejelboere? Vil vi være ved at vi er vendelboere?' (125–37); E. Haase, 'Ingen sønderjysk — ingen sønderjysk identitet' (139–45); B. Bendtsen (in a conversation with G. T. Leffers), 'Fyn er fin' (147–56); P. Westh-Jensen, 'Bornholmernes skift mellem dialekt og standard' (157–61); M. Maegaard, 'Sønderjysk i dag — holdninger og forestillinger' (163–67); D. Bleses and P. Thomsen, 'Spilt eller spilled: Spiller den fynske og sjællandske udtale en rolle for børns stavning?' (169–85); and A. Gudiksen, 'Hvor kan man læse mere?' (187–92).

Danske Talesprog, 3, includes: H. Juul, 'Børnerim der ikke rimer' (1–16); T. Kristiansen, T. B. Clausen, and M. Havgaard, 'Sprogholdninger hos unge i Nakskov' (17–70); I. Ejskjær, 'Urriset, tværriset, purrisset, perrisset — nogle adjektiver set i orddannelsesperspektiv' (71–77); F. Køster, 'Om to fynske købstadsdagbøger' (79–91); and A. Jensen, 'Pisalike — eller har en æbleskive noget til fælles med en skrøne?' (93–102). *Ord & Sag*, 22, has three relevant articles: T. Arboe, 'Skuld gammel venskab rejn forgo . . . / Auld Lang Syne — om sproget mv. i Jeppe Aakjærs og Robert Burns's velkendte vise' (16–39); I. S. Hansen, '1 brukiel for 6 sldlr., 2 gamel thin fade for 1 mk. — dialekt i 1600–tals retstekster' (40–46); and P. Michaelsen, 'Ponni, niks, alle-halve — og andre betegnelser for spil med terningepind og -top' (47–61). H. Juul, *'Conditioned spellings in Danish', pp. 97–107 of *Working Papers 50. Papers from the Third Conference on Reading and Writing*, ed. Kerstin Nauclér, Lund U.P., 123 pp.; and Id., *'Grammatisk opmærksomhed. En overset vanskelighed i skolebørns udvikling?', *Mål & Mæle*, no. 2:8–18. T. Kristiansen, *'Noget om dialekter og dialektforskning', *ib.*, 3:25–31; and Id., *'Standard language and dialects in Denmark and Norway', *Idun*, 15:335–66. M. Maegaard, *'Hvorfor er sønderjysk så svært at forstå?', pp. 93–100 of *Jallaspråk, slanguage og annet ungdomsspråk i Norden*, ed. Eli-Marie Drange, Ulla-Britt Kotsinas, and Anna-Brita Stenström, Kristianssand, 152 pp. I. L. Pedersen, *'The impact of internal or contact-induced change on weak preterites in *-et* in Danish dialects with an outlook to Norway and Sweden', pp. 269–82 of *Present-day Dialectology. Problems and Findings*, ed. Jan Berns and Jaap van Marle, Berlin–NY, Mouton de Gruyter, vii + 366 pp. V. Sørensen, 'Dialekterne — dør de? — og hvad sker der ved det?', *Vandfanget*, Institut for Sprog og Litteratur, Århus, no. 2:24–27.

De unges sprog. Artikler om sproglig adfærd, sproglige holdninger og flersprogethed hos unge i Danmark, ed. Jens Norman Jørgensen (Københavnerstudier i tosprogethed, Køgeserien, K9), Akademisk, 288 pp., has the following contributions: J. N. Jørgensen, 'Studier af flersprogethed hos unge' (9–35); J. L. Bøll, 'Etnicitet, sprog, generation og køn hos unge' (36–73); J. Møller, 'De sejes klub' (74–97); H. Eskildsen, 'Kodeskift hos unge i 8. klasse' (98–127); A.-S. Kohl, 'Ritual, musik og performance i kodeskift til fremmedsprog' (128–45); M. B. Jacobsen, 'Magtens kode' (146–71); M. Havgaard, 'Pragmatiske funktioner med kodeskrift hos tosprogede unge' (172–202);

K. Reiff, 'Tosprogede unges brug af engelsk' (203–32); J. Hansen, 'Sproglig bevidsthed hos tosprogede unge' (233–67); and M. Laursen, 'Registerskift hos børn. Frække ord og tabuord i 1. og 2. klasse' (268–88).

Multilingual Behaviour in Youth Groups. Scandinavian Studies in the Simultaneous Use of two or more Languages in Group Conversations among Children and Adolescents, ed. Jens Normann Jørgensen (Copenhagen Studies in Bilingualism, Køge Series, K11), Danish University of Education, 2001, 142 pp., includes the following articles: J. N. Jørgensen, 'Multilingual behaviour in youth groups' (5–11); J. Cromdal, Bilingual text production as task and resource: social interaction and task oriented student groups' (13–30); T. Esdahl, 'Language choice' (31–54); J. Steensig, 'Some notes on the use of conversation analysis in the study of bilingual interaction' (55–80); L. M. Madsen, 'Linguistic power wielding and manipulation strategies in group conversations between Turkish-Danish children' (99–115); and J. N. Jørgensen, 'Multi-variety code-switching in conversation 903 of the Køge Project' (117–37). Lian Malai Madsen, *De som har kan få. En undersøgelse af medbragt og forhandlet sproglig magt i gruppesamtaler mellem børn* (Københavnerstudier i tosprogethed, Køgeserien, K12), Danish University of Education, 158 pp. Lone Hegelund, *A Comparative Language Policy Analysis of Minority Mother Tongue Education in Denmark and Sweden* (Copenhagen Studies in Bilingualism, 33), Danish University of Education, 288 pp.

Hans Jørgen Boe, *Snak dansk! Suomen ja ruotsin kautta tanskaan*, Jyväskylä, 133 pp., is a course in Danish for Finnish speakers. **Fremmedsprog i den danske skole*, ed. Signe Holm-Larsen, Kolding, Kroghs, 251 pp. Uffe Ladegaard, *Sprog, holdning og etnisk identitet. En undersøgelse af holdninger over for sprogbrugere med udenlandsk accent*, Odense U.P., 112 pp. R. Brodersen, *' "Jeg føler meg mest norsk, men jeg føler meg en god del dansk også." Om national identitet og sproglig adfærd blandt danskere in Norge', *Nordica Bergensia*, 26: 139–59, and Id, *'Sproglig adfærd og identitetsopfattelser blandt danskere i Norge', *Målbryting*, 5: 135–71. H. Gottlieb, 'Hey, jeg har et navn, okay?', *Studier i Nordisk*, 191–209. I. Korzen, 'Fra sprogsystem og kontekst til tekst — og fra det lineære og praktiske dansk til det hierarkiske og poetiske/retoriske italiensk', *Sprint*, no. 2:5–36. D. Nikulitcheva, *'Основные типы синтагматпческих различий между континентальными скандинавскими языками (Статья)' (main types of syntagmatic differences between the Mainland Scandinavian languages), *Scandinavian Languages*, 6, Moscow, 2001, 279–303; and Id., 'Contrastive studies of translations: reflexivity in Danish, Norwegian and Swedish. Lingvistisk teori i oversættelsesstudier', *Copenhagen Working Papers in LSP*, Handelshøjskolen, no. 1: 120–27.

M. V. Christensen, 'Nu du skal læse om min sprog, habibi!', *Vandfanget*, Institut for Sprog og Litteratur, Århus, no. 2 : 6–9. P. Quist and J. N. Jørgensen, 'Indfødte dansktalendes vurdering af unges andetsprogsdanske talesprog', *NyS*, 29, 9–44; and Id., 'Native speakers' judgements of second language Danish', *Language Awareness*, 10.1, 2001, 41–56. P. Quist, 'Sociolingvistik i Danmark og Japan. En kursorisk oversigt og sammenligning, samt en tanke on national identitet og standardisering', *Idun*, 14, 2001, 259–80; and Id., 'Sproglig habitus, symbolsk magt og standardisering — Pierre Bourdieus begreber anvendt på sociolingvistik', *ib.*, 15 : 119–30. I. Voller, 'Die Modalpartikeln auf Deutsch and Dänisch — eine kontrastive Analyse', *Hermes*, 28 : 135–54. V. Andersen, 'Nye tiltag i grammatikundervisningen', *ib.*, 29 : 187–95.

4. Lexicography, Grammars, Stylistics, and Rhetoric

A number of dictionaries have appeared. Among them are: **Engelsk-Dansk, Dansk-Engelsk Internetordbog* (CD ROM), ed. Jens Axelsen, Gyldendal. **Fransk-Dansk, Dansk-Fransk Miniordbog*, ed. Else Juul Hansen, Gyldendal, 944 pp. **Spansk-Dansk, Dansk-Spansk Internetordbog* (CD ROM), ed. Johan Windfeld Hansen, Birthe Gawinski, and Hanne Brink Andersen, Gyldendal. **Tysk-Dansk, Dansk-Tysk Ordbog. Mediumsordbog*, ed. Ken Farø and Inge Voller, Gyldendal, 862 pp. **Engelsk-Dansk, Dansk-Engelsk Ordbog. Mediumordbog*, ed. Erik Hvid, Jane Rosenkilde Jacobsen, and Dorthe Stage, Gyldendal, 871 pp. **Retskrivningsordbog. Miniordbog*, ed. Jens Axelsen et al., Gyldendal, 1342 pp. **Farveordbog. Farvernes skjulte universelle signaler*, ed. Lene Bjerregaard, Byggecentrum, 173 pp. *Lir. Slang om sex*, ed. Christian Graugaard, Rosinante, 117 pp. **Gyldendals Slikleksikon*, Gyldendal, 119 pp. **Informationsordbogen. Ordbog for informationshåndtering, bog og bibliotek*, 3rd edn, Dansk Standard, 220 pp. **Modeleksikon. Fra couture til kaos*, ed. Mads Nørgaard, Politiken, 407 pp. *Politikens Slangordbog*, ed. Søren Anker Møller, Peter Stray Jørgensen, and Trine Ravn, Politiken, 2001, 536 pp. **Politikens Danske Ord der Driller*, ed. Gitte Hou Olsen, Politiken, 192 pp. **Med andres ord. Citater med vid, bid og humor*, Samleren, 317 pp.

J. Lund, 'Sprog og tekster — alfabetisk', *Nyt fra Sprognævnet*, no. 1 : 5–11, gives examples of the many language choices that had to be made when writing *Den Store Danske Encyklopædi*. O. Rasmussen, 'Jysk Ordbog — en 70–årig med fremtid i', *Ord & Sag*, 22 : 4–15. *NyS*, 30, is devoted to corpus linguistics and contains the following articles: S. Kirchmeier-Andersen, 'Dansk korpusbaseret forskning. Hvordan kommer vi videre?' (11–26); J. Asmussen, 'Korpus 2000. Et overblik over projektets baggrund, fremgangsmåder og perspektiver' (27–38); J. Allwood, L. Grönquist, E. Ahlsén, and M. Gunnarsson, 'Göteborgkorpusen för talspråk' (39–58); D. Haltrup, 'Danske resurser til automatisk opmærkning' (59–67); P. J. Henrichsen, 'Fyrre kilometer kryds og bolle. Metoder til grammatisk opmærkning i største skala' (68–88); D. Hardt, 'Dansk grammatikkontrol med transformation-based learning' (89–99); and B. Blom, 'Kvantitativ terminologi. En sprogstatistisk tilgang til automatisk identifikation og udtrækning af teksttypiske og -begrænsede lemmata i fagsprogstekster' (100–22). Kim Møller Jørgensen, **Sprog og Sygepleje* (Institut for Sygeplejevidenskab, 6), Aarhus U.P., 87 pp. Anna Vibeke Lindø, **Samtalen som livsform. Et bidrag til dialoganalysen*, Århus, Klim, 183 pp. Poul Majgaard, **Om at skrive bedre — tre trin på vejen. Journalistværktøj når en artikel bygges op*, Dike, 204 pp. Bent Møller and Jens Olsen, **Juridisk formidling — at skrive juridiske tekster*, Nyt Juridisk, 2001, 66 pp. Bettina Perregaard, *Forskning og undervisning i skriftsprog*, Akademisk, 202 pp. The possible influence on the standard language of text messages and computer chatting forms the topic of three articles: M. Rathje and O. Ravnholt, 'R tjat å sms 1 trusl mod skriftsprågd?', *Nyt fra Sprognævnet*, no. 2:1–8; D. Rasmussen, 'Sms — mere end en sprogtrend', *Vandfanget*, Institut for Sprog og Litteratur, Århus, no. 2:18–20; and T. T. Hougaard, 'Chat r 4 fedt ;-)', *ib.*, 21–23. J. Scheuer, *'Sandheden sekund for sekund — om flygtige og misvisende diskurser i MU-samtaler', pp. 87–122 of *Diskursanalysen til debat. Kritiske perspektiver på en populær teoriretning*, ed. Bøje Larsen and Kristine Munkgård Pedersen (Nyt fra samfundsvidenskaberne), 265 pp. **Hvordan staver studenterne? En undersøgelse af stavefejl i studentereksamensstilene 1998* (Uddannelsesstyrelsens temahæfteserie, 6), Ministry of Education, 70 pp.

5. Onomastics

V. Dalberg, *'De propriale særtræk — et diskussionsindlæg', pp. 9–19 of *Avgränsning av namnkategorier. Rapport från NORNA:s tjugonionde symposium på Svidja 20–22 april 2001*, ed. Terhi Ainiala and Peter Slotte (Forskningscentralen för de inhemska språken, 4), Tallinn, 190 pp. Id. *'Epexegesis in Danish place-names', pp. 443–48 of *Onomastik, VI. Akten des 18. Internationalen Kongresses für Namenforschung*, ed. Dieter Kremer (Patronymica Romanica, 19), Tübingen, Niemeyer, ix + 544 pp. Id., *'Name variant or new name? A discussion based on Danish toponyms', pp. 829–34 of *Actas do XX Congreso Internacional de Ciencias Onomásticas, 20–25 September 1999*, ed. Ana Isabel Boullón Agrelo, Santiago de Compostela. Id., *'Reflections on some theoretical problems in Scandinavian onomastics', *Onoma. Journal of the*

International Council of Onomastic Sciences, 37:7–19. G. Fellows-Jensen, 'Fra *Hungate* til *Finkle Street*. En vandring gennem nogle ildelugtende gader med danske navne i England', *Studier i Nordisk*, 115–25. Id., *'Nordisk bosættelse i England. Et tilbageblik efter tyve år', pp. 7–16 of *Tyvende tværfaglige vikingesymposium*, ed. Hans Bekker-Nielsen and Hans Frede Nielsen, Højbjerg, Hikuin, 2001. Id., *'Old Faroese ærgi yet again', pp. 89–96 of *Eivindarmál. Heiðursrit til Eivind Weyhe á seksti ára degi hansara 25. apríl 2002*, ed. Anfinnur Johansen et al., Tórshavn, Føroya Fróðskaparfelag. Id., *'Toponymie maritime scandinave en Angleterre, au Pays de Galles et sur l'Île de Man', pp. 401–22 of *L'héritage maritime des Vikings en Europe de l'Ouest*, ed. Élisabeth Ridel, Caen U.P., 565 pp. Id., *'Variations in naming practice in areas of Viking settlement in the British Isles', pp. 123–42 of *Naming, Society and Regional Identity*, ed. David Postles, Oxford, Leopard's Head, 294 pp. P. Gammeltoft, *'Det nordiske og nordatlantiske databasesamarbejde', *Seksjon for Namnegransking, Årsmelding 2001*, 63–68; and Id., 'Hølled — et helvedes sted!', *Fra Ribe Amt 2002*, 29, 73–79. B. Holmberg, *'Guden — et sakralt ånavn', pp. 30–34 of *Vandskel — Watershed*, ed. Erik A. Nielsen and Iben From, Silkeborg, Kunstcentret Silkeborg Bad. Id., *'Nordisk namnforskning 2001', *Namn och bygd*, 90:133–38. Id., *'Snekke-navne og andre stednavne fra vikingetid og tidlig middelalder i Storstrøms Amt', pp. 33–37 of *Venner og Fjender. Dansk-vendiske forbindelser i vikingetid og middelalder*, ed. Anna-Elisabeth Jensen, Næstved, Næstved Museum, 104 pp. B. Jørgensen, *'Kirkens navn. Danske kirkers navne gennem 1000 år', *Norna-Rapporter*, 74:145–51. Id., *'Køge Sønakke og Køge Søhuse', *Årbog for Køge Museum, 2001*, 7–14. Id., *'Storbyens stednavne', *Språkbruk*, no. 1:11–14. Id., 'Storbyens stednavne. Betyder det noget hvor vi bor?', *Studier i Nordisk*, 127–31. Id., *'Urban toponymy in Denmark and Scandinavia', *Onoma. Journal of the International Council of Onomastic Sciences*, 37:165–79. M. L. Nielsen, *'Nordisk namnforskning', *NORNA-Rapporter*, 75, Uppsala, 133–63. S. M. R. Vogt, *'Danske klosternavne — og disses holdbarhed', *ib.*, 74, 177–88; and Id., *'Skiftet efter hr. Oluf Holgersen Ulfstand til Bønnet og Örup', *Sydsvenska Ortnamnssällskapets Årsskrift*: 15–41.

LITERATURE

By Jens Lohfert Jørgensen, *Lecturer in Danish, Department of German and Nordic Studies, The University of Iceland*

1. General

Set fra sidste punktum. Tekst og udsigelse i semiotisk perspektiv, ed. Peter Allingham, Per Aage Brandt, and Bent Rosenbaum, Borgen, 404 pp., is dedicated to the memory of Harly Sonne, one of the founders of 'enunciation analysis' in Danish literary criticism, i.e analysis concerning the conditions of the statement itself. In addition to a personal introduction concerning Sonne's influence on the literary environment and a complete biography, the book consists of three parts. In the first part Sonne himself, Bent Rosenbaum, Henrik Jørgensen, and Frederik Stjernfeldt, Torben Fledelius Knap, and Per Aage Brandt discuss enunciation in five theoretical texts, each from of their point of view. The second part consists of seven exemplary analyses, for instance of Tove Ditlevsen's 'Katten' by Christian Grambye, H. C. Andersen's 'Den lille Havfrue' by Palle Schantz Lauridsen, Henrik Bjelke's 'Togplan for Otto' by René Rasmussen, and J. P. Jacobsen's 'Et Skud i Taagen' by Peter Allingham. The third part is a hitherto unpublished interpretation of J. P. Jacobsen's 'Mogens' by Erik Jerlung and Sonne.

Stoppesteder — en introduktion til historisk læsning, ed. Claus Blaaberg et al., Århus, Systime, 116 pp., is an anthology aimed at the Danish equivalent of GCSE level, published with the purpose of giving students an overview of developments in literary history over the last 1000 years. The book is divided into five periods, focusing on the organization of society and the role of the individual, and contains a number of rarely published texts by prominent authors such as Ludvig Holberg, Herman Bang, Tove Ditlevsen, and Jens Blendstrup. The book has its own homepage with supplementary text material: <www.systime.dk/stoppesteder>. Ettrup, *Bogen*, is a collection of papers, primarily on the external circumstances of literature, given at the meetings of Den Litterære Institution, *uss* ('uss' meaning 'under stadig skælven') in commemoration of Peter Seeberg, who was the force behind the institution. Bo Hakon Jørgensen, *Intentionalitet. Om litterær analyse på fænomenologisk grundlag* (University of Southern Denmark Studies in Language and Literature, 57), Odense, Southern Denmark U.P., 169 pp., attempts to deduce a model for literary analysis from the phenomenological philosophical tradition as formulated by 20th-c. thinkers such as Edmund Husserl, Martin Heidegger, and Maurice Merleau-Ponty, by drawing an analogy between the phenomenological concept of the relationship between consciousness and its surroundings and the relationship between reader and text. As the 'objects' of the surroundings are transformed into phenomena in consciousness and met by the intentions of the subject, the scenes in a work of fiction are transformed into 'pictures' in the reader's consciousness. The book includes an introduction to phenomenology, a discussion of methodical predecessors such as Roman Ingarden, Jean-Paul Sartre, and Mikel Dufrenne, a description of a model for literary analysis on a phenomenological foundation, and model analyses of a poem by Pia Tafdrup, of two short prose texts by Per Højholt and Peter Adolphsen, and of Otto Rung's novel *Den hvide Yacht.*

Virkelighedshunger, ed. Britta Timm Knudsen and Bodil Marie Thomsen, Tiderne Skifter, 252 pp., dicusses realism in contemporary art through a number of essays devoted to different artistic forms, claiming that the conception of 'reality' has to be expanded in order to enable it to meet the challenges posed by such forces as globalization and the internet. Three essays deal with literature: M. Rosendahl Thomsen, 'Hvis samfundet ikke kan findes på rådhuset, hvor så? — om Pablo Henrik Llambias' *Rådhus*' (203–20), B. Timm Knudsen, 'Teksten på overfladen. Interview med Helle Helle' (221–28), and Id., 'Realismespor i 90'ernes kortprosa — om Helle Helle, Christina Hesselholdt, Thøger Jensen og Pia Juul' (229–49). Ebbe Krogh and Finn Lykke Schmidt, *Længsel, lyst og lidenskab*, Århus, Systime, 172 pp., focuses on the theme of eroticism in Danish literature. Apart from introductory descriptive chapters on the cultural history of eroticism and the psychological concept of the term, the book consists of an anthology of texts from the Middle Ages to the present day, on the theme of eroticism. S. Hejlskov Larsen, 'Metaforsystemer', *Passage*, 42:61–70, is an investigation of the patterns that make the basis of the systematic poetry in the works of Inger Christensen, Klaus Høeck, Henrik Nordbrandt, and Jørgen Leth.

In *Mutters alene. Ensomhed som litterært tema*, Gads, 397 pp., Svend Erik Larsen discusses how fictional perceptions of solitude function in relation to the linguistic expression of them. He points out the basic paradox at the root of this relation: that solitude becomes universally accessible when it finds expression in literature. He goes on to investigate the dynamics of solitude in fictional texts using the contrast between the subject's individual perception of his/her solitude and the reader's common reaction towards it. This investigation takes place in five chapters, each concentrating on a subject connected to solitude. The first is on the historical dimension of the expression of solitude, the second on memory, the third on the monster, the fourth on metaphor, and the fifth on landscape and identity. The book includes analyses of a number of principal works of world literature. Danish texts dealt with are *Lykke-Per* by Henrik Pontoppidan, *Den afrikanske Farm*, 'Sorg-Agre', and 'Peter og Rosa' by Karen Blixen (Isak Dinesen), and the poems 'Vaaren' by Johann Herman Wessel, 'I Danmark er jeg født' by H. C. Andersen, and 'Glæde over Danmark' by Povl Martin Møller. Gerd Lütken and Johannes Fibiger, *Udsat — en bog om eksistentialisme*, Gads, 320 pp., is a well written book aimed at the Danish equivalent of GCSE and teacher training college level. Not being an anthology in a normal sense, the book contains a number of excerpts from philosophical and fictional texts dealing with the fundamental 'existentialia' in eight chapters with titles such as 'At være i verden uden Gud' and 'At være ked af verden'. While the philosophical texts are by well-known existentialist thinkers and their predecessors such as Søren Kierkegaard, Friedrich Nietzsche, Martin Heidegger, Jean-Paul Sartre, Simone de Beauvoir, and Albert Camus, the book creates surprising connections to the works of a number of younger authors such as Peter Adolphsen, Pia Juul, Carsten René Nielsen, Helle Helle, Katrine Marie Guldager, and Simon Fruelund.

Peter Lützen, *Et billede at læse med*, Akademisk, 239 pp., is a metaphor-orientated discussion of the practice of the prominent methodological movements in Danish literary criticism since New Criticism, based on the thesis that a methodological school of thought can be defined as a community of users of different metaphors. By not evaluating the methods according to the success of their results but rather to their status as constructed texts, L. manages to create connections between different movements of which we are not normally aware. In *Digterne omkring Limfjorden*, Gyldendal, 176 pp., Knud Sørensen takes readers on a round trip to the many literary places in the district around Limfjorden in a relaxed, conversational style. The trip starts in St. St. Blicher's Thorning, goes through such places as J. P. Jacobsen's Thisted and Johannes V. and Thit Jensen's Farsø, and ends on Jeppe Aakjær's farm Jenle. The authors interviewed in Thurah, *Historien*, have all played an important role in the history of European literature after World War II, in that they have been simultaneously experimental and representative of the literary movements in their countries. *På sporet af virkeligheden*, Gyldendal, 2000, 240 pp., is a collection of essays concerning the coherence between form and experience in 20th-c. literature by one of the leading Danish literary theorists, Frederik Tygstrup. The essays were previously published between 1993 and 1999.

2. The Middle Ages

Pil Dahlerup, *Dansk litteratur. Middelalder.* 1. *Religiøs litteratur.* 2. *Verdslig litteratur*, Gyldendal, 2 vols, 1998, 542, 438 pp. Jørn Jacobsen, Frits Kjærgaard-Jensen, and Jørgen Aabenhus, *Folkeviser*, Århus, Systime, 250 pp., provides a thorough introduction to the study of ballads. In the first chapter, the influence of ballads on present day literature and art is discussed, whereupon the four main genres of ballads are described via interpretations of 'Jomfruen og dværgekongen', 'Stolt Elin hævn', 'Dronning Dagmars død', and 'I bondedatterens vold'. Furthermore, the book includes chapters on the contemporary view of ballads, on the revival of the genre in the Romantic period, and on the conceptual world of the Middle Ages, on which the psychological and social conflicts of the ballads are based. The last part of the book is an anthology consisting of 43 ballads and other related fictional texts. The book has its own homepage with supplementary text material.

3. The Eighteenth Century

EWALD, J. K. Wentzel, 'Tilblivelsen af den moderne litterære institution omkring et digt af Johannes Ewald', Ettrup, *Bogen*, 92–101, is an article on 'Følelser ved den hellige Nadvere. En Ode, tilegnet hans Høiærværdighed Hr. Dr. Scønheider'.

4. The Nineteenth Century

Krydsfelt. Ånd og natur i Guldalderen, ed. Mogens Bencard (Golden Days in Copenhagen), Gyldendal, 2000, 276 pp., is a beautifully illustrated collection of essays on 'the Golden Age' — the romantic period of the first half of the 19th c. — discussing the relationship between art and science. It includes the essays 'Sand nydelse eller comisk nysgjerrighed. Om mikroskopet, H. C. Andersen og Søren Kierkegaard' by I. Kjær, 'Naturen som tegn. Om Grundtvig og naturvidenskaben' by S. Auken, and 'Huldre-Gaverne eller Ole-Navnløses Levnets-Eventyr fortalt af ham selv. Den litterære fejde mellem B. S. Ingemann og H. C. Ørsted i året 1831' by N. Kofoed. As beautiful a book is *Uden for murene. Fortællinger fra det moderne gennembruds København*, ed. Klaus P. Mortensen (Golden Days in Copenhagen), Gads, 288 pp., which deals with the role Copenhagen played in the breakthrough of realism around 1870. Worth reading are for instance K. P. Mortensen's essay 'Det uforfærdede øje. Det moderne gennembrud i kulturen', 'Nervøsitetens tidsalder' by J. Fabricius Møller, and 'Middag hos ritmesterens' by E.-M. Boyhus. Else Eva Pohl, *Blikket i spejlet* (University of Southern

Denmark Studies in Language and Literature, 34), Odense, Southern Denmark U.P., 213 pp., is a trans-aesthetic examination of self-interpretation in painting and literature from 1880 to 1914. By analysing novels about artists by, among others, Holger Drachmann, Herman Bang, and Adda Ravnkilde and a number of self portraits, P. investigates the intention of self-interpretation, its limits and the consequences for self-conception, and finally whether self-interpretation has a developing effect on the artists' work.

GJELLERUP, K. P. Houe, 'Begyndelsen på enden: Karl Gjellerups debutroman(er)', Garton, *Threshold*, 144–51.

JACOBSEN, J. P. J. Lohfert Jørgensen, 'Den repetitive slutning: Døden i J. P. Jacobsens *Niels Lyhne*', Garton, *Threshold*, 152–60.

KIERKEGAARD, S.M]J. Bøggild, 'Variationer over Guds uforanderlighed — om Søren Kierkegaards sidste opbyggelige tale og hans retorik overhovedet', *Spring*, 19:169–184. J. Bonde Jensen, 'Galleriet og gentagelsen. En Kierkegaardsk problemstillning', *ib.*, 185–209. Bo Kampmann Walther. *Øjeblik og tavshed*, Odense, Southern Denmark U.P., 260 pp., is a doctoral dissertation containing close readings of 'Forførerens Dagbog', *Gjentagelsen*, *Frygt og Bæven*, 'Skyldig — Ikke Skyldig?', *Synspunkter paa min Forfatter-Virksomhed*, *Begrebet Angest*, *Philosophiske Smuler*, and *Afsluttende Uvidenskabelig Efterskrift* which take, as their point of departure, K.'s rhetoric. Walther continues the prevalent tendency to read K.'s work in the light of the literary and philosophical deconstructive tradition. This appears, for instance, in his discussion of one of his main theses: that the relationship between religion and aesthetics in K.'s work is more complex than hitherto presumed, a complexity that Walther attempts to disclose with the recognition of what he calls 'boundary concepts' such as 'the moment' and 'silence', which reappear in the work in varying contexts, thereby gaining ambiguous and even contradictory meaning.

AARESTRUP, E. A. Gemzøe, 'Lyriske kulminationer: "Paa Maskeraden"', Garton, *Threshold*, 118–28.

5. The Twentieth Century

Torben Brostrøm, *Underspil. Litterær kritik i udvalg*, Gads, 389 pp., is a collection of B.'s reviews from 1956–2001 focusing on his articles on the generation of modernistic authors who came forward in the 1960s, for example Inger Christensen, Per Højholt, Ivan Malinowski, and Klaus Rifbjerg. The book includes a postscript by Christian Lund and Erik Skyum-Nielsen, who have edited the collection. *Fem års litteratur — 1998–2002*, ed. Stefan Emkjær et al., Århus, Systime, 170 pp., is an anthology consisting of 35 poems, short stories, and extracts from novels, written between 1998 and 2002, aimed at the

Danish equivalent of GCSE level. In addition, the anthology includes an introduction in which tendencies in the period and themes in its literature are defined. In *At notere himlen*, Gyldendal, 2000, 174 pp., the poet Niels Lyngsø analyses ten poems which were published in 2000 and, according to Lyngsø's assessment, were good. He has deliberately chosen poems by lesser known authors, among others Kristina Stoltz, Henriette Houth, Else Tranberg Hansen, Lars Skinnebach, and Mikael Josephsen. G. Mose, 'Flashes: Danish short short fiction at the turn of the twentieth century', Garton, *Threshold*, 31–51. In *Engle i sneen*, Gyldendal, 2000, 283 pp., Erik Skyum-Nielsen portrays the literature of the 1990s, his main thesis being that the decade is characterized by the coexistence of two opposing tendencies: one emphasizing minimalism, the fragment, the notion that 'less is more', thematical exclusion, and a renunciation of the transmission of meaning; the other emphasizing the encyclopedic, totality, the notion of 'the more the better', thematical inclusion and an openness towards attribution of meaning. The book is composed in three parts, each consisting of a number of essays, some of which have earlier been published. In the first part, 'Indgange', Skyum-Nielsen describes some currents in the literature of the period; in the second, 'Ansigter', he looks at works of individual outstanding authors, for instance Simon Grotrian, Pia Juul, Solvej Balle, Christina Hesselholdt, Peter Adolphsen, and Helle Helle; and in the last part, 'Åbninger', he discusses dominating themes and motives in the literature, focusing especially on the apparent religious preoccupation of some of the authors.

Erik Skyum-Nielsen, *Ordet fanger*, Gads, 602 pp., is a collection covering reviews of Danish literature from 1978 to 2001 by one of the most influential critics in Denmark. The book also includes an introduction by Øystein Rottem and an interview with Skyum-Nielsen by Christian Lund, who has edited the collection. Marianne Stidsen, *Idyllens grænser*, Samleren, 430 pp., is an annotated and partly rewritten collection of essays written between 1990 and 2000. In a direct and provocative style, Stidsen follows the history of postmodernism in Danish culture, first sceptical, then overwhelmingly enthusiastic, and finally sceptical again, but on another basis. Her thesis is that postmodernism has become an idyllic state that perceives all forms of expression as equal, and that it therefore has lost its original, critical sting. In the essay 'Idyllens grænser', this point of view is expressed in a discussion about the *raison d'être* of the avantgarde movement today. Stidsen's point of view is that it indeed has a *raison d'être*, but in the shape of a postmodern avantgarde, which is constantly seeking to exceed limits, but without following a direction given in advance.

ABELL, K. *Abell blomstrer ikke for enhver — 11 artikler om Kjeld Abell*, ed. Lisbet Jørgensen, Isabella Hercel, and Katrine Brøgger Speldt, Multivers, 174 pp., is a collection of articles on the occasion of A.'s 100th birthday in 2001. Even though the articles are written primarily from a dramaturgical point of view, the book covers all facets of A.'s work in its effort to explain why A.'s plays are rarely produced in Danish theatres today. It contains interpretations of famous dramas such as *Den blå Pekingeser*, *Dage paa en Sky*, *Skriget* and *Melodien, der blev væk*. Throughout the book, two opposite views on A. emerge: promotion of him as the father of the modernist theatre in Denmark and condemnation of him, because of his support of communism during the cold war.

ANDERSEN NEXØ, M. J. Haugan, 'Fra Askov til Moskva. Om at skrive Martin Andersen Nexøs biografi', Ettrup, *Bogen*, 242–64.

BALLE, S. H. van der Liet, 'På vej til en begyndelse: nogle poetologiske overvejelser omkring Solvej Balles forfatterskab', Garton, *Threshold*, 393–404.

BLIXEN, K. *Samtaler med Karen Blixen*, ed. Else Brundbjerg, Gyldendal, 2000, 409 pp., is a collection of interviews with B. from between 1934 and 1962, some of them given in connection with the publication of her works, others on various subjects, for instance the Nobel Prize. In *Billedets ekko*, Gyldendal, 2000, 252 pp., Charlotte Engberg presents competent interpretations of B.'s tales 'Kardinalens første Historie', 'Det ubeskrevne Blad', 'Den gamle vandrende Ridder', 'Et Familieselskab i Helsingør', 'Drømmerne', 'Alkmene', 'Sorg-Agre', and 'Babettes Gæstebud', focusing especially on visual aspects of the tales. Ivan Ž. Sørensen and Ole Togeby, *Omvejene til Pisa*, Gyldendal, 2001, 281 pp., is a new interpretation of the tale 'Vejene til Pisa', and furthermore contains an introductory chapter on how to read B., a reproduction of B.'s tale, very extensive annotations with the purpose of verifying the interpretation, and an overview of critics' responses to the tale. In continuation of this work, Ivan Ž. Sørensen has written '*Gid de havde set mig dengang*', Gyldendal 196 pp., an essay on the two tales 'Heloïse' and 'Ehrengaard'. S.'s interpretations of the tales place the emphasis, as is the case in *Omvejene til Pisa*, on their intertextual relationships, partly with the works of authors such as Heinrich Heine, William Shakespeare, Johann Wolfgang von Goethe, Choderlos de Laclos, and — of national interest — St. St. Blicher, Frederik Paludan-Müller, and Søren Kierkegaard, partly with sculptures and paintings by Michelangelo, John Collier, and in particular Titian, who is identified as B.'s most important dialogic counterpart in 'Heloïse'. The book is exemplarily illustrated.

BRØGGER, S. A. Born, 'Suzanne Brøgger's *The Jade Cat*', Garton, *Threshold*, 457–65.

CHRISTENSEN, I. *Spring*, 18, is devoted to C. It takes, as its point of origin, the poetological thoughts in C.'s collection of essays from 1989 to 1994, *Hemmelighedstilstanden*, which are discussed in relation to her works. Furthermore, the volume contains articles on most of her works, including E. Skyum-Nielsen, 'Længsel og struktur. Inger Christensens tidlige og tidligste lyrik' (35–49), M. Barlyng, 'Romerske udkast — bevægelsens poetiske tale i Inger Christensens "Vandtrapper"' (82–114), L. Wedell Pape, 'Fortælleligheder — om tal og tale som system i Inger Christensens *Det* og *Alfabet*' (126–40), R. Toft Nørgård, 'Mirakler for realister — en analyse af *Brev i april*' (141–53), B. Andreasen, 'Det ustadiges ro — en studie i *Sommerfugledalens* dødsindsigt' (154–70).

GRØNFELDT, V. Inger-Lise Hjordt-Vetlesen, *Versioner af kunstneren og romanen i Vibeke Grønfeldts forfatterskab* (University of Southern Denmark Studies in Language and Literature, 51), Odense, Southern Denmark U.P., 125 pp., is the first book on the work of G., who, in later years, has found a growing audience. On the basis of a perception of G.'s work as polycentric and postmodernistic, H.-V. focuses on a hitherto uncharted aspect of the work: its continued exploration of the conditions of writing through recurrent motifs concerning artists, metafictional reflections, and intertextual references. Via interpretations of the novels *Din tavshed er min skrift på væggen*, *Sommerens døde*, *Stenbillede*, *Dødningeuret*, and *Et godt menneske*, H.-V. characterizes the aesthetics and poetics of the work as distended between an extreme realism and an endeavour to create an ornamental form.

HANSEN, M. A. *Arvesyndens skønne Rose. Punktnedslag i Martin A. Hansens digtning*, ed. David Bugge, Gads, 116 pp., is a collection of five articles written by young critics who are concerned with the more experimental potential of H.'s work. An example is G. Wernaa Butin, who dicusses the relationship between writing and the demonic in the works of H. and Kierkegaard on the basis of the influential theories of Paul de Man in the article 'Lindormens skrig' (53–71). The other articles are 'Helten og digteren' by A. Thyrring Andersen on *Lykkelige Kristoffer* and Kierkegaard's *Frygt og Bæven* (9–38), 'Den svigefulde digter' by D. Bugge on *Løgneren* (39–52), 'En enkelt erfaring kan være bundløs' by N. Gunder Hansen on *Tanker i en Skorsten* (73–99), and 'Lyst, løgn og lys' by E. Pohl on *Løgneren* and the diary which H. wrote in hospital (101–14).

HEINESEN, W. A.-K. Skarðhamer, "Hvor begyndelse og ende mødes': mytiske motiver hos William Heinesen', Garton, *Threshold*, 354–63. M. Marnersdóttir, 'Mange begyndelser — én udsat slutning: *Tårnet ved verdens ende* af William Heinesen', *ib.*, 364–70. Ejgil Søholm, *Godheds ubændige vælde*, Gyldendal, 2000, 176 pp., is a personal, cheerful, and easily read book about (as the sub-title explains) the important Danish writer of the Faroe Islands on the occasion of his 100th birthday. It consists of three parts: in the first, Søholm discusses H.'s work from his début with *Arktiske Elegier og andre Digte* to his final book, *Laterna Magica*, on a biographical and literary historical basis; in the second part, Søholm repeats the conversations he had with H. during two visits to the Faroe Islands in 1980 and 1983 about his books and his connections to Danish and Faroese authors; the third part is an annotated reproduction of the letters Søholm received from H.

HULTBERG, P. T. Thurah, 'March for levende og døde', Thurah, *Historien*, 347–59.

HØJHOLT, P. C. Falkenstrøm, 'Den iscenesatte vildfarelse — om Per Højholts blindgyder', Garton, *Threshold*, 334–40. A. Hejlskov Larsen, 'Et essay om en ikke-eksisterende tekst. Per Højholts Turbo som en litterær kendsgerning', *Spring*, 19:229–39. T. Thurah, 'Jeg befinder mig', Thurah, *Historien*, 227–35.

JENSEN, J. V. *Spring*, 19, is devoted to J. and contains a number of articles on the themes of his work and its relation to literary history, among others: F. Harrits, 'Uden sprog. Erindringens fluktuationer i Johannes V. Jensens mytedigning, især med henblik på "Ved Livets Bred"' (47–62), L. Handesten, 'Livet er et ridt — om rejsen i Johannes V. Jensens liv og forfatterskab' (63–80), R. E. Friis, 'Dublinfolk og himmerlændinge — om dødens troper hos Johannes V. Jensen og James Joyce (81–100), E. Svendsen, 'Johannes V. Jensen — en modernist in spe' (120–41) and E. Spang Thomsen, 'Saltomortale og tom trancendens. Den unge Jensen mellem himmelstorm og modernisme' (142–56). A. V. Korovin, 'Beginning as a structural element in Johannes V. Jensens *Den lange Rejse*', Garton, *Threshold*, 232–36.

JUUL, P. S. Gottschalck Anbro, 'Ironi versus dialektik — om Pia Juuls *Forgjort* og Anne-Marie Mais læsning af den', *Spring*, 19:216–28.

JÆGER, F. Two books on J. have been published: *Skyggerne gror — et portræt af Frank Jæger*, ed. Jacob Kramhøft and Janus Kramhøft, Tiderne Skifter, 133 pp., is a well written and entertaining portrait of J.'s life, chronologically told through interviews with his colleagues connected to the magazine *Heretica*, such as Thorkild Bjørnvig, Ole Wivel, and Tage Skou-Hansen, letters between them and J., excerpts from previous interviews with J. and some of his poems. The book aims to contradict the myth about J. as the inspired, optimistic, harmless poet of his time, for instance by showing to what extent he felt pushed aside by the appearance of Klaus Rifbjerg, and claims that, rather than being a result of excess, his poetry was an expression of a deficit of vitality. In *Den magiske livskreds*, Gads, 309 pp., Finn

Stein Larsen has to some extent the same goal. The book is published as a volume in Gads Forlag's biographical series, but J.'s biography is for Larsen only a starting point for his primary object of interest: J.'s poetical work consisting of eight collections of poetry, which Larsen discusses in separate chapters. Furthermore, he deals with nine single poems from the whole range of J.'s work in thorough close-readings inspired by New Criticism. L. bases his book on the thesis that J. has built his self-understanding on a reappearing pattern of experience which places him at the centre of a circular formation of his surroundings, a pattern that implies a strong tension between what was inside and outside the circle. L.'s point is that J. transferred this pattern of experience to his poetry in the shape of a conceptual pattern, which on the one hand enlarges the subject of his poems, but on the other implies a perception of the surroundings as a constant threat.

KRISTENSEN, T. P. Stein Larsen, 'Undergangsvisionen i Tom Kristensens sene lyrik', Garton, *Threshold*, 249–60.

RIFBJERG, K. T. Thurah, 'Dørgrebets saglighed', Thurah, *Historien*, 281–95.

SAALBACH, A. M. Bach Henriksen, 'Den han er. Fiktion og postkolonialisme i Astrid Saalbachs *Fjendens land*', *Spring*, 19:251–64.

SKOU-HANSEN, T. T. Thurah, 'Ven med mørket', Thurah, *Historien*, 49–55.

SEEBERG, P. M. Juhl, 'Fra nåde til benådning', Ettrup, *Bogen*, 279–90. T. Thurah, 'Eksistensens talrække', Thurah, *Historien*, 125–39.

SONNERGAARD, J. K. Alstrup, ''Polterabend' — kravet om en ny moral?', Garton, *Threshold*, 466–76.

SOYA, C. E. Mogens Garde, *Peber, salt og Soya*, Multivers, 78 pp., is an anthology about S. with contributions by the author himself, Garde, Jarl Borgen, and others.

SØRENSEN, V. Carl Steen Pedersen, *Midtens vovestykke* Gyldendal, 2000, 180 pp., is an analysis of the essay writings of S. from *Digtere og dæmoner* to *Jesus og Kristus*.

THOMSEN, S. U. Neil Ashley Conrad, *Skønheden er en gåde. Søren Ulrik Thomsens forfatterskab*, Valby, Vindrose, 586 pp., is the first analysis of all T.'s work, with the exception of his collection of poetry *Det værste og det bedste*, which was only published in 2002, and his re-creation of dramas by Sophocles, Euripides, and Shakespeare. The book follows the progress of T.'s work in chronologically ordered chapters, each of which contains close readings of his collections of poetry and poetological essays, pointing out important themes and subject matter, and both continuity and ruptures in these, the most pronounced of which is perhaps the turning towards a religious outlook on life in the later part of T.'s career. This structure means that it is possible to read the individual chapters independently of each other. C.'s main intention throughout the book is to encircle and investigate the specific kind of beauty combined with cruelty that the reader meets in T.'s works, an investigation that leads him to a discussion of the notion of the concept of beauty, as it appears in the philosophical aesthetics of Immanuel Kant, Martin Heidegger, Hans-Georg Gadamer, and Jean-François Lyotard. In the final chapter, C. compares the work of T. to the poetic tradition and specific authors to whom he is indebted, such as Charles Baudelaire, Inger Christensen, and Gunnar Ekelöf. The book contains a complete bibliography, including translations and an incomplete list of works on T.

IV. NORWEGIAN STUDIES*

LANGUAGE

POSTPONED

LITERATURE SINCE THE REFORMATION

By Øystein Rottem, *Cand. phil., Copenhagen*

1. General

Ivar Havnevik, *Dikt i Norge. Lyrikkhistorie 200–2000*, Aschehoug, 511 pp., is the first complete history of Norwegian poetry. The approach is rather traditional, and the book has caused much discussion in Norway. However, the objections are not always to the point. As an overall survey the book is both informative and useful. Ingrid Terland, *Sørlandsforfattere gjennom tidene. Skjønnlitterære forfatterskap 800–1999*, Bergen, Vigmostad & Bjørke, 470 pp. Ø. Rottem, *Hurtigruta. En litterær reise*, Press, 229 pp., is a popular presentation of Norwegian authors who are influenced by the culture and the nature of the Norwegain coast.

2. The Sixteenth to Nineteenth Century

Laila Akslen, *Femfaldig festbarokk. Norske perikopedikt til kyrkjelege høgtider*, Sofiemyr, 401 pp. Knut O. Eliassen, '"Klarhet" i 1700–tallets romaner', *Motskrift*, 1:26–38.

HOLBERG, L. Aslaug Nyrnes, *Det didaktiske rommet. Didaktisk topologi i Ludvig Holbergs* Moralske tanker, Bergen Univ., 457 pp., is a doctoral thesis, a shrewd study of H.'s way of presenting his philosophy of ethics. P. Christensen, 'Nok sagt! Om villet vægelsind og erotisk vidensdannelse i Holbergs klassiker *Den vægelsindede* anno 2000', *Edda*: 3–21.

STORM, E. O. Solberg, 'Hyrdedikting på norsk? Edvard Storms lyriske dikting', *Nordlit*, 11:225–37.

WESSEL, J. H. Alvhild Dvergsdal, 'Johan Herman Wessel. Klassisist? Romantisk? En drøfting med utgangspunkt i hans versfortellinger', *Nordlit*, 11:37–58.

* The place of publication of books is Oslo unless otherwise stated.

3. The Nineteenth Century

BJØRNSON, B. Jan O. Gatland, *Mitt halve liv. Bjørnstjerne Bjørnsons vennskap med Clemens Petersen — og andre menn*, Kolofon, 164 pp. A. Schmiesing, 'Bjørnson and the inner plot of *A Midsummer Night's Dream*', *ScSt*, 74:465–82.

BLIX, E. A. M. Andersen, 'Elias Blix og den klassiske nynorske lyrikken', *KK*, 5–6:535–46. Bjørn K. Nicolaysen, 'Den nord-norske frelsesopplevinga i salmedikting til Elias Blix', *ib.*, 547–68.

COLLETT, C. Kristin Ørjasæter, *Selviakttakelsens poetikk. En lesning av Camilla Wergelands dagbok fra 1830–årene* (Acta humaniora, 120), Unipub — Det historisk-filosofiske fakultet, Oslo Univ., 358 pp., is a doctoral thesis. A. Heitmann, 'Anekdoter om billeder. Camilla Colletts idolatrikritik', *Edda*: 283–95.

GARBORG, A. Gudleiv Bø, *Veslemøys verden. Veiviser i* Haugtussa, Aschehoug, 199 pp. H. Gujord, 'Jærbu og indoeuropeer. Heretisk blikk på den apokryfe Garborg', *Edda*: 378–95.

HAMSUN, K. Lars F. Larsen, *Tilværelsens Udlænding. Hamsun ved gjennombruddet (1891–1893)*, Schibsted, 558 pp., is the last volume of L.'s imposing biographical trilogy about the young Hamsun, which brings much new and interesting information about the life and writings of H. In this last volume the literary programme of H. is presented accurately, as is the political and aesthetic background of his articles and books. Of special interest is L.'s presentation of the political implications of the novel *Redaktør Lynge.* The book also contains a very useful overview of the reception of H.'s works. Christian Schlüter and Sigmund Karterud, *'Selvets mysterier'*, Pax, 189 pp., analyses *Mysterier* from the point of view of the modern theory of ego-psychology. The book may be criticized for its *literary* interpretation, but the approach is fresh and original and sheds new light on the character of the protagonist Nagel. In *Hamsun og fantasiens triumf*, Gyldendal, 257 pp., Øystein Rottem is concerned with how Schopenhauer and Nietzsche influenced the work of H. The book also contains interpretations of *Sult, Pan, Markens grøde, Siste kapittel,* and *Landstrykere.* R. argues that literary fantasy overshadows the political commitment of the writer. *Nordnorske anmeldelser av Knut Hamsuns bøker 1912–1959*, ed. Nils Aagard-Nilsen, Svolvær, Anstabben, 104 pp. *Knut Hamsun og 1890–tallet. 10 foredrag fra Hamsun-dagene på Hamarøy 2002*, ed. Even Arntzen, Hamarøy, Hamsun-Selskapet, 247 pp., has the early writings of H. as its main theme. It contains articles by L. F. Larsen on the political commitment of H. (9–26), S. Karterud and C. Schlüter on *Mysterier* in the prospective of modern psychological theory (27–48), A. Farsethås on *Hunger* and the literary program of H. as a young writer (49–78), E. Østerud on the function of main names in H.'s works (79–104), J. Halberg on the problem of adapting *Mysterier* for the stage (105–26), Ø. Rottem on the novel *Redaktør Lynge* (127–50), R. N. Altinius on the influence of eastern religion on H. (151–72), M. Burima on *Pan* (173–96), R. H. Ystad on three short stories in *Siesta* (197–224) and E. Arntzen on *The Kareno trilogy* (225–46). *Les Dossiers K.H.*, ed. Régis Boyer, Lausanne, L'Age d'Homme, 319 pp., is a collection of studies on H., covering a broad scale of topics. Among the contributors are several well-known Hamsun scholars, such as. L. F. Larsen, H. S. Næss, N. M. Knutsen, O. Gouchet, M. Auchet, B. Hemmer, Ø. Rottem, E. Arntzen, and R. Boyer. E. Østerud, 'Modernitet og medialitet. Knut Hamsuns *Sult* og *Victoria* lest i lys av den tyske medieforskeren Friedrich A. Kittlers *Aufschreibesysteme 1800/1900*', *Edda*: 39–62. S. Gimnes, 'Den nostalgiske fantasien. Hamsuns novelle "Reiersen av Sydstjærnen"' (*Siesta* 1897)', *Motskrift*, 1:46–56. S. Langva, 'Masochisme i *Sult*', *Replikk. Tidsskrift for human- og samfunnsvitenskap*, 14:83–96. L. P. Wærp, 'Kulturkritikk og romandiktning i Knut Hamsuns *Den siste glæde*', *Norsk litteraturvitenskapelig tidsskrift*, 5:32–44. Wilhelm Friese, *Knut Hamsun und Halldor Kiljan Laxness. Anmerkungen zu Werken und Wirkung*, Tübingen, Francke, 103 pp. A. M. Bjorvand, 'Dekadanse hos Hamsun. Ei nærlesing av Edevart i *Landstrykere* og *August*', *Norskrift*, 105:5–17.

HOVDEN, A. Jens K. Engeset, *Anders Hovden. Diktarprest og folketalar*, Samlaget, 378 pp. Rangdi Hovden, '*Fraa far din.' Anders Hovden (1860–1943)*, Staur, 74 pp.

IBSEN, H. Atle Kittang, *Ibsens heroisme. Fra 'Brand' til 'Når vi døde vågner'*, Gyldendal, 383 pp., is a penetrating study of the idealism and heroism of I.'s plays. K. maintains that I. must be taken seriously when he claims that Brand is himself at his best. K. does not hide or overlook I.'s unveiling of the self-betrayal of the male protagonists, but he convincingly argues that they also represent values which the author himself supports. L. P. Wærp's main view of I. in *Overgangens figurasjoner. En studie i Henrik Ibsens 'Kejser og Galilæer' og 'Når vi døde vågner'*, Solum, 240 pp., is very similar to K.'s work. She rejects the traditional view on the development of I.'s drama as a change from idealism to scepticism and accentuates instead the complexity and ambiguity of each separate work. Nina S. Alnæs, *Varulv om natten. Henrik Ibsen — folketro og folkediktning* (Acta humaniora, 142), Unipub–Oslo Univ., 373 pp., is a doctoral thesis. Ross I. Coombes, *A Reception Study of 'A Doll's House'* by *Henrik Ibsen from 1879 to 1994*, Ann Arbor, Michigan U.P., 333 pp. A. M. Rekdal, 'The female *jouissance*. An analysis of Ibsen's *Et Dukkehjem*', *ScSt*, 74:149–80. Leif K. Roksund, *Henrik Ibsen og eros*, Porsgrunn, Grenland, 325 pp. K. Brynhildsvoll, 'Identitetskrisen i *Peer Gynt* — belyst fra groteskestetiske synspunkter',

Edda: 161–72. A. H. Aasland, 'En lesning av Ibsens *Hedda Gabler*', *Bøygen*, 1–2: 102–05. U. Langås, 'Fascinasjon og uhygge. Kunsten og døden som kvinne i Henrik Ibsens *Når vi døde vågner*', *TidLit*, 31.1: 28–50. J. Wiingaard, 'Henrik Ibsen and Denmark', *Ibsen Studies*, 2: 9–33. E. Özdemir, 'A Jungian reading of Ibsen's *The Lady from the Sea*', *ib.*, 34–53. T. Rem, 'Yet another honour. Ibsen and the British Scandinavian Society', *ib.*, 54–58. M. G. Lokrantz, 'Three unpublished letters by Henrik Ibsen about the first performances of *Et dukkehjem* in Italy', *ib.*, 59–74. H. Wivel, '*Når vi døde vågner*. Eksempler på det værende og ikke-værende i Vilhelm Hammershøis figurnbilleder omkring år 1900 og deres korrespondance med Henrik Ibsens sene dramatik', *Edda*: 324–35.

JUEL, D. Roar Lishaugen, *Dagny Juel*, Andresen & Butenschøn, 224 pp., is a rather traditional, but nevertheless interesting and well-informed biography.

SCHWACH, C. N. Arild Stubhaug, *Helt skal jeg ikke dø*, Aschehoug, 428 pp., is an excellent life-and-work biography, well-written and informative. It also gives a lively picture of the political, literary, and social life of Norway of the period.

KIELLAND, A. Tore Rem, *Forfatterens strategier. Alexander Kielland og hans krets*, Oslo U.P., 277 pp., presents a new picture of K., not only as an uncompromising tendentious novelist, but also as a writer who had to take into consideration what the reading public wanted from him. Gunnar A. Skadberg, *Alexander L. Kielland. 'I slekt med hele byen.' Kielland og hans nærmiljø sett fra et lokalhistorisk ståsted*, Stavanger, Wigestrand, 328 pp. T. Rem, 'Alexander L. Kiellands *Garman & Worse*. En annerledes bokhistorie', *Edda*: 173–85.

KRAG, V. Gunvald Opstad, *Fandango! En biografi om Vilhelm Krag*, Bergen, Vigmostad & Bjørke, 495 pp.

LANDSTAD, M. Ivar Bjørndal, *Magnus Brostrup Landstad. Prest, dikter og borger i Fredrikshald 1849–59*, Halden, Forum Bjørndal, 153 pp. S. Tveit, '"Fra Fjord og Fjære, fra Fjeld og dyben Dal." Magnus Brostrup Landstad — salmist og kirkesalmebokforfatter', *KK*, 107: 131–46.

LIE, J. E. Østerud, 'Jonas Lies *Familien paa Gilje* inter artes', *Edda*: 296–317. A. Aarseth, 'Jonas Lie — ein eller fleire? Kritikk av ein historiografisk tradisjon', *Nordica Bergensia*, 27: 223–44.

SKRAM, A. L. Ziukaite, 'I ordenes og bildenes vold. A reading of Amalie Skram's *Forraadt*', *Edda*: 318–23.

THORESEN, M. Elin Page, *The Real Lady from the Sea. A Study in the Authorship of Magdalene Thoresen (1819–1903)*, Øvre Ervik, Alvheim & Eide, 135 pp.

WERGELAND, H. Aslaug G. Michaelsen, *Irreparabile Tempus. Ah! En undersøkelse av Henrik Wergelands farsediktning*, Tangen, Krystalline, 168 pp.

ØSTGAARD, N. R. O. Jonsmoen, 'Nicolai Ramm Østgaards *En Fjeldbygd* — 150 år. Eit "gjennombrudd" for det lokale i norsk litteratur', *Årbok for Nord-Østerdalen*, 47–54.

4. The Twentieth Century

In *Marginalitet og myte i moderne nordnorsk lyrikk*, Gdansk U.P., 228 pp., Maria Sibinska presents the diversity of the modern poetry of Northern Norway and shows how it is marked by both regional, feminist, ethnic, and modernist impulses. The poets studied are H. Aga, A. Gaup, A. Hanssen, K. Holte, R. M. Lukkari, L. Lundberg, K. Sandvik, and H. Wassmo. Jofrid K. Smidt, *Mellom elite og publikum. Litterær smak og litteraturformidling blant bibliotekarer i norske folkebibliotek* (Acta humaniora, 13), Unipub–Oslo Univ., 389 pp., is a doctoral thesis. I. Kongslien, 'De nye stemmene i norsk samtidslitteratur. Innvandrarlitteratur i Norge', *NLÅ*: 174–90.

ASKILDSEN, K. B. I. Andersen, 'En pratsom gammel gubbe med sans for livet? Tema og norm i Kjell Askildsens "Thomas F's siste nedtegnelser til almenheten"', *Nordlit*, 12: 3–20.

BJERKE, A. Vilde Bjerke, *Du visste om et land*, Aschehoug, 198 pp., is a personal book of memories from the daughter of the writer.

BREKKE, P. Toril Brekke, *Paal Brekke. En kunstner. Et liv*, Aschehoug, 327 pp., is a well-written and well-documented biography which gives a many-sided picture of B., both as poet, critic, and politically committed essayist. As the poet's daughter T.B. draws on her experiences with her father.

EGGE, P. Helge N. Nilsen, *Temaer og historisk bakgrunn i Peter Egges trondheimsdikting*, Trondheim folkebibliotek, 102 pp.

FANGEN, R. J. I. Sørbø, 'Ronald Fangens romankunst i lys av Baktins polyfoniteori', *NLÅ*, 129–40.

FLØGSTAD, K. H. Bakken, 'En kritisk vurdering av Kjartan Fløgstads *Kron og mynt. Eit veddemål* i lys av fortellerinstansen Aa. Aavaath', *Norskrift*, 105: 81–95.

FOSSE, J. L. Wærp, 'Forsvinning og fastholdelse. Jon Fosses *Ein sommars dag* — en dramaestetisk lesning', *Edda*: 86–97. L. Sætre, 'I staden for død — i staden for guddom: Ande, røyster, lys og ord i Jon Fosses roman *Morgon og kveld*', *ib.*, 217–26. R. N. Jakobsen, '"Quiet is the new loud." Refleksjonar med utgangspunkt i resepsjonen av *Nightsongs* av Jon Fosse', *Bøygen*, 1–2: 64–70. Therese Bjørneboe, 'Absurd teater og pasjonsspill. Om Jon Fosses *Dødsvariasjonar*', *ib.*, 72–79. K. Skovholt, 'Jon Fosses realisme — om samtalen og møtet i

Mor og barn', *ib.*, 80–89. Å. M. Ommundsen, 'Du å du! Jon Fosses all-alder-litteratur for barn', *ib.*, 90–93. L. G. Granlund, 'Mytiske *Morgon og kveld*', *ib.*, 94–97. O. E. Færevåg, 'Det ubehjelpelige', *ib.*, 98–100. N. Reinhoff, 'Kven er det som skriv? Skriveren i romanen *Naustet* av Jon Fosse', *Nordlit*, 12:111–24.

HAUGE, O. H. Hadle O. Andersen, *Poetens andlet. Om lyrikaren Olav H. Hauge*, Samlaget, 247 pp. J. Brumo, 'Olav H. Hauges modernisme', *Motskrift*, 1:5–15.

HAUGEN, P.-H. K. Ørjasæter, '*Anne* — et sympoetisk kulturoppgjør', *NLÅ*, 141–54.

HAAVARDSHOLM, E. I. Holen, 'Det essayistiske subjektet i Espen Haavardsholms "Jeg er ingen"', *Nordica Bergensia*, 27:105–23.

JACOBSEN, R. L. Johansen, 'Det nordnorske stedet i Roy Jacobsens *Det nye vannet* (1987)', *Nordlit*, 12:67–93.

JENSEN, A. Petter Mæjlender, *Livet sett fra Nimbus*, Spartacus, 256 pp.

KJÆRSTAD, J. Gudmund R. Pedersen, *At tænke stort. Omkring Jan Kjærstads 'Forføreren', 'Erobreren' og 'Opdageren'. Litteratur og kristendom*, Aros, Valby, 184 pp.

LARSEN, G. Bente Aamotsbakken, 'Gunnar Larsens *Week-end i evigheten* (1934) — betydningen av eksilet', *NLÅ*: 112–28.

LØVEID, C. Bettina Baur, *Melancholie und Karneval. Zur Dramatik Cecilie Løveids* (Beiträge zur nordischen Philologie, 29), Tübingen, Francke, 234 pp. T. Thresher, 'The polymorphous female subject in Cecilie Løveid's *Barock Friise*', *Edda*:202–16. Id., 'Bringing Ibsen's *Brand* into the twentieth century. Cecilie Løveid's *Østerrike*', *ScSt*, 74:47–60.

SANDEMOSE, A. Lectures given at an 'Aksel Sandemose/Nordahl Grieg-seminar' in Risør are published in *Risørmagasinet*, 2001–2002:50–59. M. Humpál, 'The fifth commandment of the Jante Law and the theme of self-knowledge in Sandemose's *En flyktning krysser sitt spor*', *Brünner Beiträge zur Germanistik und Nordistik*, 16:191–97. S. von Schnurbein, 'Masking the trauma. Psychoanalysis and social criticisms in Aksel Sandemose's *En flyktning krysser sitt spor* (*A Fugitive Crosses his Tracks*)', *Edda*:409–18. J. Alnæs, 'Tiden er av lage — Fortiden eksisterer nå! Nytt lys på Aksel Sandemoses *Det svundne er en drøm*', *ib.*, 419–35.

SOLSTAD, D. Atle Krogstad, *Tid, landskap, erfaring — om den norske livsverden i Dag Solstads forfatterskap*, Trondheim, NTNU, 341 pp. B. Jager, 'Kvifor har ikkje Dag Solstad suksess i Tyskland? Medan Thomas Bernhard har suksess i Norge? Tankar om dei litterære diskursane i Noreg og Tyskland med blikk på tilhøvet mellom litteratur og makt', *SS*, 1:4–21. T. Holm, 'Det skjær av komikk som rammer gammel ungdom. Tanker om komikk, metafysikk og forsoning i en roman av Dag Solstad', *Bøygen*, no. 1–2: 51–57.

UNDSET, S. C. Hamm, 'Kjønn, kropp og tro. En feministisk lesning av Sigrid Undsets roman *Gymnadenia*', *Edda*: 396–407.

VESAAS, T. B. Aamotsbakken, *Det utrulege greineverket. Lesninger av Tarjei Vesaas' lyrikk*, Universitetsforlaget, 277 pp. *Kunstens fortrolling. Nylesingar av Tarjei Vesaas' forfattarskap*, ed. Steinar Gimnes, LNU–Cappelen akademiske, 206 pp., includes work on V. by L. Sætre (83–101) and A. Kittang (185–99). S. Wiland, 'Krisens rom. Innlevelse og perspektivering i Tarjei Vesaas' novelle "Det snør og snør"', *Edda*: 186–201. F. Hermundsgård, 'Depicting subjectivity in the film adaptation of Tarjei Vesaas' *Fuglane (The Birds)*', *Tijdschrift voor Skandinavistiek*, 23: 243–71.

VOLD, J. E. Henning H. Wærp, 'Jan Erik Vold og det ekspanderende diktet — *Mor Godhjerta* gjenbesøkt', *Bokvennen*, 14: 36–41.

ØRSTAVIK, H. J. Steensnæs, 'Om familien, språket og kroppen i *Like sant som jeg er virkelig*', *Norskrift*, 105: 97–111.

AAMODT, B. T. Norheim, 'Diktet og leseren. Om Bjørn Aamodts *ABC* (1994)', *NLÅ*, 155–73.

V. SWEDISH STUDIES*

LANGUAGE

POSTPONED

LITERATURE

POSTPONED

5

SLAVONIC LANGUAGES

I. CZECH STUDIES

LANGUAGE

By Marie Nováková and Jana Papcunová,
Ústav pro jazyk český Akademie věd České republiky, Prague

1. General and Bibliographical

The major work this year, *Encyklopedický slovník češtiny*, ed. Petr Karlík, Marek Nekula, and Jana Pleskalová, Prague, Nakladatelství Lidové noviny, 604 pp., is a comprehensive work recording both written and spoken variation of Czech, its varieties and their periods of development. Jan Horálek, *. . . nejde jen o slova*, Chomutov, Milenium Publ., 309 pp., is a collection of short essays first published in the monthly *Přítomnost* in the 1990s, and covers a wide spectrum of themes: lexicology, lexicography, etymology, semantics, pragmatics, sociolinguistics, and history of the language. M. Nekula and L. Uhlířová, pp. 302–10 of *Sprachkulturen in Europa*, ed. Nina Janich and Albrecht Greule, Tübingen, Narr, offer a short survey of Czech; J. Kořenský, Kučinskaja, *Vstreči*, 77–110, is a recapitulative essay on Czech as a national language; P. Sgall, *ib.*, 311–29, writes on the stratification of Czech. Two papers on general questions of the Czech language have appeared in *PLS*, 45: M. Čechová (13–21), on function of Czech from the diachronic and synchronic viewpoint (from the 10th c. until the present day) and on Czech as a means of the multiethnic communication, and F. Čermák (23–37) on common Czech, its relation to the literary language, on the present language situation and functional features of the spoken language; M. Hrdlička, *Žemličkův Vol.*, 149–54, comments on the centre, periphery, and stratification of Czech; E. Hajičová, J. Panevová, and P. Sgall, *SaS*, 63: 161–77, 241–62, concentrate on a new level of work on exploring Czech which is the work with an annotated corpus, and they discuss individual values of syntactic and morphological attributes used in the syntactic annotation.

Marie Nováková, *Bibliografie české onomastiky 1999–2000*, Prague, ÚJČ AV ČR, 103 pp., includes 701 entries.

2. History of the Language

J. Marvan, *PLS*, 45:95–116, submits a survey of the history of Czech and characterizes the tradition of the description of Czech (the first grammars and present-day historical grammars); Š. Lešnerová, *ČDS*, 10:38–42, analyses some peculiarities of humanistic Czech, especially word order and the position of enclitics, based on material from *Putování* by Kryštov Harant z Polžic a Bezdružic; in Hladká, *Čeština*, IV, 325–27, L. also refers to the position of enclitics in the same text; T. Vykypělová, *ib.*, 123–33, treats the grammatical category of number, specifically the dual in Old Czech; and in *Polyslav* 5, 251–54, contributes on the agglutinative tendencies in the Old Czech morphological system. P. Kosek, Hladká, *Čeština*, IV, 323–24, comments on the conjunctions in baroque Czech; Id., 'Interpunkce Hory Olivetské Matěje Tannera', *LFil*, 125:120–38, discusses the rules of transcription of baroque texts; and *ib.*, 280–88, follows dialectal elements in the same document; H. Koukalová, *AOn*, 43:88–100, analyses personal names in Old Czech translations of the Bible.

3. Phonetics and Phonology

J. Volín, *ČDS*, 10:7–13, deals with the changes in the pronunciation of the Czech consonant [l]; M. Nilsenová, *ib.*, 43, elucidates the alternations in the acoustic realization of the Czech syllabic sounds. P. Bímová, Saicová-Římalová, *Bádání*, 193–95, describes the phonetics and phonology of Czech sign language; and, Z. Palková, M. Laun, and P. Machač, Hladká, *Čeština*, IV, 337–42, present basic information on the Czech sound database which is constructed in the Phonetic Institute of the Charles University.

4. Morphology and Word Formation

MORPHOLOGY. R. Brabcová, *Žemličkův Vol.*, 133–39, contributes on gender oscillation of Czech nouns (illustrated on the noun *image*); J. Obrovská, *NŘ*, 85:79–89, analyses the transition of feminine nouns from the paradigm *kost* to the paradigm *píseň*; she discusses similar questions in Hladká, *Čeština*, IV, 329–331. S. Čmejrková, *SaS*, 63:263–86, follows some aspects of the relations between grammatical, natural, and cultural gender in Czech as a specific feature of the language. M. Komárek, Hladká, *Čeština*, IV, 135–40, deals with the relationship between aspect and the so-called Aktionsarten; K. Kamiš, *ib.*, 141–50, defines aspect as a grammatical category and compares aspect in Czech and Romany. M. Srpová, Krausová, *Setkání*, 119–28, offers a classification of the Czech verbs from aspectual point of view (oriented on French speakers). K. Osolsobě, Hladká, *Čeština*, IV, 333–36, focuses on variant endings of the Czech nouns; P. Karlík, *ib.*, 13–23, analyses Czech deverbal nouns from the viewpoint of valency; M. Jelínek, *ib.*, 77–84, follows simple and prepositional cases in Czech; O. Uličný, *ib.*, 233–36, refers to the development of contemporary Czech inflexion. J. Šimandl, 'K rozdílům a konkurenci mezi adjektivy na *-ící* a *-icí*', *JazA*, no. 1–2 : 28–36, is a corpus analysis of adjectives in question; L. Veselovská, Saicová-Římalová, *Bádání*, 11–37, presents some morphosyntactic characterizations of Czech adverbial and nominal quantifiers; V. Petkevič and M. Hnátková, Hladká, *Čeština*, IV, 243–52, deal with automatic morphological disambigutions of prepositional groups in the Czech National Corpus.

WORD FORMATION. F. Štícha, *ČDS*, 10 : 302–10, elucidates Dokulil's concept of word-formative productivity and compares the frequency of the names of agents with the suffix *-tel* in the Czech National Corpus and in *Tvoření slov v češtině*, vol. 2, by Miloš Dokulil; J. Klímová, *ib.*, 297–302, concentrates on the frequency of the names of agents and of nomina actoris and on their word-formative relationships; Z. Rusínová, *ib.*, 311–22, investigates word-formative adaptation of loan words (especially of nouns, adjectives, and verbs) and gives their typology and a survey of used linguistic devices. V. Staněk, *NŘ*, 85 : 57–67, analyses occasionalisms in present-day Czech journalism; M. Ziková, *SPFFBU-A*, 50 : 92–104, studies productivity and regularity in word-formative processes of neologisms; P. Šmídová, *Varia*, 9 : 217–22, follows Greek and Latin components in formation of neologisms in Czech.

5. Syntax and Text

I. Kolářová, *NŘ*, 85 : 90–97, analyses the function of the expression *takže* and of its synonyms in compound sentences and texts from the pragmatic point of view; similarly, F. Daneš, *ib.*, 113–18, focuses on the expression *naopak* from the lexical, syntactic, and textual viewpoint; M. Slezáková, *ib.*, 199–206, is a syntactic, lexical, and semantic analysis of the expression *nicméně*; L. Uhlířová, 'Zipf's notion of "economy" on the text level : a case study in Czech', *Glottometrics*, no. 3 : 39–60, studies the role of the anaphoric pronouns *tento, tato*, and *toto* in text structure.

L. Nebeský, *SaS*, 63 : 98–110, is on the word order, sentence factors, and their role in the sentence analysis; M. Jelínek, *Universitas*, no. 4 : 70–73, deals with the use of nominal adjectival forms in verbal attribute and predicate in the past and nowadays; K. Oliva jr, Hladká, *Čeština*, IV, 253–63, submits an essay on a formalism for the description of Czech syntax (with particular regard to word order); L. Veselovská, *ib.*, 199–212, discusses some examples of subject-predicate agreement in Czech; and E. Hošnová, *PLS*, 45:73–82, illustrates the development of word order in present-day Czech, starting with the identification of topic-focus articulation as a grammatical principle. M. Marková, *Žemličkův Vol.*, 79–88, focuses on the word order of transgressive condensates; M. Adamíková, *Polyslav 5*, 1–10, is a comparative study on word order in adversative complex sentences with the conjunction *ale* in Czech and Slovak; K. Ribarov, *PBML*, 78:77–99, on the rule-based parsing of Czech compared to English.

6. Orthography

N. Bermel, Krausová, *Setkání*, 1–7, sums up opinions of the Czech public on the rules of the Czech orthography from 1993. J. Šimandl, *NŘ*, 85:244–56, deals with some orthographic questions concerning foreign names and loan words in Czech; P. Kaderka, *ib.*, 108–11, is on the orthography and semantics of the verbs *vymýtit/vymítat.*

7. Lexicology and Phraseology

H. Skoumalová, *PBML*, 77:19–62, brings a detailed characterization of an electronic dictionary of Czech verbs. Two contributions concentrate on the conception of the Old Czech Dictionary: M. Vajdlová, *Varia*, 9:136–45, analyses the theoretical conception and changes, they have occured in the dictionary since 1968, while Z. Braunšteinová, *ib.*, 145–48, is on a new conception intended for a new lexicographic generation. M. Křístek, *ib.*, 102–12, deals with the ways of defining stylistic features in the lexicon.

M. Hrdlička, *NŘ*, 85:52–54, focuses on numerals and their occurance in phraseologisms in Czech and French; M. Hnátková, *SaS*, 63:117–26, covers the tagging of phrasemes and idioms in the Czech National Corpus; E. Stehlíková, *ČDS*, 10:27–30, 31–34, follows the vocabulary connected with the use of tea and coffee respectively, both from etymological and word-formative points of view.

8. Semantics and Pragmatics

V. Spousta, *Universitas*, no.2:14–16, deals with the so-called 'word pads' (the expressions *prostě, smysluplně, řádově, v časovém horizontu, zviditelňovat*) and criticizes their semantic poverty and misuse in contemporary Czech; M. Jelínek, 'O "plevelných" slovech', *ib.*,

16–19, argues with some ideas of V. Spousta. L. A. Janda, Krausová, *Setkání*, 29–35, focuses on the semantics of Czech cases. M. Dočekal, Hladká, *Čeština*, IV, 223–32, is on the semantic interpretation of some Czech anaphors. L. Janovec, *Varia*, 9:37–42, provides a semantic and frequency analysis of colours in the work of Jaroslav Seifert. D. Jerie, Saicová-Římalová, *Bádání*, 121–29, is a lexical-semantic analysis of the word *slunce* and its use in the poetry of Karel Hynek Mácha and Jan Neruda; M. Husáková, *Varia*, 9:124–28, focuses on the meaning of the word *šteft* used in fiction by Zikmund Winter.

J. Hoffmannová and O. Müllerová, *SaS*, 63:1–14, explore the speech of old generation on the lexical and morphological level, L. Hašová, *Varia*, 9:64–79, analyses Czech political discourse. S. Čmejrková, Hladká, *Čeština*, IV, 59–69, discusses the relationship between the grammar and pragmatics illustrating it with the examples of the use of personal and possessive pronouns (1st and 2nd person) in Czech. M. Vondráček, *ib.*, 265–76, focuses on the pragmatics of single-element sentences (semantic field *déšť, tma, zima, vítr, smutek*). T. Berger, *ib.*, 189–97, covers the system of adress and pragmatic mechanisms of politeness in Czech; M. Pravdová, *NŘ*, 85:177–89, analyses the language functions of advertising texts.

9. Sociolinguistics and Dialectology

K. Gammelgaard, *SEER*, 80:601–23, follows the development of standard/spoken Czech (compared to Slovak and Polish) from historical-sociolinguistic viewpoint. J. Nekvapil and I. Leudar, pp. 60–101 of *Language, Interaction and National Identity: Studies in the Social Organization of National Identity in Talk-in-Interaction*, ed. Stephen Hester and William Housley, Aldershot, Ashgate, 249 pp., define the concept of the dialogical network and analyse the picture of different ethnic groups in the Czech mass media (based on material from the Czech newspapers). F. Daneš, Hladká, *Čeština*, IV, 29–35, investigates loan words, especially Anglicisms in contemporary Czech, from a sociolinguistic point of view. H. Srpová, *Slovanské studie*, 5:37–49, discusses the code mixing in two stylistic spheres and also reflects on language endangerment. J. van Leeuwen-Turnovcová, *SaS*, 63:178–99, is on Czech diglossia from the point of view of gender studies with a comparison to Russian. J. Horálek, *WSlA*, suppl. 55:305–10, writes on the development of depreciative and pejorative words in Czech from a gender perspective. J. Valdrová, *ib.*, 247–58, follows sociolinguistic aspects of deriving feminine forms from masculine surnames. J. Hubáček, Hladká, *Čeština*, IV, 237–42, deals with onomasiological methods in Czech social dialects. J. Hála and

P. Soudková, *České vězeňství*, no.4: 5–58, outline the development of Czech prison slang completed with a vocabulary.

Jan Balhar et al., *Český jazykový atlas*, vol. 4, Prague, Academia, 626 pp., is devoted to the dialectal diversification of morphological phenomena. M. Spodareva, *Polyslav 5*, 220–28, makes several critical observations on the present state of the Czech dialectology (compared to German). J. Vojtová, *SPFFBU-A*, 50: 105–10, writes on perspectives of dialectal lexicography, specifically on the ordering of dialectal material. Z. Hlubinková, *ib.*, 111–18, presents a study on formations of adverbs derived from nouns, verbs, and numerals in East Moravian dialects.

10. Stylistics

K. Sgallová, *ČL*, 50: 606–13, describes verse, rhyme, and prosody in the period of the Czech national revival and summarizes the opinions of J. Dobrovský, A. Puchmajer, and J. Jungmann on these subjects. M. Krčmová, Kučinskaja, *Vstreči*, 329–41, gives a survey of Czech rhetorical style; J. Bartošek, *NŘ*, 85: 68–78, deals with journalistic style; A. Jaklová, *ib.*, 169–76, is on means of persuasion in journalistic style; L. Hašová, *ib.*, 207–12, defines a newly emerging style of SMSs; J. Hoffmannová, *Stil*, 143–80, presents a characterization of a style of age and of its specific features; F. Schindler, *WSlA*, suppl. 55: 153–75, analyses the language and style of personal advertisements and presents some differences between the style of heterosexuals and homosexuals. J. Hoffmannová, Hladká, *Čeština*, IV, 163–70, defines a handout as a genre; J. Světlá, *NŘ*, 85: 119–29, analyses operating instructions as a special style; M. Křístek, *SPFFBU-A*, 50: 119–39, examines the style of Karel Poláček (especially cohesion) in his pentalogy.

11. Onomastics

Miloslava Knappová, *Naše a cizí příjmení v současné češtině*, Liberec, AZ Kort, 256 pp., covers not only the origin, development, declension, and formation of feminine forms from masculine of surnames, but also the orthography, changes, frequency, and adaptation of foreign surnames into Czech, including transcription rules from some foreign languages into Czech. Jiří Zeman, *Výslovnost a skloňování cizích osobních jmen v češtině: románská osobní jména (španělština, portugalština, rumunština)*, vol. 3, Hradec Králové, Gaudeamus, 136 pp., continues analogous publications on the English and Scandinavian names and explains the pronunciation and declension of names in Romance languages. Similarly, Karel Sekvent and Dušan Šlosar, *Jak užívat francouzská vlastní jména ve spisovné češtině*, Prague, Academia, 150 pp., clarify the orthography, pronunciation, and declension of French names in Czech.

L. Olivová-Nezbedová, *NŘ*, 85:23–27, describes the adjectives *březí, dubí, bučí,* and *javoří* occuring in Czech minor place names; P. Štěpán, *ib.*, 143–49, analyses common nouns *zelinka, zelenka, zelánka* in minor place names in Bohemia; M. Vondrová, V. Klain, and V. Blažek, *SPFFBU-A*, 50:47–60, seek for Illyrian traces in the Czech toponymy and analyse the place names *Doksany* and *Doksy*; L. Klimeš, *AOn*, 43:23–28, is on names of the Czechoslovak fortifications built in 1936–38; D. Klimeš and S. Pastyřík, *ib.*, 29–38, on proper names in four plays by Alois Jirásek; J. Maleninská, *ib.*, 39–42, on the place names *Řepy, Říčany, Říčky*; and S. Svoboda, *ib.*, 84–87, on the origin of the surname *Honskus.*

12. Languages in Contact and Comparative Studies

The collective volume *InterFaces: obraz vzájemných vztahů Čechů, Poláků a Němců v jejich jazycích, literaturách a kulturách*, ed. Šárka Lešnerová, Dorothea Uhde, Alexandra Wojda, and Albert Gorzkowski, Prague, Charles University, 212 pp., contains a number of comparative essays: D. Filippovová (9–17) on Czech-Polish language contacts (based on material in the corpus SYN2000); C. Prüfer (181–87) on the so-called false friends in Czech, Polish, and German; A. Nováková (188–90) on Germanisms in Czech. J. Skácelová, pp. 111–15 of *Jazykovědná rusistika na počátku nového tisíciletí*, ed. Jiří Gazda, Brno, Masaryk Univ., 233 pp., compares the functions of the Czech and Russian infinitives, V. Šaur, *ib.*, 78–83, explains the origin of names of months in Czech and other Slavonic languages. B. Rudincová, *ib.*, 192–200, follows the process of univerbization in Czech and Russian. C. Avramova, *Slavia*, 71:23–33, focuses on word-formative tendencies and on neologisms in Czech and Bulgarian. S. M. Newerkla, *ČJL*, 53:61–68, reports on the language contacts in Central European area (Czech, German, Slovak, Hungarian). J. Kadlec, *LPr*, 12:24–39, is a comparison of expressions for blood relations in Czech, French, and Spanish. K. Skwarska, *Varia*, 9:201–08, discusses the genitive of negation in Czech, Russian, Polish, and Slovenian. A. Rechzieglová, Krausová, *Setkání*, 88–96, analyses assimilation of consonants *s/š* in Czech and Dutch. G. Neščimenko, *ib.*, 63–71, is on adaptation of loan words in Czech and Russian. H. Lehečková, *ib.*, 50–56, is on gender in Czech, Russian, English, Swedish, Hungarian, and Finnish. M. U. Fidler, Hladká, *Čeština*, IV, 285–98, compares the use of the form *ty* or *vy* in Japanese and Czech; and Eun-Hae Kin,

JazA, 39:4–27, describes basic aspectual differences between Czech and Korean.

13. Czech Abroad

A. Jaklová, *NŘ*, 85:1–10, analyses the vocabulary style of American periodicals *Slowan Amerikánský* and *Národní Noviny*. E. Eckertová, *ČMF*, 84:1–17, deals with the language of Czech emigrants recorded in the tombstone inscriptions in Texas and follows the changes in orthography and morphology.

14. Bilingual Dictionaries

Anca Irina Ionescu has compiled *Rumunsko-český slovník*, Voznice, Leda, 294 pp.; Darina Vystrčilová and Amir Taherzadeh, *Příruční slovník persko-český : Persian-Czech Desk Dictionary*, Prague, PetroChem-Eng, 361 pp. Valerij Mokienko and Alfréd Wurm, *Česko-ruský frazeologický slovník*, Olomouc, Nakladatelství Olomouc, 659 pp., submit around 9000 alphabetically ordered idioms with detailed grammatical description and stylistic notes. Rather curious is a slang dictionary by Kelley Hamilton Brineman (trans. Jana Koubová), *Get down wit'cha bad self: Rozdej si to se svým špatným já*, Prague, Mať'a, 141 pp. (*c.* 3500 items).

LITERATURE

POSTPONED

II. SLOVAK STUDIES

LANGUAGE

POSTPONED

LITERATURE

POSTPONED

III. POLISH STUDIES

LANGUAGE

By Nigel Gotteri, *University of Sheffield*

1. Bibliographies and Surveys

E. Niemkiewicz, **Bibliografia bibliografii językoznawstwa polskiego*, Lublin, KUL Press, 2000, 116 pp.; J. A. Dziewiątkowski et al., 'Przegląd polskich prac językoznawczych ogłoszonych drukiem w roku 2001', *PJ*, no.10:63–121. H. Karaś, 'Profesor Stanisław Dubisz — w trzydziestolecie pracy naukowej i dydaktycznej', *PJ*, no.7:4–14, leaves a bibliography implied. 'Bibliografia prac Prof. Władysława Kupiszewskiego', *PFil*, 45, 2000:13–22. *Towards a History of Linguistics in Poland. From the Early Beginnings to the End of the Twentieth Century*, ed. E. Koerner and A. Szwedek, Amsterdam-Philadelphia, Benjamins, 2001, xx + 335 pp., expands further on *HistL*, 25 (see *YWMLS* 61:846).

2. Phonetics, Phonology, and Orthography

A. Bergermayer, 'Die gemeinslavische Alveolarenpalatalisation ("Jotierung") und ihre Ergebnisse', *WSJ*, 47, 2001:7–24. B. Kreja, 'Problemy z akcentem w formach czasownikowych typu *robiliśmy*', *JPol*, 82:76, links increasing misaccentuation of such forms with changes in their syntax. W. Mańczak, 'Czy istnieją słowa nieakcentowane?', *ib.*, 81, 2001:303–06. K. Sikora, 'Przejście wygłosowego *-x* w *-f* pod Krakowem?', *ib.*, 82:199–200. N. Ukiah, 'O akcencie wyrażeń przyimkowych typu *na dół, na wsi*', *PJ*, no.6:3–14. M. Wolan, 'O potrzebie kształcenia ortofonicznego', *Polonistyka,* 55:551–54, may be looking at linguistic change in progress (allegro forms, spelling pronunciations, variations in accentuation) as well as pathology (shallow breathing, dysprosody, and close jaw setting). *Współczesny język polski*, ed. J. Bartmiński, Lublin, UMCS Press, 2001, 695 pp., is in most respects a second edition of a volume of *Encyklopedia kultury polskiej XX wieku*, but J. Szpyra-Kozłowska, 'Fonologia — system dźwiękowy języka' (485–502), and S. Barańczak, 'Użycie języka w poezji: zwięzłość i wieloznaczność' (147–53), are new.

Orthography and punctuation: H. Duda, 'Ortograficzne kłopoty z *internetem*', *JPol*, 81, 2001:156–58; A. Kowalska, 'Z historii kropki', *ib.*, 82:208–13; E. Polański and P. Żmigrodzki, **Leksykon ortograficzny*, Wa, Wyd. Szkolne PWN, 2001, 856 pp.; S. Rzedzicka, 'Jakiej długości jest myślnik?', *PJ*, no.4:55–59, argues for a return to clearly distinguished usage for the hyphen (*krótka kreseczka*, *dywiz*, *ćwierćpauza*), the short dash or en rule (*krótka kreska*, *en-myślnik*, *półpauza*), and the long dash or em rule (*długa kreska*, *em-myślnik*, *pauza*); *Słownik ortograficzno-gramatyczny języka polskiego z zasadami ortografii i interpunkcji*, ed. I. Kamińska-Szmaj, Ww, Europa, 936 pp., has a separate section for proper names (829–936), including some abbreviations such as *AZS* and *MFW*. Rada Języka Polskiego, 'Użycie wielkiej litery ze względów grzecznościowych. Forma żeńska rzeczownika *marynarz* – *marynarka*? Sweter. Standard. Odsetki. Czynsz', *PJ*, no.7 : 72–74; the problem with *marynarz* and its likely solution correspond to the case of *kierowca* and *dyplomata*; *standard* should be spelled only with final <d>, not <t>.

3. Morphology and Word-Formation

A. Cieślikowa, 'Różnice między fleksją nazw własnych a pospolitych', *PFil*, 45, 2000 : 83–90. K. Długosz-Kurczabowa and S. Dubisz, *Gramatyka historyczna języka polskiego*, Warsaw U.P., 2001, 458 pp., is a second edition significantly expanded with a substantial section on word-formation. B. Kreja, 'Problem oboczności: *unasienianie* // *unasiennianie* (na tle czasowników na *u-i(a)ć*)', *JPol*, 81, 2001 : 113–16;. Id., 'O *prawojazdach* (czyli o 'prawie jazdy')', *ib.*, 314–15. T. Kurdyło, 'Luksus słowotwórczy, czyli o tzw. derywatach tautologicznych i funkcjach tworzących je formantów', *ib.*, 82 : 178–87. A. Lica, *Słownik trudności językowych*, Gdańsk, Harmonia, 2001, viii + 453 pp., presents material in tabular manner, with headword, correct form, and erroneous or undesirable forms, dealing not only with grammatical difficulties but also, for example, with the misuse of *abnegat* for *nihilista*. E. Łuczyńska, 'Zagadnienie kompetencji fleksyjnej dzieci w wieku przedszkolnym (na przykładz ie rzeczownika)', *JPol*, 82 : 43–50. T. Malec, 'O poprawność odmiany nazwy miejscowej *Rachanie*', *ib.*, 81, 2001 : 158–59; Id., 'Uwagi o odmianie nazwisk typu Pańków', *ib.*, 226–27. A. Nagórko, 'Über die Rolle der Inferenz in der Wortbildungslehre (anhand des polnischen Sprachmaterials)', *ZSl*, 47 : 410–42, finds language anthropomorphic rather than anthropocentric. D. Ochmann, 'Między dezintegracją a analogią. O pewnym typie złożeń współczesnej polszczyzny', *JPol*, 82 : 322–29, discusses the like of *euro-* and *alko-*. A. Piela, 'Rzeczownikowe derywaty mutacyjne od nazw osobowych w historii języka polskiego', *ib.*, 87–95; her 'Osobowe *nomina propria* jako podstawy słowotwórcze derywatów', *PJ*, 2001, no.8 : 28–40, notes a marked increase, including many new nouns in *-alia/-alie* and *-(i)ana*. R. Przybylska, 'Struktura schematyczno-wyobrażeniowa prefiksu czasownikowego *roz-*', *Polonica*, 21, 2001 : 269–86, and K. Termińska, 'Słowotwórstwo — z porządku w chaos i z powrotem', *ib.*, 287–302, draw an unprecedented coda from I. Bobrowski, *ib.*, 303. I. Stąpor, 'Ewolucja form liczebników głównych w języku polskim', *PJ*, no.2 : 35–52, based on a detailed study of Bible translations from 1595 to 1997, presents much of her findings in tabular form. J. Szych, 'Ocena normatywna najnowszych polskich złożeń rzeczownikowych (badania ankietowe)', *PJ*, no.9 : 66–78. M. Urban, 'Czy wyróżniać homonimiczne sufiksalne formanty przymiotnikowe?', *Polonica*, 21, 2001 : 260–68, examines *-any*, *-awy* and *-alny*. E. Wójcikowska, 'Przymiotniki odprzymiotnikowe z formantem *pół-* (na materiale nowopolskim i współczesnym)', *PFil*, 45, 2000 : 655–58. P. Zbróg, 'Formy oboczne przyczyną zakłóceń w odbiorze tekstu', *JPol*, 82 : 268–72.

4. Syntax

B. Chachulska and R. L. Górski, 'Frekwencja form wyrażających kategorię bierności', *JPol*, 82 : 252–59. B. Chachulska and K. Węgrzynek, 'Propozycja syntaktycznego opisu czasowników polskich na przykładzie synonimów WYBAŁUSZAĆ/WYTRZESZCZAĆ', *Polonica*, 21, 2001 : 231–36. M. Gawełko, 'Język polski wobec tendencji analitycznej języków indoeurop ejskich', *ib.*, 11–24. A. Kępińska, 'Fleksyjna kategoria strony w polszczyźnie — jest czy jej nie ma?', *PFil*, 45, 2000 : 249–58, argues that in Polish the passive is at most a syntactic and not an inflectional category. I. Kosek, 'Charakterystyka składniow a i interpretacja gramatyczna leksemów o postaci *niby*', *Polonica*, 21, 2001 : 237–57. P. Kosta, 'Klitika im Slavischen: sind sie immer optional?', *ZSl*, 47 : 127–46, covers W. and S. Slavonic; Polish and Lusatian occupy a position intermediate between languages with clitics in the second, Wackernagel, slot and languages where the clitic cluster is attached to the verb; Kosta's Polish examples are: *Nie chcę, żebyś mi ją nim straszył. Gdzieście się go pozbyli? On uczył cię go. Pozbawiłeś go jej. Myśmy bawili się na dworze. Piotr mówi, że się go bardzo baliście jako dzieci.* Z. Krążyńska, **Staropolskie konstrukcje przyimkowe, część II*, Pń, WiS, 2001, 182 pp.; J. Malejka, 'Polskie zdania względne i pytajnozależne — podobieństwa i różnice', *Polonica*, 21, 2001 : 165–84. M. Mączyński, 'O zaimku *ten* w XVII-wiecznej księdze gromadzkiej wsi Jadowniki', *JPol*, 81, 2001 : 344–55. B. Milewska, 'Przyimki wtórne w wydawnictwach normatywnych', *ib.*, 176–82, and 'Od przyimka do przyimka wtórnego', *ib.*, 82 : 260–67. A. Niziołek, 'Warunki anaforyzacji w modelu transformacyjno-generatywnym', *Polonica*, 21, 2001 : 202–10, examines constructions with *(z)robić* and *(u)czynić*. M. Preyzner, '*Pozostałe obszary kontynentu obejmują wyże* (Pogoda TVP 1, g. 8^{15}, 6 X 2001 r.)', *PJ*, no.1 : 62–63, points out that it is co-text, context, and knowledge of the world, rather than any alleged SVO default, that disambiguate utterances of structures where both subject and object are in forms which could in theory be either nominative or accusative. M. Ruszkowski, 'Kategorie przejściowe polskiej parataksy', *PJ*, 2001, no.9:34–38, is an extract from Id., *Kategorie pośrednie w składni polskiej*, Wyd. Akademii Świętokrzyskiej, Kielce, 2001, 94 pp.; Id., 'Relacja między pojęciami "zdanie nierozwinięte" — "zdanie rozwinięte" w modelu składni tradycyjnej', *JPol*, 81, 2001:76–81; Id., 'Pośrednie konstrukcje składniowe (na przykładzie hipotaksy)', *Polonica*, 21, 2001:185–92. P. Wojdak, '"Akademicka" konstrukcja? *Mam dzisiaj dwa zajęcia* (o użyciu liczebników głównych przy rzeczownikach pluralia tantum)', *JPol*, 82:345–48; Id., 'O liczebnikach jedynkowych', *ib.*, 81, 2001:82–92. P. Zbróg, 'O *dwa tysiące pierwszym* i *dwutysięcznym pierwszym roku*', *ib.*, 82:399–400; see also *YWMLS*, 62:883; Id., 'Problemy derywacji i akomodacji w skoordynowanych frazach z niepowtórzonym składnikiem', *Polonica*, 21, 2001:211–29, examines constructions like *Janek był tam jedną lub dwie godziny* .

5. Lexicology and Phraseology

M. Bańko, 'Peryfrazy w naszym życiu', *PJ*, no.9:3–23, alludes to the title of T. Krzeszowski's Polish translation of G. Lakoff and M. Johnson, *Metafory w naszym życiu*, Wa, PIW, 1988. B. Bartnicka, 'Czy przymiotniki *chytry* i *szczery* moga być antonimami?', *PFil*, 45, 2000:35–42. J. Basara, '*Wiejaczka* i *pióro* do *spachania* kłosów oraz ich synonimy', *ib.*, 43–51. S. Bąba, '*Sprzedać coś za miskę soczewicy* i *za miskę soczewicy*', *JPol*, 81, 2001:308–11; Id., '*Przypiąć kwiatek do kożucha — kwiatek do kożucha*', *ib.*, 82:396–98; Id., '*Słoma komuś z butów wychodzi (wystaje)*', *ib.*, 319–20. S. Bąba and J. Liberek, *Słownik frazeologiczny współczesnej polszczyzny*, Wa, 1096 pp.; A. Bogusławski, 'To jest / "das ist". Unteilbare Spracheinheiten? Doch!', *WSl*, 47:131–54, 251–74. M. Borejszo, **Nazwy ubiorów we współczesnej polszczyźnie.* Pń, WiS, 2001, 220 pp.; R. Bronikowska, 'Nazwy cech percypowanych zmysłem smaku jako określenia uczuć', *PJ*, no.6:43–58. K. Czarnecka, 'Odbicie zjawisk gospodarczych we frazeologii III Rzeczpospolitej (1989–2000)', *PJ*, no.4:32–41. R. Dulian, '*Centrum florystyczne*', *JPol*, 82:399. W. Dynak, '*O filipie (Filipie), co się wyrwał z konopi.* Przyczynek od paremiologii łowieckiej', *PJ*, no.6:59–63. M. Gębka-Wolak, 'O wyrażeniach typu *identyczny jak*', *PJ*, no.3:35–42. K. Głowińska, **Popularny słownik frazeologiczny*, Wa, Wilga, 2000, 790 pp., based on a computer corpus, contains 5000 items. A. Hącia, 'Typy redundantnych połączeń wyrazowych w języku polskim', *PJ*, no.5:3–15. A. Janota, '*Podatek* w języku polskim', *PJ*, no.10:45–56. M. Janusz, *Słownik wyrazów obcych*, Ww, Europa, 2001, 925 pp., has a section

(863–925) for *sentencje, powiedzenia*, and *zwroty*. M. Karpluk, **Słownik staropolskiej terminologii chrześcijańskiej*, Kw, DWN, 2001, 390 pp.; T. Karpowicz, 'Wokół koncepcji nowoczesnego słownika ortograficznego', *PFil*, 45, 2000: 245–48, would enrich the at present unhelpfully spartan entries in orthographical dictionaries. U. Kopeć, **Rozwój słownictwa nazywającego uczucia w języku dzieci i młodzieży*, Rzeszów, Wyd. WSP, 2000, 179 pp.; K. Kleszczowa, '*Gasnące słowa*', *PFil*, 45, 2000: 267–76, examines mechanisms that encourage words to disappear from the language. D. Kopczyńska, 'Metafory nazwiskowe w konstrukcjach z pogranicza frazeologii i składni', *PJ*, no.6: 30–42, examines *X w spódnicy*, *X dla ubogich*, *gminny* or *powiatowy X*, and *drugi X*. K. Kowalik, '*Euro* i "europeizacja" polskiego słownictwa', *JPol*, 82: 81–86. I. Kraśnicka-Wilk, 'Kognitywne schematy wyobrażeniowe leżące u podstaw frazeologizmów z leksemem *głowa*', *ib.*, 81, 2001: 339–43. B. Kreja, '*(Poległym) w służbie ojczyzny* czy też ... *w służbie ojczyźnie*. Jakie powinny być światła: *preciwmgłowe* czy *przeciwmgielne*?', *ib.*, 231–33. T. Malec, '*Dokładnie, dokładnie tak*', *ib.*, 82: 75–76; Id., '*Kinonoc*', *ib.*, 154. A. Młotek, 'Refleksy życia zakonnego utrwalone w polskiej leksyce, frazeologii i przysłowiach', *PJ*, no.2: 17–24, notes that general monkishness is regarded positively in Polish, but Bernardines, Capuchins, and Jesuits tend to have less positive connotations. R. Pawelec, 'Jak Polacy mówili o upadku finansowym firmy w roku 1800, 1900 i jak mówią w 2000? Dzieje słów: *bankructwo, upadłość, plajta* i *konkurs*', *PFil*, 45, 2000: 433–44. A. Pietrzykowska, 'Leksemy przymiotnikowe a najwyższej frekwencji w propagandzie Marca 1968 roku', *PJ*, no.5: 16–25. T. Piotrowski, '*Karimata*. Słowo o pewnej metodologii', *JPol*, 81, 2001: 227–30; M. Preyzner, '*Łamy internetu*', *ib.*, 230. **Problemy frazeologii europejskiej*, Vol. 4, ed. A. M. Lewicki, Lublin, Norbertinum, 2001, 100 pp., is on Polish. R. Przybylska, 'O najnowszym słownictwie polskim', *Polonistyka*, 55: 516–20. J. Puzynina, 'Metaforyka w polskich słownikach epoki baroku', *PFil*, 45, 2000: 461–73.

On the PWN dictionary, an open letter, *PJ*, no.5: 49–51, to PWN from several dozen linguists and others, pleading for Doroszewski's 1958–69 *Słownik języka polskiego*, available on CD-ROM since 2000, to be made available on the Internet receives an encouraging response, *PJ*, no.10: 61–62. Rada Języka Polskiego, 'Umowa-zlecenie. Nazwiska dwuczłonowe. Samorząd studialny', *PJ*, no.5: 62–63. Z. Saloni, '*Poziomnica*?', *JPol*, 82: 273–76. H. Satkiewicz, 'Nazwy roślin we frazeologii współczesnego języka polskiego', *PJ*, no.7: 45–49, sees fewer and fewer plant names featuring in phraseological expressions. R. Sinielnikoff and T. Zduńczyk, 'Zaduszki, mikołajki, walentynki', *PFil*, 45, 2000: 539–53, examine the long history of such terms.

Słownik gramatyki języka polskiego, ed. W. Gruszczyński and J. Bralczyk, Wa, WSiP, 360 pp.; L. Styrcz-Przebinda, 'O trudnościach w rozpoznawaniu homonimii czasowników *rozpisywać się, rozczytywać się*', *JPol*, 81, 2001:93–97. G. Szpila, 'Minimum paremiologiczne języka polskiego — badania pilotażowe', *ib.*, 82:36–42. B. Walczak, 'Przyczynki (bardzo drobne) do problematyki staropolskich nazw i określeń kierunków i stron świata', *PFil*, 45, 2000:611–17. Z. Wanicowa, 'Tajemnicza *marszuda*', *JPol*, 82:277–81. A. Zajda, **Studia z historii polskiego słownictwa prawniczego i frazeologii*, Kw, Jagiellonian U.P., 2001, 196 pp.; P. Żmigrodzki, 'Ciągłość i przemiany w polskiej leksykografii współczesnej', *Polonica*, 21, 2001:305–327; Id., 'Leksykografia jako przedmiot uniwersyteckiej edukacji polonistycznej. Uwagi i propozycje', *PJ*, 2001, no.9:39–50.

6. Semantics and Pragmatics

S. Bortnowski, 'O retoryce — bez entuzjazmu', *Polonistyka*, 55:271–75. A. Bugaj, 'Językowy obraz domu w piosence turystycznej', *PJ*, 2001, no.9:18–33. M. Bugajski, 'Kilka uwag o współczesnej komunikacji medialnej', *PFil*, 45, 2000:75–81. A. Chudzik, *Mowne zachowania magiczne w ujęciu pragmatyczno-kognitywnym*, Kw, Universitas, 148 pp.; K. Cyra, 'Czy rzeczywiście *ktokolwiek* znaczy *każdy*?', *Polonica*, 21, 2001:69–76. K. Czarnecka, M. Rzeszutek, B. Sobczak, 'Gdy trzeba zabrać głos', *Polonistyka*, 55:279–84. A. Dobaczewski, 'Czasowniki percepcji wzrokowej z uzupełnieniem propozycjonalnym (wstęp do analizy semantycznej)', *Polonica*, 21, 2001:51–68. A. Dominiak, 'Profile pojęć: "biznes", "biznesik", "biznesmen" i "biznes-women" we współczesnym języku polskim', *PJ*, 2001, no.8:9–27. A. Engelking, *Klątwa. Rzecz o ludowej magii słowa*, Ww, Funna, 2000, 312 pp.; A. Gałczyńska, 'Niedefinicyjne funkcje performatywu *przepraszam*', *PJ*, no.4:16–24. A. Grybosiowa, '*Biznesmeni* czy *nowi kapitaliści*?', *PJ*, 2001, no.9:66–68, notes approving connotations in recent usage of the latter. R. Grzegorczykowa, 'O znaczeniach współczesnych i ewolucji semantycznej wyrazów *gorszyć (się)*, *zgorszyć (się)* i *zgorszenie*', *PFil*, 45, 2000:215–19; B. Kreja, 'O antonimicznej kategorii słowtwórcze j czasownków inceptywno-amulatywnych', *ib.*, 301–11. M. Majewska, 'Próba systematyzacji zjawisk określanych wspólnym mianem *homonimia*', *PFil*, 45, 2000:367–74. T. Malec, 'Kulturowa (lingwistyczna) przestrzeń leksemu *gwiazda*', *ib.*, 375–82. I. Mendoza, 'Nicht-referentielle Indefinitheit im Polnischen: *-kolwiek, bądź, byle* und *lada*', *ZSl*, 47:327–43. J. Nicpoń, 'Sposoby wyrażania intencji nagany w tekstach pisanych i mówionych', *PJ*, no.5:26–37. E. Nowak, 'Wybrane aspekty konceptualizacji uczuć pozytywnych w języku polskim (na przykładzie zwrotów werbo-nominalnych)', *PJ*, no.3:21–34, and her 'Opis semantyczny analitycznych konstrukcji werbo-nominalnych (na przykładzie AWN oznaczających wybrane uczucia pozytywne)', *Polonica,* 21, 2001:25–50. M. Nowosad-Bakalarczyk, 'Kobieta "typowa" i "prawdziwa" w oczach studentów (Przyczynek do stereotypu kobiety)', *JPol,* 82:25–35. T. Orłowski, 'Cierpienie w kontekście kulturowym', *PJ,* 2001, no.10:42–48, is concerned with cultural context and cultural metaphor. J. Porayski-Pomsta, 'Pragmalingwistyczne aspekty rozwoju mowy', *PJ,* no.7:36–44. R. Przybylska, *Polisemia przyimków polskich w świetle semantyki kognitywnej,* Kw, Universitas, 608 pp.; A. Rola, 'Próba opisu różnic semantycznych w grupie polskich nazw współczucia', *PJ,* no.4:42–54. A. Różyło, 'Obraz pór dnia (doby) w polszczyźnie ogólnej', *JPol,* 81, 2001:273–81, and her 'Obraz *dnia* i *nocy* w polszczyźnie', *ib.*, 82:111–18. S. Rzedzicka, 'O wyrażeniu *naprawdę*', *Polonica,* 21, 2001:85–104. M. Rzeszutko, 'Kategorialne wyznaczniki gry w tekście rozprawy sądowej', *PJ,* 2001, no.10:1–8. L. Sikora, 'Analiza aktów chwalenia się w wypowiedziach dzieci sześcioletnich', *PJ,* 2001, no.9:11–17. M. Stróżyński, 'Sztuka dobrego mówienia — dzisiaj', *Polonistyka,* 55:284–89. T. Sudujko, 'Próba opisu semantycznego wielosegmentowych jednostek leksykalnych z komponentem *tak*', *Polonica,* 21, 2001:105–40. A. Sulich, 'Obraz pojęcia *ojciec* we współczesnej polszczyźnie', *PJ,* no.3:3–20. K. Sykulska, 'Chrypka — jej stylistyczne konotacje', *PJ,* no.10:57–60. E. Walusiak, 'O *nigdzie, nigdy* i *przenigdy.* Wstępna analiza semantyczna', *Polonica,* 21, 2001:77–84. K. Waszakowa, 'Polskie podstawowe nazwy barw w roli "interpretantów" świata (na przykładzie nazwy barwy *zielonej*)', *PFil,* 45, 2000:619–32. R. Wojtach, 'Paradygmat romantyczny jako składnik autostereotypu Polaka,' *PJ,* no.1:11–17, examines the language of the Polish right-wing press at a moment when Poland's entry into the European Community seems only a matter of time. M. Wołos, *Koncepcja "gry językowej" Wittgensteina w świetle badań współczesnego językoznawstwa,* Kw, Universitas, 126 pp.; P. Wróblewski, 'Językowy obraz ludzkich zachowań w świetle metaforycznych użyć czasowników zwierzęcych i odzwierzęcych', *PFil,* 45, 2000:659–80. K. Wyrwas, 'Neosemantyzm *mrówka*', *JPol,* 81, 2001:312–13, notes the sense 'petty smuggler'. D. Załęcka, 'Reklamy papierosów a problem rozumienia', *PJ,* 2001, no.8:41–47, discusses the irrationally confused messages conveyed by tobacco advertisements. Z. Zaron, 'Właściwości semantyczne orzeczeń. Preparacje składniowe. Część I', *PFil,* 45, 2000:681–91. T. Zgółka, 'O retoryce bez uprzedzeń. Stanisławowi Bortnowskiemu w odpowiedzi', *Polonistyka,* 55:276–78.

7. Sociolinguistics and Dialectology

K. Bakuła, 'Współczesny język polski albo permanentny remanent', *Polonistyka*, 55:542–50, challenges current dogma of linguistic communication. E. Breza, 'Rzeczowniki abstrakcyjne w dostojnej tytulaturze', *JPol*, 81, 2001:161–67; K. Cicha, '*Szerokości, przyczepności . . .*, czyli o języku kierowców TIR-owych', *JPol*, 82:75; A. Czesak, 'O *ku* w gwarach śląskich', *ib.*, 349–53. K. Długosz, 'Językowy obraz kobiety i mężczyzny w polszczyźnie potocznej', *PFil*, 45, 2000:121–31, thoroughly surveys linguistic ways of not appearing 'soft'. A. S. Dyszak, 'Słownictwo gwary miejskiej mieszkańców Bydgoszczy', *JPol*, 82:100–04. S. Gajda, 'Polska wielojęzyczność', *Polonistyka*, 55:261–66, is about varieties of Polish. S. Gala, 'O pewnych wyznacznikach słowotwórstwa gwarowego', *PFil*, 45, 2000:173–78. A. Grybosiowa, 'Nowe sytuacje — nowe zachowania grzecznościowe', *PJ*, no.2:3–8, notes a re-drawing of the boundaries between *ty* and the *pan*-words. B. Guz, 'Język wchodzi w grę — o grach językowych na przykładzie sloganów reklamowych, nagłówków prasowych i tekstów graffiti', *PJ*, 2001, no.10:9–20, examines phonic, graphic, lexical, and intertextual play. W. Jurek, 'Jaki jest język polski w Internecie?', *Polonistyka*, 55:525–30. M. Karwatowska, '*Prawda i kłamstwo w języku młodzieży licealnej lat dziewięćdziesiątych*', Lublin, UMCS Press, 2001, 206 pp.; **Kaszubszczyzna — Kaszëbizna*, ed. E. Breza, Opole U.P., 2000, 354 pp.; E. Kern-Jędrychowska, 'Zjawisko aktywności metajęzykowej dzieci', *PJ*, no.9:53–65. M. B. Koleśnikow, 'Problemy interpunkcji w języku przepisów prawnych', *PJ*, 2001, no.10:49–55, notes discrepancies between *legislacja* and *język ogólny*. D. Kopertowska, 'Ostatni będą *pieszymi* — czyli o transformacji stałych połączeń wyrazowych we współczesnej reklamie', *PFil*, 45, 2000:291–99. A. Kowalska, **Studia nad dialektem mazowieckim*, Wa, WSP Wiedzy Powszechnej, 2001, 415 pp.; A. Krawczyk-Tyrpa, **Tabu w dialektach polskich*, Bydgoszcz, Akademia Bydgoska im. Kazimierza Wielkiego, 2001, 345 pp.; R. Kucharczyk, 'Gwara w ocenie jej użytkowników', *JPol*, 81, 2001:98–103. H. Kurek, 'Wariantywność fleksyjna rzeczowników we wsiach Beskida Niskiego', *PFil*, 45, 2000:337–45. W. Mańczak, 'Pogląd Steinkego na praojczyznę Słowian', *JPol*, 82:316–19. J. Mędelska and M. Marszałek, 'Z badań nad stanem kulturalnej polszczyzny kowieńskiej w dwudziestoleciu międzywojennym', *ib.*, 81, 2001:259–66. T. Mika, 'Język polski mówiony w szkole?', *Polonistyka*, 55:359–66. J. Miodek, *Słownik ojczyzny polszczyzny*, Ww, Europa, 811 pp., gathers years of advice into a single alphabetical whole. W. Moch, 'Słownictwo swoiste polskiej subkultury hiphopowej', *JPol*, 82:188–98. K. Mosiołek-Kłosińska, 'Językowy obraz nowej polskiej polityki', *Polonistyka,* 55:367–70. P. Mostowik and W. Żukowski, **Ustawa o języku polskim. Komentarz,* Wa, LexisNexis, 2001, 216 pp., is aimed primarily at lawyers. J. Nalepa, '*Burdele* w polskich górach', *JPol,* 81, 2001:117–20. K. Olesiak, 'Kilka słów o polszczyźnie konsumpcyjnej', *Polonistyka,* 55:555–58. K Ożóg, 'Metafory potoczne w języku polityki', *JPol,* 82:21–24, Id., 'Kod ograniczony wśród współczesnej polskiej młodzieży', *Polonistyka,* 55:521–24, and especially Id., *Polszczyzna przełomu XX i XXI wieku. Wybrane zagadnienia,* Rzeszów, Fraza, 2001, 263 pp., offer perceptive and mature linguistic observation. W. Paryl, 'Elementy gwarowe w mowie ludności z Tarnowicy Polnej na Pokuciu osiedlonej na Dolnym Śląsku', *PFil,* 45, 2000:423–31. H. Pelcowa, **Interferencja leksykalna w gwarach Lubelszczyzny,* Lublin, UMCS Press, 2001, 301 pp.; J. Piller, 'Recepcja reklam telewizyjnych przez najmłodszych odbiorców i jej wpływ na ich język', *PJ,* no.10:31–44. E. Polański, 'O błędach semantycznych i frazeologicznych uczniów', *PFil,* 45, 2000:453–59. Rada Języka Polskiego, '*Dwa końce włosa.* "Polszczyzna sterowana komputerowo". *Aterotromboza* — czemu nie?', *PJ,* no.6:70–71; '*Na politechnice* lepiej niż *w politechnice.* Tylko *powiat koszaliński.* Tylko *poziomica. Spółka akcyjna,* czyli *SA. Pod adresem* i *na adres.* Odmiana nazwisk włoskich', *PJ,* no.3:76–78. J. Reichan, 'Polski gwarowy wyraz *pomłoże*', *PFil,* 45, 2000:475–77. M. Sagan-Bielawa, 'Użycie elementów dialektalnych jako wskaźnik wspólnoty kulturowej (na przykładzie języka kresowian)', *JPol,* 82:105–10. H. Satkiewicz, 'O zmianach w strukturze językowej wiadomości prasowych', *PFil,* 45, 2000:507–12. S. Schmidt, 'Zagadnienie honoryfikatywności w wybranych publikacjach polonistyczny ostatnich lat', *PJ,* no.2:9–16, pays particular attention to collocations with *pan.* H. Sędziak, 'Zdania bezpodmiotowe w tekstach gwarowych', *PFil,* 45, 2000:519–27; H. Skoczylas-Stawska, 'Z historii badań gwaroznawczych na ziemi wieluńskiej', *ib.,* 555–65. **Słownik gwar śląskich,* Vols 1–3 (A–BŻDŻON), ed. B. Wyderka, Opole, PIN-IŚ, 2000, 2001, 2002, xlv + 178, xxiii + 156, xxiii + 158 pp.; K. Sobstyl, '"Czego człowiekowi do szczęścia potrzeba?" — czyli jak zmienia się nasze spojrzenie na świat. Na podstawie ogłoszeń towarzysko-matrymonialnych', *PJ,* 2001, no.10:36–41.

Texts: E. Dzięgiel, 'Z Zielonej na Podolu (obwód chmielnicki na Ukrainie)', *JPol,* 81, 2001:104–09. A. Golonka, 'Z Jeziora koło Parczewa', *ib.,* 192–95. K. Górski, 'Zagędzielec. Opowieść z ziemi łomżyńskiej', *PFil,* 45, 2000:207–13. R. Kucharczyk, 'Z Rzepiennika Strzyżewskiego', *JPol,* 82:201–05. Z. Kurzowa and M. Zabłocka, 'Teksty polskie z Krzemieńca', *ib.,* 282–87. A. Otwinowska-Kasztelanic, *Korpus języka mówionego młodego pokolenia Polaków (19–35 lat),* Wa, Dialog, 2000, 312 pp., presents transcripts, not phonetic transcriptions, of recorded Warsaw conversations.

A. Wilkoń, **Typologia odmian językowych współczesnej polszczyzny (PNUS,* 1875), Katowice, Silesian U.P., 2000, 112 pp., is an expanded second edition of his 1987 work. J. Winiarska, 'Spontaniczność dialogów w polskiej telewizji w latach siedemdziesiątych i dziewięćdziesiątych', *JPol,* 81, 2001, no. 1–2 : 32–36. I. Winiarska, 'Nazywanie Chrystusa w tradycji Kościoła ewangelicko-reformowanego', *PFil,* 45, 2000 : 633–42. E. Wolańska, "Właściwości komunikacyjne, genologiczne i językowe krótkiej wiadomości tekstowej (SMS). Wybrane zagadnienie', *PJ,* no.10 : 21–30. K. Wyrwas, 'Przytoczenia w potocznym tekście narracyjnym', *JPol,* 81, 2001 : 183–88. M. Zaśko-Zielińska, *Przez okno świadomości. Gatunki mowy w świadomości użytkowników języka,* Wrocław U.P., 179 pp. T. Zgółka, 'Jednostka uwikłana w wielości języków', *Polonistyka,* 55 : 266–71. R. Zimny, 'Mechanizmy samoidentyfikacji i autokreacji w języku wlepkarzy', *PJ,* no.6 : 15–29.

8. Individuals, Individual Works, Stylistics

ANONYMOUS LITHUANIAN GRAMMAR. H. Karaś, 'O polszczyźnie anonimowej gramatyki języka litewskiego z I ćwierci XIX wieku (przez X.D.K.P.S.). Morfologia, składnia, słownictwo', *PFil,* 45, 2000 : 225–44.

BACZYŃSKI. P. Paziak, 'Ręka błogosławi i zabija — o konotacjach semantycznych *ręki* i *dłoni* w poezji K. K. Baczyńskiego', *PJ,* no.5 : 38–45.

BARTHOLOMEW OF BYDGOSZCZ. **Słownik Bartłomieja z Bydgoszczy. Wersja polsko-łacińska. Pt I (A-G),* ed. Elżbieta Kędelska et al., Wa, Slawistyczny Ośrodek Wyd., 1999, 214 pp. + 10 reproductions (see *YWMLS,* 61 : 855).

BIBLE. S. Koziara, **Frazeologia biblijna w języku polskim,* Kw, Wyd. Naukowe AP, 2001, 343 pp.; L. Szelachowska-Winiarzowa, 'Czy Judyta rzeczywiście jadła *żemły*? Jeszcze o "zagadkowym" staropolskim *zielu*', *JPol,* 82 : 68–73; Z. Wanicowa, 'W odpowiedzi na artykuł polemiczny pt. Czy Judyta rzeczywiście jadła *żemły*?', *ib.*, 236–38; K. Herej-Szymańska, 'Czy Judyta rzeczywiście jadła *ziele*? Spojrzenie z boku', *ib.*, 238–40. M. Górna, 'Stopień znajomości biblijnych związków frazeologicznych wśród uczniów', *ib.*, 214–21. D. Bieńkowska, **Polski styl biblijny,* Łódź, Wyd. Archidiecezjalne, 2001, 160 pp.; J. Migdał, 'Określenia zwierząt i roślin wśród szesnastowiecznego osobliwego słownictwa biblijnego', *PFil,* 45, 2000 : 389–95. A. Oświeja, 'A look at biblical verse — enpassant the biblical translations of Czesław Miłosz', *SSH,* 46, 2001 : 409–12, points out that the biblical verse is a creation of translators' tradition.

BOGURODZICA. W. Rębowski, W. R. Rzepka, and W. Wydra, 'Zespół pieśniowy ze schyłku XVI wieku z rękopisu biblioteki

Klasztoru Klarysek krakowskich', *PFil*, 45, 2000:479–505, treats a collection which includes a version of *Bogurodzica*; there are photographs of the pages of Polish.

BRAUN. J. Wronicz, **Kazania cieszyńskie z XVIII wieku ks. Henryka Brauna. Tekst i analiza języka*, Cieszyn-Kw, PAN-IJP/US, 2001, 301 pp.

CHRAPOWICKI. J. Gardzińska, 'Uwagi o grafii i fonetyce inwentarzy majętności węgrowskiej i sokołowskiej z 1621 roku', *PFil*, 45, 2000:195–205.

CINCIAŁA. A. Pospiszylowa, 'O Słowniku gwarowym Andrzeja Cinciały po r az drugi', *JPol*, 81, 2001:110–12, and her 'Nazwy gatunków jabłek i gruszek w Słowniku gwarowym Andrzeja Cinciały', *ib.*, 360–62.

COMENIUS. W. Gruszczyński, 'Polski wstęp do *Orbis pictus* Komeńskiego', *PJ*, no.7:32–35.

DIDACTIC VERSE. K. Maćkowiak, 'Potoczny materiał leksykalny a styl osiemnastowiecznej dydaktyki wierszowanej', *JPol*, 82:338–44.

DZIEŃ POLSKI. J. Mędelska and M. Marszałek, 'Porady językowe kowieńskiego "Dnia polskiego"', *PJ*, no.4:6–15, looks at the interwar period.

FILM REVIEWS. E. Sękowska, 'Językowe środki wyrażania ocen w filmowych recenzjach prasowych', *PJ*, no.7:50–61.

GAZETA POLSKA. S. Mikołajczak, 'Składnia wypowiedzeń złożonych w notatkach syntetycznych na przykładzie *Przeglądu wydarzeń* w "Gazecie Polskiej"', *PFil*, 45, 2000:397–404.

GENRES. M. Kawka, 'Biogram jako gatunek tekstu', *JPol*, 81, 2001:325–30.

GRUNWALD VERSE FRAGMENT. Z. Babik. 'Nieznany słownikarzom piętnastowieczny fragment poetycki', *JPol*, 82:165–73.

GRZEPSKI. J. Biniewicz, '*Geometria* S. Grzepskiego — początki polskiej terminologii matematycznej i technicznej', *PJ*, no.4:25–31, treats *Geometryja to jest miernicka nauka*, which appeared in Kw in 1566.

GWIŻDŻ. F. Pluta, 'Stylizacja gwarowa w *Zwyrtałowej bacówce pod Wesołym Wierchem* Feliksa Gwiżdża', *PFil*, 45, 2000:445–52.

HERBERT. E. Badyda, 'Niebieskie oczy matki i błękitne oczy królowej Amazonek, czyli funkcje koloru niebieskiego w poezji Zbigniewa Herberta', *JPol*, 81, 2001:68–75.

HERLING-GRUDZIŃSKI. **Język Artystyczny, Vol. 11*, ed. A. Wilkoń and D. Ostaszewska, Katowice, Silesian U.P., 2001, 154 pp.

HOLY CROSS SERMONS. B. Taras, '*Tajnica moja mnie* . . . Zagadka nazw własnych w *Kazaniach świętokrzyskich*', *PFil*, 45, 2000:595–97.

HRABAL IN POLISH TRANSLATION. J. Baluch, '*Stryjek* (strýc, strýč, strejda), czyli *wujek*! Josef Hrabal, zwany Pepin — wujek Bohumila Hrabala', *JPol*, 82:127–28.

IWASZKIEWICZ. E. Urbańska-Mazuruk, 'Nazwy osobowe w międzywojennej poezji Jarosława Iwaszkiewicza', *PFil*, 45, 2000 : 599–609.

JAKUBOWSKI. J. Mędelska and M. Marszałek, 'Szkic Jana Jakubowskiego o polszczyźnie kowieńskiej nie zaginął!', *JPol*, 82 : 241–47.

KATYŃ MEMOIRS. Z. Gałecki, 'Osobliwości lek sykalne *Pamiętników znalezionych w Katyniu*', *PFil*, 45, 2000 : 179–85.

KORTOWICZ. Z. Leszczyński, 'Krótka relacja o puryście sprzed wieku', *PFil*, 45, 2000 : 347–52, deals with E. S. Kortowicz, the compiler of a dictionary of words which Polish could well afford to lose.

KUPISZEWSKI. M. Kucała, 'Spójnikowe wskaźniki nawiązania zewnętrznego w opisie pielgrzymki do Rzymu w r. 1900 Macieja Kupiszewskiego', *PFil*, 45, 2000 : 313–18.

LITERARY LANGUAGE. Aleksander Wilkoń, **Z dziejów języka literatury polskiej*, Katowice, Śląsk, 2001, 211 pp.

MAGAZINES. W. Kajtoch, 'O stylu popularnych pism młodzieżowych', *Polonistyka*, 55 : 531–36 follows Id., 'Odlotowe bez dwóch zdań! Kultura języka, stylu, perswazji w czasopismach dla młodzieży', *Zeszyty Prasoznawcze*, 1999, nos. 3–4 : 79–102, W. Kajtoch and J. Kołodziej, 'Dobro, zło i inne wartości w czasopismach młodzieżowych', *ib.*, 2000, nos. 1–2 : 59–80 and P. Planeta, 'Świat przedstawiony w czasopismach młodzieżowych', *ib.*, 81–104.

MICKIEWICZ. M. Białoskórska, 'Konotacje semantyczne i symboliczne wiatru w utworach Adama Mickiewicza', *JPol*, 81, 2001 : 55–67. M. Spiczakowska, 'O języku Pana Tadeusza Adama Mickiewicza', *JPol*, 82 : 12–16.

MILNE IN POLISH TRANSLATION. J. Winiarska, '*Fredzia Phi-Phi* czy *Kubuś Puchatek*', *JPol*, 81, 2001 : 334–38.

MONETA AND VOGEL. E. Worbs, 'Von Johann Moneta's *Enchiridion polonicum oder Polnisches Handbuch* (1720) zu Daniel Vogel's *Polnisch-Deutsches Lexicon* (1786) — Anmerkungen zur Genese eines Wörterbuchs', *PFil*, 45, 2000 : 643–53.

NIZIURSKI. Jerzy Głowacki, **Nazewnictwo literackie w utworach Edmunda Niziurskiego*, Gdańsk, Gdańskie Tow. Naukowe, 1999, 143 pp.; U. Nawrocka, 'Frazeologiczne innowacje modyfikujące w wybranych utworach Edmunda Niziur skiego', *JPol*, 82 : 119–26.

NORWID. D. Szagun, 'Biblijny genetivus partitivus czy forma superlatywu w poezji Norwida?', *JPol*, 82 : 17–20.

PEARL. W. J. Darasz, 'Perła po polsku, czyli próba przekładu pewnej poetyki', *JPol*, 81, 2001 : 306–08.

PILCH. A. Rejter, 'Funkcje powtórzeń w powieści *Pod Mocnym Aniołem* Jerzy Pilcha', *PJ*, no. 10 : 3–12.

POETRY. W. J. Darasz, 'Hipometria i hipermetria', *JPol*, 81, 2001 : 189–91. Id., 'Hiperkataleksa', *ib.*, 331–33. J. Franczak, 'Strategie językowe najmłodszej poezji', *Polonistyka*, 55 : 537–41, covers poets born in the 1970s or later. W. Śliwiński, 'Rzeczowniki niby-osobowe jako składniki poetyckich konstrukcji nominalnych w dziejach polskiego wiersza', *JPol*, 81, 2001 : 37–44.

PRESS. J. Smól, 'Rola środków stylistycznych w kreowaniu obrazu rzeczywistości w prasie z 1989 roku', *JPol*, 81, 2001 : 24–31.

PRUS. T. Smółkowa, 'Budowa słowotwórcza rzeczowników w *Lalce* Bolesława Prusa', *PFil*, 45, 2000 : 567–72.

SERMONS. G. Majkowski, 'Paralelizm składniowy jako wskaźnik perswazji w prozie kaznodziejskiej (na materiale kazań okresu oświecenia)', *PJ*, no.9 : 39–52.

SĘP SZARZYŃSKI. B. Wyderka, **Prawdziwy wszędzie. O stylu Mikołaja Sępa Szarzyńskiego na tle tendencji stylistycznych poezji polskiego renesansu*, Opole U.P., 251 pp.

SIENKIEWICZ. E. Sękowska, 'Stylistyczne wykładniki motywu domu w *Rodzinie Połanieckich* Henryka Sienkiewicza', *PFil*, 45, 2000 : 529–32.

SZEMIOT. K. Kupiszewska-Grzybowska, 'Kartki z historii języka polskiego', *PFil*, 45, 2000 : 319–22, on S. S. Szemiot (1657–86).

SZTRIPSZKY. I. Udvari, 'О плане венгерско-польского словаря Гиадора Стрипского', *SSH*, 47 : 35–43, examines the dictionary which ethnographer Hiador Sztripszky (1875–1946) embarked on in the 1920s.

TWARDOWSKI. M. Kabata, 'Biblijne odwołania językowe w poezji księdza Twardowskiego', *JPol*, 81, 2001 : 253–58. J. Kowalewska-Dąbrowska, 'Gdy milczenie jest mową . . . — kilka uwag o pojęciu milczeniu w języku potocznym i w poezji Jana Twardowskiego', *PJ*, no.9 : 24–38.

TRUCHANOWSKI. M. Ruszkowski, 'Epigonizm czy twórcza kontynuacja? (O stylu *Ulicy Wszystkich Świetych* Kazimierza Truchanowskiego)', *PJ*, no.10 : 13–20.

TWÓJ STYL. A. Siwek, 'Środki stylistyczne w funkcjach perswazyjnych (na materiale z "Twojego Stylu")', *PJ*, no.3 : 43–55.

VARIOUS. *Język a Kultura 14. Uczucia w języku i tekście*, ed. Iwona Nowakowska-Kempna, Anna Dąbrowska, and Janusz Anusiewicz, Wrocław U.P., 2000, 297 pp., includes B. Sieradzka-Baziur, 'Językowy obraz *serca* w polskich utworach Jana Kochanowskiego' (209–43), T. Stępień, 'O uczuciach "ideowych". Glosy do *Hymnu* Ignacego Krasińskiego' (175–86), B. Bierwiaczonek, 'Religijne subkategorie miłości' (79–115), D. Brzozowska, 'Uczucia w dowcipach' (289–97), and M. Telus, 'Konstrukcje narodowego "my", czyli dlaczego kochamy ojczyznę' (253–87). *Język a Kultura 16. Świat roślin w języku i kulturze*, ed. A. Dąbrowska and I. Kamińska-Szmaj, Wrocław U.P., 2001, 281 pp., includes K. Data and D. Janeczko, 'Świat roślin w twórczości Jana Kochanowskiego' (159–67), H. Zgółkowa and B. Sobczak, 'Rośliny w poetyckim obrazie świata Agnieszki Osieckiej' (199–205), S. Rzedzicka, 'Roślinny świat Brunona Schulza', (179–91), M. Pietrzak, 'Rośliny w porównaniach występujących w *Trylogii* Henryka Sienkiewicza' (169–91), E. Ciesielska, 'Motywy roślinne w poezji Jana Twardowskiego' (193–97), A. Dąbrowska, '*Złota dziewanna* i *biodra brzozowe*. Nazwy roślin w polskim słownictwie erotycznym (na materiale poetyckim)' (27–49), J. Woronczak, 'Rośliny w żywotach świętych' (67–70), G. Habrajska, 'Funkcjonowania nazw roślin w potocznej polszczyźnie' (207–12), M. Preyzner, 'Rodzaj i płeć w *drzewie*, czyli stosunek obrazu kategorii gramatycznej do stereotypu drzewa' (269–81), and A. Wojciechowska-Basista, 'Świat roślin w reklamie współczesnej (reklama prasowa)' (257–67).

WAŃKOWICZ. U. Sokólska, 'Językowe środki subiektywizacji świata przedstawionego w *Szczenięcych latach* Melchiora Wańkowicza', *PFil*, 45, 2000: 581–93.

WITWICKI. M. Jurkowski, 'Uwagi o *Słówniku polsko-cerkiewnosłowiańsko-ukraińskim* Teodora Witwickiego', *PFil*, 45, 2000: 221–23, treats a dictionary recently published as *Słównik polsko-cerkiewnosłowiańsko-ukraiński Teodora Witwickiego z połowy XIX wieku*, ed. J. Dzendzeliwski and J. Rieger, Wa, Wyd. Naukowe Semper, 1997, 611 pp.

WOJTYŁA. E. Laskowska, 'Wartościowanie w wypowiedziach Jana Pawła II', *JPol*, 81, 2001: 20–23.

WYSPIAŃSKI. K. Sikora, 'Gwara w Weselu — z perspektywy dialektologicznej i socjolingwistycznej', *JPol*, 81, 2001: 3–19.

ŻEROMSKI. J. Kida, 'Łacińskie słownictwo w *Dziennikach* Stefana Żeromskiego', *PFil*, 45, 2000: 259–66; P. Kupiszewski, '*Aryman mści się* — antonimia i synkretyzm i ich wyznaczniki językowe', *ib.*, 323–27; R. Kupiszewski, 'Elementy stylizacji biblijnej w *Aryman mści się* Stefana Żeromskiego', *ib.*, 329–36.

9. Polish and Other Languages

O. Baraniwska, 'O ukraińskich i polskich zdaniach przydawkowych', *JPol*, 82: 248–51. Z. Bela, 'Nieco złagodzony kompleks. O relacjach między polską i czeską literaturą botaniczno-lekarską w XVI w.', *JPol*, 82, no. 3: 174–77. F. Buffa, 'O formálnych poľsko-slovenských lexikálnych rozdieloch', *SlSl*, 37: 97–106. H. Burkhardt, 'Gruby i jego konotacje semantyczne w języku polskim i niemieckim', *PJ*, 2001, no.8: 1–8. A. Cała, H. Wegrzynek, and G. Zalewska, *Historia i kultura Żydów polskich. Słownik*, Wa, WSiP, 2000, viii + 400 pp., is encyclopedic rather than a linguist's dictionary, but contains etymological and other information of value to linguists. J. Damborský, **Polština a franština ve vzájemném vztahu. (Soubor studií)*, Ostrava, Filozofická Fakulta, 1999, 285 pp.; E. Deboveanu and D. Cojocaru, 'Культурная память фразеологии', *PFil*, 45, 2000: 101–12, compare Russian, Polish, and Romanian expressions such as *rozłożyć ręce* involving body parts. K. Długosz-Kurczabowa, 'Apokaliptyczny *zielony koń*', *ib.*, 133–42. S. Dubisz, 'Rozwój języka polskiego a integracja europejska,' *PJ*, no.1: 3–10. R. Eckert, 'Different ways of borrowing from Slavic into Old Lithuanian', *ZSl*, 47: 413–17. B. Falińska, 'Kategoria nazw młodych zwierząt w świetle map OLA', *PFil*, 45, 2000: 159–71 + two inserted maps; OLA is the *Общеславянский лингвистический атлас*. K. Gammelgaard, 'Approaching the rise of spoken standard language: the case of Polish, Czech and Slovak, 1800–1918', *SEER*, 80: 601–23. K. Geben, 'Kalki leksykalne z języka litewskiego w języku polskim uczniów polskojęzycznych szkół na Wileńszczyźnie', *PJ*, 2001, no.10: 56–63. R. L. Górski, 'Kilka uwag na temat diatezy biernej w języku polskim i łacińskim w aspekcie porównawczym', *Polonica*, 21, 2001: 141–64. J. Graczyńska 'Najdawniejsze podziały słowiańszczyzny w świetle danych językowych i archeologicznych', *PFil*, 45, 2000: 187–94. M. Guławska, **Aspektualität im Polnischen und Deutschen. Eine praktische Untersuchung am Beispiel der Übersetzungen beider Richtungen* (SB, 393), Munich, Sagner, 2000, 219 pp.; K. Herej-Szymańska, 'Славянская лексика, называющая умирание', *SSH*, 47: 269–76. L. Jászay, 'О статусе категории вида в славянских языках', *Slavica*, 31, 2001: 13–25. **Język i kultura białoruska w kontakcie z sądiadami. Studia poświęcone Antoninie Obrębskiej-Jabłońskiej w stuleciu narodzin*, ed. E. Smułkowa and A. Engelking, Wa, Wydział Polonistyki UW, 2001, 195 pp.; *Język trzeciego tysiąclecia II. Polszczyzna a języki obce: przekład i dydaktyka*, ed. W. Chłopicki, Kw, Tertium, 385 pp., contains papers on translation theory, the pragmatics of translation, literature in translation, translator competence, language teaching, and Polish and other languages. W. Kotikowa, 'Formy adresatywne we współczesnym języku rosyjskim, polskim i w amerykańskim wariancie języka angielskiego. Charakterystyka socjolingwistyczna,' *PJ*, no.1: 43–51. T. Krajewski, 'Hot-dog w fast foodzie, czyli o anglicyzmach w języku polskim', *Polonistyka*, 55: 294–95. K. Lipiński, **Vademecum tłumacza*, Kw, Idea, 2001, 188 pp.; W. Mańczak, 'Rzekomy "substrat" przedpolski', *PFil*, 45, 2000: 383–87. M. Moser, 'Zur Polszczyzna kresowa in Weißrußland und der Ukraine', *WSl*, 47: 31–56, a thorough study, with a useful bibliography (52–56) of the relationship between Polish as a minority language in neighbouring countries and the Polish of Eastern Polish dialects. B. Nowowiejski, 'Cytaty obcojęzyczne w dziejach polszczyzny jako problem badawczy', *PFil*, 45, 2000: 405–15. T. Z. Orłoś, 'Częściowo złudna czesko-polska ekwiwalencja leksykalna. Polonizmy czeskie i ich polskie odpowiedniki', *ib.*, 417–22. W. Pisarek, 'Prawne uwarunkowania rozwoju języka', *JPol*, 81, 2001: 242–52. K. Pisarkowa, 'Łac. *palatium*, *palatinus* i niem. *Pfalz* z perspektywy polskiej', *JPol*, 82: 132–33; and her 'Magia Orientu', *ib.*, 2–11. M. Podhajecka, 'Zapożyczenia polskie w języku angielskim na podstawie Oxford English Dictionary (OED)', *ib.*, 330–37. I. Ripka, 'Názvy farieb v slovenských a poľských nárečových prirovnaniach', *SSH*, 46, 2001: 317–23. J. Siatkowski, 'Słowiańskie nazwy zawodów w świetle materiałów *Atlasu ogólnosłowiańskiego*. II Nazwy kowala', *PFil*, 45, 2000: 533–38. M. Sitarz, * *Yiddish and Polish Proverbs. Contrastive Analysis Against Cultural Background*, Kw, PAU, 2000, 161 pp.; F. Sławski, 'Prasłowiańskie **nagú*, polskie *nagi*', *JPol*, 81, 2001: 2. E. Smułkowa, 'Kształt współistnienia na polsko-białorusko-litewskim pograniczu językowym', *PFil*, 45, 2000: 573–80. M. Stachowski, 'Uwagi o wybranych etymologiach węgierskich w języku polskim', *SSH*, 47: 45–52. S. Tornow, 'Zum Verhältnis Nation und Nationalsprache in Osteuropa', *ZSl*, 47: 172–80. K. Trost, 'Das System der Durativitätsarten, der Aktionsarten und des Aspekts im Russichen, Teil I', *ASP*, 30: 21–56, and N. Nübler, 'Aspekt und Aktionsart im Slovakischen', *ib.*, 171–86, both invite comparison with Polish. W. P. Turek, **Słownik zapożyczeń pochodzenia arabskiego w polszczyźnie*. Kw, Universitas, 2001, 560 pp.; Id., 'Adaptacja zapożyczeń arabskich do języka polskiego', *JPol*, 81, 2001: 267–72; Id., 'Zmiany wyrazów arabskich zapożyczonych do polszczyzny za pośrednictwem innych języków', *ib.*, 82: 96–99.

10. Onomastics

Z. Babik, 'Grünfelde-Grynwald-Grywałd-Grunwald', *JPol*, 82: 129–31, and W. Mańczak, 'Czemu *Grünfelde* > *Grunwald*?', *ib.*, 393. E. Breza, 'Imię *Niecisław* — nazwiska *Netzlaf(f)* i podobne, *Niechcic*', *PJ*, 2001, no.9: 69–72; Id., 'Nazwiska *Dubas*, *Lichtarz* i pokrewne oraz podobne', *PFil*, 45, 2000: 61–65; Id., **Nazwiska Pomorzan. Pochodzenie i zmiany*, 2 vols, Gdańsk U.P., 2000, 2002, 489, 543 pp.; Id., 'Nazwisko *Przedcieczyński*', *JPol*, 82: 77–79; Id., 'Dlaczego *Białogarda* (nie *Białogard*?)', *ib.*, 81, 2001: 313–14; Id., 'Imię *Stanigor* — historyczne i współczesne nazwisko pomorskie *S(z)tangor(ra)*', *ib.*, 82: 291–92; Id., '*Mis(z)tal* i nazwiska podobne oraz pochodne', *ib.*, 206–07; Id., 'Ulica *Nad Dworcem*', *ib.*, 81, 2001: 394; Id., 'W sprawie wskaźników liczbowo-procentowych (etymologicznie) niemieckich nazwisk na Pomorzu', *ib.*, 49–55. W. Decyk, 'Historia zapisana w nazwach — o losie obcych nazw w języku polskim', *PJ*, no.7: 15–31, examines the

Polish names for Amsterdam, Belgrade, Brussels, Budapest, Kiev, Istanbul, Lisbon, London, Luxemburg, Bratislava, and Tallinn. J. A. Dziewiątkowski, 'Wezwania kosciołów i kaplic w archidiecezji gnieźnieńskiej', *PJ*, 2001, no.10:21–35. Jerzy Głowacki, 'Raz jeszcze o nazwach własnych polskich pociągów', *JPol*, 81, 2001:356–59. J. Grzenia, **Słownik imion*, Wa, PWN, 362 pp.; B. Kreja, **Słowotwórstwo polskich nazwisk. Struktury sufiksalne*, DWN, Kw, 2001, 277 pp.; Id., 'O *Świadkach Jehowy*, czyli *jehowych*, *jehowach*, *jehowitach* itd.', *JPol*, 81, 2001:159–60. Ż. Kubiszyn-Mędrala, 'Zwroty adresatywne w polskiej telewizji w latach siedemdziesiątych i dziewięćdziesiątych', *ib.*, 168–75. M. Kucała, 'Jego Świątobliwość Ojciec Święty Jan Paweł II, papież', *ib.*, 82:161–64; and a section from the Polish Language Council, *PJ*, no.2:78–81 includes approval for the word order of *Stefan kardynał Wyszyński*; also from the Council, 'Dwuczłonowe nazwy jednostek administracyjnych. Skrótowce. *Skarb Państwa* to jednostkowa nazwa instytucji. Stanowisko Komisji Dydaktycznej Rady Języka Polskiego w sprawie dostosowania programów studiów polonistycznych do zakresu nauczania języka polskiego w reformowanej szkole', *PJ*, no.4:69–72. M. Malec, **Imię w polskiej antroponimii i kulturze*, Kw, DWN, 2001, 135 pp.; J. Miodek, '1. *Murcki*, *Kostuchna*, 2. *ściemniać* — "kręcić, mącić, gmatwać"', *PJ*, 2001, no.10:80–82. G. Seroczyński, 'Uwagi o speleonimach sudeckich', *PFil*, 45, 2000:513–18, also includes a glossary of terms connected with caving (517–18). *Słownik ortograficzno-gramatyczny języka polskiego z zasadami ortografii i interpunkcji*, ed. I. Kamińska-Szmaj, Ww, Europa, 936 pp., has a separate section for proper names (829–936), including some abbreviations such as *AZS* and *MFW*.

LITERATURE

POSTPONED

IV. RUSSIAN STUDIES

LANGUAGE

POSTPONED

LITERATURE BEFORE 1800

POSTPONED

LITERATURE, 1800–1848

By Boris Lanin, *Professor of Literature, Russian Academy of Education, Moscow*

1. General

Классический психоанализ и художественная литература, ed. V. M. Leibin, SPb, Piter, 448 pp. V. Rudnev, *Характеры и расстройства личности. Патография и метапсихология*, Mw, Klass, 264 pp., is a psychological study of writers' biographies. I. Reifman, *Ритуализованная агрессия: Дуэль в русской культуре и литературе*, Mw, NLO, 336 pp. A. Z. Krein, *Жизнь в музее*, Mw, Raduga, 608 pp., is the last volume of the trilogy about the Pushkin state museum in Moscow, written by its founder and director; previous parts were 'Рождение музея' (1969), and 'Жизнь музея' (1979). V. M. Zhivov, *Разыскания в области и предыстории русской культуры (Язык. Семиотика. Культура)* (Studia Philologica), Mw, Iazyki Slavianskoi Kul′tury, 760 pp. Iu. Barabash, '"Мой бедный protégé" (Проза Шевченко: после Гоголя)', *VL*, no.6:127–55. I. V. Gracheva, 'Жемчуг в русской литературе', *RRe*, no.3:14–20. L. L. Bel′skaya, '"Ах, как много на свете кошек . . ."', *RRe*, no.6:16–23, discusses cats in Russian poetry from Pushkin to Brodsky. V. A. Skiba, 'Мотив слухов в русской художественной литературе', *Russkaia Slovesnost*, no.1:22–29. B. Tarasov, *Куда движется история? Метаморфозы идей и людей в свете христианской традиции*, SPb, Aleteia, 348 pp., provides an excellent introduction to Russian culture. I. M. Helfant, *The High Stakes of Identity: Gambling in the Life and Literature of Nineteenth-Century Russia* (Studies in Russian Literature and Theory), Evanston, Northwestern U.P., xxv + 211 pp., is the first comprehensive study of gambling in Russian culture, concentrating on the first half of the 19th c. and on the writers Fedor Tolstoy, Pushkin, Lermontov, and the less well-known I. E. Velikopol′sky and D. Begichev.

D. Pesmen, *Russia and Soul: An Exploration*, Ithaca, Cornell U.P., 2000, xii + 364 pp., is an anthropological study of one of the most important themes in Russian literature. E. Shmeleva and A. Shmelev, *Русский анекдот: Текст и речевой жанр* (Studia Philologica), Mw, Iazyki Slavianskoi Kul'tury, 144 pp. *Образы России в научном, художественном и политическом дискурсах (история, теория, политическая практика)*, ed. I. O. Ermachenko, Petrozavodsk State Univ., 2001, 432 pp. E. V. Semenova, *Русская литература и православие*, Ulan-Ude, Buryat State Univ., 1999, 59 pp. L. I. Rubleva, *Романы В. Т. Нарежного: традиции и новаторство*, Mw, Prometei, 164 pp. V. G. Odinokov, *Литература и духовная культура*, Novosibirsk State Univ., 125 pp. *Мотив вина в литературе*, Tver' State Univ., 2001, 193 pp. A. Ochman, *Новый Парнас: русские писатели Золотого и Серебряного века на Кавказских Минеральных Водах*, Piatigorsk State Pedagogical Univ., 820 pp. *Словарь персонажей русской литературы: вторая половина 18–19 вв.*, ed. V. A. Nikitin and G. A. Gudimova, Mw–SPb, Universitetskaia kniga, 2000, 361 pp. E. Wagemans, *Русская литература от Петра Великого до наших дней*, Mw, RGGU, 554 pp. S. Gritsuk, *Метафора любви,(Философия искусства)*, Vienna, Monaco — Mw, SG-ART, 128 pp.

Serebrennikov, *Время*, contains several interesting papers: B. F. Egorov, 'Тема обмана в русской литературе' (13–17); Iu. Stennik, 'Уроки Радищева' (20–37); A. Steingol'd, 'Воспроизведение драматического текста в критической статье' (172–80), A. Zhuravleva, 'Ранние статьи Аполлона Григорьева как источник книги В. В. Виноградова "Школа сентиментального натурализма"' (181–85); F. Kanunova, '"К русскому великану" Жуковского и "Море и утес" Тютчева (об общественной и историко-культурной концепции поэтов)' (220–29); N. A. Bogomolov, 'Батюшков, Мандельштам, Гумилев. Заметки к теме' (292–310).

NZSJ, 36, publishes a *Festschrift in honour of Arnold McMillin*, ed. I. Zohrab, and includes, among others, contributions by D. Prigov, 'Стихи к 60-летию А. Макмиллина' (1–2); V. Aksyonov, 'Англичанин и Эмигранты' (3–4); V. Bykov, 'The Traum Prison' (5–8); V. Voinovich, 'Поток сознания' (9–14); Z. Zinik, 'McDonalds of the World Unite!' (15–24); A. Maldzis, 'Only a proof copy remained' (155–58); N. Meshkovskaia, 'Чем белорусы отличаются от русских?' (159–72); F. Wigzell, 'Concepts of time in East Slavonic popular visions and dreams about visiting heaven and hell' (289–302).

2. Literary History

V. Vatsuro, *Готический роман в России* (Philologicheskoe nasledie), Mw, NLO, 543 pp., presents the author's views after 40 years of study on the works of Zhukovsky, Bestuzhev-Marlinsky, Bulgarin, Lermontov, and others. V. I. Sakharov, *Русская проза 18–19 веков. Проблемы истории и поэтики. Очерки*, Mw, IMLI RAN, 216 pp., discusses Odoevsky, Bestuzhev-Marlinsky, Polevoi, Gogol, Goncharov, Garshin, and Masonic writers of the 18th c. R. N. Kleimenova, *Общество любителей российской словесности: 1811-1830*, Mw, Academia, 624 pp. I. Gurvich, *Проблематичность в художественном мышлении: конец 18-20 вв.*, Tomsk, Vodolei, 256 pp. M. V. Stroganov, *Человек в русской литературе первой половины 19 века*, Tver' State Univ., 2001, 189 pp. M. L. Maiofis and A. R. Kurilkin, *Критика первой четверти 19 века*, Mw, AST, Olimp, 525 pp. *Русская критика середины 19 века*, ed. A. V. Osipova, Mw, Klassik Stil', 320 pp. E. Valeev, *Судьбою прерванный полет ... Г. П. Каменев в русской литературе рубежа 18-19 веков*, Kazan', Nasledie, 2001, 136 pp. *Забытые и второстепенные писатели 17-19 веков как явление европейской культурной жизни*, ed. N. L. Vershinina, 2 vols, Pskov, Pskovskii Tsentr narodnogo tvorchestva, 335, 190 pp., is a very interesting book in honour of Professor E. A. Maimin. V. P. Zverev, *Федор Глинка — русский духовный писатель*, Mw, Pashkov Dom, 542 pp. E. L. Afanasiev, *На пути к 19 веку: русская литература 70–х годов 18 века - 10–х годов 19 века*, Mw, IMLI RAN, 304 pp. M. M. Dunaev, *Вера в горниле сомнений: православие и русская литература в 17-20 веках*, Mw, Izdatel'stvo Soveta Russkoi Pravoslavnoi Tserkvi, 1056 pp.

3. Theory

General. *Теория литературы: литературный процесс*, vol. 4, ed. Iu. Borev, Mw, IMLI RAN–Nasledie, 2001, 654 pp., contains chapters by N. Gey, A. Mikhailov, A. Nebol'sin, I. Podgaetskaya, and L. Sazonova. *Три века метапоэтики: Легитимация дискурса: Антология:* vol. 1 : *17-19 вв.: Барокко, Классицизм, Сентиментализм. Романтизм. Реализм*, ed. K. E. Shtain, Stavropol', Knizhnoe izdatel'stvo, 702 pp., is the first volume of a four-volume work. V. E. Khalizev, *Теория литературы*, 3rd rev. edn, Mw, Vyshaia shkola, 437 pp. V. G. Zinchenko, V. G. Zusman, and Z. I. Kirnoze, *Методы изучения литературы. Системный подход*, Mw, Flinta–Nauka, 200 pp., discusses the 'word' as 'cultural archetype' as a basis for Prigozhin's approach to the humanities. *Литературоведение как проблема: Труды научного совета 'Наука о литературе в контексте науки о культуре': Памяти А. В. Михайлова посвящается*, ed. T. A. Kasatkina and E. G. Mestergazi, Mw, Nasledie, 2001, 600 pp. *Наука о литературе в 20 веке: история, методология, литературный процесс*, ed. A. A. Reviakina, Mw, INION RAN, 2001, 376 pp.

V. A. Domansky, *Литература и культура*, Mw, Flinta–Nauka, 368 pp. *Экфрасис в русской литературе: труды Лозаннского симпозиума*, ed. L. Heller, Mw, MIK, 216 pp., contains papers by L. Heller, 'Воскрешение понятия, или Слово об экфрасисе' (5–22); O. Kling, 'Топоэкфрасис: место действия как герой литературного произведения (возможности термина)' (97–110); V. Pozner, 'Кино-экфрасис. По поводу кино-комментария в России' (152–61); Zh. Hetteni, 'Экфраза о двух концах — теоретическом и практическом. Тезисы несостоявшегося доклада' (162–66); R. Bobryk, 'Схема и описание в научных текстах о живописи. Анализ или экфрасис?' (180–89). A. B. Esin, *Литературоведение. Культурология: Избранные труды*, Mw, Flinta–Nauka, 352 pp. O. A. Mel'nichuk, *Повествование от первого лица: интерпретация текста*, Mw State Univ., 207 pp. L. N. Dushina, *Русская поэзия и проза 19 века: ритмическая организация текста*, Saratov State Univ., 217 pp.

The text of the round table discussion 'Художественный образ в литературе и литературоведении (материалы "круглого стола")', is published in *LitU*, no.1 : 79–117. The speakers were V. Guminsky, L. Chernets, N. Gey, V. Khalizev, I. Rostovtseva, V. Dudarev, M. Lukanina, Ro Chzhi Iun, Iu. Nechiporenko, L. Sakson, A. Ivanov, A. Bol'shakova, L. Boldov, and Iu. Sebina.

V. Zhivov, 'Двуглавый орел в диалоге с литературой', *NovM*, no.2 : 174–83, is a review of Andrei Zorin's book *Кормя двуглавого орла . . . Литература и государственная идеология в России в последней трети 18 – первой трети 19 века* (Mw, 2001), but goes beyond being purely a review and contains very worthwhile discussion. A. Belokurova, 'Образ читателя', *LitU*, no.1 : 201–202. T. Davydova, 'Условность', *ib.*, no.2 : 165–69. A. Varlamov, 'Воплощение образа', *ib.*, no.3 : 88–91. O. P. Ermakova, 'Ирония и проблемы лексической семантики', *ISLIa*, no.4 : 30–36. S. B. Kurash, *Метафора и ее пределы: микроконтекст — текст — интертекст*, Mozyr', MozGPI, 2001, 121 pp. O. I. Revutsky, *Основы коммуникативно-смыслового анализа художественного текста*, 2nd rev. edn, Mozyr', MozGPI, 71 pp. V. F. Rusetsky, *Ключ к слову. Беседы о языке художественной литературы*, Minsk, Ekoperspektiva, 2000, 128 pp. A. Koriakovtsev, 'Карнавал языка: афоризм как литературный жанр', *Ural*, no.3 : 94–97. G. Tsiplakov, 'Свобода стиха и свободный стих', *NovM*, no.5 : 177–84. *Архетипические структуры художественного сознания, выпуск 3*, ed. V. V. Korona and E. K. Sozina, Ekaterinburg, Ural State Univ.,

219 pp. V. G. Zusman, *Диалог и концепт в литературе: литература и музыка,* Nizhnii Novgorod, Dekom, 2001, 167 pp.

THEORY OF GENRES. T. Davydova, 'Роман', *LitU*, no.2 : 198–201. T. Davydova, 'Повесть', *ib.*, no.5 : 202–05. T. Davydova, 'Жанры и антижанры', *ib.*, no.3 : 148–51. K. Violle and E. P. Grechanaia, 'Дневник в России в конце 18 —первой половине 19 века как автобиографическое пространство', *ISLIa*, no.3 : 18–36. M. Sverdlov, 'О жанровом мифе: что воспевает пиндарическая ода?', *VL*, no.6 : 103–26. T. Davydova and V. Pronin, 'Новелла, рассказ, очерк', *LitU*, no.6, 159–61. E. M. Bondarchuk, *Лирическая проза в историко-теоретическом освещении,* Samara State Univ., 35 pp. I. L. Al'mi, *О поэзии и прозе,* 2nd rev. edn, SPb, Semantika–Skifiia, 528 pp.

4. Romanticism

A. N. Girivenko, *Из истории русского художественного перевода первой половины 19 века: Эпоха романтизма,* Mw, Flinta–Nauka, 280 pp., discusses Zhukovsky, N. I. Gnedich, I. I. Kozlov, and D. P. Oznobishin. T. L. Shumkova, *Зарубежная и русская литература XIX века: Романтизм,* Mw, Flinta–Nauka, 240 pp. V. A. Osankina, *Русский романтизм как явление культуры. Направление, типология, метод, поэтика, опыт прочтения,* Cheliabinsk State Pedagogical Univ., 86 pp. V. A. Osankina, *Религиозные истоки эстетики и поэтики русского романтизма,* Cheliabinsk State Acad. of Culture and Arts, 232 pp. *Темница и свобода в художественном мире романтизма,* ed. N. A. Vishnevskaya and E. Iu. Saprykina, Mw, IMLI RAN, 350 pp.

5. Poetry

M. L. Gasparov, *Очерк истории русского стиха: метрика, ритмика, рифма, строфика,* Mw, Fortuna, 352 pp. is the 2nd rev. edn of a highly acclaimed book. O. I. Fedotov, *Основы русского стихосложения: Теория и история русского стиха,* 2 vols, Mw, Flinta–Nauka, vol. 1: *Метрика и ритмика,* 360 pp., vol. 2: *Строфика,* 488 pp. V. Veidle, *Эмбриология поэзии: Статьи по поэтике и теории искусства* (Studia Philologica), comp. and ed. I. A. Doronchenkov, Mw, Iazyki slavianskoi kul'tury, 456 pp. V. P. Zverev, Русские *поэты первой половины 19 века: очерки жизни и творчества с приложением избранных стихов и библиографических справок,* Mw, Russkii put', 368 pp. V. E. Kholshevnikov, *Основы стиховедения. Русское стихосложение,* 4th rev. edn, Mw, Academia — SPb State

Univ., 203 pp. N. F. Alefirenko, *Поэтическая энергия слова: Синергетика языка, сознания и культуры*, Mw, Academia, 394 pp. Ia. Markovich, 'Заметки о лирической поэзии', *LitU*, no.2:51–77. A. Bubnov, '"Двояковыпуклая речь" (Этюд о палиндромии)', *ib.*, no.3:134–37. M. I. Shapir, 'Нечто о "механизме российских стихов", или Почему Онегин не мог отличить ямб от хорея', *ISLIa*, no.5:41–43. *К 200-летию Боратынского. Сборник материалов международной научной конференции*, ed. S. G. Bocharov, Mw, IMLI RAN, 367 pp. L. Lutsevich, *Псалтырь в русской поэзии*, SPb, Dmitrii Bulanin, 608 pp. V. D. Skvoznikov, *Русская лирика: развитие реализма*, Mw, IMLI RAN, 162 pp. V. P. Okeansky, *Поэтика пространства в русской метафизической лирике 19 века: Е. А. Баратынский, А. С. Хомяков, Ф. И. Тютчев*, Ivanovo State Univ., 203 pp. *Стиховедение*, ed. L. E. Liapina, Mw, Flinta–Nauka, 248 pp., is an anthology which may be useful for young scholars. The memoirs of Sologub were published a few years ago and should be noted: V. Sologub, *Воспоминания*, Mw, Slovo, 1998, 384 pp.

6. Comparative Studies

K. Iu. Lappo-Danilevsky, 'Шевырев и Винкельман', *RusL*, no.2:3–27. A. S. Petrikovskaya, *Российское эхо в культуре Австралии: XIX – первая половина XX века*, Mw, IV RAN, 200 pp.

7. Individual Authors

BATIUSHKOV. Very interesting materials are published by T. L. Latypova, 'Подробные сведения о последних днях Константина Николаевича Батюшкова', *NN*, no.61:75–79. M. V. Stroganov, 'Речь о влиянии легкой поэзии Батюшкова на язык Пушкина', Serebrennikov, *Время*, 62–69.

BELINSKY. E. Iu. Tikhonova, *Человек без маски: Личность В. Г. Белинского в его переписке*, Mw, URSS, 174 pp.

BORATYNSKY (BARATYNSKY). *К 200-летию Боратынского: Сборник материалов международной научной конференции (Москва–Мураново, 21–23 февраля 2000 г.)*, ed. I. A. Pil'shchikov, Mw, IMLI RAN, 367 pp., contains studies by M. Shapir, O. Zyrianov, L. Deriugina, A. Kushner, and I. Kyblanovsky. See also the very interesting work by Grigorii Osipovich Vinokur, 'Boratynsky i simvolisty', republished in this book (111–35) with comments by S. G. Bocharov. A. Mashevsky, 'Вопросы Боратынского', *Literatura*, no.14:7–8. V. S. Baevsky, 'О предыстории стихотворения

Баратынского "Подражателям" ("Когда печалью вдохновенный ...")', Serebrennikov, *Время*, 131–33. L. G. Frizman, 'Баратынский и крепостное право', *ib.*, 134–42.

BULGARIN. N. N. Akimova, *Ф. В. Булгарин: литературная репутация и культурный миф*, Khabarovsk State Pedagogical Univ., 183 pp.

DEL'VIG. S. Levitskaia, *Здравствуй, мой Дельвиг!*, Ekaterinburg, Bank kul'turnoi informatsii, 2001, 199 pp. A. M. Beloshchin, '"Протекших дней очарованья" (О поэтике романсов А. А. Дельвига)', *RRe*, no.4: 3–8.

DERZHAVIN. N. P. Morozova, 'О последнем стихотворении Г. Р. Державина', *RusL*, no.2: 137–68. N. L. Vasil'ev, 'Г. Р. Державин и Н. Е. Струйский (Об одном из возможных источников предсмертного стихотворения Державина)', *ISLIa*, no.2: 44–50.

GOGOL. *Трудный Путь: зарубежная Россия и Гоголь, из наследия русской эмиграции*, ed. M. D. Filin, Mw, Russkii mir, 445 pp. Iu. Mann, 'Заметки о 'неевклидовой геометрии' Гоголя, или "Сильные кризисы, чувствуемые целою массою"', *VL*, no.4: 170–200. V. A. Voropaev has written several deep studies on Gogol's spiritual life: *Гоголь над страницами духовных книг*, Mw, Makarievskii fond, 205 pp.; 'Николай Гоголь. Опыт духовной биографии', *LitU*, no.1: 118–79; *ib.*, no.2: 87–146. D. Bykov, 'Гоголевский проезд. Магистральный русский путь (К 150-летию со дня смерти Гоголя)', *Ogonyok*, no.15: 23–24. V. Guminsky, 'Гоголь. Александр I и Наполеон. К 150-летию со дня смерти писателя и к 190-летию Отечественной войны 1812 г.', *NSo*, no.3: 216–31. B. I. Matveev, 'Античные образы в произведениях Н. В. Гоголя', *RRe*, no.2: 3–9. V. Tomachinsky, 'Стилистический синтез Гоголя', *Kontinent*, 114: 372–84. V. A. Voropaev, 'Малоизвестная часть творческого наследия Н. В. Гоголя: выписки из творений святых отцов и богослужебных книг', Serebrennikov, *Время*, 162–71. N. N. Mostovskaya and Kyon Kan Yn, 'Творчество Гоголя и эстетика абсурда (некоторые наблюдения)', *ib.*, 155–61. *Н. В. Гоголь: загадка третьего тысячелетия: Первые Гоголевские чтения*, ed. V. L. Vikulova, Mw, Knizhnyi dom universitet, 296 pp. V. G. Gippius, *Гоголь: воспоминания, письма, дневники*, Mw, Agraf, 1999, 459 pp. Iu. Mann, 'Пишу и сжигаю: к 150-летию со дня смерти Гоголя', *NG*, no.50: 4–5, where the interviewer was A. Shchuplov.

V. A. Voropaev, 'Мертвые души: кто они? (О названии поэмы Н. В. Гоголя)', *RRe*, no.3: 10–13. Id., 'Пословицы и притчи в "Мертвых душах" Н. В. Гоголя', *RRe*, no.2: 96–102. L. Aizerman, 'Павел Иванович Чичиков на рубеже веков и тысячелетий',

Russkaia Slovesnost, no.3 : 21–27. A. Kh. Goldenberg, 'Традиции народной песни в поэтике "Мертвых душ"', *ib.*, no.7 : 5–18.

V. Sh. Krivonos, 'Сон Тараса в структуре повести *Тараса Бульба*', *ISLIa,* no.4 : 10–18. V. A. Voropaev, '"На зеркало неча пенять . . .": Смысл эпиграфа и "немой сцены" в комедии Н. В. Гоголя *Ревизор*', *RRe,* no.6 : 9–15. K. A. Grimstad, '"No sissy stuff!": the en-gendering significance of Polishness in Gogol's *Taras Bulba*', *NZSJ*, 36 : 115–28. I. F. Zamanova and N. V. Bardykova, *'Вечера на хуторе близ Диканьки' Н. В. Гоголя: пространство и время*, Belgorod State Univ., 2001, 160 pp. *Феномен 'Шинели' Н. В. Гоголя в свете философского миросозерцания писателя*, ed. Iu. I. Miroshnikov and O. V. Zyrianov, Ekaterinburg, UrORAN, 211 pp.

GRIBOEDOV. *'Век нынешний и век минувший . . .': комедия А. С. Грибоедова 'Горе от ума' в русской критике и литературоведении,* ed. M. Ia. Bilinkis, SPb, Azbuka-klassika, 448 pp. S. Drugoveiko-Dolzhanskaya, '"Взгляд и нечто" об искусстве компромиссов в искусстве', *Neva,* no.12: 176–79, is a new and modern interpretation of the character Chatsky. Iu. V. Lebedev, '"Загадка" "Горя от ума" А. С. Грибоедова', Serebrennikov, *Время*, 48–53. M. Hobson, 'A poem of the utmost significance: *Gore ot uma (Woe from Wit)*', *NZSJ*, 36 : 129–42. V. G. Kostomarov and N. D. Burvikova, *Читая и почитая Грибоедова*, Mw, Russkii iazyk, 1998, 78 pp.

KRYLOV. M. A. Gordin, *Жизнь Ивана Крылова,* Mw, Terra, 2001, 334 pp.

KUKOL'NIK. An extremely important publication is that of the diaries of Nestor Kukol'nik, 'Дневник', *Sklianka Chasu*, nos 21–22, published by A. Nikolaenko.

LERMONTOV. A. I. Zhuravleva, *Лермонтов в русской литературе: Проблемы поэтики*, Mw, Progress-Traditsiia, 288 pp. S. G. Semenova, 'Вестничество Лермонтова', *Chelovek*, no.1 : 169–85; no.2 : 160–78. V. I. Zagorul'ko and E. P. Abramov, *Поручик Лермонтов: Страницы военной биографии поэта*, SPb, Prosveschenie, 175 pp. S. N. Zotov, *Художественное пространство мира Лермонтова*, Tagangor State Pedagogical Univ., 2001, 321 pp. T. Mel'nikova, *И дышит непонятная святая прелесть в них . . .: Рассказы о реликвиях Лермонтовского музея-заповедника*, Penza, Penzenskaya Pravda, 176 pp. *'Этот край . . . моя Отчизна!': Лермонтовский музей-заповедник 'Тарханы'*, ed. L. Polukarova and E. Shpikalova, Mw, Voskresenie, 159 pp. *М. Ю. Лермонтов: pro et contra: Личность и творчество Михаила Лермонтова в оценке русских мыслителей и исследователей: антология (Русский путь)*, comp. and ed. V. M. Arkovich and G. E. Potapova, SPb, RkhGI, 1080 pp. P. Meyer, 'An author of his time: Lermontov rewrites

George Sand', *NZSJ*, 36:173–82. A. A. Diakina, *Духовное наследие М. Ю. Лермонтова и поэзия Серебряного века*, Mw Pedagogical Univ., 2001, 239 pp. A. A. Diakina, *Природа и человек в поэтической картине М. Ю. Лермонтова и В. В. Хлебникова*, Ielets State Univ., 2001, 102 pp.

There are three studies of '*Герой нашего времени*': V. Mil'don, 'Лермонтов и Киркегор: феномен Печорина. Об одной русско-датской параллели', *Oktjabr'*, no.4:177–86; O. E. Frolova, 'Предвиденное и непредвиденное в романе М. Ю. Лермонтова "Герой нашего времени"', *RRe*, no.2:10–16; D. A. Goldfarb, 'Lermontov and the omniscience of narrators', *Philosophy and Literature*, 20, 1996:61–74, which explores the range of constraints and the effects of the narrator's fictional power and knowledge; Lermontov's novel *A Hero of Our Time* is chosen as a test case.

ODOEVSKY. A. M. Beloshchin, 'И чувства жар, и мыслей свет . . . (О лирике А. И. Одоевского)', *RRe*, no.6:3–8.

POLEVOI. *Литературные взгляды и творчество Н. А. Полевого*, ed. A. S. Kurilov, Mw, IMLI RAN, 216 pp.

PUSHKIN. A very useful reference guide is G. G. Martynov, *Библиография пушкинской библиографии: 1846–2001*, SPb, Aton, 544 pp. O. S. Soina, 'Судьба Пушкина и судьба России', *Chelovek*, no.5:42–53. S. Nebol'sin, 'Пушкин и Россия', *NSo*, no.6:246–57. E. M. Vereshchagin and V. G. Kostomarov, 'Пушкинский Молок и ветхозаветный Молох', *RRe*, no.3:3–6. I. Ermachenko, 'Пушкин как Сталин. Метаморфозы тоталитаризма в постмодернистской поэзии', Eimermacher, *Культура*, 177–208. W. Kasack, 'Смерть в творчестве Пушкина', *NZh*, 228:259–79. N. Lobanov-Rostovsky, 'Улыбка Пушкина', *ib.*, 280–89. A. Baldin, 'Месторождение Александра Пушкина', *Oktjabr'*, no.2:117–45. J. Love, 'Parody as polemos in Pushkin's *The Shot*', *CSP*, 44:61–78, concerns Pushkin's parodic praxis: the duels as the central figuration of polemical parody. I. Budylin, *Деревенский Пушкин: Пушкинские места Псковского края*, Mw, Profizdat, 384 pp. *Пушкин и его современники*, vol. 42, ed. S. A. Fomichev, V. D. Rak, and E. O. Larionova, SPb, Akademicheskii Proekt, 443 pp. S. Iu. Poroikov, *Неизвестный Пушкин: философия писателя в свете раннехристианского наследия*, Mw, Muravei, 144 pp. A. Rogachevski, 'Hunting Pushkin's sources: a note on methodology', *NZSJ*, 36:237–42. *Пушкинский альманах (1799–2001)*, ed. A. A. Asoian, Omsk State Pedagogical Univ., 2001, 180 pp. *Пушкинские чтения — 2002*, SPb, Leningrad Regional State Univ., 247 pp. *Пушкин и Торжок*, ed. T. V. Gorokh, Tver', Liliia, 206 pp. *Пушкин на порога 21 века: провинциальный контекст, выпуск 4*, ed. E. P. Titkov, Arzamas State Pedagogical Inst., 212 pp. *Михайловская пушкиниана: по материалам конференции 'Столица и усадьба: два дома русской культуры', выпуск 23*, Mw, Infokonsalting, 187 pp. N. P. Pishchulin, *Философия А. С. Пушкина*, Mw, Zhizn' i mysl', 159 pp. R. T. Pevtsova, *А. С. Пушкин и религия*, Mw, Al'fa, 2001, 42 pp. G. P. Vdovykin, *Поездки А. С. Пушкина по Подмосковью*, Mw, Sputnik+ , 61 pp. A. P. Rassadin, *Последний из пушкинской плеяды,* Ul'ianovsk, Simbirskaia kniga, 198 pp. S. N. Broitman, *Тайная поэтика Пушкина,* Tver' State Univ., 110 pp. E. Vatsuro, *Лирика пушкинской поры: 'Элегическая школа'*, 2nd rev. edn, SPb, Nauka, 240 pp. *Пушкин через двести лет,* ed. V. S. Nepomniashchii and S. D. Selivanova, Mw, IMLI RAN, 416 pp. *Временник пушкинской комиссии, выпуск 28*, ed. V. P. Stark, SPb, Nauka, 368 pp. *А. С. Пушкин и Московский университет*, ed. V. B. Kataev, Mw State Univ., 1999, 51 pp. V. Sukailo, *Симбиряне в жизни и творчестве А. С. Пушкина,* Ulianovsk, Korporatsiia tekhnologii prodvizheniia, 2001, 621 pp. N. M. Gordeev and V. P. Peshkov, *Тамбовская тропинка к Пушкину,* 3rd rev. edn, Tambov State Univ., 1999, 219 pp. *Прогулки по пушкинской Москве,* ed. A. Ia. Nevsky, Mw, Interbuk-biznes, 1999, 79 pp. V. I. Shcherbachenko, *Пушкины в Сибири,* SPb, Istoricheskii Illiustrator, 1999, 60 pp. A. P. Zakharov, *На неведомых дорожках: Пушкин и сказочная Сибирь*, 2nd rev. edn, Tiumen' State Univ., 1999, 234 pp. *Творчество А. С. Пушкина: Вопросы содержания и поэтики,* ed. Iu. A. Dvoriashin, Surgut State Pedagogical Inst., 2001, 104 pp. *Пушкин,* ed. M. L. Remneva, Mw State Univ., 1999, 277 pp. *Пушкин А. С. Переводы и подражания: комментированное издание с текстами источников на языке оригинала,* comp. K. N. Atarova and G. A. Lesskis, Mw, Raduga, 1999, 447 pp. V. A. Grekhnev, *В созвездье Пушкина,* Nizhnii Novgorod, Begemot, 1999, 93 pp. *Наш Пушкин: юбилейный сборник статей и материалов,* ed. S. N. Tiapkov, Ivanovo State Univ., 1999, 185 pp. V. V. Chubukov, *Всенародный памятник Пушкину,* Mw, Tverskaia 13, 1999, 153 pp. V. A. Kurbatov, *Домовой: Семен Степанович Гейченко: Письма и разговоры,* Pskov, Gosudarstvennyi muzei-zapovednik Mikhailovskoe, 80 pp. I. Ustiian, *Пушкин и политэкономия: от революционного романтизма к экономическому реформизму,* Kishinev, Cartea Moldovei, 426 pp. *Московский Пушкинист–X: ежегодный сборник,* ed. V. S. Nepomniashchii, Mw, IMLI RAN, 408 pp.

Two biographies have appeared: D. N. Chernigovsky, *Проблема создания биографии А. С. Пушкина в СССР и русском зарубежье в 20–30-е годы,* Mw, Prometei, 171 pp.; and *Летопись жизни и творчества Александра Пушкина в четырех томах*, ed. M. A. Tsyavlovsky, 4 vols, 1: 1799–1824, 2: 1825–28, 3: 1829–32, 4:

1833–37, Mw, SLOVO, 1999, 875, 246, 287, 367 pp., which is probably the most complete biography of P.

A. S. Mel′nikov, *Друзья! Вам сердце оставляю . . . Хроника жизни и творчества А. С. Пушкина*, Mw, Olma, 1999, 446 pp. E. A. Riabtsev, *113 прелестниц Пушкина*, Mw, AST, 1999, 508 pp. V. Alekseev, *Графы Воронцовы, Воронцовы-Дашковы в истории России*, Mw, Tsentrpoligraf, 462 pp. V. A. Udovik, *Е. К. Воронцова и А. С. Пушкин*, SPb, Vorontsovskoe obshchestvo, 36 pp. G. Sedova and L. Soldatova, *Особняк на Мойке*, 12, SPb, Beloe i chernoe, 1999, 126 pp. I. Budylin, *Деревенский Пушкин: Пушкинские места Псковского края*, Mw, Profizdat, 384 pp. *Пушкинский трилистник*, ed. L. Romanova and V. Kal'pidi, Cheliabinsk, Cheliabinskii fond kul′tury, 1999, 299 pp. N. I. Granovskaya, *Вместе с Пушкинъм от Царского Села до Михайловского*, SPb, Notabene, 1999, 213 pp. S. Belov, *Пушкинские места Подмосковья*, Istra, MOK Tsentr, 1998, 59 pp. *Тысячелетнее древо А. С. Пушкина: корни и крона*, ed. L. A. Trubacheva, Mw, Libereia, 1998, 87 pp. V. M. Fridkin, *Дорога на Черную речку*, Mw, Vagrius, 1999, 445 pp. I. Surat and S. Bocharov, *Пушкин: Краткий очерк жизни и творчества* (Studia philologica), Mw, Iazyki Slavianskoi Kul′tury, 240 pp. A. Tyrkova-Williams, *Жизнь Пушкина*, 2 vols, vol. 1: 1799—1824, vol. 2: 1824—1837, 3rd rev. edn, Mw, MG, 471, 514 pp. V. Baevsky, 'Новые документы о жизни и смерти Пушкина', *VL*, no. 2 : 135–56.

V. I. Kuleshov, *А. С. Пушкин: научно-художественная биография*, 2nd rev. edn, Mw, MAKS, 426 pp. '*К привычкам бытия вновь чувствую любовь': гастрономические пристрастия Пушкина*, Saransk, Krasnyi Oktiabr', 126 pp. G. Mitin, *Солнце поэзии: лицейские годы в творчестве Александра Пушкина (1813–1817)*, Mw, Moscow Writers' Organization, 190 pp. V. N. Bochkov, *Костромские спутники Пушкина*, Kostroma, Gubernskii Dom, 175 pp. V. A. Kozeev, *Пушкин — питомец и ценитель чистых муз*, SPb, 2001, 103 pp. Id., *Пушкин и декабристы*, SPb, 2001, 105 pp. N. F. Shakhmagonov, *Пушкин и русские монархи: соратники или враги?*, Mw, Sokol, 1999, 47 pp. V. P. Kazarin and P. V. Kon'kov, *Памятники, памятные знаки и памятные места в Крыму, связанные с А. С. Пушкиным*, Simferopol', Krymskii arkhiv, 64 pp. V. I. Korovin, *А. С. Пушкин в жизни и творчестве*, Mw, Russkoe slovo, 88 pp. N. K. Mal′kova, *С Пушкиным по Большой Морской*, SPb, Izdatel′stvo N. Kupriianova, 222 pp.

Studies on *Evgenii Onegin* include M. I. Shapir, '*Евгений Онегин*: проблема аутентичного текста', *ISLIa*, no. 3 : 3–17, and the same author's 'Какого *Онегина* мы читаем?' *NovM*, no. 6 : 147–65. V. G. Dolgushev, 'Комическое в романе *Евгений Онегин*', *RRe*, no. 3 : 7–9. S. A. Fomichev, 'Об эпиграфах ко второй главе

Евгения Онегина', Serebrennikov, *Время*, 95–101. V. Iu. Kozmin, '"Себя в коня преобразив ...": из комментариев к *Евгению Онегину*', *ib.*, 102–109. A. A. Mushnikov, *'Евгений Онегин' как трагедия непонимания: опыт прочтения*, Mw, Triada Plius, 125 pp. There is a fabulous selection of parodies on *Evgenii Onegin*: *Судьба Онегина,* comp. V. and A. Nevskikh, Mw, Iskusstvo, 2001, 432 pp.

N. E. Miasoedov, *Пушкинские замыслы. Опыт реконструкции*, SPb, Spetslit, 279 pp., provides a commentary on Pushkin's drafts and notes on uncompleted works. N. Cornwell, '"You've heard of the Count Saint-Germain", in P.'s *The Queen of Spades* and far beyond', *NZSJ*, 36:49–66. A. Marchenko, 'Пушкин. *Осень*. Опыт медленного чтения', *LitU*, no:4:156–78. V. D. Rak, 'К датировке пушкинского стихотворения *Обвал*', *RusL*, no.3:106–12. V. Esipov, '"Необычные, неправдоподобные» ситуации в «Повестях Белкина"', *VL*, no.3:304–12. L. Kogan, '"И внял я неба содроганье ..." (О философии пушкинского "Пророка")', *VL*, no.4:201–30. B. Sarnov, 'Бывают странные сближения. "Медный всадник". Взгляд из двадцать первого века', *VL*, no.5:45–74. A. Solomin, 'Тайный смысл "маленьких трагедий"', *Pod'em*, 2001, nos.11–12:89–101; D. N. Medrish, 'Народно-поэтические мотивы в стихотворении *Зимнее утро* А. С. Пушкина', *RRe*, no.1:108–12. A. Bazhenov, '"Схождение во ад" как творческая задача Пушкина: К вопросу о "Гавриилиаде"', *NSo*, no.1:96–110. M. Altshuller, 'Незаконченная поэма Пушкина о Тазите', *NZh*, 226:205–23. M. V. Sdobnov, 'К истокам пушкинской "Русалки" (1819)', Serebrennikov, *Время*, 70–81. T. G. Mal'chukova, 'Об одном гомеровском образе в поэзии А. С. Пушкина', *ib.*, 82–94. N. L. Vershinina, 'К проблеме "эпического" и "исторического" времени в прозе А. С. Пушкина конца 1820-х —1830-х гг.', *ib.*, 110–17. A. F. Belousov, 'Источник "Вод глубоких ..."', *ib.*, 118–20. S. V. Denisenko, 'Бланманже синее, красное и полосатое, или Водевильный Пушкин (Переделки пушкинской "Барышни-крестьянки" для сцены в XIX веке)', *ib.*, 121–30.

R. V. Ovchinnikov, *По страницам исторической прозы А. С. Пушкина*, Mw, IRI RAN, 294 pp. I. A. Pil'shchikov and M. I. Shapir have edited and commented on P.'s erotic works in their *А. С. Пушкин. Тень Баркова: Тексты. Комментарии. Экскурсы* (Philologica russica et speculative, 2), Mw, Iazyki Slavianskoi Kul'tury, 497 pp. O. Proskurin, *Поэзия Пушкина, или Подвижный Палимпсест,* Mw, NLO, 1999, 462 pp., contains 5 chapters: 'Мнимая поэма: *Руслан и Людмила*', 'Юг как эксперимент', 'Роман о стихах: судьбы поэтических жанров в *Евгении*

Онегине', 'Трансформация жанров в поэзии конца 1820–х годов', 'Метаморфозы *чужого слова* в лирике 1830–х годов'. V. A. Lukov and Vl. A. Lukov, *'Маленькие трагедии' А. С. Пушкина: философия, композиция, стиль*, Mw State Pedagogical Univ., 1999, 205 pp. V. L. Savel'zon, *Пушкин и Оренбуржье: над страницами 'Капитанской дочки' и 'Истории Пугачева'*, 2nd rev. edn, Orenburg, Iuzhnyi Ural, 408 pp.

Comparative studies on P. and other writers include M. Tarlinskaya, 'Через Гете и Байрона — к Пушкину: история одной межъязыковой формулы', *ISLIa*, no.2:26–33; G. V. Krasnov, 'Два финала: *Горе от ума* и *Евгений Онегин*', Serebrennikov, *Время*, 54–61; I. V. Fomenko, *Три статьи о поэтике: Пушкин, Тютчев, Бродский*, Tver′ State Univ., 40 pp.; Iu. L. Prokushev, *Пушкин и Есенин: есенинский сборник: Новое о Есенине, выпуск 5*, Mw, Nasledie, 2001, 232 pp.; V. M. Rusakov, *О лже-потомках А. С. Пушкина: и не только о них*, Pskov, Gosudarstvennyi muzei-zapovednik Mikhailovskoe, 134 pp.; M. Lazutkina, *Самозванец Лжедмитрий I между А. С. Пушкиным и Ф. В. Булгариным: Опыт сравнительного анализа художественного образа Лжедмитрия I в трагедии 'Борис Годунов' и в романе 'Димитрий Самозванец'*, Mw, Sputnik+ , 56 pp.; *Пушкин и античность*, ed. I. V. Shtal', Mw, Nasledie, 2001, 139 pp.; V. M. Mul'tatuli, *Пушкин во французских переводах: соотношения ритмических форм русского и французского стихосложения*, SPb State Univ. for Culture and Arts, 120 pp.; V. A. Sirenok, *Радищев и Пушкин*, Sochi, RIO SGUTiKD, 51 pp.

ZHUKOVSKY. H. Gemba, 'Questions without answers? On verse melody in Zhukovskii's poetic works', *NZSJ*, 36:89–100. N. M. Kopytseva, *Душа его возвысилась до строю . . . К 220–летию со дня рождения В. А. Жуковского*, Velikii Novgorod State Univ., 80 pp.

LITERATURE, 1848–1917

By Boris Lanin, *Professor of Literature, Russian Academy of Education, Moscow*

1. General

S. Lurie, *Успехи ясновидения*, SPb, Pushkinskii Fond, 256 pp., is a brilliantly written literary 'investigation' of Zhukovsky, Del′vig, Gogol, Goncharov, Annensky, Blok, Pasternak, and others. V. B. Kataev, *Игра в осколки: судьбы русской классики в эпоху постмодернизма*, Mw State Univ., 252 pp. Chzhang Khan Ik, *Проблема мессианства в русской литературе*, Mw, Sputnik+, 107 pp. Iu. A. Fedosiuk, *Что непонятно у классиков, или Энциклопедия русского быта XIX века*, 5th rev. edn, Mw, Flinta–Nauka, 264 pp., is a very useful reference book for scholars of Russian 19th-c. literature and culture. L. Sapchenko, 'Сумасшедший дом в произведениях русской литературы (От Карамзина к Чехову)', *VL*, no.6:342–53. A. V. Gromov-Kolli, 'Путевая проза русских писателей первой трети XX века', *RRe*, no.5:24–30. O. M. Chupasheva, '"Легче держать вожжи, чем бразды правления." (О грамматической форме афоризмов Козьмы Пруткова)', *RRe*, no.2:17–21. A. V. Safronov, *Виноватые, отверженные, несчастные: проблемы преступления и наказания в русской художественной документалистике конца 19 – начала 20 века*, Riazan' State Pedagogical Univ., 2001, 123 pp. L. A. Sapchenko, *Карамзин и русская литература второй половины 19 века*, Ulianovsk State Univ., 2001, 109 pp.

Проблемы художественного миромоделирования в русской литературе: выпуск 6, ed. A. V. Urmanov and S. I. Krasovskaia, Blagoveshchensk State Pedagogical Univ., 85 pp. L. V. Zhigach, *Формула русской идеи. Опыт прочтения идеи 'народной правды' на рубеже эпох: Пушкин — Достоевский — Л. Толстой — Блок*, Tver' State Univ., 1999, 264 pp. *А. Н. Толстой: новые материалы и исследования: ранний А. Н. Толстой и его литературное окружение*, Mw, IMLI RAN, 243 pp. L. N. Savina, *Проблематика и поэтика автобиографических повестей о детстве второй половины 19 века (Л. Н. Толстой 'Детство', С. Т. Аксаков 'Детские годы Багрова-внука', Н. Г. Гарин-Михайловский 'Детство Темы')*, Volgograd, Peremena, 282 pp. A. Dolin, *Пророк в своем Отечестве: профетические, мессианские, эсхатологические мотивы в русской поэзии и общественной мысли*, Mw, Nasledie, 319 pp. *Литература и христианство: К 2000-летию христианства*, ed. N. V. Bardykova, Belgorod State Univ., 2001, 123 pp. *Словарь литературных персонажей: герои литературных произведений. Сюжетные линии,* ed. V. P. Meshcheriakov, Smolensk, Rusich, 2001, 622 pp. A. L. Iastrebov, *Богатство и бедность: поэзия и проза денег*, Mw, Agraf, 524 pp. *Тыняновский сборник: выпуск 11*, ed. M. O. Chudakova, Mw, Ogi, 992 pp. *Христианство и русская литература, выпуск 4*, ed. V. A. Kotel'nikov, SPb, Nauka, 535 pp.

G. Safran, *Rewriting the Jew: Assimilation Narratives in the Russian Empire,* Stanford U.P., 2000, 269 + xvii pp., contains four chapters: 'An unprecedented type of human being: Grigory Bogrov' (26–62), 'The nation and the wide world: Eliza Orzeszkowa' (63–107), 'Jew as a text, Jew as a reader: Nikolai Leskov' (108–46), 'Mutable, permutable, approximate, and relative: Anton Chekhov' (147–89). The book examines narratives of Jewish assimilation, and introduces English-language readers to works that were much discussed in their own time. The author situates Jewish and non-Jewish writers together in the context they shared.

2. Literary History

Летопись литературных событий в России конца 19 – начала 20 в. 1891 —октябрь 1917, выпуск 1: 1891 —1900, ed. M. G. Petrova, Mw, IMLI RAN, 528 pp., is a very useful reference book for scholars. *Литература и история: исторический процесс в творческом сознании русских писателей и мыслителей 18–20 веков,* ed. Iu. V. Stennik, SPb, Nauka, 328 pp.

On criticism: E. V. Ivanova, *Критика начала 20 века*, AST, Olimp, 432 pp. O. G. Egorov, *Дневники русских писателей 19 века*, Mw, Flinta–Nauka, 286 pp. O. V. Sergeev and V. V. Prozorov, *История русской литературной критики*, Mw, Vyshaia Shkola, 297 pp. N. A. Berdiaev, *Sub specie aeternitatis. Опыты философские, социальные и литературные. 1900–1906 гг.*, comp. and comm. V. V. Sapov, Mw, Kanon–Reabilitatsiia, 656 pp. *Критика 40-х годов XIX века,* ed. L. I. Sobolev, Mw, AST–Olimp, 413 pp. *Критика 50-х годов XIX века,* ed. L. I. Sobolev, Mw, AST–Olimp, 520 pp. *Критика русского символизма,* ed. N. A. Bogomolov, 2 vols, Mw, AST–Olimp, 396, 441 pp. *Критика 70-х годов XIX века*, ed. S. F. Dmitrenko, Mw, AST–Olimp, 464 pp.

Поэтика Л. Андреева и художественная картина мира в XX веке, SPb, Nauka, 167 pp. V. A. Keldysh, *Русская литература рубежа веков: 1890-е —начало 1920-х годов*, vol. 1, Mw, Nasledie, 2001, 688 pp. G. V. Nefed'ev, 'Русский символизм и розенкрейцерство. Статья вторая', *NLO*, 56: 149–78. A. V. Vislova, *'Серебряный век' как театр: феномен театральности в культуре рубежа 19–20 веков*, Gosudarstvennyi Institut Kul'tury, 2000, 212 pp. S. G. Isaev, *'Сознанию незнаемая мощь': Поэтика условных форм в русской литературе начала 20 века*, Novgorod Velikii, Novgorodskii Univ., 2001, 213 pp. V. V. Petrochenkov, *Драма Страстей Христовых: К. Р. 'Царь Иудейский'*, SPb, Zhurnal 'Neva', 288 pp. *Алексей Ремизов — узник снов: поэтика сновидений в прозе А. М. Ремизова 1890–1910-х годов*, Mw Pedagogical Univ., 358 pp.

3. Theory

E. Orlova, '"Меж контуром и запахом цветка" (Из истории методологических исканий 1910–х годов)', *VL*, no.4:136–69. V. V. Polonsky, 'Изучение русской литературы рубежа 19–20 веков и современная академическая наука', *ISLIa*, no.5:3–18. N. Bogomolov, 'Авантюрный роман как зеркало русского символизма', *VL*, no.6:43–56. K. Eimermacher, *Знак. Текст. Культура*, Mw, RGGU, 2001, 394 pp. I. V. Samorukova, *Дискурс — художественное высказывание — литературное произведение: типология и структура эстетической деятельности*, Samara State Univ., 203 pp. I. G. Riabii and M. M. Riabii, *Жанры народной прозы*, Khanty-Mansiisk, Poligrafist, 409 pp. V. V. Kurilov, *Теория литературы в системе литературоведения*, Mw, Ekon-inform, 63 pp. N. Z. Kokovina, *Этико-аксиологические аспекты памяти в образной структуре художественного произведения*, Kursk State Pedagogical Univ., 2001, 188 pp. O. V. Miroshnikova, *Лирическая книга: архитектоника и поэтика (на материале поэзии последней трети 19 века)*, Omsk State Univ., 139 pp. L. O. Butakova, *Авторское сознание в поэзии и прозе: когнитивное моделирование*, Barnaul, Altay State Univ., 2001, 282 pp. V. E. Vetlovskaya, *Анализ эпического произведения: проблемы поэтики*, SPb, Nauka, 213 pp. N. A. Gavrilenko, *Программа 'чистого искусства' в русской критико-эстетической мысли середины 19 века*, Mw State Open Pedagogical Univ., 2001, 249 pp. M. M. Girshman, *Литературное произведение: теория художественной целостности*, Mw, Iazyki Slavianskoi Kul′tury, 527 pp. A. B. Esin, *Психологизм русской классической литературы*, 2nd rev. edn, Mw, Flinta–Moscow Inst. for Psychology, 174 pp. E. Kurganov, *Анекдот — символ — миф*, SPb, Izdatel′stvo Zvezda, 127 pp. L. G. Kikhney, *Акмеизм: миропонимание и поэтика*, Mw, MAKS, 2001, 183 pp.

4. Poetry

O. S. Kriukova, *Италия в русской поэзии XIX века*, Mw, Editorial URSS, 144 pp. V. A. Sarychev, *Кубофутуризм и кубофутуристы: эстетика, творчество, эволюция*, Lipetsk, Lipetskoe izdatel′stvo,

2000, 254 pp. M. Shvets, *Технология русского стихосложения*, SPb, Leks Star, 96 pp.

5. Comparative Studies

S. M. Klimova, 'Эссенция и экзистенция Любви: "Дух" и "Запах" (Вл. Соловьев и "Парфюмер" П. Зюскинда)', *RusL*, no.4 : 20–29. G. A. Time, 'О "метафизике" любви: А Шопенгауэр и Вл. Соловьев', *RusL*, no.2 : 58–68. V. A. Nedzvetsky, 'Жорж Санд и русские классики 19 века (параллели и реминисценции', *ISLIa*, no.2 : 16–25. S. Povartsov, 'Мережковский, Уэллс и красная звезда', *VL*, no.6 : 168–86. S. I. Ketchian, *Keats and the Russian Poets* (Birmingham Slavonic Monographs, 33), Birmingham Univ., Department of Russian, 2001, viii + 308 pp., makes a highly significant contribution to studies on Russian poetry. K. writes about Pushkin, Fet, Annenskii, Gumilev, Briusov, Blok, and Akhmatova. *Россия и Франция: тема города в литературе, истории, культуре*, SPb State Univ., 66 pp. O. B. Kafanova, *Жорж Санд и русская литература 19 века: мифы и реальность, 1830–1860 гг*, Tomsk State Pedagogical Univ., 1998, 410 pp.

6. Major Writers

chekhov

general. *А. П. Чехов: pro et contra: творчество А. П. Чехова в русской мысли конца 19 – начала 20 веков (1887–1914): антология*, SPb, Russian Christian Univ. of the Humanities, 1072 pp., is a very useful anthology for scholars of the history of Russian literature. Z. Papernyi, *Тайна сия . . . Любовь у Чехова*, Mw, B.S.G., 334 pp., is the latest book by a well-known specialist, discussing such figures as Lidiia Mizinova, Tatiana Schepkina-Kupernik, Lidiia Avilova, Elena Shavrova, Liliia Iavorskaya, Vera Komissarzhevskaya, and Ol′ga Knipper. See also: Iu. A. Bychkov, *Тайны любви, или 'Кукуруза души моей'*, Mw, Druzhba narodov, 2001, 253 pp. S. Vasil'eva, 'Пустячок, идиома', *Oktjabr′*, no.6 : 185–90, discusses K. Ginkas's interpretation of Chekhov's works. E. S. Afanas'ev, ' "Является по преимуществу художником" (о художественности произведений А. П. Чехова', *Russkaia Slovesnost'*, no.8 : 23–27. A. Kushner, 'Почему они не любили Чехова?', *Zv*, no.11 : 193–96, discusses the views of Annensky, Khodasevich, and Akhmatova on Chekhov. E. Tolstaia, *Поэтика раздражения: Чехов в конце 1880 —начале 1890–х годов*, 2nd rev. edn, Mw, RGGU, 368 pp. N. E. Razumova, *Творчество А. П. Чехова в аспекте пространства*, Tomsk State Univ., 2001,

521 pp. T. Iu. Il′iukhina, *Антоша Чехонте, Макар Балдастов и другие*, Kemerovo, Kuzbassvuzizdat, 83 pp.

DRAMA. M. V. Teplinsky, '"Каждый пишет так, как хочет и как может." (тема искусства в чеховской "Чайке")', Serebrennikov, *Время*, 257–64. R. Freeborn, 'Absurdity and residency: an approach to Chekhov's *The Seagull*', *NZSJ*, 36:81–88. T. G. Ivleva, *Автор в драматургии А. П. Чехова*, Tver' State Univ., 2001, 123 pp. *Чеховиана. 'Три сестры' — 100 лет*, Mw, Nauka, 379 pp. A. Ia. Altshuller, *А. П. Чехов в актерском кругу*, SPb, Stroiizdat, 2001, 223 pp. S. A. Komarov, *А. Чехов — В. Маяковский: комедиограф в диалоге с русской культурой конца 19 —первой трети 20 века*, Tiumen' State Univ., 247 pp.

PROSE. N. F. Ivanova, 'Отзвуки пушкинского колокольчика в чеховской "Ведьме"', Serebrennikov, *Время*, 248–56.

DOSTOEVSKY

GENERAL. There are several works that 'read D.'s works religiously': (Rev.) D. Grigoriev, *Достоевский и Церковь: У истоков религиозных убеждений писателя*, Mw, Izdatel′stvo Pravoslavnogo Sviato-Tikhonovskogo Bogoslovskogo Instituta, 175 pp. I. Vinogradov, 'Религиозно-духовный опыт Достоевского и современность', *Oktjabr′*, no.3:163–67. See also the very interesting book *Dostoevsky and the Christian Tradition*, ed. G. Pattison and D. Oenning Thompson, CUP, 2001, xi + 281 pp., where the editors in their 'Introduction: reading Dostoevsky religiously' (1–28), insist that 'it is almost impossible *not* to read Dostoevsky religiously'. It contains M. Ziolkowski, 'Dostoevsky and the kenotic tradition' (31–40), which explores the reflections of the kenotic ideal in *The Devils* and *The Brothers Karamazov;* I. Kirillova, 'Dostoevsky's markings in the Gospel according to St John' (41–50), which offers a theological perspective on D.'s reading of the Gospel of St John; S. Ollivier, 'Icons in Dostoevsky's works' (51–68); D. Oenning Thompson, 'Problems of the biblical word in Dostoevsky's poetics' (69–99); A. Pyman, 'Dostoevsky in the prism of the orthodox semiosphere' (103–15), which gives an interesting interpretation of polyphony as 'a tragic form of *sobornost*', which remains 'unresolved'; I. Esaulov, 'The categories of Law and Grace in Dostoevsky's poetics' (116–33), which highlights the opposition between the two theological categories of Law and Grace in Dostoevsky's poetics; E. Ziolkowski, 'Reading and incarnation in Dostoevsky' (156–70), which relates incarnation to the motif of reading aloud, as found in the major novels of D.; G. Pattison, 'Freedom's dangerous dialogue: reading Kierkegaard and Dostoevsky together' (237–56), which argues that the current situation allows for fruitful new readings that are able to explore further the convergences between these two writers.

G. Kogan, 'Загадки в родословной Ф. М. Достоевского', *VL*, no.5 : 375–80. P. Kuznetsov, 'Эмиграция, изгнание, Кундера и Достоевский', *Zvezda*, no.4 : 220–23. Dm. Bykov, 'Достоевский и психология русского литературного Интернета', *Oktjabr'*, no.3 : 167–72. I. Volgin, 'Ничей современник', *ib.*, 143–49. P. Nikolaev, 'Амбивалентность художественного сознания Ф. М. Достоевского', *ib.*, 155–59; V. Kantor, 'Кого и зачем искушал черт? (Иван Карамазов: соблазны «русского пути»)', *VL*, no.2 : 157–81. V. V. Savelieva, 'Сны и циклы сновидений в произведениях Ф. М. Достоевского', *Russkaia Slovesnost'*, no.7 : 24–31. N. Ia. Berkovsky, 'О Достоевском', *Zv*, no.6 : 129–47, presents extracts from unpublished works of a famous specialist on Dostoevsky. S. Belov, 'Достоевский и оптинский старец Амвросий', *NZh*, 226 : 195–204. N. Nasedkin, *Самоубийство Достоевского. Тема суицида в жизни и творчестве писателя,* Mw, Algoritm, 448 pp. V. S. Sizov, *Русская идея в творчестве Ф. М. Достоевского*, Kirov, VSEI, 2001, 172 pp. J. P. Scanlan, *Dostoevsky the Thinker,* Ithaca, Cornell U.P., xii + 251 pp. G. Ponomareva, *Музей-квартира Ф. М. Достоевского в Москве: Путеводитель*, Mw, Palomnik, 110 pp. G. A. Skleinis, '*Двойничество' в аспекте системности художественного творчества Ф. М. Достоевского*, Magadan, Kordis, 39 pp. A. F. Sedov, *Достоевский и текст: Проблема текста с точки зрения поэтики повествования в повестях и романах Ф. М. Достоевского 60–70-х годов*, Balashov, Al'manakh Vesy, 76 pp. S. V. Belov, *Петербург Достоевского*, SPb, Aleteia, 355 pp. *21 век глазами Достоевского: перспективы человечества: материалы международной конференции, состоявшейся в университете Тиба (Япония),* ed. T. Kinoshita and K. Stepanian, Mw, Graal', 560 pp. *Письма Ф. М. Достоевского из игорного дома,* SPb, Kul'tinformpress, 2001, 158 pp. L. D. Dostoevskaya, *Достоевский в изображении его дочери,* transl. from German L. Ia. Krukovskaya, ed. A. G. Gornfel'd, Mw, SIP RIA, 2001, 96 pp. L. Volkova, *Декорации Достоевского: роман одного петербургского квартала*, SPb, Russko-baltiiskii informatsionyi tsentr BLITS, 2001, 103 pp. G. B. Ponomareva, *Достоевский: Я занимаюсь этой тайной,* Mw, Akademkniga, 2001, 304 pp. A. Dostoevsky, *Воспоминания*, Mw, Agraf, 1999, 432 pp., is a reprint of the memoirs of D.'s brother, published in 1930.

THE BROTHERS KARAMAZOV. M. Kanevskaya, 'Smerdiakov and Ivan: Dostoevsky's *The Brothers Karamazov*', *RusR*, 61 : 358–77. M. Kanevskaya, *N. K. Mikhailovsky's Criticism of Dostoevsky: The Cruel Critic* (Studies in Slavic Languages and Literature, 17), Lewiston, NY, Mellen, 2001, vii + 291 pp. S. M. Klimova, 'Агиографические элементы романа Ф. М. Достоевского *Братья Карамазовы*', *Chelovek*, no.6 : 157–65. E. Kurganov, *Достоевский и Талмуд. Штрихи к портрету Ивана Карамазова*, SPb, Izdatel′stvo zhurnala 'Zvezda', 144 pp. There are two interesting papers on this novel in Pattison, *Christian Tradition* (see above, p. 823): D. S. Cunningham, '*The Brothers Karamazov* as trinitarian theology' (134–55), which explores the multitudinous reflections of trinitarian theology in *The Brother Karamazov; and* V. Kantor, 'Pavel Smerdyakov and Ivan Karamazov: the problem of temptation' (189–225), which argues that Smerdyakov is not just the helpless tool of Ivan Karamazov, but an active manipulator who bears primary responsibility for the parricide.

CRIME AND PUNISHMENT. B. Khamvash, 'Предисловие к *Преступлению и наказанию*', *VL*, no.1 : 213–29, is an interesting article in which the Hungarian philosopher coins the term 'oskvernenie bytiia' to describe Raskol'nikov's philosophy. L. Ivanits, 'The other Lazarus in *Crime and Punishment*', *RusR*, 61 : 341–58. Two papers on 'Crime and Punishment' are published in Pattison, *Christian Tradition* (see above, p. 823): A. Johae, 'Towards an iconography of Dostoevsky's *Crime and Punishment*' (173–88), which explores the relationship between symbolism and realistic fiction in this novel; and H. M. W. Russell, 'Beyond the will: humiliation as Christian necessity in *Crime and Punishment*' (226–36), which sees several key characters of *Crime and Punishment* as exemplifying the application of the spirit of apophatic theology to the human condition.

THE IDIOT and THE DEVILS. *Роман Ф. М. Достоевского «Идиот»: современное состояние изучения*, ed. T. Kasatkina, Mw, Nasledie, 2001, 560 pp. E. Kurganov, *Роман Ф. М. Достоевского «Идиот»: опыт прочтения*, SPb, Izdatel′stvo zhurnala 'Zvezda', 144 pp.

OTHER WORKS. R. Giankuinta, '"У нас мечтатели и подлецы". О *Записках из подполья* Ф. М. Достоевского', *RusL*, no.3 : 3–18. J. Andrew, 'Same time, same place: some reflections on the chronotope and gender in D.'s *White Nights*', *NZSJ*, 36 : 25–38. V. Z. Gassieva, *Сюжетно-композиционная структура и образная система в произведениях Ф. М. Достоевского 1840 — начала 1860-х годов*, Vladikavkaz, State Univ. of North Osetiia, 262 pp.

DOSTOEVSKY AND OTHER WRITERS. E. A. Poliakova, *Поэтика драмы и эстетика театра в романе: 'Идиот' и 'Анна Каренина'*, Mw, RGGU, 324 pp. L. Maksimova and V. Danil'chenko-Danilevskaya, '"Русский максимализм" по Ф. М. Достоевскому и Н. Я. Данилевскому, носителям духа Славянства', *LitU*, no.3 : 71–80. Iu. Sokhriakov, *Творчество Ф. М. Достоевского и русская проза 20 века (70–80-е годы)*, Mw, IMLI RAN, 238 pp. I. Zolotussky, '*Записки сумасшедшего* и *Записки из подполья*',

Oktjabr', no.3 : 149–55. A. Tsvetkov, 'Достоевский и Эйн Рэнд', *ib.*, 159–63. I. A. Sukhanova, 'Кармадон альтиста Данилова и Черт Ивана Суханова', *RRe*, no.6 : 30–35. O. Sedakova, '"Неудавшаяся епифания": два христианских романа — *Идиот* и *Доктор Живаго*', *Kontinent*, 112 : 376–85. A. G. Gacheva, 'Философия истории Ф. М. Достоевского в контексте русской философской мысли 19 —начала 20 века', *Russkaia Slovesnost'*, no.5 : 11–16. N. Nasedkin, 'Поправки к лекции В. Набокова "Федор Достоевский"', *Neva*, no.12 : 164–75.

TOLSTOY

N. S. Manaev, *За гранью невидимого: в творческой лаборатории Л. Н. Толстого: от изобразительного источника — к историческому повествованию*, Kaluga, Eidos, 157 pp. O. V. Slivitskaya, 'Об эффекте жизнеподобия в *Анне Карениной*: ритм композиции', *RusL*, no.2 : 28–40. A. Bol'shakova, 'Русский "Золотой век" у Л. Толстого', *LitU*, no:4 : 112–32. L. D. Opul'skaya-Gromova, 'Текстология незавершенного (Л. Толстой)', *RusL*, no.2 : 117–21. V. N. Abrosimova and G. V. Krasnov, 'Последний секретарь Л. Н. Толстого (по материалам архива В. Ф. Булгакова', *ISLIa*, no.3 : 49–63. '"...Гений не замедлит откликнуться гению ..." Письма литераторов Л. Н. Толстому', published and trans. V. Alekseeva, *Oktjabr'*, no.9 : 184–89. S. A. Shul'ts, *Историческая поэтика драматургии Л. Н. Толстого: герменевтический аспект*, Rostov-na-Donu, Rostov State Univ.–Irbis, 238 pp. *Новые материалы о Толстом: Из архива Н. Н. Гусева*, ed. A. A. Donskov, comp. Z. N. Ivanova and L. D. Gromova, Ottawa, Slavic Research Group at the Univ. of Ottawa — Mw, L. N. Tolstoy Museum, xii + 282 pp., contains 80 of Gusev's letters to Tolstoy, and a series of memoirs of Tolstoy. *Война из-за 'Войны и мира': Роман Л. Н. Толстого в русской критике и литературоведении*, ed. M. Ia. Bilinkis, SPb, Azbuka–Klassika, 480 pp., contains papers by P. V. Annenkov, N. S. Leskov, I. S. Turgenev, D. A. Pisarev, and many others. '*Война и мир' Л. Н. Толстого: жизнь книги*, Tver' State Univ., 164 pp. A. Garborg, *Статьи о Толстом*, trans. from Norvegian, Mw, Impeto, 72 pp. A. D. Sukhov, *Яснополянский мудрец: Традиции русского философствования в творчестве Л. Н. Толстого*, Mw, IF RAN, 2001, 145 pp. V. B. Remizov, *Л. Н. Толстой: диалоги во времени*, Tula State Pedagogical Univ., 1998, 301 pp. S. V. Svetana-Tolstaya and F. E. Svetana, *Неизвестная Александра Толстая*, Mw, Ikar, 2001, 165 pp. G. D. Grachev, *С Толстым встреча через век: исповедь*, Mw, Vuzovskaia kniga, 1999, 108 pp.

N. Sankovitch, *Creating and Recovering Experience: Repetition in Tolstoy*, Stanford U.P., 1998, 245 pp., contains four chapters: 'Repetition in Tolstoy' (13–67), 'The structure of characters' experience' (68–135), 'Relationships among characters' (136–79), 'Intertextual repetition in Tolstoy' (180–224). The author argues that Tolstoy uses repetition to represent and examine the processes by which people structure and give meaning to their experience. This complex of devices is shown to be essential to T.'s style, to his understanding of psychology, and to his interaction with readers.

7. Other Individual Authors

ANNENSKY. G. V. Petrova, *Творчество Иннокентия Анненского*, Novgorod State Univ., 128 pp.

BAL'MONT. L. Andguladze, *Бальмонт и Грузия*, Mw, Agraf, 256 pp. N. A. Molchanova, *Поэзия К. Д. Бальмонта 1890–1910-х годов. Проблемы творческой эволюции*, Mw, MPGU, 146 pp., is a study of Bal'mont's works of 1890–1910. P. V. Kupriianovsky and N. A. Molchanova, *Поэт Константин Бальмонт: Биография, творчество, судьба*, Ivanov State Univ., 2001, 469 pp. P. Davidson, 'Magic, music and poetry: Prokofiev's creative relationship with Bal'mont and the genesis of *Semero ikh*', *NZSJ*, 36: 67–80.

BLOK. S. Slobodniuk, *Соловьиный сад. Трилогия вочеловечения Александра Блока: онтология небытия*, SPb, *Aleteia*, 385 pp. V. Esipov, 'Об одном трагическом заблуждении Александра Блока', *VL*, no.2: 95–103. M. Tartakovsky, 'Чувственные радости и революция', *Moskva*, no.3: 175–87. D. Bykov, 'Нерушимый Блок', *Ogonyok*, no.17: 48–51. N. Chulkova, 'Александр Блок: из воспоминаний', *NZh*, 226: 184–94.

CHERNYSHEVSKY. G. G. Shpet, 'Источники диссертации Чернышевского', *NLO*, 56: 6–48, provides an excellent publication of an unknown work by a famous Russian philosopher, edited by L. V. Fedorova. V. G. Shchukin, 'Блеск и нищета "позитивной эротологии." (К концепции любви у Н. Г. Чернышевского)', *VF*, no.1: 140–50.

DAL'. G. P. Matvievskaya and I. K. Zubkov, *Владимир Иванович Даль. 1801–1872*, Mw, Nauka, 223 pp., is a new biography of the famous Russian writer and linguist. V. Mil'don, '"Взять любой случай." (Литературная техника В. И. Даля)', *VL*, no.6: 156–67.

FET. *А. А. Фет и русская литература: материалы Всероссийской научной конференции «16-е Фетовские чтения» (28 июня – 1 июля 2001 года)*, ed. V. A. Koshelev, Kursk State Pedagogical Univ., 207 pp. *А. А. Фет: поэт и мыслитель: к 175-летию со дня рождения А. А. Фета*, ed. E. N. Lebedev, Mw,

Nasledie, 1999, 308 pp. M. L. Gasparov, 'Лирические концовки Фета, или Как Тургенев учил Фета одному, а научил другому', *NLO*, 56 : 96–113. I. Smirnova, '"Жертва жизни всей." (К 110–летию со дня смерти А. А. Фета)', *NSo*, no.11 : 277–88. A. P. Auer, 'Гротеск в поэтике А. А. Фета', Serebrennikov, *Время*, 229–34.

FOFANOV. S. Sapozhkov, 'К. М. Фофанов и репинский кружок писателей. *Статья третья.* Литературный портрет поэта в интерьере', *NLO*, 56 : 135–48.

GONCHAROV. A special issue of *Russian Literature* is devoted to Goncharov's 190th anniversary: T. B. Il'inskaya, 'Категория времени в романе *Обломов* (к истории вопроса)', *RusL*, no.3 : 38–43; S. N. Gus'kov, 'Хрустальный башмачок Обломова', *ib.*, 44–52; A. V. Romanova, 'В тени Обломова (автор и герой в сознании читателя)', *ib.*, 53–69; A. Iu. Balakin, 'О проблеме выбора основного источника текста романа И. А. Гончарова *Обрыв*', *ib.*, 70–88; E. G. Gaitseva, 'Семь писем И. А. Гончарова из Бахметевского архива', *ib.*, 89–105. See also S. L. Shtil'man, 'Книга отражений. Гоголевские мотивы в романе И. А. Гончарова *Обломов*', *Russkaia Slovesnost'*, no.3 : 28–33.

GUMILEV. V. Gubailovsky, 'Орел и ястреб', *Arion*, no.2 : 103–05, discusses two poems: Nikolai Gumilev's 'Орел' (1909) and Josef Brodsky's 'Осенний крик ястреба' (1973).

HERZEN. N. V. Dulova, *Поэтика 'Былого и дум' А. И. Герцена*, Irkutsk State Univ., 130 pp.

IVANOV, VIACH. A. G. Grek, '*Каникула* Вяч. Иванова', *RRe*, no.4 : 24–28. *Вячеслав Иванов — творчество и судьба: К 135–летию со дня рождения*, ed. E. A. Takho-Godi, Mw, Nauka, 349 pp.

LEBEDEV. L. V. Lytkina, *Художественная проза М. Н. Лебедева начала XX века*, Syktyvkar State Pedagogical Inst., 1998, 78 pp.

LESKOV. G. A. Kosykh, *Идейно-композиционное своеобразие поэмы Н. С. Лескова 'Очарованный странник'*, Volgograd, Peremena, 2001, 75 pp. N. Iu. Zavarzina, 'Оппозиция «свое» / «чужое» в рассказе Н. С. Лескова *На краю света*', *RusL*, no.2 : 174–84. E. A. Popova, 'От первого лица (Сказ у Н. С. Лескова)', *RRe*, no.5 : 9–15. I. V. Moteiunaite, 'От "Шерамура" к "Дурачку" (о восприятии юродства Н. С. Лесковым)', Serebrennikov, *Время*, 235–47.

MAMIN-SIBIRIAK. A special issue of *Ural* is devoted to Mamin-Sibiriak: G. Shchennikov, 'Непрочитанный Д. Н. Мамин-Сибиряк', *Ural*, no.11 : 29–38; L. Slobozhaninova, 'Певцы Урала', *ib.*, 39–48; A. Tyrkova-Williams, 'Воспоминание о Мамине-Сибиряке', *ib.*, 49–51; S. Beliaev, 'Судьба и музыка: музыкально-биографический этюд', *ib.*, 52–59; T. Galeeva and R. Galeeva, 'Д.

Н. Мамин-Сибиряк — художник', *ib.*, 60–63; R. Galeeva, 'Листая семейную книгу Маминых', *ib.*, 64–84; M. Riabinina-Novikova, 'Воспоминания о Д.Н. Мамине-Сибиряке', *ib.*, 85–87; E. Molchanov, 'Последнее странствие по Каме и уральские письма Чехова', *ib.*, 88–105.

MEREZHKOVSKY. D. Merezhkovsky, *Было и будет: Невоенный дневник*, Mw, Agraf, 2001, 510 pp., contains M.'s selected works on literature previously published in 'Russkoe slovo' between 1910 and 1916.

NEKRASOV. G. V. Krasnov, *Н. А. Некрасов в кругу современников*, Kolomna State Pedagogical Inst., 215 pp. T. A. Besedina, *Эпопея народной жизни: 'Кому на Руси жить хорошо' Н. А. Некрасова*, SPb, Dmitry Bulanin, 2001, 214 pp. A. Mashevsky, '"Мерещится мне всюду драма." О современном прочтении Некрасова', *Neva*, no.6:193–205. G. V. Stadnikov, 'О стихотворении "Душно! Без счастья и воли . . ." в свете проблеме "Некрасов и Гейне"', *RusL*, no.3:113–18. B. V. Mel'gunov, 'Рисунки на полях Некрасова', Serebrennikov, *Время*, 214–19. D. Bykov, 'Современник', *Ogonyok*, no.6:48–51.

OGAREV. *Огарев от 19 к 21 веку: Материалы 27 Саранских международных Огаревских чтений*, Saransk State Univ., 1999, 254 pp.

OSTROVSKY. I. Zohrab, 'Re-assessing A. N. Ostrovsky's *Groza*: from the Classical tradition to contemporary critical approaches', *NZSJ*, 36:303–20. *'Снегурочка' в контексте драматургии А. Н. Островского*, Kostroma, Departament po turizmu i kul'ture, 2001, 450 pp. I. L. Vishnevskaya, *Талант и поклонники: А. Н. Островский и его пьесы*, Mw, Nasledie, 1999, 215 pp. *Русская трагедия: Пьеса А. Н. Островского 'Гроза' в русской критике и литературоведении*, ed. M. Ia. Bilinkis, SPb, Azbuka–Klassika, 480 pp.

SALTYKOV-SHCHEDRIN. B. I. Matveev, 'Античные образы в произведениях М. Е. Салтыкова-Щедрина', *RRe*, no.4:17–23.

SOLOGUB. *О Федоре Сологубе. Критика: Статьи и заметки*, comp. A. Chebotarevskaya, SPb, Navii chary, 560 pp. M. Pavlova, '"Одиночество" и "Об одиночестве" Ф. К. Тетерникова: ранняя поэма и психофизиологический очерк Федора Сологуба', *NLO*, 55:5–13. M. Pavlova also publishes fragments of an unknown early poem by S.: F. Sologub, 'Начало поэмы "Одиночество" и некоторые отрывки', *NLO*, 55:14–31. L. V. Evdokimova, *Мифопоэтическая традиция в творчестве Ф. Сологуба*, Astrakhan' Pedagogical Univ., 1998, 222 pp.

SOLOV'EV. I. Rodnianskaya, '*Белая Лилия* как образец мистерии-буфф. К вопросу о жанре и типе юмора пьесы Владимира Соловьева', *VL*, no.3:86–102. *Вл. Соловьев: pro et contra: Личность и творчество Владимира Соловьева в оценке русских мыслителей и исследователей: антология*, vol. 2, ed. V. V. Boikov and Iu. Iu. Bulychev, SPb, RKhGI, 1072 pp.

SUKHOVO-KOBYLIN. V. Seleznev, '"Картина не может быть боевым орудием." Неизвестное письмо А. В. Сухово-Кобылина', *VL*, no.4 : 379–80.

TURGENEV. Iu. V. Lebedev, *Художественный мир романа И. С. Тургенева 'Отцы и дети'*, Mw, Klassik Stil', 288 pp. V. Ivanov, 'Евгений Васильевич Базаров', *Neva*, no.8 : 238–40. V. I. Etov, '"Их поколенье миновало": Рудин и Лаврецкий', *Russkaia Slovesnost'*, no.1 : 12–21. I. V. Gracheva, 'Роль художественной детали в романе И. С. Тургенева *Отцы и дети*', *Russkaia Slovesnost'*, no.1 : 30–35. V. Mil'don, 'Единица — вздор, единица — ноль. Тургенев и Ницше — образы нигилизма', *Oktjabr'*, no.11 : 160–71. S. M. Aiupov, *Эволюция тургеневского романа 1856–1862 гг.: соотношение метафизического и конкретно-исторического*, Kazan' State Univ., 2001, 290 pp. O. Egorov, *Романы И. С. Тургенева: проблемы культуры*, Mw State Univ., 2001, 223 pp. V. V. Shapochka, *Охотничьи тропы Тургенева*, Orel, Veshnie vody, 1998, 159 pp.

O. M. Barsukova has published several studies: 'Образ птицы в прозе И. С. Тургенева', *RRe*, no.2 : 22–28; 'Мотив тумана в прозе Тургенева', *RRe*, no.3 : 21–29; 'Мотив стихии в прозе Тургенева', *RRe*, no.4 : 9–16; 'Образ водного пространства в произведениях И. С. Тургенева', *RRe*, no.5 : 3–8.

VVEDENSKY. L. F. Katsis and M. P. Odessky, 'Барокко и авангард (*Кругом возможно Бог* А. Введенского и школьная драма *Ужасная измена сластолюбивого жития*)', *ISLIa*, no.5 : 19–34.

LITERATURE FROM 1917 TO THE PRESENT DAY

By BORIS LANIN, *Professor of Literature, Russian Academy of Education, Moscow*

1. GENERAL

O. A. Krivtsun, 'Художник 20 века: поиски смысла творчества', *Chelovek*, no.2 : 38–53; no.2 : 29–40; 'Из неизданной книги Ф. Д. Батюшкова «Около талантов» «Владимир Сергеевич Соловьев»', published by P. R. Zaborov, *RusL*, no.2 : 185–96; T. Nikol'skaia, *Авангард и окрестности*, St Petersburg, Ivan Limbakh PH, 320 pp., contains many interesting facts about Brodsky, Vaginov, Konstantin Bol'shakov, Alexei Khvostenko, and the less known Il'ia Zdanevich, Alexandr Chachikov, Ivan Likhachev, Andrei Egunov, and many others.

Из истории литературных объединений Петрограда—Ленинград 1910–1930-х годов: Исследования и материалы, ed. V. P. Muromskii, SPb, Nauka, 390 pp.; M. P. Cherednikova, *«Голос детства из дальней дали. . .»: Игра, магия, миф в детской культуре (Школа В. Я. Проппа: Разыскания в области филологии, истории и традиции культуры)*, Mw, Labirint, 224 pp.; M. N. Mikhailov and N. V. Mikhailova, 'Глаза в литературе 20 века', *RRe*, no.1 : 17–26; E. Shteiner, *Искусство советской детской книги 1920-х годов. Авангард и построение нового человека*, Mw, NLO, 256 pp.; A. A. Aronov, *Вклад России в мировую культуру: Биографический энциклопедический словарь*, Mw, IPO Profizdat, 448 pp.; I. Shaitanov, '«Бытовая» история', *VL*, no.2 : 3–24; A. Bogdanov, 'Доигрались до литературы', *LitU*, no.3 : 44–58; V. Alekseev, A. Kuznetsova, and L. Ahkenazi, 'Литература и Интернет, или Кто более матери-филологии ценен?', *DN*, no.10 : 194–206.

An excellent study of Russian and Soviet Nobel Prize winners is M. Blokh, *Советский Союз в интерьере Нобелевских премий*, SPb, Gumanistika, 2001, 342 pp. *Русские писатели, поэты (советский период): Библиографический указатель: 25: Арс. Тарковский —А. Твардовский*, ed. D. B. Aziatsev, SPb, Izdatel'stvo Rossiiskoi Natsional'noi biblioteki, 608 pp. N. G. Krasnikov, *Роковая зацепка за жизнь, или В поисках утраченного неба: жизнь и гибель Н. Гумилева, С. Есенина, Н. Рубцова, Ю. Друниной, юбилейный реквием по Шукшину*, Mw, MG-Zvonnitsa, 494 pp.

2. Literary History

GENERAL. S. Esin, *На рубеже веков. Дневник ректора*, Mw, OLMA-Press, 638 pp., written by the President of the Institute for Literature (Moscow), is a very useful source for understanding recent literary events; S. Savitsky, *Андеграунд (История и мифы ленинградской неофициальной литературы)*, Mw, NLO, 224 pp., is about Soviet 'neomodern' literature 1960–1980s. I. Kondakov, 'Адова пасть (Русская литература XX века как единый текст)', *VL*, no.1:3–70; *Русская литература первой половины 20 века: сборник авторских интерпретаций*, Ekaterinburg, Ural State Univ., 293 pp. *Русская литература 20 века: школы, направления, методы творческой работы*, ed. S. I. Timina, SPb, Logos, Vyshaia Shkola, 586 pp.; N. Leiderman, 'Траектории «экспериментирующей эпохи»', *VL*, no.4:3–47; *Русская литература 20 века*, ed. L. P. Krementsov, Mw, Akademia, vol.1: *1920 —1930-е годы*, 496 pp.; vol.2: *1940 —1990-е годы*, 464 pp; *Кафедральные записки: вопросы новой и новейшей русской литературы*, ed. N. M. Solntseva, Mw, MGU, 256 pp., has work on Remizov, Tsvetaeva, Platonov, Zamiatin, Il'f and Petrov, Sorokin, Blok, Belyi, Elena Guro, J. Brodsky, Bulgakov, L. Andreev, Annensky, Ovsianiko-Kulikovsky, Viacheslav Ivanov, and Gershenzon; *Традиции русской классики 20 века и современность*, ed. S. I. Kormilov, Mw, MGU, 336 pp.; T. N. Fominykh, *Первая мировая война в русской прозе 1920 —1930-х годов: историософия и поэтика*, Perm′ State Pedagogical U.P., 2001, 175 pp.; L. Sukhanek, 'Вождь на кончике пера. Образ Сталина в творчестве А. Солженицына, В. Максимова, Ю. Дружникова', *Vyshgorod*, no.1–2; A. Borshchagovsky, *Пустотелый монолит: документальный детектив*, Mw, MIK, 216 pp., is about the significant events in Russian literature of the 40s and 50s; *Тыняновский сборник. Вып. 11: Девятые Тыняновские чтения. Исследования. Материалы*, ed. M. O. Chudakova, Mw, OGI, 992 pp, contains work on the history of Russian literature from Lomonosov and Radishchev to the 1970s. Among the most interesting papers are those by A. Kurilkin, A. Gribanov, and A. Nemzer; S. Rassadin, *Самоубийцы: повесть о том, как мы жили и что читали*, Mw, Tekst, 478 pp., contains essays on Bulgakov, Zoshchenko, Fadeev, Olesha, Mikhalkov, Tvardovsky, Kataev, and Erdman; A. E. Kedrovsky, *Русская литература 20 века: 1917–1930 годы*, Kursk State Pedagogical Univ., 347 pp. *Русская литература 20-х годов: художественный текст и историко-культурный контекст*, Perm′ State Pedagogical Univ., 304 pp., is a volume published in memory of Professor I. A. Smirin. E. Tolstaia, *Мирпослеконца: Работы о русской литературе XX века*, Mw, RGGU, 512 pp., contains work on Akim Bolynsky, the poet

K. R., A. N. Tolstoy, M. Bulgakov, and A. Platonov. I. N. Sukhikh, *Книги 20 века: русский канон*, Mw, NG, 2001, 348 pp.

Many interesting works about Russian and Soviet academia have appeared: M. Robinson, 'Русская академическая элита: советский опыт (конец 1910–х–1920–е гг.)', *NLO*, 53:159–98; V. M. Alpatov, 'Филологи и революция', *ib.*, 199–216; A. Dmitriev and D. Ustinov, '«Академизм» как проблема отечественного литературоведения 20 века (историко-филологические беседы)', *ib.*, 217–40; A. N. Shebunin, 'Основание Академии наук', *ib.*, 54:7–28; A. Dmitriev, '«Академический марксизм» 1920–1930–х гг. и история Академии: случай А. Н. Шебунина', *ib.*, 29–60.

THE SILVER AGE. T. Davydova, 'Образ Англии в творчестве Евгения Замятина', *LitU*, no.3:81–87; E. A. Romanova, 'София Парнок и Владислав Ходасевич: к истории творческих перекличек (на материале статьи С. Я. Парнок «Ходасевич»)', *RusL*, no.2:199–215; R. Eterovich, *Особенности перевода русской лирики Серебряного века на хорватский язык*, Mw, MAKS Press, 156 pp., S. Osherov, *Найти язык эпох: от архаического Рима до русского Серебряного века*, Mw, Agraf, 2001, 336 pp.

LITERARY CULTURE . *Национальный Эрос и культура*, ed. G. D. Gachev and L. N. Titova, 2 vols, vol.1: *Исследования (Русская потаенная литература)*, Mw, Ladomir, 563 pp.; *Призраковое пространство культуры*, ed. S. M. Tolstaya (Библиотека Института славяноведения РАН), Mw, Indrik, 432 pp.; A. Dolgin, *Прагматика культуры*, Mw, Прагматика культуры, 168 pp.; Eimermacher, *Культура* , contains K. Eimermacher and G. Bordiugov, 'Культура и власть' (9–16); I. Grabowsky, '«Контроль и руководство»: литературная политика советской партийной бюрократии в 1920–е годы' (17–49); L. Erren, '«Самокритика своих собственных ошибок». Истоки покаянных заявлений в среде партийных литературных интеллектуалов' (50–65); J. Mamedova, 'Персонажи власти в литературе для детей советского времени' (131–57); N. Margulis, '«Слово наше —это сила и оружие»: литературная пропаганда в «испанском конфликте»' (158–77) on Andrei Platonov and Nikoi Zabolotsky; H. Schmidt, '«Красавица и чудовище». К вопросу взаимоотношений государства и сетевого сообщества в России' (348–60) and others. See also K. Eimermacher, *Политика и культура при Ленине и Сталине. 1917 – 1932*, Mw, AIRO-XX, 1998, 204 pp., W. Eggeling, *Политика и культура при Хрущеве и Брежневе. 1953 —1970 гг.*, Mw, AIRO-XX, 1999, 249 pp., D. Kretschmar, *Политика и культура при Брежневе, Андропове и Черненко. 1970 —1985 гг.*, Mw, AIRO-XX, 1997, 411 pp., *Трансформация и функционирование культурных моделей в русской литературе XX века (архетип, мифологема, мотив)*, ed. V. E. Golovchiner, Tomsk State Pedagogical Univ., 153 pp.; *Zwischen Anachronismus und Fortschritt. Modernisierungsprogrezesse und ihre Interferenzen in der russischen und Sowjetischen Kultur des 20. Jahrhunderts*, ed. P. Becker, K. Mundt, and D. Steinweg, Bochum U.P., 2001, 432 pp.; *Körperzeichen – Zeichenkörper. Zu einer Physiologie der russischen und sowjetischen Kultur des 20. Jahrhunderts*, ed. P. Becker, I. Grabowsky, and C. Schönegger-Zanoni, Bochum U.P., 238 pp.

B. Dubin, 'Социальные формы, знаковые фигуры, символические образцы', *Znamia*, no.12: 176–83, is about modern literary culture. P. A. Nikolaev, *Культура как фактор национальной безопасности России*, Mw, Druzhba narodov, 2001, 93 pp. I. Pomerantsev, *Радио «С»: Книга радиосюжетов*, (Современная библиотека для чтения), Mw, MK-Periodika, 288 pp., contains many scripts of the author's 'Radio Liberty' broadcasts. M. Chegodaeva, *Там за горами горя . . .: Поэты, художники, издатели, критики в 1916–1923 годах*, SPb, Dmitrii Bulanin, 424 pp.; N. Krenov, *Культура в эпоху социального хаоса*, Mw, Editorial URSS, 448 pp.; M. Ryklin, *Деконструкция и деструкция*, Mw, Logos, 270 pp.; M. Korshunov and V. Terekhova, *Тайны и легенды Дома на набережной*, 2nd rev. edn, Mw, Slovo, 400 pp.; *Художественный язык эпохи*, ed. S. A. Golubkov, Samara State Univ., 388 pp.; S. I. Timina, *Культурный Петербург*, SPb, Logos, 2001, is an electronic book on CD. V. V. Desiatov, *Прозрачные вещи: очерки по истории литературы и культуры 20 века*, Barnaul, Altay State Univ., 2001, 91 pp.

MODERN LITERATURE. Among the best books published in 2002 is A. Genis, *Два. Расследования*, Mw, Podkova, Eksmo, 492 pp., on Siniavsky, Bitov, Makanin, Dovlatov, Sasha Sokolov, Tatiana Tolstaya, Pelevin, and others. A. Nemzer, *Памятные даты: от Гаврилы Державина до Юрия Давыдова*, Moscow, Vremia, 2002, 521 pp., is a selection of critical papers by Andrei Nemzer written during the last 11 years and previously published in four popular journals. A. Iu. Merezhinskaya, *Художественная парадигма переходной культурной эпохи: русская проза 80–90–х годов 20 века*, Kiyv U.P., 2001, 433 pp.; O. Aksiutina, 'Власть и контркультура в 1980 —90–е годы. Панк как этика и эстетика противостояния', Eimermacher, *Культура*, 303–34; T. V. Igosheva, *Современная русская литература*, Novgorod State U.P., 137 pp. P. Basinsky, 'Три портрета', *Neva*, no.2: 188–203, has three essays on Victor Pelevin, Alexandr Kabakov, and Boris Akunin; I. Klekh, 'Выход героя в неглиже (некоторые спорные вопросы «художественного поведения»)', *DN*, no.3: 199–202; *Творчество Александры Марининой как отражение современной российской ментальности: Международная конференция (19–20 октября 2001 года), Институт Славяноведения, Париж*, ed. E. I. Trofimova, Mw, INION RAN, 189 pp.; L. N. Skakovskaia, *Проза Владимира Крупина: проблематика и поэтика*, Tver' State U.P., 2000, 131 pp.; M. I. Gromova, *Русская современная драматургия*, 2nd rev. edn, Mw, Flinta–Nauka, 159 pp.; Iu. I. Mineralov, *История русской литературы: 90–е годы 20 века*, Mw, Vlados, 223 pp. *Нестоличная литература. Поэзия и проза регионов России*, comp. D. Kuz'min, Mw, NLO, 2001, 342 pp., is an interesting selection of Russian provincial literature:

THE EMIGRATION. *Литературная энциклопедия русского зарубежья. 1918–1940*, vol. 3: *Книги*, ed. A. N. Nikoliukin, Mw, ROSSPEN, 712 pp.; *Литературное зарубежье: национальная литература — две или одна? выпуск 2*, ed. Iu. Ia. Barabash, Mw, IMLI RAN, 246 pp; B. K. Zaitsev, 'Две рецензии', is published by A. V. Iarkova in *RusL*, no.2:216–25; *Критика русского зарубежья (антология)*, comp. and ed. O. Korostelev and N. Mel'nikov, Mw, Olimp–AST, 471 pp; N. Evdaev, *Давид Бурлюк в Америке: Материалы к биографии*, Mw, Nauka, 340 pp.; *Русский Нью-Йорк: Антология «Нового журнала»*, ed. A. Nikoliukin, Mw, Russkii put', 448 pp.; Ia. V. Sarychev, *Религия Дмитрия Мережковского: «Неохристианская» доктрина и ее художественное воплощение*, Lipetsk, Lipetskoe izdatel'stvo, 2001, 221 pp.; E. Ponomarev, 'Распад атома в поэзии русской эмиграции (Георгий Иванов и Владислав Ходасевич', *VL*, no.4:48–81. Osorgin's diary is published: M. Osorgin, 'Что я слышал, что я видел что я делал в течение жизни', *NZh*, 225, 2001:110–47. K. Turumova publishes B. Zaitsev's and G. Adamovich's letters to Iurii Dombrovsky in: 'Из архива Юрия Домбровского', *VL*, no.2:222–28. A. Lysenko, *Голос изгнания: становление газет русского Берлина и их эволюция в 1919 —1922 гг.*, Mw, Russkaia kniga, 2000, 366 pp.; L. Kopelev, R. Orlova, 'Мы жили в Кельне', *Vestnik Evropy*, no.4, is an extract from their book published in 1996 in German; E. Taskina, 'О поэтическом творчестве дальневосточного Зарубежья (наследники)', *NZh*, 229:252–58; F. P. Fedorov, 'Пушкин в системе воззрений Георгия Адамовича', Serebrennikov, *Время*, 324–37; R. Goldt, 'Экфрасис как литературный автокомментарий у Леонида Андреева и Бориса Поплавского', Heller, *Экфрасис*, 111–22. D. P. Sviatopolk-Mirsky, *Поэты и Россия: статьи, рецензии, портреты, некрологи (Серия: Русское зарубежье)*, comp. and ed. V. V. Perkhin, SPb, Aleteia, 380 pp; K. Postoutenko, '"Я, я, я. Что за дикое слово. . ." Vladislav Khodasevich's deconstruction of the first-person personal pronoun', *NZSJ*, 36:225–36; I. Kaspe, 'Бегство от власти. Литературный журнал в эмиграции и в интернете: «Числа» (Париж) и «TextOnly»', Eimermacher, *Культура,* 335–47; Iu. V. Babicheva, *Гайто Газданов и творческие искания Серебряного века,* Vologda, Rus', 85 pp. *Диаспора: новые материалы, вып. 4,* ed. O. Korostelev, SPb, Feniks, 704 pp., contains letters by Erenburg, Annenkov, Nikulin, and some interesting papers. L. I. Bronskaya, *Концепция личности в автобиографической прозе русского зарубежья первой половины XX века (И. С. Шмелев, Б. К. Зайцев, М. А. Осоргин),* Stavropol' State U.P., 2001, 119 pp.; *Лицо и гений: из наследия русской эмиграции,* ed. M. D. Filin, Mw, Russkii mir, 2001, 317 pp.; E. R. Obatnina, *Царь Асыка и его подданные: Обезьянья Великая Палата А. Ремизова в лицах и документах,* SPb, Izdatel'stvo Ivana Limbakha, 2001, 382 pp.; *Сатира и юмор русской эмиграции,* comp S. A. Alexandrov, Mw, AIRO-XX, 1998, 334 pp.

SOCIALIST REALISM. An excellent book is a selected volume *Советское богатство: статьи о культуре, литературе и кино: К 60–летию Х. Гюнтера,* ed. M. Balina, E. Dobrenko, and Iu. Murashov, SPb, Akademicheskii proekt, 448 pp. M. Ryklin, *Пространства ликования. Тоталитаризм и различие,* Mw, Logos, 280 pp., is a selection of Ryklin's papers published in 1995–2001, including polemics with H. Arendt and A. Besançon; *Агитмассовое искусство Советской России 1918–1932. Материалы и документы,* ed. I. M. Bibikova , Mw, Iskusstvo, 299 pp.; Ia. Lotovsky, 'О последних днях Леопольда Авербаха, генерального секретаря РАПП', *VL,* no.2 : 299–309. On Stalin and the totalitarian culture see: M. Vaiskopf, *Писатель Сталин,* 2nd rev. edn, Mw, NLO, 384 pp., *Im Dschungel der Macht. Intellektuelle Professionen unter Stalin und Hitler,* ed. D. Beyrau, Goettingen, Vandenhoeck und Ruprecht, 2000, 432 pp. A very interesting memoir is written by one of the principal Communist Party functionaries responsible for ideology: A. Beliaev, 'На Старой площади', *VL,* no.3 : 243–70.

A. M. Beda, *Советская политическая культура через призму МВД: От «московского патриотизма» к идее «Большого Отечества» (1946 —1958),* Mw, Mosgorarkhiv, 272 pp.

CENSORSHIP. A. V. Blium presents his new and extremely important work: 'Index Librorum Prohibitorum русских писателей 1917–1991 (Часть 1. А – Ж)', *NLO,* 53 : 425–45; (Часть 2.) *NLO,* 56 : 418–36; Another very interesting publication is N. Volkova's interview 'Я считаю, что все это должно быть в РГАЛИ. . .', *NN,* no.61, (Interviewer: A. Man'kovsky) – about Eisenstein's, Meierkhol'd's, Tsvetaeva's, Osorgin's, Khardzhiev's, and Pasternak's archives.

3. Theory

GENERAL. Iu. N. Tynianov, *Литературная эволюция: избранные труды*, ed. Vl. Novikov, Mw, Agraf, 496 pp.; Heller, *Экфрасис*, explores the connections between narrative technique and fine arts in Russian culture. A. A. Kobrinsky, *Поэтика «Обэриу» в контексте русского литературного авангарда*, Mw, Moskovskii kul′turologicheskii litsei, 2000, 192 pp.; Iu. B. Orlitsky, *Стих и проза в русской литературе*, Mw, RGGU, 685 pp.; B. V. Tomashevskii *Теория литературы. Поэтика*, Mw, Aspekt, 334 pp.; *Russian Imago 2001. Исследования по психоанализу культуры*, ed. V. A. Medvedev, SPb, Institut Psikhologii I Seksologii, 562 pp., has papers on Venedict Erofeev, Mikhail Bulgakov and others; N. A. Nikolina, *Поэтика русской автобиографической прозы*, Mw, Flinta–Nauka, 423 pp.; V. V. Zamanskaia, *Экзистенциальная традиция в русской литературе XX века: Диалоги на границах столетий*, Mw, Flinta–Nauka, 304 pp.; *Поэтические образы: от Абажура до Яшмы: Словарь*, ed. V. B. Ferkel', Cheliabinsk, Biblioteka A. Millera, 590 pp.

There are several works on laughter in Russian culture: *Феноменология смеха: Карикатура, пародия, гротеск в современной культуре*, ed. V. A. Shestakov, Mw, Rossiiskii institut kul′turologii, 269 pp.; B. Lanin, *'Ирония и сатира в русской литературе 20 века (забытые имена)', ASJ*, 19:228–242. On narrative techniques in 20th-c. Russian literature see: A. Ulanov, 'Сквозь город', *NLO*, 56:269–73; V. Mikhailin, 'Автопортрет Алисы в Зазеркалье', *ib.*, 274–95; O. Chernoritskaya, 'Трансформация тел и сюжетов: физиология перехода в поэтике абсурда', *ib.*, 296–309.

Русский литературный портрет и рецензия в 20 веке: концепции и поэтика, ed. T. M. Vakhitova, St Petersburg State University, 150 pp.; E. V. Kliuev, *Теория литературы абсурда*, Mw, University of Russian Academy of Education, 2000, 102 pp.; A. F. Liubimova, *Жанр антиутопии в 20 веке: содержательные и поэтологические аспекты*, Perm′ State U.P., 2001, 90 pp.; M. N. Lipovetsky, *«Нет, ребята, все не так!»: Гротеск в русской литературе 1960 — 1980-х годов*, Ekaterinburg, AMB, 2001, 60 pp.; I. Shaitanov, 'Классическая поэтика неклассической эпохи. Была ли завершена «Историческая поэтика»?', *VL*, no.4:82–135; E. B. Meksh, 'Мифологический архетип в искусстве и в жизни (Всеволод Иванов и Варлам Шаламов)', *RusL*, no.2:226–33; M. L. Gasparov, 'Литературный интертекст и языковой интертекст', *ISLIa*, no.4:3–9; S. Dmitrenko, 'Беллетристика породила классику (К проблеме интерпретации литературных произведений)', *VL*, no.5:75–102; V. Gubailovsky, 'Обоснование счастья. О природе фэнтези и первооткрывателе жанра',

NovM, no.3:174–85; B. Dubin, 'Классическое, элитарное, массовое: начала дифференциации и механизмы внутренней динамики в системе литературы', *NLO*, 57:6–23; E. Berard, 'Экфрасис в русской литературе XX века. Россия малеванная, Россия каменная', Heller, *Экфрасис*, 145–51.

criticism. There are new works on Lotman : O. N. Leuta, 'Ю. М. Лотман о трех функциях текста', *VF*, no.11 : 165–73; G. Levinton, 'Заметки о критике и полемике, или Опыт отражения некоторых нелитературных обвинений (Ю. М. Лотман и его критики)', *Novaia Russkaia Kniga*, no.1:27–29. See also the exciting memoirs about Iurii Lotman and his wife Professor Zara Mints: B. F. Egorov, 'Юрмих и Зара', *Zvezda*, no.2:137–42; Iu. Lotman, 'В мире гротеска и философии', *Vyshgorod*, no. 1–2: is the first Russian publication of Lotman's paper previously published in Estonia (1978).

Works on Bakhtin include: N. D. Tamarchenko, *«Эстетика словесного творчества» М. М. Бахтина и русская религиозная философия*, Mw, RGGU, 2001, 200 pp., *М. М. Бахтин в Саранске: документы, материалы, исследования*, ed. O. E. Osovsky, Saransk, 235 pp. See also M. Bakhtin, *Собрание сочинений, Проблемы поэтики Достоевского, 1963. Работы 1960-х – 1970-х гг., Vol. 6*, Mw, Russkie slovari — Iazyki Slavianskoi Kul'tury, 800 pp., and M. Bakhtin, 'Роман —целая жизнь', *Lit Rossiia*, no.21, a publication of documents from the Mordovian State archive (Saransk).

Many works are devoted to Gukovsky's 100 anniversary: R. Zernova, 'Незабываемый', *NLO*, 55:32–39; L. Lotman, 'Он был нашим профессором', *ib.*, 40–53; Il'ia Serman, 'Пути и судьба Григория Гуковского', *ib.*, 54–65; F. Dziadko, '«Карманная история литературы»: к поэтике филологического текста Г. А. Гуковского', *ib.*, 66–76; V. Markovich, 'Концепция «стадиальности литературного развития» в работах Г. А. Гуковского 1940-х годов', *ib.*, 77–105. Gukovsky's unknown work is also published, by D. V. Ustinov, 'О стадиальности истории литературы', *ib.*, 106–31.

Also useful are A. Bem, *Исследования. Письма о литературе*, comp. and ed. S. Bocharov and I. Surat, Mw, Iazyki Slavianskoi Kul'tury, 2001, 448 pp.; L. A. Pokrovskaya, 'В. М. Жирмунский и актуальные проблемы тюркологии', *ISLIa*, no.3:64–69; B. M. Eikhenbaum, *Мой временник. Художественная проза и избранные статьи 20–30-х годов*, comp. Iu. Berezhnaya, SPb, Inapress, 2001, 653 pp.; S. I. Sukhikh, *Теоретическая поэтика А. А. Потебни*, Nizhnii Novgorod, Kitizdat, 2001, 287 pp.; G. Adamovich, *Одиночество и свобода*, ed. Oleg Korostelev, StP, Aleteia, 471 pp.; G. Adamovich, *Литературные заметки. Книга 1 («Последние новости» 1928–1931)*, ed. O. Korostelev, SPb, Aleteia, 786 pp.;

F. Raskol'nikov, *Статьи о русской литературе,* Mw, Vagrius, 351 pp.; V. Voropaev, 'Воронский и его «Гоголь»', *VL*, no.3 : 313–20; A. Kuznetsova, '«Весь» Агеев', *VL*, no.5 : 346–55; A large part of *Zvezda* no.3 is devoted to Lidiia Ginzburg's works. See also N. Kryshchuk, 'Лидия Гинзбург: в поисках жанра', *Zvezda*, no.10 : 206–10; V. I. Pliukhin, *Проблемы писательской критики сибирского региона*, Khakas State Univ., 202 pp.; O. A. Lekmanov, *Критика русского постсимволизма*, Mw, AST, Olimp, 380 pp.

MEMOIRS. M. Grobman, *Левиафан. Дневники 1963 – 1971 годов*, Mw, NLO, 544 pp., contains the interesting memoirs by émigré artist on Gennadii Aigi, Josef Brodsky, Genrikh Sapgir, Il'ia Kabakov, Igor Kholin, Eduard Limonov, Iurii Mamleev, Victor Nekrasov, Bulat Okudzhava, Alexandr Prokhanov, and others; L. Ia. Ginzburg, *Записные книжки. Воспоминания. Эссе,* introd. Alexandr Kushner, SPb, Iskusstvo, 768 pp. See also L. Ia. Ginzburg, 'Из записных книжек (1925–1934)', *Zvezda*, no.3. 104–32; V. V. Ivanov, *Дневники,* comp. M. V. Ivanov and E. A. Papkova, Mw, IMLI RAN–Nasledie, 2001, 490 pp.; V. G. Korolenko, *Дневник. 1917–1921. Письма*, Mw, Sovremennyi pisatel', 2001, 542 pp.; P. P. Pertsov, *Литературные воспоминания. 1890–1902*, Mw, NLO, 496 pp., on N. Mikhailovsky, Blok, S. Diagilev, Z. Gippius, Belyi, D. Merezhkovsky, A. Skabichevsky, F. Sologub, Rozanov, Briusov, Vladimir Soloviev, and others, and Pertsov's rare works 'Rannii Blok' (1922), 'Briusov nachala veka' (1940), has excellent commentaries by A. Lavrov. E. Gershtein, *Мемуары*, Mw, Zakharov, 761 pp.; B. Pankin, *Пресловутая эпоха в лицах и масках, событиях и казусах*, Mw, Voskresenie, 560 pp., is a very useful resourse for historians of Russian literature of 1960–1990. *Филологический факультет Санкт-Петербургского университета: Материалы к истории факультета*, ed. I. S. Lutovinov and S. I. Bogdanov, 3rd rev. edn, SPb, Philology Department of St Petersburg State University. *Дмитрий Лихачев и его эпоха*, ed. E. Vodolazkin, SPb, Logos, 424 pp., has memoirs by the Prince of Wales, Naina Yeltzina, Mikhail Gorbachev, Victor Astaf'ev, Daniil Granin, Iurii Shevchuk, and others. G. Agranovskaya, 'Отец', *VL*, no.3 : 152–76, is about one of the real authors of Leonid Brezhnev's books. A. Borin, '«Пессимистом быть пошло» (О Натане Эйдельмане)', *VL*, no.3 : 177–91; Ia. Khelemsky, 'Неуступчивая муза', *ib.*, 192–213; V. Subbotin, '«Все, что я значил и зачем я жил . . .»', *ib.*, 214–21; B. Bialik, 'Вместо дневника', *ib.*, 222–29; V. Porudominsky, 'Пишу из жизни. Заметки к ненаписанным воспоминаниям', *ib.*, 230–42; B. Zakhoder, 'Приключения Винни-Пуха (Из истории моих публикаций)', *VL*, no.5 : 197–225; M. Sinel'nikov, 'Игра в снежки. Главы из воспоминаний', *ib.*, 226–72. V. Kurbatov,

'Одна счастливая весна', *DN*, no.6: 191–200, contains memoirs on Valentin Berestov and his wife Tatiana Alexandrova. I. Zolotussky, 'У времени в плену', *Zvezda*, no.2: 209–15; L. Kopelev, R. Orlova, 'Мы жили в Кельне', *Vestnik Evropy*, no.4: 75–98; Mikhail Lobanov, 'На передовой. Опыт духовной автобиографии', *NSo*, no.2: 168–205, no. 3: 97–157, no. 4: 130–73, is a very useful source for studies in recent literary history.

Iu. Lotman's memoirs are published in *Novaia gazeta*, 74, 76, 78, 2001.

On the émigré poet Il'ia Rubin see: Iu. Krelin, 'И один в поле воин', *VL*, no.2: 322–45, about Shaginian, Maksimov, Iskander, and others; *Дмитрий Лихачев и его эпоха: Воспоминания, эссе, документы, фотографии*, ed. E. Vodolazkin, SPb, Logos, 424 pp.; E. Katseva, *Мой личный военный трофей* (Сквозь призму времени), Mw, Raduga, 232 pp; *Николай Островский —человек и писатель —в воспоминаниях современников (1904–1936) к столетию со дня рождения*, Mw, Druzhba narodov, 237 pp.; S. Tkhorzhevsky, *Открыть окно: воспоминания и попутные записи*, SPb, Aleteia, 304 pp.; L. Chukovskaya, *Памяти детства: воспоминания о Корнее Чуковском*, SPb, Limbus Press, 2001, 208 pp.; A. Saakiants, *Спасибо Вам! Воспоминания, письма, эссе*, Mw, Ellis–Lak, 1998, 608 pp., is mostly on Ariadna Sergeevna Efron, Marina Tsvetaeva's daughter; E. Gollerbakh, *Встречи и впечатления*, SPb, Inapress, 1998, 568 pp.

COMPARATIVE STUDIES. N. Bassel', 'Проблемы межлитературных отношений: вчера и сегодня', *VL*, no.6: 3–17., R. Davis, V. Keldysh, *С двух берегов: русская литература 20 века в России и за рубежом, Mw, IMLI RAN, 822 pp.*; G. G. Ishimbaeva, *Русская фаустиана XX века*, Mw, Flinta–Nauka, 304 pp.; D. Tokarev, *Курс на худшее: Абсурд как категория текста у Даниила Хармса и Сэмюэля Беккета*, Mw, NLO, 336 pp.; *Диалог писателей: Из истории русско-французских культурных связей XX века. 1920–1970*, Mw, IMLI RAN, 960 pp.; A. Ulanov, 'На развалинах разговора', *NLO*, 53: 304–13, is a comparative study in modern poetry; M. A. Litovskaya, 'Аристократия в демократические времена: «Хождение по мукам» А. Толстого и «Унесенные ветром» М. Митчелл как «народные романы»', *NLO*, 57: 41–53; M. Popovsky, 'Семидесятые', *NZh*, 228: 192–248; *Диалог писателей: из истории русско-французских культурных связей XX в. 1920 —1970*, ed. T. V. Balashova, Mw, IMLI RAN, 960 pp.

PROSE. A. Bol'shakova, *Русская деревенская проза XX века: Код прочтения*, Shumen, Aksios, 160 pp.; Ia. S. Dukhan, *Трагедия и подвиг: Великая Отечественная война в прозе 60 – 90-х годов*, St Petersburg State Pedagogical Univ., 1998, 206 pp.; E. Mestergazi,

'Документальное начало в литературе XX века', *LitU*, no.5 : 96–113; M. Remizova, 'Свежая кровь', *NovMir*, no.6 : 166–70, discusses the genre of the short story in modern Russian prose; O. Slavnikova, 'К кому едет ревизор? Проза «поколения next»', *Novmir*, no.9 : 171–81, is about Sergei Shargunov, Arkadii Babchenko, Anton Fridl'and, Alexei Lukianov, Denis Osokin; V. Kholkin, 'Грамматика жизни в обстоятельствах времени и. . . местечка', *Zvezda*, no.10: 211–17, is about Grigorii Kanovich and Asar Eppel'; L. Gursky, 'А вы – не проект?' *Neva*, no.11 : 158–70, is about modern 'literary projects'; I. Zolotussky, 'Интеллигенция: смена вех', *Neva*, no.10 : 200–11.

POETRY. I. Erenburg, *Портреты русских поэтов*, ed. A. I. Rubashkin, SPb, Nauka, 351 pp., has profound comments on Erenburg's famous works on Russian poetry. D. Sviatopolk-Mirsky, *Поэты в России: Статьи. Рецензии. Портреты. Некрологи,* ed. V. Perkhin, SPb, Aleteia, 380 pp., includes works on Nikolai Gumilev, Anna Akhmatova, Marina Tsvetaeva, Sergei Esenin, letters to Maxim Gorky and Kornei Chukovsky. V. Bondarenko, 'Богоборчество и Богоискательство в русской поэзии конца века', *LitU*, no.5 : 88–95; S. Semenova, *Русская поэзия и проза 1920 – 1930-х годов: поэтика —видение мира —философия*, Mw, IMLI RAN, Nasledie, 2001, 590 pp.

Several interesting works by I. Kukulin are published: I. Kukulin, 'Как использовать шаровую молнию в психоанализе', *NLO*, 52, 2001 : 217–29; Id., 'Актуальный русский поэт как воскресшие Аленушка и Иванушка', *NLO*, 53 : 273–97; Id., 'Фотография внутренностей кофейной чашки', *NLO*, 54 : 262–82; Id., 'Эзотерическая амнистия песни', *NLO*, 55 : 282–94; Id., 'Прорастание отдельных слов в задымленных руинах', *DN*, no.3 : 180–91. O. Lebedushkina, 'Часть пространства, которая занята Богом', *DN*, no.5 : 182–99, is about the modern Russian poets Svetlana Kekova, Gennadii Rusakov, and Victor Krivulin. L. Borodin, 'В августе 68-го', *Den' Literatury*, no.4, is memoirs on Borodin's staying at the Soviet compulsory 'Dubrovlag' camp (mostly about Andrei Siniavsky); A. Naiman, 'Поэтическая непреложность', *NovM*, no.7 : 167–69.

V. Gubailovsky became a very active critic during last year: V. Gubailovsky, 'Поверх барьеров (взгляд на русскую поэзию 2001 года)', *Arion*, no.1; Id., 'Усиление смысла. Заметки о современной поэме. Максим Амелин. Глеб Шульпяков. Дмитрий Быков', *DN*, no.4 : 182–95; Id., 'Волна и камень. Поэзия и проза. Инна Кабыш. Анатолий Гаврилов. Сергей Гандлевский', *DN*, no.7 : 190–98.

There are several works about Russian bards: I. Sokolova, *Авторская песня: от фольклора к поэзии*, Mw, Blagotvoritel′nyi fond Vladimira Vysotskogo, 292 pp. I. Sokolova, 'Авторская песня: от экзотики к утопии', *VL*, no.1 : 139–56; A. Kulagin, 'Барды и филологи (Авторская песня в исследованиях последних лет)', *NLO*, 54 : 333–55; A. Krylov, *Галич – «соавтор»*, Mw, Blagotvoritel′-nyi fond Vladimira Vysotskogo, 2001, 124 pp. See also T. Bek, 'Старые поэтические жанры на новом витке', *Literatura*, no.7 : 2–3; A. Ulanov, 'Сны о чем-то большем', *DN*, no.2 : 185–94; V. Perel'muter, 'Записки без комментариев', *Arion*, no.2 : 66–78; M. Liubomudrov, 'Русский романс в конце тысячелетия', *NSo*, no.10 : 242–47; K. Kobrin, *Письма в Кейптаун о русской поэзии и другие эссе*, Mw, NLO, 128 pp.; A. Komlev, 'Очерки встреч — разлук: Светлейший и сиятельный Леонид Оболенский; почва и космос Вячеслава Терентьева', *Ural*, no.11; I. Falikov, 'Прозапростихи. Три этюда', *DN*, no.9 : 178–88, about Grigorii Kruzhkov, Iurii R'ashentsev, Aleksei Korolev; *Павел Васильев: исследования и материалы*, ed. V. I. Khomiakov, Omsk State U.P., 119 pp.; L. Kostiukov, 'Абсолютно всерьез. О поэзии Кирилла Медведева', *DN*, no.3 : 192–98; *Русские поэты 20 века*, ed. L. P. Krementsov and V. V. Losev, Mw, Flinta–Nauka, 320 pp.; *Твой нерасшатанный мир: памяти Вадима Козового: стихи, письма, воспоминания*, Mw, Progress–Traditsiia, 2001, 248 pp., compiled by I. Emelianova, Kozovoi's widow.

DRAMA. V. I. Mil′don, *Вершины русской драмы*, Mw, MGU, 256 pp.; M. Dubnova, 'Чудо, деньги, любовь. . . Основные ценности девяностых в популярных пьесах десятилетия', *VL*, no.6 : 57–77; S. Goncharova-Grabovskaia, 'Жанровая модель комедии в русской драматургии конца XX века', *NZSJ*, 36 : 101–14; G. Ia. Verbitskaya, *Традиции поэтики А. П. Чехова в современной отечественной драматурии 80–х – 90 – х годов: пьесы Н. Коляды в чеховском контексте*, Ufa, RITs UGII, 28 pp. *Репетитор: пьесы уральских драматургов*, Ekaterinburg, Ural′skoe izdatel′stvo, 460 pp., contains 17 plays by the modern writers Ol′ga Berseneva, Tatiana Shiriaeva, Oleg Bogaev, and Vasilii Sigarev, all of them Nikolai Koliada's students. N. Sadur, 'Я еще помню, как мыла в театре полы. . .', *Trud-7*, 53, is interviewed by E. Ul'chenko.

POSTMODERNISM. I. S. Koropanova, *Русская постмодернистская литература*, 4t h rev. edn, Mw, Flinta–Nauka, 608 pp.; M. Lipovetsky, 'Конец постмодернизма?', *LitU*, no.3 : 59–70.

GENDER STUDIES. L. Berezovchuk, 'У феминизма не женское лицо', *Oktiabr'*, no.1 : 104–29.

EPISTOLARY. G. F. Blagova publishes 'Переписка В. М. Жирмунского с С. Е. Маловым', *Izv. RAN SliIA*, no.2 : 61–67.

B. Pil′niak, *Мне выпала горькая слава... Письма 1915–1937*, Mw, Agraf, 400 pp.; S. Shcheglov publishes 'Письма Константина Федина', *VL*, no.2 : 371–78. There are valuable publications of Georgii Adamovich's letters to A. V. Bakhrakh: letters written in 1954–1956 are published by Vera Kreid in *NZh*, 224, 2001 : 70–98, and *ib.*, 228 : 151–91, and those written in 1957–1965 are published in *NZh*, 225, 2001 : 148–85. Petr Bitsilli's letters to A. L. Bem are in *NZh*, 228 : 122–50; 64 letters of the Russian émigré poet Dmitry Iosifovich Klenovsky (whose real last name was Krachkovsky, 1892–1976) are published by I. Sarukhanian: 'Письма Дм. Кленовского к И. С. Топорковой', *Zvezda*, no.1 : 98–128. Letters by A. Sharov and B. Chichibabin are in: 'Судьбы, встречи, письма... Из архива А. Шарова и Б. Чичибабина', *VL*, no.1; 'Иван Шмелев: отражения в зеркале писем', *NN*, 59–60, 2001; for Ivan Shmelev's letters to N. Ia Roshchin, see in 'Писатель — это тот, кому писать дается всего труднее', ed. L. G. Golubeva, *NovM*, no.9 : 128–35; 'Письма к Игорю Чиннову', *NZh*, 226 : 157–83; Correspondence between G. P. Sruve and V. V. Veidle is published in 'Откликаюсь фрагментами из собственной биографии...', *NovM*, no.9 : 133–42, ed. E. B. Belodubrovsky; A. Rubashkin, 'Письма прошлого века', *Neva*, no.11 : 171–89, has letters by the critics A. E. Gorelov, N. N. Ianovsky, L. I. Levin, and Z. G. Mints to the critic Rubashkin.

ESSAYS. A. Bitov, *Пятое измерение: На границе времени и пространства (Эссеистика)*, Mw, Nezavisimaia gazeta, 544 pp.; M. Zolotonosov and N. Kononov, *З/К, или Вивисекция: Книга протоколов*, SPb, Modern, 208 pp.; G. Shul′piakov, *Персона grappa: Избранные эссе*, Mw, MK–Periodika; Iu. Mamleev, *Россия вечная. (Русь многоликая)*, Mw, AiF-Print, 336 pp.; V. Aksenov, 'Чудо или чудачество? Роман: путь к помойке', *Moskovskie Novosti*, no.11 : 4–5; G. Pomerants, 'Созерцатели нашего века', *Zvezda*, no.1 : 180–96; V. Shubinsky, 'Взгляд и некто', *NLO*, 52, 2001 : 272–80; K. Kobrin, *Книжный шкаф Кирилла Кобрина* (Studia philologica. Series minor), Mw, Iazyki Slavianskoi Kul′tury, 144 pp., Dm. Bykov, *Блуд труда: Эссе*, SPb, Limbus Press, 416 pp.; Iu. Stefanov, *Скважины между мирами: контекст–9*, Mw, Nauka, 430 pp.; D. Bykov, *Блуд труда*, SPb, Limbus Press, 416 pp.; G. Kruzhkov, *Ностальгия обелисков: литературные мечтания*, Mw, NLO, 2001, 704 pp.

INTERVIEWS. There are several interesting collection of interviews with modern Russian writers. A. Minchin, *Двадцать интервью*, Mw, Izografus, EKSMO-Press, 2001, 352 pp., contains interviews with V. Aksenov, I. Brodsky, V. Maksimov, L. Navrozov, and E. Neizvestny; see also V. Pimonov, *Говорят «особо опасные»*, Mw,

Detektiv-Press, 1999, 240 pp., containing interviews with L. Borodin, L. Timofeev, and V. Senderov. V. Amursky's *Запечатленные голоса*, Mw, MIK, 1998, 166 pp., contains interviews with I. Brodsky, E. Rein, V. Ufliand, A. Bitov, A. Kushner, L. Losev, N. Gorbanevskaya, V. Maksimov, B. Okudzhava, S. Zalygin, O. Volkov, A. Zinoviev, G. Aigi, V. Makanin, F. Gorenstein, E. Popov, and M. Veller. Other interviews include Lev Anninsky, 'Талантом в России никого не удивишь', *LitU*, no.3 : 37–43 (interviewer K. Paskal'); Vadim Kreid, 'Вчерашний день жив в сегодняшнем', *LitU*, no.3 : 206–12 (interviewer G. Krasnikov); Victoriia Tokareva, 'Прогулки по Вене', *LitU*, no.4 : 61–69 (interviewer N. Stremitina); I. Polianskaya, 'Литература — это послание', *VL*, no.1 : 243–60 (interviewer E. Cherniaeva); S. Kekova, 'А стихи — тонкая материя. . .', *VL*, no.2 : 200–20 (interviewer I. Kuznetsova); N. Shmelev, 'Мотив был неистребимое любопытство', *VL*, no.4 : 231–49 (interviewer T. Bek); N. Trauberg, 'Жизнь как благодарность', *ib.*, 250–63 (interviewer E. Kalashnikova); A. Marinina, 'Я пишу для людей, а не для критиков!', *Lit Rossiia*, 2001, no.41 (interviewer V. Ivanov); L. Borodin, 'Считаю себя русистом', *Den' Literatury*, no.4 (interviewer V. Bondarenko); V. P'etsukh, 'Писательский труд — редкое заболевание', *Trud-7*, no.76 (interviewer A. Starodubets); Iu. Kublanovsky, 'Россию без поэзии не мыслю', *Trud-7*, no.48 (interviewer V. Korobov); S. Shenbrunn, 'Интуитивно и непреднамеренно', *VL*, no.6 : 262–73 (interviewer T. Bek).

4. Individual Authors

AKHMATOVA. *Творчество Н. Гумилева и А. Ахматовой в контексте русской поэзии 20 века: Третьи Ахматовские чтения*, Tver' State U.P., 115 pp.; S. A. Shul'ts, 'Наблюдатель и творец истории (о «Северных элегиях» А. А. Ахматовой)', *RusL*, no.2 : 89–97. M. Kralin, '«Двух голосов перекличка» (Иван Бунин и Анна Ахматова)', *NSo*, no.6 : 258–82. M. Sinel'nikov, 'Тарковский и Ахматова', *Znamia*, no.7 : 151–76, is a chapter from a memoir *Принесенные ветром, или Таш и Тоголок* (in progress in Limbus Press). A. Naiman, *Рассказы об Анне Ахматовой*, Mw, EKSMO-Press, 448 pp. O. Berggol'ts (ed. E. Efimov), 'Военные стихи Анны Ахматовой', *Znamia*, 2001, no.10 : 139–49, is an honest appraisal of A., written on the eve of Zhdanov's well-known speech about A. and Zoshchenko. L. Losev, 'О любви Ахматовой к «Народу»', *Zvezda*, no.1 : 206–14; D. Davydov, 'Поэтика последовательного ухода', *NLO*, 57 : 195–204; E. Soshkin, 'От адамова яблока до Адамова языка: территория Анны Горенко', *ib.*,

205–19; I. Verblovskaya, *Горькой любовью любимый: Петербург Анны Ахматовой,* Zhurnal Zvezda, 336 pp.; I. N. Nevinskaya, *'В то время я гостила на земле. . .' Поэзия Ахматовой,* Mw, Prometei, 1999, 237 pp.; R. Mnikh, 'Сакральная символика в ситуации экфрасиса (стихотворение Анны Ахматовой «Царскосельская статуя»)', Heller, *Экфрасис,* 87–96; S. V. Burdina, *Поэмы Анны Ахматовой: «Вечные образы» культуры и жанр,* Perm′ State University, 310 pp.

AKSENOV. A. McMillin, 'Vasilii Aksenov in the criticism of other Russian writers', pp. 145–52 of *Balten – Slaven – Deutsche: Aspekte und Perspektiven kultureller Kontakte: Festschrift für Friedrich Scholz zum 70. Geburstag,* Münster, Lit, 2000.

AKUNIN. V. Liuty, 'Случайные черты', *Pod'em,* no.1 : 185–209, is about Akunin's 'Chaika'; O. Sulkin, 'Фандорин в Голливуде', *Itogi,* no.11 : 40–41; Iu. Samarin, 'Фандорин как представитель Гаагского трибунала', *Lit Rossiia,* no.14 : 12–13; V. V. Savel'eva, '«Чайка» Б. Акунина —«чисто английское убийство»', *RRe,* no.6 : 36–41.

ASTAF'EV. Al. Mikhailov, 'Уроки Астафьева (Памяти Виктора Астафьева)', *LitU,* no:4 : 84–90; G. Trifonov, 'Рубцы войны: памяти В. П. Астафьева', *Kontinent,* 114; G. I. Romanova, 'Сказка и быль в «Царь- рыбе» В. П. Астафьева', *Russkaia Slovesnost',* no.5 : 25–31; V. Astaf'ev, 'Без выходных. Из писем Валентину Курбатову', *Trud,* no. 130, 30 July. More complete publications are V. Astaf'ev, 'Без выходных. Из писем Валентину Курбатову', *DN,* no.8 : 3–25, and *Крест бесконечный. В.Астафьев – В.Курбатов: Письма из глубины России,* comp. and ed. G. Sapronov, Irkutsk, Izdatel' Sapronov, 512 pp,.

BABEL'. V. Kovsky, 'Исаак Бабель: неподдельная жизнь и беллетристические подделки', *VL,* no.3 : 73–85; E. Sicher, 'Babel's 'Shy Star': reference, inter-reference and interference', *NZSJ,* 36 : 259–76.

BELYI. A. Belyi, *Переписка, 1903—1919,* Mw, Progress–Pleiada, 2001, 606 pp.; L. Kolobaeva, 'Андрей Белый о символе', *LitU,* no.1 : 180–86; A. V. Lavrov, *Андрей Белый: публикации, исследования,* Mw, IMLI RAN, 363 pp. Id., '«Производственный роман» — последний замысел Андрея Белого', *NLO,* 56 : 114–34.

BITOV. O. A. Kutmina, '«Живые души» Андрея Битова', *Vestnik Omskogo Universiteta,* 2000, no.1: — about Bitov's novel 'Oglashennye' (1995); I. Sukhikh, 'Сочинение на школьную тему (1964 – 1971; 1978 —. . . «Пушкинский дом» А. Битова ', *Zvezda,* no.4 : 224–34. See also two interviews: 'Жизнь в этой жизни', *Ex*

Libris, no.18 (interviewer E. Varkan); A. Bitov, 'Попадание в резонанс', *Kontinent*, 113.

BRODSKY. *Как работает стихотворение Бродского: Из исследования славистов на Западе* (Научное приложение. Выпуск XXXVI), ed. L. V. Losev and V. P. Polukhina, Mw, NLO, 304 pp.; N. A. Bogomolov, 'О двух «рождественских стихотворениях» И. Бродского', *NLO*, 56: 192–98; A. M. Ranchin, 'Три заметки о полисемии в поэзии Иосифа Бродского', *ib.*, 199–203; A. Lonsbery (trans E. Staf'eva), 'Иосиф Бродский как американский поэт-лауреат', *ib.*, 204–12; N. Korzhavin, 'Генезис «стиля опережающей гениальности», или миф о великом Бродском', *Kontinent*, 113; *Венецианские тетради. Иосиф Бродский и другие*, comp. E. Margolis, Mw, Ogi, 256 pp., contains all Brodsky's works and essays on Venice.

BULGAKOV. L. Ianovskaya, *Записки о Михаиле Булгакове*, Mw, Paralleli, 414 pp.; L. Ianovskaya, 'Горизонтали и вертикали Ершалаима', *VL*, no.3: 291–303; D. Bykov, 'Три соблазна Михаила Булгакова', *Ogonyok*, no.19–20; V. I. Sakharov, *М. А. Булгаков в жизни и творчестве*, Mw, Russkoe slovo, 112 pp. B. Sokolov, *Булгаков: энциклопедия (Русские писатели)*, Mw, Algoritm, 608 pp., is a revised edition of a popular encyclopedia. O. Z. Kandaurov, *Евангелие от Михаила*, 2 vols, Mw, Graal', I: *Михаил Булгаков: мистика жизни*, 815 pp, II: *'Мастер и Маргарита': эзотерика текста*, 731 pp. G. M. Rebel', *Художественные мифы романов Михаила Булгакова*, Perm', Pripit, 2001, 196 pp.;T. G. Buditskaya, *Михаил Булгаков глазами Запада*, Mw, Sputnik+ , 2001, 215 pp.; *Родословия Михаила Булгакова*, ed. B. Miagkov, Mw, Apart, 2001, 94 pp. S. Ermolinsky, Mw, Agraf, 448 pp., *О времени, о Булгакове и о себе*, contains works on Bulgakov and memoirs on Ermolinsky. A. Minakov, *Символика романа М. А. Булгакова «Мастер и Маргарита»: опыт эзотерического исследования*, Mw, Parusa, 1998, 74 pp.

BUNIN. Kim Ken Te, 'Мир Востока в рассказе Бунина «Братья»', *RusL*, no.3: 19–36; V. V. Perkhin, 'И. А. Бунин в письмах корреспондентов Н. П. Смирнов (1959–1975)', *RusL*, no.3: 119–34; A. Abramiants, 'Звездные руны Ивана Бунина', *RRe*, no.2: 29–33; A. A. Diakina, *Иван Бунин —поэт Серебряного века*, Yelets State U.P., 2000, 115 pp.; G. M. Blagasova, *Иван Бунин: жизнь, творчество, проблемы метода и поэтики*, Belgorod State U.P., 2001, 232 pp.

CHICHIBABIN. N. M. Ogloblina, *'Меры жизни' поэта Бориса Чичибабина*, Komsomol'sk State Pedagogical U.P., 91 pp.

DANIEL. V. Katagoshchin, 'Юлий Даниэль', *NZh*, 229: 259–63.

DAVYDOV. E. Ermolin, 'Узы совести и зов свободы. Над страницами прозы Юрия Давыдова', *Kontinent*, 112:385–95.

DOVLATOV. D. Gillespie, 'The booze and the blues: laughter and the "real" world in the work of Sergei Dovlatov', *ASEES*, 15, 2001:21–37; V. Khait, 'Истоки музыки. О письмах Сергея Довлатова отцу из армии', *VL*, no.3:271–82; D. Ol'shansky, 'Кто виноват в шестьдесят? Юбилей Сергея Довлатова', *Novaia gazeta*, 163, 2001:11–12.

ERENBURG. B. Frezinsky, 'Эренбург и Ахматова (взаимоотношения, встречи, письма, автографы, суждения)', *VL*, no.2:243–91; A. Pirozhkova, 'Эренбург и Бабель', *VL*, no.6:274–318.

EROFEEV VEN. I. N. Marutina, 'Преломление темы «маленького человека» в поэме Вен. Ерофеева «Москва —Петушки»: традиции и новаторство', *Russkaia Slovesnost'*, no.3:34–37; N. Shmel'kova, *Последние дни Венедикта Ерофеева*, Mw, Vagrius, 320 pp.

ESENIN. N. I. Shubnikova-Guseva, *С. А. Есенин в жизни и творчестве*, Mw, Russkoe slovo, 112 pp; N. Shubnikova-Guseva, 'Девушка в белой накидке и помещица Анна Снегина', *LitU*, no.1:187–91; Alla Bol'shakova and Tatiana Davydova, 'Есениноведение сегодня: ключи к пониманию', *ib.*, 192–96; B. Gribanov, *Женщины, любившие Есенина*, Mw, TERRA – Knizhnyi Klub, 304 pp.

FADEEV. S. Zolotsev, 'Вознесенный и убитый веком. К 100-летию со дня рождения А. А. Фадеева', *Pod'em*, 2001, no.12:205–10.

GANDLEVSKY. A. K. Zholkovsky, 'К проблеме инфинитивной поэзии (Об интертекстуальном фоне стихотворения С. Гандлевского «Устроиться на автобазу. . .»)', *ISLIa*, no.1:34–42; D. Kuz'min, 'О нелюбви и неловкости', *DN*, no.8:192–94; V. Gubailovsky, 'Все прочее и литература', *NovM*, no.8:167–74; M. Zolotonosov, 'Синдром Гандлевского. Филологический роман о первой старости', *Moskovskie Novosti*, no.9; E. Ivanitskaya, 'Акела промахнулся', *DN*, no.8:195–97.

GARIN-MIKHAILOVSKY. L. N. Savina, 'Автор и герой в повести «Детство Темы»', *RRe*, no.1:3–10.

GIPPIUS. *Зинаида Николаевна Гиппиус. Новые материалы. Исследования*, ed. N. V. Koroleva, Mw, IMLI RAN, 384 pp.; L. Zvonareva, 'Зооморфный код в поэзии Зинаиды Гиппиус', *LitU*, no:4:100–11. Z. N. Gippius, *Дневники*, Mw, Zakharov, 364 pp., is well commented modern edition of well-known texts.

GIRSHOVICH. M. Lipovetsky, 'Леонид Гиршович и поэтика необарокко (Пример «Прайса»)', *NLO*, 57:220–37.

GOR. A. Laskin, 'Гор и мир', *Zvezda*, no.5: 131–34.

GORENSHTEIN. V. Shubinsky, 'Мессианский вирус. Фридрих Горенштейн, Россия и еврейство: попытка введения в тему', *Narod Knigi v mire knig*, no.38:4–5, interprets Gorenshtein as the 'Jewish Dostoevsky'. F. Gorenshtein, 'При свободе слова многим сказать нечего', *Trud*, no. 65, is interviewed by A. Starodubets.

GORKY. L. A. Sp iridonova, 'Текстология писем М. Горького', *RusL*, no.2:122–26; N. N. Primochkina, 'М. Горький в судьбе Нины Петровской', *Izv. RAN SliIA*, no.2:7–15; *Максим Горький —художник: проблемы, итоги и перспективы изучения: Горьковские чтения. 2000 год: Материалы Международной конференции*, ed. G. S. Zaitseva, Nizhnii Novgorod U.P., 492 pp.; R. T. Pevtsova, *Максим Горький и Фридрих Ницше*, Mw, Al'fa, 2001, 64 pp.; T. P. Ledneva, *Авторская позиция в произведениях М. Горького 90–х годов 19 века*, Izhevsk State Univ., 2001, 132 pp.

GRIGORIEV. E. Khvorostianova, *Поэтика Олега Григорьева*, SPb, Gumanitarnaia Akademiia, 2002, 160 pp.

GRONAS. L. Kostiukov, 'То,чего мы ждали', *DN*, no.6:201–202.

IAN. V. Oskotsky, 'Вехи судьбы, рубежи творчества (К 125–летию со дня рождения Василия Яна (В. Г. Янчевецкого)', *LitU*, no.3:123–34.

KAZAKOV . K. Saranchin, 'Странник советской литературы', *LitU*, no:4:72–78; A. Shorokhov, 'Юрий Казаков: Долгие крики на берегу Коцита', *ib.*, 79–83.

KAVERIN. Vl. Novikov, 'Он выполнил свой план', *VL*, no.5:3–9; N. Kaverin, 'Несколько случаев из жизни Вениамина Каверина', *ib.*, 10–16. An extract from Kaverin's uncompleted book is published by T. V. Berdikova: 'Оглядываясь назад', *Zvezda*, no.4:133–46.

KENZHEEV. I. Vasil'ev, 'Сопряжения (О поэзии Бахыта Кенжеева)', *Ural*, no.2:235–41.

KLUEV. K. M. Azadovsky, *Жизнь Николая Клюева: документальное повествование*, SPb, Zhurnal 'Zvezda', 365 pp.

KHILKOV. N. N. Primochkina, 'Судьба одного писателя («Большевик-князь» А. Д. Хилков)', *ISLIa*, no.4:43–48.

KHLEBNIKOV. H. Baran, *О Хлебникове. Контексты, источники, мифы*, Mw, RGGU, 416 pp., is an excellent study of Khlebnikov's oeuvre. V. V. Aristov, *В. В. Хлебников в Казани, 1898 – 1908: гимназия, университет, становление Велимира*, Kazan' U.P., 2001, 66 p; S. G. Semenova, '«Зачеловеческие» сны Велимира Хлебникова', *RusL*, no.2:69–88; J.-C. Lanne, 'О разных аспектах экфрасиса у Велимира Хлебникова', Heller, *Экфрасис*, 71–86.

KOL'TSOV. V. Fradkin, *Дело Кольцова*, Mw, Vagrius — Mezhdunarodnyi Fond 'Demokratiia', 351 pp.

KRUSANOV. K. Koksheneva, 'Империя без народа', *Moskva,* no.7.190–98

KRZHIZHANOVSKY. A very valuable publication is S. D. Krzhizhanovsky, 'Пьеса и ее заглавие', *NLO,* 52, 2001:205–16; E. Vorob'eva, 'Неизвестный Кржижановский (Заметки о киевском периоде творчества писателя)', *VL,* no.6:274–318.

KUZMIN. M. A. Kuzmin, *Дневник 1934 года,* comp. and ed. G. Morev, SPb, Izdatel'stvo Ivana Limbakha, 1998, 413 pp.

LEONOV. V. A. Petishev and A. A. Petishev, *Романное творчество Л. М. Леонова,* Birsk State Pedagogical Institute, 137 pp.; *Поэтика Леонида Леонова и художественная картина мира в XX веке: материалы международной конференции (20–21 июня 2001 г.),* SPb, Nauka, 166 pp.; T. M. Vakhitova, 'Проблемы текстологии Леонида Леонова', *RusL,* no.2:127–36; L. P. Iakimova, '«. . . Отвечающие времени формулы мифа» (некоторые особенности поэтики в произведениях Леонида Леонова)', *RusL,* no.3:184–91.

LEVITANSKY. A. N. Iavorsky, '«Окно, горящее в ночи» (О поэтическом языке Ю. Д. Левитанского)', *RRe,* no.1:27–29.

LICHUTIN. Iu. Arkhipov, 'Не годится русский в инородцы. К выходу в свет романа Владимира Личутина «Миледи Ротман»', *Den' literatury,* no.3.

MAIAKOVSKY. O. A. Lekmanov, 'В. Маяковский: поэт и публика', *RRe,* no.4:29–33. M. M. Polekhina, *Художественные искания в русской поэзии первой трети XX века: М. Цветаева и В. Маяковский,* Mw, Prometei, 304 pp.

MAKANIN. V. D. Serafimova, 'Метафорический язык произведений В. С. Маканина', *RRe,* no.2:34–41; R. Kireev, 'Контрапункт Владимира Маканина', *Literatura,* no. 29:4–5; V. Makanin, 'Против стиля', *Ex Libris,* no.9:2–3 (interviewer: E. Varkan).

MANDELSTAM. There two interesting books and several papers on Mandelstam: L. Katsis, *Осип Мандельштам: мускус иудейства,* (Прошлый век), Jerusalem, Gesharim — Mw, Mosty kul'tury, 600 pp.; G. M. Lifshits, *Многозначное слово в поэтической речи: история слова "ночь" в лирике О. Э. Мандельштама,* Mw, MAKS Press, 272 pp.; A. Bershtadt, 'Идея времени у Мандельштама', *LitU,* no.4:179–83; L. M. Vidgof, 'О «Чертежнике пустыни» О. Мандельштама', *ISLIa,* no.5:43–51; V. P. Grigoriev, 'Об одном тире в одном из «Восьмистиший» Осипа Мандельштама', *ISLIa,* no.5:52–61. *Осип и Надежда Мандельштамы в рассказах современников,* ed. O. and M. Figurnovs, Mw, Natalis, 544 pp. O. Lekmanov, 'О двух «дурацких» баснях Осипа Мандельштама', *Daugava,* 2001, nos 1–2; M. Pavlova, '«Поэзия —плуг, взрывающий время. . . Опыт внимательного чтения стихотворения О. Мандельштама «Золотистого меда струя из бутылки текла. . .»', *Literatura,* no. 22:3–4; A. Sergeeva-Kliatis, '«Из стакан в стакан». Мандельштам и Батюшков', *ib.*, 5–6; M. L. Gasparov and O. Ronen, 'О «Веницейской жизни. . .» О. Мандельштама. Опыт комментария', *Zvezda,* no.2:193–202; G. V. Zykova, 'Стихотворение Мандельштама «Нет, не луна, а светлый циферблат. . .» и «Русские ночи» В. Ф. Одоевского', Serebrennikov, *Время,* 311–13.

MARTYNOV. S. Povartsov, '«Мы старые поэты» (О Леониде Мартынове и Семене Кирсанове)', *VL,* no.3:283–90.

NABOKOV. N. Anastas'ev, *Владимир Набоков. Одинокий король,* Mw, Tsentrpoligraf, 525 pp., is a popular biography of Nabokov; E. Klepikova, *Невыносимый Набоков,* Tver', Drugie berega, 364 pp.; *Набоков о Набокове и прочем: Интервью, рецензии, эссе,* comp. and ed. N. G. Mel'nikov, Mw, Nezavisimaia gazeta, 704 pp.; I. N. Cheplygina, *Повтор как структурное средство актуализации в языковой картине мира В. Набокова,* Rostov-na-Donu, IUBIP, 131 pp.; N. S. Stepanova, *Мотив воспоминаний в русских романах В. Набокова,* Kursk, Uchitel', 2001, 204 pp.; N. V. Semenova, *Цитата в художественной прозе: на материале произведений В. Набокова,* Tver' State U.P., 200 pp.; A. V. Zlochevskaya, *Художественный мир Владимира Набокова и русская литература 19 века,* Moscow State U.P., 185 pp.; N. M. Zheltysheva, *«Пушкинская тема» в романе В. Набокова «Лолита»,* Mw, Sputnik+, 53 pp.; L. N. Riaguzova, *Концептуализированная сфера «творчество» в художественной системе В. В. Набокова,* Krasnodar, Kuban' State Univ., 2000, 184 pp.; L. N. Riaguzova, *Система эстетических и теоретико-литературных понятий В. В. Набокова,* Krasnodar, Kuban' State Univ., 2001, 140 pp.; *Набоковский сборник: искусство как прием,* ed. M. A. Dmitrovskaya, Kaliningrad State U.P., 2001, 169 pp.; M. Grishakova, 'Визуальная поэтика В. Набокова', *NLO,* 54:205–28; Sergei Kaverin, 'В. Набоков: формализация содержательного', *Moskovsky vestnik,* 2001, no.3:67–81; O. Liubimov, 'Цугцванг: Роман Владимира Набокова «Защита Лужина» как продолжение гуманистических традиций русской литературы', *Pod'em,* 2001, no.7:201–09; G. Nikitin, 'Возвращение рая', *LitU,* no.6:138–47; B. Wyllie, 'Experiments in perspective: cinematics in Nabokov's Russian fiction', *NZSJ,* 36:289–302.

NEKRASOV. V. A. Karpov, 'Виктор Некрасов, или Искусство оставаться самим собой', *LitU,* no.2:78–86. L. Lazarev, 'Верность правде. Творческий путь Виктора Некрасова', *Literatura,* no. 18:8–9.

NOSOV, E. A. E. Kedrovsky, *Земляки: творчество К. Д. Воробьева и Е. И. Носова*, Kursk State Pedagogical U.P., 154 pp., B. Ageev, 'Человек уходит. Мотив Конца Света в повести Евгения Носова «Усвятские шлемоносцы»', *NSo*, no.5 : 224–34; S. V. Molchanova, 'Слово «таинство» и таинство слова', *RRe*, no.3 : 30–34.

OKUDZHAVA. Several interesting works on Okudzhava were published in *VL*, no. 3: N. Bogomolov, 'Булат Окуджава и массовая культура' (4–14); M. Chudakova, 'Возвращение лирики' (15–42); O. Kling, '«. . .Дальняя дорога дана тебе судьбой. . .» Мифологема пути в лирике Булата Окуджавы' (43–57). See also: *Окуджава: проблемы поэтики и текстологии*, Mw, Gosudarstvennyi kul′turnyi tsentr-muzei V. S. Vysotskogo, 254 pp.

OLESHA. E. R. Men'shikova, 'Редуцированный смех Юрия Олеши', *VF*, no.10 : 75–85.

OSTROVSKY, N. *Николай Островский — человек и писатель — в воспоминаниях современников: 1904–1936: К 100-летию со дня рождения*, ed. T. I. Andronova, Mw, DN, 240 pp.

PASTERNAK. A. Gladkov, *Встречи с Пастернаком*, Mw, Art-Fleks, 288 pp., is a revised edition; A. Pasternak, *Воспоминания*, Mw, Progress–Traditsiia, 430 pp., is a memoir written by P.'s brother. V. Livanov, *Невыдуманный Борис Пастернак: воспоминания и впечатления*, Mw, Drofa, 109 pp. Evgenii Pasternak has edited and published his father's correspondence with the French novelist Romain Rolland, in 'На том берегу неба. Переписка', *Znamia*, no.11 : 167–92; See also I. Rostovtseva, 'Муза и собеседница (Природа в поэзии Пастернака и Заболоцкого)', *VL*, no.1 : 123–38. O. Kling, 'Борис Пастернак и символизм', *VL*, no.2 : 25–59. A. Samoilov, 'Пастернак без сносок', *VL*, no.2 : 350–52; L. Sova, *Борис Пастернак и его родные в Берлине*, *Neva*, no.6 : 250–52; E. Clowes, 'Pasternak's *Safe Passage* and the question of philosophy', *NZSJ*, 36 : 39–48; *Марбург Бориса Пастернака. Письма и стихотворения*, comp. E. L. Kudriavtseva, Mw, Russkii put', 2001, 244 pp.

PAUSTOVSKY. A. Izmailov, *Я был захвачен Севером сильнее: К. Г. Паустовский и Северо-Запад России*, SPb, B&K, 2001, 166 pp.

PAVLOV. K. Ankudinov, 'Манихейский вариант', *NovM*, no.5 : 166–72. E. Ermolin, 'Инстанция взгляда', *ib.*, 172–76.

PAVLOVA. K. Ragozina, 'За жен косноязычных и немых', *NLO*, 54 : 295–96; V. Rasputin, 'Самая большая беда литературы — безъязыкость', *LitG*, nos.14–15 (interviewer: N. Gorlova).

PELEVIN. D. Perevozov, 'Зарытый талант. О Владимире Маяковском и о романе Виктора Пелевина «Чапаев и Пустота»',

Pod'em, 2001, no.9: 181–87, is rather unfair to Victor Pelevin but some of the author's points are worth consideration.

PEREDREEV. A. Bazhenova, '«Еще не все потеряно, мой друг!»: К 70-летию поэта Анатолия Передреева', *NSo*, no.12: 131–37.

PETRUSHEVSKAIA. T. T. Davydova, 'Сумерки реализма: о прозе Л. Петрушевской', *Russkaia Slovesnost'*, no.7: 32–36.

PIL'NIAK. 'Письма с Востока. К пребыванию Б. Пильняка в Японии в 1932 году', is published by N. Iu. Griakalova, *RusL*, no.3: 170–83.

PLATONOV. E. A. Iablokov, *На берегу неба: роман Андрея Платонова «Чевенгур»*, SPb, Dmitrii Bulanin, 2001, 375 pp.; *Наш Платонов*, ed. R. Andreeva, Voronezh, Tsentr dukhovnogo vozrozhdeniia Chernozemnogo kraia, 1999, 382 pp. M. Iu. Mikheev, 'Андрей Платонов: между плеоназмом, парадоксом, анаколуфом и языковым ляпсусом', *ISLIa*, no.4: 19–29; S. Fediakin, '1946-й', *Literatura*, no.18: 3–4; E. Ovanesian, '«Антинародный» Платонов и безродные космополиты', *MG*, nos. 7–8: 129–34, is an openly anti-Semitic interpretation of Platonov's prose.

PRIGOV. K. Mundt, '«Мы видим или видят нас?» Сила взгляда в искусстве Д. А. Пригова', Eimermacher, *Культура*, 270–84.

PRISHVIN. A. Varlamov, 'Пришвин, или Гений жизни: биографическое повествование', *Oktiabr'*, no.1: 130–84; V. Prishvina, *Невидимый град*, ed. Ia. Grishina, Mw, MG, 529 pp.

PROKHANOV. M. Remizova, 'Ведь вы этого достойны: заметки об Александре Проханове, герое нашего времени', *Kontinent*, 113: 365–74; S. Beliakov, 'Пейзаж после взрыва — с Немзером, Бондаренко и исчезающей радугой', *Ural*, no.12: 215–25; V. Chepelev, 'Каждый охотник желает знать, где сидит фазан', *Ural*, no.12: 226–31. A lot of reviews on Prokhanov's latest novel 'Mr Hexogen' are collected on <http://www.geksogen.veshnyaki.ru>.

RASPUTIN. I. Sukhikh, 'Однажды была земля (1976. «Прощание с Матерой» В. Распутина)', *Zvezda*, no.2: 225–36; V. Oskotsky, 'Валентин Распутин в двух лицах', *Demokraticheskii vybor*, no. 18; V. D. Serafimova, 'Слово в художественном мире Валентина Распутина', *RRe*, no.6: 24–29; L. A. Kolobaeva, 'В. Распутин-рассказчик', *Russkaia Slovesnost'*, no.2: 11–17; V. Rasputin, 'Самая большая беда литературы —безъязыкость', *LitG*, no.14–15 (interviewer: N. Gorlova).

RAZGON. *Пленник эпохи. Памяти Л. Э. Разгона*, comp. and ed. Marlen Korallov, Mw, Zveniia, 334 pp., contains works by Lev Razgon, and memoirs about Razgon written by Daniil Danin, Lidiia

Libedinskaya, Anatolii Pristavkin, Kirill Koval′dzhi, Iulii Krelin, and others.

REIN. E. Izvarina, 'Наука убеждать: сентиментальные хроники Евгения Рейна', *Ural*, no.2225–34; E. Rein, 'Вся жизнь и еще «Уан бук»', *VL*, no.5 : 167–96 (interviewer: T. Bek).

ROMANOV. V. P. Meshcheriakov, 'Искать свой материал в обыкновенном (о поэтике юмористических рассказов П. Романова', Serebrennikov, *Время*, 282–91.

ROZHDESTVENSKY. Robert Rozhdestvensky, *Удостоверение личности*, ed. K. Rozhdestvenskaia, Mw, Estepona, 568 pp., contains R's selected poems and poets' and critics' memoirs about his poetry.

RUBTSOV. V. A. Zaitsev, *Николай Рубцов*, Mw, MGU, 64 pp.

RYZHII. 'Венок Борису Рыжему', comp. Iu. Kazarin, *Ural*, no.5 : 2–23.

SEDAKOVA. O. Sedakova, 'Гермес: Невидимая сторона классики', *Kontinent*, 114 : 333–61; M. Kopeliovich, 'Путешествие в глубину, или Пламенная филология Ольги Седаковой', *ib.*, 420–28.

SENCHIN. K. Koksheneva, 'Все та же любовь', *NSo*, no.7 : 270–80.

SHKLOVSKY. V. Shklovsky, 'Письма внуку', *VL*, no.4 : 264–300.

SHMELEV. T. V. Marchenko, 'Иван Шмелев и Нобелевская премия', *Izv. RAN SLIA*, no.1 : 25–33; *Шмелевские чтения: сборник научных трудов*, ed. O. N. Shotova, Simferopol', Tavriia-Plus, 2000, 212 pp. *Венок Шмелеву*, ed. L. A. Spiridonova and O. N. Shotova, Mm, Nasledie, 2001, 352 pp.

SHOLOKHOV. A. G. Makarov and S. E. Makarova, *Цветок-Татарник: в поисках автора «Тихого Дона» от Михаила Шолохова к Федору Крюкову*, Mw, AIRO-XX, 2001, 500 pp.; A. V. Venkov, *«Тихий Дон»: источниковедческая база и проблема авторства*, Rostov State University, 2000, 234 pp.; N. M. Muravieva, *"Поднятая целина" М. А. Шолохова: философско-поэтический контекст*, Borisoglebsk State PI, 123 pp.. V. Petelin, *Жизнь Шолохова: Трагедия русского гения*, Mw, Tsentrpoligraf, 895 pp., is a selection of previously published works with nothing new. See the unpleasant F. Kuznetsov, 'Неразгаданная тайна «Тихого Дона»', *NSo*, no.4 : 231–52, and also Id., 'Осторожно: профанация!' *Lit Rossiia*, 2001, no.16 : 9–10; S. Semenova, 'Философско-метафизические грани «Тихого Дона»', *VL*, no.1 : 71–122; V. N. Eremenko, 'Три встречи', *Lit Rossiia*, no.23 : 5–6.

SHUKSHIN. Ni. I. Stopchenko, *Василий Шукшин в зарубежной культуре*, Rostov State University, 2001, 183 pp.; V. I. Korobov, *В. И. Шукшин. Вещее слово*, Mw, Molodaia gvardiia, 1999, 403 pp.

SINIAVSKY. M. Rozanova, 'Синявский, Абрам Терц и я', *Vremia MN*, 2001, no.180; N. Voronel', 'Юлик и Андрей', *VL*, no.5:273–304.

SLAVNIKOVA. There were debates around Slavnikova's latest novel: E. Ivanitskaya, 'Жизнь в петле', *DN*, 2001, no.10:163–65; V. Lipnevich, 'Долгое прощание, или О, Славникова!', *ib.*, 166–69; S. Beliakov, 'Оптические эффекты. Заметки о творчестве Ольги Славниковой', *Ural*, no.4.

SOLZHENITSYN. V. Voinovich, *Портрет на фоне мифа*, Mw, EKSMO-Press, 192 pp., is the scandal of the year! Voinovich gives his personal vision of Solzhenitsyn's works and his role in Russian literature and culture. R. Medvedev, *Солженицын и Сахаров*, Mw, Prava cheloveka, 272 pp. R. Porter, ' "Us, we don't die" —notions of death and immortality in Solzhenitsyn', *NZSJ*, 36:213–24; G. Gachev, 'Россия и ее приемный сын: в связи с книгой А. И. Солженицына «Двести лет вместе (1795–1995)»', *Kontinent*, 111:389–95; O. Liubimov, 'Бесовский край', *Pod'em*, no.4:215–24.

SOROKIN. On his latest novel 'Led' see: M. Bondarenko, 'Роман-аттракцион и катафатическая конструкция', *NLO*, 56:241–48, V. Kukushkin, 'Мудрость Сорокина', *ib.*, 249–52; I. Kukulin, 'Every trend makes a brand', *ib.*, 253–68. I. Shamir, 'Наше прошлое —дело нашего будущего', *Novaia Russkaia Kniga*, 2001, nos.3–4:31–34, is about Sorokin's novel *Goluboe salo*.

SHTIL'MARK, R. F. Shtil'mark, 'Очарованный странник', *Lit Rossiia*, no.18:3–4.

SULEIMENOV. L. Frizman, 'Возмутитель спокойствия. Книга О. Сулейменова «Аз и Я» под огнем идеологической критики', *NLO*, 55:385–90.

TARKOVSKY. P. D. Volkova, *Арсений Тарковский: Жизнь семьи и история рода*, Mw, Podkova — EKSMO-Press, 224 pp. See also *Андрей Тарковский: Архивы, документы, воспоминания*, ed. P. D. Volkova, Mw, Podkova — EKSMO-Press, 224 pp.

TOLSTAYA. M. Remizova, 'Grandes Dames прошедшего сезона', *Kontinent*, 112:396–405; N. V. Balandina, 'Молчит ли автор о сущности бытия?', *RRe*, no.3:35–41, is about Tolstaya's novella 'Milaya Shura'; T. T. Davydova, 'Роман Т. Толстой «Кысь»: проблемы, образы героев, жанр, повествование', *Russkaia Slovesnost'*, no.5:25–30; G. Nefagina, 'Антиутопия в русской прозе конца XX века и роман Т. Толстой *Кысь*', *NZSJ*, 36:183–200.

A. N. TOLSTOY. S. Borovikov, 'Над головой толклись комарики. . .', *NovM*, no.7:170–76, is about the revisons and various editions of T's famous novel *Хождение по мукам*.

TSVETAEVA. Several biographies of T. have been published during the last year: I. Kudrova, *Путь кометы. Жизнь Марины Цветаевой*, SPb, Vita Nova, 768 pp., contains some new documents about T.'s husband Sergei Efron and some interesting photographs from Kudrova's private archive, see also I. V. Kudrova, *Жизнь Марины Цветаевой до эмиграции*, SPb, Izdatel'stvo zhurnala 'Zvezda', 311 pp., V. Shveitser, *Марина Цветаева (Жизнь замечательных людей)*, Mw, Molodaia Gvardiia, 591 pp., A. Saakiants, *Твой миг, твой день, твой век: жизнь Марины Цветаевой*, Mw, Agraf, 416 pp.; I. Shevelenko, *Литературный путь Цветаевой: Идеология – поэтика – идентичность автора в контексте эпохи (Научная библиотека)*, Mw, NLO, 464 pp.; A. Bobrov, '«Правда — моя последняя гордость»', *NSo*, no.11:265–76, about Marina Tsvetaeva; L. Voronin, '«Услышать... для поэта — уже ответить» (Марина Цветаева и Владимир Луговской. Версия)', *VL*, no.2:60–94; T. Gevorkian, '«Дарующий отлив» весны 1926 года (Истоки и подтексты поздних статей Цветаевой об искусстве)', *VL*, no.5:17–44; O. Ronen, 'Молвь: К 60-летию гибели Марины Цветаевой', *Zvezda*, 2001, no.9:232–38; S. V. Rudzievskaya, 'Сводные тетради и письма М. Цветаевой', *RRe*, no.5:16–19. E. O. Aisenshtein, *«Построен на созвучьях мир»: звуковая стихия М. Цветаевой*, SPb, Neva, Letnii sad, 2000, 288 pp. L. Pann, 'Сезам по складам. Вопрошая посветлевшие чернила Марины Цветаевой', *Zvezda*, no.10:195–205. M. Tsvetaeva, *Письма к Наталье Гайдукевич*, comp. and ed. L. Mnukhin, Mw, Russkii put', 146 pp.; M. I. Tsvetaeva, *Ulianovsk*, comp. E. B. Korkina Ulianovskii dom pechati, 2001, 199 pp. There are three books compiled by L. Mnukhin and L. Turchinsky: *Марина Цветаева в воспоминаниях современников: Рождение поэта*, Mw, Agraf, 352 pp., *Марина Цветаева в воспоминаниях современников: Годы эмиграции*, Mw, Agraf, 336 pp.; and *Марина Цветаева в воспоминаниях современников: книга третья*, Mw, Agraf, 304 pp. I. Z. Malinkovich, *Судьба старинной легенды: И. В. Гете, К. Зимрок, Р. Браунинг, Г. Гейне, М. Цветаева*, Mw, Sinee Iabloko, 1999, 149 pp.

TVARDOVSKY. S. Lipkin, 'Встречи с Твардовским', *VL*, no.2:237–42; M. Shapir, 'Данте и Теркин «на том свете» (О судьбах русского бурлеска в 20 веке)', *VL*, no.3:58–72; See T.'s very sincere diary: A. Tvardovsky, 'Рабочие тетради 60-х годов', *Znamia*, no.2:67–90; A. Bek, 'Встречи с Твардовским в 1940 году. Дневниковые записи', *Znamia*, 2001, no.10:131–38 (published by T. Bek); V. A. Tvardovskaya, 'Твардовский глазами М. Синельникова', *Znamia*, no.11:178–83 — polemics with Mikhail Sinel'nikov's work 'Там, где сочиняют сны'.

VAMPILOV. D. Vygorbina, 'Запрещенная и непонятная пьеса А. Вампилова «Утиная охота» — трагический фарс?', *LitU*, no.2 : 159–64; S. V. Molchanova, 'Профессиональная тайна Сарафанова', *RRe*, no.4 : 32–36; S. S. Imkhelova and O. O. Iurchenko, *Художественный мир Александра Вампилова*, Ulan-Ude, Buriat State University, 106 pp.

VIZI. O. Bakich, 'Мария Визи. Творческий путь поэта России, Китая и США', *NZh*, 227 : 198–201.

VOLOS. There are two new papers in *Znamia*, no.1, about Volos's novel *Nedvizhimost* : A. Kasymov, 'Обретение крова, или Дом, который мы потеряли' (180–83), and D. Dmitriev, 'Про нашу жизнь' (184–86).

VOLOSHIN. V. Kupchenko, *Труды и дни Максимилиана Волошина: Летопись жизни и творчества. 1877–1916*, SPb, Aleteia, 512 pp.

VOROB'EV. N. N. Arkhangel'skaya, *Проза К. Воробьева: темы, идеи, характеры*, Tambov State University, 2001, 45 pp.

VYSOTSKY. V. Zolotukhin, *Секрет Высоцкого (Дневниковая повесть)*, Mw, EKSMO-Press, 320 pp., is written by one of V.'s closest friends. V. I. Novikov, *Высоцкий* (Жизнь замечательных людей. Серия биографии: выпуск 829), Mw, Molodaia Gvardiia, 413 pp., is the best study to date on V's life and work; V. I. Batov, *Владимир Высоцкий: психогерменевтика творчества*, Mw, Rossiskii Institut Kul'turologii; Mezhdunarodnaia Pedagogicheskaia Akademiia, 224 pp.; A. V. Kulagin, *Высоцкий и другие*, Mw, Blagotvoritel'nyi fond Vladimira Vysotskogo, 200 pp.; D. Karapetian, *Владимир Высоцкий: Между словом и славой*, Mw, Zakharov, 288 pp.; N. Verderevskaya, *Двадцать лет спустя: этюды о поэзии Владимира Высоцкого*, Naberezhnye Chelny, Tatarskoe otdelenie soiuza rossiiskikh pisatelei, 2001, 90 pp.; V. Perevozchikov, *Владимир Высоцкий: Правда смертного часа. Посмертная судьба*, Mw, Vagrius, 430 pp., D. Karapetian, *Владимир Высоцкий. Между словом и славой. Воспоминания*, Mw, Zakharov, 278 pp.; V. G. Titarenko, *Прощай, Высоцкий: Документальная хроника похорон*, Tambov State University, 90 pp. See also several papers : A. Krylov, 'Заметки администратора на полях высоцковедения', *VL*, no.4 : 328–53; D. Suvorov, 'Очерки о Высоцком', *Ural*, no.7 : 181–85; S. M. Beliakova, 'Пространство и время в поэзии В. Высоцкого', *RRe*, no.1 : 30–35.

ULITIN. I. Kukulin, 'Подводный, но не вытесненный', *NLO*, 54 : 285–87.

ZAMIATIN. E. Zamiatin, *Записные книж ки*, Mw, Vagrius, 2001, 254 pp.; I. Belobrovtseva, 'Поэт R–13 и другие Государственные поэты', *Zvezda*, no.3 : 218–23, Maiakovsky in Zamiatin's novel; I. A.

Ivanova, 'Метафорические ряды в романе «Мы» Е. Замятина', *RRe*, no.5 : 20–23; T. Davydova, 'Роман Евгения Замятина «Мы» — открытие и пророчество', *LitU*, no.6 : 138–47; A. V. Lezhnev, *Повесть Е. И. Замятина «Уездное»*, Tambov State U.P., 2000, 56 pp.

ZINOVIEV. *Феномен Зиновьева*, ed. A. A. Guseinov, O. M. Zinovieva, and K. M. Kantor, Mw, Sovremennye tetradi, 400 pp.; O. Zinovieva, 'Начало: к 80–летию А. А. Зиновьева', *NSo*, no.10 : 201–6; M. Kirkwood, 'The algorithm and the kaleidoscope: metaphors for the nightmare worlds of Franz Kafka and Aleksandr Zinov'ev?', *NZSJ*, 36 : 143–54.

ZOSHSHENKO. A. Kuliapin, '«Интермедиальность» Михаила Зощенко: от звука к цвету', Heller, *Экфрасис*, 135–44; *Михаил Зощенко. Материалы к творческой биографии: книга 3*, SPb, Nauka, 318 pp.

V. UKRANIAN STUDIES

POSTPONED

VI. BELARUSIAN STUDIES

POSTPONED

VII. SERBO-CROAT STUDIES

LANGUAGE

POSTPONED

LITERATURE

POSTPONED

VIII. BULGARIAN STUDIES

POSTPONED

ABBREVIATIONS

I. ACTA, FESTSCHRIFTEN AND OTHER COLLECTIVE AND GENERAL WORKS

AHLM 8: Actas del VIII Congreso Internacional de la Asociación Hispánica de Literatura Medieval (Santander, 1999), ed. Margarita Freixas, Silvia Iriso, and Laura Fernández, 2 vols, Santander, Consejería de Cultura del Gobierno de Cantabria — Año Jubilar Lebaniego — Asociación Hispánica de Literatura Medieval, 2000, 1830 pp.

AIPI 14: '. . . E c'è di mezzo il mare': lingua, letteratura e civiltà marina. Atti del XIV Congresso dell'A.I.P.I., Spalato (Croazia), 23–27 agosto 2000, ed. Bart Van den Bossche, Michel Bastiaensen, and Corinna Salvadori Lonergan (*Cività Italiana*, n.s. 2), 2 vols, Florence, Cesati, 440, 503 pp.

Akten (Wien), III: *Akten des X. Internationalen Germanistenkongresses Wien 2000.* III, ed. Peter Wiesinger (Jahrbuch für Internationale Germanistik, Reihe A, 55), Frankfurt–Berne, Lang, 443 pp.

Akten (Wien), V: *Akten des X. Internationalen Germanistenkongresses Wien 2000.* V, *Mediävistik und Neue Philologie*, ed. Peter Wiesinger (Jahrbuch für Internationale Germanistik, Reihe A, 57), Frankfurt–Berne, Lang, 361 pp.

Allières Vol.: Hommage a Jacques Allières, ed. Michel Aurnague and Michel Roché, 2 vols, I, *Domaines basque et pyreneen*, II, *Romania sans frontières*, Anglet, Atlantica, 1–324, 325–656 pp.

Álvarez, *Dialectoloxía: Dialectoloxía e léxico*, ed. Rosario Álvarez, Francisco Dubert García, and Xulio Sousa Fernández, Santiago de Compostela, Instituto da Lingua Galega — Consello da Cultura Galega, 429 pp.

Angelini Vol.: Granteatro: omaggio a Franca Angelini, ed. Beatrice Alfonzetti, Daniela Quarta, and Mirella Saulini, Rome, Bulzoni, 591 pp.

Arambasin, *Médiations: Pour une littérature savante: les médiations littéraires du savoir, actes du colloque de Besançon (4–5 novembre 1999)*, ed. Nella Arambasin (Annales littéraires de l'Université de Franche-Comté, 737), Besançon, Presses Universitaires Franc-Comtoises, 314 pp.

Arn, *Charles d'Orléans: Charles d'Orléans in England 1415–1440*, ed. Mary-Jo Arn, Cambridge, Brewer, 2000, 231 pp.

Arnold, *Kanonbildung: Literarische Kanonbildung*, ed. Heinz Ludwig Arnold, Munich, Edition Text + Kritik, 372 pp.

Atti (Assisi): *Alle frontiere della cristianità. I frati mendicanti e l'evangelizzazione tra '200 e '300. Atti del XXVIII Convegno internazionale (Assisi, 12–14 ottobre 2000)*, Spoleto, Centro Italiano di Studi sull'Alto Medioevo — Centro Interuniversitario di Studi Francescani, 2001, x + 311 pp.

Atti (Florence): *Da Firenze all'aldilà. Atti del terzo Seminario dantesco internazionale (Firenze 9–11 giugno 2000)*, ed. Michelangelo Picone, Florence, Cesati, 2001, 383 pp.

Atti (Rome): *La cultura letteraria italiana e l'identità europea*, Rome, Accademia Nazionale dei Lincei, 2001[2002], 402 pp.

Atti (Todi): *La propaganda politica nel Basso Medioevo. Atti del XXXVIII Convegno storico internazionale (Todi, 2001)*, Spoleto, Centro Italiano di Studi sull'Alto Medioevo — Accademia Tudertina — Centro di Studi sulla Spiritualità Medievale dell'Università degli Studi Perugia, ix + 582 pp.

Atti (Verona–Ravenna): *'Per correr miglior acque . . .': bilanci e prospettive degli studi danteschi alle soglie del nuovo millennio. Atti del Convegno internazionale di Verona–Ravenna, 25–29 ottobre 1999*, 2 vols, Rome, Salerno, 2001, xvi + 734, 739–1176 pp.

Aurnhammer, *Antike-Rezeption: 'Mehr Dionysos als Apollo.' Antiklassizistische Antike-Rezeption um 1900*, ed. Achim Aurnhammer and Thomas Pittrof, Frankfurt, Klostermann, 502 pp.

Badia, *Literatura: Literatura i cultura a la Corona d'Aragó (s. XIII-XV)*, ed. Lola Badia, Miriam Cabré, and Sadurní Martí, Barcelona, Curial–PAM, 496 pp.

Baker, *Hundred Years' War: Inscribing the Hundred Years' War in French and English Cultures*, ed. Denise N. Baker, Albany, State University of New York, 2000, x + 277 pp.

Banniard, *Langages: Langages et peuples d'Europe. Cristallisation des identités romanes et germaniques (VIIe–XIe siècle). Colloque international organisé par le Centre Européen d'Art et Civilisation Médiévale de Conques et l'Université de Toulouse-Le Mirail (Toulouse-Conques, juillet 1997)*, ed. Michel Banniard, Toulouse, CNRS–Université de Toulouse-Le Mirail, 271 pp.

Barabtarlo, *Fusion: Cold Fusion. Aspects of the German Cultural Presence in Russia*, ed. Gennady Barabtarlo, New York, Berghahn, 2000, viii + 310 pp.

Barbieri, *Anonimato:* Alvaro Barbieri, Alessandra Favero, and Francesca Gambino, *L'eclisse dell'artifice: sondaggi sull'anonimato nei canzonieri medeivali romanzi*, Alessandria, Dell'Orso, 167 pp.

Bauer, *Edition*: *'Ich an Dich.' Edition, Rezeption und Kommentierung von Briefen*, ed. Werner M. Bauer, Johannes John, and Wolfgang Wiesmüller (Innsbrucker Beiträge zur Kulturwissenschaft, Germanistische Reihe, 62), Universität Innsbruck, 2001, 278 pp.

Baumgartner, *Seuils: Seuils de l'oeuvre dans le texte médiéval*, ed. Emmanuèle Baumgartner and Laurence Harf-Lancner, 2 vols, Paris, Presses de la Sorbonne Nouvelle, 254, 248 pp.

Beaulieu, *Disposition: Le simple, le multiple: la disposition du recueil à la Renaissance*, ed. Jean-Philippe Beaulieu (= *Etudes françaises*, 38.3), Montreal U. P., 40 pp.

Begemann, *Kunst: Kunst — Zeugung — Geburt. Theorien und Metaphern ästhetischer Produktion in der Neuzeit*, ed. Christian Begemann and David E. Wellbery (Reihe Litterae, 82), Freiburg, Rombach, 423 pp.

Beggiato, *Vettori: Vettori e percorsi tematici nel Mediterraneo romanzo*, ed. Fabrizio Beggiato and Sabina Marinetti, Messina, Rubbetino, 308 pp.

Bein, *Walther: Walther von der Vogelweide. Beiträge zu Produktion, Edition und Rezeption*, ed. Thomas Bein (Walther-Studien, 1), Frankfurt, Lang, 364 pp.

Bennewitz, *Genderdiskurse: Genderdiskurse und Körperbilder im Mittelalter. Eine Bilanzierung nach Butler und Laqueur*, ed. Ingrid Bennewitz and Ingrid Kasten (Bamberger Studien zum Mittelalter, 1), Münster, Lit, ii + 254 pp.

Berghahn, *Essays: Millennial Essays on Film and Other German Studies*, ed. Daniela Berghahn and Alan Bance (CUTG Proceedings, 3), Oxford–Berne, Lang, 197 pp.

Bernhart, *Song Cycle: Word and Music Studies: Essays on the Song Cycle and on Defining the Field. Proceedings of the Second International Conference on Word and Music Studies at Ann Arbor, MI, 1999*, ed. Walter Bernhart, Werner Wolf, and David Mosley, Amsterdam, Rodopi, 2001, xii + 253 pp.

Beutler, *Spuren: Spuren, Signaturen, Spiegelungen. Zur Goethe-Rezeption in Europa*, ed. Bernhard Beutler and Anke Bosse, Cologne, Böhlau, 2000, 635 pp.

Beutner, *Literatur: Literatur als Geschichte des Ich*, ed. Eduard Beutner and Ulrike Tanzer, Würzburg, Königshausen & Neumann, 2000, 364 pp.

Birkhan Vol.: Lektüren der Differenz. Studien zur Mediävistik und Geschlechtergeschichte gewidmet Ingvild Birkhan, ed. Ingrid Bennewitz, Berne, Lang, 231 pp.

Bishop, *Prose: French Prose in 2000*, ed. Michael Bishop and Christopher Elson, Amsterdam–NY, Rodopi, viii + 272 pp.

Blumenfeld-Kosinski, *Spirit: The Vernacular Spirit. Essays on Medieval Religious Literature*, ed. Renate Blumenfeld-Kosinski et al., New York, Palgrave, viii + 324 pp.

Boitani, *Circolazione: Lo spazio letterario del Medioevo, 2: Il Medioevo volgare, 2: La circolazione del testo*, ed. Piero Boitani, Mario Mancini, and Alberto Varvaro, Rome, Salerno, 756 pp.

Boggione, *Poesia:* Valter Boggione, *Poesia come citazione: Manzoni, Gozzano e dintorni*, Alessandria, Edizioni dell'Orso, 195 pp.

Böhler, *Kulturtopographie: Kulturtopographie deutschsprachiger Literaturen. Perspektivierungen im Spannungsfeld von Integration und Differenz*, ed. Michael Böhler and Hans Otto Horch, Tübingen, Niemeyer, vi + 274 pp.

Borsellino Vol.: Sylva: studi in onore di Nino Borsellino, ed. Giorgio Patrizi, 2 vols, Rome, Bulzoni, 1–466 pp., 467–902 pp.

Bouvier, *Toponymie: La Toponymie urbaine. Significations et enjeux. Actes du colloque tenu à Aix-en-Provence, 11–12 décembre 1998*, ed. Jean-Claude Bouvier and Jean-Marie Guillon, Paris, L'Harmattan, 2001, 256 pp.
Bracchi, *Alterità: L'alterità nella parola. Storia e scrittura di donne nel Piemonte di epoca moderna*, ed. Cristina Bracchi, Turin, Thélème, 185 pp.
Brand Vol.: Britain and Italy from Romanticism to Modernism. A Festschrift for Peter Brand, ed. Martin McLaughlin, Oxford, Legenda — Modern Humanities Research Association, xx + 195 pp.
Brooks, *Poetry: Poetry and Music in the French Renaissance, Proceedings of the 6th Cambridge French Renaissance Colloquium (5–7 July 1999)*, ed. Jeanice Brooks, Philip Ford, and Gillian Jondorf, Cambridge, Cambridge French Colloquia, 2001, xiv + 290 pp.
Buschinger, *Travail: Le Travail sur le modèle*, ed. D. Buschinger (Médiévales, 16), Amiens, Presses du Centre d'Etudes Médiévales, Université de Picardie-Jules Vernes, 77 pp.
Butterworth, *Borders: Shifting Borders. Theory and Identity in French Literature*, ed. Emily Butterworth and Kathryn Robson, Berne–Oxford, Lang, 2001, viii + 208 pp.
Campailla, *Controcodice:* Sergio Campailla, *Controcodice*, Naples, ESI, 262 pp.
Castein, *Images: Dream Images in German, Austrian and Swiss Literature and Culture*, ed. Hanne Castein and Rüdiger Görner, Munich, Iudicium, 183 pp.
Cazauran Vol.: Devis d'amitié. Mélanges en l'honneur de Nicole Cazauran, ed. Jean Lecointe, Catherine Magnien, Isabelle Pantin, and Marie-Claire Thomine, Paris, Champion, 976 pp.
CEFI 36: Pétrarche en Europe (XIVe–XXe siècle), actes du 36ème congrès international du CEFI (Turin Chambéry, 11–15 décembre 1995), ed. Pierre Blanc, Paris, Champion, 776 pp.
Cerboni, *Letture:* Giorgio Cerboni Baiardi, *Letture*, ed. Giudo Arbizzoni, Tiziana Mattioli, and Anna Teresa Ossani, Manziama, Vecchiarelli, 299 pp.
Cerquiglini-Toulet, *Machaut: Guillaume de Machaut 1300–2000*, ed. J. Cerquiglini-Toulet and N. Wilkins, Presses de l'Université de Paris–Sorbonne, 180 pp.
CFE 2: Actas del II Congreso de Fonética Experimental, Sevilla 5, 6 y 7 de marzo de 2001, ed. Jesús Díaz García, Seville, Universidad de Sevilla, 336 pp.
Chevalier Vol.: Modèles, dialogues et invention. Mélanges offerts à Anne Chevalier, ed. Suzanne Guellouz and Gabrielle Chamarat-Malandain, Caen U.P., 338 pp.
CIHCE 6: Libros y documentos en la Alta Edad Media. Los libros de derecho. Los archivos familiares. [Actas del] VI congreso internacional de historia de la cultura escrita, ed. Carlos Sáez, Alcalá de Henares, Calambur, 2 vols, 601, 516 pp.
CIHLE 5: Actas del V Congreso Internacional de Historia de la Lengua Española, ed. María Teresa Echenique Elizondo and Juan Sánchez Méndez, 2 vols, Madrid, Gredos, 2430 pp.
CILM 7: Actas do VIII Conferencia Internacional de Linguas Minoritarias, ed. M. Xesús Bugarín et al., Santiago de Compostela, Xunta de Galicia, 672 pp.
Cimini, *Evasione:* Mario Cimini, *L'evasione e il ritorno. Letteratura e giornalismo in Abruzzi tra Otto e Novecento*, Rome, Bulzoni, 2001, 354 pp.
Classen, *Meeting: Meeting the Foreign in the Middle Ages*, ed. Albrecht Classen, New York, Routledge, lxxiii + 274 pp.
Cogitore, *Devenir roi: Devenir roi. Essais sur la littérature adressée au prince*, ed. Isabelle Cogitore and Francis Goyet, Grenoble, Ellug, 2001, 284 pp.
Condé Vol.: Maryse Condé: Une nomade inconvenante. Mélanges offerts à Maryse Condé, ed. Madeleine Cottenet-Hage and Lydie Moudileno, Guadeloupe, Ibis Rouge, 190 pp.
Connon, *Drama: Essays on French Comic Drama from the 1640s to the 1780s*, ed. Derek Connon and George Evans (French Studies of the Eighteenth and Nineteenth Centuries, 7), Oxford–Berne–New York, Lang, 2000, 236 pp.
Contreni, *Word: Word, Image, Number. Communication in the Middle Ages*, ed. John J. Contreni and Santa Casciani, Florence, Sismel – Edizioni del Galluzzo, 458 pp.
Courcelles, *Varietas: La 'varietas' à la Renaissance*, ed. Dominique de Courcelles (Etudes et rencontres, 9), Paris, École de Chartes, 2001, 168 pp.
Danneberg, *Wissen: Wissen in Literatur im 19. Jahrhundert*, ed. Lutz Danneberg and Friedrich Vollhardt, Tübingen, Niemeyer, 385 pp.

Dell'Aquila, *Bello stilo:* Michele Dell'Aquila, *Lo bello stilo. Percorsi di letteratura*, Bari, Palomar, 194 pp.

Dell'Aquila, *Nominanza:* Michele Dell'Aquila, *L'onrata nominanza. Studi su Dante, Manzoni e altra letteratura*, Pisa, Giardini, 2001, 169 pp.

Delmas Vol.: Mythe et histoire dans le théâtre classique: hommage à Christian Delmas, ed. Fanny Népote-Desmarres and Jean-Philippe Grosperrin, Toulouse, Société de Littératures Classiques, 479 pp.

Dembowski Vol.: Philologies Old and New: Essays in Honor of Peter Florian Dembowski, ed. J. Tasker and C. Chase, Princeton, 2001, 354 pp.

Desan, *Littérature: D'un siècle à l'autre. Littérature et société de 1590 à 1610*, ed. Philippe Desan and Giovanni Dotoli, Fasano, Schena — Paris, Presses de l'Université de Paris–Sorbonne, 2001, 362 pp.

Domínguez, *Arbor Scientiae: Arbor Scientiae: der Baum des Wissens von Ramon Lull. Akten des Internationalen Kongresses aus Anlass des 40-jährigen Jubiläums des Raimundus-Lullus-Instituts der Universität Freiburg i. Br.*, ed. Fernando Domínguez Reboiras, Pere Villalba Varneda, and Peter Walter (Instrumenta Patristica et Mediaevalia, Subsidia Lulliana, 1), Turnhout, Brepols, 372 pp.

Domrös, *Judentum: Judentum und Antijudaismus in der deutschen Literatur im Mittelalter und an der Wende zur Neuzeit. Ein Studienbuch*, ed. Arne Domrös et al., Berlin, Jüdische Verlagsanstalt, 282 pp.

Dornier, *Ecriture: Ecriture et exercice de la pensée*, ed. Carole Dornier, Caen U.P., 2001, 190 pp.

Dotoli, *Méditerranées: Les Méditerranées du XVIIe siècle*, ed. Giovanni Dotoli (Biblio 17, 137), Tübingen, Narr, 347 pp.

Eimermacher, *Культура: Культура и власть в условиях коммуникационной революции XX века*, ed. K. Eimermacher, G. Bordiugov, and I. Grabowsky, Moscow, AIRO-XX, 478 pp.

ENL 4: Actas dos IV Encontros para a normalización lingüística, Santiago de Compostela, Consello da Cultura Galega, 316 pp.

Ettrup, *Bogen: Bogen eller kaos*, ed. Flemming Ettrup and Erik Skyum-Nielsen, Copenhagen, Gyldendal, 2000, 291 pp.

Fabrizio-Costa, *Phénix: Phénix: mythe(s) et signe(s), actes du colloque international de Caen (12–14 octobre 2000)*, ed. Silvia Fabrizio-Costa, Brussels, Lang, 2001, x + 444 pp.

Faivre Vol.: Esotérisme, gnoses et imaginaire symbolique. Mélanges offerts à Antoine Faivre, ed. Richard Caron, Joscelyn Godwin, Wouter J. Hanegraaff, and Jean-Louis Vieillard-Baron (Gnostica, 3), Louvain, Peeters, 2001, xii + 948 pp.

Fenster, *Gender: Gender in Debate from the Early Middle Ages*, ed. Thelma S. Fenster and Clare A. Lees, NY, Palgrave, 2001, 292 pp.

Fest. Bender: 'Das Schöne soll sein.' Aisthesis in der deutschen Literatur. Festschrift für Wolfgang F. Bender, ed. Peter Hesselmann, Michael Huesmann, and Hans-Joachim Jakob, Bielefeld, Aisthesis, 2001, 494 pp.

Fest. Berschin: Scripturus vitam. Lateinische Biographie von der Antike bis in die Gegenwart. Festgabe für Walter Berschin zum 65. Geburtstag, ed. Dorothea Walz, Heidelberg, Mattes, xvii + 1287 pp.

Fest. Brandt: Sprache und Text in Theorie und Empire. Beiträge zur germanistischen Sprachwissenschaft. Festschrift für Wolfgang Brandt, ed. Claudia Mauelshagen and Jan Seifert, Stuttgart, Steiner, 2001, ix + 230 pp.

Fest. Cherubim: Die deutsche Sprache der Gegenwart. Festschrift für Dieter Cherubim zum 60. Geburtstag, ed. Stefan J. Schierholz et al., Frankfurt, Lang, 2001, 392 pp.

Fest. Fiedler: Überschreitungen. Dialoge zwischen Literatur- und Theaterwissenschaft, Architektur und Bildender Kunst. Festschrift für Leonhard M. Fiedler, ed. Jörg Sader and Anette Wörner, Würzburg, Königshausen & Neumann, 352 pp.

Fest. Gaede: Denken und Geschichte. Festschrift für Friedrich Gaede, ed. Hans-Günther Schwarz and Jane V. Curran, Munich, Iudicium, 299 pp.

Fest. Göschel: Beiträge zu Linguistik und Phonetik. Festschrift für Joachim Göschel, ed. A. Braun (Zeitschrift für Dialektologie und Linguistik, Beihefte, 118), 463 pp.

Fest. Grözinger: Von Enoch bis Kafka. Festschrift für Karl E. Grözinger zum 60. Geburtstag, ed. Manfred Voigts, Wiesbaden, Harrassowitz, 456 pp.
Fest. Guthmüller: Metamorphosen. Wandlungen und Verwandlungen in Literatur, Sprache und Kunst von der Antike bis zur Gegenwart. Festschrift für Bodo Guthmüller zum 65. Geburtstag, ed. Heidi Marek, Anne Neuschäfer, and Suzanne Tichy, Wiesbaden, Harrasowitz, xviii + 394 pp.
Fest. Knobloch: Grenzgänge. Studien zur Literatur der Moderne. Festschrift für Hans-Jörg Knobloch, ed. Helmut Koopmann and Manfred Misch, Paderborn, Mentis, 469 pp.
Fest. Lüdtke: Sprachgeschichte als Varietätengeschichte. Beiträge zur diachronen Varietätenlinguistik des Spanischen und anderer romanischer Sprachen. Anläßlich des 60. Geburtstages von Jens Lüdtke, ed. Andreas Wesch, Waltraud Weidenbusch, Rolf Kailuweit, and Brenda Laca, Tübingen, Stauffenburg, xii + 419 pp.
Fest. Menke: Vulpis Adolatio. Festschrift für Hubertus Menke zum 60. Geburtstag, ed. Robert Peters, Heidelberg, Winter, 2001, 976 pp.
Fest. Mertens: Literarische Leben. Rollenentwürfe in der Literatur des Hoch- und Spätmittelalters. Festschrift für Volker Mertens zum 65. Geburtstag, ed. Matthias Meyer and Hans-Joachim Schiewer, Tübingen, Niemeyer, xiv + 899 pp.
Fest. Michel: Von der ars intelligendi zur ars applicandi. Festschrift für Willy Michel, ed. Dirk Winkelmann and Alexander Wittwer, Munich, Iudicium, 360 pp.
Fest. Mittenzwei: 'Spielende Vertiefung ins Menschliche': Festschrift für Ingrid Mittenzwei, ed. Monika Hahn, Heidelberg, Winter, 376 pp.
Fest. Orłowski: Literatur im Zeugenstand. Beiträge zur deutschsprachigen Literatur- und Kulturgeschichte. Festschrift zum 65. Geburtstag von Hubert Orłowski, ed. Edward Białek, Manfred Durzak, and Marek Zybura (Oppelner Beiträge zur Germanistik, 5), Frankfurt, Lang, 861 pp.
Fest. Reichmann: Das Wort — Seine strukturelle und kulturelle Dimension. Festschrift für Oskar Reichmann zum 65. Geburtstag, ed. V. Agel et al., Tübingen, Niemeyer, xv + 344 pp.
Fest. Richter: Begegnung der Zeiten. Festschrift für Helmut Richter zum 65. Geburtstag, ed. R. Fasold, C. Giel, V. Giel, M. Masanetz, and M. Thormann, Leipzig, Universitätsverlag, 1999, 419 pp.
Fest. Röll: Röllwagenbüchlein. Festschrift für Walter Röll zum 65. Geburtstag, ed. Jürgen Jaehrling et al., Tübingen, Niemeyer, x + 515 pp.
Fest. Ruberg: 'Vox sermo res'. Beiträge zur Sprachreflexion, Literatur- und Sprachgeschichte vom Mittelalter bis zur Neuzeit. Festschrift Uwe Ruberg, ed. Wolfgang Haubrichs et al., Stuttgart, Hirzel, 2001, 291 pp.
Fest. Schulze: Walther lesen. Interpretationen und Überlegungen zu Walther von der Vogelweide. Festschrift für Ursula Schulze zum 65. Geburtstag, ed. Volker Mertens and Ulrich Müller (Göppinger Arbeiten zur Germanistik, 692), Göppingen, Kümmerle, 2001, iv + 286 pp.
Fest. Seebold: Grippe, Kamm und Eulenspiegel. Festschrift für Elmar Seebold zum 65. Geburtstag, ed. W. Schindler and J. Untermann, Berlin, de Gruyter, 1999, 415 pp.
Fest. Stackmann: Studien zu Frauenlob und Heinrich von Mügeln. Festschrift für Karl Stackmann zum 80. Geburtstag (Scrinium Friburgense, 15), Fribourg U.P., viii + 275 pp.
Fest. Stickel: Ansichten der deutschen Sprache. Festschrift für Gerhard Stickel zum 65. Geburtstag, ed. U. Hass-Zumkehr, W. Kallmeyer, and G. Zifonun (Studien zur deutschen Sprache, 25), Tübingen, Narr, xxii + 699 pp.
Fest Windfuhr: Literarische Fundstücke. Wiederentdeckungen und Neuentdeckungen. Festschrift für Manfred Windfuhr, ed. Ariane Neuhaus-Koch and Gertrude Cepl-Kaufmann (Beiträge zur neueren Literaturgeschichte, 188), Heidelberg, Winter, 527 pp.
Fidora, *Llull: Ramon Llull, caballero de la fe. El Arte luliana y su proyección en la Edad Media*, ed. Alexander Fidora and José G. Higuera (Cuadernos de Anuario Filosófico, Serie de Pensamiento Español, 17), Pamplona, Universidad de Navarra, 2001, 129 pp.
Forsdick, *Travel: Travel and Exile: Postcolonial Perspectives*, ed. Charles Forsdick (ASCALF Critical Studies in Postcolonial Literature and Culture 1), Glasgow, 2001, ix + 54 pp.
García-Medall, *Aspectos: Aspectos de morfología derivativa del español*, ed. Joaquín García-Medall, Lugo, Tris Tram, 187 pp.

Gärtner, *Skripta: Skripta, Schreiblandschaften and Standardisierungstendenzen. Urkundensprachen im Grenzbereich von Germania und Romania im 13. und 14. Jahrhundert. Beiträge zum Kolloquium vom 16. bis 18. September 1998 in Trier*, ed. Kurt Gärtner, Günter Holtus, Andrea Rapp, and Harald Völker (Trierer historische Forschungen, 47), Trier, Kliomedia, 2001, 701 pp.

Garton, *Threshold: On the Threshold: New Studies in Nordic Literature*, ed. Janet Garton and Michael Robinson, Norwich, Norvik, 489 pp.

Gerlach, *Einwände:* U. Henry Gerlach, *Einwände und Einsichten. Revidierte Deutungen deutschsprachiger Literatur des 19. und 20. Jahrhunderts*, Munich, Iudicium, 302 pp.

Girardi, *Prosa:* Antonio Girardi, *Prosa in versi. Da Pascoli a Giudici*, Padua, Esedra, 2001, 238 pp.

Going Romance 2000: Romance Languages and Linguistic Theory 2000. Selected Papers from 'Going Romance' 2000, Utrecht, 30 November–2 December, ed. Claire Beyssade, Reineke Bok-Bennema, Frank Drijkoningen, and Paola Monachesi (CILT, 232), Amsterdam, Benjamins, viii + 354 pp.

González Ollé Vol.: Pulchre, Bene, Recte. Estudios en homenaje al prof. Fernando González Ollé, ed. Carmen Saralegui and Manuel Casado, Pamplona, EUNSA , xxiii + 1483 pp.

Greenfield, *Nibelungenlied: 'Das Nibelungenlied.' Actas do Simpósio Internacional 27 de Outubro de 2000*, ed. John Greenfield, Porto, Faculdade de Letras da Universidade do Porto, 2001, 183 pp.

Grell, *Egypte: L'Egypte imaginaire de la Renaissance à Champollion*, ed. Chantal Grell, Paris, Presses de l'Université de Paris–Sorbonne, 2001, 204 pp.

Grodek, *Ruse: Écriture de la ruse*, ed. Elzbieta Grodek (Faux titre, 190), Amsterdam, Rodopi, 2000, 455 pp.

Groos, *Perceval: Perceval/Parzival. A Casebook*, ed. Arthur Groos and Norris J. Lacy (Arthurian Characters and Themes, 6), New York, Routledge, viii + 312 pp.

Grossmann, *Confrontations: Confrontations. Politics and Aesthetics in Nineteenth-Century France, Selected Proceedings of the Twenty-Fourth Annual Colloquium in Nineteenth-Century French Studies, Pennsylvania State University and State College, PA, 22–25 October 1998*, ed. Kathryn M. Grossman, Michael E. Lane, Bénédicte Monicat, and Willa A. Silverman, Amsterdam, Rodopi, 2001, vi + 311 pp. + 4 pl.

Grzega, *Romania:* Joachim Grzega, *Romania Gallica Cisalpina* (*ZRP*, Beiheft 311), Tubingen, Niemeyer, 2001, viii + 342 pp.

Haenicke Vol.: University Governance and Humanistic Scholarship. Studies in Honor of Diether Haenicke, ed. Joachim Dyck, Martin M. Herman, Marvin S. Schindler, and Roslyn Abt Schindler, Würzburg, Königshausen & Neumann, 244 pp.

Hainsworth, *Companion: The Oxford Companion to Italian Literature*, ed. Peter Hainsworth and David Robey, OUP, xli + 644 pp.

Hamesse, *Lexiques: Lexiques bilingues dans les domaines philosophique et scientfique (Moyen Age, Renaissance), actes du colloque de Paris (12–14 juin 1997)*, ed. J. Hamesse and D. Jacquart (F.I.D.E.M., 'Textes et études du Moyen Age', 14), Turnhout, Brepols, 2001, xii + 240 pp.

Hanawalt, *Space: Medieval Practices of Space*, ed. Barbara Hanawalt and Michal Kobialka, Minneapolis–London, Univ. of Minnesota Press, 2000. xviii + 269 pp.

Hardman, *Identity: The Matter of Identity in Medieval Romance*, ed. Phillipa Hardman, Woodbridge, Brewer, xii + 165 pp.

Harper, *Sappho: Sappho in the Shadows. Essays on the Work of German Women Poets of the Age of Goethe (1749–1832). With Translations of their Poetry into English*, ed. Anthony J. Harper and Margaret C. Ives, Berne, Lang, 2000, 280 pp.

Heller, *Экфрасис: Экфрасис в русской литературе: труды Лозаннского симпозиума*, ed. L. Heller, Moscow, MIK, 216 pp.

Heller, *Philippe de Remy: Essays on the Poetic and Legal Writing of Philippe de Remy and his Son Philippe de Beaumanoir of Thirteenth-Century France*, ed. Sarah-Grace Heller and Michelle Reichert (Studies in French Civilisation, 21), Lewiston–Lampeter, Mellen, 2001, iv + 304 pp.

Hellgardt, *Thüringen: Literatur und Macht im mittelalterlichen Thüringen*, ed. Ernst Hellgardt et al., Cologne, Böhlau, viii + 204 pp.

Hellinger, *Gender: Gender Across Languages. The Linguistic Representation of Women and Men*, ed. Marlis Hellinger and Hadumod Bußmann, Amsterdam, Benjamins, I, 2001, xiv + 328 pp., II, 2002, xiv + 348 pp.

Hempfer, *Spielwelten: Spielwelten. Performanz und Inszenierung in der Renaissance*, ed. Klaus W. Hempfer and Helmut Pfeiffer (Text und Kontext, 16), Stuttgart, Steiner, xiv + 166 pp.

Henne Vol.: Sprache im Leben der Zeit. Beiträge zur Theorie, Analyse und Kritik der deutschen Sprache in Vergangenheit und Gegenwart. Herbert Henne zum 65. Geburtstag, ed. Armin Burkhardt and Dieter Cherubim, Tübingen, Niemeyer, 2001, xv + 512 pp.

Henry, *Beginnings: Beginnings in French Literature*, ed. Freeman G. Henry, Amsterdam–NY, Rodopi, xii + 213 pp.

Herbin, *Richesses: Richesses médiévales du Nord et du Hainaut*, ed. Jean-Charles Herbin, Centre d'Analyse du Message Littéraire et Artistique, Valenciennes U.P., 267 pp.

Hernández, *Boccaccio: La recepción de Boccaccio en España*, ed. María Hernández Esteban (*Cuadernos de Filología Italiana*, número extraordinario), Madrid, Universidad Complutense, 2001.

Herrera Vol.: Textos medievales y renacentistas de la Romania: Jornadas del Seminario Internacional en Homenaje a la Profesora María Teresa Herrera. Madrid, Universidad Nacional de Educación a Distancia 25 y 26 de junio de 1999, ed. María Teresa Navarro, John J. Nitti, and María Nieves Sánchez, New York, Hispanic Seminary of Medieval Studies, 193 pp.

Hicks, *Christine: Au Champ des escriptures: IIIe colloque international sur Christine de Pizan*, ed. Eric Hicks, Paris, Champion, 2000, 851 pp.

Hicks Vol.: 'Riens ne m'est seur que la chose incertaine'. Études sur l'art d'écrire au Moyen Age offertes à Eric Hicks par ses élèves, collègues, amies et amis, ed. Jean-Claude Mühlethaler and Denis Billiotte, Geneva, Slatkine, 2001, xxiv + 323 pp.

Hladká, *Čeština*, IV: *Čeština univerzália a specifika*, ed. Zdeňka Hladká and Petr Karlík, IV, Brno, Masaryk Univ., 369 pp.

Hodgson, *Femme: La femme au XVIIe siècle*, ed. Richard G. Hodgson (Biblio 17, 138), Tübingen, Narr, 430 pp.

Holzner, *Wechselwirkungen: Rußland-Österreich. Literarische und kulturelle Wechselwirkungen*, ed. Johann Holzner, Berne, Lang, 2000, 320 pp.

Huber, *Tristan: Der 'Tristan' Gottfrieds von Straßburg. Symposion Santiago de Compostela, 5. bis 8. April 2000*, ed. Christoph Huber and Victor Millet, Tübingen, Niemeyer, x + 408 pp.

Hulk, *Inversion: Subject Inversion in Romance and the Theory of Universal Grammar*, ed. Aafke Hulk and Jean-Yves Pollock, OUP, 2001, vii + 215 pp.

Hutchinson, *Landmarks: Landmarks in German Poetry*, ed. Peter Hutchinson (British and Irish Studies in German Language and Literature, 20), Oxford, Lang, 2000, 218 pp.

Ichim, *Identitatea: Identitatea limbii şi literaturii române în perspectiva globalizării*, ed. Ofelia Ichim and Florin-Teodor Olariu, Iaşi, Trinitas, 431 pp.

ICLC 2: Studies in Contrastive Linguistics. Proceedings of the 2nd International Contrastive Linguistics Conference, Santiago, October 2001, ed. Luis Iglesias Rábade and Susana Mª Doval Suárez, Santiago de Compostela U.P., 1082 pp.

ICLS 10: Courtly Literature and Clerical Culture. Selected Papers from the Tenth Triennial Congress of the International Courtly Literature Society, Universität Tübingen, Deutschland, 28. Juli-3. August 2001, ed. Christoph Huber and Henrike Lähnemann, Attempto, Tübingen, xi + 246 pp.

ICOS 20: Actas do XX Congreso Internacional de Ciencias Onomásticas, Santiago de Compostela, 20–25 setembro 1999, ed. A.I. Boullón Agrelo, Corunna, Fundación Barrié de la Maza, CD-ROM.

Ingen, *Gebetsliteratur: Gebetsliteratur der Frühen Neuzeit als Hausfrömmigkeit. Funktionen und Formen in Deutschland und den Niederlanden*, ed. Ferdinand van Ingen and Cornelia Niekus Moore (Wolfenbütteler Forschungen, 92), Wiesbaden, Harrassowitz, 2001, 323 pp.

Jones, *Language Change: Language Change: The Interplay of Internal, External and Extra-Linguistic Factors*, ed. Mari C. Jones and Edith Esch (Contributions to the Sociology of Language, 86), Berlin–New York, Mouton de Gruyter, x + 338 pp.

Jones, *Willehalm: Wolfram's 'Willehalm'. Fifteen Essays*, ed. Martin H. Jones and Timothy McFarland, Columbia SC, Camden House, xxii + 344 pp.

Jones-Davies, *Mémoire: Mémoire et oubli au temps de la Renaissance, actes du colloque de la Société Internationale de Recherches Interdisciplinaires sur la Renaissance (S.I.R.I.R.), 8–9 décembre 2000, 9–10 mars 2001*, ed. M. T. Jones-Davies, Paris, Champion, 210 pp.

Jones-Davies, *Oisiveté: L'Oisiveté au temps de la Renaissance*, ed. Marie-Thérèse Jones-Davies, Paris, Presses de l'Université de Paris–Sorbonne, 256 pp.

Jürgens, *Exchanges: Mutual Exchanges, II. Sheffield Münster Colloquium, II*, ed. Dirk Jürgens, Frankfurt, Lang, 1999, 417 pp.

Kahn, *Rhetoric: Rhetoric and Law in Early Modern Europe*, ed. Victoria Kahn and Lorna Hutson, New Haven–London, Yale UP, 2001, x + 356 pp.

Kaiser, *Paris: Paris? Paris! Bilder der französischen Metropole in der nicht-fiktionalen deutschsprachigen Prosa zwischen Hermann Bahr und Joseph Roth*, ed. Gerhard R. Kaiser and Erika Tunner (Jenaer germanistische Forschungen, n.s., 11), Heidelberg, Winter, viii + 487 pp.

Kasten Vol.: Two Generations: A Tribute to Lloyd A. Kasten (1905–1999), ed. Francisco Gago Jover, New York, Hispanic Seminary of Medieval Studies, 301 pp.

Kavanagh, *Exchanges: Mutual Exchanges, I. Sheffield Münster Colloquium, I*, ed. R. J. Kavanagh, Frankfurt, Lang, 1999, 334 pp.

Kennedy, *Christine: Contexts and Continuities. Proceedings of the IVth International Colloquium on Christine de Pizan*, ed. A. Kennedy, 3 vols, Glasgow U.P., xiv + 1–314, vii + 315–620, vii + 621–903 pp.

Kennedy Vol.: Christine de Pizan 2000: Studies on Christine de Pizan in honour of Angus J. Kennedy, ed. John Campbell and Nadia Margolis, Amsterdam–Atlanta, Rodopi, 2000, 429 pp.

Kircher, *Avantgarden: Avantgarden im Ost und West. Literatur, Musik und bildende Kunst um 1900*, ed. Hartmut Kircher, Maria Kłanska, and Erich Kleinschmidt, Cologne, Böhlau, 320 pp.

Klein, *Literatur: Literatur der Weimarer Republik*, ed. Michael Klein, Sieglinde Klettenhammer, and Elfriede Pölder (Innsbrucker Beiträge zur Kulturwissenschaft. Germanistische Reihe, 64), Innsbruck, 188 pp.

Klinck, *Woman's Song: Medieval Woman's Song: Cross-Cultural Approaches*, ed. Ann L. Klinck and Ann Marie Rasmussen, Philadelphia, Pennsylvania U.P., 2001, viii + 280 pp.

Knapp, *Erzählen: Historisches und fiktionales Erzählen im Mittelalter*, ed. Fritz Peter Knapp and Manuela Niesner (Schriften zur Literaturwissenschaft, 19), Berlin, Duncker & Humblot, 164 pp.

Knight, *Frontiers: Broaching Frontiers, Shattering Boundaries. On Tradition and Culture at the Dawn of the Third Millennium. Proceedings of the 21st International Congress of F.I.L.L.M. held in Harare, Zimbabwe, 26–30 July 1999*, ed. T. E. Knight, Berne, Lang, 197 pp.

Koch, *Unities: Classical Unities: Place, Time, Action*, ed. Erec R. Koch (Biblio 17, 131), Tübingen, Narr, 456 pp.

Kohl, *Words: Words, Texts, Images*, ed. Katrin Kohl and Ritchie Robertson (CUTG Proceedings, 4), Oxford, Lang, 268 pp.

Kooper, *Chronicle II: The Medieval Chronicle II. Proceedings of the 2nd International Conference on the Medieval Chronicle, Driebergen/Utrecht 16–21 July 1999*, ed. Erik Kooper (Costerus, n.s., 144), Amsterdam, Rodopi, vi + 280 pp.

Köpf, *Theologen: Theologen des Mittelalters. Eine Einführung*, ed. Ulrich Köpf, Darmstadt, Wissenschaftliche Buchgesellschaft, 249 pp.

Kovacci Vol.: Homenaje a Ofelia Kovacci, ed. Elvira N. de Arnoux and Ángela di Tullio, Buenos Aires U.P., 2001. 544 pp.

Krausová, *Setkání: Setkání s češtinou*, ed. Alena Krausová, Markéta Slezáková, and Zdeňka Svobodová, Prague, ÚJČ AV ČR, 137 pp.

Kučinskaja, *Vstreči: Vstreči etničeskich kul'tur v zerkale jazyka v sopostavitel'nom lingvokul'turnom aspekte*, ed. A. I. Kučinskaja and T. M. Skripova, Moscow, Nauka, 478 pp.,

Kuperty-Tsur, *Ecriture: Ecriture de soi et argumentation. Rhétorique et modèles de l'autoreprésentation, actes du colloque de Tel-Aviv (3–5 mai 1998)*, ed. Nadine Kuperty-Tsur, Caen U.P., 2000, 186 pp.

La Charité Vol.: A French Forum. Mélanges de littérature française offerts à Raymond C. et Virginia A. La Charité, Paris, Klincksieck, 2000, 342 pp.

Landry, *Dialogue: Le dialogue des arts, 1: Littérature et peinture du Moyen Âge au XVIIIe siècle*, ed. Jean-Pierre Landry and Pierre Servet (C.E.D.I.C., 18), Lyon, Université Jean-Moulin, 2001, 330 pp.

Langer, *Aristotle: Au-delà de la 'Poétique': Aristote et la littérature de la Renaissance / Beyond the 'Poetics': Aristotle and Early Modern Literature*, ed. Ullrich Langer (THR, 367), Geneva, Droz, 176 pp.

Laroque, *Esthétiques : Esthétiques de la nouveauté à la Renaissance*, ed. François Laroque and Franck Lessay, Paris, Presses de la Sorbonne Nouvelle, 2001, 192 pp.

Laufhütte, *Künste: Künste und Natur in Diskursen der Frühen Neuzeit*, ed. Hartmut Laufhütte et al. (Wolfenbütteler Arbeiten zur Barockforschung, 35), 2 vols, Wiesbaden, Harrassowitz, 2000, 1196 pp.

Leclerc, *Bibliothèque: La Bibliothèque de Flaubert. Inventaires et critiques*, ed. Yvan Leclerc, Rouen U.P., 2001, 356 pp.

Lieb, *Situationen: Situationen des Erzählens. Aspekte narrativer Praxis im Mittelalter*, ed. Ludger Lieb and Stephan Müller (Quellen und Forschungen zur Sprach- und Kulturgeschichte der germanischen Völker, 20 (254)), Berlin, de Gruyter, viii + 290 pp.

Liver Vol.: Italica — Raetica — Gallica. Studia linguarum literarum artiumque in honorem Ricarda Liver, ed. P. Wunderli, I. Werlen, and M. Grünert, Tübingen, Narr, 2001, 715 pp.

Long, *Masculinity: High Anxiety. Masculinity in Crisis in Early Modern France*, ed. Kathleen P. Long (Sixteenth-Century Essays and Studies, 59), Kirksville, Missouri, Truman State U.P., xviii + 238 pp.

Loster-Schneider, *Geschlecht: Geschlecht — Literatur — Geschichte*, ed. Gudrun Loster-Schneider, St. Ingbert, Röhrig, 1999, 272 pp.

LSRL 29: Current Issues in Romance Languages: Selected Papers from the 29th LSRL, Ann Arbor, 8–11 April 1999, ed. Teresa Satterfield, Christina Tortora, and Diana Cresti (CILT, 220), Amsterdam, Benjamins, viii + 403 pp.

Lutz, *Wandmalerei: Literatur und Wandmalerei I. Erscheinungsformen höfischer Kultur und ihre Träger im Mittelalter. Freiburger Colloquium 1998*, ed. Eckart Conrad Lutz et al., Tübingen, Niemeyer, x + 626 pp.

Maddox, *Alexander: The Medieval French Alexander*, ed. Donald Maddox and Sara Sturm-Maddox, Albany, SUNY U.P., xii + 293 pp.

Marchal, *Salons: Vie des salons et activités littéraires de Marguerite de Valois à Mme de Staël*, ed. Roger Marchal (Publications du Centre des Milieux Littéraires, 2), Nancy U.P., 2001, 343 pp.

Mayer Vol.: Renaissance Reflections: Essays in memory of C. A. Mayer, ed. Trevor Peach (Études et essais sur la Renaissance, 10), Paris, Champion, 250 pp.

Mazzacurati Vol.: Per Giancarlo Mazzacurati, ed. Giulio Ferroni, Rome, Bulzoni, 139 pp.

McKenna, *Libertins: Libertins et esprits forts du XVIIe siècle: quels modes de lecture?*ed. Antony McKenna (Libertinage et philosophie au XVIIe siècle, 6), Saint-Étienne U.P., 150 pp.

Meier, *Enzyklopädie: Die Enzyklopädie im Wandel vom Hochmittelalter bis zur frühen Neuzeit. Akten des Kolloquiums des Projekts D im Sonderforschungsbereich 231 (29.11 — 1.12.1996)*, ed. Christel Meier (Münstersche Mittelalter-Schriften, 78), Munich, Fink, 589 pp.

Menichetti Vol.: Carmina semper et citharae cordi: etudes de philologie et de métrique offertes à Aldo Menichetti, ed. Marie-Claire Gérard-Zai, Geneva, Slatkine, 2000, xlv + 590 pp.

Messner Vol.: Vocabula et vocabularia: études de lexicologie et de (méta-) lexicographie romanes en l'honneur du 60e anniversaire de Dieter Messner, ed. Bernard Pöll and Franz Rainer, Frankfurt, Lang, 361 pp.

Mölk, *Alexanderdichtungen: Alexanderdichtungen des Mittelalters*, ed. Ulrich Mölk, Göttingen, Wallstein, 420 pp.

Moretti, *Da Dante:* Walter Moretti, *Da Dante a Bassani. Studi sulla tradizione letteraria ferrarese e altro*, Florence, Le Lettere, 213 pp.

Morphology 2000: Morphology 2000. Selected Papers from the 9th Morphology Meeting, Vienna, 24–28 February 2000, ed. S. Bendjaballah, W. U. Dressler, O. E. Pfeiffer, and M. D. Voeikova (CILT, 218), Amsterdam, Benjamins, viii + 317 pp.

Mühlethaler, *Poétiques: Poétiques en transition: entre Moyen Age et Renaissance*, ed. Jean-Claude Mühlethaler and Jacqueline Cerquigligni-Toulet (= *Etudes de lettres*, 4), Lausanne, 166 pp.

Murphy, *Thresholds: Thresholds of Otherness / Autrement Mêmes. Identity and Alterity in French-Language Literatures*, ed. David Murphy and Aedín Ní Loingsigh, London, Grant and Cutler, xxiii + 372 pp.

Muscetta Vol.: Per Carlo Muscetta, ed. Novella Bellucci and Giulio Ferroni, Rome, Bulzoni, xiii + 345 pp.

Neuhaus, *Literatur: Engagierte Literatur zwischen den Weltkriegen*, ed. Stefan Neuhaus, Rolf Selbmann, and Thorsten Unger (Schriften der Ernst-Toller-Gesellschaft, 4), Würzburg, Königshausen & Neumann, 410 pp.

Neumann Vol.: Das Imaginäre des Fin de siècle. Ein Symposion für Gerhard Neumann, ed. Christine Lubkoll, Freiburg / Brsg., Rombach, 519 pp.

Norman, *Documentary Impulse: The Documentary Impulse in French Literature*, ed. Buford Norman (Univ. of Carolina French Literature Series, 28), Amsterdam, Rodopi, 2001, xii + 217 pp. + 13 pl.

Palandri, *Deriva:* Enrico Palandri, *La deriva romantica: ipotesti sulla letteratura e sulla scrittura*, Novara, Interlinea, 128 pp.

Paravicini Bagliani, *Chasse: La chasse au Moyen Age. Société, traités, symboles*, ed. Agostino Paravicini Bagliani and Baudouin Van den Abeele (Micrologus Library, 5), Tournhout, Brepols, 2001, 266 pp.

Pellegrini Vol.: Studi linguistici alpini in onore di Giovan Battista Pellegrini, ed. Giovanni Angelini, Florence, Istituto di Studi per l'Alto Adige, 2001, 239 pp.

Perry, *Material Culture: Material Culture and Cultural Materialisms in the Middle Ages and Renaissance*, ed. Curtis Perry, Turnhout, Brepols, xxiv + 246 pp.

Petris, *Sources: Sources et intertexte: résurgences littéraires, du Moyen Age au XXe siècle, actes du colloque de Neuchâtel (6–7 mai 1999)*, ed. Loris Petris and Marie Bornand, Geneva, Droz, 2000, 212 pp.

Pister, *Image du prêtre: L'Image du prêtre dans la littérature classique, XVIe–XVIII siècles*, ed. Danièle Pister (Recherches en littérature et spiritualité, 1), Oxford–Berne–New York, Lang, 2001, x + 278 pp.

Plachta, *Edition: Edition und Übersetzung. Zur wissenschaftlichen Dokumentation des interkulturellen Texttransfers. Beiträge der Internationalen Fachtagung der Arbeitsgemeinschaft für germanistische Edition, 8. bis 11. März 2000*, ed. Bodo Plachta and Winfried Woesler, Tübingen, Niemeyer, viii + 467 pp.

Poag, *Construction: The Construction of Textual Authority in German Literature of the Medieval and Early Modern Periods*, ed. James F. Poag and Claire Baldwin (University of North Carolina Studies in Germanic Languages and Literatures, 123), Chapel Hill, NC, 2001, xiv + 285 pp.

Polyslav 5: Beiträge der Europäischen Slavistischen Linguistik (Polyslav V), ed. Renate Blankenhorn, Sabine Dönninghaus, and Robert Marzari, Munich, Sagner, 303 pp.

Prungnaud, *La Cathédrale: La Cathédrale*, ed. Joëlle Prungnaud, Lille III U.P., 2001, 304 pp.

Radecke, *Fontane: 'Die Décadence ist da.' Theodor Fontane und die Literatur der Jahrhundertwende*, ed. Gabriele Radecke, Würzburg, Königshausen & Neumann, 200 pp.

Ramat, *Passi:* Silvio Ramat, *Il passi della poesia: argomenti da un secolo finito*, Novara, Interlinea, 247 pp.

Renzi Vol.: Current Studies in Italian Syntax. Essays offered to Lorenzo Renzi, ed. Guglielmo Cinque and Giampaolo Salvi, Oxford, Elsevier, 2001, xii + 326 pp.

Ribémont, *Études:* Bernard Ribémont, *Qui des sept arz set rien entendre: études sur le Roman de Thèbes* (Medievalia 43), Orléans, Paradigme, 212 pp.

Rickard Vol.: *Interpreting the History of French: A Festschrift for Peter Rickard on the Occasion of his Eightieth Birthday*, ed. Rodney Sampson and Wendy Ayres-Bennett, Amsterdam–NY, Rodopi, xix + 373 pp.

Robertson, *Rape: Representing Rape in Medieval and Early Modern Literature*, ed. Elizabeth Robertson, Christine M. Rose, and Christopher Cannon, NY, Palgrave, 2001, ix + 453 pp.

Rosenkreuz: *Rosenkreuz als europäisches Phänomen im 17. Jahrhundert*(Bibliotheka Philosophica Hermetica), Amsterdam, Pelikaan, 403 pp.

Rossich, *Teatre: El teatre català dels orígens al segle XVIII*, ed. Albert Rossich, Antoni Serrà Campins, Pep Valsalobre, and David Prats, Girona, Institut de Llengua i Cultura Catalanes — Kassel, Reichenberger, 2001, 512 pp.

Rouget, *L'Objet: Poétiques de l'objet. L'objet dans la poésie française du Moyen Age au XXe siècle, actes du colloque international de Queen's University (mai 1999)*, ed. François Rouget and John Stout, Paris, Champion, 2001, 552 pp.

Rubin Vol.: *The Shape of Change: Essays in Early Modern Literature and La Fontaine in honor of David Lee Rubin*, ed. Anne L. Birberick and Russell Ganim (Faux Titre, 223), Amsterdam-New York, Rodopi, x + 348 pp.

Saccenti, *Scrittoio:* Mario Saccenti, *Lo scrittoio dei classici*, Modena, Mucchi, 2001, 227 pp.

Saicová-Římalová, *Bádání*: *Bádání o jazycích a literaturách*, ed. Lucie Saicová-Římalová, Prague, Charles Univ., 207 pp.

Salisbury, *Violence: Domestic Violence in Medieval Texts*, ed. Eva Salisbury, Georgina Donvin, and Merrall Llewelyn Price, Gainesville, Florida U.P., x + 354 pp.

Sandy, *Heritage: The Classical Heritage in France*, ed. Gerald Sandy (Studies in Intellectual History, 109), Leiden–Boston–Cologne, Brill, vi + 588 pp.

Sarmiento: *Congreso sobre frei Martín Sarmiento*, Santiago de Compostela, Xunta de Galicia, 334 pp.

Saul, *Philosophy: Philosophy and German Literature 1700–1990*, ed. Nicholas Saul (Cambridge Studies in German), CUP, 324 pp.

Sautman, *Love: Same Sex Love and Desire among Women in the Middle Ages*, ed. Francesca Canadé Sautman and Pamela Sheingorn, NY, Palgrave, viii + 312 pp.

Schiewer, *Präsenz: Die Präsenz des Mittelalters in seinen Handschriften. Ergebnisse der Berliner Tagung, 6–8. April 2000*, ed. Hans-Joachim Schiewer and Karl Stackmann, Tübingen, Niemeyer, viii + 362 pp. + 40 pls.

SCHCT 6: *Actes de la VI trobada d'història de la ciència i de la tècnica*, Barcelona, SCHCT–Institut d'Estudis Catalans, 519 pp.

Schulze, *Juden: Juden in der deutschen Literatur des Mittelalters. Religiöse Konzepte — Feindbilder — Rechtfertigungen*, ed. Ursula Schulze, Tübingen, Niemeyer, vi + 290 pp.

Schütz, *Reflexe: Reflexe und Reflexionen von Modernität 1933–1945*, ed. Erhard Schütz and Gregor Streim (Publikationen zur Zeitschrift für Germanistik. neue Folge, 6), Berne, Lang, 366 pp.

Scorrano, *Carte*: Luigi Scorrano, *Carte inquiete*, Ravenna, Longo, 128 pp.

SEHL 3: *Estudios de Historiografía Lingüística: Actas del III Congreso Internacional de la Sociedad Española de Historiografía Lingüística*, ed. Miguel Ángel Esparza Torres, Benigno Fernández Salgado, and Hans-Josef Niederehe, Hamburg, Buske, 2 vols, 1005 pp.

Serebrennikov, *Время: Время и текст*, ed. N. V. Serebrennikov, St Petersburg, Akademicheskii proekt, 352 pp.,

Serrano, *Traditions:* Richard Serrano, *Neither a Borrower. Forging Traditions in French, Chinese and Arabic Poetry*, Oxford, Legenda, x + 238 pp.

SFDES 12: *Les Funérailles à la Renaissance, actes du 12ème congrès de la SFDES (Bar-le-Duc, 2–5 décembre 1999)*, ed. Jean Balsamo (THR, 356), Geneva, Droz, 536 pp.

Silva, *Lingua*: *A lingua e a literatura: algúns aspectos didácticos*, ed. Bieito Silva Valdivia, Santiago de Compostela U.P., 2001, 140 pp.

Simmler, *Textsorten: Textsorten deutscher Prosa vom 12./13. bis 18. Jahrhundert und ihre Merkmale. Akten zum Internationalen Kongress in Berlin 20. bis 22. September 1999*, ed. Franz Simmler (JIG Kongressberichte, 67), Berne, Lang, 662 pp.

Sirera, *Actor: Del Actor Medieval a Nuestros Días. Actas del Seminario celebrado los días 30 de Octubre al 2 de Noviembre de 1996, con motivo del IV Festival de Teatre i Música Medieval d'Elx*, ed. Josep Lluís Sirera, Elx, Institut Municipal de Cultura, 2001, 214 pp.

Sirera, *Teatro: Teatro medieval, teatro vivo. Actas del Seminario celebrado del 28 al 31 de Octubre de 1998 con motivo del V Festival de Teatre i Música Medieval d'Elx*, ed. Josep Lluís Sirera, Elx, Institut Municipal de Cultura, 2001, 283 pp.

Splett Vol.: Lingua Germanica. Studien zur deutschen Philologie. Jochen Splett zum 60. Geburtstag, ed. E. Schmitsdorf, N. Hartl, and B. Meurer. Münster–New York–Munich–Berlin, Waxmann, 381 pp.

Stellmacher, *Dialektologie: Dialektologie zwischen Tradition und Neuansätzen. Beiträge der internationalen Dialektologen, Göttingen, 19.–21. Oktober 1998*, ed. Dieter Stellmacher, Stuttgart, Steiner, 2000, 437 pp.

Tato Vol.: Homenaxe a Fernando R. Tato, ed. Ramón Lorenzo Vázquez, Universidade de Santiago de Compostela, 726 pp.

Thurah, *Historien:* Thomas Thurah, *Historien er ikke slut. Samtaler med 36 europæiske forfattere*, Copenhagen, Gyldendal, 2000, 474 pp.,

Uitti Vol.: Translatio Studii. Essays by his Students in Honor of Karl D. Uitti for his Sixty-Fifth Birthday, ed. Renate Blumenfeld-Kosinski, Kevin Brownlee, Mary B. Speer, and Lori J. Walters (Faux Titre, 179), Amsterdam–Atlanta, Rodopi, 2000, 349 pp.

Vazsonyi, *Searching: Searching for Common Ground. Diskurse zur deutschen Identität*, ed. Nicholas Vazsonyi, Cologne, Böhlau, 2000, x + 306 pp.

Veiga, *Historiografía: Historiografía lingüística y gramática histórica. Gramática y léxico*, ed. Alexandre Veiga and Mercedes Suárez Fernández, Frankfurt, Vervuert, 245 pp.

Viallon-Schoneveld, *Histoire: L'Histoire et les historiens au XVIe siècle, actes du 8e colloque du Puy-en-Velay*, ed. Marie Viallon-Schoneveld, Saint-Etienne U.P., 2001, 208 pp.

Viallon-Schoneveld, *Médecins: Médecins et médecine au XVIe siècle, actes du 9e colloque du Puy-en-Velay*, ed. Marie Viallon-Schoneveld, Saint-Etienne U.P., 216 pp.

Viallon-Schoneveld, *Traduction: La traduction à la Renaissance et à l'age classique*, ed. Marie Viallon-Schoneveld, Saint-Etienne U.P., 2001, 304 pp.

Watanabe-O'Kelly, *Court Culture:* Helen Watanabe-O'Kelly, *Court Culture in Dresden, From Renaissance to Baroque*, Basingstoke, Palgrave, xv + 310 pp.

Wenzel, *Beweglichkeit: Beweglichkeit der Bilder. Text und Imagination in den illustrierten Handschriften des 'Welschen Gastes' von Thomasin von Zerclaere*, ed. Horst Wenzel and Christina Lechtermann (Pictura et Poesis, 15), Cologne, Böhlau, vi + 281 pp.

Wetsel, *Pascal: Pascal — New Trends in Port-Royal Studies*, ed. David Wetsel and Frédéric Canovas (Biblio 17, 143), Tübingen, Narr, 276 pp.

Wilhelmi, *Brant: Sebastian Brant. Forschungsberichte zu seinem Leben, zum 'Narrenschiff' und zum übrigen Werk*, ed. Thomas Wilhelmi, Basle, Schwabe, 256 pp.

Wiltshire, *Romance Phonology: Romance Phonology and Variation. Selected Papers from the 30th Linguistic Symposium on Romance Languages, Gainesville, Florida, February 2000* ed. Caroline R. Wiltshire and Joaquim Camps (CILT, 217), Amsterdam, Benjamins, xii + 238 pp.

Wischer, *Grammaticalization: New Reflections on Grammaticalization*ed. Ilse Wischer and Gabriele Diewald (Typological Studies in Language, 49), Amsterdam–Philadelphia, Benjamins, xiv + 435 pp.

Woesler, *Ballade: Ballade und Historismus. Die Geschichtsballade des 19. Jahrhunderts*, ed. Winfried Woesler, Heidelberg, Winter, 2000, 317 pp.

Žemličkův Vol.: Sborník 2002. Sborník k významnému životnímu jubileu doc. PhDr. Milana Žemličky, ed. Eva Koudelková and Milada Marková, Liberec, Technická univ., 177 pp.

Zimmermann, *Auctor: Auctor et Auctoritas. Invention et conformisme dans l'écriture moderne*, ed. Michel Zimmermann (Mémoires et Documents de l'Ecole des Chartes, 59), Paris, Ecole des Chartes, 2001, 593 pp.

Zinguer, *Dionysos: Dionysos. Origines et résurgences*, ed. Ilana Zinguer ('De Pétrarque à Descartes', 69), Paris, Vrin, 2001, 198 pp.

Zink Vol.: Chanson pouvez aller pour tout le monde: Recherches sur la memoire et l'oubli dans la chant medieval (hommage a Michel Zink), ed. A. Babbi and C. Galdersi, Orleans, Paradigme, 2001, 184 pp.

II. GENERAL

abbrev.	abbreviation, abbreviated to
Acad., Akad.	Academy, Academia, etc.
acc.	accusative
AN	Anglo-Norman
ann.	annotated (by)
anon.	anonymous
appx	appendix
Arg.	Argentinian (and foreign equivalents)
AS	Anglo-Saxon
Assoc.	Association (and foreign equivalents)
Auv.	Auvergnat
Bel.	Belarusian
BL	British Library
BM	British Museum
BN	Bibliothèque Nationale, Biblioteka Narodowa, etc.
BPtg.	Brazilian Portuguese
bull.	bulletin
c.	century
c.	circa
Cat.	Catalan
ch.	chapter
col.	column
comm.	commentary (by)
comp.	compiler, compiled (by)
Cz.	Czech
diss.	dissertation
ed.	edited (by), editor (and foreign equivalents)
edn	edition
EPtg.	European Portuguese
fac.	facsimile
fasc.	fascicle
Fest.	Festschrift, Festskrift
Fin.	Finnish
Fr.	France, French, Français
Gal.-Ptg.	Galician-Portuguese (and equivalents)
Gasc.	Gascon
Ger.	German(y)
Gk	Greek
Gmc	Germanic
IE	Indo-European
illus.	illustrated, illustration(s)
impr.	impression
incl.	including, include(s)
Inst.	Institute (and foreign equivalents)
introd.	introduction, introduced by, introductory
It.	Italian
izd.	издание
izd-vo	издательство
Jb.	Jahrbuch
Jg	Jahrgang
Jh.	Jahrhundert
Lang.	Languedocien

Lat.	Latin
Lim.	Limousin
lit.	literature
med.	medieval
MHG	Middle High German
Mid. Ir.	Middle Irish
Mil.	Milanese
MS	manuscript
n.d.	no date
n.F.	neue Folge
no.	number (and foreign equivalents)
nom.	nominative
n.p.	no place
n.s.	new series
O Auv.	Old Auvergnat
O Cat.	Old Catalan
Occ.	Occitan
OE	Old English
OF	Old French
O Gasc.	Old Gascon
OHG	Old High German
O Ir.	Old Irish
O Lim.	Old Limousin
O Occ.	Old Occitan
O Pr.	Old Provençal
O Ptg.	Old Portuguese
OS	Old Saxon
OW	Old Welsh
part.	participle
ped.	педагогический, etc.
PIE	Proto-Indo-European
Pied.	Piedmontese
PGmc	Primitive Germanic
pl.	plate
plur.	plural
Pol.	Polish
p.p.	privately published
Pr.	Provençal
pref.	preface (by)
Procs	Proceedings
Ptg.	Portuguese
publ.	publication, published (by)
Ren.	Renaissance
repr.	reprint(ed)
Rev.	Review, Revista, Revue
rev.	revised (by)
Russ.	Russian
s.	siècle
ser.	series
sg.	singular
Slg	Sammlung
Soc.	Society (and foreign equivalents)
Sp.	Spanish
supp.	supplement

Sw.	Swedish
Trans.	Transactions
trans.	translated (by), translation
Ukr.	Ukrainian
Univ.	University (and foreign equivalents)
unpubl.	unpublished
U.P.	University Press (and foreign equivalents)
Vlg	Verlag
vol.	volume
vs	versus
W.	Welsh
wyd.	wydawnictwo

* before a publication signifies that it has not been seen by the contributor.

III. PLACE NAMES

B	Barcelona
BA	Buenos Aires
Be	Belgrade
Bo	Bologna
C	Coimbra
F	Florence
Gd	Gdańsk
Kw	Kraków, Cracow
L	Lisbon
M	Madrid
Mi	Milan
Mw	Moscow
Na	Naples
NY	New York
O	Oporto
Pń	Poznań
R	Rio de Janeiro
Ro	Rome
SC	Santiago de Compostela
SPo	São Paulo
SPb	St Petersburg
T	Turin
V	Valencia
Wa	Warsaw
Ww	Wrocław
Z	Zagreb

IV. PERIODICALS, INSTITUTIONS, PUBLISHERS

AA, Antike und Abendland
AAA, Ardis Publishers, Ann Arbor, Michigan
AAA, Archivio per l'Alto Adige
AAASS, American Association for the Advancement of Slavic Studies
AABC, Anuari de l'Agrupació Borrianenca de Cultura
AAC, Atti dell'Accademia Clementina
AAL, Atti dell'Accademia dei Lincei
AALP, L'Arvista dl'Academia dla Lenga Piemontèisa
AAM, Association des Amis de Maynard
AAPH, Anais da Academia Portuguesa da História
AAPN, Atti dell'Accademia Pontaniana di Napoli
AAPP, Atti Accademia Peloritana dei Pericolanti. Classe di Lettere Filosofia e Belle Arti
AARA, Atti della Accademia Roveretana degli Agiati
AASB, Atti dell'Accademia delle Scienze dell'Istituto di Bologna
AASF, Annales Academiae Scientiarum Fennicae
AASLAP, Atti dell'Accademia di Scienze, Lettere ed Arti di Palermo

AASLAU, Atti dell'Accademia di Scienze, Lettere e Arti di Udine
AASN, Atti dell'Accademia di Scienze Morali e Politiche di Napoli
AAST, Atti dell'Accademia delle Scienze di Torino
AAVM, Atti e Memorie dell'Accademia Virgiliana di Mantova
AAWG, Abhandlungen der Akademie der Wissenschaften in Göttingen, phil.-hist. Kl., 3rd ser., Göttingen, Vandenhoeck & Ruprecht
AB, Analecta Bollandiana
ABa, L'Année Balzacienne
ABÄG, Amsterdamer Beiträge zur älteren Germanistik
ABB, Archives et Bibliothèques de Belgique — Archief- en Bibliotheekswezen in België
ABC, Annales Benjamin Constant
ABDB, Aus dem Antiquariat. Beiträge zum Börsenblatt für den deutschen Buchhandel
ABDO, Association Bourguignonne de Dialectologie et d'Onomastique, Fontaine lès Dijon
ABHL, Annual Bulletin of Historical Literature
ABI, Accademie e Biblioteche d'Italia
ABN, Anais da Biblioteca Nacional, Rio de Janeiro
ABNG, Amsterdamer Beiträge zur neueren Germanistik, Amsterdam, Rodopi
ABNG, Amsterdamer Beiträge zur neueren Germanistik
ABor, Acta Borussica
ABP, Arquivo de Bibliografia Portuguesa
ABR, American Benedictine Review
ABr, Annales de Bretagne et des Pays de l'Ouest
ABS, Acta Baltico-Slavica
ABSJ, Annual Bulletin of the Société Jersiaise
AC, Analecta Cisterciensa, Rome
ACCT, Agence de Coopération Culturelle et Technique
ACer, Anales Cervantinos, Madrid
ACIS, Association for Contemporary Iberian Studies
ACo, Acta Comeniana, Prague
AColl, Actes et Colloques
Acme, Annali della Facoltà di Filosofia e Lettere dell'Università Statale di Milano
ACP, L'Amitié Charles Péguy
ACUA, Anales del Colegio Universitario de Almería
AD, Analysen und Dokumente. Beiträge zur Neueren Literatur, Berne, Lang
ADEVA, Akademische Druck- und Verlagsanstalt, Graz
AE, Artemis Einführungen, Munich, Artemis
AE, L'Autre Europe
AEA, Anuario de Estudios Atlánticos, Las Palmas
AECI, Agencia Española de Cooperación Internacional
AEd, Arbeiten zur Editionswissenschaft, Frankfurt, Lang
AEF, Anuario de Estudios Filológicos, Cáceres
AEL, Anuario de la Escuela de Letras, Mérida, Venezuela
AELG, Anuario de Literarios Galegos
AEM, Anuario de Estudios Medievales
AF, Anuario de Filología, Barcelona
AFA, Archivo de Filología Aragonesa
AfAf, African Affairs
AfC, Afrique Contemporaine
AFe, L'Armana di Felibre
AFF, Anali Filološkog fakulteta, Belgrade
AFH, Archivum Franciscanum Historicum
AFHis, Anales de Filología Hispánica
AfHR, Afro-Hispanic Review
AfL, L'Afrique Littéraire
AFLE, Annali della Fondazione Luigi Einaudi
AFLFUB, Annali della Facoltà di Lettere e Filosofia dell'Università di Bari

AFLFUC, Annali della Facoltà di Lettere e Filosofia dell'Università di Cagliari
AFLFUG, Annali della Facoltà di Lettere e Filosofia dell'Università degli Studi di Genova
AFLFUM, Annali della Facoltà di Lettere e Filosofia dell'Università di Macerata
AFLFUN, Annali della Facoltà di Lettere e Filosofia dell'Università di Napoli
AFLFUP(SF), Annali dellà Facoltà di Lettere e Filosofia dell'Università di Perugia. 1. Studi Filosofici
AFLFUP(SLL), Annali della Facoltà di Lettere e Filosofia dell'Università di Perugia. 3. Studi Linguistici-Letterari
AFLFUS, Annali della Facoltà di Lettere e Filosofia dell'Università di Siena
AFLLS, Annali della Facoltà di Lingua e Letterature Straniere di Ca' Foscari, Venice
AFLLSB, Annali della Facoltà di Lingue e Letterature Straniere dell'Università di Bari
AFLN, Annales de la Faculté des Lettres et Sciences Humaines de Nice
AFLS, Association for French Language Studies
AFP, Archivum Fratrum Praedicatorum
AFrP, Athlone French Poets, London, The Athlone Press
AG, Anales Galdosianos
AGB, Archiv für Geschichte des Buchwesens
AGF, Anuario Galego de Filoloxia
AGGSA, Acta Germanica. German Studies in Africa
AGI, Archivio Glottologico Italiano
AGP, Archiv für Geschichte der Philosophie
AH, Archivo Hispalense
AHAM, Acta Historica et Archaeologica Mediaevalia
AHCP, Arquivos de História de Cultura Portuguesa
AHDLMA, Archives d'Histoire Doctrinale et Littéraire du Moyen Âge
AHF, Archiwum Historii Filozofii i Myśli Społecznej
AHP, Archivum Historiae Pontificae
AHPr, Annales de Haute-Provence, Digne-les-Bains
AHR, American Historical Review
AHRF, Annales Historiques de la Révolution Française
AHRou, Archives historiques du Rouergue
AHSA, Archives historiques de la Saintonge et de l'Aunis, Saintes
AHSJ, Archivum Historicum Societatis Jesu
AHSS, Annales: Histoire — Science Sociales
AI, Almanacco Italiano
AIB, Annali dell'Istituto Banfi
AIBL, Académie des Inscriptions et Belles-Lettres, Comptes Rendus
AIEM, Anales del Instituto de Estudios Madrileños
AIEO, Association Internationale d'Études Occitanes
AIFMUR, Annali dell'Istituto di Filologia Moderna dell'Università di Roma
AIFUF, Annali dell'Istituto di Filosofia dell'Università di Firenze
AIHI, Archives Internationales d'Histoire des Idées, The Hague, Nijhoff
AIHS, Archives Internationales d'Histoire des Sciences
AIL, Associação Internacional de Lusitanistas
AILLC, Associació Internacional de Llengua i Literatura Catalanes
AION(FG), Annali dell'Istituto Universitario Orientale, Naples: Sezione Germanica. Filologia Germanica
AION(FL), Annali dell'Istituto Universitario Orientale, Naples: Sezione Filologico-letteraria
AION(SF), Annali dell'Istituto Universitario Orientale, Naples: Studi Filosofici
AION(SL), Annali dell'Istituto Universitario Orientale, Naples: Sezione Linguistica

AION(SR), Annali dell'Istituto Universitario Orientale, Naples: Sezione Romanza
AION(SS), Annali dell'Istituto Universitario Orientale, Naples: Sezione Slava
AION(ST), Annali dell'Istituto Universitario Orientale, Naples: Sezione Germanica. Studi Tedeschi
AIPHS, Annuaire de l'Institut de Philologie et de l'Histoire Orientales et Slaves
AIPS, Annales Instituti Philologiae Slavica Universitatis Debreceniensis de Ludovico Kossuth Nominatae — Slavica
AISIGT, Annali dell'Istituto Storico Italo-Germanico di Trento
AITCA, Arxiu informatizat de textos catalans antics
AIV, Atti dell'Istituto Veneto
AJ, Alemannisches Jahrbuch
AJCAI, Actas de las Jornadas de Cultura Arabe e Islámica
AJFS, Australian Journal of French Studies
AJGLL, American Journal of Germanic Linguistics and Literatures
AJL, Australian Journal of Linguistics
AJP, American Journal of Philology
AKG, Archiv für Kulturgeschichte
AKML, Abhandlungen zur Kunst-, Musik- und Literaturwissenschaft, Bonn, Bouvier
AL, Anuario de Letras, Mexico
AlAm, Alba de América
ALB, Annales de la Faculté des Lettres de Besançon
ALC, African Languages and Cultures
ALE, Anales de Literatura Española, Alicante
ALEC, Anales de Literatura Española Contemporánea
ALet, Armas y Letras, Universidad de Nuevo León
ALEUA, Anales de Literatura Española de la Universidad de Alicante
ALFL, Actes de Langue Française et de Linguistique
ALH, Acta Linguistica Hungaricae
ALHA, Anales de la Literatura Hispanoamericana
ALHa, Acta Linguistica Hafniensia
ALHisp, Anuario de Lingüística Hispánica
ALHist, Annales: Littérature et Histoire
ALit, Acta Literaria, Chile
ALitH, Acta Litteraria Hungarica
ALLI, Atlante Linguistico dei Laghi Italiani
ALM, Archives des Lettres Modernes
ALMA, Archivum Latinitatis Medii Aevi (Bulletin du Cange)
ALo, Armanac de Louzero
ALP, Atlas linguistique et ethnographique de Provence, CNRS, 1975–86
AlS, Almanac Setòri
ALT, African Literature Today
ALu, Alpes de Lumière, Fourcalquier
ALUB, Annales Littéraires de l'Université de Besançon
AM, Analecta Musicologica
AMAA, Atti e Memorie dell'Accademia d'Arcadia
AMAASLV, Atti e Memorie dell'Accademia di Agricultura, Scienze e Lettere di Verona
Amades, Amades. Arbeitspapiere und Materialien zur deutschen Sprache
AMAGP, Atti e Memorie dell'Accademia Galileiana di Scienze, Lettere ed Arti in Padova
AMal, Analecta Malacitana
AMAPet, Atti e Memorie dell'Accademia Petrarca di Lettere, Arti e Scienze, Arezzo
AMAT, Atti e Memorie dell'Accademia Toscana di Scienze e Lettere, La Colombaria
AMDLS, Arbeiten zur Mittleren Deutschen Literatur und Sprache, Berne, Lang
AMDSPAPM, Atti e Memorie della Deputazione di Storia Patria per le Antiche Province Modenesi

AMGG, Abhandlungen der Marburger Gelehrten Gesellschaft, Munich, Fink
AmH, American Hispanist
AMid, Annales du Midi
AmIn, América Indígena, Mexico
AML, Main Monographien Literaturwissenschaft, Frankfurt, Main
AMSSSP, Atti e Memorie della Società Savonese di Storia Patria
AN, Академия наук
AN, Americana Norvegica
ANABA, Asociación Nacional de Bibliotecarios, Arquiveros y Arqueólogos
AnAlf, Annali Alfieriani
AnEA, Anaquel de Estudios Arabes
ANeo, Acta Neophilologica, Ljubljana
ANF, Arkiv för nordisk filologi
AnI, Annali d'Italianistica
AnL, Anthropological Linguistics
AnM, Anuario Medieval
AnN, Annales de Normandie
AnnM, Annuale Medievale
ANPOLL, Associação Nacional de Pós-graduação e Pesquisa em Letras e Lingüística, São Paulo
ANQ, American Notes and Queries
ANS, Anglo-Norman Studies
AnS, L'Année Stendhalienne
ANTS, Anglo-Norman Text Society
AnVi, Antologia Vieusseux
ANZSGLL, Australian and New Zealand Studies in German Language and Literature, Berne, Lang
AO, Almanac occitan, Foix
AÖAW, Anzeiger der Österreichischen Akademie der Wissenschaften
AOn, Acta Onomastica
AP, Aurea Parma
APIFN, Актуальные проблемы истории философии народов СССР.
APK, Aufsätze zur portugiesischen Kulturgeschichte, Görres-Gesellschaft, Münster
ApL, Applied Linguistics
APL, Associação Portuguesa de Linguística
APPP, Abhandlungen zur Philosophie, Psychologie und Pädagogik, Bonn, Bouvier
APr, Analecta Praemonstratensia
AProu, Armana Prouvençau, Marseilles
APS, Acta Philologica Scandinavica
APSL, Amsterdamer Publikationen zur Sprache und Literatur, Amsterdam, Rodopi
APSR, American Political Science Review
APUCF, Association des Publications de la Faculté des Lettres et Sciences Humaines de l'Université de Clermont-Ferrand II, Nouvelle Série
AQ, Arizona Quarterly
AqAq, Aquò d'aquí, Gap
AR, Archiv für Reformationsgeschichte
ARAJ, American Romanian Academy Journal
ARAL, Australian Review of Applied Linguistics
ARCA, ARCA: Papers of the Liverpool Latin Seminar
ArCCP, Arquivos do Centro Cultural Português, Paris
ArEM, Aragón en la Edad Media
ArFil, Archivio di Filosofia
ArI, Arthurian Interpretations
ARI, Архив русской истории
ARL, Athlone Renaissance Library
ArL, Archivum Linguisticum
ArLit, Arthurian Literature
ArP, Археографски прилози
ArSP, Archivio Storico Pugliese
ArSPr, Archivio Storico Pratese
ArSt, Archivi per la Storia
ART, Atelier Reproduction des Thèses, Univ. de Lille III, Paris, Champion
AS, The American Scholar
ASAHM, Annales de la Société d'Art et d'Histoire du Mentonnais, Menton
ASAvS, Annuaire de la Société des Amis du vieux-Strasbourg
ASB, Archivio Storico Bergamasco
ASCALF, Association for the Study of Caribbean and African Literature in French
ASCALFB, ASCALF Bulletin

ASCALFY, ASCALF Yearbook
ASE, Annali di Storia dell'Esegesi
ASEES, Australian Slavonic and East European Studies
ASELGC, 1616. Anuario de la Sociedad Española de Literatura General y Comparada
ASGM, Atti del Sodalizio Glottologico Milanese
ASI, Archivio Storico Italiano
ASJ, Acta Slavonica Japonica
ASL, Archivio Storico Lombardo
ASLSP, Atti della Società Ligure di Storia Patria
ASMC, Annali di Storia Moderna e Contemporanea
ASNP, Annali della Scuola Normale Superiore di Pisa
ASNS, Archiv für das Studium der Neueren Sprachen und Literaturen
ASocRous, Annales de la Société J.-J. Rousseau
ASolP, A Sol Post, Editorial Marfil, Alcoi
ASP, Anzeiger für slavische Philologie
AsP, L'Astrado prouvençalo. Revisto Bilengo de Prouvenco/Revue Bilingue de Provence, Berre L'Etang.
ASPN, Archivio Storico per le Province Napoletane
ASPP, Archivio Storico per le Province Parmensi
ASR, Annalas da la Societad Retorumantscha
ASRSP, Archivio della Società Romana di Storia Patria
ASSO, Archivio Storico per la Sicilia Orientale
ASSUL, Annali del Dipartimento di Scienze Storiche e Sociali dell'Università di Lecce
AST, Analecta Sacra Tarraconensia
ASt, Austrian Studies
ASTic, Archivio Storico Ticinese
AŞUI, (e), (f), Analele Ştiinţifice ale Universităţii 'Al. I. Cuza' din Iaşi, secţ. e, Lingvistică, secţ. f, Literatură
AT, Athenäums Taschenbücher, Frankfurt, Athenäum
ATB, Altdeutsche Textbibliothek, Tübingen, Niemeyer
ATCA, Arxiu de Textos Catalans Antics, IEC, Barcelona
Ate, Nueva Atenea, Universidad de Concepción, Chile
ATO, A Trabe de Ouro
ATS, Arbeiten und Texte zur Slavistik, Munich, Sagner
ATV, Aufbau Taschenbuch Verlag, Berlin, Aufbau
AtV, Ateneo Veneto
AUBLLR, Analele Universităţii Bucureşti, Limba şi literatura română
AUBLLS, Analele Universităţii Bucureşti, Limbi şi literaturi străine
AUC, Anales de la Universidad de Cuenca
AUCP, Acta Universitatis Carolinae Pragensis
AuE, Arbeiten und Editionen zur Mittleren Deutschen Literatur, Stuttgart–Bad Cannstatt, Frommann-Holzboog
AUL, Acta Universitatis Lodziensis
AUL, Annali della Facoltà di Lettere e Filosofia dell'Università di Lecce
AUMCS, Annales Uniwersytetu Marii Curie-Skłodowskiej, Lublin
AUML, Anales de la Universidad de Murcia: Letras
AUMLA, Journal of the Australasian Universities Modern Language Association
AUN, Annali della Facoltà di Lettere e Filosofia dell'Università di Napoli
AUNCFP, Acta Universitatis Nicolai Copernici. Filologia Polska, Toruń
AUPO, Acta Universitatis Palackianae Olomucensis
AUS, American University Studies, Berne — New York, Lang
AUSP, Annali dell'Università per Stranieri di Perugia
AUSt, Acta Universitatis Stockholmiensis
AUTŞF, Analele Universităţii din Timişoara, Ştiinţe Filologice
AUU, Acta Universitatis Upsaliensis

AUW, Acta Universitatis Wratislaviensis
AVen, Archivio Veneto
AVEP, Assouciacien vareso pèr l'ensignamen dòu prouvençou, La Farlède
AVEPB, *Bulletin AVEP*, La Farlède
AvT, L'Avant-Scène Théâtre
AWR, Anglo-Welsh Review

BA, Bollettino d'Arte
BAAA, Bulletin de l'Association des Amis d'Alain
BAAG, Bulletin des Amis d'André Gide
BAAJG, Bulletin de l'Association des Amis de Jean Giono
BAAL, Boletín de la Academia Argentina de Letras
BaB, Bargfelder Bote
BAC, Biblioteca de Autores Cristianos
BACol, Boletín de la Academia Colombiana
BÄDL, Beiträge zur Älteren Deutschen Literaturgeschichte, Berne, Lang
BADLit, Bonner Arbeiten zur deutschen Literatur, Bonn, Bouvier
BAE, Biblioteca de Autores Españoles
BAEO, Boletín de la Asociación Española de Orientalistas
BAFJ, Bulletin de l'Association Francis Jammes
BAG, Boletín de la Academia Gallega
BAIEO, Bulletins de l'Association Internationale d'Études Occitanes
BAJR, Bulletin des Amis de Jules Romains
BAJRAF, Bulletin des Amis de Jacques Rivière et d'Alain-Fournier
BALI, Bollettino dell'Atlante Linguistico Italiano
BALM, Bollettino dell'Atlante Linguistico Mediterraneo
BalS, Balkan Studies, Institute for Balkan Studies, Thessaloniki
BAN, Българска Академия на Науките, София
BAO, Biblioteca Abat Oliva, Publicacions de l'Abadia de Montserrat, Barcelona
BAPC, Bulletin de l'Association Paul Claudel
BAPRLE, Boletín de la Academia Puertorrigueña de la Lengua Española
BAR, Biblioteca dell'Archivum Romanicum
BARLLF, Bulletin de l'Académie Royale de Langues et de Littératures Françaises de Bruxelles
BAWA, Bayerische Akademie der Wissenschaften. Phil.-hist. Kl. Abhandlungen, n.F.
BB, Biblioteca Breve, Lisbon
BB, Bulletin of Bibliography
BBAHLM, Boletín Bibliografico de la Asociación Hispánica de Literatura Medieval
BBaud, Bulletin Baudelairien
BBB, Berner Beiträge zur Barockgermanistik, Berne, Lang
BBGN, Brünner Beiträge zur Germanistik und Nordistik
BBib, Bulletin du Bibliophile
BBL, Bayreuther Beiträge zur Literaturwissenschaft, Frankfurt, Lang
BBLI, Bremer Beiträge zur Literatur- und Ideengeschichte, Frankfurt, Lang
BBMP, Boletín de la Biblioteca de Menéndez Pelayo
BBN, Bibliotheca Bibliographica Neerlandica, Nieuwkoop, De Graaf
BBNDL, Berliner Beiträge zur neueren deutschen Literaturgeschichte, Berne, Lang
BBSANZ, Bulletin of the Bibliographical Society of Australia and New Zealand
BBSIA, Bulletin Bibliographique de la Société Internationale Arthurienne
BBSMES, Bulletin of the British Society for Middle Eastern Studies

BBUC, Boletim da Biblioteca da Universidade de Coimbra
BC, Bulletin of the 'Comediantes', University of Wisconsin
BCB, Boletín Cultural y Bibliográfico, Bogatá
BCEC, Bwletin Cymdeithas Emynwyr Cymru
BCél, Bulletin Célinien
BCh, Болдинские чтения
BCLSMP, Académie Royale de Belgique: Bulletin de la Classe des Lettres et des Sciences Morales et Politiques
BCMV, Bollettino Civici Musei Veneziani
BCRLT, Bulletin du Centre de Romanistique et de Latinité Tardive
BCS, Bulletin of Canadian Studies
BCSM, Bulletin of the Cantigueiros de Santa Maria
BCSS, Bollettino del Centro di Studi Filologici e Linguistici Siciliani
BCSV, Bollettino del Centro di Studi Vichiani
BCZG, Blätter der Carl Zuckmayer Gesellschaft
BD, Беларуская думка
BDADA, Bulletin de documentation des Archives départementales de l'Aveyron, Rodez
BDB, Börsenblatt für den deutschen Buchhandel
BDBA, Bien Dire et Bien Aprandre
BDL, Beiträge zur Deutschen Literatur, Frankfurt, Lang
BDP, Beiträge zur Deutschen Philologie, Giessen, Schmitz
BEA, Bulletin des Études Africaines
BEC, Bibliothèque de l'École des Chartes
BelE, Беларуская энцыклапедыя
BelL, Беларуская лінгвістыка
BelS, Беларускі сьвет
BEP, Bulletin des Études Portugaises
BEPar, Bulletin des Études Parnassiennes et Symbolistes
BEzLit, Български език и литература
BF, Boletim de Filologia
BFA, Bulletin of Francophone Africa
BFC, Boletín de Filología, Univ. de Chile
BFE, Boletín de Filología Española
BFF, Bulletin Francophone de Finlande
BFFGL, Boletín de la Fundación Federico García Lorca
BFi, Bollettino Filosofico
BFLS, Bulletin de la Faculté des Lettres de Strasbourg
BFo, Biuletyn Fonograficzny
BFPLUL, Bibliothèque de la Faculté de Philosophie et Lettres de l'Université de Liège
BFR, Bibliothèque Française et Romane, Paris, Klincksieck
BFR, Bulletin of the Fondation C.F. Ramuz
BFr, Börsenblatt Frankfurt
BG, Bibliotheca Germanica, Tübingen, Francke
BGB, Bulletin de l'Association Guillaume Budé
BGDSL, Beiträge zur Geschichte der deutschen Sprache und Literatur, Tübingen
BGKT, Беларускае грамадска-культуральнае таварыства
BGL, Boletin Galego de Literatura
BGLKAJ, Beiträge zur Geschichte der Literatur und Kunst des 18. Jahrhunderts, Heidelberg, Winter
BGP, Bristol German Publications, Bristol U.P
BGREC, Bulletin du Groupe de Recherches et d'Études du Clermontais, Clermont-l'Hérault
BGS, Beiträge zur germanistischen Sprachwissenschaft, Hamburg, Buske
BGS, Beiträge zur Geschichte der Sprachwissenschaft
BGT, Blackwell German Texts, Oxford, Blackwell
BH, Bulletin Hispanique
BHR, Bibliothèque d'Humanisme et Renaissance
BHS, Bulletin of Hispanic Studies, Liverpool
BHS(G), Bulletin of Hispanic Studies, Glasgow (1995–2001)
BHS(L), Bulletin of Hispanic Studies, Liverpool (1995–2001)

BI, Bibliographisches Institut, Leipzig
BIABF, Bulletin d'informations-Association des bibliothécaires français
BibAN, Библиотека Академии наук СССР
BIDS, Bulletin of the International Dostoevsky Society, Klagenfurt
BIEA, Boletín del Instituto de Estudios Asturianos
BIHBR, Bulletin de l'Institut Historique Belge de Rome
BIHR, Bulletin of the Institute of Historical Research
BIO, Bulletin de l'Institut Occitan, Pau
BJA, British Journal of Aesthetics
BJCS, British Journal for Canadian Studies
BJECS, The British Journal for Eighteenth-Century Studies
BJHP, British Journal of the History of Philosophy
BJHS, British Journal of the History of Science
BJL, Belgian Journal of Linguistics
BJR, Bulletin of the John Rylands University Library of Manchester
BKF, Beiträge zur Kleist-Forschung
BL, Brain and Language
BLAR, Bulletin of Latin American Research
BLBI, Bulletin des Leo Baeck Instituts
BLe, Börsenblatt Leipzig
BLFCUP, Bibliothèque de Littérature Française Contemporaine de l'Université Paris 7
BLI, Beiträge zur Linguistik und Informationsverarbeitung
BLi, Беларуская літаратура. Міжвузаўскі зборнік.
BLJ, British Library Journal
BLL, Beiträge zur Literatur und Literaturwissenschaft des 20. Jahrhunderts, Berne, Lang
BLR, Bibliothèque Littéraire de la Renaissance, Geneva, Slatkine–Paris, Champion
BLR, Bodleian Library Record
BLVS, Bibliothek des Literarischen Vereins, Stuttgart, Hiersemann
BM, Bibliothek Metzier, Stuttgart
BMBP, Bollettino del Museo Bodoniano di Parma
BMCP, Bollettino del Museo Civico di Padova
BML, Беларуская мова і літаратура ў школе
BMo, Беларуская мова. Міжвузаўскі зборнік
BNE, Beiträge zur neueren Epochenforschung, Berne, Lang
BNF, Beiträge zur Namenforschung
BNL, Beiträge zur neueren Literaturgeschichte, 3rd ser., Heidelberg, Winter
BNP, Beiträge zur nordischen Philologie, Basel, Helbing & Lichtenhahn
BO, Biblioteca Orientalis
BOCES, Boletín del Centro de Estudios del Siglo XVIII, Oviedo
BOP, Bradford Occasional Papers
BP, Български писател
BP, Lo Bornat dau Perigòrd
BPTJ, Biuletyn Polskiego Towarzystwa Językoznawczego
BR, Болгарская русистика.
BRA, Bonner Romanistische Arbeiten, Berne, Lang
BRABLB, Boletín de la Real Academia de Buenas Letras de Barcelona
BRAC, Boletín de la Real Academia de Córdoba de Ciencias, Bellas Letras, y Nobles Artes
BRAE, Boletín de la Real Academia Española
BRAG, Boletín de la Real Academia Gallega
BRAH, Boletín de la Real Academia de la Historia
BrC, Bruniana & Campanelliana
BRIES, Bibliothèque Russe de l'Institut d'Études Slaves, Paris, Institut d'Études Slaves
BRJL, Bulletin ruského jazyka a literatury
BrL, La Bretagne Linguistique
BRP, Beiträge zur romanischen Philologie
BS, Biuletyn slawistyczny, Łódź
BSAHH, Bulletin de la Société archéologique et historique des

hauts cantons de l'Hérault, Bédarieux
BSAHL, Bulletin de la Société archéologique et historique du Limousin, Limoges
BSAHLSG, Bulletin de la Société Archéologique, Historique, Littéraire et Scientifique du Gers
BSAM, Bulletin de la Société des Amis de Montaigne
BSAMPAC, Bulletin de la Société des Amis de Marcel Proust et des Amis de Combray
BSASLB, Bulletin de la Société Archéologique, Scientifique et Littéraire de Béziers
BSATG, Bulletin de la Société Archéologique de Tarn-et-Garonne
BSBS, Bollettino Storico–Bibliografico Subalpino
BSCC, Boletín de la Sociedad Castellonense de Cultura
BSD, Bithell Series of Dissertations — MHRA Texts and Dissertations, London, Modern Humanities Research Association
BSD, Bulletin de la Société de Borda, Dax
BSDL, Bochumer Schriften zur deutschen Literatur, Berne, Lang
BSDSL, Basler Studien zur deutschen Sprache und Literatur, Tübingen, Francke
BSE, Галоўная рэдакцыя Беларускай савеюкай энцыклапедыі
BSEHA, Bulletin de la Société d'Études des Hautes-Alpes, Gap
BSEHTD, Bulletin de la Société d'Études Historiques du texte dialectal
BSELSAL, Bulletin de la Société des Études Littéraires, Scientifiques et Artistiques du Lot
BSF, Bollettino di Storia della Filosofia
BSG, Berliner Studien zur Germanistik, Frankfurt, Lang
BSHAP, Bulletin de la Société Historique et Archéologique du Périgord, Périgueux
BSHPF, Bulletin de la Société de l'Histoire du Protestantisme Français
BSIH, Brill's Studies in Intellectual History, Leiden, Brill
BSIS, Bulletin of the Society for Italian Studies
BSLA, Bulletin Suisse de Linguistique Appliquée
BSLLW, Bulletin de la Société de Langue et Littérature Wallonnes
BSLP, Bulletin de la Société de Linguistique de Paris
BSLSAC, Bulletin de la Société des lettres sciences et arts de la Corrèze
BSLV, Bollettino della Società Letteraria di Verona
BSM, Birmingham Slavonic Monographs, University of Birmingham
BSOAS, Bulletin of the School of Oriental and African Studies
BSP, Bollettino Storico Pisano
BSPC, Bulletin de la Société Paul Claudel
BSPia, Bollettino Storico Piacentino
BSPN, Bollettino Storico per le Province di Novara
BSPSP, Bollettino della Società Pavese di Storia Patria
BSR, Bulletin de la Société Ramond. Bagneres-de-Bigorre
BsR, Beck'sche Reihe, Munich, Beck
BSRS, Bulletin of the Society for Renaissance Studies
BSS, Bulletin of Spanish Studies, Glasgow
BSSAAPC, Bollettino della Società per gli Studi Storici, Archeologici ed Artistici della Provincia di Cuneo
BSSCLE, Bulletin of the Society for the Study of the Crusades and the Latin East
BSSP, Bullettino Senese di Storia Patria
BSSPHS, Bulletin of the Society for Spanish and Portuguese Historical Studies
BSSPin, Bollettino della Società Storica Pinerolese, Pinerolo, Piemonte, Italy.

BSSV, Bollettino della Società Storica Valtellinese
BSZJPS, Bałtosłowiańskie związki językowe. Prace Slawistyczne
BT, Богословские труды, Moscow
BTe, Biblioteca Teatrale
BTH, Boletim de Trabalhos Historicos
BulEz, Български език
BW, Bibliothek und Wissenschaft
BySt, Byzantine Studies

CA, Cuadernos Americanos
CAAM, Cahiers de l'Association Les Amis de Milosz
CAB, Commentari dell'Ateneo di Brescia
CAC, Les Cahiers de l'Abbaye de Créteil
CadL, Cadernos da Lingua
CAFLS, Cahiers AFLS
CAG, Cahiers André Gide
CAH, Les Cahiers Anne Hébert
CaH, Les Cahiers de l'Humanisme
CAIEF, Cahiers de l'Association Internationale des Études Françaises
CalLet, Calabria Letteraria
CAm, Casa de las Américas, Havana
CAm, Casa de las Américas, Havana
CanJL, Canadian Journal of Linguistics
CanJP, Canadian Journal of Philosophy
CanL, Canadian Literature
CanSP, Canadian Slavonic Papers
CanSS, Canadian–American Slavic Studies
CarA, Carmarthenshire Antiquary
CARB, Cahiers des Amis de Robert Brasillach
CarQ, Caribbean Quarterly
CAT, Cahiers d'Analyse Textuelle, Liège, Les Belles Lettres
CatR, Catalan Review
CAVL, Cahiers des Amis de Valery Larbaud
CB, Cuadernos Bibliográficos
CC, Comparative Criticism
CCe, Cahiers du Cerf XX
CCend, Continent Cendrars
CCF, Cuadernos de la Cátedra Feijoo
CCMe, Cahiers de Civilisation Médiévale
CCol, Cahiers Colette
CCU, Cuadernos de la Cátedra M. de Unamuno
CD, Cuadernos para el Diálogo
CDA, Christliche deutsche Autoren des 20. Jahrhunderts, Berne, Lang
CdA, Camp de l'Arpa
CDB, Coleção Documentos Brasileiros
CDi, Cuadernos dieciochistas
CDr, Comparative Drama
ČDS, Čeština doma a ve světě
CDs, Cahiers du Dix-septième, Athens, Georgia
CDU, Centre de Documentation Universitaire
CduC, Cahiers de CERES. Série littéraire, Tunis
CE, Cahiers Élisabéthains
CEA, Cahiers d'Études Africaines
CEAL, Centro Editor de América Latina
CEB, Cahiers Ethier-Blais
CEC, Conselho Estadual de Cultura, Comissão de Literatura, São Paulo
CEC, Cahiers d'Études Cathares, Narbonne
CECAES, Centre d'Études des Cultures d'Aquitaine et d'Europe du Sud, Université de Bordeaux III
CEcr, Corps Écrit
CEDAM, Casa Editrice Dott. A. Milani
CEG, Cuadernos de Estudios Gallegos
CEL, Cadernos de Estudos Lingüísticos, Campinas, Brazil
CELO, Centre d'Etude de la Littérature Occitane, Bordes.
CEM, Cahiers d'Études Médiévales, Univ. of Montreal
CEMa, Cahiers d'Études Maghrebines, Cologne
CEMed, Cuadernos de Estudios Medievales
CEPL, Centre d'Étude et de Promotion de la Lecture, Paris

CEPON, Centre per l'estudi e la promocion de l'Occitan normat.
CEPONB, CEPON Bulletin d'échange.
CER, Cahiers d'Études Romanes
CERCLiD, Cahiers d'Études Romanes, Centre de Linguistique et de Dialectologie, Toulouse
CEROC, Centre d'Enseignement et de Recherche d'Oc, Paris
CERoum, Cahiers d'Études Roumaines
CeS, Cultura e Scuola
CESCM, Centre d'Études Supérieures de Civilisation Médiévale, Poitiers
CET, Centro Editoriale Toscano
CEtGer, Cahiers d'Études Germaniques
CF, Les Cahiers de Fontenay
CFC, Contemporary French Civilization
CFI, Cuadernos de Filologia Italiana
CFLA, Cuadernos de Filología. Literaturas: Análisis, Valencia
CFM, Cahiers François Mauriac
CFMA, Collection des Classiques Français du Moyen Âge
CFol, Classical Folia
CFS, Cahiers Ferdinand de Saussure
CFSLH, Cuadernos de Filología: Studia Linguistica Hispanica
CFTM, Classiques Français des Temps Modernes, Paris, Champion
CG, Cahiers de Grammaire
CGD, Cahiers Georges Duhamel
CGFT, Critical Guides to French Texts, London, Grant & Cutler
CGGT, Critical Guides to German Texts, London, Grant & Cutler
CGP, Carleton Germanic Papers
CGS, Colloquia Germanica Stetinensia
CGST, Critical Guides to Spanish Texts, London, Támesis, Grant & Cutler
CH, Crítica Hispánica
CHA, Cuadernos Hispano-Americanos
CHAC, Cuadernos Hispano-Americanos. Los complementarios
CHB, Cahiers Henri Bosco
ChC, Chemins Critiques
CHCHMC, Cylchgrawn Hanes Cymdeithas Hanes y Methodistiaid Calfinaidd
CHLR, Cahiers d'Histoire des Littératures Romanes
CHP, Cahiers Henri Pourrat
CHR, Catholic Historical Review
ChR, The Chesterton Review
ChRev, Chaucer Review
ChrA, Chroniques Allemandes
ChrI, Chroniques Italiennes
ChrL, Christianity and Literature
ChrN, Chronica Nova
ChS, Champs du Signe
CHST, Caernarvonshire Historical Society Transactions
CHum, Computers and the Humanities
CI, Critical Inquiry
CiD, La Ciudad de Dios
CIDO, Centre International de Documentation Occitane, Béziers
CIEDS, Centre International d'Etudes du dix-huitième siècle, Ferney-Voltaire
CIEL, Centre International de l'Écrit en Langue d'Òc, Berre
CIEM, Comité International d'Études Morisques
CIF, Cuadernos de Investigación Filológica
CIH, Cuadernos de Investigación Historica
CILF, Conseil International de la Langue Française
CILH, Cuadernos para Investigación de la Literatura Hispanica
CILL, Cahiers de l'Institut de Linguistique de l'Université de Louvain
CILT, Centre for Information on Language Teaching, London
CIMAGL, Cahiers de l'Institut du Moyen Âge Grec et Latin, Copenhagen
CIn, Cahiers Intersignes
CIRDOC, Centre Inter-Régional de Développement de l'Occitan, Béziers

CIRVI, Centro Interuniversitario di Ricerche sul 'Viaggio in Italia', Moncalieri
CISAM, Centro Italiano di Studi sull'Alto Medioevo
CIt, Carte Italiane
CIUS, Canadian Institute of Ukrainian Studies Edmonton
CivC, Civiltà Cattolica
CJ, Conditio Judaica, Tübingen, Niemeyer
CJb, Celan-Jahrbuch
CJC, Cahiers Jacques Chardonne
CJG, Cahiers Jean Giraudoux
CJIS, Canadian Journal of Italian Studies
ČJL, Český jazyk a literatura
CJNS, Canadian Journal of Netherlandic Studies
CJP, Cahiers Jean Paulhan
CJR, Cahiers Jules Romains
CL, Cuadernos de Leiden
CL, Comparative Literature
ČL, Česká literatura
CLA, Cahiers du LACITO
CLAJ, College Language Association Journal
CLCC, Cahiers de Littérature Canadienne Comparée
CLCWeb, Comparative Literature and Culture, A WWWeb Journal, <http://www.arts.ualberta.ca/clcwebjournal/>
CLE, Comunicaciones de Literatura Española, Buenos Aires
CLe, Cahiers de Lexicologie
CLEAM, Coleción de Literatura Española Aljamiado-Morisca, Madrid, Gredos
CLESP, Cooperativa Libraria Editrice degli Studenti dell'Università di Padova, Padua
CLett, Critica Letteraria
CLEUP, Cooperativa Libraria Editrice, Università di Padova
CLF, Cahiers de Linguistique Française
CLHM, Cahiers de Linguistique Hispanique Médiévale
CLin, Cercetări de Lingvistica
CLit, Cadernos de Literatura, Coimbra
ClL, La Clau lemosina
CLO, Cahiers Linguistiques d'Ottawa
ClP, Classical Philology
CLS, Comparative Literature Studies
CLSl, Cahiers de Linguistique Slave
CLTA, Cahiers de Linguistique Théorique et Appliquée
CLTL, Cadernos de Lingüística e Teoria da Literatura
CLUEB, Cooperativa Libraria Universitaria Editrice Bologna
CLus, Convergência Lusíada, Rio de Janeiro
CM, Cahiers Montesquieu, Naples, Liguori — Paris, Universitas — Oxford, Voltaire Foundation
CM, Classica et Mediaevalia
CMA, Cahier Marcel Aymé
CMar, Cuadernos de Marcha
CMCS, Cambrian Medieval Celtic Studies
CMERSA, Center for Medieval and Early Renaissance Studies, State University of New York at Binghamton. Acta
ČMF (PhP), Časopis pro moderni filologii: Philologica Pragensia
CMHLB, Cahiers du Monde Hispanique et Luso-Brésilien
CMi, Cultura Milano
CML, Classical and Modern Literature
ČMM, Časopis Matice Moravské
CMon, Communication Monographs
CMP, Cahiers Marcel Proust
CMRS, Cahiers du Monde Russe et Soviétique
CN, Cultura Neolatina
CNat, Les Cahiers Naturalistes
CNCDP, Comissão Nacional para a Comemoração dos Descobrimentos Portugueses, Lisbon
CNor, Los Cuadernos del Norte
CNR, Consiglio Nazionale delle Ricerche
CNRS, Centre National de la Recherche Scientifique
CNSL, Centro Nazionale di Studi Leopardiani
CNSM, Centro Nazionale di Studi Manzoniani
CO, Camera Obscura

CoF, Collectanea Franciscana
COJ, Cambridge Opera Journal
COK, Centralny Ośrodek Kultury, Warsaw
CoL, Compás de Letras
ColA, Colóquio Artes
ColGer, Colloquia Germanica
ColH, Colloquium Helveticum
ColL, Colóquio Letras
ComB, Communications of the International Brecht Society
ComGer, Comunicaciones Germánicas
CompL, Computational Linguistics
ConL, Contrastive Linguistics
ConLet, Il Confronto Letterario
ConLit, Contemporary Literature
ConS, Condorcet Studies
CORDAE, Centre Occitan de Recèrca, de Documentacion e d'Animacion Etnografica, Cordes
CorWPL, Cornell Working Papers in Linguistics
CP, Castrum Peregrini
CPE, Cahiers Prévost d'Exiles, Grenoble
CPL, Cahiers Paul Léautand
CPr, Cahiers de Praxématique
CPR, Chroniques de Port-Royal
CPUC, Cadernos PUC, São Paulo
CQ, Critical Quarterly
CR, Contemporary Review
CRAC, Cahiers Roucher — André Chénier
CRCL, Canadian Review of Comparative Literature
CREL, Cahiers Roumains d'Études Littéraires
CREO, Centre régional d'études occitanes
CRev, Centennial Review
CRI, Cuadernos de Ruedo Ibérico
CRIAR, Cahiers du Centre de Recherches Ibériques et Ibéro-Américains de l'Université de Rouen
CRIN, Cahiers de Recherches des Instituts Néerlandais de Langue et Littérature Françaises
CRITM, Cahiers RITM, Centre de Recherches Interdisciplinaires sur les Textes Modernes, Université de Paris X-Nanterre
CRLN, Comparative Romance Linguistics Newsletter
CRM, Cahiers de Recherches Médiévales (XIIIe–XVe siècles), Paris, Champion
CRQ, Cahiers Raymond Queneau
CRR, Cincinnati Romance Review
CRRI, Centre de Recherche sur la Renaissance Italienne, Paris
CRRR, Centre de Recherches Révolutionnaires et Romantiques, Université Blaise-Pascal, Clermont-Ferrand.
CrT, Critica del Testo
CS, Cornish Studies
CSAM, Centro di Studi sull'Alto Medioevo, Spoleto
ČSAV, Československá akademie věd
CSDI, Centro di Studio per la Dialettologia Italiana
CSem, Caiete de Semiotică
CSFLS, Centro di Studi Filologici e Linguistici Siciliani, Palermo
CSG, Cambridge Studies in German, Cambridge U.P.
CSGLL, Canadian Studies in German Language and Literature, Berne — New York — Frankfurt, Lang
CSH, Cahiers des Sciences Humaines
CSIC, Consejo Superior de Investigaciones Científicas, Madrid
CSJP, Cahiers Saint-John Perse
CSl, Critica Slovia, Florence
CSLAIL, Cambridge Studies in Latin American Iberian Literature, CUP
CSLI, Center for the Study of Language and Information, Stanford University
CSM, Les Cahiers de Saint-Martin
ČSp, Československý spisovatel
CSS, California Slavic Studies
CSSH, Comparative Studies in Society and History
CST, Cahiers de Sémiotique Textuelle
CSt, Critica Storica
CT, Christianity Today
CTC, Cuadernos de Teatro Clásico

CTE, Cuadernos de Traducción e Interpretación
CTe, Cuadernos de Teología
CTex, Cahiers Textuels
CTH, Cahiers Tristan l'Hermite
CTh, Ciencia Tomista
CTJ, Cahiers de Théâtre. Jeu
CTL, Current Trends in Linguistics
CTLin, Commissione per i Testi di Lingua, Bologna
CUECM, Cooperativa Universitaria Editrice Catanese Magistero
CUER MA, Centre Universitaire d'Études et de Recherches Médiévales d'Aix, Université de Provence, Aix-en-Provence
CUP, Cambridge University Press
CUUCV, Cultura Universitaria de la Universidad Central de Venezuela
CV, Città di Vita
CWPL, Catalan Working Papers in Linguistics
CWPWL, Cardiff Working Papers in Welsh Linguistics

DAEM, Deutsches Archiv für Erforschung des Mittelalters
DaF, Deutsch als Fremdsprache
DAG, Dictionnaire onomasiologique de l'ancien gascon, Tübingen, Niemeyer
DalR, Dalhousie Review
DanU, Dansk Udsyn
DAO, Dictionnaire onomasiologique de l'ancien occitan, Tübingen, Niemeyer
DaSt, Dante Studies
DB, Дзяржаўная бібліятэка БССР
DB, Doitsu Bungaku
DBl, Driemaandelijkse Bladen
DBO, Deutsche Bibliothek des Ostens, Berlin, Nicolai
DBR, Les Dialectes Belgo-Romans
DBr, Doitsu Bungakoranko
DCFH, Dicenda. Cuadernos de Filología Hispánica
DD, Diskussion Deutsch
DDG, Deutsche Dialektgeographie, Marburg, Elwert
DDJ, Deutsches Dante-Jahrbuch
DegSec, Degré Second
DELTA, Revista de Documentação de Estudos em Lingüística Teórica e Aplicada, Šao Paulo
DESB, Delta Epsilon Sigma Bulletin, Dubuque, Iowa
DeutB, Deutsche Bücher
DeutUB, Deutschungarische Beiträge
DFC, Durham French Colloquies
DFS, Dalhousie French Studies
DGF, Dokumentation germanistischer Forschung, Frankfurt, Lang
DgF, Danmarks gamle Folkeviser
DHA, Diálogos Hispánicos de Amsterdam, Rodopi
DHR, Duquesne Hispanic Review
DhS, Dix-huitième Siècle
DI, Deutscher Idealismus, Stuttgart, Klett-Cotta Verlag
DI, Декоративное искусство
DIAS, Dublin Institute for Advanced Studies
DiL, Dictionnairique et Lexicographie
DiS, Dickinson Studies
DisA, Dissertation Abstracts
DisSlSHL, Dissertationes Slavicae: Sectio Historiae Litterarum
DisSlSL, Dissertationes Slavicae: Sectio Linguistica
DisSoc, Discourse and Society
DK, Duitse Kroniek
DkJb, Deutschkanadisches Jahrbuch
DKV, Deutscher Klassiker Verlag, Frankfurt
DL, Детская литература
DLA, Deutsche Literatur von den Anfängen bis 1700, Berne — Frankfurt — Paris — New York, Lang
DLit, Discurso Literario
DLM, Deutsche Literatur des Mittelalters (Wissenschaftliche Beiträge der Ernst-Moritz-Arndt-Universität Greifswald)
DLR, Deutsche Literatur in Reprints, Munich, Fink
DLRECL, Diálogo de la Lengua. Revista de Estudio y Creación Literaria, Cuenca
DM, Dirassat Masrahiyyat

DMRPH, De Montfort Research Papers in the Humanities, De Montfort University, Leicester
DMTS, Davis Medieval Texts and Studies, Leiden, Brill
DN, Дружба народов
DNT, De Nieuwe Taalgids
DOLMA, Documenta Onomastica Litteralia Medii Aevi, Hildesheim, Olms
DOM, Dictionnaire de l'occitan médiéval, Tübingen, Niemeyer, 1996–
DosS, Dostoevsky Studies
DoV, Дошкольное воспитание
DPA, Documents pour servir à l'histoire du département des Pyrénées-Atlantiques, Pau
DPL, De Proprietatibus Litterarum, The Hague, Mouton
DpL, День поэзии, Leningrad
DpM, День поэзии, Moscow
DR, Drama Review
DRev, Downside Review
DRLAV, DRLAV, Revue de Linguistique
DS, Diderot Studies
DSEÜ, Deutsche Sprache in Europa und Übersee, Stuttgart, Steiner
DSL, Det danske Sprog- og Litteraturselskab
DSp, Deutsche Sprache
DSRPD, Documenta et Scripta. Rubrica Paleographica et Diplomatica, Barcelona
DSS, XVIIe Siècle
DSt, Deutsche Studien, Meisenheim, Hain
DSt, Danske Studier
DT, Deutsche Texte, Tübingen, Niemeyer
DteolT, Dansk teologisk Tidsskrift
DtL, Die deutsche Literatur
DTM, Deutsche Texte des Mittelalters, Berlin, Akademie
DTV, Deutscher Taschenbuch Verlag, Munich
DUB, Deutschunterricht, East Berlin
DUJ, Durham University Journal (New Series)
DUS, Der Deutschunterricht, Stuttgart
DUSA, Deutschunterricht in Südafrika
DV, Дальний Восток
DVA, Deutsche Verlags-Anstalt, Stuttgart
DVLG, Deutsche Vierteljahresschrift für Literaturwissenschaft und Geistesgeschichte

E, Verlag Enzyklopädie, Leipzig
EAL, Early American Literature
EALS, Europäische Aufklärung in Literatur und Sprache, Frankfurt, Lang
EAS, Europe-Asia Studies
EB, Estudos Brasileiros
EBal, Etudes Balkaniques
EBM, Era Bouts dera mountanho, Aurignac
EBTch, Études Balkaniques Tchécoslovaques
EC, El Escritor y la Crítica, Colección Persiles, Madrid, Taurus
EC, Études Celtiques
ECan, Études Canadiennes
ECar, Espace Caraïbe
ECent, The Eighteenth Century, Lubbock, Texas
ECentF, Eighteenth-Century Fiction
ECF, Écrits du Canada Français
ECI, Eighteenth-Century Ireland
ECIG, Edizioni Culturali Internazionali Genova
ECL, Eighteenth-Century Life
ECla, Les Études Classiques
ECon, España Contemporánea
EconH, Économie et Humanisme
EcR, Echo de Rabastens. Les Veillées Rabastinoises, Rabastens (Tarn)
ECr, Essays in Criticism
ECre, Études Créoles
ECS, Eighteenth Century Studies
EdCat, Ediciones Cátedra, Madrid
EDESA, Ediciones Españolas S.A.
EDHS, Études sur le XVIIIe Siècle
EDIPUCRS, Editora da Pontífica Universidade Católica de Rio Grande do Sul, Porto Alegre
EDL, Études de Lettres
EDT, Edizioni di Torino

EDUSC, Editora da Universidade de Santa Catarina
EE, Erasmus in English
EEM, East European Monographs
EEQ, East European Quarterly
EF, Erträge der Forschung, Darmstadt, Wissenschaftliche Buchgesellschaft
EF, Études Françaises
EFAA, Échanges Franco-Allemands sur l'Afrique
EFE, Estudios de Fonética Experimental
EFF, Ergebnisse der Frauenforschung, Stuttgart, Metzler
EFil, Estudios Filológicos, Valdivia, Chile
EFL, Essays in French Literature, Univ. of Western Australia
EFR, Éditeurs Français Réunis
EG, Études Germaniques
EH, Europäische Hochschulschriften, Berne–Frankfurt, Lang
EH, Estudios Humanísticos
EHF, Estudios Humanísticos. Filología
EHN, Estudios de Historia Novohispana
EHQ, European History Quarterly
EHR, English Historical Review
EHRC, European Humanities Research Centre, University of Oxford
EHS, Estudios de Historia Social
EHT, Exeter Hispanic Texts, Exeter
EIA, Estudos Ibero-Americanos
EIP, Estudos Italianos em Portugal
EJJR, Études Jean-Jacques Rousseau
EJWS, European Journal of Women's Studies
EL, Esperienze Letterarie
El, Elementa, Würzburg, Königshausen & Neumann –Amsterdam, Rodopi
ELA, Études de Linguistique Appliquée
ELF, Études Littéraires Françaises, Paris, J.-M. Place — Tübingen, Narr
ELH, English Literary History
ELin, Estudos Lingüísticos, São Paulo
ELit, Essays in Literature
ELL, Estudos Lingüísticos e Literários, Bahia
ELLC, Estudis de Llengua i Literatura Catalanes
ELLF, Études de Langue et Littérature Françaises, Tokyo
ELLUG, Éditions littéraires et linguistiques de l'université de Grenoble
ELM, Études littéraires maghrebines
ELR, English Literary Renaissance
EMarg, Els Marges
EMH, Early Music History
EMS, Essays in Medieval Studies
EMus, Early Music
ENC, Els Nostres Clàssics, Barcelona, Barcino
ENSJF, École Nationale Supérieure de Jeunes Filles
EO, Edition Orpheus, Tübingen, Francke
EO, Europa Orientalis
EOc, Estudis Occitans
EP, Études Philosophiques
Ep, Epistemata, Würzburg, Königshausen & Neumann
EPESA, Ediciones y Publicaciones Españolas S.A.
EPoet, Essays in Poetics
ER, Estudis Romànics
ERab, Études Rabelaisiennes
ERB, Études Romanes de Brno
ER(BSRLR), Études Romanes (Bulletin de la Société Roumaine de Linguistique Romane)
ERL, Études Romanes de Lund
ErlF, Erlanger Forschungen
ERLIMA, Équipe de recherche sur la littérature d'imagination du moyen âge, Centre d'Études Supérieures de Civilisation Médiévale/Faculté des Lettres et des Langues, Université de Poitiers.
EROPD, Ежегодник рукописного отдела Пушкинского дома
ERR, European Romantic Review
ES, Erlanger Studien, Erlangen, Palm & Enke
ES, Estudios Segovianos

EsC, L'Esprit Créateur
ESGP, Early Studies in Germanic Philology, Amsterdam, Rodopi
ESI, Edizioni Scientifiche Italiane
ESJ, European Studies Journal
ESk, Edition Suhrkamp, Frankfurt, Suhrkamp
ESoc, Estudios de Sociolinguística
ESor, Études sorguaises
EspA, Español Actual
ESt, English Studies
EstE, Estudios Escénicos
EstG, Estudi General
EstH, Estudios Hispánicos
EstL, Estudios de Lingüística, Alicante
EstLA, Estudios de Linguística Aplicada
EstR, Estudios Románticos
EStud, Essays and Studies
ET, L'Écrit du Temps
ETF, Espacio, Tiempo y Forma, Revista de la Facultad de Geografía e Historia, UNED
EtF, Etudes francophones
EtH, Études sur l'Hérault, Pézenas
EthS, Ethnologia Slavica
ETJ, Educational Theatre Journal
ETL, Explicación de Textos Literarios
EtLitt, Études Littéraires, Quebec
EUDEBA, Editorial Universitaria de Buenos Aires
EUNSA, Ediciones Universidad de Navarra, Pamplona
EUS, European University Studies, Berne, Lang
ExP, Excerpta Philologica
EzLit, Език и литература

FAL, Forum Academicum Literaturwissenschaft, Königstein, Hain
FAM, Filologia Antica e Moderna
FAPESP, Fundação de Amparo à Pesquisa do Estado de São Paulo
FAR, French-American Review
FAS, Frankfurter Abhandlungen zur Slavistik, Giessen, Schmitz
FBAN, Фундаментальная бібліятэка Акадэміі навук БССР
FBG, Frankfurter Beiträge zur Germanistik, Heidelberg, Winter
FBS, Franco-British Studies
FC, Filologia e Critica
FCE, Fondo de Cultura Económica, Mexico
FCG — CCP, Fondation Calouste Gulbenkian — Centre Culturel Portugais, Paris
FCS, Fifteenth Century Studies
FD, Fonetică şi Dialectologie
FDL, Facetten deutscher Literatur, Berne, Haupt
FEI, Faites entrer l'infini. Journal de la Société des Amis de Louis Aragon et Elsa Triolet
FEK, Forschungen zur europäischen Kultur, Berne, Lang
FemSt, Feministische Studien
FF, Forum für Fachsprachenforschung, Tübingen, Narr
FF, Forma y Función
FFM, French Forum Monographs, Lexington, Kentucky
FGÄDL, Forschungen zur Geschichte der älteren deutschen Literatur, Munich, Fink
FH, Fundamenta Historica, Stuttgart-Bad Cannstatt, Frommann-Holzboog
FH, Frankfurter Hefte
FHL, Forum Homosexualität und Literatur
FHS, French Historical Studies
FIDS, Forschungsberichte des Instituts für Deutsche Sprache, Tübingen, Narr
FHSJ, Flintshire Historical Society Journal
FilM, Filologia Mediolatina
FilMod, Filologia Moderna, Udine –Pisa
FilN, Филологические науки
FilR, Filologia Romanza
FilS, Filologické studie
FilZ, Filologija, Zagreb
FiM, Filologia Moderna, Facultad de Filosofía y Letras, Madrid
FinS, Fin de Siglo
FIRL, Forum at Iowa on Russian Literature
FL, La France Latine

FLa, Faits de Langues
FLang, Functions of Language
FLG, Freiburger literaturpsychologische Gespräche
FLin, Folia Linguistica
FLinHist, Folia Linguistica Historica
FLK, Forschungen zur Literatur- und Kulturgeschichte. Beiträge zur Sprach- und Literaturwissenschaft, Berne, Lang
FLP, Filologia e linguística portuguesa
FLS, French Literature Series
FLV, Fontes Linguae Vasconum
FM, Le Français Moderne
FMADIUR, FM: Annali del Dipartimento di Italianistica, Università di Roma 'La Sapienza'
FMDA, Forschungen und Materialen zur deutschen Aufklärung, Stuttgart — Bad Cannstatt, Frommann-Holzboog
FMI, Fonti Musicali Italiane
FMLS, Forum for Modern Language Studies
FMon, Le Français dans le Monde
FmSt, Frühmittelalterliche Studien
FMT, Forum Modernes Theater
FN, Frühe Neuzeit, Tübingen, Niemeyer
FNDIR, Fédération nationale des déportés et internés résistants
FNS, Frühneuzeit-Studien, Frankfurt, Lang
FoH, Foro Hispánico, Amsterdam
FNT, Foilseacháin Náisiúnta Tta
FoI, Forum Italicum
FoS, Le Forme e la Storia
FP, Folia Phonetica
FPub, First Publications
FR, French Review
FrA, Le Français Aujourd'hui
FranS, Franciscan Studies
FrCS, French Cultural Studies
FrF, French Forum
FrH, Französisch Heute
FrP Le Français Préclassique
FrSoc, Français et Société
FS, Forum Slavicum, Munich, Fink
FS, French Studies
FSB, French Studies Bulletin
FSlav, Folia Slavica
FSSA, French Studies in Southern Africa
FT, Fischer Taschenbuch, Frankfurt, Fischer
FT, Finsk Tidskrift
FTCG, 'La Talanquere': Folklore, Tradition, Culture Gasconne, Nogano
FUE, Fundación Universitaria Española
FV, Fortuna Vitrea, Tübingen, Niemeyer
FZPT, Freiburger Zeitschrift für Philosophie und Theologie

GA, Germanistische Arbeitshefte, Tübingen, Niemeyer
GAB, Göppinger Akademische Beiträge, Lauterburg, Kümmerle
GAG, Göppinger Arbeiten zur Germanistik, Lauterburg, Kümmerle
GAKS, Gesammelte Aufsätze zur Kulturgeschichte Spaniens
GalR, Galician Review, Birmingham
GANDLL, Giessener Arbeiten zur neueren deutschen Literatur und Literaturwissenschaft, Berne, Lang
Garona, Garona. Cahiers du Centre d'Etudes des Cultures d'Aquitaine et d'Europe du Sud, Talence
GAS, German-Australian Studies, Berne, Lang
GASK, Germanistische Arbeiten zu Sprache und Kulturgeschichte, Frankfurt, Lang
GB, Germanistische Bibliothek, Heidelberg, Winter
GBA, Gazette des Beaux-Arts
GBE, Germanistik in der Blauen Eule
GC, Generalitat de Catalunya
GCFI, Giornale Critico della Filosofia Italiana
GEMP, Groupement d'Ethnomusicologie en Midi-Pyrénées, La Talvèra
GerAb, Germanistische Abhandlungen, Stuttgart, Metzler

GerLux, Germanistik Luxembourg
GermL, Germanistische Linguistik
GeW, Germanica Wratislaviensia
GF, Giornale di Fisica
GFFNS, Godišnjak Filozofskog fakulteta u Novom Sadu
GG, Geschichte und Gesellschaft
GGF, Göteborger Germanistische Forschungen, University of Gothenburg
GGF, Greifswalder Germanistische Forschungen
GGVD, Grundlagen und Gedanken zum Verständnis des Dramas, Frankfurt, Diesterweg
GGVEL, Grundlagen und Gedanken zum Verständnis erzählender Literatur, Frankfurt, Diesterweg
GIDILOc, Grop d'Iniciativa per un Diccionari Informatizat de la Lenga Occitana, Montpellier
GIF, Giornale Italiano di Filologia
GIGFL, Glasgow Introductory Guides to French Literature
GIGGL, Glasgow Introductory Guides to German Literature
GIP, Giornale Italiano di Psicologia
GJ, Gutenberg-Jahrbuch
GJb, Goethe Jahrbuch
GJLL, The Georgetown Journal of Language and Linguistics
GK, Goldmann Klassiker, Munich, Goldmann
GL, Germanistische Lehrbuchsammlung, Berlin, Weidler
GL, General Linguistics
GLC, German Life and Civilisation, Berne, Lang
GLCS, German Linguistic and Cultural Studies, Frankfurt, Lang
GLL, German Life and Letters
GLM, Gazette du Livre Médiéval
GLML, The Garland Library of Medieval Literature, New York –London, Garland
GLR, García Lorca Review
GLS, Grazer Linguistische Studien
Glyph, Glyph: Johns Hopkins Textual Studies, Baltimore
GM, Germanistische Mitteilungen
GML, Gothenburg Monographs in Linguistics
GMon, German Monitor
GN, Germanic Notes and Reviews
GoSt, Gothic Studies
GPB, Гос. публичная библиотека им. М. Е. Салтыкова-Щедрина
GPI, Государственный педагогический институт
GPSR, Glossaire des Patois de la Suisse Romande
GQ, German Quarterly
GR, Germanic Review
GREC, Groupe de Recherches et d'Études du Clermontais, Clermont-l'Hérault
GRECF, Groupe de Recherches et d'Études sur le Canada français, Edinburgh
GREHAM, Groupe de REcherche d'Histoire de l'Anthroponymie Médiévale, Tours, Université François-Rabelais
GRELCA, Groupe de Recherche sur les Littératures de la Caraïbe, Université Laval
GRLH, Garland Reference Library of the Humanities, New York — London, Garland
GRLM, Grundriss der romanischen Literaturen des Mittelalters
GRM, Germanisch-Romanische Monatsschrift
GrSt, Grundtvig Studier
GS, Lo Gai Saber, Toulouse
GSA, Germanic Studies in America, Berne–Frankfurt, Lang
GSC, German Studies in Canada, Frankfurt, Lang
GSI, German Studies in India
GSl, Germano-Slavica, Ontario
GSLI, Giornale Storico della Letteratura Italiana
GSR, German Studies Review
GSSL, Göttinger Schriften zur Sprach– und Literaturwissenschaft, Göttingen, Herodot
GTN, Gdańskie Towarzystwo Naukowe
GTS, Germanistische Texte und Studien, Hildesheim, Olms
GV, Generalitat Valenciana
GY, Goethe Yearbook

H, Hochschulschriften, Cologne, Pahl-Rugenstein
HAHR, Hispanic American Historical Review
HB, Horváth Blätter
HBA, Historiografía y Bibliografía Americanistas, Seville
HBG, Hamburger Beiträge zur Germanistik, Frankfurt, Lang
HDG, Huis aan de Drie Grachten, Amsterdam
HEI, History of European Ideas
HEL, Histoire, Epistémologie, Language
Her(A), Hermes, Århus
HES, Histoire, Économie et Société
HeyJ, Heythrop Journal
HF, Heidelberger Forschungen, Heidelberg, Winter
HHS, History of the Human Sciences
HI, Historica Ibérica
HIAR, Hamburger Ibero-Amerikanische Reihe
HICL, Histoire des Idées et Critique Littéraire, Geneva, Droz
HIGL, Holland Institute for Generative Linguistics, Leiden
HisJ, Hispanic Journal, Indiana–Pennsylvania
HisL, Hispanic Linguistics
HistL, Historiographia Linguistica
HistS, History of Science
His(US), Hispania, Ann Arbor
HJ, Historical Journal
HJb, Heidelberger Jahrbücher
HJBS, Hispanic Journal of Behavioural Sciences
HKADL, Historisch-kritische Arbeiten zur deutschen Literatur, Frankfurt, Lang
HKZMTLG, Handelingen van de Koninklijke Zuidnederlandse Maatschappij voor Taalen, Letterkunde en Geschiedenis
HL, Hochschulschriften Literaturwissenschaft, Königstein, Hain
HL, Humanistica Lovaniensia
HLB, Harvard Library Bulletin
HLitt, Histoires Littéraires
HLQ, Huntington Library Quarterly
HLS, Historiska och litteraturhistoriska studier
HM, Hommes et Migrations
HMJb, Heinrich Mann Jahrbuch
HP, History of Psychiatry
HPh, Historical Philology
HPos, Hispanica Posnaniensia
HPR, Hispanic Poetry Review
HPS, Hamburger Philologische Studien, Hamburg, Buske
HPSl, Heidelberger Publikationen zur Slavistik, Frankfurt, Lang
HPT, History of Political Thought
HR, Hispanic Review
HRef, Historical reflections / Reflexions historiques
HRel, History of Religions
HRev, Hrvatska revija
HRJ, Hispanic Research Journal
HRSHM, Heresis, revue semestrielle d'hérésiologie médiévale
HS, Helfant Studien, Stuttgart, Helfant
HS, Hispania Sacra
HSLA, Hebrew University Studies in Literature and the Arts
HSlav, Hungaro-Slavica
HSMS, Hispanic Seminary of Medieval Studies, Madison
HSp, Historische Sprachforschung (Historical Linguistics)
HSR, Histoire et Sociétés Rurales
HSSL, Harvard Studies in Slavic Linguistics
HSt, Hispanische Studien
HSWSL, Hallesche Studien zur Wirkung von Sprache und Literatur
HT, Helfant Texte, Stuttgart, Helfant
HT, History Today
HTe, Hecho Teatral (Revista de teoría y práctica del teatro hispánico)
HTh, History and Theory
HTR, Harvard Theological Review
HUS, Harvard Ukrainian Studies
HY, Herder Yearbook
HZ, Historische Zeitschrift

IÅ, Ibsen-Årbok, Oslo
IAP, Ibero-Americana Pragensia
IAr, Iberoamerikanisches Archiv

IARB, Inter-American Review of Bibliography
IASL, Internationales Archiv für Sozialgeschichte der deutschen Literatur
IASLS, Internationales Archiv für Sozialgeschichte der deutschen Literatur: Sonderheft
IB, Insel-Bücherei, Frankfurt, Insel
IBKG, Innsbrucker Beiträge zur Kulturwissenschaft. Germanistische Reihe
IBL, Instytut Badań Literackich PAN, Warsaw
IBLA, Institut des Belles Lettres Arabes
IBLe, Insel-Bücherei, Leipzig, Insel
IBS, Innsbrücker Beiträge zur Sprachwissenschaft
IC, Index on Censorship
ICALP, Instituto de Cultura e Língua Portuguesa, Lisbon
ICALPR, Instituto de Cultura e Língua Portuguesa. Revista
ICC, Instituto Caro y Cuervo, Bogotà
ICLMF, Istitut Cultural Ladin 'Majon de Fasegn'
ICLMR, Istitut Cultural Ladin 'Micurà de Rü'
ICMA, Instituto de Cooperación con el Mundo Árabe
ID, Italia Dialettale
IDF, Informationen Deutsch als Fremdsprache
IDL, Indices zur deutschen Literatur, Tübingen, Niemeyer
IdLit, Ideologies and Literature
IEC, Institut d'Estudis Catalans
IEI, Istituto dell'Enciclopedia Italiana
IEO, Institut d'Estudis Occitans
IEPI, Istituti Editoriali e Poligrafici Internazionali
IES, Institut d'Études Slaves, Paris
IF, Impulse der Forschung, Darmstadt, Wissenschaftliche Buchgesellschaft
IF, Indogermanische Forschungen
IFAVL, Internationale Forschungen zur Allgemeinen und Vergleichenden Literaturwissenschaft, Amsterdam–Atlanta, Rodopi
IFC, Institutión Fernando el Católico
IFEE, Investigación Franco-Española. Estudios
IFiS, Instytut Filozofii i Socjologii PAN, Warsaw
IFOTT, Institut voor Functioneel Onderzoek naar Taal en Taalgebruik, Amsterdam
IFR, International Fiction Review
IG, Information grammaticale
IHC, Italian History and Culture
IHE, Índice Histórico Español
IHS, Irish Historical Studies
II, Information und Interpretation, Frankfurt, Lang
IIa, Институт языкознания
IIFV, Institut Interuniversitari de Filologia Valenciana, Valencia
III, Институт истории искусств
IJ, Italian Journal
IJAL, International Journal of American Linguistics
IJBAG, Internationales Jahrbuch der Bettina-von-Arnim Gesellschaft
IJCS, International Journal of Canadian Studies
IJFS, International Journal of Francophone Studies, Leeds
IJHL, Indiana Journal of Hispanic Literatures
IJL, International Journal of Lexicography
IJP, International Journal of Psycholinguistics
IJSL, International Journal for the Sociology of Language
IJSLP, International Journal of Slavic Linguistics and Poetics
IK, Искусство кино
IKU, Institut za književnost i umetnost, Belgrade
IL, L'Information Littéraire
ILAS, Institute of Latin American Studies, University of London
ILASLR, Istituto Lombardo. Accademia di Scienze e Lettere. Rendiconti
ILen, Искусство Ленинграда
ILG, Instituto da Lingua Galega
ILing, Incontri Linguistici
ILTEC, Instituto de Linguistica Teórica e Computacional, Lisbon

IMA, Imagines Medii Aevi, Wiesbaden, Reichert
IMN, Irisleabhar Mhá Nuad
IMR, International Migration Review
IMU, Italia Medioevale e Umanistica
INCM, Imprensa Nacional, Casa da Moeda, Lisbon
InfD, Informationen und Didaktik
INLF, Institut National de la Langue Française
INIC, Instituto Nacional de Investigação Científica
InL, Иностранная литература
INLE, Instituto Nacional del Libro Español
InstEB, Inst. de Estudos Brasileiros
InstNL, Inst. Nacional do Livro, Brasilia
IO, Italiano e Oltre
IPL, Istituto di Propaganda Libraria
IPZS, Istituto Poligrafico e Zecca dello Stato, Rome
IR, L'Immagine Riflessa
IRAL, International Review of Applied Linguistics
IRIa, Институт русского языка Российской Академии Наук
IrR, The Irish Review
IRSH, International Review of Social History
IRSL, International Review of Slavic Linguistics
ISC, Institut de Sociolingüística Catalana
ISI, Institute for Scientific Information, U.S.A.
ISIEMC, Istituto Storico Italiano per l'Età Moderna e Contemporanea, Rome
ISIM, Istituto Storico Italiano per il Medio Evo
ISLIa, Известия Академии наук СССР. Серия литературы и языка
ISOAN, Известия сибирского отделения АН СССР, Novosibirsk
ISP, International Studies in Philosophy
IsPL, Istitut pedagogich Ladin
ISPS, International Studies in the Philosophy of Science
ISS, Irish Slavonic Studies
IsS, Islamic Studies, Islamabad
ISSA, Studi d'Italianistica nell'Africa Australe: Italian Studies in Southern Africa
ISt, Italian Studies
ISV, Informazioni e Studi Vivaldiani
IT, Insel Taschenbuch, Frankfurt, Insel
ItC, Italian Culture
ITL, ITL. Review of Applied Linguistics, Instituut voor Toegepaste Linguistiek, Leuven
ItQ, Italian Quarterly
ItStudien, Italienische Studien
IUJF, Internationales Uwe-Johnson-Forum
IULA, Institut Universitari de Lingüística Aplicada, Universitat Pompeu Fabra, Barcelona
IUP, Irish University Press
IUR, Irish University Review
IV, Istituto Veneto di Scienze, Lettere ed Arti
IVAS, Indices Verborum zum altdeutschen Schrifttum, Amsterdam, Rodopi
IVN, Internationale Vereniging voor Nederlandistiek

JAAC, Journal of Aesthetics and Art Criticism
JACIS, Journal of the Association for Contemporary Iberian Studies
JAE, Journal of Aesthetic Education
JAIS, Journal of Anglo-Italian Studies, Malta
JAMS, Journal of the American Musicological Society
JanL, Janua Linguarum, The Hague, Mouton
JAOS, Journal of the American Oriental Society
JAPLA, Journal of the Atlantic Provinces Linguistic Association
JARA, Journal of the American Romanian Academy of Arts and Sciences
JAS, The Journal of Algerian Studies

JASI, Jahrbuch des Adalbert-Stifter-Instituts
JATI, Association of Teachers of Italian Journal
JazA, Jazykovědné aktuality
JazLin, Jazykověda: Linguistica, Ostravska University
JazŠ, Jazykovedné štúdie
JAZU, Jugoslavenska akademija znanosti i umjetnosti
JBSP, Journal of the British Society for Phenomenology
JČ, Jazykovedný časopis, Bratislava
JCanS, Journal of Canadian Studies
JCHAS, Journal of the Cork Historical and Archaeological Society
JCL, Journal of Child Language
JCLin, Journal of Celtic Linguistics
JCS, Journal of Celtic Studies
JDASD, Deutsche Akademie für Sprache und Dichtung: Jahrbuch
JDF, Jahrbuch Deutsch als Fremdsprache
JDSG, Jahrbuch der Deutschen Schiller-Gesellschaft
JEA, Lou Journalet de l'Escandihado Aubagnenco
JEGP, Journal of English and Germanic Philology
JEH, Journal of Ecclesiastical History
JEL, Journal of English Linguistics
JES, Journal of European Studies
JF, Južnoslovenski filolog
JFA, Jahrbuch Felder-Archiv
JFDH, Jahrbuch des Freien Deutschen Hochstifts
JFG, Jahrbuch der Fouqué Gesellschaft
JFinL, Jahrbuch für finnisch-deutsche Literaturbeziehungen
JFL, Jahrbuch für fränkische Landesforschung
JFLS, Journal of French Language Studies
JFR, Journal of Folklore Research
JG, Jahrbuch für Geschichte, Berlin, Akademie
JGO, Jahrbücher für die Geschichte Osteuropas
JHA, Journal for the History of Astronomy
JHI, Journal of the History of Ideas
JHispP, Journal of Hispanic Philology
JHP, Journal of the History of Philosophy
JHR, Journal of Hispanic Research
JHS, Journal of the History of Sexuality
JIAS, Journal of Inter-American Studies
JIES, Journal of Indo-European Studies
JIG, Jahrbuch für Internationale Germanistik
JIL, Journal of Italian Linguistics
JILAS, Journal of Iberian and Latin American Studies (formerly *Tesserae*)
JILS, Journal of Interdisciplinary Literary Studies
JIPA, Journal of the International Phonetic Association
JIRS, Journal of the Institute of Romance Studies
JJQ, James Joyce Quarterly
JJS, Journal of Jewish Studies
JKLWR, Jahrbuch zur Kultur und Literatur der Weimarer Republik
JL, Journal of Linguistics
JLACS, Journal of Latin American Cultural Studies
JLAL, Journal of Latin American Lore
JLAS, Journal of Latin American Studies
JLH, Journal of Library History
JLS, Journal of Literary Semantics
JLSP, Journal of Language and Social Psychology
JMemL, Journal of Memory and Language
JMEMS, Journal of Medieval and Early Modern Studies
JMH, Journal of Medieval History
JMHRS, Journal of the Merioneth Historical and Record Society
JML, Journal of Modern Literature
JMLat, Journal of Medieval Latin
JMMD, Journal of Multilingual and Multicultural Development
JMMLA, Journal of the Midwest Modern Language Association
JModH, Journal of Modern History
JMP, Journal of Medicine and Philosophy

JMRS, Journal of Medieval and Renaissance Studies
JMS, Journal of Maghrebi Studies
JNT, Journal of Narrative Technique
JONVL, Een Jaarboek: Overzicht van de Nederlandse en Vlaamse Literatuur
JOWG, Jahrbuch der Oswald von Wolkenstein Gesellschaft
JP, Journal of Pragmatics
JPC, Journal of Popular Culture
JPCL, Journal of Pidgin and Creole Languages
JPh, Journal of Phonetics
JPHS, The Journal of the Pembrokeshire Historical Society
JPol, Język Polski
JPR, Journal of Psycholinguistic Research
JQ, Jacques e i suoi Quaderni
JRA, Journal of Religion in Africa
JRG, Jahrbücher der Reineke-Gesellschaft
JRH, Journal of Religious History
JRIC, Journal of the Royal Institution of Cornwall
JŘJR, Jazyk a řeč jihočeského regionu. České Budějovice, Pedagogická fakulta Jihočeské univerzity
JRMA, Journal of the Royal Musical Association
JRMMRA, Journal of the Rocky Mountain Medieval and Renaissance Association
JRS, Journal of Romance Studies
JRUL, Journal of the Rutgers University Libraries
JS, Journal des Savants
JSCS, Journal of Spanish Cultural Studies
JSEES, Japanese Slavic and East European Studies
JSem, Journal of Semantics
JSFG, Jahrbuch für schwäbisch-fränkische Geschichte
JSFWUB, Jahrbuch der Schlesischen Friedrich-Wilhelms-Universität zu Breslau
JSH, Jihočeský sborník historický
JSHR, Journal of Speech and Hearing Research
JSL, Journal of Slavic Linguistics
JSoc, Journal of Sociolinguistics
JSS, Journal of Spanish Studies: Twentieth Century
JTS, Journal of Theological Studies
JU, Judentum und Umwelt, Berne, Lang
JUG, Jahrbuch der ungarischen Germanistik
JUS, Journal of Ukrainian Studies
JV, Jahrbuch für Volkskunde
JVF, Jahrbuch für Volksliedforschung
JVLVB, Journal of Verbal Learning and Verbal Behavior
JWCI, Journal of the Warburg and Courtauld Institutes
JWGV, Jahrbuch des Wiener Goethe-Vereins, Neue Folge
JWH, Journal of World History
JWIL, Journal of West Indian Literature
JWRH, Journal of Welsh Religious History
JZ, Jazykovedný zborník

KANTL, Koninklijke Akademie voor Nederlandse Taal- en Letterkunde
KASL, Kasseler Arbeiten zur Sprache und Literatur, Frankfurt, Lang
KAW, Krajowa Agencja Wydawnicza
KAWLSK, Koninklijke Academie voor Wetenschappen, Letteren en Schone Kunsten van België, Brussels
KB, Književni barok
KBGL, Kopenhagener Beiträge zur germanistischen Linguistik
Kbl, Korrespondenzblatt des Vereins für niederdeutsche Sprachforschung
KDC, Katholiek Documentatiecentrum
KDPM, Kleine deutsche Prosadenkmäler des Mittelalters, Munich, Fink
KGOS, Kultur- und geistesgeschichtliche Ostmitteleuropa-Studien, Marburg, Elwert

KGS, Kölner germanistische Studien, Cologne, Böhlau
KGS, Kairoer germanistische Studien
KH, Komparatistische Hefte
KhL, Художественная литература
KI, Književna istorija
KiW, Książka i Wiedza
KJ, Književnost i jezik
KK, Kirke og Kultur
KKKK, Kultur og Klasse. Kritik og Kulturanalyse
KlJb, Kleist-Jahrbuch
KLWL, Krieg und Literatur: War and Literature
Klage, Klage: Kölner linguistische Arbeiten. Germanistik, Hürth-Efferen, Gabel
KN, Kwartalnik Neofilologiczny
KnK, Kniževna kritika
KO, Университетско издателство 'Климент Охридски'
KO, Книжное обозрение
KP, Книжная палата
KRA, Kölner Romanistische Arbeiten, Geneva, Droz
KS, Kúltura slova
KSDL, Kieler Studien zur deutschen Literaturgeschichte, Neumünster, Wachholtz
KSL, Kölner Studien zur Literaturwissenschaft, Frankfurt, Lang
KSt, Kant Studien
KTA, Kröners Taschenausgabe, Stuttgart, Kröner
KTRM, Klassische Texte des romanischen Mittelalters, Munich, Fink
KU, Konstanzer Universitätsreden
KUL, Katolicki Uniwersytet Lubelski, Lublin
KuSDL, Kulturwissenschaftliche Studien zur deutschen Literatur, Opladen, Westdeutscher Verlag
KZG, Koreanische Zeitschrift für Germanistik
KZMTLG, Koninklijke Zuidnederlandse Maatschappij voor Taal- en Letterkunde en Geschiedenis, Brussels
KZMTLGH, Koninklijke Zuidnederlandse Maatschaapij voor Taal- en Letterkunde en Geschiedenis. Handelingen

LA, Linguistische Arbeiten, Tübingen, Niemeyer
LA, Linguistic Analysis
LaA, Language Acquisition
LAbs, Linguistics Abstracts
LaF, Langue Française
LAILJ, Latin American Indian Literatures Journal
LaLi, Langues et Linguistique
LALIES, LALIES. Actes des sessions de linguistique et de littérature. Institut d'Etudes linguistiques et phonétiques. Sessions de linguistique. Ecole Normale Supérieure Paris, Sorbonne nouvelle
LALR, Latin-American Literary Review
LaM, Les Langues Modernes
LangH, Le Langage et l'Homme
LangLit, Language and Literature, Journal of the Poetics and Linguistics Association
LArb, Linguistische Arbeitsberichte
LARR, Latin-American Research Review
LaS, Langage et Société
LATR, Latin-American Theatre Review
LatT, Latin Teaching, Shrewsbury
LB, Leuvense Bijdragen
LBer, Linguistische Berichte
LBIYB, Leo Baeck Institute Year Book
LBR, Luso-Brazilian Review
LC, Letture Classensi
LCC, Léachtaí Cholm Cille
LCh, Literatura Chilena
LCP, Language and Cognitive Processes
LCrit, Lavoro Critico
LCUTA, Library Chronicle of the University of Texas at Austin
LD, Libri e Documenti
LdA, Linha d'Agua
LDan, Lectura Dantis
LDanN, Lectura Dantis Newberryana

LDGM, Ligam-DiGaM. Quadèrn de lingüística e lexicografía gasconas, Fontenay aux Roses
LE, Language and Education
LEA, Lingüística Española Actual
LebS, Lebende Sprachen
LEMIR, Literatura Española Medieval y del Renacimiento, Valencia U.P.; http://www.uv.es/~lemir/Revista.html
Leng(M), Lengas, Montpellier
Leng(T), Lengas, Toulouse
LenP, Ленинградская панорама
LetA, Letterature d'America
LetC, La Lettre Clandestine
LetD, Letras de Deusto
LETHB, Laboratoires d'Études Théâtrales de l'Université de Haute-Bretagne. Études et Documents, Rennes
LetL, Letras e Letras, Departmento de Línguas Estrangeiras Modernas, Universidade Federal de Uberlândia, Brazil
LetLi, Letras Libres, Mexico D.F.
LetMS, Letopis Matice srpske, Novi Sad
LetP, Il Lettore di Provincia
LetS, Letras Soltas
LevT, Levende Talen
Lex(L), Lexique, Lille
LF, Letras Femeninas
LFil, Listy filologické
LFQ, Literature and Film Quarterly
LGF, Lunder Germanistische Forschungen, Stockholm, Almqvist & Wiksell
LGGL, Literatur in der Geschichte, Geschichte in der Literatur, Cologne–Vienna, Böhlau
LGL, Langs Germanistische Lehrbuchsammlung, Berne, Lang
LGP, Leicester German Poets, Leicester U.P.
LGW, Literaturwissenschaft — Gesellschaftswissenschaft, Stuttgart, Klett
LH, Lingüística Hispánica
LHum, Litteraria Humanitas, Brno
LI, Linguistic Inquiry
LIA, Letteratura italiana antica
LIÅA, Litteraturvetenskapliga institutionen vid Åbo Akademi, Åbo Akademi U.P.
LiB, Literatur in Bayern
LIC, Letteratura Italiana Contemporanea
LiCC, Lien des chercheurs cévenols
LIE, Lessico Intellettuale Europeo, Rome, Ateneo
LiL, Limbă şi Literatură
LiLi, Zeitschrift für Literaturwissenschaft und Linguistik
LingAk, Linguistik Aktuell, Amsterdam, Benjamins
LingBal, Балканско езикознание – Linguistique Balkanique
LingCon, Lingua e Contesto
LingFil, Linguistica e Filologia, Dipartimento di Linguistica e Letterature Comparate, Bergamo
LingLett, Linguistica e Letteratura
LíngLit, Língua e Literatura, São Paulo
LinLit, Lingüística y Literatura
LINQ, Linq [Literature in North Queensland]
LInv, Linguisticae Investigationes
LiR, Limba Română
LiR(M), Limba Română (Revist ă de ştiinţ ă şi culturą), Casa limbii române, Moldova
LIT, Literature Interpretation Theory
LIt, Lettera dall'Italia
LitAP, Literární archív Památníku národního pisemnictví
LItal, Lettere Italiane
LitB, Literatura, Budapest
LitC, Littératures Classiques
LitG, Литературная газета, Moscow
LitH, Literature and History
LItL, Letteratura Italiana Laterza, Bari, Laterza
LitL, Literatur für Leser
LitLing, Literatura y Lingüística
LitM, Literární měsícník
LitMis, Литературна мисъл
LitP, Literature and Psychology
LitR, The Literary Review
LittB, Litteraria, Bratislava
LittK, Litterae, Lauterburg, Kümmerle
LittS, Litteratur og Samfund
LittW, Litteraria, Wrocław
LitU, Literaturnaia Ucheba

LiU, Літературна Україна

LivOS, Liverpool Online Series. Critical Editions of French Texts. Department of Modern Languages. University of Liverpool <http://www.liv.ac.uk/www/french/LOS/>

LJb, Literaturwissenschaftliches Jahrbuch der Görres–Gesellschaft

LK, Literatur-Kommentare, Munich, Hanser

LK, Literatur und Kritik

LKol, Loccumer Kolloquium

LL, Langues et Littératures, Rabat

LlA, Lletres Asturianes

LLC, Literary and Linguistic Computing

LlC, Llên Cymru

LlLi, Llengua i Literatura

LLS, Lenguas, Literaturas, Sociedades. Cuadernos Hispánicos

LLSEE, Linguistic and Literary Studies in Eastern Europe, Amsterdam, Benjamins

LM, Le Lingue del Mondo

LN, Lingua Nostra

LNB, Leipziger namenkundliche Beiträge

LNL, Les Langues Néo-Latines

LNouv, Les Lettres Nouvelles

LoP, Loccumer Protokolle

LOS, Literary Onomastic Studies

LP, Le Livre de Poche, Librairie Générale Française

LP, Lingua Posnaniensis

LPen, Letras Peninsulares

LPh, Linguistics and Philosophy

LPLP, Language Problems and Language Planning

LPO, Lenga e Païs d'Oc, Montpellier

LPr, Linguistica Pragensia

LQ, Language Quarterly, University of S. Florida

LQu, Lettres québécoises

LR, Linguistische Reihe, Munich, Hueber

LR, Les Lettres Romanes

LRev, Linguistic Review

LRI, Libri e Riviste d'Italia

LS, Literatur als Sprache, Münster, Aschendorff

LS, Lingua e Stile

LSa, Lusitania Sacra

LSc, Language Sciences

LSil, Linguistica Silesiana

LSNS, Lundastudier i Nordisk Språkvetenskap

LSo, Language in Society

LSp, Language and Speech

LSPS, Lou Sourgentin/La Petite Source. Revue culturelle bilingue nissart-français, Nice

LSty, Language and Style

LSW, Ludowa Spółdzielnia Wydawnicza

LTG, Literaturwissenschaft, Theorie und Geschichte, Frankfurt, Lang

ŁTN, Łódzkie Towarzystwo Naukowe

LTP, Laval Théologique et Philosophique

LU, Literarhistorische Untersuchungen, Berne, Lang

LVC, Language Variation and Change

LW, Literatur und Wirklichkeit, Bonn, Bouvier

LWU, Literatur in Wissenschaft und Unterricht

LY, Lessing Yearbook

MA, Moyen Âge

MAASC, Mémoires de l'Académie des Arts et des Sciences de Carcassonne

MACL, Memórias da Academia de Ciências de Lisboa, Classe de Letras

MAe, Medium Aevum

MAKDDR, Mitteilungen der Akademie der Künste der DDR

MAL, Modern Austrian Literature

MaL, Le Maghreb Littéraire – Revue Canadienne des Littératures Maghrébines, Toronto

MaM, Marbacher Magazin

MAPS, Medium Aevum. Philologische Studien, Munich, Fink

MARPOC, Maison d'animation et de recherche populaire occitane, Nimes

MAST, Memorie dell'Accademia delle Scienze di Torino
MatSl, Matica Slovenská
MBA, Mitteilungen aus dem Brenner-Archiv
MBAV, Miscellanea Bibliothecae Apostolicae Vaticanae
MBMRF, Münchener Beiträge zur Mediävistik und Renaissance-Forschung, Bachenhausen, Arbeo
MBRP, Münstersche Beiträge zur romanischen Philologie, Münster, Kleinheinrich
MBSL, Mannheimer Beiträge zur Sprach- und Literaturwissenschaft, Tübingen, Narr
MC, Misure Critiche
MCV, Mélanges de la Casa de Velázquez
MD, Musica Disciplina
MDan, Meddelser fra Dansklærerforeningen.
MDG, Mitteilungen des deutschen Germanistenverbandes
MDL, Mittlere Deutsche Literatur in Neu- und Nachdrucken, Berne, Lang
MDLK, Monatshefte für deutschsprachige Literatur und Kultur
MDr, Momentum Dramaticum
MEC, Ministerio de Educação e Cultura, Rio de Janeiro
MedC, La Méditerranée et ses Cultures
MedH, Medioevo e Umanesimo
MedLR, Mediterranean Language Review
MedP, Medieval Perspectives
MedRom, Medioevo Romanzo
MedS, Medieval Studies
MEFR, Mélanges de l'École Française de Rome, Moyen Age
MerH, Merthyr Historian
MerP, Mercurio Peruano
MF, Mercure de France
MFDT, Mainzer Forschungen zu Drama und Theater, Tübingen, Francke
MFS, Modern Fiction Studies
MG, Молодая гвардия
MG, Молодая гвардия
MGB, Münchner Germanistische Beiträge, Munich, Fink
MGG, Mystik in Geschichte und Gegenwart, Stuttgart-Bad Cannstatt, Frommann-Holzboog
MGS, Marburger Germanistische Studien, Frankfurt, Lang
MGS, Michigan Germanic Studies
MGSL, Minas Gerais, Suplemento Literário
MH, Medievalia et Humanistica
MHJ, Medieval History Journal
MHLS, Mid-Hudson Language Studies
MHRA, Modern Humanities Research Association
MichRS, Michigan Romance Studies
MILUS, Meddelanden från Institutionen i Lingvistik vid Universitetet i Stockholm
MINS, Meddelanden från institutionen för nordiska språk vid Stockholms universiteit, Stockholm U.P.
MiscBarc, Miscellanea Barcinonensia
MiscEB, Miscel·lània d'Estudis Bagencs
MiscP, Miscel·lània Penedesenca
MITWPL, MIT Working Papers in Linguistics
MJ, Mittellateinisches Jahrbuch
MK, Maske und Kothurn
MKH, Deutsche Forschungsgemeinschaft: Mitteilung der Kommission für Humanismusforschung, Weinheim, Acta Humaniora
MKNAWL, Mededelingen der Koninklijke Nederlandse Akademie van Wetenschappen, Afd. Letterkunde, Amsterdam
ML, Mediaevalia Lovaniensia, Leuven U.P.
ML, Modern Languages
MLAIntBibl, Modern Language Association International Bibliography
MLIÅA, Meddelanden utgivna av Litteraturvetenskapliga institutionen vid Åbo Akademi, Åbo Akademi U.P.
MLIGU, Meddelanden utgivna av Litteraturvetenskapliga

institutionen vid Göteborgs universitet, Gothenburg U.P.
MLit, Мастацкая літаратура
MLit, Miesięcznik Literacki
MLIUU, Meddelanden utgivna av Litteraturvetenskapliga institutionen vid Uppsala universitet, Uppsala U.P.
MLJ, Modern Language Journal
MLN, Modern Language Notes
MLQ, Modern Language Quarterly
MLR, Modern Language Review
MLS, Modern Language Studies
MM, Maal og Minne
MMS, Münstersche Mittelalter-Schriften, Munich, Fink
MN, Man and Nature. L'Homme et la Nature
MNGT, Manchester New German Texts, Manchester U.P.
MO, Monde en Oc. Aurillac (IEO)
ModD, Modern Drama
ModS, Modern Schoolman
MoL, Modellanalysen: Literatur, Paderborn, Schöningh–Munich, Fink
MON, Ministerstwo Obrony Narodowej, Warsaw
MonS, Montaigne Studies
MosR, Московский рабочий
MoyFr, Le Moyen Français
MP, Modern Philology
MQ, Mississippi Quarterly
MQR, Michigan Quarterly Review
MR, Die Mainzer Reihe, Mainz, Hase & Koehler
MR, Medioevo e Rinascimento
MRev, Maghreb Review
MRo, Marche Romane
MRS, Medieval and Renaissance Studies
MRTS, Medieval and Renaissance Texts and Studies, Tempe, Arizona, Arizona State University
MS, Marbacher Schriften, Stuttgart, Cotta
MS, Moderna Språk
MSB, Middeleeuwse Studies en Bronnen, Hilversum, Verloren
MSC, Medjunarodni slavistički centar, Belgrade
MSG, Marburger Studien zur Germanistik, Marburg, Hitzeroth
MSHA, Maison des sciences de l'homme d'Aquitaine
MSISS, Materiali della Società Italiana di Studi sul Secolo XVIII
MSL, Marburger Studien zur Literatur, Marburg, Hitzeroth
MSLKD, Münchener Studien zur literarischen Kultur in Deutschland, Frankfurt, Lang
MSMS, Middeleeuse Studies — Medieval Studies, Johannesburg
MSNH, Mémoires de la Société Néophilologique de Helsinki
MSp, Moderne Sprachen (Zeitschrift des Verbandes der österreichischen Neuphilologen)
MSS, Medieval Sermon Studies
MSSp, Münchener Studien zur Sprachwissenschaft, Munich
MSUB, Moscow State University Bulletin, series 9, philology
MTCGT, Methuen's Twentieth-Century German Texts, London, Methuen
MTG, Mitteilungen zur Theatergeschichte der Goethezeit, Bonn, Bouvier
MTNF, Monographien und Texte zur Nietzsche-Forschung, Berlin — New York, de Gruyter
MTU, Münchener Texte und Untersuchungen zur deutschen Literatur des Mittelalters, Tübingen, Niemeyer
MTUB, Mitteilungen der T. U. Braunschweig
MUP, Manchester University Press
MusL, Music and Letters
MusP, Museum Patavinum
MyQ, Mystics Quarterly

NA, Nuova Antologia
NAFMUM, Nuovi Annali della Facoltà di Magistero dell'Università di Messina
NAJWS, North American Journal of Welsh Studies
NArg, Nuovi Argomenti
NAS, Nouveaux Actes Sémiotiques, PULIM, Université de Limoges
NASNCGL, North American Studies in Nineteenth-Century German Literature, Berne, Lang

NASSAB, Nuovi Annali della Scuola Speciale per Archivisti e Bibliotecari
NAWG, Nachrichten der Akademie der Wissenschaften zu Göttingen, phil.-hist. Kl., Göttingen, Vandenhoeck & Ruprecht
NBGF, Neue Beiträge zur George-Forschung
NC, New Criterion
NCA, Nouveaux Cahiers d'Allemand
NCEFRW, Nouvelles du Centre d'études francoprovençales 'René Willien'
NCF, Nineteenth-Century Fiction
NCFS, Nineteenth-Century French Studies
NCL, Notes on Contemporary Literature
NCo, New Comparison
NCSRLL, North Carolina Studies in the Romance Languages and Literatures, Chapel Hill
ND, Наукова думка
NDH, Neue deutsche Hefte
NdJb, Niederdeutsches Jahrbuch
NDL, Nachdrucke deutscher Literatur des 17. Jahrhunderts, Berne, Lang
NDL, Neue deutsche Literatur
NdS, Niederdeutsche Studien, Cologne, Böhlau
NDSK, Nydanske Studier og almen kommunikationsteori
NdW, Niederdeutsches Wort
NE, Nueva Estafeta
NEL, Nouvelles Éditions Latines, Paris
NFF, Novel: A Forum in Fiction
NFS, Nottingham French Studies
NFT, Német Filológiai Tanulmányok. Arbeiten zur deutschen Philologie
NG, Nevasimaia Gazeta
NG, Nordistica Gothoburgensia
NGC, New German Critique
NGFH, Die Neue Gesellschaft/ Frankfurter Hefte
NGR, New German Review
NGS, New German Studies, Hull
NH, Nuevo Hispanismo
NHi, Nice Historique
NHLS, North Holland Linguistic Series, Amsterdam
NHVKSG, Neujahrsblatt des Historischen Vereins des Kantons St Gallen
NI, Наука и изкуство
NIJRS, New International Journal of Romanian Studies
NIMLA, NIMLA. Journal of the Modern Language Association of Northern Ireland
NJ, Naš jezik
NJb, Neulateinisches Jahrbuch
NJL, Nordic Journal of Linguistics
NKT, Norske klassiker-tekster, Bergen, Eide
NL, Nouvelles Littéraires
NLÅ, Norsk Litterær Årbok
NLD, Nuove Letture Dantesche
NLe, Nuove Lettere
NLH, New Literary History
NLi, Notre Librairie
NLLT, Natural Language and Linguistic Theory
NLN, Neo-Latin News
NLO, Novoe Literaturnoe obozrenie
NLO, Novoe Literaturnoe obozrenie
NLT, Norsk Lingvistisk Tidsskrift
NLWJ, National Library of Wales Journal
NM, Народна младеж
NMi, Neuphilologische Mitteilungen
NMS, Nottingham Medieval Studies
NN, Наше наследие
NNH, Nueva Narrativa Hispano-americana
NNR, New Novel Review
NOR, New Orleans Review
NORNA, Nordiska samarbetskommittén för namnforskning, Uppsala
NovE, Novos Estudos (CEBRAP)
NovM, Новый мир
NovR, Nova Renascenza
NOWELE, North-Western European Language Evolution. Nowele
NP, Народна просвета
NP, Nouvello de Prouvènço (Li), Avignon, Parlaren Païs d'Avignoun
NQ, Notes and Queries

NR, New Review
NŘ, Naše řeč
NRE, Nuova Rivista Europea
NRe, New Readings, School of European Studies, University of Wales, College of Cardiff
NRF, Nouvelle Revue Française
NRFH, Nueva Revista de Filología Hispánica
NRL, Neue russische Literatur. Almanach, Salzburg
NRLett, Nouvelles de la République des Lettres
NRLI, Nuova Rivista di Letteratura Italiana
NRMI, Nuova Rivista Musicale Italiana
NRO, Nouvelle Revue d'Onomastique
NRP, Nouvelle Revue de Psychanalyse
NRS, Nuova Rivista Storica
NRSS, Nouvelle Revue du Seizième Siècle
NRu, Die Neue Rundschau
NS, Die Neueren Sprachen
NSc, New Scholar
NSh, Начальная школа
NSL, Det Norske Språk- og Litteraturselskap
NSlg, Neue Sammlung
NSo, Наш современник . . . Альманах
NSP, Nuovi Studi Politici
NSS, Nysvenska Studier
NSt, Naše stvaranje
NT, Навука і тэхніка
NT, Nordisk Tidskrift
NTBB, Nordisk Tidskrift för Bok- och Biblioteksväsen
NTC, Nuevo Texto Crítico
NTE, Народна творчість та етнографія
NTg, Nieuwe Taalgids
NTQ, New Theatre Quarterly
NTSh, Наукове товариство ім. Шевченка
NTW, News from the Top of the World: Norwegian Literature Today
NU, Narodna umjetnost
NV, Новое время
NVS, New Vico Studies
NWIG, Niewe West-Indische Gids
NyS, Nydanske Studier/Almen Kommunikationsteori
NYSNDL, New Yorker Studien zur neueren deutschen Literaturgeschichte, Berne, Lang
NYUOS, New York University Ottendorfer Series, Berne, Lang
NZh, Новый журнал
NZh (StP), Новый журнал, St Petersburg
NZJFS, New Zealand Journal of French Studies
NZSJ, New Zealand Slavonic Journal

OA, Отечественные архивы
OB, Ord och Bild
OBS, Osnabrücker Beiträge zur Sprachtheorie, Oldenbourg, OBST
OBTUP, Universitetsforlaget Oslo–Bergen–Tromsø
ÖBV, Österreichischer Bundesverlag, Vienna
OC, Œuvres et Critiques
OcL, Oceanic Linguistics
Oc(N), Oc, Nice
OCP, Orientalia Christiana Periodica, Rome
OCS, Occitan/Catalan Studies
ÖGL, Österreich in Geschichte und Literatur
OGS, Oxford German Studies
OH, Ottawa Hispánica
OIU, Oldenbourg Interpretationen mit Unterrichtshilfen, Munich, Oldenbourg
OL, Orbis Litterarum
OLR, Oxford Literary Review
OLSI, Osservatorio Linguistico della Svizzera italiana
OM, L'Oc Médiéval
ON, Otto/Novecento
ONS, Obshchestvennye Nauki i Sovremennost'
OPBS, Occasional Papers in Belarusian Studies
OPEN, Oficyna Polska Encyklopedia Nezależna
OPI, Overseas Publications Interchange, London

OPL, Osservatore Politico Letterario
OPM, 'Ou Païs Mentounasc': Bulletin de la Société d'Art et d'Histoire du Mentonnais, Menton
OPRPNZ, Общество по распространению политических и научных знаний
OPSLL, Occasional Papers in Slavic Languages and Literatures
OR, Odrodzenie i Reformacja w Polsce
ORP, Oriental Research Partners, Cambridge
OS, 'Oc Sulpic': Bulletin de l'Association Occitane du Québec, Montreal
OSP, Oxford Slavonic Papers
OSUWPL, Ohio State University Working Papers in Linguistics
OT, Oral Tradition
OTS, Onderzoeksinstituut voor Taal en Spraak, Utrecht
OUP, Oxford University Press
OUSL, Odense University Studies in Literature
OUSSLL, Odense University Studies in Scandinavian Languages and Literatures, Odense U.P.
OWPLC, Odense Working Papers in Language and Communication

PA, Présence Africaine
PAc, Primer Acto
PAf, Politique Africaine
PAGS, Proceedings of the Australian Goethe Society
Pal, Palaeobulgarica — Старобългаристика
PAM, Publicacions de l'Abadia de Montserrat, Barcelona
PAN, Polska Akademia Nauk, Warsaw
PaP, Past and Present
PapBSA, Papers of the Bibliographical Society of America
PAPhS, Proceedings of the American Philosophical Society
PapL, Papiere zur Linguistik
ParL, Paragone Letteratura
Parlem!, Parlem! Vai-i, qu'as paur! (IEO-Auvergne)
PartR, Partisan Review
PaS, Pamiętnik Słowiański
PASJ, Pictish Arts Society Journal
PaT, La Parola del Testo
PAX, Instytut Wydawniczy PAX, Warsaw
PB, Д-р Петър Берон
PBA, Proceedings of the British Academy
PBib, Philosophische Bibliothek, Hamburg, Meiner
PBLS, Proceedings of the Annual Meeting of the Berkeley Linguistic Society
PBML, Prague Bulletin of Mathematical Linguistics
PBSA, Publications of the Bibliographical Society of America
PC, Problems of Communism
PCLS, Proceedings of the Chicago Linguistic Society
PCP, Pacific Coast Philology
PD, Probleme der Dichtung, Heidelberg, Winter
PDA, Pagine della Dante
PdO, Paraula d'oc, Centre International de Recerca i Documentació d'Oc, Valencia
PE, Poesía Española
PEGS(NS), Publications of the English Goethe Society (New Series)
PenP, Il Pensiero Politico
PENS, Presses de l'École Normale Supérieure, Paris
PerM, Perspectives Médiévales
PEs, Lou Prouvençau à l'Escolo
PF, Présences Francophones
PFil, Prace Filologiczne
PFPS, Z problemów frazeologii polskiej i słowiańskiej, ZNiO
PFSCL, Papers on French Seventeenth Century Literature
PG, Païs gascons
PGA, Lo pais gascon/Lou pais gascoun, Anglet
PGIG, Publikationen der Gesellschaft für interkulturelle Germanistik, Munich, Iudicium
PH, La Palabra y El Hombre
PhilosQ, Philosophical Quarterly

PhilP, Philological Papers, West Virginia University
PhilR, Philosophy and Rhetoric
PhilRev, Philosophical Review
PhLC, Phréatique, Langage et Création
PHol, Le Pauvre Holterling
PhonPr, Phonetica Pragensia
PhP, Philologica Pragensia
PhR, Phoenix Review
PHSL, Proceedings of the Huguenot Society of London
PI, педагогический институт
PId, Le Parole e le Idee
PIGS, Publications of the Institute of Germanic Studies, University of London
PiH, Il Piccolo Hans
PIMA, Proceedings of the Illinois Medieval Association
PIMS, Publications of the Institute for Medieval Studies, Toronto
PIW, Państwowy Instytut Wydawniczy, Warsaw
PJ, Poradnik Językowy
PLing, Papers in Linguistics
PLit, Philosophy and Literature
PLL, Papers on Language and Literature
PL(L), Pamiętnik Literacki, London
PLRL, Patio de Letras/La Rosa als Llavis
PLS, Přednášky z běhu Letní školy slovanských studií
PL(W), Pamiętnik Literacki, Warsaw
PM, Pleine Marge
PMH, Portugaliae Monumenta Historica
PMHRS, Papers of the Medieval Hispanic Research Seminar, London, Department of Hispanic Studies, Queen Mary and Westfield College
PMLA, Publications of the Modern Language Association of America
PMPA, Publications of the Missouri Philological Association
PN, Paraulas de novelum, Périgueux
PNCIP, Plurilinguismo. Notizario del Centro Internazionale sul Plurilinguismo
PNR, Poetry and Nation Review
PNUS, Prace Naukowe Uniwersytetu Śląskiego, Katowice
PoetT, Poetics Today
PolR, Polish Review
PortSt, Portuguese Studies
PP, Prace Polonistyczne
PPNCFL, Proceedings of the Pacific Northwest Conference on Foreign Languages
PPr, Papers in Pragmatics
PPU, Promociones y Publicaciones Universitarias, S.A., Barcelona
PQ, The Philological Quarterly
PR, Podravska Revija
PrA, Prouvenço aro, Marseilles
PraRu, Prace Rusycystyczne
PRev, Poetry Review
PRF, Publications Romanes et Françaises, Geneva, Droz
PRH, Pahl-Rugenstein Hochschulschriften, Cologne, Pahl–Rugenstein
PrH, Provence Historique
PrHlit, Prace Historycznoliterackie
PrHum, Prace Humanistyczne
PRIA, Proceedings of the Royal Irish Academy
PrIJP, Prace Instytutu Języka Polskiego
Prilozi, Prilozi za književnost, jezik, istoriju i folklor, Belgrade
PrilPJ, Prilozi proučavanju jezika
PRIS-MA, Bulletin de liaison de l'ERLIMA, Université de Poitiers
PrLit, Prace Literackie
PRom, Papers in Romance
PrRu, Przegląd Rusycystyczny
PrzH, Przegląd Humanistyczny
PrzW, Przegląd Wschodni
PS, Проблеми слов'янознавства
PSCL, Papers and Studies in Contrastive Linguistics
PSE, Prague Studies in English
PSGAS, Politics and Society in Germany, Austria and Switzerland
PSLu, Pagine Storiche Luganesi
PSML, Prague Studies in Mathematical Linguistics
PSQ, Philologische Studien und Quellen, Berlin, Schmidt
PSR, Portuguese Studies Review

PSRL, Полное собрание русских летописей
PSS, Z polskich studiów slawistycznych, Warsaw, PWN
PSSLSAA, Procès-verbaux des séances de la Société des Lettres, Sciences et Arts de l'Aveyron
PSV, Polono-Slavica Varsoviensia
PT, Pamiętnik Teatralny
PUC, Pontifícia Universidade Católica, São Paulo
PUCRS, Pontífica Universidade Católica de Rio Grande do Sul, Porto Alegre
PUE, Publications Universitaires, Européennes, NY–Berne–Frankfurt, Lang
PUF, Presses Universitaires de France, Paris
PUG Pontificia Università Gregoriana
PUMRL, Purdue University Monographs in Romance Languages, Amsterdam — Philadelphia, Benjamins
PUStE, Publications de l'Université de St Étienne
PW, Poetry Wales
PWN, Państwowe Wydawnictwo Naukowe, Warsaw, etc

QA, Quaderni de Archivio
QALT, Quaderni dell'Atlante Lessicale Toscano
QASIS, Quaderni di lavoro dell'ASIS (Atlante Sintattico dell'Italia Settentrionale), Centro di Studio per la Dialettologia Italiana 'O. Parlangèli', Università degli Studi di Padova
QCFLP, Quaderni del Circolo Filologico Linguistico Padovano
QDLC, Quaderni del Dipartimento di Linguistica, Università della Calabria
QDLF, Quaderni del Dipartimento di Linguistica, Università degli Studi, Firenze
QDLLSMG, Quaderni del Dipartimento di Lingue e Letterature Straniere Moderne, Università di Genova
QDSL, Quellen zur deutschen Sprach- und Literaturgeschichte, Heidelberg, Winter
QFCC, Quaderni della Fondazione Camillo Caetani, Rome
QFESM, Quellen und Forschungen zur Erbauungsliteratur des späten Mittelalters und der frühen Neuzeit, Amsterdam, Rodopi
QFGB, Quaderni di Filologia Germanica della Facoltà di Lettere e Filosofia dell'Università di Bologna
QFIAB, Quellen und Forschungen aus italienischen Archiven und Bibliotheken
QFLK, Quellen und Forschungen zur Literatur- und Kulturgeschichte, Berlin, de Gruyter
QFLR, Quaderni di Filologia e Lingua Romanze, Università di Macerata
QFRB, Quaderni di Filologia Romanza della Facoltà di Lettere e Filosofia dell'Università di Bologna
QFSK, Quellen und Forschungen zur Sprach- und Kulturgeschichte der germanischen Völker, Berlin, de Gruyter
QI, Quaderni d'Italianistica
QIA, Quaderni Ibero-Americani
QIGC, Quaderni dell'Istituto di Glottologia, Università degli Studi 'G. D'Annunzio' di Chieti, Facoltà di Lettere e Filosofia
QIICM, Quaderni dell'Istituto Italiano de Cultura, Melbourne
QILLSB, Quaderni dell'Istituto di Lingue e Letterature Straniere della Facoltà di Magistero dell'Università degli Studi di Bari
QILUU, Quaderni dell'Istituto di Linguistica dell'Università di Urbino
QINSRM, Quaderni dell'Istituto Nazionale di Studi sul Rinascimento Meridionale
QJMFL, A Quarterly Journal in Modern Foreign Literatures
QJS, Quarterly Journal of Speech, Speech Association of America

QLII, Quaderni di Letterature Iberiche e Iberoamericane
QLL, Quaderni di Lingue e Letterature, Verona
QLLP, Quaderni del Laboratorio di Linguistica, Scuola Normale Superiore, Pisa
QLLSP, Quaderni di Lingua e Letteratura Straniere, Facoltà di Magistero, Università degli Studi di Palermo
QLO, Quasèrns de Lingüistica Occitana
QM, Quaderni Milanesi
QMed, Quaderni Medievali
QP, Quaderns de Ponent
QPet, Quaderni Petrarcheschi
QPL, Quaderni Patavini di Linguistica
QQ, Queen's Quarterly, Kingston, Ontario
QR, Quercy Recherche, Cahors
QRCDLIM, Quaderni di Ricerca, Centro di Dialettologia e Linguistica Italiana di Manchester
QRP, Quaderni di Retorica e Poetica
QS, Quaderni di Semantica
QSF, Quaderni del Seicento Francese
QSGLL, Queensland Studies in German Language and Literature, Berne, Francke
QSt, Quaderni Storici
QStef, Quaderni Stefaniani
QSUP, Quaderni per la Storia dell'Università di Padova
QT, Quaderni di Teatro
QuF, Québec français
QuS, Quebec Studies
QV, Quaderni del Vittoriale
QVen, Quaderni Veneti
QVer, Quaderni Veronesi di Filologia, Lingua e Letteratura Italiana
QVR, Quo vadis Romania?, Vienna

RA, Romanistische Arbeitshefte, Tübingen, Niemeyer
RA, Revista Agustiniana
RAA, Rendiconti dell'Accademia di Archeologia, Lettere e Belle Arti
RABM, Revista de Archivos, Bibliotecas y Museos
RAct, Regards sur l'Actualité
Rad, Rad Jugoslavenske akademije znanosti i umjetnosti
RAE, Real Academia Española
RAfL, Research in African Literatures
RAG, Real Academia Galega
RAL, Revista Argentina de Lingüística
RAN, Regards sur l'Afrique du Nord
RANL, Rendiconti dell'Accademia Nazionale dei Lincei, Classe di scienze morali, storiche e filologiche, serie IX
RANPOLL, Revista ANPOLL, Faculdade de Filosofia, Letras e Ciências Humanas, Univ. de São Paulo.
RAPL, Revista da Academia Paulista de Letras, São Paulo
RAR, Renaissance and Reformation
RAS, Rassegna degli Archivi di Stato
RASoc, Revista de Antropología Social
RB, Revue Bénédictine
RBC, Research Bibliographies and Checklists, London, Grant & Cutler
RBDSL, Regensburger Beiträge zur deutschen Sprach- und Literaturwissenschaft, Frankfurt–Berne, Lang
RBG, Reclams de Bearn et Gasconha
RBGd, Rocznik Biblioteki Gdańskiej PAN (Libri Gedanenses)
RBKr, Rocznik Biblioteki PAN w Krakowie
RBL, Revista Brasileira de Lingüística
RBLL, Revista Brasileira de Lingua e Literatura
RBN, Revista da Biblioteca Nacional
RBPH, Revue Belge de Philologie et d'Histoire
RBS, Rostocker Beiträge zur Sprachwissenschaft
RC, Le Ragioni Critiche
RCat, Revista de Catalunya

RČAV, Rozpravy Československé akademie věd, Prague, ČSAV
RCB, Revista de Cultura Brasileña
RCCM, Rivista di Cultura Classica e Medioevale
RCEH, Revista Canadiense de Estudios Hispánicos
RCEN, Revue Canadienne d'Études Néerlandaises
RCF, Review of Contemporary Fiction
RCL, Revista Chilena de Literatura
RCLL, Revista de Crítica Literaria Latino-Americana
RCo, Revue de Comminges
RCSF, Rivista Critica di Storia della Filosofia
RCVS, Rassegna di Cultura e Vita Scolastica
RD, Revue drômoise: archéologie, histoire, géographie
RDE, Recherches sur Diderot et sur l''Encyclopédie'
RDM, Revue des Deux Mondes
RDsS, Recherches sur le XVIIe Siècle
RDTP, Revista de Dialectología y Tradiciones Populares
RE, Revista de Espiritualidad
REC, Revista de Estudios del Caribe
RECat, Revue d'Études Catalanes
RedLet, Red Letters
REE, Revista de Estudios Extremeños
REEI, Revista del Instituto Egipcio de Estudios Islámicos, Madrid
REH, Revista de Estudios Hispánicos, Washington University, St Louis
REHisp, Revista de Estudios Hispánicos, Puerto Rico
REI, Revue des Études Italiennes
REJ, Revista de Estudios de Juventud
REJui, Revue des Études Juives, Paris
REL, Revue des Études Latines
RELA, Revista Española de Lingüística Aplicada
RelCL, Religion in Communist Lands
RELI, Rassegna Europea di Letteratura Italiana
RELing, Revista Española de Lingüística, Madrid
RelLit, Religious Literature
ReMS, Renaissance and Modern Studies
RenD, Renaissance Drama
RenP, Renaissance Papers
RenR, Renaissance and Reformation
RenS, Renaissance Studies
RER, Revista de Estudios Rosalianos
RES, Review of English Studies
RESEE, Revue des Études Sud-Est Européennes
RESS, Revue Européenne des Sciences Sociales et Cahiers Vilfredo Pareto
RevA, Revue d'Allemagne
RevAl, Revista de l'Alguer
RevAR, Revue des Amis de Ronsard
RevAuv, Revue d'Auvergne, Clermont-Ferrand
RevEL, Revista de Estudos da Linguagem, Faculdade de Letras, Universidade Federal de Minas Gerais
RevF, Revista de Filología
RevHA, Revue de la Haute-Auvergne
RevG, Revista de Girona
RevIb, Revista Iberoamericana
RevL, Revista Lusitana
RevLex, Revista de Lexicografía
RevLM, Revista de Literatura Medieval
RevLR, Revista do Livro
RevO, La Revista occitana, Montpellier
RevP, Revue Parole, Université de Mons-Hainault
RevPF, Revista Portuguesa de Filosofia
RevR, Revue Romane
RF, Romanische Forschungen
RFE, Revista de Filología Española
RFe, Razón y Fe
RFHL, Revue Française d'Histoire du Livre
RFLI, Rivista de Filologia e Letterature Ispaniche
RFLSJ, Revista de Filosofía y Lingüística de San José, Costa Rica

RFLUL, Revista da Faculdade de Letras da Universidade de Lisboa
RFLUP, Línguas e Literaturas, Revista da Faculdade de Letras, Univ. do Porto
RFN, Rivisti di Filosofia Neoscolastica
RFo, Ricerca Folklorica
RFP, Recherches sur le Français Parlé
RFR, Revista de Filología Románica
RFr, Revue Frontenac
RG, Recherches Germaniques
RGand, Romanica Gandensia
RGCC, Revue du Gévaudan, des Causses et des Cévennes
RGG, Rivista di Grammatica Generativa
RGI, Revue Germanique Internationale
RGL, Reihe Germanistische Linguistik, Tübingen, Niemeyer
RGo, Romanica Gothoburgensia
RGT, Revista Galega de Teatro
RH, Reihe Hanser, Munich, Hanser
RH, Revue Hebdomadaire
RHA, Revista de Historia de America
RHAM, Revue Historique et Archéologique du Maine
RHCS, Rocznik Historii Czasopiśmiennictwa Polskiego
RHDFE, Revue Historique de Droit Français et Étranger
RHE, Revue d'Histoire Ecclésiastique
RHEF, Revue d'Histoire de l'Église de France
RHel, Romanica Helvetica, Tübingen and Basle, Francke
RHFB, Rapports — Het Franse Boek
RHI, Revista da Historia das Ideias
RHis, Revue Historique
RHL, Reihe Hanser Literaturkommentare, Munich, Hanser
RHLF, Revue d'Histoire Littéraire de la France
RHLP, Revista de História Literária de Portugal
RHM, Revista Hispánica Moderna
RHMag, Revue d'Histoire Maghrébine
RHMC, Revue d'Histoire Moderne et Contemporaine
RHPR, Revue d'Histoire et de Philosophie Religieuses
RHR, Réforme, Humanisme, Renaissance
RHRel, Revue de l'Histoire des Religions
RHS, Revue Historique de la Spiritualité
RHSc, Revue d'Histoire des Sciences
RHSt, Ricarda Huch. Studien zu ihrem Leben und Werk
RHT, Revue d'Histoire du Théâtre
RHTe, Revue d'Histoire des Textes
RI, Rassegna Iberistica
RIA, Rivista Italiana di Acustica
RIa, Русский язык
RIAB, Revista Interamericana de Bibliografía
RIaR, Русский язык за рубежом
RICC, Revue Itinéraires et Contacts de Culture
RICP, Revista del Instituto de Cultura Puertorriqueña
RicSl, Ricerche Slavistiche
RID, Rivista Italiana di Dialettologia
RIE, Revista de Ideas Estéticas
RIEB, Revista do Instituto de Estudos Brasileiros
RIL, Rendiconti dell'Istituto Lombardo
RILA, Rassegna Italiana di Linguistica Applicata
RILCE, Revista del Instituto de Lengua y Cultura Españoles
RILI, Revista Internacional de Lingüística Iberoamericana
RILP, Revista Internacional da Língua Portuguesa
RIM, Rivista Italiana di Musicologia
RIndM, Revista de Indias
RInv, Revista de Investigación
RIO, Revue Internationale d'Onomastique
RIOn, Rivista Italiana di Onomastica
RIP, Revue Internationale de Philosophie

RIS, Revue de l'Institute de Sociologie, Université Libre, Brussels
RiS, Ricerche Storiche
RITL, Revista de Istorie şi Teorie Literară, Bucharest
RivF, Rivista di Filosofia
RivL, Rivista di Linguistica
RJ, Romanistisches Jahrbuch
RKHlit, Rocznik Komisji Historycznoliterackiej PAN
RKJŁ, Rozprawy Komisji Językowej Łódzkiego Towarzystwa Naukowego
RKJW, Rozprawy Komisji Językowej Wrocławskiego Towarzystwa Naukowego
RLA, Romance Languages Annual
RLaR, Revue des Langues Romanes
RLB, Recueil Linguistique de Bratislava
RLC, Revue de Littérature Comparée
RLD, Revista de Llengua i Dret
RLet, Revista de Letras
RLettI, Rivista di Letteratura Italiana
RLex, Revista de Lexicologia
RLF, Revista de Literatura Fantástica
RLFRU, Recherches de Linguistique Française et Romane d'Utrecht
RLH, Revista de Literatura Hispanoamericana
RLI, Rassegna della Letteratura Italiana
RLib, Rivista dei Libri
RLing, Russian Linguistics
RLiR, Revue de Linguistique Romane
RLit, Revista de Literatura
RLJ, Russian Language Journal
RLLCGV, Revista de Lengua y Literatura Catalana, Gallega y Vasca, Madrid
RLLR, Romance Literature and Linguistics Review
RLM, Revista de Literaturas Modernas, Cuyo
RLMC, Rivista di Letterature Moderne e Comparate
RLMed, Revista de Literatura Medieval
RLMexC, Revista de Literatura Mexicana Contemporánea
RLMod, Revue des Lettres Modernes
RLModCB, Revue des Lettres Modernes. Carnets Bibliographiques
RLSer, Revista de Literatura Ser, Puerto Rico
RLSL, Revista de Lingvistică şi Ştiinţă Literară
RLT, Russian Literature Triquarterly
RLTA, Revista de Lingüística Teórica y Aplicada
RLV, Revue des Langues Vivantes
RLVin, Recherches Linguistiques de Vincennes
RM, Romance Monograph Series, University, Mississippi
RM, Remate de Males
RMAL, Revue du Moyen Âge Latin
RMar, Revue Marivaux
RMC, Roma Moderna e Contemporanea
RMEH, Revista Marroquí de Estudios Hispánicos
RMH, Recherches sur le Monde Hispanique au XIXe Siècle
RMI, Rivista Musicale Italiana
RMM, Revue de Métaphysique et de Morale
RMon, Revue Montesquieu
RMRLL, Rocky Mountain Review of Language and Literature
RMS, Reading Medieval Studies
RMus, Revue de Musicologie
RNC, Revista Nacional de Cultura, Carácas
RNDWSPK, Rocznik Naukowo-Dydaktyczny WSP w Krakowie
RO, Revista de Occidente
RoczH, Roczniki Humanistyczne Katolickiego Uniw. Lubelskiego
RoczSl, Rocznik Slawistyczny
ROl, Rossica Olomucensia
RoM, Rowohlts Monographien, Reinbek, Rowohlt
RomGG, Romanistik in Geschichte und Gegenwart
ROMM, Revue de L'Occident Musulman et de la Méditerranée
RoN, Romance Notes
RoQ, Romance Quarterly

RORD, Research Opportunities in Renaissance Drama
RoS, Romance Studies
RoSl, Роднае слова
RP, Радянський письменник
RP, Revista de Portugal
RPA, Revue de Phonétique Appliquée
RPac, Revue du Pacifique
RPC, Revue Pédagogique et Culturelle de l'AVEP
RPF, Revista Portuguesa de Filologia
RPFE, Revue Philosophique de la France et de l'Étranger
RPh, Romance Philology
RPL, Revue Philosophique de Louvain
RPl, Río de la Plata
RPLit, Res Publica Litterarum
RPM, Revista de Poética Medieval
RPN, Res Publica nowa, Warsaw
RPol, Review of Politics
RPP, Romanticism Past and Present
RPr, Raison Présente
RPS, Revista Paraguaya de Sociologia
RPyr, Recherches pyrénéennes, Toulouse
RQ, Renaissance Quarterly
RQL, Revue Québécoise de Linguistique
RR, Romanic Review
RRe, Русская речь
RRL, Revue Roumaine de Linguistique
RRou, Revue du Rouergue
RRR, Reformation and Renaissance Review
RS, Reihe Siegen, Heidelberg, Winter
RS, Revue de Synthèse
RSBA, Revista de studii britanice şi americane
RSC, Rivista di Studi Canadesi
RSCI, Rivista di Storia della Chiesa in Italia
RSEAV, Revue de la Société des enfants et amis de Villeneuve-de-Berg
RSF, Rivista di Storia della Filosofia
RSH, Revue des Sciences Humaines
RSh, Радянська школа
RSI, Rivista Storica Italiana
RSJb, Reinhold Schneider Jahrbuch
RSL, Rusycystyczne Studia Literaturoznawcze
RSl, Revue des Études Slaves
RSLR, Rivista di Storia e Letteratura Religiose
RSPT, Revue des Sciences Philosophiques et Théologiques
RSR, Rassegna Storica del Risorgimento
RSSR, Rivista di Storia Sociale e Religiosa
RST, Rassegna Storica Toscana
RSt, Research Studies
RSTe, Rivista di Studi Testuali
RStI, Rivista di Studi Italiani
RT, Revue du Tarn
RTAM, Recherches de Théologie Ancienne et Médiévale
RTLiM, Rocznik Towarzystwa Literackiego im. Adama Mickiewicza
RTr, Recherches et Travaux, Université de Grenoble
RTUG, Recherches et Travaux de l'Université de Grenoble III
RUB, Revue de l'Université de Bruxelles
RUC, Revista de la Universidad Complutense
RuLit, Ruch Literacki
RUM, Revista de la Universidad de Madrid
RUMex, Revista de la Universidad de México
RUOt, Revue de l'Université d'Ottawa
RUS, Rice University Studies
RusH, Russian History
RusL, Русская литература, ПД, Leningrad
RusM, Русская мысль
RusMed, Russia Medievalis
RusR, Russian Review
RUW, Rozprawy Uniwersytetu Warsawskiego, Warsaw
RV, Revue Voltaire
RVB, Rheinische Vierteljahrsblätter
RVF, Revista Valenciana de Filología
RVi, Revue du Vivarais
RVQ, Romanica Vulgaria Quaderni
RVV, Romanische Versuche und Vorarbeiten, Bonn U.P.

RVVig, Reihe der Villa Vigoni, Tübingen, Niemeyer
RZLG, Romanistische Zeitschrift für Literaturgeschichte
RZSF, Radovi Zavoda za slavensku filologiju

SA, Studien zum Althochdeutschen, Göttingen, Vandenhoeck & Ruprecht
SAB, South Atlantic Bulletin
Sac, Sacris Erudiri
SAG, Stuttgarter Arbeiten zur Germanistik, Stuttgart, Heinz
SAH, Studies in American Humour
SANU, Srpska akademija nauka i umetnosti
SAOB, Svenska Akademiens Ordbok
SAQ, South Atlantic Quarterly
SAR, South Atlantic Review
SAS, Studia Academica Slovaca
SaS, Slovo a slovesnost
SASc, Studia Anthroponymica Scandinavica
SATF, Société des Anciens Textes Français
SAV, Slovenská akadémia vied
SAVL, Studien zur allgemeinen und vergleichenden Literaturwissenschaft, Stuttgart, Metzler
SB, Slavistische Beiträge, Munich, Sagner
SB, Studies in Bibliography
SBAW, Sitzungsberichte der Bayerischen Akad. der Wissenschaften, phil-hist. Kl., Munich, Beck
SBL, Saarbrücker Beiträge zur Literaturwissenschaft, St. Ingbert, Röhrig
SBL, Старобългарска литература
SBR, Swedish Book Review
SBVS, Saga-Book of the Viking Society
SC, Studia Celtica, The Bulletin of the Board of Celtic Studies
SCB, Skrifter utgivna av Centrum för barnkulturforskning, Stockholm U.P.
SCC, Studies in Comparative Communism
SCen, The Seventeenth Century
SCES, Sixteenth Century Essays and Studies, Kirksville, Missouri, Sixteenth Century Journal
SCFS, Seventeenth-Century French Studies
SchG, Schriftsteller der Gegenwart, Berlin, Volk & Wissen
SchSch, Schlern-Schriften, Innsbruck, Wagner
SchwM, Schweizer Monatshefte
SCJ, Sixteenth Century Journal
SCL, Studii şi Cercetări Lingvistice
SCl, Stendhal Club
ScL, Scottish Language
ScM, Scripta Mediterranea
SCN, Seventeenth Century News
SCO, Studii şi Cercetări de Onomastică
ScO, Scriptoralia, Tübingen, Narr
ScPo, Scientia Poetica
SCR, Studies in Comparative Religion
ScRev, Scandinavian Review
ScSl, Scando-Slavica
ScSt, Scandinavian Studies
SD, Sprache und Dichtung, n.F., Berne, Haupt
SD, Современная драматургия.
SdA, Storia dell'Arte
SDFU, Skrifter utgivna genom Dialekt- och folkminnesarkivet i Uppsala
SDG, Studien zur deutschen Grammatik, Tübingen, Stauffenburg
SDL, Studien zur deutschen Literatur, Tübingen, Niemeyer
SDLNZ, Studien zur deutschen Literatur des 19. und 20. Jahrhunderts, Berne, Lang
SdO, Serra d'Or
SDOFU, Skrifter utgivna av Dialekt-, ortnamns- och folkminnesarkivet i Umeå
SDS, Studien zur Dialektologie in Südwestdeutschland, Marburg, Elwert
SDSp, Studien zur deutschen Sprache, Tübingen, Narr
SDv, Sprache und Datenverarbeitung
SE, Série Esludos Uberaba
SeC, Scrittura e Civiltà

SECC, Studies in Eighteenth-Century Culture
SECCFC, Sociedad Estatal para la Conmemoración de los Centenarios de Felipe II y Carlos V
SEDES, Société d'Éditions d'Enseignement Supérieur
SEEA, Slavic and East European Arts
SEEJ, The Slavic and East European Journal
SEER, Slavonic and East European Review
SEES, Slavic and East European Studies
SEI, Società Editrice Internazionale, Turin
SELA, South Eastern Latin Americanist
SemL, Seminarios de Linguística, Universidade do Algarve, Faro
SEN, Società Editrice Napoletana, Naples
SEP, Secretaría de Educación Pública, Mexico
SeS, Serbian Studies
SEz, Съпоставително езикознание
SF, Slavistische Forschungen, Cologne — Vienna, Böhlau
SFAIEO, Section Française de l'Association Internationale d'Études Occitanes, Montpellier
SFI, Studi di Filologia Italiana
SFIS, Stanford French and Italian Studies
SFKG, Schriftenreihe der Franz–Kafka–Gesellschaft, Vienna, Braumüller
SFL, Studies in French Literature, London, Arnold
SFL, Studi di Filologia e Letteratura
SFPS, Studia z Filologii Polskiej i Słowiańskiej PAN
SFR, Stanford French Review
SFr, Studi Francesi
SFRS, Studia z Filologii Rosyjskiej i Slowiańskiej, Warsaw
SFS, Swiss-French Studies
SFUŠ, Sborník Filozofickej Fakulty Univerzity P. J. Šafárika, Prešov
SG, Sprache der Gegenwart, Düsseldorf, Schwann
SGAK, Studien zu Germanistik, Anglistik und Komparatistik, Bonn, Bouvier
SGECRN, Study Group on Eighteenth-Century Russia Newsletter
SGEL, Sociedad General Española de Librería
SGesch, Sprache und Geschichte, Stuttgart, Klett-Cotta
SGF, Stockholmer Germanistische Forschungen, Stockholm, Almqvist & Wiksell
SGG, Studia Germanica Gandensia
SGGed, Studia Germanica Gedanensia
SGI, Studi di Grammatica Italiana
SGLL, Studies in German Language and Literature, Lewiston-Queenston-Lampeter
SGLLC, Studies in German Literature, Linguistics, and Culture, Columbia, S.C., Camden House, Woodbridge, Boydell & Brewer
SGP, Studia Germanica Posnaniensia
SGS, Stanford German Studies, Berne, Lang
SGS, Scottish Gaelic Studies
SGU, Studia Germanistica Upsaliensia, Stockholm, Almqvist & Wiksell
SH, Slavica Helvetica, Berne, Lang
SH, Studia Hibernica
ShAn, Sharq al-Andalus
SHCT, Studies in the History of Christian Thought, Leiden, Brill
SHPF, Société de l'Histoire du Protestantisme Français
SHPS, Studies in History and Philosophy of Science
SHR, The Scottish Historical Review
SI, Sprache und Information, Tübingen, Niemeyer
SIAA, Studi di Italianistica nell'Africa Australe
SiCh, Слово і час
SIDES, Société Internationale de Diffusion et d'Édition Scientifiques, Antony

SIDS, Schriften des Instituts für deutsche Sprache, Berlin, de Gruyter
Siglo XX, Siglo XX/20th Century
SILTA, Studi Italiani di Linguistica Teorica ed Applicata
SiN, Sin Nombre
SINSU, Skrifter utgivna av institutionen för nordiska språk vid Uppsala universitet, Uppsala U.P.
SIR, Stanford Italian Review
SISMEL, Società Internazionale per lo Studio del Medioevo Latino, Edizioni del Galluzzo, Florence
SIsp, Studi Ispanici
SISSD, Società Italiana di Studi sul Secolo XVIII
SJLŠ, Slovenský jazyk a literatúra v škole
SKHAW, Schriften der phil.-hist. Klasse der Heidelberger Akademie der Wissenschaften, Heidelberg, Winter
SkSt, Skandinavistische Studien
SKZ, Srpska Književna Zadruga, Belgrade
SL, Sammlung Luchterhand, Darmstadt, Luchterhand
SL, Studia Linguistica
SLÅ, Svensk Lärarföreningens Årsskrift
SlaG, Slavica Gandensia
SlaH, Slavica Helsingensia
SlaL, Slavica Lundensia
SlavFil, Славянска филология, Sofia
SlavH, Slavica Hierosolymitana
SlavLit, Славянските литератури в България
SlavRev, Slavistična revija
SlaW, Slavica Wratislaviensia
SLeg, Studium Legionense
SLeI, Studi di Lessicografia Italiana
SLESPO, Suplemento Literário do Estado de São Paulo
SLF, Studi di Letteratura Francese
SLG, Studia Linguistica Germanica, Berlin, de Gruyter
SLI, Società di Linguistica Italiana
SLI, Studi Linguistici Italiani
SLIGU, Skrifter utgivna av Litteraturvetenskapliga institutionen vid Göteborgs universitet, Gothenburg U.P.
SLILU, Skrifter utgivna av Litteraturvetenskapliga institutionen vid Lunds universitet, Lund U.P.
SLinI, Studi di Lingua Italiana
SLit, Schriften zur Literaturwissenschaft, Berlin, Dunckler & Humblot
SLit, Slovenská literatúra
SLitR, Stanford Literature Review
SLIUU, Skrifter utgivna av Litteraturvetenskapliga institutionen vid Uppsala universitet, Uppsala U.P.
SLK, Schwerpunkte Linguistik und Kommunikationswissenschaft
SLL, Skrifter utg. genom Landsmålsarkivet i Lund
SLM, Studien zur Literatur der Moderne, Bonn, Bouvier
SlN, Slovenský národopis
SLO, Slavica Lublinensia et Olomucensia
SlO, Slavia Orientalis
SlOc, Slavia Occidentalis
SlOth, Slavica Othinensia
SlPN, Slovenské pedagogické nakladateľstvo
SlPoh, Slovenské pohľady
SlPr, Slavica Pragensia
SLPS, Studia Linguistica Polono-Slovaca
SLR, Société de Linguistique Romane
SLR, Second Language Research
SLRev, Southern Literary Review
SLS, Studies in the Linguistic Sciences
SlSb, Slezský sborník
SlSl, Slavica Slovaca
SlSp, Slovenský spisovateľ
SLu, Studia Lulliana
SLWU, Sprach und Literatur in Wissenschaft und Unterricht
SM, Sammlung Metzler, Stuttgart, Metzler
SM, Studi Medievali
SMC, Studies in Medieval Culture
SME, Schöninghs mediävistische Editionen, Paderborn, Schöningh
SMer, Студенческий меридиан

SMGL, Studies in Modern German Literature, Berne – Frankfurt – New York, Lang
SMHC, Studies in Medieval History and Culture, New York, Routledge
SMI, Stilistica e metrica italiana
SMLS, Strathclyde Modern Language Studies
SMRT, Studies in Medieval and Reformation Thought, Leiden, Brill
SMS, Sewanee Medieval Studies
SMu, Советский музей
SMV, Studi Mediolatini e Volgari
SN, Studia Neophilologica
SNL, Sveučilišna naklada Liber, Zagreb
SNM, Sborník Národního muzea
SNov, Seara Nova
SNTL, Státní nakladatelství technické literatury
SÖAW, Sitzungsberichte der Österreichischen Akademie der Wissenschaften, phil.-hist. Klasse
SOBI, Societat d'Onomastica, Butlleti Interior, Barcelona
SoCR, South Central Review
SOH, Studia Onomastica Helvetica, Arbon, Eurotext: Historisch-Archäologischer Verlag
SoK, Sprog og Kultur
SopL, Sophia Linguistica, Tokyo
SoRA, Southern Review, Adelaide
SoRL, Southern Review, Louisiana
SOU, Skrifter utgivna genom Ortnamnsarkivet i Uppsala
SP, Sammlung Profile, Bonn, Bouvier
SP, Studies in Philology
SPat, Studi Patavini
SpC, Speech Communication
SPCT, Studi e Problemi di Critica Testuale
SPES, Studio per Edizioni Scelte, Florence
SPFB, Sborník Pedagogické fakulty v Brně
SPFFBU, Sborník prací Filosofické fakulty Brněnské Univerzity
SPFFBU-A, Sborník prací Filosofické fakulty Brněnské Univerzity, A - řada jazykovědná
SPGS, Scottish Papers in Germanic Studies, Glasgow
SPh, Studia philologica, Olomouc
SPi, Serie Piper, Munich, Piper
SPIEL, Siegener Periodicum zur Internationalen Empirischen Literaturwissenschaft
SPK, Studia nad polszczyzną kresową, Wrocław
SpLit, Sprache und Literatur
SpMod, Spicilegio Moderno, Pisa
SPN, Státní pedagogické nakladatelství
SPol, Studia Polonistyczne
SPR, Slavistic Printings and Reprintings, The Hague, Mouton
SpR, Spunti e Ricerche
SPRF, Société de Publications Romanes et Françaises, Geneva, Droz
SPS, Specimina Philologiae Slavicae, Munich, Otto Sagner
SPS, Studia Philologica Salmanticensia
SPSO, Studia Polono–Slavica–Orientalia. Acta Litteraria
SpSt, Spanish Studies
SPUAM, Studia Polonistyczna Uniwersytetu Adama Mickiewicza, Poznań
SR, Slovenská reč
SRAZ, Studia Romanica et Anglica Zagrabiensia
SRev, Slavic Review
SRF, Studi e Ricerche Francescane
SRL, Studia Romanica et Linguistica, Frankfurt, Lang
SRLF, Saggi e Ricerche di Letteratura Francese
SRo, Studi Romanzi
SRom, Studi Romeni
SRoP, Studia Romanica Posnaniensia
SRP, Studia Rossica Posnaniensia
SRU, Studia Romanica Upsaliensia
SS, Symbolae Slavicae, Frankfurt–Berne–Cirencester, Lang
SS, Syn og Segn
SSBI, Skrifter utgivna av Svenska barnboksinstitutet
SSB, Strenna Storica Bolognese
SSCJ, Southern Speech Communication Journal

SSDSP, Società Savonese di Storia Patria
SSE, Studi di Storia dell'Educazione
SSF, Studies in Short Fiction
SSFin, Studia Slavica Finlandensia
SSGL, Studies in Slavic and General Linguistics, Amsterdam, Rodopi
SSH, Studia Slavica Academiae Scientiarum Hungaricae
SSL, Studi e Saggi Linguistici
SSLF, Skrifter utgivna av Svenska Litteratursällskapet i Finland
SSLP, Studies in Slavic Literature and Poetics, Amsterdam, Rodopi
SSLS, Studi Storici Luigi Simeoni
SSMP, Stockholm Studies in Modern Philology
SSPHS, Society for Spanish and Portuguese Historical Studies, Millersville
SSR, Scottish Studies Review
SSS, Stanford Slavic Studies
SSSAS, Society of Spanish and Spanish-American Studies, Boulder, Colorado
SSSlg, Sagners Slavistische Sammlung, Munich, Sagner
SSSN, Skrifter utgivna av Svenska språknämnden
SSSP, Stockholm Studies in Scandinavian Philology
SST, Sprache — System und Tätigkeit, Frankfurt, Lang
SSt, Slavic Studies, Hokkaido
ST, Suhrkamp Taschenbuch, Frankfurt, Suhrkamp
ST, Studi Testuali, Alessandria, Edizioni dell'Orso
StB, Studi sul Boccaccio
StBo, Studia Bohemica
STC, Studies in the Twentieth Century
StCJ, Studia Celtica Japonica
STCL, Studies in Twentieth Century Literature
StCL, Studies in Canadian Literature
STCM, Sciences, techniques et civilisations du moyen âge à l'aube des temps modernes. Paris, Champion
StCrit, Strumenti Critici
StD, Studi Danteschi
StF, Studie Francescani
StFil, Studia Filozoficzne
STFM, Société des Textes Français Modernes
StG, Studi Germanici
StGol, Studi Goldoniani
StH, Studies in the Humanities
StI, Studi Italici, Kyoto
StIt, Studi Italiani
StL, Studium Linguistik
StLa, Studies in Language, Amsterdam
StLI, Studi di Letteratura Ispano-Americana
StLi, Stauffenburg Linguistik, Tübingen, Stauffenburg
StLIt, Studi Latini e Italiani
StLM, Studies in the Literary Imagination
StLo, Studia Logica
STM, Suhrkamp Taschenbuch Materialien, Frankfurt, Suhrkamp
StM, Studies in Medievalism
STMFN, Studien und Texte zum Mittelalter und zur frühen Neuzeit, Münster, Waxmann
STML, Studies on Themes and Motifs in Literature, New York, Lang
StMon, Studia Monastica
StMus, Studi Musicali
StMy, Studia Mystica
StN, Studi Novecenteschi
StNF, Studier i Nordisk Filologi
StO, Studium Ovetense
StP, Studi Piemontesi
StPet, Studi Petrarcheschi
StR, Studie o rukopisech
StRLLF, Studi e Ricerche di Letteratura e Linguistica Francese
StRmgn, Studi Romagnoli
StRo, Studi Romani
StRom, Studies in Romanticism
StRu, Studia Russica, Budapest
StS, Studi Storici
StSec, Studi Secenteschi
StSem, Studia Semiotyczne
StSen, Studi Senesi
StSet, Studi Settecenteschi
STSG, Schriften der Theodor-Storm-Gesellschaft, Heide in Holstein, Boyens

StSk, Studia Skandinavica
STSL, Studien und Texte zur Sozialgeschichte der Literatur, Tübingen, Niemeyer
StSp, Studies in Spirituality
StT, Studi Tassiani
STUF, Sprachtypologie und Universalienforschung
StV, Studies on Voltaire and the 18th Century
STW, Suhrkamp Taschenbücher Wissenschaft, Frankfurt, Suhrkamp
StZ, Sprache im technischen Zeitalter
SU, Studi Urbinati
SUBBP, Studia Universitatis Babeş-Bolyai, Philologia, Cluj
SUDAM, Editorial Sudamericana, Buenos Aires
SuF, Sinn und Form
SUm, Schede Umanistiche
SUP, Spisy University J. E. Purkyně, Brno
SupEz, Съпоставително езикознание, Sofia
SV, Studi Veneziani
SVEC, Studies in Voltaire and the Eighteenth Century, Oxford, Voltaire Foundation (formerly *StV*)
SZ, Studia Zamorensia

TAL, Travaux d'Archéologie Limousine, Limoges
TAm, The Americas, Bethesda
TAPS, Transactions of the American Philosophical Society
TB, Tempo Brasileiro
TBL, Tübinger Beiträge zur Linguistik, Tübingen, Narr
TC, Texto Critico
TCBS, Transactions of the Cambridge Bibliographical Society
TCERFM, Travaux du Centre d'Études et de Recherches sur François Mauriac, Bordeaux
TCL, Twentieth-Century Literature
TCLN, Travaux du Cercle Linguistique de Nice
TCMA, Traductions des Classiques du Moyen Age, Paris, Champion
TCWAAS, Transactions of the Cumberland and Westmorland Antiquarian and Archaeological Society
TD, Teksty Drugie
TDC, Textes et Documents pour la Classe
TEC, Teresiunum Ephemerides Carmeliticae
TECC, Textos i Estudis de Cultura Catalana, Curial — Publicacions de l'Abadia de Montserrat, Barcelona
TeK, Text und Kontext
TELK, Trouvaillen — Editionen zur Literatur- und Kulturgeschichte, Berne, Lang
TeN, Terminologies Nouvelles
TeSt, Teatro e Storia
TE(XVIII), Textos y Estudios del Siglo XVIII
TF, Texte zur Forschung, Darmstadt, Wissenschaftliche Buchgesellschaft
TFN, Texte der Frühen Neuzeit, Frankfurt, Keip
TGLSK, Theorie und Geschichte der Literatur und der Schönen Künste, Munich, Fink
TGSI, Transactions of the Gaelic Society of Inverness
THESOC, Thesaurus Occitan
THL, Theory and History of Literature, Manchester U.P.
THM, Textos Hispánicos Modernos, Barcelona, Labor
THR, Travaux d'Humanisme et Renaissance, Geneva, Droz
THSC, Transactions of the Honourable Society of Cymmrodorion
TI, Le Texte et l'Idée
TidLit, Tidskrift för Litteraturvetenskap
TILAS, Travaux de l'Institut d'Études Latino-Américaines de l'Université de Strasbourg
TILL, Travaux de l'Institut de Linguistique de Lund
TJ, Theatre Journal
TK, Text und Kritik, Munich
TK, Text und Kritik
TKS, Търновска книжевна школа, Sofia

TL, Theoretical Linguistics
TLF, Textes Littéraires Français, Geneva, Droz
TLit, Travaux de Littérature
TLP, Travaux de Linguistique et de Philologie
TLQ, Travaux de Linguistique Québécoise
TLTL, Teaching Language Through Literature
TM, Les Temps Modernes
TMJb, Thomas Mann-Jahrbuch
TMo, O Tempo e o Modo
TMS, Thomas-Mann Studien, Frankfurt, Klostermann
TN, Theatre Notebook
TNA, Tijdschrift voor Nederlands en Afrikaans
TNT, Towarzystwo Naukowe w Toruniu
TOc, Tèxtes Occitans, Bordeaux
TODL, Труды Отдела древнерусской литературы Института русской литературы АН СССР
TP, Textual Practice
TPa, Torre de Papel
TPS, Transactions of the Philological Society
TQ, Theatre Quarterly
TR, Телевидение и радиовещание
TravL, Travaux de Linguistique, Luxembourg
TRCTL, Texte-Revue de Critique et de Théorie Littéraire
TRI, Theatre Research International
TRISMM, Tradition — Reform — Innovation. Studien zur Modernität des Mittelalters, Frankfurt, Lang
TrK, Трезвость и культура
TrL, Travaux de Linguistique
TrLit, Translation and Literature
TRS, The Transactions of the Radnorshire Society
TS, Theatre Survey
TSC, Treballs de Sociolingüística Catalana
TSDL, Tübinger Studien zur deutschen Literatur, Frankfurt, Lang
TSJ, Tolstoy Studies Journal
TSL, Trierer Studien zur Literatur, Frankfurt, Lang
TSLL, Texas Studies in Literature and Language
TSM, Texte des späten Mittelalters und der frühen Neuzeit, Berlin, Schmidt
TsNTL, Tijdschrift voor Nederlandse Taal- en Letterkunde
TSRLL, Tulane Studies in Romance Languages and Literature
TsSk, Tijdschrift voor Skandinavistiek
TsSV, Tijdschrift voor de Studie van de Verlichting
TSWL, Tulsa Studies in Women's Literature
TT, Tekst en Tijd, Nijmegen, Alfa
TT, Travail Théâtral
TTAS, Twayne Theatrical Arts Series, Boston–New York
TTG, Texte und Textgeschichte, Tübingen, Niemeyer
TTr, Terminologie et Traduction
TUGS, Texte und Untersuchungen zur Germanistik und Skandinavistik, Frankfurt, Lang
TVS, Theorie und Vermittlung der Sprache, Frankfurt, Lang
TWAS, Twayne's World Authors Series, Boston–New York
TWQ, Third World Quarterly

UAB, Universitat Autònoma de Barcelona
UAC, Universidad de Antioquia, Colombia
UAM, Uniwersytet Adama Mickiewicza, Poznań
UB, Universal-Bibliothek, Stuttgart, Reclam
UBL, Universal-Bibliothek, Leipzig, Reclam
UCLWPL, UCL Working Papers in Linguistics
UCPL, University of California Publications in Linguistics
UCPMP, University of California Publications in Modern Philology

UDL, Untersuchungen zur deutschen Literaturgeschichte, Tübingen, Niemeyer
UDR, University of Dayton Review
UERJ, Universidade Estadual do Rio de Janeiro
UFPB, Universidade Federal da Paraiba
UFRGS, Univ. Federal do Rio Grande do Sul (Brazil)
UFRJ, Universidade Federal do Rio de Janeiro
UFSC, Universidade Federal de Santa Catarina
UFSM, Universidade Federal de Santa Maria
UGE, Union Générale d'Éditions
UGFGP, University of Glasgow French and German Publications
UGLD, Union generala de Ladins dles Dolomites
UL, Українське літературознавство, Lvov U.P.
UM, Українська мова і література в школі
UMCS, Uniwersytet Marii Curie-Skłodowskiej, Lublin
UMov, Українське мовазнавство
UNAM, Universidad Nacional Autónoma de Mexico
UNC, Univ. of North Carolina
UNCSGL, University of North Carolina Studies in Germanic Languages and Literatures, Chapel Hill
UNED, Universidad Nacional de Enseñanza a Distancia
UNESP, Universidade Estadual de São Paulo
UNMH, University of Nottingham Monographs in the Humanities
UPP, University of Pennsylvania Press, Philadelphia
UQ, Ukrainian Quarterly
UR, Umjetnost riječi
USCFLS, University of South Carolina French Literature Series
USFLQ, University of South Florida Language Quarterly
USH, Umeå Studies in the Humanities, Stockholm, Almqvist & Wiksell International
USLL, Utah Studies in Literature and Linguistics, Berne, Lang
USP, Universidade de São Paulo
UTB, Uni-Taschenbücher
UTET, Unione Tipografico-Editrice Torinese
UTPLF, Università di Torino, Pubblicazioni della Facoltà di Lettere e Filosofia
UTQ, University of Toronto Quarterly
UVAN, Українська Вільна Академія Наук, Winnipeg
UVK, Universitätsverlag Konstanz
UVWPL, University of Venice Working Papers in Linguistics
UWCASWC, The University of Wales Centre for Advanced Studies in Welsh and Celtic
UZLU, Ученые записки Ленинградского университета

VAM, Vergessene Autoren der Moderne, Siegen U.P.
VAS, Vorträge und Abhandlungen zur Slavistik, Giessen, Schmitz
VASSLOI, Veröffentlichungen der Abteilung für Slavische Sprachen und Literaturen des Osteuropa–Instituts (Slavistiches Seminar) an der Freien Universität Berlin
VB, Vestigia Bibliae
VBDU, Веснік Беларускага дзяржаўнага ўніверсітэта імя У. І. Леніна. Серыя IV
VCT, Les Voies de la Création Théâtrale
VDASD, Veröffentlichungen der Deutschen Akademie für Sprache und Dichtung, Darmstadt, Luchterhand
VDG, Verlag und Datenbank für Geisteswissenschaften, Weimar
VF, Вопросы философии
VGBIL, Всесоюзная государственная библиотека иностранной литературы
VH, Vida Hispánica, Wolverhampton
VHis, Verba Hispanica
VI, Военно издателство
VI, Voix et Images
VIa, Вопросы языкознания

VIN, Veröffentlichungen des Instituts für niederländische Philologie, Erftstadt, Lukassen
ViSH, Вища школа
VIst, Вопросы истории
Vit, Вітчизна
VKP, Всесоюзная книжная палата
VL, Вопросы литературы
VLet, Voz y Letras
VM, Время и мы, New York — Paris — Jerusalem
VMKA, Verslagen en Mededelingen, Koninklijke Academie voor Nederlandse Taal- en Letterkunde
VMUF, Вестник Московского университета. Серия IX, филология
VMUFil, Вестник Московского университета. Серия VII, философия
VÖAW, Verlag der Österreichischen Akademie der Wissenschaften, Vienna
Voz, Возрождение
VP, Встречи с прошлым, Moscow
VPen, Vita e Pensiero
VR, Vox Romanica
VRKhD, Вестник Русского христианского движения
VRL, Вопросы русской литературы
VRM, Volkskultur am Rhein und Maas
VS, Вопросы семантики
VSAV, Vydavateľstvo Slovenskej akadémie vied
VSh, Вышэйшая школа
VSh, Визвольний шлях
VSPU, Вестник Санкт-Петербургского университета
VSSH, Вечерняя средняя школа
VV, Византийский временник
VVM, Vlastivědný věstník moravský
VVSh, Вестник высшей школы
VWGÖ, Verband der wissenschaftlichen Gesellschaften Österreichs
VySh, Вища школа
VysSh, Высшая школа
VyV, Verdad y Vida
VZ, Vukova zadužbina, Belgrade
WAB, Wolfenbütteler Arbeiten zur Barockforschung, Wiesbaden, Harrassowitz
WADL, Wiener Arbeiten zur deutschen Literatur, Vienna, Braumüller
WAGAPH, Wiener Arbeiten zur germanischen Altertumskunde und Philologie, Berne, Lang
WAiF, Wydawnictwa Artystyczne i Filmowe, Warsaw
WaT, Wagenbachs Taschenbücherei, Berlin, Wagenbach
WB, Weimarer Beiträge
WBDP, Würzburger Beiträge zur deutschen Philologie, Würzburg, Königshausen & Neumann
WBG, Wissenschaftliche Buchgesellschaft, Darmstadt
WBN, Wolfenbütteler Barock-Nachrichten
WBS, Welsh Book Studies
WF, Wege der Forschung, Darmstadt, Wissenschaftliche Buchgesellschaft
WGCR, West Georgia College Review
WGY, Women in German Yearbook
WHNDL, Würzburger Hochschulschriften zur neueren Deutschen Literaturgeschichte, Frankfurt, Lang
WHR, The Welsh History Review
WI, Word and Image
WIFS, Women in French Studies
WJMLL, Web Journal in Modern Language Linguistics
WKJb, Wissenschaftskolleg. Institute for Advanced Study, Berlin. Jahrbuch
WL, Wydawnictwo Literackie, Cracow
WŁ, Wydawnictwo Łódzkie
WLub, Wydawnictwo Lubelskie
WLT, World Literature Today
WM, Wissensliteratur im Mittelalter, Wiesbaden, Reichert
WNB, Wolfenbütteler Notizen zur Buchgeschichte
WNT, Wydawnictwa Naukowo-Techniczne
WoB, Wolfenbütteler Beiträge

WoF, Wolfenbütteler Forschungen, Wiesbaden, Harrassowitz
WP, Wiedza Powszechna, Warsaw
WPEL, Working Papers in Educational Linguistics
WPFG, Working Papers in Functional Grammar, Amsterdam U.P.
WRM, Wolfenbütteler Renaissance Mitteilungen
WS, Wort und Sinn
WSA, Wolfenbütteler Studien zur Aufklärung, Tübingen, Niemeyer
WSiP, Wydawnictwa Szkolne i Pedagogiczne, Warsaw
WSJ, Wiener Slavistisches Jahrbuch
WSl, Die Welt der Slaven
WSlA, Wiener Slawistischer Almanach
WSP, Wyższa Szkoła Pedagogiczna
WSp, Word and Spirit
WSPRRNDFP, Wyższa Szkoła Pedagogiczna w Rzeszowie. Rocznik Naukowo-Dydaktyczny. Filologia Polska
WSS, Wiener Studien zur Skandinavistik
WUW, Wydawnictwo Uniwersytetu Wrocławskiego
WuW, Welt und Wort
WW, Wirkendes Wort
WWAG, Woman Writers in the Age of Goethe
WWE, Welsh Writing in English. A Yearbook of Critical Essays
WZHUB, Wissenschaftliche Zeitschrift der Humboldt-Universität, Berlin: gesellschafts- und sprachwissenschaftliche Reihe
WZPHP, Wissenschaftliche Zeitschrift der pädagogischen Hochschule Potsdam. Gesellschafts- und sprachwissenschaftliche Reihe
WZUG, Wissenschaftliche Zeitschrift der Ernst-Moritz-Arndt- Universität Greifswald
WZUH, Wissenschaftliche Zeitschrift der Martin-Luther-Universität Halle-Wittenberg: gesellschafts- und sprachwissenschaftliche Reihe
WZUJ, Wissenschaftliche Zeitschrift der Friedrich-Schiller-Universität Jena/Thüringen: gesellschafts-und sprachwissenschaftliche Reihe
WZUL, Wissenschaftliche Zeitschrift der Karl Marx Universität Leipzig: gesellschafts- und sprachwissenschaftliche Reihe
WZUR, Wissenschaftliche Zeitschrift der Universität Rostock: gesellschafts- und sprachwissenschaftliche Reihe

YaIS, Yale Italian Studies
YB, Ysgrifau Beirniadol
YCC, Yearbook of Comparative Criticism
YCGL, Yearbook of Comparative and General Literature
YDAMEIS, Yearbook of the Dutch Association for Middle Eastern and Islamic Studies
YEEP, Yale Russian and East European Publications, New Haven, Yale Center for International and Area Studies
YES, Yearbook of English Studies
YFS, Yale French Studies
YIP, Yale Italian Poetry
YIS, Yearbook of Italian Studies
YJC, Yale Journal of Criticism
YM, Yearbook of Morphology
YPL, York Papers in Linguistics
YR, Yale Review
YSGP, Yearbook. Seminar for Germanic Philology
YSPS, The Yearbook of the Society of Pirandello Studies
YWMLS, The Year's Work in Modern Language Studies

ZÄAK, Zeitschrift für Ästhetik und allgemeine Kunstwissenschaft
ZB, Zeitschrift für Balkanologie
ZBL, Zeitschrift für bayerische Landesgeschichte
ZbS, Zbornik za slavistiku
ZCP, Zeitschrift für celtische Philologie

ZD, Zielsprache Deutsch
ZDA, Zeitschrift für deutsches Altertum und deutsche Literatur
ZDL, Zeitschrift für Dialektologie und Linguistik
ZDNÖL, Zirkular. Dokumentationsstelle für neuere österreichische Literatur
ZDP, Zeitschrift für deutsche Philologie
ZFKPhil, Zborník Filozofickej fakulty Univerzity Komenského. Philologica
ZFL, Zbornik za filologiju i lingvistiku
ZFSL, Zeitschrift für französische Sprache und Literatur
ZGB, Zagreber germanistische Beiträge
ZGer, Zeitschrift für Germanistik
ZGKS, Zeitschrift der Gesellschaft für Kanada-Studien
ZGL, Zeitschrift für germanistische Linguistik
ZGS, Zürcher germanistische Studien, Berne, Lang
ZK, Zeitschrift für Katalanistik
ZL, Zeszyty Literackie, Paris
ZMS(FL), Zbornik Matice srpske za filologiju i lingvistiku
ZMS(KJ), Zbornik Matice srpske za književnost i jezik
ZMS(Sl), Zbornik Matice srpske za slavistiku
ZNiO, Zakład Narodowy im. Ossolińskich, Wrocław
ZnS, Знание — сила
ZNTSh, Записки Наукового товариства ім. Шевченка
ZNUG, Zeszyty Naukowe Uniw. Gdańskiego, Gdańsk
ZNUJ, Zeszyty Naukowe Uniw. Jagiellońskiego, Cracow
ZNWHFR, Zeszyty Naukowe Wydziału Humanistycznego. Filologia Rosyjska
ZNWSPO, Zeszyty Naukowe Wyższej Szkoly Pedagogicznej w Opolu
ZO, Zeitschrift für Ostforschung
ZPŠSlav, Zborník Pedagogickej fakulty v Prešove Univerzity Pavla Jozefa Šafárika v Košiciach-Slavistika, Bratislava
ZR, Zadarska revija
ZRAG, Записки русской академической группы в США
ZRBI, Зборник радова бизантолошког института, Belgrade
ZRL, Zagadnienia Rodzajów Literackich
ZRP, Zeitschrift für romanische Philologie
ZS, Zeitschrift für Sprachwissenschaft
ZSJ, Zápisnik slovenského jazykovedca
ZSK, Ze Skarbca Kultury
ZSL, Zeitschrift für siebenbürgische Landeskunde
ZSl, Zeitschrift für Slawistik
ZSP, Zeitschrift für slavische Philologie
ZSVS, Zborník Spolku vojvodinských slovakistov, Novi Sad
ZT, Здесь и теперь
ZV, Zeitschrift für Volkskunde
ZvV, Звезда востока
ZWL, Zeitschrift für württembergische Landesgeschichte

INDEX

Aabenhus, J., 766
Aagard-Nilsen, N., 775
Aakjær, Jeppe, 758, 765
Aamodt, Bjørn, 780
Aamotsbakken, B., 779, 780
Aarestrup, Emil, 767
Aarseth, A., 777
Aasland, A. H., 777
Aavaath, A., 778
Abardo, R., 372
Abassi, A., 184
Abate, G., 425, 435
Abba, Marta, 484
Abbadie, Jacques, 158
Abbrugiati, P., 434, 438
Abdala, B., (Jr.), 344
Abeillé, A., 24
Abel, A., 723
Abelard, Peter, 399
Abell, Kjeld, 769
Abels, N., 424
Abouda, L., 25
Abraham, C., 144
Abramiants, A., 846
Abramov, E. P., 813
Abrams, M. H., 293
Abreu, Caio Fernando, 348
Abrosimova, V. N., 826
Abu-Haidar, J. A., 233
Abuín González, A., 269
Accart, X., 515
Accetto, Torquato, 160
Acciai, G., 236
Acerbi, Giuseppe, 352
Acereda, A., 335–36
Achnitz, W., 600, 601, 606
Achugar, H., 337
Achugar, M., 262
Acosta, José de, 266
Acterian, Haig, 515
Actis-Grosso, M., 480
Adam de la Halle, 57, 58, 65–66
Adam, G., 513
Adam, I., 513
Adam, J.-M., 20
Adam, V., 135
Adam, W., 621
Adameşteanu, Gabriela, 514
Adami, Anton Filippo, 404
Adamíková, M., 784
Adamo, G., 481
Adamo, S., 490
Adamovich, Georgii, 835, 838, 843
Adams, A., 107, 128
Adams, T., 71, 81, 82
Addeo, G., 403
Adelson, L. A., 736
Adelung, Johann Christoph, 551, 566
Adiego, I.-X., 16
Adini, G., 373
Adolphsen, Peter, 764, 765, 768
Adorno, F. P., 164
Adorno, Luisa, 467
Adorno, Theodor W., 658, 707, 718, 719, 721, 723, 724, 743, 749
Adrien, H. M., 39
Aesop, 114, 120, 418, 620
Afanasiev, E. L., 808
Afanasiev, E. S., 822
Affigné, C. A., 320
Afribo, A., 385, 467
Aga, Hanne, 778
Ageev, B., 851
Ágel, V., 562, 863
Agnesi, E., 419
Ago, L. M., 383
Agonigi, M., 361
Agopian, Ştefan, 508
Agosín, M., 337
Agosti, S., 494
Agostini, T., 421
Agoult, Marie d', 686
Agranovskaya, G., 839
Agreda y Vargas, Diego de, 148
Agreiter, Antoine, 509
Agresti, G., 238
Agrippa von Nettesheim, Heinrich Cornelius, 630
Aguiar, F., 349
Aguinis, Marcos, 340
Agustín, Antonio, 266
Ahkenazi, L., 831
Ahlsén, E., 761
Ahlsen, Leopold, 642
Ahn, M.-H., 726
Aigi, Gennadi, 839, 844
Aikin, J. P., 640, 645
Ailes, M. J., 38
Aillaud, Jean-Antoine, 408
Aiol, 392
Aira González, R., 307, 310
Airoldi Namer, F., 468
Aisenshtein, E. O., 855
Aiupov, S. M., 830
Aizenberg, E., 339
Aizerman, L., 812
Ajello, R., 405
Akehurst, F. R. P., 53
Akhmatova, Anna Andreevna, 822, 841, 844–45
Akimova, N. N., 812
Aksakov, Ivan Sergeevich, 819
Aksakov, Sergei Timofeevich, 819
Aksenov, Vasilii, 843, 845
Aksiutina, O., 834
Akslen, L., 774
Aksyonov, V., 807
Akunin, Boris, 834, 845
Al'mi, I. L., 810
Ala, Fabio, 405
Alacevich, A., 415
Alain de Lille, 51
Alarcos Llorach, E., 3
Albanese, R. (Jr.), 134
Albanis, E., 705
Alber, B., 558
Alberdi, Juan Bautista, 318, 319
Albergati Capacelli, Francesco, 411
Albéric, 49
Alberni, A., 297
Albert the Great (*Saint*), 77
Albert, C., 718
Albertanus Brixensis (A. of Brescia), 618
Albertelli, E., 431
Alberti, Leon Battista, 96, 109
Alberti, P., 429, 442
Alberti, Rafael, 282, 283–84, 292
Alberto, C., 414
Albinati, Edoardo, 459
Alboreto, L., 445
Albrecht (author of *Der jüngere Titurel*), 596, 597, 601
Albrecht von Bonstetten, 620

Albrecht von Eyb, 582, 609
Albrecht, M., 741
Albrecht, W., 673
Albrico, 397
Albright, A., 353
Albu, L. C., 504
Albu, R., 504
Albuquerque, P. G. B. de, 348
Alciato, Andrea, 271
Alcina, J. F., 303
Alcover, M., 150
Alcripe, Philippe d', 123
Aldobrandino da Toscanella, 391
Aldric del Vilar, 235
Alefirenko, N. F., 811
Alekseev, V., 816, 831
Alekseeva, V., 826
Alén Garabato, M. C., 242
Alencar, José de, 343, 344, 345
Aleramo, Sibilla, 467
Aleran, Thomas d', 72
Alessio, G. C., 374
Alet, M., 156
Alexander I (*Tsar of Russia*) 812
Alexander, romances of, 36, 49–51, 77–78, 639, 867
Alexandre de Paris, 50
Alexandre, P., 171
Alexandre, S., 180
Alexandrov, S. A., 836
Alexandrova, Tatiana, 840
Alexis, Paul, 204, 206
Alexius V (*Emperor of Constantinople*), 64
Aleza Izquierdo, M., 263
Alfie, F., 374, 387, 391
Alfieri, Vittorio, 400, 406–09, 411, 422, 428, 430
Alfonso de' Liguori (*Saint*), 400
Alfonso X (*el Sabio, King of Castile and León*), 248, 249, 251, 252, 253, 254, 313
Alfonzetti, B., 448, 859
Alfonzetti, G., 363
Algarotti, Francesco, 400, 404
Algazi, L. G., 184
Aliaga Jiménez, J. L., 259
Alibert, L., 224, 227
Alighieri, Pietro, 369
Alinei, M., 16, 221
Alioth, Gabrielle, 741
Allaire, G., 65
Allam, S., 125
Allan, S., 719
Allard, J., 210, 213
Allatson, P., 326
Allegretti, P., 374
Allende, Isabel, 338, 340
Alleva, Annalisa, 459
Allières, J., 4, 859
Allingham, P., 763
Alloatti Boller, S., 386
Allwood, J., 761
Almafuerte *v.* Palacios
Almansi, G., 470
Alma-Tadema, Lawrence, 701
Almeida, A., 547
Almeida, M. C. F. de, 343
Almeida, Manuel Antônio de, 345
Almquist, K., 165
Alnæs, J., 779
Alnæs, N. S., 776
Alomar Canyelles, A. I., 303
Alonge, R., 466
Alonso, Dámaso, 279, 281, 287
Alonso Marks, E., 247
Alonso Núñez, A. S., 305
Alonso-Ovalle, L., 12
Alonso Pintos, S., 307
Alonso Raya, R., 256
Alonso Seoane, M. J., 276
Alpa, G., 417
Alpatov, V. M., 833
Alpetragus, 368
Alpharts Tod, 590
Alstrup, K., 772
Alt, P.-A., 650
Altenberg, T., 319
Althaus, T., 627, 639, 687
Altinius, R. N., 776
Altmann, B., 80, 82, 85
Altmann, H., 565
Altoviti, Bindo, 389
Altrock, S., 611
Altshuller, A. I., 823
Altshuller, M., 817
Altuna, E., 320
Alvarez, A., 262
Álvarez, R., 859
Álvarez, X. M., 315
Álvarez Barrientos, J., 275
Álvarez Blanco, R., 304, 307, 308, 309, 310
Álvarez Chanca, Diego, 270
Álvarez de la Granja, M., 309
Álvarez de Miranda, P., 255, 276
Álvarez Rodríguez, A., 251
Alvarez Varó, E., 258
Alvaro, Corrado, 452, 465, 467, 483
Alves, J. C. M., 347
Alyn-Stacey, S., 118
Amacker, R., 20
Amadis de Gaule, 103, 150
Amaduzzi, Giovanni Cristofano (*abate*), 412
Amaduzzi, I., 412
Amanshauser, Gerhard, 741
Amăriuţei, Constantin, 507, 5
Amatangelo, S., 478
Amboise, Catherine d', 117
Amboise, François d', 112
Ambroise, 63
Ambrose (*Saint*), 488
Ambrosoli, L., 429
Amelang, J. S., 267
Amelin, Maksim, 841
Amenta, L., 363
Amer, S., 61
Améry, Jean, 549, 705
Amigoni, F., 480
Ammerlaan, T., 225
Ammon, U., 546
Amonoo, R. F., 137
Amoroso, G., 461
Amos, T., 430
Amrein, U., 706
Amtstätter, M. E., 604
Amursky, V., 844
Amyot, Jacques, 98, 103
Anacreon of Theos, 274
Anastas'ev, N., 850
Anbro, S. G., 771
Ancelot, Virginie, 177
Anceschi, G., 491
Anceschi, Luciano, 452
Ancrenat, A., 213
Andersch, Alfred, 747, 751
Andersen, A. M., 775
Andersen, A. T., 770
Andersen, B. I., 778
Andersen, H., 42
Andersen, H. B., 760
Andersen, H. O., 779
Andersen, Hans Christian, 76 765, 766
Andersen, N. M., 755
Andersen, V., 760
Andersen Nexø, Martin, 769
Anderson, A. A., 281, 285
Anderson, M. M., 721
Anderson, P., 453
Anderson, S. C., 735
Andersson, D. C., 116
Andguladze, L., 827
Andrade, A. L. V. de, 347
Andrade, Carlos Drummond 346, 349
Andrade, Mario de, 343
Andrade, Oswald de, 343–44, 347, 349
Andrea da Barberino, 392
Andreae, Johann Valentin, 64
Andreas Capellanus, 231
Andreas-Salomé, Lou, 707
Andreasen, B., 770
Andreev, Leonid, 820, 832, 83
Andreeva, R., 852

ndreoli, A., 430, 431, 432
ndréoli, M., 175
ndreose, A., 388
ndrès, B., 210
ndrés, Juan, 405
ndrès, P., 181
ndresen, K., 697
ndrew, J., 825
ndrian, Leopold von, 700, 704
ndrieux-Reix, N., 56
ndronova, T. I., 851
ndropov, Iurii Vladimirovich, 833
ndroutspoulos, J. K., 567
neau, Barthélemy, 634
ngeli, G., 81, 94, 451
ngelini, F., 411, 414, 473, 859
ngelini, G., 521, 868
nghel, I., 496
nghelescu, M., 507, 510, 512, 516
ngiolieri, Cecco, 387, 391
nglani, B., 407
nglet, A., 644, 706, 712
ngueira, A., 315
njou, Réal d', 215
nkudinov, K., 851
nne de Graville, 70
nnenkoff, Georges, 712
nnenkov, I., 836
nnenkov, P. V., 826
nnensky, I., 832
nnensky, Innokentii Fedorovich, 819, 822, 827
nninsky, Lev, 844
nnolied, 584
nnoni, G. M., 494
nokhina, O., 28
nreiter, P., 519
nsaldi, Innocenzio, 401
nsel, Y., 182, 183
ntenhofer, C., 573
nthony of Padua (*Saint*), 611
ntoine, André, 181
ntoine, R., 218
nton von Pforr, 620
nton Ulrich, Herzog von Braunschweig-Wolfenbüttel, 646
nton, M., 498
ntonelli, A., 386
ntonelli, Luigi, 467
ntonelli, R., 367
ntonelli, S., 426
ntonio Francesco (*Prince of Piombino*), 401
ntrim, N. M., 13
nusiewicz, J., 801
nz, T., 672, 701, 718
Apollinaire, Guillaume (Wilhelm Apollinaris de Kostrowitsky), 456, 700
Apollonius of Tyre, 236
Apothéloz, D., 29
Appel, H.-W., 568
Appelfeld, Aharon, 705
Aprile, M., 360, 362
Aptroot, M., 547
Aquien, M., 220
Aquilecchia, G., 440
Aquin, Hubert, 210
Aragon, Louis, 193
Aragonnès, Jeanne Legendre, madame, 155
Arambasin, N., 859
Arambel-Guinazu, C., 318
Aranci, G., 390
Aranda, F. J., 269
Aranovich, R., 12
Araquistain, Luis, 280
Arato, F., 404
Araujo-Mendieta, O., 341
Arbasino, Alberto, 461, 466
Arbasino, Giovanni, 461
Arbaud, Joseph d', 242
Arbizzoni, G., 861
Arboe, T., 758
Arbogast, H., 688
Arbuthnot, S., 539
Arcamone, M. G., 14
Arcangeli, M., 356
Archibald, E., 43
Arden, H. M., 54, 82
Ardissino, E., 443
Arduini, F., 406
Arduino, Giovanni, 403
Arduino, Pietro, 403
Arêas, V., 349
Arellano, I., 271, 274
Arenas, F., 348
Arend, S., 548
Arendt, Hannah, 465, 666, 705, 836
Arens, K., 714
Argensola, Bartolomé Leonardo de, 274
Argenter, J. A., 522
Argetoianu, C., 517
Arghezi, Tudor, 514, 517
Arguedas, José María, 341
Argüello, 338
Arias Cabal, A., 258
Arias Montano, Benito, 268
Aricescu, Constantin D., 510
Ariosto, Ludovico, 109
Aris, D., 127
Aristotle, 50, 103, 112, 126, 365, 368, 374, 375, 380, 617, 634, 867
Aristov, V. V., 848
Ariza Viguera, M., 249, 250
Ariztondo, J., 258
Arkhangel'skaya, N. N., 856
Arkhipov, I., 849
Arkovich, V. M., 813
Arlt, W., 91
Armas, C., 313
Armas, F. A. de, 271
Armas Wilson, D. de, 273
Armstrong, A., 100, 106
Armstrong, E., 101
Armstrong, M.-S., 203
Armstrong, N., 19, 26
Arn, M.-J., 79, 80, 859
Arnal Purroy, M.-L., 259
Arnaldi, G., 379
Arnaldus de Villanova, 221, 299
Arnall Juan, M. J., 297
Arnaudin, F., 226
Arnaudo, M., 443
Arnauld, Antoine, 158, 164
Arnauld, Jacqueline Angélique Marie de Sainte-Magdeleine, 146
Arnauld d'Andilly, Robert, 133, 158, 159, 164
Arnaut de Carcasses, 232
Arnaut Daniel, 235, 236, 374
Arnaut de Maruelh, 235
Arndal, S., 727
Arndt, K. J. R., 694
Arniches, Carlos, 295
Arnim, Achim von, 650, 651, 655
Arnim, Bettina von, 649, 669, 672, 686
Arnold, Gottfried, 641
Arnold, H. L., 743, 744, 745, 749, 859
Arnold, I., 63
Arnould, J.-C., 113, 150
Arnous, E., 247
Arnoux, E. N. de, 866
Arntzen, E., 775, 776
Aronoff, M., 560
Arpadelle, Arnaud, 77
Arpagaus, N., 523
Arpaia, P., 428
Arrigucci, D. (Jr.), 346
Arrizabalaga, J., 299
Arrous, M., 183
Arsenault, J., 93
Arsenault, S., 210
Arslan, A., 429
Artaud, Antonin, 287
Arteel, I., 748
Artifoni, E., 388
Artigas-Menant, G., 149
Arvers, Félix, 169

Arvieux, Laurent d', 125
Arvigo, T., 479
Arvinte, V., 502, 504
Ascenzo, F. d', 150
Aschenberg, H., 17
Aschieri, E., 442
Ascoli, A., 375
Ashcroft, J., 596
Aske, C. E., 751
Aski, J. M., 9
Askildsen, Kjell, 778
Askins, W., 79
Asmussen, J., 760
Asnès, M., 25
Asoian, A. A., 814
Asor Rosa, A., 461
Asperti, S., 232, 233, 236
Assaf, F., 125
Asselin, Olivar, 210
Assens, M., 221
Assis, Joaquim Maria Machado de, 343, 344, 345, 346
Assoucy, Charles Coipeau d', 147
Assoun, P.-L., 181
Astaf'ev, Victor, 839, 845
Astengo, D., 479
Asturias, Miguel Ángel, 333
At de Mons, 236
Atanasov, P., 506
Atarova, K. N.., 815
Atrocianus, Johannes, 624
Attori, E., 356
Atwood, C., 91
Aub, Max, 289, 290–91
Auberi le Bourgoin, 65
Aubert de Gaspe, Philippe, 210
Aubert, David, 78
Aubert, P., 107
Aubert-Gillet, S., 109
Aubery, Claude, 634
Aubignac, François Hédelin, abbé d', 130, 136, 137, 138, 147–48
Aubigné, Agrippa d', 96, 97, 107–08, 117, 119, 121, 147
Aubigné, Constant d', 107
Aubin, Napoléon, 210
Aucassin et Nicolette, 38, 45, 57, 59
Auchet, M., 776
Auden, W[ystan] H[ugh], 285
Audet, Noël, 210
Audisio, F., 428
Auer, A. P., 828
Auer, P., 550, 567
Auerbach, Berthold, 672, 674
Auger, J., 30
Augieri, C. A., 482
August (*Elector of Saxony*), 638
August the Strong, (*Elector of Saxony, King of Poland*), 638
Augustus I (*Elector of Saxony*), 622
Augustine of Hippo (*Saint*), 81, 84, 101, 112, 127, 130, 133, 137, 152, 157, 158, 167, 271, 301, 368, 397, 399
Augustyn, P., 584
Auhuber, F., 656
Auken, S., 766
Aulnoy, Marie Catherine, comtesse d', 147, 148
Aulotte, R., 127
Aumale, Suzanne d', 147
Aureau, B., 170
Aurell, M., 233
Aurnague, M., 26, 859
Aurnhammer, A., 640, 701, 859
Aust, H., 676, 680, 689, 711
Austin, J. L., 348
Austorc de Galhac, 235
Auteri, L., 637
Automne, Bernard, 112
Auton, Jean d', 106
Auzzas, G., 391
Avenel-Cohen, P., 718, 731
Averroes, 365, 374, 395
Aversano, M., 372
Averton *v.* Belin
Avery, G. C., 719
Avesani, C., 353
Avesnes, Jean d', 74
Aveto, A., 481
Avicenna, 379
Avila Muñoz, A. M., 259
Avilova, L., 822
Avram, A., 496, 499, 506
Avram, L., 500, 501
Avram, M., 498, 499, 501
Avramova, C., 787
Avrămuţ, Horia, 517
Awbery, G. M., 534
Axeitos, X. L., 304
Axel, K., 562
Axelsen, J., 760
Ayala, Francisco, 289, 290
Aymard, R., 225
Ayo, A. A., 290
Ayres-Bennett, W., 22, 869
Ayzanneau, M., 33
Azadovsky, K. M., 848
Azaustre Galiana, A., 269, 274
Aziatsev, D. B., 831
Azorín (J. Martínez Ruiz), 279, 280, 289, 291, 316
Azorín Fernández, D., 259
Azouvi, F., 162
Azparren Giménez, L., 342
Azzam, W., 68
Baardewijk-Rességuier, J. van, 33
Baasner, R., 672
Bab, Julius, 705, 707
Bąba, S., 792
Babbi, A. M., 57, 870
Babchenko, Arkadii, 841
Babel, Isaac, 845
Babenko, N., 552
Babicheva, I. V., 836
Babik, Z., 799, 804
Babrius, 120
Bacaud, F., 716
Baccar, A., 125
Baccarini, E., 488
Bacchelli, Riccardo, 467, 493
Bacchetta, F., 432
Bacci, Marco, 718
Bach, Johann Sebastian, 371
Bach, R., 616
Bachleitner, N., 707
Bachmann, Ingeborg, 733, 737, 741
Bachofen, Johann Jakob, 672
Bächtold, H. U., 631, 633, 635
Backes, M., 598
Backhouse, J., 80
Bäckström, K., 682
Backus, I., 625
Bacon, Anthony, 112
Bacon, Roger, 374
Bacovia, George, 514
Baczyński, Krzysztof Kamil, 79
Bada, V., 218
Bader, M., 562
Badia, L., 236, 237, 298, 300, 860
Badia Margarit, A. M., 302
Badini Confalonieri, L., 443, 47
Baerentzen, P., 561
Baernstein, P. R., 272
Baeskow, H., 560
Baevsky, V. S., 811, 816
Báez de Aguilar González, F., 258
Bagnoli, P., 487
Bagnoli, V., 459
Bahr, E., 703
Bahr, Hermann, 707, 866
Baïf, Jean-Antoine de, 21, 104, 119, 120
Baillie, Joanna, 675
Bailly, J.-C., 191
Bailly, S., 19
Baines, M., 535
Baisch, M., 595
Bajani, A., 464
Baker, D. N., 860
Baker, J. M. (Jr.), 663
Baker, M., 71, 79, 85, 87

Baker, S. R., 149
Bakhrakh, A. V., 843
Bakhtin, Mikhail Mikhailovich, 165, 211, 530, 746, 748, 755, 778, 838
Bakich, O., 856
Bakken, H., 778
Bakker, D., 262
Bakuła, K., 796
Balakin, A. I., 828
Balandina, N. V., 854
Bălan-Mihailovici, A., 498
Balashova, T. V., 840
Balavoine, C., 103
Balbi, Giovanni, 391
Balbiani, L., 644
Balcom, P., 31
Baldacci, L., 486
Balderston, D., 337–38
Baldi, G., 468
Baldi, P., 4
Baldin, A., 814
Baldinger, K., 26, 113, 221
Baldini, Raffaello, 459
Baldovinetti, Antonio, 403
Baldwin, C., 868
Baldzuhn, M., 582, 605, 606
Balestrini, N., 456, 458
Balhar, J., 786
Balina, M., 836
Balle, Solvej, 768, 769
Ballestra-Puech, S., 171
Ballor, A., 69
Ballot, Marcel, 206
Bally, Charles, 20
Bal'mont, Konstantin, 827
Balotă, Nicolae, 513
Balsamo, J., 99, 100, 105, 112, 396, 869
Baltensweiler, T., 696
Baluch, J., 799
Balzac, Honoré de, 96, 169, 174–79, 183, 195, 444, 689
Balzac, Jean-Louis Guez de, 126, 148
Bamberg, Felix, 684
Bammesberger, A., 553, 555, 558
Bancaud, F., 718, 745
Bance, A., 721, 860
Banderier, G., 96, 106, 107, 108, 118, 119, 131, 132, 148
Bandiera, E., 492
Bandini, Angelo Maria, 409
Bandini, Fernando, 467
Bandle, O., 756
Bang, Herman, 763, 767
Bańko, M., 792
Banniard, M., 5, 860
Bannister, M., 150
Bannrasch, B., 710
Banoun, B., 706
Bansa, H., 580
Bănulescu, Ştefan, 508, 509, 514
Banville, Théodore de, 193
Baquero, G., 287
Bär, J. A., 549, 563
Barabash, I. I., 835
Barabash, Iurii, 806
Barabtarlo, G., 860
Barahona de Soto, Luis, 273
Baran, H., 848
Barańczak, S., 789
Baranda Leturio, C., 273
Barandun, P., 523
Baraniwska, O., 802
Baranowski, A.-M., 714
Barański, Z. G., 369, 373
Baratinsky/Boratynsky, E. A., 811–12
Barbagallo, A., 471
Barban, J., 54, 61
Barbarisi, G., 410, 416
Barbarulli, C., 429
Barbeito Carneiro, M. I., 273
Barbély, A., 505
Bárberi Squarotti, G., 446
Barbetta, M. C., 752
Barbey d'Aurevilly, Jules-Amédée, 195, 196, 205
Barbian, J.-P., 704
Barbiellini Amidei, B., 235, 374
Barbier, H.-A., 448
Barbier, J. P., 105
Barbierato, F., 401
Barbierato, P., 521
Barbieri, A., 860
Barbieri, G. L., 459
Barbieri, G. M., 236
Barbieri, Giovanni M., 85
Barbieri, Giuseppe, 447
Barbieri, L., 235
Barbieri, T., 428
Barbina, A., 483
Barbolani, C., 406
Barbosa, A., 348
Barbosa, P., 11
Barbu, Eugen, 508
Barbuto, A., 441
Bardell, M., 231
Bardykova, N. V., 813, 819
Barenghi, M., 460, 469, 470
Barga, Corpus, 445
Bargalló Escrivá, M., 257
Bargues Rollins, Y., 203
Barignano, Pietro, 398
Barile, Angelo, 479
Barilli, A., 493
Bárkányi, Z., 247
Barlach, Ernst, 707
Barlera, P., 443
Barletti, Carlo, 402–03
Barlyng, M., 770
Barnaby, P., 428
Barner, W., 637
Barnes, J. C., 436
Baroja, Pío, 280, 289, 291
Baron, A.-M., 178
Baron, L., 725
Baroni, G., 452, 456, 485
Baronius, Cesare, 121
Barra Jover, M., 252
Barral (*vicomte de Marseille*), 392
Barral, Carlos, 337
Barre, A., 59
Barreto, A. A., 260
Barroero, L., 401
Barron, W. R. J., 232, 302
Barsi, M., 122
Barsotti, A., 473
Barsotti, F., 425
Barsukova, O. M., 830
Barth, K., 663
Barthel, E., 545
Barthes, Roland, 39, 179, 200, 203
Bartholomew of Bydgoszcz, 798
Bartl, G., 699
Bartmiński, J., 789
Bartnaes, M., 697
Bartnicka, B., 792
Bartoldus, T., 614
Bartoli, Daniello, 477
Bartolomeo di Iacovo di Valmontone, 384
Bartolomeo Zorzi, 235
Bartolozzi, G., 368
Bartolucci, L., 392
Bartošek, J., 786
Bartoszewicz, I., 547
Bartsch, E., 681
Bartsch, K., 715
Bary, René, 138
Barz, I., 559, 560
Barzantny, T., 719
Basara, J., 792
Bascelli, M. S., 357
Bascetti, E., 357
Bascialli, F., 406
Basco, Virginia, 432
Bascuas López, E., 309
Basile, B., 370
Basilio, K., 202
Basinsky, P., 834
Basnage de Beauval, Henri, 160
Bassani, A., 403
Bassani, Giorgio, 456, 468, 867
Bassel, N., 840
Bassi, A., 424
Bassler, H., 549

Bassler, M., 734
Bassola, P., 561
Bassompierre, François de, 148
Bastert, B., 588
Bastiaensen, M., 859
Bastress-Dukehart, E., 626
Batiushkov, Konstantin Nikolaevich, 807, 811
Batov, V. I., 856
Batt, C., 69
Battafarano, I. M., 642, 643, 644, 645, 682
Battaglia, G., 475
Battaglia Ricci, L., 369, 376
Battignani, M., 412
Battistini, A., 370, 410, 482, 494
Batushkov, F. D., 831
Baude Fastoul, 58
Baudelaire, Charles, 189, 190, 191–93, 204, 205, 206, 280, 286, 421, 457, 697, 701, 745, 773
Baudoin, Jean, 129, 148
Baudouin de Sebourc, 65
Bauer, B., 621, 626, 637, 641
Bauer, Felice, 716
Bauer, K., 678, 712
Bauer, M., 692
Bauer, R., 519, 520, 523, 701
Bauer, S., 674
Bauer, W. M., 860
Bauer-Roesch, S., 645
Baufeld, C., 617
Baum, Oskar, 704
Baum, Vicki, 707, 741
Baumann, A., 644
Baumann, Hans, 642
Baumann, K., 565
Baumann, S., 557
Baumann-Koch, A., 625
Baumgartner, E., 50, 60, 64, 92, 860
Baumgartner, K., 662
Baur, B., 779
Baur, R. S., 547
Bausch, K.-H., 571
Bauschke, R., 603
Bausen, M., 633
Baussan, 235
Bautista, A., 286
Bauvois, C., 19
Bay, H., 658
Bayer, Konrad, 731, 742
Bayerdörfer, H.-P., 671, 704
Bayle, Pierre, 157, 158, 160, 161
Bayley, P., 147
Bazalgues, G., 223, 227
Bazhenov, A., 817
Bazhenova, A., 852
Bazlen, R., 479
Bazzocchi, M. A., 436, 441, 457, 471, 494
Beardsley, Aubrey, 200
Beardsmore, B., 78
Beauchamp, V. W., 272
Beaudet, M.-A., 211
Beaugrand, Honoré, 211
Beaulieu, É., 197
Beaulieu, J.-P., 101, 111. 117, 860
Beaulieu, L., 31
Beaulieu, Victor-Lévy, 211
Beaumarchais, Pierre Augustin Caron de, 412
Beaune, C., 74
Beausoleil, Claude, 211
Beauvoir, Simone de, 765
Bec, P., 226
Beccari, Antonio, 399
Beccaria, Cesare, 400, 404
Beccaria, G. L., 236, 444, 456
Beceiro, C., 288
Becher, Johannes R., 642, 704, 707
Becher, P., 703
Beck, G., 590
Beck, Marco, 468
Beck, W., 583
Becke, A., 693
Becker, C., 202
Becker, Jurek, 742, 744
Becker, P., 834
Becker, S., 679, 703, 730
Becker-Ho, A., 33
Beckett, Samuel, 185, 341, 371, 456, 708, 709, 840
Bécquer, Gustavo Adolpho, 285
Beda, A. M., 836
Beddow, M., 721
Bede (*the Venerable*), 271
Bedia, M. M., 292
Bedon, E., 487
Beeching, K., 19, 33
Beekman, K., 680
Beer, J., 82
Beer, Johann, 641
Beer, M., 427
Beer-Hofmann, Richard, 700, 704, 707
Beerbohm, Max, 200
Begemann, C., 671, 691, 695, 860
Beggiato, F., 235, 237, 860
Begichev, D., 806
Béhar, R., 682
Beheim, Michael, 609
Behler, E., 691
Behne, M., 658
Behr, H.-J., 583
Behring, E., 513
Beigel, F., 280
Bein, T., 580, 582, 603, 860
Beise, A., 646, 749, 753
Bek, A., 855
Bek, T., 842, 844, 853, 855
Bekker-Nielsen, H., 762
Bel, B., 361
Bel, J., 727, 731, 743
Bel Bravo, M. A., 272
Bela, Z., 802
Belei, S. L. P., 343
Beliaev, A., 836
Beliaev, S., 828
Beliakov, S., 852, 854
Beliakova, S. M., 856
Belin, C., 157
Belin, Jean François de Faudoas *dit* 'l'Averton', comte de, 127
Belinsky, Vissarion Grigorievich, 811
Bell, D. F., 178
Bell, S., 82
Bell, T., 633
Belleau, Rémy, 104, 115, 116, 118
Bellei, R., 426
Bellemin-Noël, J., 189, 199
Bellenger, Y., 115, 117
Belletti, A., 11
Bellezza, Dario, 468
Belli, Giuseppe Gioachino, 427
Bellina, A. L., 416
Bellini, G., 338
Bellini, Vincenzo, 424
Bellio, A., 422, 437, 485
Bellmann, G., 561, 564, 570
Bellmann, W., 742
Bellomo, S., 370
Bellon-Méguelle, H., 61
Bellosi, Giuseppe, 459
Bellucci, N., 429, 436, 868
Bellver, C. G., 283
Belobrovtseva, I., 856
Belodubrovsky, E. B., 843
Belokurova, A., 809
Belon, Pierre, 122
Beloshchin, A. M., 812, 814
Belosselski, Alexander (*prince*), 409
Belousov, A. F., 817
Belov, S. V., 816, 824
Belpoliti, M., 488
Bel'skaya, L. L., 806
Belski Crespi, F., 426
Beltrami, P. G., 234, 352, 456
Belyi, Andrei, 725, 832, 839, 8[illegible]
Bem, A. L., 838, 843
Bemberg, María Luisa, 339
Bénabou, M., 469
Benatti, S., 429

enavente, J., 292
enay, J., 737
encard, M., 766
ender, W. F., 862
ender, W. J. A., 689
endi, C., 418
endick, C., 612
endjaballah, S., 868
endtsen, B., 757
ene, Carmelo, 466–67
enech de Cantenac, Jean, 127
enedeit, 55
enedetti, C., 451, 464
enedetti, Mario, 341
enedetti Stow, S., 395
enedetto, G., 404, 411
enedict (*Saint*), 584, 613
enedini, L., 480
enedix, Roderich, 670
eneš, J., 641
enfiglio, T. P., 705
enhamou, N., 206
enini Sforza, L., 459
eniscelli, A., 411
eniston, J., 714, 728
enitez, M., 149
enjamin, A., 707
enjamin, Benjamin (Bardd Coch), 534
enjamin, Walter, 165, 192, 653, 658, 699, 702, 703, 704, 707–08, 709, 714, 729
enkov, E., 81, 84
enn, Gottfried, 549, 684, 708, 743
enne, C., 679, 706
ennett, B. J., 714
ennett, P. E., 596
ennewitz, I., 578, 593, 597, 603, 606, 860
enoist, Élie, 160
enoît de Sainte-Maure, 48, 62, 64, 69, 72, 391
enoit, E., 193
enoit, M.-S., 720, 745
entivogli, B., 387
entivoglio d'Aragona, Cornelio (*cardinal*), 406, 409
entley, D., 363
ento, M., 33
entzinger, R., 555, 675
enucci, E., 389, 440, 441
enucci, F., 12
enussi, C., 452
enveniste, É., 20
envenuti, G., 438, 475
envenuto da Imola, 369, 382, 488
envenuto, A., 433
envenuto, B., 447
Benvoglienti, Uberto, 415
Benzecry, C. E., 338
Benzi, E., 416
Bepler, J., 638
Berard, E., 838
Berardinelli, A., 461, 472
Berbig, R., 680
Berchet, Giovanni, 427
Berchthold, S. M., 523
Berdiaev, N. A., 820
Berdikova, T. V., 848
Berejan, S., 497
Berend, N., 547
Berentelg, W., 718
Berestov, Valentin, 840
Berezhnaya, I., 838
Berezovchuk, L., 842
Berg, C., 199
Bergel, H., 736
Berger, E[berhard], 713
Berger, E[lfriede], 713
Berger, G., 145, 156
Berger, T., 785
Bergermayer, A., 789
Berggolts, O., 844
Berghahn, D., 736, 860
Berghahn, K. L., 733
Berghausen, B., 620
Bergmann, G., 571
Bergmann, R., 559
Bergounioux, G., 7
Bergson, Henri, 492
Bergvall, Å., 101
Berhorst, R., 663
Bering, D., 552, 691
Berkovsky, N. I., 824
Berlan, F., 143
Berlau, Ruth, 709, 710
Berlin, J. F., 728
Berman, N., 714
Berman, R. A., 701, 716
Bermbach, U., 697
Bermel, N., 784
Bermúdez, S., 315, 319
Bermúdez, T., 313, 317
Bernanos, Georges, 194
Bernard, C., 177
Bernard, Catherine, 145
Bernard, Harry, 211
Bernard-Griffiths, S., 186
Bernárdez, C. L., 314
Bernardino da Siena, 390, 391
Bernardus Silvestris, 399
Bernáth, Á., 691
Bernauer, M., 708
Bernd, C. A., 673
Bernd, Z., 349
Bernhard, Thomas, 735, 737, 739, 740, 742, 750, 779
Bernhardi, Karl, 550
Bernhardt, R., 674
Bernhart, W., 860
Berns, J. J., 643
Berns, J., 758
Berns, T., 97, 113
Béroalde de Verville, François, 120, 122, 148
Béroul, 597
Berréby, G., 436
Berregard, S., 134
Berroth, D., 569
Berruto, G., 4
Bersani, C., 436
Berschin, W., 542, 862
Berseneva, Olga, 842
Bershtadt, A., 849
Bersuire, Pierre, 73
Bertacchini, R., 431
Bertaux, Félix, 720
Bertelli, I., 427, 452
Bertelli, S., 373
Bertelsmeier-Kierst, C., 582
Bertheau, J., 722
Berthelot, A., 45, 46
Berthiaume, P., 149
Berthier, P., 174, 176, 183, 184, 199
Berthold von Holle, 601
Berthold von Regensburg, 612
Bertinetto, P. M., 10, 354, 361
Bertini, S., 478
Bertola, Aurelio de' Giorgi, 409
Bertolani, C., 397
Bertoldo, R., 473, 476, 483, 487
Bertoletti, N., 388
Bertolucci, A., 423
Bertolucci, Attilio, 456
Bertolucci-Pizzorusso, V., 74
Bertone, G., 466
Bertoni, A., 450, 475
Bertoni, C., 428
Bertran de Born, 398
Bertran Carbonel, 231
Bertrand, Aloysius, 196
Bertrand, D., 99, 111, 115, 134, 151
Bertrand, J.-P., 199
Bertrand, L., 212
Bertrand, R., 228, 243
Bérulle, Pierre de (*cardinal*), 157, 159
Besançon, A., 836
Besch, W., 564
Besedina, T. A., 829
Besozzi di Castelbarco, Margherita, 432
Bessat, H., 230
Besse, M., 520
Bessette, Gérard, 212
Bessing, Joachim, 734

Bessire, F., 149, 189
Besslich, B., 699, 723
Besson, Diego, 270
Best, K.-H., 565
Bestuzhev-Marlinsky, Alexander Alexandrovich, 808
Bétemps, I., 90
Béthemont, J., 244
Betocchi, Carlo, 457, 468
Bettarini, R., 390
Bettella, P., 421
Betten, A., 549, 557, 563
Betti, M. P., 231
Bettinelli, Saverio, 405, 409, 418
Bettini, M., 15
Bettinzoli, A., 486
Bettoni, A., 106
Beugnot, B., 148
Beurrier, Paul (*Fr.*), 167
Beutin, W., 580, 671
Beutler, B., 860
Beutner, E., 860
Beuve de Hantone, 51, 63, 528
Beuys, Joseph, 745
Bevan, G. A., 525
Beverley, J., 337
Beverley Smith, J., 529
Beverley Smith, L., 529
Bevilacqua, Alberto, 366, 464
Bevilacqua, G., 493
Beyer, K., 549
Beyer, M., 702
Beyer, Marcel, 733, 743
Beyersdorf, H., 745
Beyle *v.* Stendhal
Beyrau, D., 836
Beyssade, C., 864
Beyssade, J.-M., 162
Bèze, Théodore de, 98, 108
Bezzel, I., 633
Bezzini, L., 429
Bézzola, G., 443
Biagini, E., 412, 479
Białek, E., 863
Bialik, B., 839
Białoskórska, M., 800
Biamonti, Alberto, 455
Biamonti, Francesco, 466
Biancardi, G., 417
Bianchi, A., 482
Bianchi, Augusto Guido, 446
Bianchi, F., 231
Bianchi, M. L., 622
Bianchi, N., 373
Bianchini, Francesco, 409
Bianchini, Giuseppe, 404
Bianco, M., 398
Biasi, P.-M. de, 197
Biasin, Gian-Paolo, 424
Biasutti, F., 410
Bibescu, Martha, 514, 517
Bibikova, I. M., 836
Bible moralisée, 76
Bibliander, Theodor, 556
Bichel, I., 683
Bichel, U., 683
Bidault (*Maître*), 196
Bideaux, M., 124
Bidian, V., 506
Bidu-Vrănceanu, A., 504
Bieder, M., 283
Biendarra, A. S., 747
Bienek, Horst, 753
Bieńkowska, D., 798
Bierbach, C., 258
Bierwiaczonek, B., 801
Bierwirth, S., 686
Biet, C., 129, 137, 138
Biglione di Viarigi, L. A., 446
Bignamini, M., 459
Bigongiari, Piero, 468
Bigot, J.-Y., 224
Bikov, Dmitri, 841
Bilenchi, Romano, 461, 464
Bilinkis, M. I., 813, 826, 829
Billanovich, G., 384
Billard de Courgenay, Claude, 127
Billaut, A., 103
Billiote, D., 865
Billone, A., 192
Billotte, D., 92
Billy, D., 235
Billy, P.-H., 221, 225, 227, 230
Bilous, D., 193
Bímová, P., 782
Binazzi, N., 361
Binchois, Gilles, 606
Binder, Georg, 623
Binet, Léon, 492
Binetti, V., 482
Bini, D., 424
Biniewicz, J., 799
Binni, Walter, 453
Binns, N., 337
Biondi, M., 406, 463, 475, 481, 485
Bioy Casares, Adolfo, 339
Birberick, A. L., 134, 869
Birch, D., 205
Birch-Pfeiffer, Charlotte, 670
Birgfeld, J., 746
Birken, Sigmund von, 641
Birkhan, H., 576
Birkhan, I., 860
Bîrleanu, I.-H., 506
Biron, M., 199
Birus, H., 691
Biscardi, L., 412, 430
Bischoff, J.-L., 166
Biser, E., 690
Bishop, M., 860
Bishop, P., 721
Bismarck, Otto, Prinz von, 551, 710
Biterolf und Dietleib, 590
Bito, H., 573
Bitov, Andrei, 834, 843, 844, 845–46
Bitsilli, Peter, 843
Bivort, O., 195
Bizer, M., 109, 241
Bjaï, D., 116
Bjelke, Henrik, 763
Bjerke, André, 778
Bjerke, V., 778
Bjerregaard, L., 760
Björkman, S., 239, 243
Bjørndal, I., 777
Bjørneboe, T., 778
Bjørnson, Bjørnstjerne, 775
Bjørnstad, H., 165
Bjørnvig, Thorkild, 771
Bjorvand, A. M., 776
Blaaberg, C., 763
Blacatz, 234
Black, P., 39
Blaga, Lucian, 513
Blagasova, G. M., 846
Blagova, G. F., 842
Blair, A., 100
Blair, H., 651
Blais, Marie-Claire, 213
Blake, R., 251
Blamires, A., 53
Blanc, P., 396, 861
Blanche, Émile, 190
Blanche, Esprit, 189
Blanche-Benveniste, C., 19, 32
Blanchet, P., 228, 229, 242
Blanco, C., 316
Blanco-Amor, Eduardo, 313
Blanco Garcia, P., 243
Blanco Martínez, R., 277
Blankenhorn, R., 868
Blannbekin, Agnes, 610
Blänsdorf, J., 631
Blas Arroyo, J. L., 264
Blasberg, C., 704, 732, 733
Blaschitz, G., 608
Blasco Ferrer, E., 363
Blass, Ernst, 704, 711
Blasucci, L., 377, 378, 411, 422, 437, 439, 440, 479
Blau, H., 708
Blayer, I. M. F., 337
Blažek, V., 787
Bléchet, F., 131
Bleck, R., 604
Blecua, A., 269

Blei, Franz, 699
Blendstrup, Jens, 763
Bleses, D., 758
Blicher, Steen Steensen, 765, 769
Bligger von Steinach, 588
Blioumi, A., 735
Blium, A. V., 836
Blix, Elias, 775
Blixen, Karen (Isak Dinesen), 765, 769
Bloch, Albert, 726
Bloch, B., 732
Bloch, Ernst, 708, 738
Bloch, O., 140
Bloh, U. von, 591, 602
Blok, Alexander Alexandrovich, 819, 822, 827, 832, 839
Blokh, M., 831
Blom, B., 761
Blood, S., 190, 192
Bloom, Harold, 198, 284, 657
Bloom, M. E., 203
Bloy, Léon, 196, 204, 210
Blühdorn, A., 736
Bluhm, L., 718
Blum, L., 653
Blum-Cuny, P., 121
Blume, H., 557
Blumenberg, Hans, 657, 679
Blumenfeld-Kosinski, R., 71, 78, 82, 860, 870
Blumenthal, P., 26, 34
Blumesberger, S., 667
Blumreich, K., 44
Bo, Carlo, 452
Bø, G., 775
Boa, E., 709, 716
Boaglio, M., 443
Boaistuau, Pierre, 99, 101, 110
Boal, Augusto, 347
Boario, A., 357
Boatto, A., 410
Bobinac, M., 689
Bobrov, A., 855
Bobrowski, I., 791
Bobrowski, Johannes, 742
Bobryk, R., 809
Boca, L.-N., 65
Boccaccio, Giovanni, 36, 82, 86, 302, 352, 372, 392–96, 431, 618, 865
Boccioni, Umberto, 451, 458
Boch, J., 158
Bocharov, S. G., 811, 816, 838
Bochkov, V. N., 816
Bock, H. M., 699
Bocquet (*les demoiselles*), 155
Bodel, Jean, 58, 60, 62, 68
Bodenmann, R., 635
Bodenstein von Karlstadt, Andreas, 630
Bodin, Jean, 97, 104, 123
Bodini, V., 460
Bodon (Boudou), Joan (Jean), 237, 238
Boe, H. J., 759
Boenig, R., 91
Boethius, Anicius Manlius Torquatus Severinus, 73, 82, 91, 92, 302, 386, 584–85, 608
Bogaev, Oleg, 842
Bogdanov, A., 831
Bogdanov, S. I., 839
Bogdanow, F., 47
Böger, A., 694
Bøggild, J., 767
Boggione, V., 442, 456, 475, 860
Bogner, R. G., 719
Bogomolov, N. A., 807, 820, 821, 846, 851
Bogrov, Grigory, 820
Bogurodzica, 798–99
Bogusławski, A., 792
Böhl von Faber, Cecilia, 667
Böhl von Faber, Johann Nikolas, 652
Böhlau, Helene, 708
Böhler, M., 860
Böhling, F., 641
Bohm, Hark, 735
Böhm, R., 606
Böhme, Jakob, 622
Böhme, W., 752
Böhmer, R., 604
Bohn, W., 282
Bohnen, K., 724
Boikov, V. V., 830
Boileau-Despréaux, Nicolas, 132, 148, 158
Boine, Giovanni, 464, 468
Boisgontier, J., 226
Boissard, Jean-Jacques, 101
Boitani, P., 232, 236, 297, 365, 380, 860
Boitano, J. F., 166
Boito, Arrigo, 422, 427–28
Boito, Camillo, 422, 428
Boivin, J.-M., 114
Bok, V., 616
Bok-Bennema, R., 501, 864
Bokdam, S., 122
Boland, M., 54
Bold, S. C., 165
Boldensele, Guillaume de, 74
Boldori de Baldussi, R., 337
Boldov, L., 809
Boldt, B., 730
Bolduc, M., 45
Bolívar, A., 261
Böll, Heinrich, 642, 742
Bøll, J. L., 758
Boll, K., 748
Böll, V., 742
Bollard de Broce, K., 271
Bollinger, A., 690
Bologna, C., 367
Bol'shakov, Konstantin, 831, 840, 847
Bol'shakova, A., 809, 826, 840, 847
Bolster, R., 184
Bolterauer, A., 748
Bolzoni, L., 390
Bombal, María Luisa, 338
Bombosch, R., 410
Bomers, J., 640
Bompaire-Evesque, C., 204
Bompiani, Ginevra, 451, 465, 480
Bonacchi Gazzarrini, G., 476
Bonaccorsi, E., 455
Bonagiunta da Lucca, 386
Bonanni, Laudomia, 423
Bonaparte, Joseph (*King of Naples, then of Spain*), 416
Bonaventura (*pseudonym*), 651
Bonaviri, Giuseppe, 465
Bonavita, R., 438, 441
Bond, Z., 247
Bondarchuk, E. M., 810
Bondarenko, M., 854
Bondarenko, V., 841, 844
Bonenfant, L., 196
Bonet, E., 10
Bonghi, Ruggero, 421, 422
Bonhomme, M., 19
Boni, Deo, 389
Bonicatti, M., 378
Bonichi, Bindo, 391
Boniface VIII (*Pope*), 377
Bonifacino, G., 474
Bonifazi, N., 450
Bonin, M., 31
Bonino, G. D., 466
Bonitz, A., 730
Bonjour, F., 159
Bonn, K., 731, 742
Bonnaud, L., 229
Bonnaud, P., 230
Bonnefoy, Y., 192, 194, 436
Bonnel, Emilo, 240
Bonner, A., 298
Bonnet, C., 241
Bonnet, G., 199
Bonnier, X., 118
Bonnifet, P., 396
Bonora, E., 490
Bonstetten, Albrecht von, 623
Bontempelli, Massimo, 468, 483

Boogaart, J., 89
Booth, W., 114
Bopp, Raul, 347
Boratynsky *v.* Baratynsky
Borchardt, Rudolf, 684, 699, 708, 711
Borchmeyer, D., 647
Borcilă, M., 496
Bordas, E., 174, 175, 184
Bordei-Boca, R., 510
Bordelon, Laurent, 147
Borderie, R., 177
Bordessoule, N., 69
Bordier, J.-P., 66, 137
Bordin, M., 459
Bordiugov, G., 833, 862
Borejszo, M., 792
Borenstein, W., 291
Boretti, E., 446
Borev, I., 808
Borgard, T., 726
Borgen, J., 763, 772
Borges, Jorge Luis, 318, 327, 339, 452, 470, 478, 488
Borges Morán, P., 272
Borgese, Giuseppe Antonio, 422, 468
Borghello, G., 409
Borghi Cedrini, L., 236
Borin, A., 839
Bormann, A. von, 647
Born, A., 769
Born, Nicolas, 742
Bornand, M., 868
Börne, Ludwig, 669, 671, 685
Borneto, C. S., 565
Borodin, Leonid, 841, 844
Borovikov, S., 854
Borrego, J., 246
Borrell, A., 31
Borrelli, C., 475
Borsa, P., 386
Borsellino, N., 440, 450. 465, 483, 484, 860
Borshchagovsky, A., 832
Borsje, J., 538, 539, 541
Bortnowski, Stanisław, 794
Bortolini, U., 359
Borza, E., 626
Böschenstein, R., 722
Boschi Rotiroti, M., 373
Bosco, G., 131
Bosco, Henri, 245
Bose, M., 85
Bosley, V., 167
Bosquet, M.-F., 410
Bosse, A., 860
Bossé-Andrieu, J., 32
Bossong, G., 258
Bossuet, Jacques Bénigne, 148–49, 157, 161
Bossy, M.-A., 88
Bost, H., 160
Bot, I., 510, 511
Bothorel-Witz, A., 569
Botl, M.-L., 746
Bots, W. J. A., 97, 113
Botta, A., 469
Bottée de Toulmon, 91
Bottenberg, J., 714
Botti, F. P., 439
Botticelli, Sandro, 395
Bouchage *v.* Joyeuse
Bouchard, N., 474
Boucher, J., 97
Bouchet, Jean, 116
Bouchilloux, H., 167
Boucicaut, Jean le Meingre, maréchal de, 93
Boudou *v. also* Bodon
Boudou, B., 101
Bouhélier, Saint-Georges de (Stéphane-Georges Lepelletier de Bouhélier), 191
Bouhours, Dominique, 125
Bouillon, R., 697
Bouillon-Mateos, C., 176
Bouix, D.-L., 24
Boulanger, J.-C., 14
Boullón Agrelo, A. I., 305, 761, 865
Boulton, J. D'A., 81
Boulton, M., 75, 82
Bouquet, S., 20
Bour, I., 169
Bourdieu, Pierre, 197, 318, 760
Bourdin, Nicolas, 162
Bourdoise, Adrien, 159
Bourgain, P., 232
Bourges, Élémir, 190
Bourget, Paul, 200, 725
Bouriau, C., 162
Bourin, M., 14
Bourke, C., 538
Bourke, E., 680
Bourre, J.-P., 194. 202
Boursault, Edmé, 130
Bousch, D., 729
Boussart, M., 710
Bousy, Pierre de, 106
Boutan, P., 7
Boutcher, W., 112
Bouterwek, Friedrich, 651
Boutier, M.-G., 23
Boutin, A., 170, 171
Bouvet, D., 33
Bouvier, J.-C., 7, 30, 223, 228, 229, 243, 244, 861
Bouvier, L., 170
Bouwsma, W. J., 96
Bouzada, X. M., 311
Bovari, C., 229
Bovelles, Charles de, 117
Bowen, B., 122
Bowen, D. J., 531
Bowman, F., 180
Bowman, P. J., 679
Bowsher, K., 340
Boyde, P., 365
Boyer, Abel, 27
Boyer, H., 312
Boyer, R., 776
Boyhus, E.-M., 766
Boysonné, Jean de, 115
Boysset, Bertran, 299
Bozza, M., 642
Bozzolo, C., 81
Braasch-Schwesmann, U., 574
Brabant, R., 144
Brabcová, R., 782
Brabois, O. de, 199
Bracchi, C., 403, 861
Brachart, Charlotte de, 161
Brachet, J.-P., 16
Bracken, P., 57, 236
Brackert, H., 596
Brady, M., 716
Braese, S., 734
Braga, M., 425
Bragança Júnior, A. A., 580
Brahms, Johannes, 691
Braider, C., 142
Bralczyk, J., 794
Brall-Tuchel, H., 586
Branca, V., 392, 393, 407, 440, 452
Brancale, D., 471
Brancaleoni, F., 428
Brancati, Vitaliano, 465, 467
Brâncuş, G., 496
Brand, P., 861
Brandão, R. S., 349
Brandão, T., 347
Brandellero, S., 346
Brandenberger, T., 82
Brandes, Georg, 723
Brandes, H., 683
Brandes, W., 751
Brandín Feijoo, C., 311
Brandis, T., 580
Brändle, F., 635
Brändle, R., 720
Brandsma, F., 43
Brandstetter, G., 697, 700
Brandt, G., 552
Brandt, P. A., 763
Brandt, W., 556, 862
Branscombe, P., 689
Brant, Sebastian, 582, 619, 870

Brantôme, Pierre de, 97
Braselmann, P., 546
Bratvogel, F., 681
Braudel, Fernand, 337
Braun, A., 557, 862
Braun, C. von, 679
Braun, Henryk, 799
Braun, M., 743, 747
Braun, P., 655
Braun, Volker, 739, 743
Braune, Rudolf, 708
Braune, W., 554
Braungart, W., 712
Braunšteinová, Z., 784
Braunwarth, P. M., 707
Bravo, D., 261, 262
Bravo, J., 287
Bray, B., 152
Braybrook, J., 120
Bréal, M., 7
Breatnach, C., 541
Breatnach, M., 204, 697
Breatnach, P. A., 540
Brecht, Bertolt, 347, 456, 642, 685, 699, 708–10, 725, 729, 749
Brecht, M., 641
Bredel, U., 561
Breeze, A., 530
Breger, C., 727
Breitenbach, Josef, 702
Breithaupt, F., 658
Brekke, Paal, 778
Brekke, Toril, 778
Bremer, T., 683
Brémond, Henri, 433
Brendel-Perpina, I., 686
Brenner, M., 547
Brenner, P. J., 687
Brentano, Clemens, 650, 651, 652, 655
Bresciani, Caterina, 414
Breton, André, 451
Bretonnayau, René, 99
Breuer, D., 642, 643, 645
Breuer, U., 734
Breul-Kunkel, W., 636
Brewer, C., 665
Breyl, J., 644
Breza, E., 796, 804
Brezhnev, Leonid, 833, 839
Bricchi, M., 477
Brick, N., 29
Briçonnet, Guillaume, 111
Bridge, H., 738
Bridgeman, T., 198
Briegleb, K., 685
Briese, O., 672, 683
Brigato, S., 361
Brigit (*Saint*), 541
Brin, F., 180
Brin, Irene, 465
Brineman, K. H., 788
Brink, M., 82
Brinker-Von der Heyde, C., 596, 608, 609
Brinkmann, Rolf Dieter, 743
Brinson, C., 728
Brioschi, F., 411
Briot, F., 153
Brisset, Jean-Pierre, 204
Britnell, J., 106
Britting, Georg, 710
Brittnacher, H. R., 666, 715
Britton, C., 216, 219
Briusov, Valerii Iakovlevich, 822, 839
Brival, Roland, 216
Brix, M., 174, 189, 192
Brizuela, Mateo de, 267
Brizzi, Enrico, 462
Broce, M., 260
Broch, Hermann, 702, 704, 706
Brochu, A., 215
Brockmann, S., 752
Brod, Max, 704, 710
Brodersen, R., 759
Brodsky, Joseph, 806, 818, 828, 831, 832, 839, 843, 844, 846
Brody, J., 112, 133
Broeders, A. P. A., 557
Brøgger, Suzanne, 769
Broicher, U., 685
Broitman, S. N., 815
Brombert, V., 490
Bronikowska, R., 792
Bronskaya, L. I., 836
Brontë, Charlotte, 678
Brook, C., 479
Brook, L. C., 53, 65, 68
Brooke, A., 529
Brooks, C. N., 657
Brooks, J., 861
Brooks, T., 630
Brooks, W., 142
Broomhall, S., 99
Brors, C., 662
Brossard, Nicole, 209, 210
Brossette, Claude, 148
Brostrøm, T., 767
Brousson, Claude, 160
Brown, C., 87
Brown, E. A., 106
Brown, H., 652
Brown, K., 7, 234
Brown, M. L., 81
Brown-Grant, R., 82, 86, 92
Brownlee, K., 81, 88, 90, 870
Bruce, I., 716
Bruchhold, U., 615
Brucker, C., 72, 83
Brückner, Christine, 753
Bruckner, Ferdinand, 704
Bruckner, M., 68
Bruckner, M. T., 58
Brugè, L., 12
Brüggen, E., 585, 597
Brugnoli, G., 376, 387, 442
Brugnolo, F., 352, 386, 389, 481
Bruguera, J., 300
Brumme, J., 249, 255
Brumo, J., 779
Brun-Trigaud, G., 7
Brundbjerg, E., 769
Brunel, J., 119, 120
Brunel, P., 176, 195
Brunelleschi, Betto, 395
Brunet, F., 31
Brunet, M., 208
Brunetti, G., 386
Brunetto Latini, 57, 70, 382, 389
Brunfels, Otto, 625
Bruni, A., 406, 411
Bruni, F., 300, 351, 406, 484
Brunner, H., 599, 603, 604, 606
Brunngraber, Rudolf, 706
Bruno, F., 432
Bruno, Giordano, 440
Brunori, F., 442
Brüns, E., 684
Brunschwig, J., 161
Bruscambille, Deslauriers, *dit*, 138
Brusegan, R., 61
Brussig, Thomas, 743, 748
Bruy, C., 538
Bruzzone, B., 544, 545
Bruzzoni, G. L., 446
Bryant-Quinn, M. P., 536
Brydone, Patrick, 403
Brynhildsvoll, K., 776
Brzović, K., 740
Brzozowska, D., 801
Bub, S., 710, 744
Bubenheimer, U., 630
Buber, Martin, 705
Bubis, Ignatz, 752
Bubnov, A., 811
Bucer, Martin, 630
Büch, K. B., 753
Buchanan, George, 112, 118
Buchedd Dewi, 526
Buchenau, B., 338
Bucher, A.-L., 143
Buchi, E., 503
Büchner, Georg, 668, 670, 674, 689, 743, 753
Buciumeanu, D., 509
Buck, T. J., 699, 721, 743, 747
Budai-Deleanu, Ion, 510

Budde, B., 681
Budé, Guillaume, 102
Buditskaya, T. G., 846
Budylin, I., 814, 816
Buesa Oliver, T., 258
Buffa, F., 802
Buffalmacco, Buonamico, 390
Buffaria, P.-C., 407, 433, 434
Buffon, Georges Louis Leclerc, comte de, 436
Bugaj, A., 794
Bugajski, M., 794
Bugarín, M. X., 861
Bugenhagen, Johannes, 631
Bugge, D., 770
Buglione, S., 490
Bühler, P., 712
Bui, V., 176
Buiatti, M., 454
Bulgakov, Mikhail Afanasievich, 826, 832, 833, 837, 846
Bulgakov, V. F., 826
Bulgarin, Faddei Venediktovich, 808, 812, 818
Bulitta, B., 555
Bull, M., 233
Bullen, J. B., 205
Bullinger, Heinrich, 631, 635
Bullivant, K., 735
Bulychev, I. I., 830
Bunin, Ivan A., 846
Bunners, C., 694
Bunsen, Christian Carl Joias von, 672, 673
Buñuel, Luis, 282, 286, 410
Bunzel, W., 672
Buonarroti, Michaelangelo, 769
Burani, C., 358
Burban, C., 311
Burch, T., 581
Burchiello, (*il*), (Domenico di Giovanni), 391
Burckhardt, Jakob, 668, 674
Burckhardt, L., 674
Burdina, S. V., 845
Burger, Hermann, 737
Bürger, P., 281
Burgess, G. S., 55, 62, 232, 302,
Burgmüller, Norbert, 682
Burgos, Carmen de, 283
Burima, M., 776
Burkhardt, A., 545, 556, 686, 865
Burkhardt, H., 802
Burl, A., 95
Burlacu, A., 513
Burley, Walter, 374
Burliuk, David Davidovich, 835
Burmistrov, K., 644
Burns, E. J., 40, 58
Burns, J., 465
Burns, Robert, 758
Buron, E., 113
Burr, K. L., 52
Burrell, M., 232, 302
Burrini, G., 493
Burrow, J. A., 36
Burrows, D., 73
Burry, D. B., 567
Burt, E. S., 192
Burt, R. L., 737
Burton, R. D. E., 190
Burvikova, N. D., 813
Bury, E., 148, 163
Busby, K., 36, 51
Busch, A., 548
Busch, Wilhelm, 674–75
Büsching, Johann Gustav Gottlieb, 686
Buschinger, D., 42, 47, 82, 587, 598, 861
Busse, D., 552
Busse, U., 546
Bustamante Zamudio, G., 341
Bustos Gisbert, E., 249
Bustos Tovar, F., 255
Bustos Tovar, J. J. de, 252
Busuioceanu, Alexandru, 513
Butakova, L. O., 821
Butcher, J., 479
Butin, G. W., 770
Butinyà, J., 301
Butler, D., 341
Butler, J., 578
Butler, Judith, 200
Butor, Michel, 203
Buttazzi, G., 402
Butterfield, A., 57
Butterworth, E., 861
Büttner, W., 680
Buvet, P.-A., 26
Buvick, P., 199
Buzura, A., 516
Buzzati, Dino, 466, 468–69
Bychkov, I. A., 822
Bykov, D., 812, 824, 827, 829, 843, 846
Bykov, V., 807
Byres, James, 402
Byron, George Gordon, Lord, 426, 427, 430, 818

Caball, M., 540
Cabañas, P., 293
Cabanès, J.-L., 202
Cabirol-Lacan, B., 199
Cabré, L., 297, 301
Cabré, M., 296, 297, 860
Caccia, E., 415
Cacciaglia, N., 376, 443
Cacciapuoti, F., 432, 436, 441
Cacciari, C., 357
Cachey, T. (Jr.), 378
Cacho Blecua, J. M., 301
Cacho Millet, G., 471, 478
Cadalso, José, 277
Cadioli, A., 423, 451, 462
Cadiot, P., 25
Caduff, I., 523
Caemmerer, C., 645, 734
Caesar, A., 423
Caesar, M., 370
Caffiero, M., 401
Cagnat-Deboeuf, C., 160
Cahm, E., 204
Caillebotte, Gustave, 202
Caira Lumetti, R., 416
Cairo, R., 400
Cała, A., 802
Calabria, N., 436
Calabrò, Corrado, 457, 469
Calamai, S., 353, 360, 361
Calamel, S., 225
Caldari Bevilacqua, F., 106
Calenda, C., 370
Calepino, A., 26
Calero *v.* Carballo Calero
Calero Fernández, M. A., 257
Caliaro, I., 431
Calin, W., 92, 237–38
Călinescu, George, 514
Călinescu, M., 515
Callahan, C., 45, 58
Callahan, L. A., 81
Callejón Callejón, L., 666
Callot, Jacques, 655, 656
Calobrezi, E. T., 349
Caloprese, Gregorio, 405
Calven, Victor von, 622
Calvente, T. J., 268
Calvesi, M., 451
Calvet, A., 231
Calvin, Jean, 97, 100, 110, 634, 638
Calvino, Italo, 451, 455, 456, 462, 463, 466, 469–71, 488
Calvo, Fabio, 109
Calzavara, E., 459
Camacho, J. L., 338
Camaldo, A., 445
Câmara, Isabel, 347
Camara Bastos, M. H., 269
Cambiès, D., 242
Camerarius, Joachim, 624, 626, 631
Camerini, Eugenio, 425
Camerino, G. A., 407
Camerlengo, Marietta, 431
Camilleri, Andrea, 463, 465, 47

Caminer Turra, Elisabetta, 409
Caminha, Pero Vaz de, 345
Camões, Luís de, 396
Camois, Camel de, 88
Campa, C., 405
Campailla, S., 861
Campana, Dino, 456, 471
Campanella, Tommaso, 476
Campangne, H., 107, 115, 118
Campano of Novara, 368
Campbell, I., 426
Campbell, J., 866
Campe, Joachim Heinrich, 652
Campe, R., 662
Campion, Henri de, 147
Campistron, Jean-Galbert de, 138
Campo, Cristina, 465, 471
Campo, R., 115, 118
Campo, Rossana, 463
Campos, H., 246
Campos, Haraldo de, 346
Campos, V., 322
Camprós (Camproux), Carles, 239
Camprubi, M., 29
Camps, A., 471
Camps, J., 870
Camuffo, P., 478
Camus, Albert, 693, 765
Camus, Jean-Pierre, 127, 145, 146, 149
Canaparo, C., 318, 338
Canaye, Philippe, 634
Cancarini Petroboni, M., 429
Cândea, V., 509, 510
Candel, D., 27
Candela, E., 428
Cândido, A., 343
Canetti, Elias, 706, 710, 737
Canetti, Veza, 710
Canettiere, P., 234, 237
Cani-Wanegfflen, I., 172
Cañizares Bundorf, N., 294
Cannon, C., 869
Cano, Melchor, 634
Cano, Thomé, 270
Cano Aguilar, R., 253
Canonici, C., 401
Canova, Antonio, 402, 425
Canova, G., 470
Canova-Green, M. C., 129, 141
Canovas, F., 870
Cant de la Sibil.la, 303
Cantagrel, L., 170
Cantarella, G. M., 381
Cantarutti, G., 412
Cantavenera, E., 436
Cantemir, Antioche, 510
Cantemir, Dimitrie, 509–10
Cantigas de Santa María, 313
Cantù, Cesare, 422
Canty-Quinlan, S., 348
Capati, M., 450
Capellani, Albert, 181
Capelli, F., 417
Capitani, O., 374
Capito, Wolfgang, 625
Capo, L., 384
Capoferri, F., 446
Caporossi, C., 493
Capovilla, G., 445
Cappeau, P., 10
Cappelli, G., 268
Cappi, D., 384
Capra, C., 418
Capriolo, Paola, 463
Caproni, Giorgio, 445, 454, 456, 457, 471–72, 475
Capuana, Luigi, 422, 423, 428
Capusso, M. G., 236
Caputo, F., 433
Carabin, D., 120, 153
Caraffi, P., 81, 82
Caragiale, Ion Luca, 503, 504, 507, 508, 510, 511, 513, 514
Caragiale, Mateiu, 514
Caraion, Ion, 513
Carapezza, F., 235
Caratozzolo, V., 468
Caratù, P., 362
Carballo Calero, Ricardo, 314–15
Carbognin, F., 494
Carbone, A., 428
Carbonell, Pere Miquel, 302
Carbonero Cano, P., 246
Carbotte, Marcel, 214
Carburi, Marco, 403
Cardano, Girolamo, 104
Cardarelli, Vincenzo, 457, 472, 493
Cardinaletti, A., 12, 354
Cardini, R., 476
Cardon, Jacquet, 94
Cardona, R., 286
Cardoso, Lúcio, 343
Cardoso, W., 30
Carducci, Giosuè, 426, 428–29
Carducci, Michele, 429
Cardwell, R. A., 280
Cardy, M., 208
Carena, C., 444
Careri, M., 232
Carey, J., 538, 539, 541
Carini, E., 435, 441
Carla, V., 223
Carlebach, E., 622
Carli, A., 447
Carlin, C. L., 146
Carlino, M., 465
Carlsen, I., 757
Carlson, M., 66
Carlston, E. G., 204
Carlyle, Thomas, 426
Carmarthen, Black Book of, 526
Carmignani, Giovanni, 406
Carnazzi, G., 410, 411
Câmeci, M., 515
Carnero, G., 278
Carnero, Guillermo, 284, 285
Carnero, R., 473, 491
Carniani Malvezzi, Teresa, 416, 426
Caron, Louis, 208,
Caron, P., 22, 211
Caron, R., 862
Caron, V., 215
Carosella, M., 363
Carp, U., 744
Carpenter, S., 182
Carpenter, V., 321, 330
Carpentier, Alejo, 217, 327, 333, 426
Carpi, U., 434, 453, 454
Carrà, Carlo, 472
Carrà, M., 472
Carrai, S., 434
Carranza de Miranda, Bartolo, 266
Carrasco, I. M., 340
Carré, A., 298
Carré, M., 727
Carrer, Luigi, 429
Carrera, A., 491
Carreras Artau, J., 296
Carreras Artau, T., 296
Carreri, Raffaele, 460, 472
Carricaburo, N., 258
Carrier, Roch, 211
Carrizo, S., 345
Carroll, B., 81
Carroll, C., 70
Carron, J.-C., 115
Carruthers, M., 300
Cartagena, Antonio de, 270
Cartmill, C., 155
Carton, J.-P., 39
Cartwright, J., 528
Carugati, G., 375–76
Carvalho, L. F. M. de, 348
Casado, M., 864
Casado, P., 223, 228
Casado Velarde, M., 246, 257, 258
Casagrande, B., 452
Casagrande, G., 377
Casangiu, L., 514
Casanova, Giacomo Girolamo, 185, 409–10

Casanòva, Joan-Ives, 241
Casanovas Catalá, M., 257
Casaretto, A.-D., 720
Casas, A., 314
Casas Rigall, J., 269
Casati Stampa, Luisa, 432
Casaubon, Isaac, 98
Cascardi, A. J., 273
Casciani, S., 861
Casella, P., 483
Casellato, S., 403
Caselli, C., 359
Casgrain, Henri-Raymond, 208
Casini, P., 455
Casoli, G., 431, 438
Caspari, M., 648, 745, 749
Casprini, M., 417
Cassano, M., 423
Cassata, L., 388
Cassell, A., 368
Cassigoli, Renzo, 481
Cassiodorus, 271
Cassola, Carlo, 464
Castagne, E., 10
Castagnola, R., 431, 432
Castaldi, M., 464
Castaldini, A., 383
Castan, Felix, 240
Castañega, Martín de, 270
Castaño, J., 303
Castarède, J., 148
Castein, H., 861
Castel, Jean, 86
Castelao *v.* Rodríguez Castelao
Castellana, R., 453, 492
Castellani, A., 352
Castellani Pollidori, O., 356
Castellanos, Rosario, 334
Castellino, M. E., 340
Casti, Giambattista, 410, 426
Castiglione, Giuseppe, 429
Castillo, D., 327
Castillo Gómez, A., 266, 269, 273
Castoldi, M., 445
Castonguay Bélanger, J., 117
Castrillo González, C., 266
Castro, A., 339
Castro, J. E. de, 337
Castro, Rosalía de, 315
Castro-Klaren, S., 341
Castronuovo, A., 471, 488
Casu, P., 363
Catalá Torres, N., 257
Catalano, E., 433
Cataldi, P., 479
Catanzaro, G., 422
Cátedra, P. M., 267, 270
Cathen (*Saint*), 527
Catherine de Bourbon, duchesse de Bar, 126–27
Catherine de Medici (*Queen of France*), 96
Catherine of Siena (*Saint*), 391
Cattafi, Bartolo, 460, 472
Cattaneo, Carlo, 429
Cattaneo, M., 401
Catullus, 485
Cauhapé, A., 222
Caurres, Jean des, 122
Caussat, P., 20
Cavaillé, J.-P., 160
Cavalca, Domenico, 391, 394
Cavalcanti, Guido, 365, 366, 367, 377, 387, 394, 395, 396, 397
Cavalho, Bernardo, 344
Cavallini, G., 378, 393, 433, 437, 442, 476
Cavallotti, Felice, 429
Cavaluzzi, R., 433
Cavaluzzo, R., 433
Cavarra, A., 417
Cavazzoni, Ermanno, 461
Cavazzuti, S., 428
Cave, T., 112
Cavicchioli, Luigi, 467
Caxton, William, 298
Caylus, Anne Claude de Tubières, comte de, 134
Cayre, Henri, 240
Cazaban, T., 513
Cazauran, N., 110, 861
Cazenave, M., 179
Cazes, H., 101, 119
Cazotte, Jacques, 188, 404
Ceballos, Jerónimo de, 269
Ceballos, R., 339
Cecchetti, D., 115
Cecchi, Emilio, 453, 480, 493
Cecchini, E., 372
Cecconi, E., 390
Čechová, M., 781
Cecovini, M., 452
Cedrola, M., 465
Celan, Paul, 515, 685, 743, 744
Celati, Gianni, 461, 463, 470, 472
Celato, C., 353
Céline (Louis-Ferdinand Destouches), 198
Celtis, Conrad, 631
Cenarbe, Ramón Ximénez de, 405
Cenati, G., 474
Cennamo, M., 362
Cenni, A., 485
Cent nouvelles nouvelles, 78–79
Cepl-Kaufmann, G., 704, 863
Cepollaro, Biagio, 457
Ceporin, Jacob, 623
Ceppi, M., 425
Cepraga, D. O., 235
Ceragioli, F., 436, 440
Cerboni Baiardi, G., 861
Cercamon, 235
Cercignani, F., 656
Cerfontaine, R., 689
Cerisola, P. L., 446
Čermák, F., 781
Cernovodeanu, P., 510
Cernuda, Luis, 281, 284–85
Cerquiglini, B., 20
Cerquiglini-Toulet, J., 70, 81, 86, 91, 861, 868
Cerro Malagón, R. del, 294
Cerruti, M., 407
Cervantes Saavedra, Miguel de, 150, 156, 266, 271, 273, 276, 280, 343, 443, 460, 467, 473, 594
Cerverí de Girona, 234, 237, 297, 298
Cesa, C., 653
Césaire, Aimé, 216, 217–18
Césaire, Ina, 218
Cesaretti, E., 423, 438
Cesaro, G., 438
Cesarotti, Melchiorre, 404, 410–11, 422
Ceserani, R., 462
Cessolis, Jacobus de, 382
Cetrangolo, Enzio, 485
Ceuppens, J., 751
Ceva, L., 450, 455
Cevasco, G. A., 200
Cézanne, Paul, 202
Chabert, G., 204
Chabrant, C., 225
Chacel, Rosa, 289, 290
Chachikov, Alexander, 831
Chachulska, B., 791
Challe, Robert, 147, 149
Chamarat-Malandain, G., 861
Chambers, H., 694, 695
Chambon, J.-P., 14, 30, 222, 223, 228, 230
Chamisso, Adalbert von, 650
Chamoiseau, Patrick, 216, 218, 220
Chamorro, M. I., 265
Champagne, R. A., 197
Champigny, S., 171
Champlain, Samuel de, 126
Champollion, Jean-François, 179, 864
Champourcin, Ernestina, 283
Chancé, D., 216
Chance, J., 82

Chandler, K., 530
Chanet, J.-F., 243
Chanet, Pierre, 128
Chang, S.-H., 547
Chanson d'Antioche, 40
Chanson de Guillaume, 39
Chanson de Roland, 36–37, 38–39, 69, 591
Chanson de la Sainte-Foy, 236
Chantal, Jeanne Françoise de (*Saint*), 158
Chaouche, S., 138
Chapelain, Jean, 126, 132, 137
Chaperon, D., 203
Chaplain, E., 225
Char, René, 192
Charbon, R., 673
Charbonneau, F., 146, 154
Charcot, Jean-Martin, 190
Chareyron, N., 81
Charles V (*Emperor*), 105, 553
Charles V (*King of France*), 82, 86
Charles VI (*King of France*), 88
Charles VII (*King of France*), 85
Charles III (*King of Spain*), 275
Charles IV (*King of Spain*), 275, 276
Charles le Noble (*King of Navarre*), 86
Charles le Téméraire (*Duke of Burgundy*), 89, 187
Charles of Aragon (*Prince of Viana*), 297
Charles d'Orléans, 43, 57, 79–80, 859, 868
Charles de Valois, 71
Charles, Prince of Wales, 839
Charlotte Elisabeth de Bavière, princesse Palatine, 129, 153
Charon, A., 131
Charpentier, F., 110
Charpentier, Georges, 199
Charron, F., 212
Charron, Pierre, 127
Chartier, Alain, 67, 71, 82, 102
Chartier, D., 207
Chartier, R., 267, 669
Chase, C., 862
Chase, J., 669
Chase, S.-E., 709
Chastelain, George, 73
Chastelain de Coucy, 72
Chastelaine de Vergi, 70
Chateaubriand, François-René de, 170, 175
Chatelain, J.-M., 128
Châtellier, H., 711
Chaubet, D., 72
Chaucer, Geoffrey, 36, 67, 69, 84, 92
Chaurette, Normand, 209
Chauveau, François, 133
Chauveau, J.-P., 135
Chebotaresvskaya, A., 825
Checa Puerta, J. E., 295
Chédozeau, B., 159
Cheesman, T., 736
Chegodaeva, M., 834
Chekhov, Anton Pavlovich, 819, 820, 822–23, 829, 842
Chen, Ying, 208, 209
Chenet-Faugeras, F., 171
Cheney, L., 82
Cheney, P., 271
Chepelev, V., 852
Cheplygina, I. N., 850
Cherbuliez, J., 151
Cherchi, P., 88, 102, 391
Cherednikova, M. P., 831
Chernenko, K., 833
Chernets, L., 809
Cherniaeva, E., 844
Chernigovsky, D. N., 815
Chernoritskaya, O., 837
Chernyshevsky, Nikolai Gavrilovich, 827
Cherubim, D., 550, 862, 865
Chesneaux, J., 201
Chestov, Léon, 515
Cheung, C.-Y., 690
Chevalerie Vivien, 39
Chevalier du Papegau, 68
Chevalier, A., 861
Chevallier, C., 181
Chevallier, R., 114
Chevassus-Marchioni, V., 727
Chevrolet, T., 109
Chiappini, L., 349
Chiara, F., 487
Chiarelli, Luigi, 467
Chiari, Pietro, 403, 404, 411
Chiarini, Giuseppe, 429
Chiarini, P., 648
Chiavacci Leonardi, A. M., 364–65, 369
Chichibabin, Boris, 843, 846
Chichikov, Pavel Ivanovich, 812
Chicote, Enrique, 295
Chiellino, C., 466
Childeric II, 74
Chinard-Rater, Ildephonse, 401
Chinca, M., 596
Chinnov, Igor, 843
Chiodo, C., 415, 472
Chirico, G., 493
Chirio, J., 229
Chitoran, I., 499
Chiummo, C., 484
Chivu, G., 497, 498, 503
Chłopicki, W., 803
Chodorowska-Pilch, M., 261
Choi, J., 263
Choisy, François Timoléon, abbé de, 129, 147
Cholakian, R., 80, 234
Cholewka, N., 29
Choluj, B., 661
Chomarat, J., 161
Chomsky, Noam, 5, 20, 543, 560
Choné, P., 127, 128
Chong, J.-S., 744
Choquette, L., 211
Choquette, Robert, 211
Chrapowicki, Adam, 799
Chrétien de Troyes, 35, 36, 37, 40, 41–43, 45, 47, 50, 51, 52, 68, 69, 84, 396, 864
Christen, Ada, 668
Christen, H., 567, 569
Christensen, Inger, 764, 767, 770, 773
Christensen, M. V., 760
Christensen, P., 774
Christians, I., 690
Christiansen, H., 197
Christine de Pizan, 67, 69, 70, 80–87, 89, 92, 865, 866
Christophersen, C., 666
Chubukov, V. V., 815
Chudakova, M. O., 820, 832, 851
Chukovskaya, L., 840
Chukovsky, Kornei, 840, 841
Chulkova, N., 827
Chupasheva, O. M., 819
Ciaia, Ignazio, 442
Cian, V., 408
Ciani, I., 446
Ciarlantini, P., 441
Cicala, R., 429, 486
Ciccarelli, A., 421
Ciccia, C., 366
Ciccuto, M., 377, 489
Cicero, Marcus Tullius, 116, 123, 126, 301, 382, 633
Cicha, K., 796
Cicognara, Leopoldo, 425
Cidrás Escáneo, F., 308
Cierbide, R., 221
Ciesielska, E., 802
Cieślikowa, A., 790
Cifarelli, P., 104, 120
Cifoletti, G., 121
Cifuentes Comamala, L., 299
Cigada, S., 522
Cigliana, S., 448, 451
Cigni, F., 236
Cima, C., 520
Cimini, M., 425, 431, 861
Cimpoi, M., 513

Cinciała, Andrzej, 799
Cincinnius, Johannes, 631–32
Cingolani, S., 301
Cini, M., 361
Cino da Pistoia, 395, 399
Cinque, G., 868
Cinque, P., 405
Cinquina Pari, A., 493
Cintra, L. F. Lindley, 306
Ciobanu, A., 497
Ciobanu, V., 500
Ciobanu-Tofan, A., 513
Ciocârlie, L., 516
Ciolac, M., 505
Ciopraga, C., 517
Cioran, Emil, 482, 510, 515
Ciorănescu, A., 502
Cipollone, A., 386
Ciprés Palacín, M. A., 243
Cipriani, A., 412
Cipriani, S., 489
Cisek, Oskar Walter, 735
Cislagh, G., 415
Citro, E., 475
Cixous, Hélène, 662, 753
Cladel, Léon, 196
Claesges, U., 691
Clahsen, H., 358
Clamages, Nicolas de, 81
Clamor, A., 198
Claricio, Girolamo, 393
Clarín (Leopoldo Alas), 294, 678
Clark, R. L. A., 44, 61
Clark-Evans, C., 82
Clas, A., 27, 28
Classen, A., 579, 587, 600, 620, 627, 861
Clauberg, Johann, 556
Claudius, Hermann, 683
Claudon, F., 176
Clausen, T. B., 758
Clement V (*Pope*), 378
Clement XII (*Pope*), 418
Clemente, P., 441, 448
Clerici, Fabrizio, 472
Clerici, L., 480
Cloulas, I., 96
Cloutier, C., 213
Clowes, E., 851
Clyne, M., 547
Čmejrková, S., 782, 785
Cobben, P., 655
Cobeña, Carmen, 294
Cobley, E., 724
Cobos Fajardo, A., 297
Cocea, Sofia, 508
Cocteau, Jean, 144, 700
Coda, E., 447, 490
Code, D. J., 194
Codebò, M., 463
Codignola, Tristano, 455
Codoñer Merino, C., 266
Coen, P., 402
Cofano, Domenico, 371
Coffa da Noto, Marianna, 429
Cogitore, I., 861
Coglievina, L., 370
Cogman, P. M. W., 200
Cogman, P., 186, 195
Cogoi, G., 421
Cohen, H., 144
Cojocaru, D., 803
Col, Pierre, 87
Colaiacomo, P., 460
Colangelo, S., 494
Colard, J.-M., 102
Colasanti, A., 475
Colbert, Jean-Baptiste, 126, 137
Coldiron, A. E. B., 79
Coleman, J., 90
Coligny, Gaspard de Coligny, *dit* l'amiral de, 121
Colin, J.-P., 21, 24
Colin, M., 423
Colinas, A., 283
Colines, Simon de, 101
Collet, A., 76
Collett, Camilla, 775
Collette, C., 92
Collier, John, 769
Collina, S., 358
Collini, P., 656
Collins, M. S., 280
Cölln, J., 600
Collodi, Carlo (C. Lorenzini), 429
Collomp, D., 65
Collot, M., 169
Collura, M., 488
Colombani, F. C., 78
Colomba-Timelli, M.,73
Colombi, Marchesa (M. A. Torriani), 429–30
Colombo, A., 411
Colombo, L., 358
Colombo, V., 407, 408
Colón, G., 296
Colón Doménech, G., 248, 254, 255
Colonna, A. F., 482
Colonna, Giovanni, 398
Coloşenco, M., 514, 517
Coltun, G., 502
Coluccia, R., 363, 385
Colummi Camerino, M., 444
Colussi, D., 439
Colvin, S., 667
Combarieu du Grès, M. de, 65
Combes, A., 46
Comellas Aguirrezábal, M., 293
Comenius (Jan Amos Komenski), 638, 799
Cometa, M., 656
Comi, Girolamo, 459
Comisso, Giovanni, 472
Commynes, Philippe de, 82
Compagna Perrone Capano, A. M., 297
Compagni, Dino, 384, 395, 396
Compagnon, A., 218
Compagnoni, Giuseppe, 411, 422, 430
Company, C., 253
Company, R., 697
Compère, D., 179, 201
Comte, Auguste, 204
Conan, Laure, 211
Conconi, B., 97
Conde, Alfredo, 315
Conde, Carmen, 283
Condé, Louis II, prince de (Le Grand Condé), 161
Condé, Maryse, 216, 217, 218–19, 861
Condorcet, Marie Jean Antoine Nicolas de Caritat, marquis de, 288
Conihout, I. de, 100
Conley, T., 94, 97, 99, 113
Connochie-Bourgne, C., 60
Connon, D., 861
Conocchia, S., 435
Conrad, Joseph, 280, 469, 470, 475
Conrad, N. A., 772
Conreni, J. J., 5
Conrieri, D., 448
Conroy, D., 157
Consarelli, B., 159
Consbruch, B. von, 724
Consolo, Vincenzo, 465, 472
Constantin-Weyer, Maurice, 20
Constantine, D., 709, 716
Constantinescu-Podocea, M., 513, 517
Conta, Vasile, 515
Contarini, S., 419, 467
Conte, A., 390
Conte, Giuseppe, 456
Conter, C. D., 747
Conti, A., 426
Conti, Angelo, 425
Conti, Antonio, 406
Conti, E., 493
Conti, Guido, 463
Conti, Primo, 478
Contini, A., 464
Contini, Gianfranco, 453, 479
Contò, A., 457
Contorbia, F., 423

Contreni, J. J., 861
Contreras, Gonzalo, 340
Convenevole da Prato, 397
Cook, R. F., 65, 686
Cooke, P., 203
Coombes, R. I., 776
Cooper, R., 104, 111, 112
Copernicus, Nicolaus, 438
Coppée, Denys, 138
Coppel, G., 410
Coppini, R. P., 426
Corà, B., 483
Corazzini, Sergio, 457
Corbea, A., 680
Corbea-Hoisie, A., 750
Corbellari, A., 52, 60
Corbière, Tristan, 193
Corbineau-Hoffman, A., 713
Corcheş, V., 508
Cordati, B., 445
Cordelli, Franco, 461, 472
Cordero, J., 270
Cordibella, G., 494
Cordie, A. M., 637
Cordin, P., 355, 357
Corella *v.* Roís de Corella
Coretti, M., 452
Corilla Olimpica (Maria Maddalena Morelli), 411–12
Corleto, Manuel, 328
Corlito, G., 453
Cormeau, C., 604
Cormier, J., 149
Cormier, M. C., 14, 27, 28
Cornea, A., 501
Corneille, Pierre, 126, 129, 130, 136, 137, 138–40, 144, 147, 195
Corneille, Thomas, 140
Cornelissen, G., 571
Cornford, B., 85
Corngold, S., 716, 717, 718
Cornilescu, A., 500
Cornillat, F., 117
Cornu, J., 255
Cornu, J.-M., 170
Cornwell, N., 817
Corominas, J., 255
Corradini, Enrico, 455
Correa Ramón, A., 319
Correia, M. de C., 346
Corsinovi, G., 455
Cort d'amor, 231
Cortázar, Julio, 327, 332, 340
Cortelazzo, M., 360, 388
Cortella, R., 481
Cortellessa, A., 452, 486, 489, 491, 494
Corti, M., 367, 432, 452, 470, 472
Cortijo Ocaña, A., 3
Cortijo, A., 313
Corum, R. T. (Jr.), 132
Corver, N., 501
Cosaşu, R., 516
Coşbuc, George, 507
Coscia, F., 405
Coşeriu, E., 8, 496
Cospito, G., 420
Cossard, C., 40
Cossío, José María de, 287
Costa, D., 112
Costa, G., 419, 479
Costa, Giacomo, 425
Costa, J., 11
Costa, O. R., 319
Costa, S., 406
Costabile-Heming, C. A., 747, 751
Costantini, A. M., 366, 393
Costa-Zalessow, N., 416, 426
Costas González, X. H., 307
Costentin, C., 149
Côté, J.-F., 207
Cotelnic, T., 500
Cotolendi, Ignace, 161
Cotrone, R., 434
Cotruş, Aron, 514
Cottenet-Hage, M., 218, 861
Cotticella, F., 405
Cottignoli, A., 444
Cottonaro, A., 443
Cottone, M., 640
Cottret, B., 160
Courbet, Gustave, 202
Courcelles, D. de, 861
Courcy, N., 208
Courouau, J.-F., 236, 241
Courtès, N., 136
Courtilz de Sandras, Gatien de, 130, 145, 149
Coutier, M., 29
Coutinho, Sonia, 348
Couturier-Heinrich, C., 664
Couzinet, M.-D., 97, 104, 123
Covacich, M., 464
Covarrubias y Leiva, Diego de, 266
Coveney, A., 26
Coward, D., 37
Cowling, D., 73
Cox, F., 180
Coxon, S., 595
Coye, Jean-Baptiste, 242
Cozic, A., 743
Cracco, G., 384
Crăciun, V., 516
Craffonara, L., 519, 521
Craig, H. E., 331
Crăineceanu, I., 500
Cramer, Daniel, 625
Cramer, J., 755
Cramer, T., 579, 602, 603
Cramer Vos, M., 39
Crane, S., 71, 72
Craşoveanu, D., 500
Cravens, T. D., 8, 249
Cré, M., 93
Creangă, Ion, 504, 511, 513
Creasman, A. F., 629
Cremaschi, Inìsero, 472
Cremona, J. A., 3, 7, 17
Crenne, Hélisenne de, 103, 123
Crépon, M., 690
Crépu, M., 188
Crescenzo, R., 96
Crespet, Pierre, 117
Crespi, Luigi, 401
Crespo, R., 59
Cresti, D., 867
Creţan, R., 503
Creţu, N., 512
Crini, G., 471
Crinò, R., 363
Crippa, S., 183
Criscione Stuparich, G., 452
Crise, S., 490
Crispin, J., 281, 289
Crispino, F., 481
Crist, L. S., 65
Cristaldi, S., 364, 437
Cristea, D., 502
Cristea, T., 501
Cristobalina Moreno, M., 252–53
Cristofolini, C., 453
Crivelli, T., 404
Croatto, E., 520
Croce, Benedetto, 450, 452, 453, 455, 468, 486
Croenen, G., 89
Croese, M., 371
Croisille, C., 186, 187
Croizy-Naquet, C., 48, 51, 63, 74
Cromdal, J., 759
Cronk, N., 133
Cropp, G. M., 29, 73, 82, 83
Cropper, C. L., 174
Cròs, E., 240
Crossley, C., 187
Crosta, S., 217
Crotti, I., 472, 484
Crovi, A., 493
Crovi, Raffaele, 371
Crow, D., 706
Crowther-Heyek, K., 629
Cruciger, Elisabeth, 627
Crudeli, Tommaso, 418
Cruz, A., 271, 273

Cubleşan, C., 510, 511
Cucchi, Maurizio, 460
Cuccioletta, D., 207
Cucinotta, C., 430
Cuénin-Lieber, M., 139
Cuetos, F., 247
Culianu, Ioan Petru, 507, 511, 513, 515
Culicea, G., 508
Cullhed, A., 651
Cullière, A., 126
Cultrera, G., 425
Cunha, Euclides da, 344, 349
Cuniţă, A., 501
Cunningham, D. S., 825
Cunqueiro, Álvaro, 313, 315
Cuoco, Vincenzo, 412, 430
Cuppone, R., 414
Cura Curà, G., 382
Curcetti, A., 488
Curcó, C., 261
Cureau de la Chambre, Marin, 128
Curi, F., 438, 458
Curran, J. V., 862
Curreli, M., 426
Curros Enríquez, Manuel, 306, 315, 319
Curschmann, M., 608
Curti, E., 377
Curtius, A. D., 218
Curtius, Ernst Robert, 577
Curto, Francesco, 472
Cusson, M., 214
Cynog (*Saint*), 527
Cyra, K., 794
Cyrano de Bergerac, Savinien de Cyrano, *dit*, 132, 149–50, 159
Czapla, R. G., 642, 730
Czarnecka, K., 792, 794
Czarnecki, T., 552
Czesak, A., 796

Dąbrowska, A., 801, 802
Daça, Benito, 270
D'Achille, P., 356
Dacier, Anne, 130
D'Afflitto, C., 446
Dafydd y Coed, 527
Dafydd Epynt, 527
Dafydd ap Gwilym, 530
Dafydd, Ifor ap, 535
Dafydd ab Ieuan ab Einion, 529
Dafydd Llwyd ap Dafydd, 529
Dafydd Nanmor, 529
D'Agostini, M. E., 655
D'Agostino, M., 356
Dahlerup, P., 766
Dahlke, B., 701
Dahmen, L., 45
Dahn, Felix, 675, 710
Dainat, H., 711
Dal, Vladimir Ivanovich, 827
Dalbera-Stefanaggi, M.-J., 361
Dalberg, V., 761
Dal Bianco, S., 494
Dalcher, P., 569
D'Alessandrio, F., 485
D'Alessio, C., 478, 480
Dali, Salvador, 286
Dali, S[hen], 177
Dalisson, R., 188
Dall'Aglio, M., 361
Dall'Aglio, W., 383
Dal Negro, S., 357
Dalpé, Jean Marc, 209
Damborský, J., 803
Damiani, C., 445
Damiani, R., 440, 465
D'Amico, S., 117
Damien, R., 164
Damm, Sigrid, 738
Dandelet, T. J., 265
Dandrey, P., 142
Daneš, F., 783, 785
Dangeau, L., 21
Dangel-Pelloquin, E., 663, 714
Daniel, Iurii, 846
Daniel, R. I., 527
Danielczyk, J., 689
Daniele, A., 387, 481
Danieli, N., 490
Dănilă, E., 501
Danil'chenko-Danilevskaya, V., 825
Danilevsky, Nikolai Iakovlevich, 825
Daniliuc, L., 495
Daniliuc, R., 495
Danin, Daniil, 852
Danna, B., 432
Danneberg, L., 650, 861
Danner, R., 133
D'Annunzio, Gabriele, 422, 430–32, 460, 475, 655, 716
Dantas, V., 343
Dante Alighieri, 36, 42, 43, 86, 236, 364–80, 385, 386, 387, 389, 393, 395, 396, 397, 398, 406, 411, 426, 443, 444, 467, 469, 476, 488, 489, 492, 745, 862, 867
Danzi, L., 411
Danzi, M., 407
Da Ponte, Lorenzo, 412
Da Pozzo, G., 414, 434
D'Aquino, A., 430
Darasz, W. J., 800, 801
D'Arco Avalle, S., 454
Dardano, M., 352
Dardel, R. de, 11
Daret, Pierre, 128
Darío, Rubén, 279, 318, 319, 335–36
Darmon, J.-C., 159
D'Arrigo, Stefano, 465
Darwin, Charles, 669
D'Arzo, Silvio, 473
Dascălu-Jinga, L., 499
Dash, M., 219
Data, K., 802
Datcu, I., 507
Däubler, Theodor, 701
Daude de Pradas, 232
Daudet, Alphonse, 196, 245
Daudin, Jean, 85
Daunais, I., 197
Daussy, H., 121
Dauvois, N., 117
Davatz, S., 572
Da Veiga, M., 652
Davenport, W. A., 67
Daviau, D. G., 707, 728
Davico Bonino, G., 414, 415, 466
Davidsen-Nielsen, N., 755
Davidson, A., 744
Davidson, P., 827
Davidson, S., 115
Davidson, William, 292
Davies, C., 730
Davies, M. P., 670
Davies, P., 81, 85, 702, 707, 736
Davies, S., 532
Davin, Félix, 174, 175
Davis, R., 840
Davydov, D., 844
Davydov, Iurii, 847
Davydova, T., 809, 810
Davydova, T. T., 833, 847, 852, 854, 857
Dawidowski, C., 691
Dawson, A., 30
Day, P. L., 191
Dayan, P., 205
Dayre, É., 169
Daza Pinciano, Bernardino, 271
Deacon, P., 277
De Amicis, Anna, 406
De Amicis, Edmondo, 432
De Angelis, Salvatore, 425
De Angelis, Vincenzo, 473
De Angelis, Vincenzo (Jr.), 473
Debenedetti, Giacomo, 453, 487
Debenedetti, M. E., 482
De Blasi, N., 362, 433
Debon, G., 558
Deboveanu, E., 803
Debus, F., 573

Debussy, Claude, 206, 701
De Camilli, D., 448
Decamps, S., 20
Decante, S., 340
De Caprio, C., 426
De Carlo, Andrea, 462, 463
De Chirico, Giorgio, 451
Décimo, M., 7, 223
Decke, G., 713
Decke-Cornill, R., 595
Decker, C., 740
Decloedt, L. R. G., 706, 728
De Conca, M., 231, 232, 235, 236
De Costa, E., 337
De Coureil, Giovanni, 406
Décourt, M., 183
De Crescenzo, A., 484
De Cristofaro, F., 443, 448
Decuble, H., 692
Decurtins, A., 523
Decyk, W., 804
Dedenaro, R., 459
Dédéyan, C., 103
Dedola, R., 429
Dees, A., 23
Defaux, G., 100, 111, 113, 115, 117
De Federicis, L., 461
Defendi, A. S., 434
De Ferra, D., 463
De Filippo, Eduardo, 466, 467, 473
Defoe, Daniel, 155
De Francesco, A., 412
Deghenghi Oluji, E., 491
De Gioia, M., 14
De Giovanni, N., 465
Degler, F., 657
Degli Alessandri, Giovanni, 407
Deguy, M., 192
De Heinrico, 584
Dei, A., 481
Deichsler, Heinrich, 559
Deidier, R., 483
Deinert, W., 712
Deiters, F.-J., 700
Dejond, A., 33
Delacroix, Eugène, 181, 184
De Lange, A., 630
De Laude, S., 443
Delavouët, Mas-Felipe, 237, 242
Delavrancea, Barbu, 507
Del Balzo, Carlo, 421
Delcò-Toschini, S., 441
Del Colle, Paolo, 459
Delcorno, C., 381, 394
Del Corno, N., 423
Delden, M. van, 321
Deledar, J., 228
Delègue, Y., 194
Deleuze, Gilles, 197, 292, 348, 691
Delforge, F., 167
Delgado Morales, M., 286
Del Garbo, Dino, 395
Del Gatto, A., 438
Del Giudice, Daniele, 461, 477
Del Gobbo, F., 9
D'Elia, Gianni, 371
Delianidou, S., 717
De Libero, Libero, 460, 473
Delin, J., 261
Delius, Friedrich Christian, 743
Dell'Aquila, M., 379, 413, 442, 452, 492, 862
Dell'Aquila, M. M.,427
Della Casa, Giovanni, 422, 439
Della Neva, J. A., 117
Della Porta, Giovan Battista, 644
Della Terza, D., 370, 453
Della Valle, Federico, 439
Della Valle, Pietro, 125
Della Volpe, Galvano, 450
Delle Donne, F., 382
Del Litto, V., 184
De Luca, Erri, 463, 473
Del Lungo, I., 384, 429
Delmas, C., 136, 862
Delmas, Jean-Jacques, 240
Del Negro, P., 414
Deloffre, F., 152
Deloince-Louette, C., 114, 122
Delporte, C., 159
Del Re, G., 426
Del Serra, Maura, 473
Delsing, L.-O., 756
Delsol, C., 510
Deluz, C., 75
Del Vento, C., 407, 411, 434
Del'vig, Anton Antonovich, 812, 819
De Marchi, Emilio, 432
De Marchi, P., 480
De Marco, G., 368
DeMarco, P., 71
Demaría, L., 319
Demarolle, P., 93
Demartini, A.-E., 173
De Martino, D., 453
De Martino, M., 8
Dembowski, P. F., 862
Demello, G., 247
Demerson, G., 116, 118
Demetriescu, A., 511
Demetz, P., 716
Demey, E., 549
Demonet, M.-L., 103, 634
Dencker, K. P., 602
De Nicola, F., 455, 464
Denina, Carlo, 405
Denis, D., 155
Denisenko, S. V., 817
Denisot, Nicolas, 123
De Nittis, Giuseppe, 424
Dennis, H. M., 95
Dennis, N., 281, 284
Dennison, M. J., 189
Densusianu, A., 511
De Palchi, Alfredo, 473
De Pascale, G., 455
Depestre, René, 218
Depiante, M. A., 354
D'Episcopo, F., 434, 474, 485
D'Eramo, Luce, 473
De Rentiis, D., 396
Deriugina, L., 811
De Robertis, D., 365, 372, 389, 397
De Roberto, Federico, 421, 422, 432
De Roberto, Giuseppe, 467
Deroint-Allaire, O., 104
De Rosa, F., 438
Derradji, Y., 32
Derrida, Jacques, 219, 348, 658, 690, 724, 743, 746, 749
Derron, M., 605
Derschka, H. R., 615
Derşidan, I., 510
Déruelle, A., 176
Derusha, W., 335–36
Derzhavin, Gavrila Romanovich, 812
Desan, P., 111, 112, 862
De Sanctis, Francesco, 419, 421, 432–33, 441, 452
De Sande, M. G., 464
De Santi, G., 441
Desbordes-Valmore, Marceline, 171, 195
Descartes, René, 127, 128, 129, 130, 150, 155, 157, 161–63, 167, 870
Deschamps, Eustache, 69, 81, 82, 87, 90
Deschapper, C., 58
Deschepper, C., 68
Deshouliers, Antoinette, 135
Desiatov, V. V., 834
Desideri, L., 425
Desjardins *v.* Villedieu
Desjardins, L., 145
Desjardins, N., 210
Desmarets de Saint-Sorlin, Jean, 126, 127, 132, 137
Des Masures, Louis, 103, 106
Des Périers, Bonaventure, 104
Desportes, M., 197

Desportes, Philippe, 117, 118, 119
Desroches, V., 211
Des Rosiers, Joël, 211
Dessì, Giuseppe, 473
Dessì, R. M., 381
Destro, A., 656
De Swart, H., 12
Detering, H., 696
Detken, A., 711
De Troja, E., 406
Dettori, A., 363
De Vendittis, L., 431
Devesa, J.-M., 239
Devescovi, A., 359
Devincenzo, G., 113
Dewaele, J.-M., 19
Dewhurst, J., 602
Diaconu, M. A., 511
Diaghilev, Sergei, 839
Diakina, A. A., 814, 846
Diana, R., 430
Dias, A. M., 346
Dias, Antônio Gonçalves, 344
Dias, J.-L., 174
Dias, Willy, 464
Diatesseron, 613
Diaz, B., 183
Díaz, Diego, 268
Díaz, G. J., 340
Diaz, Juan, 621
Díaz, N., 263
Díaz, O. A., 318
Díaz, R. I., 323
Díaz Fernández, José, 282
Díaz García, J., 861
Díaz de Mendoza, Fernando, 294
Dib, Mohammed, 219
Di Benedetto, A., 406, 407, 426, 428, 433, 453, 490
Di Benedetto, V., 434
Di Biase, M. L., 362
Di Brazzà, Antonio, 422
Di Brazzà, F., 422
Di Carlo, E., 432
Di Ciolla McGowan, N., 463
Dicke, G., 597, 602
Dickens, Charles, 198
Dickey, E., 11
Dickinson, Emily, 475
Dickson, M., 51
Diderot, Denis, 130
Didier, B., 410
Didier de Iungman, N., 337
Di Donna Principe, C., 427
Didot (*family*), 406
Dieminger, S., 690
Dierick, A. P., 744
Diérickz, C., 202
Dierks, M., 723, 725
Dieterle, R., 676
Diethe, C., 693
Diethelm, M.-B., 177
Dietl, C., 585, 599
Dietrich und Wenezlan, 590
Dietrich, Veit, 559
Dietrich, W., 497
Dietrichs Flucht, 590
Dietz, K., 559
Dietz, L., 699
Dietzsch, S., 691
Dieudonné de Hongrie, 65
Diewald, G., 870
Díez, E., 295
Díez, Miguel Ángel, 293
Díez de Revenga, F. J., 283, 289
Di Fonzo, C., 373
DiGiacomo, S., 4
Di Giacomo, Salvatore, 433, 460, 473
Di Girolamo, C., 236, 385
Di Grado, A., 475
Digulleville, Guillaume de, 75
Di Leva, I., 416
Diliberto, O., 417
Dillon, E., 70
Di Lorena Carignano, Giuseppina, 413
Di Mauro, D., 106
Di Mauro, L., 406
Di Meola, C., 353–54
Dimitrescu, F., 503, 504
D'Imperio, M., 353
Dingeldein, H. J., 550
Dini, P., 424
Dino, O., 485
Dinzelbacher, P., 610
Diogenes Laertius, 163
Dion, J.-N., 211
Di Pino, G., 377
Di Ricco, A., 404, 412
Dîrul, F., 500
Dische, Irene, 735
Disegni, S., 202, 204
Di Silvestro, A., 447
Disselkamp, M., 639
Disselkötter, A., 718
Disteli, Martin, 681
Di Tizio, F., 431
Ditlevsen, Tove, 763
Di Trocchio, F., 410
Divers, G., 739
Dix, Otto, 730
Djassemy, I., 719
Djomo, E., 700
Długosz-Kurczabowa, K., 790, 803
Długosz, K., 796
Dmitrenko, S. F., 820, 837
Dmitriev, A., 833
Dmitriev, D., 856
Dmitrovskaya, M. A., 850
Dobaczewski, A., 794
Dobarro, X. M., 315, 316
Döblin, Alfred, 703, 704, 710–11, 745
Dobre-Bogdan, C., 509
Dobrenko, E., 836
Dobrescu, A., 511
Dobrovský, J., 786
Dočekal, M., 785
Dodd, B., 716
Doderer, Heimito von, 546
Doering, S., 712
Dohm, Hedwig, 708
Doiron, N., 127
Dokulil, M., 783
Dolet, Etienne, 100
Dolfi, A., 457, 468, 473
Dolfin, Antonio, 401
Dolgin, A., 833
Dolgushev, V. G., 816
Dolin, A., 819
Dolle-Weinkauff, B., 715
Dollinger, R., 751
Domansky, V. A., 809
Domascnew, A., 572
Dombrovsky, Iurii, 835
Dombrowski, R., 453
Domenici, C., 407
Domergue, L., 276
Domingo Malvadi, A., 266
Domínguez, A., 247
Domínguez, F., 237, 298
Domínguez García, M., 310
Domínguez Reboiras, F., 862
Dominiak, A., 794
Dominic (*Saint*), 280
Dominte, C., 496, 499
Dommes, G., 752
Domrös, A., 862
Dona, C., 42
Donadello, A., 388
Donadoni Omodeo, M., 467
Donald, S. G., 743
Donaldson, R. P., 673
Donaldson-Evans, L. K., 114, 121
Donatelli, B., 198
Donati, C., 353
Donato, M. P., 401
Dondaine, C., 31
Dondero, M., 445
Dondi dall'Orologio, Giovanni, 391
Dondi dall'Orologio, Jacopo, 391
Donetzkoff, D., 159
Doneux, J. L., 24

Doni, C., 406
Donnarel, E., 467
Donnarumma, R., 470, 491
Donneau de Visé, Jean, 142
Dönninghaus, S., 868
Donnini, A., 428
Donovan, P. J., 525
Donskov, A. A., 826
Donvin, G., 869
Dopont, E., 750
Doppler, A., 695, 702, 726
Doran, R., 691
Dorat, Jean, 116, 122
Dord-Crouslé, S., 198
Doremus, A., 326, 327
Doria, Paolo Mattia, 415
Döring, B., 550
Döring, J., 747
Döring, N., 560
Dorléans, Louis, 123
Dornier, C., 862
Dorninger, M. E., 580
Doronchenkov, I. A., 810
Doroszewski, W., 793
Dorowin, H., 706, 737
Dörrich, C., 577
Dörrie, Doris, 735
D'Ors, E., 281
D'Ors, M., 279
Dorsch, H., 519
D'Ortenzi, S., 481
Dossi, Carlo, 433, 447, 468
Dostie, G., 31
Dostoevskaya, L. D., 824
Dostoevsky, A., 824
Dostoevsky, Fedor Mikhailovich, 444, 819, 823–26, 848
Dotoli, G., 96, 862
Dotti, U., 421, 460
Douceline, (*Saint*), 76
Douceline of Digne, 237
Doval Suárez, S. M., 865
Dovlatov, Sergei, 834, 847
Dowden, S. D., 705
Drach, Albert, 704
Drachmann, Holger, 767
Dragnat, M., 215
Drago, A. G., 453
Drago, M., 464
Dramé, M., 209
Drange, E.-M., 758
Drees, H., 753
Dreike, B. M., 750
Drendorf, Heinrich, 695
Drescher, M., 32
Dressel, R., 708
Dressler, W. U., 868
Dreyfus, Alfred, 190, 203, 204–05
Drigo, Paola, 464
Drijkoningen, F., 864
Drimba, L., 512
Drincu, S., 500
Dronke, P., 376
Droste, W., 731
Droste-Hülshoff, Annette von, 667, 669, 671, 672, 674, 675–76, 686, 694
Drouet, Juliette, 186
Drude, O., 676
Drügh, H. J., 644
Drugoveiko-Dolzhanskaya, S., 813
Drumm, E., 283
Drunina, I., 831
Duarte, C. L., 345
Du Bartas, Guillaume de Salluste, sieur, 105, 108, 117
Dubé, Marcel, 209
Dubel, S., 201
Du Bellay, Joachim, 97, 103, 105, 109, 115, 117, 118, 241
Dubert García, F., 304, 305, 312, 859
Dubin, B., 834, 838
Dubisz, S., 789, 790, 803
Dubnova, M., 842
Du Boccage, Anne Marie, 135
Duboile, C., 202
Dubois, A., 197
Dubois, J., 199
Du Bos, Jean-Baptiste, 129, 157, 405
Du Bosc, Pierre Thomine, 157
Duboucher, G., 159
Du Breuil, Jean, 127
DuBruck, E., 66, 73
Dubuis, R., 93
Dubuisson, P., 31
Ducharme, Réjean, 211, 212, 214
Duché, V., 123
Duchêne, R., 126
Duclert, V., 204
Ducrey, A., 190
Duda, H., 789
Dudarev, V., 809
Dudash, S., 82
Duden, Anne, 733
Duekilde, A., 757
Dufault, R. L., 209
Duffaut, R., 737
Duffy, L., 189
Dufief, P.-J., 199
Dufief-Sanchez, V., 181
Du Fossé, Pierre Thomas, 159
Dufour, A., 108
Dufour, H., 182
Dufourcet Hakim, M.-B., 90
Dufournet, J., 42, 53, 82
Dufrenne, Mikel, 764
Dufresne, M., 741
Du Gallas, Jean, 127
Du Guesclin, Bertrand, 75
Du Guillet, Pernette, 118
Duhl, O. A., 67
Duke, P. R., 177
Dukhan, I. S., 840
Dulac, L., 81, 83, 87
Dulfu, Petre, 507
Dulian, R., 792
Dulova, N. V., 828
Dumas, Alexandre (*père*), 96, 172, 179
Dumas, C., 144
Dumas, V., 230
Dumistrăcel, S., 505
Dumitrescu, M., 491
Du Monin, Jean-Édouard, 106, 118–19
Dumont, Fernand, 211–12
Dumora-Mabille, F., 128
Dumville, D., 539
Dunaev, M. M., 808
Duncker, D., 756
Dunker, A., 657
Dunphy, G., 639
Duns Scotus, John, 368
Dupèbe, J., 114
Du Perron, Jacques Davy, 118
Dupleix, Scipion, 126
Duplessis-Mornay, Philippe, 121
Duport, D., 98
Dupouy, J.-P., 119
Du Pré, Galliot, 99, 110, 117
Dupré dal Poggetto, M. G., 365
Duprilot, J., 204
Dupuis, D., 175, 176
Duran, S., 199
Durán Barceló, J., 270
Durán López, F., 277
Durand, Catherine, 135
Durand, P., 194, 199
Durand-Le-Guern, I., 172
Durand de Villegagnon, Nicolas, 123
Durante, F., 426
Duranti, Francesca, 463
Dürer, Albrecht, 559, 617, 619, 632
Durer, S., 20
Dürinc, 602
Durling, R. M., 367
Durrani, O., 716
Durrell, M., 546, 552
Dürrenmatt, Friedrich, 732, 743
Dürrenmatt, J., 182, 184
Dürrschmidt, B., 568
Dürscheid, C., 561
Durst, D. C., 708

Durvye, C., 181
Du Ryer, Pierre, 140
Durzak, M., 661, 863
Dusar, I., 741
Duse, Eleonora, 425
Dushina, L. N., 809
Duso, E. M., 388, 389
Du Souhait, François, 127
Dutton, D., 149
Duţu, A., 514
Du Vair, Guillaume, 122
Duval, E. M., 111, 115
Duval, F., 73
Duval-Arnould, L., 222
Duve, Karen, 743
Du Verdier, Gilbert Saulnier, sieur, 150
Düwel, K., 553, 585
Dvergsdal, A., 774
Dvorak, P. F., 736
Dvoriashin, I. A., 815
Dworkin, S. N., 246, 251, 254
Dyck, J., 864
Dynak, W., 792
Dyszak, A. S., 796
Dzendzeliwski, J., 802
Dziadko, F., 838
Dziedzic, A., 84
Dzięgiel, E., 797
Dziewiątkowski, J. A., 789, 805
Dzikowska, E. K., 727
Dziuba, Helmut, 736

Earle, B., 679
Earp, L., 91
Ebani, N., 446
Ebenbauer, A., 592
Eberhard von Cersne, 603
Eberhard, W., 576
Eberhardt, J., 741
Ebers, Georg, 701
Ebersbach, V., 692
Ebguy, J.-D., 175
Ebisch-Burton, K., 662
Ebles II de Ventadorn, 234, 235
Ebner, Margarete, 611
Ebner-Eschenbach, Marie von, 667, 668
Ebrahim, H., 220
Ebrecht, K., 749
Echenique Elizondo, M. T., 861
Echevarría Goñi, P. L., 272
Echeverría, Esteban, 318
Echtermann, A., 81
Ecker, H.-P., 672
Eckert, R., 803
Eckertová, E., 788
Eckhart (*Meister*), 610
Eco, Umberto, 379, 451, 452, 462, 463, 473–74
Eddington, D., 247, 358
Edel, D., 540
Edel, Peter, 743–44
Edighoffer, R., 639
Edlinger, C. von, 701
Edsall, M. A., 89
Edward I (*King of England*), 74
Edwards, C. W., 583
Edwards, E., 535
Edwards, H. M., 530
Edwards, H. T., 534, 536
Edwards, J. B., 533
Effinger, M., 582
Efimov, E., 844
Efron, Ariadna Sergeevna, 840
Efron, Sergei, 855
Egbert, M., 562
Egge, Peter, 778
Eggeling, W., 833
Egger, K., 522
Eggers, E., 552, 567
Eggerts, J., 742
Egidi, M., 599, 603, 605, 606
Egido, A., 268
Egorov, B. F., 807, 838
Egorov, O. G., 820, 830
Egunov, Andrei, 831
Ehlers, K.-H., 6
Ehlich, K., 545, 547, 564, 677
Ehness, J., 727
Ehrenstein, Albert, 705
Ehrismann, O., 588
Ehrman, A., 131
Ehrsam, T., 730
Ehrstine, G., 625, 636, 645
Eibl, K., 669
Eichel-Lojkine, P., 96, 98, 104
Eichendorff, Joseph von, 647, 648, 649, 650, 651, 675, 676
Eichhoff, J., 546
Eichinger, L. M., 357, 547, 559, 561, 567
Eichler, E., 575
Eigler, F., 748
Eigler, J., 722
Eijirô, I., 545
Eike von Repgow, 555, 615
Eikhenbaum, B. M., 838
Eikon Basilike, 533
Eilert, H., 642, 643, 723
Eilhart von Oberge, 598
Eimeric, Nicolau, 299
Eimermacher, K., 814, 821, 833, 834, 862
Einstein, Carl, 700, 711
Eisenbeis, M., 675
Eisenberg, P., 546
Eisenstein, Sergei Mikhailovich, 836
Eisermann, F., 620
Eiximenis, Francesc, 299–300
Ejskjær, I., 758
Eke, N. O., 681, 682, 688
Ekelöf, Gunnar, 773
Ekstein, N., 139
Eladan, J., 172
Elben, C., 746
Elbogen, Paul, 711
Elda Funaro, L., 426
Eleonora Magdalena Theresia von Pfalz-Neuburg, 645
Eley, P., 47, 51
Elf, M. J., 756
Eliade, Mircea, 511, 513, 515
Eliassen, K. O., 774
Eliot, T[homas] S[tearns], 285, 476
Elisabeth of Braunschweig-Calenberg, 627
Elisabeth von Nassau-Saarbrücken, 591
Elisabeth von Schönau, 610, 61
Elizaincín, A., 11
Ellena, O., 89
Elli, E., 446
Ellis, M., 534, 536
Ellis, R. R., 338
Ellis, Y., 23
Elmalan, S., 123
Elmarsafy, Z., 143
Elsaghe, Y., 721, 723, 724
Elsen, H., 565
Elslande, J.-P. van, 147, 153, 15
Elson, C., 860
Elspass, S., 556
El-Tibi, Z., 20
Eltink, I., 674
Eltit, Diamela, 325, 340
Éluerd, R., 19, 24
Embach, M., 576
Emden, C. J., 691
Emelianova, I., 842
Emery, E., 202
Emig, G., 683, 686
Eminescu, Mihai, 511, 512, 513
Eming, J., 599, 600
Emkjær, S., 767
Emma *v.* Ferretti
Emo, Andrea, 471
Emont, B., 134
Emptaz, F., 197
Enache, A., 503
Enciso Recio, L.-M., 275
Enders, J., 66, 138
Endo, N. F., 194
Endres, J., 661
Engammare, M., 115

Engberg, C., 769
Engel, D. M., 25
Engel, M., 650
Engelbert (*Archbishop of Cologne*), 676
Engelhard, M., 436
Engelhardt, D. von, 722
Engelking, A., 794, 803
Engerer, V., 757
Engeset, J. K., 776
Engler, M. R., 752
Englier, R., 20
Enguita Utrilla, J. M., 263
Enikel, Jans, 580, 600, 617
Enklaar, J., 679
Enselmino (*Fra*), 459
Ensenyat, G., 303
Enslin, A. P., 742
Entrée d'Espagne, 65
Enzensberger, Hans Magnus, 744
Epée, F., 104
Epicurus, 158, 163
Eppel, Asar, 841
Equicola, Mario, 236
Erasmus, Desiderius, 96, 100, 114, 269, 632
Eraúso, Catalina de, 265
Erba, Luciano, 371, 474
Erbertz, C., 194
Erdman, Nikolai Robertovich, 832
Eremenko, V. N., 853
Erenburg, Ilia, 836, 841, 847
Erfurter Judeneid, 615
Erhart, W., 701
Erler, G., 676
Ermachenko, I. O., 807, 814
Ermakova, O. P., 809
Ermini, F., 456
Ermolin, E., 847, 851
Ermolinsky, S., 846
Ernst, G., 23
Ernst, P., 521, 523, 572, 574
Ernst, Paul, 711
Ernst, T., 636
Ernst, U., 575, 584, 593, 595, 630
Erofeev, Venedict, 837, 847
Eroms, H.-W., 561
Erren, L., 833
Esaulov, I., 823
Escartin, J., 223
Escartín Gual, M., 288, 291
Esch, E., 866
Escher, G., 695
Escobar, A. M., 249
Escola, M., 140
Escourido Pernas, A. B., 310
Escudé, P., 241
Escudero-Alie, M. E. L., 341
Esdahl, T., 759
Esenin, Sergei Alexandrovich, 818, 831, 841, 847
Esgueva Martínez, M. A., 259
Esin, A. B., 809, 821
Esin, S., 832
Esipov, V., 817, 827
Eskénazi, A., 52
Eskildsen, H., 758
Eskin, M., 745
Esmarch, Constanze, 696
Espadaler, A., 236, 297
Espagne, G., 663
Esparza Torres, M. A., 869
Espejo-Saavedra, R., 289
Espert, N., 286
Espina, Antonio, 281
Espinosa Elorza, R. M., 252
Esposito, V., 459
Espronceda, José, 291
Esquier, S., 183
Esselborn, H., 645, 663, 708
Essen, G. von, 680, 720
Essig, Hermann, 699
Estella, Diego de, 274
Ester, H., 679
Esterhammer, A., 338
Estévez, C., 315
Estienne, Henri (I), 101
Estienne, Henri (II), 98, 101, 104, 123
Estienne, Henri, 274
Estoire de Merlin, 46
Estoire del Saint Graal, 46
Etensel-Ildem, A., 200
Eterovich, R., 833
Étienne II (*bishop of Clermont*), 223
Etienne de Fougères, 61
Eto, M., 719
Etov, V. I., 830
Ette, O., 320
Ette, W., 724
Ettner von Eiteritz, Johann Christoph, 644
Ettrup, F., 763, 862
Eulenspiegel, 555, 863
Eulenspiegelbuch, 632
Eulogio of Cordoba, 5
Euripides, 143, 772
Eusebi, M., 232
Evangelisti, P., 300
Evans, Beriah Gwynfe, 534
Evans, D. F., 527
Evans, G., 861
Evans, H. M., 528
Evdaev, N., 835
Evdokimova, L. V., 829
Everard of Gateley, 55
Eversberg, G., 696, 697
Evrard, F., 180, 181
Evrard, I., 25
Evseev, I., 504
Ewald, Johannes, 766
Ewenz, G. L., 712
Ewers, Hanns Heinz, 715
Ewers, Hans-Heino, 715
Ewert, M., 677, 678
Eximeno y Pujades, Antonio, 276
Expilly, Claude, 112
Eygun, J., 223
Ezzolied, 586

Fabbri, M., 411
Fabbri, P., 406, 429
Faber, B., 674
Faber, R., 653
Faber, S., 290
Fabiani, P., 420
Fabre, François-Xavier, 406, 407
Fabri, Felix, 612
Fabrizi, A., 400, 407, 408
Fabrizio-Costa, S., 862
Facques, B., 25
Fadeev, Alexander Alexandrovich, 832, 847
Færevåg, O. E., 779
Faggin, Giuseppe, 481
Fagioli, K., 474
Faiciuc, E., 496
Faitinelli, Pietro de', 387, 391
Faitrop-Porta, A. C., 467
Faits des Romains, 51
Faivre, A., 862
Faivre-Duboz, B., 210, 211, 212, 214
Fajen, R., 69
Falcetto, B., 470
Falikov, I., 842
Falileyev, A., 530, 538
Falińska, B., 803
Falissard, R., 224
Falke, G., 691
Falkenstrøm, C., 771
Falkner, S. R., 741
Fallacara, Luigi, 459, 475
Fallada, Hans, 700, 711
Fancello, S., 479
Fanfani, M., 355
Fangen, Ronald, 778
Fanlo, J.-R., 107, 108
Fanning, S., 158
Fanon, Frantz, 216, 217, 239
Fantato, G., 483
Fantato, M., 410
Fantoni, M., 73
Fantuzzi, M., 355
Faraco, Sergio, 343

Fargue, Léon-Paul, 713
Farhoud, Abla, 207
Farina, A., 31
Farina, E., 411
Farina, Salvatore, 433
Farnetti, M., 454, 465
Farø, K., 760
Farquhar, S. W., 112
Farrant, T., 175, 178
Farrell, J., 4
Farrère, Claude (Frédéric Bargone), 200
Farsethås, A., 775
Fasani, R., 377, 442
Fasano, P., 421, 440
Fasbender, C., 588, 596, 606, 615
Fasold, R., 696, 863
Fassbinder, Rainer Werner, 720, 744
Fassel, H., 517
Fasulo, A., 355
Faucheux, A., 181
Faulkner, William, 219, 338, 693, 725
Faustini, G., 465
Faustini, Margherita, 474
Fauvel, D., 196
Fava Guzzetti, L., 436
Favaro, F., 411, 444
Favero, A., 860
Favre, Antoine, 121, 123
Fayolle, V., 33
Fazio degli Uberti, 389, 391
Fazio, M., 484
Fea, Carlo, 402
Feal, R. G., 340
Featherston, S., 561
Febbraro, P., 483
Febel, G., 116
Fechner, Gustav, 726
Fedele, D., 425
Federici Vescovini, G., 368
Fedi, B., 232
Fedi, F., 410
Fedi, L., 205
Fedi, R., 430, 448
Fediakin, S., 852
Fedin, Konstantin, 843
Fedorova, L. V., 827
Fedosiuk, I. A., 819
Fedotov, O. I., 810
Fehervary, H., 729
Feigenbaum, S., 25
Feilchenfeldt, K., 677
Fein, D., 78
Felder, Franz Michael, 676
Felecan, N., 500
Félibien, André, 129
Felici, L., 440, 441
Fellows-Jensen, G., 762
Fénelon, François de Pons de Salignac de la Mothe, 125, 130, 147, 150, 157
Fénié, J.-J., 226
Fenoglio, Beppe, 456, 461, 474
Fenster, T., 81, 82, 84, 87, 862
Fenu Barbera, R., 394
Fenzi, E., 373, 399
Feo, M., 412
Feraru, M., 516
Féraud, Henri, 242
Ferdinand of Aragon (*King of Spain*), 268
Ferguson, A.-M., 43
Ferguson, F., 198
Ferguson, S., 685
Feriani, G., 473
Ferioli, A., 388
Ferkel, V. B., 837
Ferlampin-Acher, C., 43, 69
Ferlenga, A., 470
Fermi, Enrico, 451
Fernandes, R. de, 349
Fernández, F., 246
Fernández, L., 859
Fernández, M., 258
Fernández, Macedonio, 339
Fernández, X. A., 316
Fernández Ariza, G., 337
Fernández Dobao, A. M., 311
Fernández Gracia, R., 272
Fernández de Heredia, Juan, 302
Fernández Juncal, C., 258
Fernández de Madrigal, Alfonso, 270
Fernández de Moratín, Nicolás, 277
Fernández Mosquera, S., 274
Fernández-Ordóñez, I., 248
Fernández Rei, F., 306, 310, 312
Fernández Retamar, R., 319
Fernández Rivera, E., 268
Fernández Salgado, B., 305, 869
Fernández Salgado, X. A., 305
Fernández Sanchez, C., 208
Feroldi, D., 464
Ferran, O., 282
Ferrandis d'Herèdia, Joan, 296, 303
Ferrando, A., 300, 302
Ferraresi, G., 24
Ferrari, Curzia, 486
Ferrari, Giuseppe, 419
Ferrari, I., 464
Ferrari, S., 401, 403
Ferraris, A., 462
Ferraris, D., 443, 482
Ferraris Cornaglia, F., 421
Ferraro, B., 491
Ferrazzi, Cecilia, 113
Ferreira, D. R. S., 348
Ferrer, Francesc, 297
Ferrer, Joan Ramon, 297
Ferrer, V., 108
Ferrer, Vicent (*Saint*), 300
Ferrero, Carlo Vincenzo, 402
Ferretti, Emilia Viola ('Emma'), 426
Ferretti, Giancarlo, 462
Ferreyrolles, G., 157, 166, 167
Ferri, F., 481
Ferrières, M., 228, 229
Ferro, Marise, 465
Ferron, Jacques, 212
Ferrone, S., 414
Ferroni, G., 398, 405, 427, 867, 868
Ferrucci, Franco, 371, 373
Fet, Afanasii Afanasievich, 822, 827–28
Fétis, François-Joseph, 91
Fetrenheuer, K., 636
Feuchtwanger, Lion, 704
Feuerbach, Ludwig, 161
Feuerwehrbuch von 1420, 616
Feulner, A. H., 583
Feyerabend, W., 678
Feyl, Renate, 738
Fibiger, J., 765
Fichte, Hubert, 744
Fichte, Johann Gottlieb, 187, 650, 652–53, 658
Ficino, Marsilio, 102
Fidalgo, E., 313
Fiddian, R., 318
Fiddler, A., 740, 746
Fidler, M. U., 787
Fido, F., 407, 440, 448, 460
Fidora, A., 863
Fiedler, L. M., 862
Fiehler, R., 550
Field, T., 224, 225, 226
Fielding, Henry, 594
Fierabras, 39, 223
Figg, K. M., 88
Figl, J., 692
Figueiredo, M. L., 341–42
Figueiredo, Rubens, 349
Figurnov, M., 849
Figurnov, O., 849
Fijman, Jacobo, 339
Filangieri, Gaetano, 400, 413
Filimon, Nicolae, 514
Filin, M. D., 812, 836
Filippi, P. M., 460
Filippo di Novara, 383
Filipponi, S., 471
Filippovová, D., 787

Fille du Comte de Pontieu, 71
Filmer-Davies, C., 537
Fina, A. de, 261
Finazzi-Agrò, E., 344
Fingerhut, K., 685, 686
Fink, G.-L., 651, 653, 658
Finkch, R., 600
Finke, M. C., 694
Finoli, A. M., 74
Finotti, F., 412, 433
Fiol-Matta, L., 340
Fiore, Elio, 371, 441
Fiorentino, C. M., 443
Fiorentino, F., 175
Fiorentino, M., 480
Fiori, G., 480
Fiorucci, N., 229
Firaza, J., 744
Fischart, Johann, 623, 627
Fischart, Sebastian, 114
Fischer, B., 660
Fischer, B.-J., 723
Fischer, D., 609
Fischer, G., 699, 734, 740
Fischer, H., 602, 677, 679
Fischer, I., 496
Fischer, J. M., 729
Fischer, K., 691
Fischer-Lichte, E., 660, 669
Fisher, R. W., 602, 604
Fishman, J. A., 547
Fita, F., 302
Fitz, E. E., 337, 343
Fitzon, T., 701
Fiumi, Lionello, 458
Flacius Illyricus, Matthias, 622, 632–33
Flaiano, Ennio, 472
Flaubert, Gustave, 169, 176, 190, 192, 195, 196–99, 200, 424, 448, 668, 670, 678, 867
Flavia, L., 400
Flecchia, P., 483
Flechtenmacher, Maria, 508
Fleck, Konrad, 599
Fleck, S. H., 142
Flègès, A., 117
Fleischer, W., 543
Fleisser, Marieluise, 712
Fleming, J., 395
Fleming, Paul, 639, 641
Flex, Walter, 710
Fliedl, K., 728
Fløgstad, Kjartan, 778
Floirac, Marcelin Prosper, 223
Floire et Blancheflor, 57
Flood, J. L., 639
Flor, F. R. de la, 270
Florack, R., 731
Florea, I. A., 505
Florès, Juan de, 100
Flores Farfán, F., 262
Florescu, C., 504
Florescu, N., 513
Floresta, Nílsia, 345–46
Flórez Miguel, C., 270
Floricic, F., 363
Florus, Hèrcules, 303
Flöss, L., 355
Fo, Dario, 466, 473
Fobbe, E., 560
Fochi, A., 507
Foehr, Y., 79
Foehr-Jannsens, Y., 61
Foerster, F., 673
Fofanov, Konstantin Mikhailovich, 828
Fogazzaro, Antonio, 433
Fohlen, J., 381
Fohrmann, J., 681, 688, 733
Foigny, Gabriel de, 147, 159
Földes, C., 546, 547
Fole, Ánxel, 313
Folena, G., 385
Folgar, C., 250
Folin, A., 435, 437
Föllner, U., 568
Folquet de Lunel, 231, 232
Folquet de Marseille, 236
Folz, Hans, 614
Fomenko, I. V., 818
Fomichev, S. A., 814, 816
Fominykh, T. N., 832
Fondane *v.* Fundoianu
Fonnesu, L., 653
Fontaine, Nicolas, 147, 158
Fontana, Gregorio, 403
Fontane, Emilie, 676–77
Fontane, Martha, 676
Fontane, Theodor, 667, 668, 669, 670, 676–80, 694, 701, 719, 868
Fontanelli, G., 467
Fontanini, Giusto, 404
Fontenelle, Bernard Le Bovier de, 159, 160
Forcadela, M., 314, 315
Force, P., 164, 166
Ford, P., 112, 115, 116, 541, 861
Forel, A., 20
Forestier, G., 144
Forêt, Joan-Claudi, 225, 237, 238, 239
Forgács, E., 548
Forhan, K. L., 81, 86
Forment, M., 257
Formentin, V., 360, 361, 384, 388
Fornasetti, A., 427
Fornasiero, J., 194
Forner, Juan Pablo, 276
Fornesi, D., 438
Forni, M., 520, 521
Forrestal, A., 159
Forsdick, C., 863
Forssman, B., 561
Forster, Georg, 665
Forster, M. H., 334
Förster-Nietzsche, Elisabeth, 712
Forth, C. E., 204
Forti, M., 486
Fortichiari, V., 480
Fortini, Franco, 453, 474
Fortunato, Giustino, 427
Fortunato, Mario, 465
Fortunatus, 620, 627
Foschi, F., 441
Foscolo, Ugo, 369, 411, 422, 426, 430, 433–34, 440, 449, 485
Fossat, J.-L., 224
Fossati, V., 455
Fosse, Jon, 778–79
Fossetier, Julien, 105
Foster, I., 728
Fothergill-Payne, L., 268
Fothergill-Payne, P., 268
Fotiade, R., 515
Foucault, Michel, 330, 331, 332, 577, 657, 659, 660, 685, 691, 749
Fouke le Fitz Waryn, 63
Fouquet, Nicolas, 133
Fouriè, J., 243
Fourier, Charles, 194
Fournel, P., 469
Fournier, H.-F., 42
Fox, J., 80
Fozzer, G., 471
Fracassa, U., 476
Fracassi, F., 464
Fracchia, Umberto, 453
Fradkin, V., 848
Frago Gracia, J. A., 248, 263
Fraiman, S., 732
Fraimout-Auda, M., 118
Fraioli, D., 72
Fraisse, L., 189
Franceschini, B., 47
Franceschini, R., 357
Francese, J., 470
Franchini, E., 473
Francioso, M., 462
Francis of Assisi (*Saint*), 161, 234, 383, 479, 492, 611
Francis Xavier (*Saint*), 271
Franck, G., 634
Franck, Johann, 640
Franck, Sebastian, 633
Franckel, J.-J., 28

Franckenberg, Abraham von, 641
Franco, B., 172
Franco, J., 325
Franco Figueroa, M., 263
Francoeur, L., 209
François de Sales (*Saint*), 121, 130, 150, 157, 158
François I (*King of France*), 99, 102, 120
Frâncu, C., 499
Franczak, J., 801
Frandini, P., 487
Frank, G., 669, 672, 683, 684
Frank, Hubert Konrad, 642
Frank, I., 572
Franke, W., 192
Frankl, Ludwig August, 680
Franklin Grout-Flaubert (*Madame*), 196
Franz II (*Emperor*), 409
Franz, Robert, 685, 688
Franz, T. R., 291, 293
Franzinelli, M., 489
Franzos, Karl Emil, 668, 680
Frappier-Mazur, L., 177, 196
Frasca, Gabriele, 457
Frasca, Gabriella, 461
Frasca-Spada, M., 100
Fraser, H., 426
Frassica, P., 486
Frassineti, L., 411, 416, 444
Frath, P., 33
Fratnik, M., 492
Fratta, A., 297
Frattini, A., 435, 452, 456
Frauenlob (Heinrich von Meissen), 605–06, 863
Fréart de Chambray, Roland, 127
Freccero, C., 110
Freder, Johannes, 633
Frederick II (*Emperor*), 384, 385
Freeborn, R., 823
Freeman, M., 94
Frégnac-Clave, F., 220
Frei, Henri, 20
Freidank, 582
Freiligrath, Ferdinand, 673 680
Freise, D., 614
Freitäger, A., 631
Freiwald, B. T., 208
Freixas, M., 859
Frelick, N., 117, 150
Frémiot, A., 196
French, J. L., 340
Freud, Sigmund, 52, 185, 189, 190, 192, 197, 200, 216, 428, 453, 468, 490, 491, 551, 600, 667, 714, 722, 724
Freudenberg, R., 549
Freund, W., 696
Freund-Spork, W., 687
Frey, W., 614
Freyeisen, A., 703
Freyre, Gilberto, 344, 348
Freytag, Gustav, 672, 681
Freytag, H., 575, 586
Frezinsky, B., 847
Frias, J. M., 346
Fridkin, V. M., 816
Fridland, Anton, 841
Fried, Erich, 710
Friedberg, L., 741
Friedemann, J., 172, 173
Friedl, H., 694
Friedlaender, Salomo, 702
Friedrich (*Magister*), 617–18
Friedrich von Hausen, 602
Friedrich von Nürnberg, 617
Friedrich von Schwaben, 601
Friedrich Wilhelm IV (*King of Prussia*), 672
Friedrich, Caspar David, 438
Friedrich, H., 192
Friedrich, M., 672, 673
Friedrich, T., 661
Friedrich, U., 630
Fries, Fritz Rudolf, 739
Fries, Johannes, 623
Fries, M., 62
Fries, N., 561
Fries, U., 747
Friese, W., 776
Friesen, E., 76
Frietsch, W., 745
Friis, R. E., 771
Friis, R., 334
Frisch, Efraim, 704
Frisch, Johann Leonhard, 643
Frisch, Max, 739, 740, 744, 747, 750
Fritsch, Ahasuerus, 638
Fritsch, Gerhard, 744
Fritsch, Werner, 744
Fritz, J.-M., 43, 58
Frizman, L. G., 812, 854
Fröhlich, Abraham Emanuel, 681
Fröhlich, M., 749
Froissart, Jean, 36, 69, 70, 71, 80, 82, 88–89
Frølich, J., 175, 176
Frolova, O. E., 814
From, I., 762
Froment-Meurice, M., 194
Fromentin, Eugène, 199
Fromm, H., 553
Fromm, W., 695
Fröschle, H., 648
Fruelund, Simon, 765
Frugoni, C., 381
Früh, E., 732
Frühe, U., 578–79
Fruquièra, R., 225
Fruttero, Carlo, 474
Fruyt, M., 15
Frýba-Reber, A.-M., 7, 20
Fubini, M., 408, 453
Fuchs, A., 716, 752
Fuchs, B., 271
Fuchs, G., 737
Fuchs, Leonhardt, 622, 629
Fuchs-Jolie, S., 596
Fuentes, Carlos, 287, 322, 323
Fuentes, V., 282
Füetrer, Ulrich, 599
Fugazza, M., 429
Fuguet, Alberto, 340
Fühmann, Franz, 744
Fuhrhop, N., 560
Fujita, S., 195
Fuksas, A. P., 232, 234
Fuld, D., 719
Fulgentius, 397
Fulhet, J., 227
Füllner, B., 672, 697
Fulton, H., 532
Fulvio, Andrea, 109
Fumagalli, E., 383
Fumaroli, M., 98
Fundoianu, Benjamin, 515
Fürbeth, F., 616
Furer, J.-J., 523
Furetière, Antoine, 145
Furno, V., 426
Furtado, E. M., 213
Furtwängler, Wilhelm, 339
Furukawa, N., 25
Fusaro, E., 428
Fusco, Florinda, 457
Fuss, P., 627

Gàbici, F., 474
Gabriel, E., 523, 570
Gabriel-Stheeman, L., 8, 260
Gabriele, J. P., 293
Gabriele, T., 478
Gabrieli, V., 427
Gabrielle de la Tour, 74
Gabrielle, R., 228
Gac-Artigas, P., 338
Gace Brulé, 57
Gachev, G. D., 833, 854
Gacheva, A. G., 826
Gadamer, Hans-Georg, 214, 658, 773
Gadda, Carlo Emilio, 451, 452, 474, 663–64

Gaede, F., 642, 862
Gaeta, L., 561
Gaetano *v.* Tizzone
Gaetano, R., 429, 437
Gafton, A., 497
Gafurova, N., 550
Gagan, R., 655
Gagliardi, Gaetano Maria, 413
Gagliolo, J.-L., 229
Gago Jover, F., 254, 866
Gago Rodó, A., 294
Gaiba, C., 445
Gaidukevich, Natalia, 855
Gaier, U., 669
Gaillard, A., 128
Gaillard, F., 199
Gaillard, M., 43
Gaimar, Geoffrey, 63
Gaines, J. F., 141
Gaisbauer, S., 568
Găitănaru, S., 503, 505
Gaitseva, E. G., 828
Gajda, S., 796
Gala, S., 796
Galaction, Gala, 515
Galand-Hallyn, P., 102, 121
Gałczyńska, A., 794
Galderisi, C., 80, 870
Galdi, Matteo Angelo, 413
Galdós, Benito Pérez, 289, 295
Galeazzi, G., 435
Gałecki, Z., 800
Galeeva, R., 828, 829
Galeeva, T. 828
Galeran de Bretagne, 52
Galiani, Ferdinando, 404, 691
Galignani, P., 448
Galileo Galilei, 415
Galimberti, G. C., 437
Gallagher, M., 216, 220
Galland-Szymkowiak, M., 152
Galle, H. J., 700
Galli, M., 656
Gallina, B., 106
Gallina, Giacinto, 434
Gallinaro, I., 469
Gallone, A. O., 339
Gallucci, J. A., 158
Gally, M., 60
Gambaro, F., 470
Gambaro, Griselda, 339
Gambart, Adrien, 150
Gambini, D., 293
Gambino, F., 234, 860
Gammelgaard, K., 785, 803
Gammeltoft, P., 762
Gamon, Christofle de, 108
Gană, G., 511
Gandini, Teresa, 414
Gandlevsky, Sergei, 841, 847
Ganeri, M., 462
Ganim, R., 134, 143, 869
Ganivet, Ángel, 279, 287
Gansel, C., 739
Gantelet, M., 161
Gaos, V., 288
Garapon, J., 153
Garasse, François, 163
Garay, K., 76
Garbe, J., 740
Garber, K., 623
Garbiglia, R., 435
Garboli, C., 445
Garborg, A., 826
Garborg, Arne, 775
Garcés, M. A., 273
Garcia, A., 296
García, C., 261
García, E. C., 10
García, I., 338
García, M. A., 288
García Alonso, J. L., 526
García Ares, M. C., 309
García Ballester, L., 299
García Barrientos, J. L., 294
García Gallarín, C., 253
García López, J., 300, 302
García Lorca, Conchita, 286
García Lorca, Federico, 281, 282, 285–87
García Lorca, Isabel, 285, 286
García Márquez, Gabriel, 328, 341
García Martín, J. M., 248
García-Medall, J., 863
García Montero, L., 286
García Sánchez, José Luis, 293
Garcia Sempere, M., 298
García Turnes, B., 305
García Valdés, C. C., 274
García Valle, A., 255
García Velasco, J., 286
Garde, M., 772
Gardini, N., 494
Gardt, A., 563
Gardy, P. (F.), 238, 239, 241
Gardzińska, J., 799
Gareffi, Andrea, 483
Gargiulo, G., 410, 463
Garí, B., 298
Garidel, D. de, 154
Garin le Loherain, 39
Garin de Monglane, 65
Garin-Mikhailovsky, Nikolai Georgievich, 819, 847
Garneau, François-Xavier, 212
Garneau, Hector de Saint-Denys, 212
Garnier, Charles, 294–95
Garnier, Robert, 99, 106, 127
Garnier, S., 116
Garofalo, P., 448
Garovi, A., 523
Garrido Medina, J., 258
Garrido Valls, J. D., 300
Garriga Escribano, C., 257
Garròs, Pèir de, 241
Garry, J., 224
Garshin, Vsevolod Mikhailovich, 808
Gärtner, K., 4, 555, 585, 593, 864
Garton, J., 864
Gasbarrone, L. M., 212
Gaspar, S., 313
Gasparov, M. L., 810, 828, 837, 850
Gasquet, A., 318
Gassendi, Pierre, 140, 158, 159, 163
Gasser, M., 715
Gassieva, V. Z., 825
Gast, W., 720, 742
Gaston de France, duc d'Orléans, 134
Gaston Phébus (*Count of Foix*), 88
Gastreich, V., 649
Gather, A., 15
Gatland, J. O., 775
Gattamorta, L., 371, 476
Gatto, Alfonso, 434, 438, 456, 459, 474, 485
Gaucher, E., 93
Gaudenz, D., 522
Gaudenzi, C., 434
Gaudenzi, T., 349
Gaudin, F., 27
Gaudreau, G., 211
Gauguin, Paul, 200
Gaulard, B., 128
Gaullier-Bougassas, C., 49, 50, 63
Gaunt, S., 234
Gaup, Ailo, 778
Gautier d'Arras, 41, 52–53, 57
Gautier de Coinci, 36, 56–57
Gautier le Leu, 393
Gautier, L., 548
Gautier, Théophile, 169, 171, 177, 189, 192, 195, 199, 204, 205, 515
Gauvard, C., 35, 89
Gavagnin, C., 487
Gavrilenko, N. A., 821
Gavrilov, Anatolii, 841
Gawain and the Green Knight, 36
Gawełko, M., 6, 791
Gawinski, B., 760
Gay, P., 198
Gayà, J., 298

Gaylord, M., 273
Gazda, J., 787
Gazzellini, S., 358
Gazzola, A. L., 337
Gazzola Stacchini, V., 488
Geben, K., 803
Gebert, S., 718
Gêbka-Wolak, M., 792
Geckeler, H., 7
Geeraerts, D., 562
Geeshin, K., 247
Gehl, H., 571
Geichenko, Semen Stepanovich, 815
Geier, A., 748
Geier, R., 548
Geiler von Kaysersberg, Johannes, 612, 620, 623
Geisenhanslüke, A., 648, 743
Geiss, J., 619, 628
Geistlicher Rosengarten, 612
Gelinas, Pierre, 212
Gellermann, H., 746
Gelli, Licio, 474
Gelli Mureddu, D., 436
Gellianu, G., 511
Gellunek, C., 726
Gelu, Jacques, 85
Gemba, H., 818
Gemert, G. van, 638, 643
Gemzøe, A., 767
Genco, G., 445
Genet, Jean, 200
Genetelli, C., 440, 441
Génetiot, A., 135
Genette, Gérard, 375, 657
Genevois, E., 432
Genis, A., 834
Genna, G., 464
Gennaro, E., 435
Gennaro, R., 492
Genot, G., 422, 436
Genovesi, Antonio, 413, 415
Genovesi, F., 468
Gensini, S., 405
Gentile, C., 460
Gentile, Giovanni, 455
Gentili, S., 373, 455
Genton, H., 108
Geoffrey of Monmouth, 63, 593
Geonget, S., 115
George, A., 516
George, Stefan, 194, 430, 658, 712
Georgescu, M., 497
Gephart, I., 603
Geppert, H. V., 693
Gérard de Liège, 92
Gérard-Sai, M.-C., 86, 867
Gerbert de Montreuil, 52
Gerchunoff, Alberto, 339
Gereint ac Enid, 42
Gerhardt, C., 612
Gerhartz, L. K., 424
Gerigk, H.-J., 725
Gerlach, B., 10
Gerlach, H., 864
Gerlach, U. H., 682, 684, 688, 697, 731
Germain, J., 225
Germi, C., 230
Gerok-Reiter, A., 588, 598
Gerratana, V., 450
Gershenzohn, Mikhail, 832
Gershtein, E., 839
Gerson, Jean, 81, 85, 89
Gervais, A., 212
Gervais, M.-M., 19
Gessinger, J., 547
Gessner, Conrad, 556, 621, 630
Gesta Romanorum, 533
Gethner, P., 126, 135
Getty, L. J., 42
Geulen, E., 719
Geunich, D., 573
Gevorkian, T., 855
Gey, N., 808, 809
Geyer, A., 695
Gfereis, H., 713
Ghanime, J., 313
Ghelardi, M., 674
Gheran, N., 516
Gheţie, I., 497, 498
Ghetta, F., 520
Ghiazza, S., 487, 492
Ghidetti, E., 436, 441, 484
Ghidetti, L., 453
Ghiga, G., 504
Ghiotto, E., 415
Giachery, E., 492
Giachery, N., 492
Giachetti, C., 201
Giachino, M., 429, 446
Giacobazzi, C., 655
Giacomino da Verona, 388
Giacopo da Lentini, 236
Gialdroni, T. M., 405
Giambonini, C., 425
Giandino (*maestro*), 386
Gianelli, L., 360, 361
Giankuinta, R., 825
Giannantonio, V., 430, 431
Giannetti, V., 444
Giannini, G., 236
Giannini, Maria, 451
Giannini, S., 484
Giannone, A. L., 451, 489
Giannone, Pietro, 405, 413
Giannoni, D. S., 354
Giardinazzo, F., 440
Giarrizzo, G., 405
Giavarini, L., 157
Gibbons, D., 375
Gibbons, M. W., 82
Gibbs, M. E., 596, 675–76
Gibbs, S. V., 82
Gibellini, P., 430
Gide, André, 191, 642
Giel, C., 863
Giel, V., 673, 680
Gièly, Bernard, 242
Gies, D. T., 276
Giesing, M., 671
Gigante, M., 439
Giger, F., 523
Gigli, Piero, 474–75
Gigli Berzolari, A., 415
Gigliucci, R., 482
Gignoux, A.-C., 203
Gil, M., 72
Gil-Albert, Juan, 285
Gilbert de Tournai, 300
Gilbert, Gabriel, 153
Gilbert, P., 213
Gilbert, P. R., 209
Gilcriest, Margaret, 536
Gili Fivela, B., 361
Gilleir, A., 738
Gilles, P., 547, 567
Gillespie, D., 847
Gilliéron, J., 16
Gillman, A., 728
Gilly, C., 639, 641
Gilman, S. L., 717, 734
Giménez Caballero, Ernesto, 281
Giménez Micó, J. A., 341
Gimeno Blay, F. M., 296
Gimma, Giacinto, 405
Gimnes, S., 776, 780
Ginanni, Maria, 458
Gingras, F., 37, 76
Ginguené, Pierre-Louis, 426
Ginkas, K., 822
Ginsberg, Allen, 335
Ginzburg, L. I., 839
Ginzburg, Lidia, 839
Ginzburg, Natalia, 475, 483
Gioanola, E., 421, 437, 485
Gioberti, Vincenzo, 421, 441
Giocanti, S., 161, 163
Giono, Jean, 189, 240, 245
Giordanengo, G., 48
Giordani, Pietro, 425, 434, 441
Giordano da Pisa, 390
Giordano, C., 338
Giordano, E., 437
Giordano, N., 438
Giorgetti Vichi, A. M., 429
Giorgi, G., 150

Giovanardi, S., 460, 481
Giovanni del Virgilio, 397
Giovanuzzi, S., 456
Giovio, Paolo, 98
Gippius, V. G., 812
Gippius, Zinaida Nikolaevna, 839, 847
Giralt, S., 221
Girard, A., 193
Girard, René, 292, 464
Girardi, A., 430, 864
Girardi, E. N., 433, 437, 446, 483
Girardin, Émile de, 186
Girart de Roussillon, 40, 233
Giraud, Y., 117, 120
Girauld, Antoni, 225
Giraut de Borneil, 234
Girivenko, A. N., 810
Girndt, H., 652
Girolametto, L., 358
Girón Alconchel, J. L., 253
Girot, J.-E., 103
Girou Swiderski, M.-L., 149
Girshman, M. M., 821
Girshovich, Leonid Moiseevich, 847
Gissi Bustos, J., 337
Giudici, Giovanni, 475, 864
Giuli, P., 412
Giuliani, A., 456, 458
Giuliani, Veronica, 413
Giuliotti, Domenico, 475
Giunta, C., 386, 387
Giuriato, D., 707
Giusti, G., 13, 352
Giusti, Giuseppe, 434
Gjellerup, Karl, 767
Gladkov, A., 851
Glahn, R., 546
Glanemann, C., 15
Glaser, E., 567
Glaser, H. A., 410
Glassner, C., 582
Glatzer Rosenthal, B., 691
Glaudes, P., 204
Glauert-Hesse, B., 712, 726
Glauser, Friedrich, 712
Gledhill, C., 24
Gleit, Maria, 703
Gleizes, D., 180
Glenn, K., 282
Glessgen, M.-D., 23
Glidden, H., 114
Glinka, Fedor Nikolaevich, 808
Glissant, Edouard, 216, 217, 219
Gloning, T., 618
Głowacki, J[erzy], 800, 805
Głowińska, K., 792
Glück, H., 544, 545, 556
Glunk, F. R., 589
Gluscevic, Z., 741
Glynn, R., 463, 477
Gmeyner, Anna, 700, 703
Gnedich, N. I., 810
Gnocchi, A., 429
Gnüg, H., 669
Göbbel, E., 9
Göbel, H., 710
Gobert, F., 28
Gobetti, Pietro, 383, 407, 408
Gobrecht, B., 653
Goch, K., 690
Goci, A., 517
Godard, D., 24
Godard de Donville, L., 163
Godbout, Jacques, 208
Gödde, C,. 721
Gödde, G., 692
Gödden, W., 674, 750
Godenne, R., 201
Godfrey, S., 192
Gödicke, S., 694, 695
Godin, Gérald, 212
Gododdin, 526
Godoli, E., 451
Godolin, Pèire, 241, 242
Godwin, J., 862
Goebel, R. J., 716, 717
Goebl, H., 16, 23, 26, 518, 519, 520
Goedert, G., 690
Goehr, L., 206
Goes, S., 548
Goethe, Johann Wolfgang von, 187, 285, 288, 403, 407, 422, 426, 430, 647, 648, 650, 652, 655, 657, 658, 665, 666, 671, 681, 682, 685, 687, 688, 702, 708, 714, 724, 735, 769, 818, 860, 864
Goette, J.-W., 725
Goetz, A., 176
Goetz, Rainald, 744
Goetze, M., 652
Goeury, J., 115
Goffin, R., 28
Gogol, Nikolai Vasilievich, 172, 806, 808, 812–13, 819, 825, 828
Gohin, Y., 180
Göhler, P., 603
Gohory, Jacques, 103
Goicu, S., 503, 504
Golato, A., 561
Goldammer, P., 697
Goldbach, M., 24
Goldberg, Oskar, 704
Goldenberg, A. K., 813
Goldfarb, D. A., 814
Goldin Folena, D., 411
Goldmann, S. T., 446
Goldoni, Carlo, 400, 412, 414–15
Goldschmidt, G. A., 686
Goldstein, Moritz, 705
Goldt, R., 835
Golino, E., 477
Goll, Claire, 726
Goll, Yvan, 712
Gollerbakh, E., 840
Golonka, A., 797
Golovchiner, V. E., 834
Goltschnigg, D., 674, 719
Goltz, R., 683
Golubeva, L. G., 843
Golubkov, S. A., 834
Golz, J., 663
Goma, Paul, 513, 515
Gomberville, Marin Le Roy de, 125, 128, 145, 150
Gombocz, I., 688
Gomes, R. C., 349
Gómez, F. J., 301
Gómez, J. L., 286
Gómez, M. A., 283
Gómez Abalo, Á., 294
Gómez Manzano, P., 246
Gómez Muntané, M., 303
Gómez-Pérez, A., 289
Gómez de la Serna, Ramón, 281, 290
Gómez de Tudanca, R., 287
Goncharov, Ivan Alexandrovich, 808, 819, 828
Goncharova-Grabovskaia, S., 842
Goncourt, Edmond de, 199, 206
Gong, Alfred, 705, 712
Gong, S., 710
Góngora y Argote, Luis de, 287, 492
Gontero, V., 41, 47
Gontier de Soignies, 57
González, A., 327
González, J. E., 318
Gonzalez, P.-G., 30, 230
González, S., 316
González, X., 314
González Aranda, Y., 256
González González, M[anolo], 304
González González, M[aría], 306
González Guerra, A., 304
González Hebrán, J. M., 269
González Ollé, F., 249, 864
González Rey, I., 33
González Seoane, E., 305, 309

González del Valle, L. T., 280, 286
González Velasco, M., 265
Gooding-Williams, R., 690
Goodkin, R. E., 142
Goodyear, William, 533
Goossens, J., 553
Gor, Gennadii, 839, 848
Gorbachev, Mikhail, 839
Gorbanevskaya, Natalia Evgenievna, 844
Gordeev, N. M., 815
Gordin, M. A., 813
Gordon, B., 631
Gordon, S., 334
Gorelov, A. E., 843
Gorenshtein, Fridrikh, 844, 848
Goria, C., 359
Gorini, Paolo, 447
Gorky, Maxim, 841, 848
Gorlova, N., 851, 852
Górna, M., 798
Görner, R., 660, 684, 705, 861
Gornfel'd, A. G., 824
Gorni, G., 372, 376, 378–79, 395, 396, 432
Gorokh, T. V., 814
Görres, Joseph, 664
Gorris Camos, R., 103, 112
Gorriti, Juana Manuela, 319
Górski, K., 797
Górski, R. L., 791, 803
Gorzkowski, A., 787
Göschel, J., 862
Gosman, M., 77
Gosser-Esquilín, M. A., 323
Gossip, C. J., 139, 140
Gössmann, W., 686
Got, O., 202, 203
Gottdang, A., 598
Gottfried von Strassburg, 47, 579, 586, 592, 597–98, 865
Gottlieb, H., 759
Gottschall, D., 607
Göttsche, D., 741
Gottsched, Johann Christoph, 556
Götz, U., 553
Goubet, J.-F., 653
Gouchet, O., 776
Goudaillier, J.-F., 33
Goulart, Simon, 109
Gould Levine, L., 340
Goulesque, F., 193
Goulet, A., 174
Goupillaud, L., 132
Gourdin, H., 167
Gourmont, Rémy de, 190, 199
Gournay, Marie Le Jars de, 103, 112, 113, 146, 150–51
Gouvéa, André de, 112
Gouverneur, S., 167
Gouville, Lucie de Cotentin, marquise de, 154
Govoni, Corrado, 457, 475
Gowans, L., 43
Gower, John, 71, 84
Goya y Lucientes, Francisco, 284
Goyet, F., 103, 861
Gozzano, Guido, 422, 456, 475, 860
Gozzi, Carlo (*Count*), 400, 409, 415, 655
Grabbe, Christian Dietrich, 671, 674, 681–82
Grabovszki, E., 705
Grabowsky, I., 833, 834, 862
Gracchus, Fritz, 216
Grachev, G. D., 826
Gracheva, I. V., 806, 830
Gracián, Baltasar, 268
Gracq, Julien (Louis Poirier), 189
Graczyńska, J., 803
Grădinaru, D., 511
Grădişteanu, P., 511
Graevenitz, G. von, 696
Graf von Savoyen, 607
Graf, A., 699
Graf, Arturo, 422, 434–35
Graf, E. C., 340
Graf, K., 578
Grafton, A., 100
Grama, A., 511
Grambye, C., 763
Gramfort, V., 206
Gramigna, G., 461, 483
Grammont, M., 7
Gramsci, Antonio, 450, 462
Gramuglio, M. T., 338
Granados, P., 341
Granda, G. de, 249, 257, 262
Grande, N., 154, 155
Grandesso, E., 441
Grandi, N., 16
Grandmontagne, Francisco, 318
Grandson, Oton de, 90
Granese, A., 413, 422
Granier, Pau-Loís, 239
Granièr, S., 227
Granin, Daniel, 839
Granisso, M. P., 467
Granlund, L. G., 779
Granovskaya, N. I., 816
Gras, Felix, 243
Grăsoiu, D., 510
Grass, Günter, 642, 711, 718, 726, 733, 744–45
Grassau, C. S., 661
Grasso, Silvana, 475
Grätz, K., 729
Grauby, F., 199
Graugaard, C., 760
Graur, A., 496
Graves, P., 736
Gravina, Gianvincenzo, 404, 405
Grawe, C., 677, 679
Gray, D., 85
Gray, F., 97, 116
Gray, John, 199, 200
Gray, R. T., 717
Graziano, C., 481
Gréban, Arnoul, 66
Grechanaia, E. P., 810
Greci, R., 383
Gréciano, G., 548, 565
Green, D. H., 41, 553, 591–92, 594, 595
Green, D. W., 557
Green, L. D., 634
Greene, V., 43, 45
Greenfield, J., 589, 595, 596, 86
Gregori, I., 511, 515
Gregory (*Saint*), 593
Gregory of Tours, 6
Gregson, J., 736
Greiffenberg, Catharina Regina von, 639, 641–42
Greimas, A. J., 746
Greiner, B., 660
Greiner, F., 131
Grek, A. G., 828
Grekhnev, V. A., 815
Grell, C., 864
Gremler, C., 723
Grenaille, François de, 144
Grente-Méra, B., 177
Grenville, A., 703
Gresti, P., 235
Greub, Y., 222
Greule, A., 523, 545, 547, 553, 555, 574, 781
Grewe, A., 97
Greyerz, K. von, 635
Griakalova, N. I., 852
Gribanov, A., 832
Gribanov, B., 847
Gribnitz, B., 659
Griboedov, Alexander Sergeevich, 813
Grice, H., 329
Grice, M., 557
Grideanu, C., 508
Grieg, Nordahl, 779
Griffini Rosnati, G. M., 444
Griffiths, Ann, 535
Grignan, Françoise Marguerite de Sévigné, comtesse de, 155
Grignani, M. A., 456

Grignon, Claude-Henri, 212
Grigoriev, Apollon Alexandrovich, 807
Grigoriev, D., 823
Grigoriev, Oleg, 848
Grigoriev, V. P., 849
Grijzenhout, J., 10
Griley, Y., 258
Grill, H., 553
Grillon, L., 222
Grillparzer, Franz, 670, 671, 682–83, 706, 751
Grimaldi, Domenico, 415
Grimaldi, G., 444
Grimalt, J. A., 299
Grimarest, Jean Léonor Le Gallois, sieur de, 138
Grimberg, M., 679
Grimm, E., 744
Grimm, Hans, 712
Grimm, Herman, 683
Grimm, J., 111
Grimm, Jacob, 551, 653–54
Grimm, Melchior (*Baron*), 187
Grimm, Wilhelm, 653–54
Grimmelshausen, Hans Jacob Christoffel von, 155, 642–43
Grimstad, K. A., 724, 813
Grisé, C. M., 133, 156
Griselini, Francesco, 415
Grishakova, M., 850
Grishina, I., 852
Grisko, M., 711
Gritsuk, S., 807
Grivel, C., 144
Gröber, Gustav, 233
Grobet, A., 33
Grobman, M., 839
Groddeck, W., 731
Grodek, E., 864
Groethuysen, Bernhard, 702
Grohmann, K. K., 562
Grolimund, C., 574
Gromov-Kolli, A. V., 819
Gromova, L. D., 826
Gromova, M. I., 835
Gronas, A., 848
Gronda, G., 438
Grønfeldt, Vibeke, 770
Grönquist, L., 761
Grønvik, O., 755
Groodt, S. de, 562
Groos, A., 864
Groos, A. T., 594, 603
Groppe, C., 711
Gros, J.-M., 161
Grosjean, F., 23
Grosperrin, J.-P., 136, 138, 148, 862
Gross, Erhard, 609
Gross, G., 28, 667, 701
Gross, M., 522
Gross, R. V., 716, 717
Grosse, R., 571
Grosse, S., 547, 551, 674
Grosse, W., 674
Grossel, M.-G., 55, 76
Grossi, A., 401
Grossi, P., 426
Grossi, Tommaso, 435
Grossman, K. M., 172, 180, 864
Grossman, U., 720
Grosz, George, 730
Groth, Klaus, 683
Grotius, Hugo, 645
Groto, Luigi, 398
Grotowski, J., 294
Grotrian, Simon, 768
Grove, L., 128, 135
Groza, G., 512
Grozdanic, G.-D., 730
Grözinger, K. E., 863
Gruber, A., 572
Grubitz, C., 715
Grubmüller, K., 580, 602
Grucza, F., 549
Gruffat, S., 133
Gruffudd Hiraethog, 531
Gruffydd, Hywel, 534
Gruffydd, R. G., 528, 531
Gruget, Claude, 110
Grün, Max von der, 745
Grünbein, Durs, 745
Grundtvig, Nikolai Frederik Severin, 766
Grünert, M., 867
Grüninger, I., 708
Grunwald, M., 699
Gruszczyński, W., 794, 799
Grutman, R., 172
Grüttemeier, R., 680
Gruuthuse, Louis de, 89
Grybosiowa, A., 794, 796
Gryphius, Andreas, 644, 699
Gryphius, Sébastien, 100
Grywatsch, J., 750
Grzega, J., 15, 518, 864
Grzegorcyk, M., 319
Grzegorczykowa, R., 794
Grzenia, J., 805
Grzepski, S., 799
Grzywka, K., 683
Guagni, E., 452
Guagnini, E., 464
Gualbes, Melcior de, 297
Gualdo, R., 385
Guarinonius, Hippolytus, 643
Guarnieri, B., 451
Guarnieri, Gianfrancesco, 347
Guarnieri, Luigi, 475
Guarracino, V., 440
Guastella, Serafino Amabile, 423
Guasti, M. T., 12
Guay, P., 213
Gubailovsky, V., 828, 837, 841, 847
Gubatz, T., 589
Guberti, M. C., 480
Gudayol, A., 296
Gudiksen, A., 758
Gudimova, G. A., 807
Guégan, S., 185
Guellouz, S., 861
Guelpa, P., 539
Guénon, René, 515
Guenthner, F., 28
Guéret, Gabriel, 137
Guéret-Laferté, M., 74
Guérin, M.-A., 209
Guermès, S., 202
Guernes de Pont-Sainte-Maxence, 55
Guerra, Tonino, 459
Guerracino, V., 459
Guerrero, María, 294
Guerricchio, R., 481
Guerrier, O., 112
Guerrin, C., 225
Guerrini, L., 415
Guerrini, Olindo, 435
Guevara, Antonio de, 266, 271
Guèvremont, Germaine, 212, 215
Guglielmi, G., 457, 461
Guglielmi, L., 520
Guglielmi, S., 456
Guglielminetti, Amalia, 465
Guglielminetti, M., 370, 396, 454, 465
Gui de Cavaillon, 233
Gui de Warewick, 63
Guiati, A., 468
Guibert de Tournai, 92
Guibert, F., 230
Guicciardini, Francesco, 438
Güida, E.-M., 254
Guida, S., 231
Guidacci, Margherita, 475
Guiderdoni-Bruslé, A., 150
Guidin, M. L., 345
Guido de Adam, 384
Guilhem de Baus, 392
Guilhem Molinier, 232
Guilhem de la Tor, 232
Guillaume X (*Duke of Aquitaine*), 235
Guillaume de Lorris, 36, 38, 41, 44, 53, 54, 395
Guillaume de Palerne, 52
Guillaume, G., 24

Guillaume, Jacquette, 161
Guilleminot-Chrétien, G., 106
Guillén, C., 288
Guillén, Jorge, 281, 287
Guillén, T., 286
Guilleragues, Gabriel de Lavergne, vicomte de, 151, 152
Guillerm, J.-P., 205
Guillon, J.-M., 30, 228, 229, 861
Guimarães, Bernardo, 343, 344, 349
Guimarães, R., 345, 349
Guimarães Rosa, João, 343, 344, 349
Guinizelli, Guido, 377, 385, 386–87
Guion, B., 130, 158, 164
Güiraldes, Ricardo, 332
Guiraut de Bornelh, 235
Guiraut Riquier, 231
Guiron le Courtois, 69
Guisan, J., 315
Guittone d'Arezzo, 386, 387, 395, 399
Guixeras, D., 299, 300
Gujord, H., 775
Gukovsky, Grigorii, 838
Gulawska, M., 803
Guldager, Katrine Marie, 765
Gumbel, E. J., 730
Gumilev, Nikolai Stepanovich, 807, 822, 828, 831, 841, 844
Guminsky, V., 809, 812
Gummelt, V., 631
Günderrode, Karoline von, 649
Gundersen, K., 183
Gunnarsson, M., 761
Gunnemann, K. V., 720
Günter, A. L., 712
Güntert, G., 439
Günthart, R., 635
Günther, H., 565, 630
Günther, S., 562
Günzel, S., 690
Guran, P., 509
Gurgel, G. L., 348
Guro, Elena, 832
Gursky, L., 841
Gürtler, C., 706
Gurvich, I., 808
Guseinov, A. A., 857
Gusev, N. N., 826
Gus'kov, S. N., 828
Gusmani, R., 555
Gussalli, Antonio, 441
Gustavsson, J., 757
Gutenberg, Johannes, 267
Guthke, K., 670
Guthmüller, B., 863
Gutiérrez, Juan, 266
Gutiérrez, S., 313
Gutiérrez-Bravo, R., 9
Gutiérrez Carou, J., 440
Gutiérrez Cerezo, A., 255
Gutiérrez Cuadrado, J., 257
Gutiérrez Muñón, M., 265
Gutiérrez Nájera, Manuel, 327
Gutiérrez Ordóñez, S., 3
Gutiérrez-Rexach, J., 246
Gutscher-Schmid, C., 611
Guţu Romalo, V., 505
Gutwald, T., 621
Gutwirth, M., 126
Gutzkow, Karl, 668, 672, 683–84
Guyaux, A., 199
Guyon du Chesnoy, Jeanne-Marie Bouvier de la Motte, Dame de, 146, 158
Guyot-Bachy, I., 71
Guyot-Rouge, G., 196
Guz, B., 796
Gwallog (*King of Elmet*), 530
Gwalther, Rudolf, 633, 635
Gwilym Fychan, 531
Gwilym ap Gruffydd, 531
Gwilym Hiraethog (William Rees), 534
Gwiżdż, Feliks, 799
Gyp (Sybille-Gabrielle Marie-Antoinette de Riquetti de Mirabeau, comtesse de Martel de Joinville), 199
Gyssels, K., 219, 220

Haac, O., 187
Haarmann, H. D., 545, 546
Haas, B., 700
Haas, W., 569, 572
Haase, E., 757
Haase, M., 226
Haavardsholm, Espen, 779
Habeck, R., 709
Haberkamm, K., 643
Haberkern, E., 610
Habermann, M., 556, 558, 618, 629
Habermas, Jürgen, 579
Habers, H., 748
Habicht, P., 619
Habrajska, G., 802
Hachmeister, G. L., 648
Hącia, A., 792
Häcki-Buhofer, A., 567
Hackländer, Friedrich Wilhelm, 670
Hacks, Peter, 745
HaCohen, R., 705
Hadamar von Laber, 581
Hadlock, P. G., 192, 200
Haeckel, Ernst, 669
Haefs, W., 726
Haenicke, D., 864
Haferland, H., 584, 589, 603
Haffemayer, S., 131
Häfner, R., 640
Hage, A., 185
Hägele, G., 299
Hageman, E. H., 272
Häggkvist, C., 261
Hahn, B., 675
Hahn, G., 603
Hahn, H. J., 663
Hahn, M., 689, 863
Hahn, R., 588
Hahn, T., 710
Hahn, U., 239
Haider, Jörg, 746
Haigh, S., 217, 218
Haimerl, E., 519
Haines, B., 749
Hainsworth, P., 364, 400, 421, 450, 864
Hainz, M., 743
Hajek, J., 355
Hajičová, E., 781
Häker, H., 660, 661
Hála, J., 785
Halbe, Max, 712
Halberg, Jonny, 776
Halder, W., 704
Hall, H. G., 132
Hall, K., 82
Hall, T. A., 557
Haller, H. W., 359
Hallward, P., 219
Hallyn, F., 162
Halperín-Donghi, T., 337
Haltrup, D., 761
Halub, M., 686
Hamblin, V., 66
Hambly, P., 193
Hamburger, A., 757
Hamburger, J. F., 610
Hamburger, Käte, 737
Hamel, J.-F., 214
Hamel, R., 209
Hamelin, Louis, 208
Hamesse, J., 76, 864
Hamilton, J. F., 171
Hamm, C., 780
Hamm, J., 623
Hamm, M., 607
Hammacher, K., 652
Hammel, A., 732
Hammer, T. A., 523
Hammershøi, Vilhelm, 777
Hammond, N., 142, 165, 166

Hamon, B., 182
Hamrick, L. C., 192
Hamsun, Knut, 775–76
Hanamann, R., 613
Hanawalt, B., 864
Handesten, L., 771
Handke, Peter, 745
Händl, C., 580, 591
Handoca, M., 515
Hanegraaff, W. J., 862
Hanganu, L., 514
Hanlin, T. C., 737
Hans von Bühel, 618
Hansen, A. B., 23
Hansen, E., 757
Hansen, E. J., 760
Hansen, E. W., 755
Hansen, Else Tranberg, 768
Hansen, I. S., 758
Hansen, J., 759
Hansen, J. A., 345
Hansen, J. W., 760
Hansen, Martin A., 770
Hansen, N. G., 770
Hansen, R., 683
Hanslick, Eduard, 692
Hanssen, Arvid, 778
Häntzschel, G., 677, 711
Häntzschel, H., 677, 708
Happé, P., 66
Hara, T., 193
Harant z Polžic a Bezdružuc, Kryštov, 782
Harbaoui, C., 187
Hardin, J., 705
Harding, C., 84
Hardman, P., 864
Hardt, D., 761
Hardy, C., 28
Hardy, Thomas, 280
Harel, S., 207
Harf-Lancner, L., 38, 49, 78, 88, 860
Harig, Ludwig, 642, 745, 751
Harismendy-Lony, S., 189
Hârlav, C., 510
Harm, V., 555
Harman, M., 716, 717
Harmat, M., 585
Harms, W., 621, 623
Harnisch, R., 553, 561, 567
Harnischfeger, J., 660
Harper, A. J., 676, 686, 864
Harrington, T. M., 165
Harris, J., 141
Harris, N., 576, 596
Harris, Wilson, 216
Harris-Northall, R., 252
Harrits, F., 771
Harsdörffer, Georg Philipp, 645
Hart, K., 194
Hart, S., 340
Hartau, J., 619
Härtl, H., 652
Hartl, L. A., 706
Hartl, N., 619, 870
Hartlaub, Felix, 712
Hartlieb, Johannes, 600, 617
Härtling, Peter, 736
Hartman, L., 253
Hartmann von Aue, 579, 586, 592–93, 603
Hartmann, D., 567
Hartmann, H., 595
Hartmann, Karl Amadeus, 642
Hartmann, Lukas, 737
Hartmann, P., 671
Hartmann, R., 572
Hartmann, S., 580, 606
Hartung, G., 711
Hartung, S., 191
Hartwich, W.-D., 704, 721
Harvey, C., 53, 67
Harvey, R., 233, 235
Hasdeu, Bogdan Petriceicu, 511
Hasebrink, B., 586, 600
Hasenclever, Walter, 699, 712
Hasenkamp, W., 29
Hasenohr, G., 3, 5, 76, 110
Hasler, Eveline, 738
Hašová, L., 785, 786
Hasse, D. N., 629
Hassel, U., 668
Hasselman, M., 90
Hassen, B., 707
Hassenpflug, Ludwig, 654
Hassler, G., 10
Hass-Zumkehr, U., 562, 863
Hastings, R., 362
Hasty, W., 586
Hasubek, P., 683, 687
Hatoum, Milton, 344
Hätzlerin, Clara, 602
Haubrichs, W., 616, 863
Hauf, A. G., 298
Hauff, Wilhelm, 654, 672
Haug, C., 683
Haug, W., 586, 589, 592, 598
Haugan, J., 769
Hauge, Olav H., 779
Haugen, Paal-Helge, 779
Haupt, B., 587
Haupt, S., 649, 657
Hauptmann, Carl, 713
Hauptmann, Gerhart, 713
Hauschild, J.-C., 684, 685
Hauschild, V., 726
Hausdorff, Felix, 692
Häusler, L., 550
Hausmann, A., 604
Hausmann, F., 6
Hausmann, Raoul, 713
Hausner, I., 521, 523
Haustein, J., 605
Hautcoeur, G., 148
Hautefeuille, Jean, abbé de, 154
Havemann, D., 690
Havgaard, M., 758
Havnevik, I., 774
Hawthorne, M. C., 201
Hayes, N., 629
Hazlett, W. I. P., 630
Heaney, Seamus, 456
Heap, D., 16
Heathcote, O., 174
Hebbel, Friedrich, 668, 669, 672, 684
Hebel, Johann Peter, 653, 654–55
Heberger, A., 746
Hébert, Anne, 208, 209, 212–13
Heck, C., 80
Heck, K., 630, 636
Heeke, U., 675
Heereboord, Adriaan, 162
Heftrich, E., 721, 725
Hegarty, T. J., 4
Hegel, Georg Wilhelm Friedrich, 169, 655
Hegelund, L., 759
Hehle, C., 584–85, 679, 680
Heidegger *(family)*, 625
Heidegger, Martin, 438, 461, 488, 658, 690, 707, 743, 745, 763, 765, 773
Heidermann, H., 686
Heidermanns, F., 553
Heijkant, M.-J., 392
Heil, A., 377
Heimann, Moritz, 704
Hein, Christoph, 742
Hein, J., 689, 694
Hein, S., 582
Heine, A., 561
Heine, Heinrich, 426, 648, 666, 668, 669, 672, 684–86, 769, 829
Heinen, R., 693
Heinesen, William, 770–71
Heinrich von Morungen, 602–03
Heinrich von Mügeln, 605–06
Heinrich von München, 596, 616
Heinrich von Neustadt, 601
Heinrich der Teichner, 609
Heinrich von dem Türlin, 598–99
Heinse, Wilhelm, 649
Heinsius, Daniel, 645

Heintzelmann, M. Z., 614
Heinz, S., 526, 532
Heinzer, F., 609
Heinzle, J., 577, 582, 597
Heinzmann, J.-M., 636
Heise, H.-J., 744
Heitmann, A., 677, 775
Heitsch, D., 93
Hekking, E., 262
Helbig, H., 747
Helfant, I. M., 806
Helfer, M. B., 682
Heliade Rădulescu, Ion, 508, 512, 513
Heliand, 576, 584
Hell, J., 746, 747
Helle, Helle, 764, 765, 768
Heller, K., 546
Heller, L., 809, 864
Heller, P., 737
Heller, S.-G., 53, 59, 77, 91, 864
Hellfritzsch, V., 574
Hellgardt, E., 597, 865
Hellinger, M., 13, 865
Helmreich, C., 663, 664
Helms, L., 200
Helmstetter, R., 714
Heloïse, 87
Hemecker, W. W., 727
Hemingway, Ernest, 493
Hemmer, B., 776
Hémon, Louis, 213
Hempel, N., 751
Hempen, D., 719
Hempfer, K. W., 97, 109, 865
Hemprich, G., 532
Hengartner, T., 633
Hénin, E., 136
Henisch, Peter, 737, 745
Henne, H., 566, 669, 865
Hennequin, Jeanne, 109
Hennessy, S. S., 203
Hennig, T., 660
Hennig von Lange, C., 612
Hennings, T., 585
Henri III (*King of France*), 97, 106, 122
Henri IV (*King of France*), 106, 121, 167
Henri de Ferrières, 77
Henrich, R., 631, 635
Henrichsen, P. J., 761
Henriette-Anne Stuart, duchesse d'Orléans, *dite* Henriette d'Angleterre, 126, 137
Henriksen, M. B., 772
Henry IV (*King of England*), 71
Henry of Saltry, 56
Henry, F. G., 865
Henscheid, Eckard, 752
Hensel, Fanny, 688
Hensel, Luise, 686
Henshaw, A., 130
Hentschel, U., 648, 668
Henze, Hans Werner, 741
Hepfer, C., 396
Hepp, N., 126
Herberay des Essarts, Nicolas, 103
Herberg, D., 566
Herbermann, C.-P., 566
Herberstein, Sigmund von, 629
Herbert, M., 541, 542
Herbert, Zbigniew, 799
Herbin, J.-C., 39, 49, 55, 56, 865
Hercel, I., 769
Herder, Johann Gottfried, 187, 648, 649, 663
Heredia, José María, 193, 319
Herej-Szymańska, K., 798, 803
Hériché, S., 72
Hérilier, C., 230
Herling-Grudziński, Gustaw, 799
Herlinghaus, H., 338
Herman, J., 6
Herman, M. M., 864
Hermand, J., 709
Hermann von Sachsenheim, 609
Hermann, Daniel, 628
Hermann, Georg, 704
Hermann, Judith, 743
Hermann, R., 726
Hermanns, F., 551
Hermida de Blas, F., 292
Hermlin, Stephan, 743–44, 746
Hermsdorf, K., 715, 717
Hermundsgård, F., 780
Hernández, B., 465
Hernández, Felisberto, 339
Hernández, M., 285
Hernández, R. J., 270
Hernández Alonso, C., 265
Hernández Esteban, M., 865
Hernández-Rodríguez, R., 281
Hernando Delgado, J., 296
Héroët, Antoine, 118
Herr von Braunschweig, 576
Herrand von Wildonie, 582
Herrenkind, S., 673
Herrera, Fernando de, 273
Herrera, J. N., 341
Herrera, M. T., 865
Herreras, J. C., 4
Herrero, A., 315
Herrero, G., 257
Herrero-Velarde, G. I., 284
Herrgen, J., 570
Herrmann, G., 284
Herrmann, J., 712
Herrnleben, T., 553
Herrschel, M., 710
Herry, G., 414
Hershberger, R. P., 291
Hertel, François, 213
Herviz de Metz, 39
Herweg, M., 584
Herwegh, Georg, 680, 686
Herwig, M., 724
Herz, Marcus, 654, 656
Herz, R., 617
Herzen, Alexander Ivanovich, 187, 828
Herzinger, R., 708
Herzl, Theodor, 713
Herzog Ernst, 576, 577, 587–88
Herzog Herpin, 591
Herzog, A., 705
Herzog, H. H., 706
Herzog, T., 706
Herzog, Wilhelm, 700
Hesdin, Acart de, 69
Hesketh, G., 76
Hess, P., 637
Hesse, Hermann, 280, 702, 713
Hessel, Franz, 704, 713
Hesselholdt, Christina, 764, 768
Hesselmann, P., 642, 643, 862
Hess-Lüttich, E. W. B., 548
Hester, S., 785
Hettche, W., 678, 701
Hetteni, Z., 809
Hetzner, M., 660
Heussler, Leonhard, 633
Heuvel, G. van den, 643
Hewitt, L. D., 219
Heydebrand, R. von, 675
Heyden, Sebald, 545
Heydenreich, T., 320, 457
Heyer-Caput, M., 480
Heym, Georg, 656, 743
Heym, Stefan, 746
Heyme, Hansgünther, 684
Heyns, Pierre, 106
Heyse, Paul, 686
Heysel, G. R., 200
Heyworth, G., 42
Hick, Jochen, 736
Hicks, E., 83, 865
Hidalgo, M., 249
Hiddleston, J. A., 179, 180
Hiebler, H., 714
Hierro, José, 285
Higgins, J., 341
Highfill, J., 282
Higley, S., 532
Higman, F., 100
Higuera, J. G., 299, 863
Hilbig, Wolfgang, 746
Hildebrand, R., 207

Hildebrandslied, 579, 583, 585
Hildebrandt, A., 650
Hildebrandt, H., 687
Hildebrandt, R., 557
Hildegard von Bingen, 576, 578, 610
Hildesheimer, Wolfgang, 746, 750
Hilgar, M.-F., 154
Hill, V., 500
Hillard, D., 692
Hillenbrand, R., 643, 688, 720
Hiller von Gaertringen, J., 680, 682, 698
Hiller, Kurt, 704
Hillesheim, J., 725
Hillgarth, J. N., 296
Hillman, James, 478
Hillman, R., 150
Hillmann, H., 670
Hilmes, C., 753
Hilscher, E., 603
Hiltalingen von Basel, Johannes, 610–11
Hilty, G., 248, 522
Himelfarb, G., 23
Hinck, W., 669
Hîncu, D., 514
Hindelang, G., 556
Hinderer, W., 647
Hindret, J., 21
Hiner, S., 203
Hinojosa, José María, 282
Hintz, E. R., 600
Hintze, M.-A., 30
Hinz, M., 690
Hippel, Theodor Gottlieb von, 655, 656
Hirakawa, K., 687
Hirdt, W., 445
Hirsch, R., 713
Hirsch, S., 720
Hirschfeld, U., 557
Hirt, Alois, 402
Hirte, C., 725
Histoire ancienne jusqu'à César, 391
Histoire du royaume d'Antangil, 154, 159
Historia de Preliis, 49
Hitler, Adolf, 703, 709, 730, 746
Hjordt-Vetlesen, I.-L., 770
Hladká, Z., 865
Hlubinková, Z., 786
Hnátková, M., 783, 784
Ho, C., 84
Hoberg, R., 545, 546
Hobson, M., 813
Hochhuth, Rolf, 740
Hochstrasser, G., 503
Hock, W., 553
Hoddis, Jakob von, 704
Hodgson, R. G., 164, 865
Høeck, Klaus, 764
Hoefert, S., 713
Hof, A. M., 690
Hoffman, D. L., 43
Hoffmann, B., 641, 682
Hoffmann, D., 704
Hoffmann, E[rnst] T[heodor] A[madeus], 649, 650, 651, 655–57
Hoffmann, G., 111, 112, 113
Hoffmann, H., 496
Hoffmann, M., 550
Hoffmann, V., 672
Hoffmann, W., 552, 573
Hoffmann, Y., 706
Hoffmann von Fallersleben, August Heinrich, 686–87
Hoffmannová, J., 785
Hoffmeister, G., 685
Hofmann, D., 546
Hofmann, F., 708
Hofmann, Gert, 746
Hofmann, P., 713
Hofmannsthal, Hugo von, 663, 691, 701, 704, 706, 711, 713–15
Hofmeister, W., 603, 620
Hogan-Brun, G., 546
Hogenbirk, M., 43
Hohensinner, K., 568, 572, 573
Hohler, K., 726
Hohnerlein-Buchinger, T., 360
Hoinkes, U., 15
Højholt, Per, 764, 767, 771
Holberg, Ludvig, 756, 763, 774
Holden, A. J., 62
Hölderlin, Friedrich, 194, 285, 494, 652, 653, 657–58, 712
Holderness, J. S., 81, 86
Holen, I., 779
Holian, G. C., 53
Holitscher, Arthur, 715
Hollander, R., 393
Hollard, C.-F., 222
Hollender, M., 681
Höller, H., 670, 695
Holly, W., 547, 552, 556
Hollywood, A., 93
Holm, I. W., 717
Holm, T., 779
Holm-Larsen, S., 759
Holmberg, B., 756, 762
Holmberg, H., 755, 756
Holte, Knut, 778
Holtei, Karl von, 687
Holton, M., 95
Holtus, G., 23, 864
Holub, R. C., 734
Holz, Arno, 701
Hölz, Max, 730
Holzapfel, O., 569
Holzkamp, H., 710
Holznagel, F.-J., 577, 610
Holzner, J., 865
Homer, 130, 143, 201, 273, 410, 411, 417, 438
Hondorff, Andreas, 633
Honemann, V., 576
Hong, K.-P., 731
Hong, R. E., 141
Honigmann, Barbara, 746
Honold, A., 701
Honoré, Pierre, 71
Honorius Augustodunensis, 388, 607, 608
Hoock-Demarle, M.-C., 648
Hope, Q. M., 152
Höpel, I., 640
Hopgyn ap Tomas, 527
Hopil, Claude, 157
Horace (Quintus Horatius Flaccus), 395, 397, 403–04
Horálek, J., 781, 785
Horcajo, A., 181
Horcajo, C., 181, 202
Horch, H. O., 705, 860
Horia, Vintilă, 509, 513, 517
Horkheimer, Max, 749
Horn, E., 657
Hörner, P., 610
Hornsby, D., 30
Horodincă, G., 514
Horozco, Agustín de, 270
Hörsch, N., 221
Horst, C. auf der, 684
Hort von der Astronomie, 606
Horvat, D., 689
Horváth, Ödön von, 689, 700, 703, 706, 715, 731
Hošnová, E., 784
Hössli, Heinrich, 669
Houbert, J., 183
Houdard, S., 136, 158
Houdebine-Gravaud, A.-M., 29
Houe, P., 767
Houellebecq, Michel, 204
Hougaard, T. T., 761
Housley, W., 785
Houth, Henriette, 768
Hovden, Anders, 776
Hove, I., 546
Howe, A., 134
Howells, R., 165
Howes, G. C., 706
Hoyer, G., 523
Hoyer, T., 692
Hoyo, A. del, 286
Hrabal, Josef, 799

Hrdlička, M., 781, 784
Hualde, J. I., 9, 247
Huarte de San Juan, Juan, 266
Hubáček, J., 785
Huber, A., 235, 688
Huber, C., 597, 600, 606, 620, 865
Huber, F., 81
Huber, M., 742
Hubert (*Saint*), 280
Hubert, J. D., 133
Hübinger, G., 701
Hubrath, M., 611
Huchon, M., 21, 103
Huck, D., 569
Hudabiunigg, I., 547
Hudde, H., 712
Hudon, J.-G., 214
Hue de Rotelande, 51
Hüe, D., 43, 76, 91, 116
Huebner, S., 203
Huerkamp, J., 682
Huesmann, M., 862
Huet, Pierre Daniel, 127, 147, 158
Hufnagel, E., 692
Hufnagel, I., 680
Hug, A., 574
Hug, Johannes, 576
Huge Scheppel, 591
Hugeburc von Heidenheim, 578
Hugh of St Victor, 608
Hughes, B., 258
Hughes, E. J., 200
Hughes, H., 536, 716
Hughes, J., 727
Hughes, T. R., 536
Hügli, M. E. S., 346
Hugo von Langenstein, 611
Hugo von Trimberg, 609
Hugo, Abel, 172
Hugo, Victor, 169, 171–73, 174, 175, 179–82, 185, 186, 191, 192, 193, 203, 424
Hugo Cruz, V., 328
Huguccio of Pisa, 391
Hugues, R., 299
Hühn, P., 670
Hulk, A., 11, 865
Hülsenbeck, A., 675
Hultberg, Peer, 771
Humboldt, Wilhelm von, 20
Hume, David, 161, 409
Huml, A., 705
Hummel, C., 742
Humpál, M., 779
Hunbaut, 68
Hundsnurscher, F., 564
Hundt, M., 552, 559
Hunt, T., 55, 56
Hunter, J., 535
Huon d'Auvergne, 65
Huonder, Silvio, 738
Huot, G., 212
Huot, M. C., 208
Huot, S., 47, 70, 72, 86, 88, 91
Huppert, G., 98
Hürlimann, Thomas, 746
Hurworth, A., 91
Hus, Auguste, 408
Husáková, M., 785
Huschenbett, D., 608
Husserl, Edmund, 763
Hussherr, C., 171
Huszai, V., 725
Hutcheon, L., 289, 424
Hutcheon, M., 424
Hutchinson, P., 670, 709, 746, 753, 865
Hutson, L., 866
Hutten, Ulrich von, 633
Huws, D., 529, 532
Huysmans, Charles-Marie-Georges, *dit* Joris-Karl, 190, 199–200, 203
Hvid, E., 760
Hyams, B., 694
Hywel Cilan, 531
Hywel Swrdwal, 531

Iablokov, E. A., 852
Iacuzzi, P. F., 468
Iakimova, L. P., 849
Ianchevetskovy, Vasilii Grigorievich, 848
Iancu, M., 512, 514
Iannaccone, G., 481
Iannucci, A. A., 366, 367
Ianoş, I., 517
Ianovskaya, L., 846
Ianovsky, N. N., 843
Iastrebov, A. L., 820
Iatromathematisches Corpus, 576
Iavorskaya, L., 822
Iavorsky, A. N., 849
Ibáñez, Juan, 293
Iberville, Pierre Lemoyne d', 158
Ibsen, Henrik, 678, 746, 776–77, 779
Ichim, O., 865
Icíar, Juan de, 269
Iermano, T., 423, 432
Ierunca, V., 513
Ieuan Llwyd ab y Gargam, 527
Ifans, R., 534
Ife, B. W., 273
Ifkovits, K., 711
Iglesia, C., 339
Iglesias Álvarez, A., 311
Iglesias Rábade, L., 865
Igosheva, T. V., 834
Ihrie, M., 283
Ik, C. K., 819
Ilarregui, G., 322
Il'f, Ilya Arnol'dovich, 832
Ilin, S., 510
Il'inskaya, T. B., 828
Il'iukhina, T. I., 823
Illiano, A., 423, 448
Illies, Florian, 734
Iluk, J., 549
Image du monde, 60
Imbach, R., 371
Imberal del Balzo, 392
Imberty, C., 476, 482
Imbriani, Vittorio, 435
Imkhelova, S. S., 856
Immermann, Karl, 668, 672, 687
Inauen, Y., 749
Indizio, G., 378
Infantes, V., 267
Ingarden, Roman, 764
Ingemann, Bernhard Severin, 766
Ingen, F. van, 638, 641, 644, 8
Inglese, A., 464
Inglese, G., 386
Innerhofer, Franz, 746
Innocent III (*Pope*), 612
Inomata, K., 116
Intras, Jean d', 127
Ioli, G., 479
Iolo Goch, 527
Ionesco, Eugene, 456, 515
Ionescu, A. I., 788
Ionescu, Nae, 515–16
Ionescu-Ruxăndoiu, L., 495
Ioniţă, V., 504
Iorga, Nicolae, 513, 517
Iovănel, I., 514
Iovino, S., 652
Ippolito, C., 198
Iravedra, A., 288
Ireton, S., 720
Iriso, S., 859
Irler, H., 621
Irving, Washington, 666
Isaac, G. R., 525, 526, 528, 529, 530, 531, 532
Isabelle d'Angoulême, 234
Isabelle-Claire-Eugénie (*Infanta of Spain*), 134
Isaev, S. G., 820
Isasi, C., 250
Isella, D., 433, 442, 489
Isenberg, N., 707
Ishimbaeva, G. G., 840

Isidore of Seville (*Saint*), 397, 576, 583
Iskander, Fazil Abdulovich, 840
Isopescu, Claudiu, 516
Isotti Rosowsky, G., 478, 482
Istrati, Panait, 517
Italia, P., 442
Itinerarium regis Ricardi, 63
Itoda, S., 687
Iun, R. C., 809
Iurchenko, O. O., 856
Ivănescu, G., 496
Ivanits, L., 825
Ivanitskaya, E., 847, 854
Ivanov, A., 809
Ivanov, M. V., 839
Ivanov, V., 830, 844
Ivanov, Viacheslav Vsevolodovich, 828, 832, 839
Ivanov, Vsevolod, 837
Ivanova, E. V., 820
Ivanova, I. A., 856–57
Ivanova, N. F., 823
Ivanova, Z. N., 826
Ives, M. C., 864
Ivleva, T. G., 823
Iwaskiewicz, Jarosław, 800
Izmailov, A., 851
Izvarina, E., 853
Izzi Benedetti, G., 390
Izzo, L., 422, 457

Jaberg, K., 7
Jabès, Edmond, 194
Jablkowska, J., 752
Jackson, D., 696
Jacob *v.* Montfleury
Jacob, R., 77
Jacob, Suzanne, 213
Jacobbi, Ruggero, 347
Jacobi, K., 298
Jacobs, H. C., 276
Jacobs, N., 529, 530
Jacobsen, E., 697
Jacobsen, J., 765
Jacobsen, Jens Peter, 763, 765, 767
Jacobsen, M. B., 758
Jacobsen, M. C., 123
Jacobsen, Roy, 779
Jacobson Schutte, A., 113
Jacobus de Voragine, 394
Jacomuzzi, V., 427
Jacopo da Bologna, 391
Jacopone da Todi, 383, 390, 391
Jacquart, D., 864
Jacquemart, 228
Jaeger, C. S., 586
Jæger, Frank, 771–72
Jaehrling, J., 863
Jaeschke, W., 675
Jaffe, A., 4
Jager, B., 778
Jäger, E., 730
Jäger, L., 20
Jagow, B. von, 669
Jahier, Piero, 458, 475
Jahn, B., 630, 636, 640, 646
Jahnn, Hans Henny, 715
Jahr, S., 549
Jahraus, O., 718
Jaitner, K., 643
Jaklová, A., 786, 788
Jakob, H.-J., 676, 862
Jakobsen, R. N., 778
Jakobson, R., 9
Jakubowski, Jan, 800
Jal, Auguste, 185
Jama, S., 112
James I (*King of Aragon*), 237, 300
James, E., 157, 161, 166
James, E. W., 534, 535
James, Henry, 677
James, T., 191
James, William, 455
Jameson, F., 290, 344
Jamison, A., 192
Jan, Vasilii (V. G. Janchevetskii), 848
Jancke, G., 619
Janda, L. A., 785
Janeczek, E., 464
Janeczko, D., 802
Janés, A., 697
Janet, Pierre, 492
Janich, N., 523, 781
Janiga-Perkins, C., 345
Jannidis, F., 677
Janota, A., 792
Janota, J., 613, 614
Janovec, L., 785
Janse, M., 518
Jansen, Cornelius (Jansenius), 130, 165, 167, 400
Jansen, M., 462
Janson, S., 678, 729
Janusz, M., 792, 801
Janvier, Ambroise, 206
Jardine, N., 100
Jarnés, Benjamín, 281, 291
Jarry, Alfred, 279–80, 682
Jasmin, N., 148
Jaśtal, K., 750
Jaubert, A., 19
Jaufre, 236–37
Jaufre Rudel, 235
Jáuregui, Juan de, 269
Jauslin, K., 681, 683, 692
Javel, D., 225
Jean d'Angoulême, 79, 80
Jean d'Arras, 66, 72, 78
Jean-Bart, A., 215
Jean de Meun, 36, 38, 40, 41, 44, 53, 54, 69, 80, 82, 87, 90, 91–92, 395
Jean Paul *v.* Richter
Jean Renart, 41, 57
Jeandillou, J.-F., 186
Jeanneret, S., 80
Jeay, M., 70, 76, 78, 237
Jehasse, J., 98
Jelinek, Elfriede, 670, 737, 740, 746
Jelínek, M., 783, 784
Jenal-Ruffner, K., 523, 572
Jenckes, K., 339
Jenkins, G. H., 533
Jenny, B. R., 635
Jenny, Zoë, 738
Jens, I., 722
Jensen, A., 758
Jensen, A.-E., 762
Jensen, Axel, 779
Jensen, E. S., 757
Jensen, J. B., 767
Jensen, J. H. C., 288
Jensen, J. N., 757
Jensen, Johannes Vilhelm, 765, 771
Jensen, M., 451
Jensen, P. A., 756
Jensen, Thit, 765
Jensen, Thøger, 764
Jensen, Wilhelm, 687
Jentsch, T., 710
Jeong, M., 743
Jeremiah, E., 734
Jerie, D., 785
Jerlung, E., 763
Jernej, J., 354
Jerome (*Saint*), 271, 469
Jesi, Furio, 476
Jesus, Carolina Maria de, 348
Jeu d'Adam, 62
Jeziorkowski, K., 695
Jianhua, Z., 545
Jiménez, D., 341
Jiménez, Juan Ramón, 279, 287–88
Jiménez Ríos, E., 257
Jiménez Ruiz, J. L., 259
Jirásek, Alois, 787
Joachim of Fiore, 364, 391
Joachimsthal, J., 724
Joan de Castellnou, 236
Joan of Arc (*Saint*), 71, 72, 81, 85, 138, 699
Joch, M., 720
Jodelle, Etienne, 117

Johae, A., 825
Johanek, P., 616
Johann von Konstanz, 608
Johann von Würzburg, 601
Johannes de Alta Silva, 618
Johannes von Frankenstein, 580
Johannes Gobi (Jr.), 618
Johannes von St. Lambrecht, 576
Johansen, A., 762
Johansen, Hanna, 738
Johansen, L., 779
John Chrysostom (*Saint*), 576
John Climacus (*Saint*), 159, 576
John of Capua, 298
John of Gaunt (*Duke of Lancaster*), 90
John of Salisbury, 393
John, J., 695, 860
Johnson, Charles, 219
Johnson, L. P., 595
Johnson, L. R., 649, 660
Johnson, M., 792
Johnson, S., 557
Johnson, S. M., 596
Johnson, Uwe, 739, 746–47, 748
Johnston, G. S., 637
Johnston, P. G., 288
Joisten, K., 692
Jokinen, U., 24
Jolles, C., 680
Joly, Richard, 212
Jomphe, C., 115
Jonard, N., 436
Jonasson, K., 239, 243, 352
Jondorf, G., 106, 861
Jones, A. R., 533
Jones, B. L., 534
Jones, D. G., 535
Jones, G. A., 536
Jones, J. G., 533
Jones, John (Jac Glan-y-Gors), 533
Jones, John (Tegid), 534
Jones, M., 79
Jones, M. C., 30, 31, 866
Jones, M. H., 596, 866
Jones, M. L., 165
Jones, N. A., 52
Jones, R. M., 534
Jones, T. S., 88
Jones, Tegwyn, 533
Jones-Davies, M. T., 866
Jonge, B. de, 247
Jonsmoen, O., 778
Jordan de l'Isla de Venessi, 232
Jordan, C., 113
Jordan, J., 730
Jörg, R., 631
Jørgensen, B., 762
Jörgensen, B. E., 340
Jørgensen, B. H., 763
Jørgensen, H., 756, 763
Jørgensen, J. L., 763, 767
Jørgensen, J. N., 758, 759, 760
Jørgensen, K. M., 761
Jørgensen, L., 769
Jørgensen, P. S., 760
Jori, G., 383
Joseph II (*Emperor*), 409, 412
Joseph, S., 214
Josephsen, Mikael, 768
Josephson, O., 755
Jost, P., 697
Jost, V., 699, 734
Jouannaud, L., 203
Joubert, Laurent, 105
Joudoux, R., 221
Jouffroy, A., 195
Joufroi de Poitiers, 54
Jouhaud, C., 100, 126, 145
Joulin, C., 161
Jourde, P., 199
Jouval, C., 242
Joyce, D. A., 714
Joyce, James, 200, 211, 280, 332, 490
Joyeuse, Henri de, comte du Bouchage (Père Ange de Joyeuse), 145
Juan Bolufer, A. de, 294
Juan-Navarro, S., 322
Juan y Santacilia, Jorge, 277
Jud, Leo, 623
Jüdel, 612
Judge, A., 30
Juel, Dagny, 777
Juge, J.-P., 223
Juge, M. L., 14
Juhl, M., 772
Julian of Norwich, 93
Jumelais, Y., 171
Juminer, Bertène, 219
Jung, Carl Gustav, 471, 477, 478, 488, 515, 727, 745, 777
Jung, M.-R., 117
Jung, S., 689
Jung, T., 734
Jung, W., 175, 745
Jung-Hofmann, C., 700
Jünger, Ernst, 642, 699, 702, 715, 747, 751
Jüngerer Sigenot, 591
Jungmann, J., 786
Jungmayr, J., 611, 627
Junod, S., 108
Jurek, W., 796
Jürgens, D., 660, 752, 866
Jurieu, Pierre, 163
Jurkowski, M., 802
Jurzik, H., 582
Juul, H., 758
Juul, Pia, 764, 765, 768, 771
Juvenal (Decimus Junius Juvenalis), 196, 411

'K. R.', 833
Kabakov, Alexander, 834
Kabakov, Ilya, 839
Kabata, M., 801
Kabish, Inna, 841
Kadare, Ismail, 508
Kaderka, P., 784
Kadlec, J., 787
Kaenel, P., 621
Kaestli, J.-D., 541
Kafanova, O. B., 822
Kafitz, D., 678
Kafka, Franz, 279, 341, 552, 685, 704, 706, 710, 715–18, 735, 743, 745, 857, 863
Kahn, D., 99, 110, 113
Kahn, V., 866
Kailuweit, R., 14, 17, 863
Kaiser, C., 669
Kaiser, G., 746
Kaiser, G. R., 699, 866
Kaiser, Georg, 699, 719
Kaiser, Joachim, 752
Kaiserchronik, 587
Kajino, K., 182
Kajtoch, W., 800
Kalashnikova, E., 844
Kalb, J., 709
Kalkuhl, C., 643
Kallendorf, C., 274, 379
Kallendorf, H., 274, 379
Kaller, P., 615
Kallmeyer, W., 550, 863
Kal'pidi, V., 816
Kaltemback, M., 215
Kaltz, B., 560
Kamath, R., 744
Kambas, C., 703
Kamenev, G. P., 808
Kamińska-Szmaj, I., 790, 802, 805
Kaminski, N., 643, 651, 750
Kaminsky, C., 694
Kamiš, K., 782
Kämpchen, M., 745
Kämper, H., 549, 551
Kanatli, F., 548
Kandaurov, O. Z., 846
Kandinsky, Wassili, 702, 719
Kane, M., 734
Kane, Sarah, 744
Kaneko, T., 564
Kanevskaya, M., 824

Kanovich, Grigorii, 841
Kant, Immanuel, 161, 162, 438, 511, 658, 659, 660, 691, 773
Kant, R. M., 727
Kantor, K. M., 857
Kantor, V., 824, 825
Kanunova, F., 807
Kany-Turpin, J., 201
Kanz, C., 718, 734
Kanzog, K., 709, 728
Kaplan, E. K., 187
Kappler, E., 163
Kapsoli Escudero, W., 292
Karamzin, Nikolai Mikhailovich, 819
Karapetian, D., 856
Karaś, H., 789, 798
Karg, I., 595
Karge, H., 687
Karker, A., 756
Karlhuber, P., 742
Karlík, P., 781, 783, 865
Karlsson, B.-M., 110
Karnabatt, Dimitrie, 517
Karoui, A., 160
Karpiak, R., 179
Karpluk, M., 793
Karpov, V. A., 850
Karpowicz, T., 793
Karterud, S., 775
Kartschoke, D., 587, 592, 596, 603
Kartschoke, E., 587
Karwatowska, M., 796
Kasack, W., 814
Kasatkina, T. A., 808, 825
Kaschnitz, Marie Luise, 700
Kaspe, I., 835
Kasten, I., 588, 611, 614, 860
Kasten, L. A., 254, 866
Kasties, B., 642
Kästner, Erich, 715
Kastovsky, D., 559
Kasuya, Y., 182
Kasymov, A., 856
Kataev, V. B., 815, 819
Kataev, Valentin Petrovich, 832
Katagoshchin, V., 846
Katritzky, M. A., 645
Katseva, E., 840
Katsis, L. F., 830, 849
Kattan, Naïm, 213
Kattenbusch, D., 518
Katz, E., 25, 26
Katz, Leo, 735
Katz Crispin, R., 289
Kauffeld, C., 250
Kauffeldt, R., 704, 725
Kauffmann, K., 708
Kaufmann, D., 707
Kaufmann, K., 694
Kaufmann, S., 707
Kaufringer, Heinrich, 581, 601–02
Kaul de Marlangeo, S. B., 256
Kaus, R. J., 718
Kavanagh, R. J., 866
Kaverin, Benjamin, 848
Kaverin, N., 848
Kaverin, S., 850
Kawakami, A., 200
Kawasaki, Y., 584
Kawka, M., 799
Kay, R., 374
Kay, S., 35, 233, 234
Kayne, R. S., 10, 11, 12
Kazakov, Iurii, 848
Kazantsákis, Nikos, 508
Kazarin, I., 853
Kazarin, V. P., 816
Kaznelson, Siegmund, 680
Keats, John, 822
Kebir, S., 709
Keck, A., 598
Kędelska, E., 798
Keding, Paul, 700
Kedrovsky, A. E., 832, 851
Keffer, K., 111
Kehr, K., 571
Kehrein, R., 562
Kekova, Svetlana, 841, 844
Keldysh, V. A., 820, 840
Keller, A., 637
Keller, Gottfried, 668, 670, 672, 687, 694, 696
Keller, H. E., 65, 617
Keller, J., 615
Kellermann, K., 597, 616
Kellermeier, B., 568
Kelley, D. D., 151
Kellner, B., 600, 606
Kellogg, J., 82
Kelly, D., 41, 50
Kelly, V. V., 192
Kemedjio, C., 217, 218, 219
Kemp, W., 21, 100
Kempff, Diana, 735
Kendrick, L., 233
Kennedy, A., 81, 86, 866
Kennedy, W., J., 396
Kenzheev, Bakhyt, 848
Kępińska, A., 791
Keppler, S., 595
Kern, M., 592, 602
Kern, P., 595, 604
Kern-Jędrychowska, E., 796
Kerth, S., 591
Kessler, E., 621
Kessler, Engelbert, 676
Kessler, Harry (*Graf*), 719
Kesten, Hermann, 703
Kesting, H., 674
Ketchian, S. I., 822
Ketelsen, U.-K, 726
Kettler, W., 620, 623
Keun, Irmgard, 700, 703
Keyserling, Eduard von, 667, 678, 701, 719
Khait, V., 847
Khalfa, J., 217
Khalizev, V. E., 808, 809
Khamvash, B., 825
Khardzhiev, Nikolai, 836
Kharms, Daniil Ivanovich, 840
Khaznadar, E., 29
Khelemsky, I., 839
Khilkov, A. D., 848
Khlebnikov, Velimir (Victor Vladimirovich), 814, 848
Khodasevich, Vladislav Feltsanovich, 822, 833, 835
Kholin, Igor, 839
Kholkin, V., 841
Kholshevnikov, V. E., 810
Khomiakov, Alexei Stepanovich, 811
Khomiakov, V. I., 842
Khruschev, Nikita Sergeevich, 833
Khvorostianova, E., 848
Khvostenko, Alexei, 831
Kibbee, D. A., 22
Kibler, W. W., 50
Kida, J., 802
Kiefer, S., 745
Kiehl, C., 82
Kielland, Alexander, 777
Kiening, C., 576, 595, 601
Kierkegaard, Søren, 461, 666, 674, 765, 766, 767, 769, 770, 823
Kiesel, H., 704
Kikhney, L. G., 821
Kilian, J., 551
Kilwardby, Robert, 374
Kimbell, D., 426
Kimm, D., 215
Kimmich, D., 668
Kimpel, D., 688
Kin, E.-U., 787
Kindt, T., 709
Kinefuchi, H., 745
King, I., 730
Kinkel, Gottfried, 680
Kinoshita, S., 44
Kinoshita, T., 824
Kipphardt, Heinar, 740
Kiràly, E., 731
Kircher, H., 866
Kircher, T., 394

Kirchmeier-Andersen, S., 760
Kirchner, V., 738
Kireev, R., 849
Kirillova, I., 823
Kirkness, A., 546
Kirkpatrick, G., 338
Kirkwood, M., 857
Kirnbauer, Martin, 607
Kirnoze, Z. I., 808
Kirsanov, Simen, 850
Kirsch, F. P., 225
Kirsch, K., 674
Kirsop, W., 100
Kisch, Egon Erwin, 727
Kissler, A., 708
Kitchener Davies, James, 535
Kitova-Vasileva, M., 256
Kittang, A., 776, 780
Kittler, Friedrich A., 776
Kittstein, U., 654
Kjær, I., 766
Kjærgaard-Jensen, F., 766
Kjærstad, Jan, 779
Klabund (Alfred Heuschke), 719
Klage, 589, 590, 591
Klain, V., 787
Kłanska, M., 727, 732, 866
Klar, K., 528
Klare, A., 608
Klatovsky, Ondrej, 544
Klatte, H., 544, 545
Klausenburger, J., 4, 7, 10
Klausmann, H., 523, 570
Kleiber, W., 569, 574
Kleimenova, R. N.,808
Klein, C., 746
Klein, D[orothea], 593
Klein, Georg, 747
Klein, Gerhard, 736
Klein, J., 547, 551
Klein, K[urt], 590
Klein, M., 715, 866
Klein, R., 617
Klein, T., 558
Klein, W., 691
Klein, W. P., 557
Klein-Andreu, F., 259
Kleinschmidt, E., 866
Kleinschmidt, S., 747
Kleinwechter, Valentin, 640
Kleist, Heinrich von, 650, 659–62, 686
Klekh, I., 834
Klemm, Wilhelm, 700
Klenovsky (Krachkovsky), Dmitri Josifovich, 843
Klepikova, E., 850
Kleppin, K., 549
Kleszczowa, K., 793
Klettenhammer, S., 866
Kley, A., 688
Kliebenstein, G., 188
Kliege-Biller, H., 600
Klier, M., 656
Klimeš, D., 787
Klimeš, L., 787
Klímova, J., 783
Klimova, S. M., 822, 824
Klinck, A. L., 866
Kling, O., 809, 851
Kling, Thomas, 743
Klingebiel, K., 221, 224
Klinger, J., 580
Klingner, J., 612
Klinkenberg, J.-M., 19
Kliuev, E. V., 837
Klopf, K.-H., 695
Klosa, A., 572
Klösch, C., 703
Klötzer, S., 748
Kluev, Nikolai, 848
Kluge, Alexander, 747
Kluge, G., 687
Kluge, R., 573
Klüger, Ruth, 747
Klugkist, T., 723
Klussmann, P. G., 676
Kluwe, S., 704
Knafl, A., 746
Knaller, S., 707
Knap, T. F., 763
Knape, J., 617, 618
Knapp, F. P., 595, 607, 866
Knapp, U., 741
Knappová, M., 786
Knebel, H., 684
Knefelkamp, U., 577
Knight, T. E., 702, 866
Knipf-Komlósi, E., 547, 571
Knipper, O., 822
Knirsch, R., 548
Knischewski, N., 620
Knittel, A. P., 683
Knobloch, H.-J., 863
Knopf, J., 708
Knorr von Rosenroth, Christian, 643–44, 645, 646
Knudsen, B. T., 764
Knütel, W., 736
Knutsen, N. M., 776
Koban, S., 194
Köbele, S., 597, 610
Kobialka, M., 864
Kobrin, K., 842, 843
Kobrinsky, A. A., 837
Kobus, Kathi, 642
Koch, A., 673
Koch, E. R., 164, 866
Koch, G., 568
Koch, H.-G., 717, 718
Kochanowski, Jan, 801, 802
Kochanske Stock, L., 44
Kochhar-Lindgren, G., 751
Kock, T., 101, 609
Koelb, C., 716, 717
Koenig, Alma Johanna, 719
Koepke, W., 710
Koeppen, Wolfgang, 699, 733, 747
Koerner, E., 789
Koerner, E. F. K., 7
Kofoed, N., 766
Kogan, G., 824
Kogan, L., 817
Kogan, V., 188
Kogler, S., 741
Kohl, A.-S., 758
Kohl, K., 736, 866
Köhler, J., 690
Kohlhaase, Wolfgang, 736
Kohlheim, R., 552, 574, 575
Kohlheim, V., 552, 574, 575
Köhlmeier, Michael, 737, 747
Köhn, L., 675, 680
Kohnen, J., 655
Kokis, Sergio, 215
Kokoschka, Oskar, 706
Kokott, H., 620
Kokovina, N. Z., 821
Koksheneva, K., 849, 853
Kolago, L., 675
Kolářová, I., 783
Kolb, Annette, 719
Kolde, G., 565
Koler von Soest, Konrad, 576
Koleśnikow, M. B., 796
Koliada, Nikolai, 842
Koll, B., 582
Kollatz, A., 645
Kolleritsch, Alfred, 706
Köllhofer, H., 744
Kölligan, D., 553
Kollmann, C., 520
Kolmar, Gertrud, 719
Kolobaeva, L. A., 845, 852
Kołodziej, J., 800
Kolski, S., 467
Kol'tsov, Mikhail Efimovich, 848
Komada, A., 76
Komárek, M., 782
Komarov, S. A., 823
Komissarzhevskaya, V., 822
Komlev, A., 842
Kommerell, Max, 719
Kondakov, I., 832
Kong, K., 38
Kongslien, I., 778
König Rother, 587, 601
Königin Sibille, 591

Königsdorf, Helga, 738
Kon'kov, P. V., 816
Kononov, N., 843
Konrad von Fussesbrunnen, 613
Konrad von Megenberg, 618
Konrad von Regensburg (Pfaffe Konrad), 576, 588, 596
Konrad von Soltau, 576
Konrad von Würzburg, 600, 602, 606
Kontzi, R., 17
Konze, B., 748
Konzett, M., 742
Kooper, E., 866
Koopmann, H., 722, 863
Koopmans, J., 70, 94
Koos, L. R., 189
Kopczyńska, D., 793
Kopeć, U., 793
Kopelev, L., 835, 840
Kopeliovich, M., 853
Kopertowska, D., 796
Köpf, U., 866
Kopp, D., 681, 683
Kopytseva, N. M., 818
Korallov, M., 852
Körber, T., 723
Kořenský, J., 781
Koriakovtsev, A., 809
Korkina, E. B., 855
Kormilov, S. I., 832
Kornbech, J., 757
Körner, A., 23
Korobov, V. I., 844, 853
Korolenko, V. G., 839
Korolev, Alexei, 842
Koroleva, N. V., 847
Korona, V. V., 809
Korostelev, O., 835, 836, 838
Korovin, A. V., 771
Korovin, V. I., 816
Korshunov, M., 834
Korte, H., 713
Kortländer, B., 671, 672, 675
Kortowicz, E. S., 800
Korzen, I., 759
Korzhavin, N., 846
Koschorke, A.,729
Kosek, I., 791
Kosek, P., 782
Koshelev, V. A., 827
Koss, G., 574
Kosta, P., 791
Køster, F., 758
Köster, U., 671
Kostiukov, L., 842, 848
Kostomarov, V. G., 813, 814
Kostroun, D. J., 146
Kosykh, G. A., 828
Koszyk, K., 677
Kotel'nikov, V. A., 820
Kotikowa, W., 803
Kotin, M. L., 552
Kotin Mortimer, A., 195
Kotrikadze, T., 727
Kotsinas, U.-B., 758
Koubová, J., 788
Koudelková, E., 870
Koukalová, H., 782
Kovacci, O., 866
Kovach, T. A., 713, 714
Kovàcs, E., 731, 742
Kovács, I., 410
Kovàcs, L., 303
Koval'dzhi, Kirill, 853
Kovsky, V., 845
Kowalewska-Dąbrowska, J., 801
Kowalska, A., 789, 796
Kozeev, V. A., 816
Koziara, S., 798
Kozlov, I. I., 810
Kozmin, V. I., 817
Kôzô, H., 580
Kozovoi, Vadim, 842
Kracauer, Siegfried, 699, 704, 727
Krachkovsky *v.* Klenovsky
Kracht, Christian, 734, 747
Kracht, K. G., 702
Kraft, H., 717
Krag, Vilhelm, 777
Kragl, F., 681
Krah, H., 669, 671, 681, 683
Krahmer, E., 353
Krajewski, T., 803
Kralin, M., 844
Kramer, A., 702
Kramer, B., 730
Kramer, J., 522
Kramer, M., 28, 544, 545
Krämer-Neubert, S., 567, 568, 574
Kramhøft, J[acob], 771
Kramhøft, J[anus], 771
Krasiński, Ignacy, 801
Kraśnicka-Wilk, I., 793
Krasnikov, G., 844
Krasnikov, N. G., 831
Krasnov, G. V., 818, 826, 829
Krasovskaia, S. I., 819
Krass, A., 606
Kratzsch, K., 726
Kraus, Karl, 546, 699, 705, 706, 719
Krause, A., 575
Krause, F. U., 681
Krause, K. M., 44, 52
Krause-Braun, C., 565
Krausová, A., 866
Krauss, A., 720
Krauss, C., 396
Krawarik, H., 572
Krawczyk, Stephan, 746
Krawczyk-Tyrpa, A., 796
Krèmová, M., 786
Kreid, Vadim, 843, 844
Krein, A. Z., 806
Kreja, B.,
Krelin, Iulii, 840, 853
Krell, M., 25
Krementsov, L. P., 832, 842
Kremer, D., 14, 655, 761
Kremnitz, G., 23, 225
Krenek, Ernst, 706, 719
Krenov, N., 834
Kretschmann, C., 729
Kretschmar, D., 833
Kreutner, R., 694
Kreutzer, H.-J., 660
Kreuzer, J., 652, 657
Krieb, S., 501
Kries, F. W. von, 608
Krippendorff, E., 682
Krisch, A., 752
Krispin, A., 223, 241
Křístek, M., 784, 786
Kristensen, K., 756
Kristensen, Tom, 772
Kristeva, Julia, 35, 192, 197, 292
Kristiansen, T., 758
Kriukova, O. S., 821
Krivonos, V. S., 813
Krivtsun, O. A., 831
Krivulin, Victor, 841
Krobb, F., 728
Krogh, E., 764
Krogstad, A., 779
Kroha, L., 468
Krohn, C.-D., 703
Kroll, R., 593
Kronenberger, K., 558
Kronning, H., 239, 352
Krotz, E., 583
Krueger, C., 192
Krueger, R. L., 38
Krüger, D., 574
Krüger, Michael, 747
Krüger, R., 96, 589
Krukov, Fedor, 853
Krukovskaya, L. I., 824
Krumm, E., 483
Krump, S., 645
Krupin, Vladimir, 835
Krusanov, Pavel, 849
Kruse, J. A., 672, 684, 686
Kruzhkov, Grigorii, 842, 843
Krylov, A., 842, 856
Krylov, Ivan, 813
Kryshchuk, N., 839
Krysinska, Marie, 193

Krzeszowski, T., 792
Krzhizhanovsky, Sigizmund Dominikovich, 849
Kubati, Ron, 465
Kubé, C., 614
Kubin, Alfred, 719, 727
Kubiszyn-Mêdrala, Z., 805
Kublanovsky, Iurii, 844
Kubrick, Stanley, 728, 729
Kucała, M., 800, 805
Kucharczyk, R., 796, 797
Kucher, P.-H., 694, 695
Kučinskaja, A. I., 781, 786, 866
Kuckart, Judith, 748
Kudriavtseva, E. L., 851
Kudrova, I., 855
Kudrun, 590
Kuechen, U.-B., 621
Kuhlmann, R., 675
Kühlmann, W., 563, 701
Kühn, C., 608
Kuhn, J., 572
Kühn, R., 748
Kuhn, T., 709
Kühne, U., 606
Kuhnle, T. R., 713
Kuizenga, D., 155
Kukol'nik, Nestor, 813
Kukulin, I., 841, 854, 856
Kukushkin, V., 854
Kulagin, A. V., 842, 856
Kuleshov, V. I., 816
Kuliapin, A., 857
Kundera, Milan, 824
Kunert, Günter, 747
Kunieda, T., 196
Kunkler, S., 631
Kunøe, M., 755, 756
Kunz, E. A., 748
Kunze, K., 572
Kunze, Reiner, 747
Künzel, C., 728
Künzel, H. J., 557
Kuon, P., 372, 470
Kupchenko, V., 856
Kuperty-Tsur, N., 112, 122, 867
Kupferman, L., 25
Kupiszewska-Grzybowska, M., 801
Kupiszewski, Maciej, 800
Kupiszewski, P., 802
Kupiszewski, R., 802
Kupiszewski, W., 789
Kupriianovsky, P. V., 827
Kurash, S. B., 809
Kurbatov, V. A., 815
Kurbatov, Valentin, 839–40, 845
Kurdyło, T., 790
Kurek, H., 796
Kurganov, E., 821, 825
Kurilkin, A., 832
Kurilkin, A. R., 808
Kurilov, A. S., 814
Kurilov, V. V., 821
Kürnberger, Ferdinand, 668
Kuropka, N., 633
Kurth, A.-E., 736
Kurz, S., 695
Kurzke, H., 721
Kurzowa, Z., 797
Kuschel, K.-J., 684
Kushner, A., 811, 822
Kushner, Alexander Semenovich, 839, 844
Kushner, E., 118, 213
Küsters, U., 611
Kusukawa, S., 100, 634
Kutmina, O. A., 845
Kutschke, A., 532
Kutzmutz, O., 681
Kuzmics, H., 682
Kuz'min, D., 835, 847
Kuzmin, Mikhail Alekseevich, 849
Kuznetsov, F., 853
Kuznetsov, P., 824
Kuznetsova, A., 831, 839
Kuznetsova, I., 844
Kwakernaak, E., 549
Kyblanovsky, I., 811
Kyeser, Konrad, 616
Kyora, S., 753

Laage, K. E., 696, 724
Labastida, J., 334
Labbé, A., 65
Labé, Louise, 117, 118, 240
Labeau, E., 25, 30
Labelle, F., 25
Łabeński, Ksawery, 448
Laberge, Marie, 209
La Boderie *v.* Le Fèvre de la Boderie
La Boétie, Etienne de, 112–13
Labombarda, F., 429
Labouret, D., 206
Labouret, M., 175
Labov, William, 7, 9, 23
Labriola, Antonio, 434
La Bruyère, Jean de, 125, 127, 151
Laca, B., 863
La Calprenède, Gautier de Costes, sieur de, 145
Lacan, Jacques, 35, 178, 192, 219, 292
La Capria, Raffaele, 462, 476
Lacassagne, M., 81, 82, 87
Lacchini, A., 432
Lacenaire, Pierre-François, 173
La Ceppède, Jean de, 130, 157
La Charité, C., 116
La Charité, R. C., 867
La Charité, V. A., 867
La Chassaigne, Geoffroy de, 112
Lachâtre, Maurice, 27
Lachmann, Karl, 604
Lackey, M., 743
Laclos, Pierre-Ambroise-François Choderlos de, 769
Lacombe, Patrice, 215
Lacoste, F., 198
Lacrosil, Michèle, 217
Lactantius, 397
Lacy, N. J., 43, 72, 94, 864
Ladegaard, U., 759
Ladenthin, V., 730
Lades, G., 240
Ladolfi, G., 421
La Fauci, N., 9, 491
La Fayette, Marie-Madeleine Pioche de la Vergne, comtesse de, 129, 130, 145, 146, 147, 151, 156
Laferrière, Dany, 208
Lafitte, J., 224, 225, 226, 227
Laflamme, M.-O., 410
Lafont, R., 225
Lafont, Robert, 231, 237, 238, 239, 240
La Fontaine, Jean de, 128, 129, 130, 131, 132–34, 147, 157, 211, 869
La Force, Charlotte-Rose de Caumont, 151
La Forge, Georges de, 104
Laforgue, P., 169, 172, 175, 183 187, 192, 193, 205
La France, Micheline, 213
La Garanderie, M.-M. de, 102
Lagarda, A., 224, 227, 229
Lagarda, C., 223
Lagarde, C., 239
Lagazzi, P., 483
La Gessée, Jean de, 105
Lagorio, Gina, 371
Laguzzi, A., 402
Lahaise, R., 208
Lahann, B., 713
La Harpe, Jean-François de, 18
Lähnemann, H., 598, 620, 865
Lahouati, G., 410
Lai d'Aristote, 50
Laidlaw, J., 81, 86, 87
Laignel-Lavastine, A., 515
Laín Entralgo, Pedro, 279
Laisney, V., 169
Lajarrige, J., 750

Lake, A. C., 531, 533, 534
Lakoff, G., 792
Laks, B., 19
Lalande, D., 93
Lallemand, M.-G., 155
Lalomia, G., 396
Lama, M. X., 315
Lamacz, S., 108
Lamarche, J., 29
Lamart, M., 181, 199
Lamartine, Alphonse de, 169, 171, 442, 510
Lamb, M., 532
Lamb, S., 720
Lamb-Faffelberger, M., 737
Lambert, P.-Y., 525, 529
Lamblin, A., 746
Lambrecht (*Pfaffe*), 587, 600
Lambrecht, K., 13, 624
La Mesnardière, Hippolyte Jules Pilet de, 136, 146
Lamiroy, B., 14
Lamonde, Y., 209
Lamothe, J., 19
La Mothe Le Vayer, François de, 160, 163
La Motte, Antoine Houdard de, 136
Lamport, F. J., 670
Lamy, Bernard, 151–52
Lamy, François, 158
Lancelot, Claude, 158
Lancelot-Graal, 42, 43, 45, 46, 47, 69
Lancillotti, Francesco, 395
Landauer, Gustav, 704, 719, 725
Landerer, C., 692
Landfried, K., 712
Landi, Gaspare, 402
Landi, P., 436
Landini, A., 473
Landino, Cristoforo, 372–73
Lando, Ortensio, 102
Landolfi, A., 750
Landolfi, G., 468, 474
Landolfi, Tommaso, 452, 465, 468, 471, 476
Landoni, E., 437
Landreau, J., 260
Landrum, D. W., 473
Landry, J.-P., 140, 149, 867
Landshoff-Yorck, Ruth, 703
Landshuter, S., 683
Landstad, Magnus Brostrup, 777
Landucci, S., 454
Landwehr, H., 685
Landwehr, J., 654
Lane, M. E., 864
Langås, U., 777
Langbroek, E., 607
Lange, Hartmut, 747, 750
Lange, N., 292
Lange-Kirchheim, A., 729
Lange-Müller, Katja, 746, 747
L'Angelier, Abel, 99
Langella, G., 443, 458
Langella, P., 484
Langenhorst, G., 742
Langer, O., 610
Langer, U., 103, 110, 122, 867
Langevin, André, 208
Langva, S., 776
Lanin, B., 831, 837
Lanini, K., 127
Lanne, J.-C., 848
Lanoue, O. de, 21
Lanza, M. T., 427
Lanza Tomasi, G., 491
Lapesa, R., 251
Laplace, Pierre Simon, marquis de, 179
La Placette, Jean de, 158
La Porta, F., 469, 482
Lappo-Danilevsky, K. I., 811
Laqueur, T., 578
Lara, la Contessa (E. C. Mancini), 435
Larbaud, Valéry, 280
Larcati, A., 702
Larchey, Lorédan, 204
Lardon, S., 122
Larionova, S. I., 814
La Rochefoucauld, François VI, duc de, 129, 152, 205
Laroque, F., 105, 867
Larose, K., 212
Larra, Mariano José, 294
Larrivée, P., 25, 29
Larsen, A. H., 771
Larsen, B., 761
Larsen, E. V., 756
Larsen, F. S., 771–72
Larsen, Gunnar, 779
Larsen, L. F., 775, 776
Larsen, N., 323–24, 325
Larsen, P. S., 772
Larsen, S. E., 764
Larsen, S. H., 764
Larson, S., 282
Lartiga, H., 225
Larubia-Prado, F., 292
Laruffa, F., 363
Larzac, Jean (Joan), 238
La Sablière, Marguerite Ilessein, madame de, 152
La Sale, Antoine de, 70, 93–94
Lascar, A., 176, 177
Las Casas, Bartolomé de (*Fray*), 266
Las Casas, Cristóbal de, 266
Lasch, A., 586
Laschen, G., 746
La Serre, Jean Puget de, 157
Lasker-Schüler, Else, 720
Laskin, A., 848
Laskowska, E., 802
Lasnier, L., 210
Lassabatère, T., 82
Lassahn, N., 65, 91
Lassberg, Friedrich Leonhard Anton, Freiherr von, 615
Lastilla, L., 477
Lateş, G., 511
Latif, Nadine, 207
Latif-Ghattas, Mona, 207
Latini *v.* Brunetto
Latini, F., 446
Latour, Bruno, 469
La Tour Landry, Geoffroy de, 77
Latry, G., 226
Lattanzio, A., 460
Lattarulo, L., 427
Latypova, T. L., 811
Laube, Heinrich, 668, 672
Lauber, Diebolt, 615
Laudanna, A., 358
Laude, C., 618
Laudin, G., 753
Laudonnière, René de, 158
Lauer, G., 677
Lauf, R., 557
Laufhütte, H., 641, 672, 867
Laughlin, James, 493
Laun, M., 782
Laur, W., 573
Lauranson-Rosaz, C., 223
Laurens, P., 102
Laurent, F., 56, 77, 187
Lauridsen, P. S., 763
Laursen, M., 759
Laus *v.* Laux
Lauster, M., 684
Lauta, G., 352
Lautréamont, Isadore Ducasse, comte de, 193
Lauwers, P., 20
Laux (Laus), C., 227
Laux, H., 130
Laval, Antoine de, 112
Lavalade, Y., 229
Lavallée, Ronald, 207
Lavater, Ludwig, 623
Lavault, M., 183
Lavezzi, G., 425, 457
Lavinio, C., 351, 359
Lavocat, F., 149
Lavrov, A. V., 839, 845
Law, V., 7
Lawrence, M., 43
Lawson, S., 82

Lawson Lucas, A., 447
Laxness, Halldor Kiljan, 776
Laye, Camara, 220
Lazamon, 530
Lazard, M., 122
Lazard, S., 14
Lazare, Bernard, 205
Lazarescu, M. V., 728
Lazarev, L., 850
Lăzăroiu, A., 499
Lazutkina, M., 818
Lazzarini, S., 491
Lazzerini, L., 231
Leach, E., 90
Lear, Edward, 427
Lebedev, E. N., 827
Lebedev, I. V., 813, 830
Lebedev, M. N., 828
Lebedushkina, O., 841
Lebert, Benjamin, 743
Le Blanc, Richard, 104
Le Bris, M., 169
Le Briz-Orgeur, S., 66
Le Calvez, E., 197
Lecercle, F., 142
Lechanteur, J., 30
Lechat, D., 70, 81, 82
Lechner, J., 266
Lechtermann, C., 608, 870
Leclerc, Y., 196, 197, 198, 867
Lecointe, J., 111, 861
Leconte de Lisle, Charles-Marie Leconte, *dit*, 193
Le Corbusier (Charles Edouard Jeanneret), 281
Lécuyer, S., 77
Ledda, E., 432
Ledda, G., 375
Ledegen, G., 24
Leder, H.-G., 631
Ledneva, T. P., 848
Ledo-Lemos, F. J., 15
Leduc, A. G., 28
Lee, C., 236
Lee, H., 748
Lee, K.-H., 627
Lee, S., 178, 197
Lee, S.-J., 546
Leech-Wilkinson, D., 90
Leeder, K., 709, 751
Leeker, J., 110
Lees, C. A., 862
Leeuwen-Turnovcová, J. van, 785
Le Faucheur, Michel, 138
Lefebvre, A.-M., 176
Lefebvre, C., 17
Lefebvre, J., 696
Lefebvre Filleau, J.-P., 168
Le Fèvre, Jean, 68, 70
Lefèvre, S., 57, 69, 81, 90, 110
Le Fèvre de la Boderie, Guy, 102
Leffers, G. T., 757
Lefrère, J.-J., 195
Lefter, I. B., 512
Legaré, A.-M., 75
Legault, M., 151
Le Gendre, Marie, 161
Leggett, B. J., 198
Léglu, C., 58, 236, 237
Legrand, M.-D., 115, 122
Legros, A., 112
Le Guern, M., 167
Le Guillou, L., 188
Lehečková, H., 787
Lehmann, M., 363
Lehnen, L., 194
Lehner, P. U., 717
Lehnert, H., 724
Lehnus, L., 410
Leibacher-Ouvrard, L., 146, 153
Leibin, V. M., 806
Leibniz, Gottfried Wilhelm, 6, 161, 165, 437, 643, 661
Leiderman, N., 832
Leip, Hans, 720
Leirbukt, O., 561
Leiris, Michael, 744
Leisten, G., 687, 748
Leiter, B., 690
Leitgeb, C., 706
Leitner, Maria, 700, 703
Lejárraga, María de la O., 295
Lekmanov, O. A., 839, 849
Lemaire, J., 82, 105
Lemaire de Belges, Jean, 105, 106, 116
Le Maistre, Antoine, 159
Lemaître, Frédérick, 176
Lemaître, J.-L., 222
Le Men, J., 259
Le Mercier, Joseph, 126
Lemirre, E., 148
Lemius, Gottfried, 645
Lemke, A., 691, 743
Le Moyne, Pierre, 152, 157
Le Nan, F., 43
Lenau, Nikolaus, 688, 706
Lenepveu, V., 24
Lénet, Pierre, 147
Leng, R., 615
Lengauer, H., 688
L'Engle, S., 77
Lenin (Vladimir Ilyich Oulianov), 833
Lennon, T. M., 161
Lentini *v.* Giacopo
Lenz, Siegfried, 747
León, Lucrecia de, 270, 272
León, María Teresa, 283, 284, 292
Leonard, L. B., 359
Leonardi, L., 367
Leonardo, L., 458
Leonardo de Argensola, Bartolomé, 276
Leonardo de Argensola, Lupercio, 276
Leone, A., 351, 363
Leone, F., 402
Leone, G., 422, 426
Leone de Castris, A., 450
Leonelli, G., 483
Leonhard, J.-F., 545
Leonhardt, J., 626, 630
Leoni, M., 182, 185
Leonov, Leonid M., 849
Leopardi, Giacomo, 352, 411, 422, 429, 430, 435–41, 445, 449, 453, 457, 490, 492, 493
Leopardi, Paolina, 441
Leopold I (*Emperor*), 645
Lepage, F., 215
Lepel, Bernhard von, 679
Leplatre, O., 132
Leppin, V., 633
Le Prince de Beaumont, Jeanne Marie, 147
Lepschy, A. L., 351, 354
Lepschy, G., 354
Lequain, M., 74
Lequin, L., 207
Lerchner, G., 556
Lerchner, K., 608
Leri, C., 408, 442
Le Rider, J., 647, 750
Lermen, B., 747
Lermontov, Mikhail Iurievich, 806, 808, 813–14
Lerner, M. G., 200
Leroux, Gaston, 24
Leroy, A., 410
Le Roy, Louis, 102
Leroy, M., 186, 189
Léry, Jean de, 108
Lesage, Alain-René, 412
Lescarbot, Marc, 123, 134, 208, 213
Lesemann, F., 207
Leskov, Nikolai Semenovich, 820, 826, 828
Lešnerová, Š., 782, 787
Lessard, Camille, 211
Lessay, F., 105, 867
Lessing, Gotthold Ephraim, 129, 647, 665
Lessing, Theodor, 704, 705
Lesskis, G. A., 815
Lestel, A., 228

L'Estoile, Pierre de, 122–23
Lestringant, F., 174
Leszczyński, Z., 800
Le Talleur, Guillaume, 74
Leterrier, S.-A., 188
Letexier, G., 157
Leth, Jørgen, 764
Leto, G., 486
Leuchte, Hans-Jörg, 580
Leudar, I., 785
Leuker, T., 372
Leurquin-Labie, A.-F., 76
Leuschner, P. E., 472
Leuta, O. N., 838
Leutenegger, Gertrud, 738
Levato, V., 482
Le Vayer de Boutigny, René-Roland, 127
Leveau, E., 151
Levers, T., 375
Levi, Carlo, 460, 487
Levi, Primo, 368, 441, 476, 549
Lévi-Strauss, Claude, 349, 600
Levin, L. I., 843
Levinton, G., 838
Levitansky, Iurii D., 849
Levitskaia, S., 812
Levorato, M. C., 357
Levy, B. J., 60
Levy, G. A., 170
Lewald, Fanny, 688
Lewark, Heinz, 700
Lewicki, A. M., 793
Lewis, A., 748
Lewis, A. M., 8
Lewis, B., 531
Lewis, John Saunders, 535
Lewis, P., 74
Lewys Daron, 531
Lewys Glyn Cothi, 528, 531
Lewys Môn, 531
Ley, K., 396, 424
Leydecker, K., 699, 728
Lezama Lima, José, 331, 332
Lezhnev, A. V., 857
Lezziero, P., 483
L'Hermite, Jean-Baptiste, 135 *v. also* Tristan L'Hermite
Lhermitte, A., 201
L'Hospital, Michel de, 121
Liapina, L. E., 811
Libedinskaya, Lidia, 852–53
Liber Scalae Mahometi, 368
Libera, A. de, 35
Liberek, J., 792
Lica, A., 790
Licastro, E., 484
Lichutin, Vladimir, 849
Lie, Jonas, 777
Lieb, C., 656
Lieb, H.-H., 558
Lieb, L., 586, 595, 867
Liébault-Estienne, Nicole, 119
Lieber, C., 180
Liebig, B., 586
Liebscher, M., 692
Lied von Deggendorf, 620
Liedtke, F., 547
Liedtke, H., 564
Lienert, E., 595
Liessmann, K. P., 691
Liet, H. van der, 769
Lieutard, H., 243
Liffol, Pierre de, 89
Lifshits, G. M., 849
Ligatto, D., 260
Ligonier, Lady Penelope, 408
Ligotti, G. E., 487
Likhachev, Ivan, 831
Lilao Franca, O., 266
Lim, J.-H., 25
Lima, D. D., 349
Lima, F. F. de, 345
Lima, L. C., 344
Lima Barreto, Afonso Henriques de, 343
Limat-Letellier, N., 199
Limentani, U., 426
Limonov, Eduard, 839
Lincio, F., 395
Lind, Jakov, 748
Lindau, Rudolf, 688, 720
Linde, Otto zur, 701
Lindemann, D., 595
Lindemann, K., 681
Lindemann-Stark, A., 655
Lindenberg, Udo, 736
Lindgren, L., 352
Lindner, D., 746
Lindner, M., 671
Lindø, A. V., 761
Lindon, J. M. A., 407, 421, 434, 448
Lindqvist, C., 33
Linguaglossa, Giorgio, 476
Link, J., 671
Linke, A., 669
Linkès, S., 183
Lins, Paulo, 349
Linsmayer, C., 703
Lintvelt, J., 208
Liphardt, E., 552
Lipiński, K., 803
Lipkin, S., 855
Lipnevich, V., 854
Lipovanu, I., 516
Lipovetsky, M. N., 837, 842, 847
Lipsius, Justus (Joost Lips), 268
Lipski, J. M., 6, 262
Lipsky, A., 561
Lishaugen, R., 777
Lispector, Clarice, 333, 344, 348, 349
Lissauer, Ernst, 705, 720
Litovskaya, M. A., 840
Little, R., 219
Littré, Émile, 27
Liubimov, O., 850, 854
Liubimova, A. F., 837
Liubomudrov, M., 842
Liuty, V., 845
Livanov, V., 851
Liver, R., 383, 867
Livera, M., 144
Livi, F., 436, 437
Livy (Titus Livius), 73
Llabrés, P., 298
Llambias, Pablo Henrik, 764
Llandâf, Book of, 526
Llewelyn Price, M., 869
Llibre de Consolat de Mar, 296
Llompart, G., 303
Llorca, F., 316
Lloyd, C., 199
Lloyd, R., 192, 194
Lluís Font, P., 296
Llwyd, A., 535
Llwyd, Angharad, 536
Llwyd, R., 534
Llywelyn Siôn, 533
Llywelyn, Robin, 536
Lobanov, M., 840
Lobanov-Rostovsky, N., 814
Lobenstein-Reichmann, A., 551, 557, 563
Lo Castro, G., 447, 448
Locher, Jakob, 619
Locke, John, 658
Lodato, S., 675
Lodge, A., 22
Loeb, P. S., 692
Loehneyss, Georg Engelhard, 638
Loehr, J., 203
Loeper, H., 709
Loewenson, Erwin, 704
Loewenstein, J., 660
Löffler, H., 546, 566, 567
Loget, F., 121
Logié, P., 48
Logier, E., 33
Logique de Port-Royal, 159
Loheide, B., 652
Lohenstein, Daniel Caspar von, 645
Loher und Maller, 591
Lohmeier, D., 696
Lohnstein, H., 561
Lohr, C., 298
Loi, Franco, 371, 459

Lokaj, R. J., 443
Lökös, P., 612
Lokrantz, M. G., 777
Lollini, M., 438
Lombard, A., 496
Lombardi, G., 463
Lombardo, G., 437
Lombroso, Cesare, 423
Lommatzsch, E., 26
Lommer, M., 643
Lomonaco, F., 405, 409, 420
Lo Monaco, Francesco, 411
Lomonosov, M. V., 832
Long, C. P., 707
Long, K. P., 867
Longevialle-Salha, A. de, 171
Longhurst, C. A., 279
Longley, A. P., 46
Longo, N., 421, 460
Longobardi, M., 470
Longoni, F., 408, 434
Lonicer, Johann, 104
Lönker, F., 725
Lonsbery, A., 846
Lonzi, Carla, 465
Looper, J., 46
Loos, H., 645
López Calahorro, I., 302
López-Calvo, I., 340
López de Corella, Alonso, 270
López Franco, Y. G., 227
López Morales, H., 246, 247
López Moreda, S., 268
López Silva, I., 314
López-Vidrieiro, M.-L., 268, 275
Loporcaro, M., 355, 360
Loquai, F., 655
Lorant, A., 175
Lorcin, M.-T., 82
Lord, M., 213
Loreaux-Kubler, C., 203
Lorenz, A., 601
Lorenz, D. C. G., 705, 716
Lorenz, E., 726
Lorenz, M. N., 753
Lorenzini, N., 456, 461, 492, 494
Lorenzo, G., 262
Lorenzo, P., 313
Lorenzo Vázquez, R., 307
Lorgna, Anton Maria, 403
Loria, Arturo, 476
Lorrain, Jean (Paul Duval), 190, 200
Lorvellec, Y., 290
Losada Goya, J. M., 171
Lösch, W., 571
Löscher, B. S., 749
Lösel, F., 689
Löser, F., 606, 610
Losev, L. V., 844, 846
Losev, V. V., 842
Loskoutoff, Y., 132, 147
Loşonţi, D., 503, 506
Loster-Schneider, G., 867
Lothe, J., 717
Loti, Pierre (Julien Viaud), 195, 200
Lotman, Iurii Mikhailovich, 283, 587, 838, 840
Lotman, L., 840
Lotovsky, I., 836
Lotze, Hermann, 726
Louâpre, M., 187
Loubayssin de Lamarca, F., 265
Loubier, P., 177
Louis XIV (*King of France*), 129, 130, 131, 132, 137, 141, 142, 143, 152, 162
Louis de France, *dit* Le Grand Dauphin, 129
Louis d'Orléans, 83
Louis de Mâle (*Count of Flanders*), 90
Louison, L., 93
Loustau, L. R., 337
Loutchitskaja, S., 63
Louth, C., 727
Louvain, Françoise, 99
Louvat-Molozay, B., 139
Loüys, Pierre, 200
Love, J., 814
Løveid, Cecilie, 779
Lovinescu, Eugen, 512, 516, 517
Lowell, Robert, 95
Löwenstein, S., 727
Löwy, M., 707
Lübecker, N., 194
Lubich, F. A., 721, 735
Lubkemann Allen, S., 198
Lubkoll, C., 648, 868
Lucan (Marcus Annaeus Lucanus), 382
Lucas, Vrain-Denis, 186
Lucas-Fiorato, C., 473
Lucchini, G., 425
Lucena, Juan de, 268
Lucentini, Franco, 474
Lucero, Juan Draghi, 340
Lucero, L., 302
Lucian of Samosata, 138, 269
Luciani, G., 409, 415
Luciani, P., 406
Lucidarius, 607, 608
Lucini, Gian Pietro, 458
Lücke, B., 746
Luckscheiter, R., 664
Lucretius (Titus Lucretius Carus), 108, 163, 201, 415
Łuczyńska, E., 790
Lüderssen, K., 676
Ludewig, Johann Peter, 638
Ludszuweit, C., 730
Lüdtke, J., 863
Ludwig von Eyb (the Elder), 61[illegible]
Ludwig von Eyb (the Younger), 616
Ludwig, K.-D., 547, 571
Ludwig, R., 263
Ludwig, W., 633
Ludwigslied, 584
Ludwin, D. M., 166
Luff, R., 602, 604
Lugones, Leopoldo, 318, 339
Lugovskoy, Vladimir, 855
Lühe, I. van der, 710
Luhmann, Niklas, 579
Lühr, R., 561
Luis de Granada, 266, 274
Lukács, Georg, 289, 324, 729
Lukanina, M., 809
Lukas, W., 670, 671, 683
Lukianov, Alexei, 841
Lukkari, Rauni Magga, 778
Lukov, V. A., 818
Lull, Ramon, 237, 296, 298–99, 862, 863
Lully, Jean-Baptiste, 143
Lumetti, R. C., 441
Luna, J.-J., 276
Luna, M.-F., 409
Lund, C., 767, 768
Lund, J., 758, 760
Lundberg, Liv, 778
Lundt, B., 618
Lunelli Spinoza, Benedetta Clotilde, 415
Lunn-Rockliffe, K., 193
Lupack, A., 43
Luperini, R., 448, 450, 452, 45[illegible] 454, 461
Lupi, F. W., 435
Lupinetti, M. Q., 397
Lupis, A., 15
Lupo, G., 449, 473, 489
Lupo di Casarano, Adele, 442
Luporini, Cesare, 439
Lurie, S., 819
Lusignan, Pierre de, 91
Lussu, Emilio, 450
Luther, Martin, 556, 564, 566, 622, 623, 624, 625, 631, 632, 633, 635, 638
Luther, S., 573
Luti, G., 422, 436, 461
Lütken, G., 765
Lutkus, A., 85
Lutovinov, I. S., 839
Lutsevich, L., 811
Luttazzi, S., 427
Lutz, A., 559

Lutz, E. C., 598, 861, 867
Lutz, W., 688
Lützeler, P. M., 659, 660
Lützen, P., 765
Luukkainen, M., 549
Luxemburg, Rosa, 642
Luzi, A., 435, 437, 477
Luzi, M., 436, 441
Luzi, Mario, 371, 456, 457, 469, 476–77, 479
Luzzi, C., 355
Luzzi, Giorgio, 477, 483, 486
Lyngsø, Niels, 768
Lyons, J. D., 132, 136, 155
Lyotard, Jean-François, 749, 773
Lysenko, A., 835
Lytkina, L. V., 828

Maack, U., 665, 730
Maber, R., 163
Mabillon, Jean, 159
Mabinogion, 529, 530, 531, 532
Mac Cana, P., 538, 540
Macchia, G., 443
Mac Craith, M., 540
MacDonald, K. M., 109
Macdonald, P. S., 162
Macedo, Joaquim Manuel de, 345
Macedonski, Alexandru, 512
Mach, Ernst, 725
Macha, J., 553, 572
Mácha, Karel Hynek, 785
Machač, P., 782
Machado, Antonio, 280, 285, 288
Machado, Leonor Izquierdo de, 288
Machado, Manuel, 279, 280
Machado de Assis *v.* Assis
Machaut, Guillaume de, 36, 57, 69, 70, 80, 89–91, 861
Macher, H., 730
Machiavelli, Niccolò, 103, 113, 407, 425, 443, 463, 509
Machon, Louis, 160
Maciel, M. E., 346
Mack, P., 634
Mack Smith, D., 426
Mackay, W. F., 4
Mackenzie, I., 246, 256
MacKenzie, L., 165
Maćkowiak, K., 799
Maclean, I., 103, 621, 634
Mac Mathúna, L., 540
Mac Niocaill, G., 538
Macovei, G., 503
Macrì, Oreste, 457, 477
Macrì Tronei, A., 464
Macrin, Salmon, 121
Maddox, D., 49, 55, 61, 867
Madeira, W. L., 345
Madou, J.-P., 219
Madrignani, C. A., 433, 454, 471
Madsen, L. M., 759
Maegaard, M., 758
Mæjlender, P., 779
Maeterlinck, Maurice, 206
Maffei, Scipione, 408
Maffia Scariati, I., 387
Maggi, Grazia, 475
Maggioni, G. P., 382
Magnanini, M., 361
Magnarelli, P., 435
Magner, C., 581
Magnien, C., 109, 112, 861
Magnien, M., 119
Magny, Olivier de, 117
Magot, A.-M., 230
Magrelli, Valerio, 457
Magrini, C., 244
Magris, Claudio, 457, 463, 477
Mahler, Gustav, 701
Mai und Beaflor, 600
Mai, A.-M., 771
Mai, E., 669
Maiakovsky, Vladimir, 823, 849, 851, 856
Maiden, M., 495, 500
Maier, B., 452, 480
Maignont, C., 539
Maillart, Jean, 70
Maimbourg, Louis, 160
Maimin, E. A., 808
Maiofis, M. L., 808
Maione, P., 405
Maiorescu, Titu, 512, 513, 514
Maiorini, M. G., 403
Maira, D., 115
Mairet, Jean, 127, 130, 242
Maistre, Joseph de, 198, 441
Majewska, I. M., 794
Majgaard, P., 761
Majkowski, G., 801
Majorano, M., 125
Makamina, J. B., 24
Makanin, Vladimir S., 834, 844, 849
Makarov, A. G., 853
Makarova, S. E., 853
Maksimov, V., 840, 843, 844
Maksimova, L., 825
Malagis, 591
Malaparte, Curzio, 463
Malaria, F., 466
Malato, E., 368
Mal'chukova, T. G., 817
Maldonado, Juan, 112
Maldonado, R., 256
Maldzis, A., 807
Malebranche, Nicolas, 127, 157, 159, 163
Malec, M., 805
Malec, T., 790, 793, 794
Malecarni, Francesco di Bonanno di, 395
Malejka, J., 791
Malenfant, M.-C., 634
Malenfant, P. C., 213
Maleninská, J., 787
Malerba, A., 427
Malerba, Luigi, 454, 466, 472, 477
Malet, M., 703, 728
Malherbe, François de, 105, 131
Malinkovich, I. Z., 855
Malinowski, Ivan, 767
Malkiel, Y., 7, 251
Mal'kova, N. K., 816
Mallarmé, Stéphane, 185, 191, 192, 193–94, 205, 206, 281, 457
Mallet, D., 224
Malm, U., 234
Malory, Sir Thomas, 36, 41, 69
Malot, Hector, 200
Malov, S. E., 842
Malvezzi, Virgilio, 637
Mamedova, J., 833
Mamiani, M., 402
Mamin-Sibiriak, Dmitrii Narkisovich, 828–29
Mamleev, Iurii, 839, 843
Man, Paul de, 707, 770
Manacorda, G., 422, 455, 465
Manaev, N. S., 826
Manavit, Aquiles, 243
Manca, D., 433
Mancho Duque. M. J., 270
Manciet, Bernat, 237, 238, 239
Mancini, M., 42, 427, 443, 860
Mańczak, W., 11, 789, 796, 803, 804
Mandach, A. de, 42
Mandel, J., 41
Mandelbaum, A., 491
Mandelbrote, G., 131
Mandel'shtam, Osip, 745, 807, 849–50
Mander, M., 464
Mandeville, Bernard, 426
Mandeville, Sir John, 74, 75, 617
Mandolini Pesaresi, M., 436
Mandosio, J.-M., 105
Mañé, N., 254
Manea, L., 501
Manea, Norman, 513
Manet, Édouard, 189, 192, 202

Manetta, Giacomo (*padre*), 435
Manetti, B., 452
Manetti, R., 389
Manganelli, Giorgio, 470, 477–78
Mangrané, Daniel, 697
Manica, R., 494
Manicom, Jacqueline, 217
Manin, Daniele, 421
Maniu, L., 517
Man'kovsky, A., 836
Manley, J., 106
Mann, Heinrich, 702, 703, 720
Mann, I., 812
Mann, Katia, 724
Mann, Klaus, 703, 720–21
Mann, Thomas, 198, 549, 667, 680, 684, 690, 699, 701, 702, 703, 704, 721–25, 727, 735
Mannack, E., 642
Mannheim, Karl, 290
Manning, J., 107
Manno, Giuseppe, 425
Mano, R., 187
Manolescu, Nicolae, 516
Manotta, M., 477, 494
Manrique, Jorge, 285
Mansau, A., 134
Mantegazza, Paolo, 432
Mantero, A., 152
Manuel Antonio *v.* Pérez Sánchez
Manuel, Niklaus, 625, 626, 633
Manzoni, Alessandro, 290, 372, 411, 422, 430, 442–44, 445, 493, 860, 862
Marabini, C., 464
Maragoni, G. P., 428
Maraini, Dacia, 478
Maraini, Fosco, 458
Maral, A., 129
Marana, Giovanni Paolo, 152
Mărănduc, C., 504
Marantz, E. G., 205
Maravall, José Antonio, 270
Marcabru, 232, 235
Marcadé, B., 193
Marcato, C., 356, 387
Marcato, G., 13, 362
March, Ausiàs, 236, 301
March, K., 315
Marchal, B., 194
Marchal, G. P., 636
Marchal, R., 867
Marchand, Clément, 211
Marchegiani Jones, I., 478
Marcheix, D., 213
Marchenko, A., 817
Marchenko, T. V., 853
Marcheschi, D., 483
Marchesini, C., 486
Marchetti, Alessandro, 415
Marchi, G. P., 432, 447
Marchi, M., 492
Marchigiani, Giovanni, 446
Marchiori, F., 472
Marchisio, M., 483
Marcialis, M. T., 405, 413
Marco Polo, 74, 75, 78, 470
Marcolini, S., 358
Marcon, L., 438
Marcos Marín, F., 3
Marcoux, N., 208
Marcozzi, L., 397
Mărdărescu-Teoderescu, M., 499
Marder, E., 192
Marechaux, P., 118
Mared, G., 536
Marek, H., 863
Mareş, A., 497, 498
Margaret of Burgundy, 70
Mărgărit, I., 505, 506
Margarit, Joan, 302
Margaritha, Antonius, 622
Margellos, C., 102
Margetts, J., 586
Margitić, M. R., 138, 140
Margolin, J.-C., 117, 118
Margolis, E., 846
Margolis, N., 81, 82, 85, 87, 866
Marguerite de Navarre (M. d'Angoulême), 92, 110–11, 114
Marguerite de Valois (*Queen of France*), 111, 152, 160, 867
Marguerite Porete, 92–93
Margulis, N., 833
Mari, A., 486
Mari, M., 411, 438, 447
María Jesús de Agreda (*Sor*), 272–73
María de San José Salazar, 272
Mariacci, C., 228
Mariana, Juan de, 266
Mariani, U., 484
Mariátegui, José Carlos, 324
Mariátegui, Juan Carlos, 280
Marichalar, Antonio, 281
Marichy, C., 225
Marie de Champagne, 55, 56
Marie de France, 35, 36, 37, 38, 40, 41, 51, 54, 56, 61
Marie de l'Incarnation, Mère (Marie Guyard), 146, 158
Mariette, A., 424
Mării, I., 505
Marillac, Louise de, 159
Marin, Biagio, 457, 478
Marin, F., 122
Marin, M., 505, 506
Marineo Sículo, Lucio, 268
Mariner, F., 167
Marinetti, Filippo Tommaso, 451, 456, 458, 478
Marinetti, S., 860
Marini, C., 429
Marini, L., 725
Marinina, Alexandra, 834, 844
Marino, A., 516
Marino, Giambattista, 355
Mariño, R., 316
Mariño, X. R., 314
Mariño Paz, R., 304, 307
Marinotti, A., 438
Mariotti, C., 435
Mariuz, P., 425
Marivaux, Pierre Carlet de Chamblain de, 136, 410
Marková, M., 784, 870
Markovich, I., 811
Markovich, V., 838
Markus, G., 707, 731
Marle, J. van, 758
Marliani, Giovanni Bartolomeo 109
Marlien, I., 361
Marmi, Anton Francesco, 415
Marmontel, Jean-François, 137
Marnersdóttir, M., 770
Marnette, S., 13, 21, 26
Marniti, Biagia, 478
Marnix de Sainte-Aldegonde, Philippe de, 121
Marolles, Michel de, 147
Maron, Monika, 748
Marot, Clément, 99, 100, 105, 111, 116
Marotta, G., 5, 361
Marpeau, E., 136
Marquard von Stein, 620
Marquets, Anne de, 134
Márquez, Juan, 265
Márquez Reiter, R., 261
Marquina, Eduardo, 279
Marr, M. J., 292
Marrache, M., 114
Marrella, L., 442
Marrone, G., 489
Marroni, F., 371
Marsal, E., 692
Marshall, Nini, 289, 295
Marshall, Paule, 219
Marsico, R., 427
Marszałek, M., 796, 799, 800
Martel, C., 228
Martel, P., 7, 223, 240, 244
Martelli, M., 435
Martello, C., 236
Martens, G., 691

Martens, P., 568
Martí, José, 319–20, 323, 338
Marti, M., 440
Martí, S., 297, 299, 300, 860
Martial d'Auvergne, 69
Martignoni, C., 480, 489
Martin le Franc, 70
Martin, C. E., 318
Martin, D., 115, 714
Martin, H.-J., 99
Martín, J. M., 289
Martin, J.-P., 39
Martin, L., 667
Martin, M., 511
Martin, P., 118
Martín Abad, J., 267
Martin-Lau, P., 200
Martin Ruano, M. R., 209
Martín y Soler, Vincente, 412
Martín Zorraquino, M. A., 253
Martineau, A., 68
Martineau-Génieys, C., 111
Martinell, E., 257
Martinelli, B., 436, 437
Martinelli, R., 464
Martinelli, V., 431
Martinengo, A., 274
Martinet, A., 7
Martinet, J.-L., 99
Martínez, A., 247, 292
Martínez, C. P., 314
Martínez, G. B., 271
Martínez, J. M., 319
Martínez, V., 339
Mártinez, Z. N., 340
Martínez Baleirón, M., 307, 312
Martínez Celdrán, E., 310
Martínez Gil, F., 246
Martínez-Gil, V., 297
Martínez-Gutierrez, J., 283
Martínez Linares, M. A., 259
Martínez de Llorach, J., 3
Martínez Romero, T., 300
Martínez Sierra, Gregorio, 295
Martínez Torrón, D., 287
Marting, D. E., 333, 348
Martino, A., 644
Martins, Cyro, 343
Martinuzzi, P., 431
Martirano, M., 419, 420
Martone, A., 419
Martorell, Joanot, 301
Marty, E., 195
Marty-Bazalgues, J., 223
Martynov, G. G., 814
Martynov, Leonid, 850
Marucci, V., 369, 422
Marutina, I. N., 847
Marvan, J., 782
Marx, F., 721
Marx, Karl, 294, 324, 680
Mary of Hungary, 627
Mary Tudor (*Queen of France, 1515*), 101
März, C., 606
Marzari, R., 868
Masanetz, M., 863
Mascagni, Pietro, 424
Mascanzoni, L., 383
Mascato Rey, R., 294
Mascheroni, Lorenzo, 415–16
Mascitelli, G., 464
Maselli, Carlo, 426
Masereel, Franz, 715
Mashevsky, A., 811, 829
Masi, Tommaso, 404
Masiakowska, D., 664
Masiello, F., 337
Masiello, V., 447
Masina, L., 343
Masino, Paola, 465
Maslard, V., 196
Maslowski, M., 510
Masoero, M., 482
Massaron, Stefano, 463
Massebeuf, A., 230
Masser, A., 584
Massip, F., 303
Mast, T., 644
Mastretta, Ángeles, 336
Mastronardi, Lucio, 478
Masüger, P., 572
Matala de Mazza, E., 691
Matarrese, T., 411
Mateos Miera, E., 283
Mateu Serra, R., 257
Matfre Ermengaut, 237, 298
Mathäs, A., 752
Mathau Brwmffild, 531
Mathesius, Johann, 628
Mathey-Maille, L., 62, 63
Mathieu de Boulogne, 393
Mathieu, M.-J., 29
Mathieu-Castellani, G., 104, 110, 118, 119
Mathieu-Colas, M., 27
Matignon, Jacques Goyon de (*maréchal*), 112
Matlová, J., 641
Matsubara, M., 182
Matsumura, T., 55
Matt, L., 355
Matt, W., 570
Mattauch, H., 183
Mattei, Saverio, 405
Matteucci, G., 420
Mattheier, K. J., 4
Matthias (*Emperor*), 640
Matthiassen, S., 463
Matthieu-Castellani, G., 135
Mattioda, E., 407
Mattioli, T., 861
Matto de Turner, Clorinda, 320
Matuschek, S., 648
Matussek, P., 714
Matveev, B. I., 812, 829
Matvievskaya, G. P., 827
Matzat, W., 156
Mauelshagen, C., 862
Mauelshagen, F., 621
Maulpoix, J.-M., 169
Maulucci Vivolo, F. P., 440
Maupassant, Guy de, 189, 195, 200–01
Maurer, C., 286
Maurer, P., 262
Mauri, D., 122
Mauriac, François, 177, 239
Maurice (*Elector of Saxony*), 622
Maurice, F., 13
Mauro, W., 492
Maurois, André, 281
Mauron, C., 243
Maury, J.-F., 230
Mauser, P., 563
Mauthner, Fritz, 669
Max, F. R., 581
Maximilian I (*Emperor*), 620, 630, 631
Maximin, Daniel, 217, 218, 219
May, Y., 715
Maya, Alcides, 343
Mayans y Siscar, Gregorio, 275
Mayer, C. A., 867
Mayer, C. O., 116
Mayer, M., 691, 714
Mayer, P., 78
Mayer-Iswandy, C., 744
Maynard, François, 132
Maynier, Jean, 104
Mayröcker, Friederike, 737, 748
Mazarin, Jules (*cardinal*), 132, 147
Mazilu, Dan Horia, 507, 509
Mazouer, C., 106
Mazza, A., 431, 482
Mazzacurati, G., 867
Mazzini, Giuseppe, 421
Mazzio, C., 94
Mazzocca, F., 411
Mazzocchi Alemanni, M., 427
Mazzoni, C., 423
Mazzoni, F., 365, 377
Mazzoni Peruzzi, S., 393
Mazzotta, G., 366
McCarthy, G., 140
McCash, J. H., 56
McClelland, J., 117
McClennen, S. A., 337
McCormick, R., 702

McCuaig, W., 123
McCulloch, J., 290
McFarland, T., 596, 866
McGrady, D., 81
McIntosh, F., 172, 196
McKenna, A., 142, 166, 867
McKenna, C., 541
McKinley, K. L., 73
McKinley, M. B., 110
McLary, L. A., 726
McLaughlin, M., 469, 470, 471, 861
McLean, M., 522
McLeod, N., 539
McLuhan, Marshall, 289
McManus, D., 540
McMillin, A., 807, 845
McMullan, T., 281, 288
McMullin, G. P., 722
McMunn, M., 80
McNally, J., 702
McNamara, M., 541
McNee, M. K., 344
McQuillan, P., 541
McVaugh, M., 299
McVeigh, J., 741
McWebb, C., 81
Meacher, S., 736
Mechthild von Hackeborn, 611
Mechthild von Magdeburg, 610
Meckel, Christoph, 733
Mecklenburg, M., 590
Mecklenburg, N., 677, 680
Mecu, N., 514
Medeiros-Lichem, M. T., 338
Mêdelska, J., 796, 799, 800
Medici (*dynasty*), 425
Medina, J., 302
Medina Granda, R. M., 15
Meding, T., 154, 156
Medrish, D. N., 817
Medvedev, Kirill, 842
Medvedev, R., 854
Medvedev, V. A., 837
Meerhoff, K., 98, 634
Megenny, W., 263
Mehl, E., 162
Mehring, Walter, 704
Meid, V., 581, 643
Meier, A., 720
Meier, C., 867
Meier, J., 556, 572, 627, 630
Meierkhold, V. E., 836
Meigret, L., 21
Meillet, A., 7
Meindl-Weiss, J., 611
Meinecke, E., 553
Meireles, Cecília, 346
Meise, H., 637, 638, 646
Meisel, J. M., 6
Mejri, S., 28
Meksh, E. B., 837
Melanchthon, Philipp, 98, 104, 622, 625, 633–35
Mel'gunov, B. V., 829
Meliga, W., 232
Melis, F., 698
Melis, I., 480
Melli, G., 411, 422
Melliti, Mohsen, 465
Mello, A. M. L. de, 346
Mel'nichuk, O. A., 809
Mel'nikov, A. S., 816
Mel'nikov, N. G., 835, 850
Melnikova, T., 813
Melo Neto, João Cabral de, 344, 346
Melosi, L., 406, 434, 436, 441
Melville, Herman, 161, 172
Melzer, S. E., 126, 144
Ménage, Gilles, 163
Ménager, D., 104, 112, 115, 117, 118
Ménard, P., 37, 75
Menarini, P., 286
Menasse, Robert, 706, 737
Menchú, Rigoberta, 331
Mendelson, D., 32
Mendes, Murilo, 346
Méndez, Concha, 283
Méndez Fernández, L., 309
Méndez Ferrín, Xosé Luis, 315
Mendoza, I., 794
Menechella, G., 477
Meneghelli, Antonio (*abate*), 425
Meneghello, Luigi, 478–79
Meneghetti, M. L., 233, 234, 235, 392
Menéndez Pidal, R., 255, 260
Menetti, A., 463, 478
Meney, L., 32
Mengal, P., 410
Mengaldo, P. V., 386, 444, 453
Menghini, Mario, 428
Menhennet, A., 699
Menichetti, A., 235, 236, 383, 386, 867
Méniel, B., 120
Menke, B., 664
Menke, C., 751
Menke, H., 568, 863
Menke, T., 751
Menozzi, D., 403
Mensa, J., 296
Men'shikova, E. R., 851
Mentzel-Reuters, A., 580
Menz, F., 548
Menzini, Benedetto, 404
Merceron, J., 70
Merchiers, D., 747
Mercier, L., 32
Mercurius van Helmont, Franciscus, 643
Merendoni, S., 412
Mereszhinskaya, A. I., 834
Merezhkovsky, Dmitrii Sergeevich, 722, 829, 835, 839
Mergenthaler, V., 645, 668
Mérimée, Prosper, 96, 174, 182, 186, 195
Merini, Alda, 479, 483
Merlanti, F., 423, 465
Merle, P., 29
Merle, R., 242
Merleau-Ponty, Maurice, 763
Merlin, H., 135
Merlin, M., 459
Mermet, Claude, 106
Merola, N., 427
Merrilees, B., 73
Merseburger Zaubersprüche, 583
Merswin, Rulman, 611
Mertens, B., 708
Mertens, V., 602, 603, 607, 612, 633, 863
Mesa, G., 457, 464
Meschonnic, H., 172
Meshcheriakov, V. P., 820, 853
Meshkovskaia, N., 807
Mesmes, Henri de, 109
Mesmes, Jean-Pierre de, 109
Mesnard, J., 164, 165
Messerli, A., 621, 669
Messina, Tommaso da, 467, 485
Messner, D., 867
Mestergazi, E. G., 808, 840–41
Mestica, G., 441
Metastasio, Pietro, 400, 405–06, 416
Metge, Bernat, 300–01
Methani, Salah, 465
Métivier, Jean-Léon de, 127
Metz, J., 695
Metzeltin, M., 495
Metzidakis, S., 185
Meun, Jean de, 69, 79, 86, 91, 9
Meurer, B., 870
Meurer, T., 695
Meurig ab Iorwerth, 527
Meyer, A.-R., 668
Meyer, Conrad Ferdinand, 688
Meyer, M., 601, 602, 692, 863
Meyer, P., 648, 813
Meyer, Paul, 7
Meyer, R., 406
Meyer, S. A., 402
Meyer, W., 635
Meyer-Kalkus, R., 557
Meyfart, Johannes Matthäus, 644

Ieylac, M., 221
Ieymeyr, B., 639
Iezdrea, D., 515
Iézières, Philippe de, 81, 92
Iezzetta, E., 485
Iiagkov, B., 846
Iiasoedov, N. E., 817
Iiccolis, S., 434
Iichaelsen, A. G., 778
Iichaelsen, P., 758
Iichaud, S., 707
Iichel von Ehenheim, 616
Iichel, A., 175, 178, 363
Iichel, Francisque, 37
Iichel, Jean, 66
Iichel, Louise, 194
Iichel, P., 682
Iichel, W., 863
Iichelangelo *v.* Buonarroti
Iichelet, Jules, 186–88
Iichelfeit, J., 724
Iichelstaedter, Carlo, 457, 479
Iichetti, Francesco Paolo, 431
Iichon, H., 166
Iickiewicz, Adam, 187, 800
Iicle, Veronica, 511
Iicó, J. M., 287
Iicone, Marco, 207
Iiddleboe, P., 532
Iidgley, D., 709, 732
Iiedema, N., 576
Iieder, W., 577
Iiehling, S., 544, 545
Iielke, C., 685
Iigdał, J., 798
Iigli, Ambrogio, 83
Iiglietta, A., 362
Iiglio, L., 369
Iiglio, M., 367
Iiglioli, Lorenzo, 463
Iignini, F., 436
Iiguel, J., 697
Iiguez Vilas, C., 294
Iihail, Z., 503
Iihăilă, G., 495, 498, 502, 510
Iihăilă, R., 516
Iihăilescu, F., 512
Iihăilescu, G., 509
Iihăilescu, S., 508
Iihm, A., 556
Iihura, Miguel, 294, 295
Iika, T., 796
Iikeilitis-Winter, A., 555
Iikesell, M., 272
Iikhailin, V., 837
Iikhailov, A., 845
Iikhailov, A. V., 808
Iikhailov, M. N., 831
Iikhailova, N. V., 831
Mikhailovsky, Nikolai Konstantinovich, 824, 839
Mikhalkov, S. V., 832
Mikheev, M. I., 852
Miklautsch, L., 591, 600
Mikołajczak, S., 799
Milani, N., 491
Milanini, A. C., 474
Milanini, C., 439
Milano, P., 470
Milcent, B., 177
Milde, V., 587
Mil'don, V. I., 814, 827, 830, 842, 854
Miles, E., 531
Milescu Spâtarul *v.* Spâtarul
Milewska, B., 791
Milland-Bove, B., 43
Millardet, G., 7
Millefiorini, F., 432
Miller, N. J., 629, 636
Miller, Y. E., 340
Millet, O., 97, 104, 110, 634
Millet, V., 598, 865
Millot, H., 205
Millward, E. G., 534
Milne, A. A., 800
Milne, L., 218
Milner, M., 191
Milone, P., 488
Miłosz, Cseław, 798
Milton, John, 108, 434
Min, L., 685
Minakov, A., 846
Minchin, A., 843
Minden, M., 721, 753
Mineo, N., 434
Miner, M., 192
Miner, R. C., 419
Mineralov, I. I., 835
Minerva, N., 201
Minervini, F. S., 409
Minervini, L., 248
Minet-Mahy, V., 68
Minkova, R., 742
Minnis, A. J., 92, 375
Minter, C. J., 664
Mints, Zara G., 838, 843
Minuţ, A.-M.,
Miodek, J., 796, 805
Miotti, M., 106
Mir, Aquiles, 243
Mirás, F., 305
Miraux, J.-P., 181
Mirbeau, Octave, 201, 205
Mircea, Corneliu, 507
Miremont, Jacqueline de, 161
Miro, J., 226
Miron, Gaston, 210, 213
Miroshnikov, I. I., 813
Miroshnikova, O. V., 821
Misch, M., 863
Mischi, G., 521
Mistère du siège d'Orléans, 66
Mistral, Frédéric, 223, 227, 242, 243, 244
Mistral, Gabriela, 340
Mitchell, M., 840
Mitin, G., 816
Mittelmann, H., 705
Mittenzwei, I., 863
Mitterand, H., 202
Mittermeyer, M., 742
Mitternacht, Johann Sebastian, 637
Mitu, M., 502, 510
Mix, Y.-G., 678, 701, 739
Mizinova, L., 822
Mizraje, M. G., 339
Mizuno, H., 205
Młotek, A., 793
Mnikh, R., 845
Mnukhin, L., 855
Moangă, E., 515
Moates, D., 247
Mocanu, N., 496
Moceanu, O., 509
Moch, W., 796
Moderne, Jacques, 100
Modesti, M., 476
Modick, Klaus, 733
Moeller van den Bruck, A., 551
Mohr, J., 599
Mohr, T., 539
Mohr, W., 594
Möhren, F., 8
Moisan, C., 207
Moisan, J.-C., 634
Mokienko, V., 788
Mola, M., 435
Molchanov, E., 829
Molchanova, N. A., 827
Molchanova, S. V., 851, 856
Moldovan, D., 509–10
Mole, G. D., 60
Molendijk, A., 25
Molière, Jean-Baptiste Poquelin, *dit*, 125, 126, 129, 130, 136, 140–42, 714
Molin, Vittore, 401
Molina, I., 257
Molinelli, P., 357
Molinet, Jean, 117
Molinié, G., 141, 145
Molinier, C., 24
Molinos Castro, R., 310
Molitor, Joseph, 708
Mölk, U., 867
Moll, J., 267, 268
Møller, B., 761

Möller, E., 682
Möller, Eberhard Wolfgang, 700
Møller, H., 755
Møller, J., 758
Møller, J. F., 766
Möller, K.-P., 679
Møller, Povl Martin, 765
Møller, S. A., 760
Mollier, J.-Y., 205
Möllmann, U., 556, 613, 627
Moloney, B., 490
Mombello, G., 85
Momigliano, Attilio, 451
Mommsen, Theodor, 680
Monachesi, P., 864
Monahan, J., 81, 82
Monaldo, Giuseppe, 437, 440
Monardes, Nicolás, 266
Monastra, R. M., 437
Mönch von Werden, 610
Moncond'huy, D., 140
Mondini, S., 358
Mondor (*brother of* Tabarin), 144
Mondor, L., 181
Moneta, Johann, 800
Monferran, J.-C., 111
Monforte, E., 489
Monfrin, J., 3
Monicat, B., 864
Monicelli, Furio, 479
Monjour, A., 5, 23
Monluc, Blaise de, 120
Monod, Gabriel, 187
Monot, A.-G., 181
Monschein, M., 736
Monsiváis, Carlos, 322
Montagne, V., 110, 118
Montaigne, Michel Eyquem de, 97, 98, 99, 103, 111–13, 114, 127, 146, 150, 158, 159
Montale, Eugenio, 422, 454, 456, 457, 469, 476, 479–80, 490
Montalto, S., 474, 483
Montanari, R., 464
Montandon, A., 190
Montanhòl, F., 239
Montausier, Julie d'Angennes, madame de, 147
Monteagudo Romero, H., 304, 306, 311, 315, 316
Montecchi, G., 401
Montefoschi, P., 492
Montengón y Paret, Pedro, 277–78
Monter, W., 97
Montero Curiel, P., 250, 255
Montesquieu, Charles de Secondat, baron de, 409
Montessori, N. M., 247
Montferrant, Jean de, 73
Montfleury, Antoine Jacob, *dit*, 138
Montfleury, Zacharie Jacob, *dit*, 137
Monti, Vincenzo, 411, 416, 422, 439, 444
Montibelli, M., 446
Montluc, Adrien, 241–42
Montobbio, L., 425
Montpensier, Anne-Marie Louise d'Orléans, duchesse de, 153
Montreuil, Jean de, 87
Montreux, Nicolas de, 124
Monye, L. P., 220
Monzetti, Joannes Benedictus, 101
Moore, George, 200
Moore, M., 341
Moosmüller, S., 557, 558
Mora, F., 51
Morabito, R., 442
Morace, A. M., 418, 447, 467
Moraes, Vinicius de, 347
Moraldo, S. M., 655
Morales, A., 263
Morales Folguera, J. M., 271
Moran Ocerinjauregui, J., 301
Morando, S., 475
Morant, R., 257
Morariu, L., 511
Moraru, A., 498
Moravia, Alberto, 465, 480
Morawe, B., 686
Morazzoni, Marta, 480
Moré, B., 260, 342
More, Henry, 643
Moréas, P., 726
Moreau, Gustave, 203
Moreau, I., 150, 164
Moreira, D. A., 309
Moreiras, A., 324, 326
Morel, M.-A., 33
Morelli, G., 425
Morelli, L., 411, 412
Moreni, C., 435
Moreno, Louis, 240
Moreno, M. P., 285, 438
Moresco, Antonio, 451, 462, 464
Moretti, F., 460
Moretti, Marino, 480
Moretti, W., 867
Morev, G., 849
Morgado García, A., 270
Morgan, B., 746
Morgan, D. D., 535
Morgan, H., 540
Morgan-Guy, J., 528
Morgana, S., 426
Morgante, J., 133, 155
Morgenstern, Soma, 725
Morgenthaler, W., 687
Morgner, Irmtraud, 648, 738, 739, 748–49
Moriconi, I., 347
Mörike, Eduard, 688–89, 712
Morimoto, Y., 256
Morin, Y. C., 21
Morín Rodríguez, A., 259
Morini, Damaso, 401
Moritz, Karl Philip, 656, 658
Morlet-Chantalat, C., 155
Morlicchio, E., 565
Morlino, D., 412
Moro, A., 12
Moro, Aldo, 488
Moroder, E., 520
Moroder, G., 520
Moroni, G., 445
Morosetti, T., 481
Morozova, N. P., 812
Morpurgo-Tagliabue, Guido, 417
Morreale, M., 439
Morrien, R., 696
Morris, L., 741
Morris, Lewis, 533
Morrison, I., 110
Morrison, I. R., 488
Morrison, S.E., 182
Morrison, Toni, 219
Morselli, Guido, 480
Mort Artu, 45
Mortara Garavelli, B., 452
Mortensen, K. P., 766
Mortimer, A. K., 110
Morton, T., 257
Morvan, F., 54
Moscherosch, Johann Michael, 637
Mose, G., 768
Mosegaard Hansen, M.-B., 25
Moser, M., 803
Moser, S., 744
Moser-Verrey, M., 208
Mosiołek-Kłosińska, K., 796
Mosl, G., 673
Mosley, D., 860
Moss, A., 99, 115, 634
Mostovskaya, N. N., 812
Mostowik, P., 797
Mota, L. D., 344
Mota, M. A. Coelho da, 306
Motapanyane, V., 500
Mote, Jean de la, 78
Moteiunaite, I. V., 828
Mothus, A., 150
Motsch, W., 560
Motta, A., 488

Motte Fouqué, Caroline de la, 652, 662
Motte Fouqué, Friedrich de la, 697
Mottel, H., 715
Moudileno, L., 218, 861
Moulis, A., 227
Mounin, Georges (Louis Leboucher), 5
Moura, J.-M., 190
Mouren, R., 104
Mourey, M.-T., 645
Moutet, M., 172
Moutier, Louis, 244, 245
Mouveaux, Jean de, 101
Moya, P., 329
Moyano Andrés, I., 267
Moyer, M., 262
Mozart, Wolfgang Amadeus, 486
Mozet, N., 177
Mozzi, G., 464
Mozzillo-Howell, E., 374
Mueller-Vollmer, K., 655
Mügeln, Heinrich von, 863
Mühlemann, J., 593
Mühlethaler, J.-C., 79, 80, 82, 865, 868
Mühlherr, A., 582, 598
Mühling, A., 631
Mühsam, Erich, 642, 725
Muir, M., 210
Mula, P., 384
Muljacic, Z., 553
Mullan, B., 686
Müller, B., 254
Müller, C., 70, 82, 92, 694
Müller, E., 691, 692
Müller, G., 561, 662, 736
Müller, H., 674
Müller, H.-H., 709
Müller, Heiner, 674, 709, 745, 749, 753
Müller, Herta, 735, 749
Müller, I., 747
Müller, J.-D., 589, 597
Müller, L., 713
Müller, M. H., 748
Müller, N., 359, 549, 660
Müller, P. O., 555, 558
Müller, Robert, 700
Müller, S., 587, 590, 867
Müller, T. C., 668
Müller, U., 602, 603, 697, 863
Müller, W., 23, 574
Müller-Bergh, K., 336
Müller-Salget, K., 659
Müller-Seidel, W., 677, 680
Müller-Sievers, H., 691
Müllerová, O., 785
Mulon, M., 221, 228
Multatuli, V. M., 818
Mumm, P.-A., 565
Munari, S., 145
Münchhausen, Börries von, 725
Mundt, K., 834, 852
Mundt, Theodor, 689
Mundt-Espìn, C., 396
Muñiz Muñiz, M. de las N., 439, 440
Munn, A., 12
Muñoz Llorente, José Esteban Isaac, 280
Muñoz Párraga, M. C., 272
Munro, M., 217
Munske, H. H., 558
Münster, Sebastian, 635
Munteanu, E., 497
Münter, Frederick, 403
Müntzer, Thomas, 624
Murashov, I., 836
Murat, L., 189
Muratori, Ludovico Antonio, 417
Muravieva, N. M., 853
Murayama, I., 653
Murcia Bielsa, S., 261
Murdoch, H. A., 218
Muresu, G., 366, 378
Muret, Marc-Antoine, 115, 116
Muromskii, V. P., 831
Murphy, D., 868
Murphy, K., 280
Murphy, S., 108, 115
Murray, K., 538, 539
Musan, R., 562
Musarra, F., 473
Musarra Schrøeder, U., 463
Muscardini, G., 433
Muscariello, M., 447
Muscatine, C., 92
Muscetta, C., 868
Muschg, Adolf, 738
Muschitiello, N., 432
Muscia da Siena, 377
Musculus, Andreas, 625, 644
Musculus, Wolfgang, 635
Mushnikov, A. A., 817
Musil, Robert, 279, 690, 699, 701, 702, 706, 725–26, 735
Musolino, G., 485, 486
Muspilli, 583
Mussafia, A., 384
Mussato, Albertino, 393
Musset, Alfred de, 169, 174
Mussi, Teresa, 417
Mussini, G., 486
Mussolini, Benito, 451
Mustè, M., 441
Muthu, M., 508
Mutterle, A. M., 446, 482
Muysken, P., 262
Muzi, Silva, 480
Muzikant, M., 572
Myers, N., 113
Myfenydd, 534

Nabert, N., 81
Nabl, Franz, 706
Nabokov, Vladimir, 608, 826, 850
Nacinovich, A., 411
Nada, N., 425
Nadeau, C. A., 273
Nadherny, Sidonie, 726
Nadiani, Giovanni, 459
Næss, H. S., 776
Nagel, S., 81
Nagelschmidt, I., 734
Nagórko, A., 790
Naguschewski, D., 19
Nagy, J. F., 540
Nagy, R., 497
Nährlich-Slatewa, E., 727
Naiditsch, L., 571
Nail, N., 556, 573
Naiman, A., 841, 844
Najjar, A., 190
Nakam, G., 111
Nakatenus, Wilhelm, 638
Nalepa, J., 797
Nancy, C., 126, 143
Nandorfy, M. J., 287
Naogeorg, Thomas, 626
Napoléon I Bonaparte (*Emperor*), 184, 416, 433, 442, 449, 654, 699, 812
Napoléon III (*Emperor*), 171
Napoli, A., 474
Napoli, M., 363
Narbona Jiménez, A., 252
Narcisus et Dané, 47
Narezhnyi, Vasilii Trofimovich, 807
Nariòo, G., 224, 226
Naro, M., 454
Nascimento, E., 343
Nascimento, J. L. de, 349
Nasedkin, N., 824, 826
Nash, J. C., 114, 115
Nasi, F., 460
Nassar, Raduan, 349
Nassi, F., 445
Nassichuk, J., 105
Nässl, S., 552, 553
Năstase, V., 504
Natali, G., 441
Nath, H., 547
Naubert, Benedikte, 652

Naudé, Gabriel, 158, 160, 163, 164
Naumann, D., 684
Nava, G., 445
Nava, Pedro, 349
Navarro, G., 302
Navarro, M. T., 865
Navarro Durán, R., 286
Navas Ocaña, I., 281
Navaza, G., 313
Navaza Blanco, G., 306, 312
Naves, Rodrigo, 349
Navigatio Sancti Brendani, 232, 302, 588
Navrozov, Lev, 843
Nawrocka, U., 800
N'Dakon, W. U., 745
N'Diaye, A.-R., 149
Neagoe Basarab, 509
Neagoe, V., 505, 506
Nebeský, L., 783
Nebol'sin, S., 808, 814
Nebrija, Antonio de, 8, 255, 266
Nechiporenko, I., 809
Nederman, C., 81
Nedzvetsky, V. A., 822
Née, P., 169
Neeman, H., 153
Nefagina, G., 854
Nefed'ev, G. V., 820
Negri, A., 232, 438
Negrici, E., 512
Négroni, N., 127, 134, 135
Negruzzi, Costache, 514
Neidhart 'von Reuenthal', 604
Neiescu, P., 506
Neiland, M., 197
Neira, J., 287
Neira Palacio, E. D., 341
Neira Vilas, Xosé, 313
Neizvestny, Ernst, 843
Nekrasov, Nikolai Alexeevich, 829
Nekrasov, Victor, 839, 850
Nekula, M., 552, 781
Nekvapil, J., 785
Nelken, Margarita, 283
Nelli, René, 237, 239
Nelligan, Emile, 214
Nellmann, E., 581
Nellner, K., 680, 682, 698
Nelson, A. A., 340
Nelson, D., 67
Nemzer, A., 832, 834
Nencioni, Enrico, 447
Nencioni, G., 352, 354, 440, 452
Nenz, C., 694
Nephew, J., 81
Nepomniashchii, V. S., 815
Népote-Desmarres, F., 141, 862
Neppi, E., 434
Nerdrum, G., 410
Neri, Giuseppe, 450, 465
Nerlich, M., 184
Neruda, Jan, 785
Neruda, Pablo, 335
Nerval, Gérard de (Gérard Labrunie), 169, 188, 189, 194–95, 205
Nervèze, Suzanne de, 161
Néry, A., 200
Neščimenko, G., 787
Nesi, A., 360, 361
Nesi, C., 452
Nesson, Pierre de, 76
Nestroy, Johann Nepomuk, 668, 689, 719
Neudeck, O., 608, 693, 729
Neuendorff, D., 612
Neuhaus, M., 679, 718
Neuhaus, S., 654, 685, 712, 718, 730, 868
Neuhaus-Koch, A., 863
Neuhoff, B., 714
Neukirchen, T., 603, 750
Neuland, E., 567
Neumann, C., 696
Neumann, G., 647, 677, 691, 717, 868
Neumann, M., 676, 721, 724
Neumann, T., 686
Neumeister, S., 436
Neuschäfer, A., 863
Neuss, E., 572, 574
Nevinskaya, I. N., 845
Nevskikh, A., 817
Nevskikh, V., 817
Nevsky, A. I., 815
Newerkla, S. M., 787
Newman, John Henry (*cardinal*), 444
Newmark, K., 192
Newton, Sir Isaac, 179
Neymeyr, B., 730
Nibelungenlied, 579, 586, 588–91, 864
Nicastro, G., 412, 424
Nic Dhonnchadha, A., 542
Niceron, Jean-Pierre, 127
Nicetas Choniates, 64
Nicholas III (*Pope*), 378
Nicholson, M., 339
Nickel, G., 732
Nickel, J., 672
Nickel-Bacon, I., 753
Nickolaus, K., 40
Niclas von Wyle, 618, 620
Nicodemi, V., 450
Nicodemo, R., 365
Nicolae, I., 496, 500, 503
Nicolaisen, W. F., 14
Nicolaus Cusanus (N. of Cusa), 619
Nicolas Oresme, 81, 96
Nicolaysen, B. K., 775
Nicole, Pierre, 137, 158, 159, 164
Nicoletti, G., 403, 406
Nicollier, B., 108
Nicpoń, J., 794
Ni Cuilleanáin, E., 486
Nida-Rfimelin, J., 545
Nider, V., 274
Niderst, A., 131
Ní Dhonnchadha, M., 540, 542
Niebaum, P., 662
Niederehe, H.-J., 869
Niederoest, M., 81
Niefanger, D., 637
Niehoff, R., 715
Niekerk, C., 660, 694
Niekus Moore, C., 638, 865
Nielsen, Carsten René, 765
Nielsen, E. A., 762
Nielsen, H. F., 762
Nielsen, M. F., 757
Nielsen, M. L., 762
Niemkiewicz, E., 789
Niemöller, K. W., 642
Nières-Chevrel, I., 190, 195, 20
Nies, F., 103
Niesner, M., 576, 866
Niethammer, O., 675, 676
Nieto Jiménez, L., 255
Nietzsche, Carl Ludwig, 692
Nietzsche, Friedrich August Ludwig, 692
Nietzsche, Friedrich, 192, 193, 210, 287, 461, 472, 551, 658, 668, 669, 679, 689–93, 695, 701, 706, 708, 712, 714, 721, 722, 723, 725, 765, 775, 830
Nieuwenuisjen, D., 253
Nievo, Ippolito, 422, 426, 444–45
Nikitin, G., 850
Nikitin, V. A., 807
Nikolaenko, A., 813
Nikolaev, P. A., 824, 834
Nikolaeva, N., 538
Nikolaus von Flüe, 610
Nikolina, N. A., 837
Nikoliukin, A. N., 835
Nikol'skaia, T., 831
Nikulin, Lev Veniaminovich, 836
Nikulitcheva, D., 759
Ní Loingsigh, A., 868
Nilsen, H. N., 778
Nilsenová, M., 782

Ní Mhaonaigh, M., 539
Nimis, J., 467
Nissen, U. K., 13
Nissim, L., 198
Nitti, Alfonso, 491
Nitti, J. J., 254, 865
Niven, B., 733
Nix, M., 599
Niziołek, A., 791
Niziurski, Edmund, 800
Noakes, S., 366
Nobili, F., 464
Noble, C. A. M., 731
Noble, P., 74, 212
Noble, P. S., 43, 64
Nocchi, N., 361
Nodier, Charles, 169
Noe, A., 646
Noe, M., 347
Noël, A., 30
Noetinger, E., 180
Noferi, A., 397, 494
Nogueira, M. A. L., 348
Nogueira, M. X., 315
Nogués, Juan, 268
Noia, C., 313, 316
Noica, Constantin, 515
Nolasco, E. C., 348
Nolke, H., 42
Noll, João Gilberto, 348
Nölle, V., 684
Nolte, T., 603
Nonnenturnier, 602
Nonot, J.-J., 67
Norat, G., 340
Nordau, Max, 195, 199
Nordbrandt, Henrik, 764
Nørgaard, M., 760
Norheim, T., 780
Nori, Paolo, 463, 464
Norman, B., 143, 868
Normand, C., 20
Northey, A., 716
Norton, R. E., 712
Norwid, Cyprian, 800
Nosov, Evgenii, 851
Nossini, Giovanni Maria, 622
Nostradamus, Jean de, 392
Nota, Alberto, 445
Notker Teutonicus (Notker der Deutsche, Notker Labeo), 584–85
Nottelmann, N., 707, 741
Novak, Helga, 735
Nováková, A., 787
Nováková, M., 781
Novalis (Friedrich von Hardenberg), 293, 647, 649, 650, 662–63, 708
Novara, Mario, 481
Novas de l'heretge, 237
Novelli, M., 491
Novello, N., 482
Novikov, V. I., 837, 848, 856
Novo, Olga, 316
Nowak, E., 794
Nowakowska-Kempna, I., 801
Nowicki, J., 510
Nowosad-Bakalarczyk, M., 795
Nowowiejski, B., 803
Nubert, R., 735
Nübler, N., 804
Nuix y Perpiñá, Juan, 276
Núñez de Guzmán, Hernán (*el Pinciano*), 266
Núñez-Méndez, E., 255
Nunn, F., 321
Nürnberger, H., 677, 680
Nussbaumer-Benz, U., 690
Nusser, P., 622
Nutting, S., 209
Nutt-Kofoth, R., 675
Nuzzo, E., 420
Nyada, G., 726
Nyffenegger, E., 572
Nyrnes, A., 774

Oakes, L., 33
Oakley, H., 338
Oancă, T., 506
Obatnina, E. R., 836
Obediente, E., 262
Oberender, T., 751
Obermaier, S., 620
Objartel, G., 556
Obolensky, D., 509
Obolensky, Leonid, 842
Ó Briain, M., 540
O'Brien, J., 103
O'Brien, W., 663
Obrovská, J., 782
Ocampo, Silvina, 338, 340
Ocampo, Victoria, 332
Ó Cathasaigh, T., 539
Ó Ceallacháin, E., 487
Ochman, A., 807
Ochmann, D., 790
Ockenden, R., 709
Ó Corráin, D., 539, 542
Ó Cróinín, D., 538
Ó Cuilleanáin, C., 486
Ó Cuív, B., 541
Oddo, N., 145
Odessky, M. P., 830
Odier-Fraisse, D., 180
Odinokov, V. G., 807
Odo of Cheriton, 235
Odobescu, Alexandru, 507, 514
Ó Dochartaigh, C., 538
O'Dochartaigh, P., 680
Odoevsky, Alexander Ivanovich, 808, 814
O'Donnell, Red Hugh, 540
Odoric de Pordenone, 74, 388
Oehler, V. F., 641
Oehm, H., 681
Oehming, S., 630
Oellers, N., 709, 720
Oenning Thompson, D., 823
Oesterle, G., 647, 651, 654, 675
Oesterle, I., 647
Offenbach, Jacques, 719
Ó Fiannachta, P., 541
Ogarev, Nikolai Platonovich, 829
Ogden, D. H., 61
Ogier von Dänemark, 591
Ogloblina, N. M., 846
O'Gorman, F., 205
Ogris, T., 572
O'Halloran, E., 565
Ó hAodha, D., 539
Ó Héalaí, P., 540
Öhlschläger, C., 715
Ó hUiginn, R., 538
Oişteanu, A., 508
Okeansky, V. P., 811
Okey, Thomas, 426
Okudzhava, Bulat, 839, 844, 851
Ó Laoghaire, D., 541
Olariu, F.-T., 865
Olberg, G. von, 616
Oldani, G., 456
Oldcorn, A., 445
Olds, M. C., 198
Olesha, Iurii, 832, 851
Olesiak, K., 797
Olgemann, S., 620
Olier, Jean-Jacques, 159
Oliva, G., 423, 428, 431
Oliva, K. (Jr.), 783
Oliveira, C. de, 346
Oliveira, V. L. de, 346
Olivella, P., 235
Oliver, Federico, 294
Olivi, A., 423
Olivi, F., 372
Olivi, Pietro di Giovanni, 364
Olivier de la Marche, 74
Olivieri-Godet, R., 344
Olivová-Nezbedová, L., 787
Ollier, M.-L., 43
Ollivier, Emile, 214
Ollivier, S., 823
O'Loughlin, T., 541
Olsen, G. H., 760
Olsen, J., 761
Olsen, M., 79
Ol'shansky, D., 847

Olson, O. K., 632
Oltrogge, D., 595
Ó Madagáin, B., 540
Omar Khan, R., 44
Omăt, G., 516
Ommundsen, A. M., 779
Ó Mórdha, E., 540
Ó Muraíle, N., 540
Ó Murchadha, D., 540
O'Neill, J., 111
Onetti, Juan Carlos, 338, 341
Ongaro, Vinicio, 480
Ong-Van-Cung, K. S., 161
Ono, U., 182
Onofri, Arturo, 480
Onofri, M., 476
Onorati, F., 427
Onu, L., 509
Oono, K., 187
Opava, Z., 544, 545
Opel, A., 744
Ophuls, Max, 728
Opitz, Martin, 639, 640
Oprea, I., 496, 497
Oprişan, I., 511
Opstad, G., 777
Opul'skaya-Gromova, L. D., 826
Orden, K. van, 115
Ördögh, E., 437
Orduña López, J., 257
O'Reilly, C. C., 4
Orelli, Giorgio, 480
Ören, Aras, 735
Orengo, Nico, 480
Ó Riain, P., 540, 541, 542
Orii, H., 111
Orioles, V., 352
Ørjasæter, K., 775, 779
Orjuela, H. H., 341
Orlitsky, I. B., 837
Orłoś, T. Z., 804
Orlova, E., 821
Orlova, R., 835, 840
Orłowski, H., 863
Orłowski, T., 795
Ormsby, E., 94
Ornea, Zigu, 516
Orozco, Alonso de, 265
Orozco, Olga, 339
Orringer, N. R., 279, 286
Orsetti, S. d', 230
Orsini, D., 130
Orsini, Luigi, 471
Orson de Beauvais, 39–40
Ørstavik, Hanne, 780
Ørsted, H. C., 766
Ort, C.-M., 672
Ort, N., 718
Ortega, J., 336
Ortega, Soledad, 286
Ortega y Gasset, José, 280, 281, 286, 289, 290, 294, 316
Ortese, Anna Maria, 465, 466, 480–81
Ortiz López, Luis. A., 263
Orzeszkowa, Eliza, 820
Osankina, V. A., 810
Osborne, R., 272
Oschlies, W., 571
Osherov, S., 833
Oshita, Y., 176
Osiecka, Agnieszka, 802
Osinski, J., 671
Osipova, A. V., 808
Oskotsky, V., 848, 852
Osokin, Denis, 841
Osolsobě, K., 783
Osorgin, Mikhail Andreevich, 835, 836
Osorio, José Antonio, 341
Osovsky, O. E., 838
Ossani, A. T., 861
Ossian (James MacPherson), 411, 422, 661
Ossola, C., 365, 383, 404, 422
Ossowski, Leonie, 753
Ostaszewska, D., 799
Ostermann, T., 547
Østerud, E., 775, 776, 777
Østgaard, Nicolai Ramm, 778
Ostheimer, M., 749
Ostler, N., 225
Ostrovská, S., 409
Ostrovsky, Alexander Nikolaevich, 829
Ostrovsky, Nikolai, 840, 851
Oswald von Wolkenstein, 606–07
Oświeja, A., 798
Otaka, Y., 25
Otero Pedraio, Ramón, 304–05, 316
Otfrid von Weissenburg, 584, 588
Otsuka, S., 751
Ott, C.-M., 718
Ott, N. H., 579, 608
Ott, U., 708
Otte, W.-D., 641
Ottieri, A., 490
Ottmann, D., 648
Otto von Botenlauben, 604
Otto, S., 420
Otto-Peters, Louise, 693
Ottokar von Steiermark, 616
Ottolini, A., 446
Otwinowska-Kasztelanic, A., 797
Ouanès, S., 224
Oudart, J., 409
Oudry, Jean-Baptiste, 133
Ouellet, P. J., 211
Ouy, G., 80, 82, 83, 89
Ovanesian, E., 852
Ovid (Publius Ovidius Naso), 42, 61, 69, 73, 84, 91, 92, 115, 155, 156, 235, 273, 371, 393, 589, 627, 634, 750
Ovide moralisé, 69, 90, 73
Ovsianiko-Kulikovsky, Dmitrii Nikolaevich, 832
Owain Glyndŵr, 530, 534
Owen, Daniel, 534
Owen, Siôn, 533
Ozanam, F., 370
Özdemir, E., 777
Oznobishin, D. P., 810
Ożóg, K., 797

Paasche, Hans, 726
Paatz, A., 338
Pacca, V., 399
Pache, R., 172
Pacheco, José Emilio, 334
Pachura, E., 753
Pacini, B., 360, 361
Pacioni, M., 486
Paco, M. de, 285
Paden, W. D., 232
Padoan, G., 366, 393
Padovani, G., 423
Padula, Vincenzo, 363, 445
Paepe, C. de, 285
Pagano, Francesco Maria, 413
Pagano, T., 472
Page, C., 68
Page, E., 777
Pagetto, R., 466
Pagliaro, A., 432
Pagnotta, L., 389
Paillard, D., 26
Pailler, J.-M., 221
Paine, Tom, 533
Pairet, A., 69
Paisiello, Giovanni, 416, 424
Palabazzer, V., 520
Palacio, J. de, 190
Palacios, Pedro Bonifacio, 320
Palafox y Mendoza, Don Juan de, 271
Palandri, E., 462, 463, 868
Palatine (*princesse*) *v.* Charlotte Elisabeth
Palazzeschi, Aldo, 480, 481
Palazzolo, M. I., 410
Palcy, Euzhan, 220
Palen Pierce, G., 443
Paleologu, Alexandru, 516
Palermo, A., 447

Palissy, Bernard, 99, 122
Palková, Z., 782
Palladio, Andrea, 109
Pallarés, P., 315
Pallavicini, P., 464
Palli Baroni, G., 423
Pallier, D., 100
Pallister, J. L., 212
Pallotta, A., 443
Palma, L., 447
Palmaro, M., 429
Palmer, N. F., 576, 612
Palmer, R. B., 88
Palmieri, G., 430
Palmieri, P., 439
Paludan-Müller, Frederick, 769
Palumbo, M., 434, 440
Pampaloni, Geno, 444, 452, 470, 480
Pan, D., 659
Pană Dindelegan, G., 499, 501
Panagl, O., 558, 682, 697
Panajia, A., 408
Panchieri, A., 480
Panello, G., 454
Panero, Leopoldo, 288
Panevová, J., 781
Paniagua, J. A., 299
Panicali, A., 431
Pankin, B., 839
Pankow, E., 651, 656
Pann, L., 855
Panofsky, Erwin, 621
Panozzo, U., 428
Pantazakos, M., 39
Pantin, I., 111, 119, 120, 634, 861
Pao, M. T., 281, 282
Paolini, G., 444, 447
Paolini, P., 485
Paolini Massimi, Petronilla, 417
Paolino di Venezia, 300
Paolone, M., 478
Paolucci, M., 431
Papadat-Bengescu, Hortensia, 516
Papahagi, M., 507
Papasogli, B., 130, 167
Pape, K., 687
Pape, L. W., 770
Papernyi, Z., 822
Papetti, V., 478
Papias, 14
Papini, Giovanni, 451, 455, 464, 472, 480, 481
Papkova, E. A., 839
Papp, E., 556
Pappalardo La Rosa, F., 477
Pappenheim, Marie, 706, 726
Papu, E., 512
Papuc, L., 511
Paque, J., 199
Paracelsus (Theophrastus Bombastus von Hohenheim), 622, 627
Paradin, Guillaume, 97
Paraschkewow, B., 566
Paravicini Bagliani, A., 868
Parayre, C., 238
Pardo, M. C. V., 350
Pardo, X., 317
Paré, F., 208
Paredes, A. V. de, 267
Parent, B., 140
Parent-Charon, A., 110
Pargner, B., 670, 671
Parinet, E., 131
Parini, Giuseppe, 400, 404, 407, 417, 422
Paris, Gaston, 7
Parise, Goffredo, 481
Parisi, L., 443, 444
Parker, S., 702, 736
Parker, T. R., 165
Parkes, S., 733
Parkin, J., 114
Parkinson, A., 733
Parmentier, B., 149
Parnok, Sophia, 833
Parodi, C., 249
Parr, R., 677
Parra, Teresa de la, 327, 338
Parra Membrives, E., 595
Parris, D., 208
Parronchi, Alessandro, 471, 481
Parry, C., 745
Parry, G., 526
Parry Owen, A., 527
Partonopeus de Blois, 35, 40
Partsch, E. W., 688
Parussa, G., 82
Paryl, W., 797
Pascal, Blaise, 127, 129, 130, 146, 157, 158, 159, 163, 164–67, 436, 437, 473, 662, 870
Pascal, Françoise, 135, 167
Pascal, J.-N., 138
Pascal, Jacqueline, 167
Pascarella, Cesare, 426
Pasci de' Bardi, Lippo, 387
Pasco, A. H., 174, 197
Pascoli, Giovanni, 422, 445–46, 469, 493, 864
Pasewalck, S., 726
Paskal, K., 844
Pasolini, Pier Paolo, 445, 451, 457, 462, 466, 476, 481–82, 494
Pasqual, L., 286
Pasquier, Etienne, 112, 119–20, 153
Pasquier, Nicolas, 120, 153
Pasquini, E., 365, 422
Pasquini, L., 428
Pasquini, P., 229
Passalacqua, M., 236
Passavanti, Jacopo, 391, 394
Passion plays, 613–15, 625–26
Pasta, J. A. (Jr.), 349
Pasta, R., 406
Pasternak, A., 851
Pasternak, Boris, 819, 826, 836, 851
Pasternak, Evgenii, 851
Pastior, Oskar, 658
Pastyřík, S., 787
Patella, G., 462
Paterno, Lodovico, 398
Paterson, L., 233
Patka, M. G., 703
Pato, Chus, 316
Patocka, F., 567, 568
Patota, G., 351
Patrizi, Francesco, 634
Patrizi, G., 479, 860
Patti, Ercole, 465
Pattison, G., 823, 825
Patty, J., 205
Patzer, G., 674, 676
Paul (*Saint*), 368
Paul, H., 566
Paul, R., 213
Paulikat, F., 30
Paulillo, M. C. R. de A., 346
Pauls, A., 339
Paulson, M. G., 96
Paulus Diaconus, 583
Paupert, A., 81, 82
Pausch, O., 544, 545
Pausewang, Gudrun, 733
Paustovsky, Konstantin Georgievich, 851
Pavel, E., 498
Pavel, L., 515
Pavel, V., 506
Pavese, Cesare, 368, 482, 710
Pavlov, Oleg, 851
Pavlov, V., 558
Pavlova, Karolina Karlovna, 851
Pavlova, M., 829, 849
Pavone, M. A., 406
Pawelec, R., 793
Paz, C., 316
Paz, Octavio, 323, 330, 334, 335
Paz-Soldán, E., 327, 340
Paziak, P., 798
Pazó, N., 314
Pazos Alonso, C., 348, 349
Pazzaglia, M., 446

Pazzi, Roberto, 371, 463
Pazzini Carli, Vincenzo, 406
Peach, T., 100, 120, 867
Peacock, N., 112
Pearsall, D., 80
Pecchio, Giuseppe, 427
Pécheux, Laurent, 402
Pecock, Reginald, 85
Pecora, E., 468, 483
Pedersen, C. S., 772
Pedersen, G. R., 779
Pedersen, I. L., 755, 756, 757, 758
Pedersen, K. M., 761
Pedrera González, A., 263
Pedriali, G., 474
Pedullà, G., 473
Peer, W. van, 677
Peeters, B., 20, 29
Pegatzky, S., 722
Pego Puigbó, A., 291
Péguy, Charles, 205, 210
Peil, D., 621
Peirats, A. I., 298
Peirce, C. S., 584
Peire d'Alvernha, 236, 237
Peire Cardenal, 232, 234, 235
Peire de Corbiac, 237
Pelcowa, H., 797
Pele, A., 503
Peletier du Mans, Jacques, 120–21, 123
Pelevin, Victor, 834, 851–52
Pelland, J., 212
Pellecchia, R., 465
Pellegrin, M.-F., 163
Pellegrini, G. B., 519, 520, 521, 868
Pellegrino, E., 467, 479
Pellegrino, P., 422
Pellerin, G., 208
Pelletier, Pol, 209
Pelletier-Baillargeon, H., 210
Pellicer y Saforcada, Juan Antonio, 276
Pellini, P., 448, 480
Peltzer, F., 288
Pelucani, C., 391
Pena, X. R., 313
Peña Diaz, M., 267
Pena-Ruiz, H., 173
Penna, Sandro, 456, 460, 482–83
Pennati, Camillo, 483
Pennone, F., 743
Penny, R. J., 248, 251, 252
Pensado Tomé, X. L., 304
Pensom, R., 143, 192
Penzkofer, G., 154
Pepe, P., 447
Pepoli, Carlo (*conte*), 437, 440
Pepperle, I., 673, 686
Peraita, C., 265, 274
Perarnau, J., 300
Perceforest, 78
Peredreev, Anatoli, 852
Pereira, M., 298
Pereiro-Otero, J. M., 294
Perella, N. J., 439
Perel'muter, V., 842
Perels, C., 549
Perevozchikov, V., 856
Perevozov, D., 851
Perez, J., 283
Pérez de Ayala, Ramón, 290
Pérez Bayer, Francisco, 275
Pérez Cascales, Francisco, 270
Pérez de Chinchón, B., 268
Pérez Cuenca, I., 274
Perez de Hita, Ginés, 125
Pérez Ibáñez, I., 273
Pérez Magallón, J., 277
Pérez Sánchez, Manuel Antonio (Manuel Antonio), 315
Peri Rossi, Cristina, 338
Périer, Gilberte, 167
Perilli, P., 482
Perinet, Joachim, 670, 740
Perini, L., 425
Perini, R., 162
Perkhin, V. V., 835, 841, 846
Perkinson, S., 98
Perl, M., 262
Perlesvaus, 45–46
Perli, A., 479
Perne, Gabriel, 91
Perodi, Emma, 448
Perón, Eva, 340
Perotti, P. A., 443
Pérouse, G.-A., 105, 123
Péroz, P., 29
Perrault, Charles, 128, 129, 132, 147, 153, 159
Perregaard, B., 761
Perret, M., 21
Perret, P., 33
Perrin, Pierre (*abbé*), 132, 148
Perrone-Moisés, L., 193
Perrot, J.-P., 67
Perrot, M., 205
Perrus, C., 491
Perry, C., 868
Persels, J., 118
Persiani, P., 403
Pertsov, P. P., 839
Perugi, M., 236
Perullo, N., 419
Peruzzi, Bindo Simone, 417–18
Peruzzo, F., 388
Pes di Villamarina, Paola, 428
Peschel, D., 600
Pesenti, T., 391
Pesenti Campagnoni, D., 191
Peshkov, V. P., 815
Pesmen, D., 806
Pestarino, R., 440
Pétain, Philippe (*maréchal*), 167
Peţan, A., 15, 496
Pete, L., 428
Petelin, V., 853
Peter the Great (*Tsar of Russia*), 807
Peter Alfonsi (Moses Sephardi), 61
Peters, G., 67
Peters, H. G., 697
Peters, J., 568
Peters, M., 556
Peters, R., 555, 863
Petersen, Clemens, 775
Petersen, J. H., 735
Petersen, Julius, 279
Petey-Girard, B., 119, 122
Petishev, A. A., 849
Petishev, V. A., 849
Petit, A., 48
Petit, L., 346
Petitier, P., 174
Petito, Antonio, 425
Petkevič, V., 783
Petrarch (Francesco Petrarca), 84, 85, 101, 100, 104, 109, 115, 118, 119, 236, 301, 368, 371, 372, 375, 385, 386, 394, 395, 396–99, 426, 439, 445, 492, 619, 628–29, 870
Petreanu, L., 510
Petrella, A., 471
Petrescu, A., 516
Petrescu, Radu, 516
Petrescu, V., 512
Petrikovskaya, A. S., 811
Petris, L., 121, 868
Petrobelli, P., 424
Petrocchi, G., 443
Petrocchi, S., 481
Petrochenkov, V. V., 821
Petrolini, G., 355
Petroni, F., 492
Petronio, Giuseppe, 462
Petronio, U., 417
Petronius (Caius Petronius Arbiter), 201, 393
Petrov, T., 832
Petrova, G. V., 827
Petrova, M. G., 820
Petrovska, Nina, 848
Petrus von Ainstetten, 612
Petrushevskaia, Liudmila Stefanovna, 852

Petsukh, Viacheslav Alekseevich,
Petzinna, B., 708
Pevtsova, R. T., 815, 848
Peyrache-Leborgne, D., 169, 171, 172, 664
Peyremaure, J., 229
Pezzin, C., 456
Pezzini, I., 429
Pfänder, S., 263
Pfeffer, W., 231
Pfefferkorn, Johannes, 622
Pfeiffer, H., 865
Pfeiffer, O. E., 868
Pfister, M., 15, 23
Pfizer, J., 705
Pharies, D., 251
Phelan, A., 709
Phelps, Anthony, 207
Philieul, Vasquin, 104
Philip III 'the Bold' (*King of France*), 77, 90
Philip II (*King of Spain*), 271
Philip IV (*King of Spain*) 270, 272
Philip, duke of Flanders, 50
Philipowski, K.-S., 599
Philipp, M., 569
Philippe le Bon (*Duke of Burgundy*), 72
Philippe de Beaumanoir, 53, 77, 864
Philippe de Croÿ (*comte de Chimay*),76
Philippe de Namur, 55
Philippe de Novare, 383
Philippe de Rémi, 53–54, 59, 67, 70, 77, 864
Philippe, J., 205
Philippide, A., 496
Philippide, Alexandru A., 516
Philipsen, H., 749
Phillips, D., 526
Philomena, 52
Philpotts, M., 702, 736
Philps, D., 30
Physiologus, 613
Piacentini, A., 471
Piatti, Guglielmo, 406
Piazza, Antonio, 404, 418
Piccat, M., 231
Picchi, L., 472
Piccini, D., 456, 469, 477, 485, 493
Piccione, M.-L., 215
Piccolomini, Francesco, 634
Picconi, G. L., 493
Picenoni, M., 522, 523
Picherit, J. L., 70
Pichois, C., 191
Pickens, R. T., 50, 56, 94, 232
Picoche, J., 27
Picón Febres, Gonzalo, 320
Picone, M., 379, 386, 448, 859
Piedra, A., 287
Piela, A., 790
Pieper, H.-J., 693, 725
Pier della Vigna, 385
Pierdominici, L., 93
Pieri, P., 481
Pierobon, E., 426, 430
Pieroni, S., 6
Pierrard, M., 26
Pierre de Béarn, 88
Pierre, C., 290
Pierreville, C., 52
Pierro, Albino, 460
Pietrini, S., 381
Pietrzak, E., 639
Pietrzak, M., 802
Pietrzykowska, A., 793
Pietzsch, E., 582
Piglia, Ricardo, 339
Piiliilainen, M.-L., 550
Piirainen, E., 546
Piirainen, I. T., 555, 580
Pikulik, L., 656
Pilch, H., 525
Pilch, Jerzy, 800
Pilcher, Caroline, 652
Piles, Roger de, 127, 129
Piller, J., 797
Pil'niak, B., 843, 852
Pil'shchikov, I. A., 811, 817
Pimenova, N. B., 554, 558
Pimonov, V., 843
Pinard, Ernest, 190
Pincet, Y., 200
Pinchard, B., 114
Pincikowski, S. E., 592
Pindar, 103, 104
Pindemonte, Ippolito, 422, 439, 446
Piñeros, C.-E., 255
Pinfold, D., 688
Pinkert, A., 744
Pinna, G., 423
Pinochet, Augusto (*General*), 340
Piñon, Nélida, 350
Pintal, Lorraine, 211
Pintariè, M., 69, 97, 108
Pintaudi, R., 409
Pinto-Mathieu, E., 57
Pintor, Giaime, 450–51
Pinvidic, M.-J., 65
Piotrowski, T., 793
Piotti, A., 464
Piotti, Pier Luigi, 483
Piovene, Guido, 470, 483
Piqué, J., 299
Pirandello, Luigi, 279, 421, 423, 450, 453, 460, 461, 465, 466, 468, 483–84, 488, 489, 655
Pirckheimer, Caritas, 578
Pirckheimer, Willibald, 635
Pires, M., 28
Pirozhkova, A., 847
Pisano, L., 421, 425
Pisarek, W., 804
Pisarev, Dmitrii Ivanovich, 826
Pisarkowa, K., 804
Piscator, E., 294
Piscator, Erwin, 700
Pishchulin, N. P., 815
Piske, T., 352
Pister, D., 868
Pitrè, Giuseppe, 446
Pittrof, T., 675, 708, 859
Piţu, L., 512
Pitz, M., 23, 30
Pius VI (*Pope*), 401, 402
Pizarnik, Alejandra, 339
Pizarro, A., 340
Pizer, J., 685
Pizzamiglio, G., 410
Pizzetti, I., 483
Pizzorusso, A., 356
Placella, V., 417, 435
Placencia, M. E., 261, 262
Plachta, B., 679, 681, 868
Placke, H., 726
Placoly, Vincent, 216
Plaisirs de l'île enchantée, 129
Planeta, P., 800
Plangg, G. A., 520
Planta, Robert von, 572
Plata, F., 274
Plate, R., 555
Platen, August, Graf von, 648, 671
Plathow, M., 635
Plato, 118, 157, 280, 292, 469, 648, 658
Platonov, Andrei, 832, 833, 852
Platter, Thomas, 635–36
Plazenet, L., 103, 152
Pleau, J.-C., 210
Pleitner, B., 668
Plenzdorf, Ulrich, 749
Pleskalová, J., 781
Plett, B., 680, 700
Pliny the Elder (Caius Plinius Secundus), 398
Ploner, E., 520
Ploog, K., 32
Plöschberger, D., 751
Plotinus, 157
Plüddemann, Hermann F., 669
Pluta, E., 671
Pluta, F., 799

Plutarch, 98, 103
Poag, J. F., 868
Pocci, Franz von, 670
Pöder, E., 730
Podewski, M., 685
Podgaetskaya, I., 808
Podhajecka, M., 804
Poe, E. W., 232, 236
Poe, Edgar Allen, 169, 189, 192, 510, 657, 664, 730
Poehlmann, H., 440
Poellnitz, Rudolf von, 711
Poemer, Johann Abraham, 643
Poggi Salani, T., 360
Poggiali, Gaetano, 404
Poggio, Giulio, 398
Pohl, E. E., 766, 770
Pohl, H. D., 521
Poirier, C., 32
Poirier, P., 212
Poisson, J.-P., 97
Poisson, Jean, 138
Pokrovskaya, L. A., 838
Poláček, Karel, 786
Polański, E., 789, 797
Polato, L., 487
Pölder, E., 866
Pole, William de la (*Duke of Suffolk*), 79–80
Polekhina, M. M., 849
Polenz, P. von, 550, 559
Poletto, C., 519
Polevoi, Nikolai Alekseevich, 808, 814
Poli, S., 125
Poliakova, E. A., 825
Polianskaya, Irina, 844
Polišenský, J., 409
Politycki, Matthias, 750
Politzer, Heinz, 726
Poliziano, Angelo (Politian), 102
Polizzi, G., 435
Poljakov, R., 629
Pöll, B., 867
Pollard, G., 131
Polledri, E., 658
Pollock, J.-Y., 11, 865
Polo, Estanislao, 267
Polo Friz, L., 429
Polonsky, V. V., 821
Polukarova, L., 813
Polukhina, V. P., 846
Pomel, F., 75
Pomerants, G., 843
Pomerantsev, I., 834
Pomerantz, A., 261
Pompa, L., 420
Ponge, Francis, 118, 480
Poniatowska, Elena, 338
Poniatowski, Stanislaus Augustus, 402
Ponis, R., 452
Ponomarev, E., 835
Ponomareva, G. B., 824
Pons Fuster, F., 268
Ponte, G., 454
Pontesilli, Giselda, 459
Pontiggia, Giuseppe, 461, 480
Pontón, G., 269
Pontoppidan, Henrik, 765
Pontormo, Jacopo, 477
Poole, G., 424
Pooley, T., 19, 30, 31
Pop, Vasile G., 512
Popa, N. I., 514, 516
Popescu, M., 503
Popescu, T., 513, 517
Popescu-Cadem, C., 512
Popescu Marin, M., 502
Popescu-Telega, Alexandru, 507
Poplavsky, Boris, 835
Popov, Evgenii Anatolievich, 844
Popova, E. A., 828
Popovsky, M., 840
Poppe, E., 526, 528
Popper, H., 598
Porayski-Pomsta, J., 795
Porcelli, B., 448
Porociuc, A., 497
Poroikov, S. I., 814
Porrmann, M., 670, 681
Porro Andriuoli, L., 474
Porta, Antonio, 485
Porta, Carlo, 446
Porter, L. M., 179, 189, 192
Porter, R., 854
Porudominsky, V., 839
Pospiszylowa, A., 799
Posse, Abel, 340
Possumato, T., 430
Post, M., 262
Posthofen, R. S., 737
Postl *v.* Sealsfield
Postles, D., 762
Postoutenko, K., 835
Posturzynnska, M., 82
Pot, O., 109
Potapova, G. E., 813
Potebnia, Alexander Afanasievich, 838
Pothen, P., 690
Pott, H.-G., 658
Pott, S., 744
Pottelberge, J. van, 561
Pötters. W., 368
Potts, D. C., 154
Pouchain, G., 186
Pouey-Mounou, A.-P., 115
Poulin, Jacques, 208
Poullain de la Barre, François, 126, 167
Poulouin, G., 199
Pound, Ezra, 95, 708
Pounder, A., 560
Pousa Ortega, H., 306
Poust, A. J., 286
Pouvreau, R., 649–50
Povartsov, S., 822, 850
Powell, A., 272
Powell, D. A., 182, 194
Powell, M., 55
Pozner, V., 809
Pozo, Luz, 316
Pozza, Neri, 450
Pozzi, Antonia, 485
Pozzi, G. (*Padre*), 383
Pozzo, F., 447
Pozzo, R., 634
Praloran, M., 398
Prasch, Johann Ludwig, 553
Prat, E., 296
Prato, Dolores, 465
Pratolini, Vasco, 463, 464
Prats, D., 869
Pratt, K., 43, 68, 82
Pravdová, M., 785
Preda, A., 112
Preda, Marin, 516
Predigtmärlein, 605
Preece, J., 716, 733
Preisendanz, Wolfgang, 719
Preisig, F., 111
Preiss, N., 186
Prest, J., 142
Prete, A., 441
Preti, Francesco Maria, 402
Prévost, M., 173, 179
Preyzner, M., 791, 793, 802
Prezzolini, Giuseppe, 455, 464, 480, 485
Price, A., 525, 532, 535, 536
Price, B. R., 298
Price, Thomas (Carnhuanawc), 536
Prichard, Caradog, 535
Prieto, E. L., 217
Prieto, J., 339
Prieto, M., 247
Prigov, D., 807
Prigov, Dimitri Alexandrovich, 852
Prigozhin, I., 808
Prill, U., 715
Primo de Rivera, Miguel (*General*), 291
Primochkina, N. N., 848
Pring-Mill, R., 299
Pringy, Madame de, 161

Printz, Wolfgang Caspar, 640, 644
Prinz, M., 552
Priscian, 374
Prishvin, Mikhail Mikhailovich, 852
Prishvina, V., 852
Pristavkin, Anatolii, 853
Privat, Jaumes, 238
Probes, C. M., 153
Probus, 9, 11
Procaccioli, P., 372
Proclus, 162
Proietti, P., 466
Prokhanov, Alexander, 839, 852
Prokofiev, Sergei, 827
Prokushev, I. L., 818
Promies, U., 672, 683
Pronin, V., 810
Propp, V. Y., 831
Prosa-Lancelot, 599–600
Prosio, P. M., 427
Proskurin, O., 817
Pross, C., 729
Prossliner, J., 690
Protze, H., 574
Proulx, Monique, 214
Proust, G., 111
Proust, Marcel, 171, 179, 188, 195, 201, 204, 205, 280, 331–32, 464
Prouteau, M.-H., 180
Providenti, E., 484
Prozorov, V. V., 820
Prüfer, C., 787
Prungnaud, J., 172, 190, 206, 868
Prus, Bolesław, 801
Prutkov, Cosmo, 819
Pruvost, J., 26
Prys, D., 526
Przybylska, R., 790, 793, 795
Przybyszewski, Stanislaus, 726
Przychodzen, J., 209
Pseudo-Dionysius, 166
Pseudo-Turpin, 231
Pucci, Antonio, 389
Puccini, Giacomo, 351
Puccini, Mario, 464
Puccini, Niccolò, 446
Puchmajer, A., 786
Pückler-Muskau, Hermann von, 680, 693
Puggioni, R., 454
Pugh, A. R., 164
Puglisi, G., 466
Puhlfürst, S., 734
Puig, A., 300
Puig, J. de, 296, 299
Puig Tàrrech, A., 302
Pujol, J., 297, 301
Pujol Payet, I., 252
Pukelsheim, F., 299
Pulci, D., 441
Pulci, Luigi, 395
Pulgar, Fernando del, 269
Pulsoni, C., 234
Pumnul, Aron, 512
Pumplun, C. M., 639, 641
Punte, M. J., 339
Pupino, A. R., 455, 484
Pupo, I., 484
Purdela Sitaru, M., 502
Pure, Michel de, 137, 153
Puşcariu, S., 15, 496
Pusch, C. D., 226
Püschel, U., 556
Pushkin, Alexander Sergeevich, 806, 811, 814–18, 819, 822, 835
Pusterla, F., 452
Pütz, P., 702, 722, 723
Puzynina, J., 793
Pyman, A., 823
Pynchon, Thomas, 469
Pyrczak, R., 177
Pyrrho, 165

Quadrio, Francesco Saverio, 405
Quarenghi, P., 467
Quarta, D., 859
Quartermaine, L., 436
Quartieri, F., 369
Quasimodo, Salvatore, 434, 456, 459, 469, 483, 485–86
Quast, B., 577, 590, 593
Quayson, A., 460
Queffélec, A., 32
Quer, J., 12
Quereuil, M., 81
Quéruel, D., 74, 93
Quesnel, C., 150
Quesnel-Chalèlh, H., 225, 230
Queste del Saint Graal, 36, 47
Quevedo y Villegas, Francisco de, 268, 271, 273–74, 289
Quillet, J., 82
Quilliet, B., 98
Quinault, Philippe, 136, 137, 142–43
Quiñones, Juan de, 266
Quinze Joies de Mariage, 68
Quirini, Giovanni, 388, 389
Quiroga, Horacio, 340
Quist, P., 757, 760

Raabe, Wilhelm, 668, 687, 693–94
Rabanus, S., 548
Rabatti, I., 475
Rabau, S., 201
Rabbitt, K. M., 182
Rabboni, R., 406, 409, 474
Rabelais, François, 94, 96, 97, 98, 99, 100, 105, 113–15, 174
Rabenschlacht, 590
Raboni, Giovanni, 483, 486, 488
Racan, Honorat de Bueil, seigneur de, 136
Rachilde (Marguerite Eymery), 190, 201
Racine, I., 23
Racine, Jean, 125, 126, 129, 136, 137, 138, 140, 143–44, 146, 147
Racioppi, P. P., 401
Ract-Madoux, P., 100
Rad, I., 512
Radatz, H.-I., 13
Radecke, G., 678, 719, 868
Radishchev, Alexander Nikolaevich, 818, 832
Radtke, E., 7
Radványi, László, 729
Rafel, J., 12
Raffa, G. P., 368
Raffaele, G., 437
Raffalovich, André, 200
Raffel, E., 727
Ragg-Kirkby, H., 695
Ragni, S., 424
Ragotzky, H., 614
Ragozina, K., 851
Rahmsdorf, S., 629
Raihala, L., 660
Raimbaut d'Aurenga, 234, 235
Raimo, C., 464
Raimondi, E., 439, 442, 444, 452
Raimondi, G., 91
Raimondi, S., 489
Raimund, Ferdinand, 668, 670, 694
Rainer, F., 867
Rainsford, D., 190
Raiziss, S., 473
Rajch, M., 673
Rajna, P., 370, 373
Rajotte, P., 209
Rak, V. D., 814, 817
Ralea, M., 517
Rama, Ángel, 324, 325, 326, 330
Ramat, Silvio, 456, 474, 481, 486, 487, 868
Ramazzini, Bernardo, 418
Rambaud, H., 21
Rambelli, P., 404, 408, 418, 438
Ramel, J.-L., 244
Ramey, L. T., 38

Ramge, H., 574
Ramírez Ribes, M., 337
Ramm, B., 46
Rammstadt, A., 711
Ramondino, Fabrizia, 465
Ramos, Graciliano, 344
Ramos Ortega, M. J., 284
Ramsay, A., 82
Ramus, Pierre de la Ramée, *dit*, 21, 103, 634
Rancé, Armand-Jean Le Bouthillier de, 159, 167
Ranchetti, Michele, 486
Ranchin, A. M., 846
Rancière, J., 169
Rand, A., 826
Randall, C., 97
Randhartinger, Benedict, 688
Randino, S., 438
Rangognini, Enzo, 405
Ranieri, Antonio, 437
Rankl, M., 742
Ransmayr, Christoph, 735, 737, 749–50
Ranz Yubero, J. A., 309
Ranzato Santin, F., 433
Ranzini, P., 411, 414
Raoul de Cambrai, 49
Rapin, Nicolas, 119
Rapin, René, 145
Rapp, A., 864
Rapp Buri, A., 607
Rappenecker, M., 705
Rasch, W., 679, 683
Raschke, Martin, 726
Raser, T., 192, 201
Rash, F., 356, 546
Rashentsev, Iurii, 842
Rask, K., 755
Rask, Rasmus, 755
Raskol'nikov, F., 839
Rasmussen, A. M., 604, 608, 866
Rasmussen, D., 761
Rasmussen, J., 756
Rasmussen, O., 760
Rasmussen, R., 763
Rasputin, Valentin, 851, 852
Rassadin, A. P., 815
Rassadin, S., 832
Rastier, F., 20
Rathje, M., 761
Rathjen, F., 751
Rau, G., 548, 563
Rauch, Neo, 746
Raulino, B., 347
Rausell Guillot, H., 269
Rautenberg, U., 582
Ravagli, F., 471
Ravegnani, Giuseppe, 480
Ravier, X., 221, 222, 228
Ravn, T., 760
Ravnholt, O., 756, 757, 761
Ravnkilde, Adda, 767
Ravy, G., 750
Rawles, S., 107, 128
Rawlings, H., 265
Raya, G., 429
Raymond of Capua, 612
Raynard, S., 147
Raynaud de Lage, G., 52
Razgon, Lev E., 852–53
Raznovich, D., 339
Razumova, N. E., 822
Re, L., 469
Rebejkov, J.-C., 488
Rebel, G. M., 846
Rebora, Clemente, 441, 457, 486
Rębowski, W., 798
Rebreanu, Liviu, 513, 515, 516, 517
Recalcati, Claudio, 486
Rechzieglová, A., 787
Recknagel, Rolf, 730
Reda, V., 473
Redaelli, E., 401
Redfern, W., 204
Redondo, A., 274
Reed, T. J., 721
Reershemius, G., 568
Rees, D. B., 534, 535
Reeve, W. C., 674
Regazzoni, S., 339
Régent, A., 164
Regis, R., 361
Regler, Gustav, 726
Regn, G., 398, 424
Regnard, Jean-François, 129
Regnaud, Robert, 67
Regnicoli, A., 361
Régnier, Marie de, 432
Regnier, Mathurin, 242
Rego, José Lins do, 343, 344
Regoliosi, M., 476
Regosin, R., 109
Regueira Fernández, X. L., 308, 310
Reguig-Naya, D., 155
Reguş, C., 503
Rehage, G. P., 700
Rehbock, H., 562
Rehfisch, Hans José, 704
Rehme-Iffert, B., 665
Rehn, M.-E., 508
Reich-Ranicki, M., 709
Reichan, J., 797
Reichardt, L., 573, 574, 575
Reichart, Elisabeth, 733
Reichel, K.-H., 230
Reichensperger, R., 706
Reichert, H., 594, 608
Reichert, M., 53, 864
Reichmann, E., 704, 732
Reichmann, O., 551, 559, 562, 863
Reid, A., 200
Reid, M., 184, 185
Reiff, K., 759
Reiffenstein, I., 553
Reifman, I., 806
Reimers, K., 700
Rein, Evgenii, 844, 853
Rein, K., 567
Reina, L., 450
Reinbot von Durne, 611
Reinecke, W., 548
Reinfried von Braunschweig, 601
Reinhardt, H., 677, 684, 687
Reinhardt, Max, 484
Reinheimer Rîpeanu, S., 500
Reinhoff, N., 779
Reinhold, F., 574
Reininghaus, F., 671
Reinmar von Hagenau, 603
Reinmar von Zweter, 605
Reinthal, A., 711
Reisch, Gregor, 630
Reisinger, R., 81, 83
Reiss, T. J., 143
Reitani, L., 658
Reiter, A., 747
Reitzel, Robert, 673
Rejter, A., 800
Rekdal, A. M., 776
Rella, G., 486
Rem, T., 777
Remak, H. H. H., 680
Remarque, Erich Maria, 702, 726
Rembrandt van Rijn, 176
Remizov, Aleksei Mikhailovich, 821, 826, 832
Remizov, V. B., 826
Remizova, A., 836
Remizova, M., 841, 852, 854
Remneva, M. L., 815
Rempnoux, François, 241
Ren, W., 717
Renart, Jean, 70
Renaud, M., 120, 148
Renaudot, Théophraste, 131
Renaut de Beaujeu, 46, 47
Renaut de Montauban, 65
René d'Anjou, 70, 71
Renedo, X., 299, 301
Renedo Sinovas, M. M., 251
Renevey, D., 93
Renn, Ludwig, 751
Renner-Henke, U., 726
Reno, C., 81, 82, 83, 87
Renou, K., 173

Renouvier, Charles, 205
Rentocchini, Emilio, 459
Renzi, G., 427
Renzi, L., 3, 5, 12, 13, 868
Requeixo, A., 316
Resch, Y., 207, 213
Resende, B., 349
Resina, J. R., 260
Resplandin, André, 243
Resta, G., 483
Restaino, F., 421
Rétat, C., 187
Rettelbach, J., 606
Retz, Jean-François Paul de Gondi, cardinal de, 146, 153
Reuchlin, Johannes, 623, 636
Reusch, J. J. K., 664
Reuss, R., 743
Reuter, Fritz, 694
Reuver, A. de, 638
Revaz, G., 136, 137
Reverdy, Pierre, 281
Reviakina, A. A., 809
Révigny, 77
Reviriego, B., 222
Revutsky, O. I., 809
Reward, S. P., 103
Rey, J.-C., 228
Rey, P.-L., 183, 184
Reynke de vos, 586, 620
Reynolds-Cornell, R., 119
Rezeanu, A., 503
Rezzori, Gregor von, 750
Rhisart ap Hywel ap Dafydd ab Einion, 530
Rhodes, Alexandre de, 154
Rhys Goch Eryri, 531
Rhys ap Gruffydd (*Sir*), 527
Rhys, M., 535
Ria, A., 487
Riabii, I. G., 821
Riabii, M. M., 821
Riabinina-Novikova, M., 829
Riabtsev, E. A., 816
Riaguzova, L. N., 850
Ribard, J., 37
Ribarov, K., 784
Ribas, P., 292
Ribbat, E., 675, 676
Ribeiro, Darcy, 349
Ribeiro, Dora, 344
Ribeiro, João Ubaldo, 349
Ribeiro, M., 346
Ribémont, B., 48, 73, 83, 87, 868
Ribero, Gaspar de, 270
Ricaldone, L., 413, 419, 433
Ricardo, Cassiano, 347
Ricas Zancarrón, M., 8
Ricci, A., 352, 355
Ricci, F., 476, 479
Ricci, L., 357
Ricciardi, A., 469
Ricciarelli, Tommaso, 446
Riccio, M., 420
Riccobaldo da Ferrara, 383
Riccoboni, Antoine-François, 138
Riccoboni, Luigi, 138
Riccobono, M. G., 447
Richard de Fournival, 58, 59, 82
Richard I (‘*Coeur de Lion*’), 63
Richard II (*King of England*), 71
Richard, E., 229
Richards, A., 708
Richards, E. J., 81, 82, 83, 84, 87, 89
Richards, M. N., 206
Richarz, M., 82
Richelieu, Armand Jean du Plessis, cardinal de, 126, 132, 148, 157
Richlick, E., 667
Richter, Gerhard, 751
Richter, H., 863
Richter, Jean Paul Friedrich (Jean Paul), 169, 172, 650, 652, 663–64, 731, 742
Richter, M., 193, 481
Rickard, P., 21, 869
Ricketts, P. T., 232
Rico, F., 268, 397
Ricoeur, Paul, 239, 289, 290, 724
Ricuperati, G., 402, 405, 406, 413
Ridder, K., 592, 595
Ridel, E., 762
Rideout, D. L., 25
Ridley, H., 681
Ridolfi, Cosimo, 426
Ridoux, C., 78, 199
Ridruejo, Dionisio, 288
Ridruejo, E., 251, 252
Rieck, G., 717
Rieck, W., 679
Riecke, J., 553
Riedesel, Johann Hermann von, 403
Riedmann, B., 728
Rieger, A., 43
Rieger, D., 396
Rieger, J., 802
Riemer, Johann(es), 644
Riemer, W., 706
Riendeau, P., 215
Rifbjerg, Klaus, 757, 767, 771, 772
Riffaterre, Michel, 198
Righini, Vincenzo, 412
Rigobello, G., 493
Rigolot, F., 96, 97, 103, 105, 114, 115, 118
Rigomer, 36
Rigoni, M. A., 437, 439
Rigoni Stern, Mario, 487
Rigosta, J., 225
Rigotti, F., 465
Riley, A. W., 711
Rilke, Rainer Maria, 700, 701, 706, 726–27, 743, 744
Rimbaud, Arthur, 191, 192, 195, 220, 471
Rinaldi, R., 474
Rinck, Melchior, 636
Ringel, S., 743
Ringeler, F., 604
Ringelnatz, Joachim, 642
Rings, A., 611
Ringuet (Philippe Panneton), 214
Rink, A., 712
Rinke, G., 711
Rinner, F., 750
Rinuccio d'Arezzo, 120
Río, Martín del, 270
Ríos, M. C., 316
Ríos Carratalá, J. A., 295
Rioux, Marcel, 212
Rioux, R., 187
Ripa, Cesare, 129
Ripellino, Angelo Maria, 487
Ripka, I., 804
Rippman, P., 731
Rippmann, I., 685, 689, 693
Risaliti, R., 412
Risco, Vicente, 315, 316
Risset, J., 444
Risso, E., 455
Rist, Johann, 644
Ritman, J. R., 639
Ritrovato, S., 487
Rittaud-Hutinet, C., 30
Ritter, A., 694
Ritter, E., 714
Ritter, Johann Wilhelm, 656
Ritter, M., 688
Rittey, J., 46
Ritz, M.-E., 25
Ritzer, M., 684, 695, 728
Riva, M., 422, 469
Rivas, J., 308
Rivas Rojas, M. R., 319
Rivers, K., 300
Rixte, J.-C., 243, 244
Rizzante, M., 483
Rizzi, G., 427
Rizzoni, G., 484
Roa Bastos, Augusto, 341
Roana, F., 487
Robelin, Jean, 106

Röber, T., 700
Robert (*Brother*), 598
Robert de Blois, 69, 77
Robert de Boron, 46
Robert le Bougre, 58
Robert de Clari, 64
Robert, F., 203
Robert, J., 627, 631
Robert, R., 147
Robertet, Jean, 73
Roberti, Giambattista, 418
Roberto, E., 214
Roberts, A., 87
Roberts, B. F., 529
Roberts, D., 734
Roberts, Kate, 536
Roberts, R. P., 32
Roberts, Y., 119
Robertshaw, A., 606
Robertson, A. W., 89
Robertson, E., 869
Robertson, R., 701, 710, 716, 721, 866
Robey, D., 864
Robin, Régine, 207, 214
Robinson, M., 833, 864
Robinson, R., 533
Roboly, D., 169
Robson, K., 861
Roca, A., 247
Rocard, M., 215
Rocca, P., 339
Rocca, R., 229
Roccati, G. M., 90
Roch (*Saint*), 280
Roche, I., 94
Roché, M., 16, 29, 859
Roche-Mahdi, S., 43
Rocher, D., 597
Röcke, W., 593
Roda, V., 447, 448
Rodenbach, Georges, 190, 200
Röder, B., 656
Rodnianskaya, I., 829
Rodó, José Enrique, 320, 339
Rodrigues, J. P. C. de S., 344
Rodrigues, Nelson, 347
Rodríguez, F., 257, 320
Rodríguez, I., 325
Rodríguez, L., 315, 316
Rodríguez, O., 316
Rodríguez Añón, M. M., 309
Rodríguez Banga, E., 310
Rodríguez Castelao, Alfonso Daniel, 315
Rodríguez González, E., 309
Rodriguez Monegal, E., 193
Rodríguez Montederramo, X. L., 307
Rodríguez Neira, M. A., 312
Rodríguez Risquete, F. J., 297
Rodríguez de Veiga, Tomás, 270
Rodway, S., 532
Roe, I. F., 670
Roeck, B., 674
Roelcke, T., 548, 564
Roelcke, V., 722
Roeleveld, A., 607
Roellenbleck, G., 378
Roes, Michael, 750
Roessler, K., 680
Roessler, P., 630
Roffmann, A., 721
Rogachevski, A., 814
Roger-Taillade, N., 187
Rogers, B. G., 205
Rogers, John, 635
Rogers, K. H., 518
Rogers, N. B., 185
Roggia, C. E., 404
Roglieri, M. A., 371
Rohde, B., 717
Rohlf, S., 703
Rohls, J., 622
Rohmer, Eric, 660
Rohou, J., 129
Rohr, W. G., 601, 617
Rohs, K., 562
Rohse, E., 686, 687
Rohwetter, C., 102
Roig, Jaume, 298
Roís de Corella, Joan, 301
Rojas, Fernando de, 269
Roksund, L. K., 776
Rola, A., 795, 801
Rolfi, S., 402
Roli, M. L., 695
Rolin, Antoine, 75
Roll, B., 617
Röll, W., 863
Rolla, C., 145
Rolland, J.-C., 27
Rolland, Romain, 450, 851
Rölleke, H., 653, 696
Rolleston, J. R., 716
Rolli, Domenico, 418
Rolli, Paolo, 416
Roloff, H.-G., 636, 641
Romagnoli. P., 81
Roman d'Aiquin, 40
Roman d'Eneas, 36
Roman de Fauvel, 57, 70, 71
Roman de Horn, 51, 63
Roman de Renart, 36, 57, 59–60, 70
Roman de Silence, 38, 43–45
Roman de Thèbes, 48–49, 87, 868
Roman de la Violette, 52
Romani, Felice, 424
Romanini, F., 382
Romano, C., 162
Romano, Lalla, 487
Romanov, Konstantin (*Prince*), 821
Romanov, Panteleimon, 853
Romanova, A. V., 828
Romanova, E. A., 833
Romanova, G. I., 845
Romanova, L., 816
Romboli, F., 434
Romeo, L., 435
Romero, M. V., 258
Romero Crego, R., 294
Romero Triñanes, M., 306
Romeu i Figueras, J., 296, 302
Romeyke, S., 608
Rommel, F., 614
Rónaky, E., 494
Roncuzzi Roversi Monaco, V., 436
Rondelet, Guillaume, 105
Rondini, A., 423, 462, 476
Ronen, O., 850, 855
Ronjat, J., 7, 223
Ronneberger-Sibold, E., 558
Ronsard, Pierre de, 97, 99, 103, 104, 105, 112, 115–16, 117, 118, 122
Ronzeaud, P., 131, 141
Rootseler, M. van, 532
Röper, U., 679
Roques, G., 72
Roqueta (Rouquette), Ives, 221, 238
Roqueta (Rouquette), Max, 238, 239
Rorato, L., 462, 463
Rosales, Luis, 288
Rosales Juega, E., 265
Rösch, H., 680
Rose, C. M., 869
Rosellini, M., 156
Rosello, M., 218
Rosén, H., 11
Rosen, K., 582–83
Rosenbaum, B., 763
Rosenbaum, Jenny, 705
Rosenberg, A., 157
Rosenberg, S. N., 59, 67
Rosengarten, F., 201
Rosenkilde Jacobsen, J., 760
Rosenmeyer, P., 104
Rosenplüt, Hans, 615
Rosenroth, Christian von, 682
Rosenstock, G., 486
Rosenthal, E., 71
Rosenzweig, Franz, 690
Rosetti, A., 496
Rosetti, Radu, 507
Roshchin, N. I., 843

Rosier, L., 19, 26
Roskothen, J., 702
Rösler, D., 549
Rösler, I., 555, 573
Rosmini, Antonio, 422
Rosner, A., 146
Rossbacher, B., 746
Rossbacher, K., 714
Rossebastiano, A., 544, 545
Rossell, A., 235
Rosselli, Amelia, 457, 487
Rosset, François, 146
Rossetti, C. A., 507
Rossetti, Christina, 371
Rossetti, Gabriele, 368
Rossetto, P., 156
Rossi, Ernesto, 450
Rossi, F., 351
Rossi, Giuseppe, 425
Rossi, L., 234, 386, 393, 434
Rossi, L. C., 382
Rossi-Gensane, N., 24
Rossich, A., 234, 297, 302, 303, 869
Rossini, Gioacchino, 184, 424
Rossinyol, A., 300
Rosso de San Secondo, Pier Maria, 465
Rosteau, Charles, 127
Rostovtseva, I., 809, 851
Roth, Gerhard, 706, 737
Roth, Joseph, 704, 727, 732, 866
Roth, K. S., 548
Rothe, Johannes, 580, 620
Rothenbühler, D., 687
Rother, Johannes, 587
Rothschild, T., 728
Rothwell, W., 26
Rotrou, Jean, 127, 136, 144
Rötscher, Heinrich Theodor, 670
Rottem, Ø., 768, 774, 775, 776
Rouanet, J.-C., 180
Rouault de La Vigne, René, 196
Roudaut, F., 101, 109
Rouffiat, F., 193
Rouget, C., 32
Rouget, F., 111, 115, 119, 869
Roulin, J.-M., 190
Rouquette *v.* Roqueta
Rouse, M., 71, 89
Rouse, R., 71, 89
Rousseau, Jean-Jacques, 126, 169, 182, 278, 648, 653, 658
Roussel, H., 702, 703
Routledge, M., 231
Roux, C., 230
Rovani, Giuseppe, 446–47
Roveda, L., 151
Rovere, G., 353
Rovira, S., 297
Rowinsky, M., 342
Rowlands, J., 536
Rowley, A., 571
Roy, B., 67
Roy, Gabrielle, 214
Roy, Maurice, 87
Roy, R., 127, 146
Roy-Reverzy, E., 171
Royano, L., 319
Royer, J., 213
Royo, A., 337
Rozanov, Vasilii Vasilievich, 839
Rozanova, M., 854
Rozhdestvenskaia, K., 853
Rozhdestvensky, Robert Ivanovich, 853
Różyło, A., 795
Rubashkin, A. I., 841, 843
Ruberg, U., 863
Rubin, D. L., 130, 869
Rubin, Ilya, 840
Rubin Suleiman, S., 204
Rubino, C., 224
Rubino, N., 198
Rubio, J. E., 299
Rubio Navajas, José, 295
Rubio Vela, A., 297
Rubleva, L. I., 807
Rubtsov, Nikolai, 831, 853
Rückert, Friedrich, 694
Rudes, B., 225
Rüdiger, J., 233
Rudincová, B., 787
Rudloff, H., 718
Rudnev, V., 806
Rudolf von Ems, 588, 600
Rudzievskaya, S. V., 855
Rüetschi, K. J., 633, 635
Ruffato, Cesare, 487
Ruffi, Robert, 241
Ruffilli, Paolo, 487
Ruge, J., 567
Rugolo, R., 402
Ruh, K., 576
Ruhe, D., 81
Rühl, J. S., 587
Rühle-Gerstel, Alice, 703
Ruhrberg, C., 581
Ruiz Gusils, J., 336
Ruiz Pérez, P., 267
Ruiz Simon, J. M., 296, 301
Ruja, A., 514
Rulfo, Juan, 338
Rung, Otto, 764
Runge, Phillip Otto, 664
Runnalls, G., 66
Runte, H. R., 208
Rupert of Deutz, 632
Rupp, M., 619
Ruprecht von Würzburg, 582
Rus, M., 75
Rusakov, Gennadii, 841
Rusakov, V. M., 818
Rüsel, M., 660
Rusetsky, V. F., 809
Rushing, R. A., 434
Rusínová, Z., 783
Ruskin, John, 205, 426
Russ, C. V. J., 543, 556, 569
Russell, D., 128
Russell, H. M. W., 825
Russo, G., 487
Russo, L., 417, 433, 443, 453, 480
Russo, M., 362
Ruşti, D., 507
Rusticien de Pisa, 74
Rusu, G., 506
Rusu, V., 496
Ruszkowski, M., 792, 801
Rüte, Hans von, 625, 626, 636
Rutebeuf, 53, 67, 69, 70
Rütten, T., 722
Rüttiger, A., 694
Ruus, H., 756
Ruysch, Friedrich, 438
Ryan, J. L., 716, 721
Rycaut, Paul, 143
Rychlo, P., 705
Ryklin, M., 834, 836
Ryzhii, Boris, 853
Rzedzicka, S., 789, 795, 802
Rzeszutko, M., 794, 795
Rzewuski, Stanislaw, 179

Saakiants, A., 840, 855
Saalbach, Astrid, 772
Saar, M., 695
Saba, Linuccia, 487
Saba, Umberto, 456, 457, 482, 487
Sabbatino, P., 376
Sabel, J., 561, 700, 711
Sabinus, Georg, 634
Sabio, F., 32
Sablé, Madeleine de Souvré, marquise de, 147
Sabler, W., 728
Sabolová, D., 436
Saccenti, M., 428, 869
Sacchetti, A., 407
Saccone, A., 451
Saccone, E., 448
Sacher-Masoch, Leopold von, 694
Sacher-Masoch, Wanda von, 668
Sachs, Hans, 605, 617, 625, 636

Sächsische Weltchronik, 616
Sackett, R. E., 711, 742
Sade, Donatien-Alphonse-François, marquis de, 444
Sader, J., 862
Sadoveanu, Izabela, 508, 516
Sadoveanu, Mihail, 508, 517
Sadur, N., 842
Sáenz-Badillos, A., 268
Saer, Juan José, 339
Sætre, L., 778, 780
Sáez (Sánchez), C., 309
Sáez, C., 861
Saffi, E., 431
Safina, R., 564
Safran, G., 820
Safranski, R., 690
Safronov, A. V., 819
Sag, I. A., 12
Sagan-Bielawa, M., 797
Sagarra, E., 680, 682
Sager, A., 579
Sagmo, I., 672
Sahagún, Bernardino de, 322
Sahl, Hans, 704
Sahlfeld, W., 423, 465
Sahm, H., 632
Saicová-Římalová, L., 869
Said, E., 657
Said, Edward, 280
Saint-Amant, Marc Antoine Girard, sieur de, 125, 131, 134
St Brendan, Voyage of, 232, 302, 588
Saint-Cyran, Jean Duvergier de Hauranne, abbé de, 130, 158, 159
Saint-Denys Garneau *v.* Garneau
Saint-Évremond, Charles de Marguetel de Saint-Denis, seigneur de, 137, 154, 161
Saint-Gelais, Octavien de, 73, 103
Saint-Gérand, J.-P., 21
St. John, M., 69
Saint-John Perse (Alexis Leger, *dit* Alexis Saint-Leger Leger), 217, 219, 220
Saint-Martin, L., 214
Saint-Réal, César Vichard de, 137
Saint Sauveur-Henn, A., 702, 703
Saint-Simon, Louis de Rouvroy, duc de, 129, 147, 154
Saint-Yves, G., 32
Sainte-Albine, Pierre-Raymond de, 138
Sainte-Beuve, Charles Augustin, 169, 188, 198, 205
Sainte-Marthe, Scévole de, 109, 120
Sakellaridou, E., 709
Sakharov, V. I., 808, 846, 854
Sakson, L., 809
Sala, M., 495, 496
Sala, Pierre, 120
Sala di Felice, E., 405, 416, 454
Salari, Tiziano, 488
Salat, Johannes, 631
Salazar, Ambrosio de, 266
Salazar, Juan Clímaco de, 276
Salazar, P.-J., 127
Salcher, P., 546
Salek, R., 485
Salel, Hugues, 105, 117
Salfi, Francesco Saverio, 400
Salgado, C. A., 332
Salgado, X. M., 315, 316
Salgari, Emilio, 447
Salhi, K., 20
Salibra, E., 445
Salieri, Antonio, 412
Salimbene de Adam, 383–84
Salin, D., 130
Salinas, Pedro, 279, 281, 282, 287, 288–89
Salisbury, E., 869
Salmeri, G., 403
Salomon, Bernard, 97
Salon, A. T., 546
Saloni, Z., 793
Salpietro, A., 482
Salten, Felix, 727
Saltykov-Shchedrin, Mikhail Evgrafovich, 829
Salvadori Lonergan, C., 859
Salvaneschi, E., 483
Salvatores, Gabriele, 468
Salvi, G., 5, 522, 868
Salvini, Anton Maria, 404
Salzmann, B., 735
Sama, C. M., 409
Samarin, I., 845
Samoilov, A., 851
Sampson, R., 21, 869
San Román, G., 320
Sancha, Antonio de, 276
Sánchez, M., 337
Sánchez, M. N., 255, 865
Sánchez-Barbudo, A., 288
Sánchez-Blanco, F., 275
Sánchez Ciruelo, Pedro, 270
Sánchez González de Herrero, M. N., 249
Sánchez Lancis, C., 253
Sánchez Méndez, J., 861
Sánchez-Miret, F., 4
Sánchez-Prieto Borja, P., 250
Sánchez Romeralo, A., 288
Sánchez Trigueros, A., 289
Sand, George (Aurore Dupin, baronne Dudevant), 182, 678, 814, 822
Sandberg, B., 717
Sandberg, H.-J., 724
Sandemose, Aksel, 779
Sanders, W., 555
Sandersen, V., 757
Sandonà, G. B., 418
Sandøy, H., 756
Sandras, M., 193
Şandru Mehedinţi, T., 502
Sandvik, Kjell, 778
Sandy, G., 102, 869
Sangirardi, G., 438
Sanguineti, Edoardo, 454, 455, 456, 457, 488
Sanguineti, F., 372, 379
Sanjinés, Jorge, 340
Sanjust, M. G., 430
Sankovich, N., 827
St. Trudperter Hohelied, 576
Sanmartín, G., 313
Sanmartín Sáez, J., 258
Sannelli, Massimo, 457
Sannia Nowé, L., 454
Sannino, A. L., 403
Sanson, H., 354
Santagata, M., 430, 445
Santamarina Fernández, A., 304, 309, 311
Santanach, J., 299
Santanelli, Manlio, 467
Santato, G., 407
Santi, F., 459, 485
Santiago, R., 249
Santiago, S., 337
Santiago, Silviano, 348
Sant Jordi, Jordi de, 297
Santini, G., 236
Santoni, S., 58
Santoro, M., 209
Santoro, P., 293
Santos, I. M. F. dos, 350
Santos, L., 246
Santos Cunha, M. T., 269
Santos Puerto, J., 278
Santos Suárez, L., 306
Santucci, A. A., 419
Santucci, M., 93
Sanyal, D., 193
Sanz, M., 358
Sanz Alonso, B., 265
Sanz Hermida, J., 270
Sapala, B., 688
Sapchenko, L. A., 819
Sapegno, N., 383

Sapgir, Genrikh, 839
Saphir, Moritz Gottlieb, 669
Sapov, V. V., 820
Sapozhkov, S., 828
Sapronov, G., 845
Saprykina, E. I., 810
Saralegui, C., 864
Saramago, J., 306
Saramandu, M., 503
Saramandu, N., 496
Saranchin, K., 848
Sarasin, Jean-François, 126
Saravia de la Calle, Luys, 270
Sarcher, W., 565
Sardo, R., 363
Sarduy, Severo, 219
Saredo, Luisa, 423
Sargent-Baur, B. N., 53, 54, 59
Sarlo, B., 349
Sarlo, Beatriz, 338
Sarmiento, Domingo Faustino, 318, 320
Sarmiento, Martín (*frei*), 278, 304, 316, 869
Sarnov, B., 817
Sarnowsky, J., 616
Sarteschi, S., 366, 386
Sartre, Jean-Paul, 461, 764, 765
Sarukhanian, I., 843
Sarychev, I. V., 835
Sarychev, V. A., 821
Sasaki, S., 83
Sasse, D., 635
Sasse, H.-J., 10
Sasso, G., 365, 379
Sasso, L., 435
Sasso, S., 489
Sasu, A., 507
Satkiewicz, H., 793, 797
Satta, Salvatore, 488, 491
Satterfield, T., 867
Saul, N., 734, 869
Saulini, M., 411, 859
Saunders, A., 100, 107, 128
Šaur, V., 787
Saurma-Jeltsch, L. E., 595
Saussure, Ferdinand de, 8, 20, 289
Sautman, F. C., 869
Sauvadet, M.-R., 230
Sauzet, P., 224
Saval, J.-V., 337
Savarese, G., 438
Savaric de Mauleon, 234
Savater, F., 339
Savelieva, V. V., 824, 845
Savel'zon, V. L., 818
Savi, F., 412
Savina, L. N., 819, 847
Savini, M., 411, 430
Savinio, Alberto (Andrea Alberto De Chirico), 451, 466, 483, 488
Savitsky, S., 832
Savoca, G., 436, 482
Savoia, F. L. M., 356
Savoie, C., 208
Savolainen, T., 560
Savorini, Luigi, 432
Say, T., 358
Sazaki, K. R., 674
Sazonova, L., 808
Sbarbaro, Camillo, 454, 457
Sberlati, F., 442
Sbiera, I. G., 512
Scaccabarozzi, Orrico, 388
Scaff, S. von R., 721
Scaliger, Joseph-Juste, 98
Scalvini, B., 418
Scanlan, J. P., 824
Scappaticci, T., 418
Scardeone, Bernardino, 391
Scarfatti, Margherita, 465
Scarpa, D., 469, 470
Scarpa, Tiziano, 464
Scarpetta, Eduardo, 425
Scarrocchia, S., 440
Scarron, Paul, 127, 134, 138, 154
Scève, Maurice, 79, 105, 117, 118
Schaap, S., 690
Schaber, I., 703
Schabus, W., 571
Schädlich, Hans Joachim, 747
Schäfer, M., 742
Schäfer, W., 565
Schaffner, S., 583
Schaller, B., 740
Schaller, H. M., 385
Schaller Wu, S., 61
Schallück, Paul, 750
Schambony, J., 353
Schanze, H., 642
Schapira, C., 11, 26
Schärf, C., 710
Scharff, T., 616
Scharfman, R., 219
Schassan, T., 582
Schedel, A., 710
Schedel, Hartmann, 607, 617
Schedel, Hartmut, 607, 617
Schedel, S., 718
Scheffel, M., 682, 718
Schehr, L. R., 178
Scheible, H., 410, 635, 728
Scheichl, S. P., 682, 687, 750
Scheidgen, A., 579–80
Scheidt, G., 729
Schein, Johann Hermann, 641
Scheirich, R. M., 707
Scheitler, I., 740, 741
Schelling, Friedrich Wilhelm Joseph von, 187, 437, 651, 655, 664
Schemmel, B., 656
Schendel, M. van, 207, 213
Schenke, M. F., 743
Schenzinger, Aloys, 700
Schepkina-Kupernik, T., 822
Scherbaum, I., 600
Scherf, F.-P., 574
Scherffer von Scherffenstein, Wencel, 639–40
Scheuer, J., 761
Scheuermann, U., 573, 575
Scheuringer, H., 568
Schiavo, L., 294
Schickele, René, 727
Schickling, M., 713
Schiel, R., 614
Schiendorfer, M., 604, 606
Schierbaum, M., 662, 691
Schierholz, S. J., 862
Schiewer, H.-J., 580, 593, 604, 612, 863, 869
Schiewer, R. D., 611
Schikorsky, I., 557, 669
Schildt, J., 564
Schiller, D., 711
Schiller, Friedrich, 285, 424, 556, 649, 658, 665, 681, 684, 699
Schilling, D., 680
Schilling, K. von, 739, 744
Schilling, M., 620, 621, 640
Schilz, G., 23
Schindler, A., 631
Schindler, F., 786
Schindler, M. S., 864
Schindler, R. A., 864
Schindler, S. K., 660
Schindler, W., 556, 863
Schirnding, A., 725
Schirok, B., 595
Schlawin, S., 703
Schlechtweg-Jahn, R., 600, 609
Schlegel, August Wilhelm, 187, 647, 651, 652, 664
Schlegel, Dorothea, 665
Schlegel, Friedrich Wilhelm, 172, 423, 647, 648, 649, 651, 652, 665, 690
Schlegel, Wilhelm, 288
Schlenstedt, D., 727
Schlesewsky, M., 562
Schlich, J., 649
Schlicht, C., 750
Schlieben-Lange, B., 225
Schlink, Bernhard, 733, 750–51

Schlömer, A., 29
Schlumberger, Gustave, 196
Schlusemann, R., 620
Schlüter, C., 775
Schlutt, M., 723
Schmeller, Johann Andreas, 567
Schmelzer, H.-J., 713
Schmid, C., 595
Schmid, E., 592, 597, 600
Schmid, G., 750
Schmid, H.-U., 553
Schmid, M. E., 713
Schmid, W. P., 562
Schmid-Bortenschläger, S., 706
Schmidt, A., 694
Schmidt, Afonso, 346
Schmidt, A[rmin], 615
Schmidt, Arno, 682, 751
Schmidt, B., 751
Schmidt, F. L., 764
Schmidt, H., 551, 564, 565, 570
Schmidt, H., 833
Schmidt, H. J., 692
Schmidt, Hermann, 644
Schmidt, J., 639
Schmidt, J. E., 557
Schmidt, Julian, 673
Schmidt, Kathrin, 743
Schmidt, S., 600, 603, 695, 797
Schmidt, W. G., 661, 697, 713, 714
Schmidt-Biggemann, W., 637, 641
Schmidt-Dengler, W., 706
Schmidt-Ott, A. C., 700
Schmidt-Welle, F., 320
Schmidt-Wiegand, R., 555, 615
Schmiesing, A., 775
Schmitsdorf, E., 870
Schmitt, C., 12, 21
Schmitt, G., 727
Schmitt, K., 590, 593
Schmitt, R., 550
Schmitz, B., 590
Schmitz, Ettore, 490
Schmitz, G., 680
Schmitz, H., 733, 751
Schmitz, Oscar A. H., 727
Schmitz, S., 587
Schmitz-Emans, M., 739
Schnabel, M., 557
Schnabel, W. W., 638
Schnecker, C., 24
Schnedecker, C., 26
Schneider, A., 693
Schneider, G., 688
Schneider, G. K., 728
Schneider, H. J., 733
Schneider, J., 584
Schneider, L., 193
Schneider, M., 675
Schneider, Peter, 751
Schneider, S., 354
Schneider, T., 676
Schneider, T. F., 725
Schneider, U., 748
Schneider Handschin, E., 702
Schneider Soltanianzadeh, A., 493
Schnell, R., 577, 612, 685, 707
Schnitzler, Arthur, 642, 667. 678, 699, 701, 704, 706, 707, 728–29
Schnitzler, G., 695
Schnurbein, S. von, 779
Schnyder, M., 592, 593, 595, 602
Schödel, K., 371
Schoeck, Othmar, 688
Scholar, R., 127
Scholdt, G., 726
Scholl, D., 377
Schöll, J., 703
Scholz, F., 845
Scholz, M. G., 603
Scholze-Stubenrecht, W., 564
Schomberg, Jeanne de, 87
Schomers, W., 724, 725
Schön, J., 27
Schönberg, Alexander von, 734
Schönberg, Arnold, 706, 723, 724
Schönegger-Zanoni, C., 834
Schönert, J., 672
Schönfeld, C., 688
Schöning, Matthias, 665
Schönleber, M., 614
Schopenhauer, Arthur, 199, 426, 441, 691, 694, 708, 721, 722, 775, 822
Schopenhauer, Johanna, 665
Schopf, W., 702
Schorta, Andrea, 572
Schøsler, L., 5, 21
Schössler, F., 713, 742
Schottelius, Justus Georg, 640
Schottmann, H., 564
Schoysman, A., 106
Schrage, M., 388
Schreiner, E., 81, 82
Schrenck, G., 122, 152
Schreuder, S., 705
Schröder, P., 720
Schröder, V., 151
Schrön, J., 732
Schrott, Raoul, 751
Schu, C., 594
Schubart, D., 640
Schubert, J., 742
Schubert, K., 733
Schubert, M. J., 595, 606, 613
Schücking, Levin, 675, 688
Schuerewegen, F., 177, 178
Schuh, R., 574
Schuhmann, R., 583
Schuldt-Britting, I., 710
Schuler, Alfred, 729
Schüler, D., 344
Schuller, W., 708
Schulman, I. A., 319
Schulman, P., 201
Schultz, J. A., 595
Schultze, C., 548
Schulz, A., 587, 590
Schulz, Bruno, 802
Schulz, M., 559, 587
Schulze, Ingo, 746
Schulze, U., 576, 590, 612, 863, 869
Schulze-Belli, P., 606
Schumacher, H., 750
Schumacher, M., 608
Schumann, A., 719
Schumann, Gottlieb, 638
Schumann, Robert, 685, 688
Schünicke, S., 619
Schunk, G., 567
Schupp, V., 577
Schuppener, G., 548
Schürr, D., 523
Schuster, G., 708
Schuster, M.-O., 692
Schutjer, K., 658
Schütt, R., 720
Schütz, E., 702, 707, 869
Schütz, Helga, 738
Schütz, Stefan, 746
Schütze, P., 681, 682
Schwabe, Carlos, 203
Schwabe von der Heyde, Ernst, 640
Schwabenspiegel, 615
Schwach, C., 777
Schwahl, M., 731
Schwam-Baird, S., 70
Schwander, H.-P., 734
Schwartz, D., 324
Schwartz, D. B., 47
Schwartz, J., 338
Schwartz, L., 268, 273, 274
Schwartz, M. E., 337–38
Schwartz, R., 344
Schwarz, A., 552, 627
Schwarz, C., 628
Schwarz, H.-G., 862
Schwarz, M., 665
Schwarz-Bart, André, 216, 220
Schwarz-Bart, Simone, 216, 220
Schwarzburg-Rudolstadt, Aemilie Juliane von, 640

Schwarze, C., 6
Schwarzenbach, Annemarie, 703
Schwegler, A., 257, 262
Schwegler, M., 629
Schweickard, W., 14
Schweikert, R., 727
Schweikert, Ruth, 738
Schwerdt, J., 553
Schwilk, Heimo, 752
Schwitters, Kurt, 702
Schwob, A., 606
Schwob, Marcel, 186, 195, 201
Schwob, U. M., 606
Scialoja, Toti, 488
Sciascia, Leonardo, 454, 465, 488–89, 491
Scientella, A., 470
Scognamiglio, G., 414
Scolari, A., 382
Sconocchia, S., 435
Scorrano, L., 365–66, 442, 472, 478, 485, 869
Scot, J.-P., 173
Scotellaro, Rocco, 489
Scott, Dennis, 218
Scott, Sir Walter, 172, 177, 178
Scotti, M., 370
Scotto d'Aniello, L., 408
Scribe, Eugène, 176
Scribner, C., 753
Scrivano, R., 452
Scrope, Stephen, 85
Scuderi, A., 473
Scudéry, Georges de, 127, 155
Scudéry, Madeleine de, 125, 126, 127, 128, 129, 130–31, 145, 146, 147, 154–55, 157
Sdobnov, M. V., 817
Sealsfield, Charles (Karl Postl), 694–95
Seara, T., 313, 314
Searle, John R., 348
Sebald, Winfried Georg, 733, 751
Sebastian, Mihail, 517
Sebastio, L., 379
Sebbah, A., 410
Šebestová, I., 738
Sebina, I., 809
Sebold, R. P., 276
Sechehaye, Albert, 20
Seco Orosa, A., 305
Seco Serrano, C., 272
Secrieru, M., 501
Sedakova, O., 826
Sedakova, Olga, 853
Sedano, M., 246, 257
Sedov, A. F., 824
Sedova, G., 816
Sędziak, H., 797
Seeba, H. C., 661, 714, 726
Seebacher, J., 180
Seeber, U., 732
Seeberg, Peter, 763, 772
Seeberg, S., 578
Seebold, E., 554, 558, 863
Segalen, Victor, 191, 195
Segarra, I., 302
Segebrecht, W., 655
Seggern, G. von, 693
Seghers, Anna, 704, 705, 729, 730, 751
Segrais, Jean, 153, 155
Segre, C., 376, 390, 392, 404, 422, 454
Segui, J., 247
Ségur, Sophie Rostopchine, comtesse de, 201
Séguy, M., 46
Seibicke, W., 14
Şeicaru, Pamfil, 517
Seidel, K. O., 602
Seidensticker, B., 734
Seidensticker, P., 553
Seiderer, U., 743
Seifert, J., 862
Seifert, Jaroslav, 785
Seifert, Johan, 644
Seifert, L. C., 126
Seiffert, A., 560
Seifrit, 600
Seignobos, C., 32
Seillan, J.-M., 199
Seknadje-Askénazi, E., 181
Sękowska, E., 799, 801
Sekvent, K., 786
Selbmann, R., 678, 718, 730, 868
Selderhuis, H. J., 635
Seleznev, V., 830
Selig, M., 4, 22
Selivanova, S. D., 815
Selting, M., 558
Selvatico, R., 434
Semacchi Gliubich, G., 452
Semenjuk, N., 556
Semenova, E. V., 807
Semenova, N. V., 850
Semenova, S., 841, 853
Semenova, S. G., 813, 848
Semprún, Jorge, 549
Senabre, R., 246
Senaldi, M., 464
Senardi, F., 463
Senchin, Roman, 853
Sender, Ramon José, 290
Senderov, V., 844
Seneca, Lucius Annaeus (*the Younger*), 112, 364, 381, 407, 645
Senff, Johann, 618
Sennewald, J. E., 653
Şenocaks, Zafer, 751
Seongho, S., 545
Sęp Szarzyński, Mikołaj, 801
Sept sages de Rome, 393, 618
Sequeri, P. A., 433
Serafimova, V. D., 849, 852
Serao, Matilde, 447
Şerban, G., 516, 517
Şerbănescu, A., 501, 504
Serebrennikov, N. V., 869
Serena, A., 426
Serena, L., 426
Sereni, Vittorio, 366, 457, 479, 483, 485, 489
Sergeev, O. V., 820
Sergeeva-Kliatis, A., 850
Serianni, L., 351
Serkowska, H., 463
Serlio, Sebastiano, 109
Sermain, Jean-Paul, 147
Serman, I., 838
Sermon sur Jonas, 56
Sermonti, Vittorio, 371
Seroczyński, G., 805
Sérodes, S., 183
Serra, F., 410
Serra, Renato, 450
Serrà Campins, A., 869
Serrano, J., 294
Serrano, R., 191, 194, 195, 869
Serrano Alonso, J., 294
Serrano Asenjo, E., 281
Serrano de Osma, Carlos, 697
Serrarius, Petrus, 643
Serres, Olivier de, 120, 167
Serri, M., 450, 464
Serroy, J., 141
Sertoli, G., 417
Servet, P., 93, 867
Şesan, D., 509
Sestini, Bartolomeo, 447
Settembrini, Luigi, 447
Settler, H., 679
Seubert, H., 690
Seuse, Heinrich, 610, 611
Sevestre, C., 115
Sévigné, Marie de Rabutin-Chantal, marquise de, 152, 155, 157
Sevin, D., 702
Seyfi, S., 693
Seyhan, A., 660
Seys, P., 206
Sgall, P., 781
Sgallová, K., 786

Sgroi, S. C., 353
Shafi, M., 737
Shaginian, Marietta Sergeevna, 840
Shaitanov, I., 831, 837
Shakespeare, William, 172, 173, 176, 184, 185, 267, 406, 418, 424, 442, 531, 769, 772
Shakhmagonov, N. F., 816
Shalamov, Varlam, 837
Shamir, I., 854
Shapin, S., 162
Shapir, M., 855
Shapir, M. I., 811, 816, 817
Shapochka, V. V., 830
Shargunov, Sergei, 841
Sharman, G. M., 699
Sharov, A., 843
Sharpe, R., 542
Shattuck, R., 195
Shavit, Z., 705
Shavrova, E., 822
Shaw, D. L., 338
Shaw, F., 596
Shaw, P., 374
Shcheglov, S., 843
Shchennikov, G., 828
Shcherbachenko, V. I., 815
Shchukin, V. G., 827
Shchuplov, A., 812
Shebunin, A. N., 833
Shedletzky, I., 685
Sheingorn, P., 869
Shek, B.-Z., 213
Shelley, Mary, 172
Shenbrunn, Svetlana, 844
Sheppard, G., 210
Shestakov, V. A., 837
Shevchenko, Taras Grigorievich, 806
Shevchuk, Iurii, 839
Shevelenko, I., 855
Shevyrev, Stepan Petrovich, 811
Shillington, J. W., 327
Shiokawa, T., 165
Shiriaeva, Tatiana, 842
Shitanda, S., 613
Shklovsky, Victor, 853
Shmelev, A., 807
Shmelev, Ivan, 836, 843, 853
Shmelev, N., 844
Shmeleva, E., 807
Shmel'kova, N., 847
Shockey, G. C., 599
Sholem, Gershom, 707, 708
Sholokhov, Mikhail, 853
Shorokhov, A., 848
Shotova, O. N., 853
Shpet, G. G., 827
Shpikalova, E., 813
Shtain, K. E., 808
Shtal, I. V., 818
Shteiner, E., 831
Shtil'man, S. L., 828
Shtil'mark, Robert F., 854
Shubinsky, V., 843, 848
Shubnikova-Guseva, N. I., 847
Shukshin, Vasilii, 853
Shulpiakov, Gleb, 841, 843
Shul'ts, S. A., 826, 844
Shumkova, T. L., 810
Shveitser, V., 855
Shvets, M., 822
Siani, C., 492
Siatkowski, J., 804
Sibbald, K. M., 279, 295
Sibinska, M., 778
Sibote, 582
Sica, P., 451, 458, 479
Sicher, E., 845
Siciliano, E., 461
Sicotte, G., 190, 199
Sieben Weisen Meister, 393, 618
Siebenhaar, B., 569
Siebenhaar, K., 707
Sieber, A., 600
Sieberg, B., 561
Sieburg, Friedrich, 729
Sieburg, H., 558
Siefken, H., 721
Siege of Caerlaverock, 74
Siemsen, Hans, 711
Siemund, P., 568
Sienkiewicz, Henryk, 801, 802
Sieradska-Baziur, B., 801
Sievers, W., 748
Siewert, K., 567
Sifuentes Jáuregui, Ben, 331
Sigal, P. A., 82
Sigarev, Vasilii, 842
Sigl, G. A. M., 565
Signer Codoñer, J., 266
Signorini, S., 435
Siguan, M., 549
Sikora, K., 789, 802
Sikora, L., 795
Silone, Ignazio, 461, 463, 489
Silorata, Pietro Bernabò, 442
Silva, J. N. de S. e, 343
Silva, José Asunción, 320
Silva Domínguez, C., 305, 308
Silva Valdivia, B., 311, 869
Silvano Nigro, S., 442
Silveira, F. M., 346
Silverman, W. A., 864
Şimăndan, E., 513
Šimandl, J., 783, 784
Simecková, A., 544, 545
Simion, E., 513, 514, 515, 516, 517
Simmel, Georg, 292, 691, 704, 711
Simmel, Gertrud, 704, 711
Simmler, F., 558, 562, 613, 869
Simmons, S., 702
Simon, A., 622
Simon, R., 714
Simon, S., 669
Simone da Cascina, 391
Simonek, S., 706
Simonetti, G., 479
Simonide di Amorgo, 438
Simonin, M., 99, 110, 112
Simonis, L., 692, 719
Simons, O., 701
Simpson, A. P., 557
Simpson, J., 657
Simpson, J. A., 206
Simpson, L., 94
Sims-Williams, P., 525, 528
Sinel'nikov, Mikhail, 839, 844, 855
Singerman, Berta, 294
Singh, S., 684
Singleton, D., 21
Siniavsky, Andrei Donatovich (Abram Terts), 834, 841, 854
Sinielnikoff, R., 793
Sinisgalli, Leonardo, 459, 489–90
Sinisi, S., 466
Siôn Ceri, 531
Siracusa, M., 460, 493
Siraisi, N. G., 622
Sîrbu, Ion D., 507
Sirenok, V. A., 818
Sirera, J. L., 870
Sirera, R., 303
Sirois, A., 209
Sisi, C., 407
Sismondi, Léonard Simonde de, 426
Sisti, L., 482
Sitarz, M., 804
Sitran Rea, L., 403
Sitta, C. A., 459
Sitter, M., 745
Siwek, A., 801
Sizov, V. S., 824
Skabichevsky, Alexander Mikhailovich, 839
Skácelová, J., 787
Skadberg, G. A., 777
Skadhauge, P. R., 756
Skakovskaia, L. N., 835
Skála, E., 553, 555, 574
Skalnik, J. V., 103
Skenazi, C., 115, 118
Skiba, V. A., 806
Skinnebach, Lars, 768

Sklar, E. S., 43
Skleinis, G. A., 824
Sklodowska, E., 331
Skoczylas-Stawska, H., 797
Skolnik, J., 669
Skou-Hansen, Tage, 771, 772
Skoumalová, H., 784
Skovholt, K., 778
Skowron, M., 692
Skram, Amalie, 777
Skripova, T. M., 866
Skvoznikov, V. D., 811
Skwarska, K., 787
Skyum-Nielsen, E., 767, 768, 770, 862
Slataper, Scipio, 457, 490
Slavnikova, Olga, 841, 854
Sławski, F., 804
Slezáková, M., 783, 866
Slivitskaya, O. V., 826
Śliwiński, W., 801
Slobodniuk, S., 827
Slobozhaninova, L., 828
Šlosar, D., 786
Sloterdijk, Peter, 693
Smeets, M., 200
Smet, I. A. R. de, 112
Smets, A., 77
Šmídová, P., 783
Smidt, J. K., 778
Smirin, I. A., 832
Smirnov, N. P., 846
Smirnova, I., 828
Smith, A., 26
Smith, D. L., 654
Smith, D. M., 533
Smith, E. E., 728
Smith, G., 65, 81
Smith, N., 17
Smith, P. J., 109
Smith, Thorne, 751
Smith, V., 757
Smól, J., 801
Smółkowa, T., 801
Smułkowa, E., 803, 804
Smykowski, A., 685
Snaith, G., 138
Sneddon, C. R., 21, 75
Sneeringer, K. K., 597
Sobatta, K., 549
Sobczak, B., 794, 802
Sobejano, G., 286, 290
Soberanas, A. J., 300
Sobolev, L. I., 820
Sobrero, A., 362
Sobstyl, K., 797
Socrates, 98
Soffici, Ardengo, 451, 481, 490
Sofia Albertina (*princess of Sweden*), 402
Søholm, E., 770, 771
Soina, O. S., 814
Sokel, W. H., 716, 717
Sokhriakov, I., 825
Sokolija, A., 33
Sokolov, B., 846
Sokolov, Sasha, 834
Sokolova, I., 842
Sokólska, U., 802
Solana Pujalte, J., 267
Solatie, R., 33
Solbach, A., 643, 693
Solberg, O., 774
Soldatova, L., 816
Sole, A., 437, 438
Solé, C. A., 336
Solé, J., 409
Soler, A., 254
Solèr, C., 522
Soler-Espiauba, D., 247
Soler Pascual, E., 277
Solervicens, J., 303
Solies, D., 693
Solimena, A., 384
Solmi, Sergio, 490
Solms, H.-J., 546, 558
Solms, W., 643
Solntseva, N. M., 832
Sologub, Fedor Kuz'mich, 829, 839
Sologub, V., 811
Solomin, A., 817
Soloviev, Vladimir Sergeevich, 822, 829–30, 831, 839
Solstad, Dag, 779–80
Solterer, H., 67
Solzhenitsyn, Alexander, 854
Somaize, Baudeau de, 126
Sombart, Werner, 711
Sommer, D., 331
Sommer, Ernst, 705
Sonderegger, S., 555, 563
Søndergaard, G., 757
Sonne, H., 763
Sonnenschein, Hugo, 729
Sonnergaard, Jan, 772
Sophocles, 626, 772
Şora, Mariana, 513
Sorbière, Samuel, 167–68
Sørbø, J. I., 778
Sorel, Charles, 125, 126, 142, 145, 155–56
Sorella, A., 439
Sørensen, B. A., 699
Sørensen, I. Ž., 769
Sørensen, K., 757, 765
Sørensen, S. P., 756
Sørensen, V., 758
Sørensen, Villy, 772
Sorescu, Marin, 517
Soresina, M., 368–69
Sorge, P., 432
Sorge Delfico, Vinca, 432
Soria Olmedo, A., 286
Sorianello, P., 361
Soriano, A., 286
Sormani, E., 447
Sornicola, R., 17
Sorohan, E., 510
Sorokin, Vladimir Georgievich, 832, 854
Soron, A., 210
Soshkin, E., 844
Sosien, B., 195
Soto, Domingo de, 266
Soucy, Gaétan, 214
Soudková, P., 786
Soufas, C. C. (Jr.), 279, 287
Soulié, M., 110
Soupel, S., 230
Sourdot, M., 33
Sousa, Gabriel Soares de, 344
Sousa Fernández, X., 304, 305–06, 308, 859
Souza, L. S. de, 344
Sova, L., 851
Soya, Carl Erik, 772
Sozina, E. K., 809
Sozzi, L., 98, 448
Spácilová, L., 545
Spadaro, A., 463
Spaggiari, A., 417
Spaggiari, W., 411
Spandri, F., 183
Spang-Hanssen, E., 755
Spangenberg, Cyriakus, 628, 636
Spanily, C., 578
Sparapani Boccapaduli, Margherita Gentili, 402
Spătarul, N. Milescu, 509
Späth, Gerold, 751
Spaziani, Maria Luisa, 457, 469
Spear, T. C., 208
Spearing, A. C., 80
Spechtler, F. V., 603
Speculum humanae salvationis, 613
Spedicato, E., 663
Spee von Langenfeld, Friedrich, 640, 644
Speer, H., 563
Speer, M. B., 870
Speier, H. M., 743
Speirs, R., 709
Speldt, K. B., 769
Spencer, C., 728
Spender, Stephen, 285
Spengler, N., 615, 620
Spengler, Oswald, 723
Sperber, Manès, 705

Spevak, O., 11
Spica, A.-E., 128, 148
Spiczakowska, M., 800
Spiegel, H., 714
Spiekermann, H., 549
Spielhagen, Friedrich, 683
Spielmann, M., 735
Spier, Samuel, 490
Spiess, R. F., 695
Spinaru, S., 504
Spinazzola, Vittorio, 462
Spingler, A., 730
Spires, J., 198
Spiridon, C. M., 512. 514
Spiridon, O., 736
Spiridonova, L. A., 848, 853
Spittler, H., 734
Spitz, H.-J., 555
Spitzer, L., 20
Spitzmüller, J., 546
Spivak, G., 218
Splett, J., 870
Spodareva, M., 786
Sponde, Jean de, 118, 119, 121, 122
Spörk, I., 668
Spousta, V., 784, 785
Spranz Fogasy, T., 550
Sprecher, T., 721, 722
Spreitzer, B., 578
Sprengel, P., 688, 702, 713
Springer, Julius, 679
Springeth, M., 580, 603
Sprunger, D. A., 88
Spunta, M., 463
Spyri, Johanna, 695
Squartana, L., 414
Squartini, M., 353
Squillacioti, P., 232
Srámek, R., 574
Srpová, H., 785
Srpová, M., 782
Sruve, G. P., 843
Staal, Marguerite-Jeanne de, 135
Stabile, G., 435
Stach, R., 715, 716
Stachowski, M., 804
Stackmann, K., 605, 863, 869
Stadler, H., 611
Stadnikov, G. V., 829
Staehelin, M., 607
Staël, Anne-Louise-Germaine, Mme de, 170, 412, 437, 662, 867
Staengle, P., 662
Staf'eva, E., 846
Stafford, A., 217
Stafford, B. M., 637
Stage, D., 760
Stage, L., 13
Stahl, P. H., 509
Stähli, M., 625
Staib, B., 518
Staiti, C., 584
Stalin, Joseph (Iosif Vissarionovich Djougashvili), 833, 836
Stamatu, Horia, 513, 517
Stancu, V. P., 510
Stancu, Zaharia, 508
Staněk, V., 783
Stanesco, M., 43
Stănescu, Nichita, 517
Stanescu, S., 547
Stanomir, I., 513
Stanton, A., 334
Stanzel, F. K., 735, 737
Staples, A., 114
Stąpor, I., 791
Starets, M., 31
Stark, E., 352
Stark, V. P., 815
Starkey, K., 596, 608
Starodubets, A., 844, 848
Stasi, Gabriele, 400
Stasi, Michele, 400
Statius, 274, 379, 391, 409
Stedman, G., 82
Steeb, D., 611
Steensig, J., 759
Steensnæs, J., 780
Steer, G., 607, 610, 618
Ştefan, Simion (*bishop*), 509
Stefanakova, J., 546
Ştefănescu, C., 517
Ştefănescu, I., 501
Ştefănescu, S., 510
Stefani, M., 410
Stefanin, A., 369
Stefanini, R., 361
Stefanov, I., 843
Stefanovska, M., 153
Steffin, Margarete, 709
Stefornio, Bernardino, 144
Stegbauer, K., 621
Stegmaier, W., 692
Stehlíková, E., 784
Steiger, H., 711
Stein, A., 26
Stein, Bartholomaeus, 624
Stein, Edith, 465
Stein, Gertrude, 493
Stein, P., 720
Steinbeck, John, 493
Steinecke, H., 655, 688, 706, 734
Steiner, F., 551
Steiner, George, 294
Steiner, Rudolf, 702
Steiner, T., 574
Steiner, U., 707
Steingol'd, A., 807
Steinhilber, A., 661
Steinhoff, Hans-Hugo, 585
Steinhöwel, Heinrich, 620
Steinkamp, F., 664
Steinnkrauss, R., 679
Steinrück, Heinrich, 616
Steinweg, D., 834
Stekeler-Weithofer, P., 692
Stella, A., 425
Stella, G., 358
Stellmacher, D., 549, 556, 870
Stelzer, W., 576
Stenbock, Eric, 200
Stendhal (Henri Marie Beyle), 169, 176, 182–85, 195, 444, 668
Stennik, I. V., 807, 820
Steno, Flavia, 464
Stenström, A.-B., 758
Stenzel, H., 156
Štěpán, P., 787
Stepanian, K., 824
Stepanova, N. S., 850
Stephens, A., 660
Stephens, S., 191
Stephens, W. P., 631
Stępień, T., 801
Stepina, C. K., 742
Steppich, C. J., 593
Stere, Constantin, 517
Sterling-Hellenbrand, A., 592
Stern, G., 720
Stern, M., 689, 703
Stern, Selma, 705
Sternberg, Alexander von, 670
Sterne, Laurence, 594
Sternheim, Carl, 702, 730
Sternheim, Thea, 730
Sternkopf, J., 575
Sterpos, M., 406, 429
Stetter, C., 20
Stettinius, Edward R., 751
Stevens, Wallace, 198
Stevenson, B., 84
Stevenson, Robert Louis, 469
Stewart, J., 705, 728, 737
Stewart, M., 246, 247, 713
Stewart, P., 149
Steyer, K., 565
Stiblin, Kaspar, 629
Štícha, F., 783
Stickel, G., 547, 755, 863
Stickelberger, H., 631
Stickney, A., 232
Stidsen, M., 768
Stieg, G., 737, 750
Stiegler, B., 713
Stieler, Caspar, 638, 640, 646

Stiening, G., 658
Stierle, K., 42, 379
Stifter, Adalbert, 671, 672, 695–96
Stiker-Metral, S.-O., 133
Stillmark, A., 730
Stingelin, M., 691
Stival, M., 425
Stjernfeldt, F., 763
Stöber, T., 669
Stock, L., 88
Stock, M., 587
Stocker, G., 738, 741
Stockhorst, S., 694
Stockinger, L., 681
Stoermer, F., 658, 661
Stoichiţu-Ichim, A., 504
Stoker, Bram, 189
Stoll, D., 331
Stolojan, Sanda, 513
Stolt, B., 627
Stoltz, Kristina, 768
Stolz, M., 582, 595, 606
Stolz, T., 262
Stopchenko, N. I., 853
Stoppelli, P., 370
Storchi, S., 462, 463
Störl, K., 341
Storm, Edvard, 774
Storm, Theodor, 669, 696–97, 724
Störmer-Caysa, U., 591, 611
Storni, Alfonsina, 318, 339
Storost, J., 6
Stosic, D., 26
Stott, R., 739
Stout, J., 869
Stowe, Harriet Beecher, 320
Strachey, Lytton, 281
Stracuzzi, R., 494
Stramm, August, 700
Strasser, A., 747
Strässle, T., 642, 656
Strässle, U., 659
Straub, E., 410
Straub, Georg, 645
Straub, W., 737
Strauss, A., 609
Strauss, Botho, 708, 751
Strauss, G., 565
Strauss, Ludwig, 705
Strauss, M.-L., 695
Strauss, Richard, 714
Strecker, B., 562
Streeruwitz, Marlene, 742, 751–52
Streim, G., 706, 708, 869
Streller, S., 643
Stremitina, N., 844
Strich, Hans, 628
Stricker (*Der*), 599, 610
Stricker, H., 572
Stricker, S., 559
Strickhausen, W., 704
Strijbosch, C., 588
Strittmatter, Erwin, 735
Strobel, J., 684
Strocka, V. M., 686
Stroev, A., 409
Stroganov, M. V., 808, 811
Strohmeyr, A., 719
Strohschneider, P., 603, 604, 611
Stróżyński, M., 795
Strubel, A., 37, 77
Strubell, M., 258
Struisky, N. E., 812
Struzyk, Brigitte, 738
Stubhaug, A., 777
Stuckmal, V., 247
Stuckrad-Barre, Benjamin von, 734, 743
Studnitz, R. E. von, 557
Stumpf, Johannes, 623
Stuplich, B., 614
Sturges, R. S., 44
Sturm-Maddox, S., 49, 115, 867
Stussi, A., 352, 377, 388, 448
Styrcz-Przebinda, L., 794
Suard, F., 50, 72
Suárez, Francisco, 266
Suárez Fernández, M., 870
Suassuna, Ariano, 347, 348, 350
Subbotin, V., 839
Subrenat, J., 66
Suchenwirt, Peter, 601
Suchon, Gabrielle, 161
Suciu, E., 498
Sudan, P., 109, 191
Sudhof, D., 731
Suditu, B., 503
Sudujko, T., 795
Suerbaum, A., 577, 596
Suffolk *v.* Pole
Sugaya, N., 197
Suglia, J., 658, 712
Suh, Y.-S., 749
Suhl, N., 729, 751
Suk, J., 216
Sukailo, V., 815
Sukhanek, L., 832
Sukhanov, Ivan, 826
Sukhanova, I. A., 826
Sukhikh, I. N., 833, 845, 852
Sukhikh, S. I., 838
Sukhov, A. D., 826
Sukhovo-Kobylin, Alexander Vasilievich, 830
Suleimenov, Olzhas, 854
Sulich, A., 795
Sulkin, O., 845
Sully, Maximilien de Béthune, baron de Rosny, duc de, 167
Sulzer, Johann Georg, 651, 664
Summers, K. M., 108
Sünden Widerstreit, 610
Suppa, S., 157
Supple, J. J., 112
Surat, I., 816, 838
Surdel, A.-J., 77
Surdich, L., 454, 491
Surmann, E., 707
Surre-Garcia, Alein, 238
Surynt, I., 681
Susinno, S., 401
Süskind, Patrick, 752, 822
Susman, Margarete, 704, 730
Sussman, H., 717
Suvorov, D., 856
Svaier, Amadeo, 403
Svendsen, E., 771
Sverdlov, M., 810
Svetana, F. E., 826
Svetana-Tolstaya, S. V., 826
Světlá, J., 786
Svevo, Italo, 279, 460, 490–91
Sviatopolk-Mirsky, D. P., 835, 841
Svoboda, S., 787
Svobodová, Z., 866
Swahn, S., 243
Swales, M., 728
Swanson, K. A., 220
Sweetser, E., 528
Sweetser, M.-O., 131, 132
Swerts, M., 353
Swiggers, P., 7
Switten, M., 90
Sykulska, K., 795
Sylvester, L., 84
Sylvius (Jacques Dubois), 102
Symmank, M., 746
Symons, Arthur, 200
Szabó, C., 731, 742
Szabó, C.-A., 572
Szagun, D., 800
Szardi, P., 294
Szász, F., 731
Szelachowska-Winiarzowa, L., 798
Szemiot, S. S., 801
Szijj, I., 308
Szkilnik, M., 68, 71, 78
Szmetan, R., 320
Szondi, Peter, 658, 743
Szpila, G., 794
Szpyra-Kozłowska, J., 789
Sztripszky, Hiador, 801
Szwedek, A., 789
Szych, J., 791
Szymani, E., 745

Tabah, M., 753
Tabarin, Antoine Gerard, *dit*, 144
Taberner, S., 733, 747, 752
Tabet, X., 434
Tabori, George, 642, 740
Tabossi, P., 358
Tabucchi, Antonio, 463, 491
Tacitus, Publius Cornelius, 112, 266
Tafdrup, Pia, 764
Taherzadeh, A., 788
Tahureau, Jacques, 98, 117
Taillandier, René (*dit* Saint-René), 189
Taine, Hippolyte, 193, 198, 205–06
Taioli, R., 475
Takaki, F., 698
Takayama, T., 177
Takeda, A., 752
Takho-Godi, E. A., 828
Talarico, K. M., 52
Talbot, E. J., 211, 214
Taliesin, 529, 530
Tallemant des Réaux, Gédéon, 127, 137
Tamarchenko, N. D., 838
Tamaro, Susanna, 463
Tamburini, A., 463
Tamburini, L., 447
Tamine, M., 224
Tamiozzo Goldmann, S., 446, 491
Tănase, S., 516
Tanner, Matěj, 782
Tansey, J., 67
Tanteri, D., 433
Tanturli, G., 367
Tanzer, U., 860
Taormina, M., 126
Taraldsen, K. T., 11
Tarantino, C., 363
Taras, B., 799
Tarasov, B., 806
Tarchetti, Igino Ugo, 422, 423, 447
Tardif, Jean-Pierre, 238
Tarkovsky, Arsenii, 831, 844, 854
Tarlinskaya, M., 818
Tarnowski, A., 81, 83
Tarozzi, Bianca, 491
Tarrête, A., 122
Tarrío, A., 313
Tartakovsky, M., 827
Tartaro, A., 377, 379
Tasende, M., 294
Tasker, J., 862
Taskina, E., 835
Tasmowski, L., 500
Tasso, Bernardo, 115
Tasso, Torquato, 112, 430, 438, 439
Tassoni, L., 397, 494
Tătaru, I., 510
Tate, R. B., 302
Tatlock, L., 660, 681
Tatlow, A., 708
Tato, F. R., 870
Tatti, M., 402
Tatzreiter, H., 567
Taubes, Susan, 705
Tauler, Johann, 633
Taunay, Alfredo d'Escragnolle, visconde de, 345
Taupiac, J., 224, 225, 226, 227
Tauss, M., 715, 747
Taussig, S., 159, 163
Tavani, G., 231, 232
Taviani, F., 415
Taviani, G., 484
Tavilla, C. E., 417
Tavola Ritonda, 392
Tavoni, M., 372
Tax, P. W., 555, 585
Taylor, A., 36
Taylor, D., 339
Taylor, J. H. M., 78, 85, 86, 94
Taylor, R., 76
Te, K. K., 846
Teaha, T., 506
Tebaldi-Flores, Carlo, 424
Tebben, K., 669, 679
Tebutt, S., 733, 736
Tedaldi, Pieraccio, 387, 391
Tedesco, N., 486
Teitler, N., 318, 339
Teleman, U., 756
Telle, J., 563
Tellechea Idígoras, J. I., 272
Telles, N., 347
Tellier, C., 213
Tellini, G., 406, 424, 454, 481
Telus, M., 801
Telve, S., 352, 355
Tempesta, I., 362
Tenenti, A., 123
Tentori, Francesco, 457
Teodonio, M., 427
Teodorescu, Leonida, 507
Ţepeneag, Dumitru, 513
Teplinsky, M. V., 823
Terekhova, V., 834
Terence (Publius Terentius Afer), 408, 619
Terentev, Viacheslav, 842
Teresa of Ávila (*Saint*), 151, 272
Terland, I., 774
Termińska, K., 790
Ternaux, J.-C., 106, 131
Ternes, C. M., 541
Terracini, Benvenuto, 452
Terramagnino da Pisa, 236
Terrones del Caño, Francisco, 274
Terry, A., 288
Terts, Abram *v.* Siniavsky
Terzoli, M. A., 394, 411, 422, 433, 434
Tesè, S. N., 484
Tesnière, M.-H., 73
Tessa, Delio, 491
Tessier, J., 207
Tessitore, F., 412, 420, 430
Testa, Enrico, 460, 491
Tetel, M., 121
Teternikov, F. K., 829
Teuffenbacherin, Barbara, 612
Teulat, R., 224, 229
Teyssandier, B., 128
Tgahrt, R., 708
Thabet, S., 747
Thacker, A., 542
Thaler, D., 215
Thaler, J., 676
Thali, J., 579
Thayer, A. T., 624
Thébault, J., 196
Theisen, B., 717
Theisen, J., 582
Thelander, M., 756
Théolas, Amadée, 244
Théoret, France, 209
Théorides, J., 184
Thérenty, M.-E., 186
Thériault, Yves, 212, 214–15
Thevenet, H. A., 339
Thévenot, Jean de, 125
Thevet, André, 98
Thibaut de Champagne, 57, 58
Thiéblemont-Dollet, S., 205
Thiele, A., 145
Thiele, S., 519
Thielking, S., 684, 693, 723
Thierry, E., 123, 134, 213
Thiher, A., 179, 195
Thim-Mabrey, C., 548
Thiolier-Méjean, S., 243, 299
Thirouin, L., 137
Thiry, C., 68
Thiry-Stassin, M., 76
Tholen, T., 735
Thomas Aquinas (*Saint*), 66, 83, 157, 371–72, 388–89, 391, 713
Thomas à Becket (*Saint*), 55
Thomas (of Britanny), 47, 51, 55, 597, 598
Thomas de Kent, 50, 64

Thomas, Adrienne, 703
Thomas, B., 559
Thomas, C., 526
Thomas, G., 530, 536
Thomas, G. E., 536
Thomas, J., 7
Thomas, J.-F., 16
Thomas, J. T. E., 55
Thomas, M. G., 534
Thomas, M. W., 535, 536
Thomas, N., 598–99
Thomas, O., 527
Thomas, R. S., 737
Thomas, W., 268, 271
Thomasberger, A., 714
Thomasin von Zerclaere, 608, 870
Thomassin, Louis, 158
Thomé, H., 671, 711
Thomine, M.-C., 115, 123, 861
Thomke, H., 619, 644
Thompson, C. W., 180
Thompson, R., 76
Thomsen, B. M., 764
Thomsen, E. S., 771
Thomsen, H., 684
Thomsen, M. R., 764
Thomsen, P., 758
Thomsen, Søren Ulrik, 772–73
Thönges-Stringaris, R., 745
Thorau, H., 347
Thorel-Cailleteau, S., 202
Thoresen, Magdalene, 777
Thormann, M., 863
Thou, Jacques-Auguste de, 112
Thouvenin, P., 158
Thresher, T., 779
Thumser, R., 703
Thüne, E.-M., 13
Thurah, T., 765, 771, 772, 870
Thurmair, M., 550, 572
Thurzó, John, 624
Tiapkov, S. N., 815
Tibi, A., 184
Tiboni, E., 431
Tichy, S., 863
Tieck, Ludwig, 649, 650, 652, 665–66
Tieder, I., 187
Tiefenbach, H., 552, 613
Tietz, M., 276
Tietz, U., 692
Tiittula, L., 550
Tikhonova, E. I., 811
Tilby, M., 177
Till Eulenspiegel v. Eulenspiegel
Tillich, Paul, 704
Tilling, C., 756
Time, G. A., 822
Timelli, M. C., 72
Timina, S. I., 832, 834
Timm, E., 581
Timm, L., 4
Timmermann, I., 638
Timofeev, L., 844
Timotin, A., 508
Timotin, E., 499, 508
Timpanaro, Sebastiano, 453–54
Tini, G., 437
Tinsley, D. F., 579
Tiozzo, E., 405
Tiraboschi, Girolamo, 405
Tissut, A., 181
Titarenko, V. G., 856
Titian (Tiziano Vecellio), 769
Titkov, E. P., 814
Titova, L. N., 833
Tittel, S., 26
Titzmann, M., 650, 671, 672
Tiugan, M., 505
Tiutchev, Fedor Ivanovich, 807, 811, 818
Tizzone, Gaetano di Pofi, 393
Tkhorzhevsky, S., 840
Tobin, R., 750
Tobler, A., 6, 26, 384
Tobler, E., 682
Toesca, C., 179
Togeby, O., 755, 757, 769
Tohăneanu, G., 503
Tokarev, D., 840
Tokareva, Victoria, 844
Tol, S., 518
Tolan, J. V., 40
Tolberg, Agnes, 696
Tolberg, Wilhelm, 696
Toldrà, M., 300
Toller, Ernst, 720, 730
Tolstaia, E., 822, 832
Tolstaya, Tatiana, 833, 834, 854
Tolstoy, A., 840
Tolstoy, Alexandra, 819, 826
Tolstoy, Alexei Nikolaevich, 833, 854
Tolstoy, Leo Nikolaevich, 198, 670, 678, 806, 819, 825, 826–27
Toma, A. F., 571
Toma, R.-F., 502
Tomachinsky, V., 812
Tomarken, A., 138
Tomasek, T., 586, 597
Tomasello, M., 549
Tomashevskii, B. V., 837
Tomasi di Lampedusa, Giuseppe, 491
Tomasin, L., 352, 355, 360, 416
Tomescu, D., 503
Tomizza, Fulvio, 491
Tommaseo, Niccolò, 421, 447
Tommaso di Giunta, 389
Ton That, T.-V., 171
Tondelli, Vittorio, 463, 491
Tongiorgi, D., 411, 416
Tonna, G., 383
Tophinke, D., 567
Toporkova, I. S., 843
Toppan, B., 436
Tordi Castria, R., 479
Torelli, F., 377
Tornow, S., 804
Torre, Alfonso de la, 302
Torre, Guillermo, 282
Torre, Josefina de la, 283
Torreblanca, M., 250, 251
Torrego, E., 12
Torres, E., 314
Torres, G., 271
Torres, Xohana, 317
Torres Cacoullo, R., 247, 260, 261
Torres Naharro, Bartolomé, 287
Torroella, Pere, 297
Tortonese, P., 191
Tortora, C., 13, 867
Tortorelli, G., 401
Toscano, M., 413
Tosi, A., 351
Tosi, G. M., 424, 476, 491
Tosin, L., 388
Tosto, E., 432
Totaro, P., 453
Töteberg, M., 744
Touborg, K., 757
Toulet, M., 223
Tourneux, H., 32
Tournon, A., 112
Touze, R., 227
Townson, M., 549
Tozzi, Federico, 453, 492
Traba, Marta, 340
Trabant, J., 20
Trachsler, R., 61, 82
Traina, G., 472
Trake, 456
Trakl, Georg, 699, 701, 730
Trama, P., 476
Trandafir, C., 510
Tranel, B., 9
Traninger, A., 645
Tranströmer, Tomas, 456
Trapp, F., 719
Trappen, S., 711, 745
Trastoy, B., 339
Trauberg, N., 844
Traven, Ben, 730
Trawny, P., 655
Treece, D., 345
Treichel, Hans-Ulrich, 752
Tremblay, Lise, 209

Tremblay, M., 211
Tremblay, Michel, 208, 209, 213, 215
Tremblay, V.-L., 211
Trenkle, F., 690
Trépanier, H., 146
Tresme, René Pothier,duc de, 127
Treves, Emilio, 431
Trevi, E., 447, 459
Trevor, D., 94
Triaire, S., 197
Triau, C., 139
Trichet, Pierre, 127
Trier, J., 4, 8, 14
Trifonov, G., 845
Trigo, B., 330
Trigo, L., 345
Tristan en prose, 37, 40, 43, 47, 51, 69, 72
Tristan L'Hermite (François L'Hermite, *dit*), 125, 128, 131, 132, 134–35, 144, 156 *v. also* L'Hermite
Tristany de Leonis, 301
Trithemius, Johannes, 636
Tritone, M. S., 476
Trivero, P., 407, 414
Trivisani Moreau, I., 151
Trofimova, E. I., 835
Tronc, Michel, 242
Tropea, M., 423
Trost, K., 804
Trotta, N., 432
Trouvé, A., 193
Trubacheva, L. A., 816
Trubetzkoy, N. S., 9
Trublot *v.* Alexis
Truchanowski, Kazimierz, 801
Truchot, C., 4
Trudeau, Pierre Elliot, 210
Truffaut, François, 174
Trumper, J. B., 363
Truwant, M., 715
Tschense, A., 688
Tschirner, E., 549
Tschopp, S. S., 621, 639
Tsiplakov, G., 809
Tsutsui, Y., 114
Tsutui, N., 112
Tsvetaeva, Marina, 832, 836, 840, 841, 849, 855
Tsvetkov, A., 826
Tsyavlovsky, M.A., 815
Tuaillon, G., 240
Tucher, Hans (the Elder), 617
Tucher, Katharina, 610
Tucholsky, Kurt, 730
Tucker, H., 148
Tudor-Anton, E., 516
Tudur Aled, 531
Tudur Ddall, 527
Tudur ap Gwyn Hagr, 527
Tudur Penllyn, 531
Tufiş, D., 502
Tugendhafte Schreiber, 606
Ţugui, P., 512, 516
Tullio, A. di, 866
Tully, C., 647, 652, 653, 667
Tumanov, V., 724
Tunberg, T., 116
Tunner, E., 866
Ţurcanu, F., 513
Turchetti, M., 97
Turchi, R., 406, 418
Turchinsky, L., 855
Turci, R., 450
Turcot, M.-P., 209
Turcotte, Elise, 215
Turculeţ, A., 506
Turek, W. P., 804
Turell, M. T., 261
Turgenev, Ivan Sergeevich, 826, 828, 830
Turi, G., 455
Turner, Victor, 593
Turpin, B., 33
Turquéty, Édouard, 169
Turró, J., 297, 301
Turumova, K., 835
Tuscano, P., 445
Tusiani, Joseph, 492
Tuten, D. N., 248
Tvardovskaya, V. A., 855
Tvardovsky, Alexander Trifonovich, 831, 832, 855
Tveit, S., 777
Twardowski, Jan, 801, 802
Tweraser, F. W., 728
Tyard, Pontus de, 118
Tygstrup, F., 765
Tymoczko, M., 540
Tynianov, I. N., 837
Tyrkova-Williams, A., 816, 828
Tyson, D., 74
Tyssens, M., 59
Tzara, Tristan, 451

Uberti, Fazio degli, 396
Ubertino da Casale, 364
Uc de Saint Circ, 234, 392
Ucelay, M., 286
Udolph, J., 565, 575
Udovik, V. A., 816
Udry, S., 77
Udvari, I., 801
Uebelhart, J., 619
Uechtritz, Friedrich von, 684
Uecker, K., 740
Uecker, M., 752
Ufliand, Vladimir, 844
Uguccione *v.* Huguccio
Uhde, D., 787
Uhlířová, L., 781, 783
Uhrig, R., 155, 642
Uhse, Bodo, 751
Uitti, K. D., 870
Ujma, C., 688
Ukena-Best, K. E., 613
Ukiah, N., 789
Ulanov, A., 837, 840, 842
Ul'chenko, E., 842
Uličný, O., 783
Ulitin, Pavel Pavlovich, 856
Ulivi, A., 506
Ulivi, F., 450
Ülkü, V., 550
Ulloa, Antonio de, 277
Ulm Sandford, G., 737
Ulmschneider, H., 616
Ulrich (*duke of Mecklenburg*), 630
Ulrich (*duke of Württemberg*), 633
Ulrich von Etzenbach, 581, 600
Ulrich von Pottenstein, 620
Umgelter, Fritz, 642
Unamuno, Miguel de, 279, 280, 291, 292, 304, 318, 474
Undset, Sigrid, 780
Ungar, Hermann, 731
Ungaretti, Giuseppe, 422, 434, 457, 483, 492–93
Unger, Erich, 704
Unger, Karoline, 688
Unger, T., 708, 868
Ungern-Sternberg, Rolf von, 726
Unglaub, E., 726
Unnold, Y. S., 340
Unruh, Fritz von, 699, 731
Untermann, J., 863
Unwin, T., 198
Unzeitig, M., 600, 603
Urban, B., 713
Urban, M., 791
Urbańska-Mazuruk, E., 800
Ureni, P., 492
Urfé, Honoré d', 103, 128, 130, 156–57
Uriţescu, D., 504
Urmanov, A. V., 819
Urscheler, A., 594
Ursu, N., 497, 503
Ustiian, I., 815
Ustinov, D. V., 833, 838
Uşurelu, C., 501
Uteza, F., 349
Utrera Torremocha, M. V., 283
Uytfange, M. van, 5

Vacante, N., 447
Văcărescu, Iancu, 512
Vaccaeus, Joannes, 102
Vaccarini, I., 437
Vaccarino, G. L., 423
Vachon, S., 175, 178
Vadeboncoeur. Pierre, 212
Vadian, Joachim, 636
Vaginov, Konstantin, 831
Vailati, Giovanni, 455
Vaillancourt, D., 125
Vaillant, A., 186
Vaiskopf, M., 836
Vaissière, M., 224
Vajdlová, M., 784
Vakhitova, T. M., 837, 849
Valcárcel Riveiro, C., 305
Valdman, A., 17
Valdrová, J., 785
Valduga, Patrizia, 493
Valeev, E., 808
Valeiras Viso, J. M., 262
Valender, J., 284
Valente, M., 405
Valenti, E., 519, 521
Valentin et Orson, 70
Valenzuela, Luisa, 337, 338, 340
Valera, Juan, 318
Valera y Alcalá Galiano, Juan, 293
Valeri, Diego, 493
Valerius Maximus, 81, 382
Valéry, Paul, 280, 281, 490, 743
Valesio, P., 460
Valla, Lorenzo, 268
Valle, J. del, 8, 246, 260
Valle, S., 436
Valle-Inclán, J., 292
Valle-Inclán, Ramón del, 279, 280, 289, 292–94
Vallero, N., 257
Vallès, Jules, 206
Vallet, Achille, 159
Valli, D., 459
Valli, Luigi, 368
Valsalobre, P., 869
Vampilov, Alexander, 856
Vanchena, L., 673
Van Damme, S., 162
Van Delft, L., 101
Vandeloise, C., 24
Van Den Abbeele, G., 158
Van den Abeele, B., 868
Van den Berghe, D., 438
Vanden Berghe, K., 321
Van den Bossche, B., 463, 482, 859
Vanderbeke, Birgit, 752
Van der Rohe, Mies, 289
Van Deyck, R., 94
Van Hemelryck, T., 81
Van Ingen, F., 865
Vanini, Giulio Cesare, 150, 160
Vann, R., 260
Vanni, V., 403
Vannucci, M., 410
Vanoncini, A., 175
Van Peteghem, M., 501
Varanini, G., 390
Vârban, F., 498
Varela Barreiro, X., 307
Varela Jácome, B., 269
Varela Pombo, S., 304
Varela Vázquez, B., 306
Varga, A. K., 637
Varga, D., 522
Vargas Llosa, Mario, 333
Vârgolici, T., 511, 515
Varkan, E., 846, 849
Varlamov, A., 809, 852
Varnhagen, F. A., 305
Varnhagen (von Ense), Rahel Levin, 666
Varry, D., 131
Varsamopoulou, E., 753
Vartic, I., 510
Varty, K., 84
Varvaro, A., 51, 301, 392, 860
Vasari, Giorgio, 98
Vasil'ev, I., 848
Vasil'ev, N. L., 812
Vasil'eva, S., 822
Vasiliev, Pavel, 842
Vasiliu, E., 496, 500
Vasiliu, G., 506
Vasiluţă, L., 502
Vasoli, C., 374
Vásquez, M., 290
Vasselin, M., 100
Vassen, F., 670
Vassilev, K., 179
Vassiliev, G., 707
Vătăşescu, C., 498
Vatsuro, E., 815
Vatsuro, V., 807
Vatteroni, S., 232, 234
Vattimo, Gianni, 463
Vaucher Gravili, A. de, 207
Vaucheret, E., 97
Vaugelas, Claude Favre de, 121
Vaughan, Rowland, 533
Vauquelin des Yveteaux, Nicolas, 157
Vauthier, M., 42
Vavra, E., 607
Vayase, J.-M., 653
Vaydat, P., 749
Vázquez, R. L., 870
Vázquez Medel, M. Á., 289
Vázquez de Menchaca, Fernando, 266
Vazsonyi, N., 870
Vazzana, S., 366
Vdovykin, G. P.,815
Vecchione, E., 473
Vedel, Émile, 200
Vedovelli, M., 357
Veenstra, T., 17
Vega, A., 298
Vega, Ana Lydia, 323
Vega, R. R., 315
Vega Carpio, Félix Lope de, 267
Vegaro, C., 355
Vegetius (Flavius Vegetius Renatus), 73, 616
Vegliante, J. C., 476
Veidle, V., 810
Veidle, V. V., 843
Veiga, A., 247, 256, 870
Veiga Grandal, M. P., 294
Veiras, Denis, 157, 159
Veit, L., 747
Veit, P., 638
Veland, R., 354
Velando Casanova, M., 253
Velázquez, Diego Rodríguez de Silva y, 270
Velázquez de Azevedo, Juan, 270
Velculescu, C., 509
Velikopol'sky, I. E., 806
Velleman, B. L., 260
Veller, Mikhail Iosifovich, 844
Vena, M., 467
Venancio Mignot, A. C., 269
Venesoen, C., 149, 151
Venier, Cristoforo, 409
Venkov, A. V., 853
Vennemann gen. Nierfeld, T., 565
Venturelli, A., 693
Venturi, F., 400
Venturi, G., 411
Veny, J., 225
Verani, C., 490
Vérard, Antoine, 79, 80
Verbaro, C., 423
Verbitskaya, G. I., 842
Verblovskaya, I., 845
Vercellin, G., 401
Verdenelli, M., 441
Verderevskaya, N., 856
Verdevoye, P., 339
Verdi, Giuseppe, 351, 424
Verdier, M.-F., 118
Verdino, S., 454, 474, 476, 493
Verdirame, R., 423
Verdonk, R. A., 268
Verebceanu, G., 499

Vereshchagin, E. M., 814
Verga, Giovanni, 421, 422, 423, 424, 428, 447–48
Verga, Giuseppe, 484
Vergiolesi, Francesco, 399
Verino, Ugolino, 302
Veríssimo, Érico, 349
Verlaine, Paul, 194, 199, 701, 712
Vermandere, D., 13
Verne, Jules, 201–02
Vernet, Florian, 238
Vernier, R., 301
Verny, M.-J., 223
Veronesi, Sandro, 462–63
Veronesi Pesciolini, L., 408
Verreault, C., 32
Verri, Alessandro, 400, 402, 418, 420, 448, 449
Verri, Pietro, 400, 418–19
Vershinina, N. L., 808, 817
Verville *v.* Béroalde de Verville
Vervliet, H. D. L., 101
Vesaas, Tarjei, 780
Vescovini, G. F., 162
Vescovo, P., 434
Veselovská, L., 783, 784
Vessey, M., 271
Vetlovskaya, V. E., 821
Veyrac, J.-L., 227
Viala, A., 100, 125, 141, 145
Viale, Lucia Cattarina, 419
Vialleton, J.-Y., 137
Viallon-Schoneveld, M., 870
Viallon-Schoneveld, M.-F., 409
Vianu, Tudor, 517
Viaro, M. E., 523
Viau, Théophile de, 130, 131, 135, 163
Viaut, A., 223, 227
Vicken, Nicolaus von, 628
Vickers, B., 622
Vico, Giambattista, 405, 410, 419–20
Victoria (*Queen of England*), 534
Victorin, P., 78
Vida, Girolamo, 120
Vidal Bolaño, Roberto, 316, 317
Vidal Gavidia, M. A., 272
Vidal Maza, M., 294
Vidau, E., 383
Videsott, P., 518, 519, 521, 522
Vidgof, L. M., 849
Vie de saint Alexis, 55
Vie des pères, 36, 55
Viegnes, M., 193
Vieillard-Baron, J.-L., 862
Vieira, M. A. da C., 343
Vielliard, F., 63, 73, 222, 232, 233
Viera, D. J., 299
Vieregge, W. H., 557
Vierhufe, A., 567
Vieri, F., 475
Viertel, Berthold, 704
Vietor-Engländer, D. J., 732
Vieusseux, Giovan Pietro, 425, 436, 441
Viganò, Renata, 456
Vigara, A., 257
Vigh, A., 213
Vighi, F., 482
Vignay, Jean de, 74
Vignes, J., 120
Vignoli, P., 425
Vignolles, Bertrand de, sieur de La Hire, 147
Vigny, Alfred de, 185–86
Vigo, Lionardo, 423, 428
Vigolo, Giorgio, 493
Vigolo, M. T., 521
Vikulova, V. L., 812
Vila, P., 296, 297, 303
Vila Rubio, M., 257
Vilain, R., 670
Vilallonga, M., 302
Vilavedra, D., 313, 314
Villa, A. I., 427
Villa, C., 369
Villalba Varneda, P., 862
Villalta, Gian Maria, 459, 464, 494
Villani, Matteo, 394
Villani, P., 421
Villanueva, D., 315
Villard, A., 159
Villard, Nina de (Nina Callias), 189
Villata, R., 417
Villedieu, Marie-Catherine-Hortense Desjardins, *dite* madame de, 129, 130, 135, 146, 147, 157
Villegas, Esteban Manuel de, 273
Villehardouin, Geoffrey de, 64
Villena, Enrique de, 270
Villena, Fernández Pacheco, marquis of, 269
Villena, J., 258
Villena, Luis Antonio de, 284
Villeneuve, L., 210
Villiers de l'Isle-Adam, Jean-Marie-Mathias-Philippe-Auguste, comte de, 195, 202
Villinger, I., 742
Villon, François, 37, 67, 69, 73, 94–95, 111
Villoutreix, M., 229
Villwock, J., 691
Villwock, P., 687
Vincensini, J.-J., 45, 59
Vincent de Paul (*Saint*), 159, 168
Vincent, A., 14, 30
Vincent, M., 133
Vinken, B., 109
Vinogradov, I., 823
Vinogradov, Viktor Vladimirovich, 807
Vinokur, Grigorii Osipovich, 811
Viola, G. E., 458
Violante, F., 385
Violante, I., 190
Violle, K., 810
Viramonte, Helena Maria, 330
Virchow, C., 613, 722
Virelade, Salomon de, 127
Virgil (Publius Vergilius Maro), 103, 109, 113, 114, 115, 134, 374, 376–77, 378, 379, 387, 397, 399, 442
Virginal, 591
Virtue, N., 71
Visani, O., 381
Visconti, Ermes, 449
Visentin, H., 136
Vishnevskaya, I. L., 829
Vishnevskaya, N. A., 810
Vislova, A. V., 820
Vitae Patrum, 55
Vitaglione, D., 245
Vitale, M., 392, 421
Vitali, L., 481
Vitali, P., 400
Vitelli, F., 486, 489. 490
Vitiello, C., 452
Vitiello, J., 459
Vitner, Ion, 511
Vitores, Feliciano, 282
Vittorelli, Jacopo, 422
Vittorini, Elio, 464, 493
Vitz, E. B., 66, 71
Vivanco, Luis Felipe, 288
Vivanti, Annie, 464, 493
Vives, Juan Luis, 272
Viviani, Cesare, 371, 493
Viviani, Q., 411
Vivoli, C., 446
Vizi, Maria, 856
Vlad, L., 509, 513
Vlad, Petru, 505
Vodolazkin, E., 839, 840
Voeikova, M. D., 868
Voetius (Gilbert Voet), 162
Voeux du héron, 72
Vogel, Daniel, 800
Vogel, Henriette, 662
Vogel, M., 635
Vögele, F., 654

Voghera, M., 358
Vogt, M., 681, 682
Vogt, S., 742
Vogt, S. M. R., 762
Vöhler, M., 734
Voia, V., 511
Voigts, M., 704, 718, 863
Voilley, P., 203
Voinovich, V., 807, 854
Vojtová, J., 786
Volante, M., 417
Vold, Jan Erik, 780
Volek, E., 337
Volfing, A., 596, 606
Volgin, I., 824
Volín, J., 782
Völker, H., 23, 864, 867
Volkert, D., 672
Volkov, Oleg Vasilievich, 844
Volkova, L., 824
Volkova, N., 836
Volkova, P. D., 854
Vollendorf, L., 282
Voller, I., 760
Vollhardt, F., 650, 861
Volli, U., 471
Vollmann, B. K., 611
Vollmann, R., 558
Volobeuf, K., 656
Voloj, J., 580
Volos, Andrei Germanovich, 856
Voloshin, Maximilian, 856
Volovici, L., 515
Völpel, A., 705
Volpi, A., 425
Volpi, Giannantonio, 404
Volponi, Paolo, 456, 493–94
Volsunga Saga, 597
Volta, Alessandro, 402
Voltaire (François Marie Arouet), 133, 134, 158, 160, 161, 410, 411, 476, 488
Voltolini, Dario, 464
Volynsky, Akim, 832
Volz, P. D., 692
Von der juden jrrsal, 576
Vona, Alexandru, 513
Vondel, Joost von, 108
Vondráček, M., 785
Vondrová, M., 787
Vonhoff, G., 683, 698
Voorwinden, N., 589
Vorbrugg, M., 729
Vordtriede, Käthe, 705
Vordtriede, Werner, 705
Vorob'ev, Konstantin Dmitrievich, 851, 856
Vorob'eva, E., 849
Voronel, N., 854
Voronin, L., 855
Vorontsova, E. K., 816
Voropaev, V., 812, 813, 839
Vosburgh, N., 283
Voss, R., 599, 604
Vossius, Gerhard Johannes, 645
Vosskamp, W., 647
Vowe, K. W., 750
Vrabie, E., 502
Vulcan, Iosif, 512
Vulcan, R. I., 123
Vulpe, M., 506
Vvedensky, Alexander Ivanovich, 830
Vygorbina, D., 856
Vykypělová, T., 782
Vysotsky, Vladimir, 856
Vystrèilová, D., 788

Wace, 62–63, 87, 593
Wachinger, B., 598
Wachsmann, C., 685
Wackenroder, Wilhelm Heinrich, 649
Wade, M. R., 638
Wærp, H. H., 780
Wærp, L. P., 776, 778
Wagemans, E., 807
Wagenbach, K., 717
Wagener, P., 567
Wagner, B., 83
Wagner, B., 715, 717
Wagner, C., 749
Wagner, F., 179
Wagner, K., 267
Wagner, N., 553
Wagner, N. R., 555
Wagner, Richard, 194, 204, 668, 670, 672, 692, 697, 704, 721, 724, 735
Wagner-Egelhaaf, M., 675
Wagner Oettinger, R., 624
Wagnerová, A., 718
Wahl, H. R., 710
Walcott, Derek, 216
Walczak, B., 794
Wald, L., 496, 497
Waldef, 63
Walden, Herwarth, 719
Waldie, D. J., 194
Waldinger, Ernst, 704
Waldo (Waldo Williams), 535
Wales, M. L., 25
Walker, C., 680
Walker, D., 203
Walker, D. C., 23
Walker, J., 81, 85
Walla, F., 689
Wallas, A. A., 705
Wallmann, J., 638
Walser, Martin, 733, 740, 748, 752–53
Walser, Robert, 731, 742
Walsh, P., 540
Walter, Otto F., 737
Walter, P., 94, 634, 862
Waltereit, R., 355
Walters, L., 68, 81, 83, 84, 86, 92
Walters, L. J., 870
Walther von der Vogelweide, 579, 580, 581, 582, 602, 603–04, 860, 863
Walther, B. K., 767
Walther, H., 575
Walusiak, E., 795
Walz, D., 862
Walzel, Oskar, 686
Wand-Wittkowski, C., 606, 611
Wandhoff, H., 579, 592, 608
Wandruszka, N., 81, 82
Wang, J., 684
Wanicowa, Z., 794, 798
Wańkowicz, Melchior, 802
Wanning, B., 688
Wanzeck, C., 555
Wappmann, V., 643
Ward, M. G., 682
Ward, P., 714
Ward, P. A., 191, 192
Warens, Louise-Eléonore de la Tour du Pil, baronne de, 182
Warner-Vieyra, Myriam, 218
Warning, R., 677, 701, 727
Warren, J., 740
Warren, J.-P., 212
Warren, M. R., 51, 62
Wasa, A., 260
Waser, E., 574
Wassermann, Jakob, 704, 731
Wassmo, Herbjørg, 778
Waszakowa, K., 795
Watanabe-O'Kelly, H., 622, 638, 870
Waterson, K., 141
Watriquet de Convins, 71
Watson, R. A., 163
Watteau, Antoine, 125
Watthée-Delmotte, M., 68
Watzlawick, H., 409
Wauchier de Denain, 49, 55
Waugh, Evelyn, 200
Wauquelin, Jehan, 72
Way, P., 101
Webb, K. E., 737
Webber, A., 667, 670
Webber, A. J., 721
Weber, A., 272
Weber, A., 627
Weber, E., 713
Weber, H., 568

Weber, L., 488
Weber, T., 550, 632
Weddige, H., 591
Wedekind, Frank, 731–32, 743
Weder, C., 656
Weder, K., 743
Weeda, R., 100
Weerth, Georg, 672, 674, 697–98
Wegener-Stratmann, M., 727
Wegera, K.-P., 558, 563
Wegmann, P., 79
Węgrzynek, K., 791, 802
Wehle, W., 437, 701
Weibel, V., 574
Weichselbaumer, R., 608
Weidemeier, K.-H., 571
Weidenbusch, W., 863
Weidenhaupt, H., 724
Weider, E., 569
Weigand, E., 564
Weigand, K., 593, 609
Weigel, A., 661
Weigel, R. G., 725
Weigel, S., 592, 659
Weil, Simone, 471
Weill, I., 65
Weinberg, F., 114
Weinberger, G. J., 728
Weineck, S.-M., 658, 661
Weinmann, F., 743
Weinrich, H., 545
Weinstein, J., 83
Weise, Christian, 638, 644
Weise, Karl, 680
Weisgerber, Jean, 108, 129
Weiss, J[ason], 337
Weiss, J[udith], 63
Weiss, Peter, 674, 740, 753
Weiss, T., 590
Weiss, U., 732
Weiss, W., 682
Weiss Adamson, M., 617
Weissberg, L., 659, 695
Welch, E., 514
Wellbery, D. E., 647, 691, 860
Wellershoff, Dieter, 753
Wells, D. A., 596
Welsch, U., 707
Weltsch, Felix, 718
Wende, Frank, 703
Weng, G., 635
Wengeler, M., 548, 551
Weninger, R., 751
Wentzel, K., 766
Wenzel, F., 593, 600, 606, 608
Wenzel, H., 586, 608, 870
Wenzel, U. J., 691
Werfel, Franz, 704, 732
Wergeland, Camilla *v.* Collett
Wergeland, Henrik, 778
Werlén, E., 567
Werlen, I., 867
Werner, M., 685
Werner, M. C. G., 705
Werner, Markus, 750
Wernher der Gartenaere, 579
Werth, G., 672
Wesch, A., 863
Weschenfelder, E. V., 345
Wesener, T., 557
Wessel, Johann Herman, 765, 774
Wessobrunner Gebet, 583
West, J., 552
West, K. R., 473
Westgate, G., 748
Westh-Jensen, P., 757
Westmoreland, M., 221
Westphal, B., 750
Wetherill, P. M., 198
Wetsel, D., 870
Wetstein, Henrik, 163
Wetzel, R., 616
Wetzels, W. L., 9
Weyand, B., 699
Weyers, C., 757
Whalan, L. A., 56
Whalley, F., 731
Wheeler, E., 86
White, H., 289
White, N., 196, 206
White, R., 689
White, S. D., 50
Whitehead, C., 93
Whitinger, R. G., 657
Whitman, Walt, 283
Whittle, R., 688
Wichmann von Arnstein, 611
Wichter, S., 548, 564
Wick, Johann Jacob, 621
Wicke, A., 644
Wickham-Crowley, K. M., 530
Wickram, 627
Widell, P., 755
Wieczorek, J. P., 748
Wiese, Benno von, 659
Wiese, J., 568
Wiesel, J., 670
Wiesel, P., 666
Wieser, D., 195
Wiesinger, P., 563, 567, 859
Wiesmüller, W., 860
Wiesner-Bangard, M., 707
Wiethaus, U., 611
Wigamur, 599
Wigbers, M., 657, 736
Wigmore, J., 733
Wigzell, F., 807
Wihl, Ludwig, 683
Wiingaard, J., 777
Wiktorowicz, J. F., 552
Wiland, S., 780
Wild, A., 701
Wild, R., 654
Wilde Alexander, Der, 606
Wilde, A., 289
Wilde, D., 729
Wilde, Oscar, 199, 200
Wildenbruch, Ernst von, 710
Wildfeuer, A., 568
Wilhelm, F., 171
Wilhelmi, T., 619, 630, 870
Wiliam, D. W., 533
Wilke, T., 663
Wilkins, N., 861
Wilkoń, A., 798, 799, 800
Wilks, C., 29
Willard, C. C., 83, 86
Wille, L., 745
Willeke, A. B., 734
Willeke, M., 620
Willems, Paul, 642
Willemsen, E., 604
Willer, S., 747
Willers, M., 601–02
William of Conches, 399
William of Ockham, 66
William, Dafydd, 534
Williams, A., 733
Williams, C., 348
Williams, G., 324, 326
Williams, G., 534, 536, 537
Williams, G. A., 529
Williams, H., 194, 205
Williams, J., 711
Williams, L., 526
Williams, P., 533
Williams, R. L., 338
Williams, R. W., 752
Williams, Rhydwen, 535, 536
Williams, Tennessee, 655
Williams-Krapp, W., 611
Willis, E., 247
Wilmet, M., 21, 24
Wilson, C., 203
Wilson, R., 371
Wiltshire, C. R., 3, 9, 870
Wimmer, R., 550, 724, 725
Winckelmann, Johann Joachim, 402
Winckler, L., 702, 703
Windberger-Heidenkummer, E., 573
Windfuhr, M., 863
Winge, V., 545
Winiarska, J., 798, 800
Winkelmann, D., 719, 863
Winkler, M., 703
Winkler, S., 9

Winn, C. H., 115, 120, 123, 160
Winsheim, Veit, 626
Winsloe, Christa, 703
Winter, C., 578
Winter, U., 635
Winter, Zikmund, 785
Wireback, K. J., 8, 249–50
Wirkner, W., 573
Wirnt von Grafenberg, 599
Wischer, I., 10, 870
Wisman, J., 84
Witt, T., 676
Witte, K. H., 610
Wittek, A., 549
Wittenwiler, Heinrich, 579, 588, 618
Wittgenstein, Ludwig von, 681, 736–37
Wittlin, C., 301
Wittlin, Jozef, 732
Wittmann, L., 489
Wittwer, A., 731, 863
Witwicki, Teodor, 802
Wivel, H., 777
Wivel, Ole, 771
Wizisla, E., 709
Wizlav von Rügen, 604
Woesler, W., 675, 739, 868, 870
Wogan-Browne, J., 92
Wohmann, Gabriele, 735
Wojciechowska-Basista, A., 802
Wójcikowska, E., 791
Wojda, A., 787
Wojdak, P., 792
Wojtach, R., 795
Wojtyła, Karol, 802
Wolan, M., 789
Wolańska, E., 798
Wolf, B., 23, 585, 690, 693, 747
Wolf, Christa, 738, 739, 753
Wolf, H., 556
Wolf, J., 580, 582
Wolf, K., 613–14
Wolf, M., 614
Wolf, N. R., 550, 552
Wolf, S., 719
Wolf, W., 860
Wolfdietrich, 591
Wolfenstein, Alfred, 704
Wolfram von Eschenbach, 577, 579, 581, 582, 586, 592, 594–97, 599, 600, 601, 864, 866
Wolfskehl, Karl, 704, 732
Wolfsohn, Wilhelm, 679
Wollenberg, Erich, 730
Wollschläger, H., 694
Wołos, M., 795
Wolpert, G., 679
Wolzogen, H. D. von, 679
Wood, S., 475
Woodford, C., 639
Woodhouse, J. R., 432
Wooldridge, R., 115
Woolf, Virginia, 280, 281
Woolford, M., 546
Worbs, E., 800
Worden, W., 336
Worley, S., 665
Wörner, A., 862
Woronczak, J., 802
Worstbrock, F. J., 576
Worth-Stylianou, V., 102
Wotjak, G., 246
Wright, B., 199
Wright, R. H. P., 5, 249
Wrisley, D. K., 53
Wróblewski, P., 795
Wronicz, J., 799
Wronikowska, D., 402
Wruck, P., 679
Wu, X., 684
Wüest, J., 4, 22
Wühr, Paul, 753
Wünderli, P., 383, 867
Wunderlich, W., 620
Wünsch, M., 672, 683
Wurm, A., 788
Wyczynski, P., 214
Wyderka, B., 797, 801
Wygant, A., 147
Wyllie, B., 850
Wyllt, Manod, 534
Wynkyn de Worde, 533
Wynn, M., 589, 595
Wyre, Llinos, 534
Wyrwas, K., 795, 798
Wyspiański, Stanisław, 802
Wyss, Laure, 738
Wyss, R., 730
Wyss, U., 589, 597
Wyszyński, Stefan (*cardinal*), 805

Xenopol, Adela, 508
Xove Ferreiro, X., 308
Xun, Lu, 690

Y Mab Cryg, 527
Y Proll, 527
Yaguello, M., 29
Yanacopoulo, A., 210
Yandell, C., 115, 118
Yates, W. E., 670, 689, 714, 728, 740
Yavneh, N., 629, 636
Yeager, R. F., 71
Yeandle, D. N., 581, 596
Yeats, William Butler, 200
Yeltzina, Naina, 839
Yn, K. K., 812
Yoshijima, S., 550
Young, C., 596, 598
Young, R. M., 185
Young, T. R., 322
Ysaÿe le Triste, 68, 78
Ystad, R. H., 776
Yuk, H.-S., 752

Zabagli, F., 389, 444, 445
Zabarella, Jacopo, 634
Zabłocka, M., 797
Zabolotsky, Nikolai Alekseevich, 833, 851
Zaborov, P. R., 831
Zaccaria, V., 439, 447
Zachmann, G., 194
Zachriat, W. G., 690
Zaciu, M., 507
Zaercher, V., 114, 123
Zafra, R., 271
Zagaevschi, V., 496
Zagari-Marinzoli, R., 448
Zagolin, Bianca, 207
Zagona, K., 256
Zagorul'ko, V. I., 813
Zaguri, Pietro, 409
Zahn, P., 616
Zaitsev, B. K., 835, 836
Zaitsev, V. A., 853
Zaitseva, G. S., 848
Zajda, A., 794
Zakharine, D., 552
Zakharov, A. P., 815
Zakhoder, B., 839
Zale, S., 73
Załęcka, D., 795
Zalewska, G., 802
Zalygin, Sergei Pavlovich, 844
Zamanova, I. F., 813
Zamanskaia, V. V., 837
Zambon, F., 43
Zamboni, A., 522
Zambrano, María, 289, 465
Zamfirescu, D., 509, 511
Zamiatin, Evgenii, 832, 833, 856–57
Zamora, F. J., 4
Zamora Bonilla, J., 290
Zamuner, I., 233
Zanato, T., 444
Zane, Giacomo, 398
Zanetti, S., 336
Zangrandi, A., 423
Zangrilli, F., 465, 484
Zaniboni, L., 409
Zanni Ulisse, P., 437
Zannoni, P. A., 464

Zantop, S., 659
Zanzotto, Andrea, 456, 457, 459, 494
Zappert, Georg, 583
Zappia, A., 467
Zaragoza, G., 171
Zarcone, S., 403
Zaron, Z., 795
Zaśko-Zielińska, M., 798
Zăstroiu, R., 516
Zavarzina, N. I., 828
Zavattini, Cesare, 459
Zayani, M., 691
Zayas, Maria de, 154
Zbróg, P., 791, 792
Zdanevich, Ilya, 831
Zduńczyk, T., 793
Zecher, C., 107
Zeffirelli, Franco, 424
Zegowitz, B., 697
Zehetner, L., 553
Zehm, Günter, 752
Zehnder-Tischendorf, K., 682
Zeliqzon, L., 31
Zeller, B., 689
Zeller, C., 743
Zeller, R., 642, 643, 688
Zeman, H., 689
Zeman, J., 786
Žemličküv, M., 870
Zendrini, Bernardino, 426
Zenge, Wilhelmine von, 662
Zeno, Apostolo, 404, 416
Zeno Gandia, Manuel, 327
Zenobi, S., 363
Zernadas y Castro, Diego A. de, 317
Zernova, R., 838
Żeromski, Stefan, 802
Zesen, Philipp von, 644
Zgółka, T., 795, 798
Zgółkowa, H., 802
Zgraon, F., 498, 509
Zhang, X., 81
Zhdanov, A. A., 844
Zheltysheva, N. M., 850
Zhigach, L. V., 819
Zhirmunsky, V. M., 838, 842
Zhivov, V. M., 806, 809
Zhokov, I., 550
Zholkovsky, A. K., 847
Zhukovsky, Vasilii Andreevich, 807, 808, 810, 818, 819
Zhuravleva, A. I., 807, 813
Zidaric, W., 467
Ziegeler, H.-J., 576, 597, 611
Ziegler, A., 552
Ziegler, E., 551, 567, 677
Ziegler, R., 200
Zielske, H., 671
Zifonun, G., 565, 863
Zignai, E., 476
Zigo, P., 573
Ziino, A., 405
Ziino, F., 302
Ziková, M., 783
Zilberman, R., 344
Zilcosky, J., 717
Zilli, L., 106
Zillig, W., 565
Zilly, B., 349
Zimbone, A., 426
Zimmermann, C. von, 719, 720–21
Zimmermann, D., 179
Zimmermann, E., 713
Zimmermann, H., 708
Zimmermann, H. D., 660, 718
Zimmermann, K., 257, 262, 617
Zimmermann, M., 70, 81, 83, 233, 741, 870
Zimmern, Froben Christoph von, 626–27
Zimmern, Wilhelm Werner von, 626–27
Zimny, R., 798
Zimorski, W., 697
Zinchenko, V. G., 808
Zinckernagel, P., 757
Zinelli, F., 233, 234
Zinguer, I., 104, 114, 122, 870
Zinik, Z., 807
Zink, M., 35, 49, 870
Zinoviev, Alexander, 844, 857
Zinovieva, O. M., 857
Zinser, H., 541
Zinsli, P., 633
Zinszner, D., 200
Zint-Dyhr, I., 546
Ziolkowski, E., 823
Ziolkowski, J., 70
Ziolkowski, J. M., 300
Ziolkowski, M., 823
Zipf, George Kingsley, 783
Zittel, C., 693
Zitterbart, J. P., 562
Ziukaite, L., 777
Zlochevskaya, A. V., 850
Žmegač, V., 711
Żmigrodzki, P., 789, 794
Zobel, Joseph, 216, 220
Zohrab, I., 807, 829
Zola, Émile, 171, 188, 191, 195, 196, 202–03, 204, 205, 206, 484, 702
Zolli, P., 409
Zollino, A., 480
Zolotonosov, M., 843, 847
Zolotsev, S., 847
Zolotukhin, V., 856
Zolotussky, I., 825, 840, 841
Zons, R., 681
Zorin, A., 809
Zorrilla y Moral, José, 286
Zorzi, Bortolo, 401
Zoshshenko, Mikhail, 832, 844, 857
Zotov, S. N., 813
Zotz, N., 597
Zovoli, P., 454
Zuber, R., 136
Zubizaretta, M. L., 9, 11
Zubkov, I. K., 827
Zuccarelli, U., 443
Zuccato, Edoardo, 459
Zucchermaglio, C., 355
Zucco, R., 411
Zuckmeyer, Carl, 732
Zugun, P., 504
Żukowski, W., 797
Zuleta, R., 320
Zulueta, C., 286
Zumbült, B., 59
Zur Mühlen, Hermynia, 732
Zürn, Unica, 753
Zürrer, P., 569
Zusman, V. G., 808, 810
Zverev, V. P., 808, 810
Zvonareva, L., 847
Zweig, Arnold, 727
Zweig, Max, 732
Zweig, Stefan, 281, 642, 702, 704, 705, 732
Zwinger, Theodor, 103, 630
Zwingli, Huldrych, 104, 623, 636
Zybura, M., 863
Zykova, G. V., 850
Zyrianov, O. V., 811, 813